THE ART OF NICKELODEON RISE OF THE TEENAGE MUTANT NINJA TURTLES™

BY THE CREW AND CAST OF RISE OF THE TEENAGE MUTANT NINJA TURTLES
WITH COLIN STEIN
FOREWORD BY ANDY SURIANO AND ANT WARD

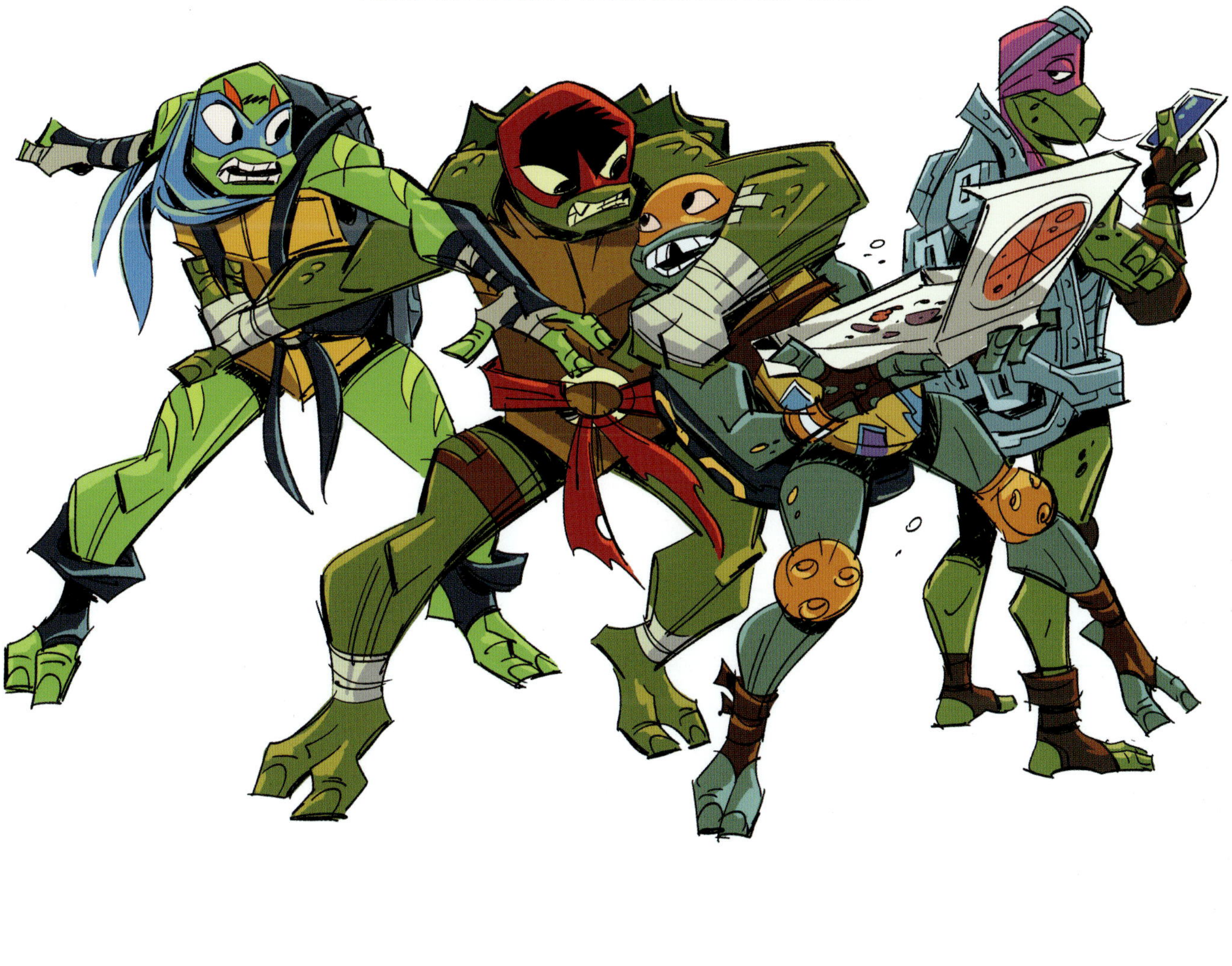

ISBN: 979-8-88724-364-1 29 28 27 26 2 3 4 5

EU RP (for authorities only)
eucomply OÜ
Pärnu mnt. 139b – 14
11317 Tallinn, Estonia
hello@eucompliancepartner.com
+33757690241

Contracting Partner: Tara McCrillis, IDW Publishing | EU RP Partner: Marko Novkovic, CEO

Special thanks to Amy Jarashow, Benjamin Harper, Jeff Whitman, and Micol Hiatt for their invaluable assistance.

Thank you to Nikki Price, Jason McConnell , Lianna Cohen, Hershel Davis, Roxanne Escatel, and Em Gomez.

Produced by Ctrl+N Studios, LLC
Written, designed, and compiled by Colin Stein
Cover illustration by Andy Suriano

THE ART OF NICKELODEON RISE OF THE TEENAGE MUTANT NINJA TURTLES™

TABLE OF CONTENTS

FOREWORD

LIKE ALL GREAT AND LASTING THINGS, *RISE* DOES AND WILL FOREVER CONTINUE TO RESONATE.

I always said history will be kind to *Rise*, and this book is proof of that sentiment. The amount of creative "candle burning," whether hours or sacrifice, is evident in these pages. But moreover, the pure *joy* we as a crew felt while making *Rise* pops out from each page, from the designs, screenshots, and testimonies of those whose job it was to have fun while crafting such a timeless series. From the beginning, Ant and I set out to make a genuine, honest portrayal of friendship and family—especially those you make. That is what the crew was, a chemistry experiment whose ingredients were just the right number of masters at storyboarding incredible action sequences, wickedly sharp comedic writers, an untested Australian animation studio, a collection of unlikely voice actors, a flexible and nimble production team, and supportive executives that initially backed our wild take on an evergreen franchise like Teenage Mutant Ninja Turtles.

It took us a while to win over the fans, but those who supported us "got" our world-breaking vision, connecting to the heart, humor, and spectacle we brought to each episode. We took huge swings, breathing new life into a then 30-year-old property. The fans who showed up continued to lift us up when we'd encounter the hurdles of any series, let alone one fraught with so much baggage and turmoil we had to overcome. The amount of fan art, talent, and passionate outcrying blew us away—so much so that some were even hired on to the show, and I'd often take to Etsy or some other creator selling platform to buy key chains, stickers, 3D prints, and cookie cutters. That is how I first discovered the author of this compendium, Colin Stein. His attention to detail and superb design skills far surpassed those of most of our official consumer products. Colin has been one of the biggest advocates for *Rise* since the beginning, and as I've gotten to know him further, I've continued to collaborate with him on multiple personal projects, relying on his keen eye, professionalism, and design skills.

The book you hold in your hands now was born from an unrelenting support, carried by new and old fans alike. Their continued fervor and excitement for what we did—and have yet to do—has touched every one of us on the crew. When we were given the opportunity to ride out the rest of what time we had left after we'd been put on "hard pause" or finish (albeit in abbreviated form) the story we'd always wanted to tell, we chose the more creative but harder path. We did it for the fans. We grew with these characters at the same time as they did and wanted to give the Mad Dogs the most satisfying send-off we could, and the fans' support was the fire that gave us the passion to do so. We could've taken it easy those last few months of production, but we worked hard until the bitter end for the fans and for the family we created, both reptile and nonshelled beings alike.

Andy Suriano
Series Co-Creator

RISE WAS A HUGE EXPERIMENT THAT SHOULD NOT HAVE WORKED, BUT IT DID. NOT ONLY DID IT WORK, IT EXCELLED.

Andy and I stepped onto the project with some very clear goals for the show. It had to be funny, bizarre, genre-crossing, dynamic, wholly unique, and beautiful. Taking the reins of this beloved franchise, coming on the heels of Ciro Nieli's incredible *Teenage Mutant Ninja Turtles* (2012), was a daunting task. So we used this as an opportunity to create a world unique to itself, a complete reimagining of TMNT rather than a traditional reboot.

We gathered a team of comedy-focused writers and action-focused storyboard artists, threw them into a blender, and unleashed the madness that ensued into the wild. The result demanded some of the highest quality of art and animation seen on television.

Oh my, did our incredible art department rise to the occasion! A massive thank-you to Carl Beu, our color supervisor, and Ben Lee, our background design supervisor. Thank you to our entire art team, who are undoubtedly some of the best in the business. Thank you, everyone at Flying Bark Studios. You embraced the challenges, were incredible creative partners, and produced groundbreaking animation that has shattered the preconceived notions of what can be achieved in hand-drawn TV animation. This show would not have been possible without the support of Megan Casey, Dana Vasquez-Eberhardt, and the rest of our Nickelodeon support team. And, of course, thank you, Mr. Andy Suriano, our brilliant art director and my partner in crime running the show. I knew we were on to something special when we started this collaborative journey together, but I am still blown away by what our team created. Thank you, Kevin Eastman and Peter Laird; your genius gave birth to one of the most iconic and incredible franchises ever. Thank you, Colin Stein, for putting this book together and for your endless patience. Last but not least, thank you to the legions of unwavering *Rise of the Teenage Mutant Ninja Turtles* fans around the world. Your passion for the show is humbling. You're the best!

This art book represents more than just beautiful drawings—it's a testament to collaboration, creativity, and the power of taking risks.

Ant Ward
Series Co-Creator

INTRODUCTION

CREATING THE DEFINITIVE ART BOOK FOR *RISE* HAS BEEN A DREAM COME TRUE.

As a lifelong Ninja Turtles fan, I never thought I would be a part of the TMNT franchise in any official capacity, but somehow...I am! What you hold in your hands is years of hard work with many sleepless nights of giving everything I've got. I've never worked harder for anything in my life, and I'm incredibly proud to be able to share this celebration of my favorite pizza-eating crime fighters.

The Turtles have always been a part of my life—there's not a time I can think of when they weren't there. Ever since the 1987 animated series, I have been a TMNT fan. Cartoons, toys, video games, comics, movies...I was hooked! Every birthday and Christmas was filled with Turtles, and I wouldn't have it any other way. So I better thank my mom, dad, and family for encouraging this obsession.

Out of all the versions of TMNT, there was something special about the 2018 series *Rise of the Teenage Mutant Ninja Turtles*. After 35 years of Turtles, I knew what I wanted from TMNT, but *Rise* had what I needed. After loving Ciro Nieli's *Teenage Mutant Ninja Turtles* (2012), which solidified itself as the definitive take on the cartoon Turtles, Andy Suriano and Ant Ward brought something I've never seen before: a wildly new direction that pushed the boundaries of what TMNT was and what it could be while still keeping what the Turtles are at their core.

Rise is a show about family, and I found my family in the community. This book is for you, the die-hards who will forever champion this series till the very end! For those who make fan art, post memes, create merch, write fanfiction, draw comics, cosplay, animate, re-animate, and so much more—you're the backbone of this series. You're keeping the love for these silly Turtles alive. You've all made an incredible impact on my life; it was a wild time that I think about every day. This community oozes with culture. Shout-out to the culture!

I'd like to give a special thanks to the cast and crew of *Rise*. The entire team was lightning in a bottle for the little series that could. To Andy Suriano, you've made a great impression on my life not only as a role model but as a friend. I hope this book makes you proud! Thank you to Ant Ward, JJ Conway, Tony Gama-Lobo, Dale Malinowski, Russ Carney and Ron Corcillo, Josh Riley Brown, Kevin Molina-Ortiz, Sheldon Vella, Ian Busch, Tom Barkel, Sarah Harper, Ashe Jacobson, Thanh Dang, Bryce Collins, Jermaine Jose, Ida Hem, Jeffry Chozon, and everyone else I poked and bothered countless times. I couldn't have done any of this without all of you. We've created an archive of that short period of time that we all shared together. It was a very special time that meant so much to so many people. This is more than a book—this is a celebration of what you all accomplished and the mark you left on these Turtles we care so deeply about.

Thank you to my work husbands, Galen Christy, Andy Swanson, Chris Hoyt, and Josh McKamie. Without you guys, I wouldn't...couldn't have been able to make this dream of mine come true. Thank you to Alonzo Simon, Bobby Curnow, and Jeff Whitman for helping me get this over the finish line. Thank you, Mackenzie, for being there throughout this entire journey and supporting me the whole time—you made sure I was fed and filled with caffeine.

Now grab a slice, get comfortable, and enjoy. Hot Soup!

Colin Stein
October 2025

PRE-PRODUCTION

For over 40 years, the *Teenage Mutant Ninja Turtles* have been a defining force in pop culture, capturing the hearts of fans across multiple generations. When animation veterans Andy Suriano and Ant Ward took on the challenge of reimagining the Heroes in a Half-Shell for a new era, they didn't just rise to the occasion—they reinvented it. Their fresh take on the pizza-loving mutants injected bold new energy into the franchise while staying true to its core spirit.

Following the success of *Teenage Mutant Ninja Turtles* (2012) by Ciro Nieli, Nickelodeon wanted to take the Turtles in a new direction—one that would honor their legacy while introducing them to a modern audience. The result was a dynamic reimagining that pushed the boundaries of what the Turtles could be, blending the familiar with the unexpected.

This iteration of the Turtles was unlike anything fans had seen before. With new weapons, mystic powers, and a shake-up in leadership roles, these brothers are a fresh take on the classic team—right down to their unique species. Alongside a rich new backstory, the Turtles navigate a world filled with familiar allies and villains as well as exciting new characters. Together, they uncover the secrets of a hidden mystic city beneath New York, taking their adventures to thrilling new heights.

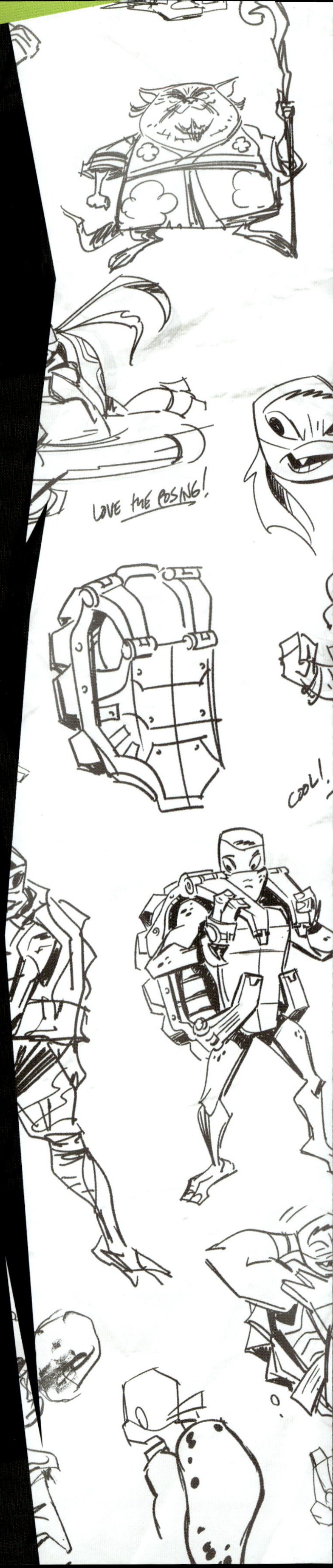

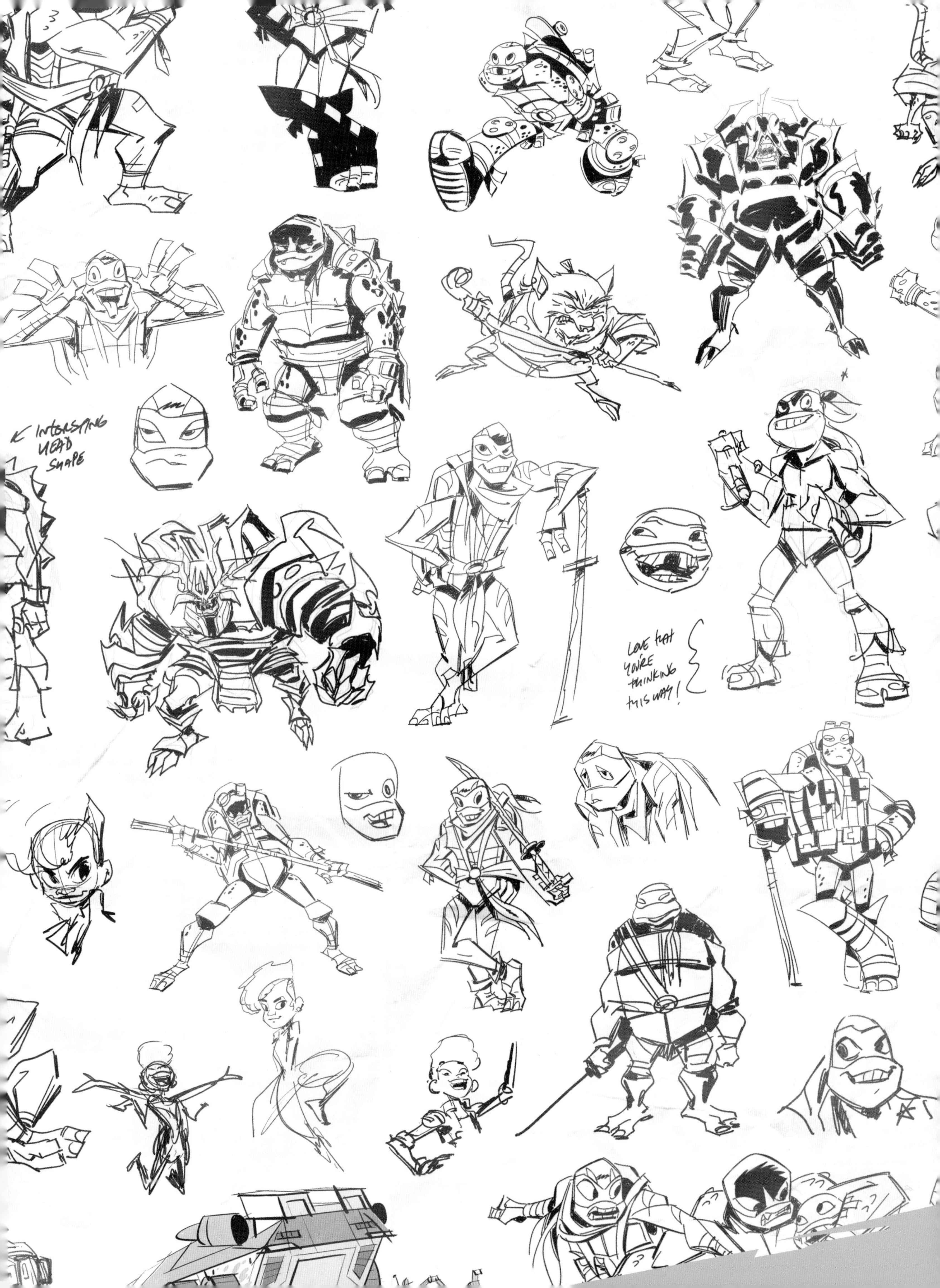
← INTERSTING HEAD SHAPE
LOVE THAT YOU'RE THINKING THIS WAY!

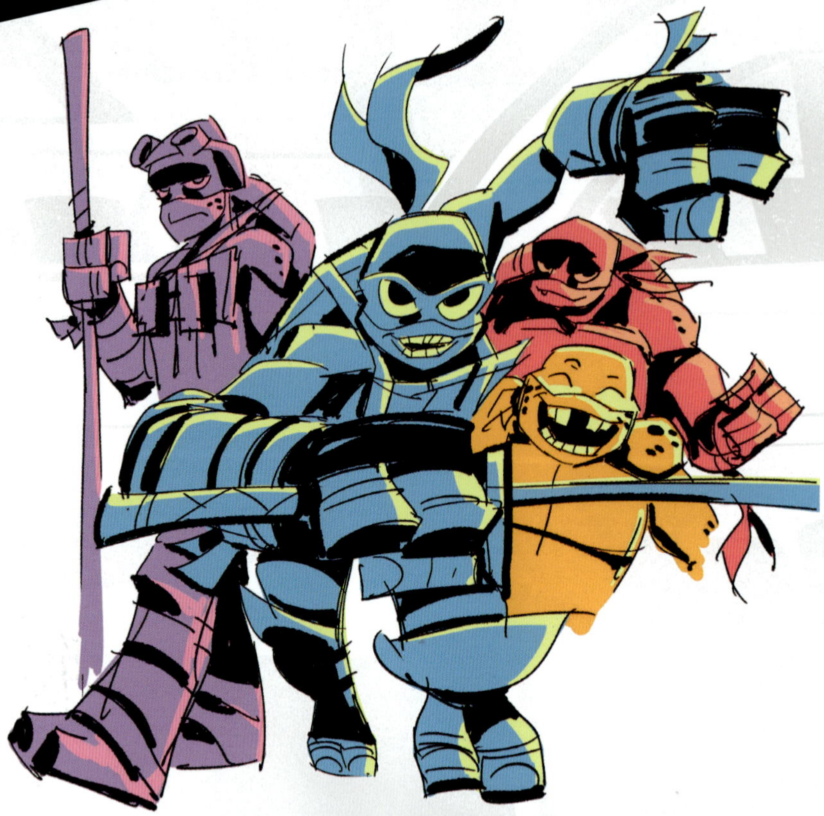

HEROES REBORN

THE RISE OF A NEW ERA

ANT WARD: I have worn many hats in the animation industry over the last 20 years or so. From storyboarding and animating to writing and directing, I played a key role in the development of Nickelodeon's CGI pipeline. I spent the better part of that time in a producing capacity, acting as supervising producer on *The Penguins of Madagascar* (2008), *Teenage Mutant Ninja Turtles* (2012), and then executive producer on *Rise of the Teenage Mutant Ninja Turtles* (2018) and *Transformers: EarthSpark* (2022). I currently live in Los Angeles with my family and a cat, a dog, two snakes, a gecko, and a panther chameleon.

ANDY SURIANO: During my 25-plus years in animation, I've done everything from storyboards to character designs, writing, directing, and any other opportunities I had on productions such as *Spider-Man: Beyond the Spider-Verse* (2027), *Rise of the Teenage Mutant Ninja Turtles* (2018), *Samurai Jack* (2001), *Spider-Man: Across the Spider-Verse* (2023), *Star Wars: Clone Wars* (2003), *Wonderful World of Mickey Mouse* (2020), *The Fairly OddParents* (2001), and at least a few dozen more. Originally hailing from Detroit, Michigan, I illustrated the Little Caesars "Pizza! Pizza!" guy, performed in sketch-comedy shows, and toured the globe for seven years with a magic-comedy show as a two-foot-tall Elvis. I've also enjoyed working in comics, illustrating creator-owned graphic novels like *Lost Company: Into the Everneath*, *Cosmic Scoundrels*, *Doc Bizarre, M.D.*, *Charlatan Ball*, and other titles like *Batman: The Brave and the Bold* and *Samurai Jack* comic runs.

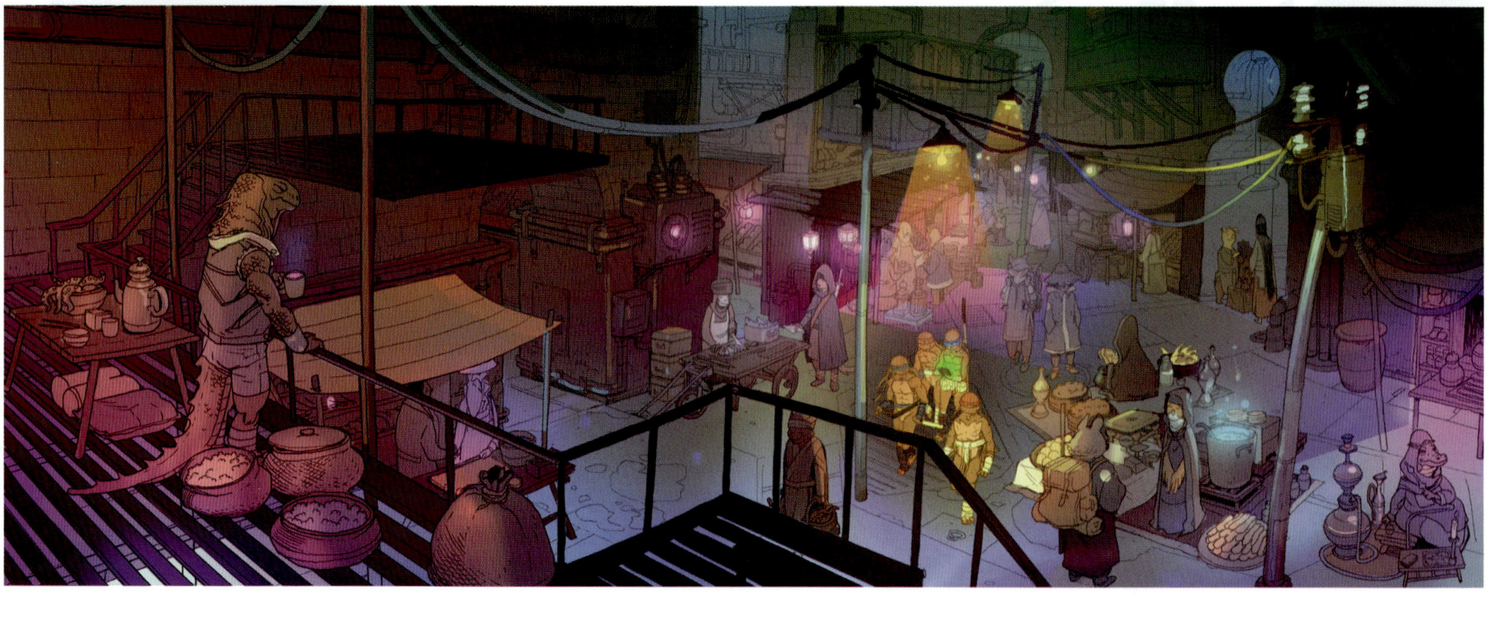

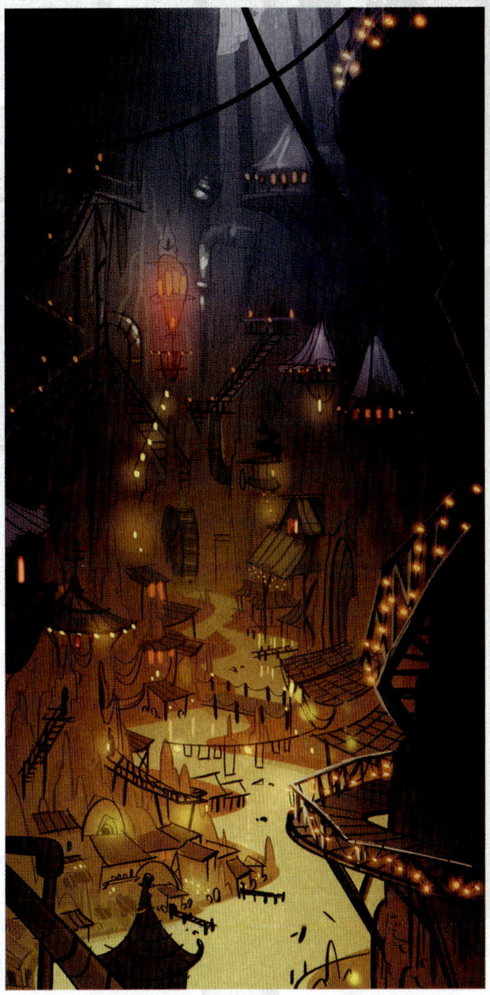

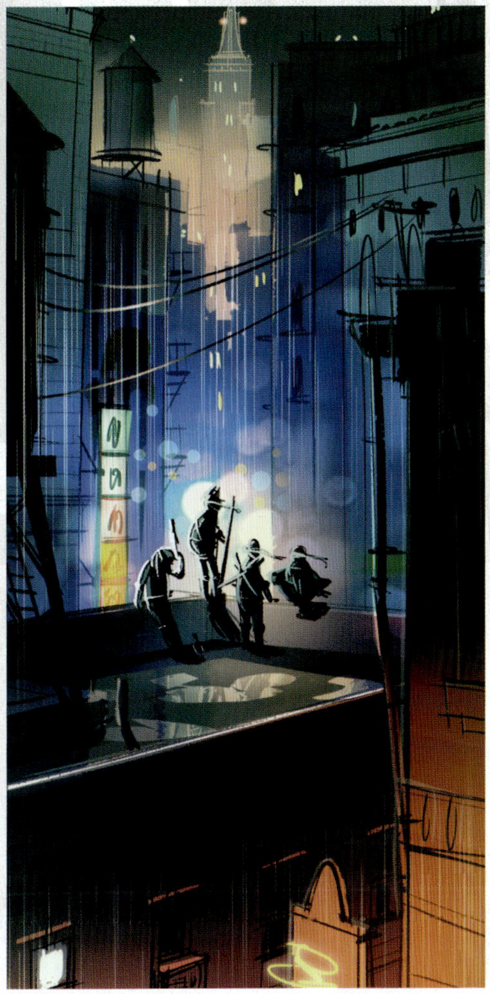

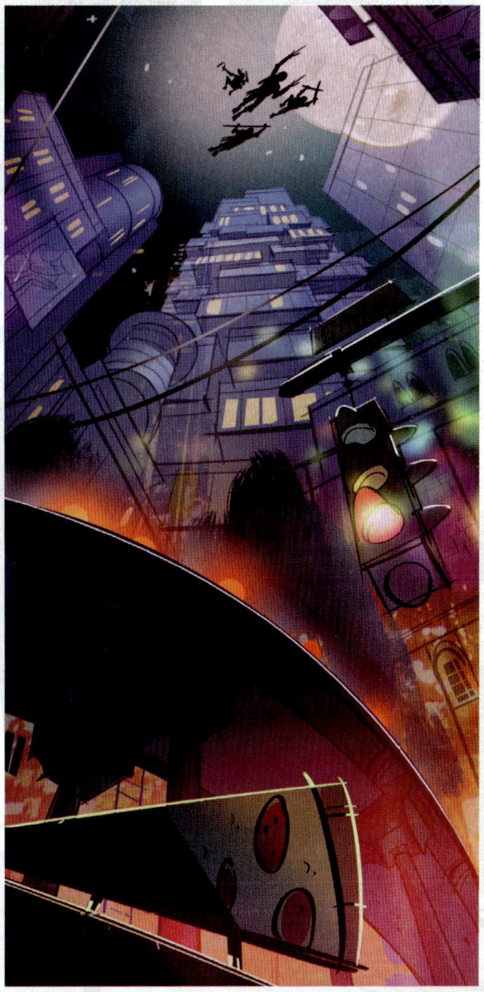

ANT WARD: I've always been a fan of TMNT. My friends and I wore out a VHS copy of the Fred Wolf show's pilot. I have very fond memories of going to see the second live-action movie in theaters with my dad and sneaking a peek of the Mirage comic at our local bookstore (which was deemed too violent for me by my mum—truly the forbidden fruit).

ANDY SURIANO: While I was working on Disney's *Mickey Mouse* (2013), I was also doing pretty consistent freelance for Nickelodeon and drawing the 2012 Turtles. With Ciro Nieli's *Teenage Mutant Ninja Turtles* (2012) coming to a close, Nick had been attempting to develop a new TMNT series for a number of years without success—that was until Megan Casey and Phil Rynda asked if I wanted to pitch one. I came up with some crazy ideas: a barbarian Raph and a young April, a futuristic take involving Bebop and Rocksteady needing to take care of Leo the "golden child..." Those were slightly too big of swings! Haha! I just had no interest in drawing Turtles skateboarding in NYC again!

ANT WARD: We were starting to wrap up season 5 of Ciro's Turtles, where I had been supervising producer for close to a decade, when Megan Casey (our Nickelodeon executive) called me, asking me to take a look and offer insight into a new TMNT pitch being developed by Brandon Auman. Brandon was leaving that development to work on *Star Wars: Resistance* (2018) at Lucasfilm. I read the pitch and latched on to one element in particular: the notion of an invisible realm hidden from humans that was home to a vast menagerie of mutants and other unique characters. Megan loved that take as well and asked me to develop a pitch based on that angle. Nick liked my pitch, and I was invited to pitch again. This time, Andy was in the room to pitch his take, and much to our surprise and excitement, we both had almost exactly the same pitch and visual references.

ANDY SURIANO: We had almost identical pitches—down to the same obscure 1970s science fiction art and French comics references!

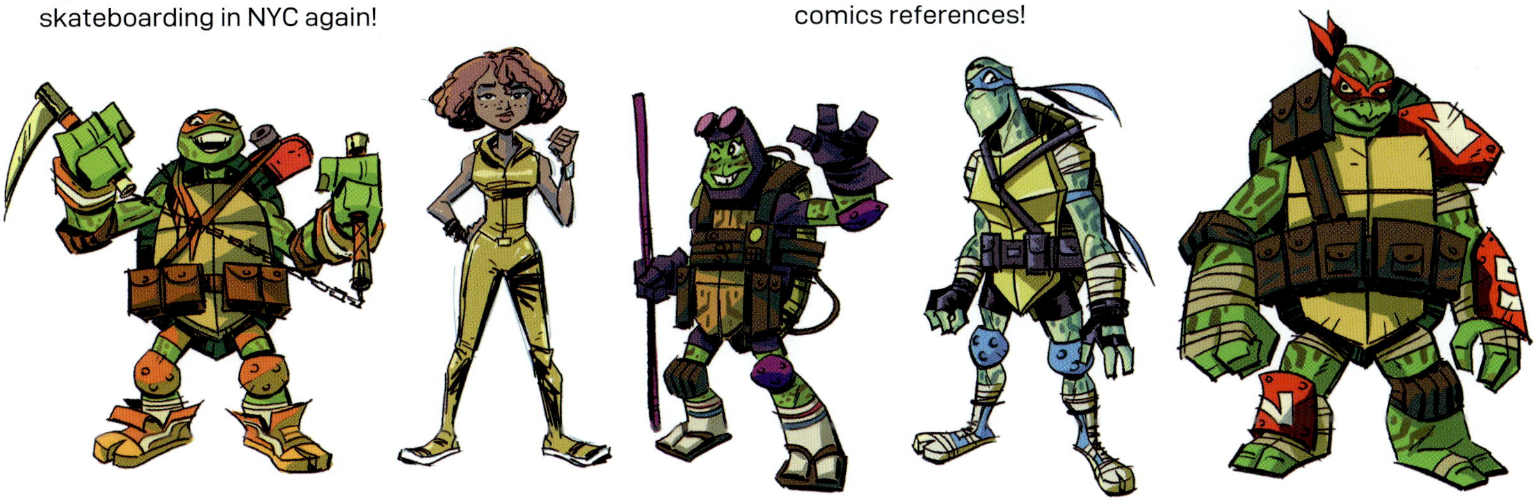

CHARACTER DESIGNS BY ANDY SURIANO (JULY 2016)

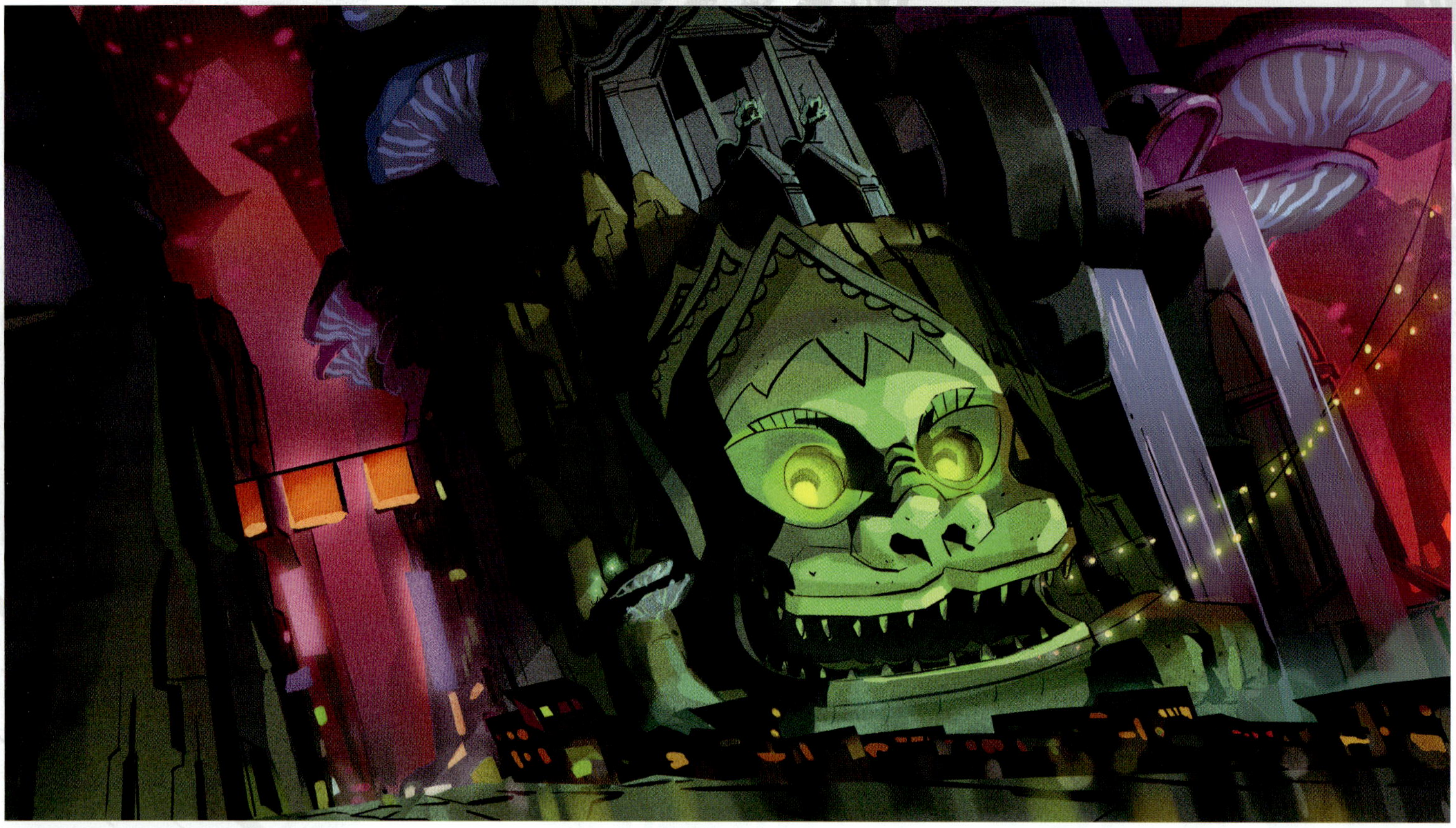

ANT WARD: We were tasked with working together, combining pitches, creating a new [story] bible, and proceeding with visual development. Nickelodeon really liked the direction we were going in, and we were off to the races.

ANDY SURIANO: Ant and I both worked on the 2012 series in different capacities. It was such a great series that when Nickelodeon came to us to make a new one, we said we very deliberately weren't interested in retreading that same material. We were also faced with the issue of timing: Ciro's series hadn't even been finished when they announced *Rise*. We needed to be a clear separate series, instead of a continuation of the former. We asked ourselves, "What haven't we seen the Turtles do yet?" and really leaned into that. We cited *Big Trouble in Little China* (1986) and *Hellboy* (2004) as inspiration.

ANT WARD: Andy and I were both fascinated by the idea of a hidden world or a hidden reality. We loved the notion of a secret fantasy realm that exists alongside humans and the direct juxtaposition of the bustle of New York, allowing kids to wonder what incredible things could be beneath each sewer lid and behind every corner. We were inspired by folk stories and myths from around the world. Elements of these would form the backbone of the Hidden City and our Yōkai. The initial inspiration came from some of Guillermo del Toro's work as well as classic adventures like *Big Trouble in Little China* (1986). Visually, as the show found its voice, we moved slightly away from the direct folklore and opened the possibilities of who the Yōkai of the Hidden City were.

ANDY SURIANO: Ant and I both have an affinity for science-fantasy art from the 1970s and '80s, and a complete obsession with Franco-Belgian comic *(bande dessinée)* art and artists from that relative time period as well. Knowing this was going to be a much lighter, humorous take on the franchise, we opted for brighter palettes vs. traditionally "dark and gritty" ones. The realism we sought came from the honest and emotional ways the characters interacted, giving our design approach an opportunity to be stylized and ambitious.

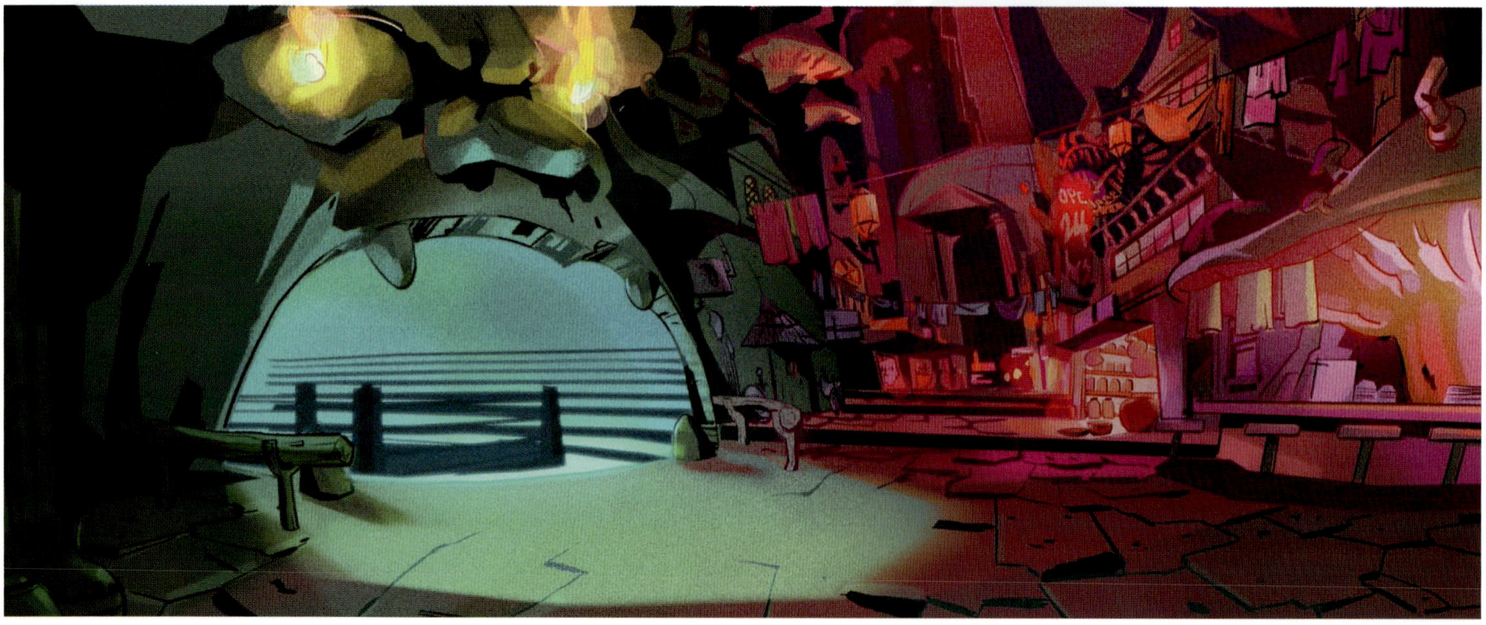

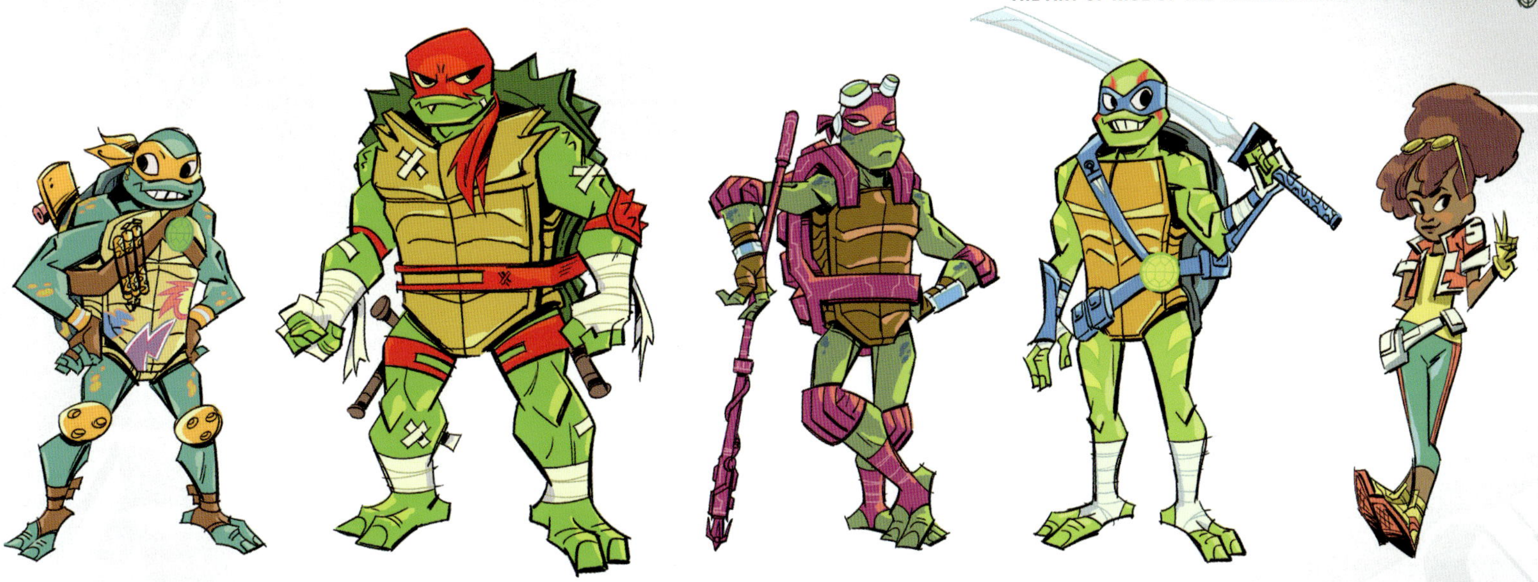

CHARACTER DESIGNS BY ANDY SURIANO (JANUARY 2017)

ANT WARD: Andy and I wanted *Rise* to be visually striking and distinct from the 2012 *TMNT*. We embraced a vibrant, modern New York color palette that married modernity with the traditional New York skyline. We wanted every frame to pop and be kinetic, even when there was no movement. We both loved European comics like *Valérian and Laureline* and '70s high fantasy artists like Philippe Druillet. Line quality, inking, and dynamic shapes were very important, as well as the heavy use of solid shadows to help lead the eye and frame action.

ANDY SURIANO: Approaching it from a design perspective, we thought that it would be great to separate the Turtles further beyond bandana colors. We wanted to make sure each brother was easily identifiable whether without color or even in complete silhouette. From a story perspective, this also helped us to separate each of their personalities even more by leaning into what were common associated traits with the specific species they were.

ANT WARD: Having spent many years as supervising producer on Ciro's *TMNT* and having a deep respect for Ciro, as well as a fondness for *Teenage Mutant Ninja Turtles* (2012), I wanted to ensure that almost every element of *Rise* would feel different and unique while still feeling inherently TMNT. The tone had to be different, as well as the color palette, format, medium, packaging in the toy aisle, and dynamics of the main cast. We wanted humor and brotherly banter to be front and center, especially in the early seasons—teenagers first, who would grow into being heroes.

ANDY SURIANO: From the outset, we sought to create a version of TMNT where the characters seemed like a genuine family, with a casualness and honesty to how they communicated with one another—using *It's Always Sunny in Philadelphia* as our north star, which also meant leaning into the comedy more, not just "action cartoon" funny. This sent us initially seeking out more comedic storyboard artists vs. action ones, but attempting to staff up like that was a disaster, because all of the directors and board artists we approached didn't believe their filmmaking styles would mesh with a franchise like TMNT. So, after exhausting all of those options, we had to pivot, which we did by hiring more traditionally action-focused board teams, then stacking a writers room with all comedy writers. These were the secret ingredients—visually incredible, groundbreaking action sequences, supported by the heart and humor we set out to make. It all comes down to chemistry, and by all rights, our little experiment shouldn't have worked as well as it did, but we ended up with just the right ingredients of skill and talent to create the series we did.

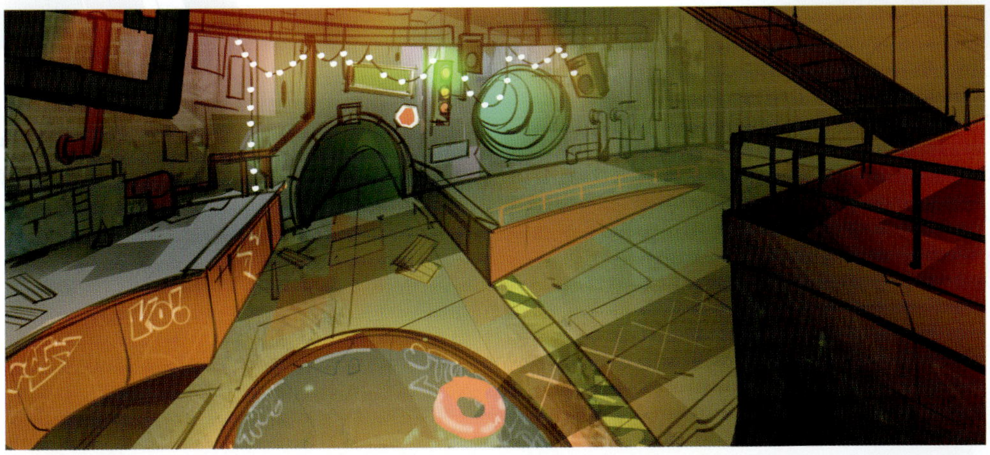

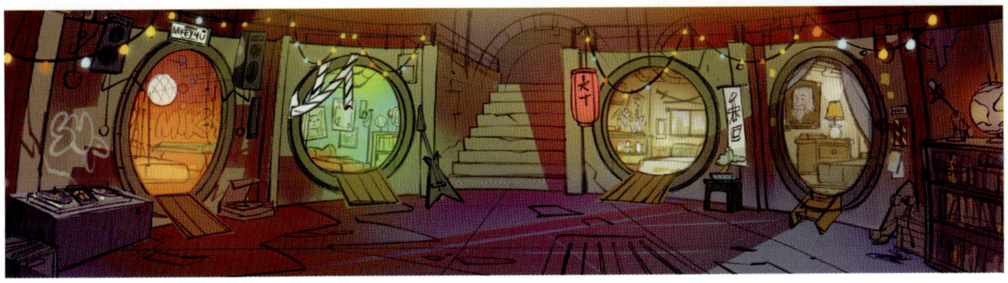

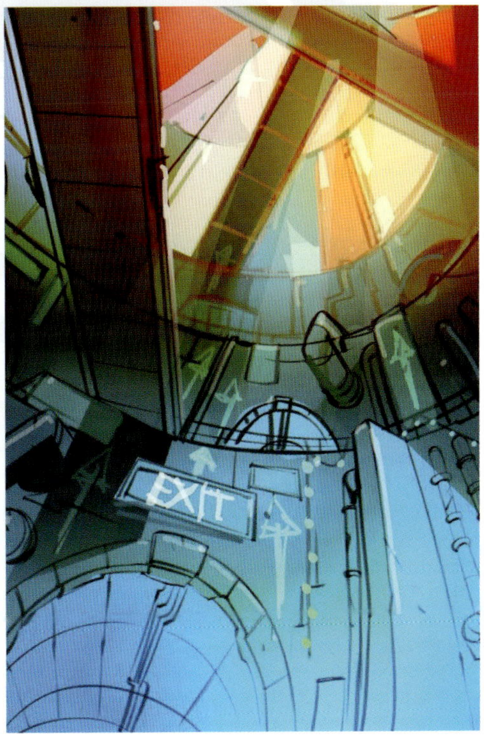

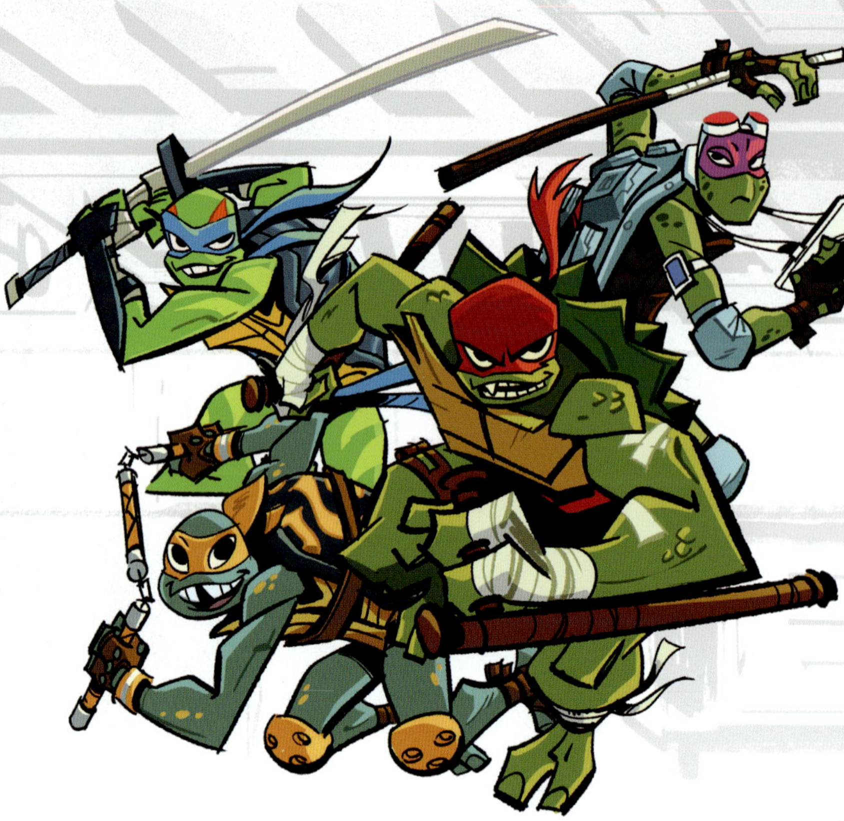

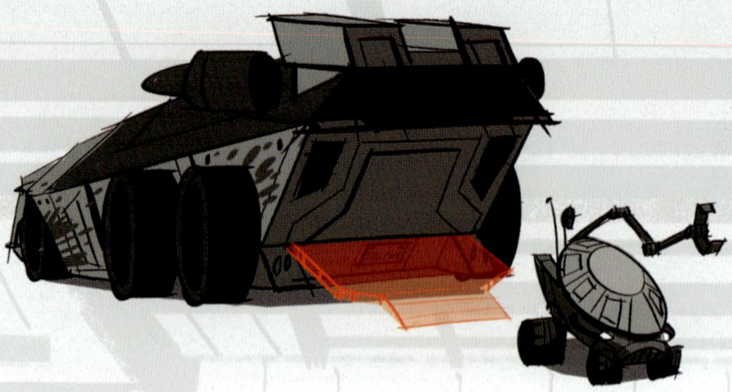

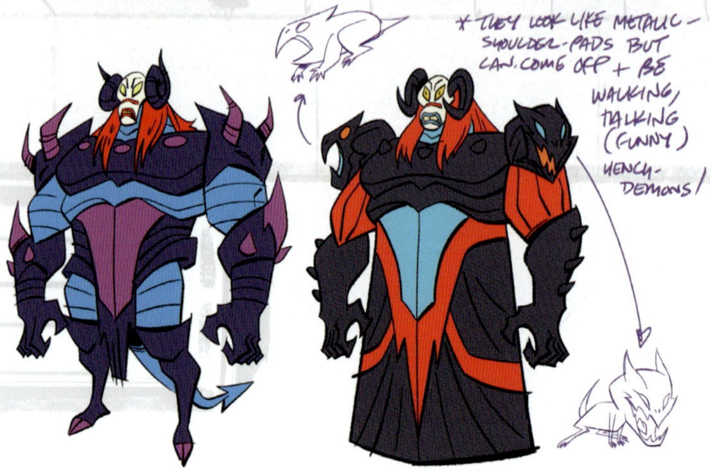

The early concept for Baron Draxum went by a different name: 'Moraxax.'

ANT WARD: Nickelodeon was excited about the new direction and was very supportive of what Andy and I wanted to do. They understood that this iteration needed to stand apart from previous iterations, especially since it was following the 2012 show so closely. We approached the show with the attitude that we did not want to repeat anything from previous iterations of TMNT, and that TMNT had already established the notion of multiverses between iterations. We were not strictly "rebooting" TMNT, we were reimagining it. All the other versions still exist and are each wonderful for different reasons.

ANDY SURIANO: I think the only major pushbacks we got were from the toy company, Playmates Toys—but our executives at Nickelodeon were very interested in a fresh take and departure from the status quo. I believe we had to make some assurances early on that they would all end up with the traditional weapons they're typically associated with. Ant and I had always intended for them to "graduate" to getting their contemporary weapons, as well as showing Leo's maturation to leadership (another thing that we weren't able to do with the show's sudden cancellation).

ANT WARD: The decision for each Turtle to be a different species was actually very organic. As soon as we had locked in on the Turtles' personalities and roles in the team, the species just started to make sense: With Raph being a snapping turtle—giant, spiky, aggressive looking—he would look like an intimidating big brother, but he was a softy on the inside. Donnie being a softshell turtle, having to build his tech and use his brain to compensate for his physical vulnerability and build out his shell. Mikey being a box turtle, able to put all his limbs completely inside his shell, it's very fun and playful. And Leo being a red-eared slider because of just his sheer sassiness.

ANDY SURIANO: We created two cast lists: one that would be expected, that fit within the previous lore, that sounded like the heroes you already knew...and then we had our second list. These were actors with such incredible range and personality, yet completely unexpected choices within the action genre. They were racially diverse as well as coming from several different backgrounds and disciplines. They were the found family we had sought to create from the beginning—a new, fresh take on 30-year-old characters. Since the beginning, Ant and I sought this diversity and ambition, out-of-the-box experimenting, and now I cannot imagine these characters any other way. These performers brought so much fresh nuance and individuality to the characters that we wrote to the actors' strengths, their

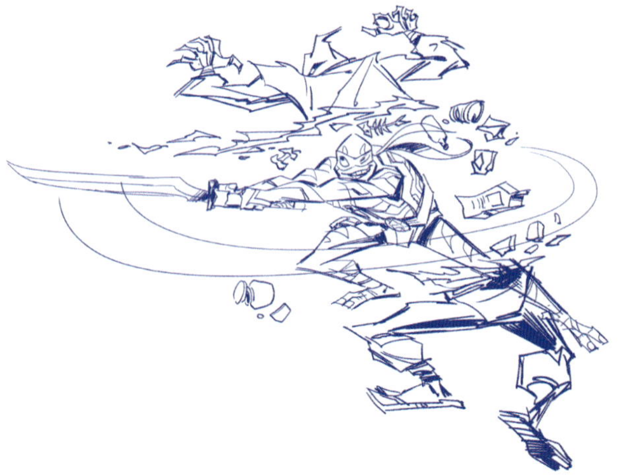

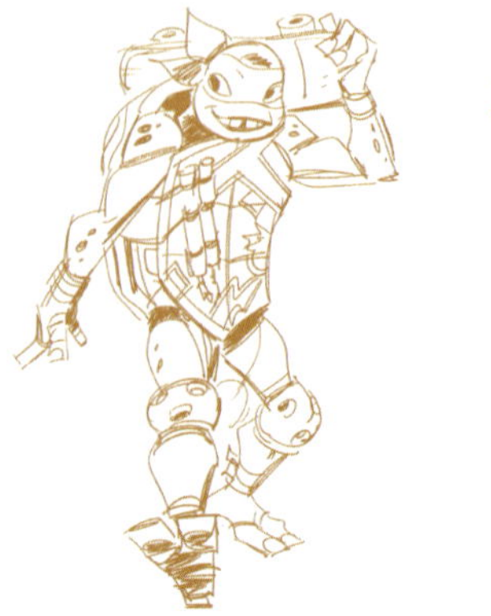

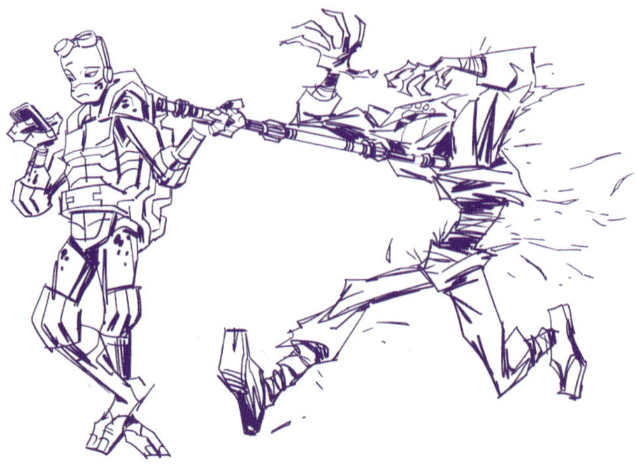

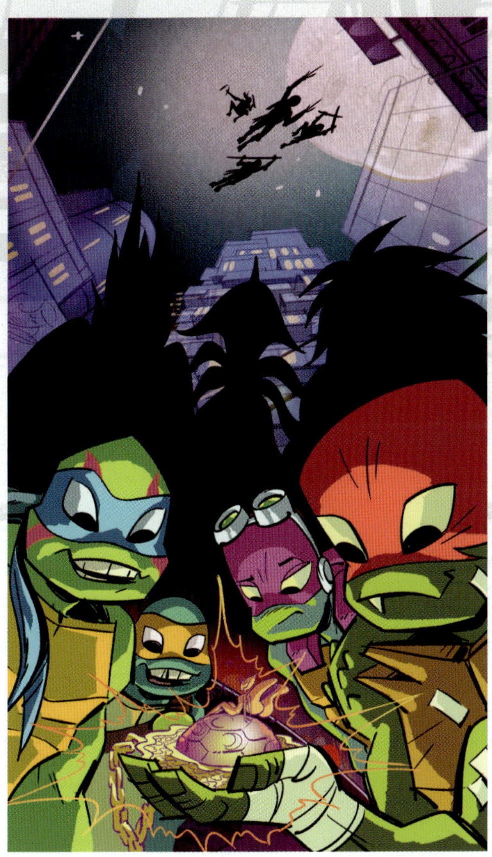

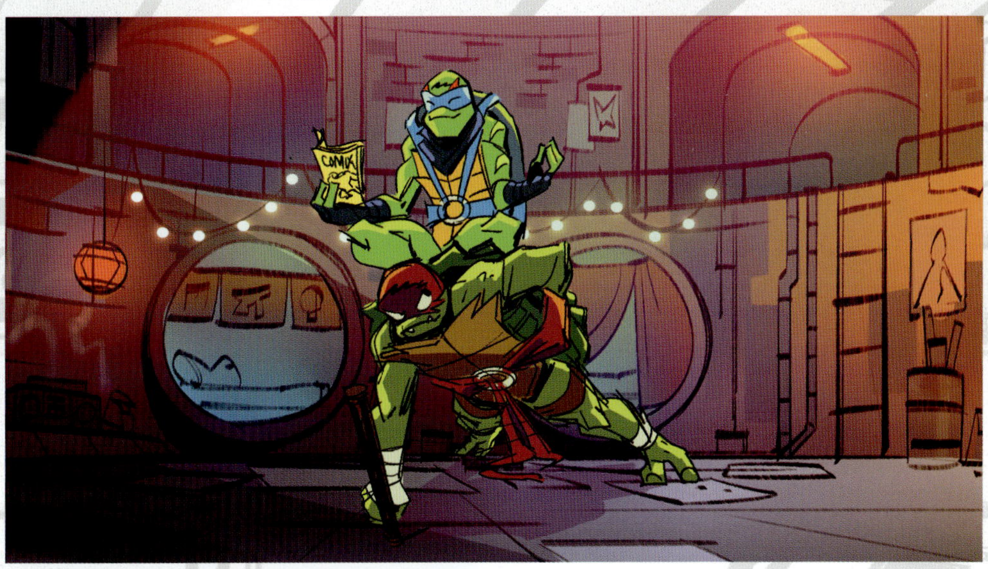

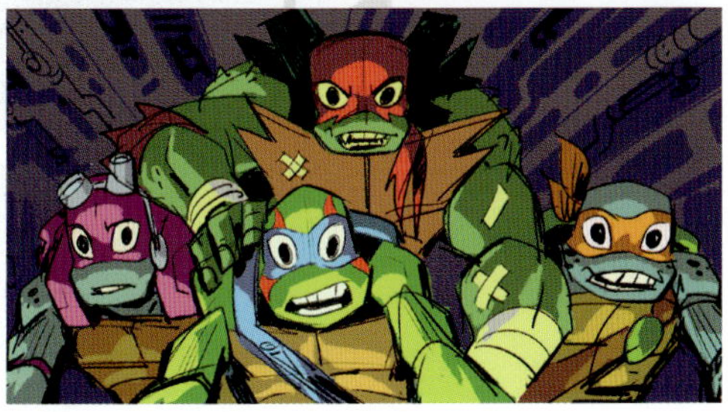

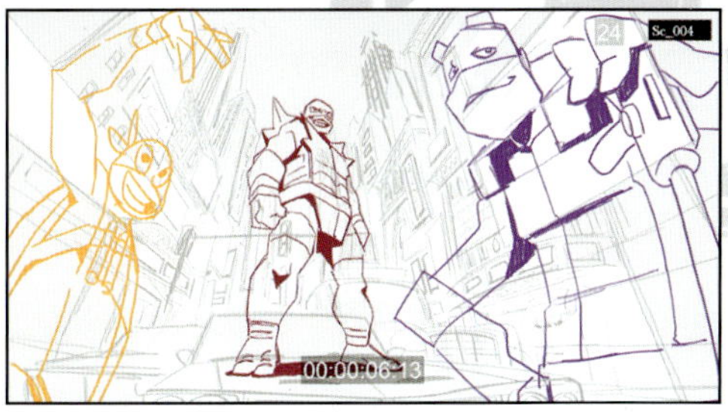

improvisational talents, suggestions they each brought, and vocal skills—informing us storytellers and propelling these characters into situations we hadn't yet even thought of.

ANDY SURIANO: As a designer, it was my dream to create new characters for such an evergreen property and contribute to that sandbox. As a writer, deviating from the classic series villains gave us an opportunity to keep our stories fresh, the outcomes unknown, and integrate these new creations so they seemed like they'd been in the franchise forever. Characters like Repo Mantis, Sloppy Joseph, Big Mama, Bullhop, and Meat Sweats (named after my appearance post–meatball eating contest) were all completely brand-new designs, yet hopefully timeless and seamless enough to feel like they've always been with the Turtles universe since Day One. We created Baron Draxum to be a troubled warrior scientist that was directly connected to the Turtles' (and Splinter's) mutations and as a way to prolong the inevitable appearance (and showdown) with "the" Shredder. We always knew we were going to reveal him eventually. That being said, Shredder was one of my first and almost completely untouched designs (I think I gave him a tail at one point) from our initial series pitch: "more monster than man"—a being so powerful that a 4v1 fight would be more than warranted. We always knew we wanted his armor to tie into a Krang past/future plot, so I was pleased we got to at least hint and show a bit of that head canon.

ANT WARD: We were more interested in creating new and unique characters for *Rise*. The TMNT library of characters is extensive, but we only drew from that library when it felt natural to take our own unique approach to the characters.

ANDY SURIANO: Each ability tells a story, so we started with their personalities to match their new mystic power. In our version, Leo was a fast-talking hustler, so teleportation seemed an apt fit. Raph being our huge "protector" brother, what better way to visually support that than armor? Mikey has a go-with-the-flow, bouncy personality, so his power has the ability to make even the heaviest objects movable. Donnie was our one holdout, choosing tech over mystic. We had an idea that Donnie was actually the most adept at mysticism but just never tried—whereas Leo's false confidence would lead to his powers being unpredictable.

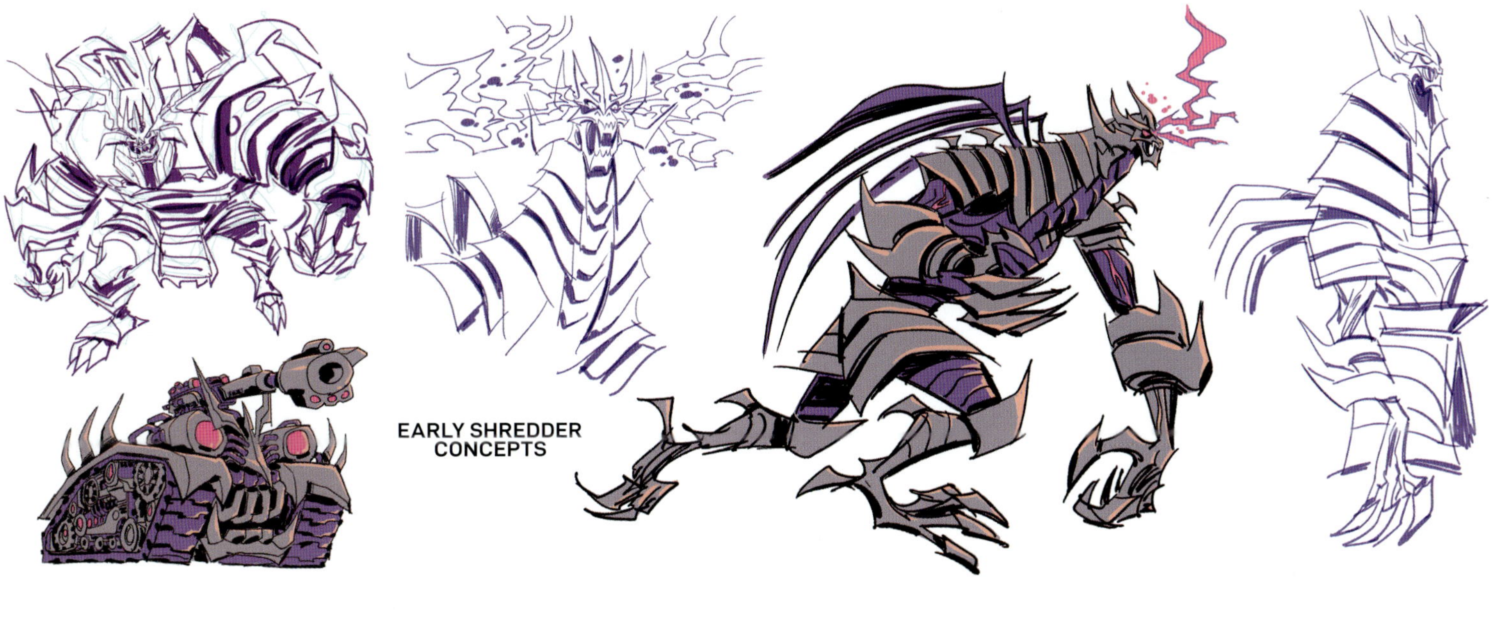

EARLY SHREDDER CONCEPTS

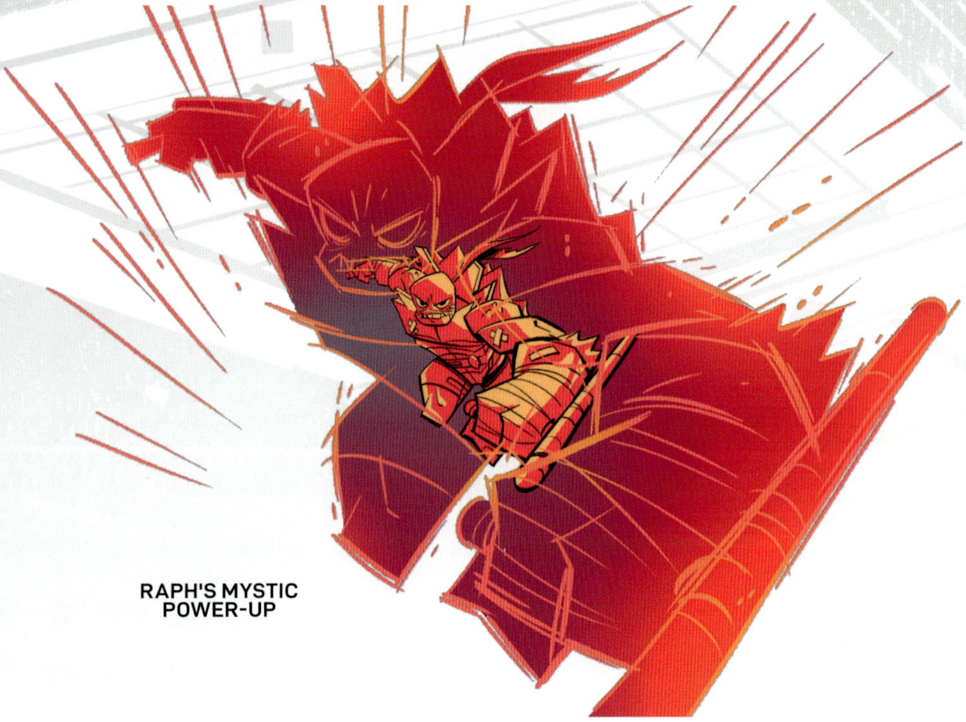

RAPH'S MYSTIC POWER-UP

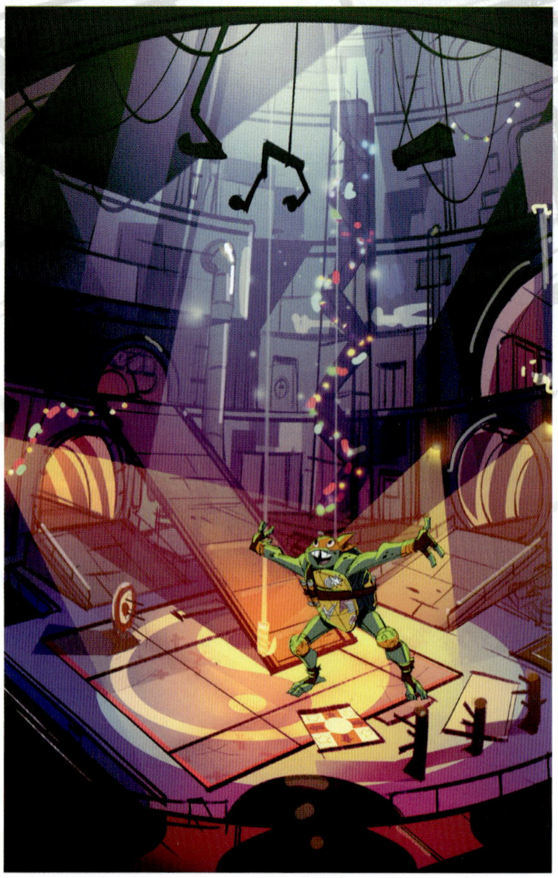

ANT WARD: Raph's tonfas would give him the ability to create a larger-than-life construct of himself, highlighting his protectiveness over his brothers and his role as the elder brother. Donnie utilizes his genius to create the most elaborate tech imaginable through his Tech-Bō. Mikey with the kusari-fundō being incredibly playful, again highlighting the youngest and most exuberant aspects of his personality. Leo being able to teleport with his sword felt right. He's sassy and someone who you can't quite keep down in one place; he's popping in and out, wisecrack after wisecrack. You can never quite catch him. It's very Bugs Bunny.

ANDY SURIANO: Both Ant and I are fathers of two boys, so I think in some ways it was our own experiences that lent to Splinter's. From Day One, we had always planned on having his character evolve to what he became. It was funny and endlessly frustrating seeing the fandom react to Splinter like they did at the beginning, because we always knew where he'd end up, so it was like, "Just wait! You will see!"

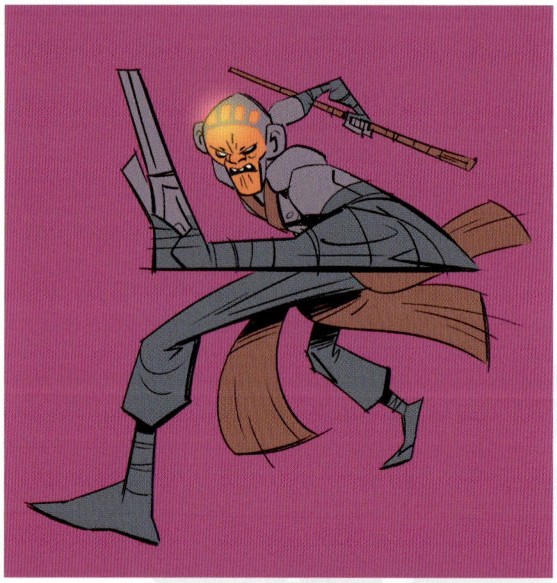

ANT WARD: To be honest, from a selfish perspective, Splinter's arc was a huge part of *Rise*'s story for me, and I am so grateful we were able to finish telling it. I had pursued my passion for animation from a very young age, using it as a distraction from some of the things happening at home. It was my escapism and my drive. Later, when I was to have kids, there was a lot of self-reflection and questioning of my identity. If my pursuit of a career in animation had been a sole defining characteristic, how would this extended family play a role in my identity? And it was learning to become a father that helped me grow beyond my identity as my career. Much like Splinter, he became Lou Jitsu to escape the trauma of his mother leaving him, thinking that Lou Jitsu was his defining identity, only to realize the importance of family.

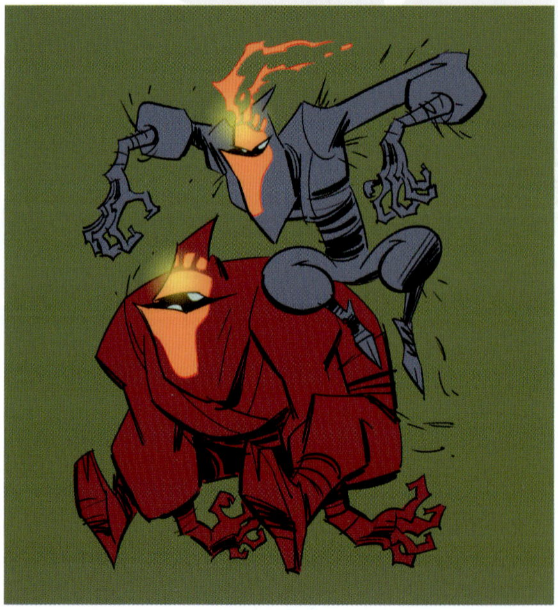

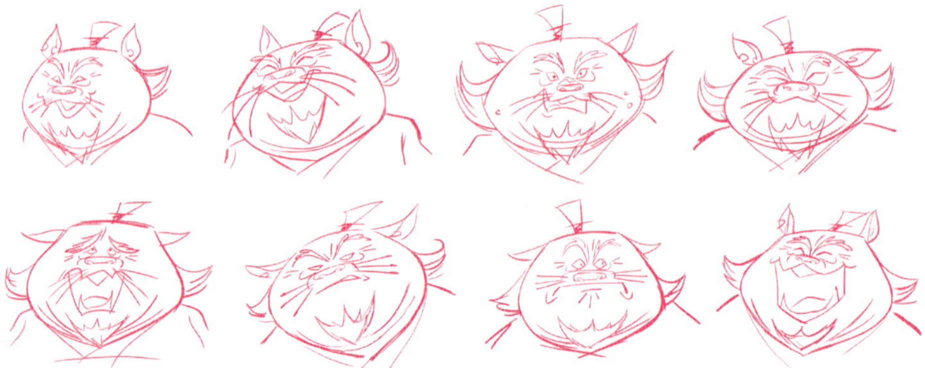

SPLINTER EXPRESSION SHEET

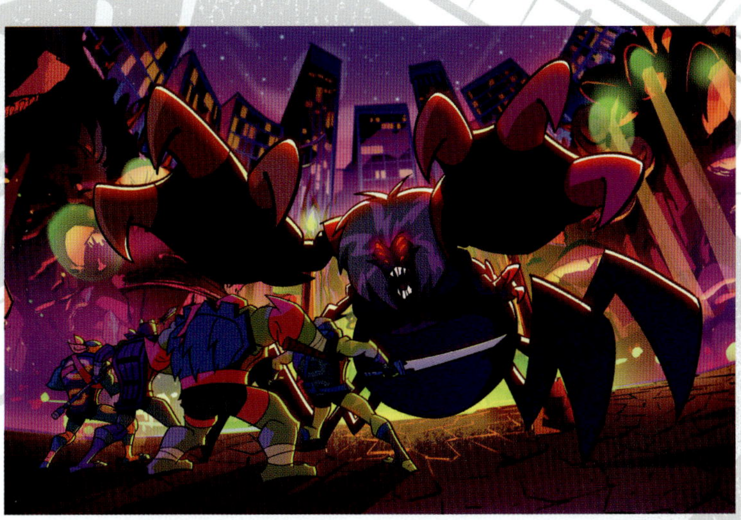

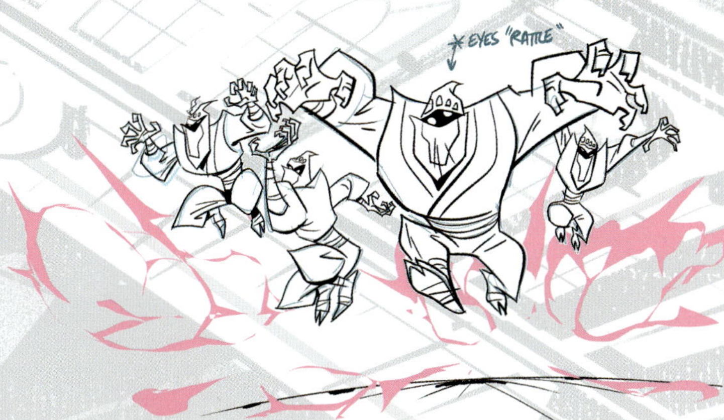

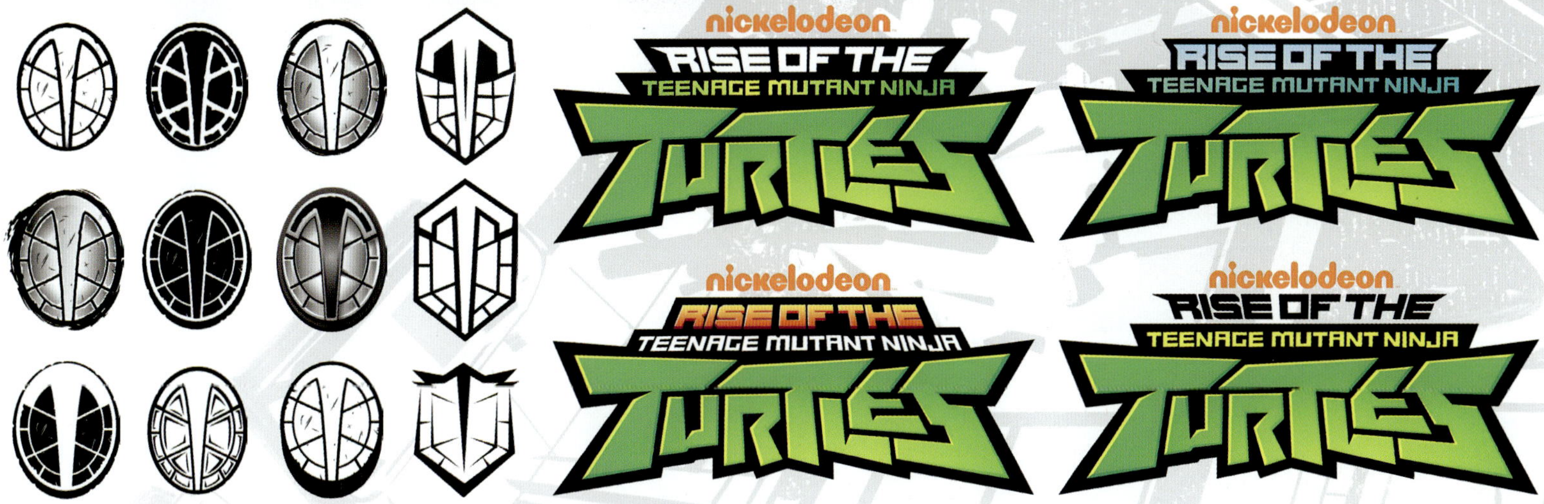

UNUSED LOGO CONCEPTS

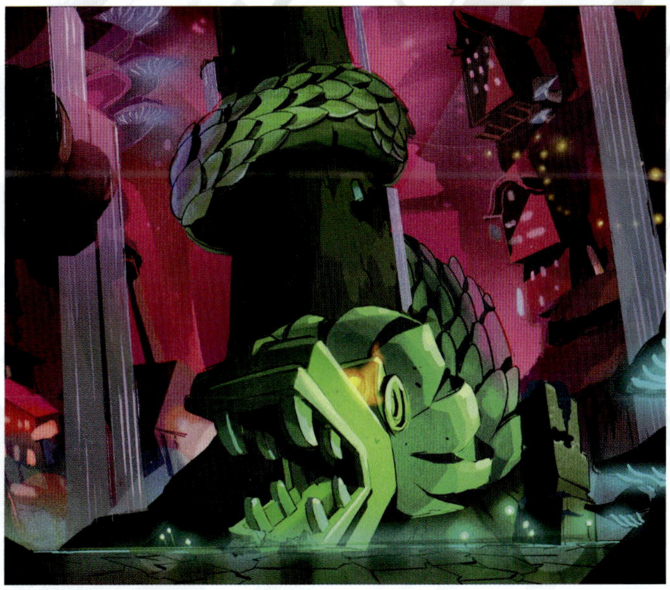

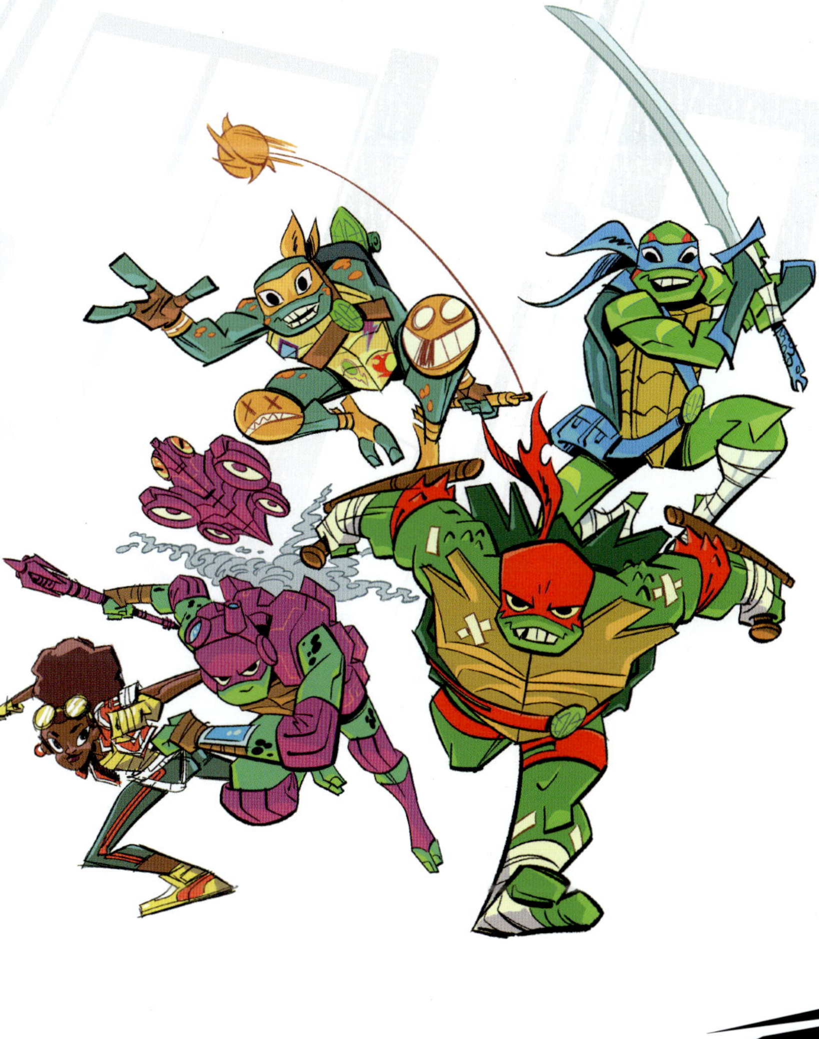

ANDY SURIANO: I feel so grateful to be able to tell the story we wanted to (albeit a much more truncated version), to be able to bring a fresh take to such an evergreen property, and to make something with the heart, humor, and spectacle it did have.

ANT WARD: The development of *Rise* was really a once-in-a-lifetime opportunity. Andy and I were on the same page from the beginning of what we wanted to do. We were able to assemble one of the best teams in the industry to help us create it, and we had incredible support during development from Nickelodeon, which allowed us to have fun, be playful, and take the franchise in a unique direction. Mad Dogs for life!

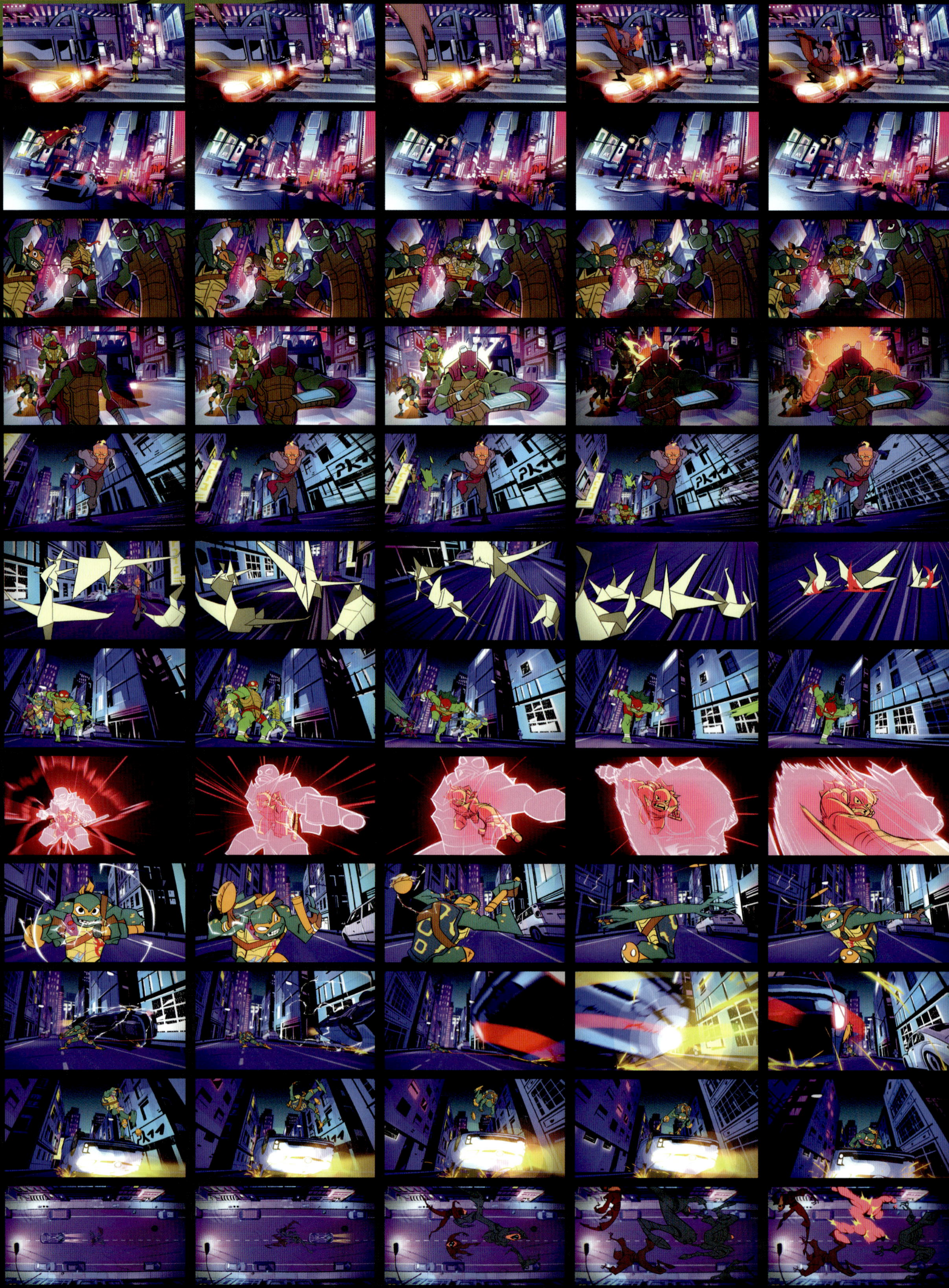

ANIMATION BY **THE LINE**

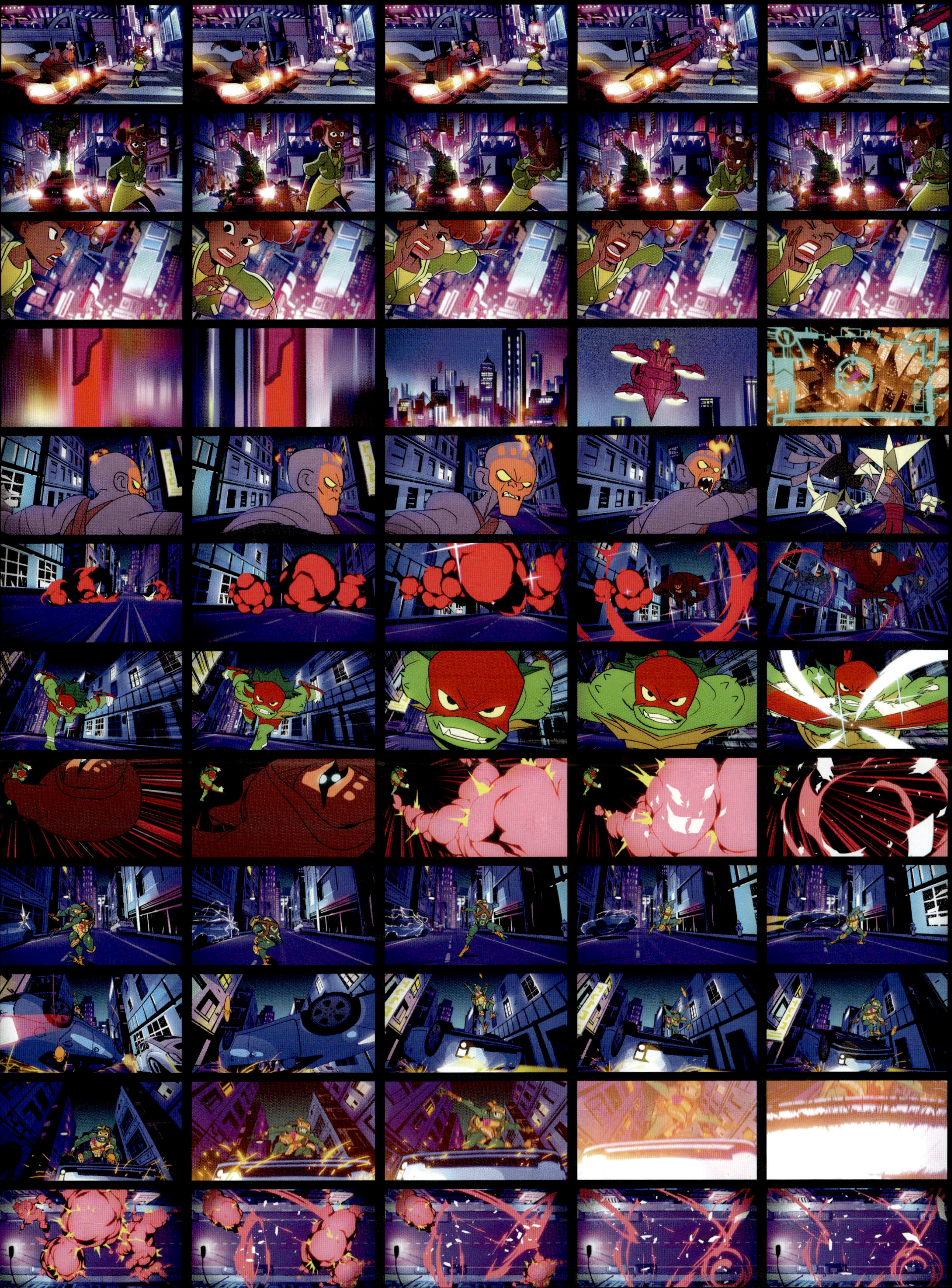

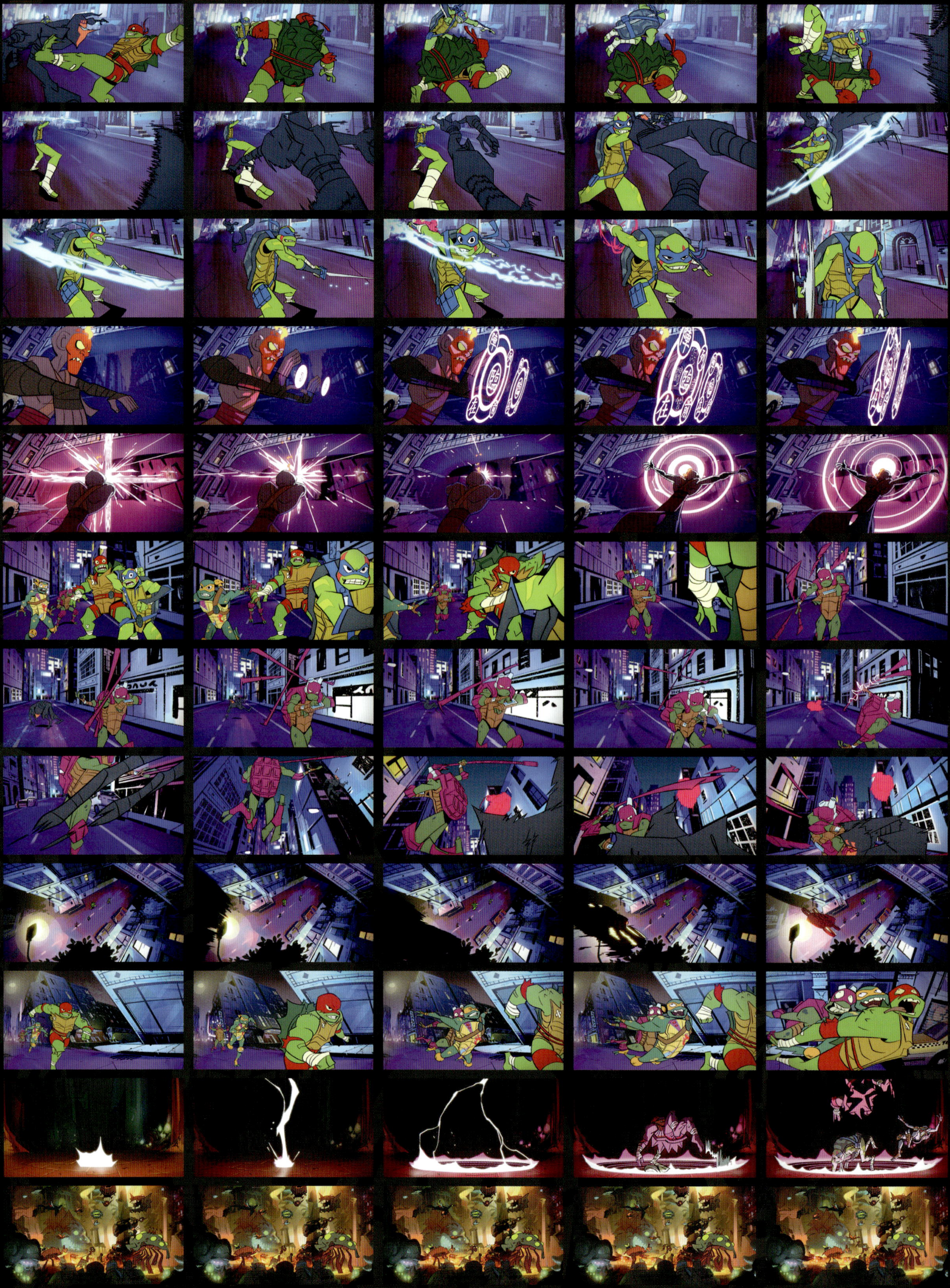

ANIMATION BY **THE LINE**

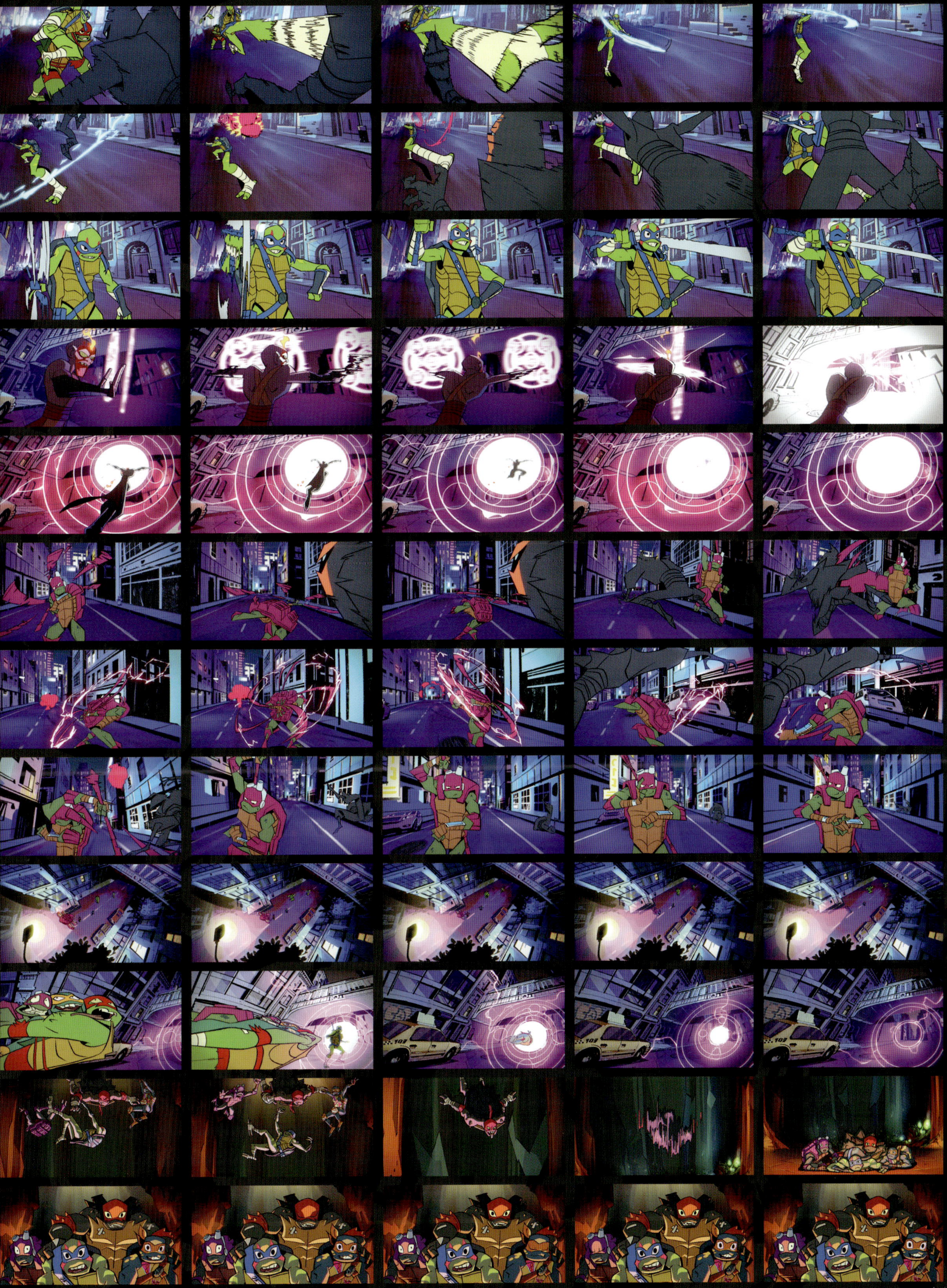

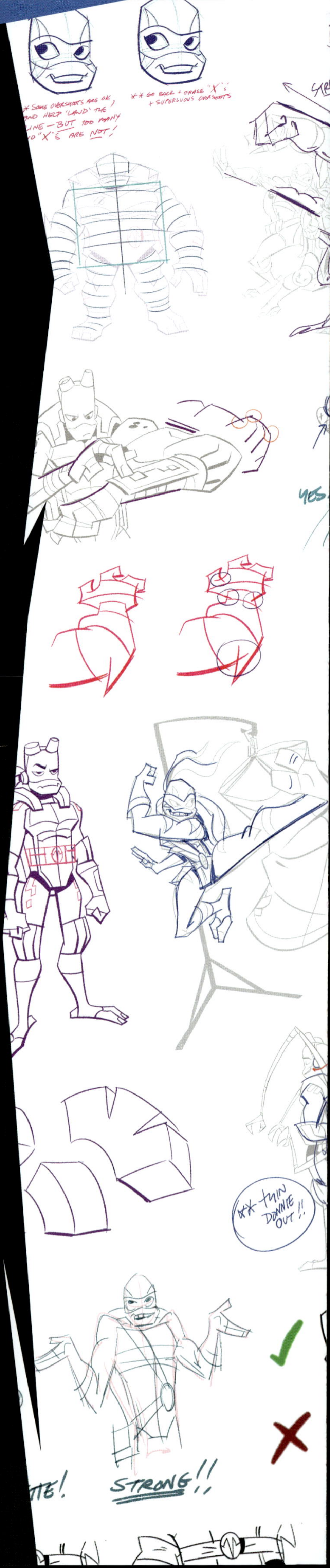

nickelodeon
RISE OF THE TEENAGE MUTANT NINJA TURTLES

THE *RISE* STYLE GUIDE

Andy Suriano's character designs are instantly recognizable—bold, dynamic, and full of personality. From *The Powerpuff Girls* (1998) and *Samurai Jack* (2001) to *Star Wars: Clone Wars* (2003), *My Life as a Teenage Robot* (2002), *Mickey Mouse* (2013), *DuckTales* (2017), and many more, he has left his mark on some of animation's most iconic series and characters. His work is a master class in creating designs that are not only visually striking but tell a story all on their own, blending bold shapes, dynamic poses, and a sense of humor that leaps off the screen.

So, how do you craft a style that leaps off the screen? In this chapter, we're pulling back the curtain to show you the rules, guidelines, and creative decisions that shaped the unique look of *Rise of the Teenage Mutant Ninja Turtles*. From distinctive silhouettes to expressive poses, you'll get an inside look at how Suriano and the team brought this vibrant vision to life. Whether you're a fan or an artist, these materials are a great resource for studying the design choices that made *Rise* stand out from the rest.

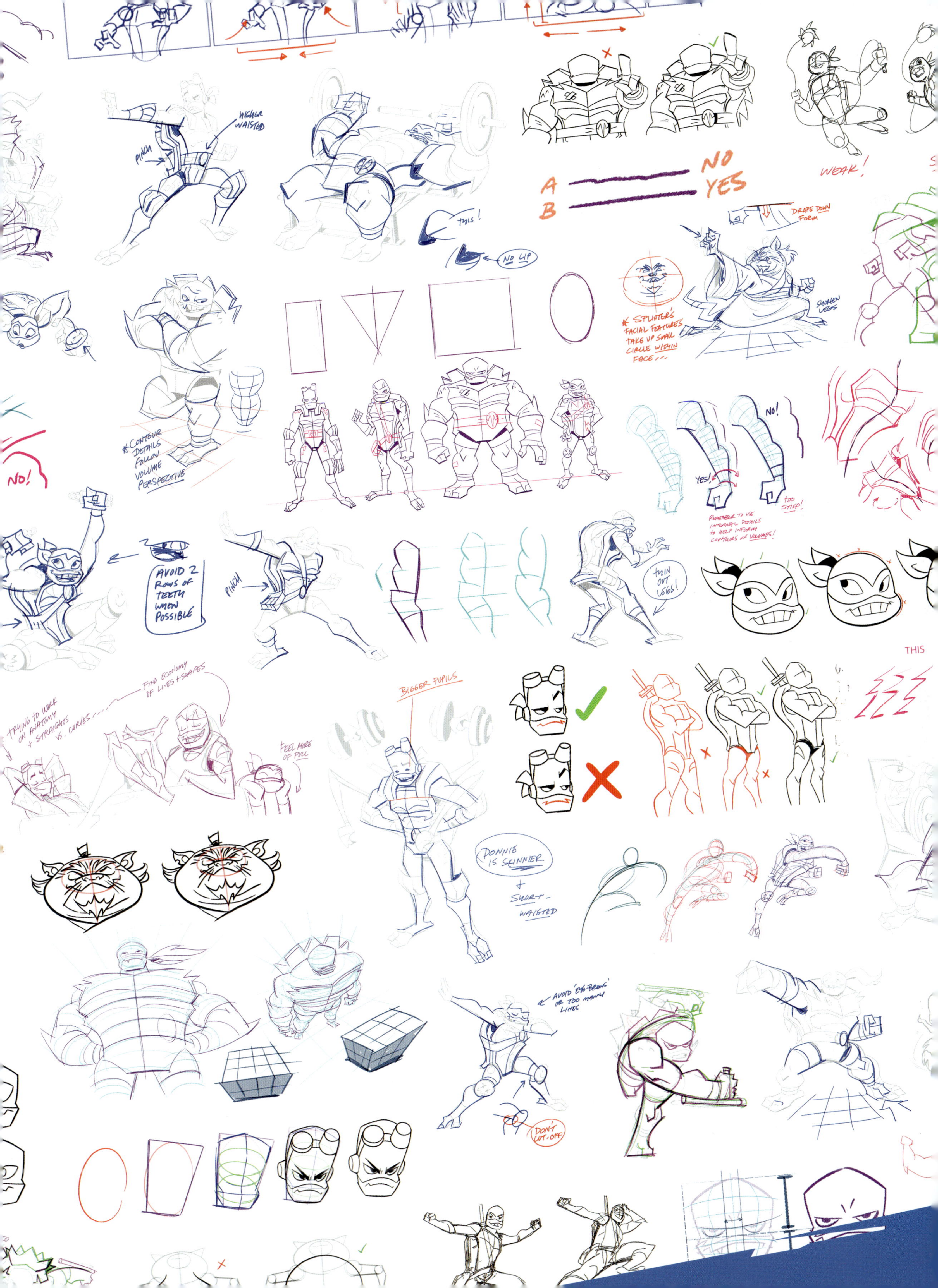

HIGHER WAISTED
PINCH
THIS!
NO LIP
A
B
NO
YES
WEAK!
DRAPE DOWN FORM
* SPLINTER'S FACIAL FEATURES TAKE UP SMALL CIRCLE WITHIN FACE...
SHORTEN LEGS
* CONTOUR DETAILS FOLLOW VOLUME PERSPECTIVE
NO!
NO!
YES!
TOO STIFF!
REMEMBER TO USE INTERNAL DETAILS TO HELP INFORM CONTOURS OF VOLUMES!
AVOID 2 ROWS OF TEETH WHEN POSSIBLE
PINCH
THIN OUT LEGS!
THIS
TRYING TO WORK ON ANATOMY + STRAIGHTS VS. CURVES.....
FIND ECONOMY OF LINES + SHAPES
FEEL MORE OF PULL
BIGGER PUPILS
DONNIE IS SKINNIER + SHORT-WAISTED
AVOID 'EYEBROWS' OR TOO MANY LINES
DON'T CUT OFF

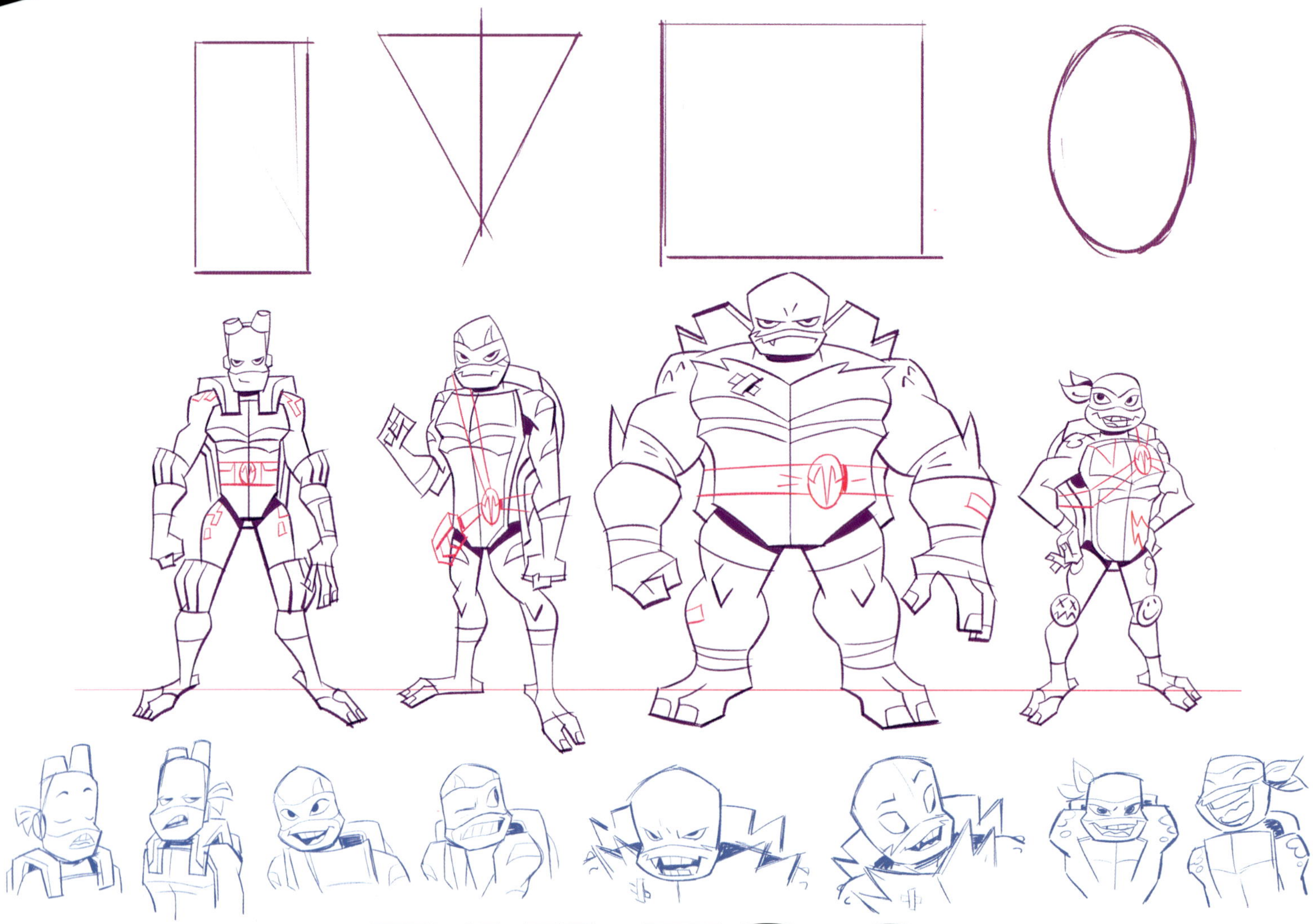

RULES & GUIDELINES

A BEHIND-THE-SCENES LOOK AT THE RULES USED BY THE CREW

This next section will cover specific design rules and principles that defined the unique visual look of *Rise of the Teenage Mutant Ninja Turtles*. Think of these as the essential cheat sheets, the core style guide, or even the show's visual bible. We'll break down the recurring elements—from line quality and shape usage to dynamic posing and environment integration—that ensured consistency and captured the show's distinct, energetic spirit across every frame.

ANDY SURIANO: Simpler, cleaner designs were definitely possible for the *Rise* Turtles—ones using far fewer lines packed with detail. But the final designs you see survived a brutal process of feedback, revisions, and deliberate additions. Much to the toy company's chagrin, we replaced the typical bulging muscles with more sophisticated lines, oblique, sharp angles, and an overall sleeker aesthetic. Utilizing shape language theory, we assigned each Turtle a distinct, easily identifiable overall shape that matched their core personality traits. While viewers might not be overtly aware of the philosophy of shape language, they nevertheless "feel" and respond to the subconscious emotion each shape evokes by association.

Raph was the eldest, strongest, and most reliable, hence the sturdiness of a square. Leo's sharp wit, quips, and barbs are supported by recurring triangles in his design, while Mikey's kinetically frenetic attitude bounces around like the circles he's built with. Donnie's rectangles were meant to evoke symmetric microchips, along with his short-waisted leanness.

When we first revealed the series' designs, the reaction was instant and loud: "What?! Hell no!" Immediate comparisons to *Teen Titans Go!* (2013) flooded in, with many assuming the show would ditch action for pure comedy. Yet that initial shock wave quickly gave way to something incredible: a surge of fan passion. The bold, stylized look, once questioned, became a rallying point. Fans didn't just accept it, they embraced it—dissecting the shape language, celebrating the expressiveness, and fueling an endless wave of fan art that proved these unique turtles had found their fiercely devoted audience.

LINE QUALITY

Rise is a fairly line-heavy show—a lot of linework will show in the painted backgrounds. Therefore, it is important to try your best to maintain a consistent approach to shape and line quality.

We are primarily using only one brush for background design. We like our lines to be confident and calligraphic. For straights, it is okay to Shift + drag the brush for some lines. Every so often we try to freehand some lines to loosen up the drawing and to avoid the backgrounds looking too rigid.

40pt

Make sure your brush size is large enough to see the texture. That will allow you to have a good amount of variation in a brushstroke.

10pt

Using too small of a brush size tends to create uniform lines. Artists have gotten overly fussy or "scratchy" with their drawings when using too small of a brush.

Quick and Confident vs. Slow and Wobbly

When possible, try to make curves a smooth, confident line. If needed, you can use "chisel" or use more than one stroke to create a curve. Sometimes a French curve is used to ensure a smooth curve and confident line.

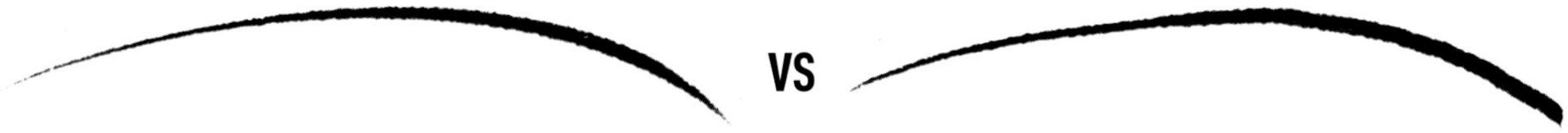

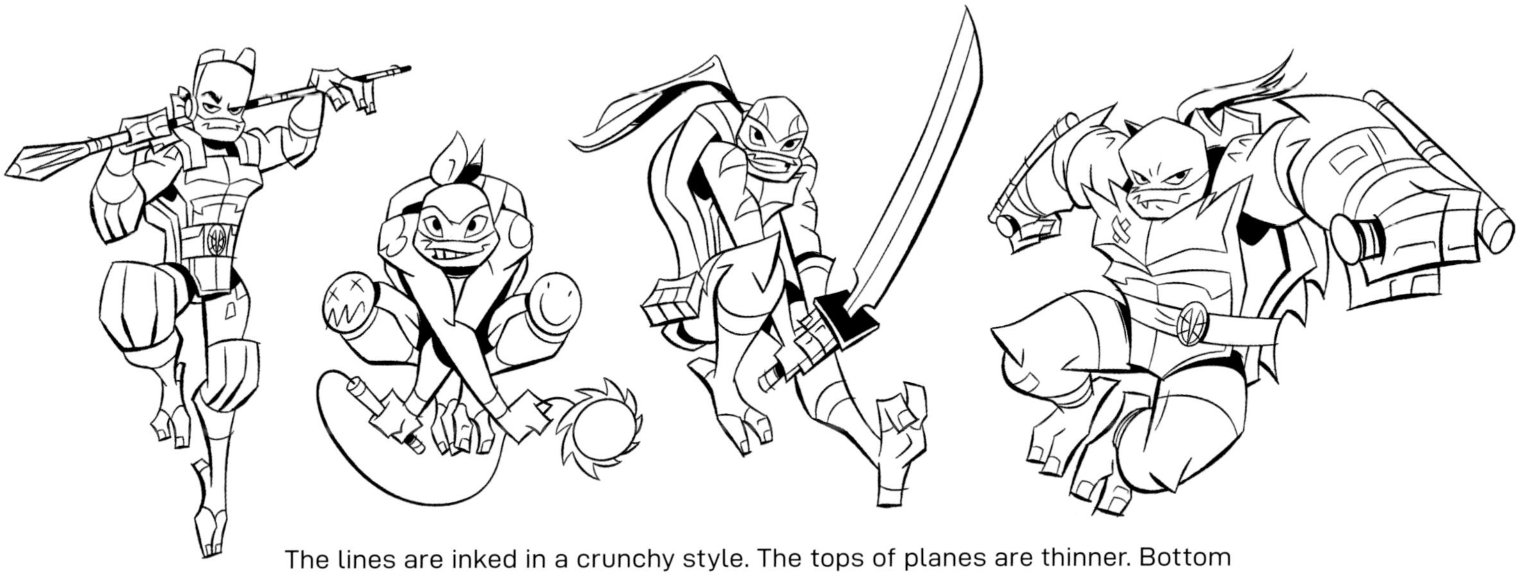

The lines are inked in a crunchy style. The tops of planes are thinner. Bottom areas are bolder to signify weight. All interior lines should be the thinnest. Apply some overshoot lines, but keep this to a minimum. Facial detailing is thin and delicate. Avoid getting too bold.

Line Detail

Depending on the size of the detail in a layout, sometimes we use a thick line to describe information that would require a lot of linework so as not to look "scratchy."

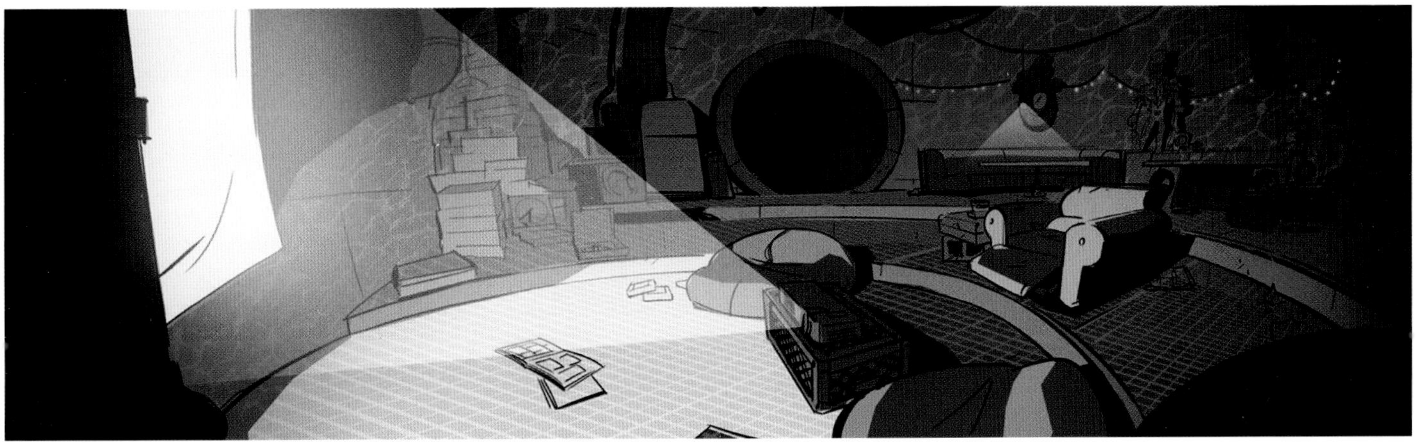

TONE

Layout artists are occasionally responsible for giving a tone pass for painters to key off of. Not every background has to have a tone pass. We mainly use the large black shapes in our tone pass to hide and minimize line mileage in the background. We also use tone as a compositional tool to lead the viewer's eyes to the center of attention.

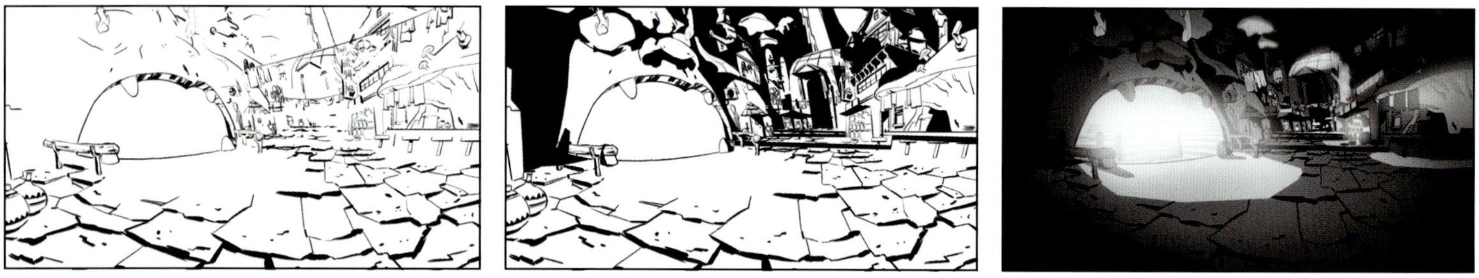

Here is an example of the three stages of a tone pass. For a major key, layout artists will go as far as doing a lighting and FX pass. For the most part, avoiding gradients in a tone pass helps to keep the background graphics and with a clear read.

Lighting

A good thing to attempt when designing a background is creating interesting lighting schemes that help frame the center of focus. Think of a stage light hitting a film set and how the light affects the surfaces facing the light, surfaces turned away from the light and interesting shadows.

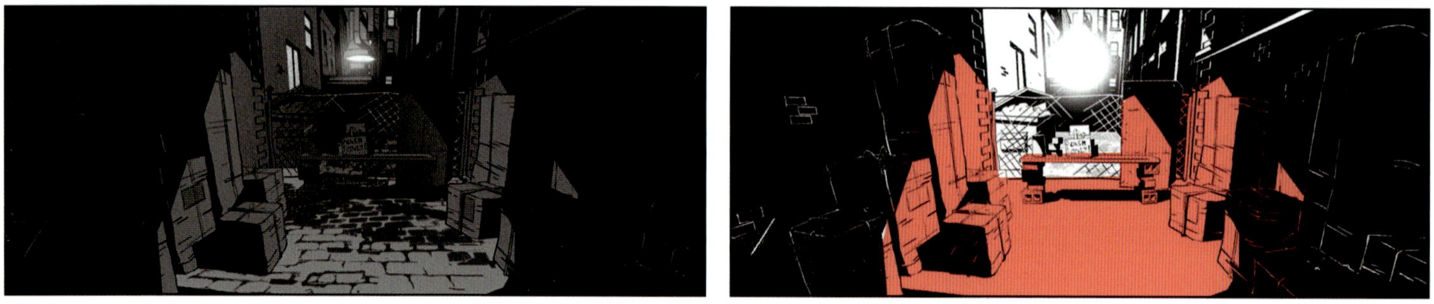

"Stylized" vs. "Wonk"

We are trying to stylize our backgrounds by publishing perspectives. What we are trying to avoid is an arbitrary perspective, which we call "wonk."

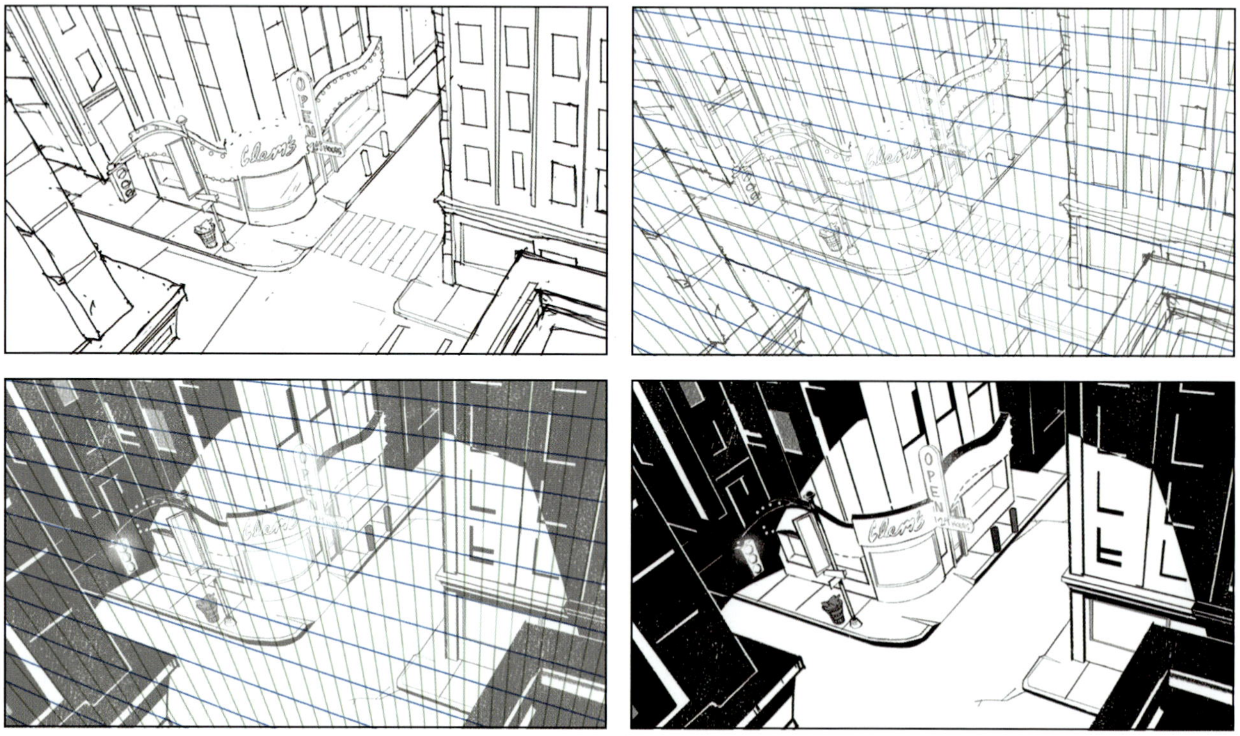

Above is an artist's rough pass at the background, which had too many skewed angles (especially in the windows) and too much detail falling off the perspective grid. The perspective was corrected in the cleanup/inking stage.

COLOR AND TEXTURE

We try to keep color and texture fairly simple, letting the bold choices and fun lighting FX do the heavy lifting. Focus on keeping color choices for backgrounds minimal: three to four colors, keeping some dominant, with the extras peppered throughout to accent and ground the scene.

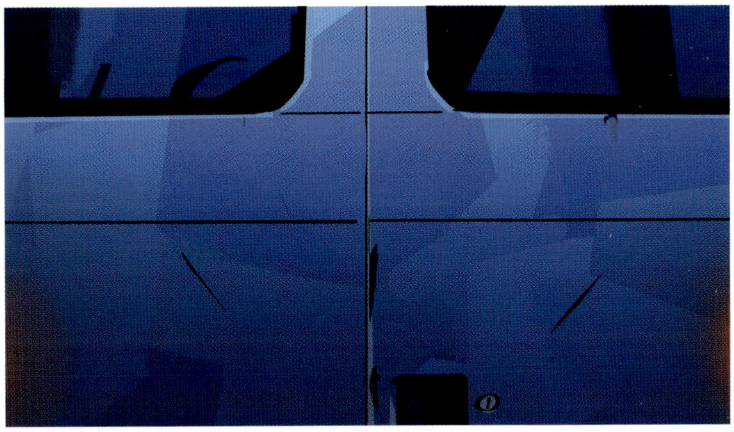

Block Plane Blender

For an easy way of adding variation to flat surfaces, such as wells, floors, ceilings, tables, car doors, etc. It can even be used as a nice lighting flare—just set it to Overlay or Color Dodge.

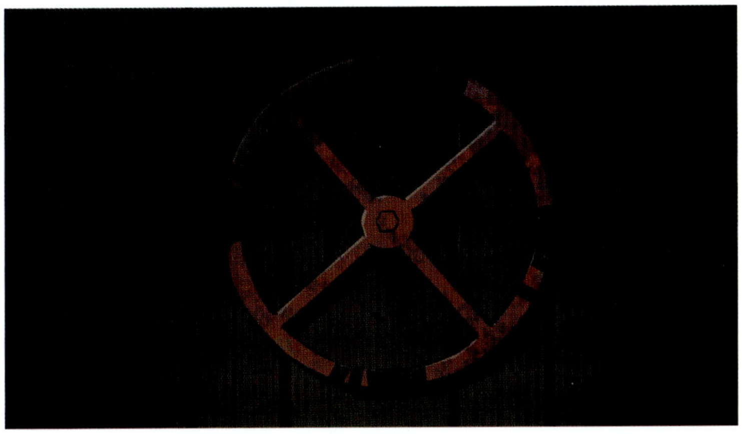

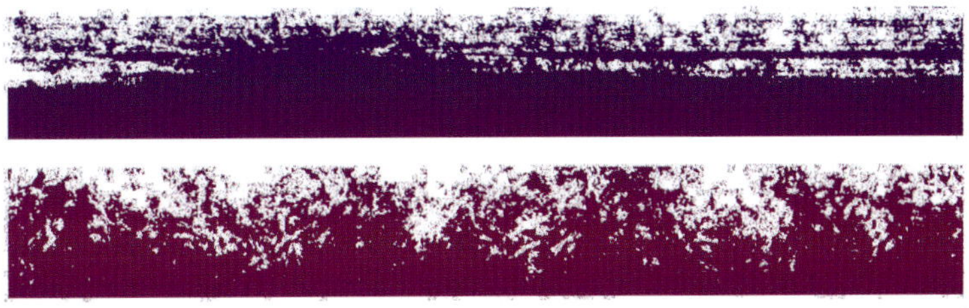

Scatter Brushes

Be sure to soften/blend some of the edges to indicate some texture for surface materials like concrete, wood, metals, etc. It can also be used for general wear and tear. Try to keep textures subtle so things don't look too busy.

BRICKS, GRAFFITI, STAINS, DUST, ETC.

To help sell the different surfaces, these are just some of the special brushes we use to make the world feel lived in.

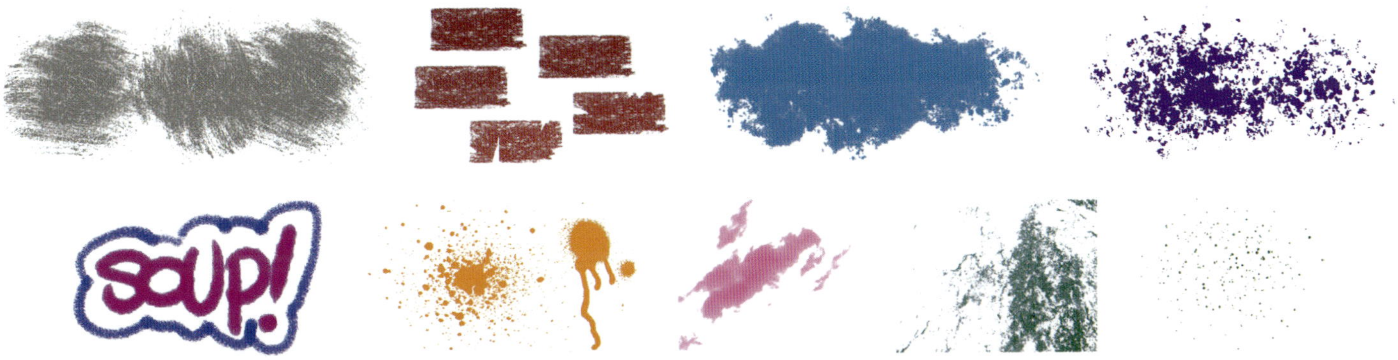

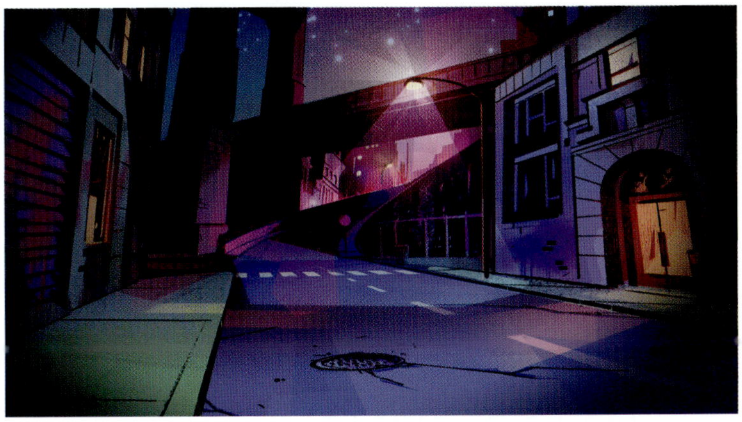

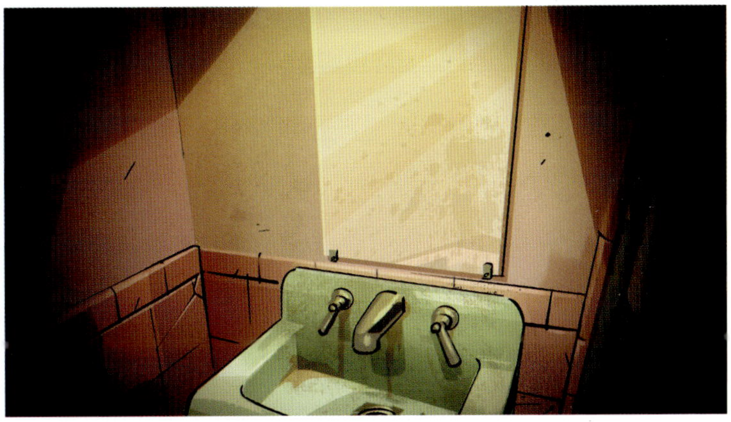

LIGHTING AND FX

Keep lighting in a separate folder for a nondestructive paint workflow. Experiment with interesting light shapes and avoid adjustment layers to keep colors and lighting deliberate. Try out different blending modes to help bring out the contrast. We usually use Screen, Overlay, and Color Dodge.

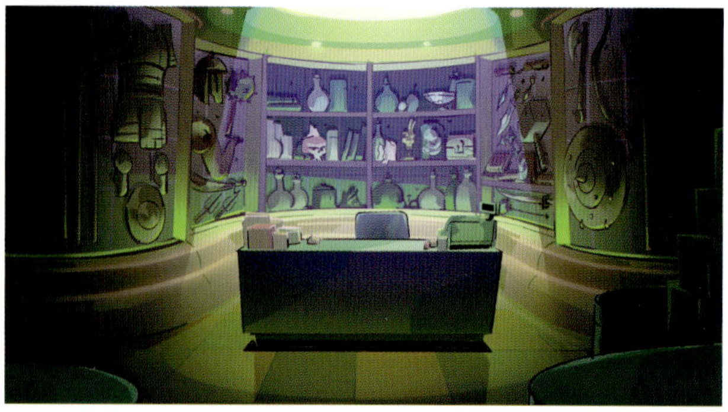

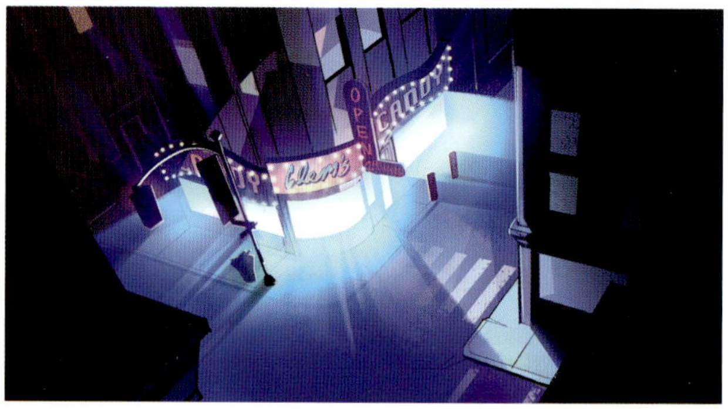

LIGHT FLARES

Use these brushes to add a bit of "flair" to the scene! Experiment with blend modes to get the best result and help things pop! Try using a mask and erasing out part of the flare to give it some transparency. Apply a motion blur to the lights to give the FX some life!

LIGHT RAYS

Use the Lasso or Pen tool to create shapes for light rays. Soften the edges by applying a motion blur. This technique can be used for any light source or reflection.

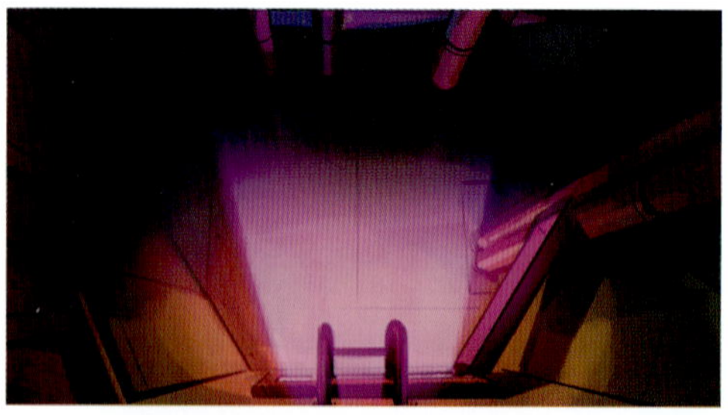

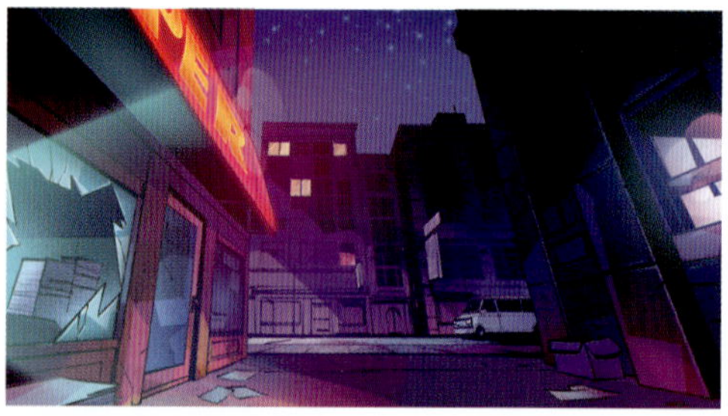

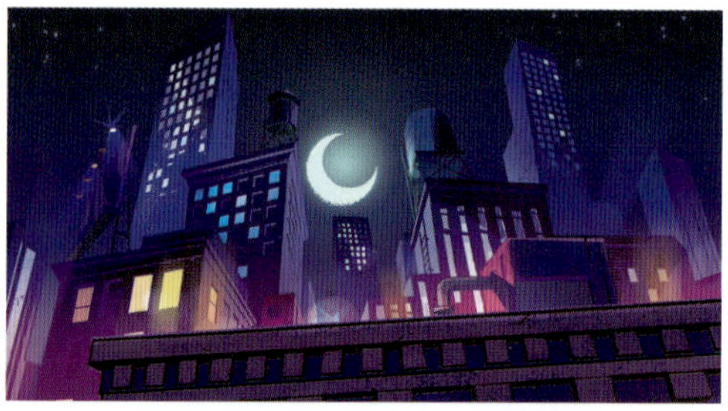

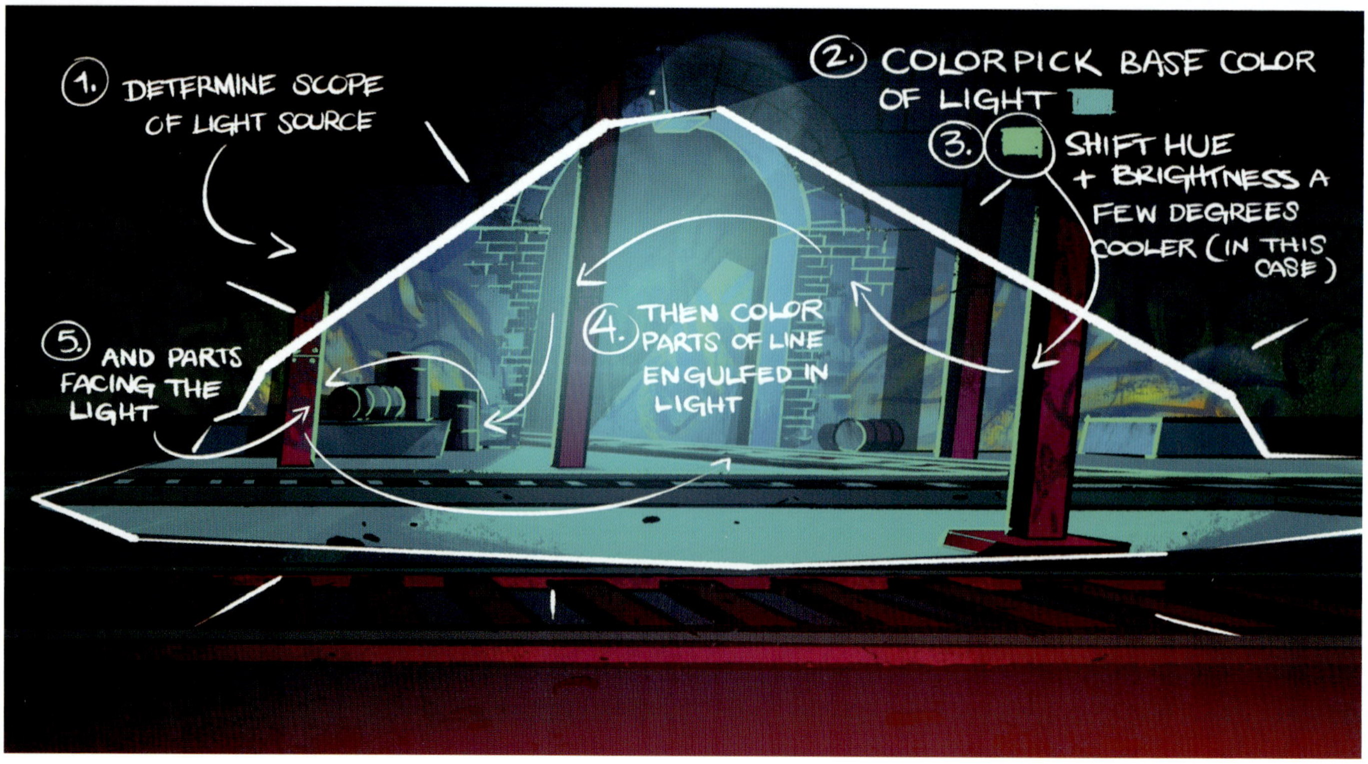

TURTLE TIPS!

These "Turtle Tips" were shared during production to keep visual consistency across the show. These tips covered a variety of guidelines from character-specific details and anatomy to posing rules and animation techniques, these tips are essential *Rise* guardrails.

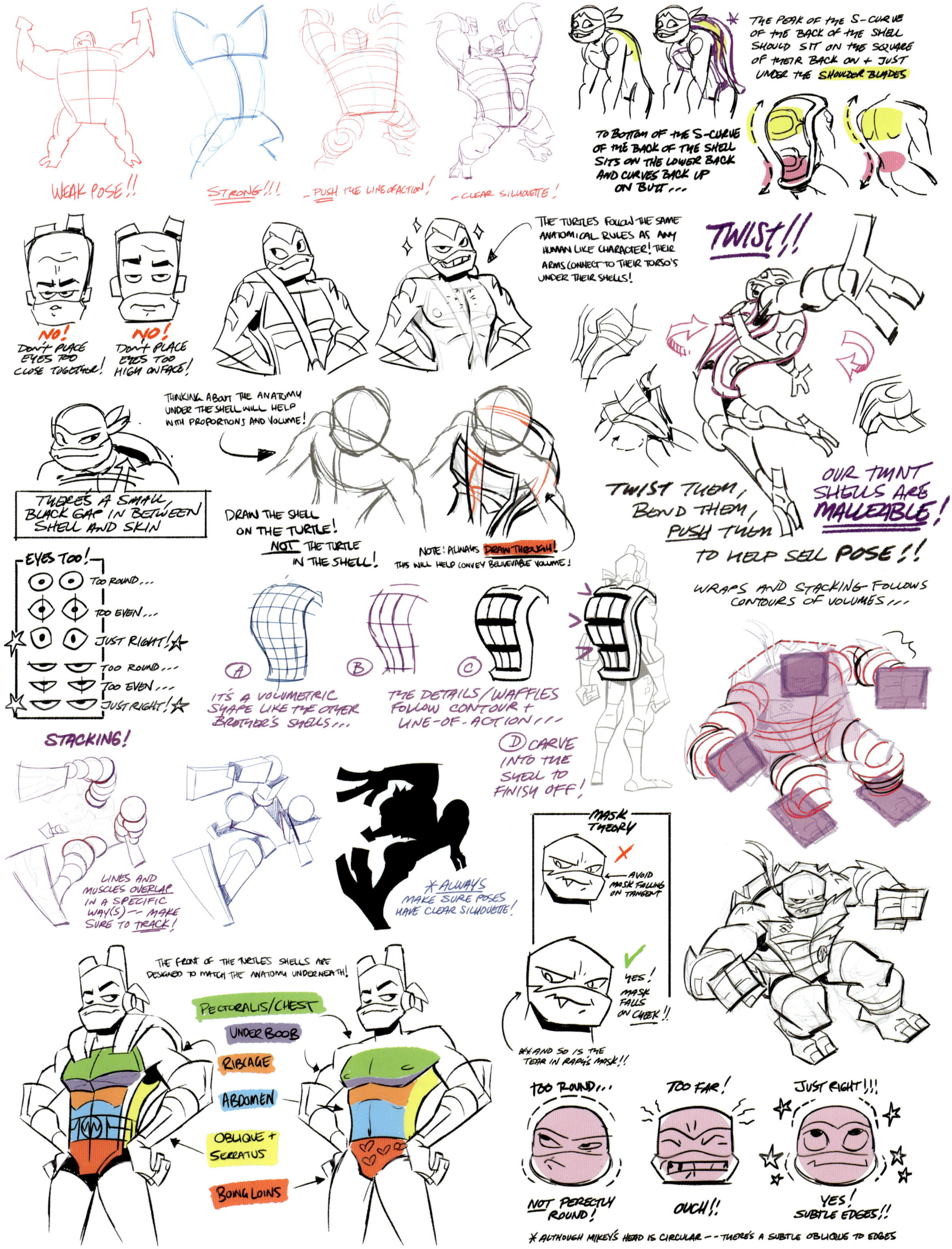

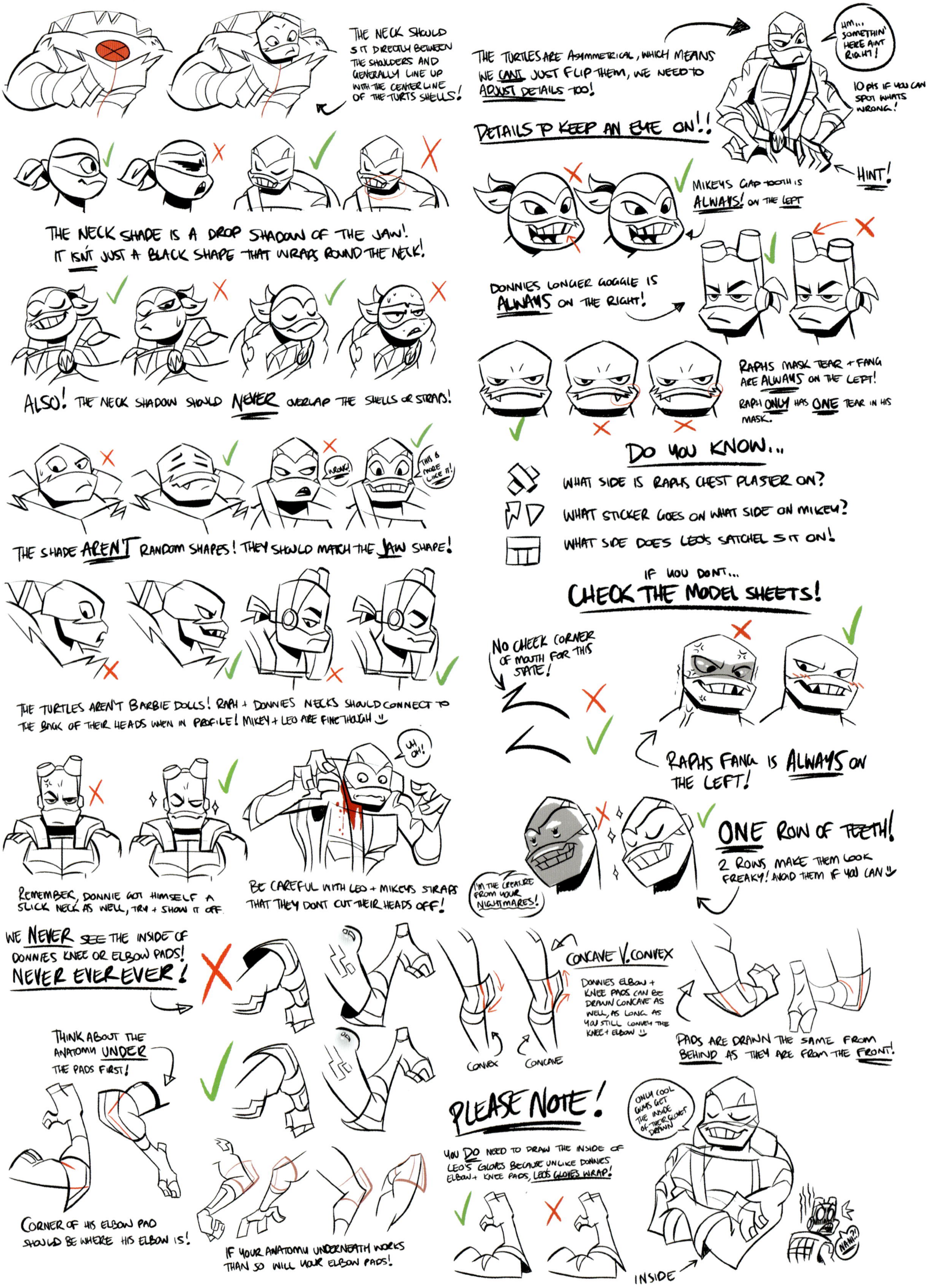
THE NECK SHOULD SIT DIRECTLY BETWEEN THE SHOULDERS AND GENERALLY LINE UP WITH THE CENTER LINE OF THE TURTS SHELLS!
THE TURTLES ARE ASYMMETRICAL, WHICH MEANS WE CANT JUST FLIP THEM, WE NEED TO ADJUST DETAILS TOO!
HM... SOMETHIN' HERE AINT RIGHT!
10 pts IF YOU CAN SPOT WHATS WRONG!
DETAILS TO KEEP AN EYE ON!!
HINT!
THE NECK SHAPE IS A DROP SHADOW OF THE JAW! IT ISN'T JUST A BLACK SHAPE THAT WRAPS ROUND THE NECK!
MIKEYS GAP TOOTH IS ALWAYS! ON THE LEFT
DONNIES LONGER GOGGLE IS ALWAYS ON THE RIGHT!
ALSO! THE NECK SHADOW SHOULD NEVER OVERLAP THE SHELLS OR STRAPS!
RAPHS MASK TEAR + FANG ARE ALWAYS ON THE LEFT!
RAPH ONLY HAS ONE TEAR IN HIS MASK.
DO YOU KNOW...
WHAT SIDE IS RAPHS CHEST PLASTER ON?
WHAT STICKER GOES ON WHAT SIDE ON MIKEY?
WHAT SIDE DOES LEOS SATCHEL SIT ON!
WRONG!
THIS IS MORE LIKE IT!
THE SHADE AREN'T RANDOM SHAPES! THEY SHOULD MATCH THE JAW SHAPE!
IF YOU DONT...
CHECK THE MODEL SHEETS!
NO CHEEK CORNER OF MOUTH FOR THIS STATE!
THE TURTLES AREN'T BARBIE DOLLS! RAPH + DONNIES NECKS SHOULD CONNECT TO THE BACK OF THEIR HEADS WHEN IN PROFILE! MIKEY + LEO ARE FINE THOUGH
RAPHS FANG IS ALWAYS ON THE LEFT!
UH OH!
ONE ROW OF TEETH!
2 ROWS MAKE THEM LOOK FREAKY! AVOID THEM IF YOU CAN
REMEMBER, DONNIE GOT HIMSELF A SLICK NECK AS WELL, TRY + SHOW IT OFF.
BE CAREFUL WITH LEO + MIKEYS STRAPS THAT THEY DONT CUT THEIR HEADS OFF!
I'M THE CREATURE FROM YOUR NIGHTMARES!
WE NEVER SEE THE INSIDE OF DONNIES KNEE OR ELBOW PADS! NEVER EVER EVER!
CONCAVE V. CONVEX
DONNIES ELBOW + KNEE PADS CAN BE DRAWN CONCAVE AS WELL, AS LONG AS YOU STILL CONVEY THE KNEE + ELBOW
THINK ABOUT THE ANATOMY UNDER THE PADS FIRST!
CONVEX
CONCAVE
PADS ARE DRAWN THE SAME FROM BEHIND AS THEY ARE FROM THE FRONT!
PLEASE NOTE!
ONLY COOL GUYS GET THE INSIDE OF THEIR GLOVES DRAWN
YOU DO NEED TO DRAW THE INSIDE OF LEO'S GLOVES BECAUSE UNLIKE DONNIES ELBOW + KNEE PADS, LEO'S GLOVES WRAP!
CORNER OF HIS ELBOW PAD SHOULD BE WHERE HIS ELBOW IS!
IF YOUR ANATOMY UNDERNEATH WORKS THAN SO WILL YOUR ELBOW PADS!
INSIDE
NANI?!

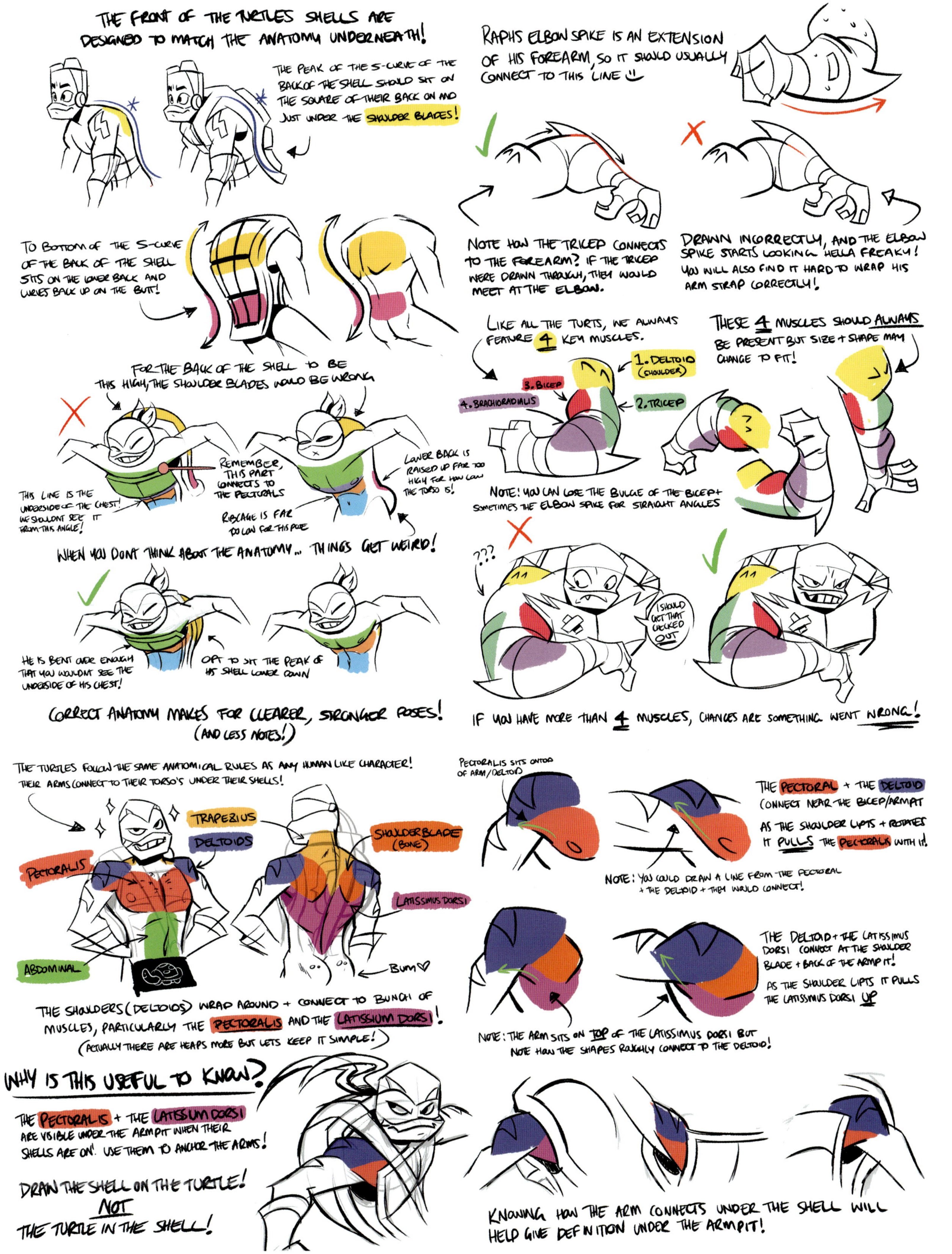
THE FRONT OF THE TURTLES SHELLS ARE DESIGNED TO MATCH THE ANATOMY UNDERNEATH!
THE PEAK OF THE S-CURVE OF THE BACK OF THE SHELL SHOULD SIT ON THE SQUARE OF THEIR BACK ON AND JUST UNDER THE SHOULDER BLADES!
TO BOTTOM OF THE S-CURVE OF THE BACK OF THE SHELL SITS ON THE LOWER BACK AND CURVES BACK UP ON THE BUTT!
FOR THE BACK OF THE SHELL TO BE THIS HIGH, THE SHOULDER BLADES WOULD BE WRONG
REMEMBER, THIS PART CONNECTS TO THE PECTORALS
THIS LINE IS THE UNDERSIDE OF THE CHEST! WE SHOULDNT SEE IT FROM THIS ANGLE!
RIBCAGE IS FAR TOO LOW FOR THIS POSE
LOWER BACK IS RAISED UP FAR TOO HIGH FOR HOW LOW THE TORSO IS!
WHEN YOU DONT THINK ABOUT THE ANATOMY... THINGS GET WEIRD!
HE IS BENT OVER ENOUGH THAT YOU WOULDNT SEE THE UNDERSIDE OF HIS CHEST!
OPT TO SIT THE PEAK OF HIS SHELL LOWER DOWN
CORRECT ANATOMY MAKES FOR CLEARER, STRONGER POSES! (AND LESS NOTES!)
RAPHS ELBOW SPIKE IS AN EXTENSION OF HIS FOREARM, SO IT SHOULD USUALLY CONNECT TO THIS LINE :)
NOTE HOW THE TRICEP CONNECTS TO THE FOREARM? IF THE TRICEP WERE DRAWN THROUGH, THEY WOULD MEET AT THE ELBOW.
DRAWN INCORRECTLY, AND THE ELBOW SPIKE STARTS LOOKING HELLA FREAKY! YOU WILL ALSO FIND IT HARD TO WRAP HIS ARM STRAP CORRECTLY!
LIKE ALL THE TURTS, WE ALWAYS FEATURE 4 KEY MUSCLES.
1. DELTOID (SHOULDER)
2. TRICEP
3. BICEP
4. BRACHIORADIALIS
THESE 4 MUSCLES SHOULD ALWAYS BE PRESENT BUT SIZE + SHAPE MAY CHANGE TO FIT!
NOTE! YOU CAN LOSE THE BULGE OF THE BICEP + SOMETIMES THE ELBOW SPIKE FOR STRAIGHT ANGLES
???
I SHOULD GET THAT CHECKED OUT
IF YOU HAVE MORE THAN 4 MUSCLES, CHANCES ARE SOMETHING WENT WRONG!
THE TURTLES FOLLOW THE SAME ANATOMICAL RULES AS ANY HUMAN LIKE CHARACTER! THEIR ARMS CONNECT TO THEIR TORSO'S UNDER THEIR SHELLS!
TRAPEZIUS
DELTOIDS
PECTORALIS
ABDOMINAL
SHOULDER BLADE (BONE)
LATISSIMUS DORSI
BUM ♡
THE SHOULDERS (DELTOIDS) WRAP AROUND + CONNECT TO BUNCH OF MUSCLES, PARTICULARLY THE PECTORALIS AND THE LATISSIUM DORSI! (ACTUALLY THERE ARE HEAPS MORE BUT LETS KEEP IT SIMPLE!)
PECTORALIS SITS ONTOP OF ARM/DELTOID
THE PECTORAL + THE DELTOID CONNECT NEAR THE BICEP/ARMPIT
AS THE SHOULDER LIFTS + ROTATES IT PULLS THE PECTORALIS WITH IT!
NOTE: YOU COULD DRAW A LINE FROM THE PECTORAL + THE DELTOID + THEY WOULD CONNECT!
THE DELTOID + THE LATISSIMUS DORSI CONNECT AT THE SHOULDER BLADE + BACK OF THE ARMPIT!
AS THE SHOULDER LIFTS IT PULLS THE LATISSIMUS DORSI UP
NOTE: THE ARM SITS ON TOP OF THE LATISSIMUS DORSI BUT NOTE HOW THE SHAPES ROUGHLY CONNECT TO THE DELTOID!
WHY IS THIS USEFUL TO KNOW?
THE PECTORALIS + THE LATISSIUM DORSI ARE VISIBLE UNDER THE ARMPIT WHEN THEIR SHELLS ARE ON! USE THEM TO ANCHOR THE ARMS!
DRAW THE SHELL ON THE TURTLE! NOT THE TURTLE IN THE SHELL!
KNOWING HOW THE ARM CONNECTS UNDER THE SHELL WILL HELP GIVE DEFINITION UNDER THE ARMPIT!

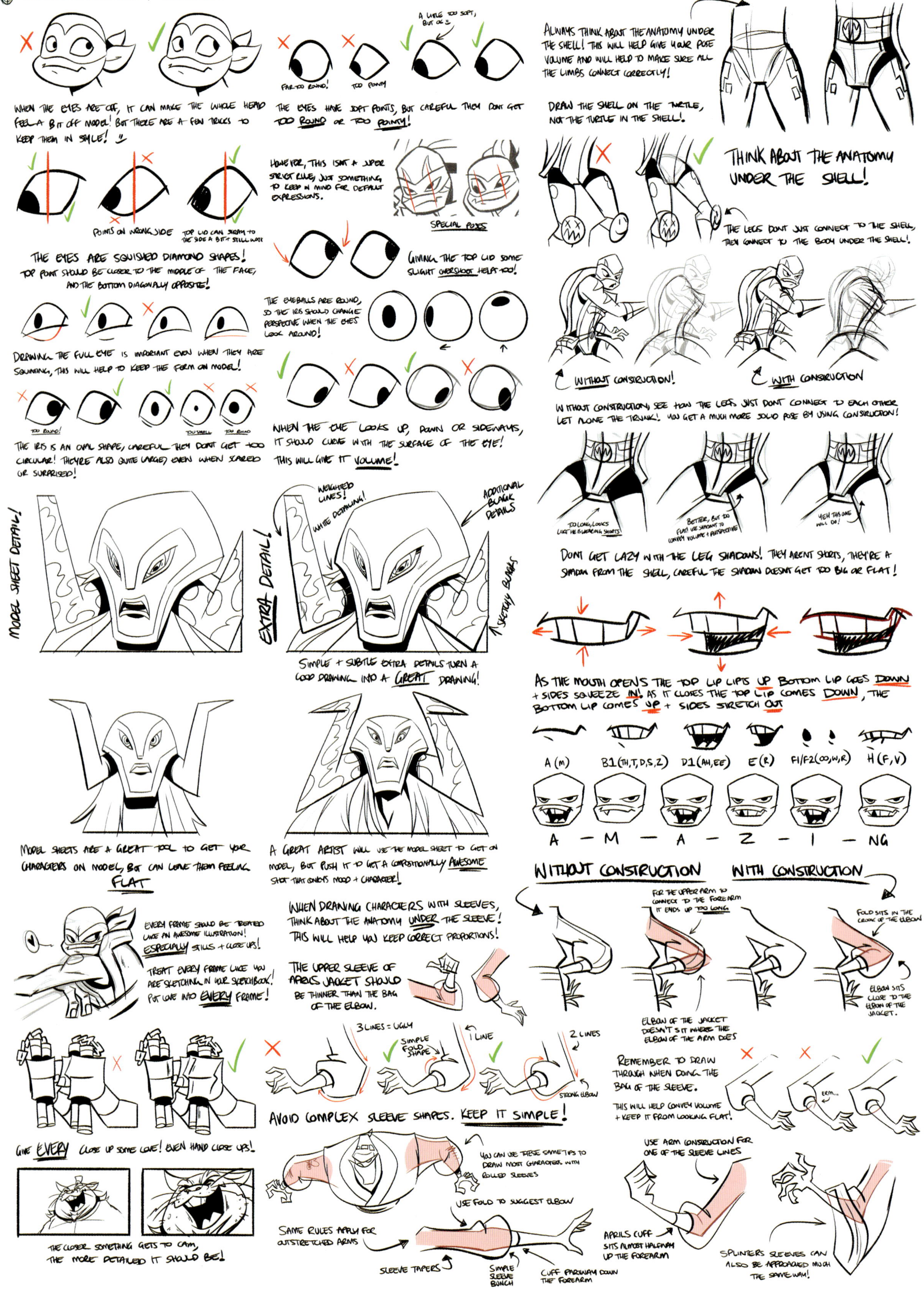
A LITTLE TOO SOFT, BUT OK
FAR TOO ROUND!
TOO POINTY
WHEN THE EYES ARE OFF, IT CAN MAKE THE WHOLE HEAD FEEL A BIT OFF MODEL! BUT THERE ARE A FEW TRICKS TO KEEP THEM IN STYLE!
THE EYES HAVE SOFT POINTS, BUT CAREFUL THEY DONT GET TOO ROUND OR TOO POINTY!
ALWAYS THINK ABOUT THE ANATOMY UNDER THE SHELL! THIS WILL HELP GIVE YOUR POSE VOLUME AND WILL HELP TO MAKE SURE ALL THE LIMBS CONNECT CORRECTLY!
DRAW THE SHELL ON THE TURTLE, NOT THE TURTLE IN THE SHELL!
POINTS ON WRONG SIDE
TOP LID CAN STRAY TO THE SIDE A BIT STILL WORK
THE EYES ARE SQUISHED DIAMOND SHAPES! TOP POINT SHOULD BE CLOSER TO THE MIDDLE OF THE FACE, AND THE BOTTOM DIAGONALLY OPPOSITE!
HOWEVER, THIS ISNT A SUPER STRICT RULE, JUST SOMETHING TO KEEP IN MIND FOR DEFAULT EXPRESSIONS.
SPECIAL POSES
GIVING THE TOP LID SOME SLIGHT OVERSHOOT HELPS TOO!
THINK ABOUT THE ANATOMY UNDER THE SHELL!
THE LEGS DONT JUST CONNECT TO THE SHELL, THEY CONNECT TO THE BODY UNDER THE SHELL!
DRAWING THE FULL EYE IS IMPORTANT EVEN WHEN THEY ARE SQUINTING, THIS WILL HELP TO KEEP THE FORM ON MODEL!
THE EYEBALLS ARE ROUND, SO THE IRIS SHOULD CHANGE PERSPECTIVE WHEN THE EYES LOOK AROUND!
WITHOUT CONSTRUCTION!
WITH CONSTRUCTION
WITHOUT CONSTRUCTION, SEE HOW THE LEGS JUST DONT CONNECT TO EACH OTHER LET ALONE THE TRUNK! YOU GET A MUCH MORE SOLID POSE BY USING CONSTRUCTION!
TOO ROUND!
TOO SMALL
TOO ROUND
THE IRIS IS AN OVAL SHAPE, CAREFUL THEY DONT GET TOO CIRCULAR! THEY'RE ALSO QUITE LARGE, EVEN WHEN SCARED OR SURPRISED!
WHEN THE EYE LOOKS UP, DOWN OR SIDEWAYS, IT SHOULD CURVE WITH THE SURFACE OF THE EYE! THIS WILL GIVE IT VOLUME!
TOO LONG, LOOKS LIKE HE IS WEARING SHORTS
BETTER, BUT TOO FLAT. USE SHADOWS TO CONVEY VOLUME + PERSPECTIVE
YEH THIS ONE WILL DO!
DONT GET LAZY WITH THE LEG SHADOWS! THEY ARENT SHORTS, THEY'RE A SHADOW FROM THE SHELL, CAREFUL THE SHADOW DOESNT GET TOO BIG OR FLAT!
MODEL SHEET DETAIL!
WEIGHTED LINES!
WHITE DETAILING!
ADDITIONAL BLACK DETAILS
EXTRA DETAIL!
SKETCHY BLACKS
SIMPLE + SUBTLE EXTRA DETAILS TURN A GOOD DRAWING INTO A GREAT DRAWING!
AS THE MOUTH OPENS THE TOP LIP LIFTS UP, BOTTOM LIP GOES DOWN + SIDES SQUEEZE IN! AS IT CLOSES THE TOP LIP COMES DOWN, THE BOTTOM LIP COMES UP + SIDES STRETCH OUT
A (M)
B1 (TH,T,D,S,Z)
D1 (AH,EE)
E (R)
F1/F2 (OO,W,R)
H (F,V)
A — M — A — Z — I — NG
MODEL SHEETS ARE A GREAT TOOL TO GET YOUR CHARACTERS ON MODEL, BUT CAN LEAVE THEM FEELING FLAT
A GREAT ARTIST WILL USE THE MODEL SHEET TO GET ON MODEL, BUT PUSH IT TO GET A COMPOSITIONALLY AWESOME SHOT THAT CONVEYS MOOD + CHARACTER!
WITHOUT CONSTRUCTION
WITH CONSTRUCTION
FOR THE UPPER ARM TO CONNECT TO THE FOREARM IT ENDS UP TOO LONG
FOLD SITS IN THE CROOK OF THE ELBOW
ELBOW SITS CLOSE TO THE ELBOW OF THE JACKET.
ELBOW OF THE JACKET DOESN'T SIT WHERE THE ELBOW OF THE ARM DOES
EVERY FRAME SHOULD BE TREATED LIKE AN AWESOME ILLUSTRATION! ESPECIALLY STILLS + CLOSE UPS!
TREAT EVERY FRAME LIKE YOU ARE SKETCHING IN YOUR SKETCHBOOK! PUT LOVE INTO EVERY FRAME!
WHEN DRAWING CHARACTERS WITH SLEEVES, THINK ABOUT THE ANATOMY UNDER THE SLEEVE! THIS WILL HELP YOU KEEP CORRECT PROPORTIONS!
THE UPPER SLEEVE OF APRILS JACKET SHOULD BE THINNER THAN THE BAG OF THE ELBOW.
3 LINES = UGLY
SIMPLE FOLD SHAPE
1 LINE
2 LINES
STRONG ELBOW
AVOID COMPLEX SLEEVE SHAPES. KEEP IT SIMPLE!
REMEMBER TO DRAW THROUGH WHEN DOING THE BAG OF THE SLEEVE.
THIS WILL HELP CONVEY VOLUME + KEEP IT FROM LOOKING FLAT!
ERM...
GIVE EVERY CLOSE UP SOME LOVE! EVEN HAND CLOSE UPS!
THE CLOSER SOMETHING GETS TO CAM, THE MORE DETAILED IT SHOULD BE!
YOU CAN USE THESE SAME TIPS TO DRAW MOST CHARACTERS WITH ROLLED SLEEVES
USE FOLD TO SUGGEST ELBOW
SAME RULES APPLY FOR OUTSTRETCHED ARMS
SLEEVE TAPERS
SIMPLE SLEEVE BUNCH
CUFF PARTWAY DOWN THE FOREARM
USE ARM CONSTRUCTION FOR ONE OF THE SLEEVE LINES
APRILS CUFF SITS ALMOST HALFWAY UP THE FOREARM
SPLINTERS SLEEVES CAN ALSO BE APPROACHED MUCH THE SAME WAY!

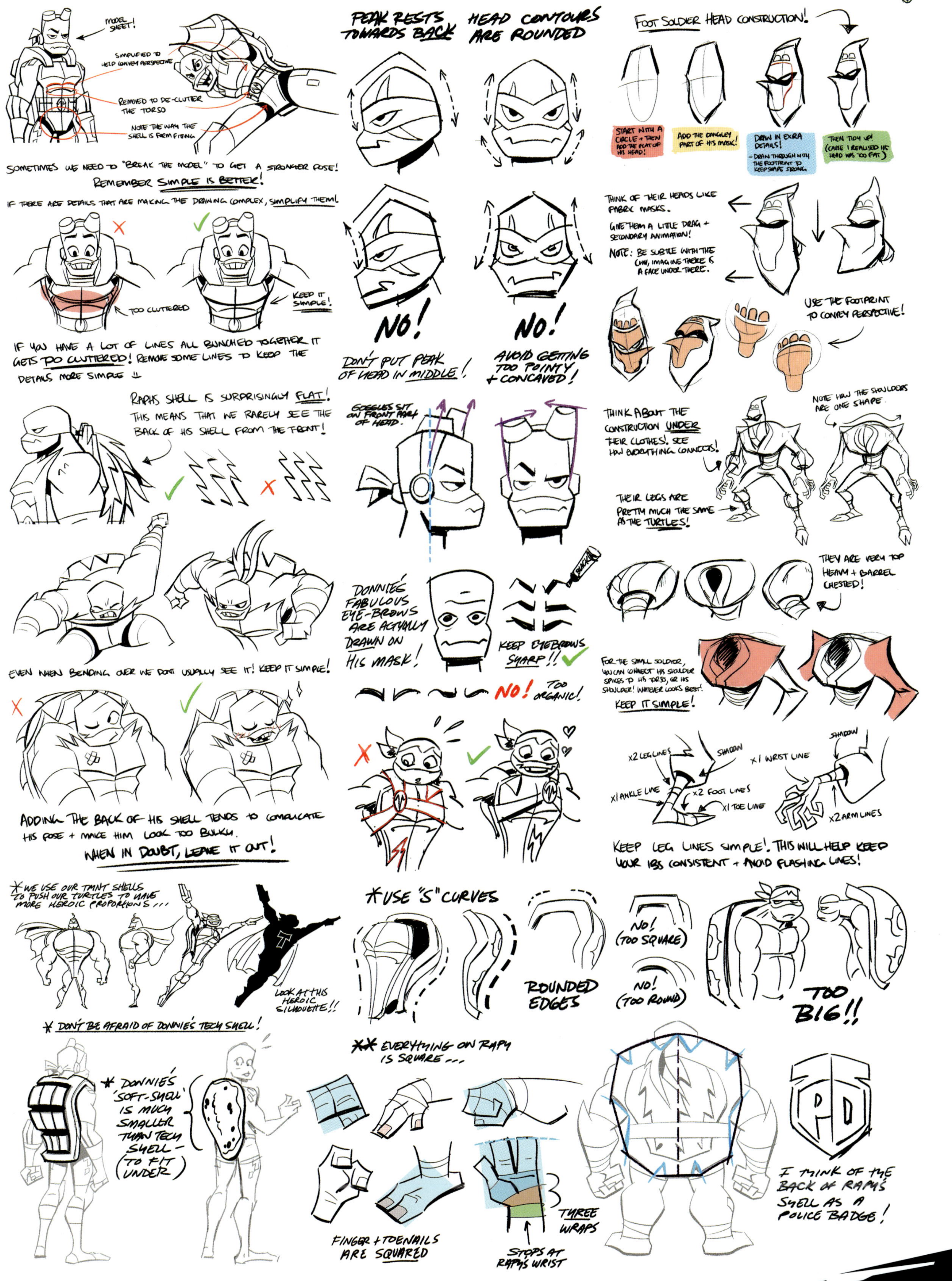
MODEL SHEET!
SIMPLIFIED TO HELP CONVEY PERSPECTIVE
REMOVED TO DE-CLUTTER THE TORSO
NOTE THE WAY THE SHELL IS FORM FITTING
SOMETIMES WE NEED TO "BREAK THE MODEL" TO GET A STRONGER POSE!
REMEMBER SIMPLE IS BETTER!
IF THERE ARE DETAILS THAT ARE MAKING THE DRAWING COMPLEX, SIMPLIFY THEM!
TOO CLUTTERED
KEEP IT SIMPLE!
IF YOU HAVE A LOT OF LINES ALL BUNCHED TOGETHER IT GETS TOO CLUTTERED! REMOVE SOME LINES TO KEEP THE DETAILS MORE SIMPLE !!
RAPH'S SHELL IS SURPRISINGLY FLAT! THIS MEANS THAT WE RARELY SEE THE BACK OF HIS SHELL FROM THE FRONT!
EVEN WHEN BENDING OVER WE DON'T USUALLY SEE IT! KEEP IT SIMPLE!
ADDING THE BACK OF HIS SHELL TENDS TO COMPLICATE HIS POSE + MAKE HIM LOOK TOO BULKY.
WHEN IN DOUBT, LEAVE IT OUT!
*WE USE OUR TMNT SHELLS TO PUSH OUR TURTLES TO HAVE MORE HEROIC PROPORTIONS...
LOOK AT THIS HEROIC SILHOUETTE!!
* DON'T BE AFRAID OF DONNIE'S TECH SHELL!
* DONNIE'S 'SOFT-SHELL' IS MUCH SMALLER THAN TECH SHELL - (TO FIT UNDER)
PEAK RESTS TOWARDS BACK
HEAD CONTOURS ARE ROUNDED
NO!
NO!
DON'T PUT PEAK OF HEAD IN MIDDLE!
AVOID GETTING TOO POINTY + CONCAVED!
GOGGLES SIT ON FRONT PART OF HEAD.
DONNIE'S FABULOUS EYE-BROWS ARE ACTUALLY DRAWN ON HIS MASK!
KEEP EYEBROWS SHARP!!
NO! TOO ORGANIC!
*USE "S" CURVES
ROUNDED EDGES
** EVERYTHING ON RAPH IS SQUARE...
FINGER + TOENAILS ARE SQUARED
STOPS AT RAPH'S WRIST
THREE WRAPS
FOOT SOLDIER HEAD CONSTRUCTION!
START WITH A CIRCLE + THEN ADD THE FLAT OF HIS HEAD!
ADD THE DANGLEY PART OF HIS MASK!
DRAW IN EXTRA DETAILS! - DRAW THROUGH WITH THE FOOTPRINT TO KEEP SHAPE STRONG
THEN TIDY UP! (CAUSE I REALISED HIS HEAD WAS TOO FAT)
THINK OF THEIR HEADS LIKE FABRIC MASKS.
GIVE THEM A LITTLE DRAG + SECONDARY ANIMATION!
NOTE: BE SUBTLE WITH THE CHIN, IMAGINE THERE IS A FACE UNDER THERE.
USE THE FOOTPRINT TO CONVEY PERSPECTIVE!
THINK ABOUT THE CONSTRUCTION UNDER THEIR CLOTHES! SEE HOW EVERYTHING CONNECTS!
NOTE HOW THE SHOULDERS ARE ONE SHAPE
THEIR LEGS ARE PRETTY MUCH THE SAME AS THE TURTLES!
THEY ARE VERY TOP HEAVY + BARREL CHESTED!
FOR THE SMALL SOLDIER, YOU CAN CONNECT HIS SHOULDER SPIKES TO HIS TORSO, OR HIS SHOULDER! WHATEVER LOOKS BEST!
KEEP IT SIMPLE!
X2 LEG LINES
SHADOW
X1 WRIST LINE
SHADOW
X1 ANKLE LINE
X2 FOOT LINES
X1 TOE LINE
X2 ARM LINES
KEEP LEG LINES SIMPLE! THIS WILL HELP KEEP YOUR LBS CONSISTENT + AVOID FLASHING LINES!
NO! (TOO SQUARE)
NO! (TOO ROUND)
TOO BIG!!
I THINK OF THE BACK OF RAPH'S SHELL AS A POLICE BADGE!

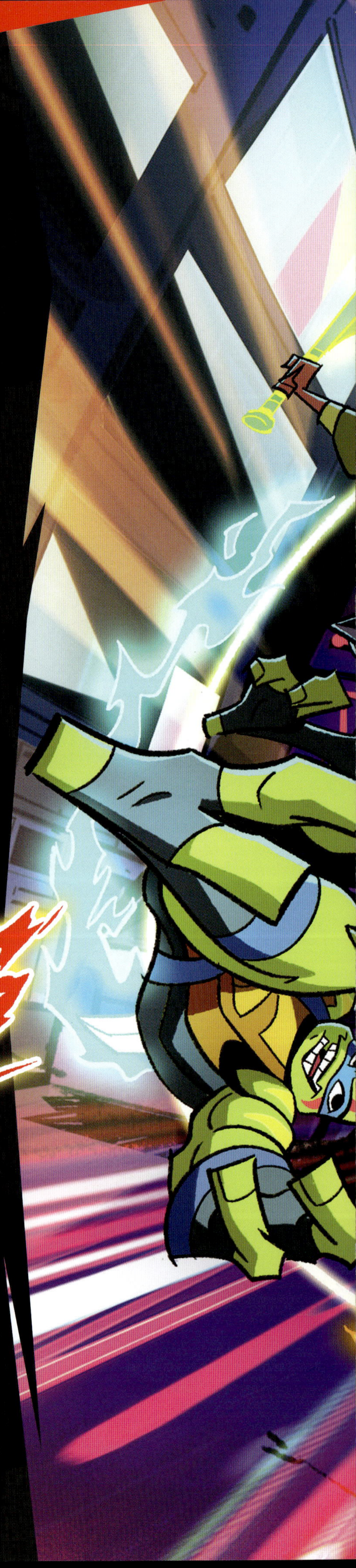

MAD DOGS

In this new origin story, the Teenage Mutant Ninja Turtles are back, and they're stronger than ever. They're armed with new weapons, mystic powers, and a unique twist on their brotherhood—now as different species. Leadership roles have also changed, bringing a new dynamic to these classic characters.

Raph, Leo, Donnie, Mikey, and April O'Neil are ready to defend New York like never before as the Mad Dogs! But they're more than just a team—they're the Hamato Clan, a family bound by courage, loyalty, and a shared passion for pizza.

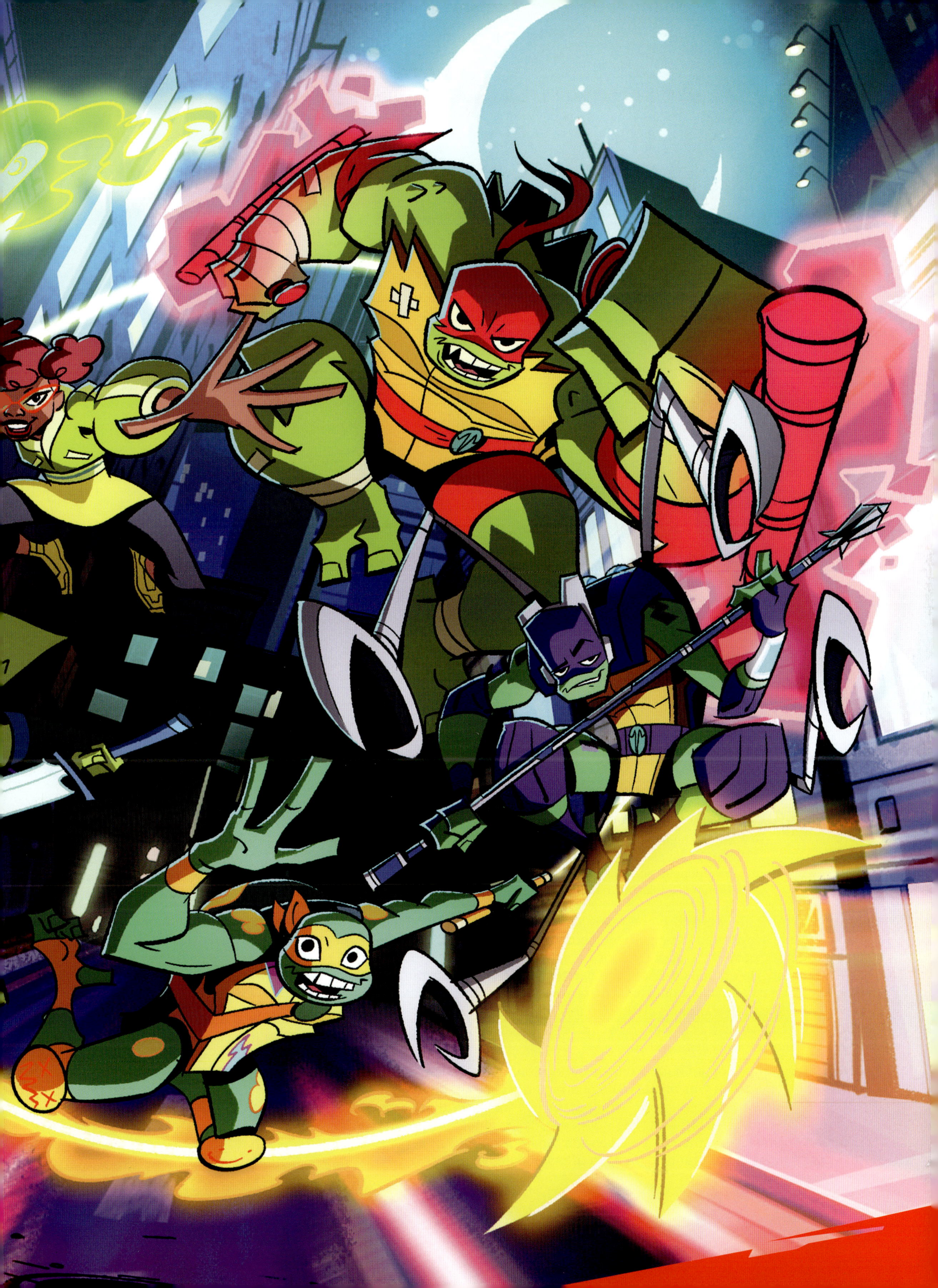

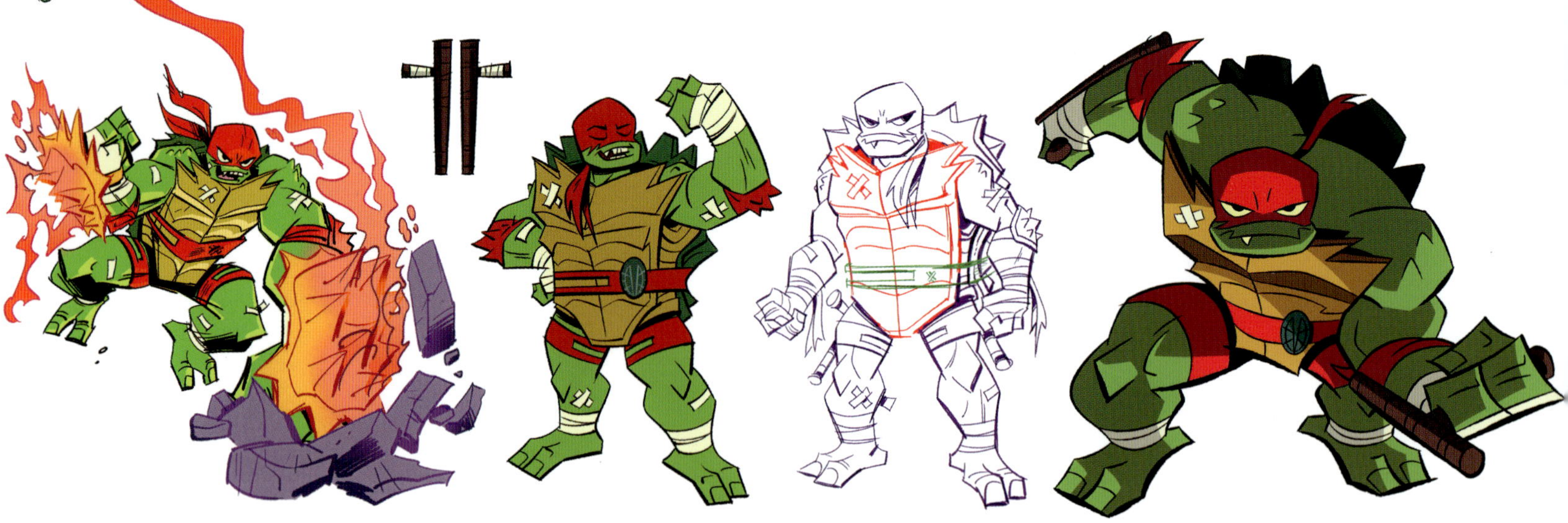

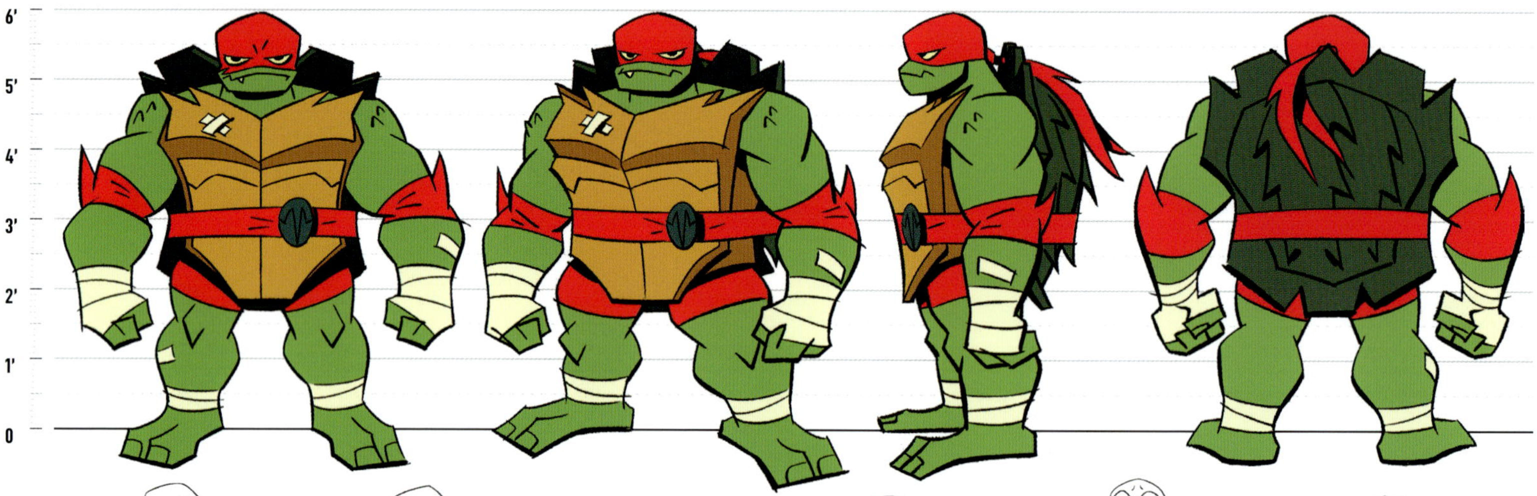

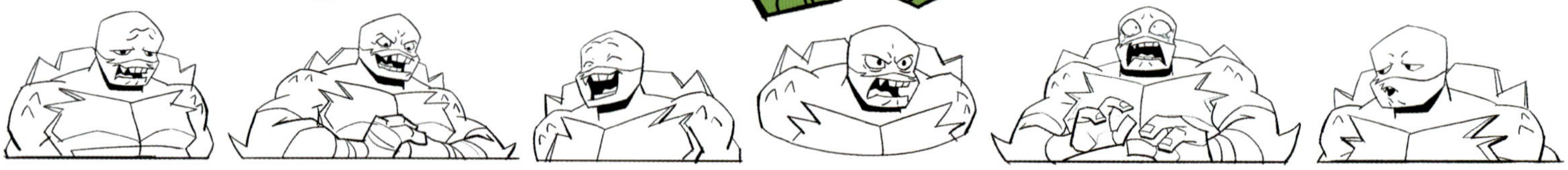

RAPH

VOICED BY OMAR BENSON MILLER

SPECIES: SNAPPING TURTLE **WEAPONS:** TWIN TONFAS **POWER:** SMASH-JITSU

As the biggest and eldest brother, Raph is the leader of the group. He thinks he can use his fists to get himself out of any situation, which is usually why he's pretty much always covered in bandages. But while Raph's muscles may be bigger than his brain, his heart is even bigger. He never backs down from a fight and always tries his best to save the day.

ANDY SURIANO: If I were to buy a teddy bear right now, I'd name it Omar. Never had I met someone so gracious, loving, and altogether positive wrapped up inside such a powerful hulk of a man. He embodied Raph, and Omar's loving heart was Raph's heart. Omar was able to turn from humor to heroic on a dime—like a boss! Omar is all these parts, unfathomably strong and still a lovable caretaker. I would let Omar lead my team, terrible catchphrases and all!

ANT WARD: Omar brought such a unique dimension to Raph during the auditions. It was an absolute charm and pleasure to hear his take on the character. His range was incredible—the frustrated older brother trying to keep his younger brothers in check even though it was almost an impossible task. He brought an outstanding balance of playfulness and tempered frustration.

OMAR BENSON MILLER: I have loved Teenage Mutant Ninja Turtles since they came out. When I was a kid I used to sing the theme song to the original series on the way to school on the bus. It was like a G-rated karaoke with my friends and classmates.

I auditioned for the role over a long period and was finally chosen to play Raph in *Rise*. It was like eating ice cream every day but never gaining weight! I was so honored and humbled to voice Raph and took it very seriously because I remember how much the cartoon impacted me as a child, and I wanted that same positivity to flow from my interpretation.

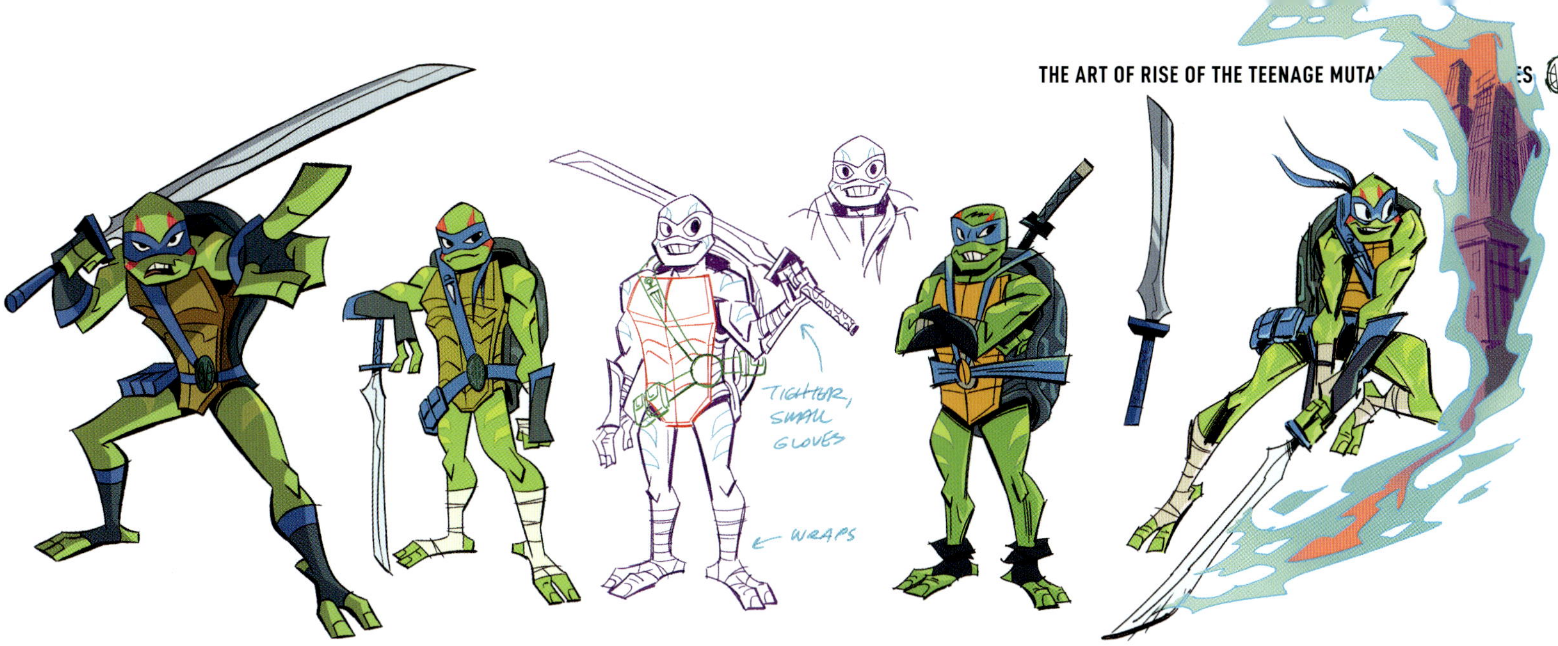

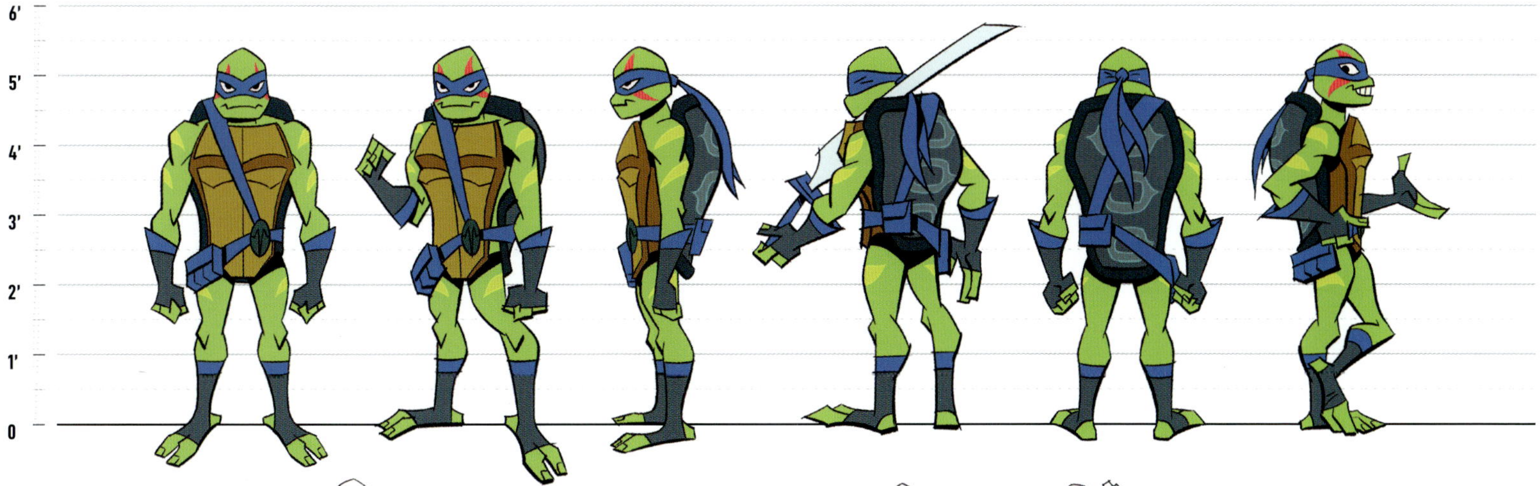

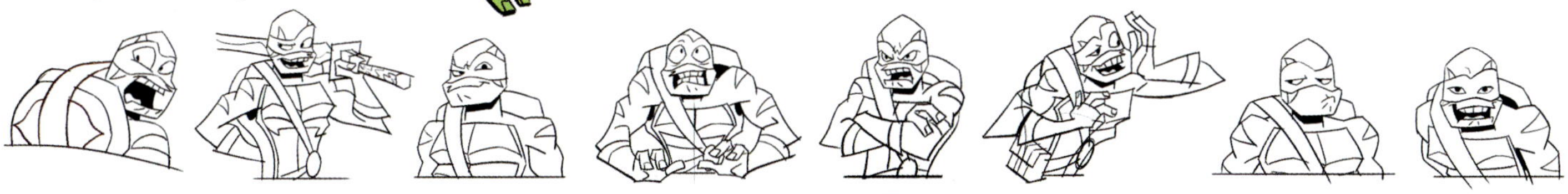

LEO

VOICED BY BEN SCHWARTZ

SPECIES: RED-EARED SLIDER WEAPON: ŌDACHI SWORD POWER: PORTAL POWER

Leo is intelligent, clever, and hilarious. He can easily figure out any situation and uses his quick-witted skills to beat opponents, clear obstacles, or land one of his many one-liners. Leo likes to think of himself as the "cool guy" on the team – a rascal with a wink and a sly grin. He's a rebel through and through and isn't afraid to break the rules when he thinks he's right. He could be a strong leader, but he'd rather go for high jinx than take the high road.

ANDY SURIANO: One of our biggest character experiments was attempting to figure out just who Leo would be outside of the typically generic "leader" role. This opened so many more fresh story opportunities and gave us a chance to see each of the characters' personalities resonate beyond their familiar and designated roles. Leo was our wild card, a hustler that could talk his way out of any situation just as smoothly as his mouth got him in trouble to begin with. Anyone that's seen Ben's improv and role in *Parks and Rec* (2009) would agree with this casting choice. Ben's wicked, rapid-fire humor and passion brought a refreshing energy to Leo that even far exceeded our expectations.

ANT WARD: Ben brought the sheer sass of Leo, the know-it-all attitude, and the constant smirk in such a unique way that I don't think we could have asked for a better performance. His Leo was overconfident, often too sure of himself, yet subtly vulnerable. It was always fun to hear Ben frequently confused by the takes we had chosen. We often went with very unique reads and not what you would expect for this kind of show.

BEN SCHWARTZ: I was an enormous Teenage Mutant Ninja Turtles fan growing up. I watched every episode of the original animated show, watched all the movies, played the arcade game, the SNES game *Turtles in Time*, and the NES game with the impossible water level, which I was proud I could beat. I also collected the action figures. For one birthday I was lucky enough to get the pizza-throwing vehicle, a huge highlight of my childhood.

So it was an absolute joy to play Leo in *Rise of the Teenage Mutant Ninja Turtles*. I got chills the first time I got to say "Cowabunga!" I had so much fun playing the drama in scenes (especially in the movie) and loved, loved, loved how much everyone let me play around and push the comedy wherever we could. I don't remember exactly how I got the role—I assume I auditioned for it—but man, did I love being a Turtle!

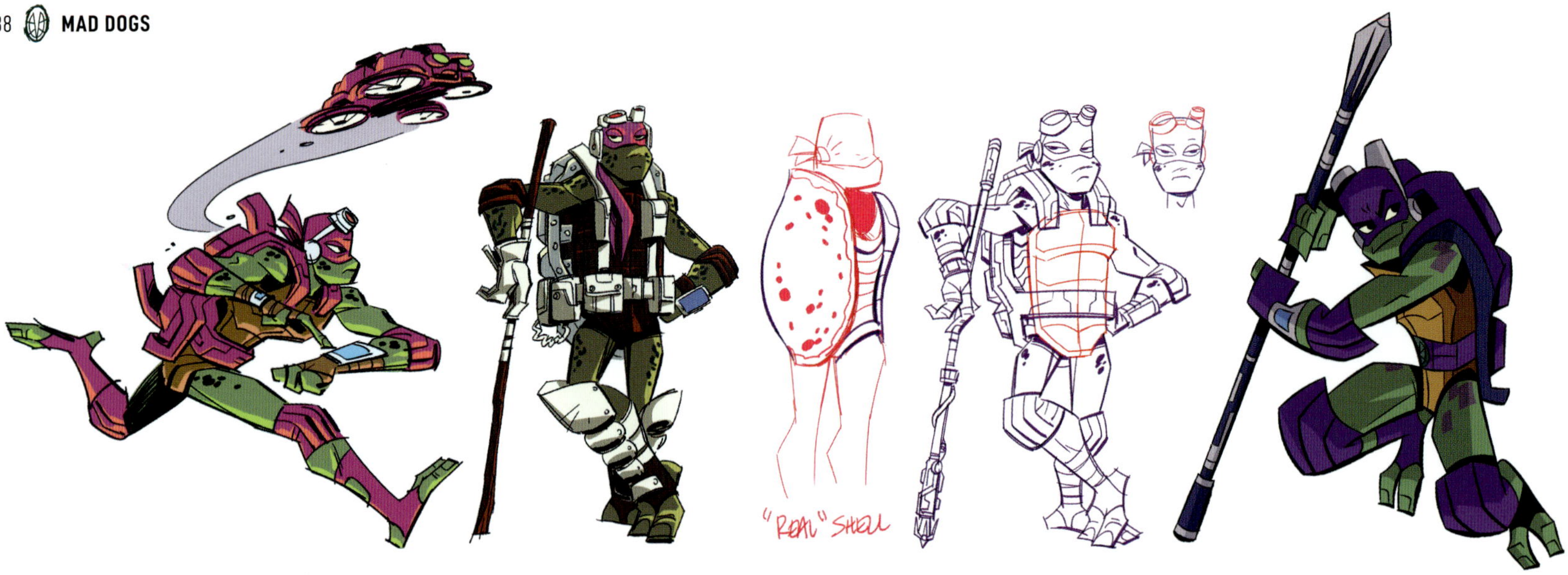

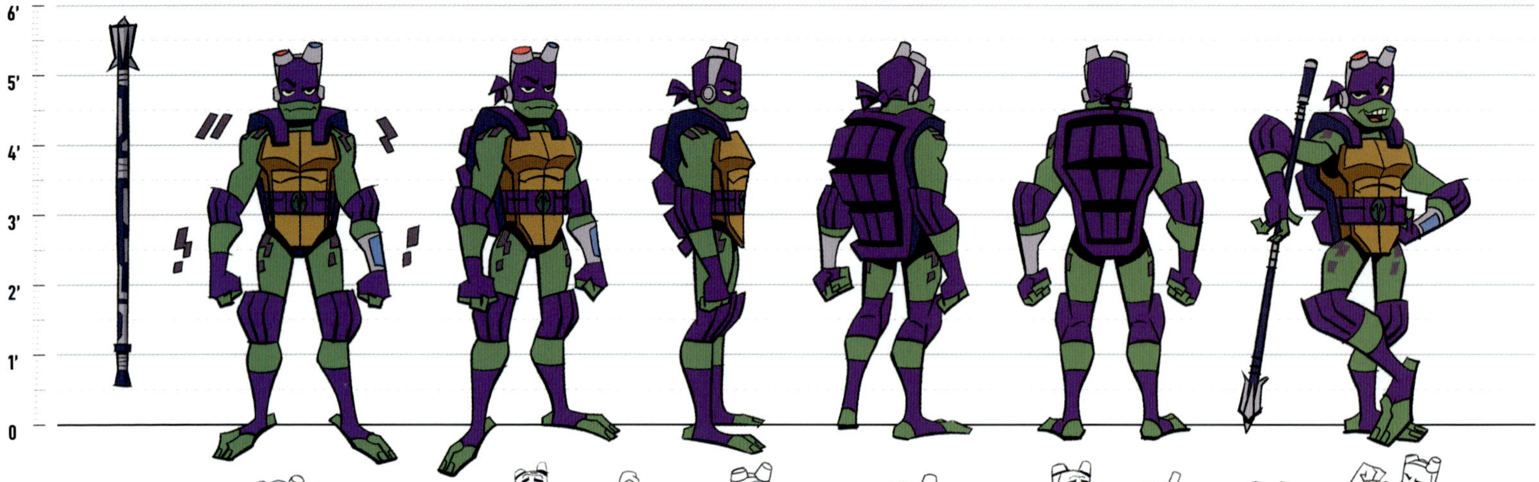

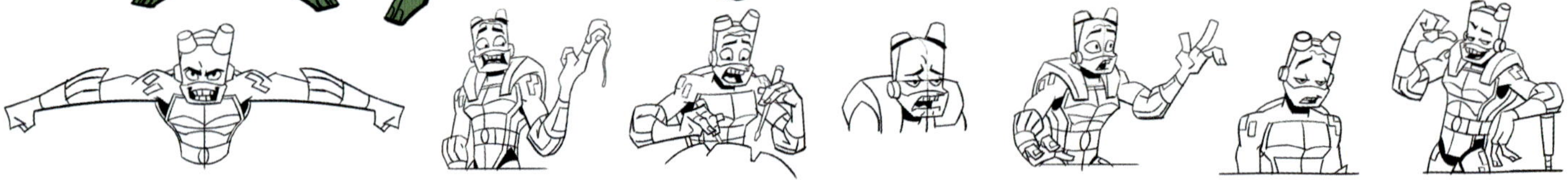

DONNIE

VOICED BY JOSH BRENER

SPECIES: SOFTSHELL TURTLE WEAPON: TECH-BŌ POWER: TRANSFORMING TECH-BŌ

Donnie is the coolest tech wiz you'll ever meet. Understandably proud of his smarts, he *may* sometimes be accused of having a bit of a big head. Donnie uses his mechanical genius to construct a series of amazing battle shells and uses his transforming Tech-Bō and robotic drone S.H.E.L.L.D.O.N. to take on any foe.

ANDY SURIANO: To be honest, there was only one actor we sought out to play Donnie. We were huge fans of his "Big-Head" character on *Silicon Valley* (2014) and so we reached out to Josh, and boy, did he deliver! Josh is not only super funny, but also crazy smart—often correcting our sloppy math errors in the scripts. He always came prepared, humbly offering alts and improvisation that almost always elevated the story and made it to screen.

ANT WARD: Josh brought wonderful deadpan humor to Donnie. There was an underlying smugness to his Donnie, someone who knew he was the most intelligent person in the room and was proud of it. Josh also brought an endearing sensitivity and soft side to Donnie as the show progressed, showing that while he knows he's the smartest of his brothers, he still holds them dear to his heart. He may have a somewhat unconventional way of showing it sometimes. When we had the chance to record all the brothers at the same time, something magical took place that stripped the characters away, leaving you with these four incredible actors who almost reacted to themselves and were very authentic. We were often crying with laughter at the records.

JOSH BRENER: I grew up watching the original animated *Teenage Mutant Ninja Turtles* series from 1987, so I had a pretty specific idea of who Donatello (my favorite Turtle as a kid) was in my head. Nerdy, reserved, maybe a little awkward. So that was the character I was preparing as I sat in the audition waiting room at Nickelodeon in March of 2017. Then, casting director Gene Vassilaros came and sat beside me and said, "So Andy and Ant don't want him to be the stereotypical dorky science guy...they think this Donnie is kind of intellectually superior, maybe even a little acerbic. He's the smartest guy in the room and he knows it." And I actually laughed out loud just thinking about Donnie being sort of aloof and sarcastic and impatient with his feeble-minded brothers. The creative team did such an amazing job bringing that eye-rolly character to life in both writing and design—I was just psyched to be along for the ride. And I really owe that to Gene. What a guy!

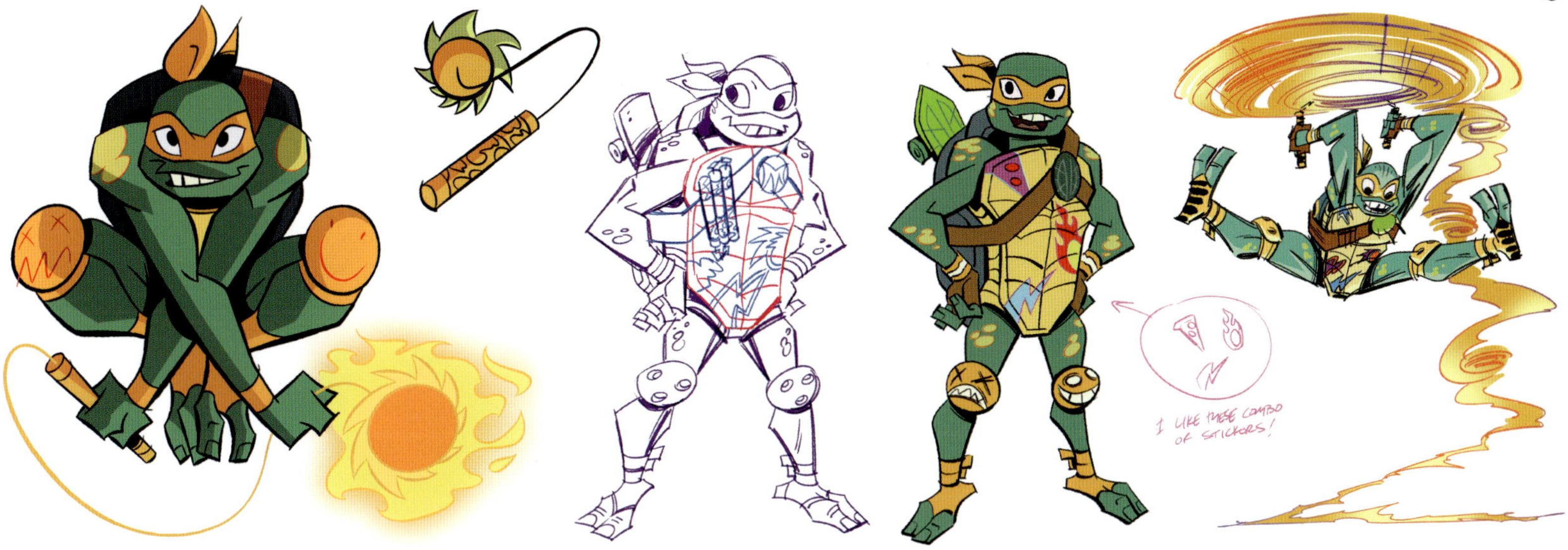

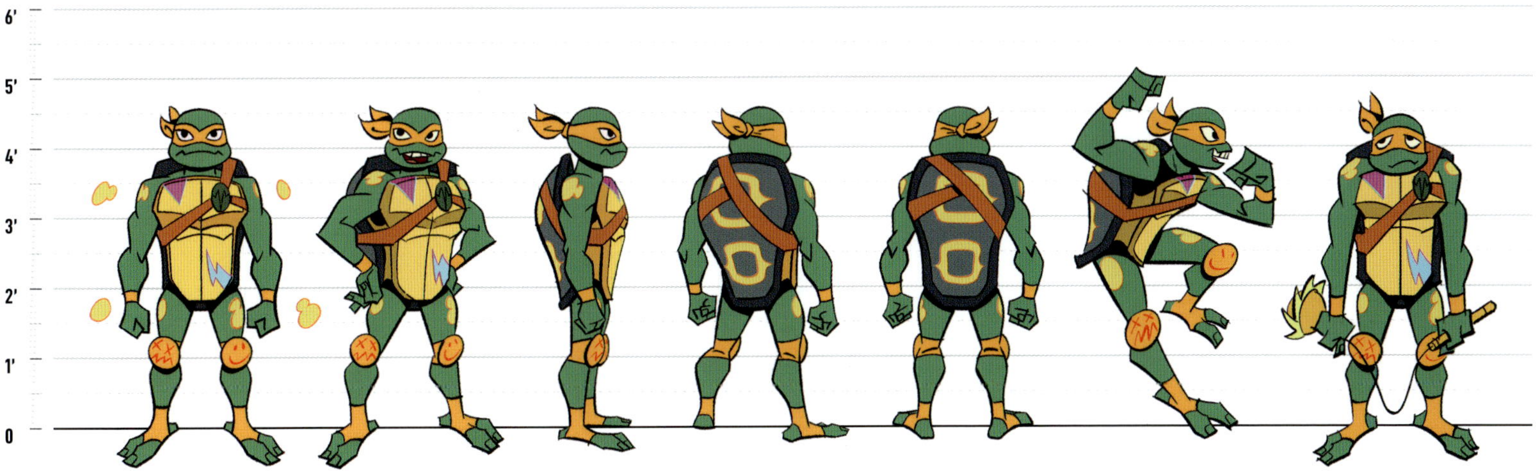

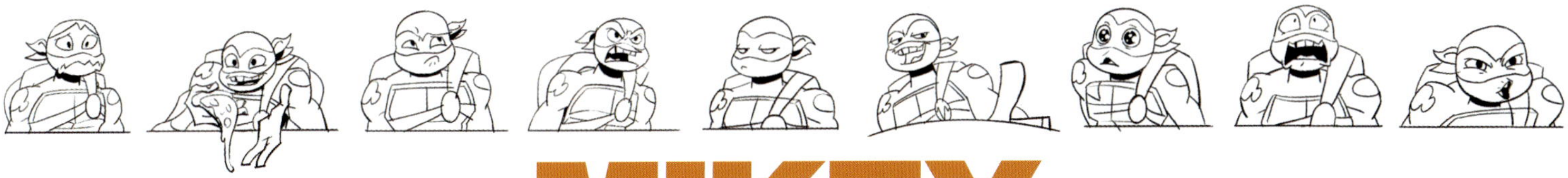

MIKEY

VOICED BY BRANDON MYCHAL SMITH

SPECIES: BOX TURTLE **WEAPON:** KUSARI-FUNDŌ **POWER:** MYSTIC WHIP

Mikey is the youngest of the four Turtles and has a wild and colorful personality. He finds the fun in any situation—and if there is no fun, he'll make it! Mikey is an artist and spends his time tagging the Turtles' lair with graffiti or decking out his shell with an ever-changing assortment of awesome stickers. Mikey is always gung-ho for adventure, which can sometimes get him into trouble. But above all else, he is an eternal optimist and kicks total butt at ninjutsu with his flaming kusari-fundō.

ANDY SURIANO: Mikey was an interesting challenge: How could we find a voice that was layered with innocence and wide-eyed optimism yet had a bit of the naughtiness of someone that's "lived" a bit? Brandon was our bull's-eye. He's such a beautiful, open human whose playfulness and eye twinkle translated to our Mikey, with having just enough "devil" in him for the audience to wonder if Mikey's not as naive as some might think.

ANT WARD: Brandon was entertaining to have in the booth. Brandon's reads are always authentic and brought a fun, playful, and youthful carefree attitude to Mikey. His Mikey was also ready for adventure and had a subtle, childlike wonder that never came off as naive but was always hilarious.

BRANDON MYCHAL SMITH: "Cowaaaabungaaaaa!" would be the quintessential word to describe my life-changing experience playing my first superhero in *Rise of Teenage Mutant Ninja Turtles*! It was a pinch-me moment the day I got the call that I had been cast as Michelangelo in *Rise*, and I knew at that moment with a face full of tears that this humbling opportunity would forever be an integral signature staple of my legacy I'm still trying to build in the entertainment industry.

My relationship with Andy Suriano and Ant Ward, truly two outliers in their field, is nothing short of a true brotherhood. Andy and Ant truly embraced me, almost identical to the way Splinter embraced the Turtles as sons! We became a family instantly and I was truly honored to be a small part of the immense, unparalleled talent we were able to dance with: Kat Graham, a true superstar, Eric Bauza, a voice legend and icon, Ben Schwartz, a rock star and comedic genius, Josh Brener, a comedy titan, and Omar Benson Miller, one of the most talented humans I've ever met on the planet and someone I've idolized since I was a kid. We had the true *Rise of the Teenage Mutant Ninja Turtles* dream team!

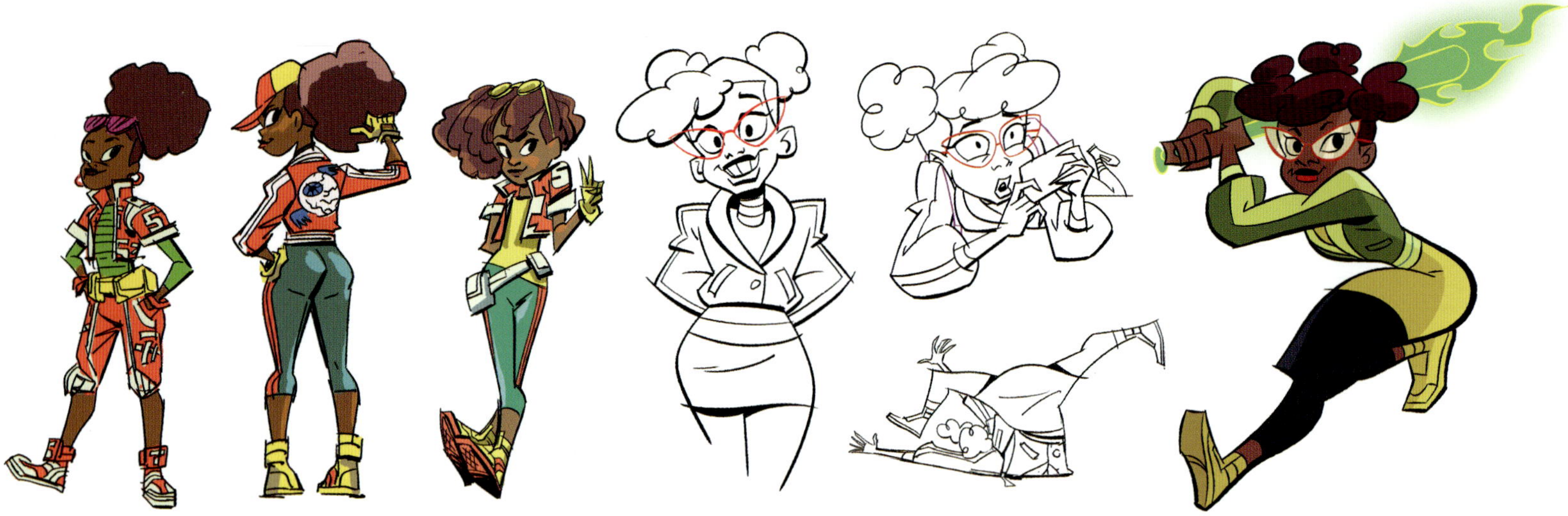

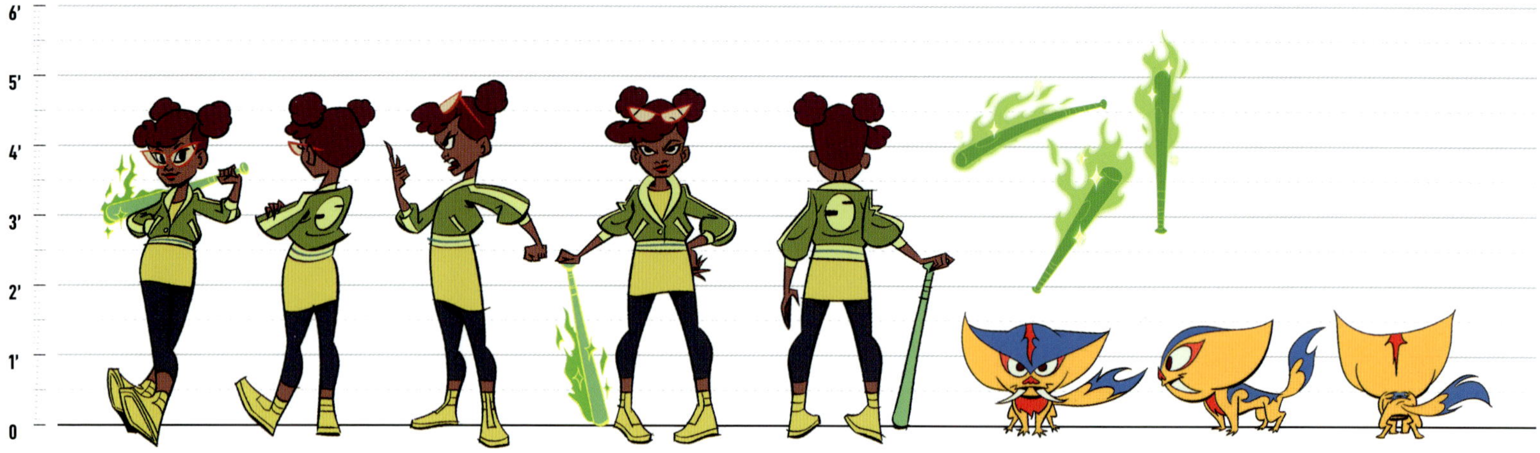

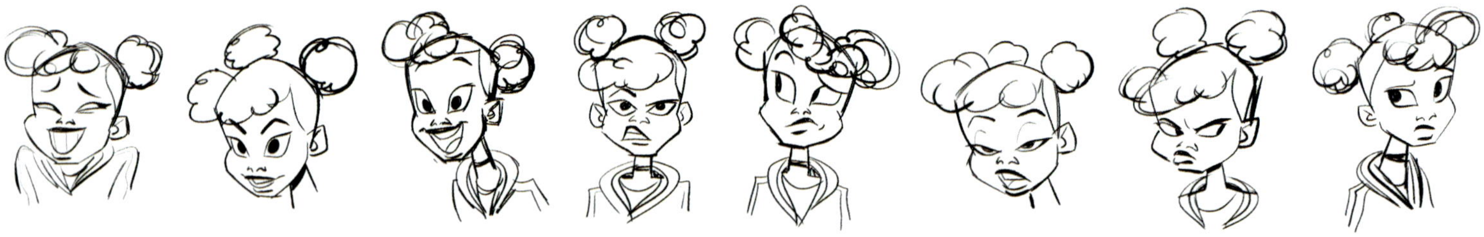

APRIL O'NEIL

AND MAYHEM

VOICED BY KAT GRAHAM

SPECIES: HUMAN **WEAPON:** MYSTIC BAT

April is a true New Yorker and a real firecracker: upbeat, wisecracking, and confident. As the Turtles' only human ally, she loves them like brothers and joins them on all their epic adventures.

ANDY SURIANO: April was the hardest to cast for us and required the most extensive search. We'd almost exhausted all hope of threading that needle on finding someone that could dish it out and take it as much as one of the brothers. She needed to be the tough but adorable older sister that gave the boys a hard time as well as being their fiercest defender.

Finally, Kat walked in. By the end of her very first read-through, Ant and I looked at each other almost in tears. We'd found our April. Kat balanced the cute with an edge we'd been endlessly searching for.

ANT WARD: Kat's range for April was outstanding. She could be zany, loud, one of the gang one minute, then a heartfelt big sister the next. She brought April's unhinged exuberance to life. We were very fortunate to cast Kat, and we knew from the auditions that she would bring a unique side to April—definitely part of the Mad Dogs.

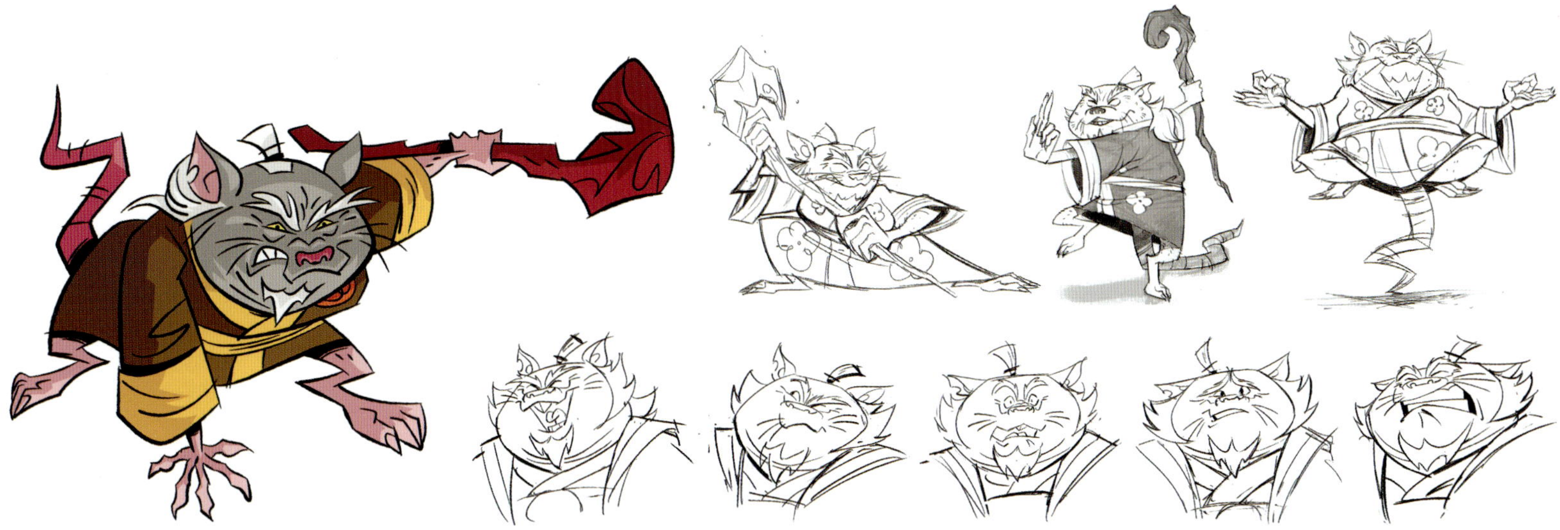

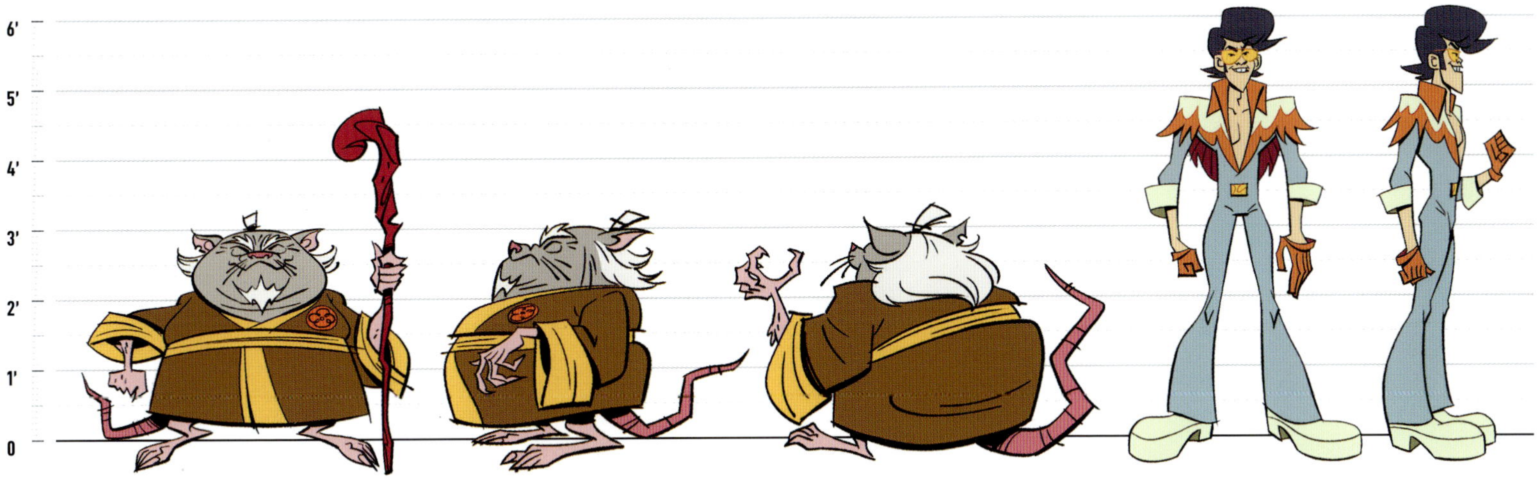

SPLINTER

HAMATO YOSHI/LOU JITSU

VOICED BY ERIC BAUZA

SPECIES: HUMAN-BORN MUTANT RAT POWER: FORMER MARTIAL ARTS MOVIE STAR

Once human, now a mutant rat, Splinter is an eccentric mentor to his turtle sons, training them in the art of ninjutsu. Well, when he's not watching game shows and Lou Jitsu movie marathons.

ANDY SURIANO: We didn't need to have any auditions for our favorite rat dad. Eric is an old friend, and I've always wanted to work with him. His amazing range, especially comedic timing, made casting him a no-brainer.

ANT WARD: We had both worked with Bauza in the past, and he was our first choice for Splinter. As we crafted Splinter's arc, Eric's voice was at the forefront, and we knew that he would bring the humor Splinter needed and the dramatic chops the character would develop—from the gross, burbling couch potato who had all but given up on life to the noble warrior, leading the charge to save the world.

ERIC BAUZA: I've been beyond lucky to be a part of two fantastic reimaginings in the TMNT universe—first being the 2012 reboot by Ciro Nieli and Brandon Auman, then *Rise of the Teenage Mutant Ninja Turtles* by Andy Suriano and Ant Ward.

I was the last to audition for Raph in the 2012 series before Sean Astin. The best thing about voiceover and working with such great casting folks as Andrea Romano and Pete Hastings: They remembered me, gave me a shot at a new original character, Tiger Claw. He soon became a fan favorite—enough of a favorite to earn his own action figure!

Time had passed after *Teenage Mutant Ninja Turtles* (2012) ended and I was approached by Andy Suriano about possibly reading for the role of Master Splinter for a new version of TMNT. Another classic role that I actually never in my wildest dreams thought I'd ever have the opportunity to play.

What I loved most about this take on TMNT was that it was different, not just in amazing character design, but different in the way we knew the characters all together. It depicted Raph as the fearless leader, Leo as the wise guy, and Splinter as a less-than-present father figure who was more interested in watching his TV programs than guiding his children. It gave the fans a fantastic fresh take rather than give just another version of what we already knew.

In time, the fans fell in love with these characters once again with *Rise of the Teenage Mutant Ninja Turtles: The Movie* (2022) made for Netflix by Nickelodeon Animation. It was a beautiful film that got to finally tie the series up in such a major way. I still to this day get such a warm reception from TMNT fans about how much they loved *Rise*. I will always be thankful for being a part of this wonderful franchise.

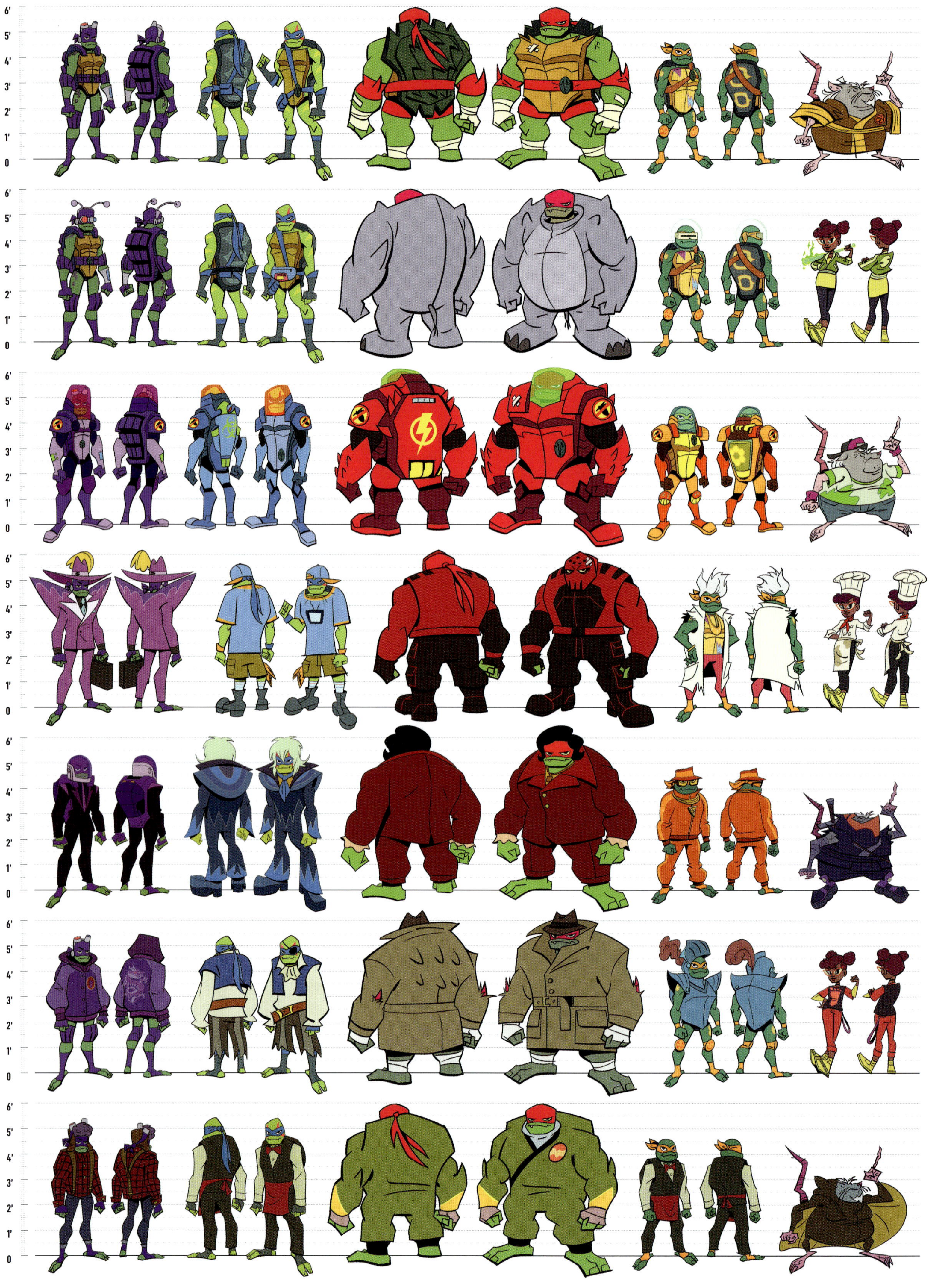
6'
5'
4'
3'
2'
1'
0
6'
5'
4'
3'
2'
1'
0
6'
5'
4'
3'
2'
1'
0
6'
5'
4'
3'
2'
1'
0
6'
5'
4'
3'
2'
1'
0
6'
5'
4'
3'
2'
1'
0
6'
5'
4'
3'
2'
1'
0

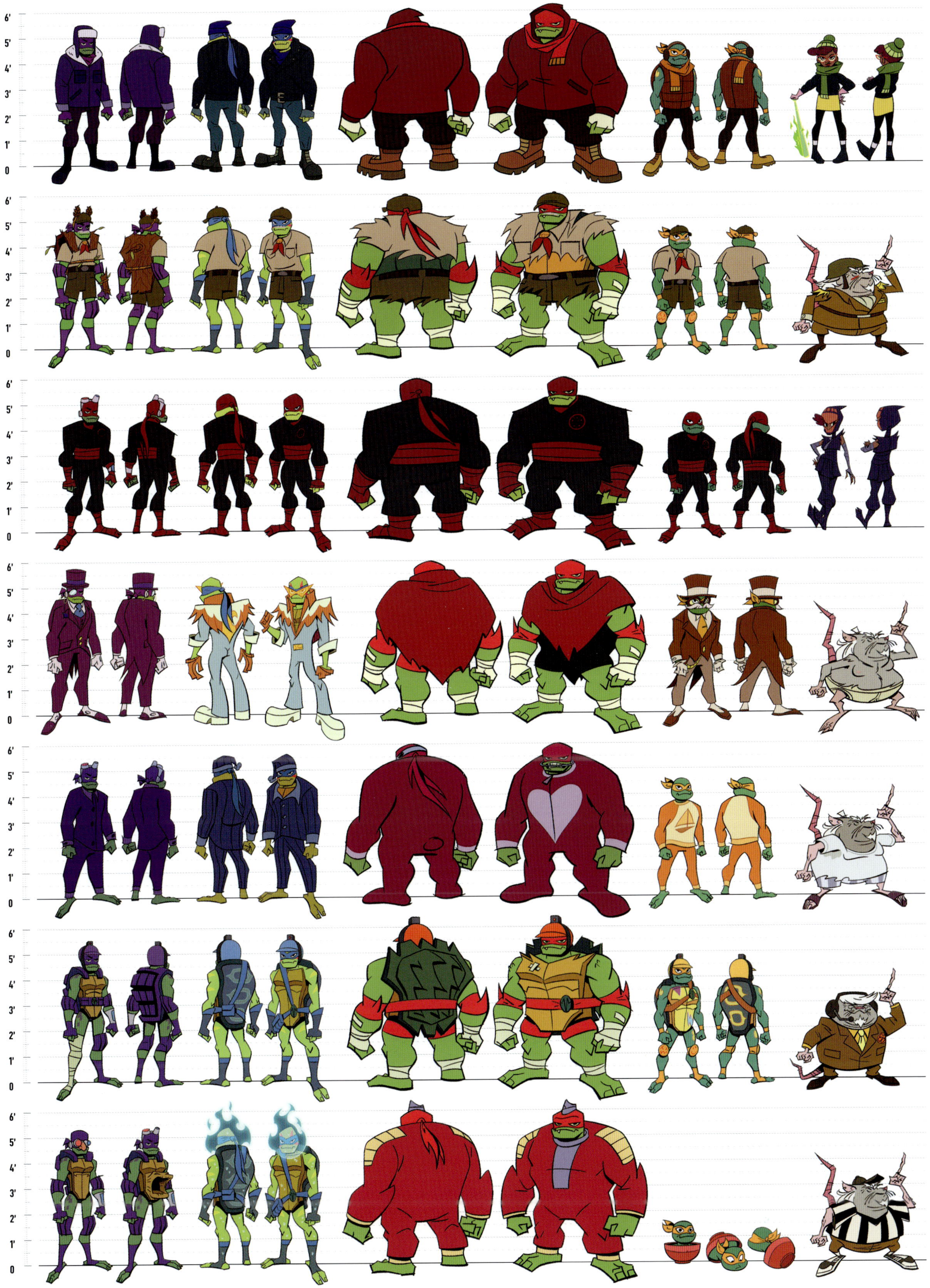
6'
5'
4'
3'
2'
1'
0
6'
5'
4'
3'
2'
1'
0
6'
5'
4'
3'
2'
1'
0
6'
5'
4'
3'
2'
1'
0
6'
5'
4'
3'
2'
1'
0
6'
5'
4'
3'
2'
1'
0
6'
5'
4'
3'
2'
1'
0

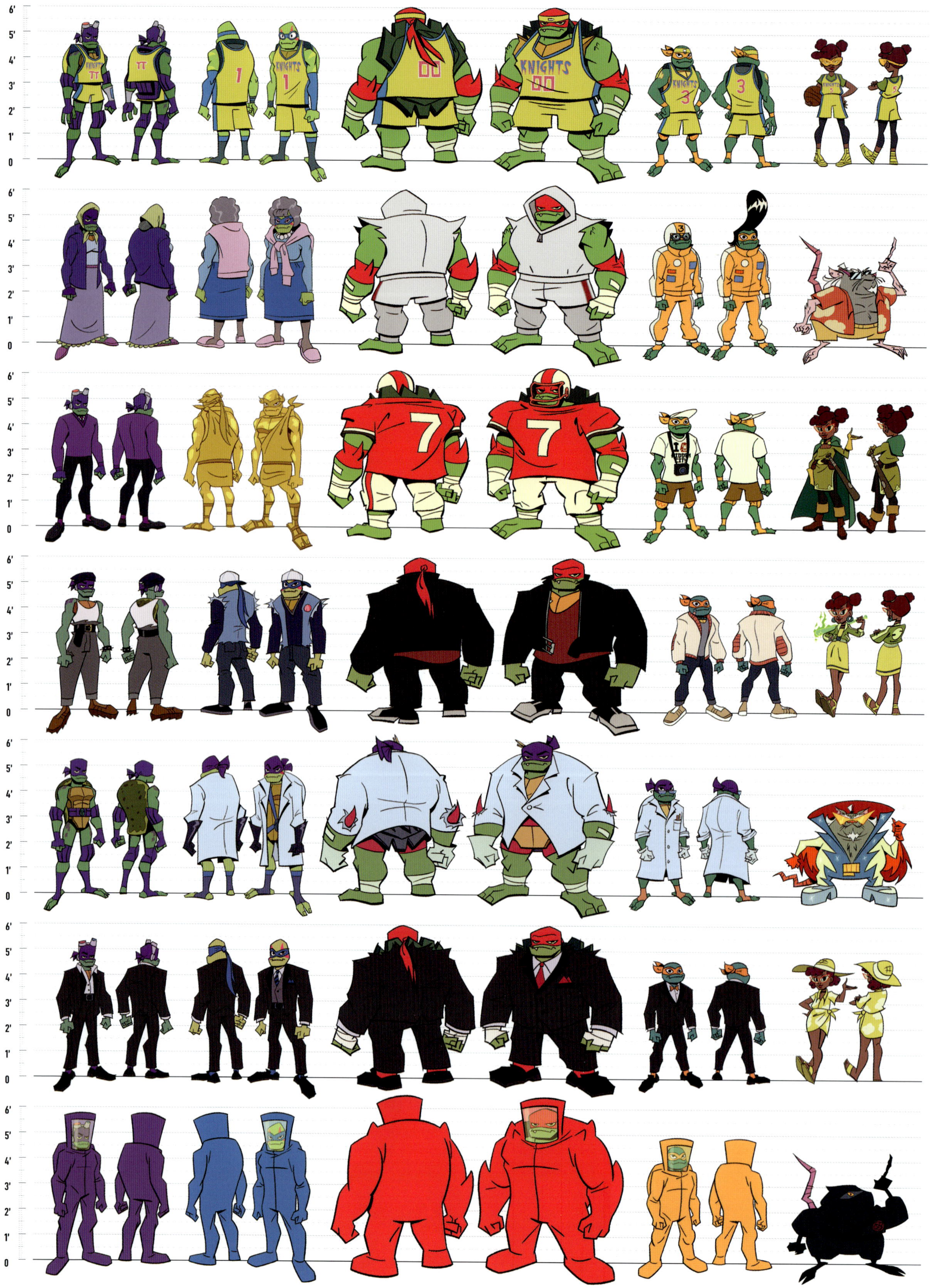
6'
5'
4'
3'
2'
1'
0
KNIGHTS
00
7

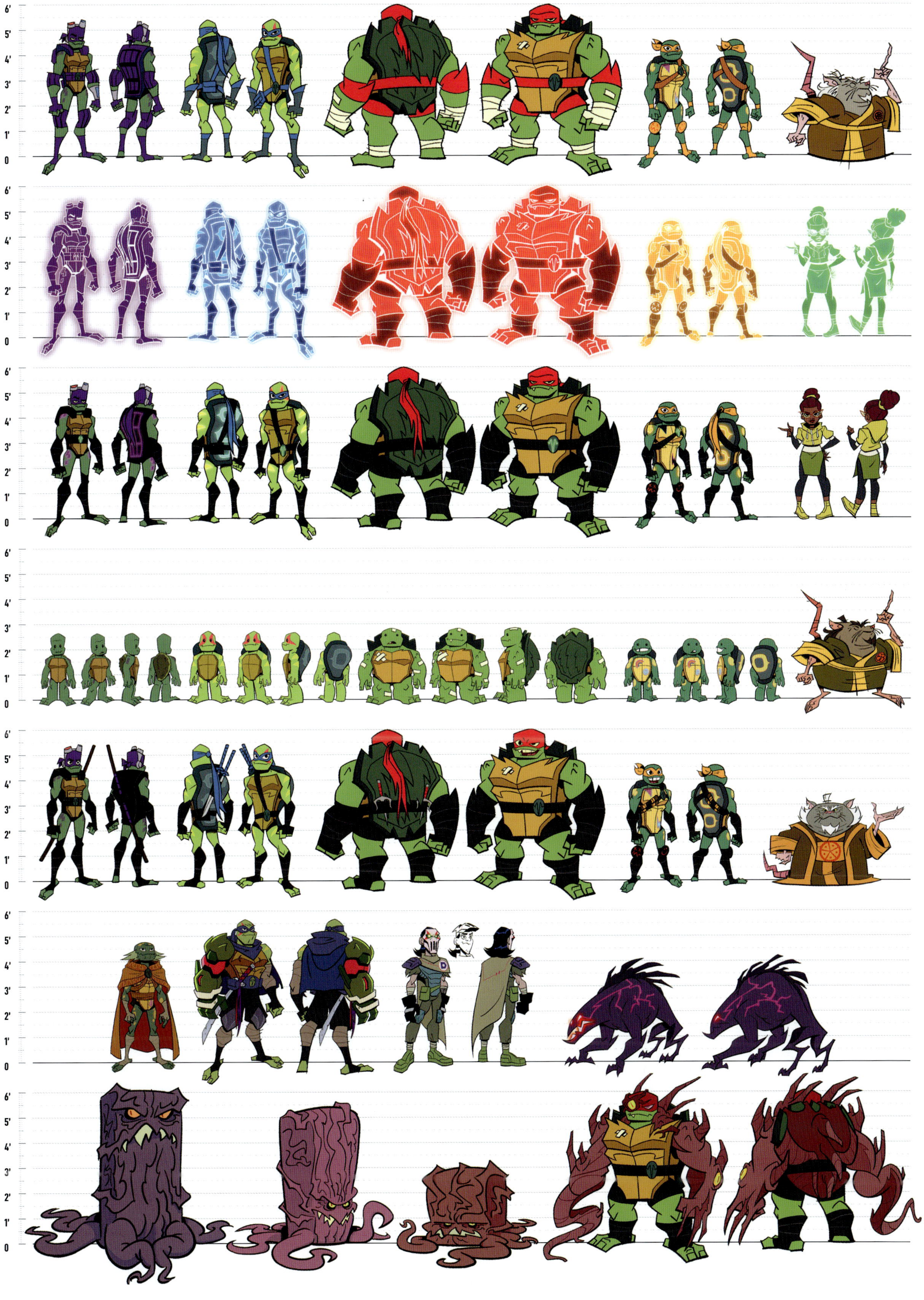
6' 5' 4' 3' 2' 1' 0
6' 5' 4' 3' 2' 1' 0
6' 5' 4' 3' 2' 1' 0
6' 5' 4' 3' 2' 1' 0
6' 5' 4' 3' 2' 1' 0
6' 5' 4' 3' 2' 1' 0
6' 5' 4' 3' 2' 1' 0
6' 5' 4' 3' 2' 1' 0

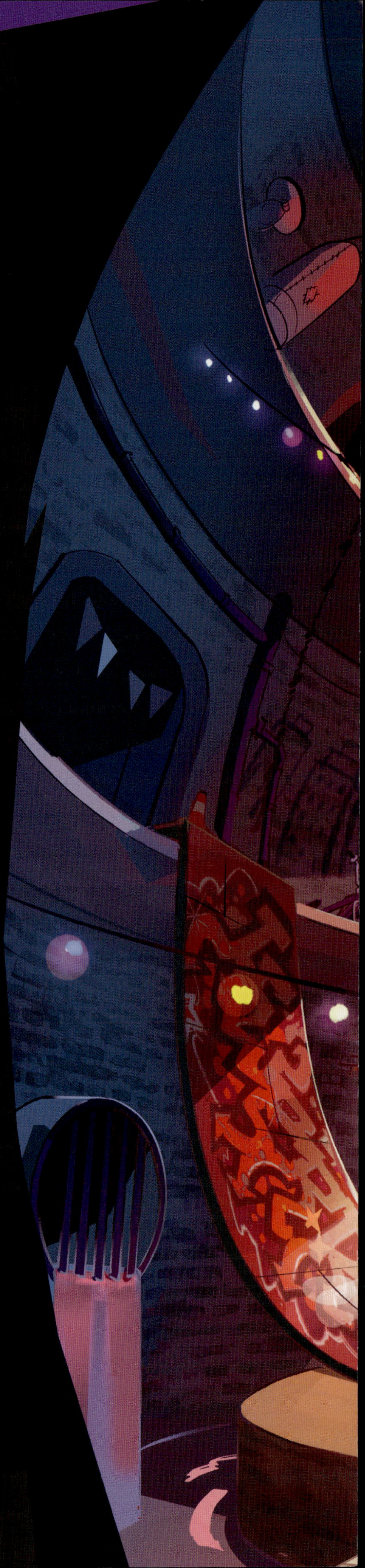

nickelodeon
RISE OF THE TEENAGE MUTANT NINJA TURTLES™

THE EPISODES

With 70 individual stories, *Rise of the Teenage Mutant Ninja Turtles* delivered a nonstop barrage of action, humor, and heart. From the Turtles' first steps into the Hidden City to their final showdown against the Shredder, each episode delivers nuanced layers, incredible fight sequences, and unforgettable moments.

This chapter provides an exclusive, behind-the-scenes exploration of the series' creation through commentary from the writers, artists, and crew. The episodes are presented in their intended story order, offering the most cohesive narrative flow. Explore the development of key scenes, the designs of new mutants, and the Turtles' evolving dynamics—this is your all-access pass to the making of Rise.

Packed with never-before-seen production art, insider insights, and hidden details, this is the ultimate companion for your journey through the Rise universe. Whether you're revisiting the series or discovering it for the first time, prepare to deepen your appreciation for every frame, relive the action, and fall in love with one of the franchise's boldest reimaginings all over again.

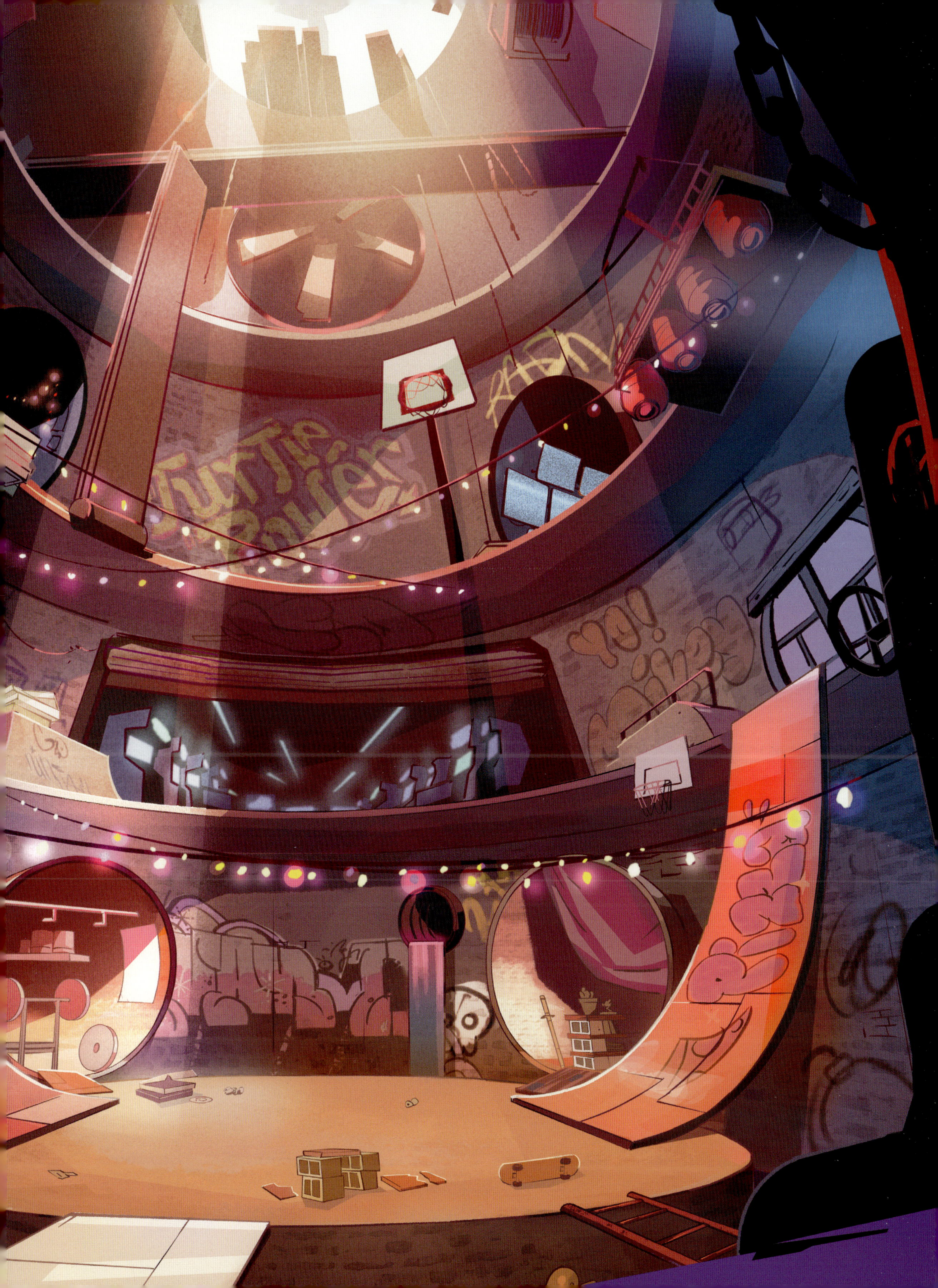
Turtle Roller

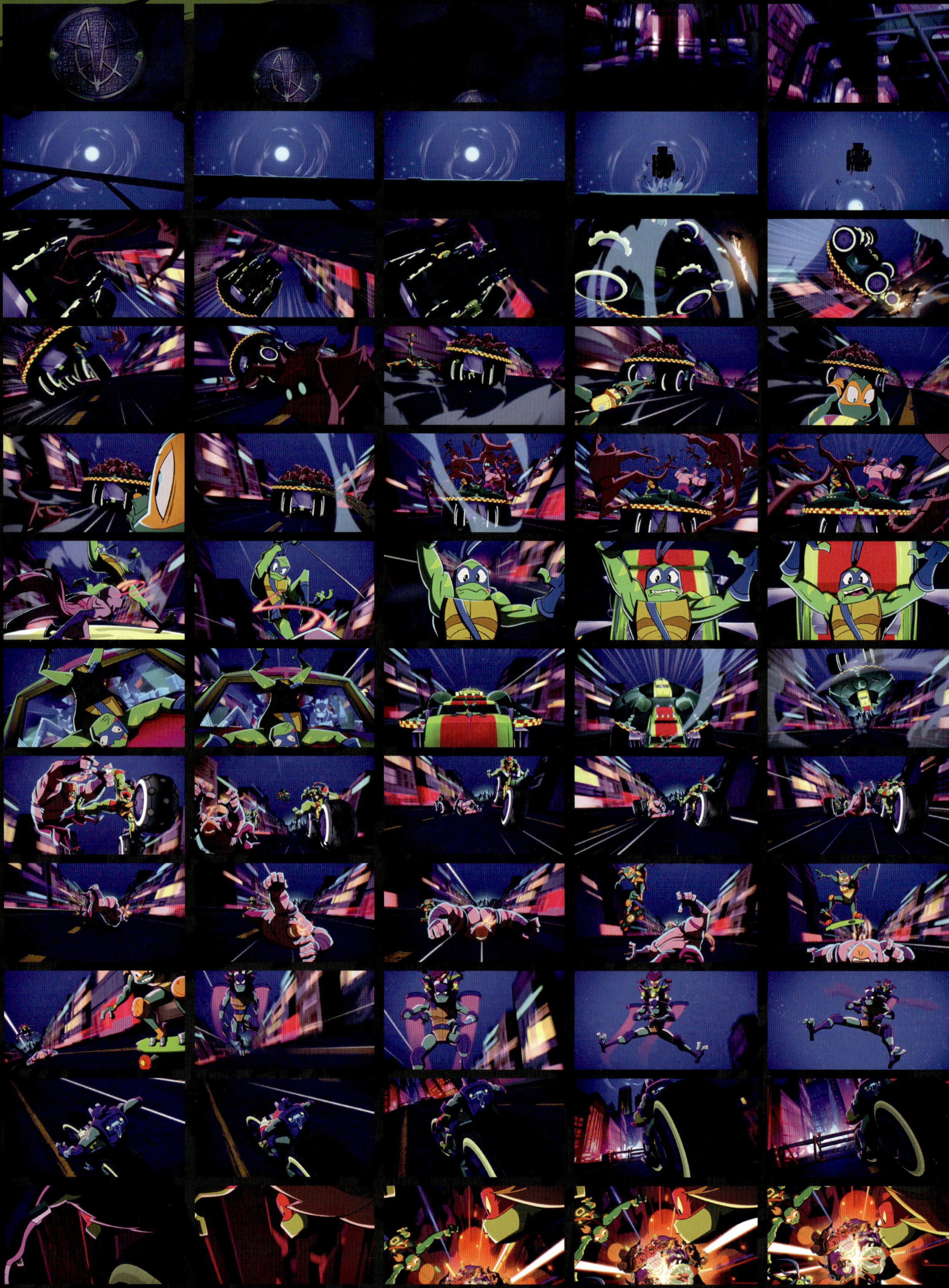

STORYBOARD ARTISTS: **KEVIN MOLINA-ORTIZ, ALAN WAN, ANT WARD, CHRISTIAN BARKEL, TOM BARKEL, SARAH HARPER**

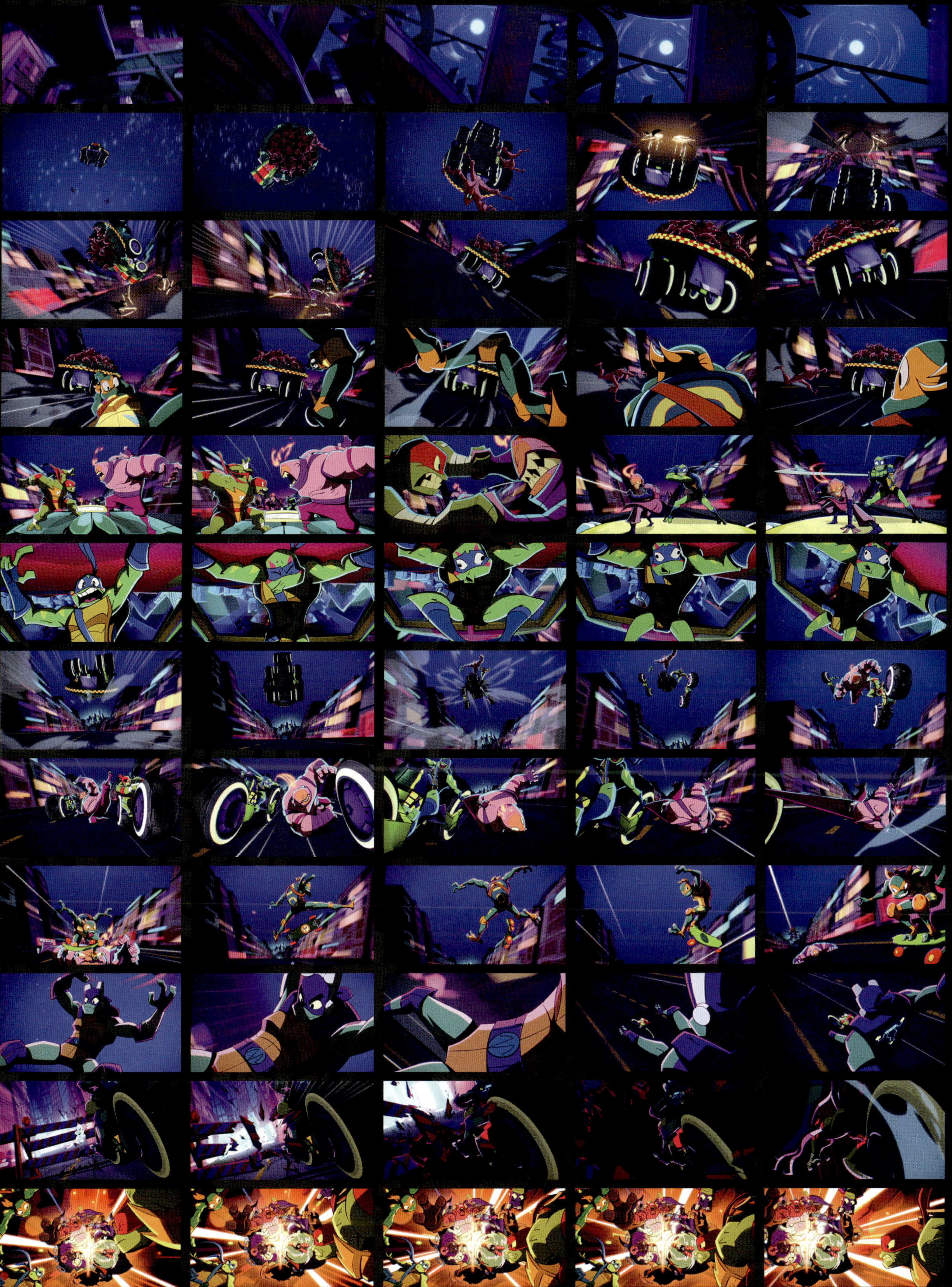

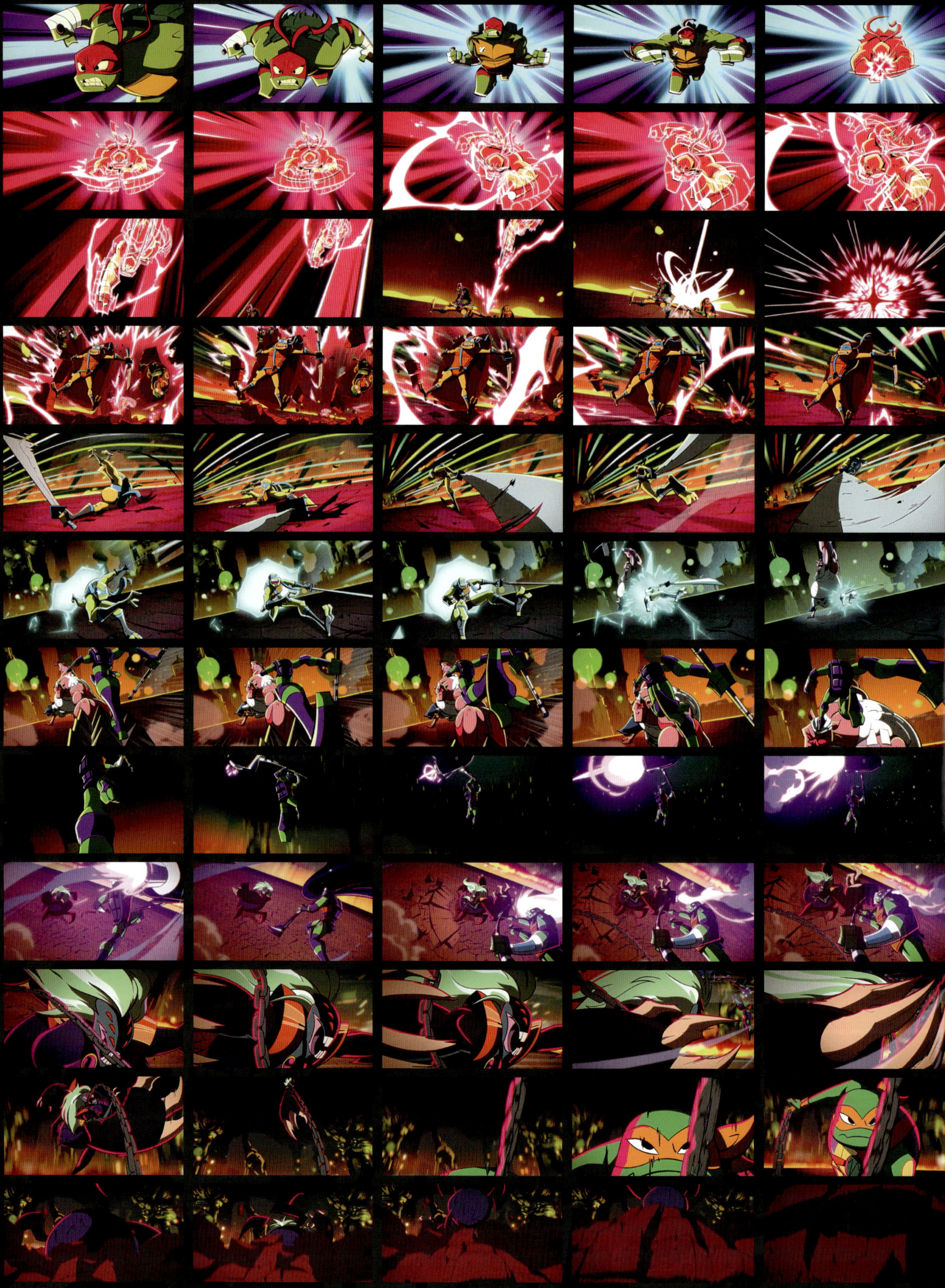

STORYBOARD ARTISTS: **KEVIN MOLINA-ORTIZ, ALAN WAN, ANT WARD, CHRISTIAN BARKEL, TOM BARKEL, SARAH HARPER**

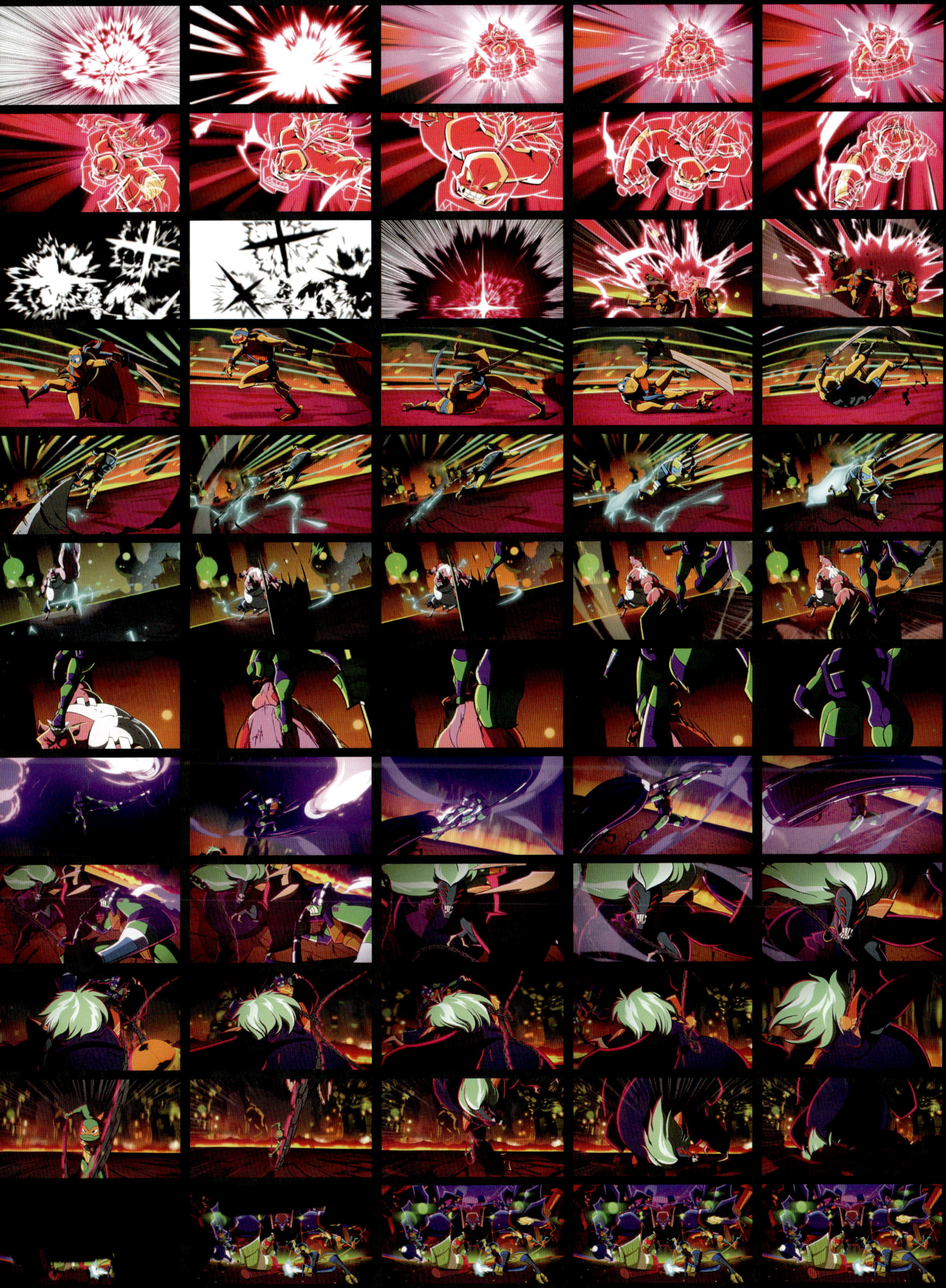

MYSTIC MAYHEM

SNEAK PEEK: JULY 20, 2018
ORIGINAL AIR DATE: SEPTEMBER 17, 2018
PRODUCTION CODE: 001-002

WRITTEN BY **IAN BUSCH, RUSS CARNEY, RON CORCILLO & JESSE GORDON**
STORYBOARDS BY **JULIA BRAID, KEVIN MOLINA-ORTIZ**
DIRECTED BY **BRENDAN CLOGHER & SEBASTIAN MONTES**

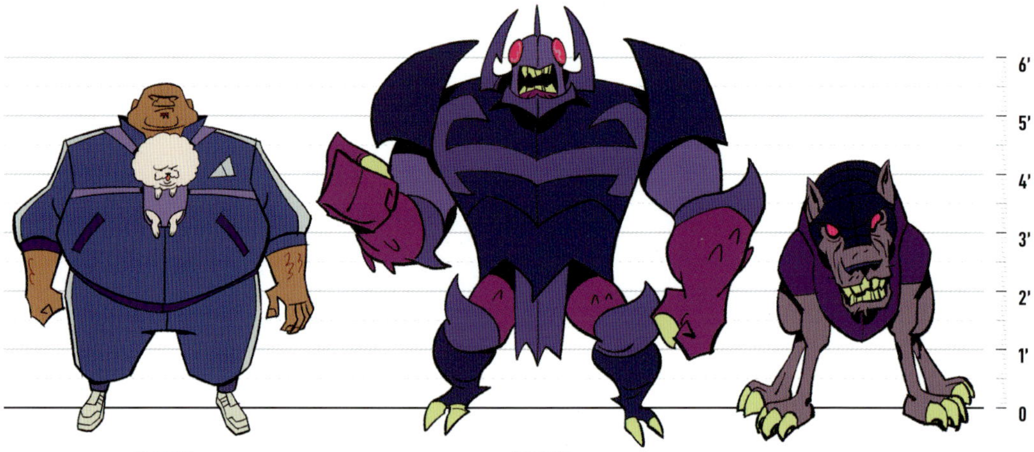

GARM
HUMAN FORM

GARM
GUARDSMAN

GUARDSMEN'S HOUNDS

RUSS CARNEY: This episode goes by *sooo* quickly because we had to cram so much stuff into the first episode. We were fresh into a new series, and the network and everybody else involved had *soooo* many wants. We want to explore New York! We want to explore the Hidden City! We want to understand the fun dynamic between the boys and April! We want kids to feel like they could find a portal to the Hidden City out in the wild! We want *toys*!

RON CORCILLO: But while we were struggling to write this first episode, *nothing* had been solidified. We didn't know the rules of the series. We didn't know how the mysticism worked. We didn't know how the mutagen and transformations worked. We knew nothing. What we did know is that we wanted our opening reveal of the Turtles and April to be epic fun, and so we did our best.

RUSS CARNEY: When Splinter is watching TV, we originally had him engrossed in a Filipino telenovela, where he was waiting for Letty to divulge her recipe to her famous moose adobo. This was a nod to Eric Bauza's Canadian and Filipino heritage. Instead, we spent time with Splinter watching *Soapy Treadmill*, a nod to a number of outlandish Japanese action-based game shows that were popular on YouTube at the time.

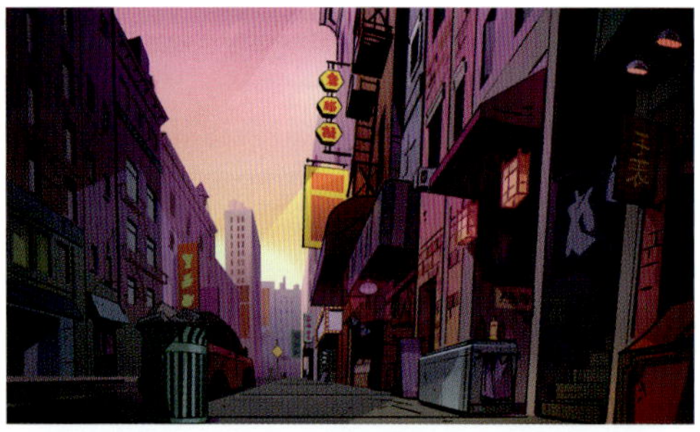

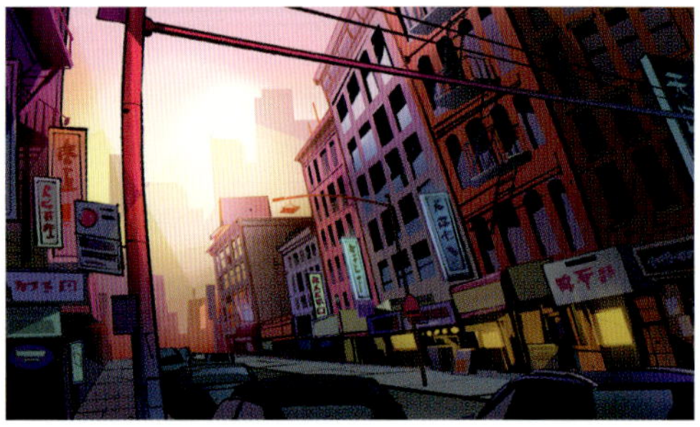

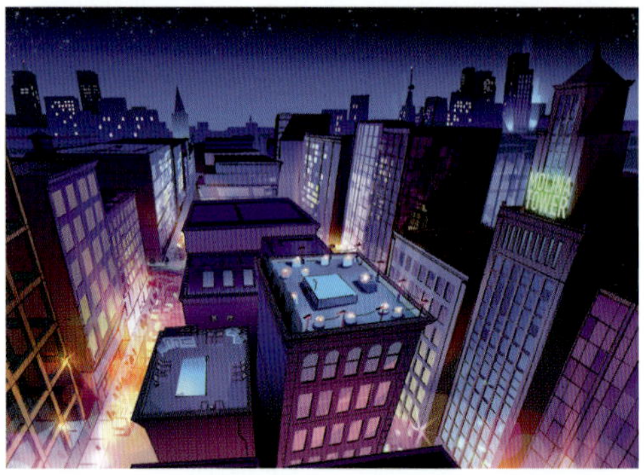

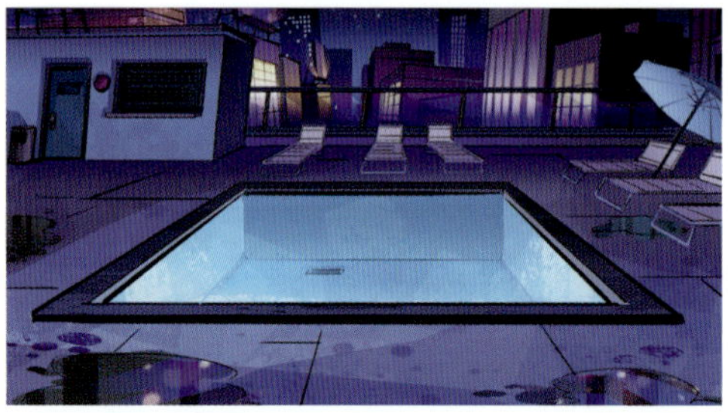

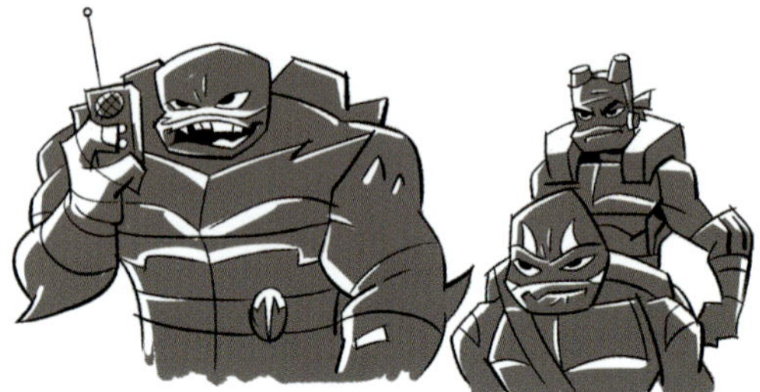

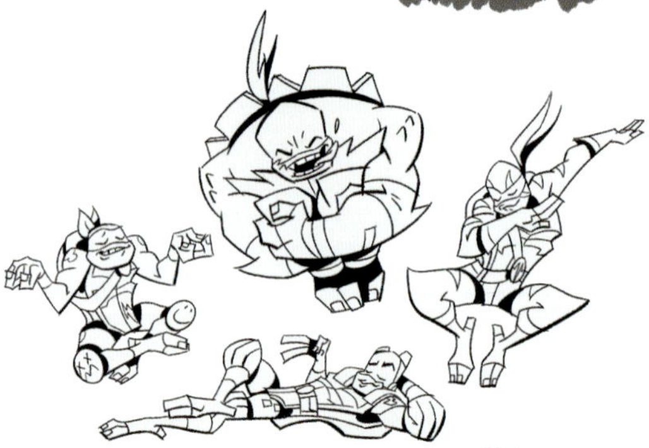

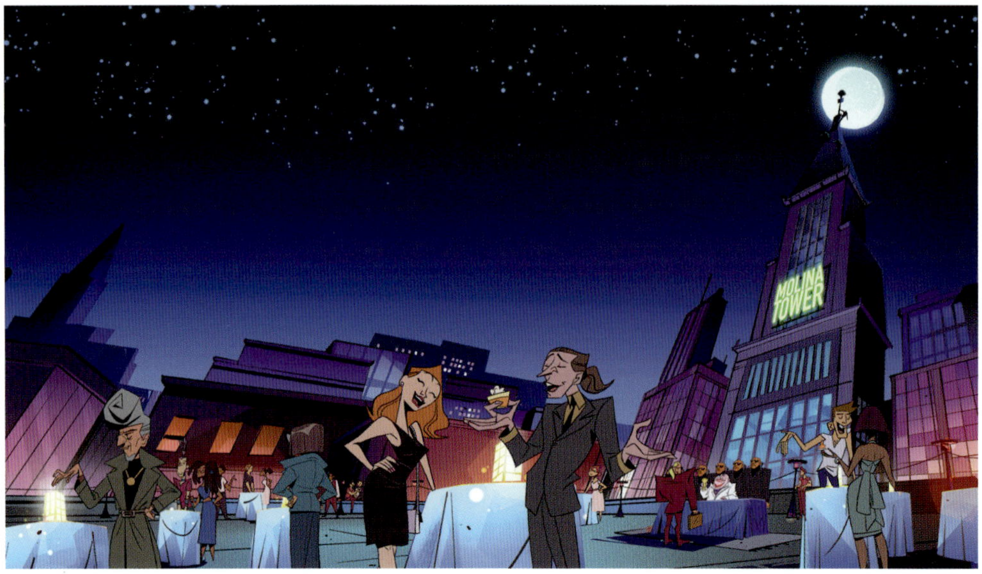

CARL BEU (COLOR SUPERVISOR): Background painter Chu-Hui Song's work establishing the skylines in our show gave us an amazing blueprint we continued to follow throughout the series.

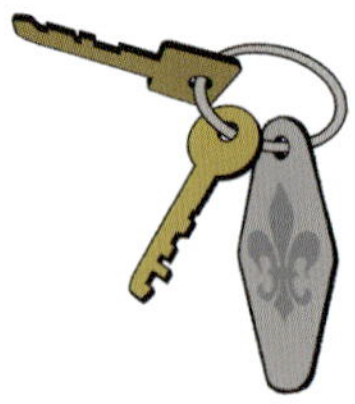

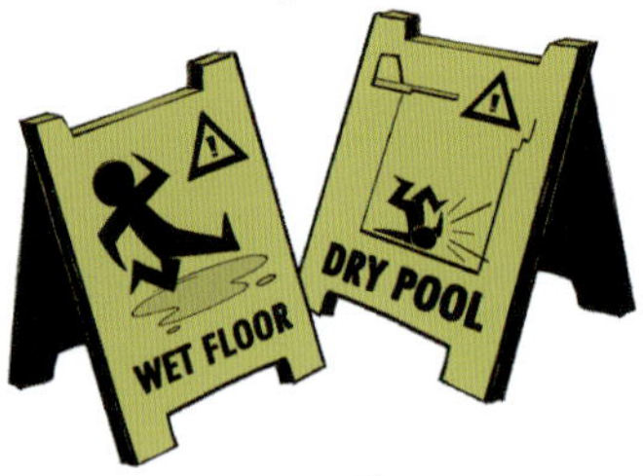

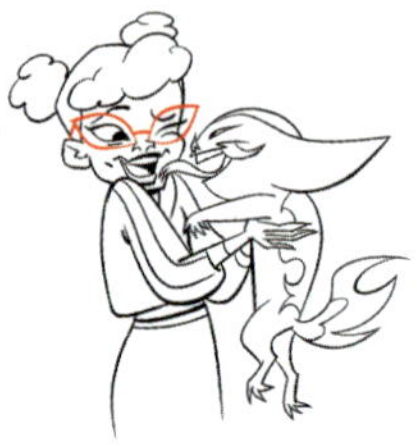

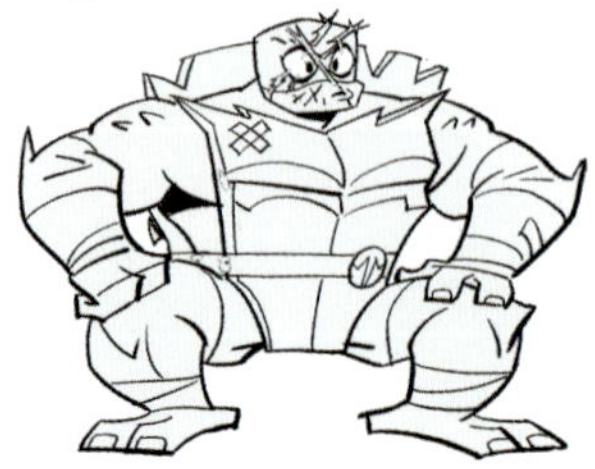

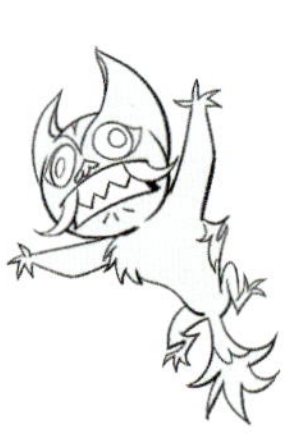

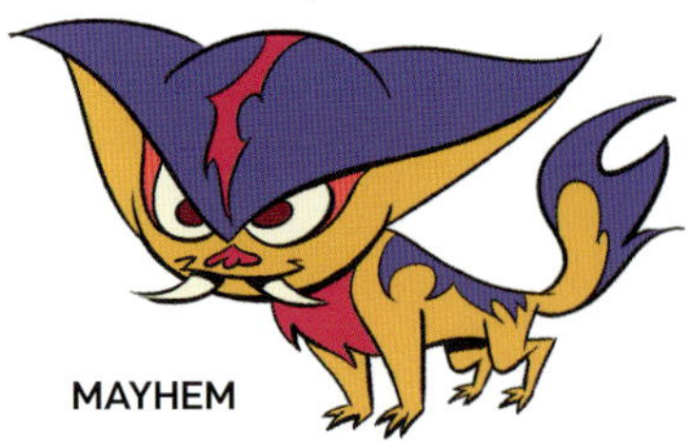

MAYHEM

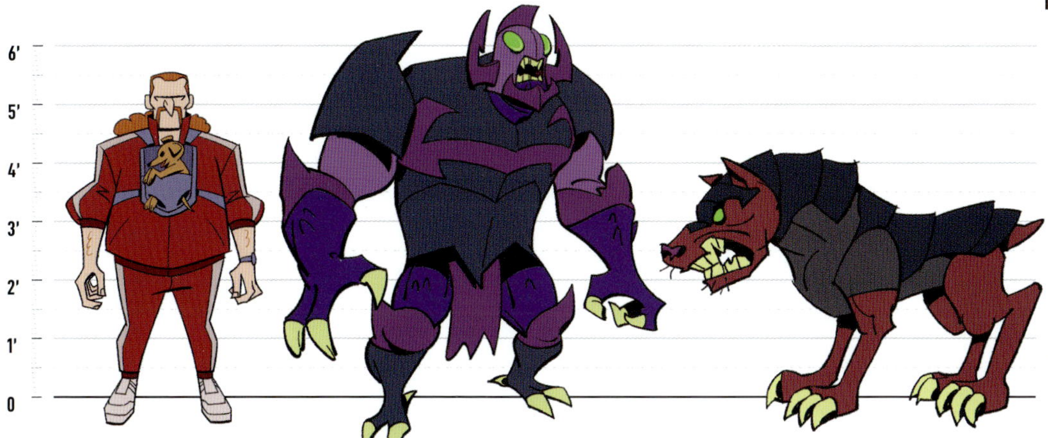

FREKI
HUMAN FORM

FREKI
GUARDSMAN

GUARDSMEN'S HOUNDS

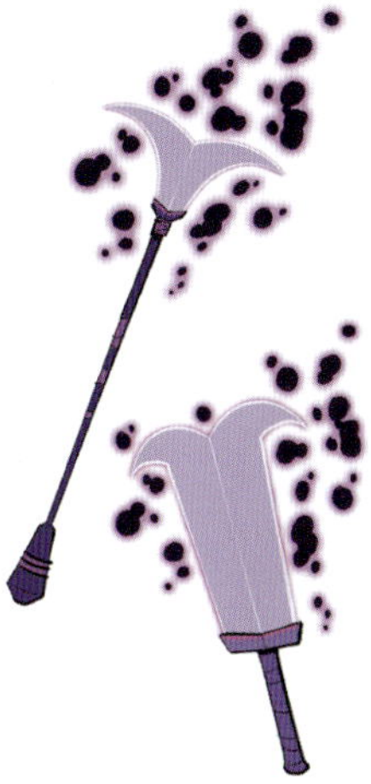

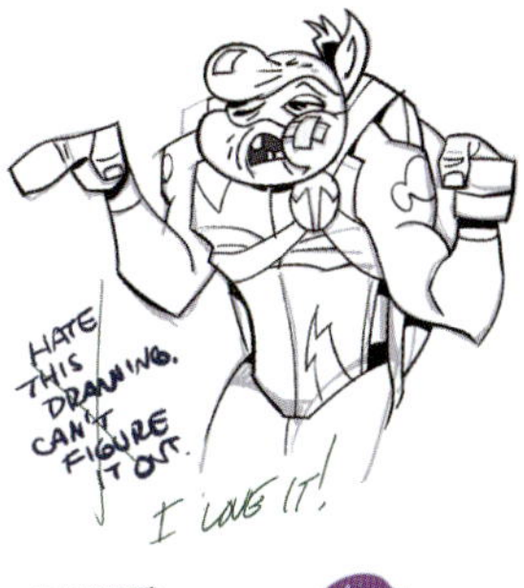

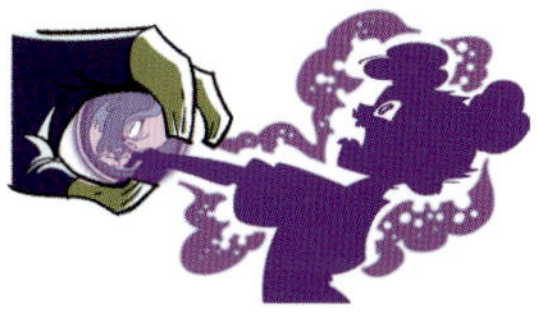

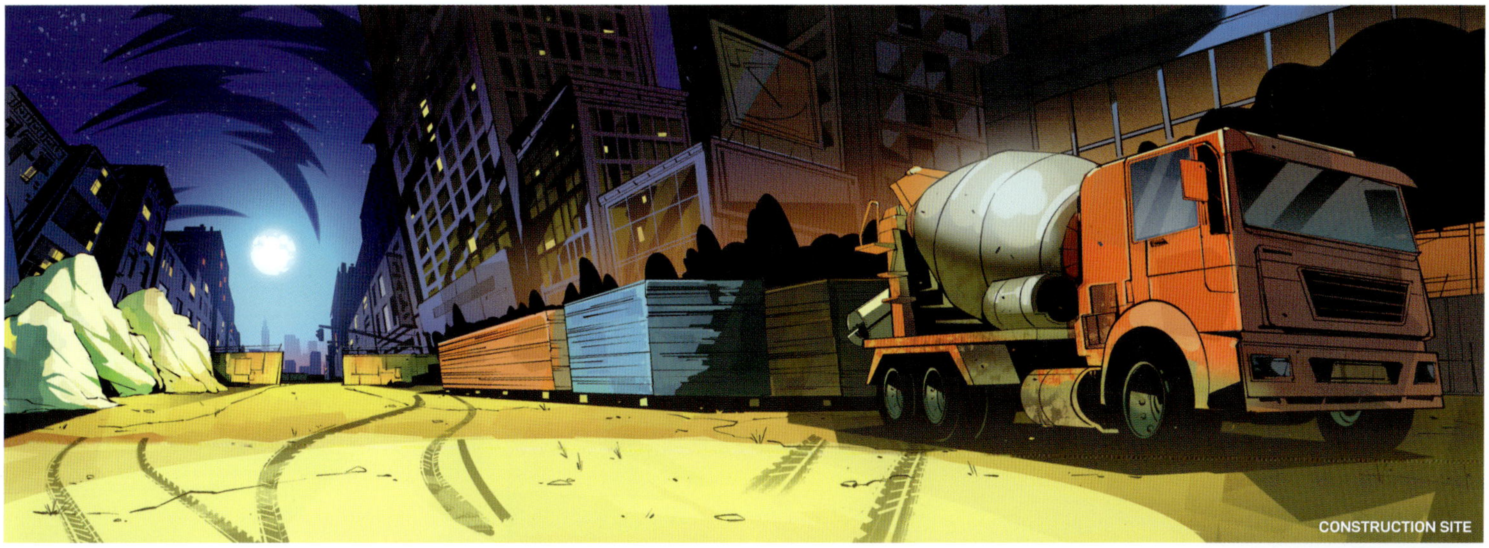

CONSTRUCTION SITE

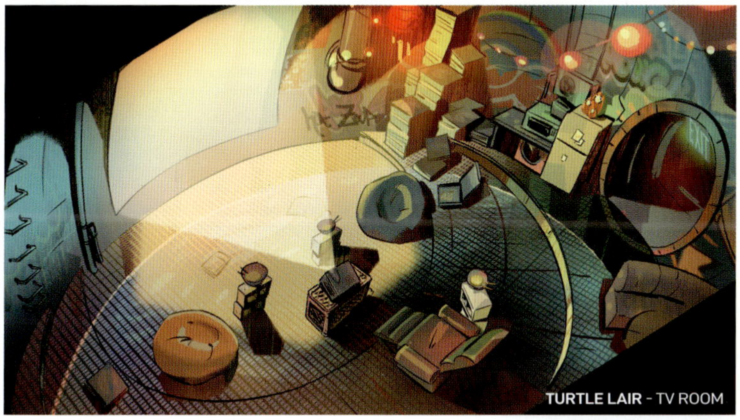

TURTLE LAIR - TV ROOM

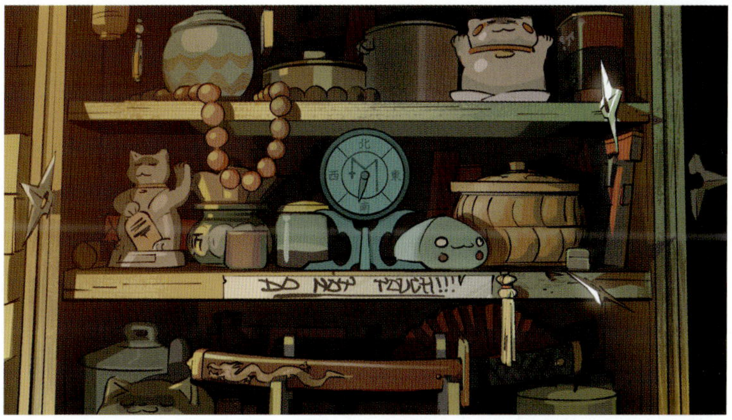

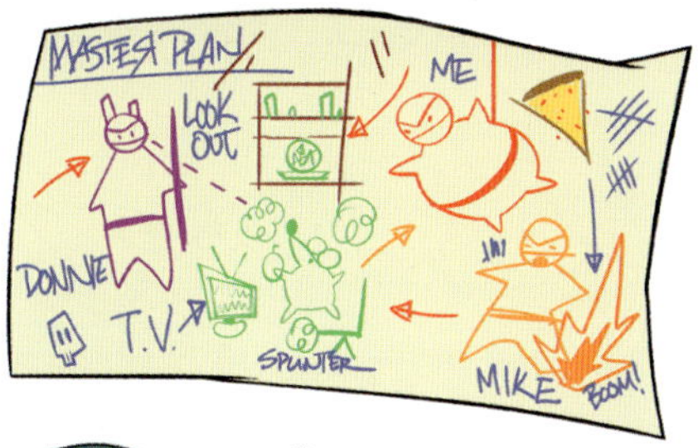

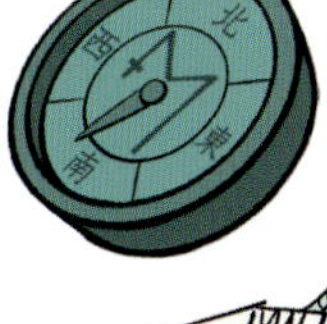

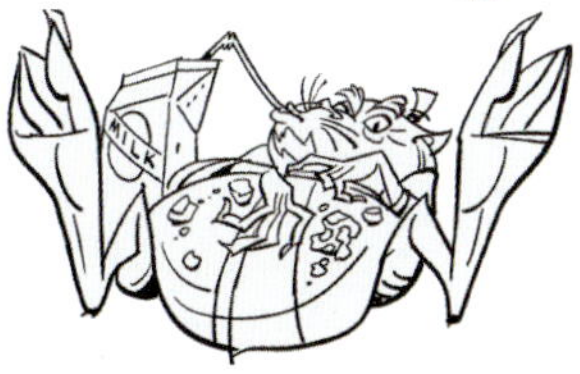

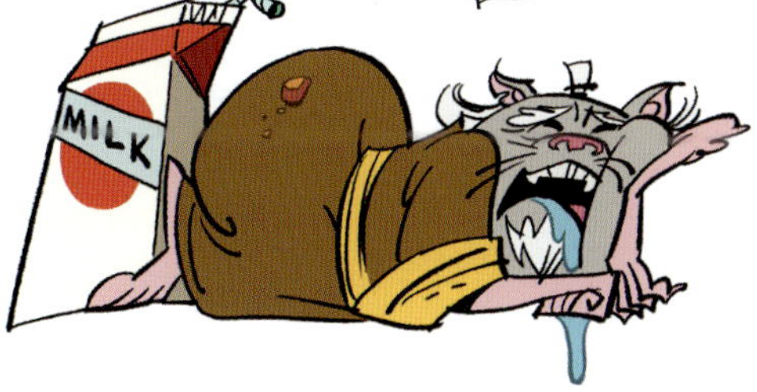

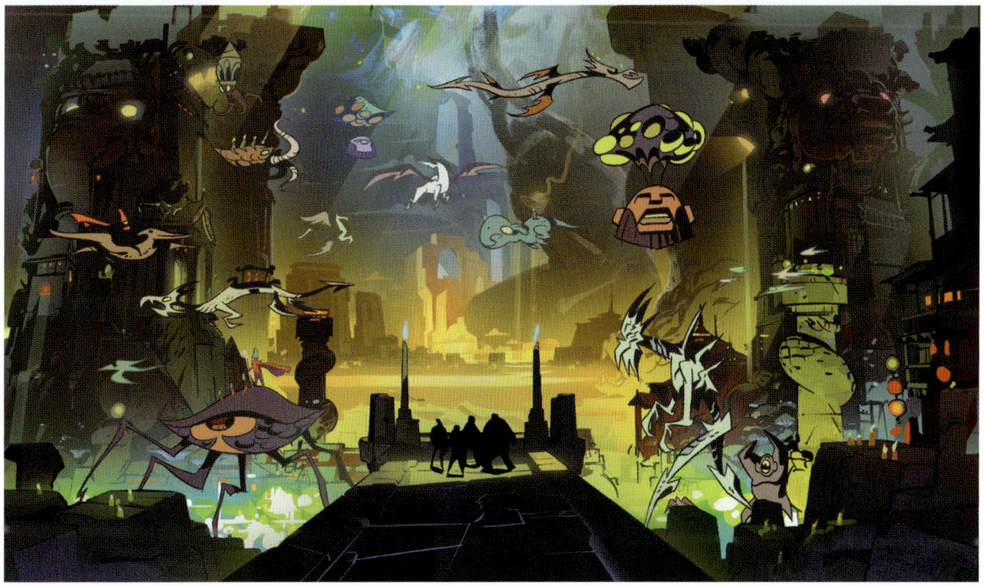

RON CORCILLO: This was the first episode where we acknowledged Raph's various stinks—fear being the first, then amazement.

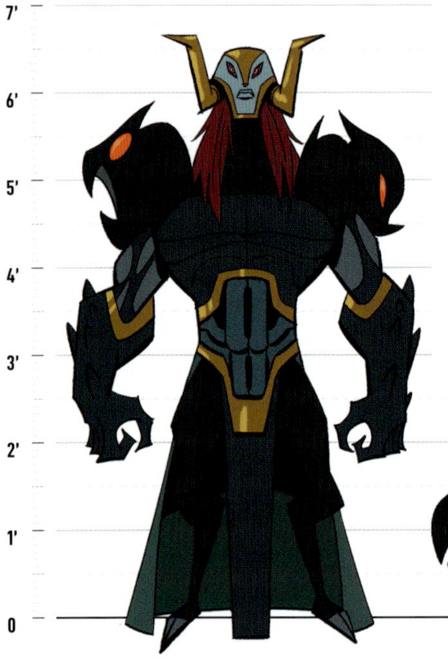

BARON DRAXUM MUNINN HUGINN OOZESQUITO

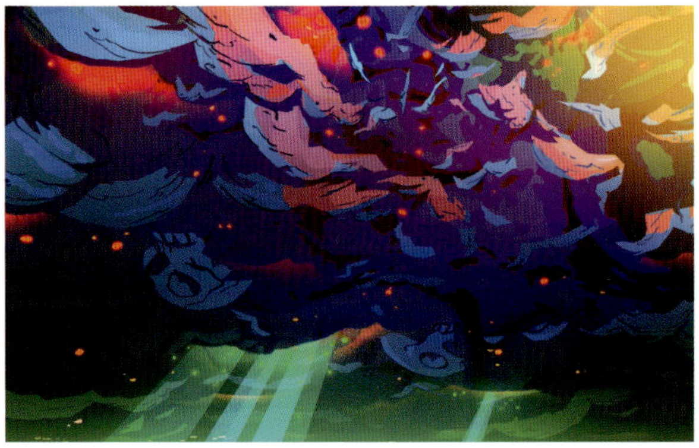

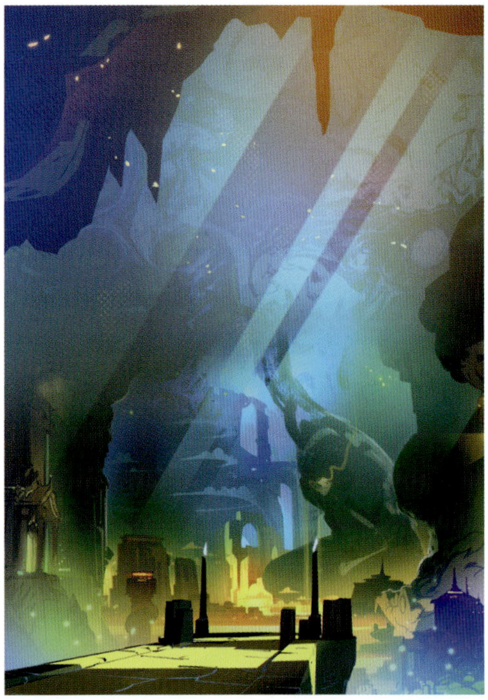

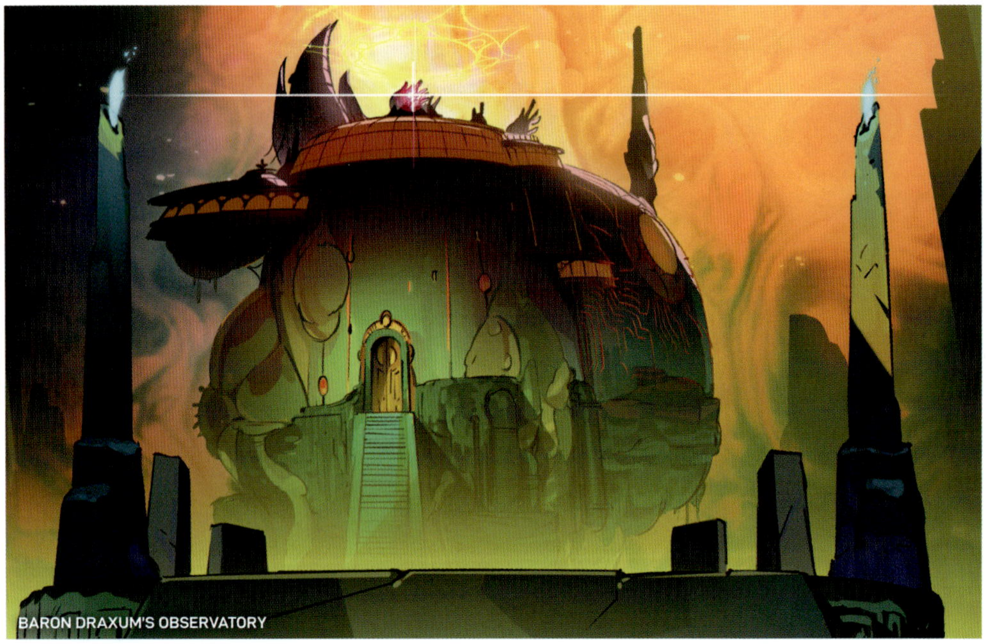

BARON DRAXUM'S OBSERVATORY

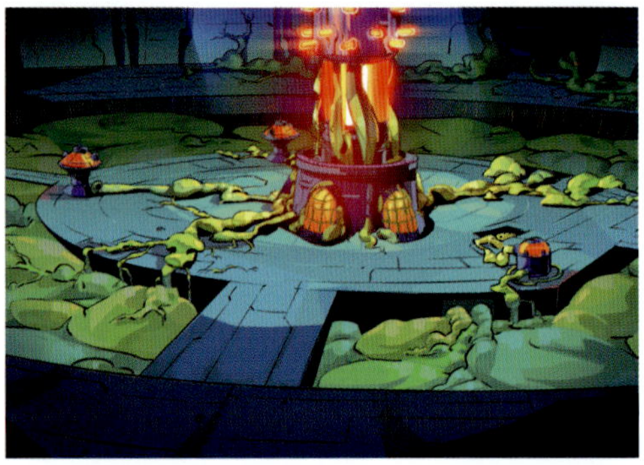

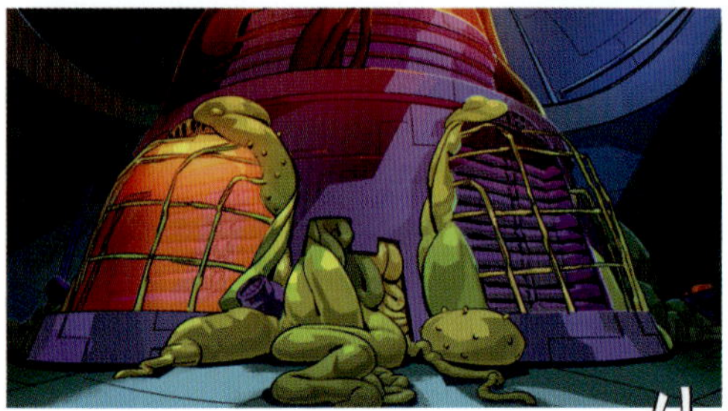

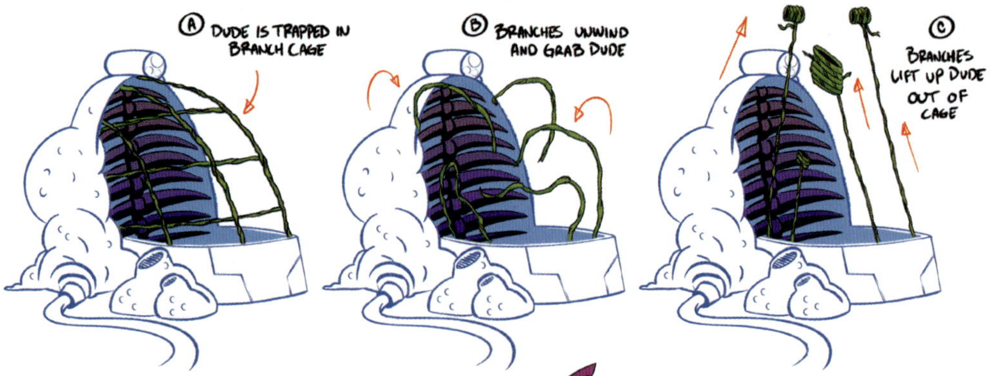

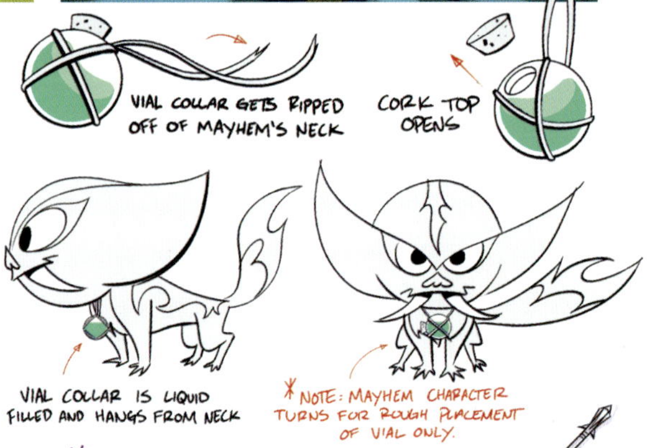

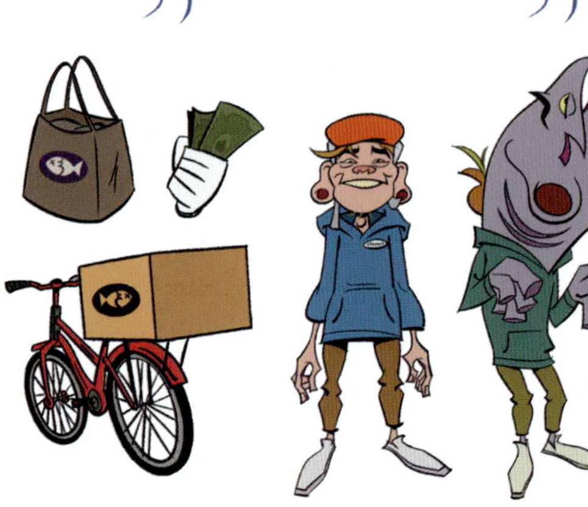

STEWART

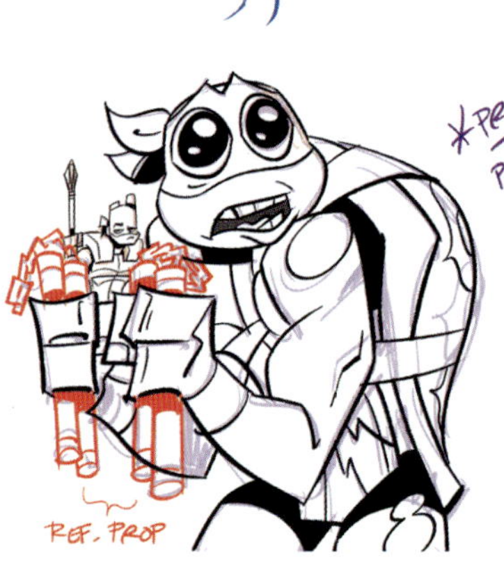

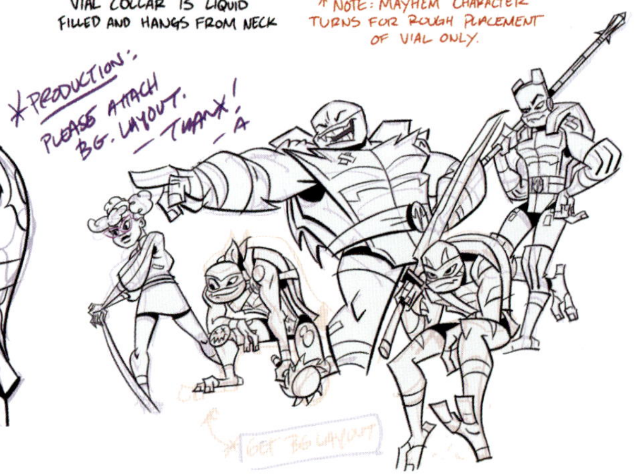

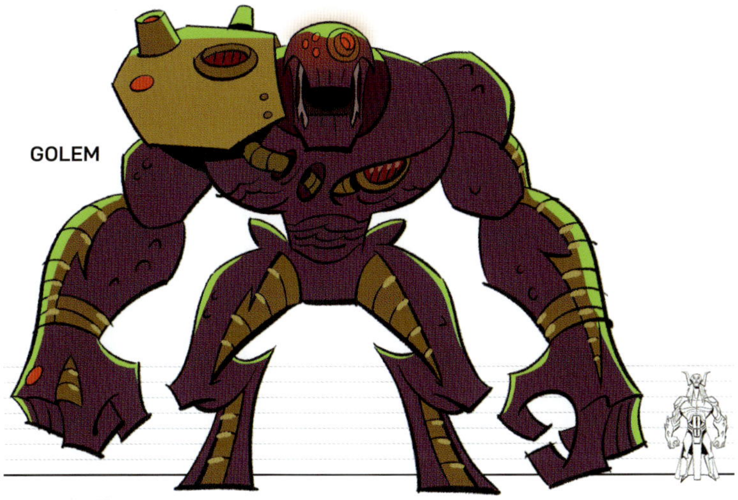
GOLEM

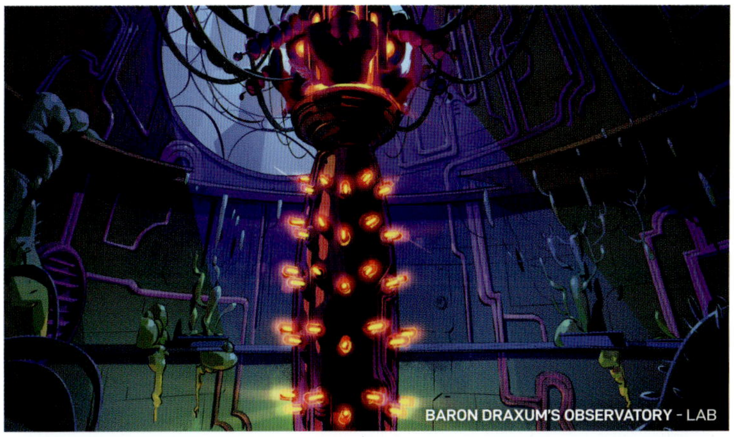
BARON DRAXUM'S OBSERVATORY - LAB

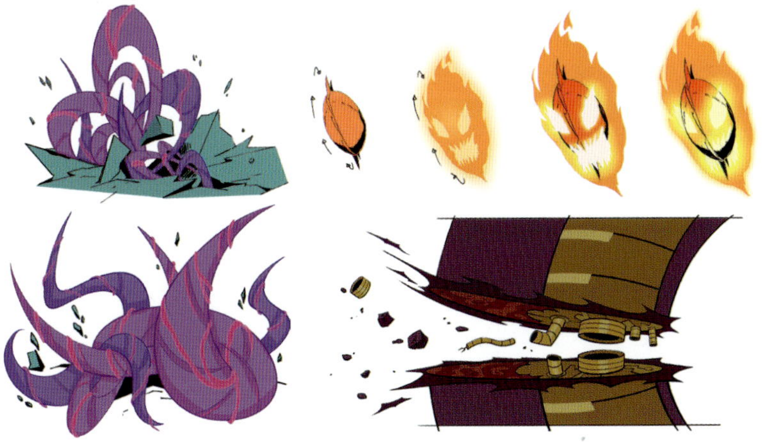

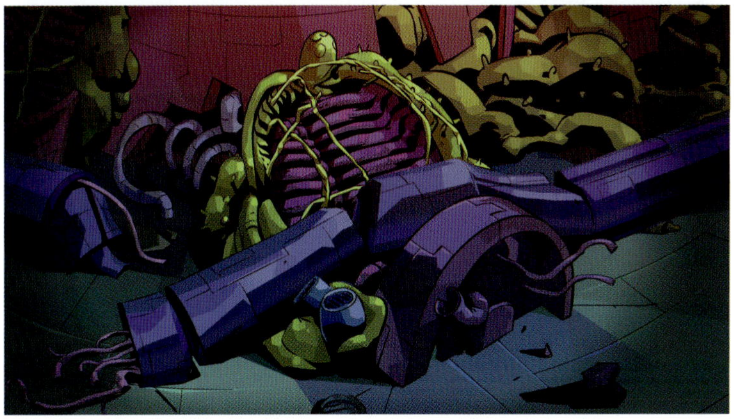

RUSS CARNEY: April jumping into battle and shouting *"April O'Neillll!"* was a direct nod to Leeroy Jenkins—the classic *World of Warcraft* meme where a player charges in recklessly shouting his name. That old-school internet lore perfectly matched April's go-getter personality.

RON CORCILLO: In the pilot, we wanted Mikey to exclaim *"omigosh,"* shorthand for *"oh my gosh,"* but Brandon Mychal Smith accidentally pronounced it *"omeegosh."* The innocence of his delivery—like a kid who'd only read the phrase in comics—was so spot-on for Mikey that we kept it. *"Omeegosh!"* became his thing.

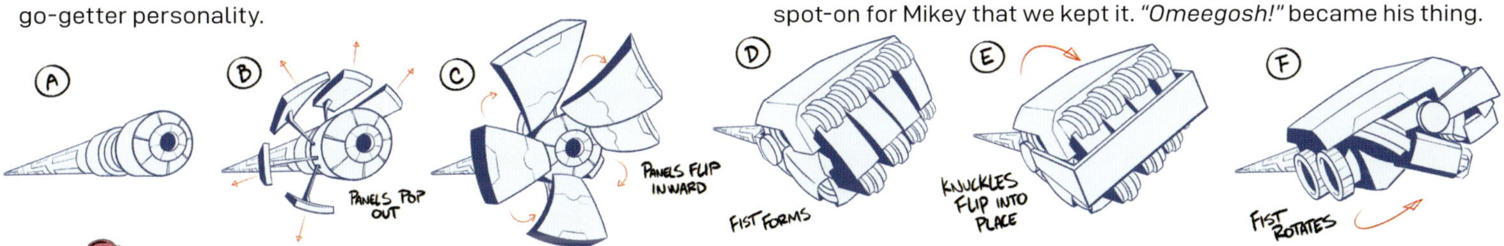

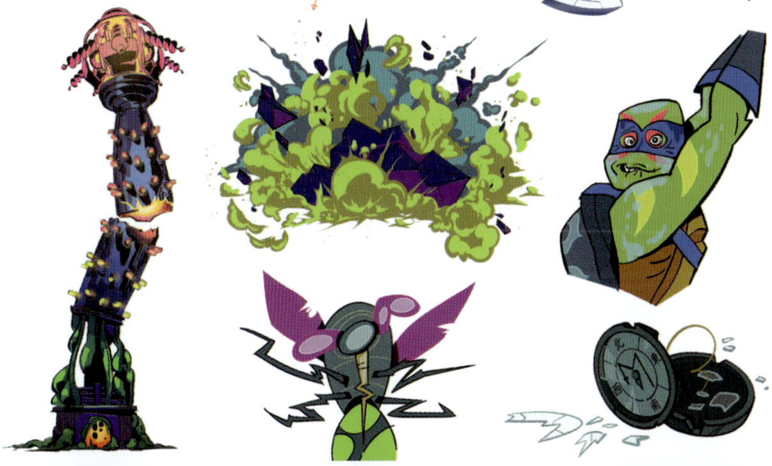

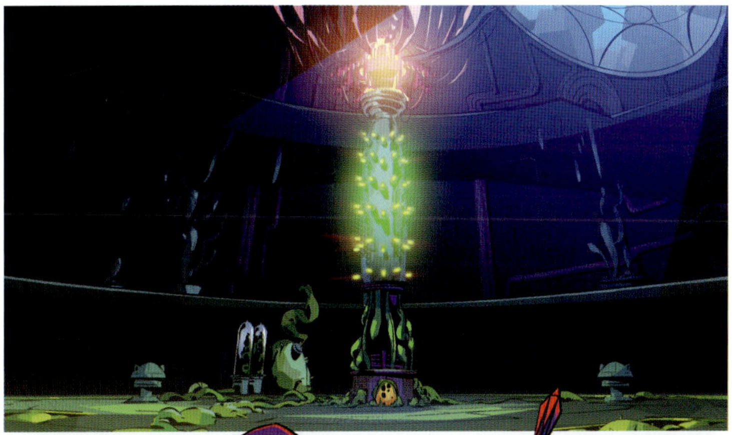

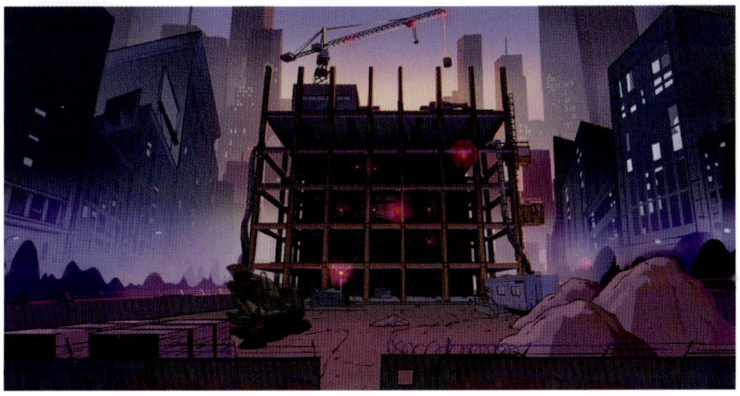

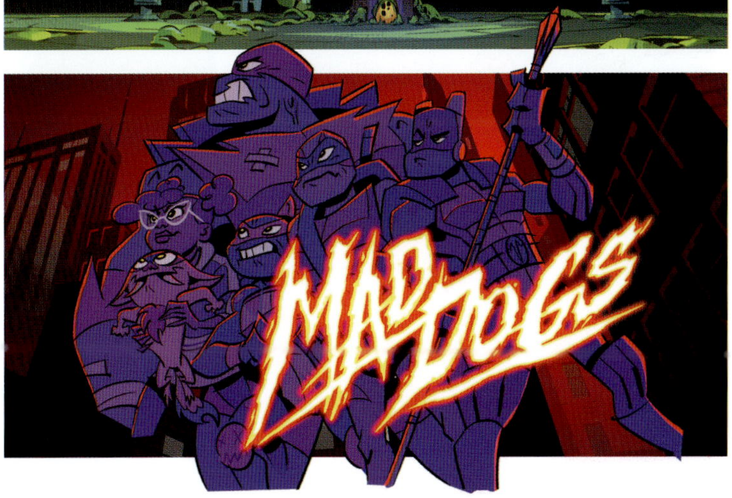

NEWSWORTHY

ORIGINAL AIR DATE: SEPTEMBER 27, 2018
PRODUCTION CODE: 003

WRITTEN BY **JESSE GORDON**
STORYBOARDS BY **KEVIN MOLINA-ORTIZ**
DIRECTED BY **SEBASTIAN MONTES**

JESSE GORDON: This was the first episode I ever wrote for the show, and it was the first episode ever written. This was before any of the Turtles had been cast. And so a lot of stuff from that episode would go on to be runners, and random things like the hippo suit would come back.

I remember saying "jazzy," which I feel like was just something dumb that we thought of that became this element of the Turtles where they would every so often use this old-timey speak and try to make it sound cool.

I remember being at a story retreat where we were pitching ideas. I've always loved villains, and it was so fun to come up with new villains. There was this idea that caught traction of a villain who thought he was their greatest enemy of all time, and he would be this tiny little worm that the Turtles would never be able to remember. And I remember even this early on that the idea was he would be a runner, where he ends up with one of the gauntlets that unleashes the Shredder. I think it was always so funny that this character was sort of just in the background that the Turtles never paid attention to.

But it needed another villain, which is where Hypno comes from. It's amazing that Hypno and Warren Stone would be this odd-couple pairing that would last throughout the series. I love magic, so combining that with a hippo—Hypno-Potamus—it just sort of made sense to make his superpower hypnotism.

John Michael Higgins was always my first choice for Warren Stone, and getting him was amazing. I don't know whose idea it was to get Rhys Darby for Hypno, but when he was so funny, I wrote a bunch of Hypno episodes just to get him to come back. Both of them together were so good.

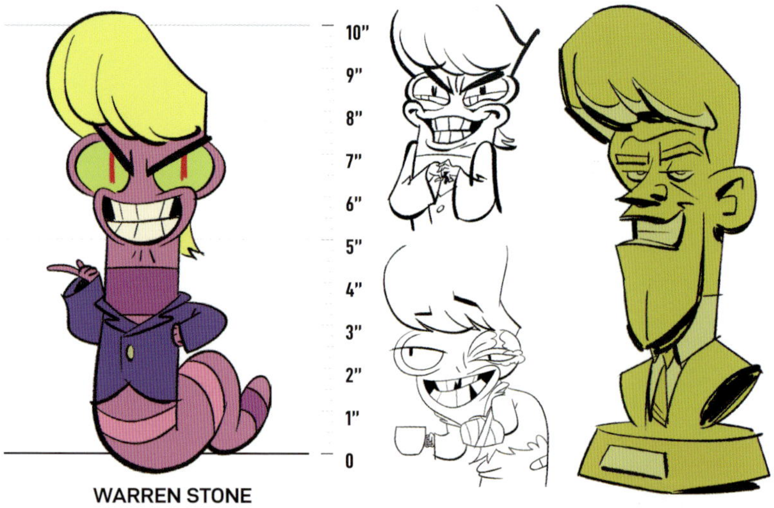

WARREN STONE

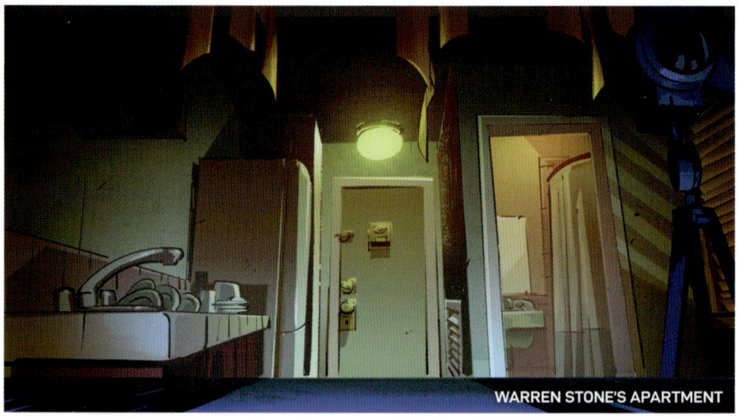
WARREN STONE'S APARTMENT

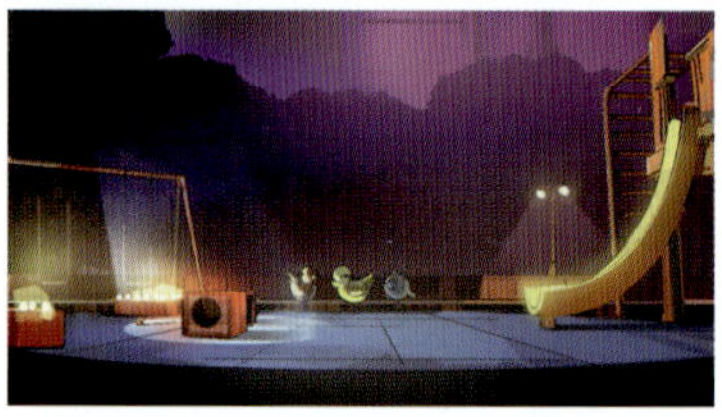

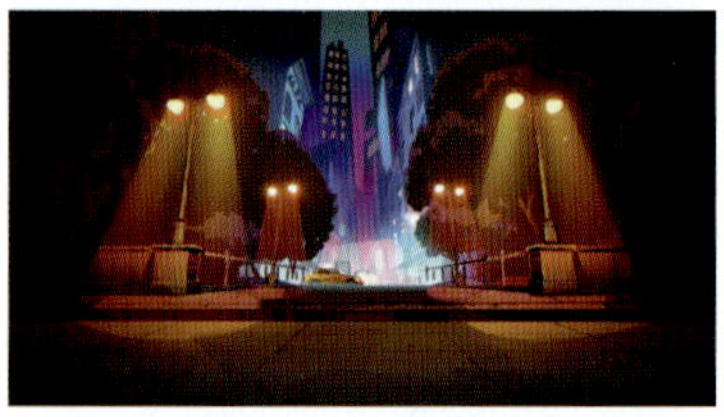

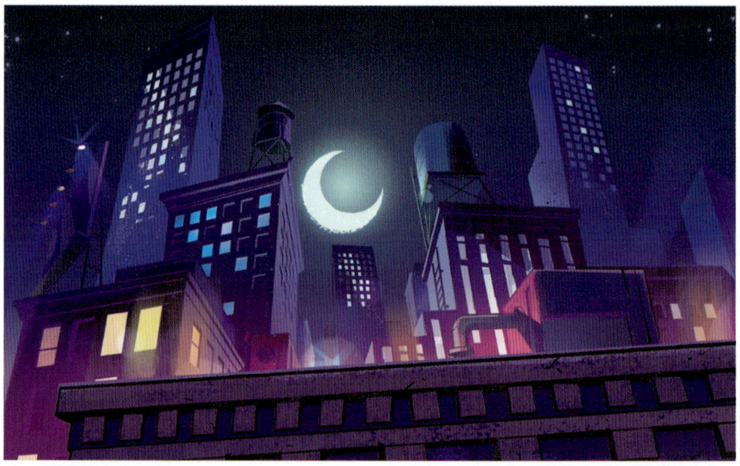

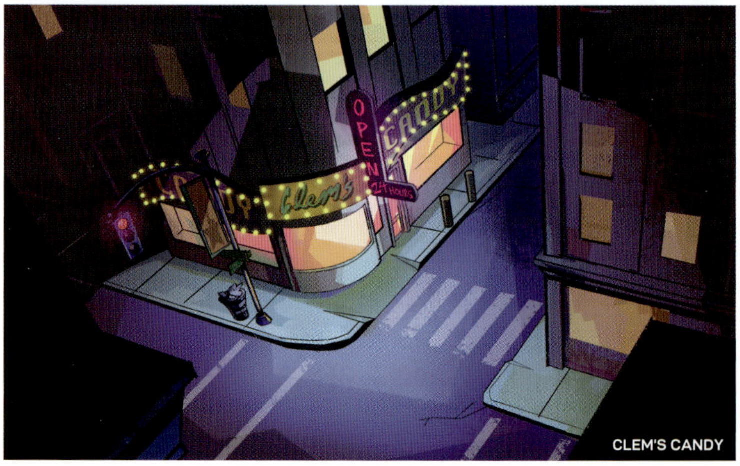

CLEM'S CANDY

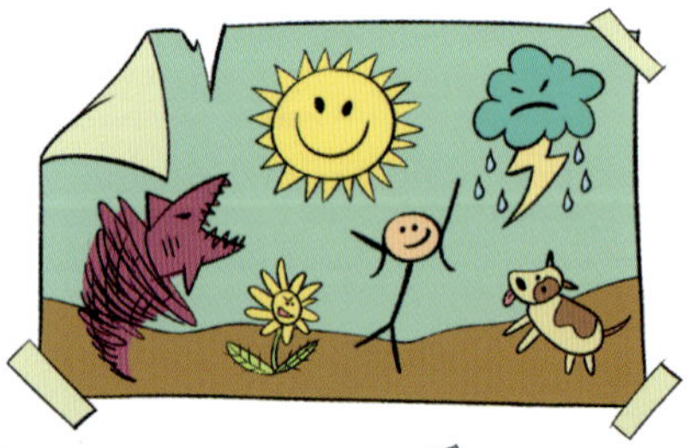

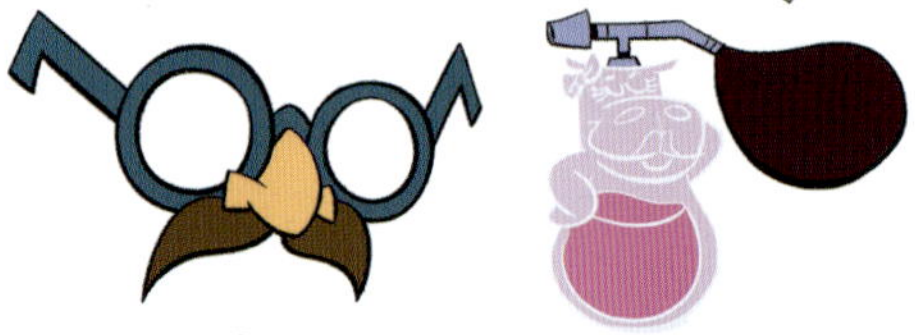

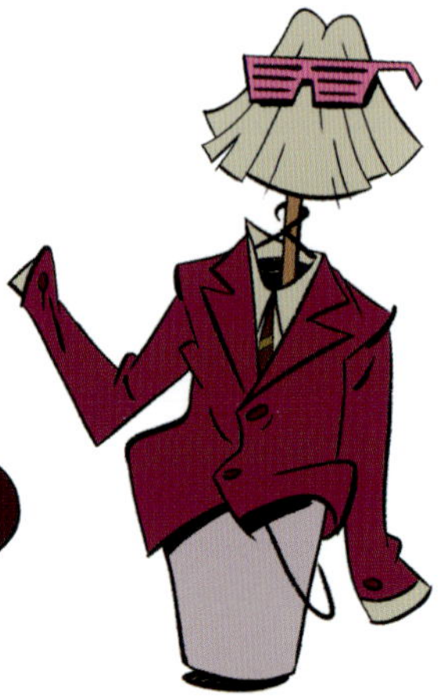

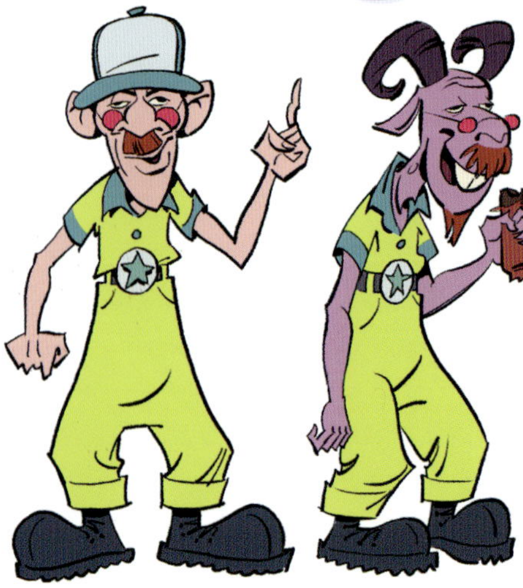
CLEM

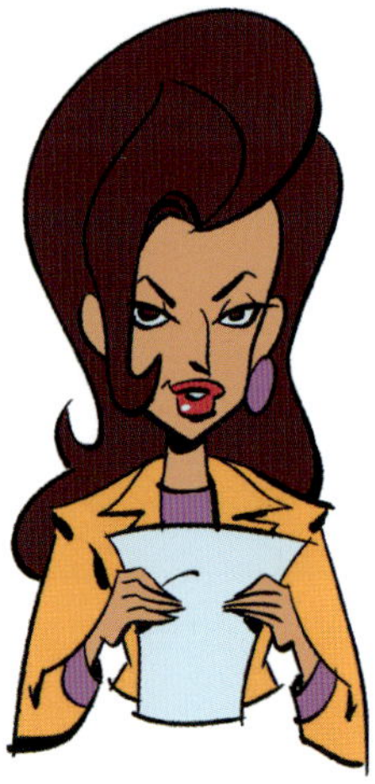
CARLY BALMACEDA

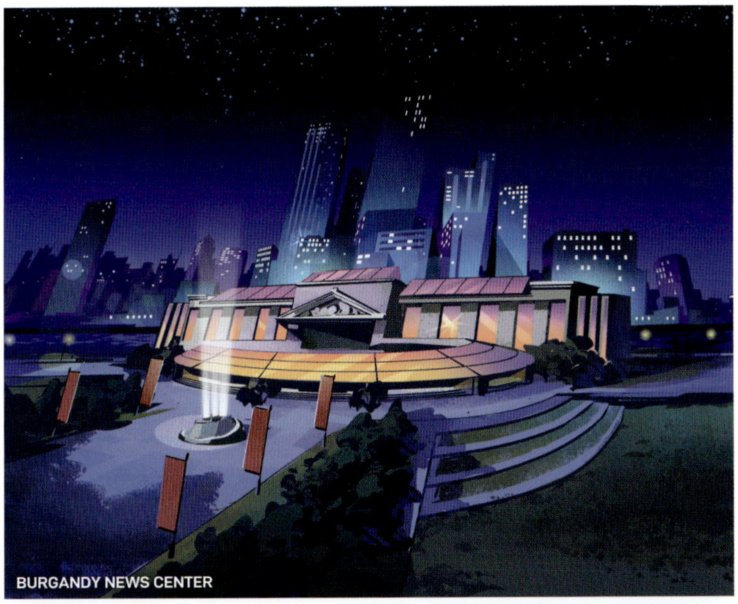
BURGANDY NEWS CENTER

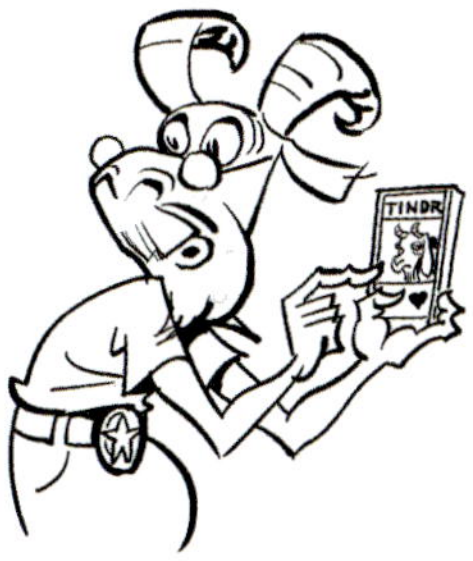

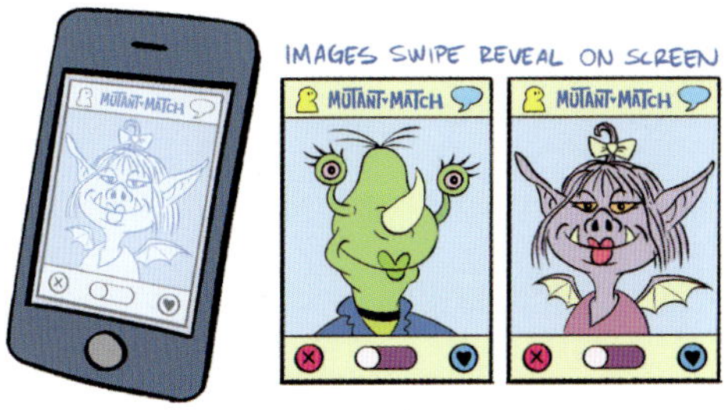

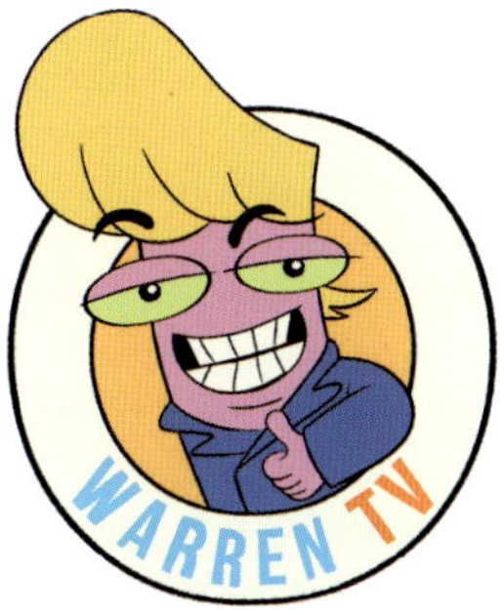

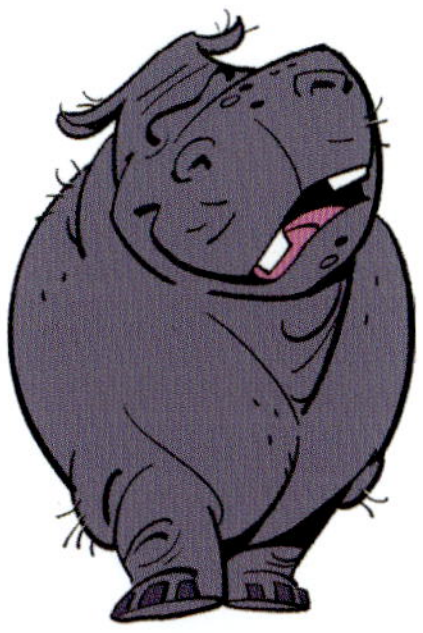
DOUG

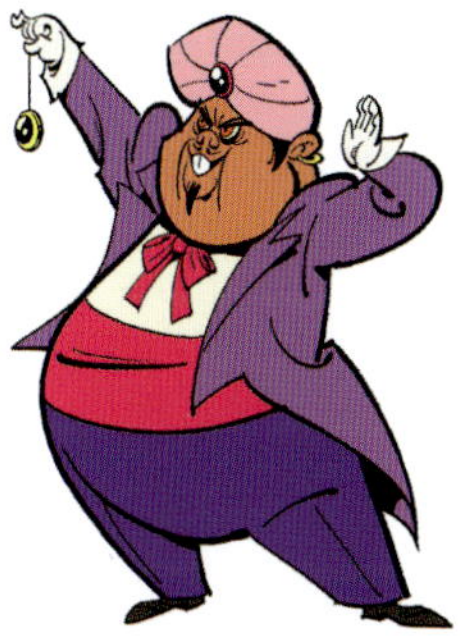
MEZMER-RON

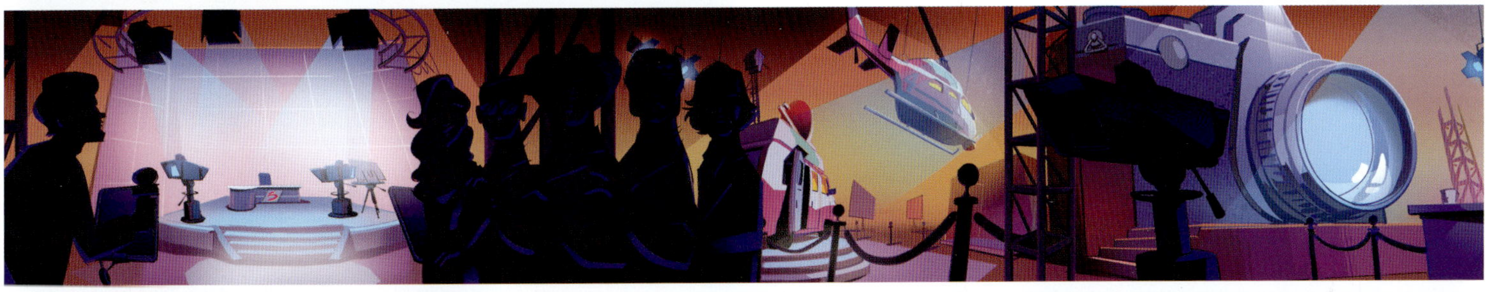

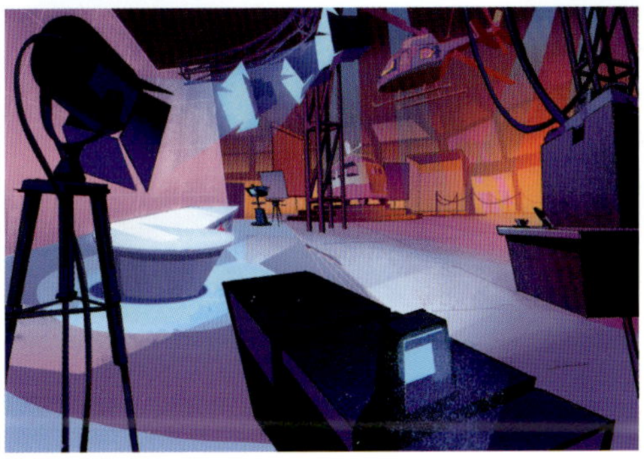

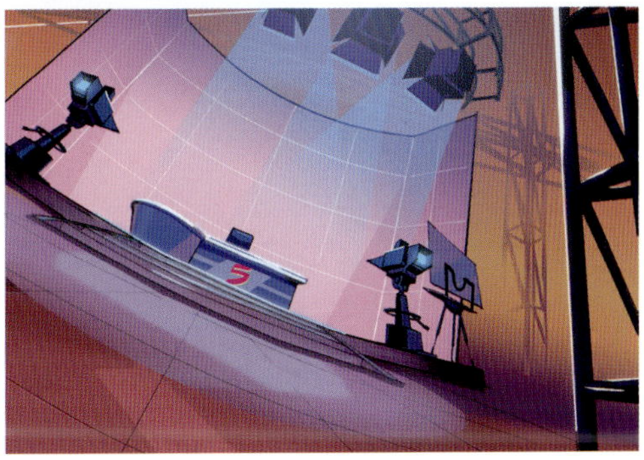

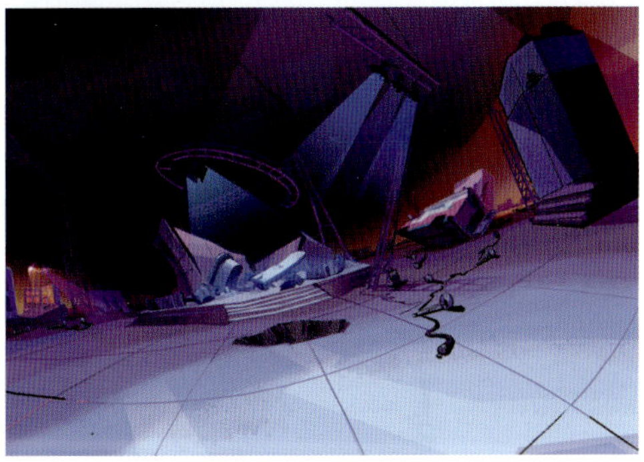

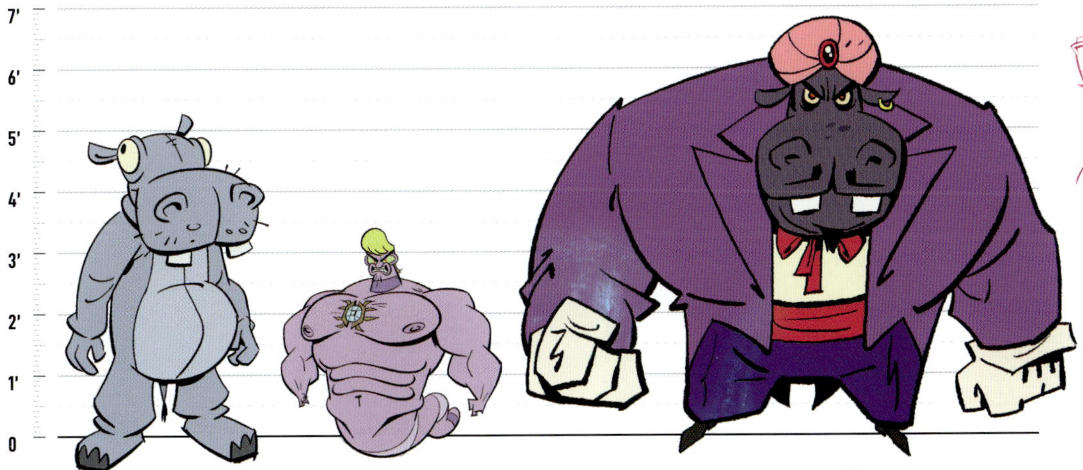

MIKEY
HIPPO SUIT
"CURRENT OCCUPANT"
WARREN STONE
HYPNO-POTAMUS

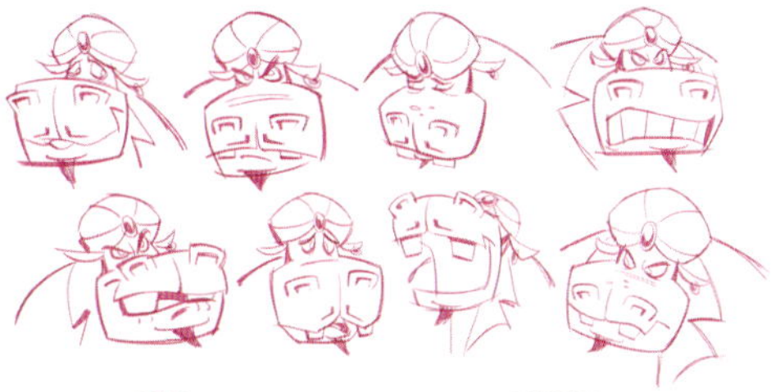

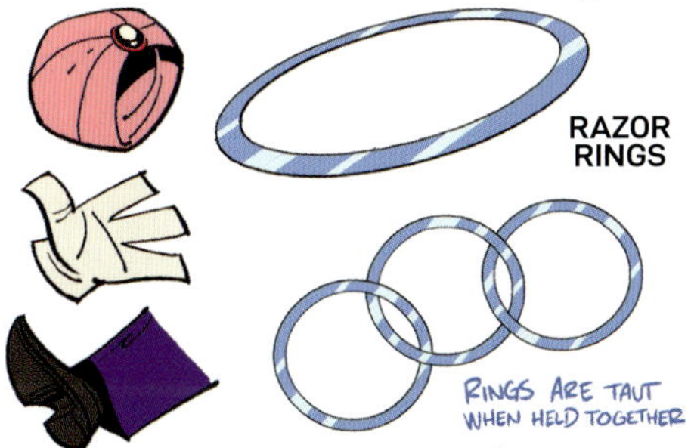

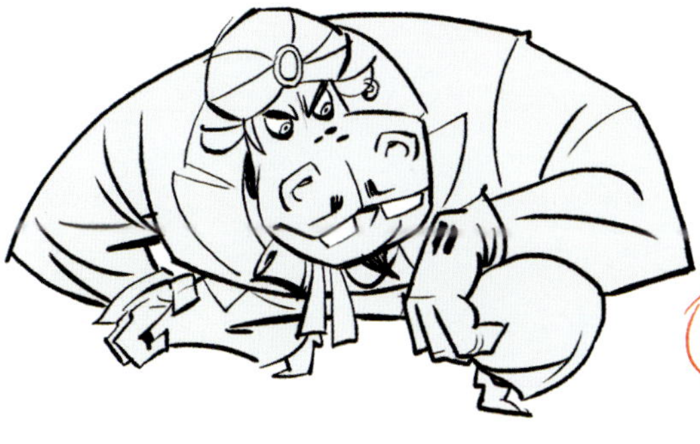

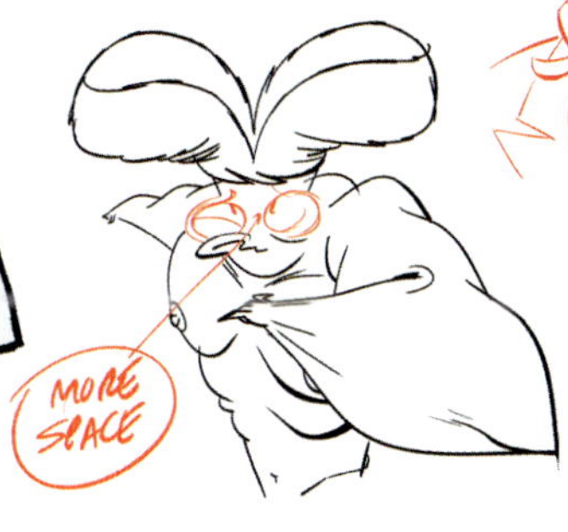

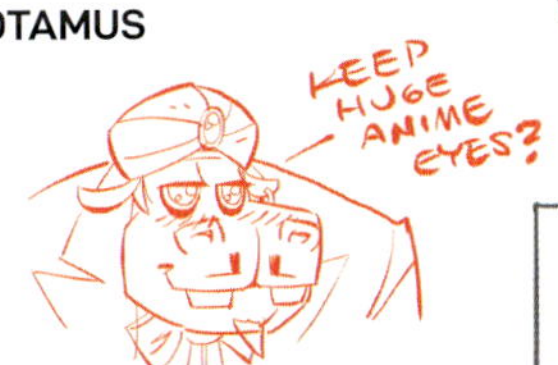

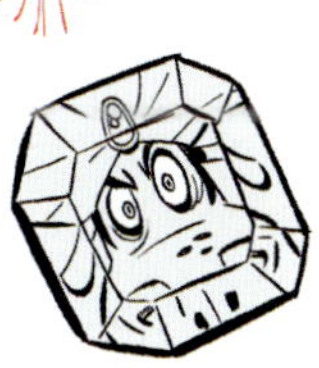

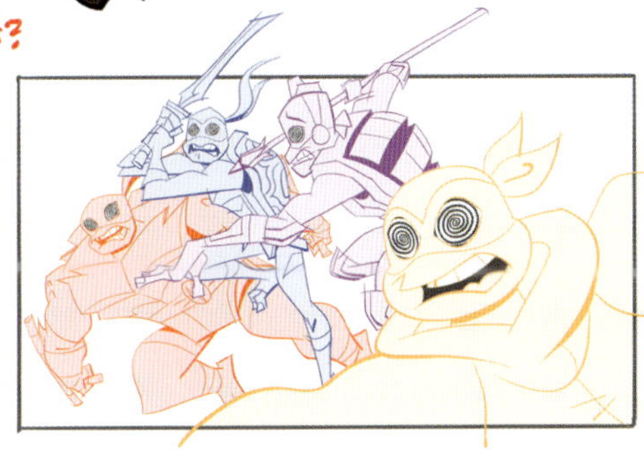

WAR AND PIZZA

ORIGINAL AIR DATE: SEPTEMBER 17, 2018
PRODUCTION CODE: 004

WRITTEN BY **IAN BUSCH**
STORYBOARDS BY **JULIA BRAID**
DIRECTED BY **BRENDAN CLOGHER**

RUSS CARNEY: This was one of the first episodes written, so we were still trying to figure out exactly what the show was about. One aspect of April's character from the original show bible was that she would keep having new, crazy jobs that would be the launching point for some sort of adventure. For instance, a job as a magician's assistant might lead to a discovery of some real magic going on, etc. But like many ideas that come up in the development of a show, it pretty much fell by the wayside once we got into production. This was the one episode that really made use of it. It's alluded to in the premiere, as April is in charge of the hotel pool that the boys cannonball into, and also in "Origami Tsunami" when she comes to the fake paper store for a job interview, but once the show became more serialized, it was harder to keep the bit going.

This episode went through a lot of changes because we were still learning how to write the show. It really came together when Ian Busch had the idea to center the story around the fact that April had never once gotten to perform the entire Albearto birthday song.

RON CORCILLO: This was also the first time that we got to meet the über-talented Tom Kenny, who gave great life to Albearto, and who also happens to be a super-cool cat who truly loves what he does. He once said casually to us, *"Ain't no job too small for Tom Kenny,"* which is such a phenomenal and inspiring attitude to have for someone as successful as he is. You rock, Tom!

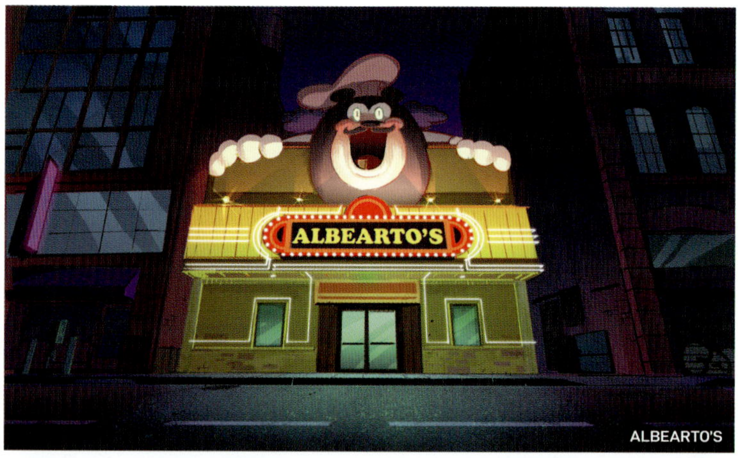

ALBEARTO'S

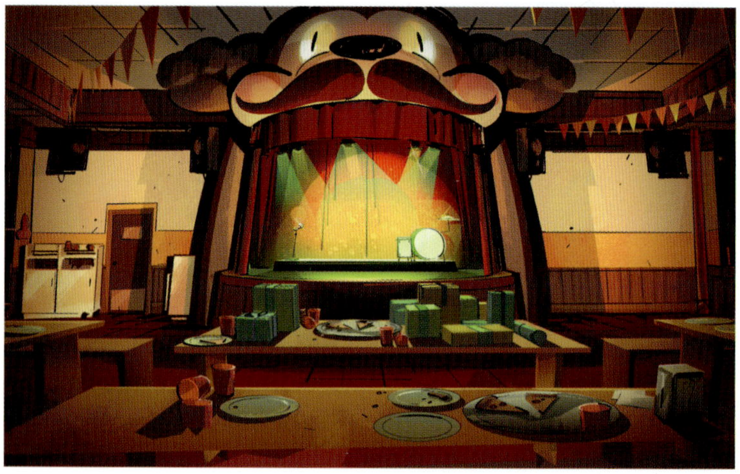

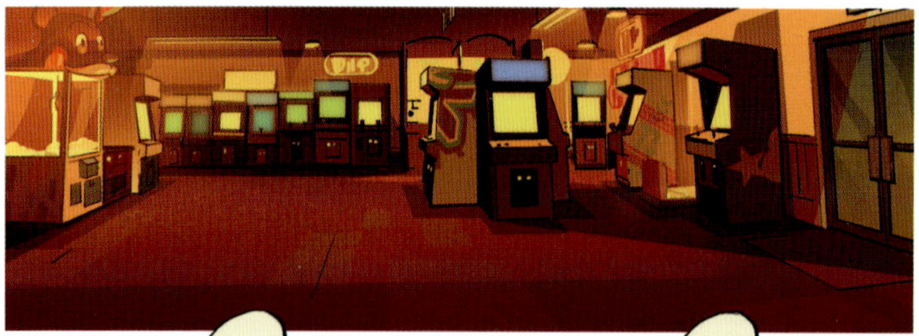

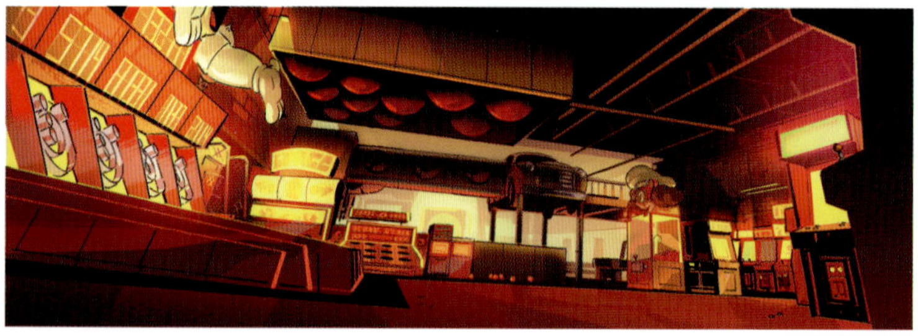

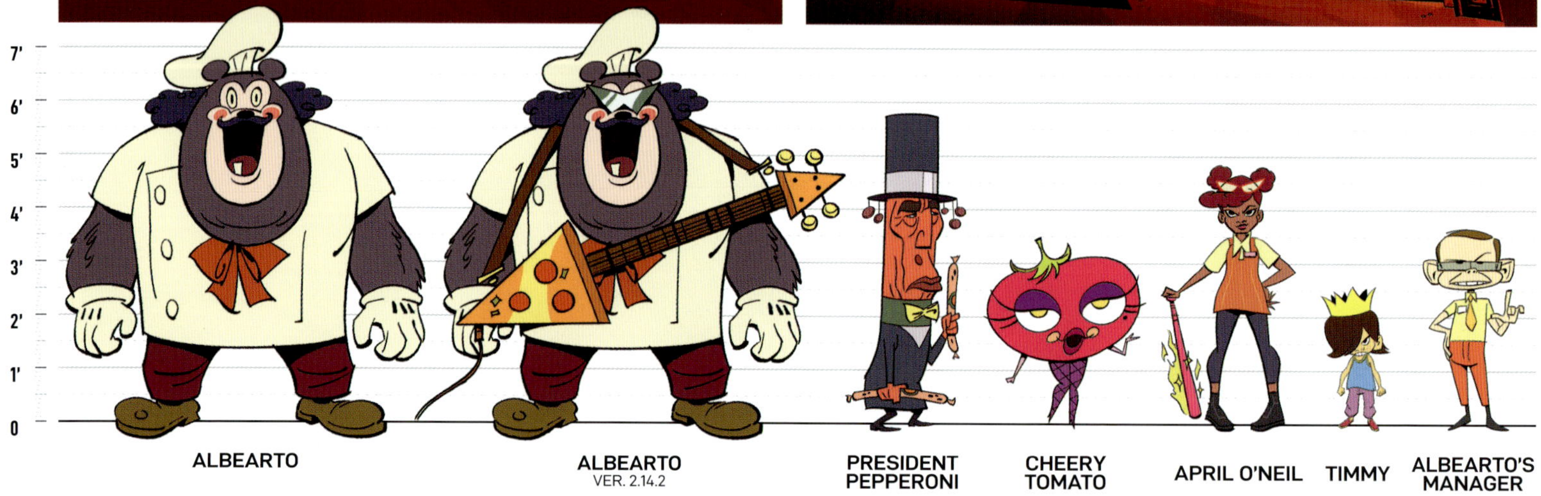

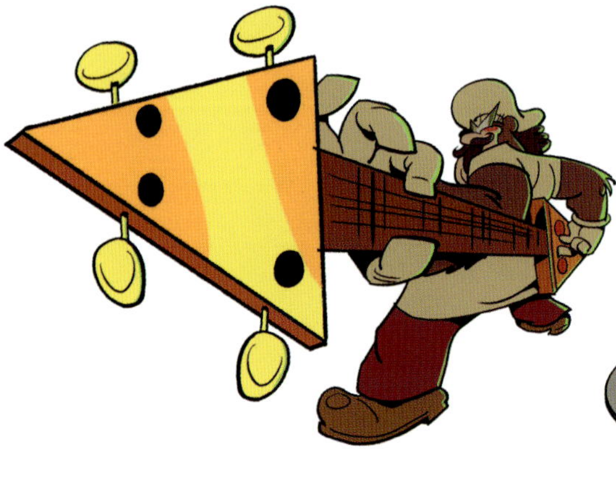

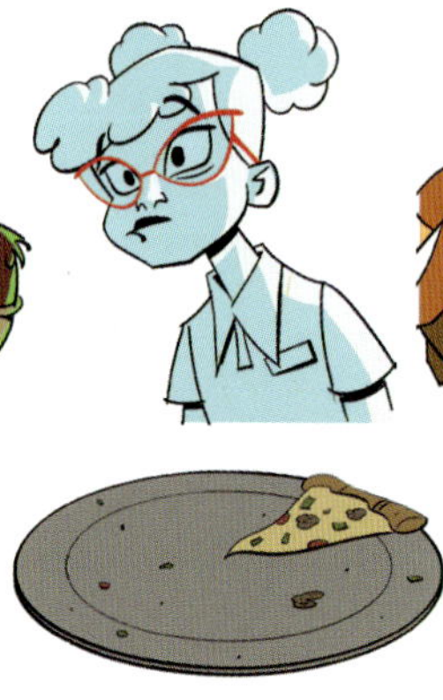

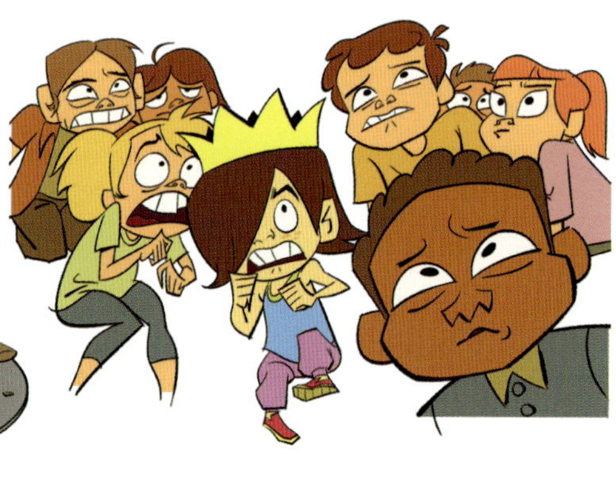

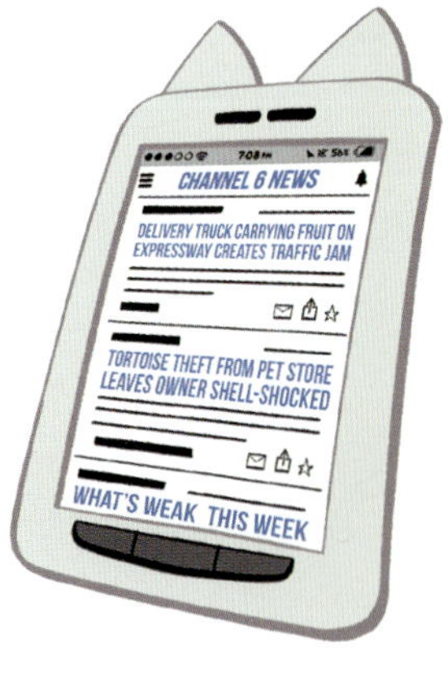

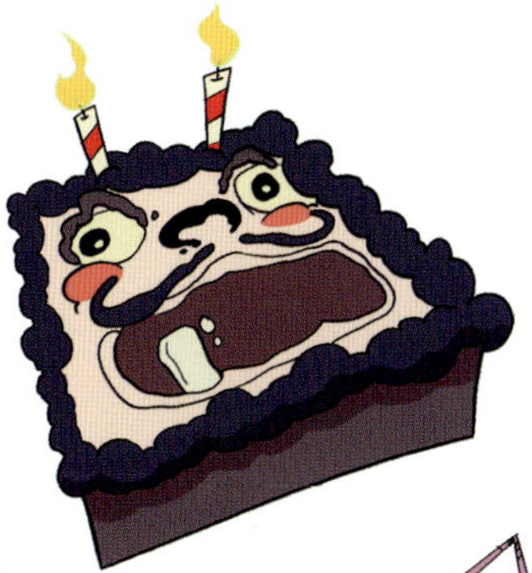

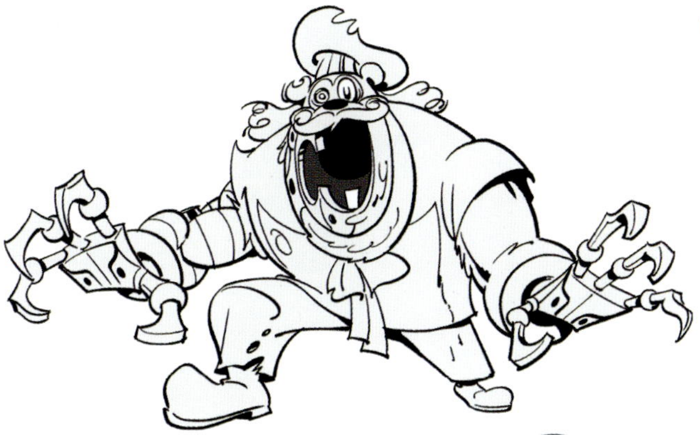

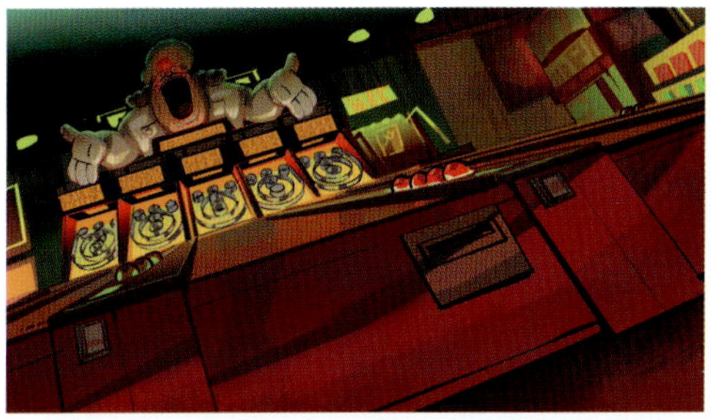

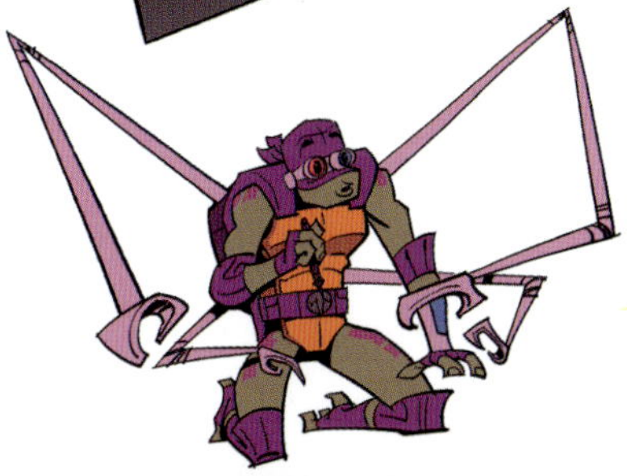

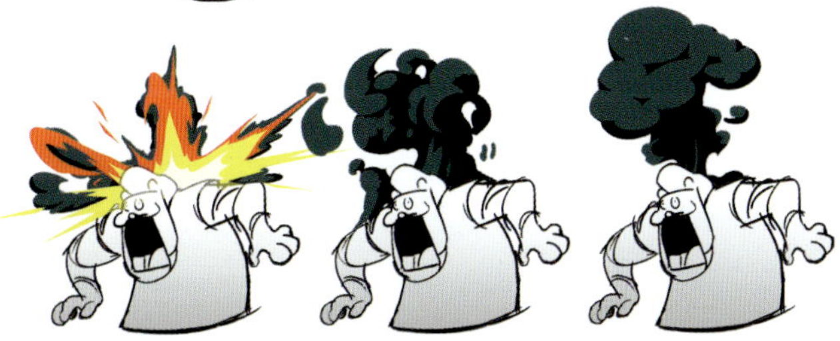

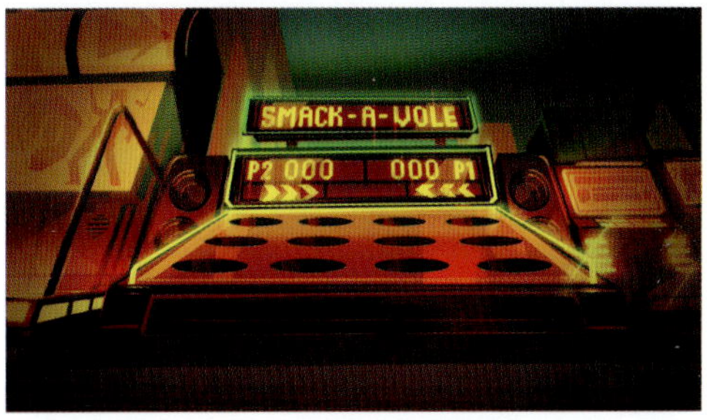
SMACK-A-VOLE
P2 000
000 P1

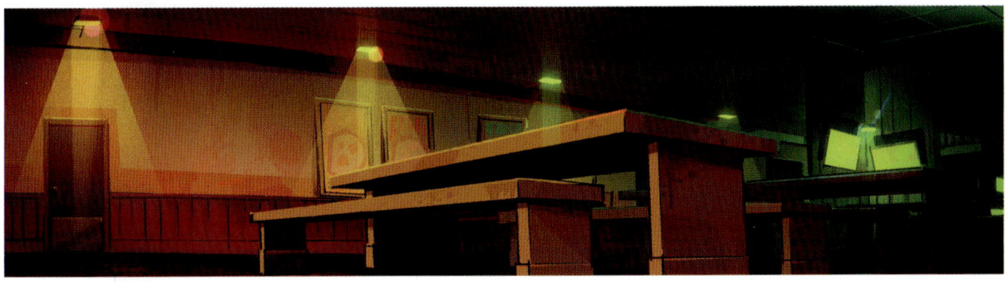

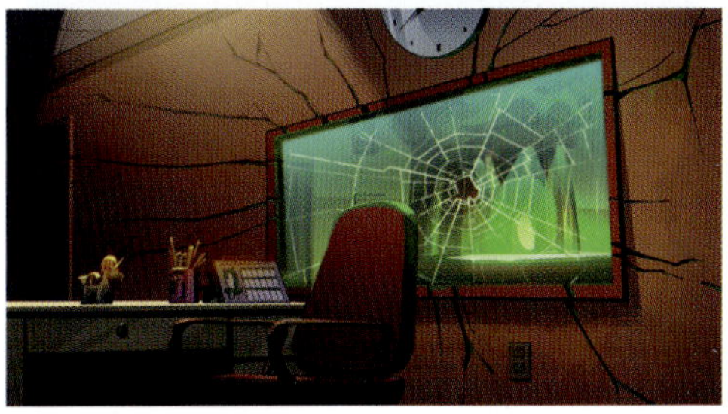

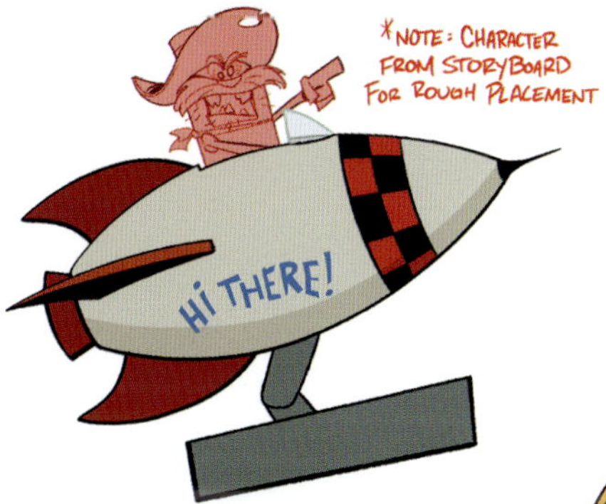
*NOTE: CHARACTER FROM STORYBOARD FOR ROUGH PLACEMENT
HI THERE!

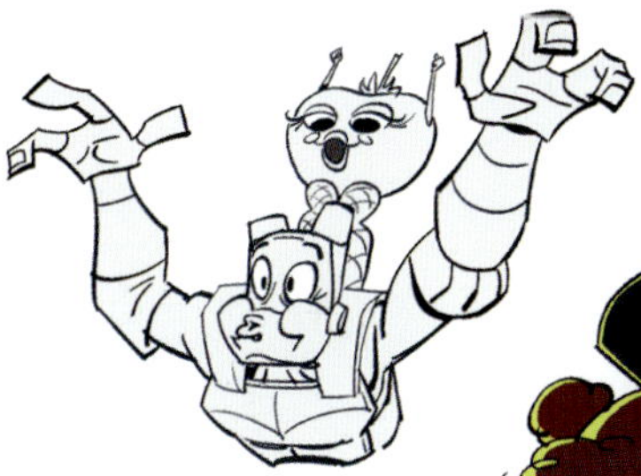

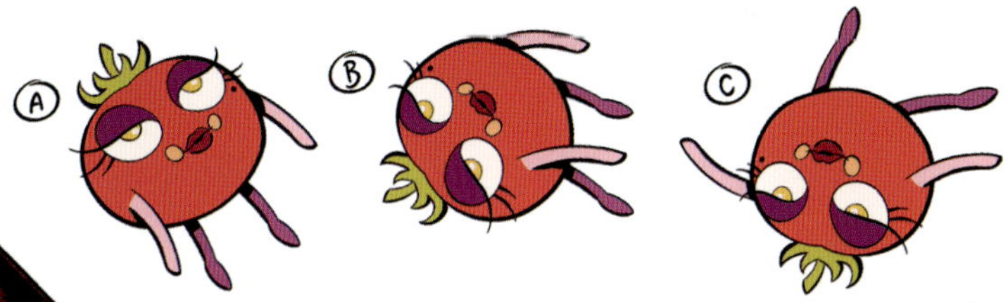
A
B
C

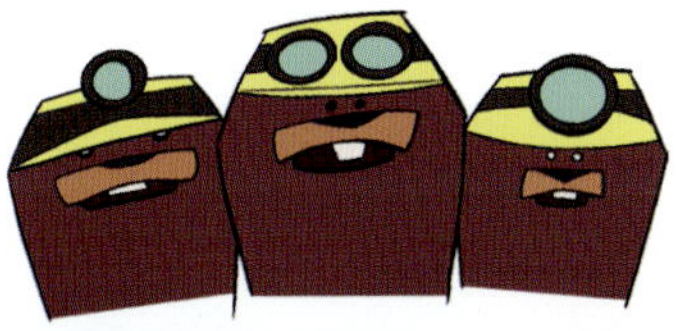

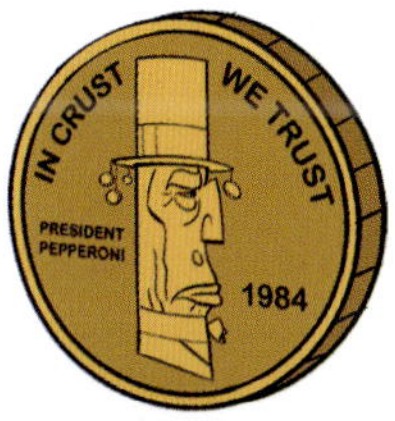
IN CRUST WE TRUST
PRESIDENT PEPPERONI
1984

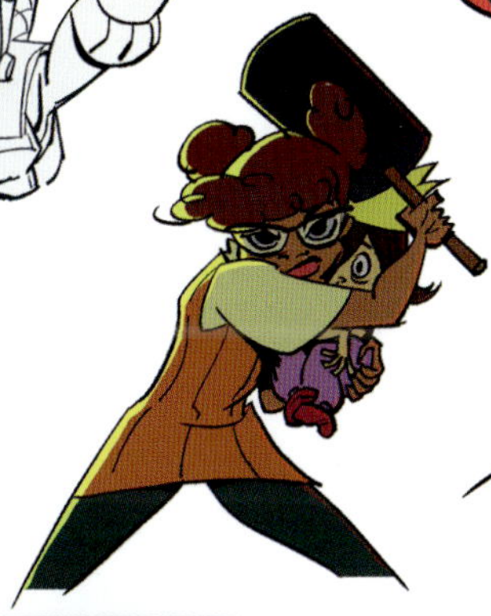

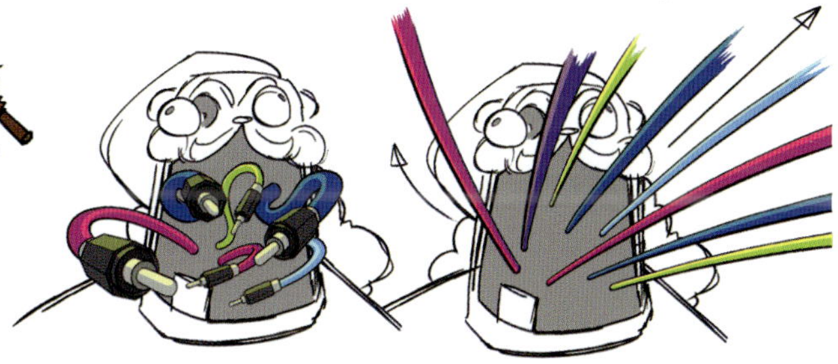

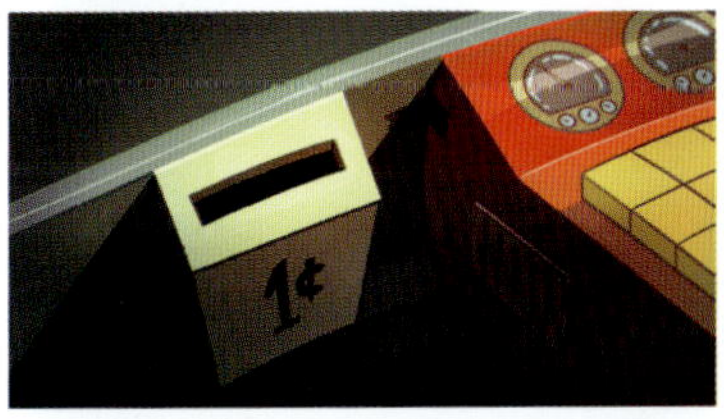
1¢

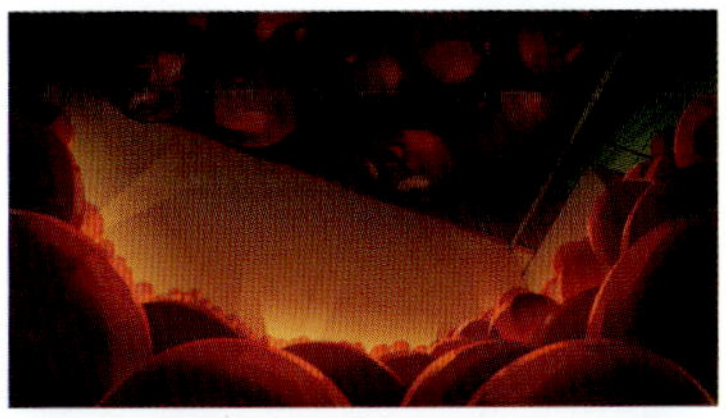

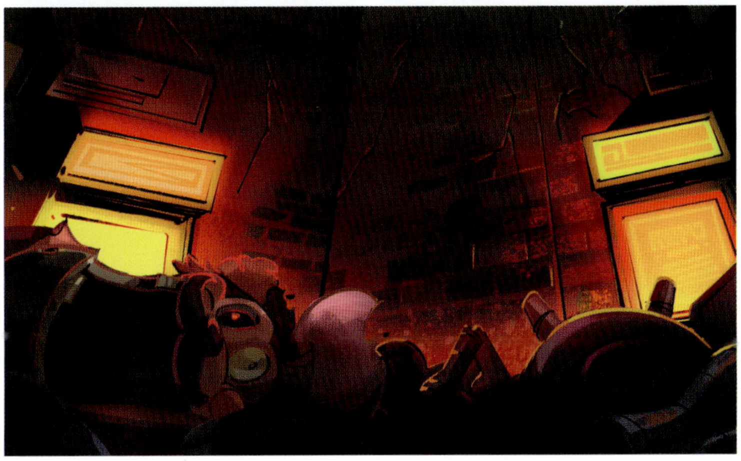

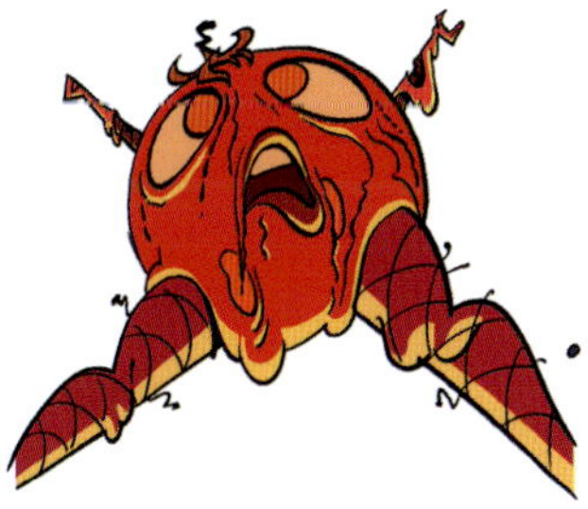

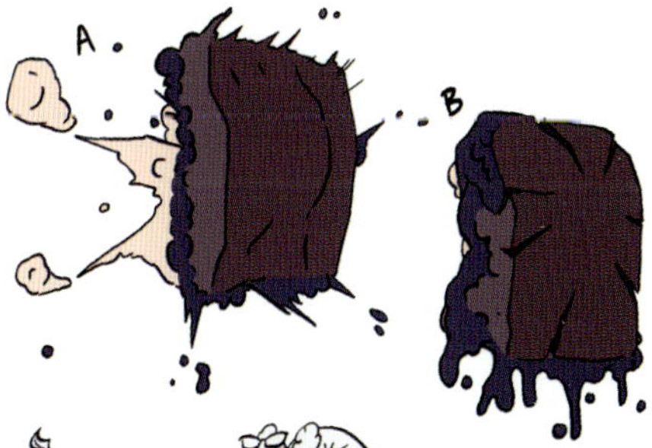
A
B

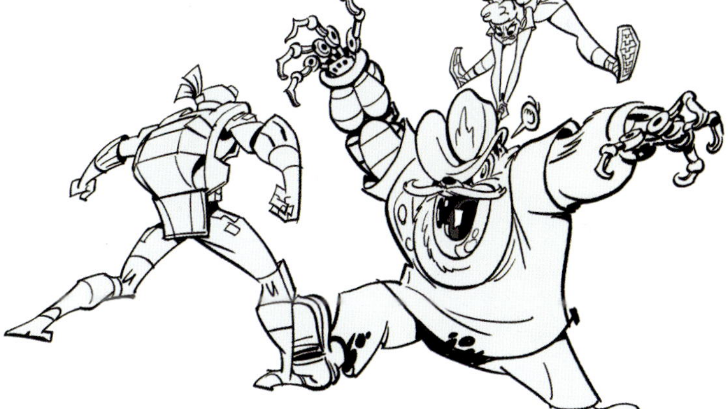

ORIGAMI TSUNAMI

ORIGINAL AIR DATE: SEPTEMBER 25, 2018
PRODUCTION CODE: 005

WRITTEN BY **RUSS CARNEY & RON CORCILLO**
STORYBOARDS BY **CHRISTOPHER LUC**
DIRECTED BY **JAMIE VICKERS**

RON CORCILLO: During development, one item on our agenda was to come up with a new catchphrase for the Turtles. We started a list, but ultimately we felt that a catchphrase should arise organically. In this episode, the boys are geeking out at Lou Jitsu's *Teriyaki Shakedown*, in which Lou Jitsu shoves a couple of thugs' heads into a bowl of ramen. *"How 'bout a little hot soup?!"* We liked it so much that we made it the boys' final battle cry, hoping that it would stick. Sometimes you have to take a big swing, and in this case everybody seemed to like it, so we got lucky! Of course, that could be because we never came up with anything else.

RUSS CARNEY: Similarly, as we were pitching on Splinter's stage name, we knew that we wanted it to be goofy and reminiscent of 1970s exploitation films. *Vicious Lee, Kung Fuji*...stuff like that. Well, we were both writing super late at night and we had to turn in our draft the next morning. Out of frustration and just so we could go home, Ron pitched the silliest name he could think of: *Lou Jitsu*. We figured everybody would hate it and change it before the next draft, but Ant and Andy dug it, and nobody pushed back on it, and ta-da! History was made.

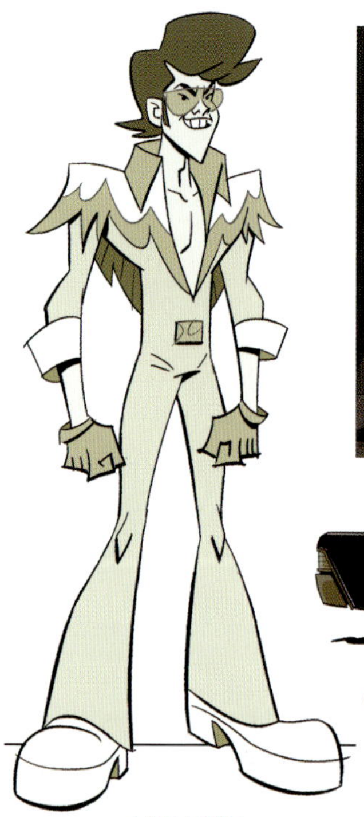

LOU JITSU

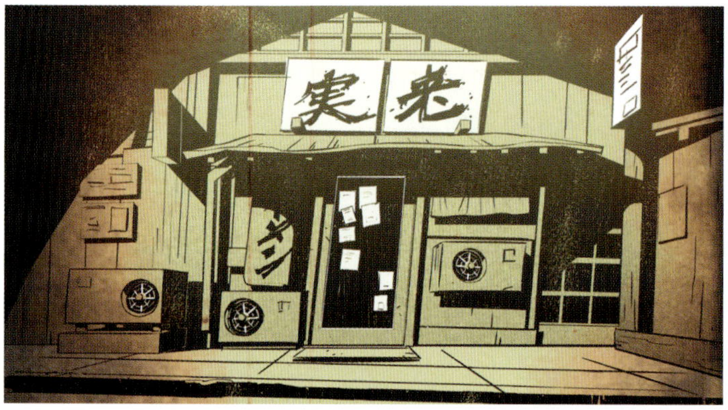

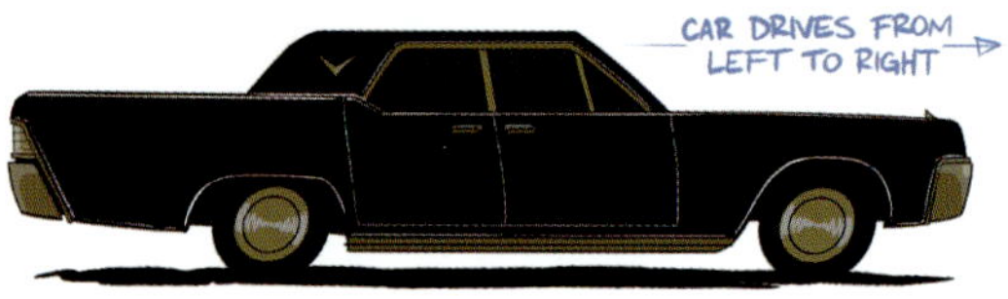

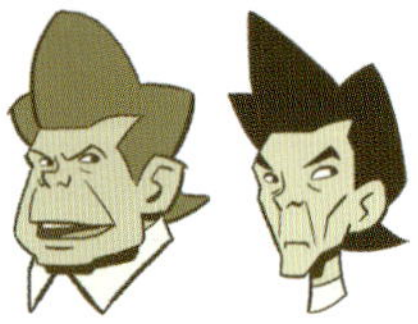

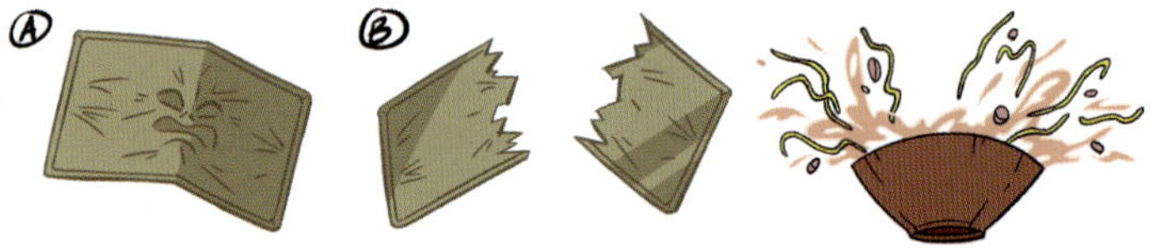

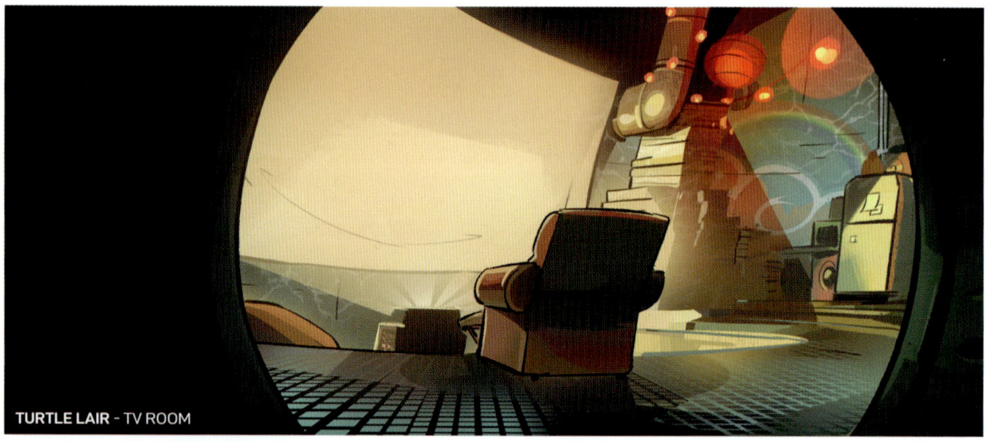

TURTLE LAIR - TV ROOM

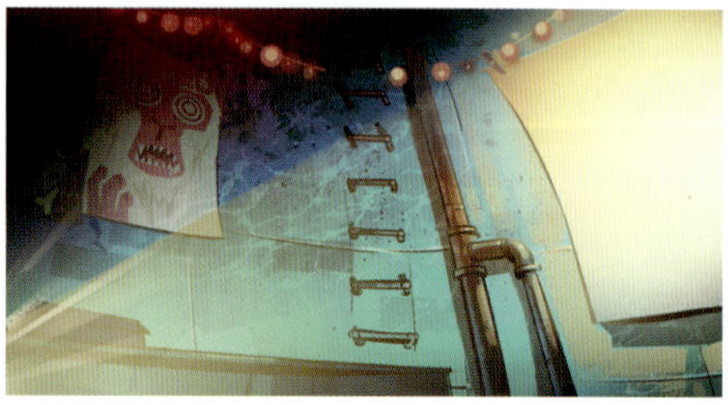

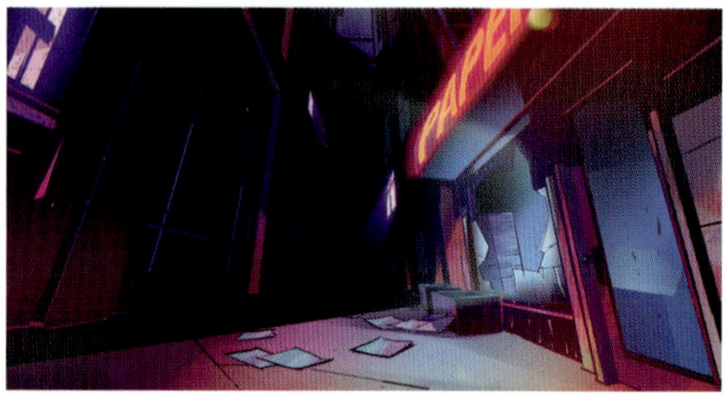

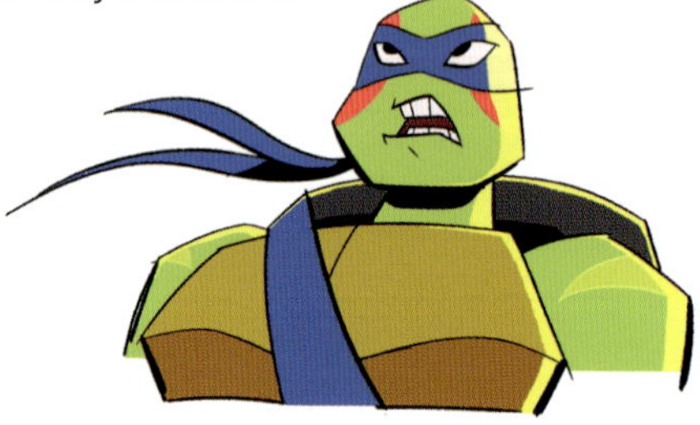

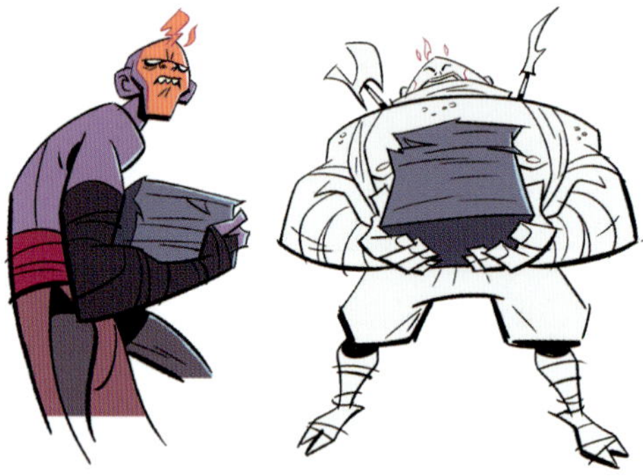

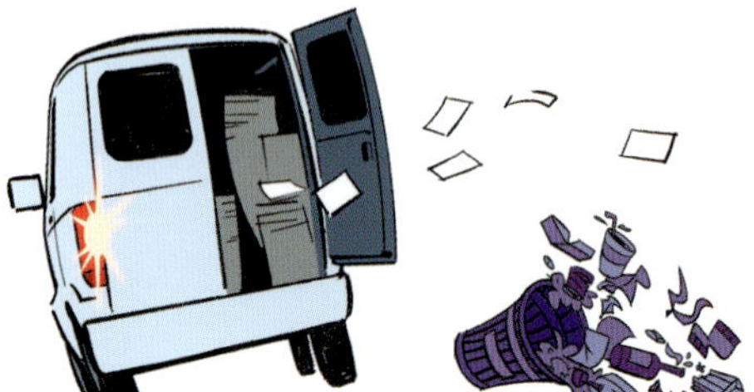

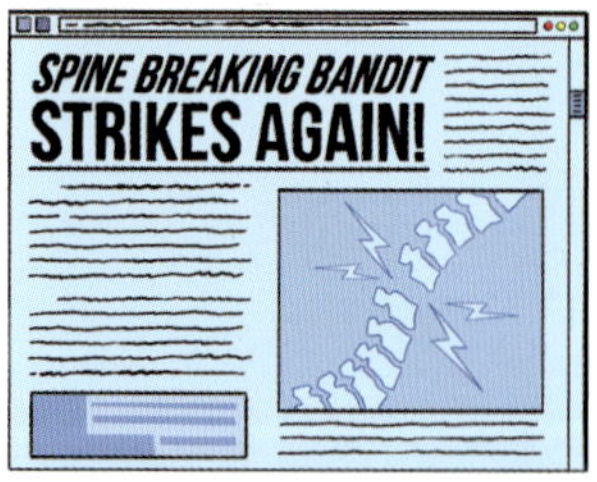

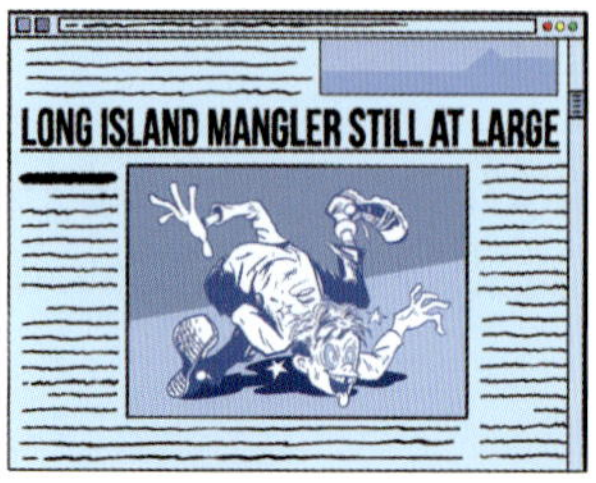

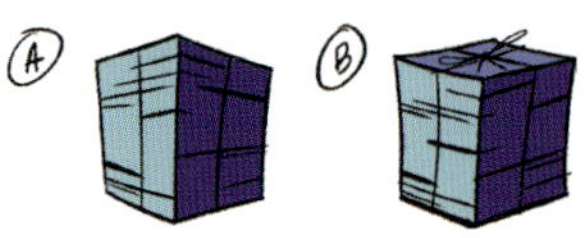

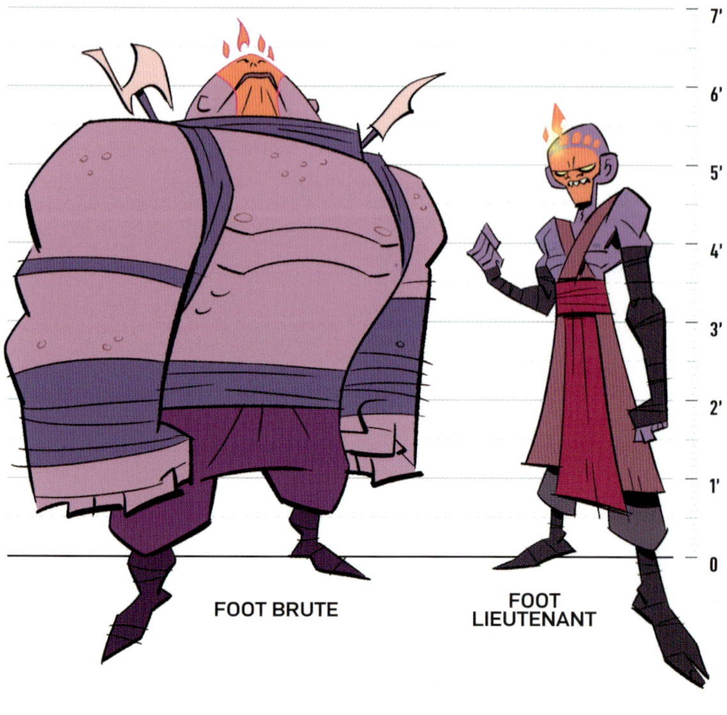

FOOT BRUTE

FOOT LIEUTENANT

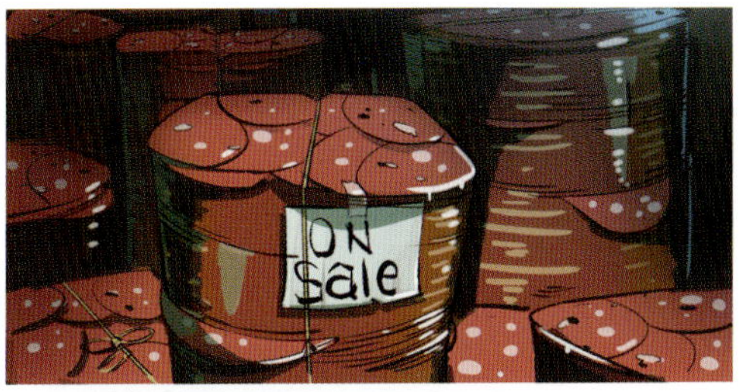

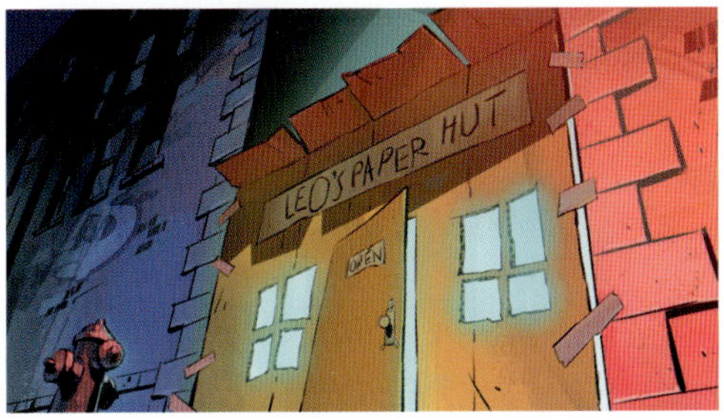

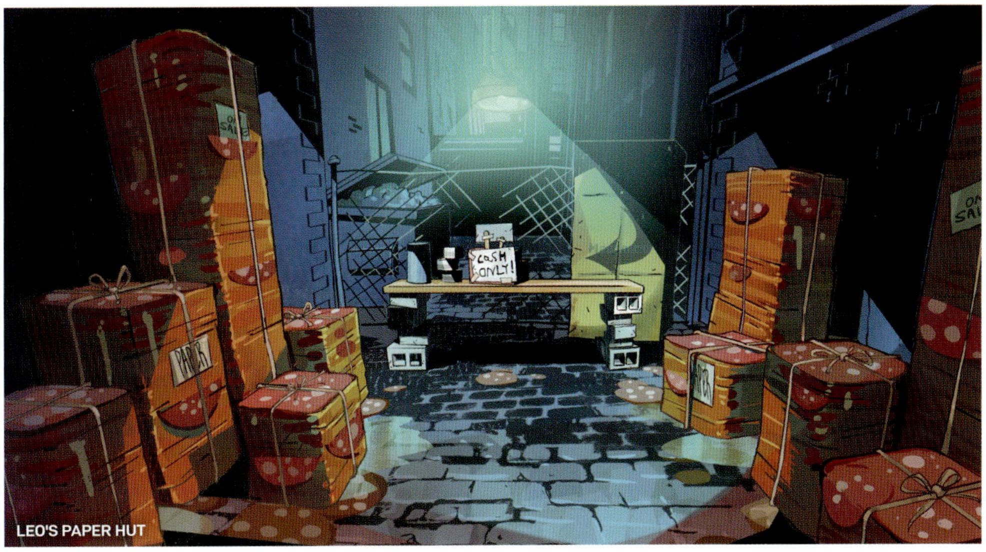

LEO'S PAPER HUT

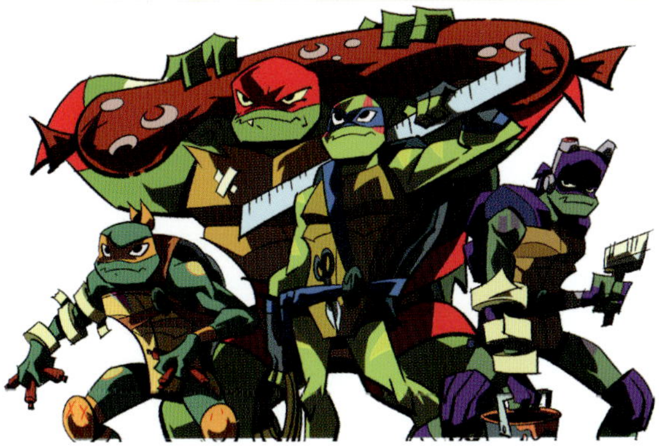

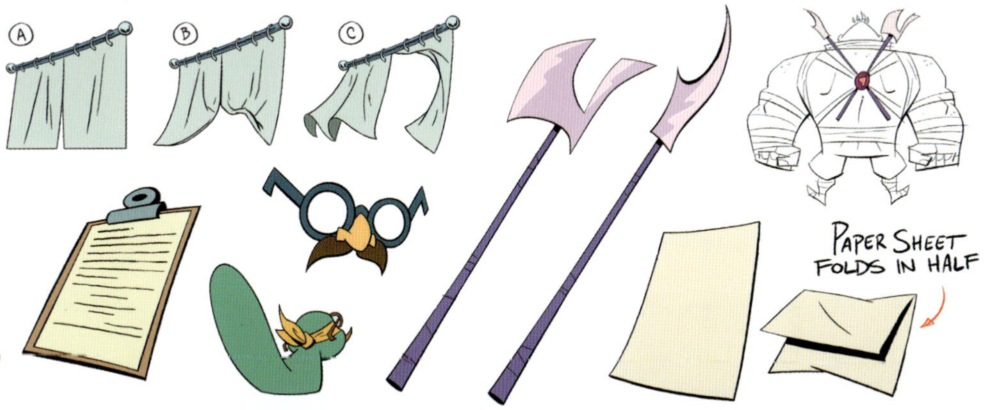

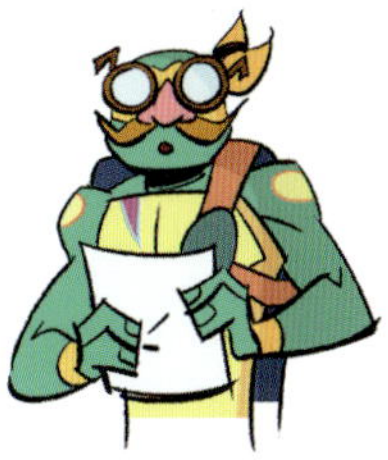

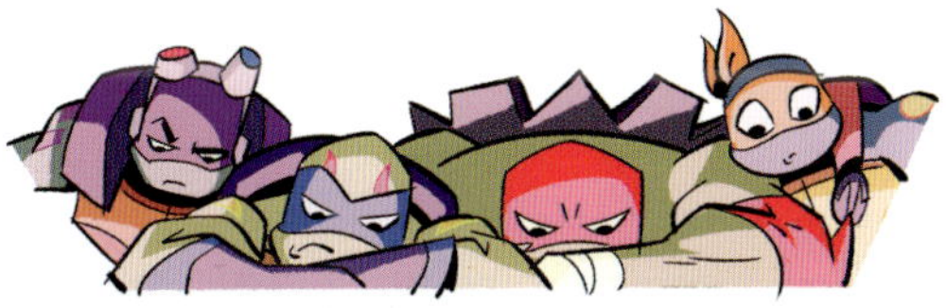

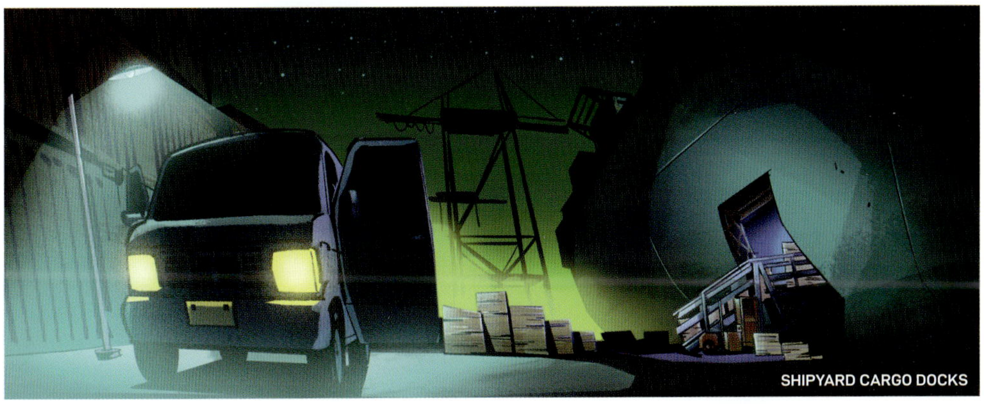
SHIPYARD CARGO DOCKS

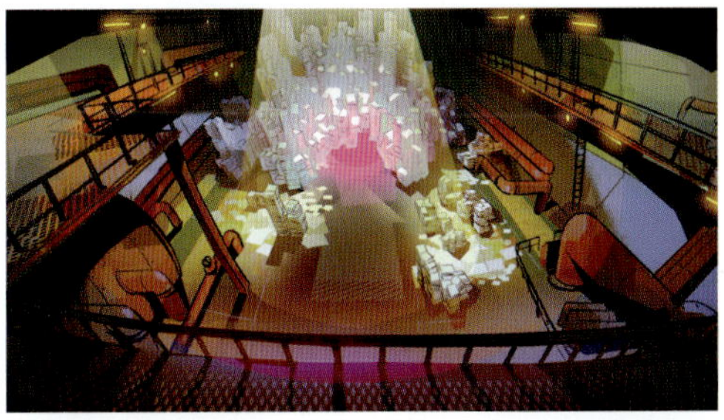

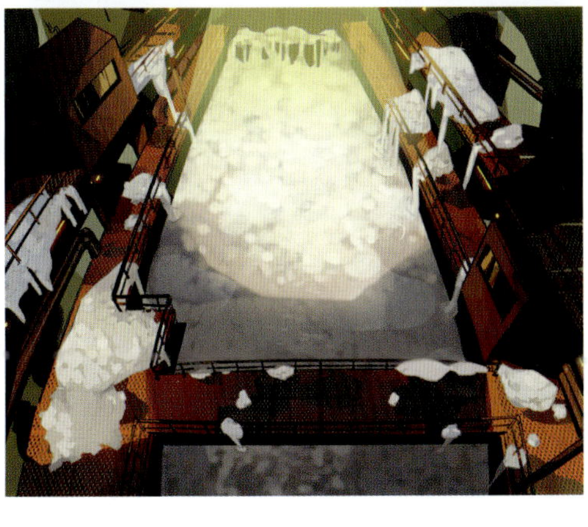

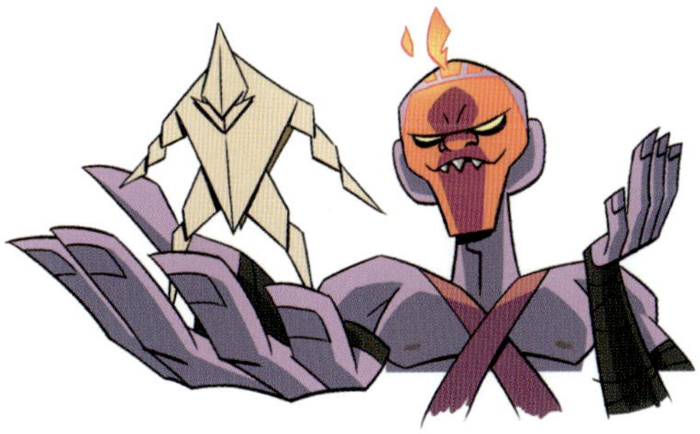

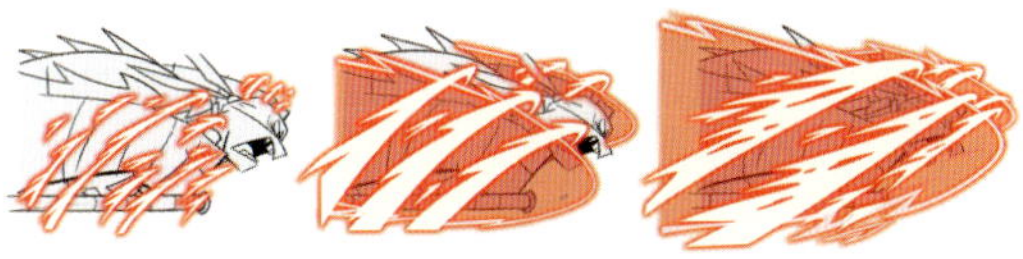

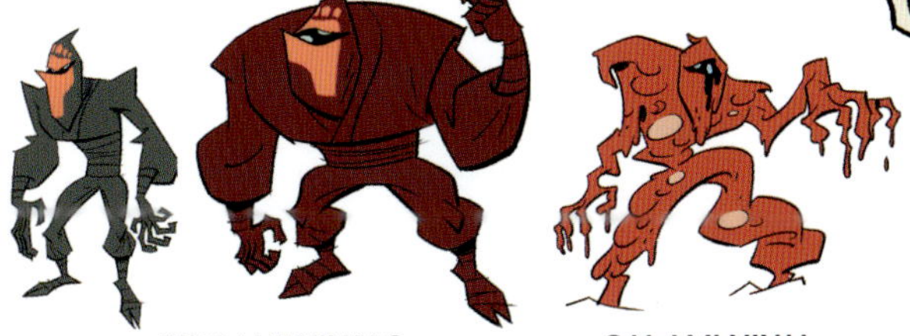
ORIGAMI NINJAS

SALAMI NINJA

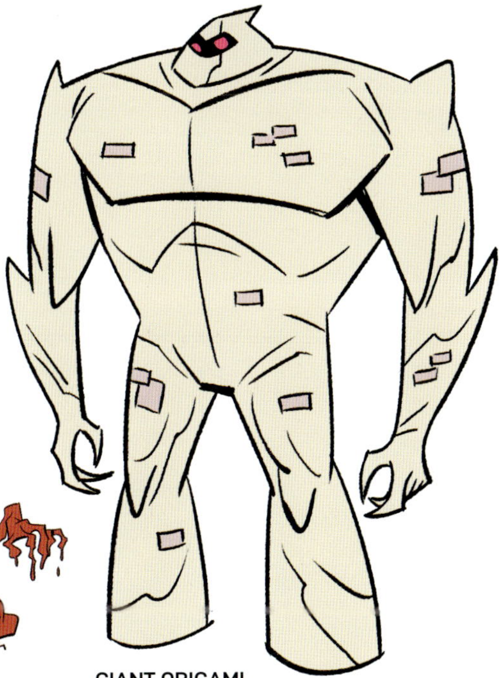
GIANT ORIGAMI NINJA

DONNIE'S GIFTS

ORIGINAL AIR DATE: SEPTEMBER 17, 2018
PRODUCTION CODE: 006

WRITTEN BY **RUSS CARNEY & RON CORCILLO**
STORYBOARDS BY **JESSICA ZAMMIT**
DIRECTED BY **SEBASTIAN MONTES**

RUSS CARNEY: While Andy was noodling around with villain character designs for the series, he came up with a meat-tenderizer-wielding mutant pig chef, Meat Sweats, as one of the big bads on the series. The term "meat sweats" describes a rumored condition in which the consumption of excessive meat causes sweating.

We writers were then tasked with coming up with some voice actor pitches for the role. Famed chef Gordon Ramsay seemed a little on the nose as a hostile British chef, and we weren't sure that Alton Brown could inspire terror. We kept kicking around ideas, and one morning before work, I was in the shower (where most good ideas originate) when the idea hit me: What about John Lydon, a.k.a. Johnny Rotten, the over-the-top lead singer of the legendary punk band the Sex Pistols?! What a delightfully stupid idea!

RON CORCILLO: Russ was a huge fan of Lydon, and he knew that Lydon's provocative and confrontational persona over the decades was largely theatrics. Johnny Rotten was built for a villain role! It took a lot of convincing to get everybody on board—à la "Is he even an actor?" —but eventually the last few people conceded and we got him!

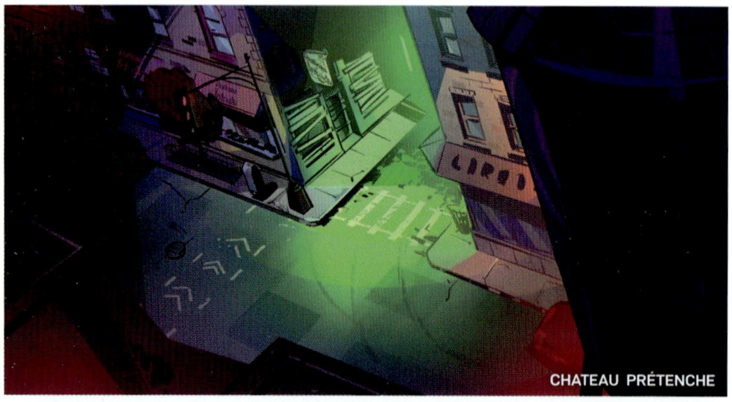
CHATEAU PRÉTENCHE

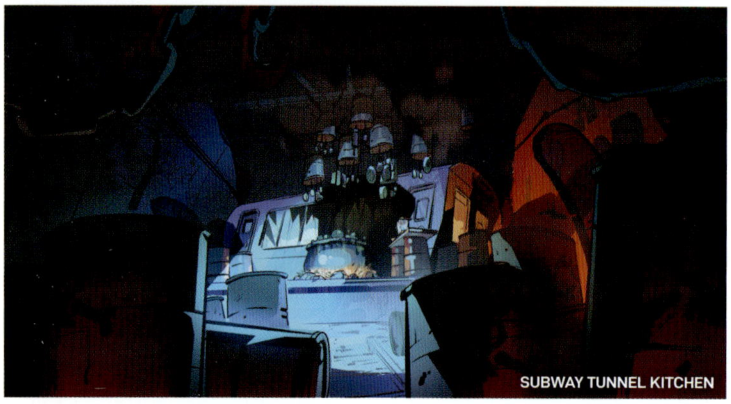
SUBWAY TUNNEL KITCHEN

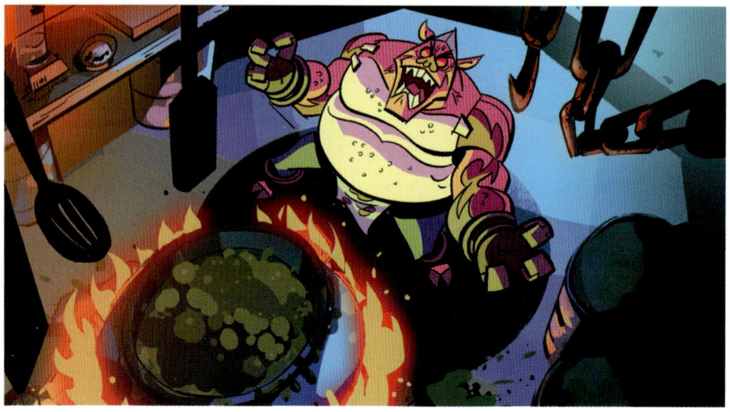

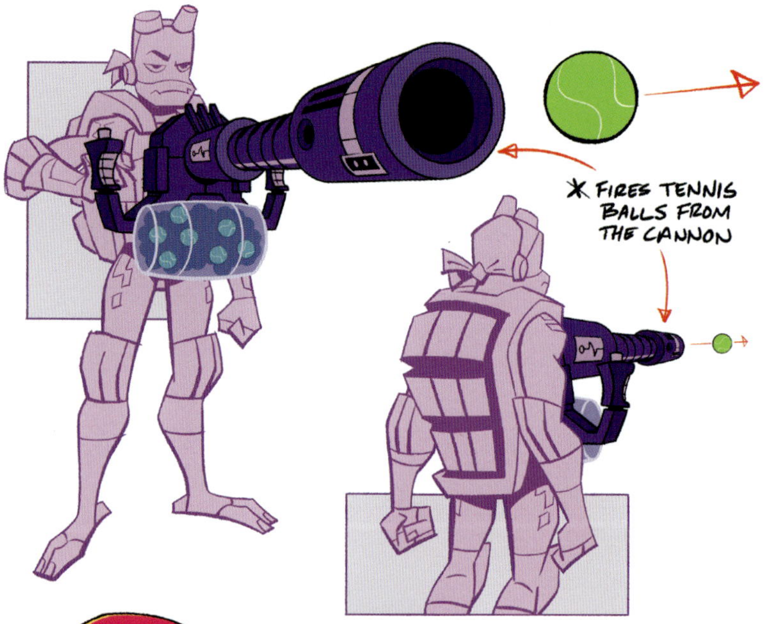

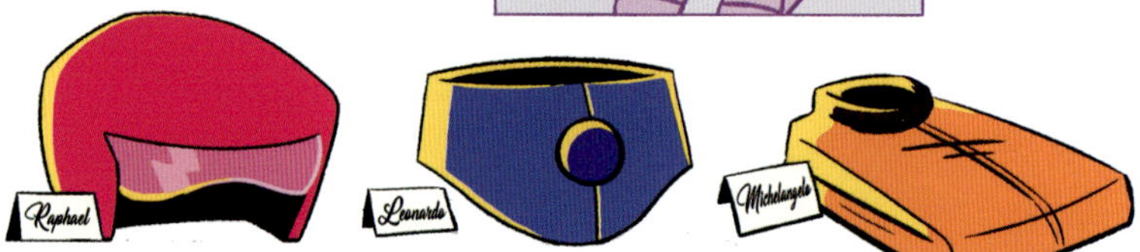

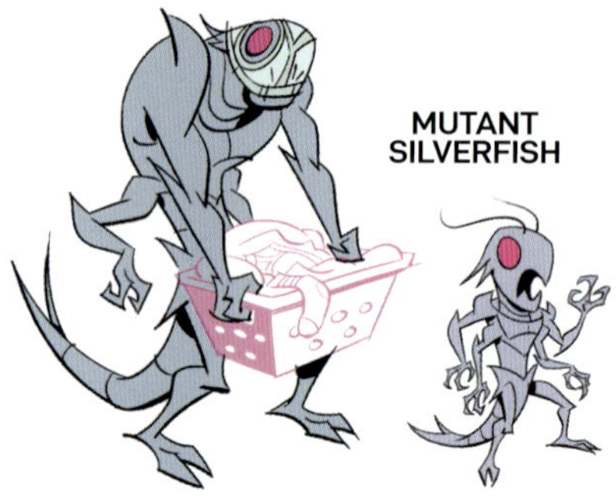
MUTANT SILVERFISH

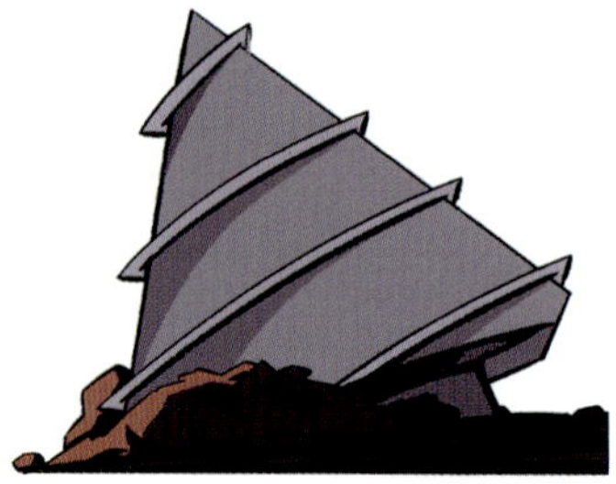
DRILL
(IN BETA)

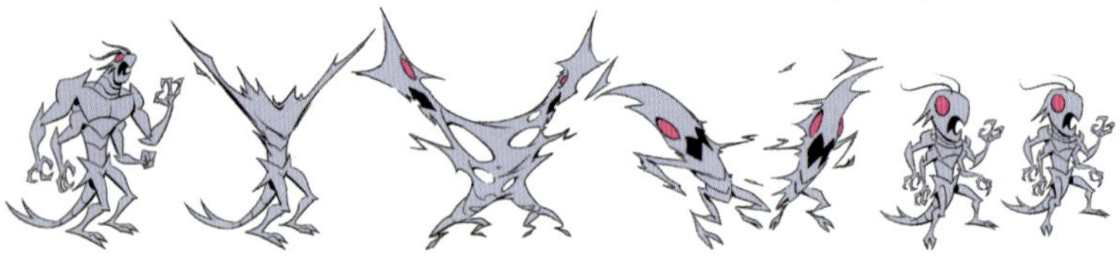

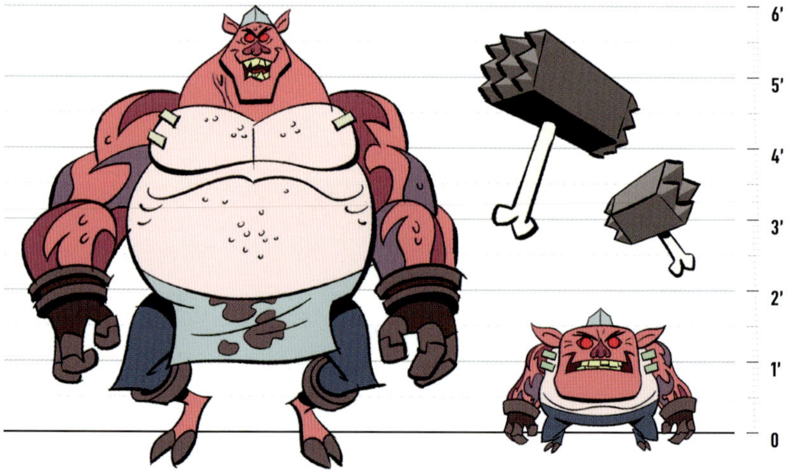

MEAT SWEATS
MINI MEATS

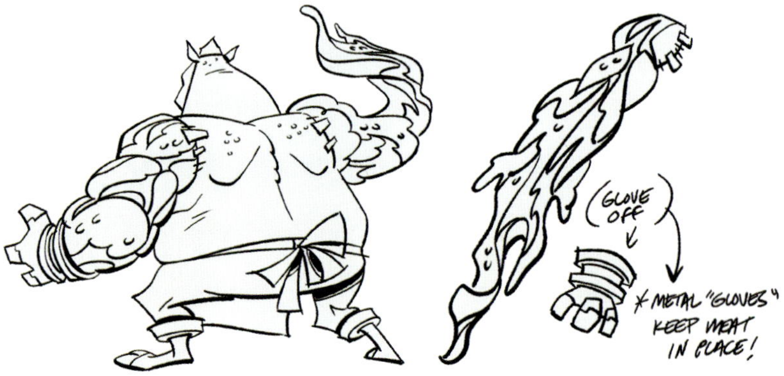

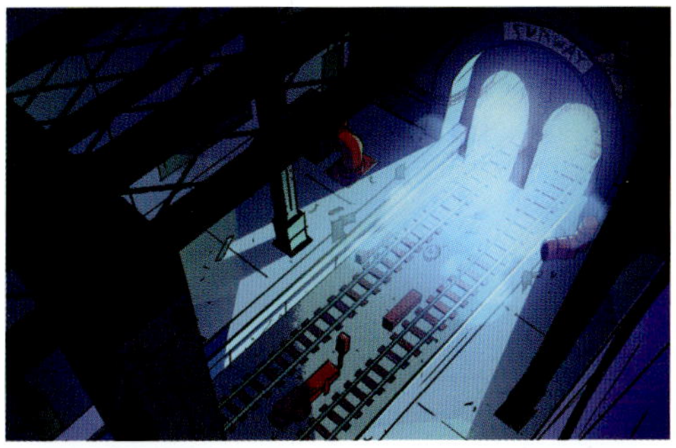

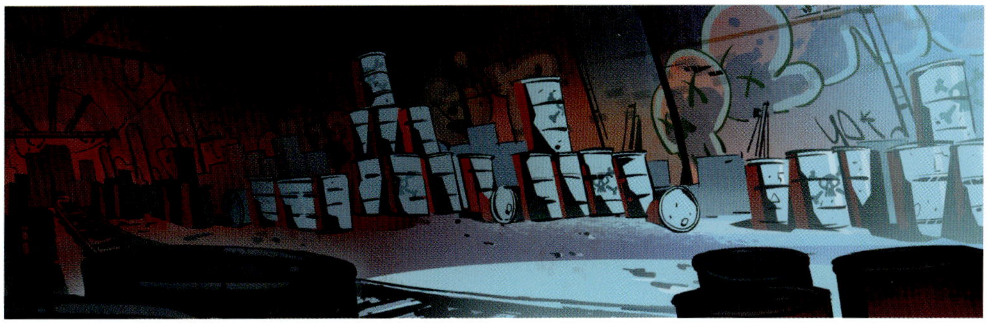

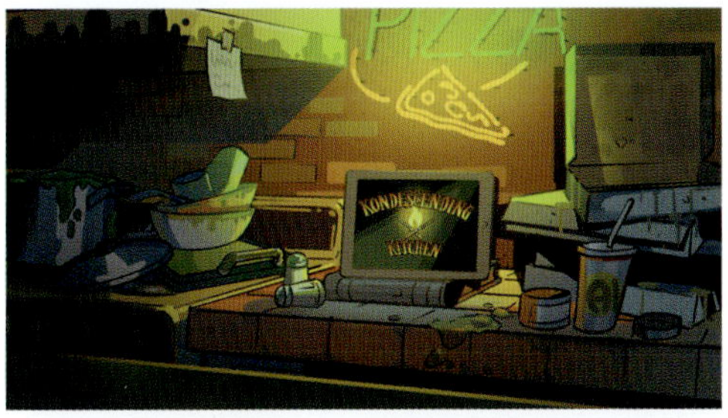

RUSS CARNEY: John showed up late at the studio on his first day. He noted that he was nervous and he needed to have his manager (and longtime friend/bodyguard, John "Rambo" Stevens) in the booth with him. All this was making Ron a little worried until John delivered his first line, and Ron suddenly realized, *"Oh wait, he's literally a rock star!"* True to his legend, Lydon slayed, continually delivering phenomenal, villainous performances. He and Rob Paulsen (voice director and the voice of Foot Lieutenant) bonded together over their appreciation of opera and other elevated musical artistry. It should also be noted that despite his infamous public persona, John was kind, self-effacing, intelligent, quick-witted, funny, welcoming, and an absolute pleasure to work with. And our mate sure does love his cappuccinos!

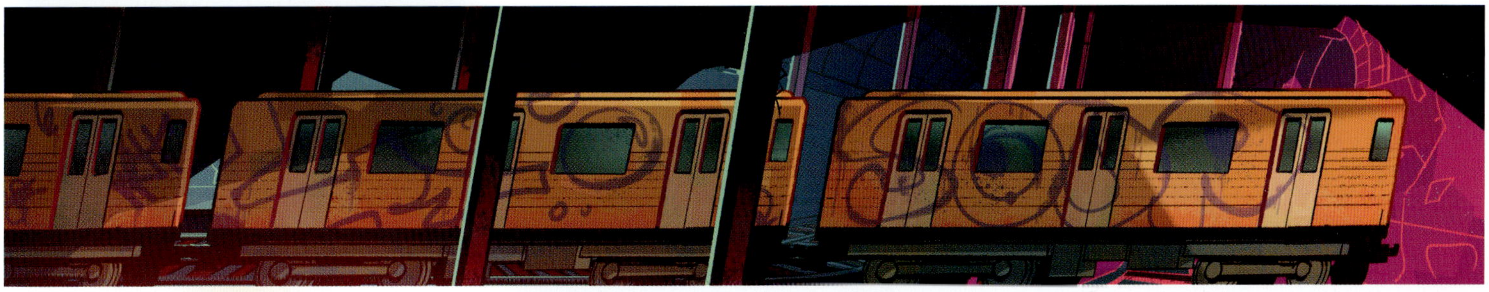

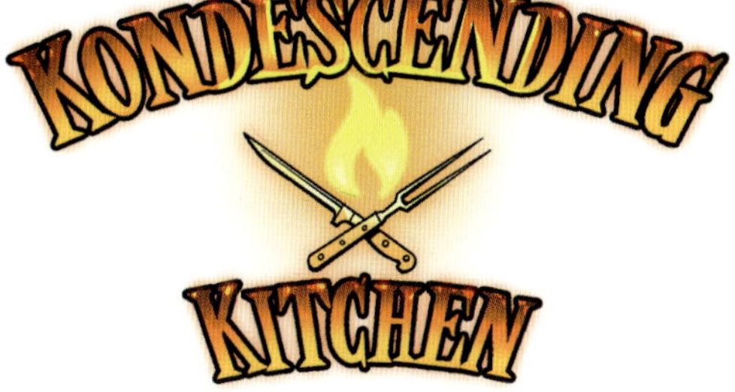

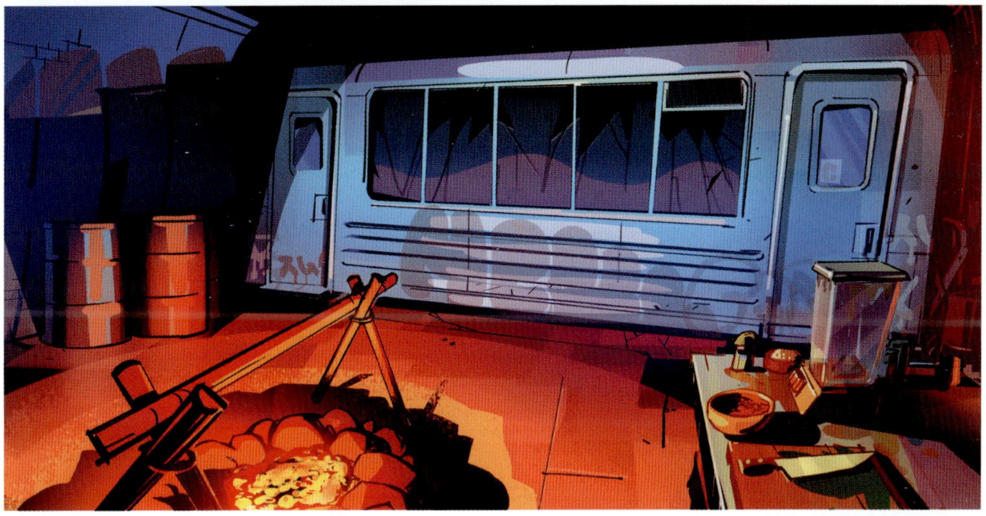

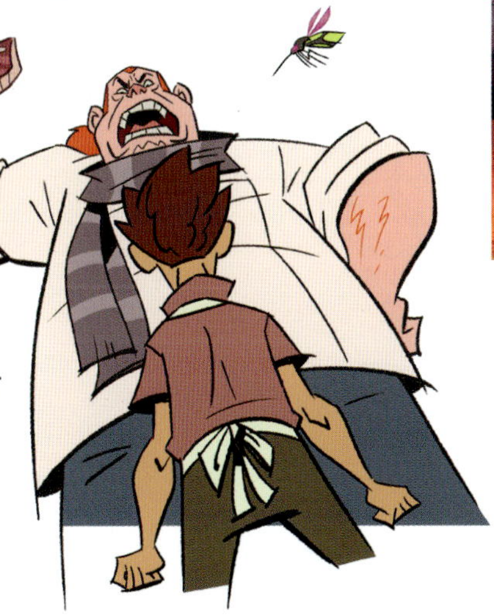

RUPPERT SWAGGART

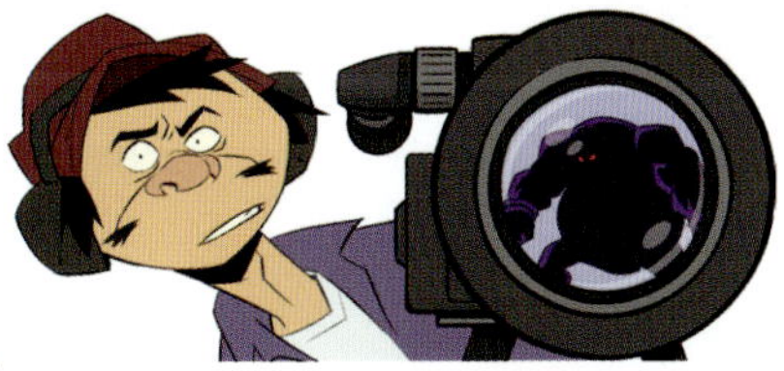

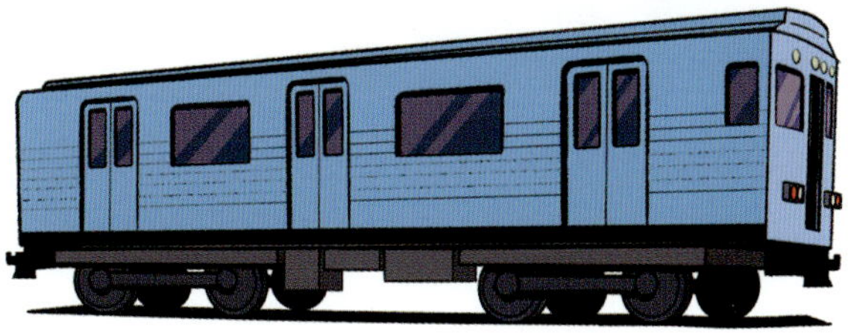

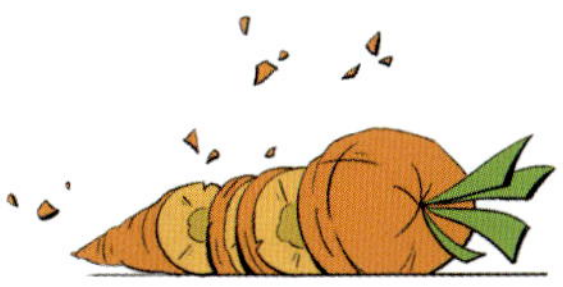

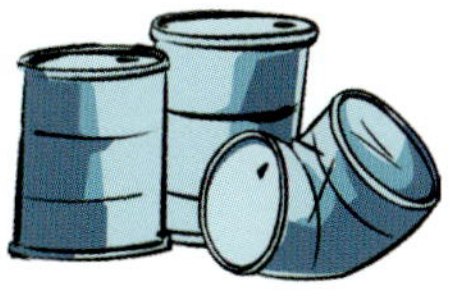

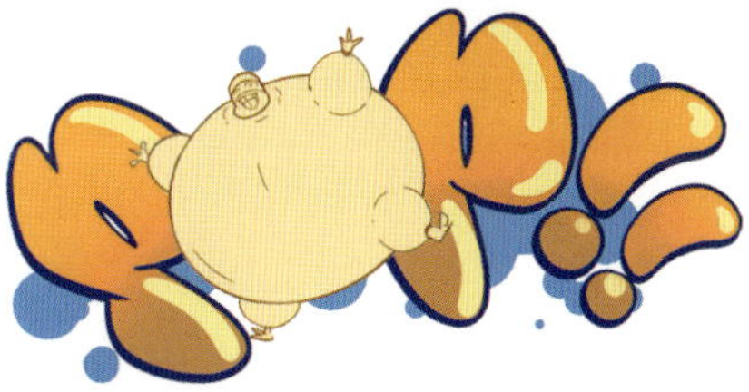

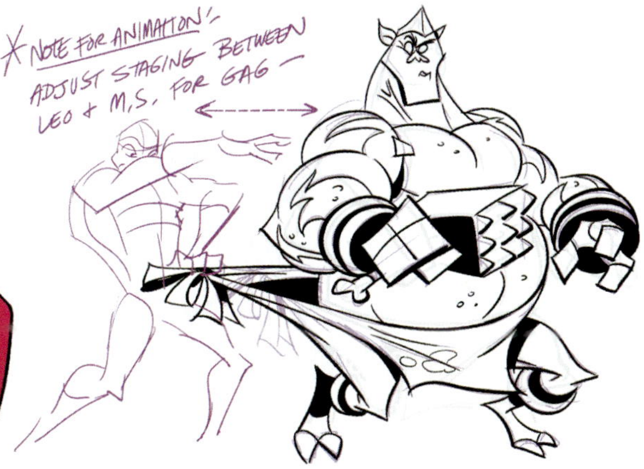

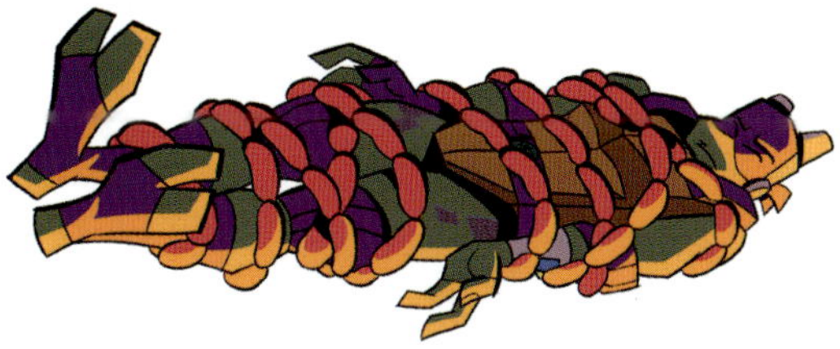

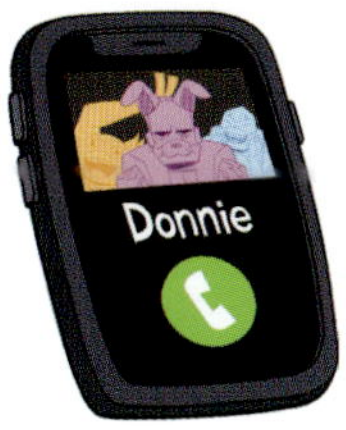

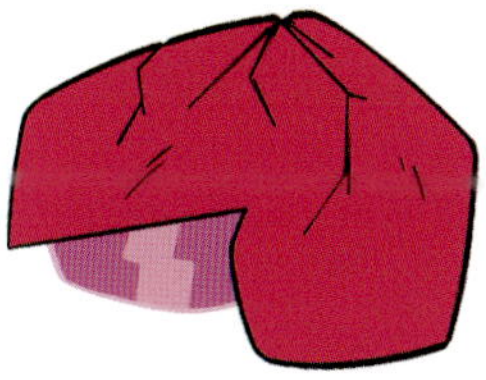

MINOTAUR MAZE

ORIGINAL AIR DATE: OCTOBER 6, 2018
PRODUCTION CODE: 007

WRITTEN BY **JESSE GORDON**
STORYBOARDS BY **CHRISTINE LIU**
DIRECTED BY **BRENDAN CLOGHER**

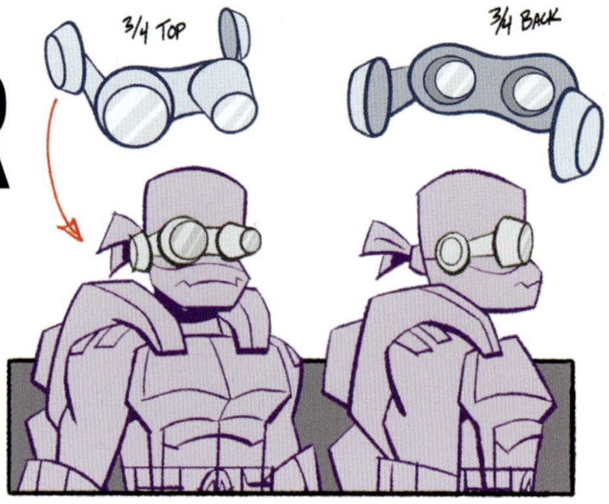

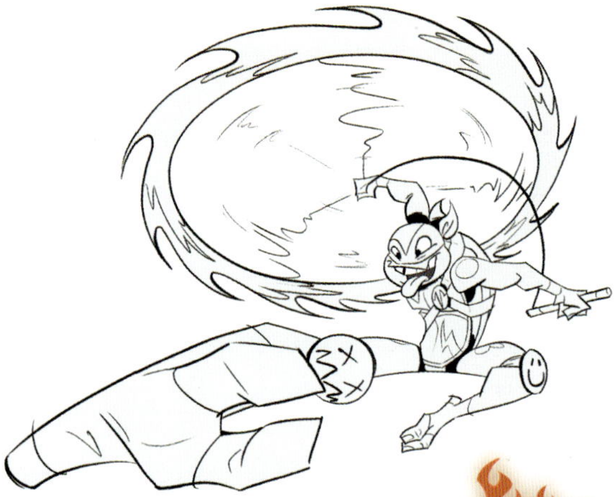

JESSE GORDON: This was one of the early episodes where we were establishing character dynamics, with Leo wanting to take shortcuts and Raph being the leader, while also setting up the Hidden City and magical quality of the show. We were wanting to set up that there was a world within that has different mythologies that exist. We had this idea that a minotaur was an early mutant—I'm not sure how far we got with that idea. The minotaur is a character from classic Greek mythology, but we wanted to combine it with something more modern, so that's why it's a pizza place. Obviously the Turtles love pizza, so it was a way to blend elements of things you knew from previous iterations of Turtles with something new and different for *Rise*.

We were finding our footing with what the Hidden City was—this was one of the early stabs at what it was like. The maze has a touch of *Harry Potter and the Goblet of Fire* (2005) in that the maze would create different challenges, giving opportunities for fun action things for them to do.

I love Señor Hueso. He has an awesome design and it was great to have him interact with the Turtles.

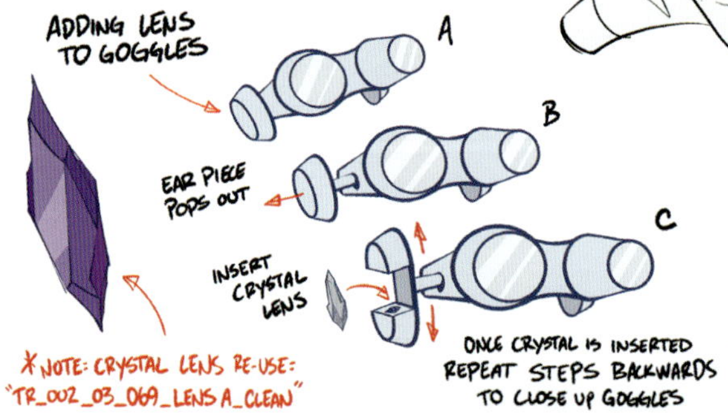

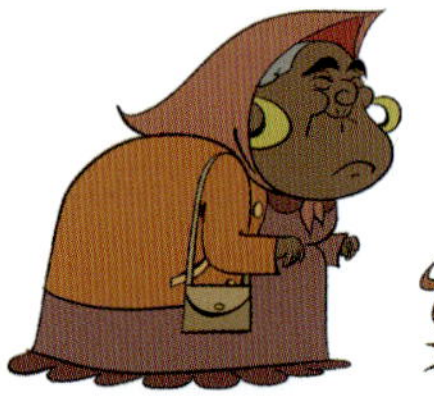
HUMAN FORM

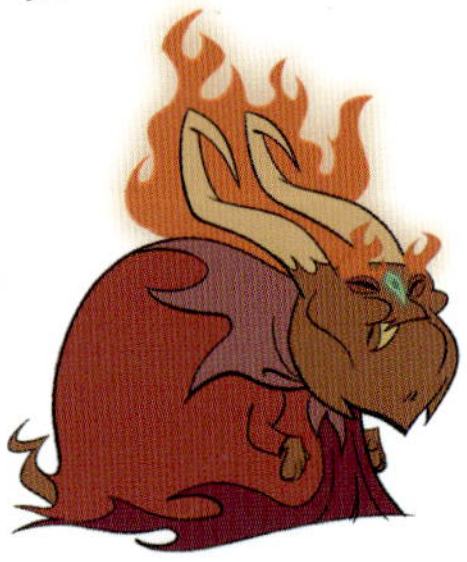
FIRE YŌKAI

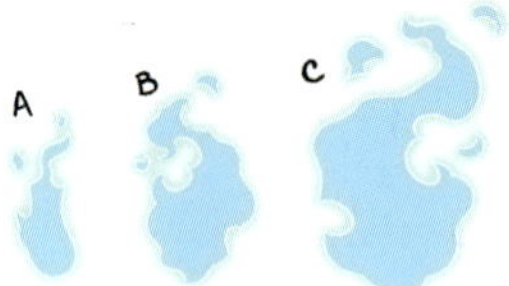

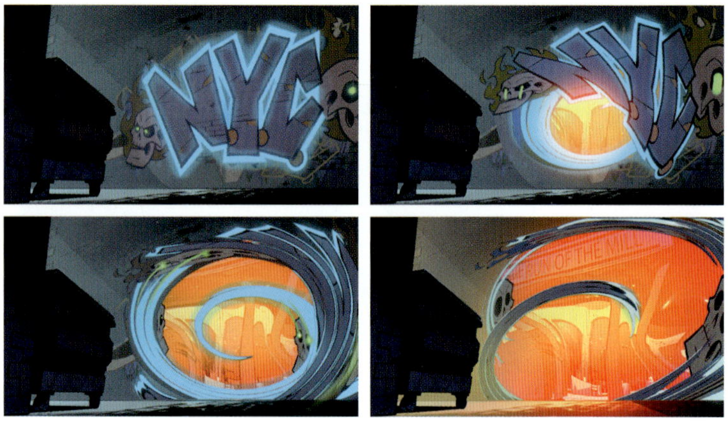

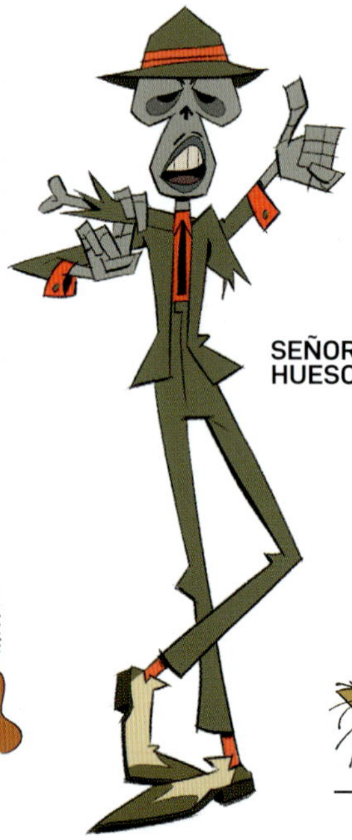
SEÑOR HUESO

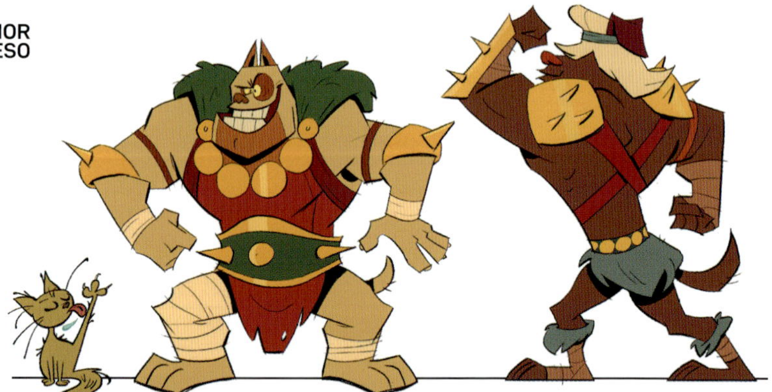
CHAMPION DUDES

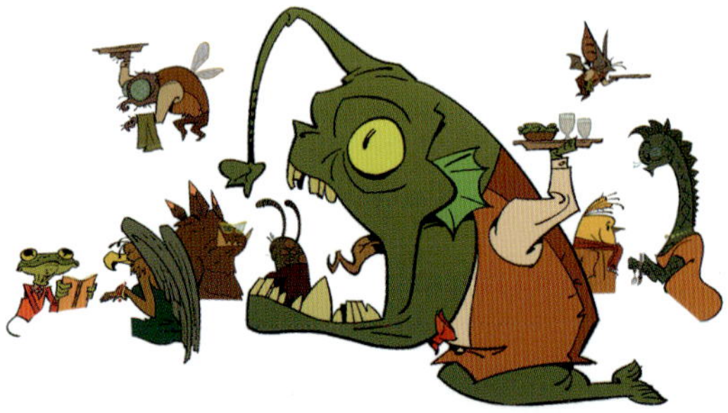

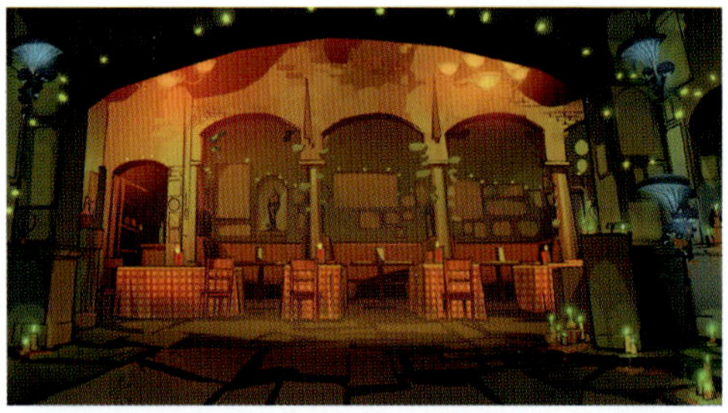

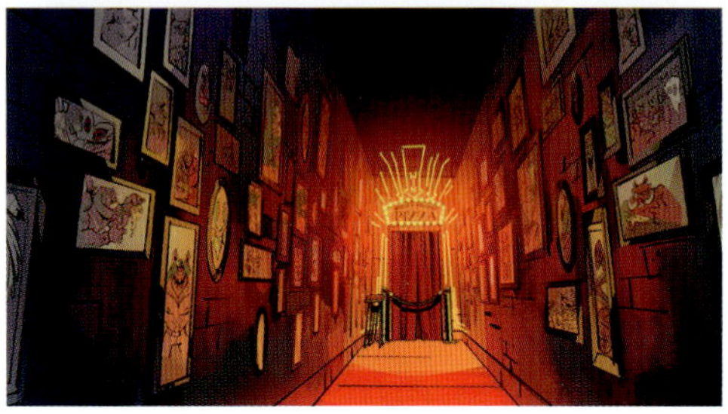

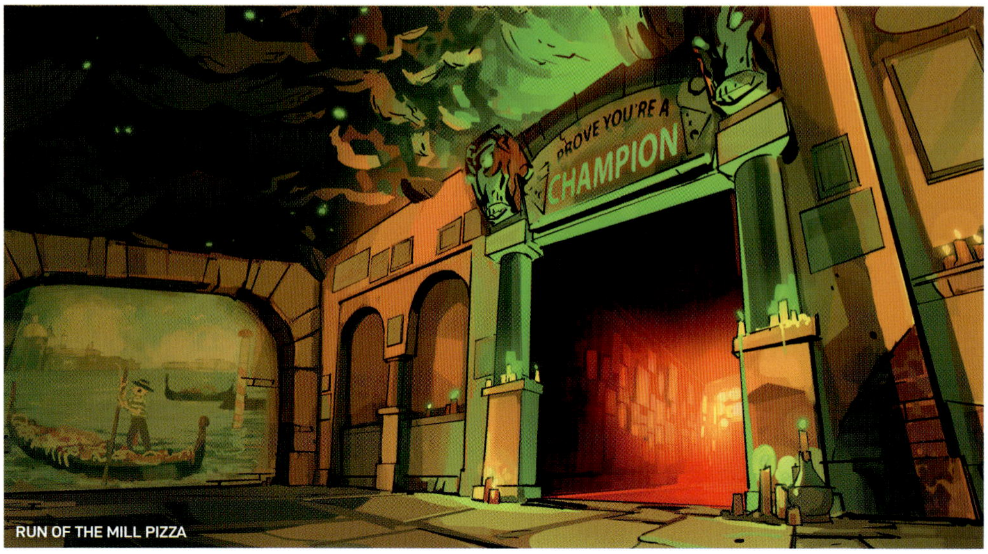

RUN OF THE MILL PIZZA

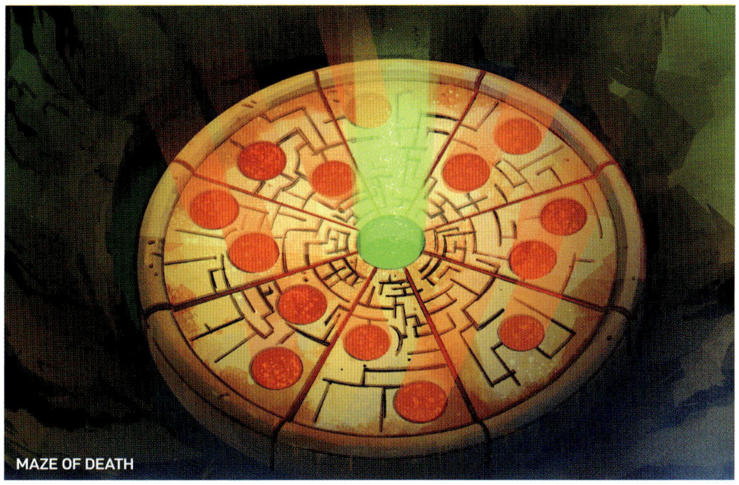

MAZE OF DEATH

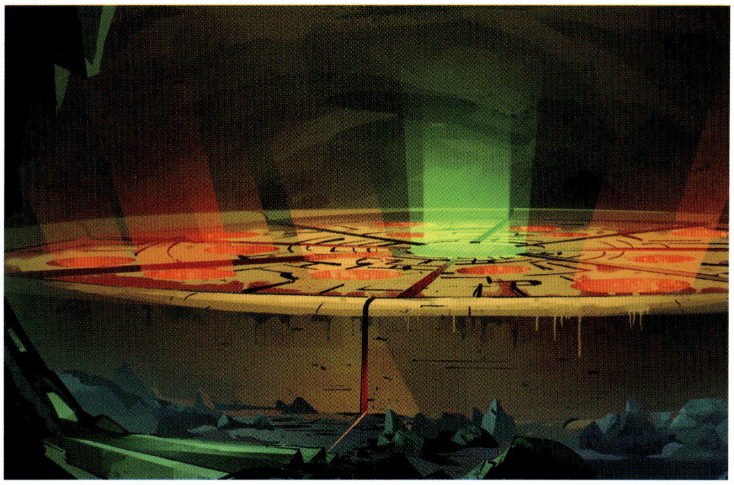

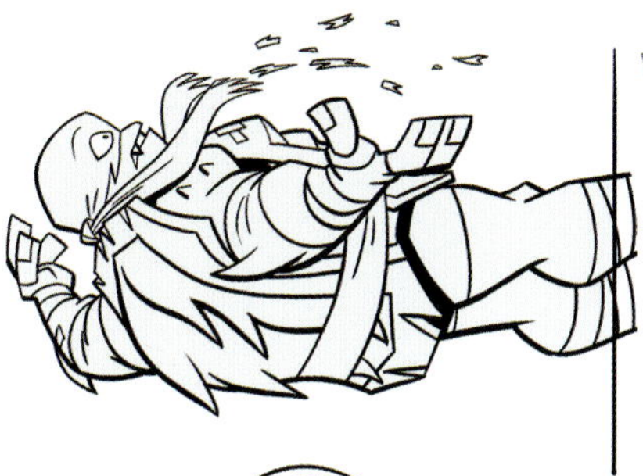

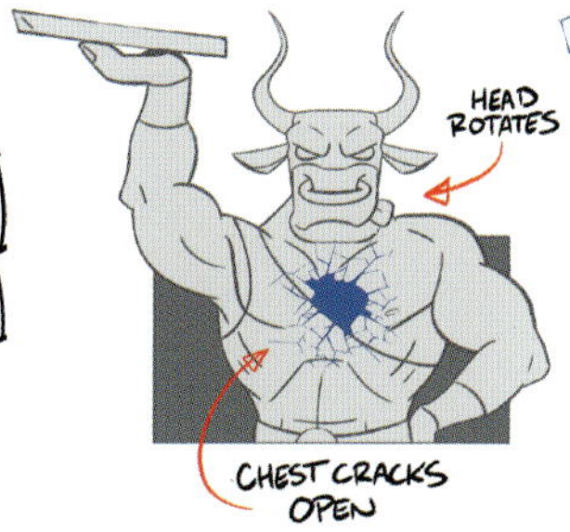

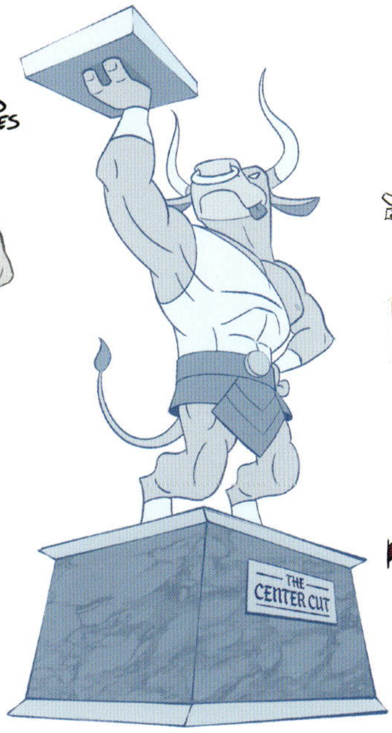

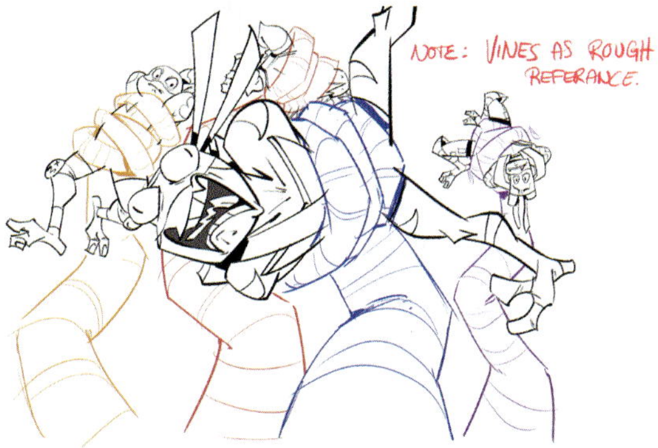

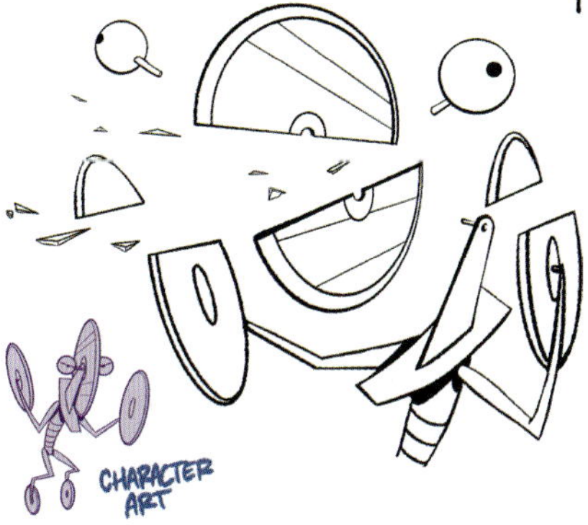

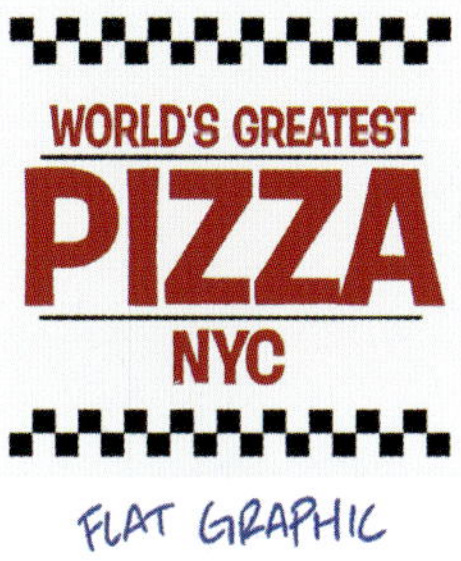

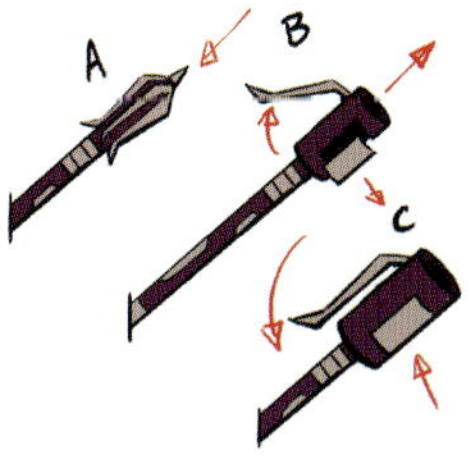

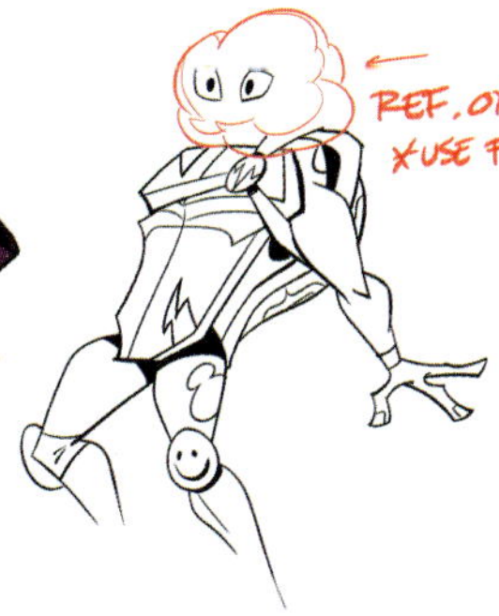

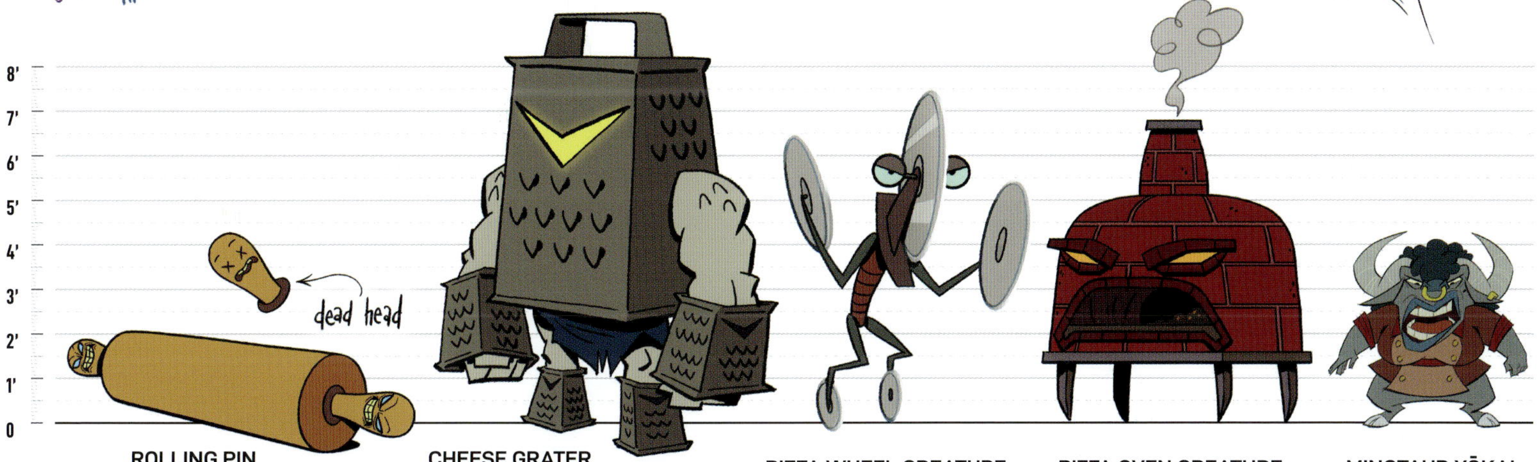

ROLLING PIN CREATURE

CHEESE GRATER CREATURE

PIZZA WHEEL CREATURE

PIZZA OVEN CREATURE

MINOTAUR YŌKAI

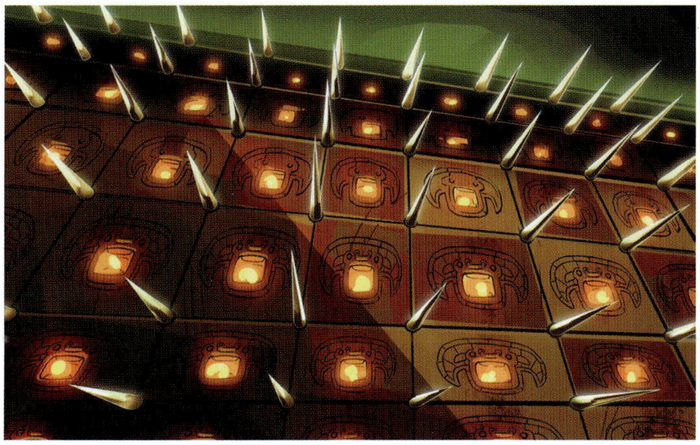

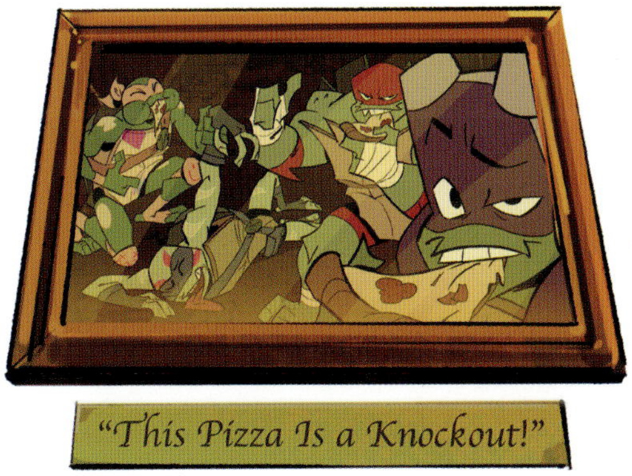

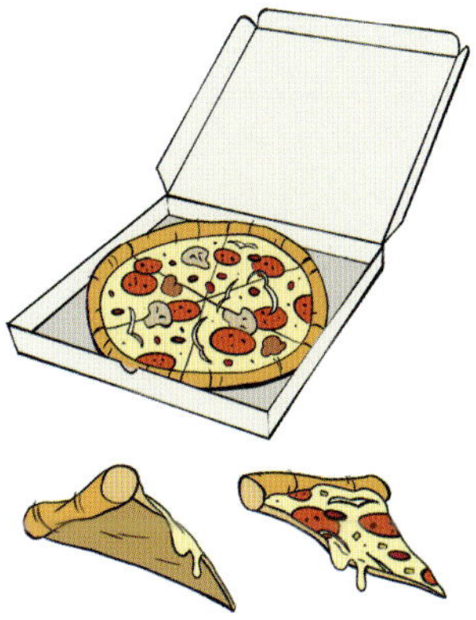

It's only fitting that the Turtles end up on the wall of shame.

DOWN WITH THE SICKNESS

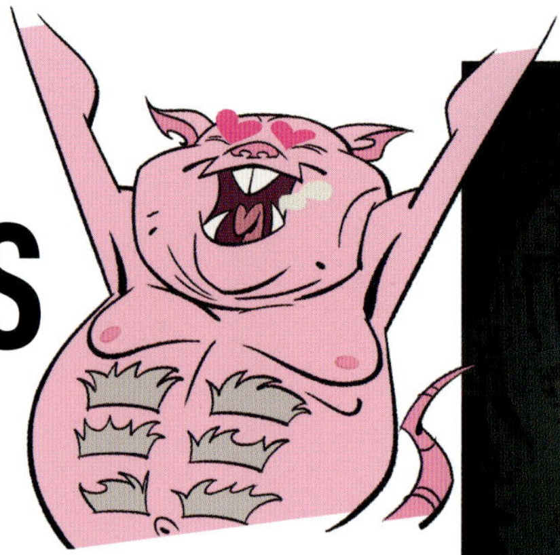

ORIGINAL AIR DATE: SEPTEMBER 18, 2018
PRODUCTION CODE: 008

WRITTEN BY **JESSE GORDON**
STORYBOARDS BY **CHRISTINA "KIKI" MANRIQUE**
DIRECTED BY **BRENDAN CLOGHER**

JESSE GORDON: I have no memory of where this idea came from—it's weird, so I'm inclined to think it was my idea. One thing I loved to do on the show was movie parodies. This was supposed to be a zombie movie where characters can't stay still and must keep running from the infected. Honestly, I don't know where the seven stages came from or why they were all so weird.

This episode sort of introduces the idea that Donnie is a bit of a mad scientist, and it was something I could have never predicted. But when he's talking about uranium, it was just a thing I put in the script, and then the boards came back and he has a giant mech behind him, the sort of inspired madness that the show did that I think was so great. I remember at the time I thought "That's too ridiculous," and now I watch it and it feels so right.

I should also mention that the title of the episode is actually a reference to this band from the early 2000s called Disturbed. The "Oh, ah-ah-ah-ah" on the final title is a direct nod to their song "Down with the Sickness."

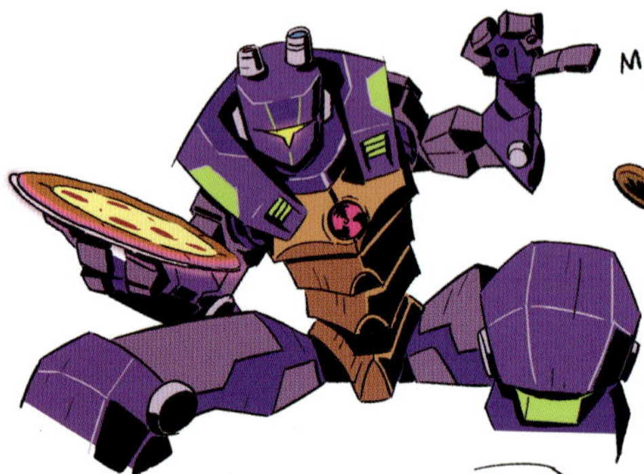

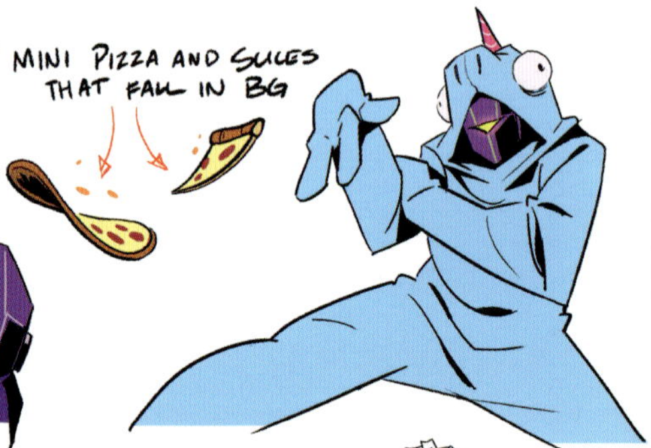

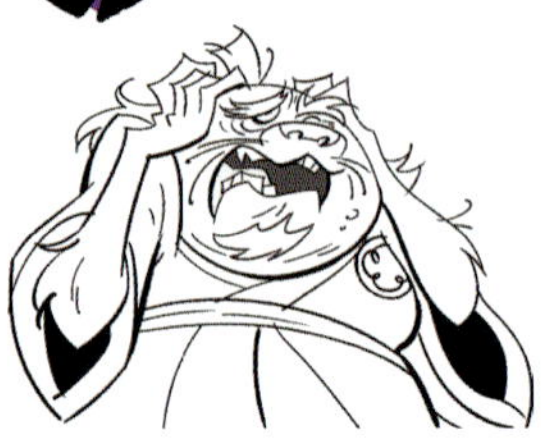

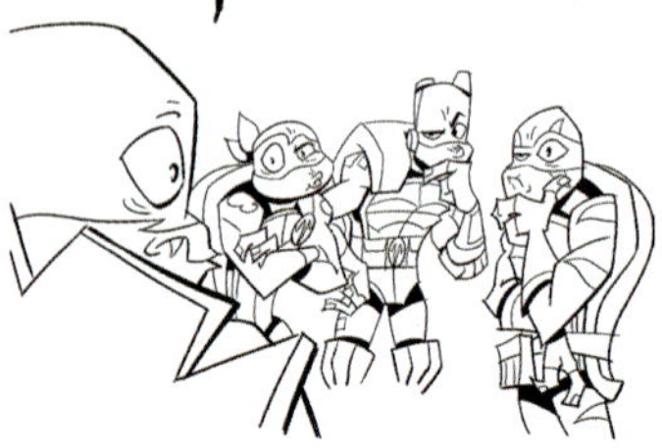

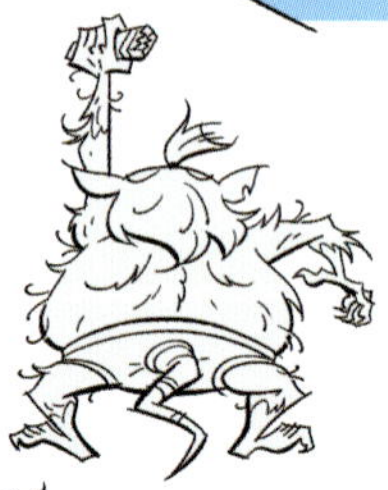

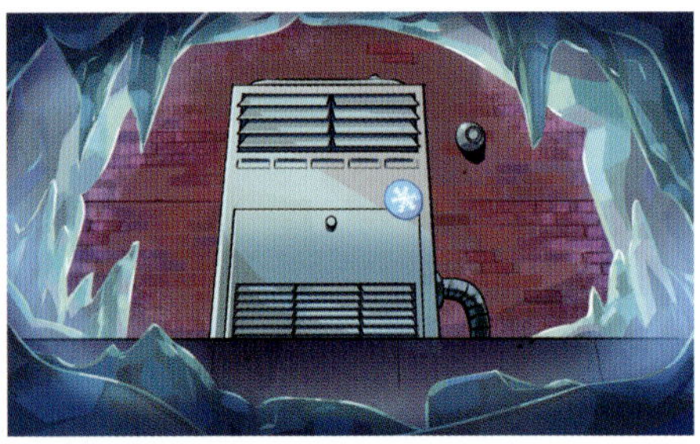

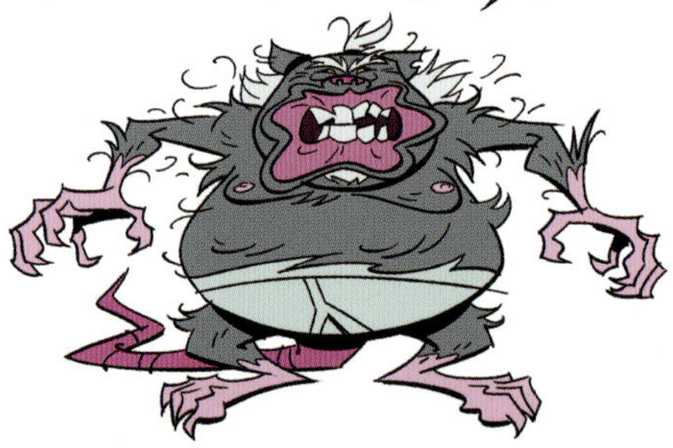

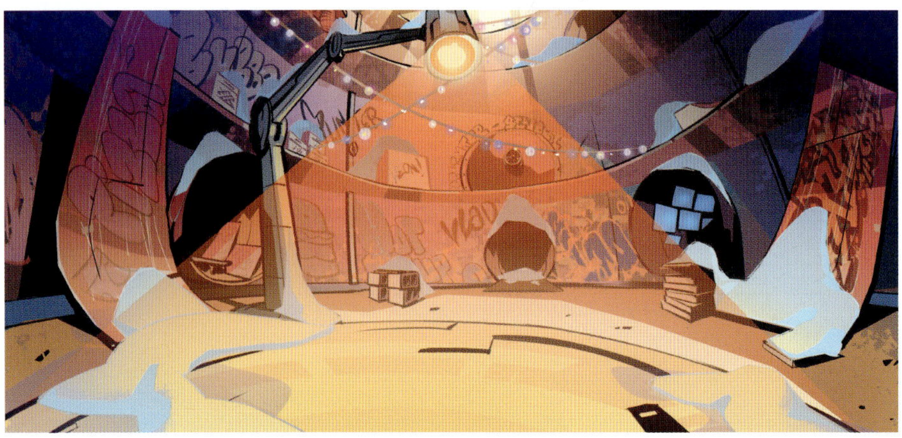

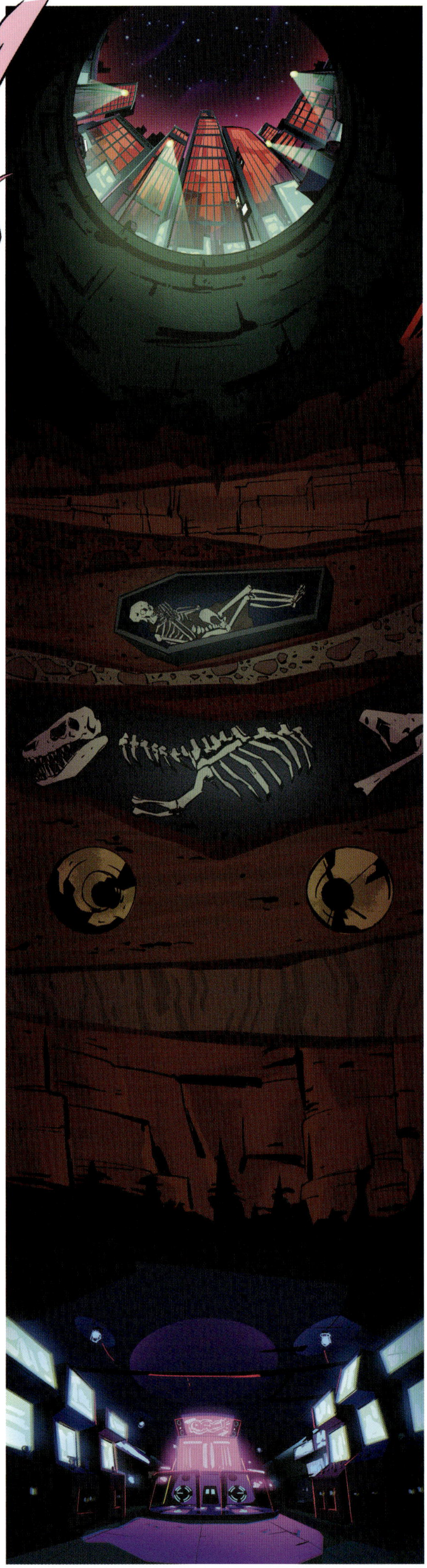

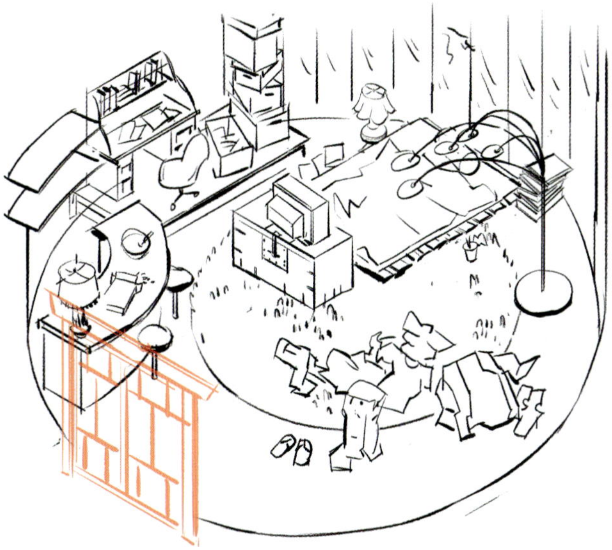

DOWNSHOT OF SPLINTER'S ROOM

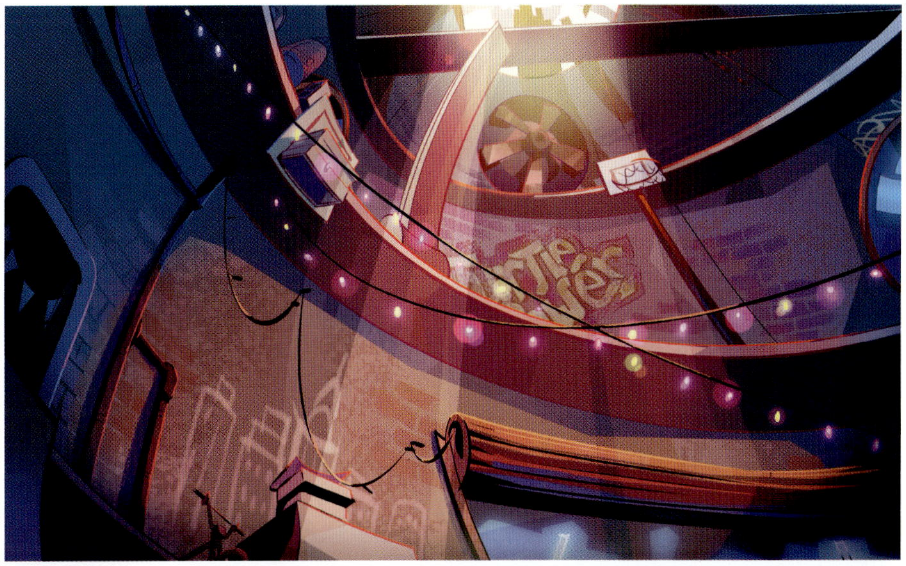

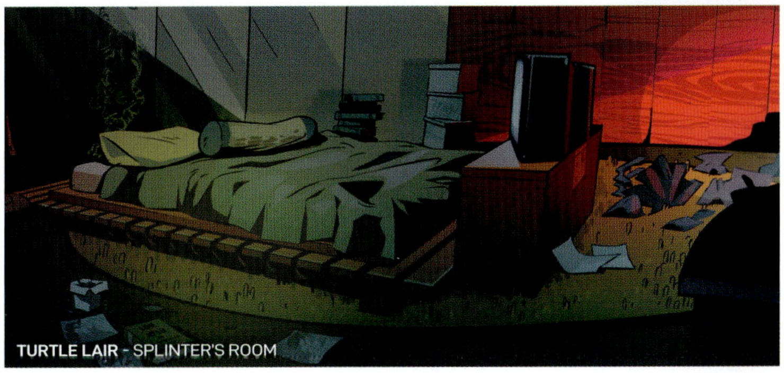

TURTLE LAIR - SPLINTER'S ROOM

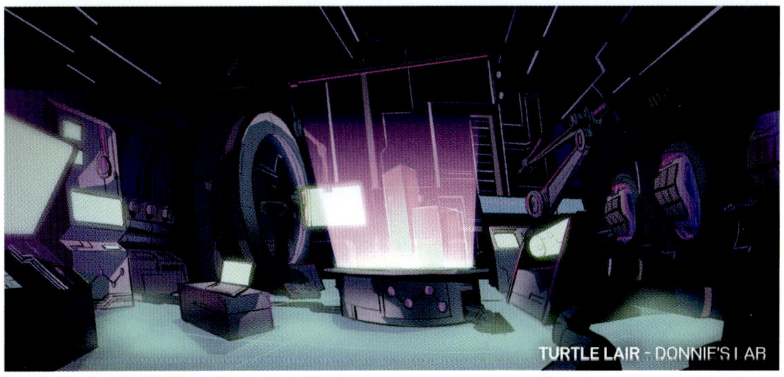

TURTLE LAIR - DONNIE'S LAB

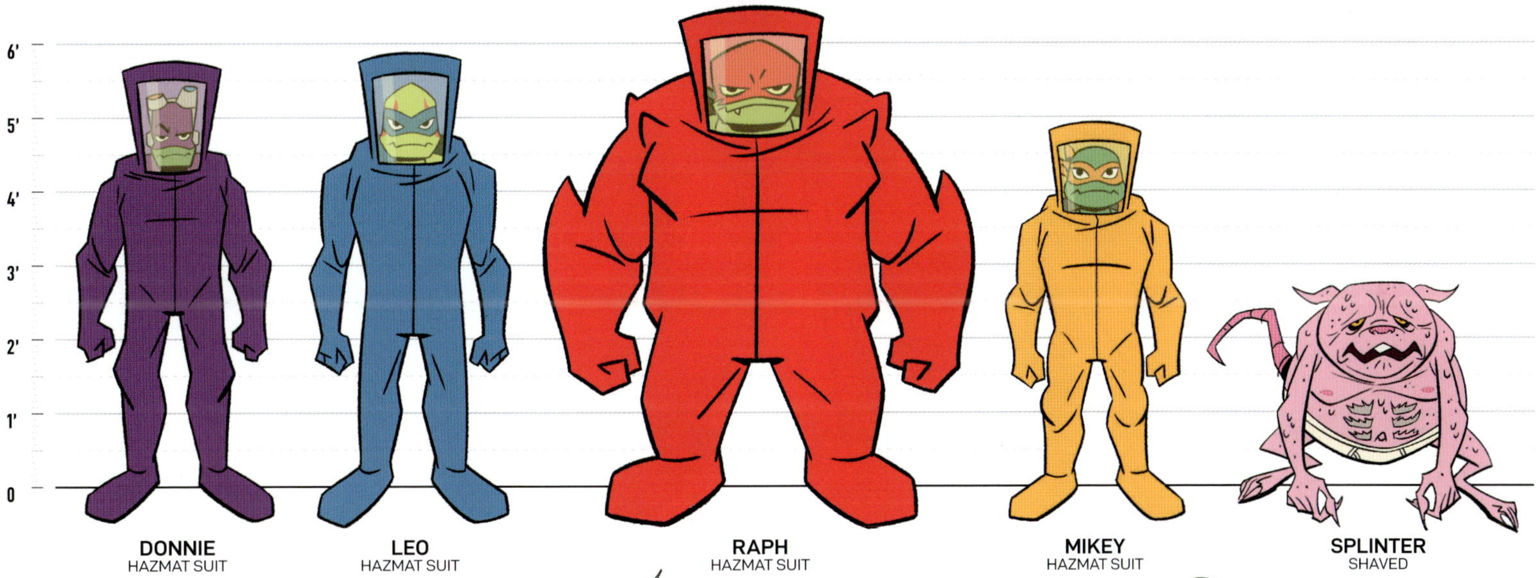

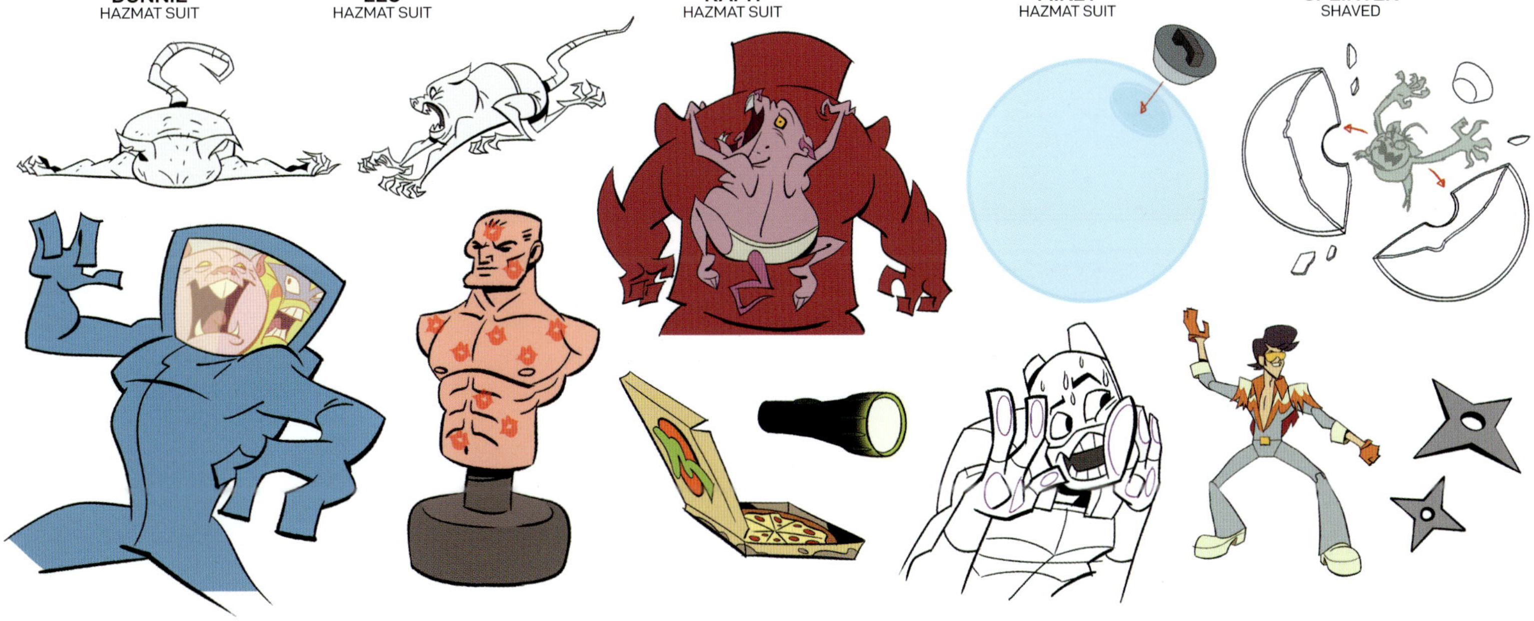

REPO MANTIS

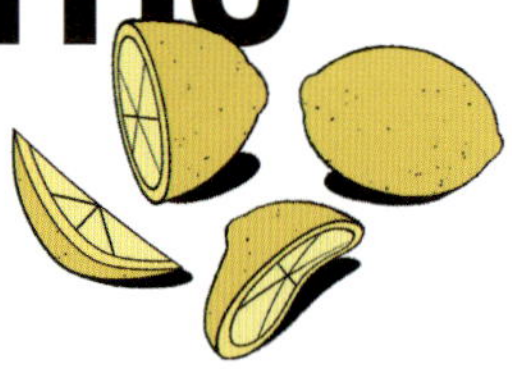

ORIGINAL AIR DATE: SEPTEMBER 20, 2018
PRODUCTION CODE: 009

WRITTEN BY **RUSS CARNEY & RON CORCILLO**
STORYBOARDS BY **CHRISTOPHER LUC**
DIRECTED BY **JAMIE VICKERS**

RON CORCILLO: This episode was a lot of fun to write, particularly because we got to introduce everyone's favorite sweet-as-pie capybara, Todd! This may have been the first episode we wrote that had two Turtles paired together instead of all four. This was done not only to get fun dynamics between two brothers, but also because it can be difficult to service four characters in an 11-minute episode. This episode was supposed to take place at the same time as "Hypno! Part Deux," where Raph and Leo had teamed up. We were going to have a phone call in each episode that connected the two missions, but it was ultimately cut for time.

RUSS CARNEY: Christopher Luc did a fantastic job boarding the episode. Our favorite shot is when Donnie is at the picnic table and he keeps rolling a puppy away, only for the puppy to happily roll back.

RON CORCILLO: Russ, who spends most of his day talking in different voices just to entertain himself, performed much of the "scratch" (a.k.a. temporary) dialogue for the series' animatics, including that of Repo Mantis. His performance as the gravelly voiced New York salvage con man was so well loved that he was officially hired to be the voice of the new character! That is, until 15 minutes later, when it was revealed that casting already hired a voice actor with actual talent, Fred Tatasciore. RIP Repo Russ!

RUSS CARNEY: Todd's puppies, Melvin, Miho, and Willis, were named after crew members Melvin Young, Miho Tomimasu, and Ellen Willis.

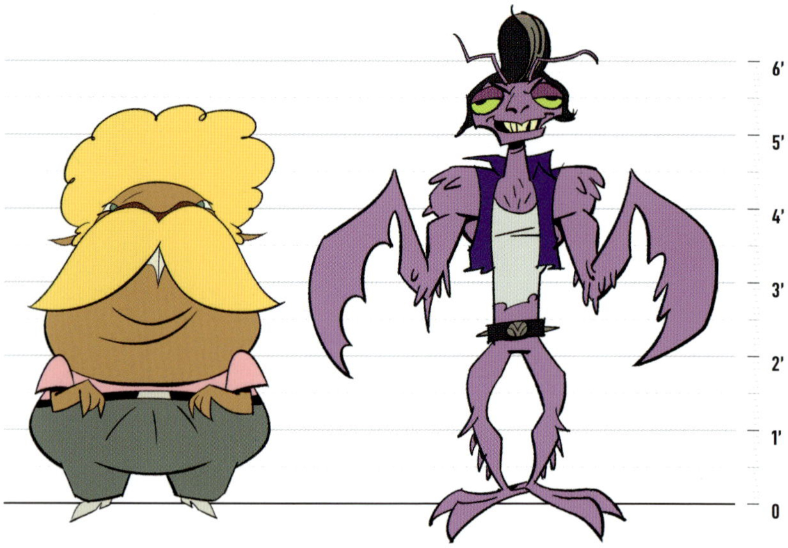

TODD CAPYBARA

REPO MANTIS

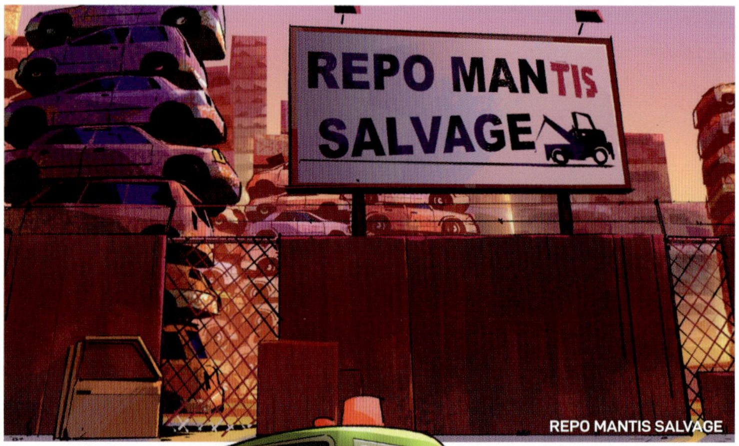

REPO MANTIS SALVAGE

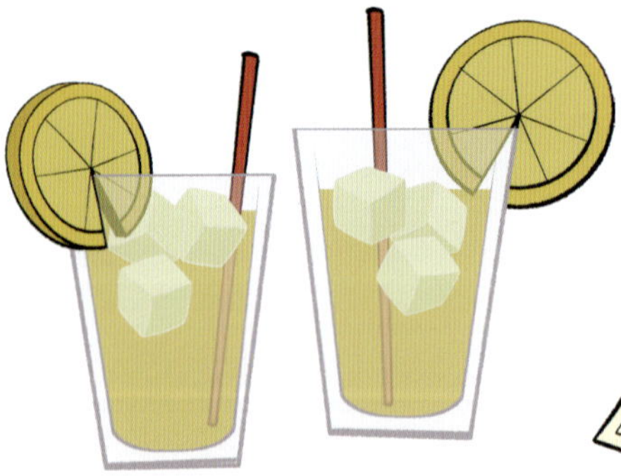

TODD'S INTERNET-FAMOUS HOMEMADE LEMONADE

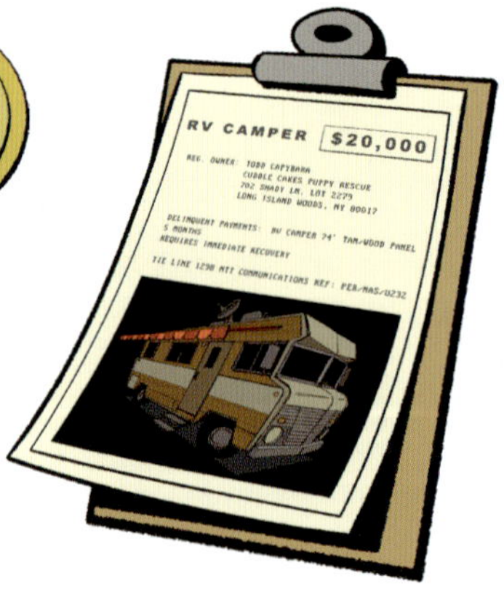

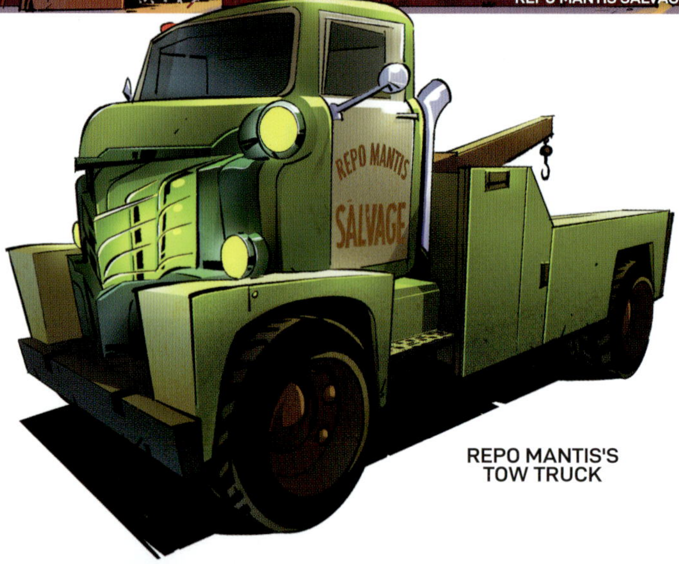

REPO MANTIS'S TOW TRUCK

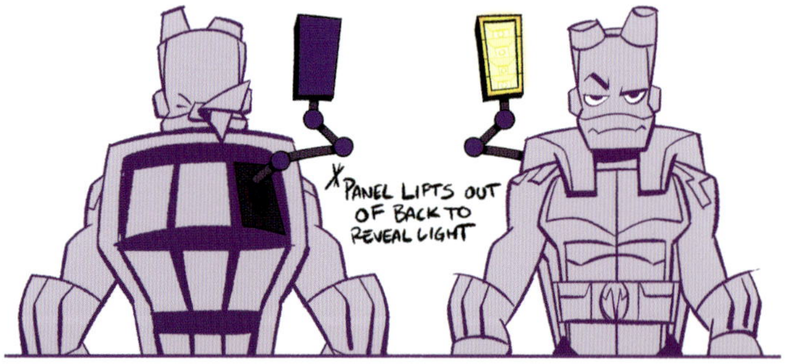

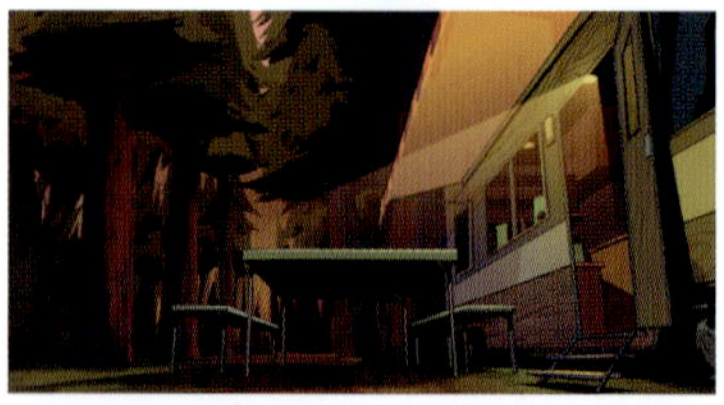

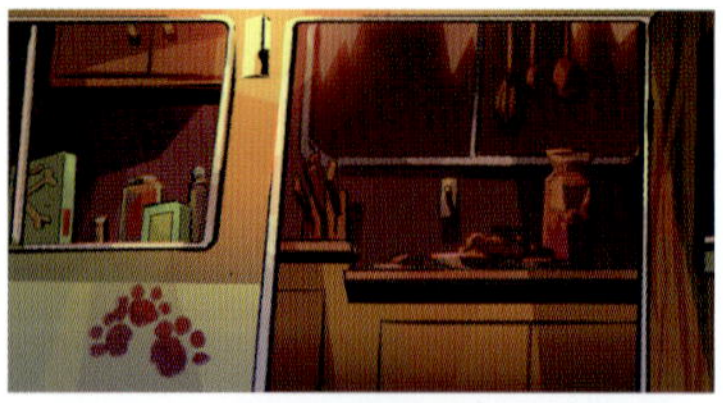

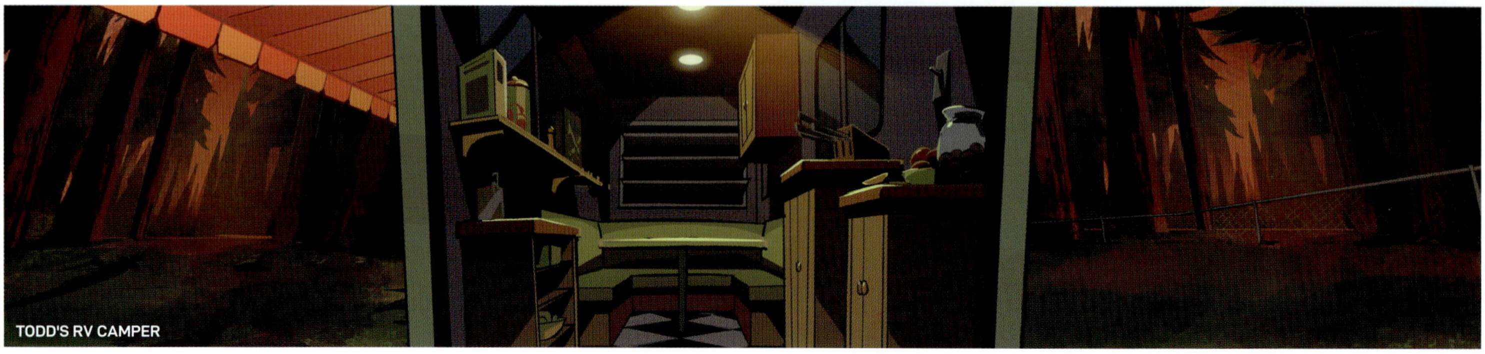

TODD'S RV CAMPER

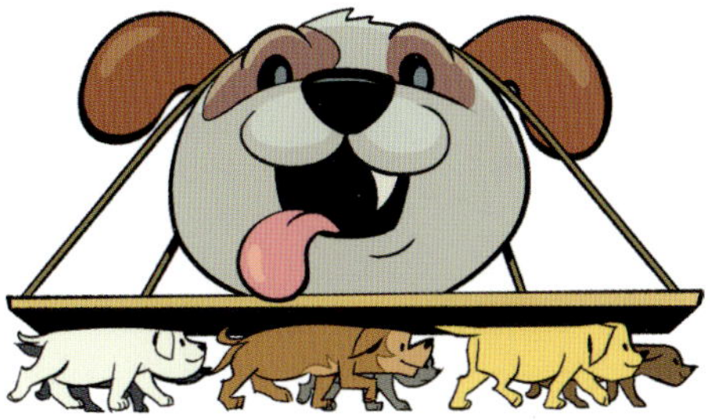

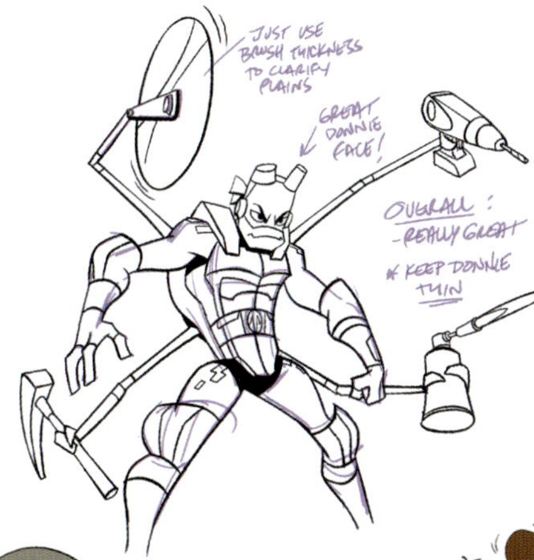

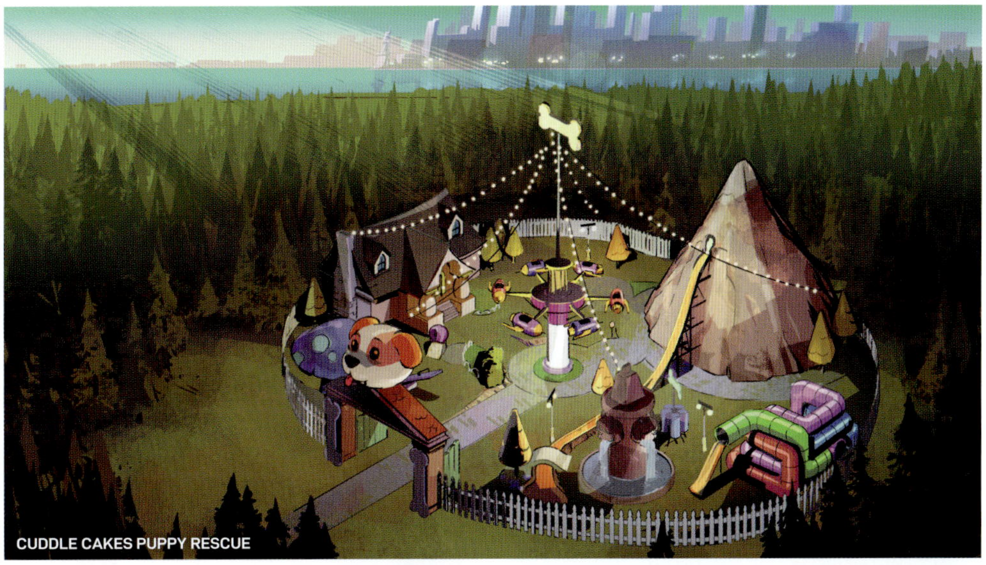
CUDDLE CAKES PUPPY RESCUE

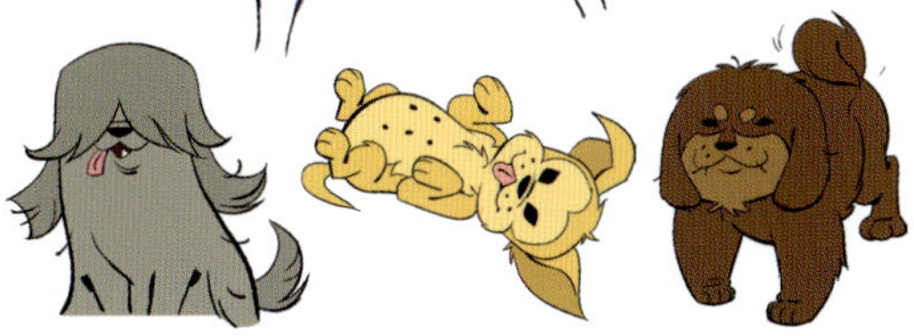

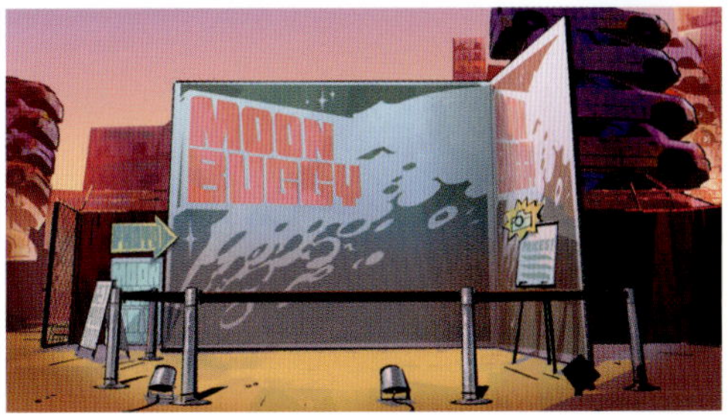

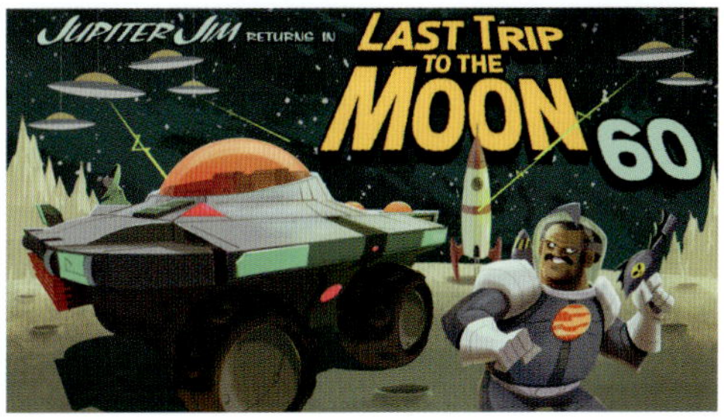

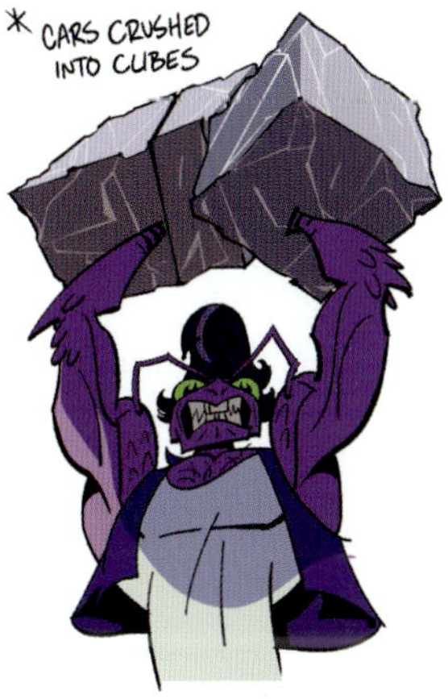

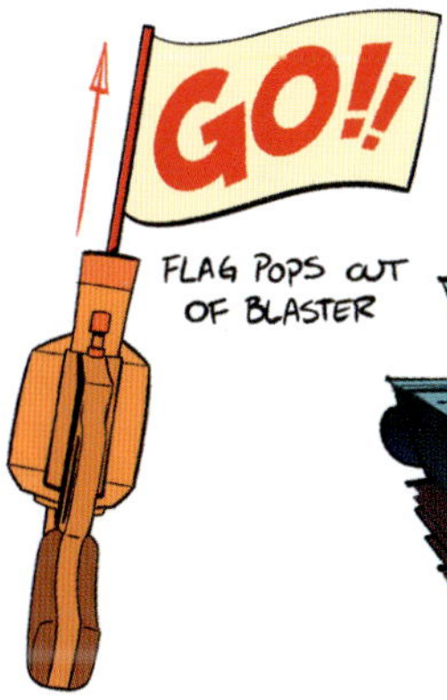

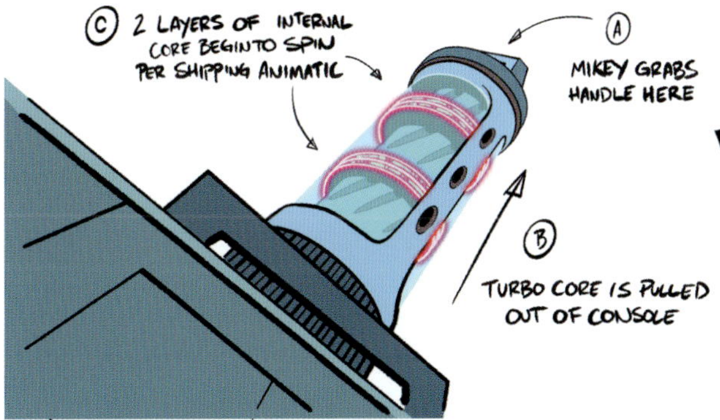

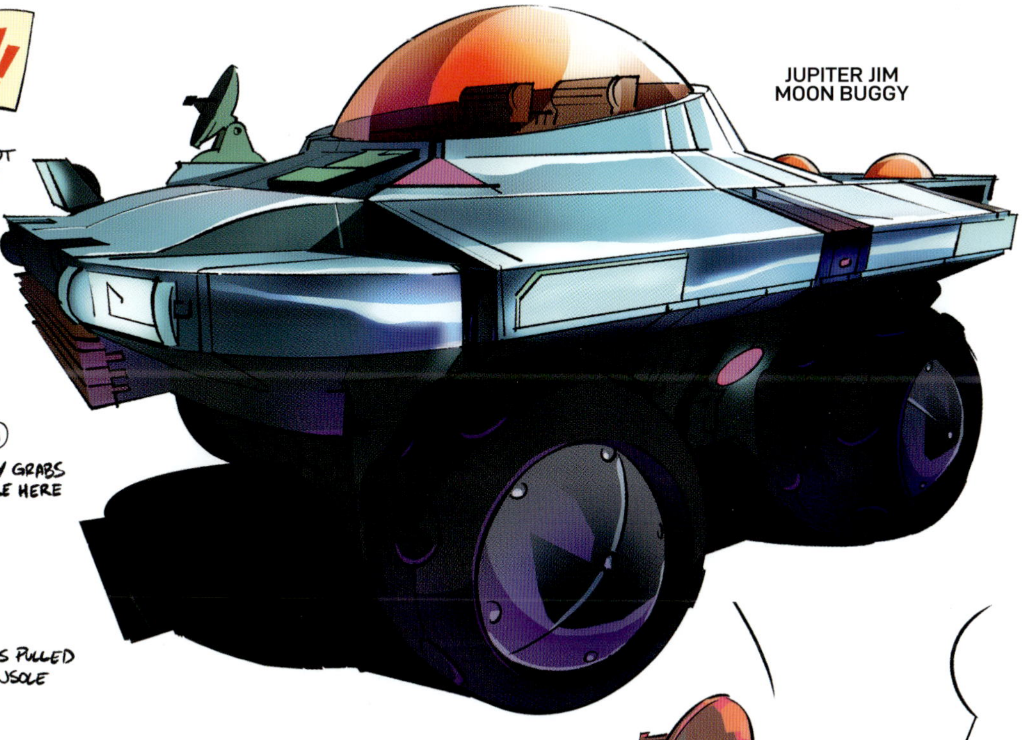
JUPITER JIM MOON BUGGY

MOON BUGGY DASHBOARD

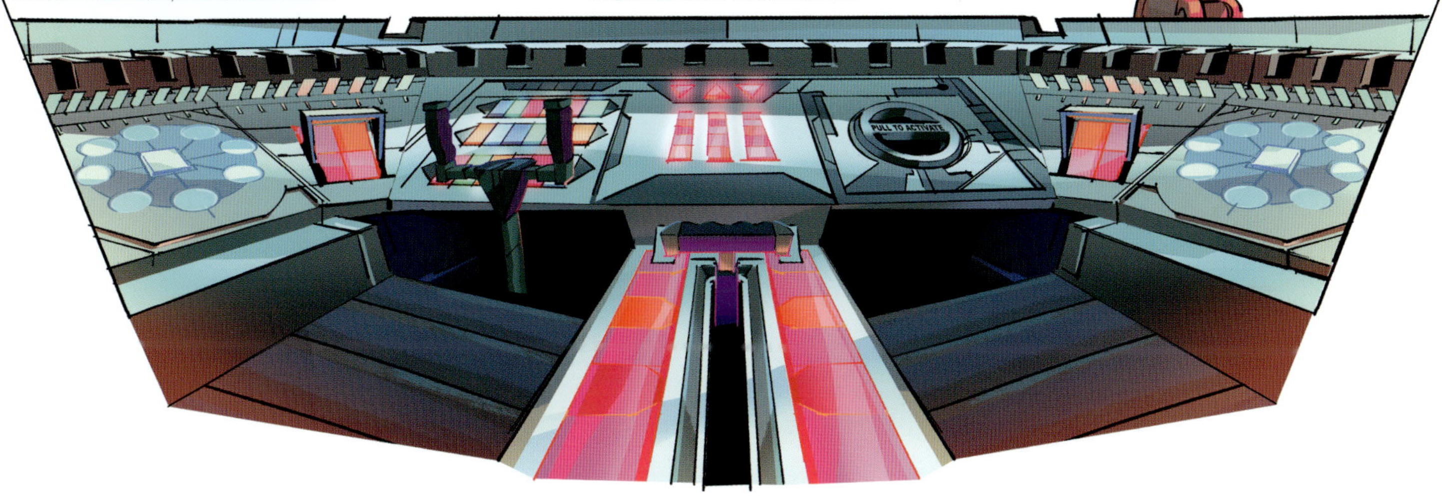

MASCOT MELEE

ORIGINAL AIR DATE: SEPTEMBER 26, 2018
PRODUCTION CODE: 010

WRITTEN BY **IAN BUSCH**
STORYBOARDS BY **JJ CONWAY**
DIRECTED BY **SEBASTIAN MONTES**

JJ CONWAY: Finding the story is essential to any action scene—otherwise it gets stale really fast—but this was the first time I had to find a story through dance. I tried to ramp up the tension by making the dancing faster, and by having everyone jump in to respond faster and faster, while most importantly tracking how the Turtles were winning over the audience.

The dance-off ended up being a huge challenge for the animation team because it was three minutes of pure choreographed movement (with an actual fight afterwards). Flying Bark did a great job stepping up, but going forward we worked with them to ensure everything we storyboarded was producible on their end.

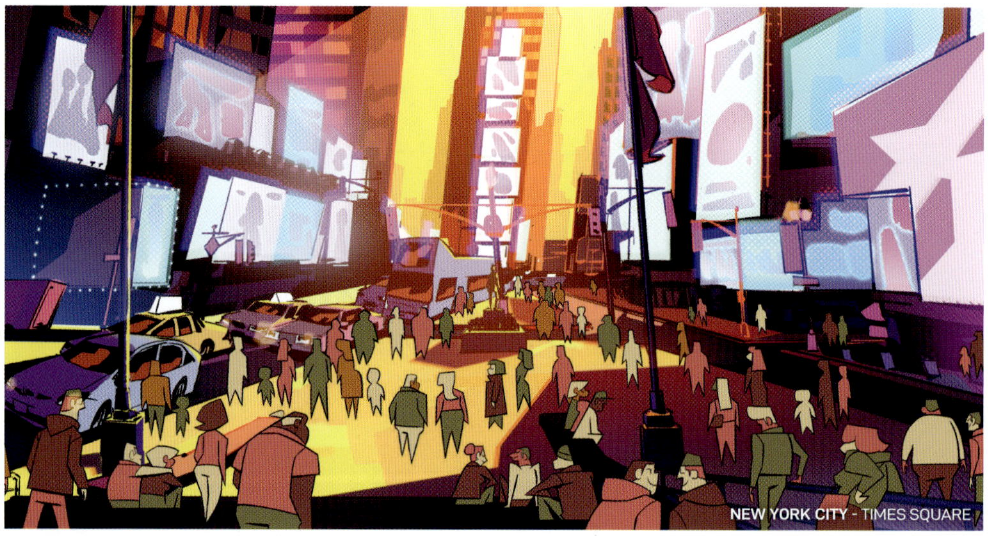
NEW YORK CITY - TIMES SQUARE

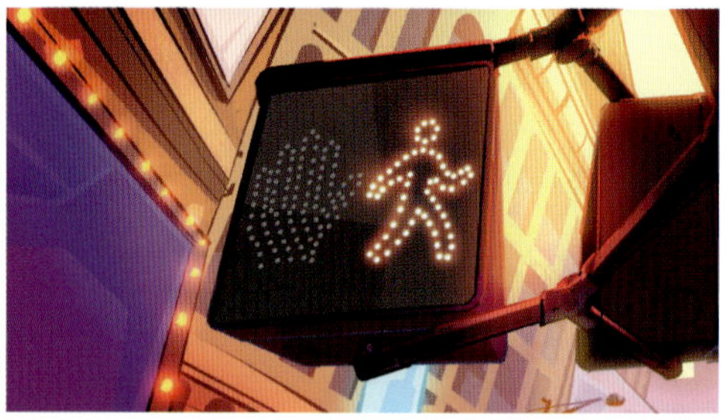

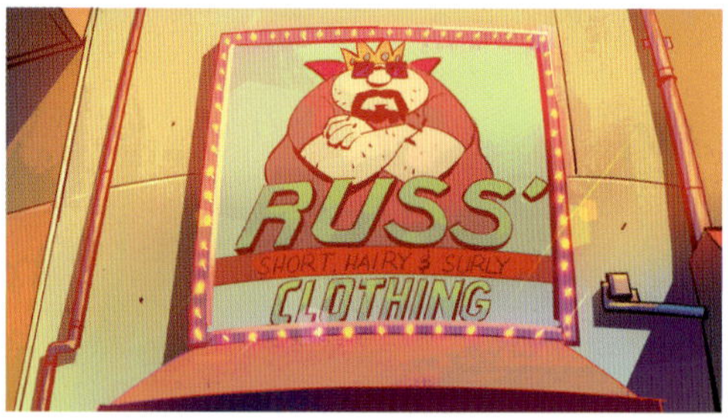

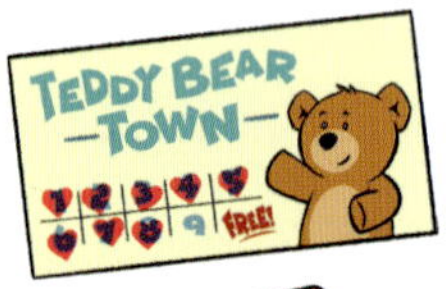

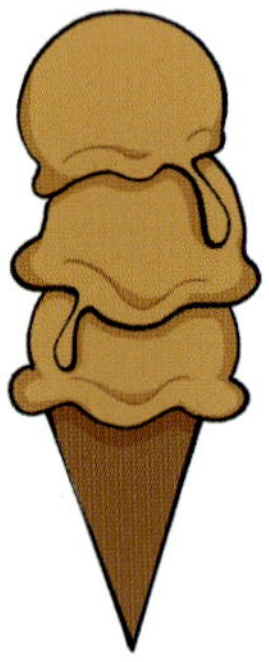

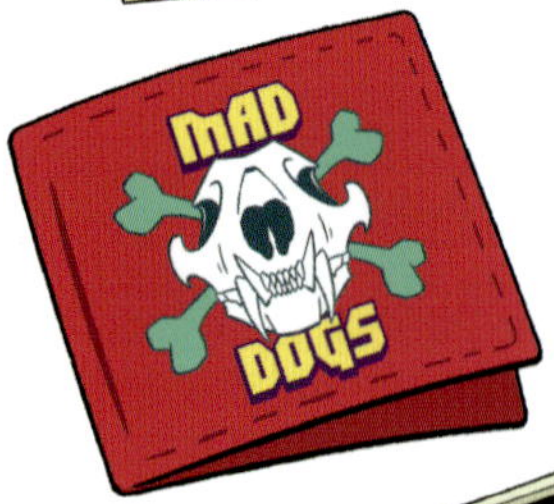

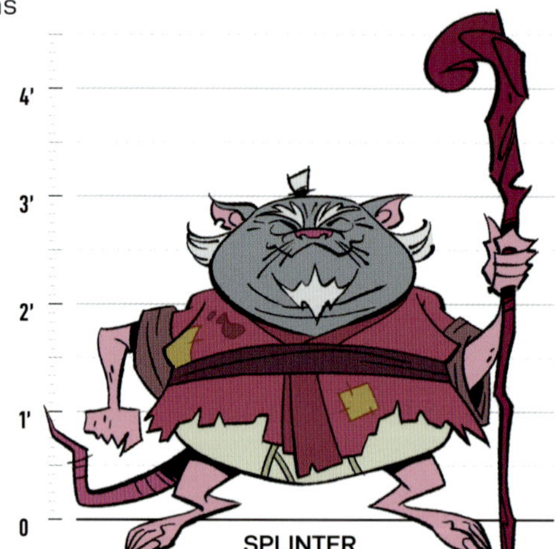

SPLINTER
TATTERED ROBE

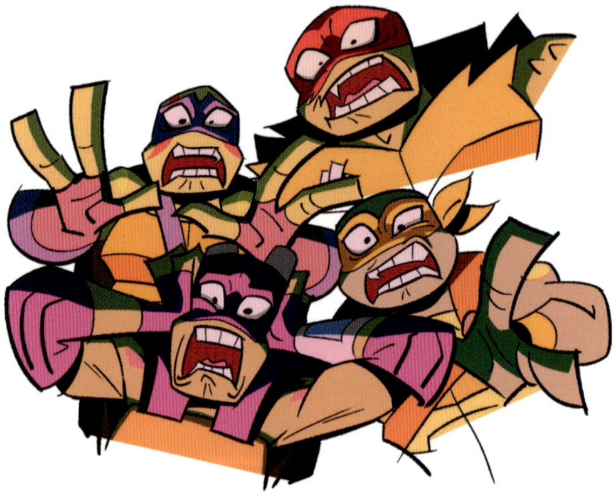

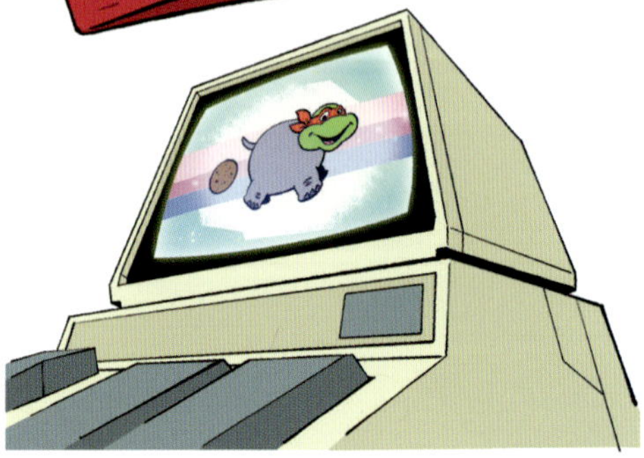

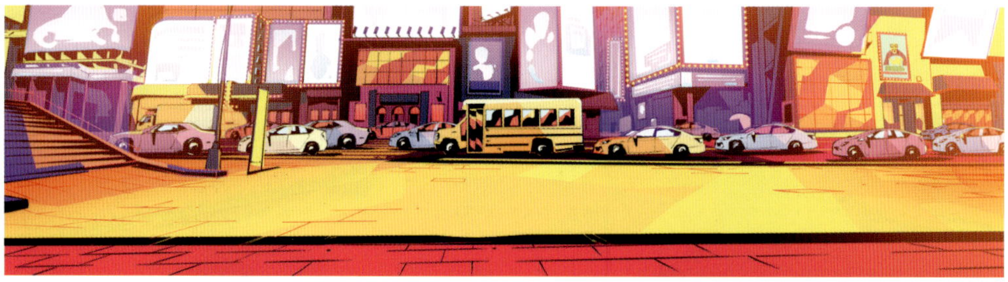

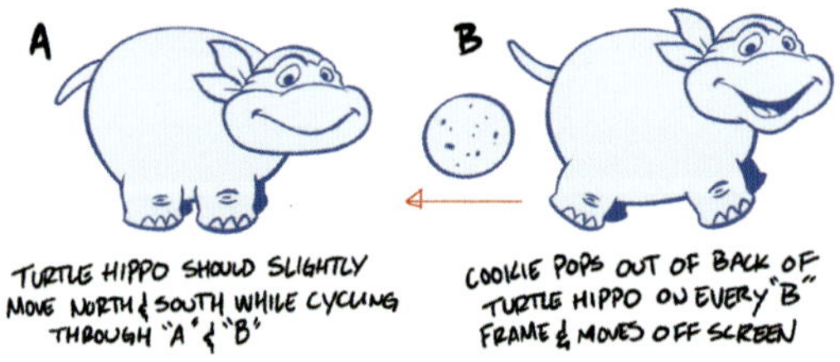

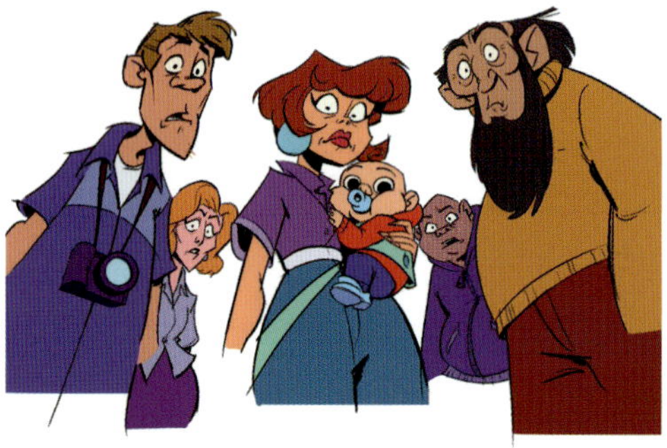

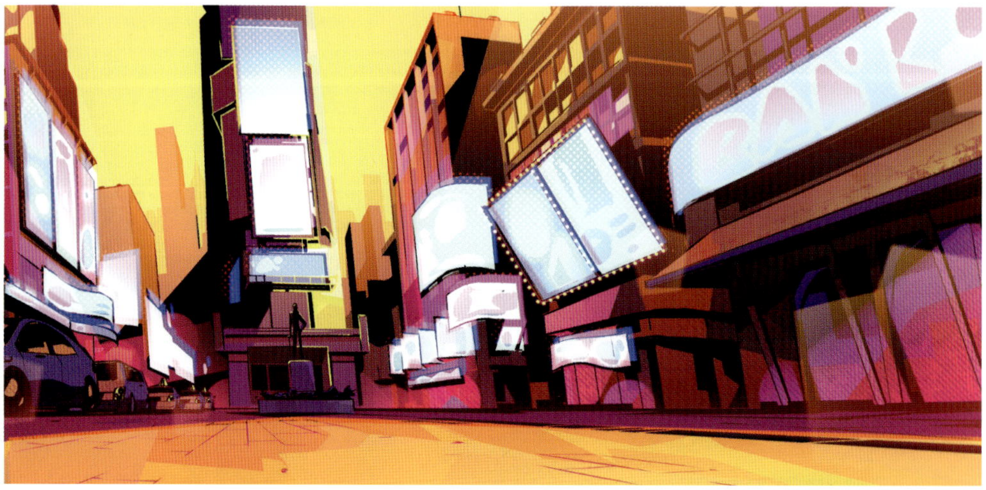

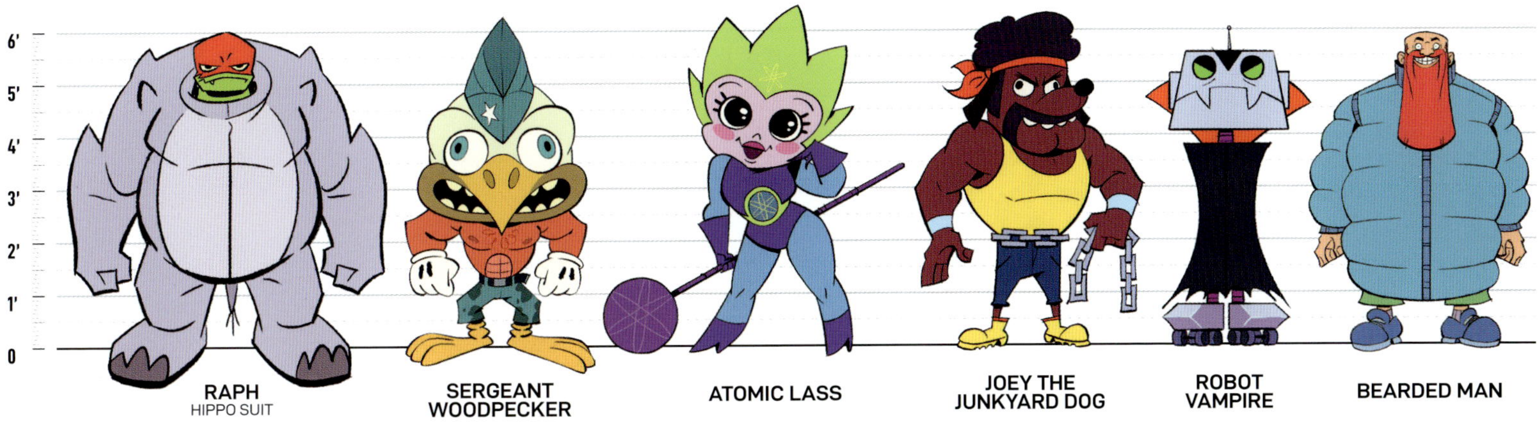
6'
5'
4'
3'
2'
1'
0
RAPH
HIPPO SUIT
SERGEANT WOODPECKER
ATOMIC LASS
JOEY THE JUNKYARD DOG
ROBOT VAMPIRE
BEARDED MAN

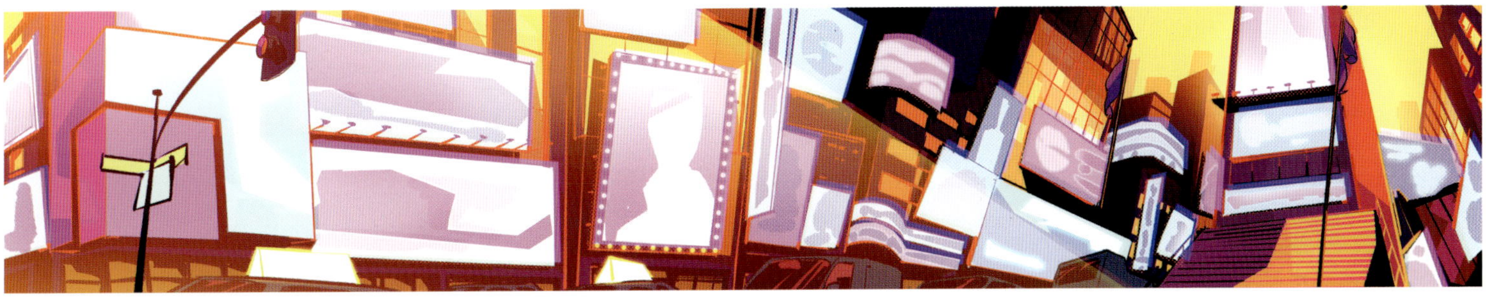

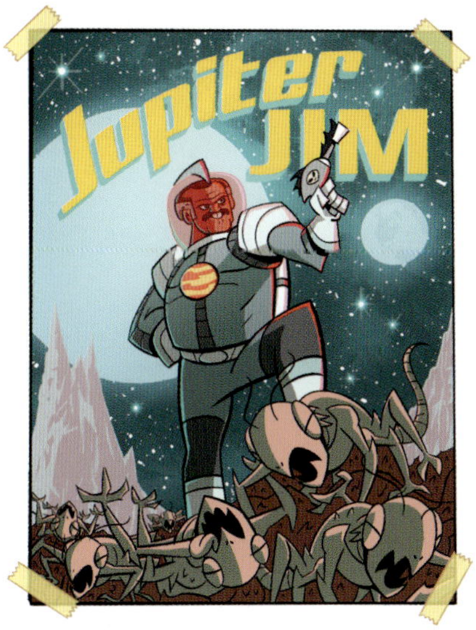
Jupiter JIM

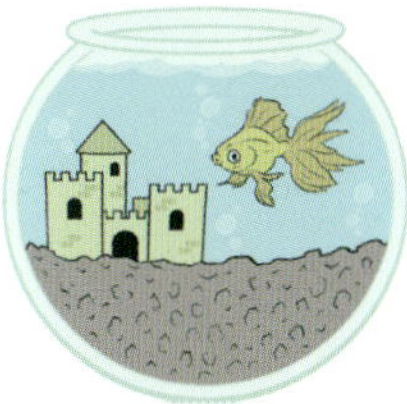

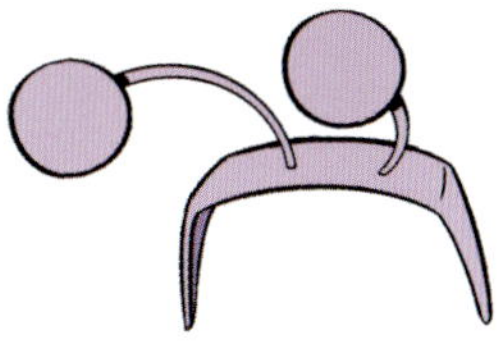

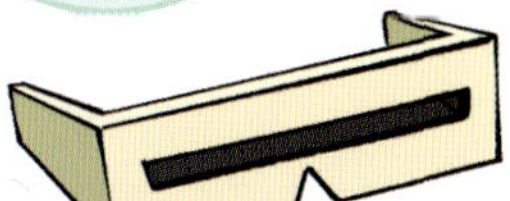

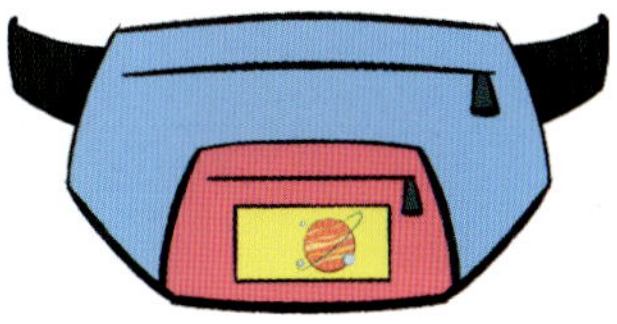

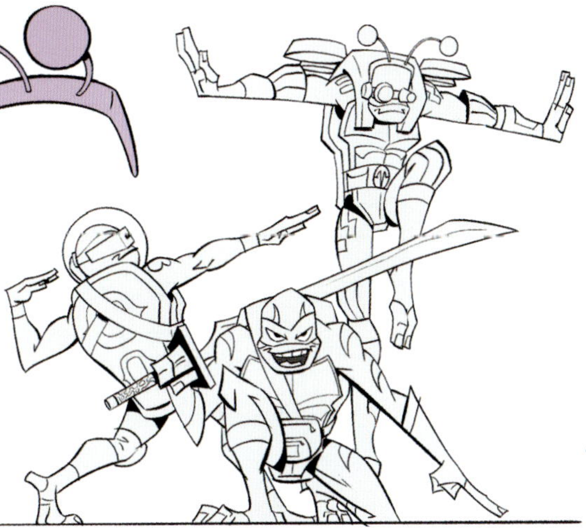

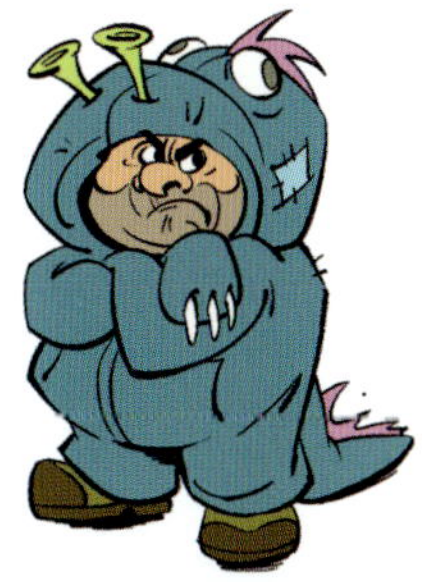

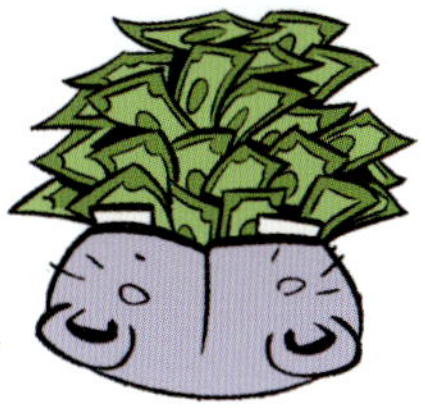

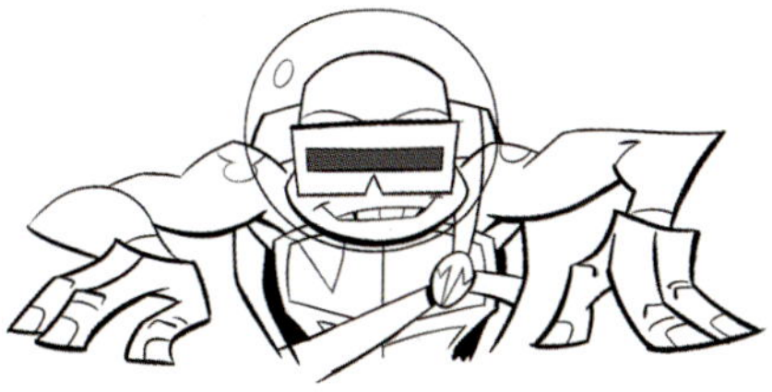

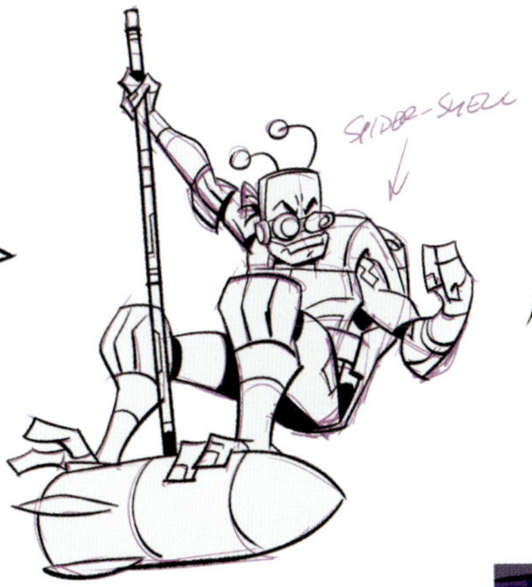
SPIDER-SHELL

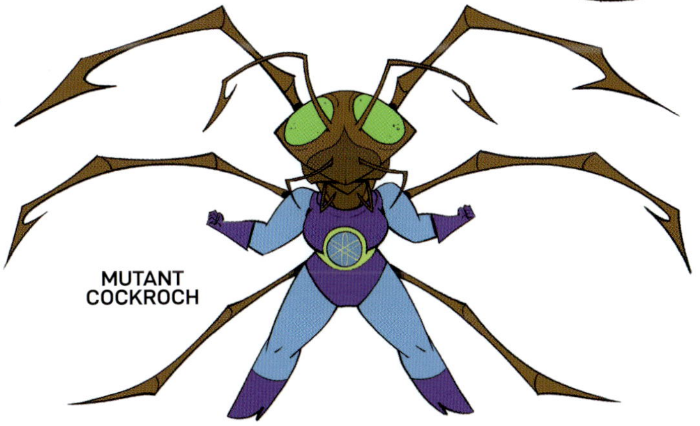
MUTANT COCKROCH

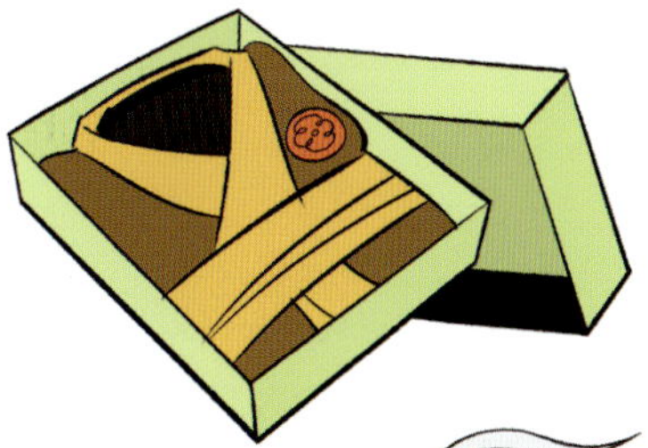

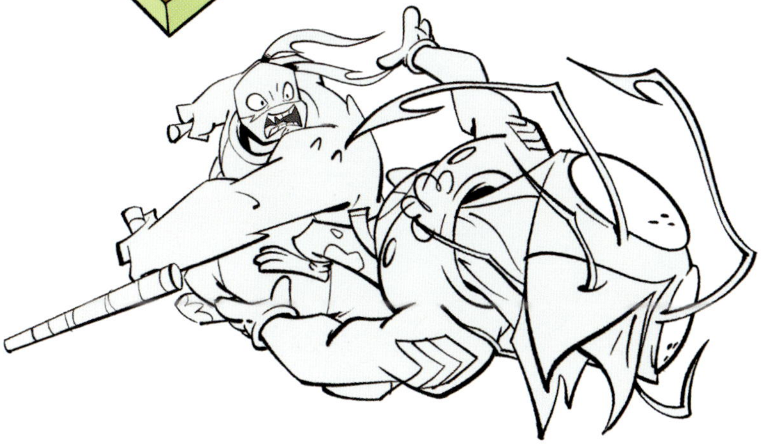

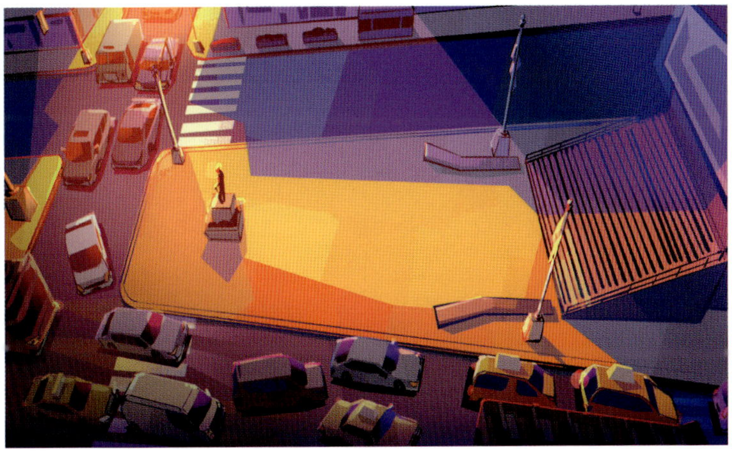

THE FAST AND THE FURRIEST

ORIGINAL AIR DATE: SEPTEMBER 24, 2018
PRODUCTION CODE: 011

WRITTEN BY **RUSS CARNEY & RON CORCILLO**
STORYBOARDS BY **CHRISTINE LIU**
DIRECTED BY **BRENDAN CLOGHER**

RUSS CARNEY: The idea of Splinter stealing the Turtle Tank was probably the easiest pitch we had to make. Trying to get people on board with a scene where teenaged Donnie busts up a restaurant like Steven Seagal in *Out for Justice* (1991) was a much harder sell.

Eagle-eyed fans might notice that while this is the episode where Donnie reveals the Turtle Tank, the vehicle appears first in "Mascot Melee." This is because the network aired the episodes out of order.

RON CORCILLO: At the end of the episode, Donnie punishes Splinter by sentencing him to a litany of math educational shows, including the *Memorizing Pi Channel.* ("Spoiler alert: The 99th digit is 7!") Since Josh Brener is a math nerd, and because we really like him, we went to the internet, found a large readout of pi, and meticulously counted to the 99th decimal. We are ride or die for Josh!

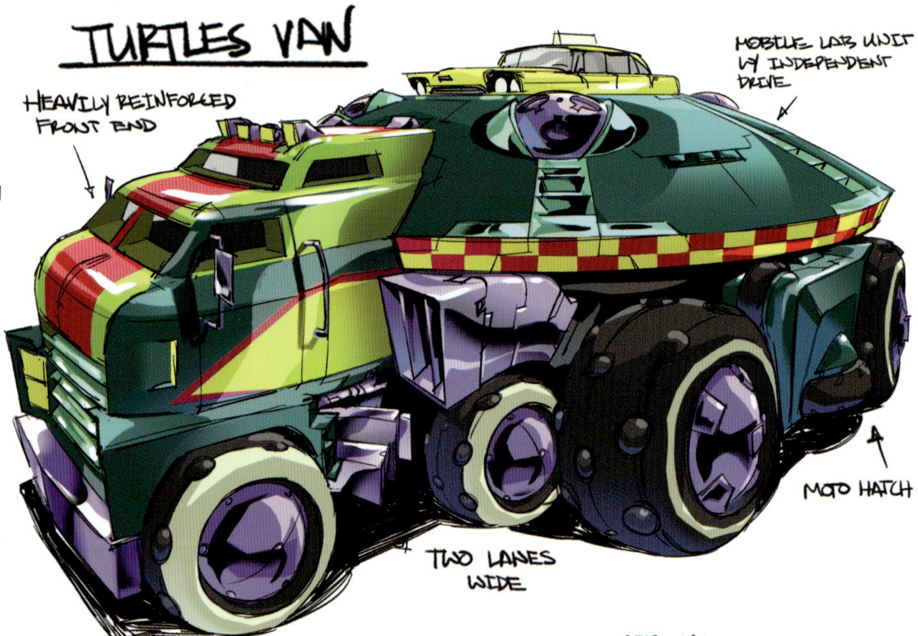

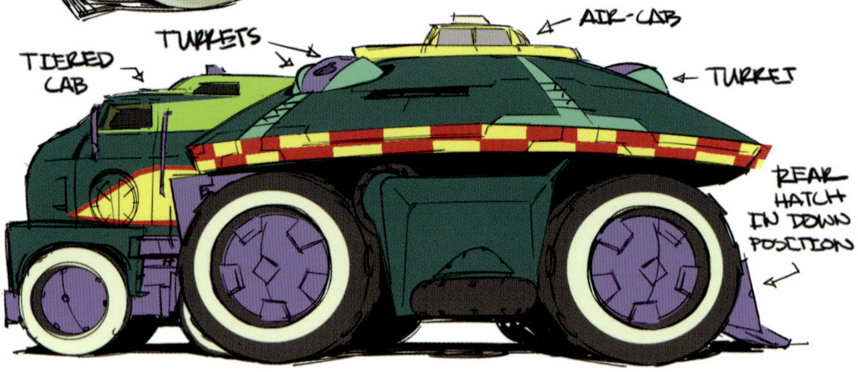

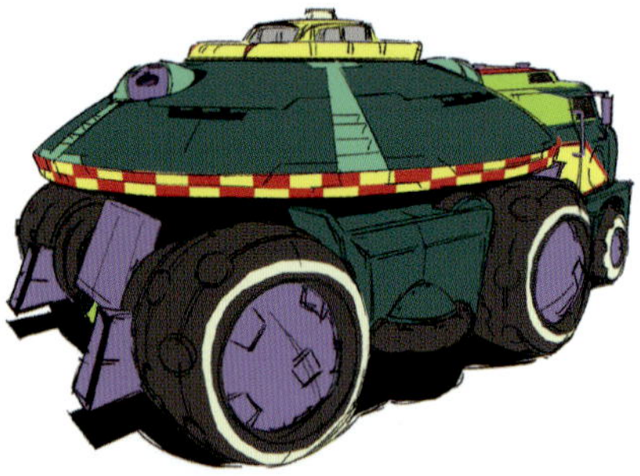

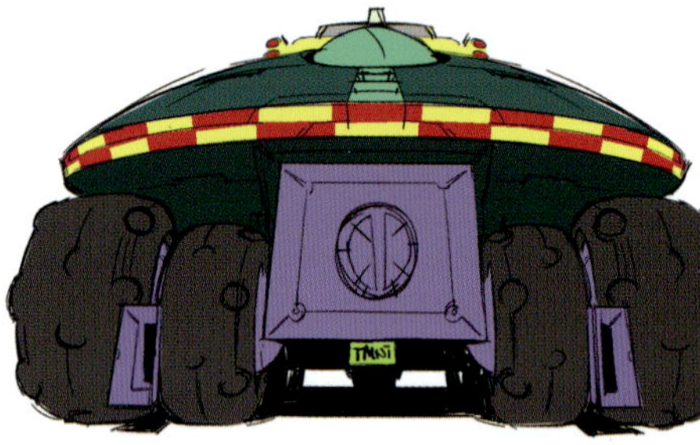

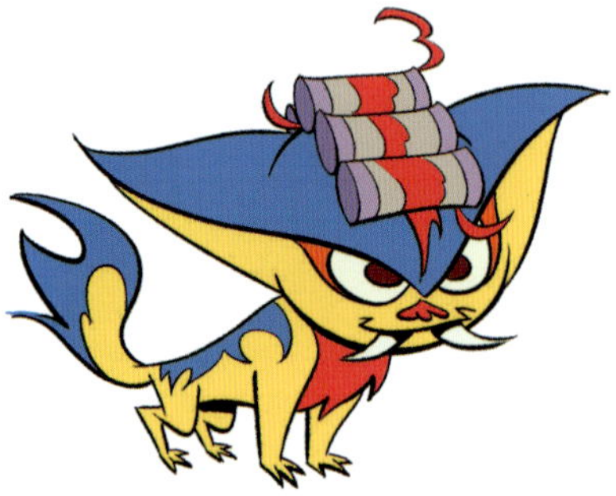

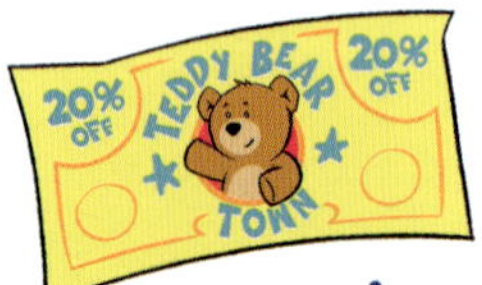

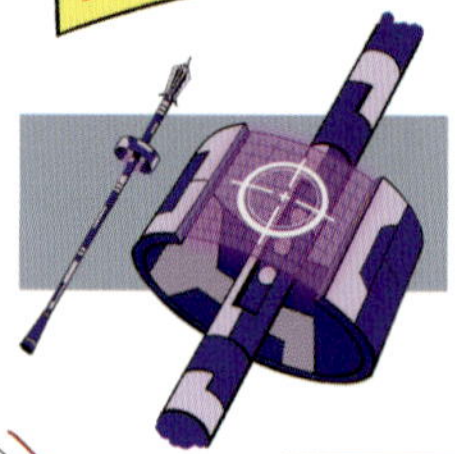

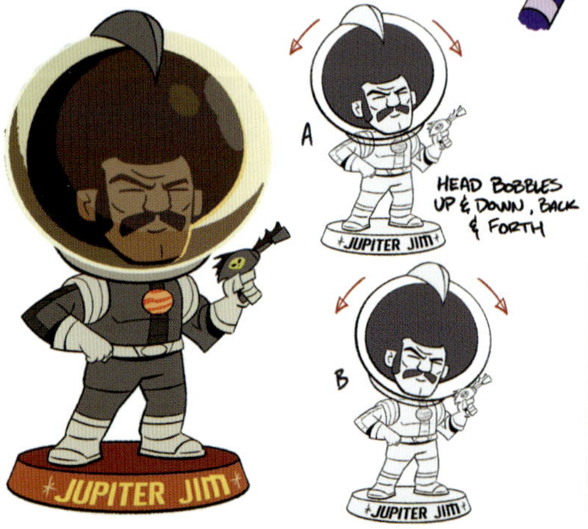

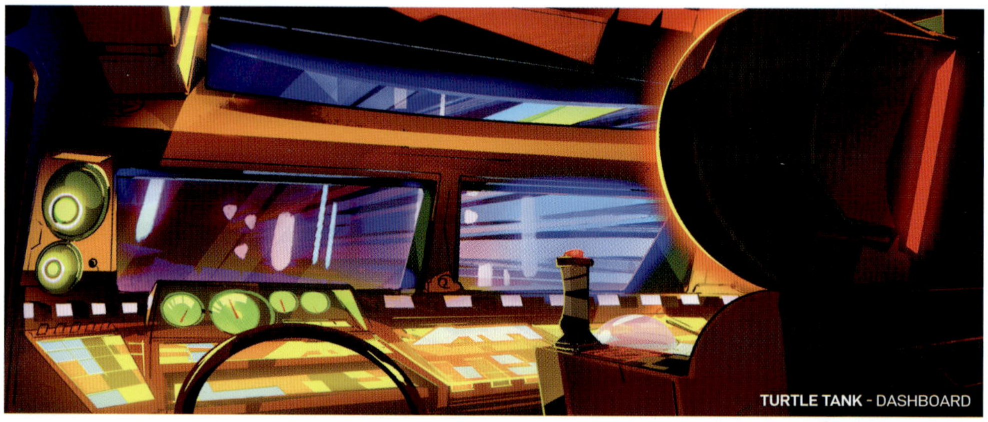
TURTLE TANK - DASHBOARD

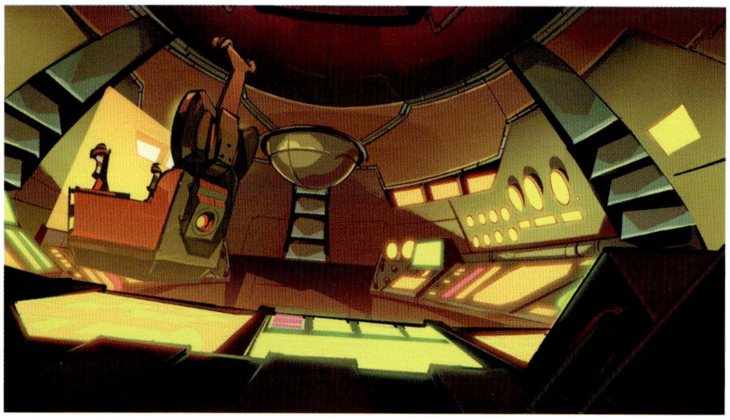

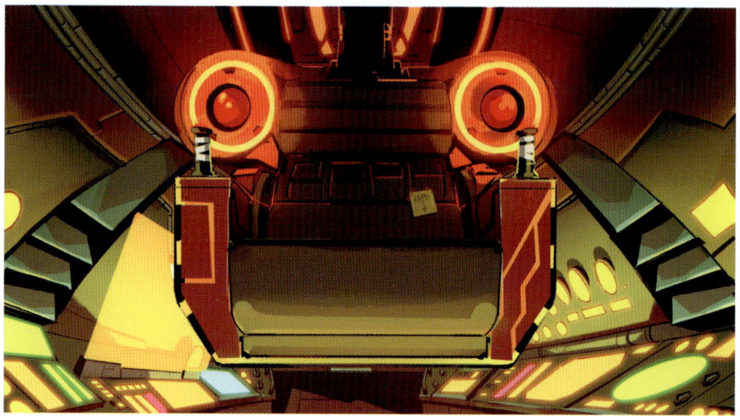

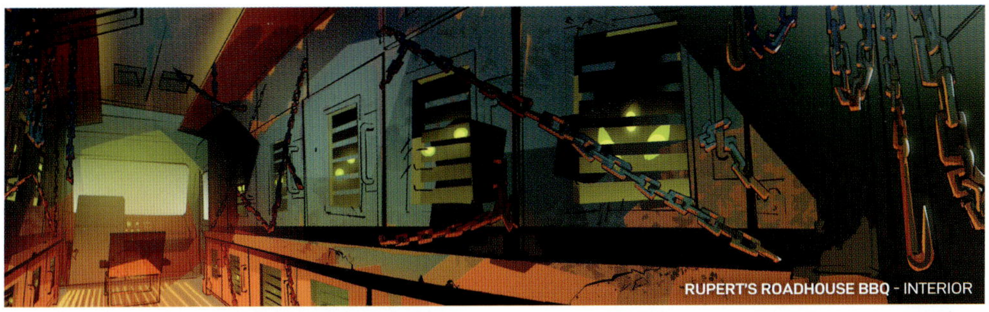
RUPERT'S ROADHOUSE BBQ - INTERIOR

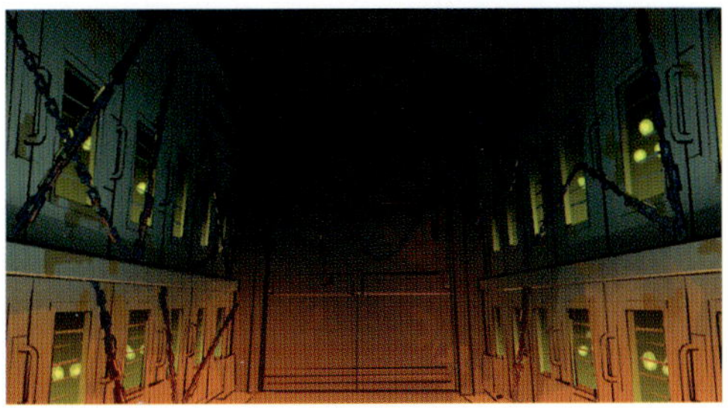

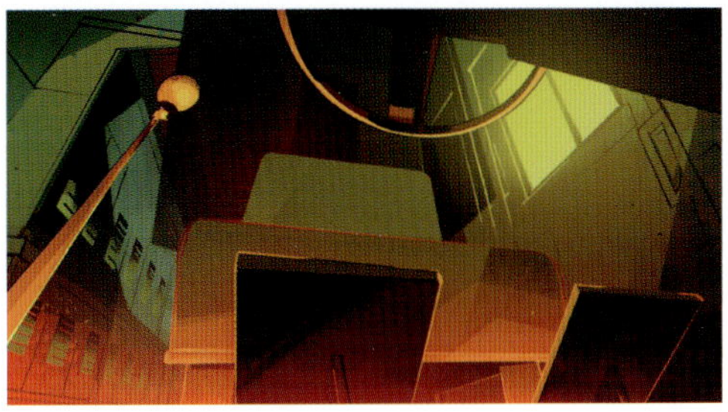

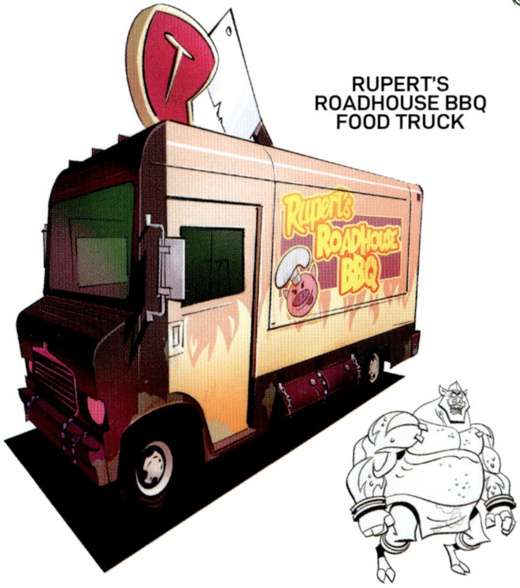

RUPERT'S ROADHOUSE BBQ FOOD TRUCK

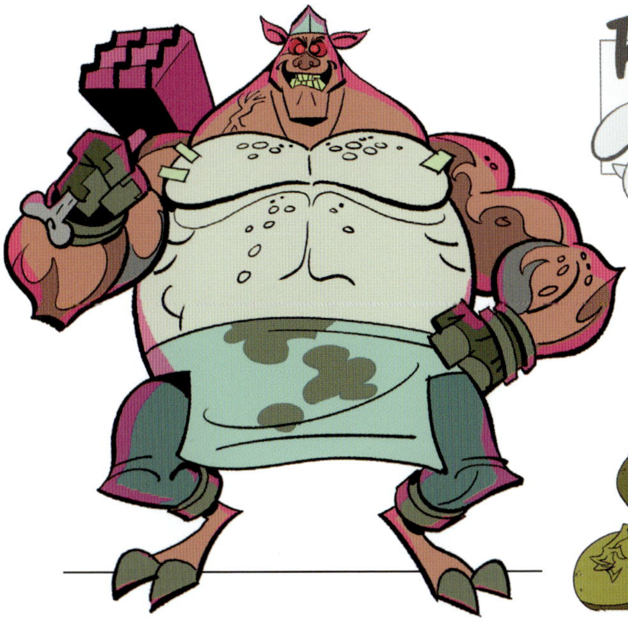

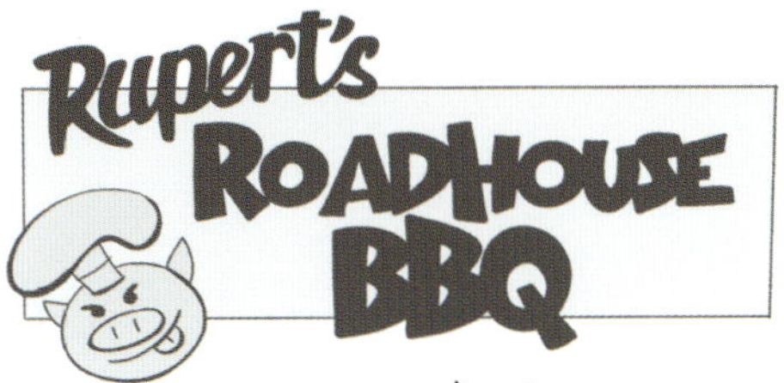

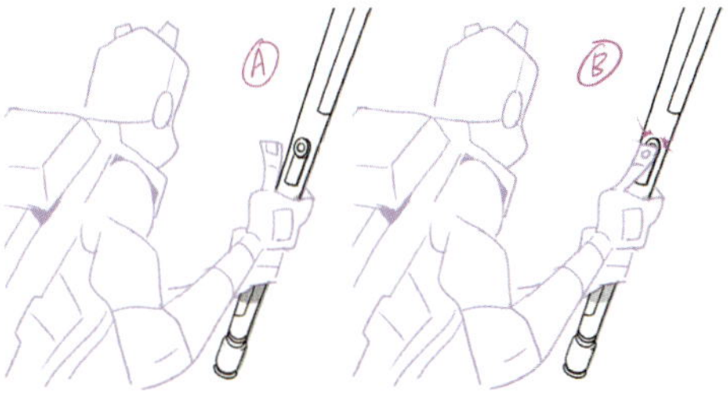

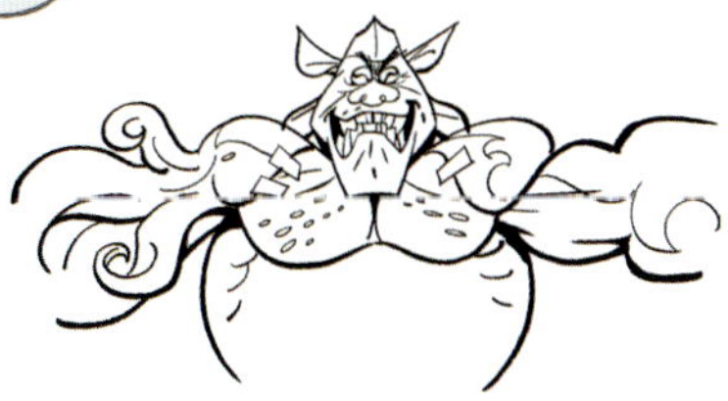

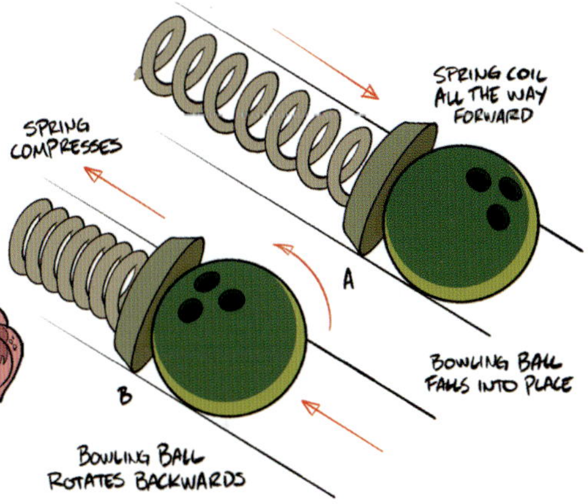

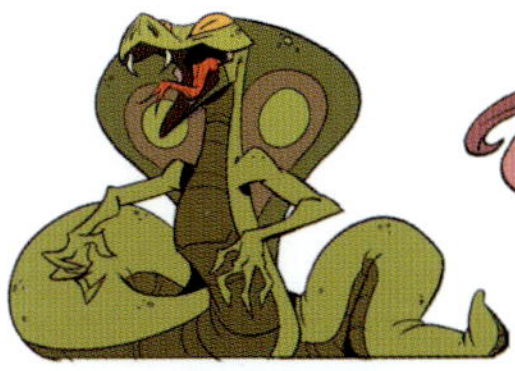

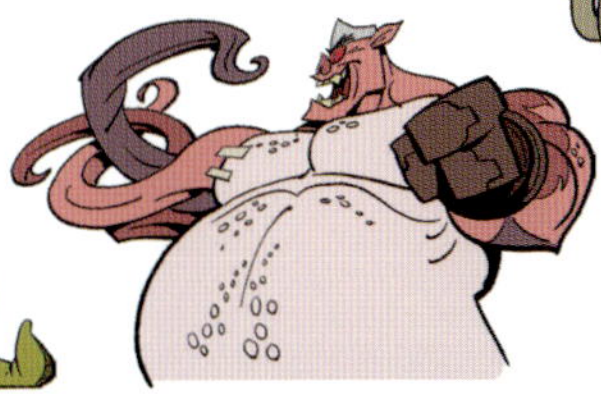

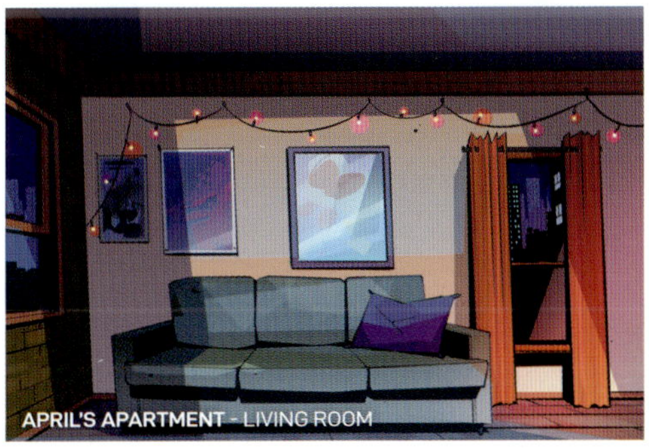
APRIL'S APARTMENT - LIVING ROOM

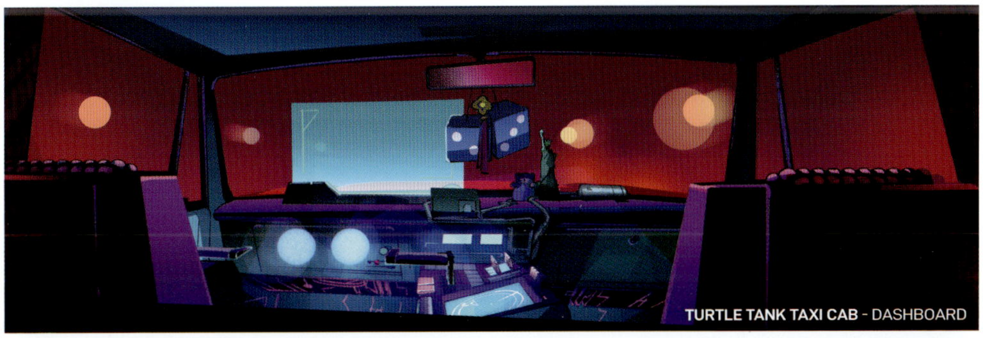
TURTLE TANK TAXI CAB - DASHBOARD

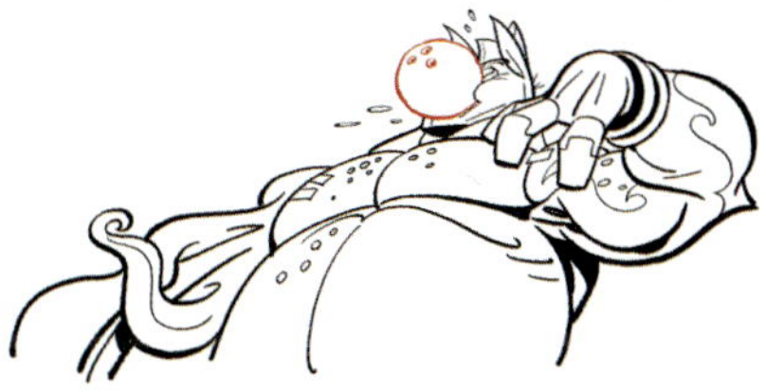

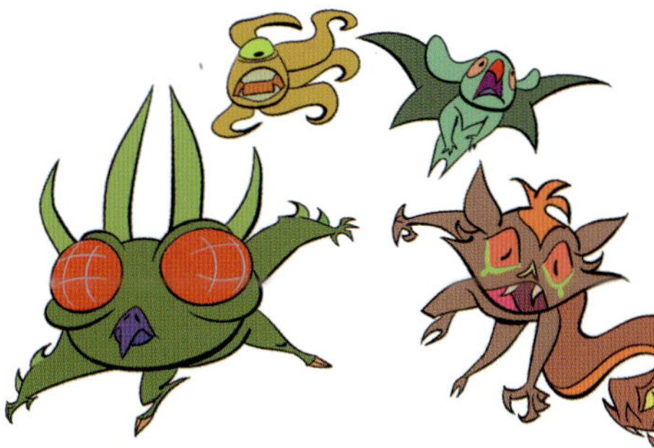

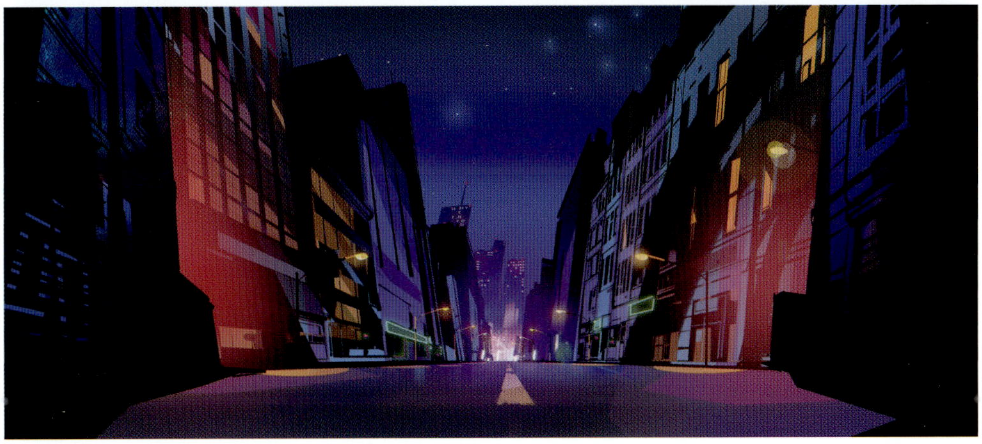

RUSS CARNEY: The Science of Chairs channel was something Ian came up with, and Ron liked it so much that he got a custom T-shirt that said "The Science of Chairs."

HYPNO! PART DEUX

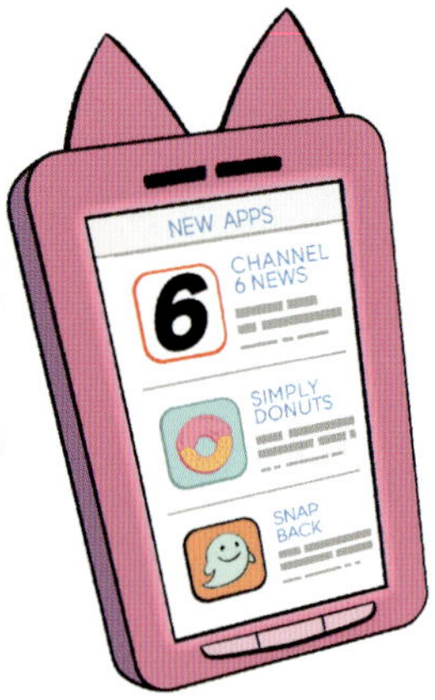

ORIGINAL AIR DATE: NOVEMBER 3, 2018
PRODUCTION CODE: 012

WRITTEN BY **JESSE GORDON**
STORYBOARDS BY **CHRISTINA "KIKI" MANRIQUE**
DIRECTED BY **JAMIE VICKERS**

JESSE GORDON: Hypno was immediately amazing in part because of Rhys Darby (Hypno), so coming up with more stuff for him to do was always fun. We always tried to split the Turtles off into different pairings, so this was a Leo/Raph slot but also an April slot. We wanted to make sure her character was well served on the show because she's a huge part of it. When using her, she has access to the world of high school, which up until that point was different from a lot of other versions of the Turtles where she was a news reporter.

I wanted to do a movie set in this high school, a classic *Invasion of the Body Snatchers* (1978) or *The Faculty* (1998) type thing where everyone at school feels a little off because they're hypnotized by this phone app.

The character Dale is named and modeled after Dale Malinowski, who was our writer's assistant at the time. A very good friend of mine named Taylor Martin has kids who watch the show and they really love that their mom's name is in the show.

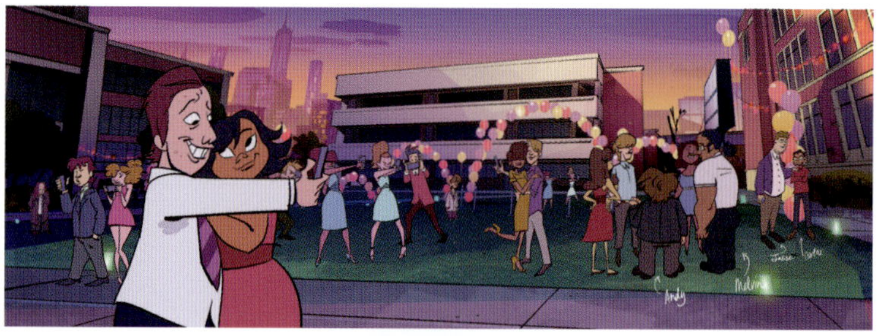

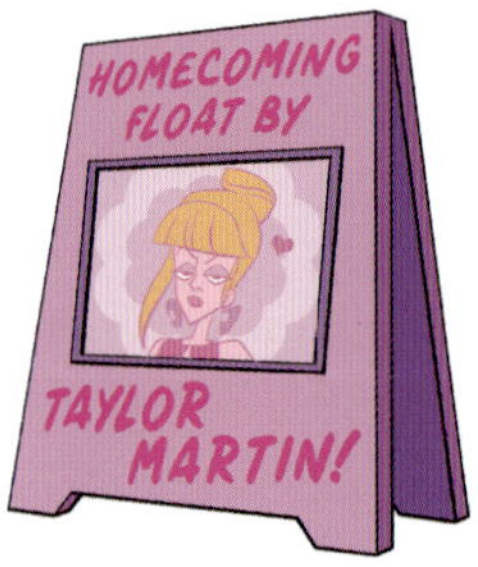

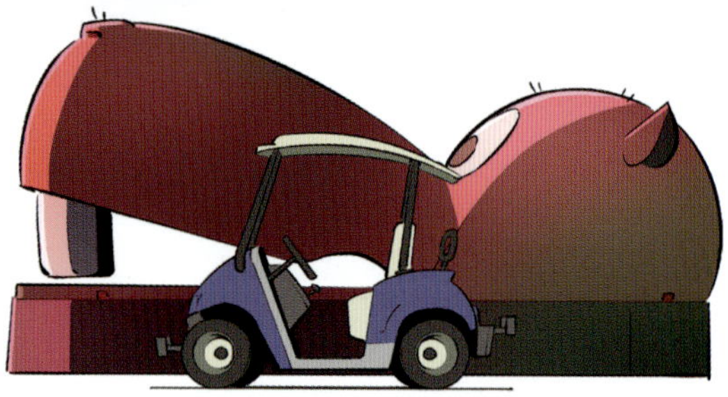

HIPPO FLOAT

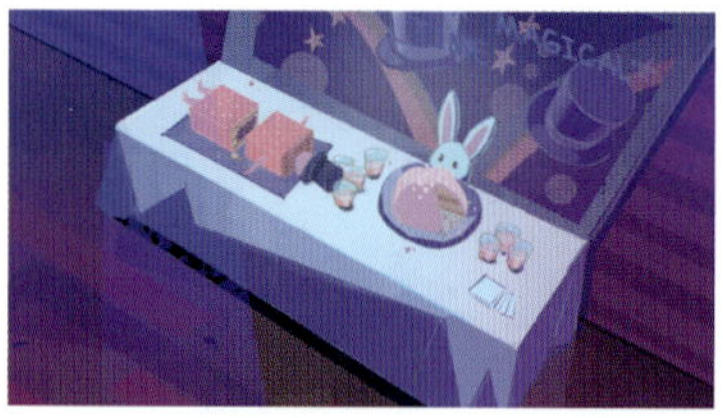

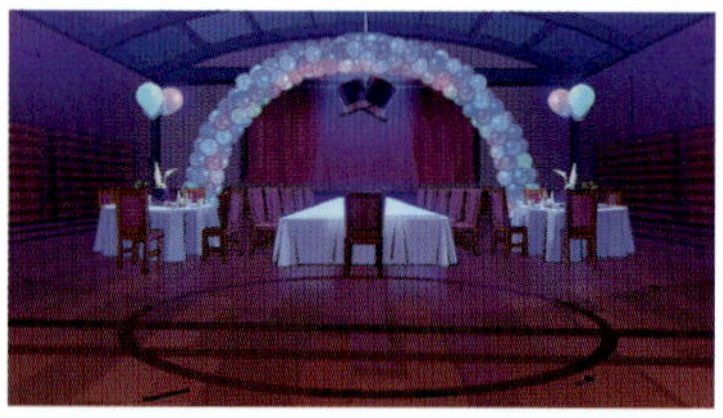

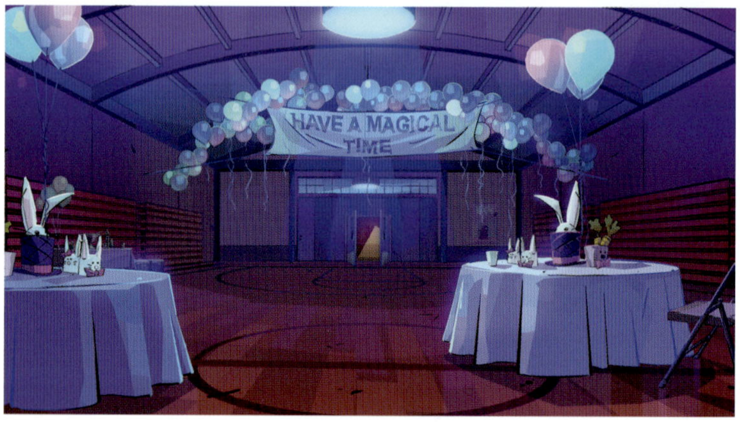

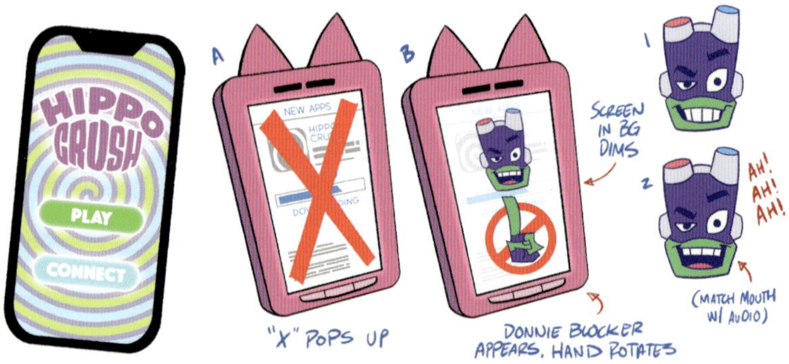

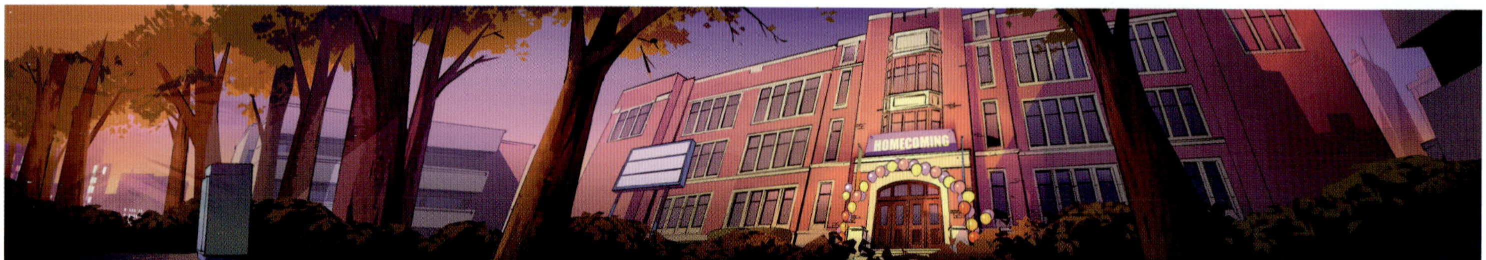

WASHINGTON IRVING HIGH SCHOOL (DECORATED FOR HOMECOMING)

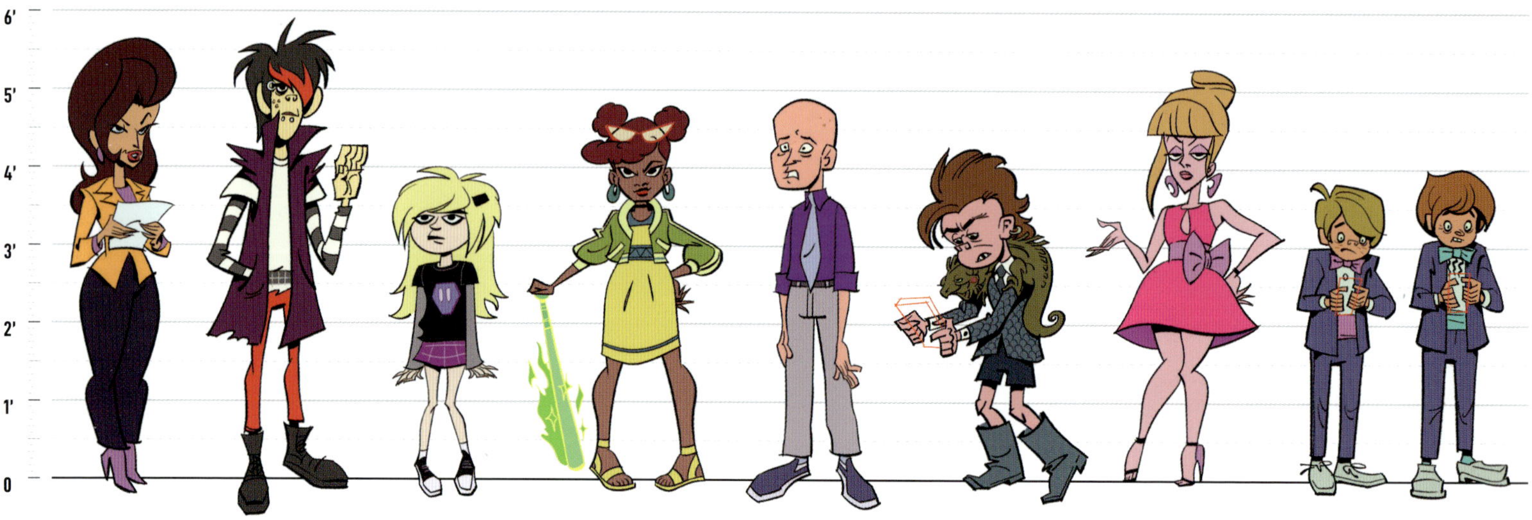

CARLY VALDEZ | NOAH SHECK | FAN GIRL | APRIL O'NEIL | DALE | SIEGEL | TAYLOR MARTIN | TAYLOR'S LACKEYS

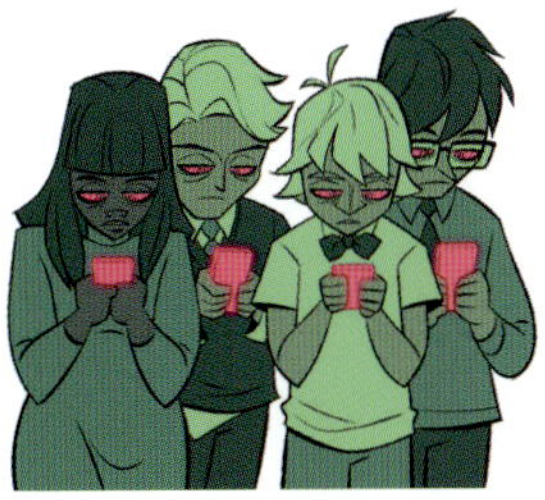

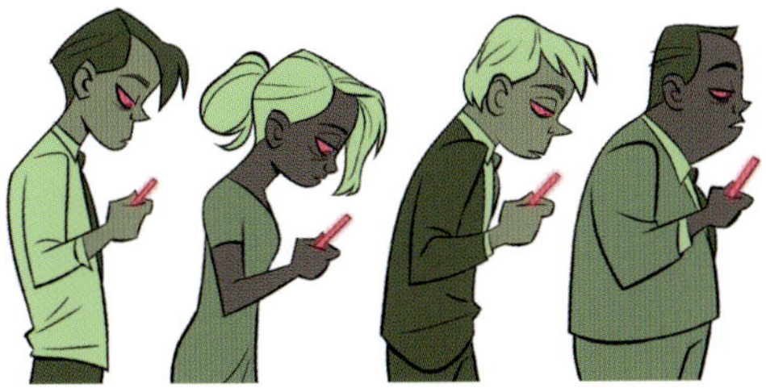

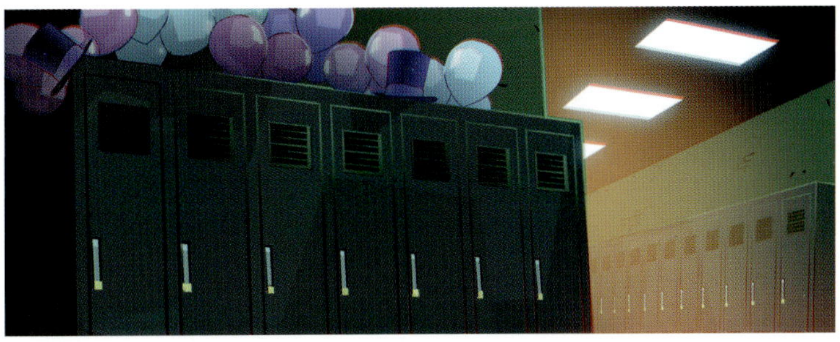

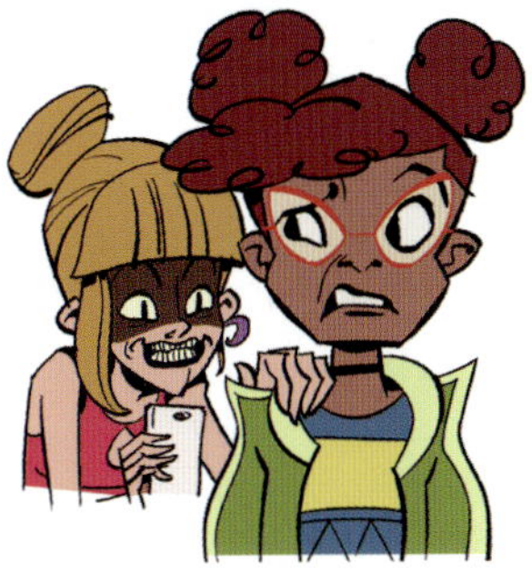

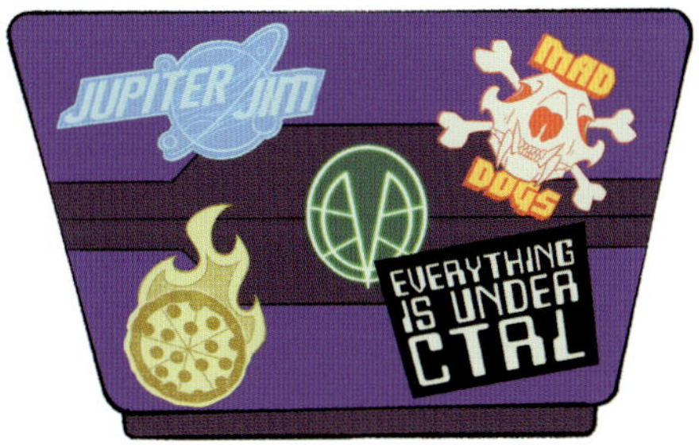

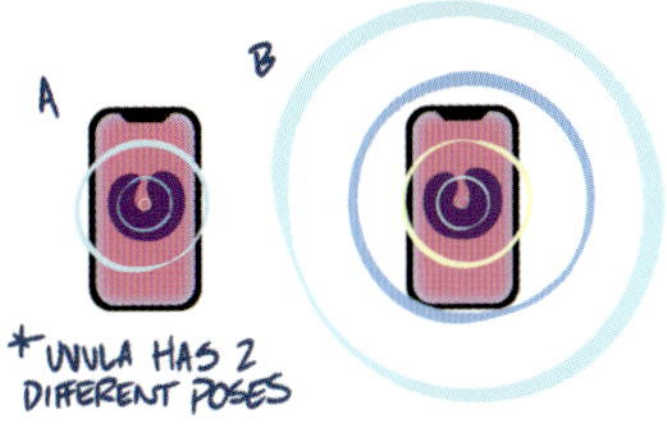

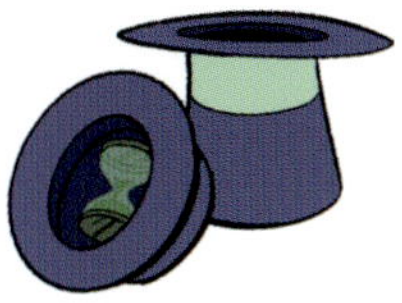

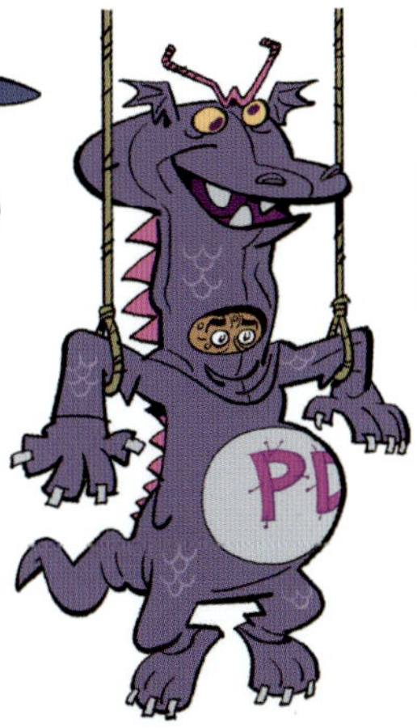

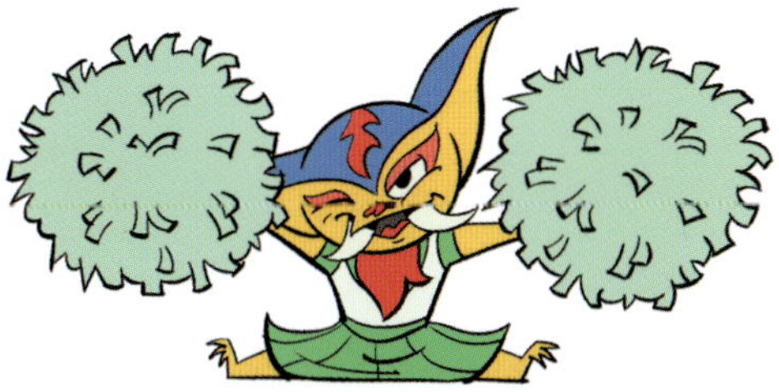

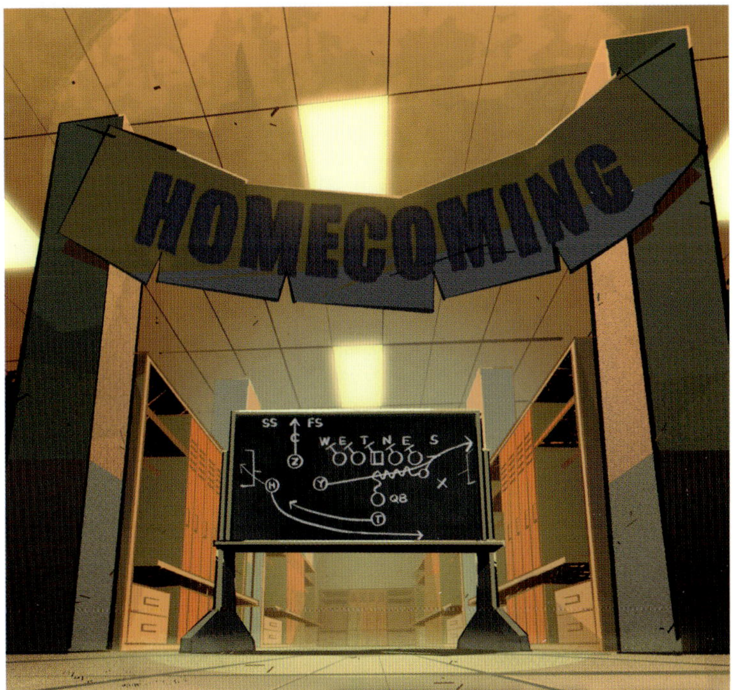

WASHINGTON IRVING HIGH SCHOOL – LOCKER ROOM

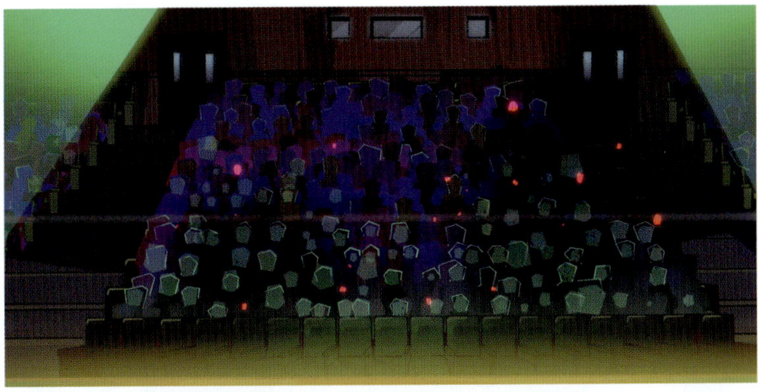

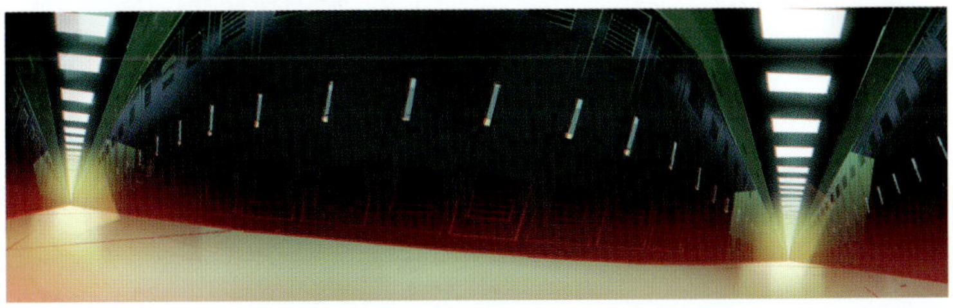

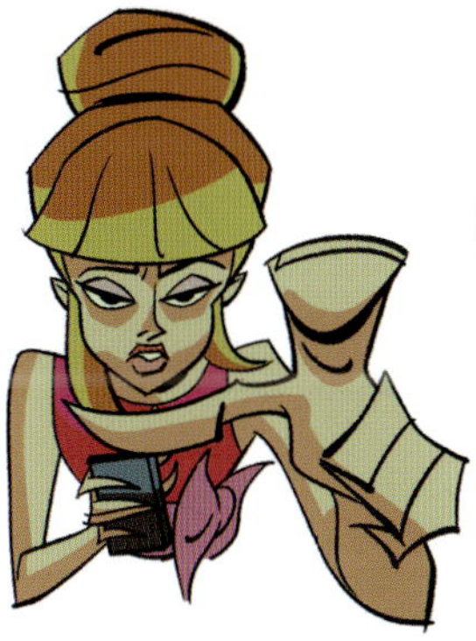

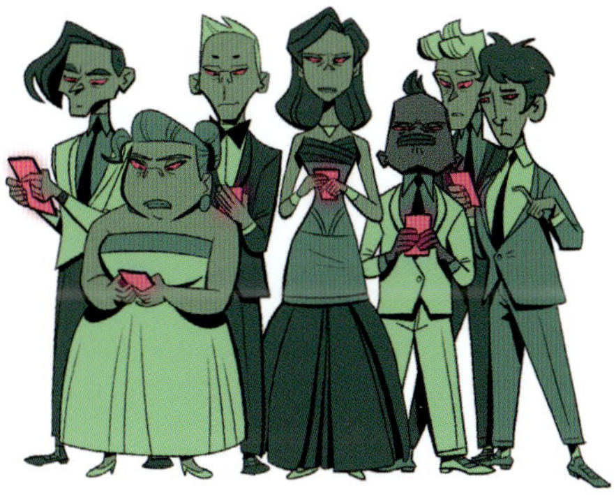

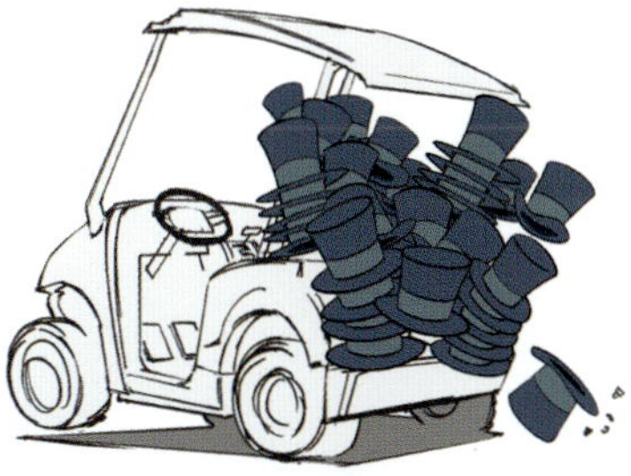

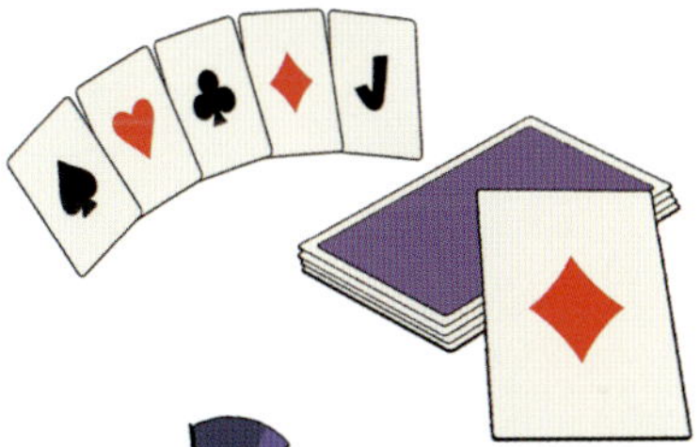

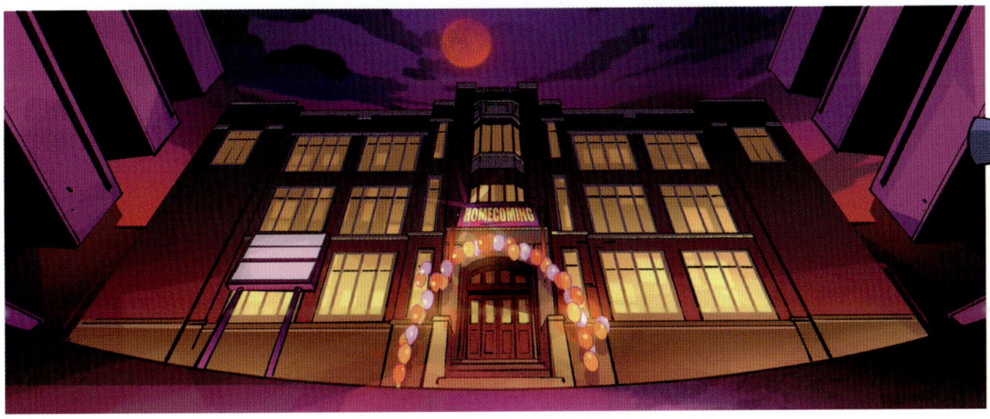

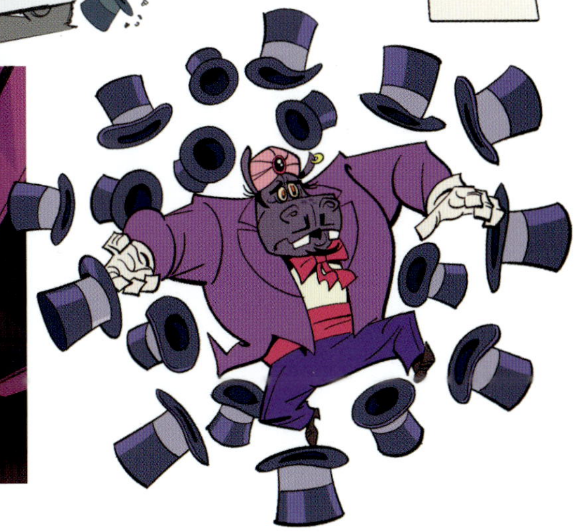

BUG BUSTERS

ORIGINAL AIR DATE: NOVEMBER 17, 2018
PRODUCTION CODE: 013-014

WRITTEN BY **IAN BUSCH, RUSS CARNEY, RON CORCILLO & JESSE GORDON**
STORYBOARDS BY **JULIA BRAID, CHRISTOPHER LUC**
DIRECTED BY **ABE AUDISH, BRENDAN CLOGHER & JAMIE VICKERS**

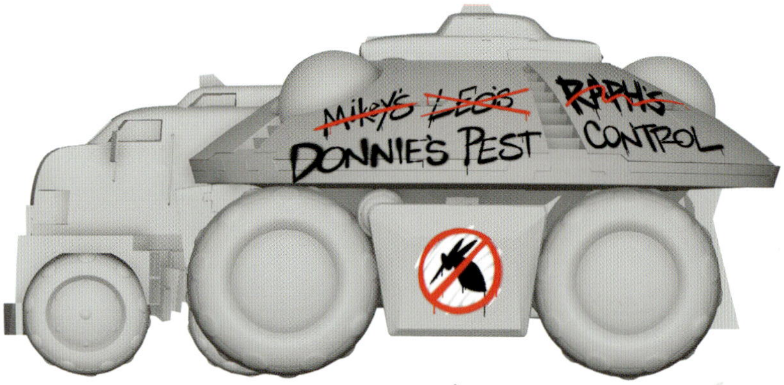

RON CORCILLO: Andy seems to know a lot of actors. Not only is he friends with Lena Headey *(Game of Thrones)* and Dave Foley *(Kids in the Hall)*, but he is also friends with Brian Posehn *(Mr. Show with Bob and David)*, and all three of these people were vital to this episode coming together.

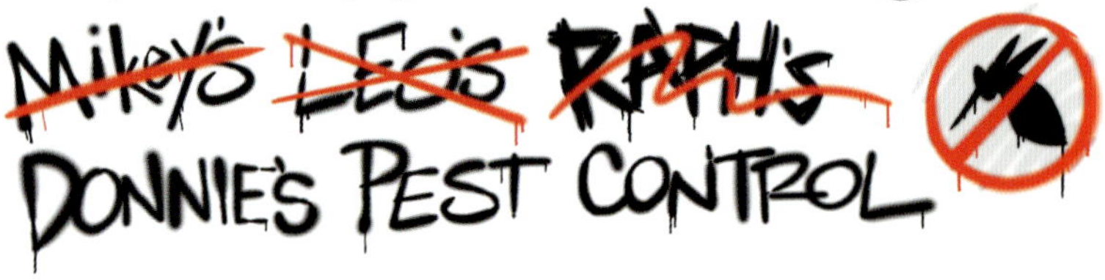

"Bug Busters" began life as a Big Mama adventure in the Hidden City, but we ultimately pivoted to a story centered in New York. Andy had designed the mutant-human bull Bullhop in preproduction, and he thought Foley would be a great choice for the character. Andy wanted Headey to play Big Mama, because she's phenomenal at playing heavies, like Ma-Ma in *Dredd* (2012).

RUSS CARNEY: Posehn was in the writers room, pitching a freelance episode he would later work on. Since he also knew Headey, we asked him what her personality was like. He told us that she has a fun, nutty sense of humor, and as a result, our dialogue for her included a quasi-nonsensical, Mary Poppins–esque style of speech.

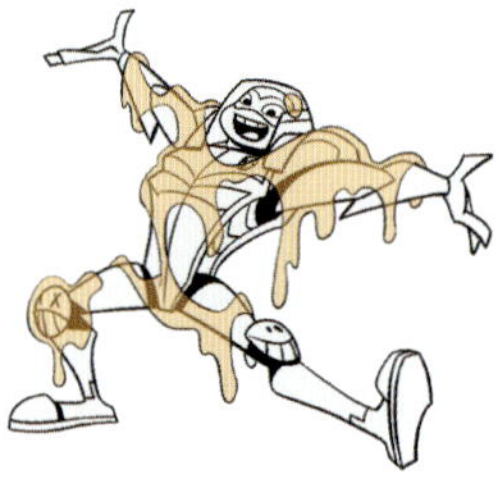

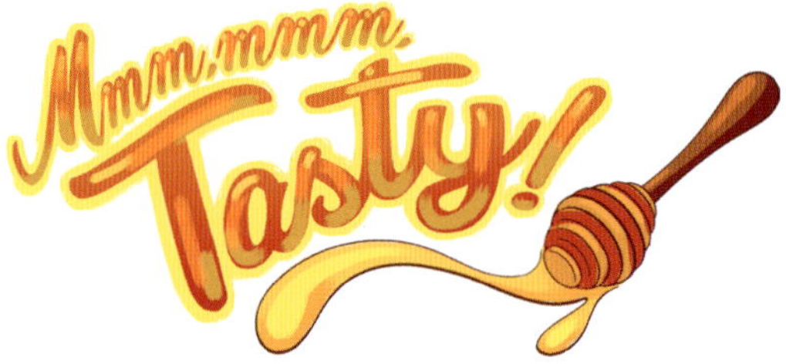

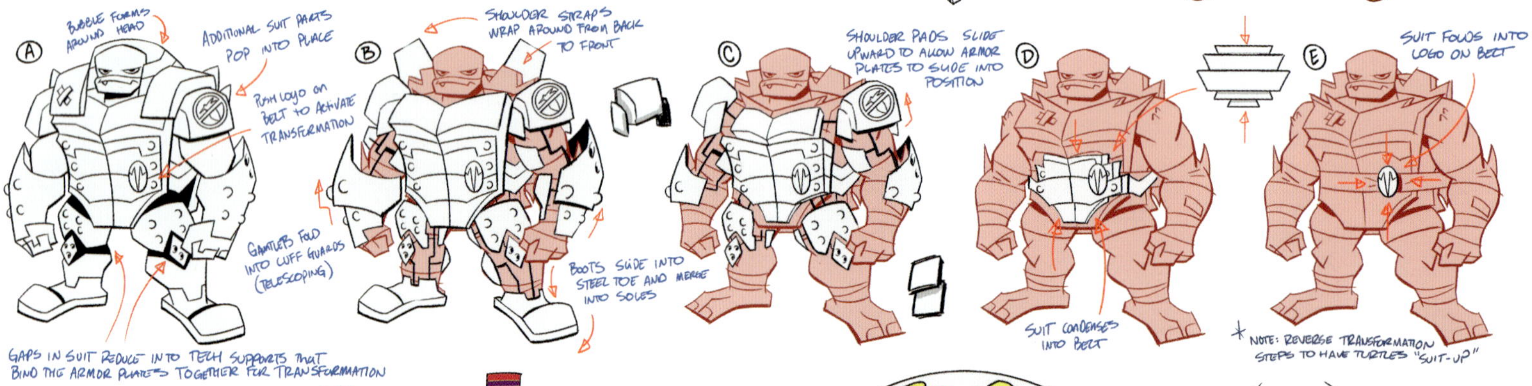

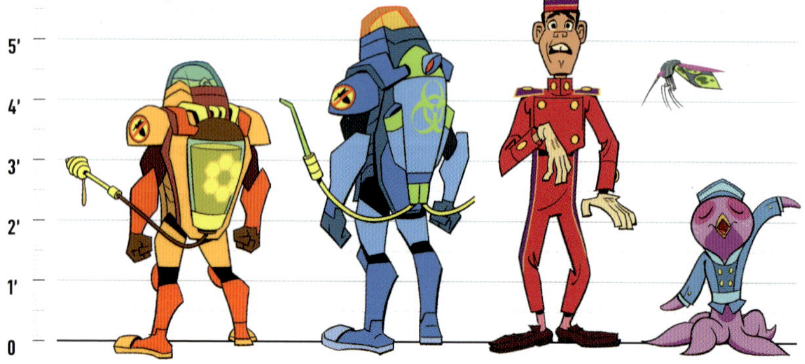

MIKEY
BUG BUSTER SUIT

LEO
BUG BUSTER SUIT

STANLEY

CHEERY

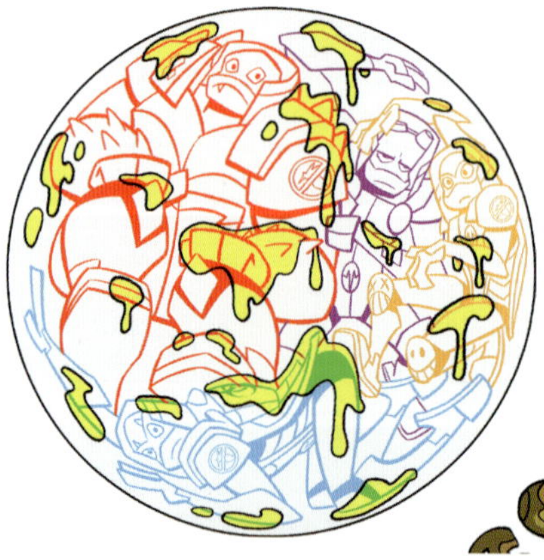

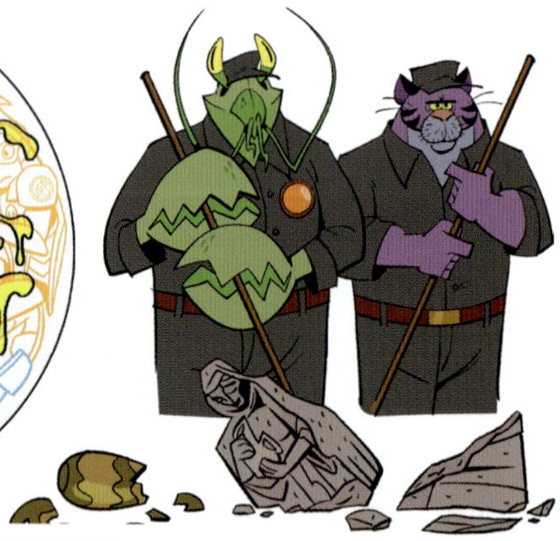

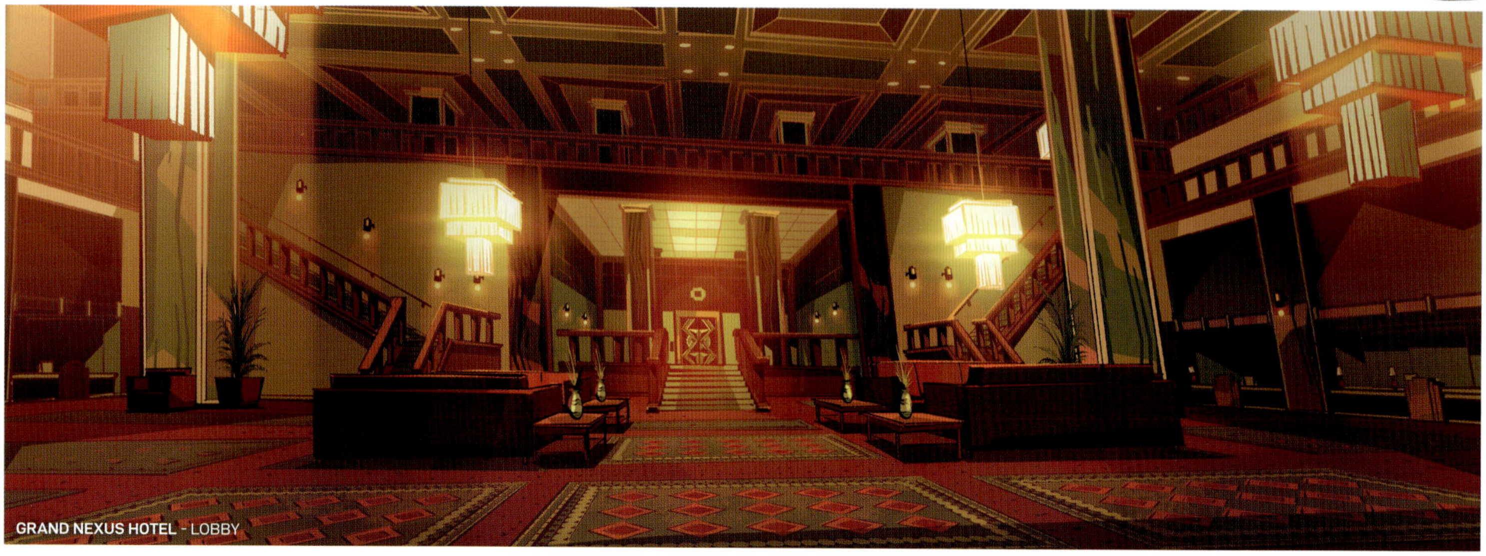

GRAND NEXUS HOTEL - LOBBY

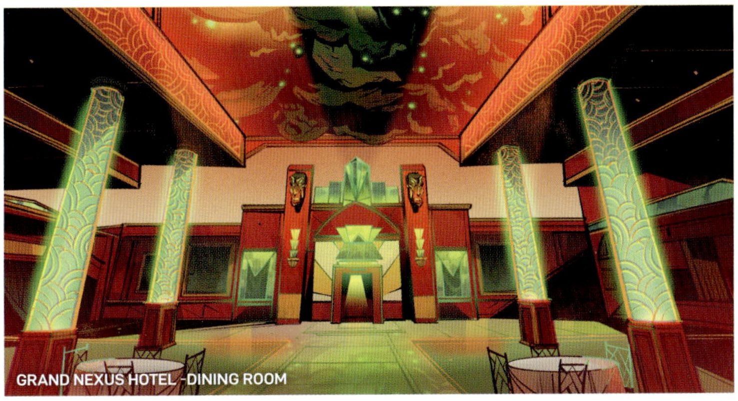
GRAND NEXUS HOTEL -DINING ROOM

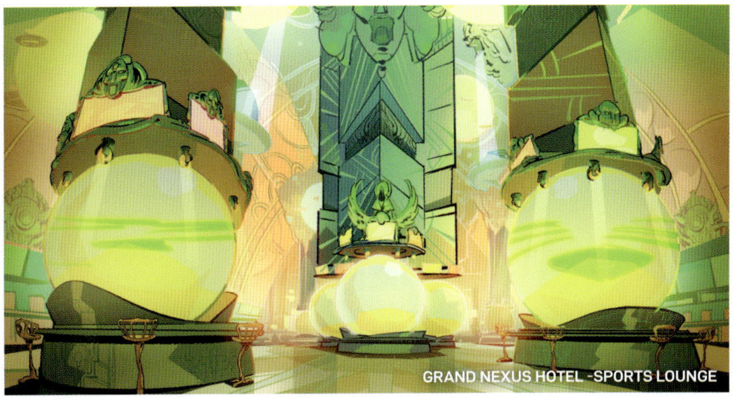
GRAND NEXUS HOTEL -SPORTS LOUNGE

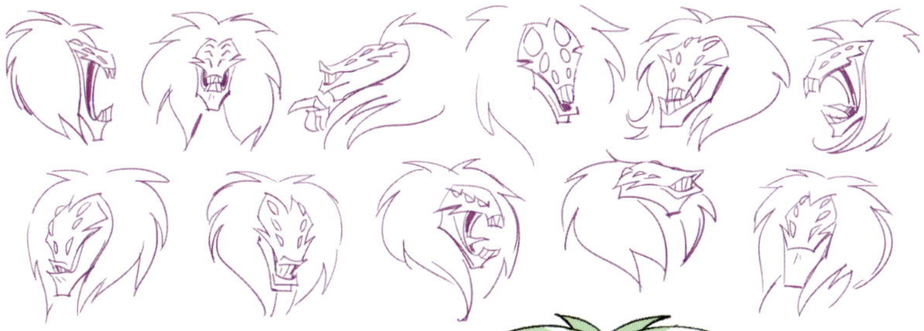

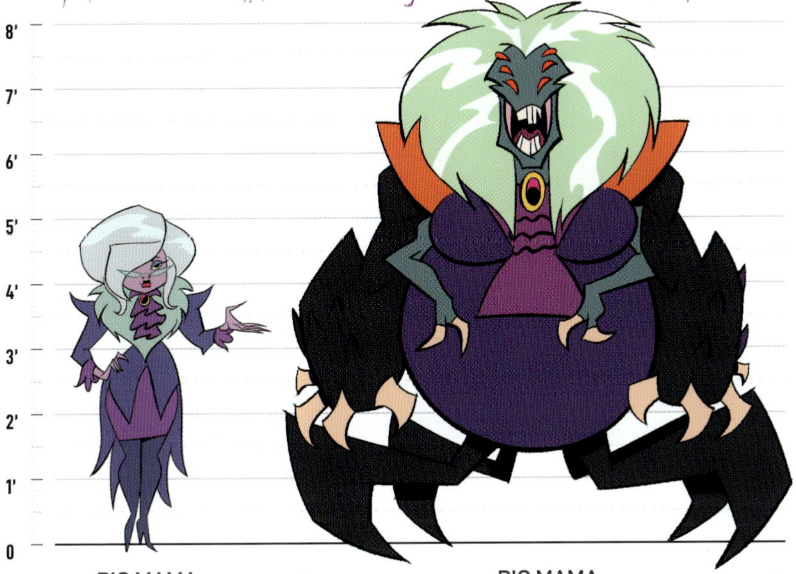

BIG MAMA
HUMAN FORM

BIG MAMA
JOROGUMO FORM

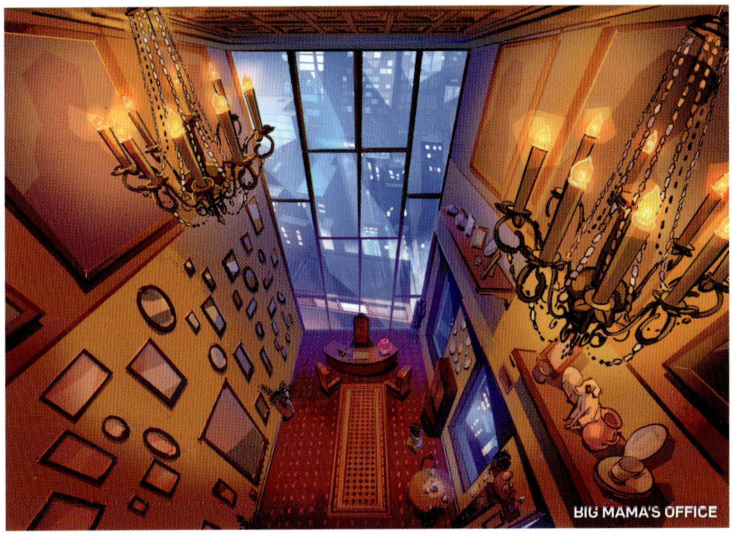
BIG MAMA'S OFFICE

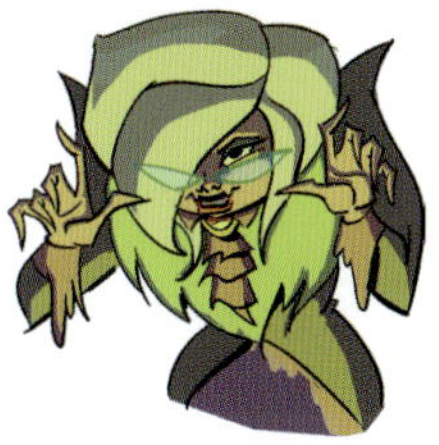

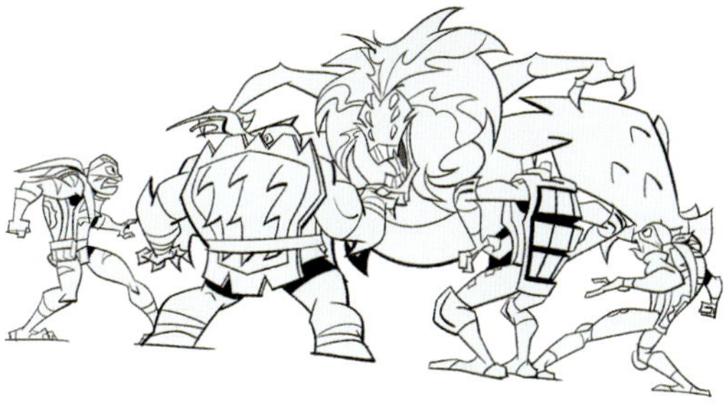

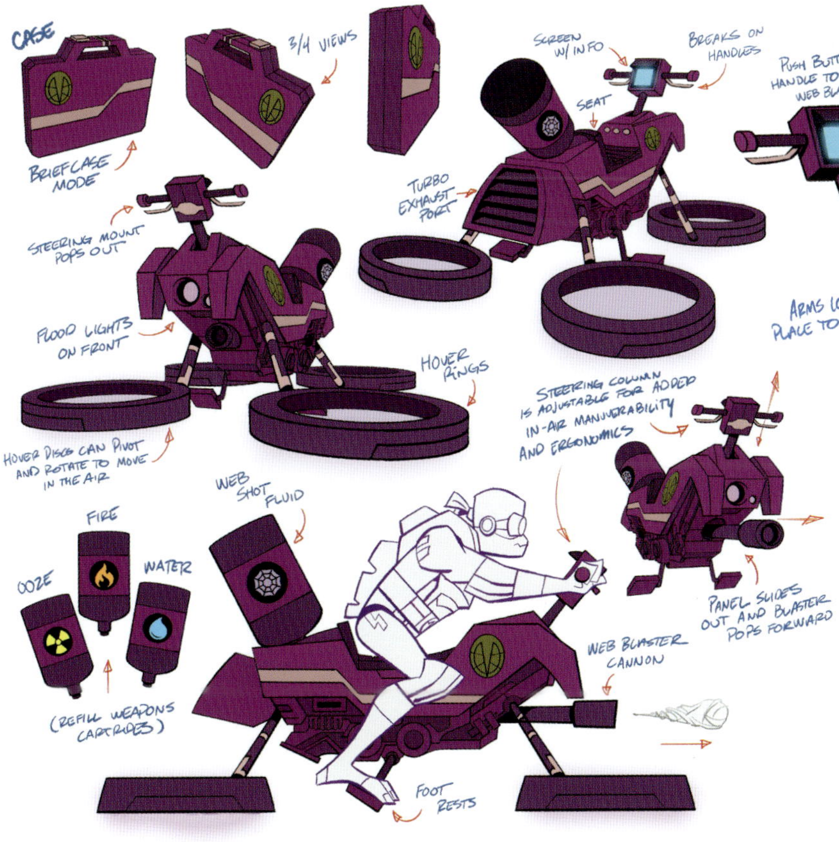

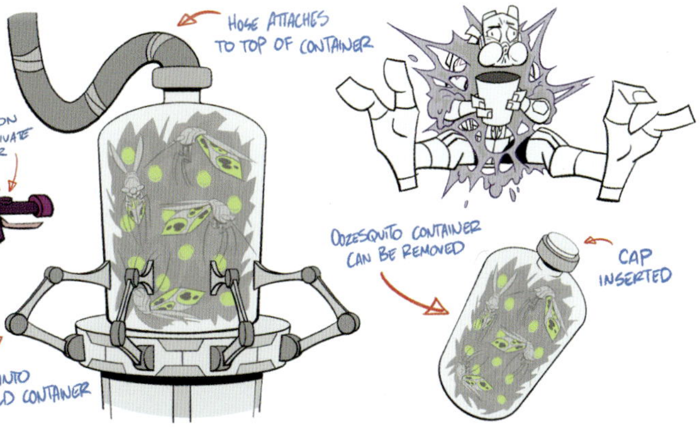

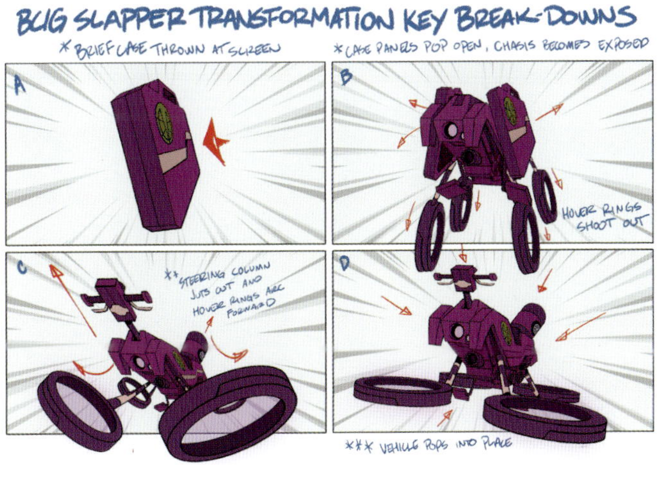

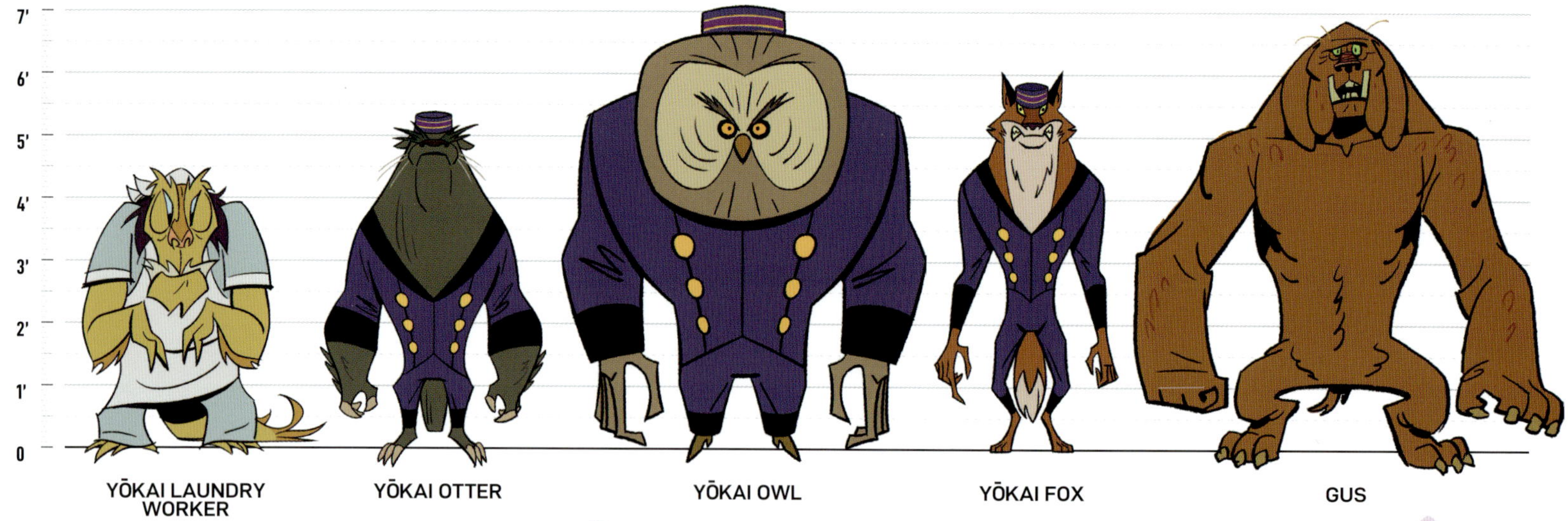

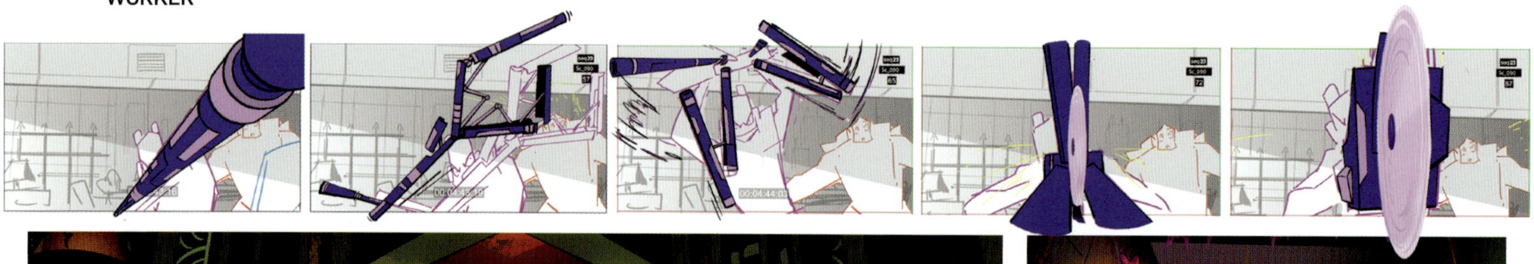

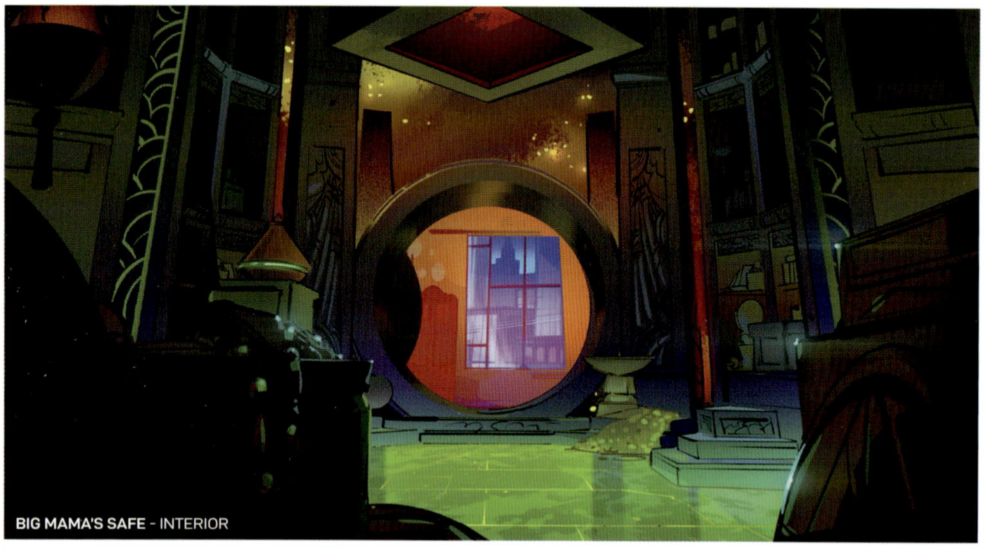
BIG MAMA'S SAFE - INTERIOR

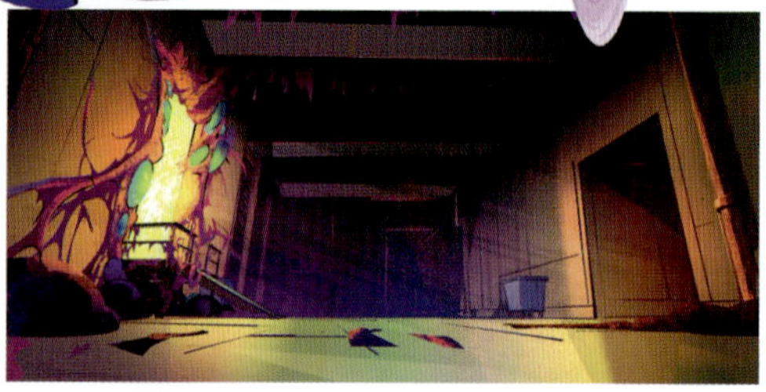

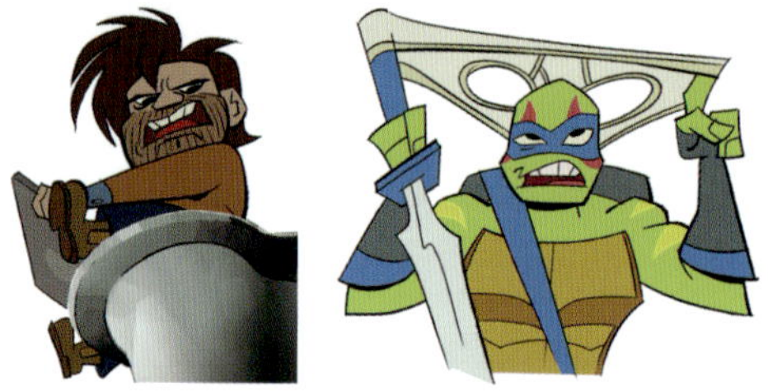
That's Andy Suriano on the toilet after Leo generates a portal through the hotel.

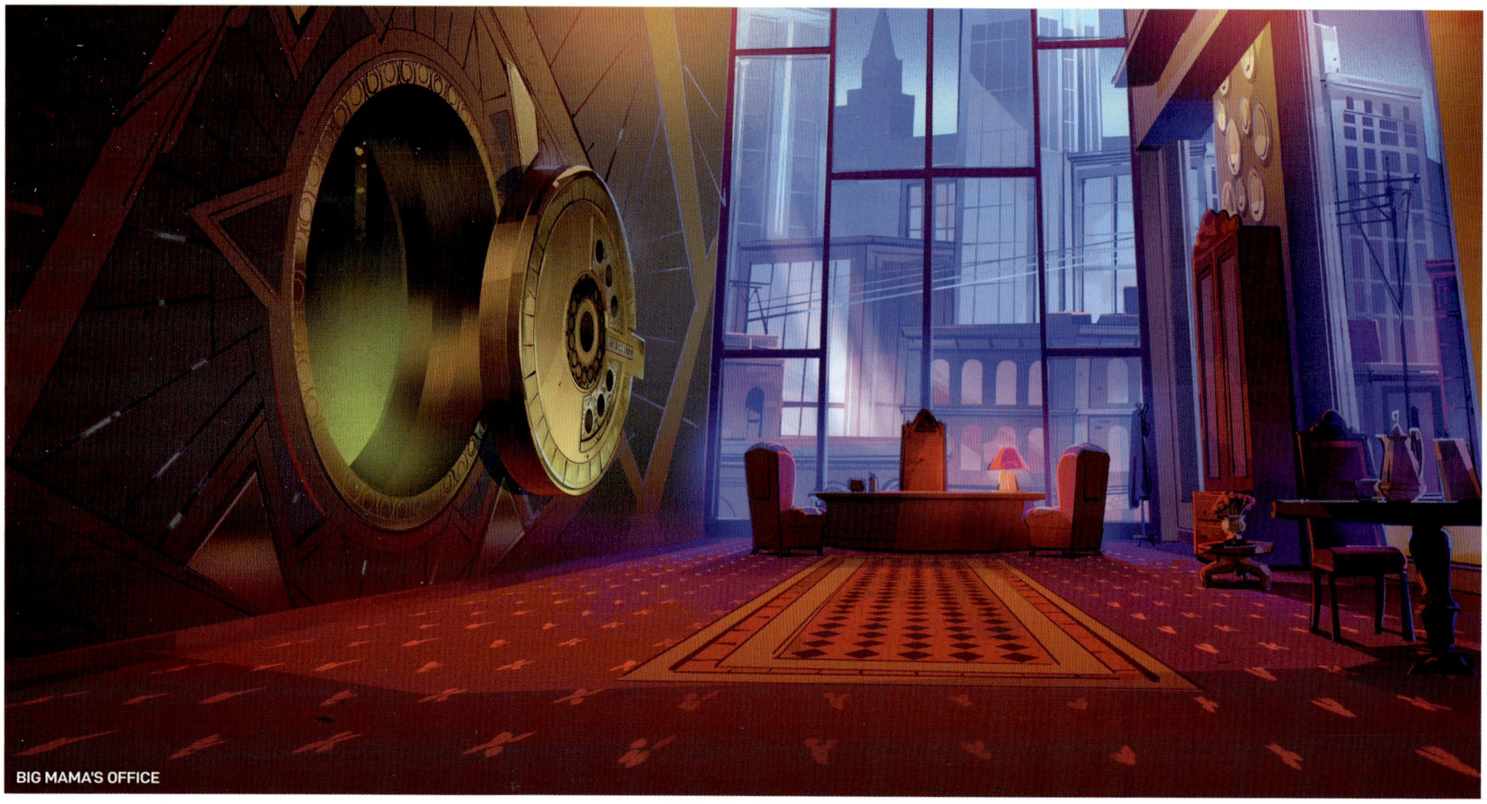
BIG MAMA'S OFFICE

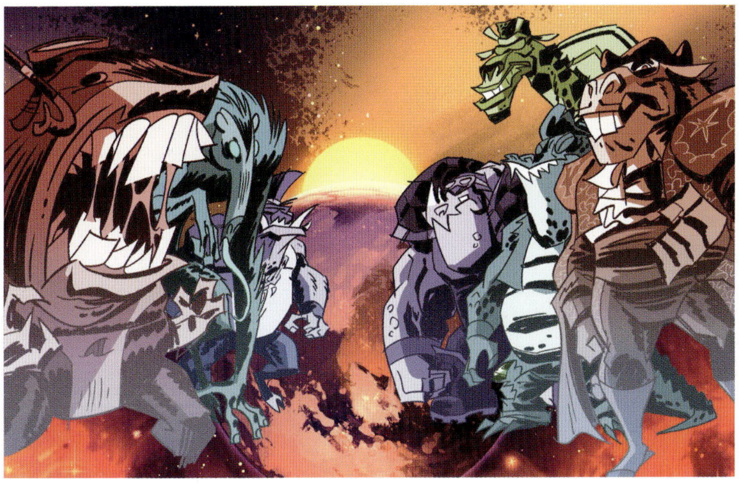

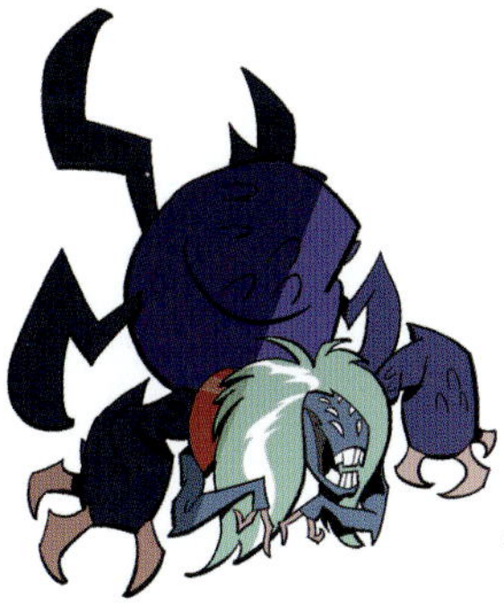

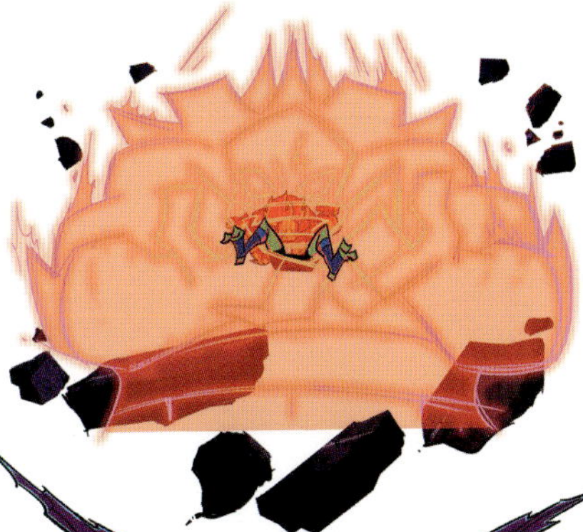

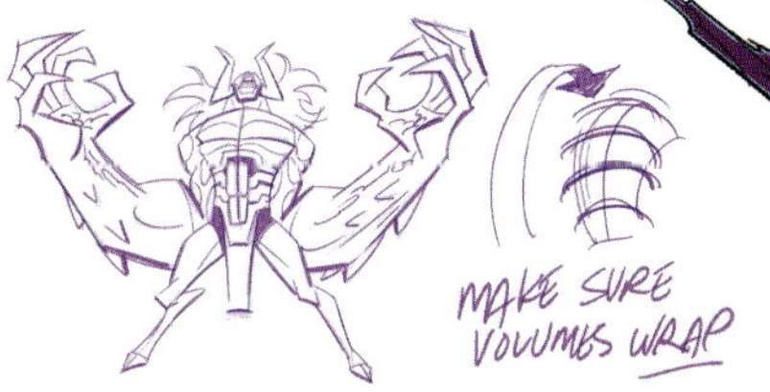

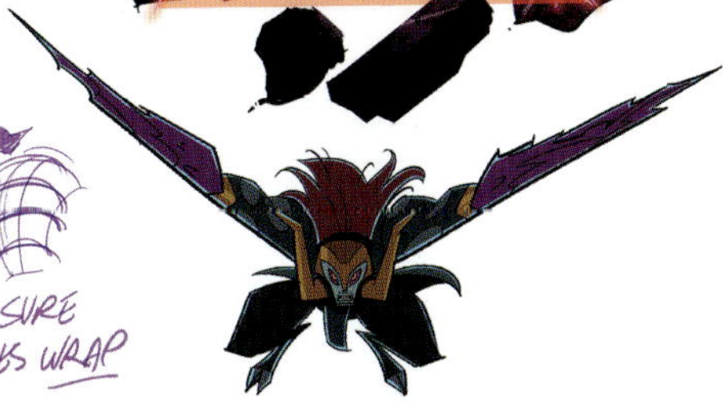

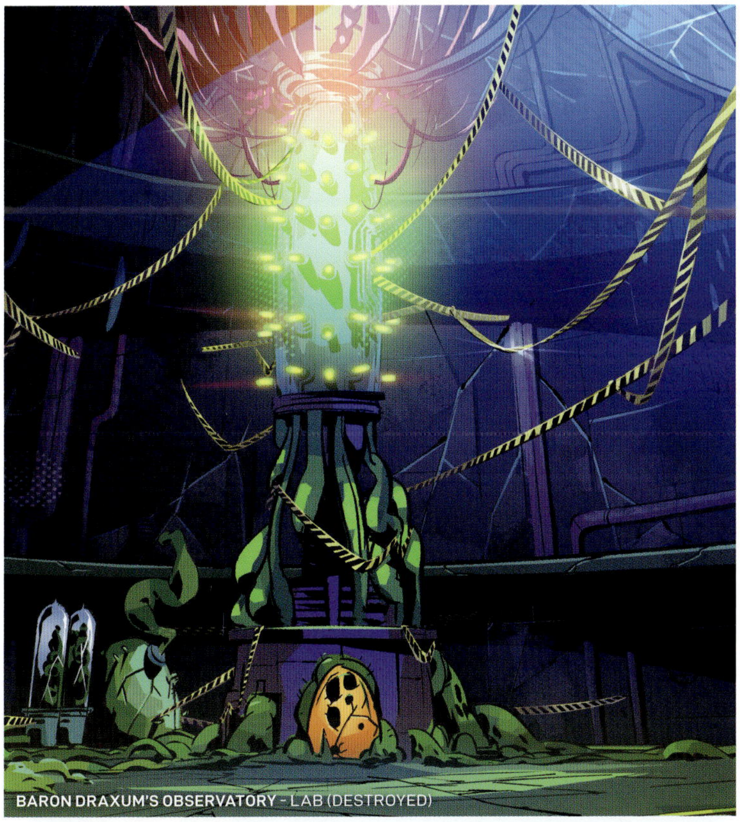

BARON DRAXUM'S OBSERVATORY - LAB (DESTROYED)

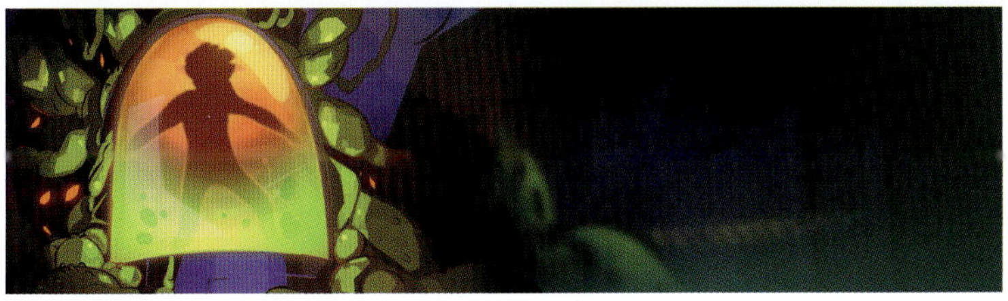

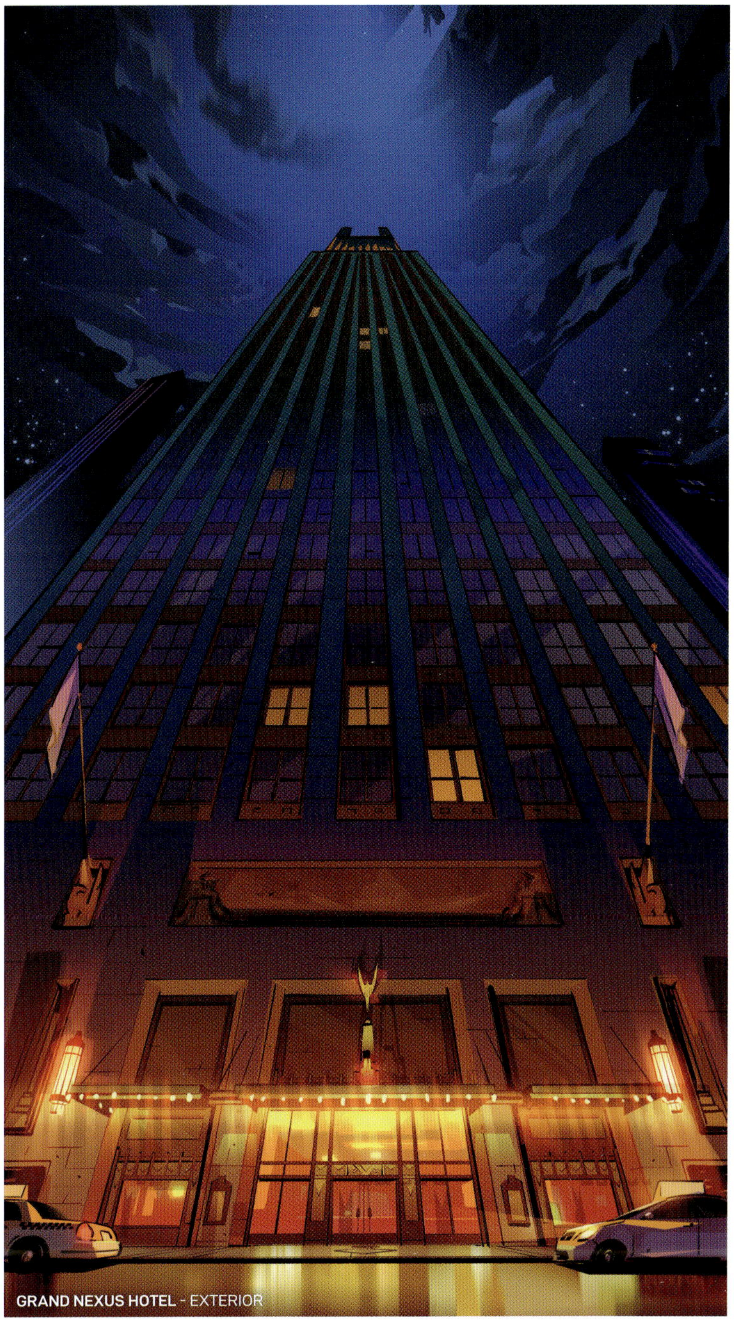

GRAND NEXUS HOTEL - EXTERIOR

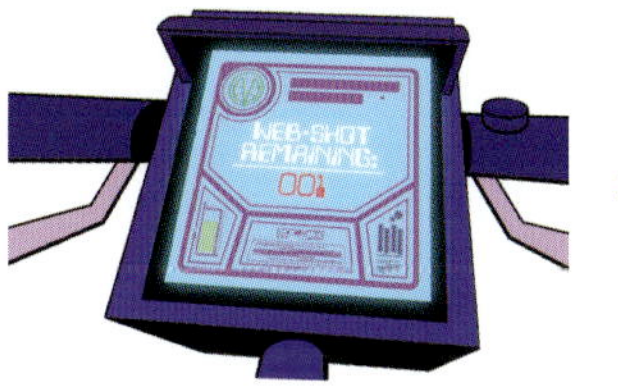

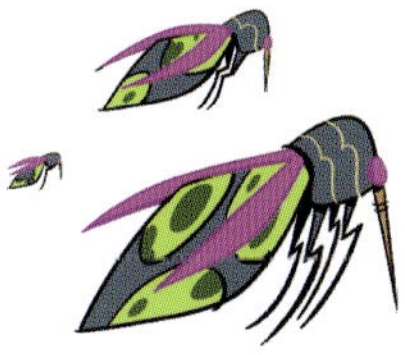

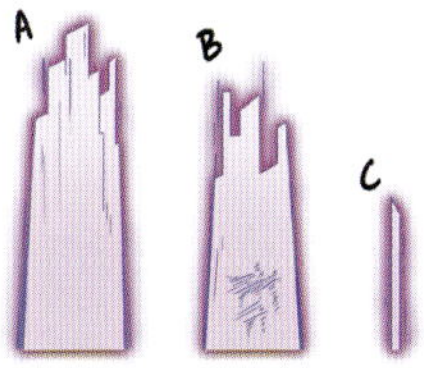

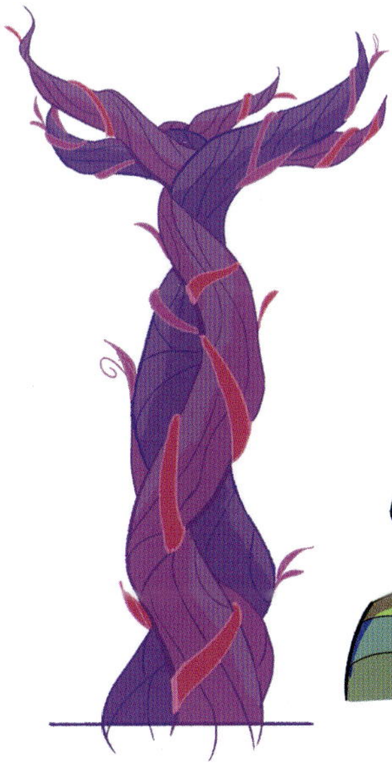

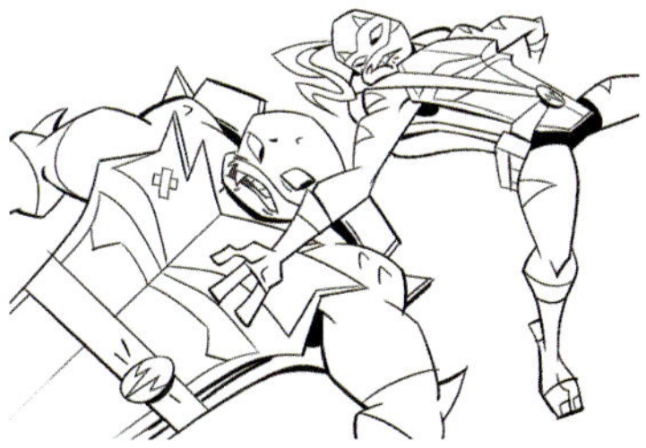

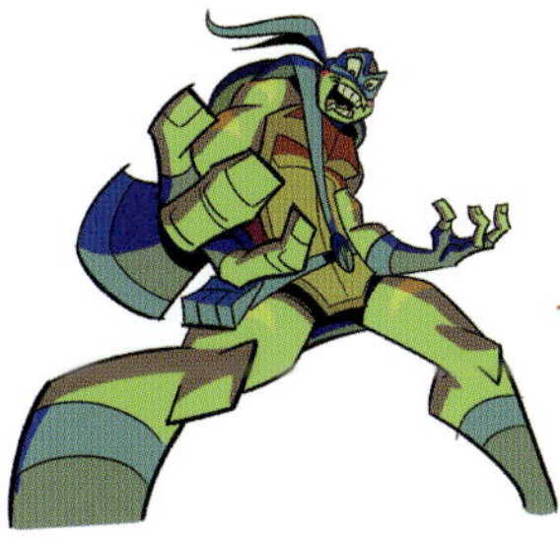

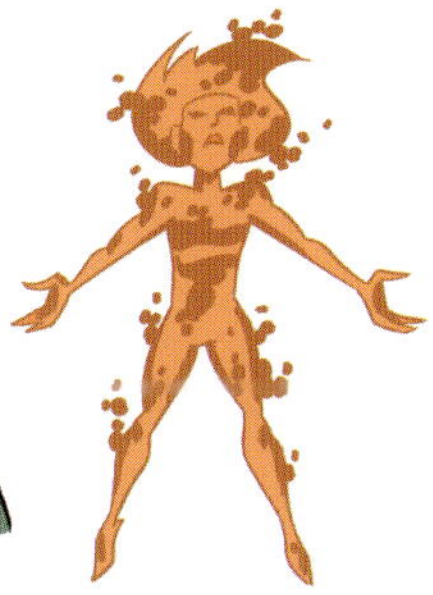

SHELL IN A CELL

ORIGINAL AIR DATE: SEPTEMBER 19, 2018
PRODUCTION CODE: 015

WRITTEN BY **DALE MALINOWSKI**
STORYBOARDS BY **KEVIN MOLINA-ORTIZ**
DIRECTED BY **SEBASTIAN MONTES**

DALE MALINOWSKI: This was my first professional screenwriting opportunity. My job on the series was script coordinator, but I had a list of stories and characters I was eager to pitch if the moment ever presented itself. Pretty soon, that happened, and Raph's love for pro wrestling became the setup for a story about brotherhood, meeting your heroes, and life often being unfair. Andy and the design team did a fantastic job of visualizing the Turtles' wrestling personas, and Sebastian and Kevin elevated every story beat, every joke, and all the action to new heights well beyond what I wrote on the page. Early in the writing process, I really wanted to mutate Ghostbear in the third act to escalate his threat level for a final fight inside the cage, but Ant was excited about the Turtles having a recurring human villain in the show, so we didn't mutate Ghostbear this time. That was a great note because it gave more space to the brothers, their conflicts, and their resolutions.

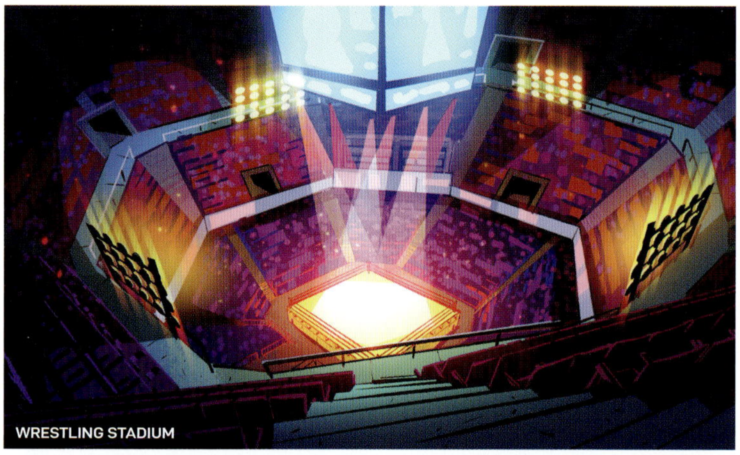
WRESTLING STADIUM

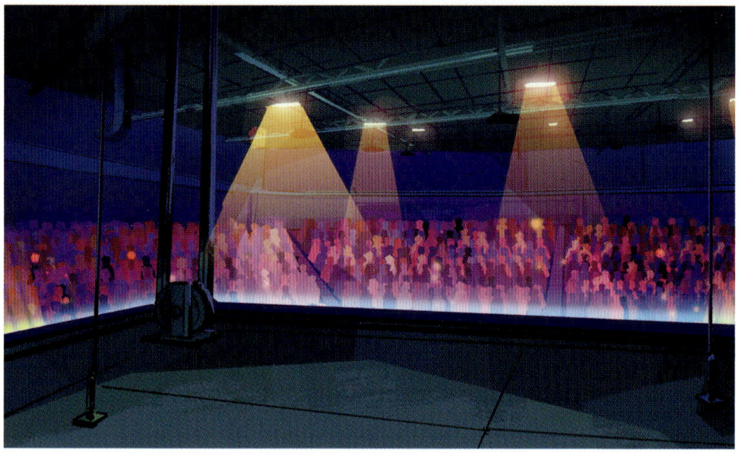

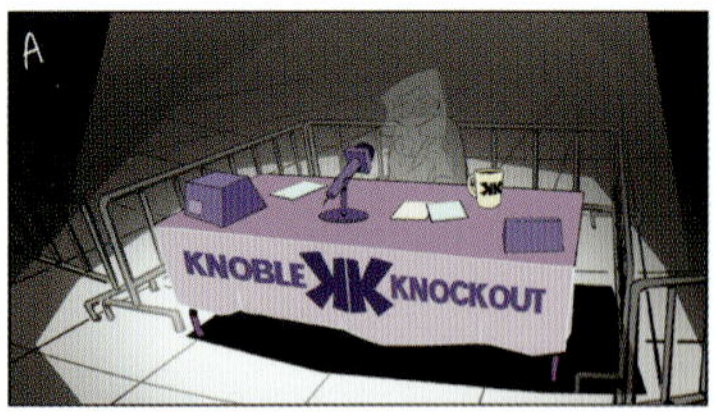

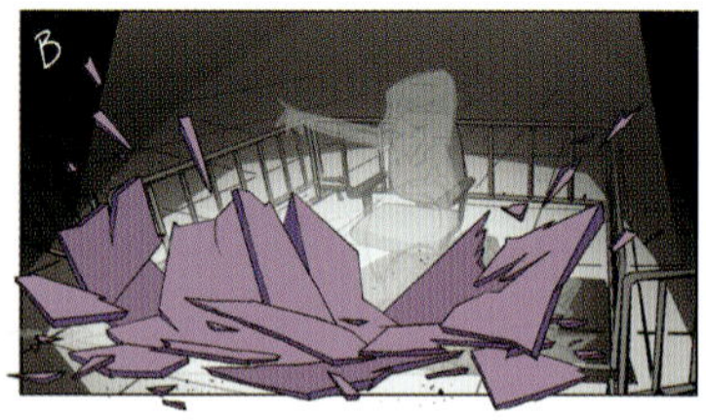

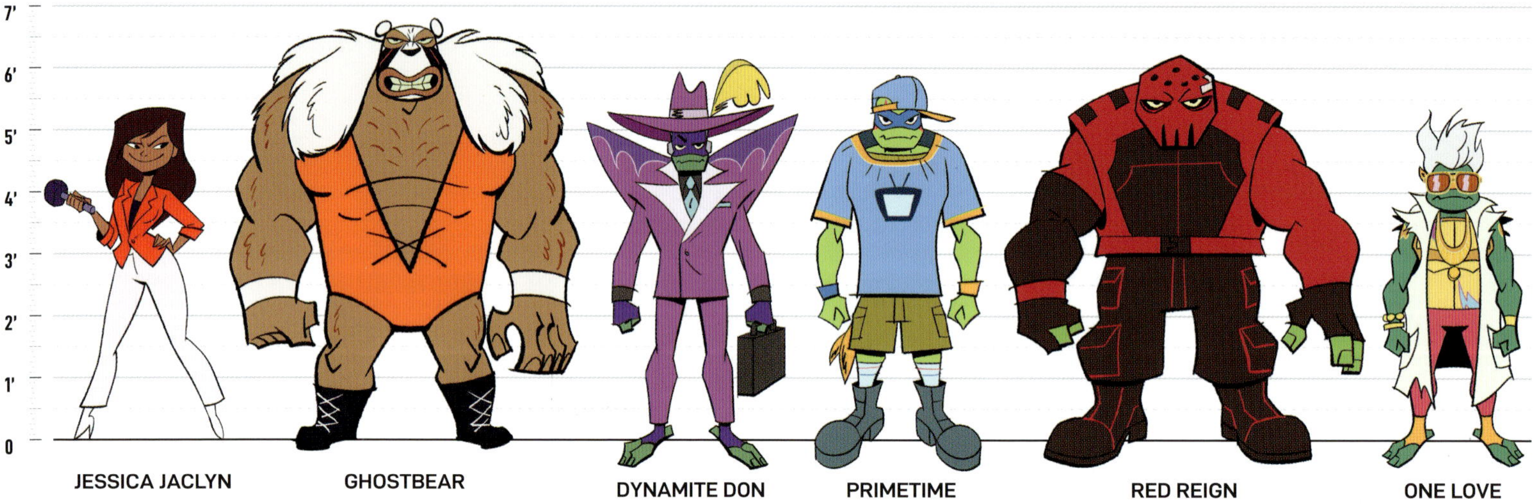

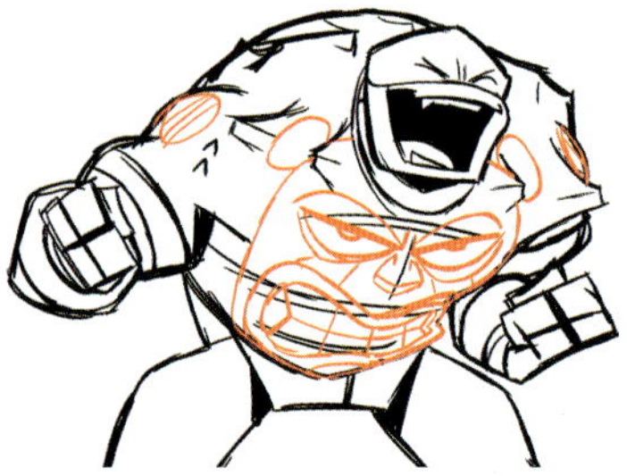

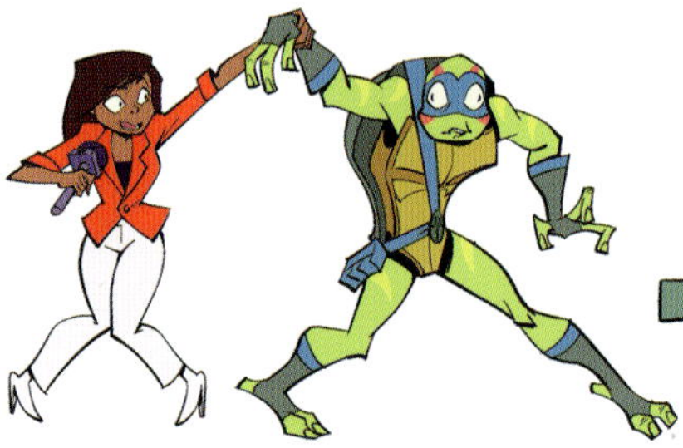

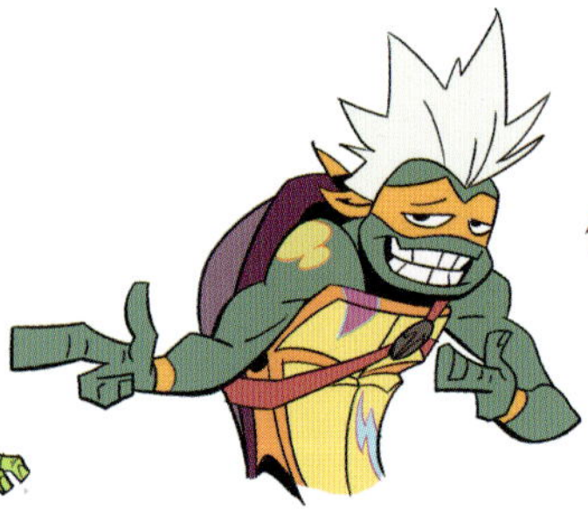

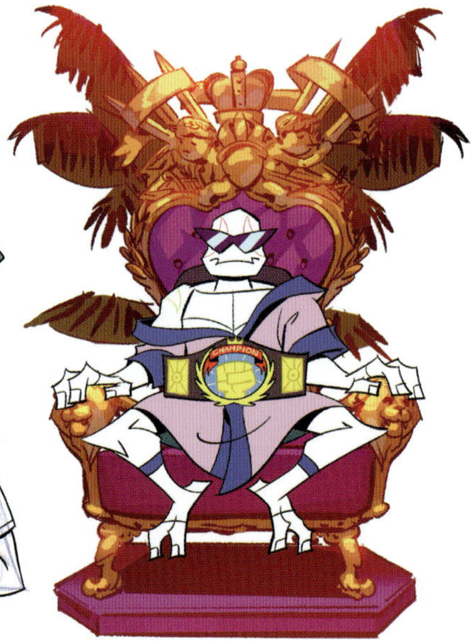

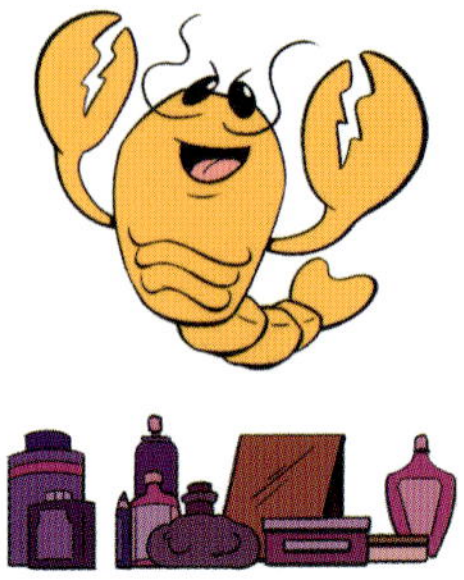

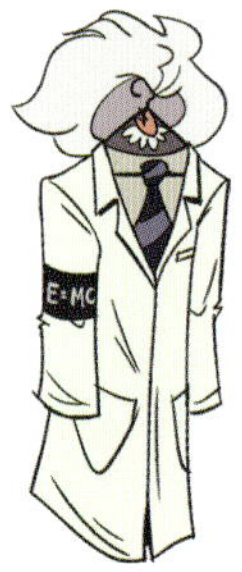

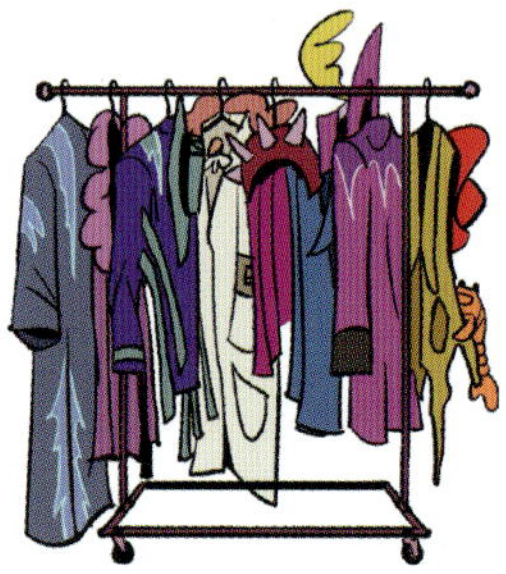

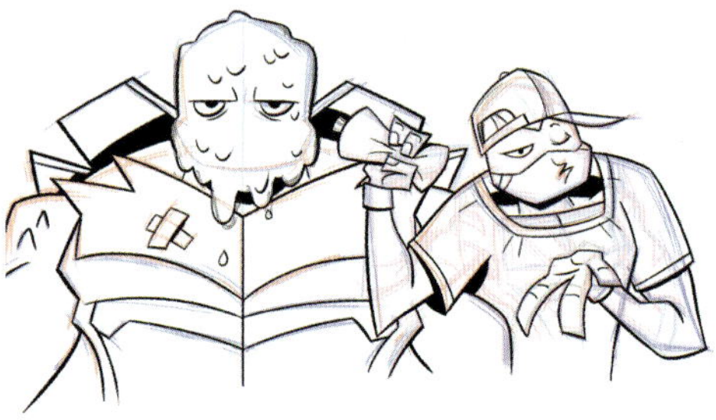

DALE MALINOWSKI: I grew up on TMNT, so I often worked Easter eggs into the show. For example, inside Leo's locker room, the Down Under Hunter costume Mikey calls attention to is, in fact, Leatherhead's outfit—complete with lobster accessory!

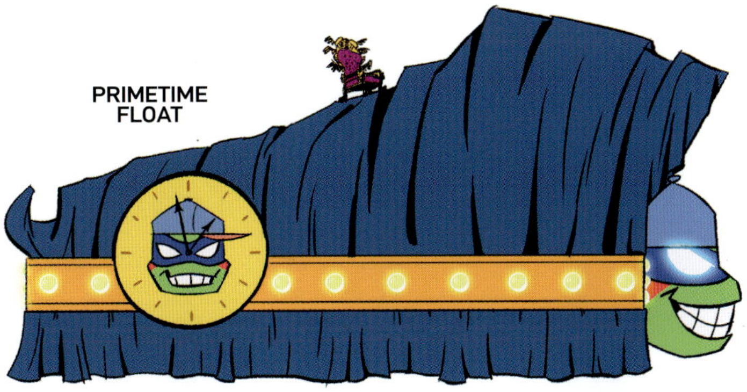

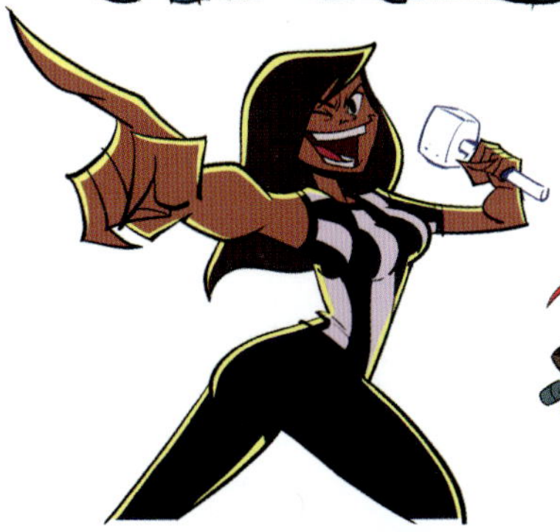

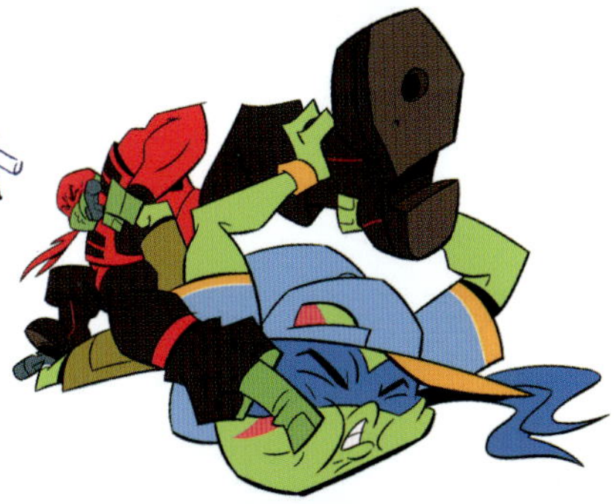

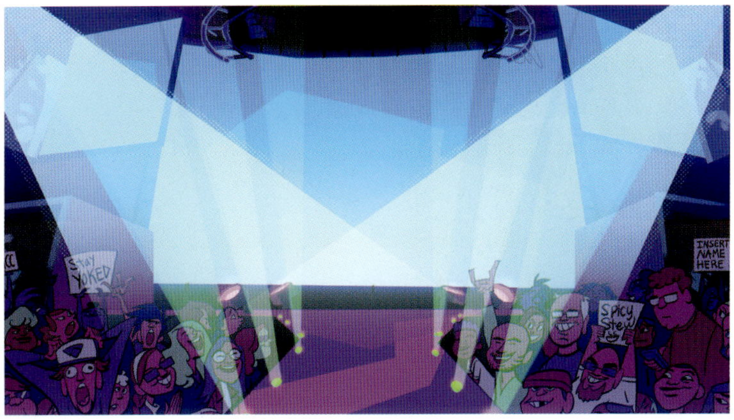

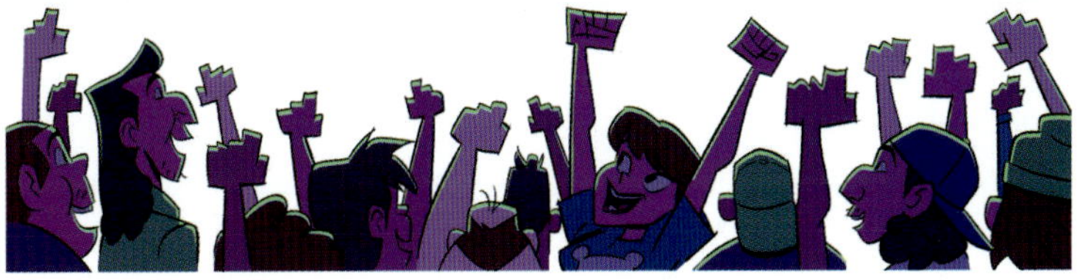

DALE MALINOWSKI: Some of the writers and story teams appear in the crowd right before Primetime Leo makes his grand entrance.

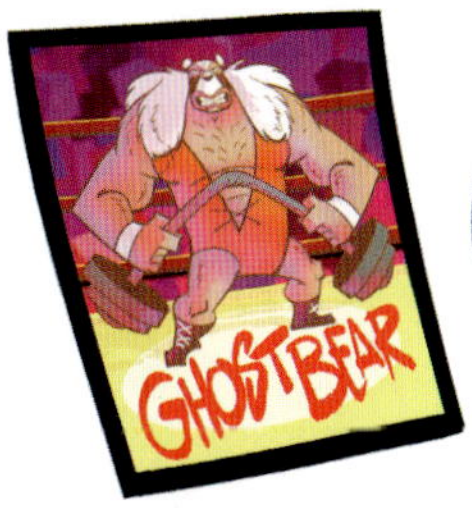

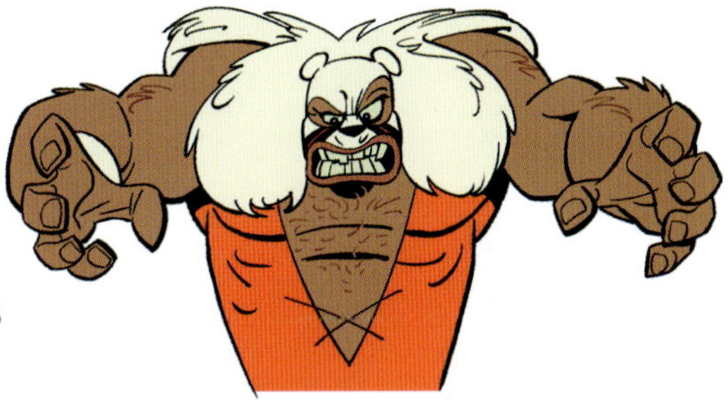

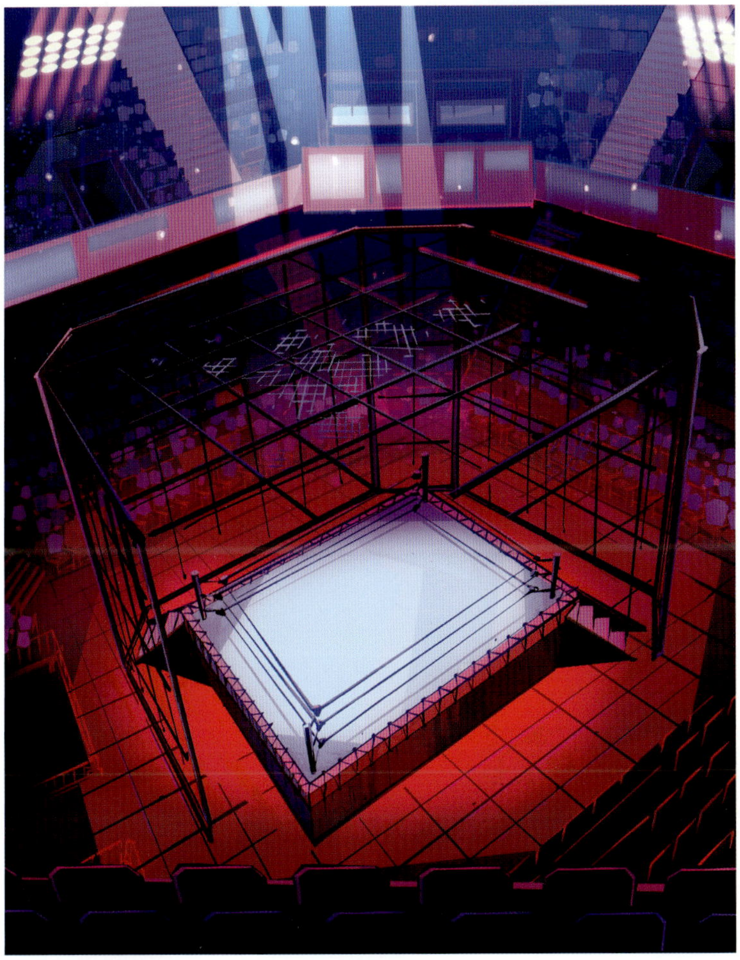

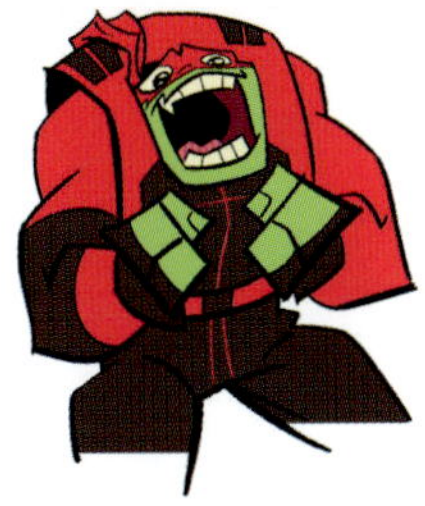

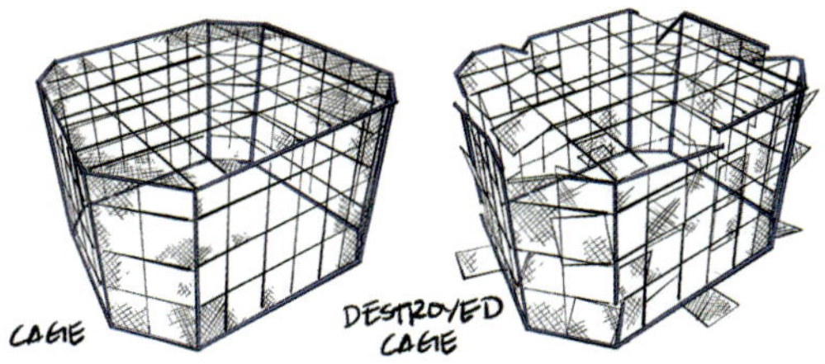

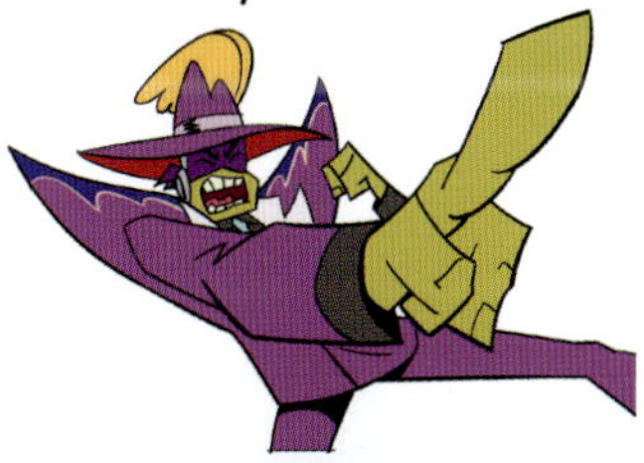

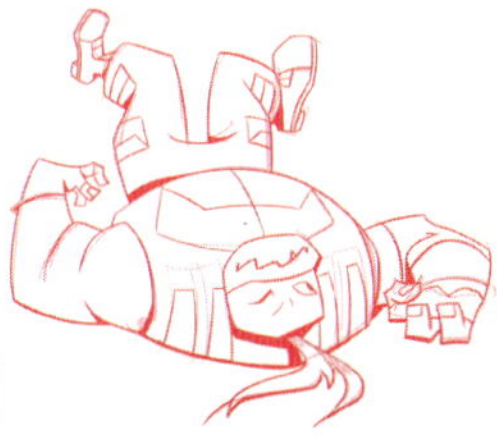

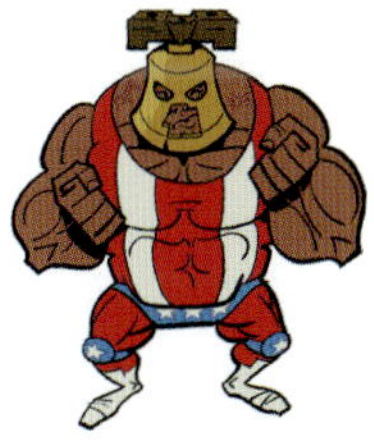

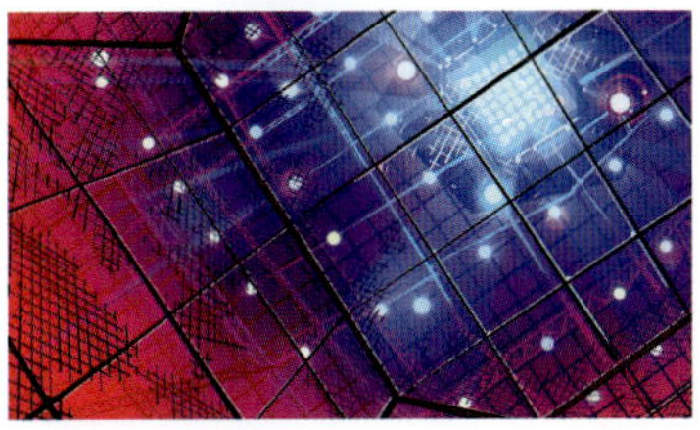

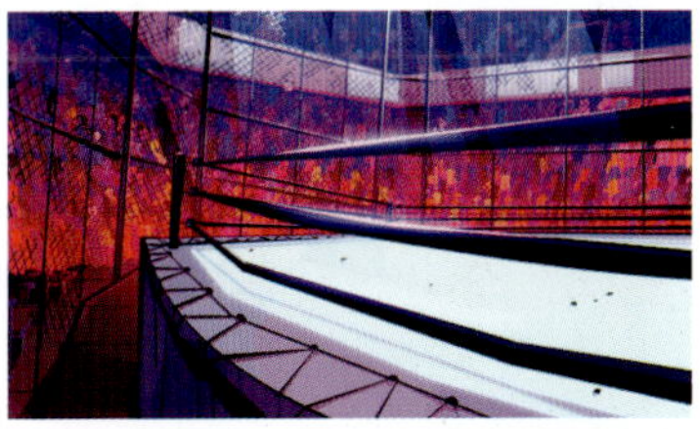

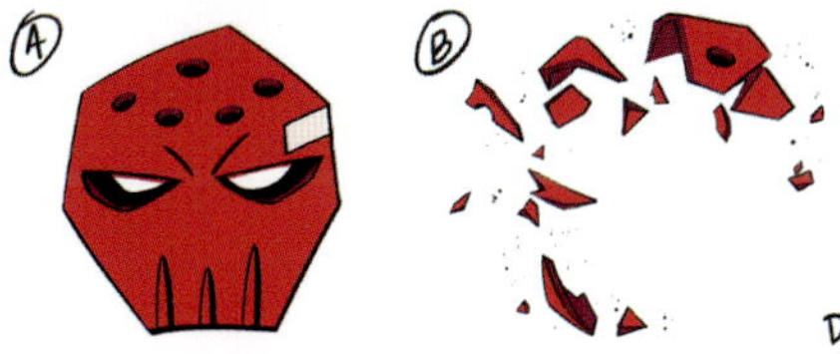

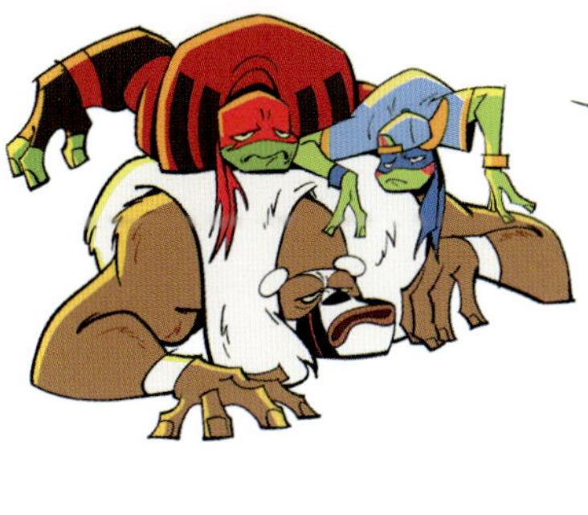

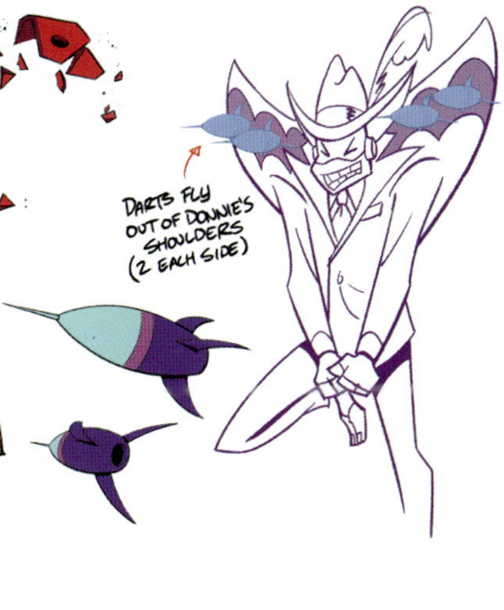

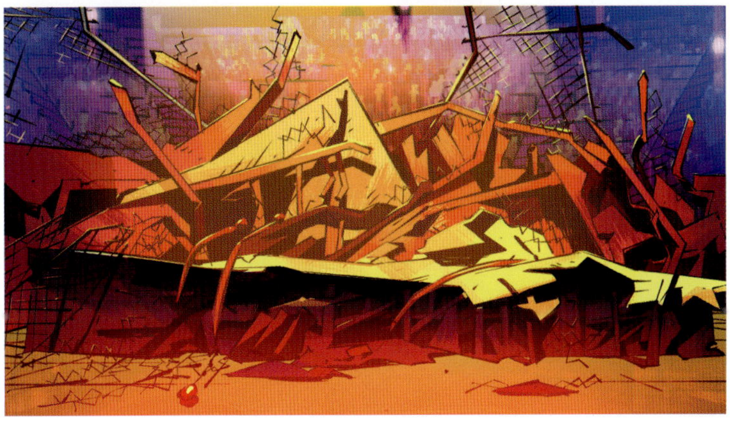

THE LONGEST FIGHT

ORIGINAL AIR DATE: OCTOBER 6, 2018
PRODUCTION DODE: 016

WRITTEN BY **IAN BUSCH**
STORYBOARDS BY **BRANDON MCKINNEY, SHAWNA MILLS**
DIRECTED BY **SEBASTIAN MONTES**

IAN BUSCH: We wanted to break the teenage boy mold by giving the boys a female hero to emulate. That's how we created their favorite skateboarder, Sydney Allen. She's actually named after two of my favorite Milwaukee Bucks basketball players, Sidney Moncrief and Ray Allen.

The origin of the story started because I wanted to break our usual story structure where we usually ended in a fight…so I aimed to get us into a fight as soon as possible and stay in that fight as long as possible.

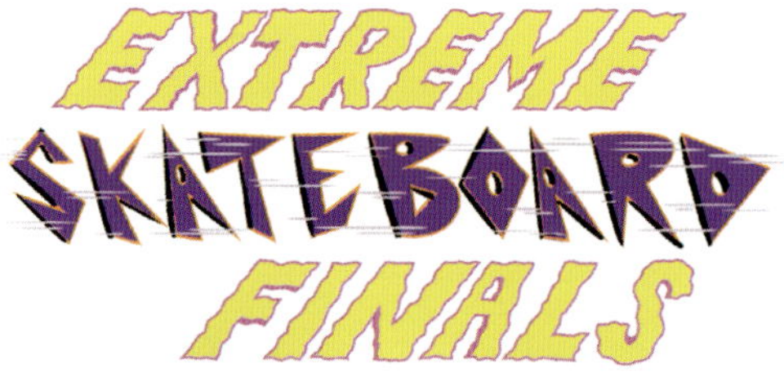

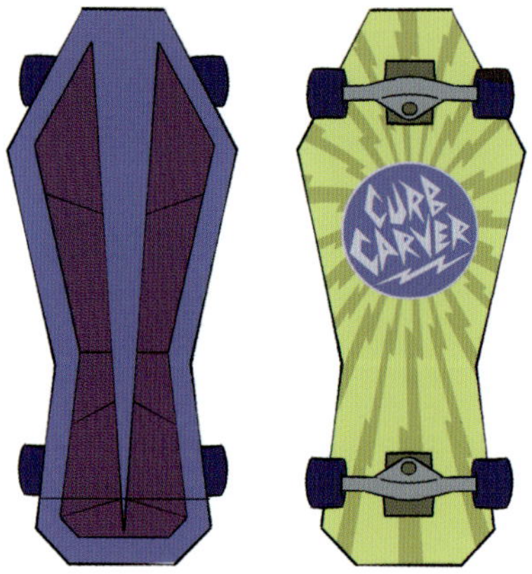

LEO'S SKATEBOARD

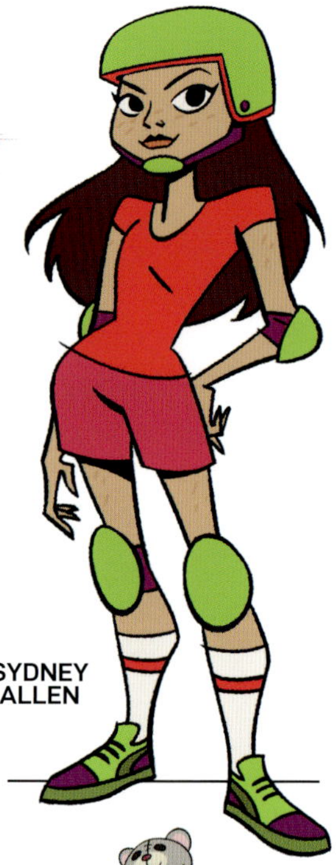
SYDNEY ALLEN

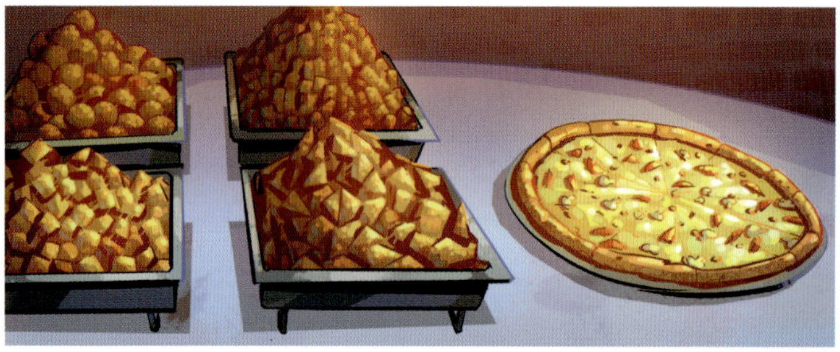

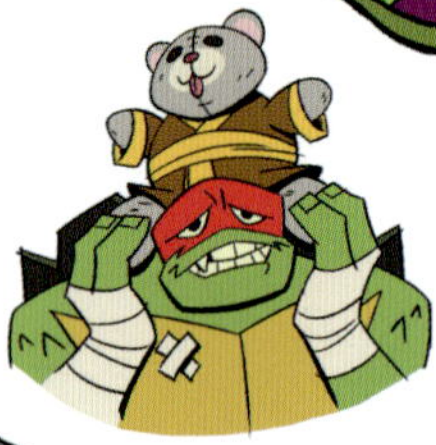

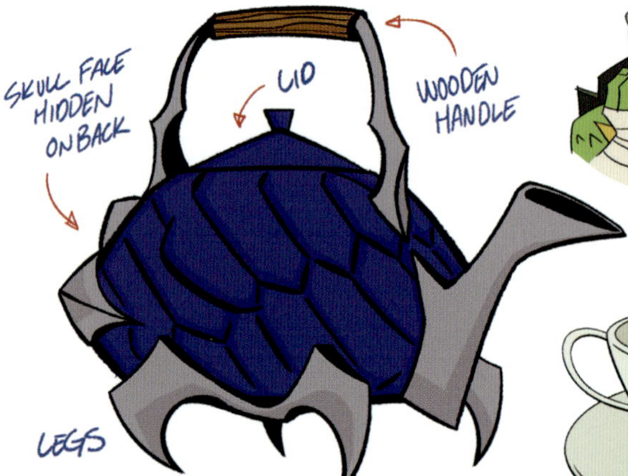

KUROI YŌROI
FACEPLATE / "SKULLY"

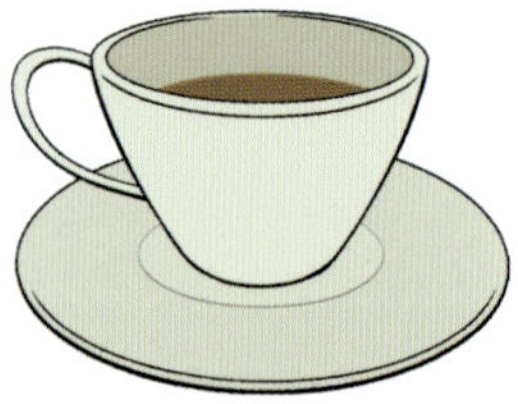

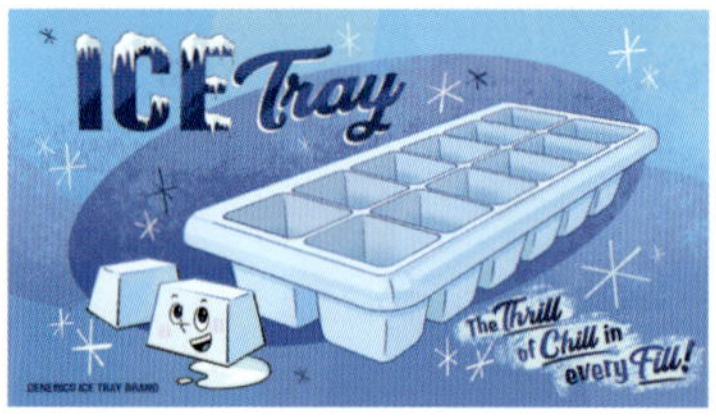

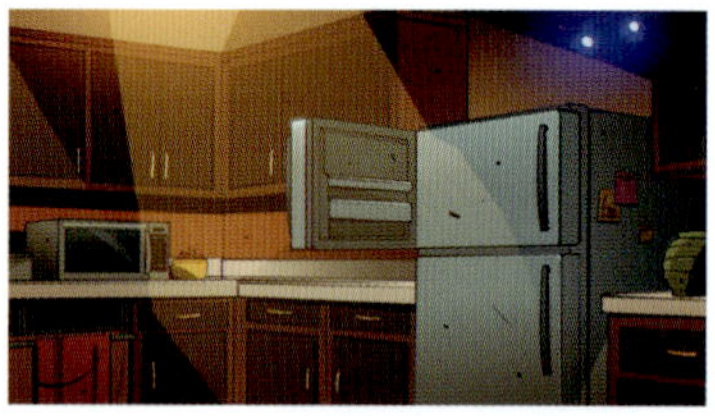

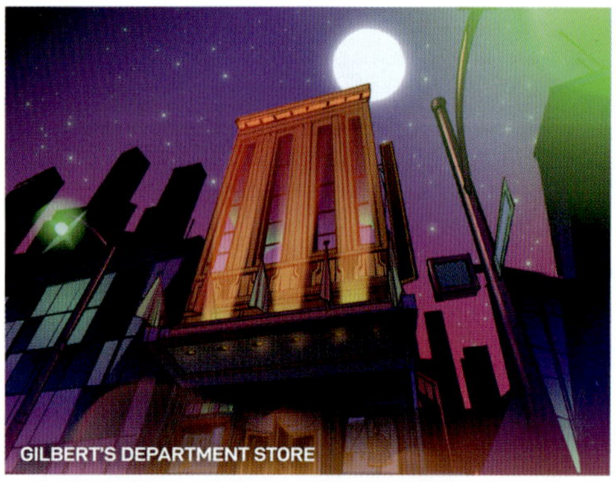
GILBERT'S DEPARTMENT STORE

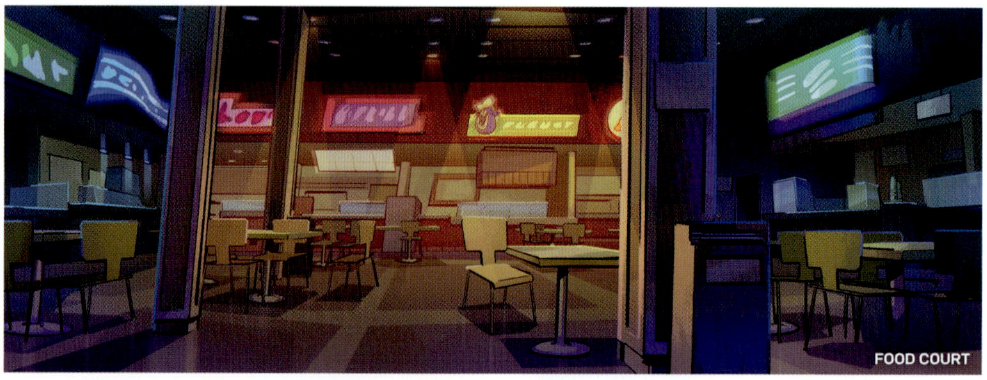
FOOD COURT

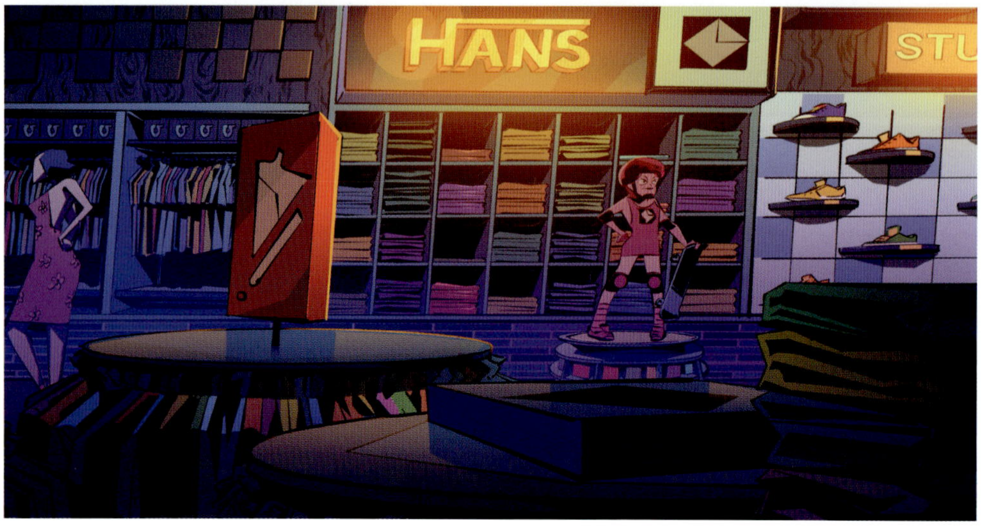

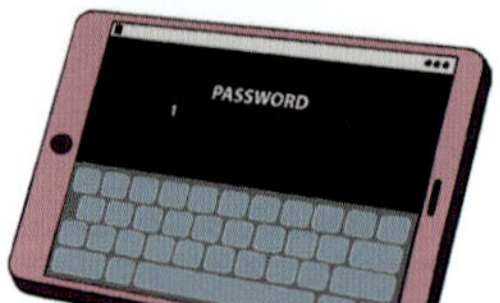

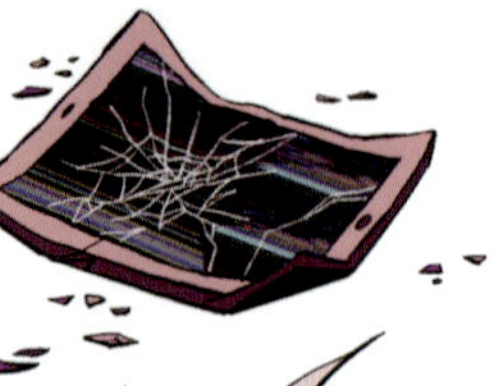

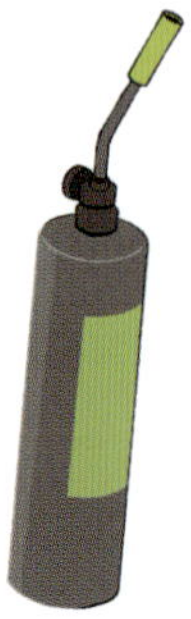

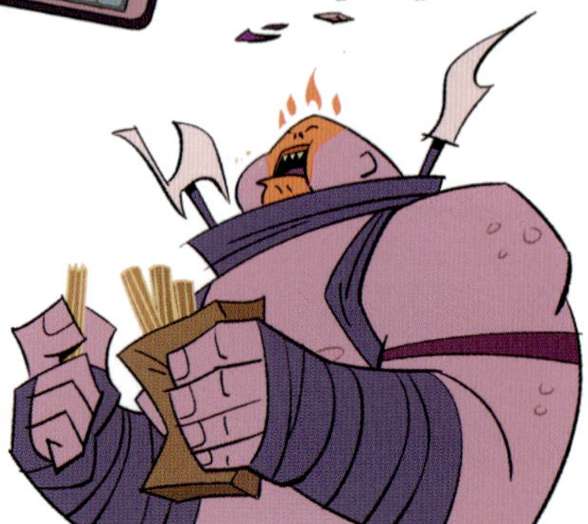

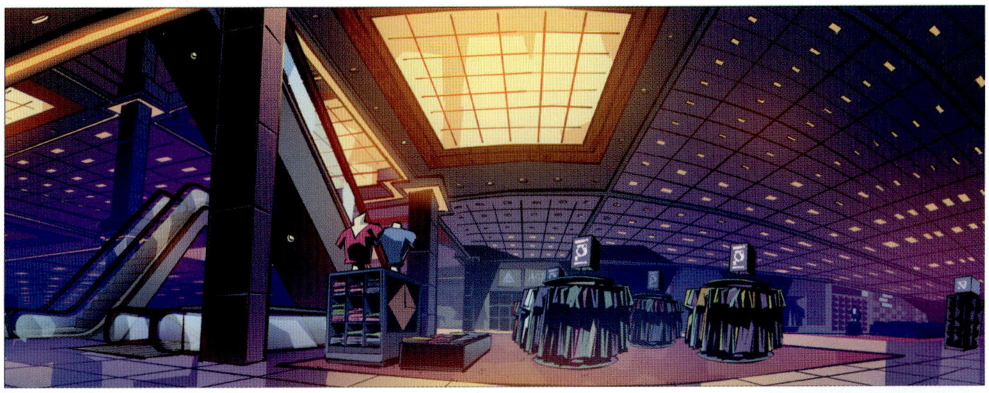

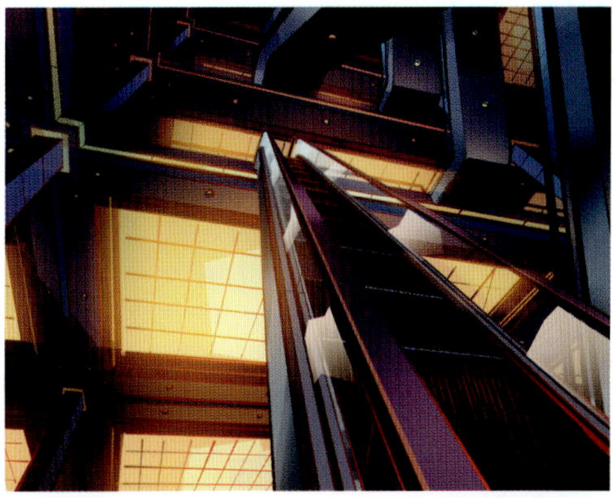

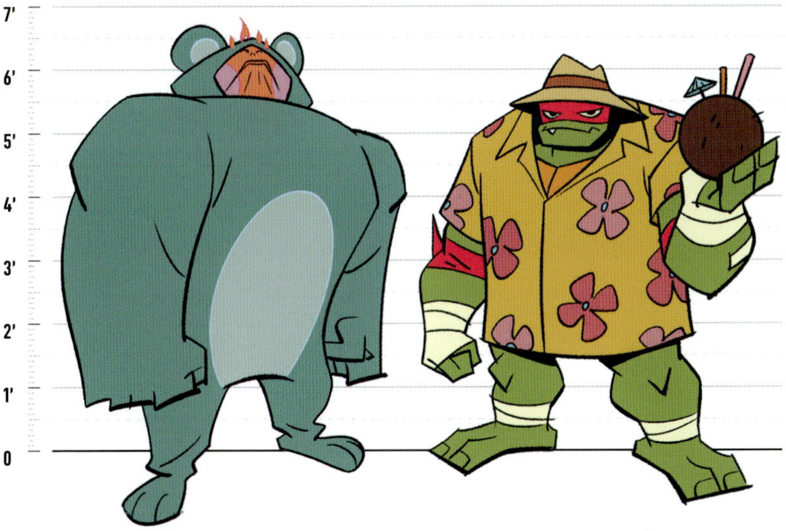

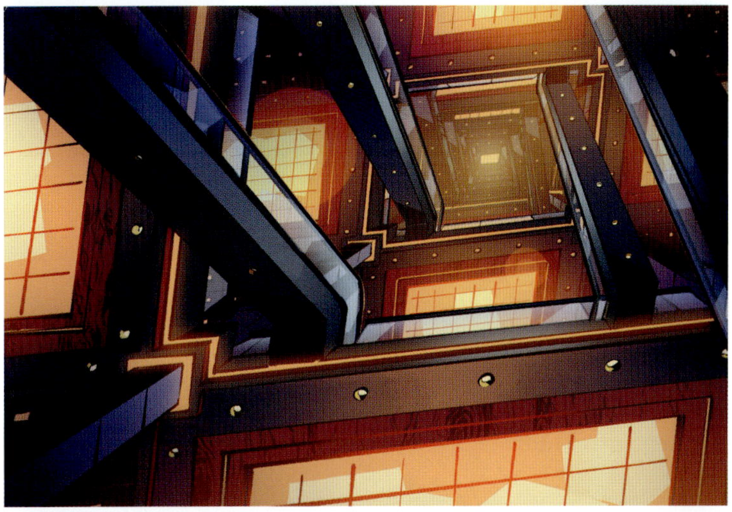

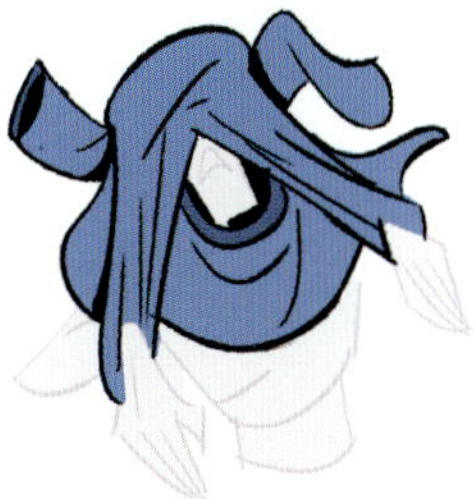

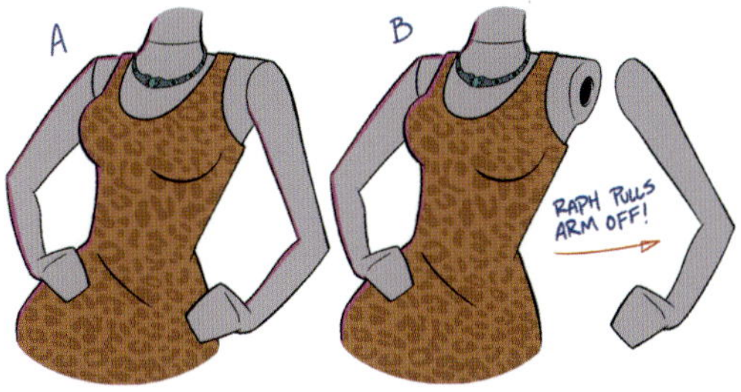

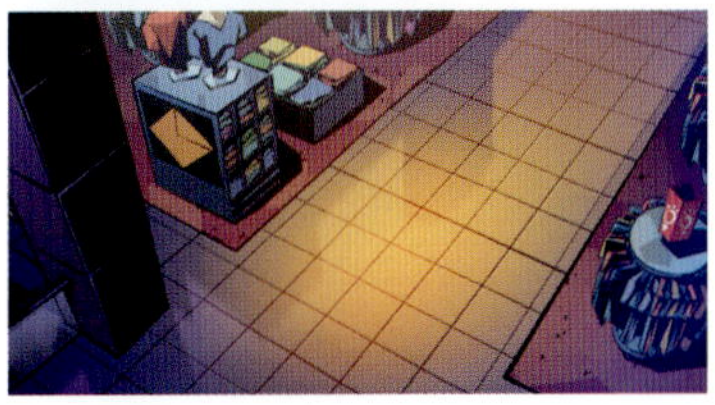

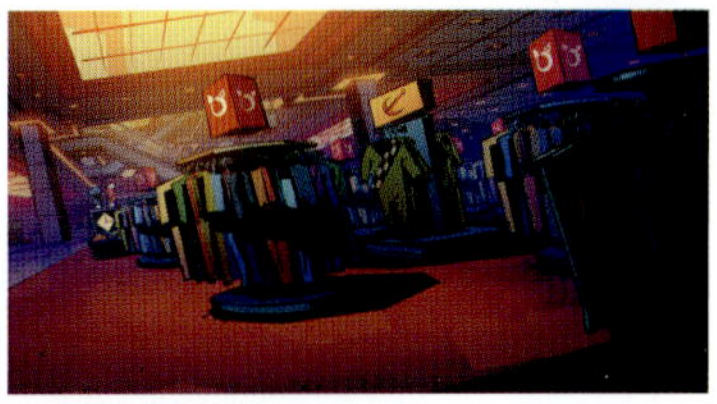

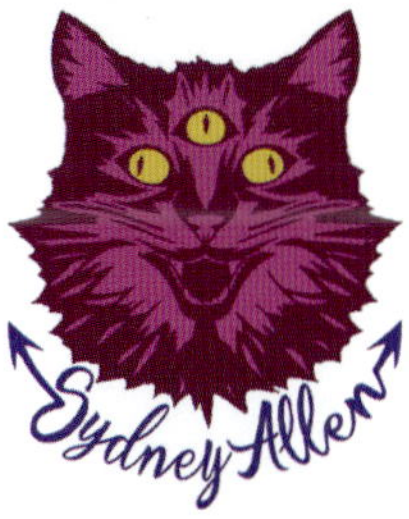

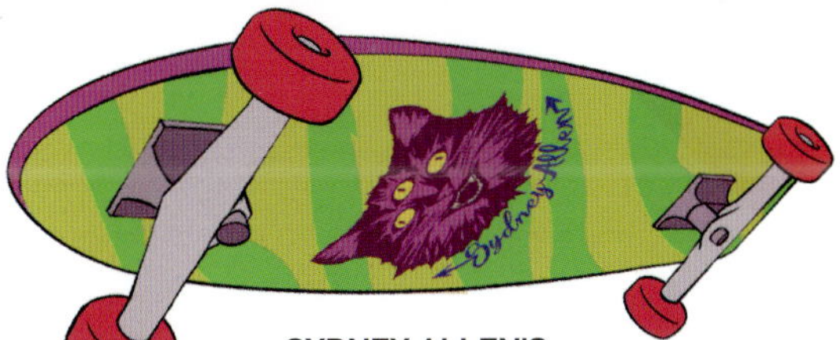

SYDNEY ALLEN'S SKATEBOARD

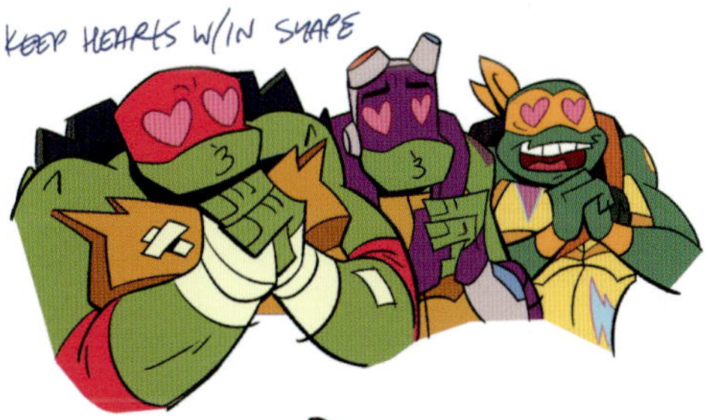

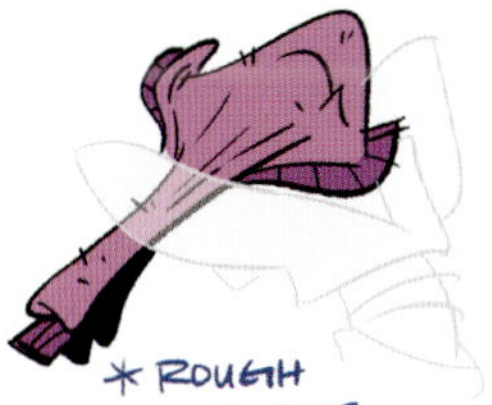

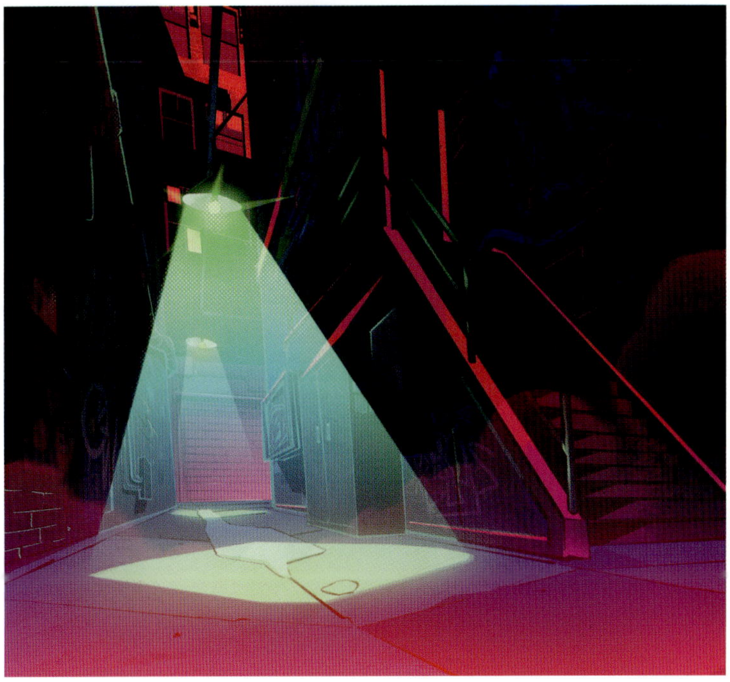

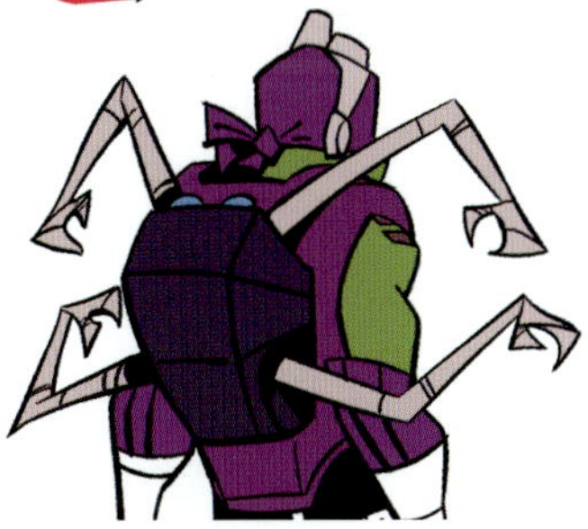

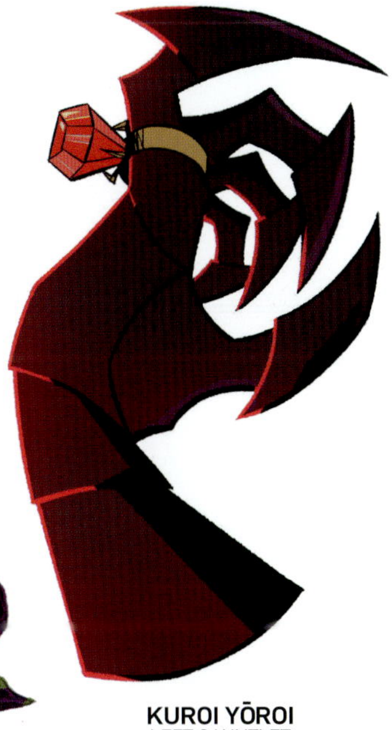

KUROI YŌROI
LEFT GAUNTLET

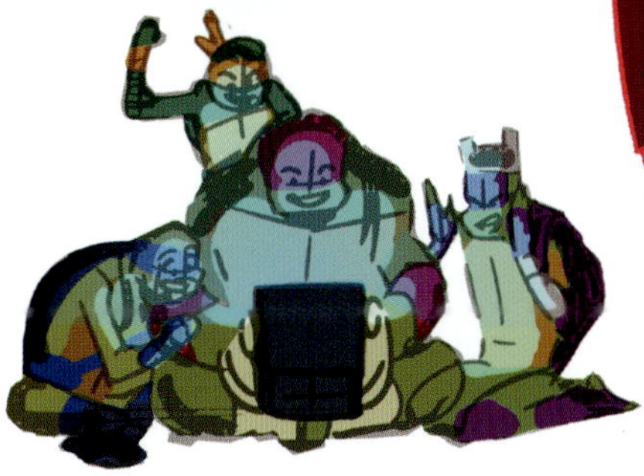

AL BE BACK

ORIGINAL AIR DATE: DEC 1, 2018
PRODUCTION CODE: 017

WRITTEN BY **F.M. DE MARCO**
STORYBOARDS BY **CHRISTINE LIU**
DIRECTED BY **BRENDAN CLOGHER**

RON CORCILLO: The storyboard pitch for this episode made our entire crew laugh raucously as all the Albeartos self-destruct over how bad the boys' music is. Christine Liu did an amazing job on that sequence!

RUSS CARNEY: Stockboy's appearance at the beginning was meant to foreshadow a future team-up between the two, which ultimately happened in "T-Hex," one of the lost episodes. The idea is that he found Albearto's head and restored him to functionality in exchange for future considerations. The birthday song sung by the animatronic Albearto in that first scene is a tribute to our illustrious production manager and color stylist Tanya Melendez. It was pretty much written in the ADR (postproduction recording) booth by the two of us, Rob Paulsen (voice director, Foot Lieutenant) and Tom Kenny (Albearto).

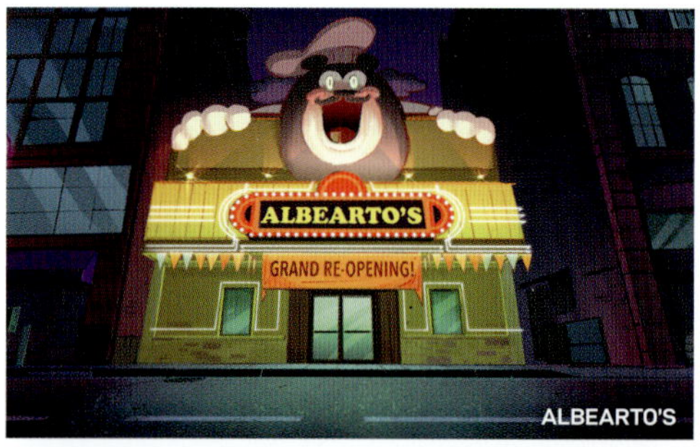

ALBEARTO'S

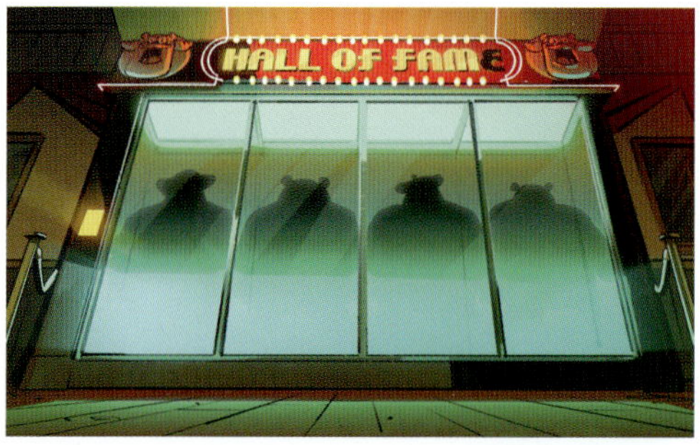

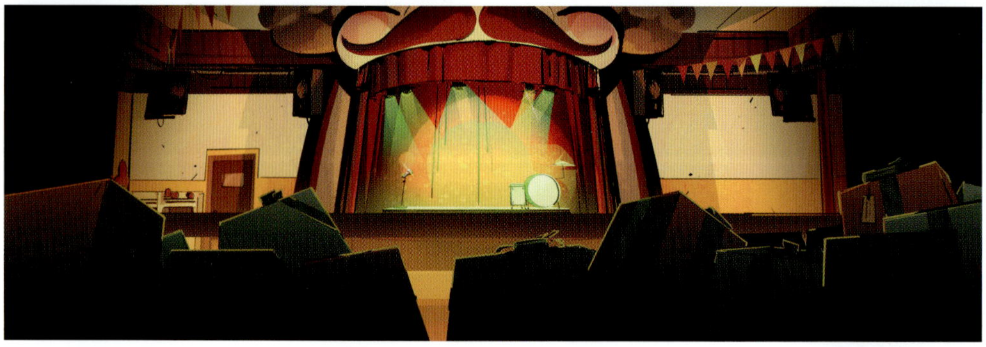

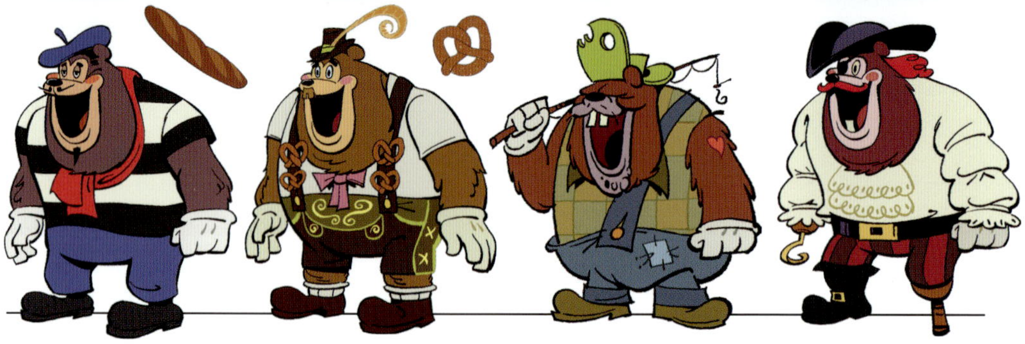

CHEF ALBÉAR

OTTO VON BEARTO

BAYOU 'BEARTO

AL-BEARDO THE PIRATE

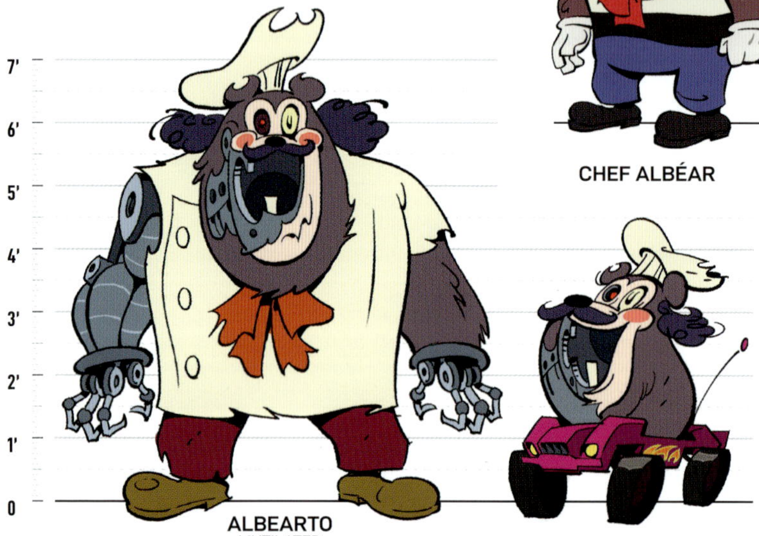

ALBEARTO
MUTILATED

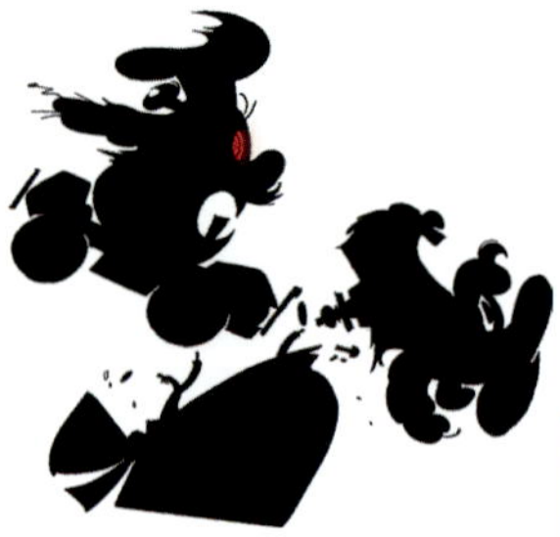

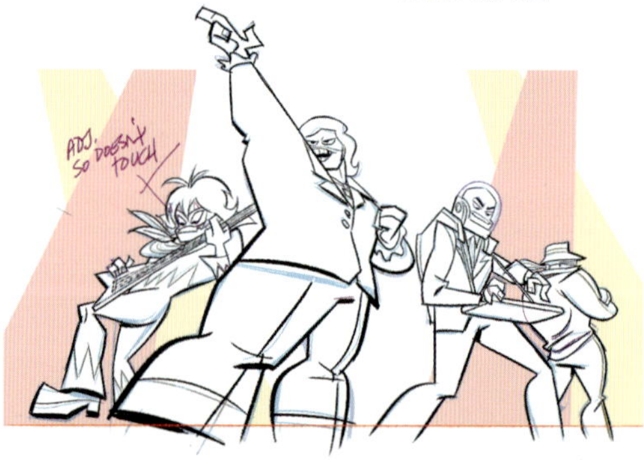

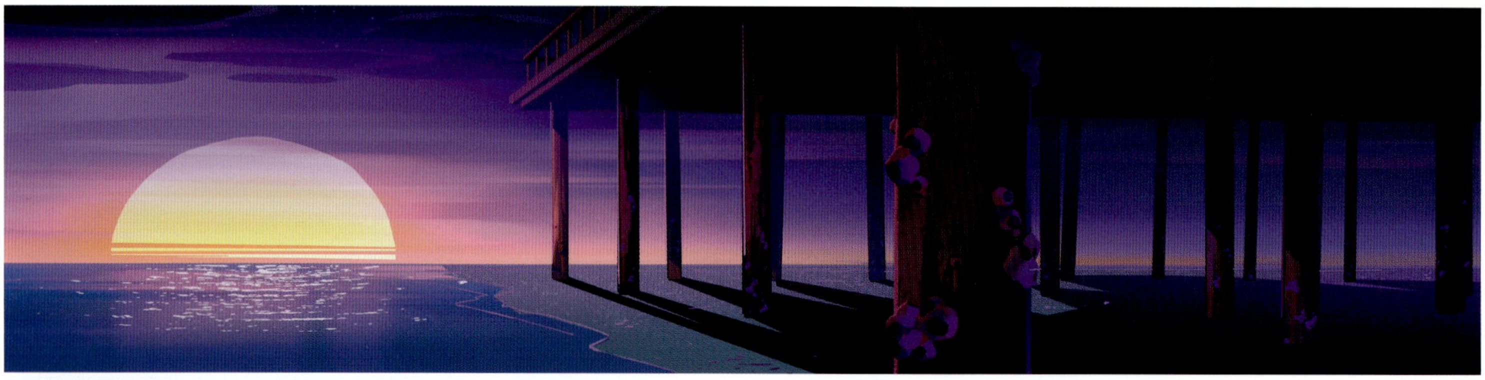

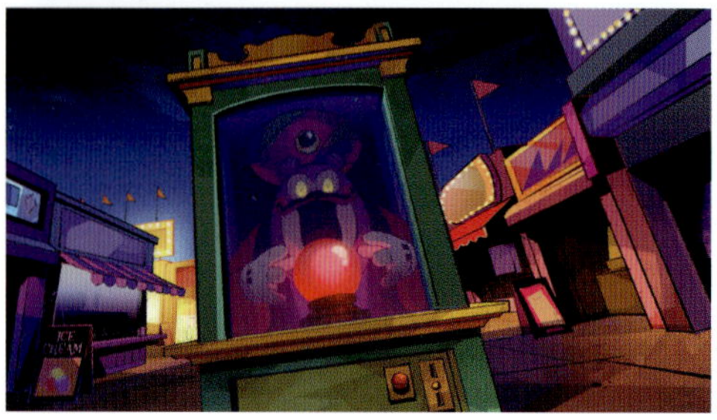

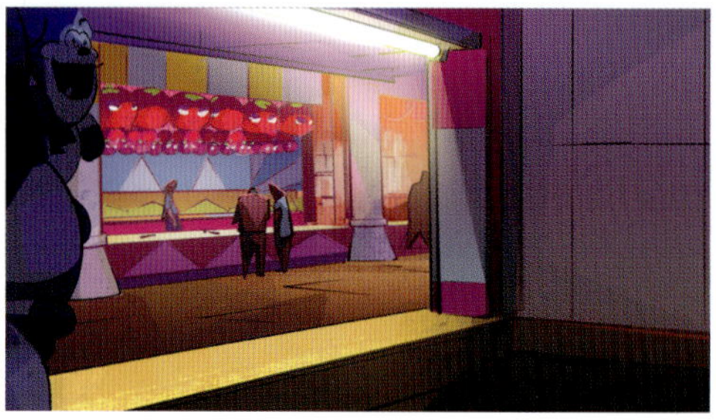

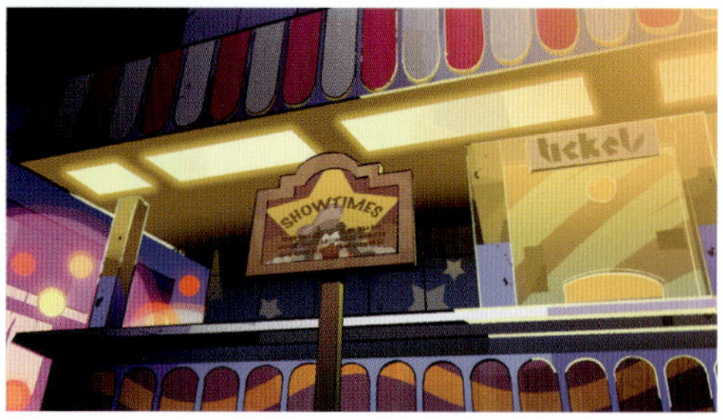

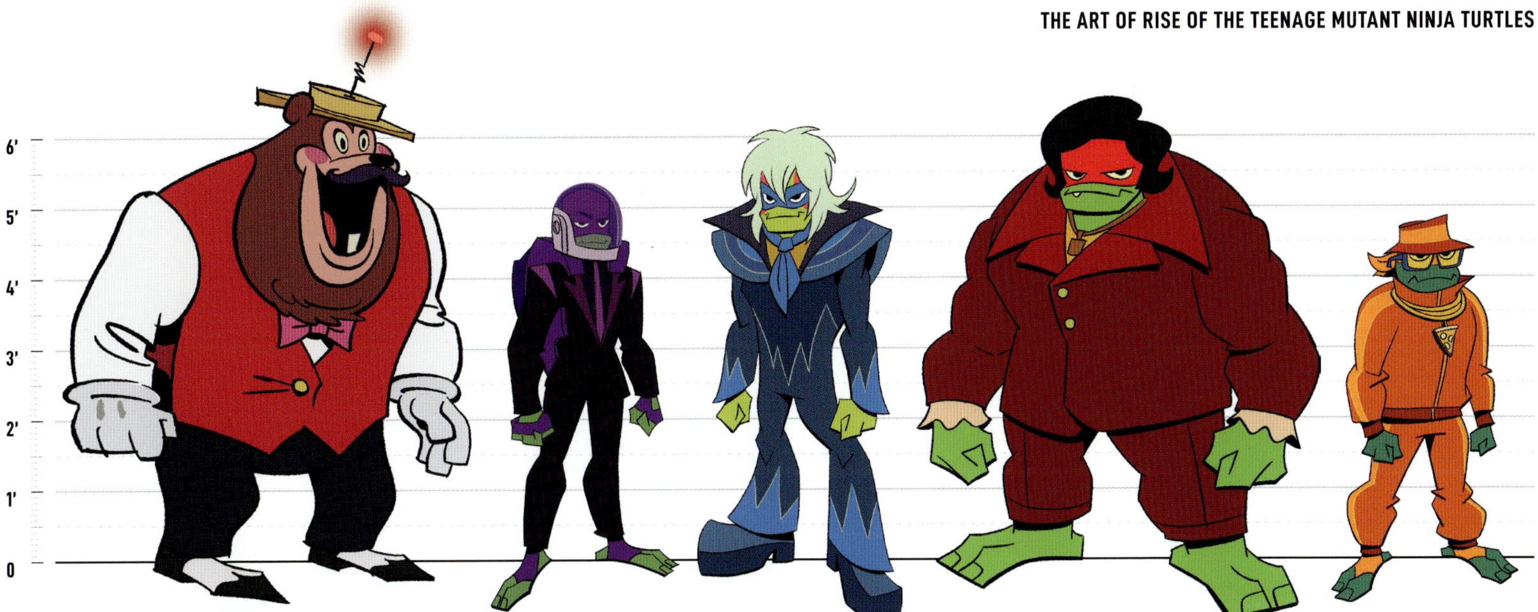

CARNIVAL ALBEARTO

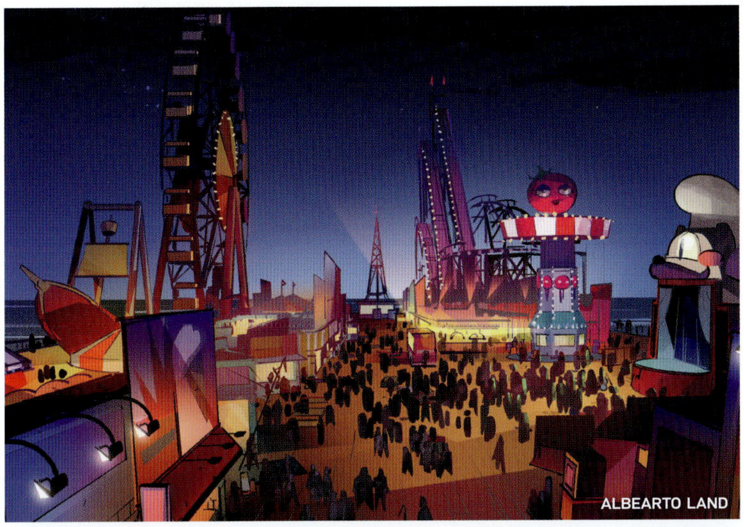

ALBEARTO LAND

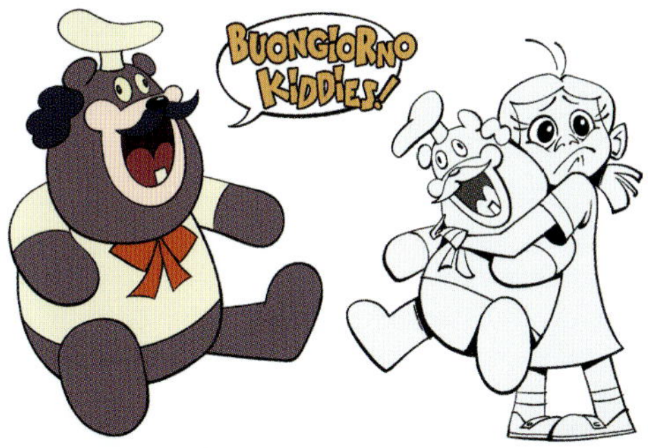

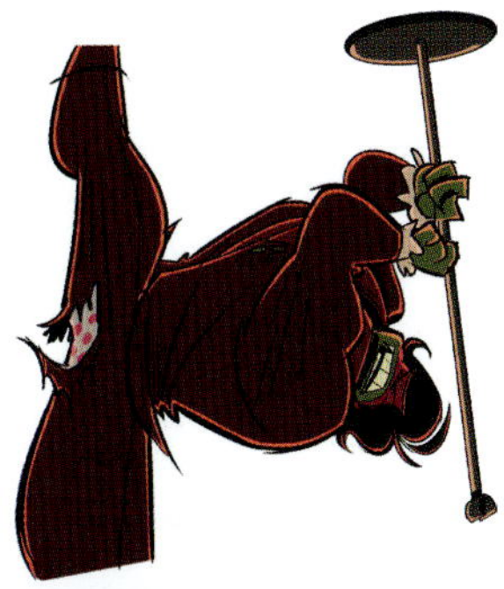

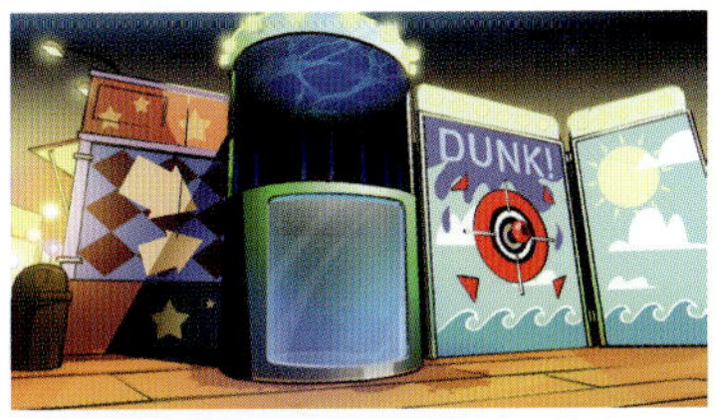

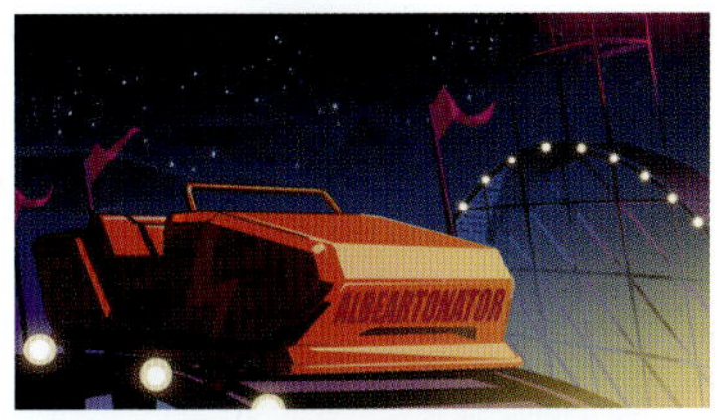

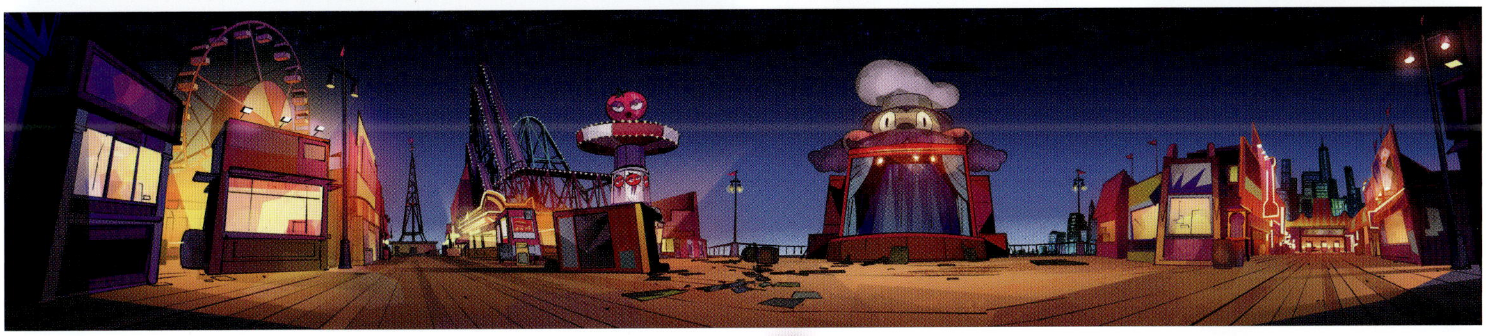

RON CORCILLO: As we were all punching up the first draft, we thought it would be funny if three of the Turtles believed in a celestial body named Moon Jr. As the boys play their instruments, we hear the following play out:

Raph: What're you guys doing?

Leo: Sendin' people's minds on a rocket ship to Moon Junior!

Donnie: Dude, there's no Moon Junior. Only the Moon.

Raph: Let's agree to disagree on whether or not there is a tiny little Moon that orbits the big Moon--

Donnie: There is not.

RUSS CARNEY: The idea cracked us writers up, but Ant and Andy thought we had lost our minds, so we cut it. But to honor the idea, Ron bought himself a custom T-shirt that read "Moon Jr." on the front and "Agree to disagree" on the back. And then I, being the impish man-child that I am, posted a variety of pro–Moon Jr. signs throughout the office, including on the inside of Andy's office door. The image featured a cloudy nighttime sky with a full moon, and a smaller moon peeking out from behind it. Some captions read "Behold Moon Jr.," "Moon Jr. is real," and "She will not be ignored." It is now up to you to decide whether or not you believe...

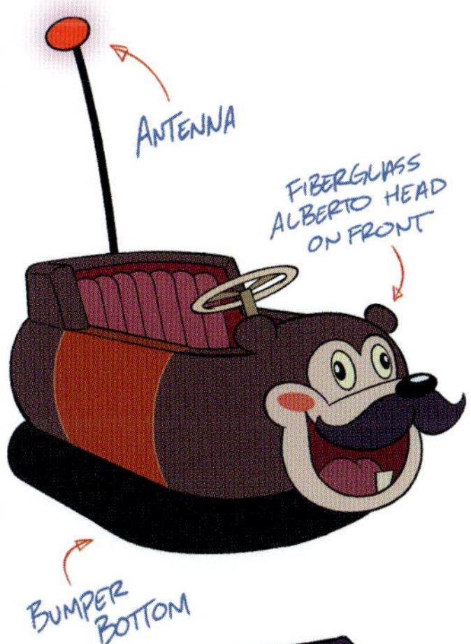

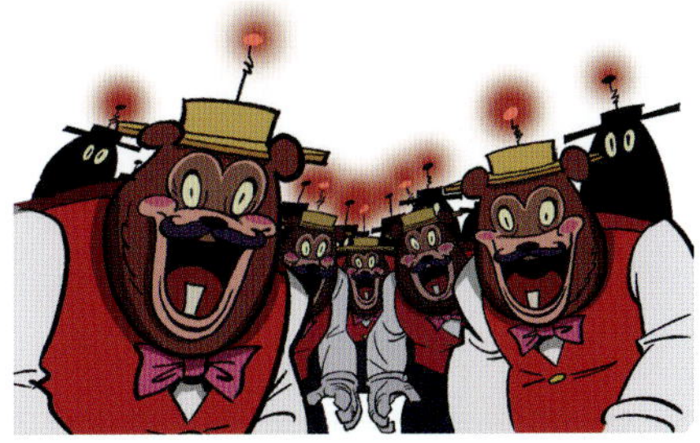

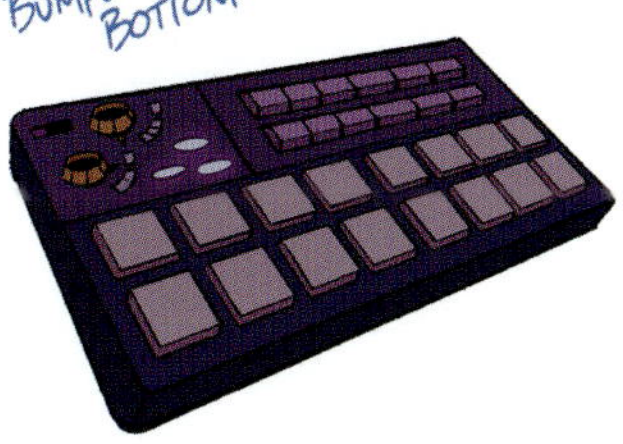

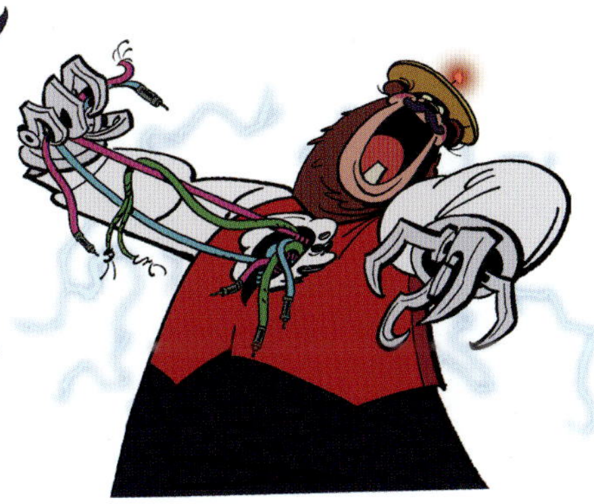

THE GUMBUS

ORIGINAL AIR DATE: OCTOBER 13, 2018
PRODUCTION CODE: 018

WRITTEN BY **RUSS CARNEY & RON CORCILLO**
STORYBOARDS BY **KEVIN MOLINA-ORTIZ**
DIRECTED BY **SEBASTIAN MONTES**

RUSS CARNEY: Sometimes cool ideas coincide. We took a huge swing when we pitched to Ant and Andy the absurd idea that this series' Baxter Stockman was a child working at a supermarket and was thusly named *Baxter Stockboy*. To our surprise, they didn't fire us, and they even thought that it was a funny idea! What?! We retroactively fire *them!* Traditionally, Stockman has utilized tech to battle the Turtles, and we wanted to keep that idea alive, so we incorporated his tech into the world of supermarkets.

RON CORCILLO: Stockboy works at his parents' store, which is heavily inspired by Stew Leonard's, a popular supermarket that I used to frequent in Connecticut. It's billed as *"the World's Largest Dairy Store"* and is basically the Disneyland of supermarkets. They had a petting zoo, animatronic creatures, a model train that circled the store, and a mesmerizing automated milk packaging machine.

RUSS CARNEY: The Gumbus was the name of a mythical evil mountain man who was said to live in the mountains above Buena Vista, Colorado. But this legend only existed at the sleepaway summer camp I attended when I was a teen. "Chain-laden Gumbus" just sounds spookier, because a Gumbus seems way more threatening when laden with chains!

RON CORCILLO: During a crew meeting about the episode, Andy asked if anyone had any thoughts on who Stockboy might look like. Russ pitched Egghead Jr. from the Foghorn Leghorn cartoons, and Andy laughed. Maybe you see the resemblance?

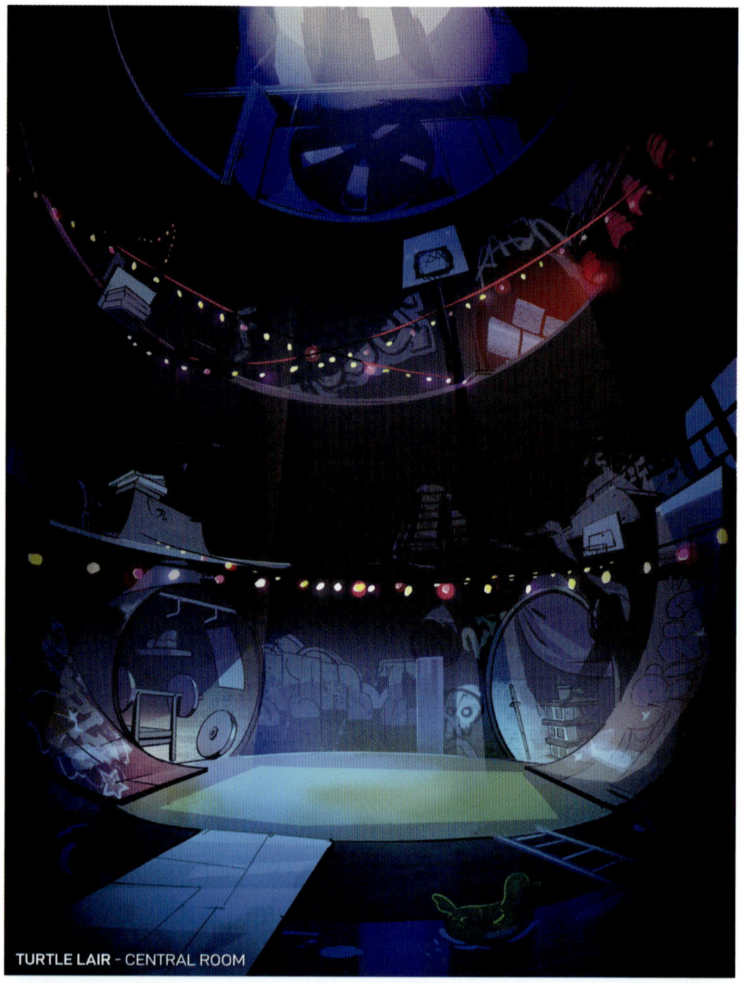
TURTLE LAIR - CENTRAL ROOM

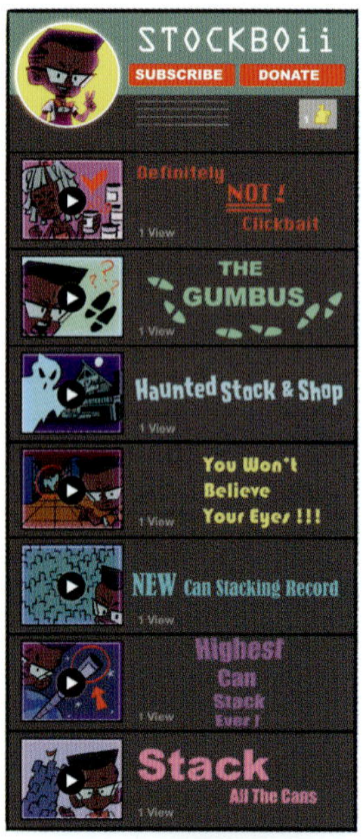

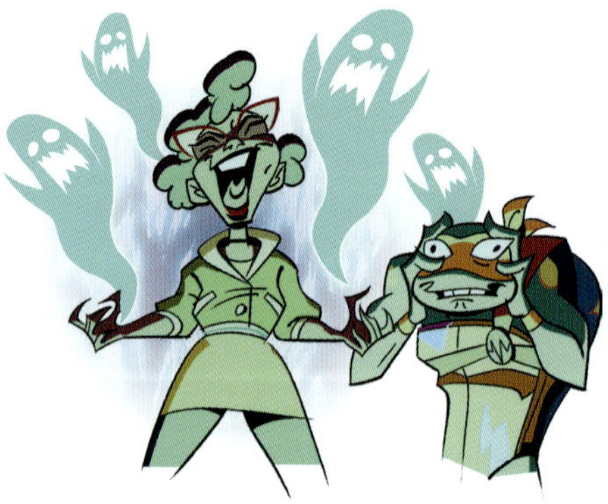

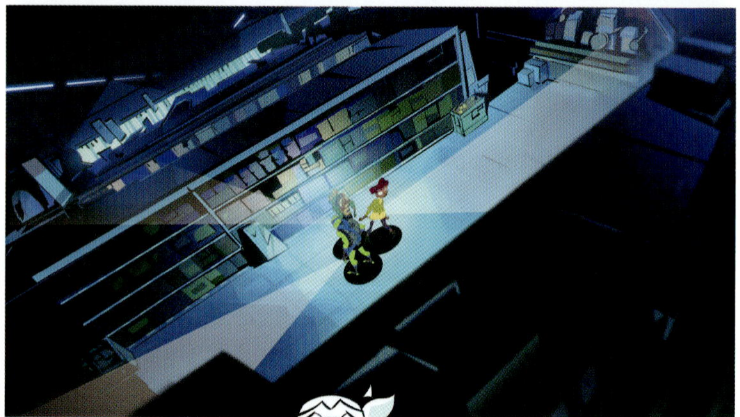

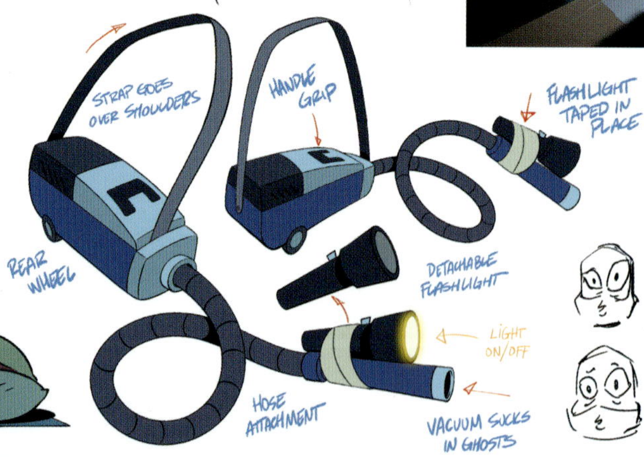

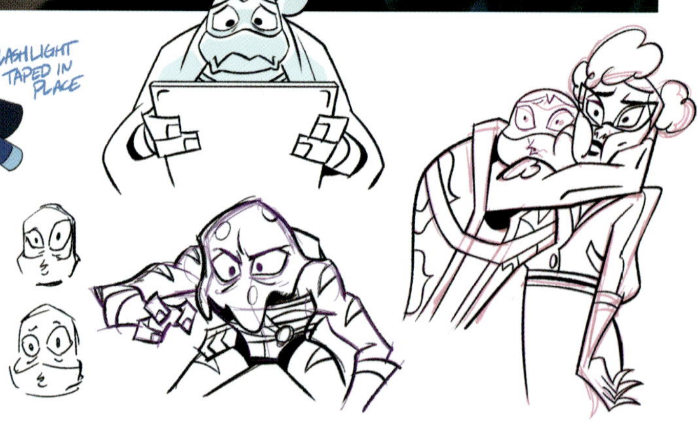

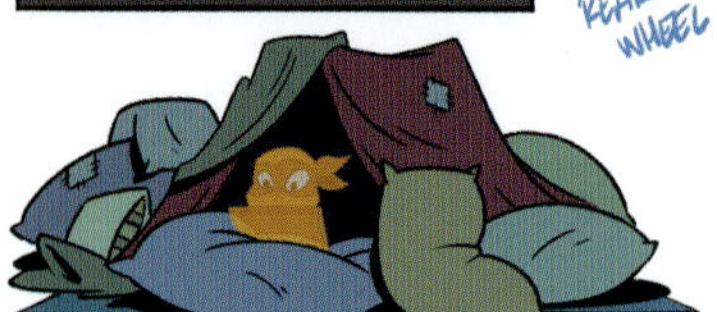

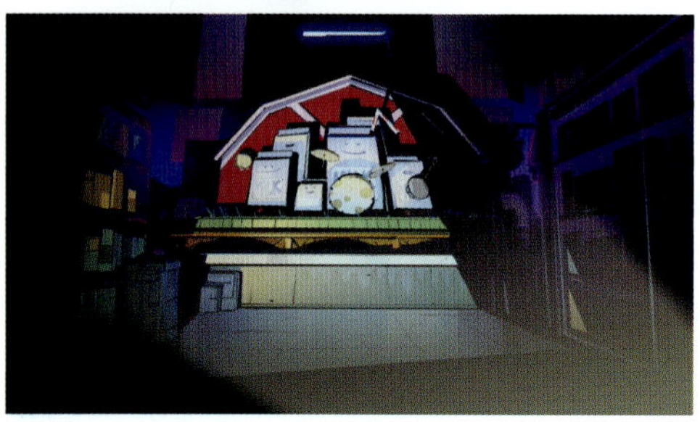

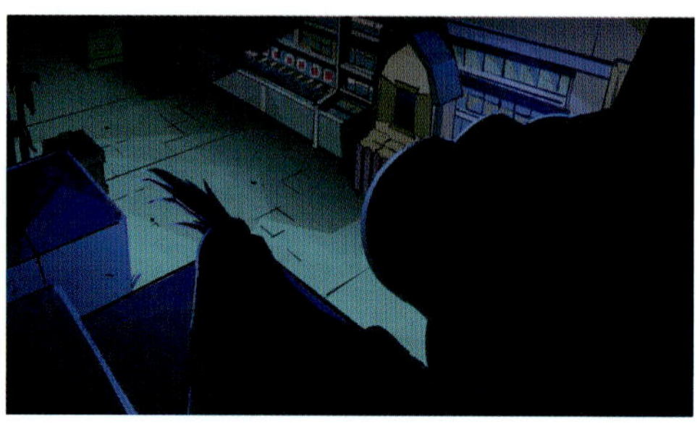

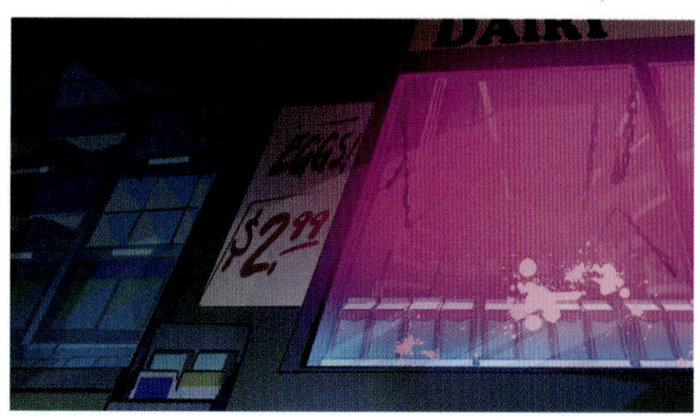

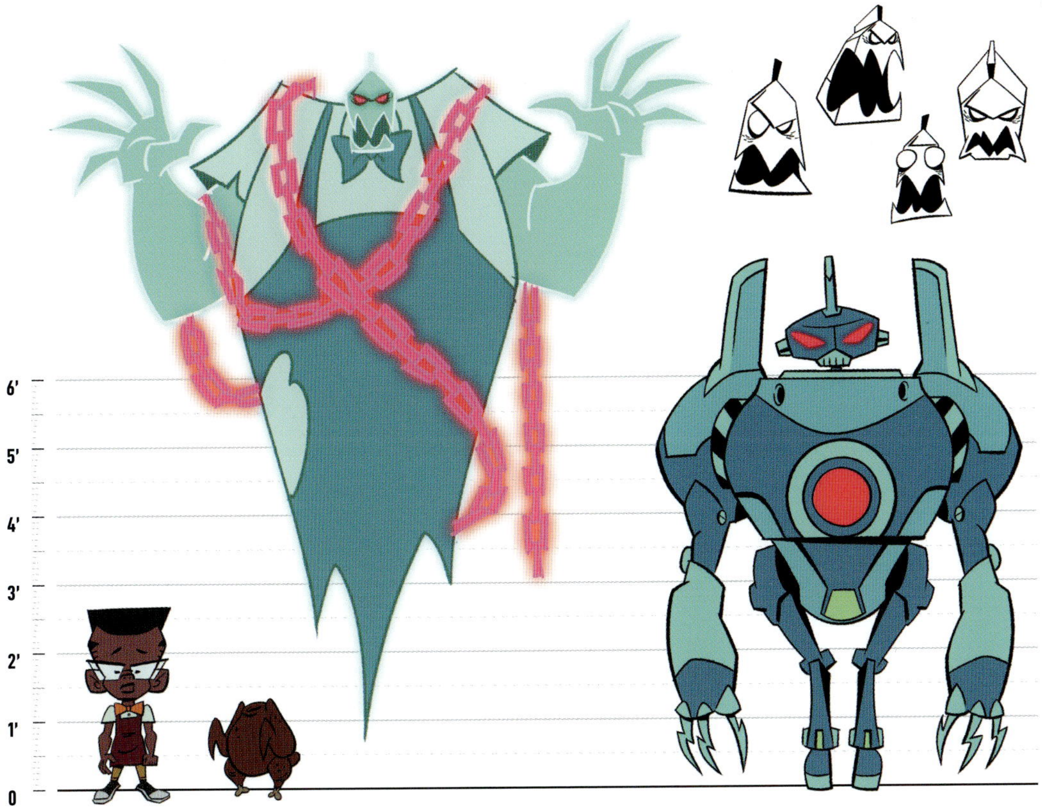

BAXTER STOCKBOY

TURKEY

THE GUMBUS

GUMBUS MECH

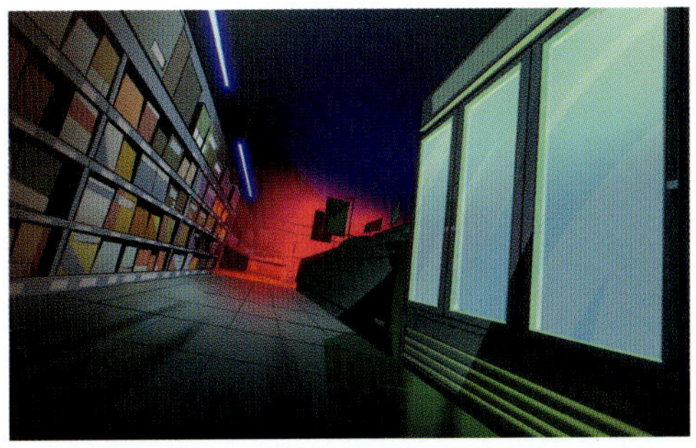

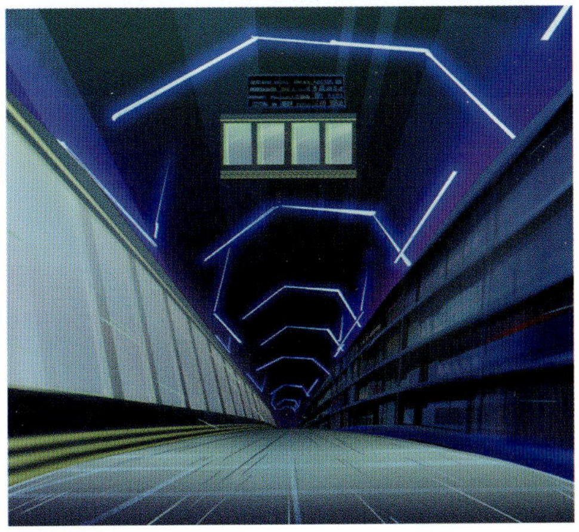

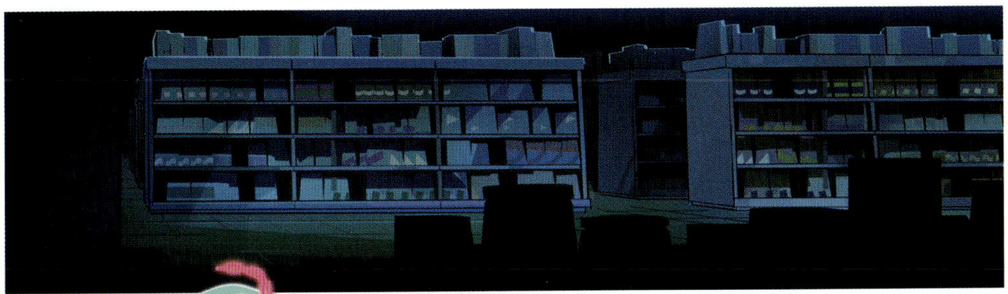

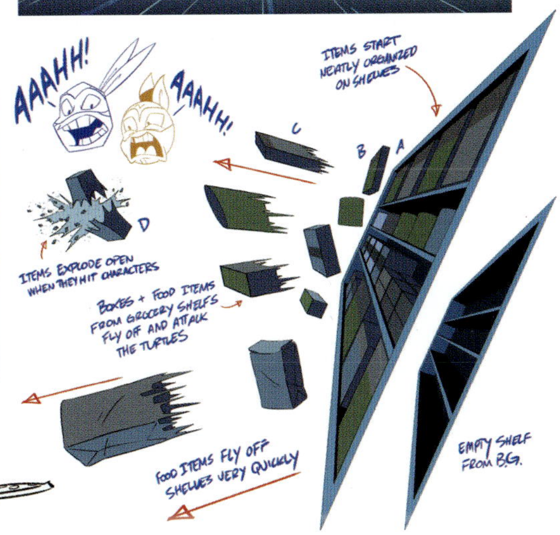

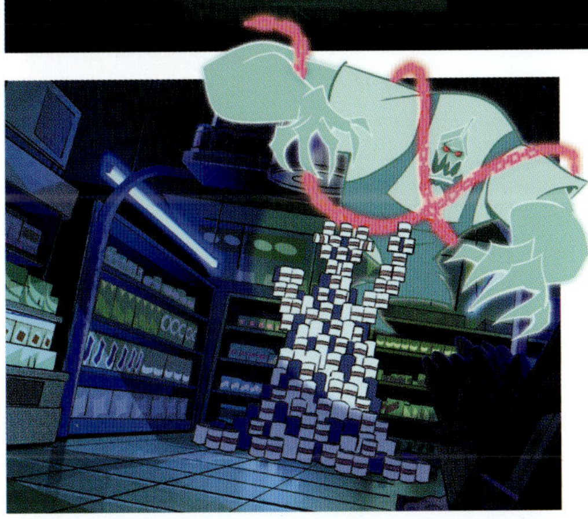

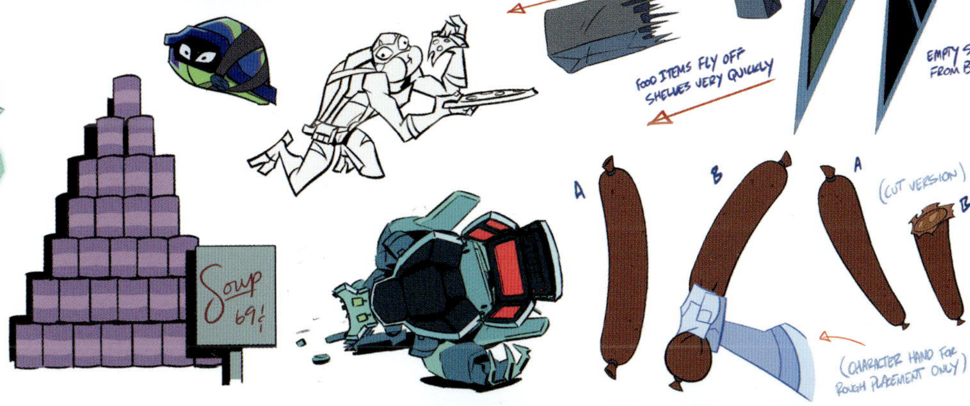

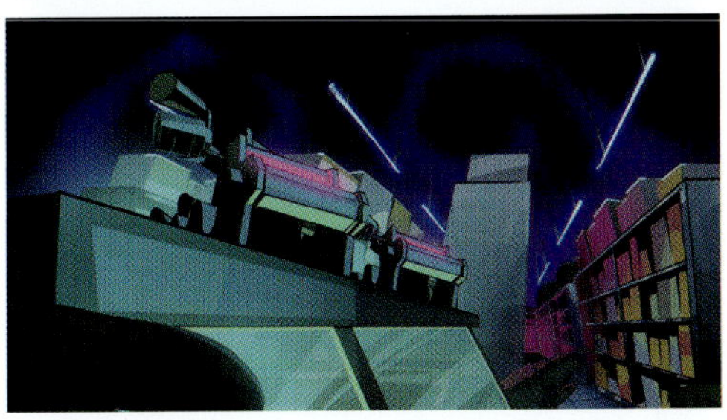

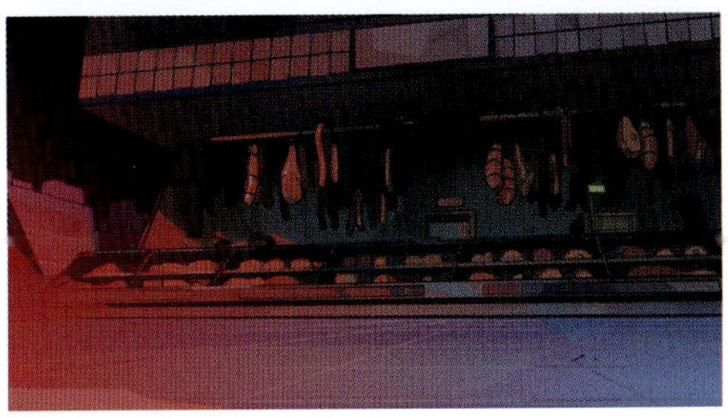

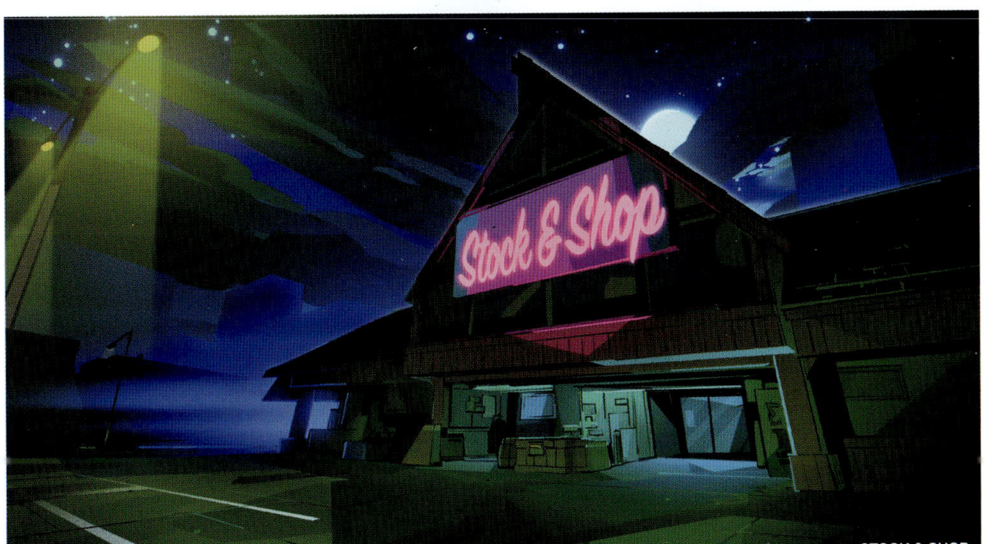

STOCK & SHOP

MRS. CUDDLES

ORIGINAL AIR DATE: OCTOBER 20, 2018
PRODUCTION CODE: 019

WRITTEN BY **IAN BUSCH**
STORYBOARDS BY **CHRISTINA "KIKI" MANRIQUE**
DIRECTED BY **ABE AUDISH & JAMIE VICKERS**

IAN BUSCH: The origin of the idea came from one of my best friends (and a staff member on *Rise* who shall remain nameless) having a childhood fear of a puppet from the late '70s and early '80s. The puppet always freaked my friend out, who is usually not afraid of such things. I felt it was a nice thing to put the usually brave Raph through.

IDA HEM (CHARACTER DESIGNER): Mrs. Cuddles is such a special character to me, because it was the first design I ever did from scratch to final turnaround. When you work as a designer in TV, it's common to turn characters that someone else designed, but this was the first one that was uniquely mine from beginning to end, and I learned so much from it! Seeing her moving and animated was even cooler!

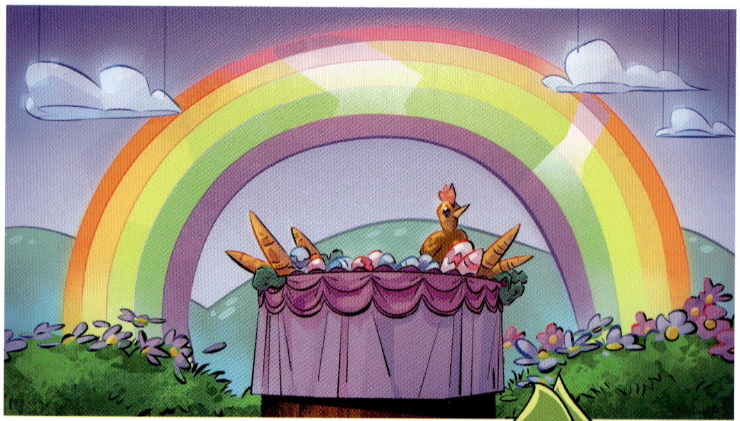

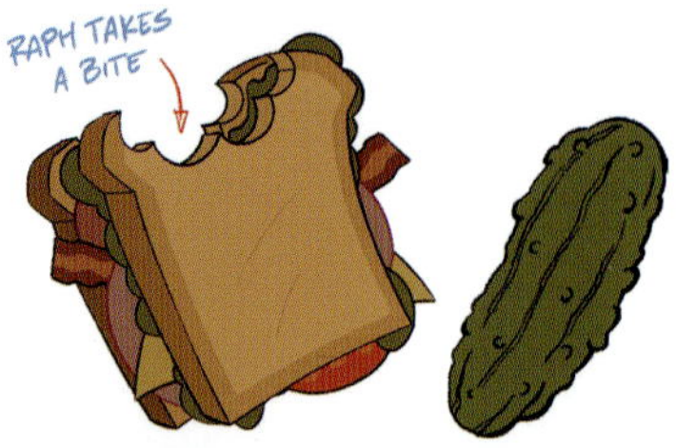

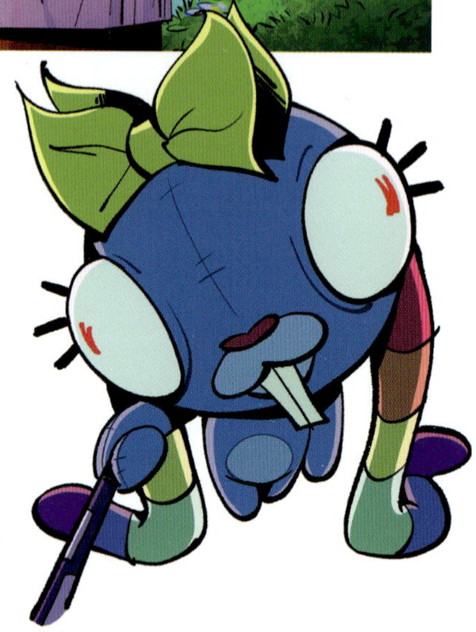

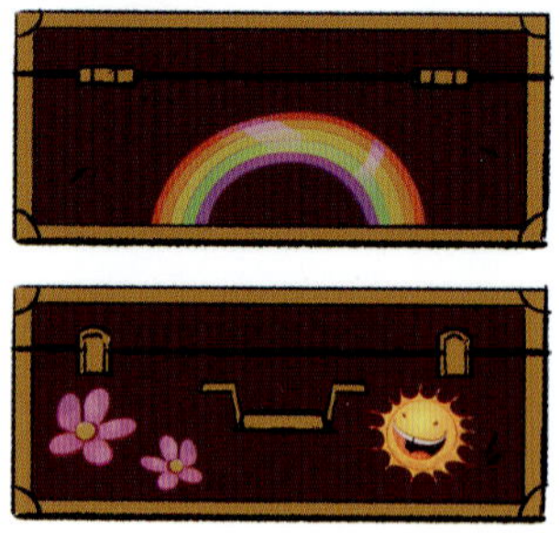

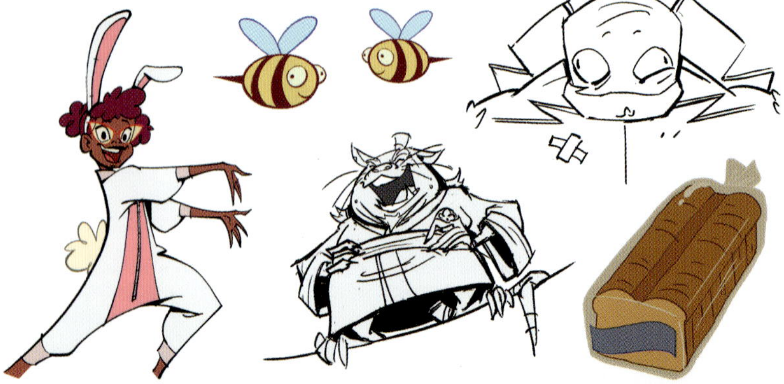

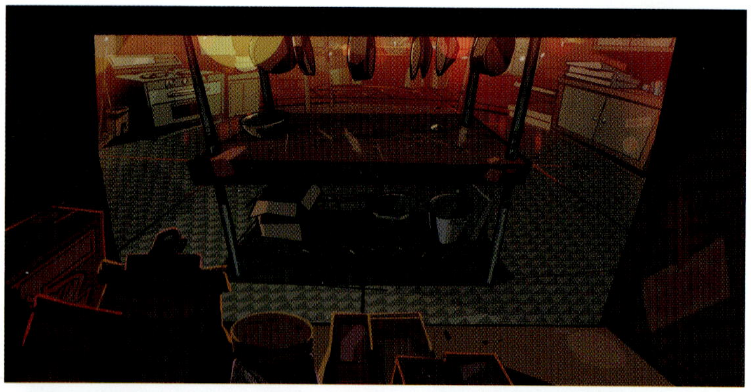

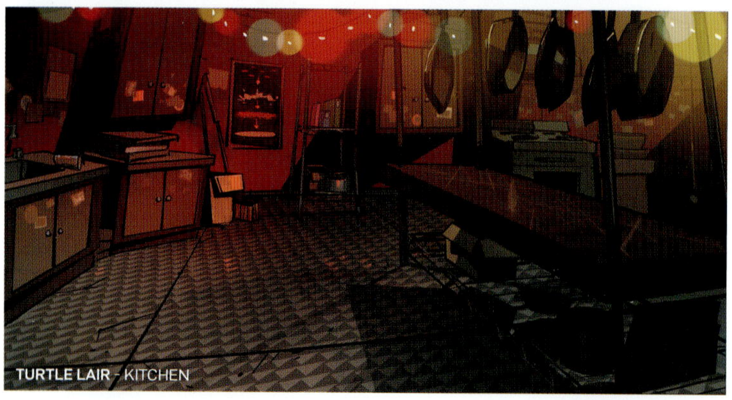

TURTLE LAIR - KITCHEN

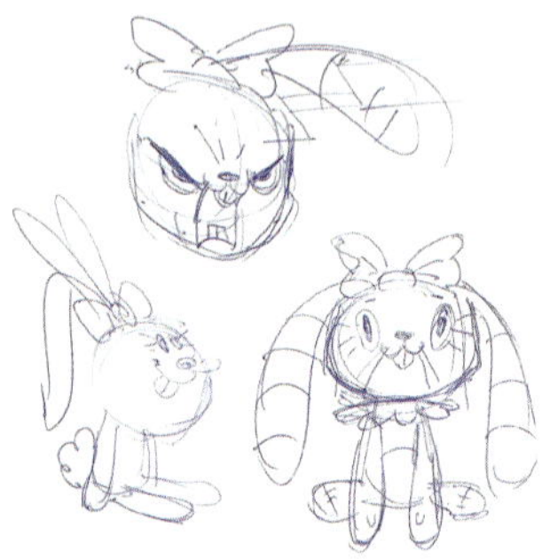

MRS. CUDDLES CONCEPT SKETCHES

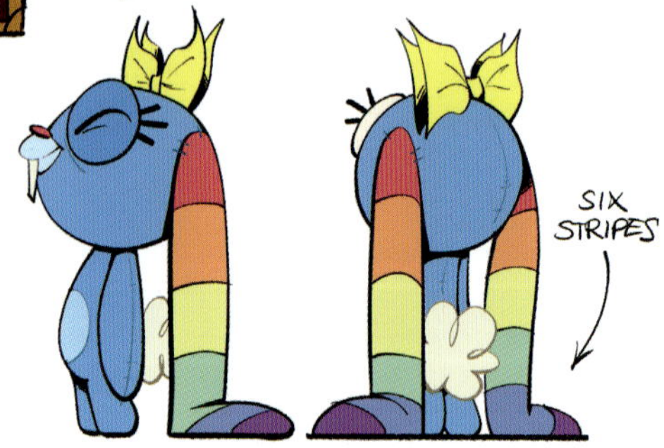

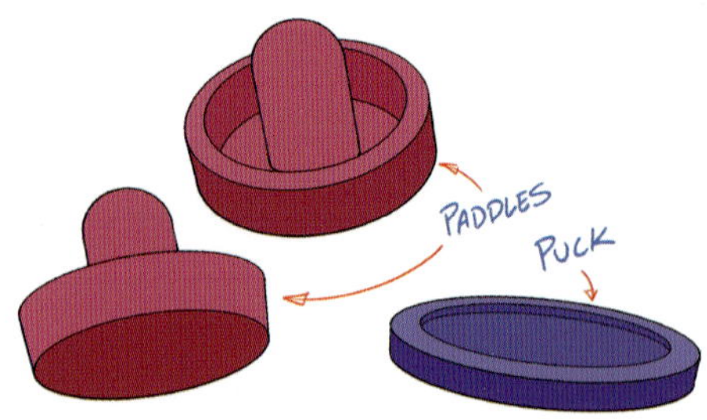

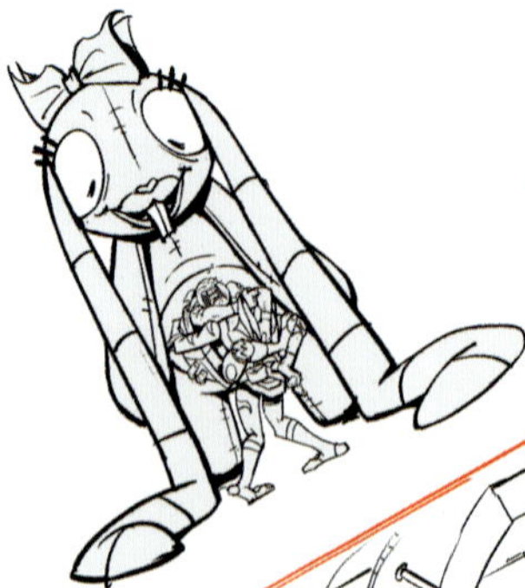

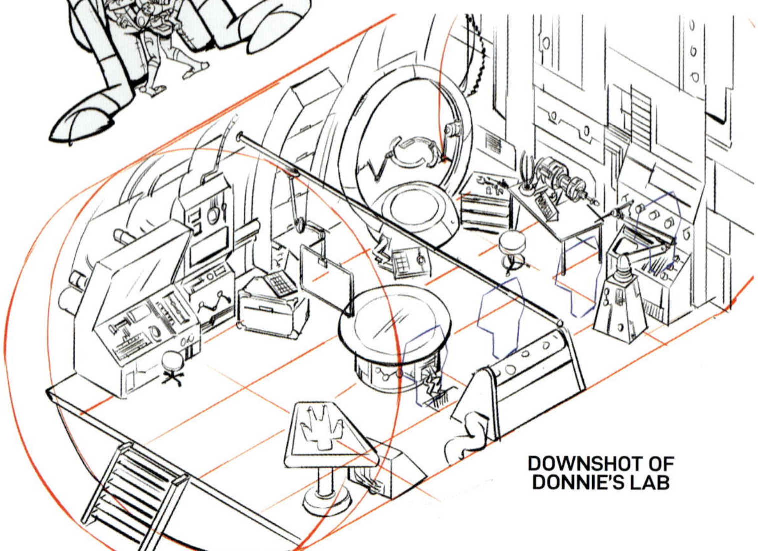

DOWNSHOT OF DONNIE'S LAB

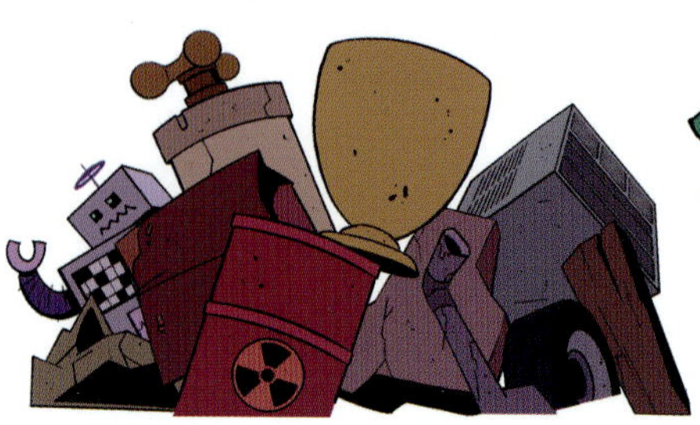

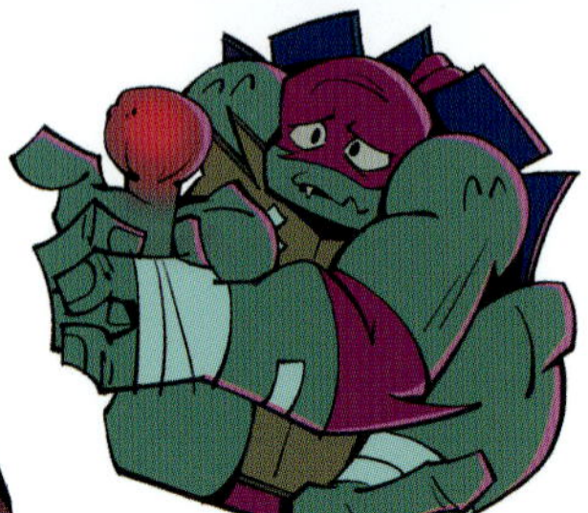

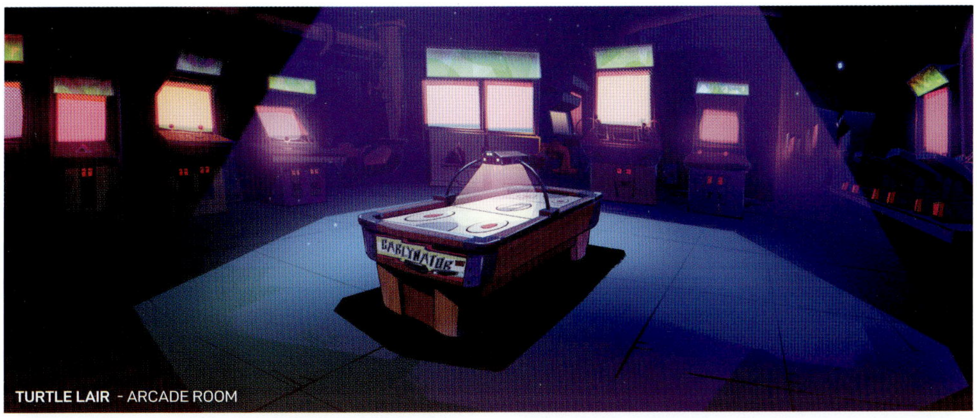

TURTLE LAIR - ARCADE ROOM

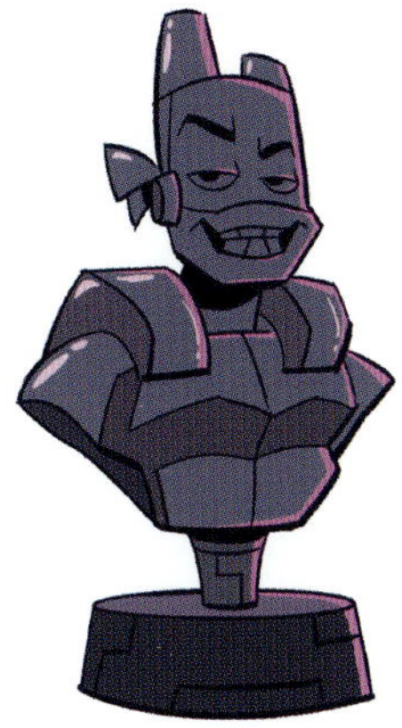

DONNIE'S TITANIUM BUST

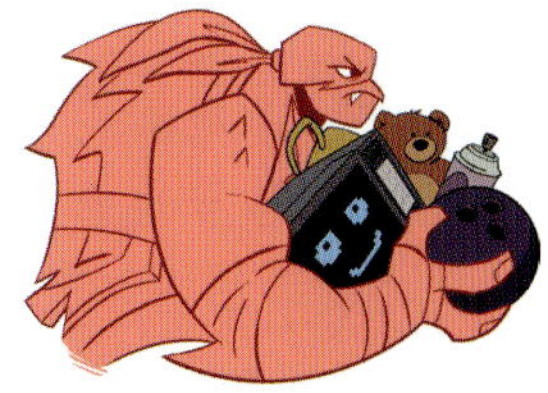

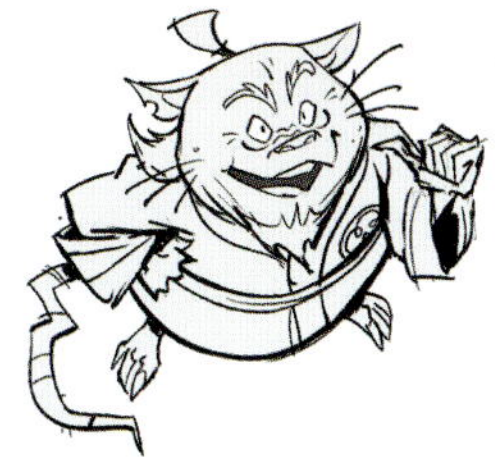

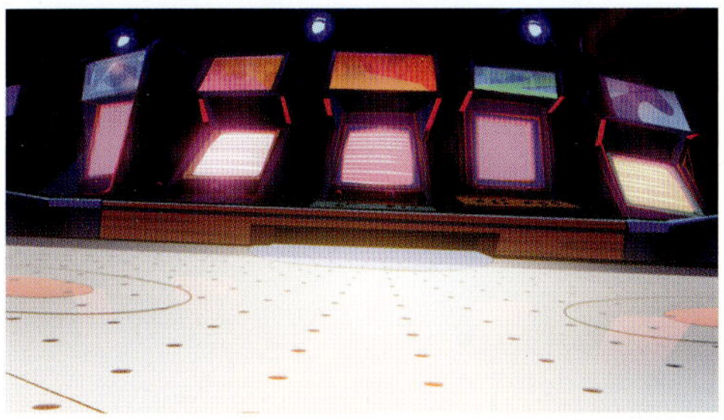

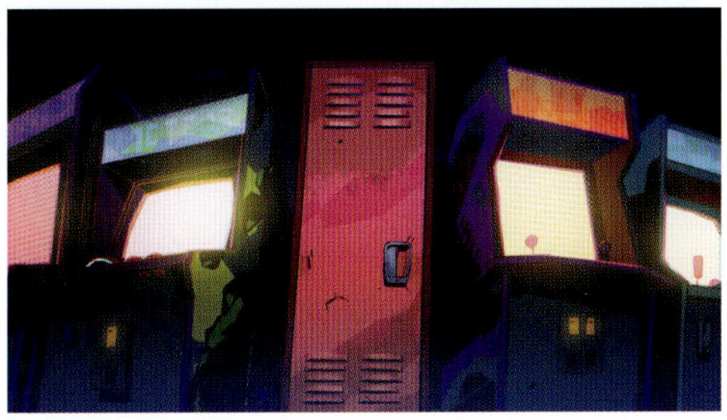

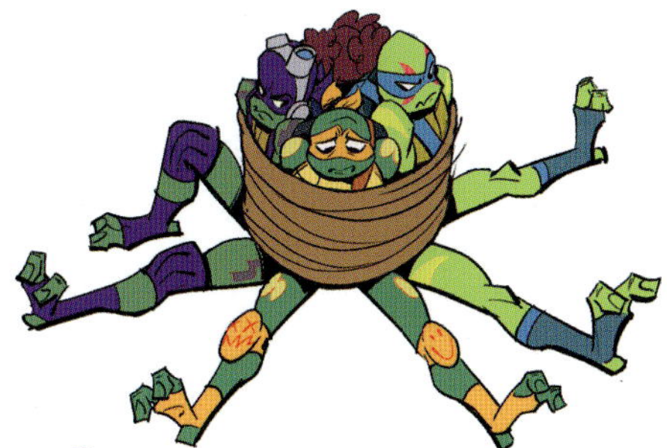

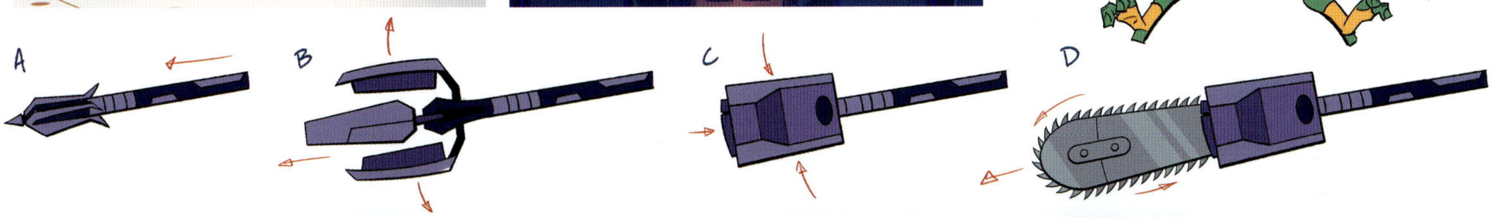

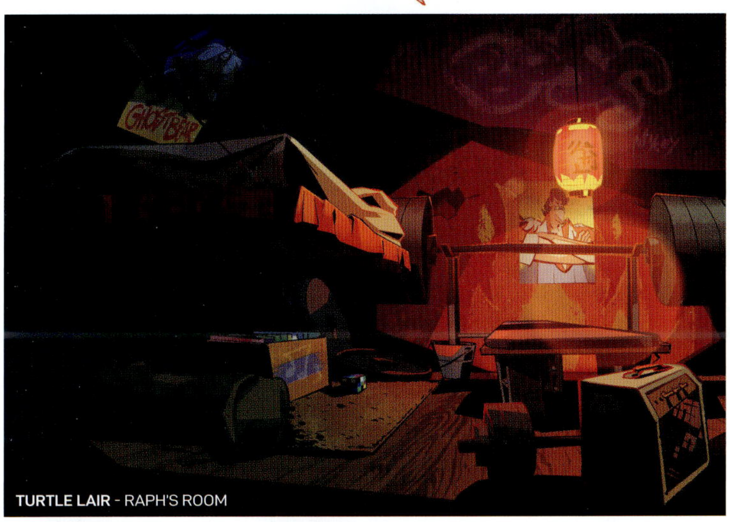

TURTLE LAIR - RAPH'S ROOM

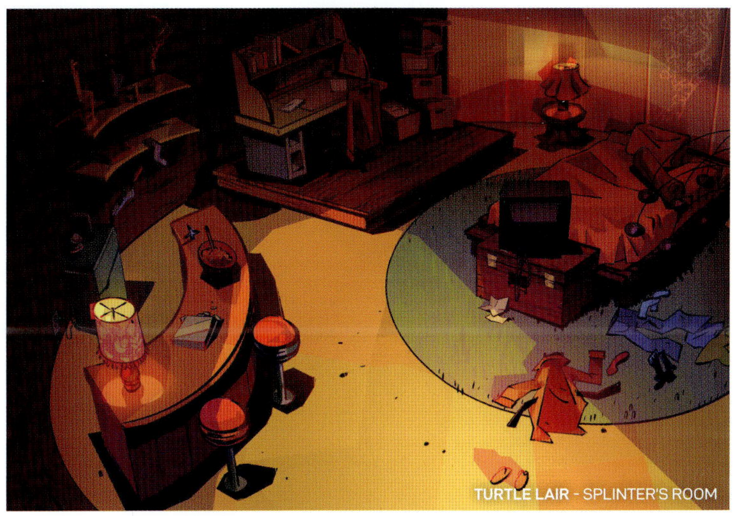

TURTLE LAIR - SPLINTER'S ROOM

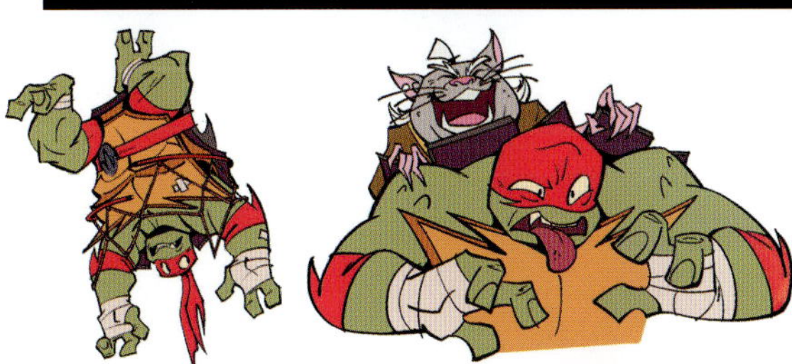

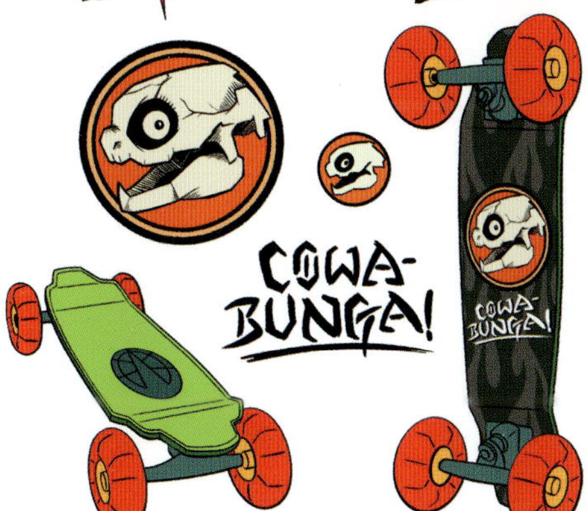

MIKEY'S SKATEBOARD

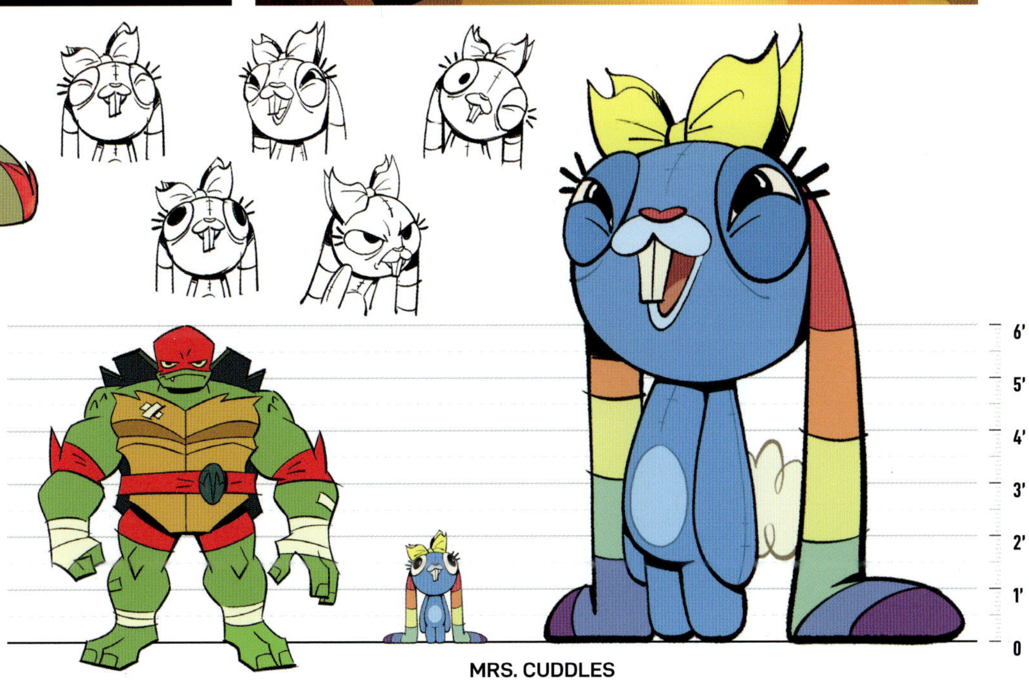

MRS. CUDDLES

STUCK ON YOU

ORIGINAL AIR DATE: NOVEMBER 10, 2018
PRODUCTION CODE: 020

WRITTEN BY **JESSE GORDON**
STORYBOARDS BY **JULIA BRAID**
DIRECTED BY **BRENDAN CLOGHER**

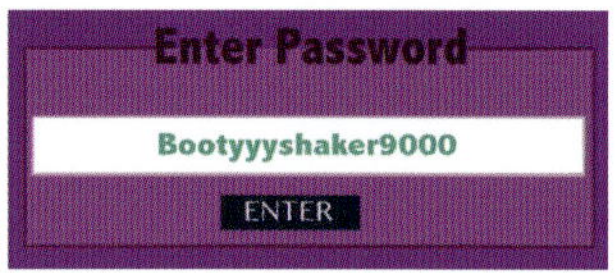

JESSE GORDON: This might be one of my better episodes—I'm pretty proud of this one. It's a very clean story showing how the Turtles work together. These are the Turtles before they're the lean, mean fighting machine we know they become, and it was always the point to show them in their early stages of failing and figuring things out. So Raph is the leader, which is new and different for our show, and this was a classic team-building exercise, like a three-legged race but done to the extreme by gluing them all into this giant ball. It was also done because production-wise, it should have been easier to animate the ball thing than four different characters, but I don't know, maybe it was harder.

This was one of those episodes that was also pushing forward the story with the gauntlet, which became important towards the end of the season, but at the same time sort of a self-contained story where the Turtles learn to work together to defeat the bad guys. It's funny to me that the characters start off hating being in the fab, but they realize that their crazy leader isn't so crazy.

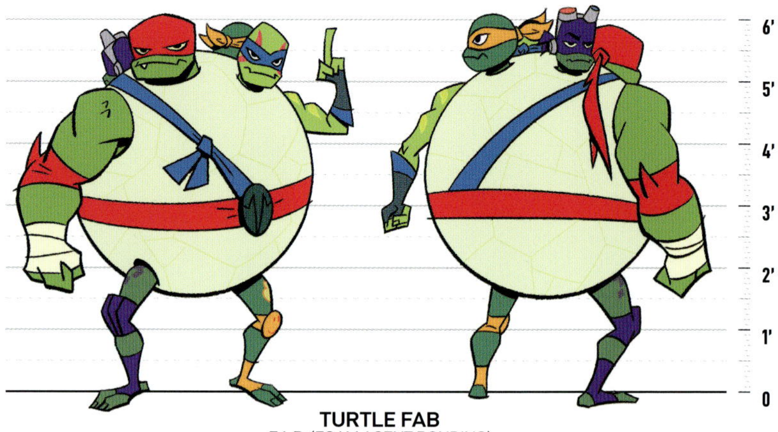

TURTLE FAB
F.A.B. (FOAM AGENT BONDING)

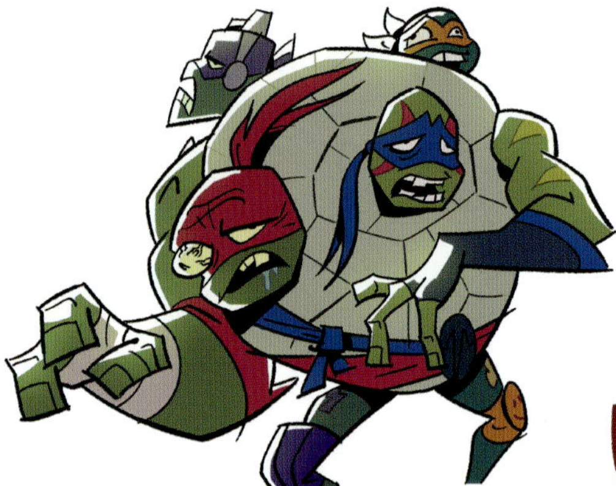

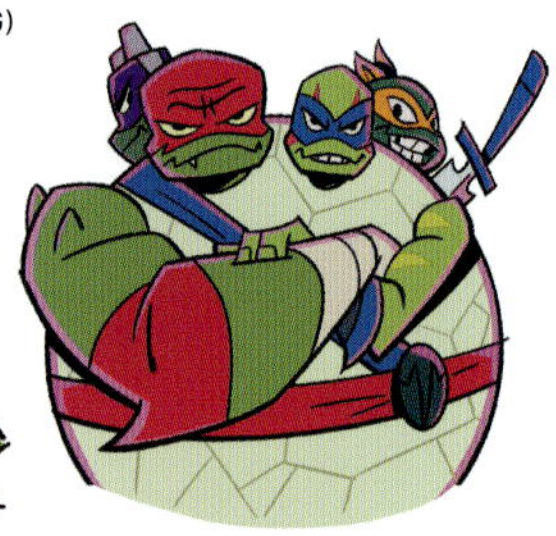

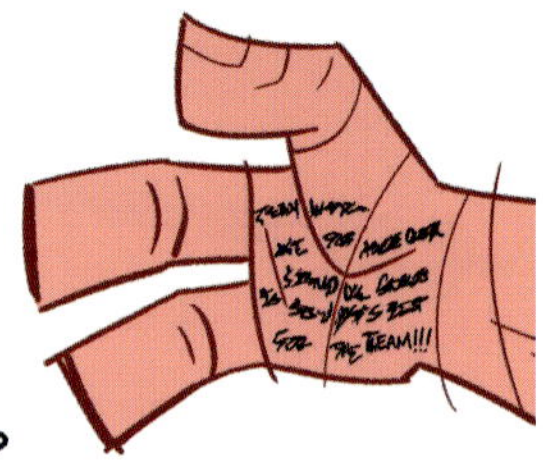

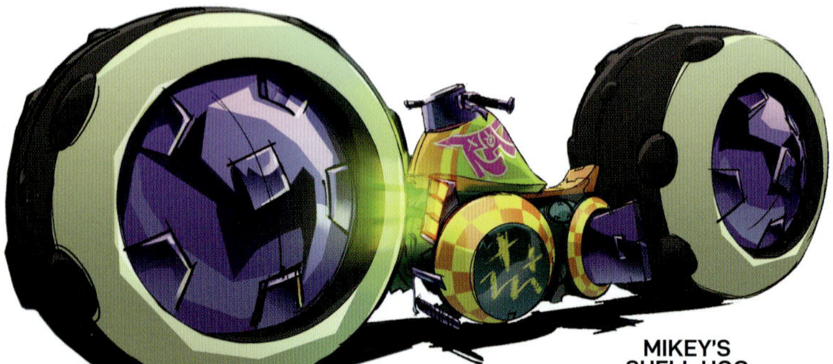

MIKEY'S SHELL HOG

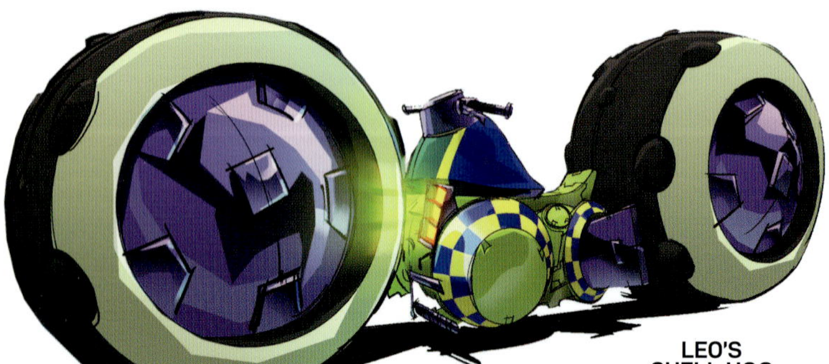

LEO'S SHELL HOG

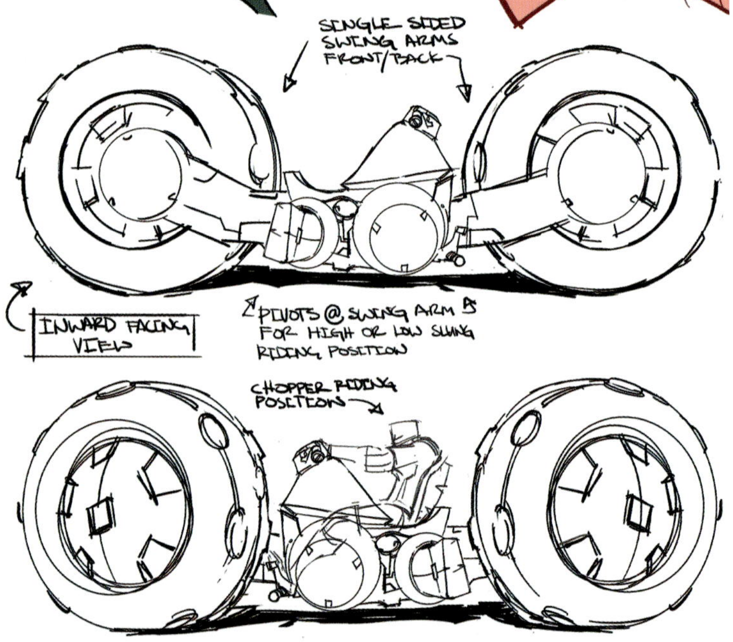

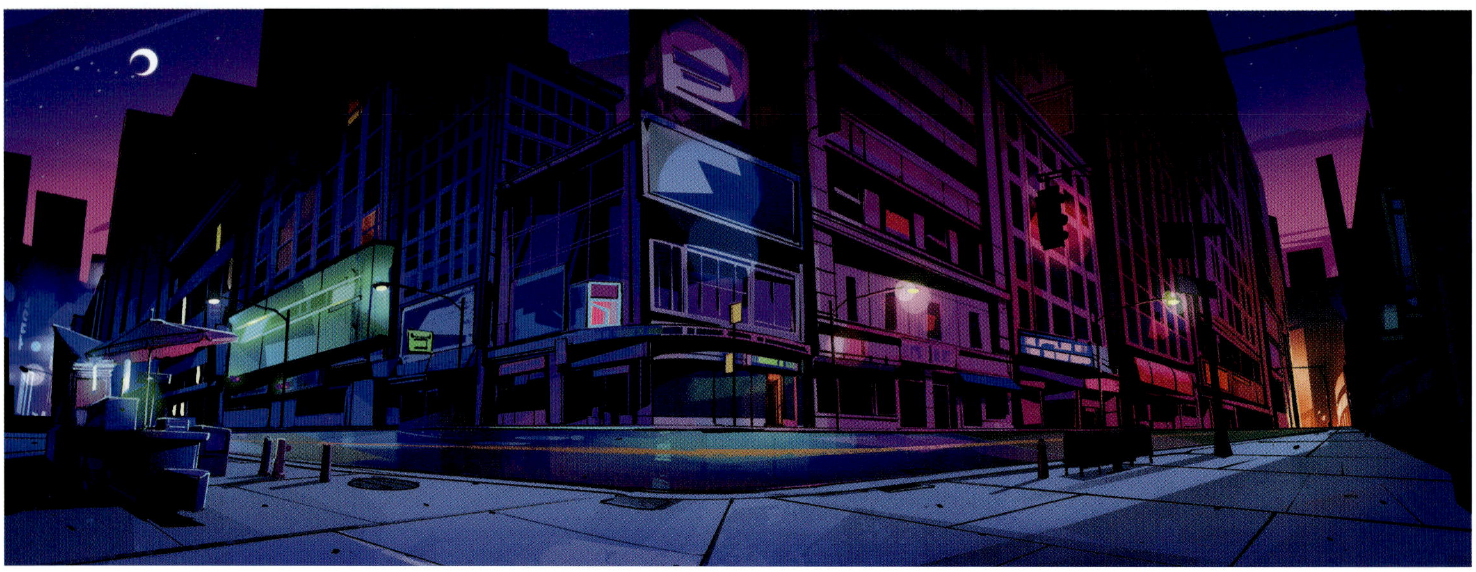

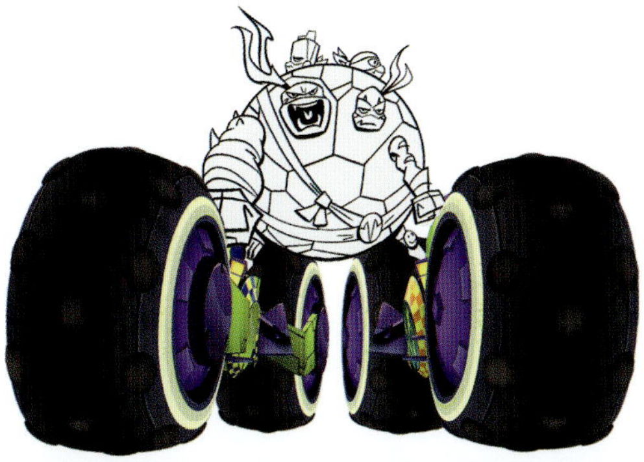

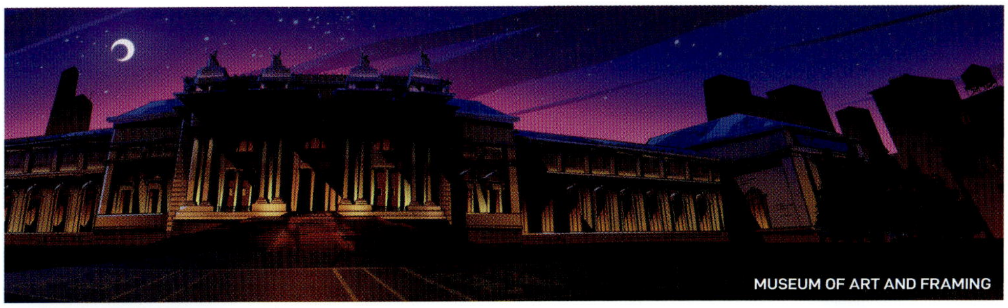

MUSEUM OF ART AND FRAMING

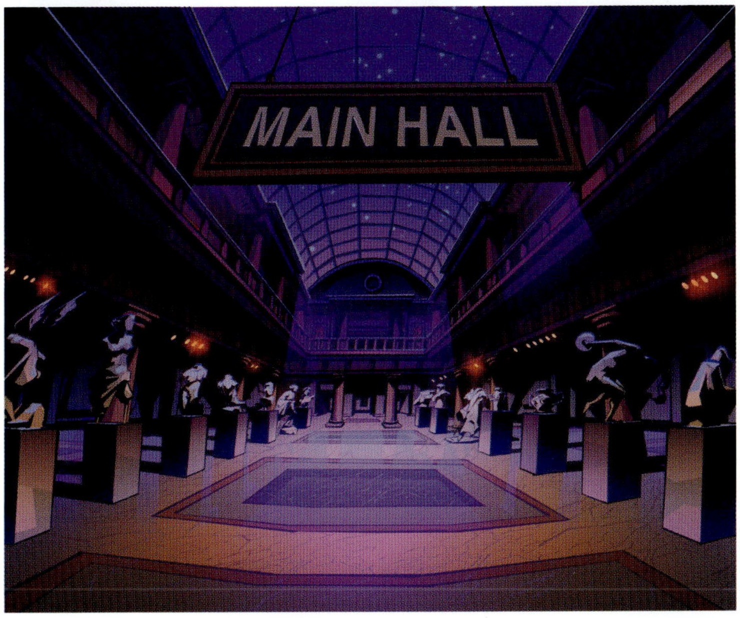

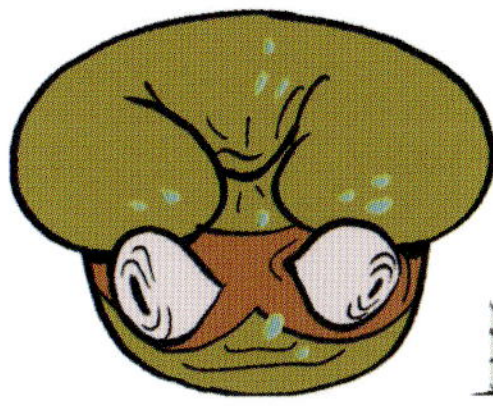

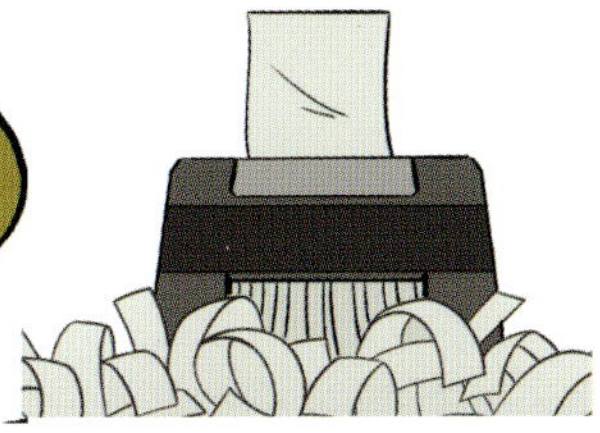

PAPER SHREDDER

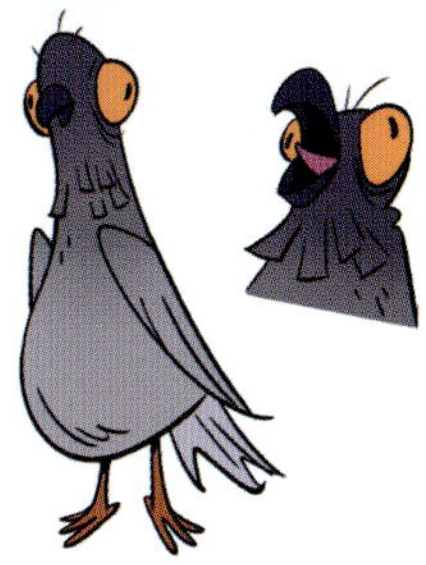

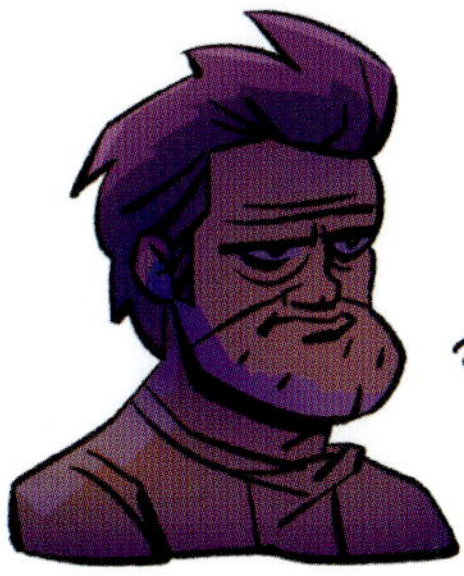

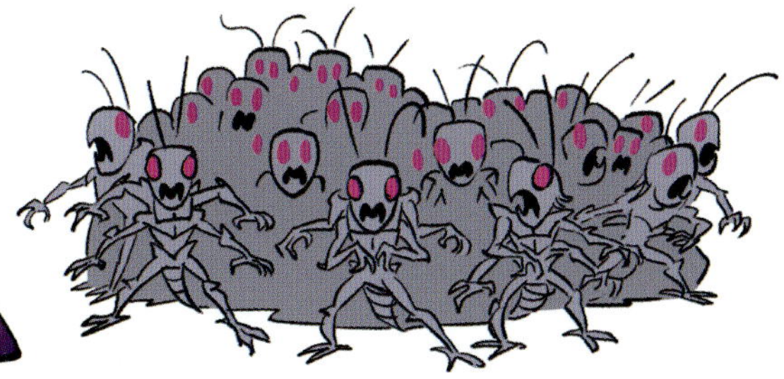

JESSE GORDON: The bust in the main hall the Turtles knock down is based on series co-creator and art director Andy Suriano.

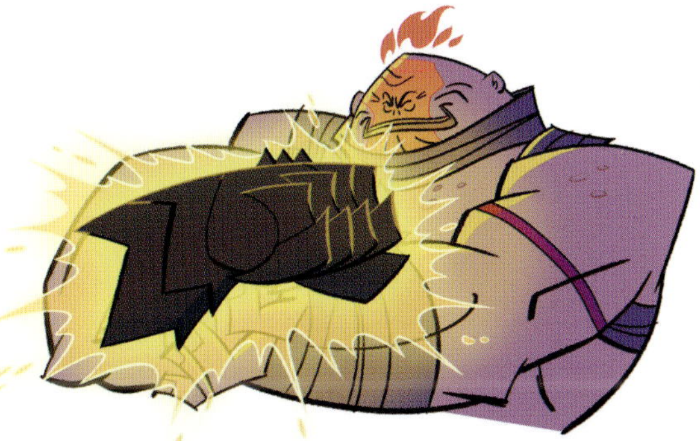

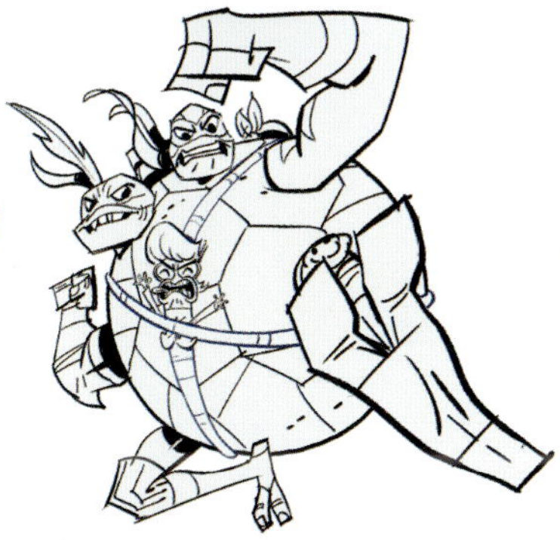

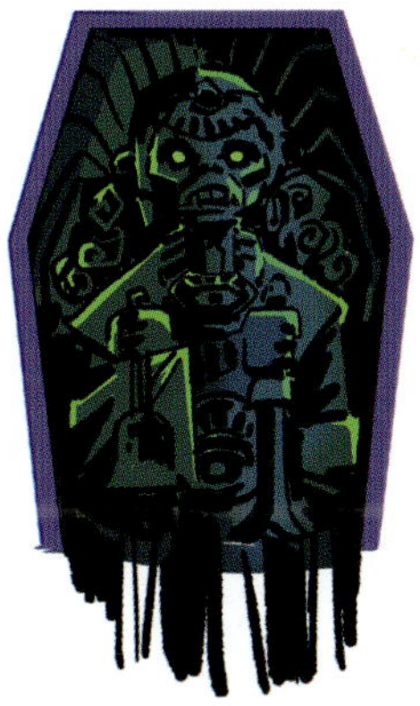

THE FIRST WITCH CASKET

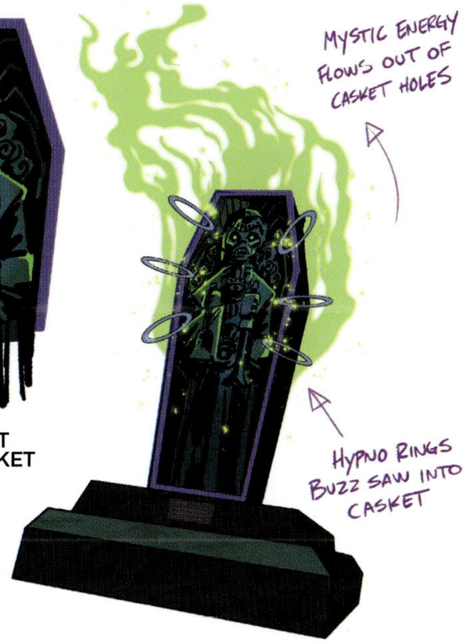

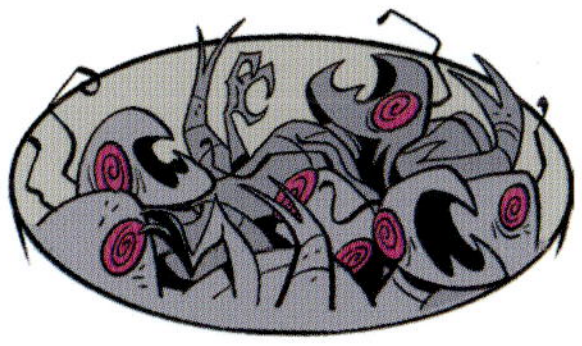

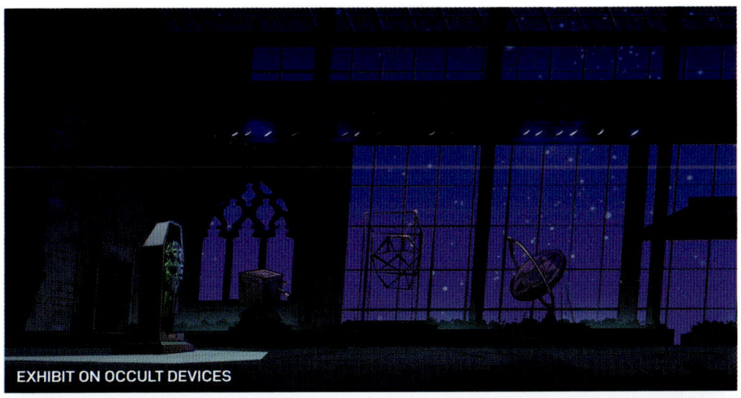

EXHIBIT ON OCCULT DEVICES

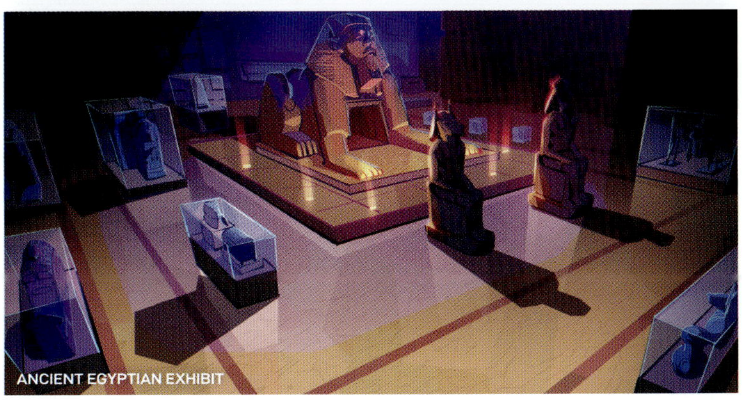

ANCIENT EGYPTIAN EXHIBIT

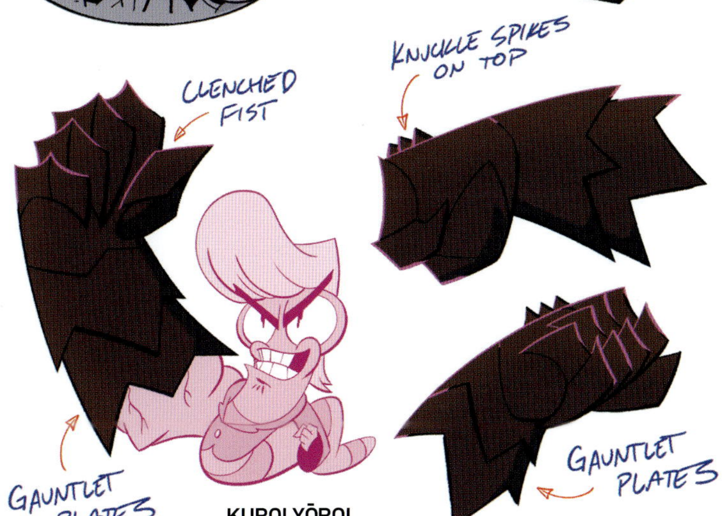

KUROI YŌROI
RIGHT GAUNTLET / "CHARLOTTE"

THE PURPLE JACKET

ORIGINAL AIR DATE: JANUARY 26, 2019
PRODUCTION CODE: 021

WRITTEN BY **RUSS CARNEY & RON CORCILLO**
STORYBOARDS BY **CHRISTOPHER LUC**
DIRECTED BY **ABE AUDISH**

RON CORCILLO: This was a fun episode to write because we got to pair April and Donnie together and establish a strong platonic friendship. And we got to explore Donnie's flaws in a classic tale about a good purple kid who falls in with the wrong purple crowd. Shakespeare wrote that first, no?

RUSS CARNEY: We had previously worked with Eugene Byrd on *LEGO Star Wars: The Freemaker Adventures* (2016), so we knew he'd be great as Jase, and we wanted to cast Tania Gunadi because she has amazing energy, she conveys toughness, and she has a great Indonesian accent!

RON CORCILLO: At the conclusion of our first season, each member of the crew was given an amazing purple satin replica of the jackets worn in the series. You'd better grab some toast, friends, because you are all jelly! We all wore them to the local pizza joint, and we looked like Burbank's dorkiest street gang.

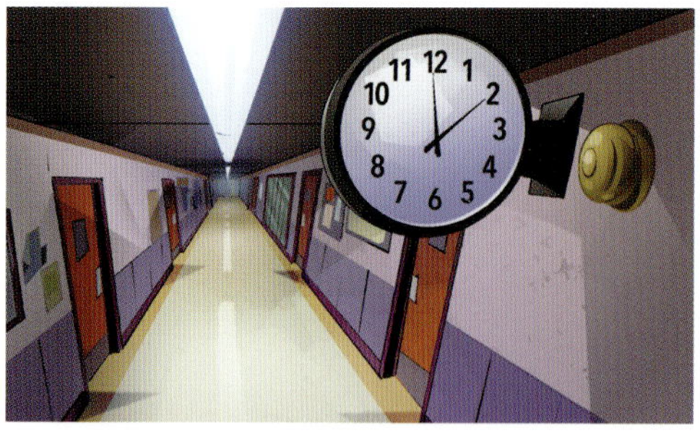

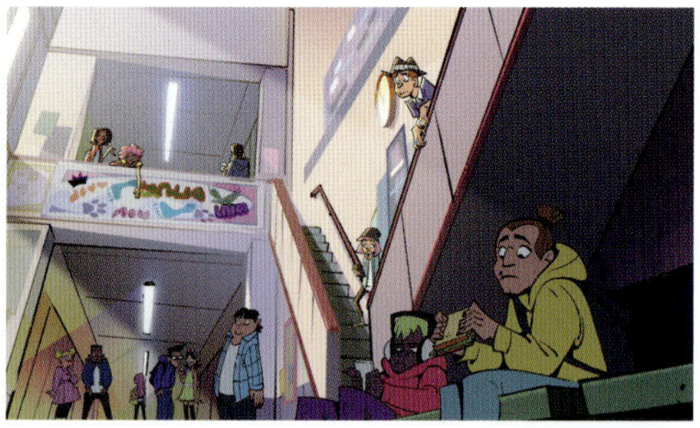

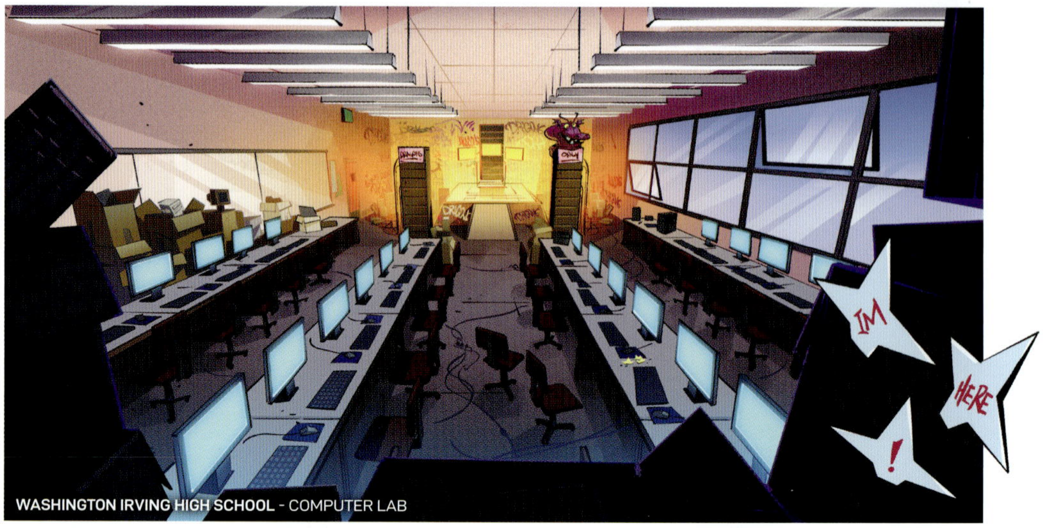

WASHINGTON IRVING HIGH SCHOOL - COMPUTER LAB

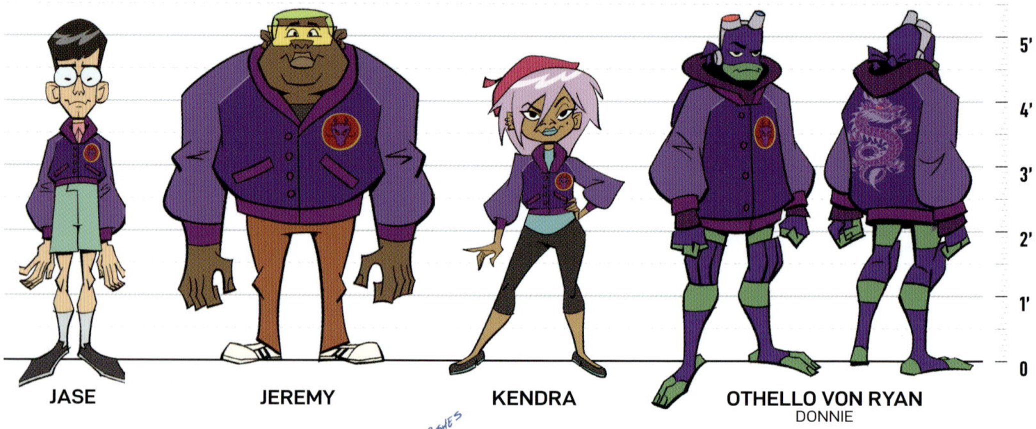

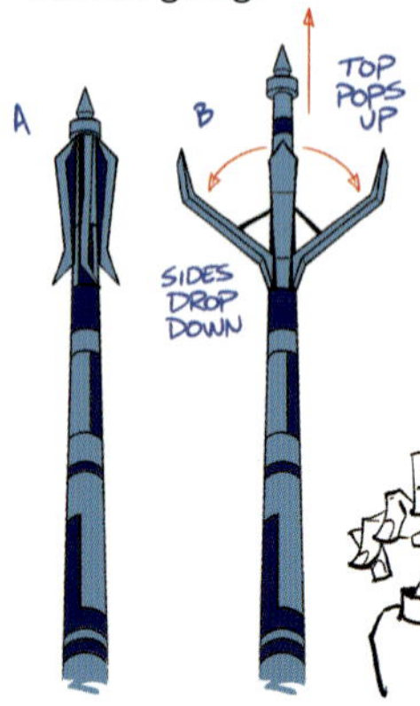

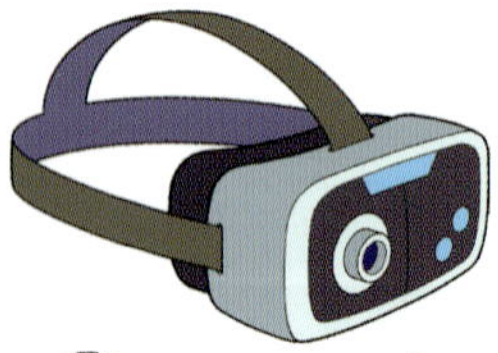

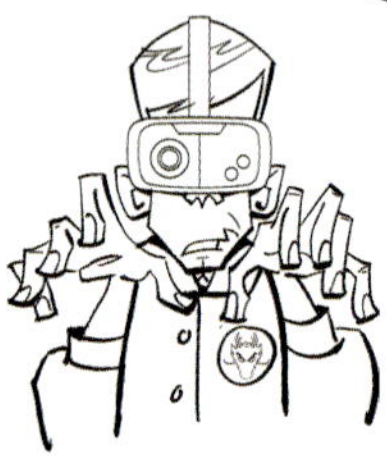

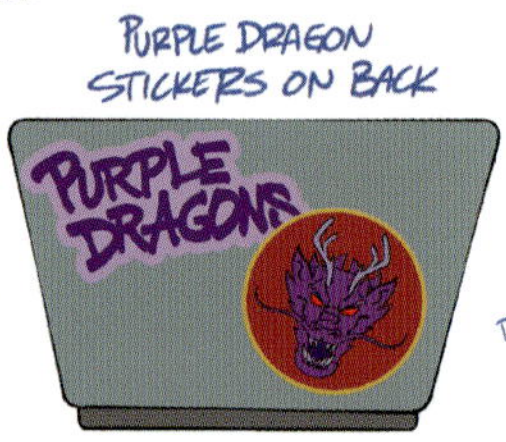

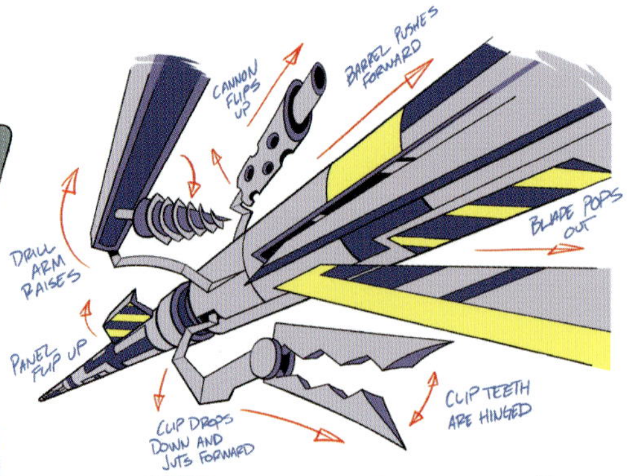

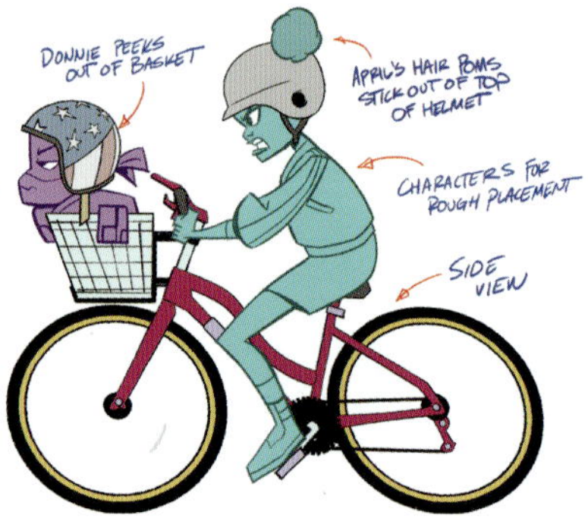

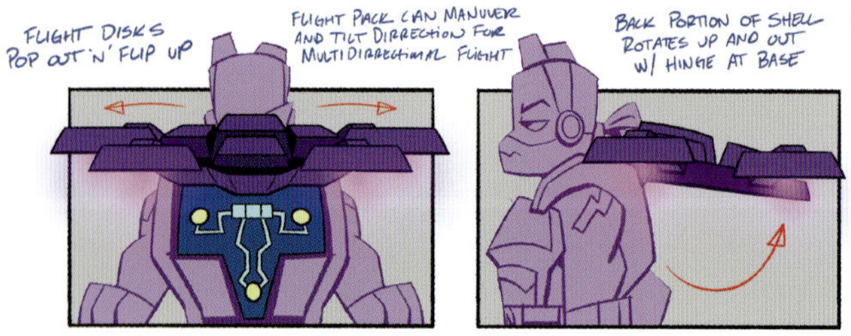

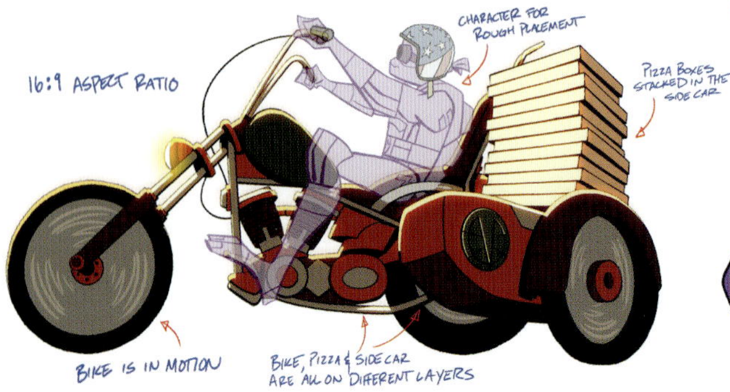

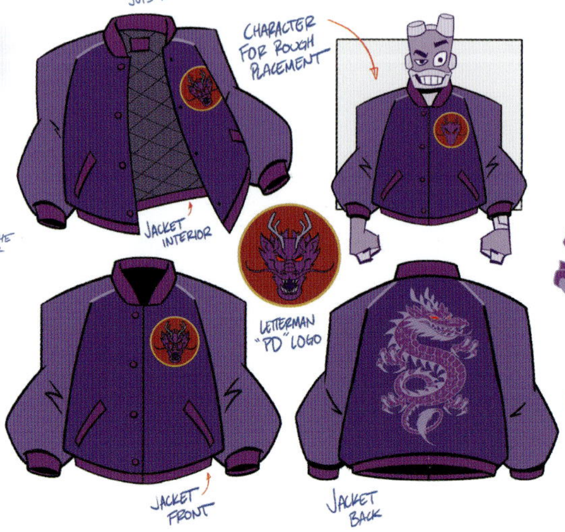

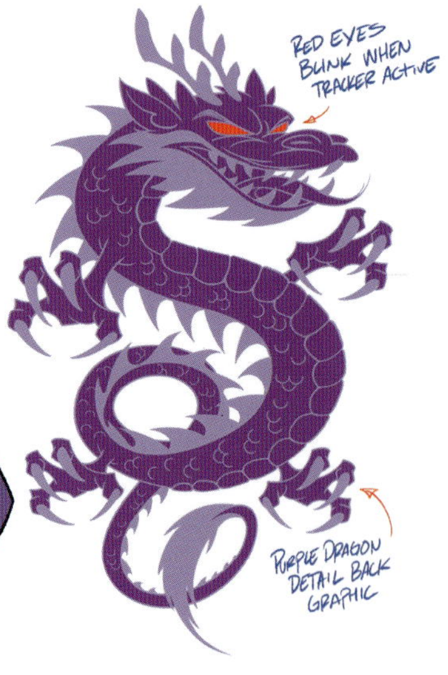

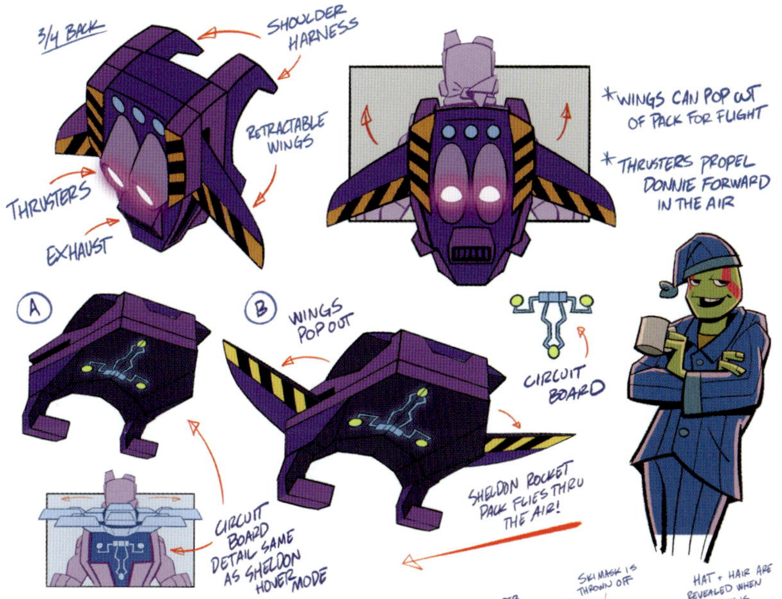

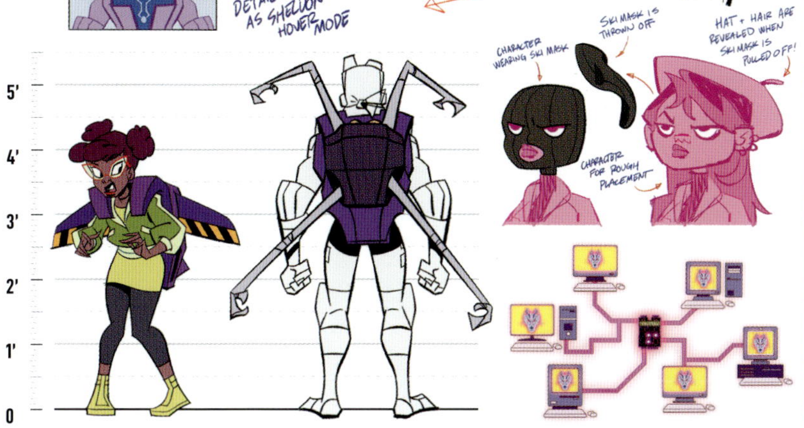

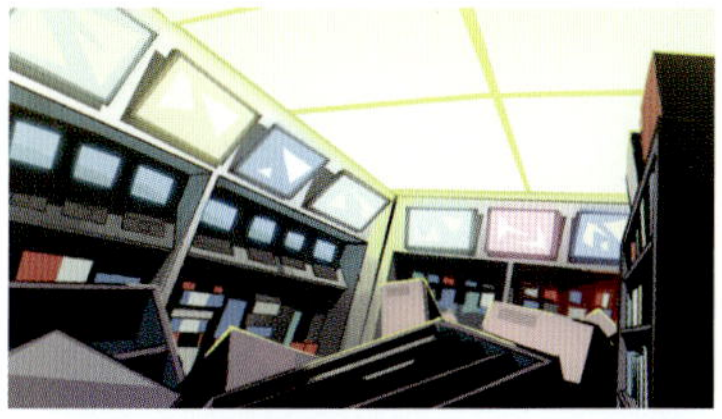

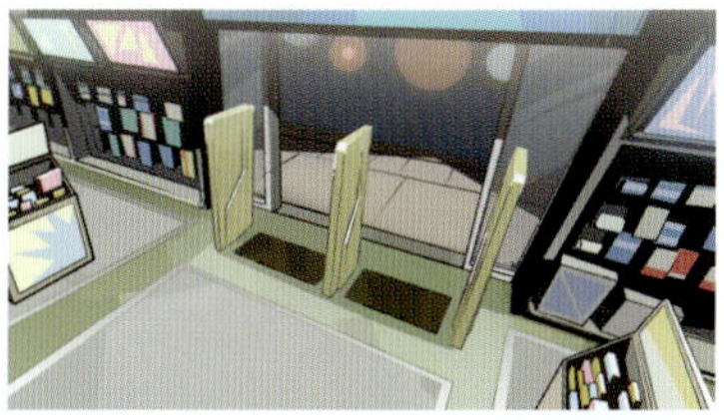

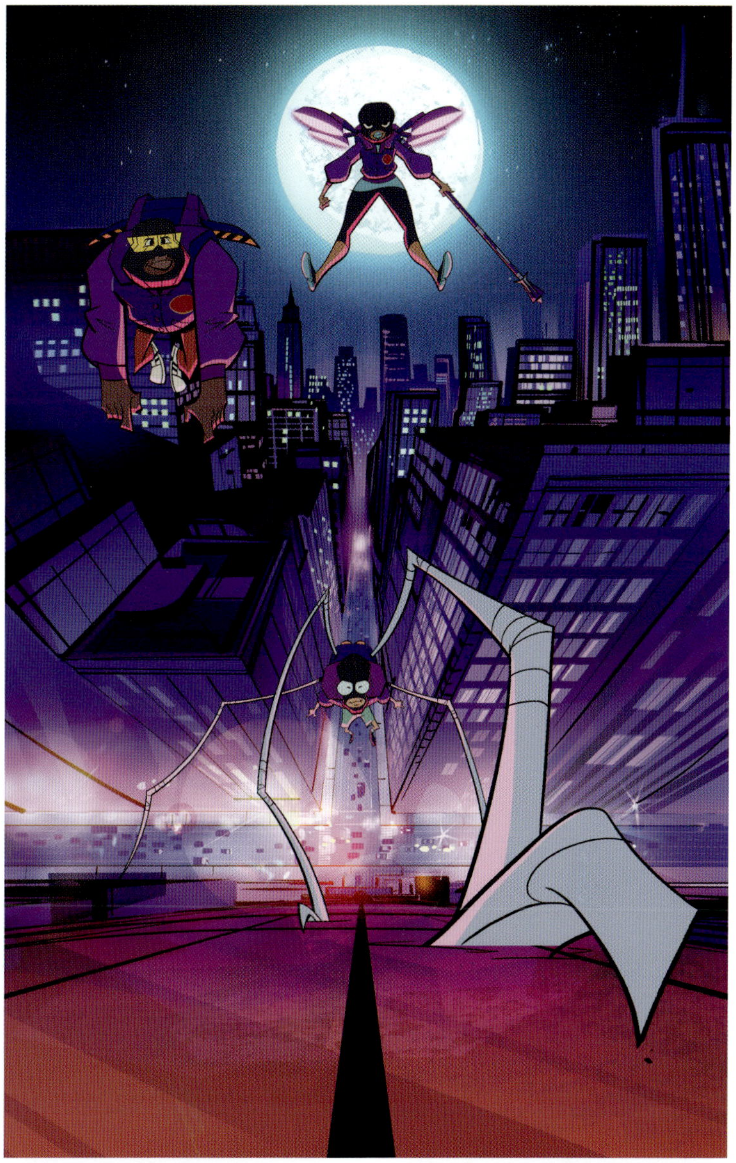

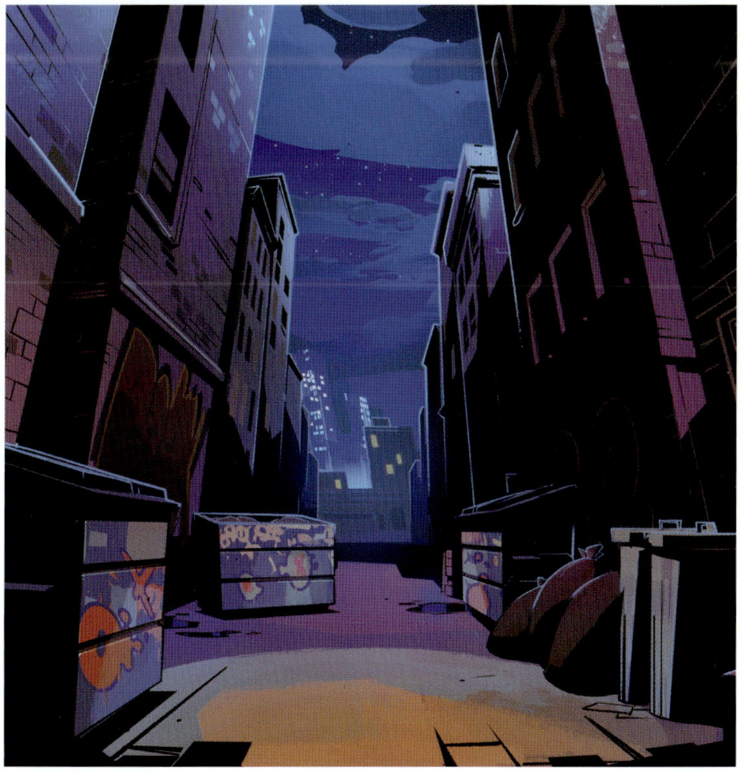

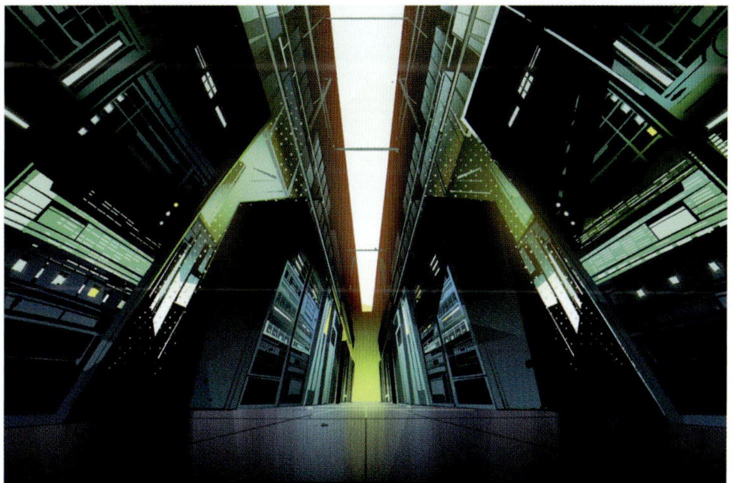

NAKAMURA CORPORATION - MAINFRAME

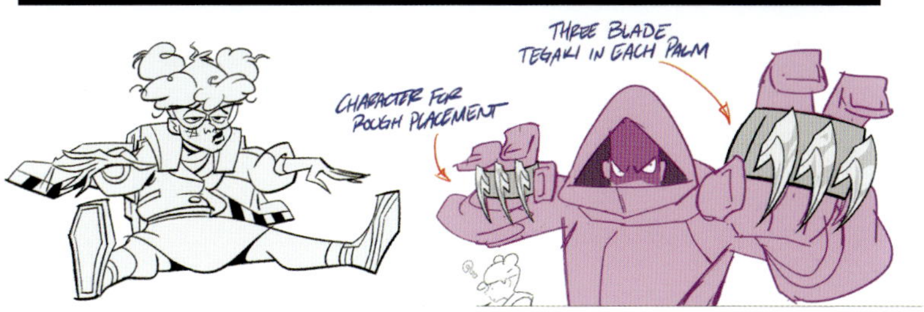

RUSS CARNEY: Donnie's code name, Othello Von Ryan, was a reference to an obscure, bizarre Elizabeth Taylor White Diamonds perfume commercial from the 1990s, which includes the line *"Not so fast, Von Ryan."* Google it sometime and see if it makes any sense to you whatsoever.

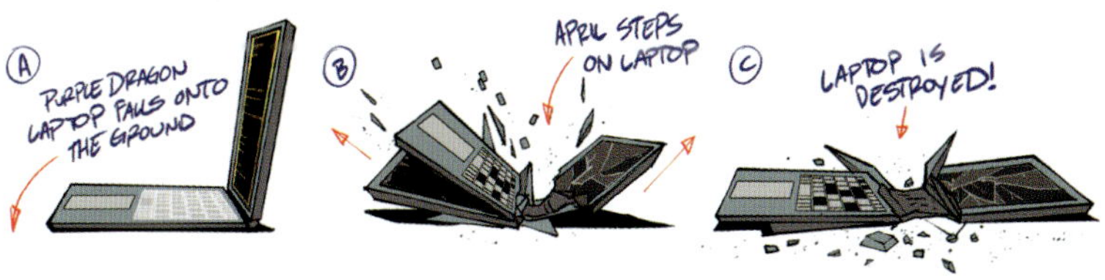

PIZZA PIT

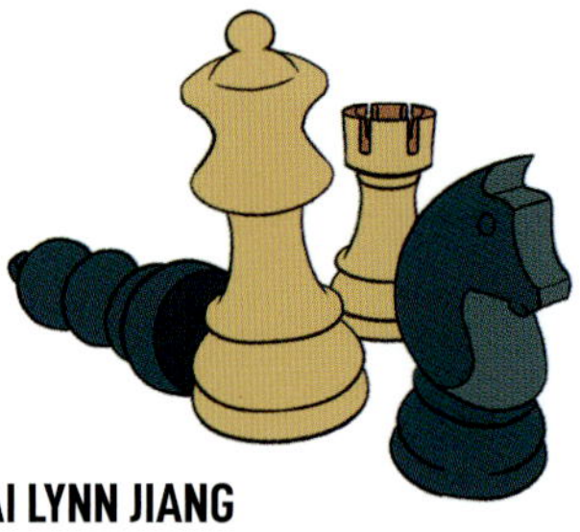

ORIGINAL AIR DATE: FEBRUARY 2, 2019
PRODUCTION CODE: 022

WRITTEN BY **BRIAN POSEHN**
STORYBOARDS BY **GLADYFAITH ABCEDE, KAI LYNN JIANG**
DIRECTED BY **SEBASTIAN MONTES**

SEBASTIAN MONTES: This was the "ugly duckling" episode but I think it came out to be a wonderfully bizarre little goose of a show.

If I remember correctly, Raph's internal dialogue was not in the original script. But it made its way in and now seems such a natural part of the episode. Credit goes to storyboard artists Gladyfaith Abcede and Kai Lynn Jiang for hitting the character beats perfectly to really bring out the comedy.

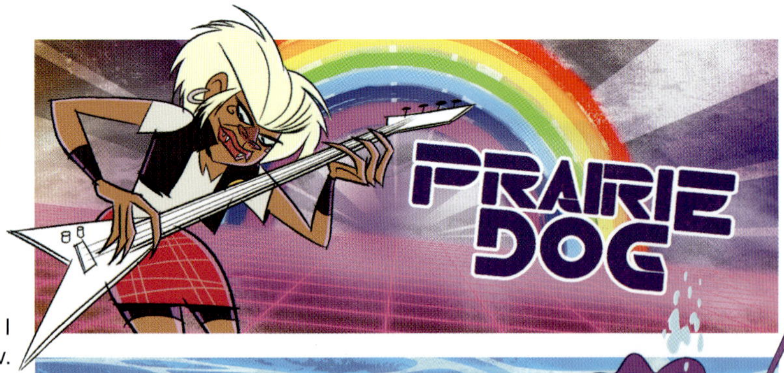

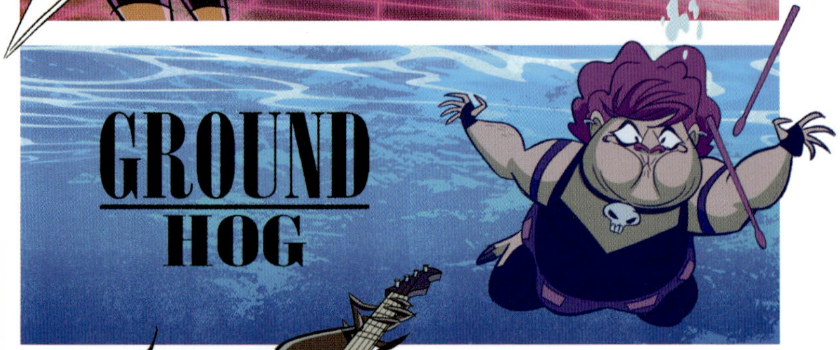

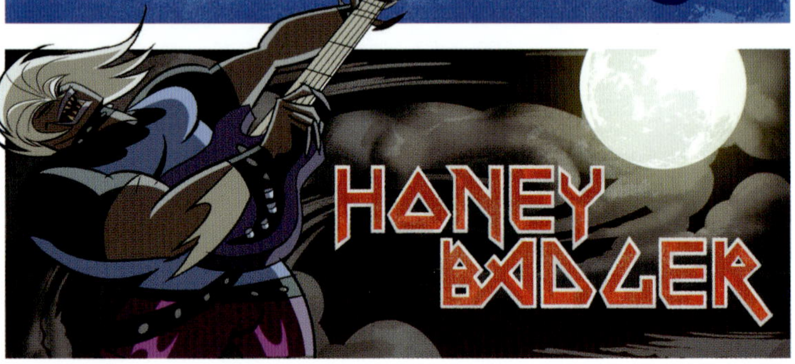

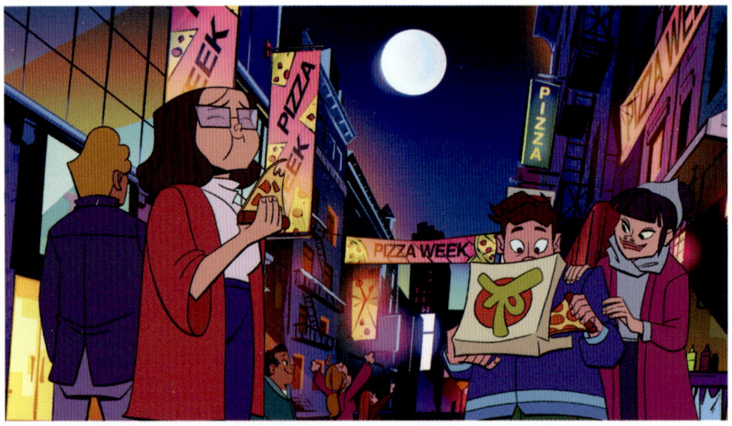

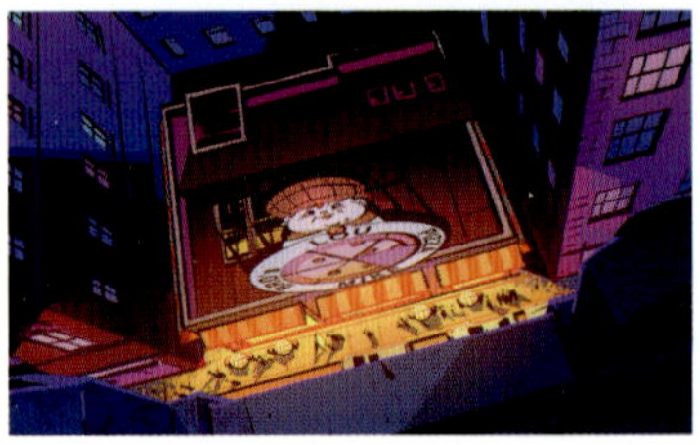

LOU MIKE-TONEY'S PIZZA

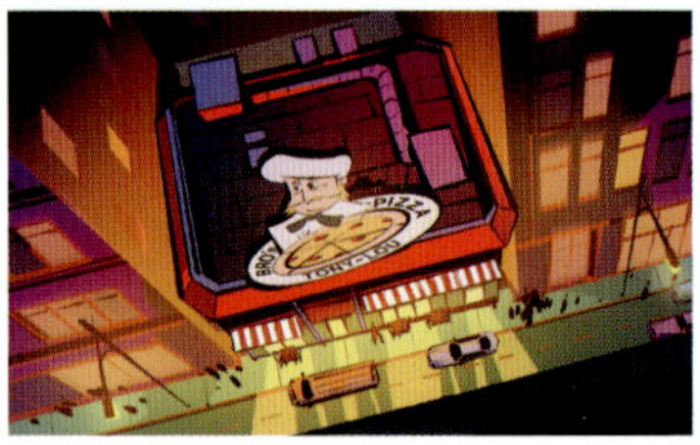

TONY LOU'S PIZZA

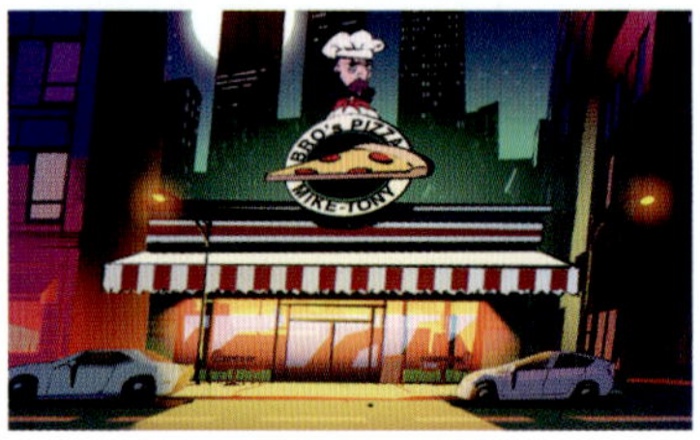

MIKE-TONY'S FAVORITE LOU PIZZA

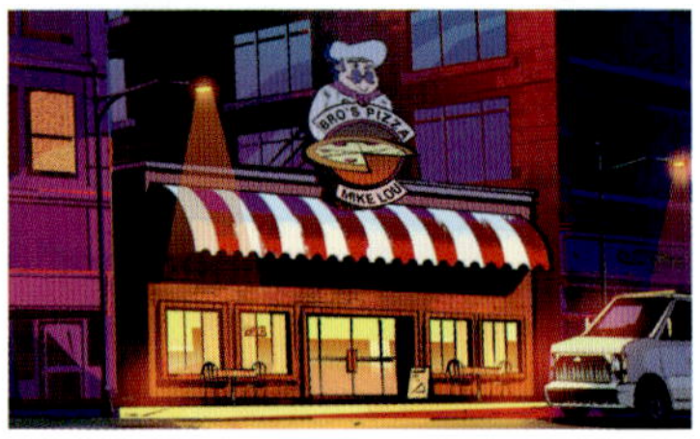

MIKE AND LOU: THE BROTHERS TONY PIZZA

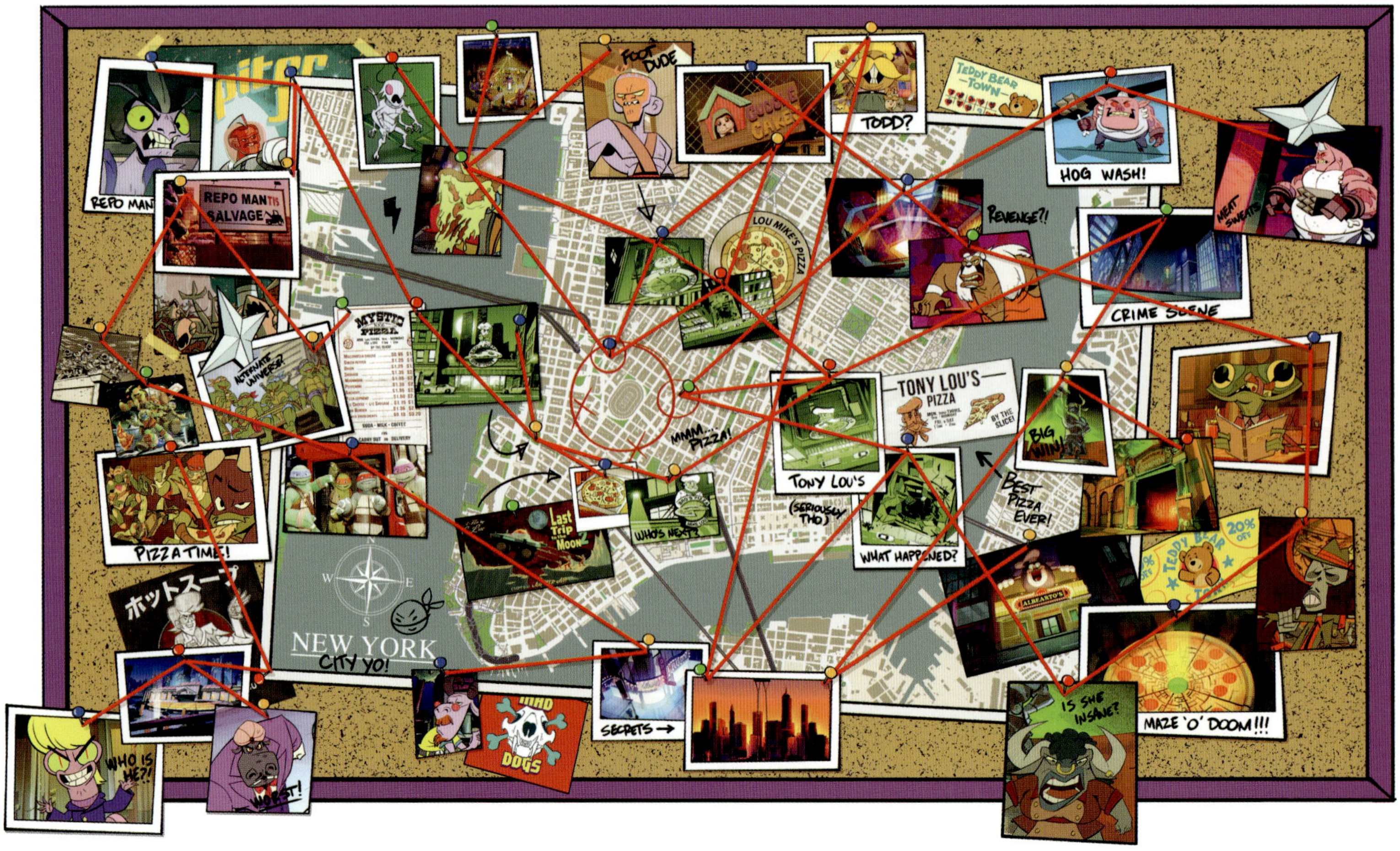

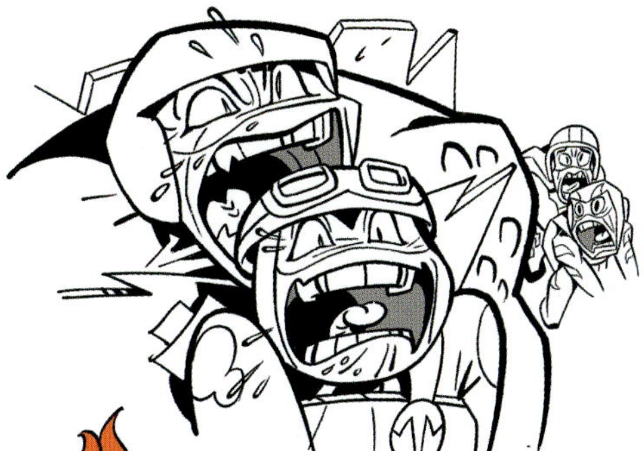

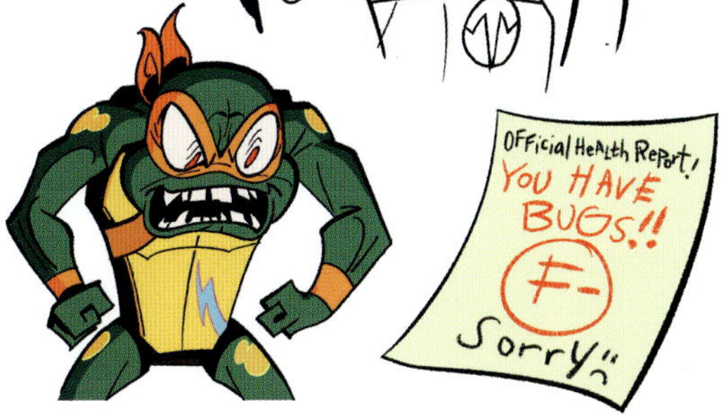

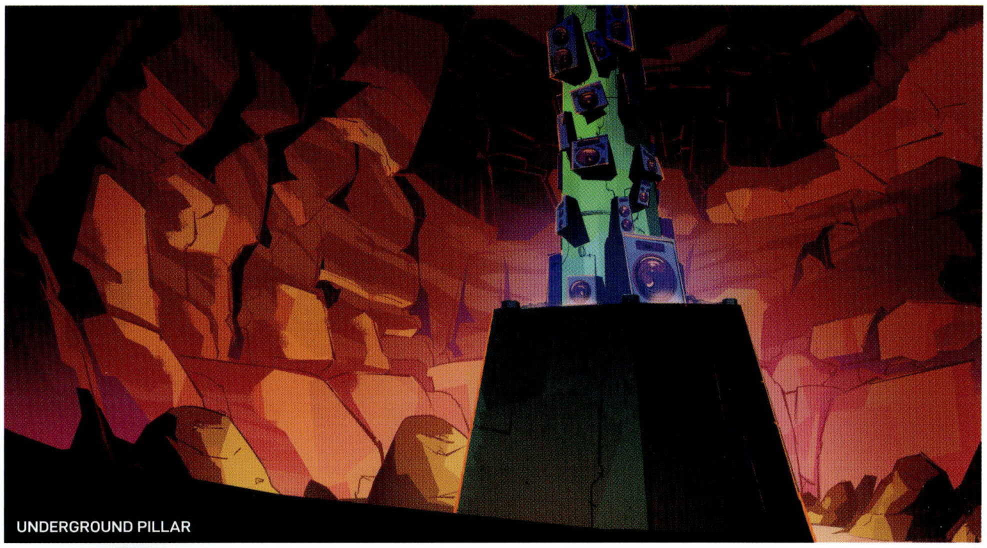
UNDERGROUND PILLAR

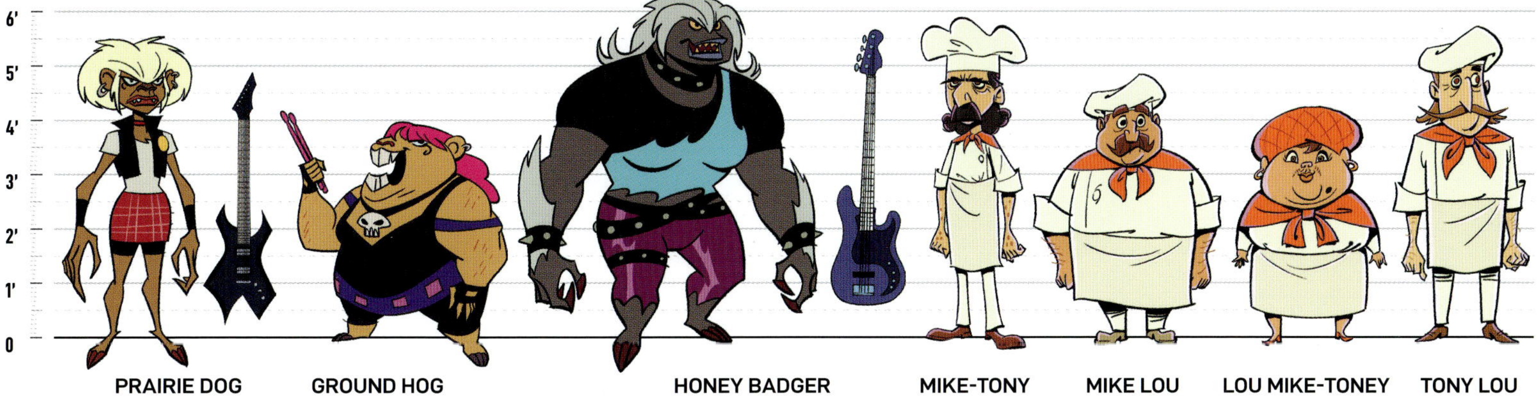

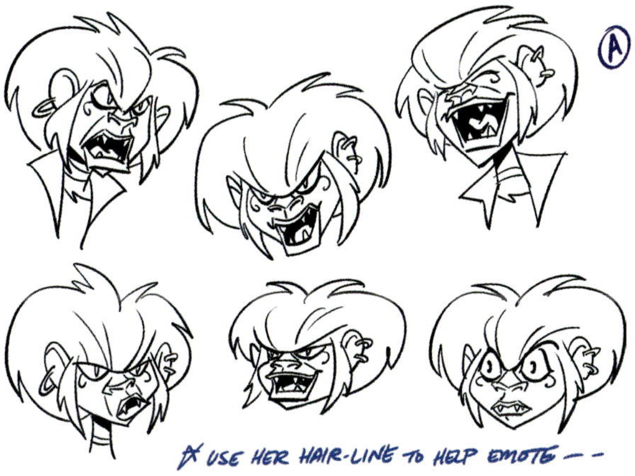

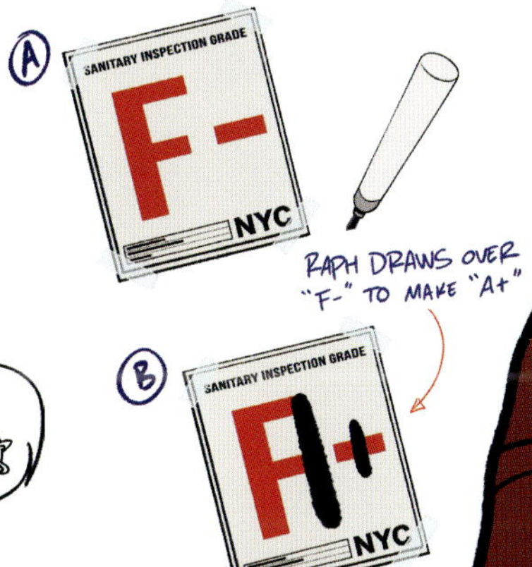

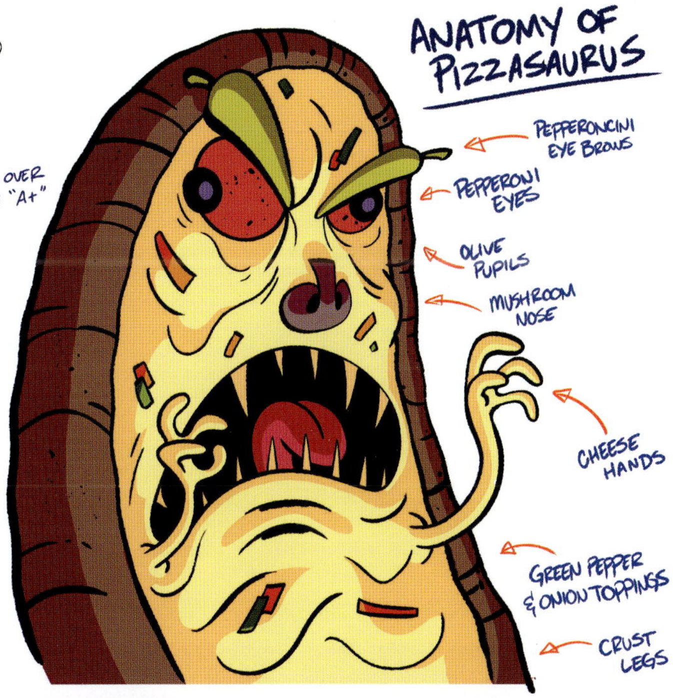

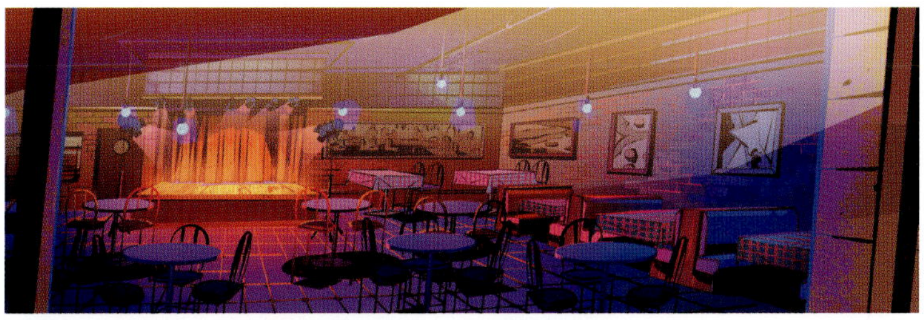

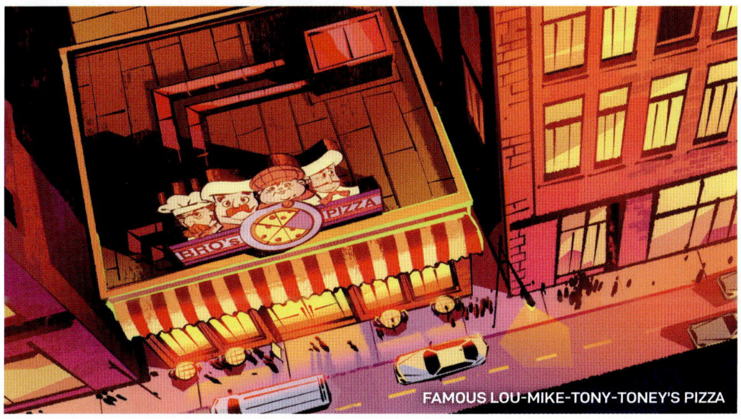
FAMOUS LOU-MIKE-TONY-TONEY'S PIZZA

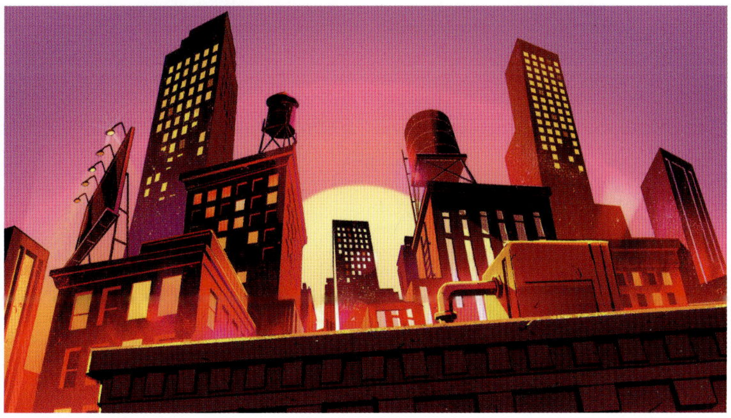

SMART LAIR

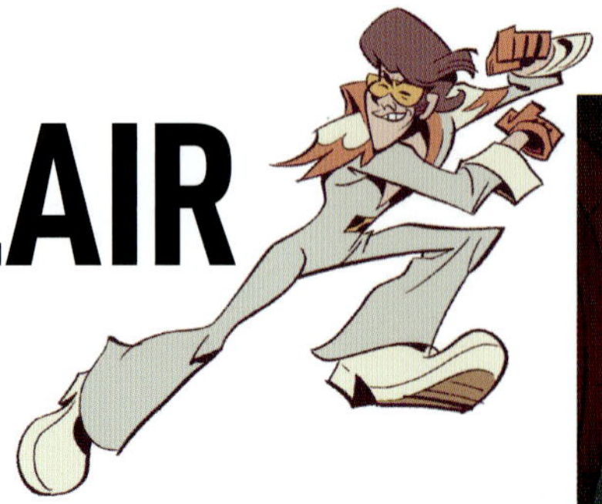

ORIGINAL AIR DATE: FEBRUARY 9, 2019
PRODUCTION CODE: 023

WRITTEN BY **IAN BUSCH**
STORYBOARDS BY **CHRISTINE LIU**
DIRECTED BY **BRENDAN CLOGHER**

IAN BUSCH: Christine and Brendan did such an amazing job of upping the tension at the end by creating the much larger Roomba as the final obstacle to overcome. Originally it was a lot of tinier Roombas, and the idea to go super big at the end gave the boys a more fearsome foe to battle.

The TMNT franchise is always paying tribute to what has come before it, honoring the legacy and bringing back familiar voices. The voice of S.H.E.L.L.D.O.N. was Greg Cipes, who many of you might know was also the voice of Michelangelo from the 2012 *TMNT* series. He would reprise his role of S.H.E.L.L.D.O.N. throughout the series from version 1.0 to Metalhead in the finale.

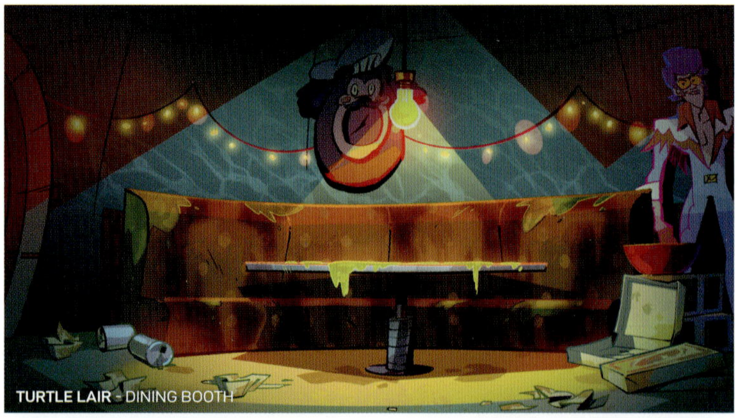

TURTLE LAIR - DINING BOOTH

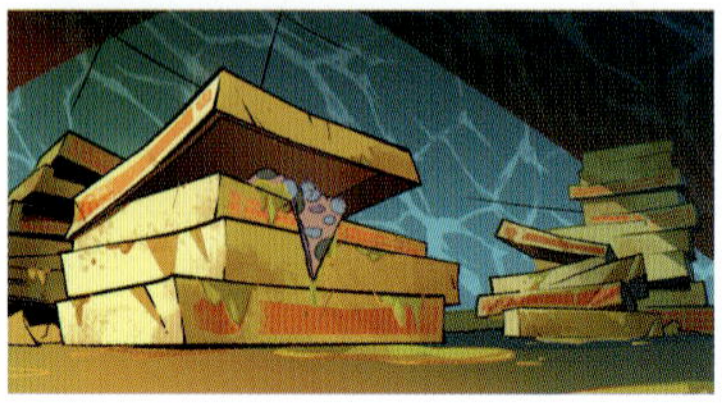

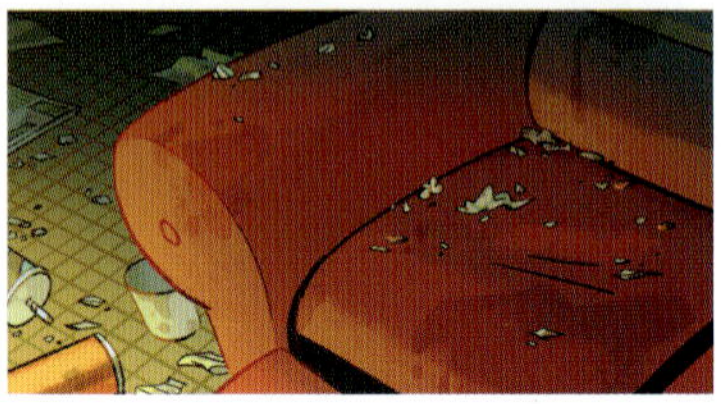

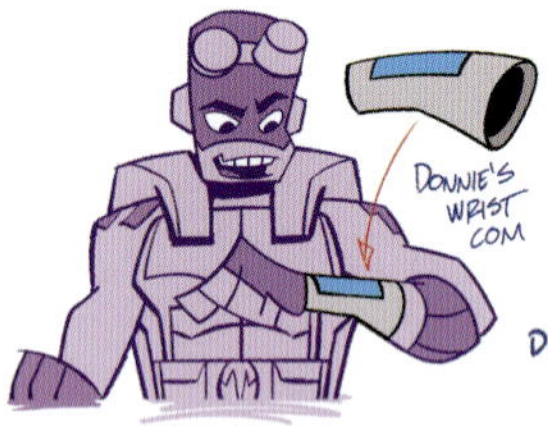

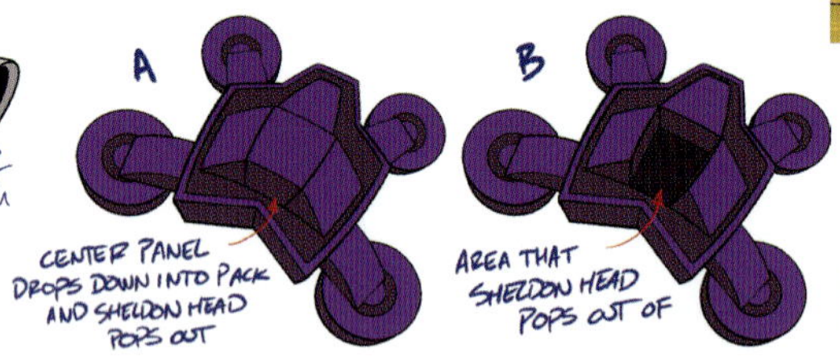

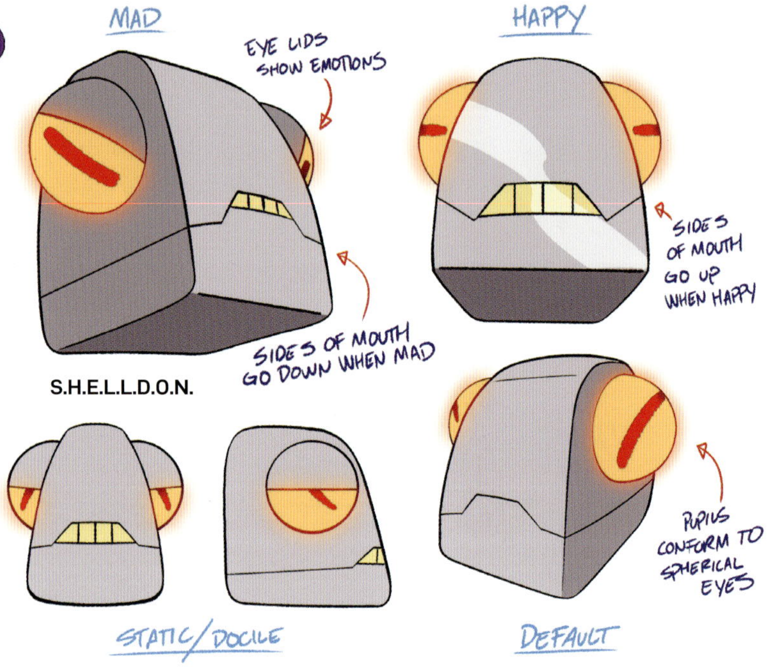

S.H.E.L.L.D.O.N.

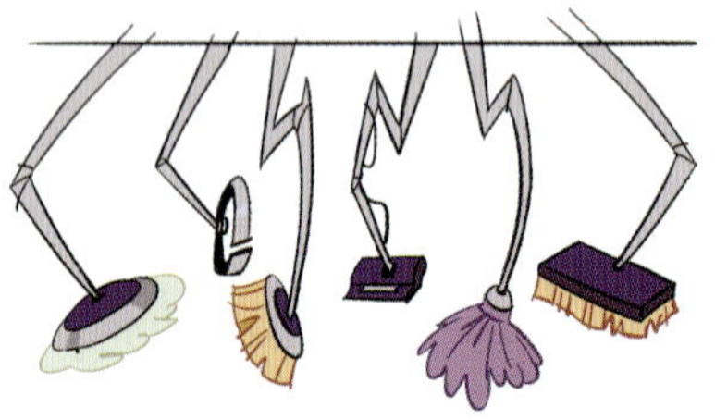

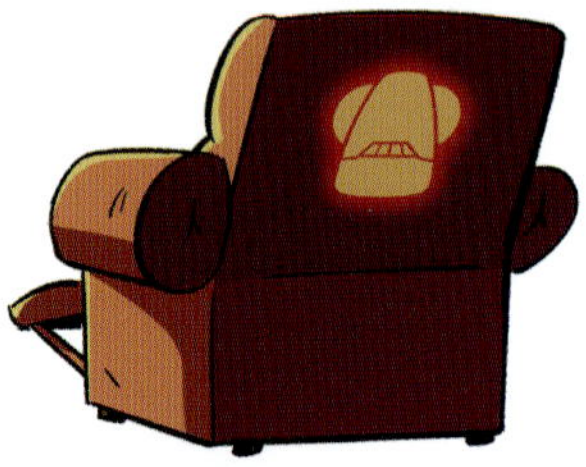

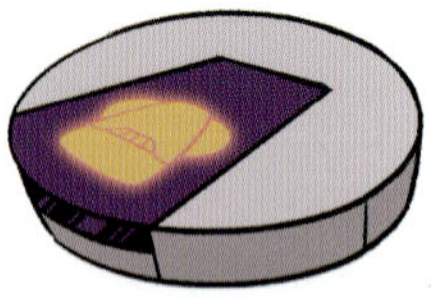

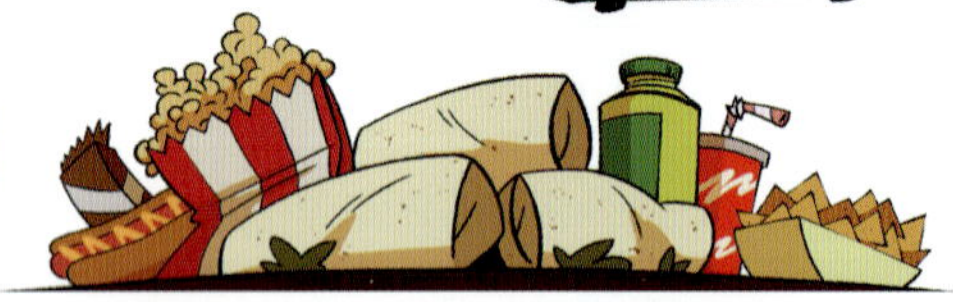

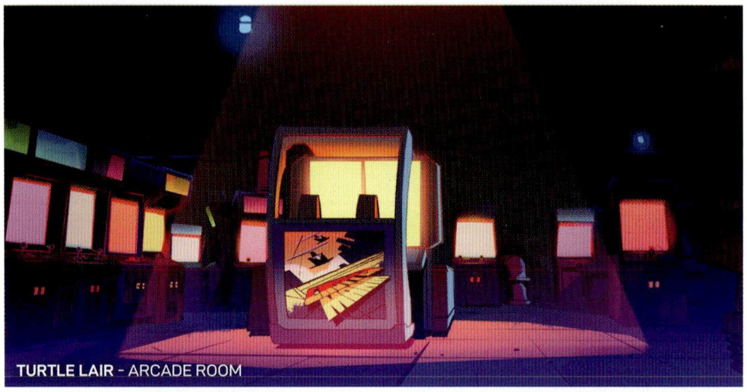

TURTLE LAIR - ARCADE ROOM

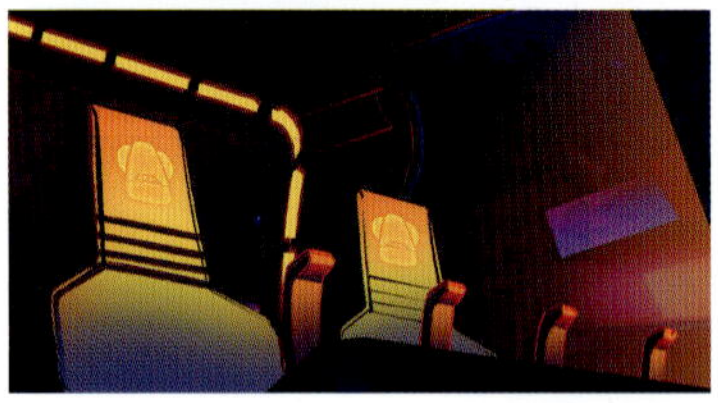

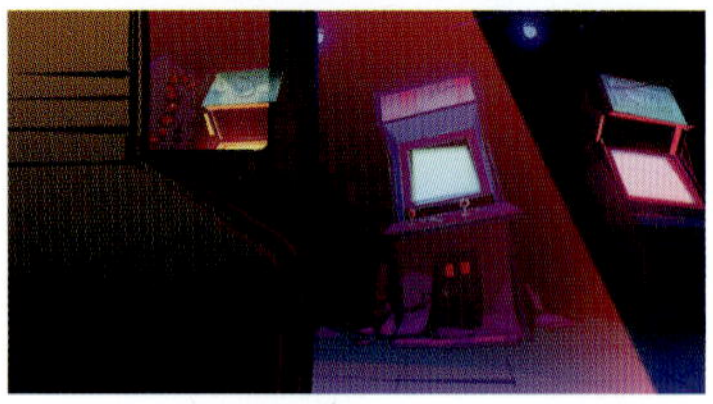

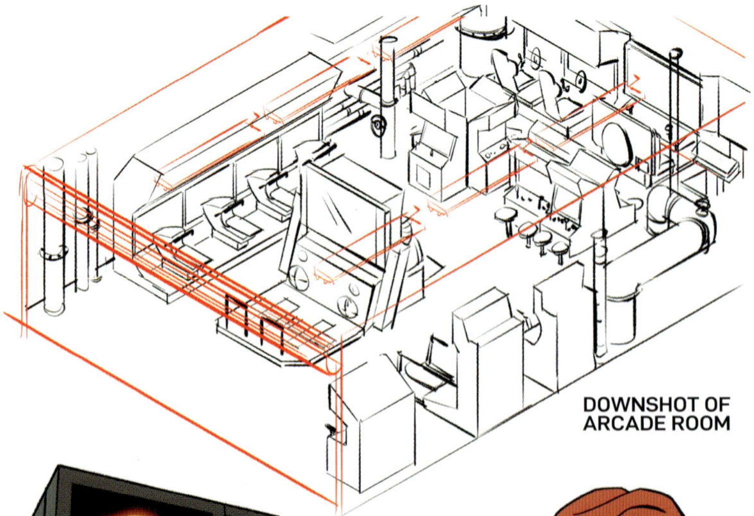

DOWNSHOT OF ARCADE ROOM

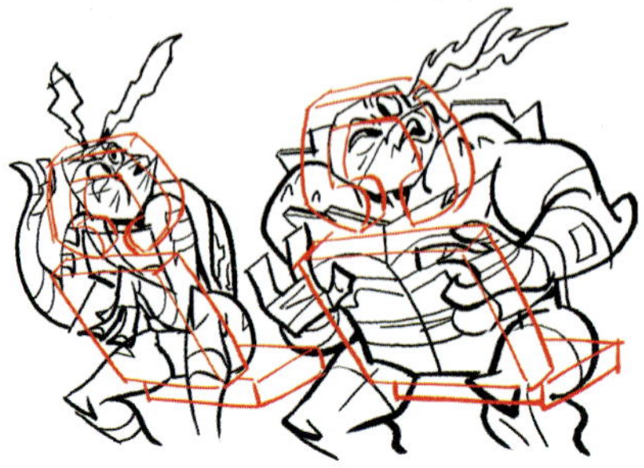

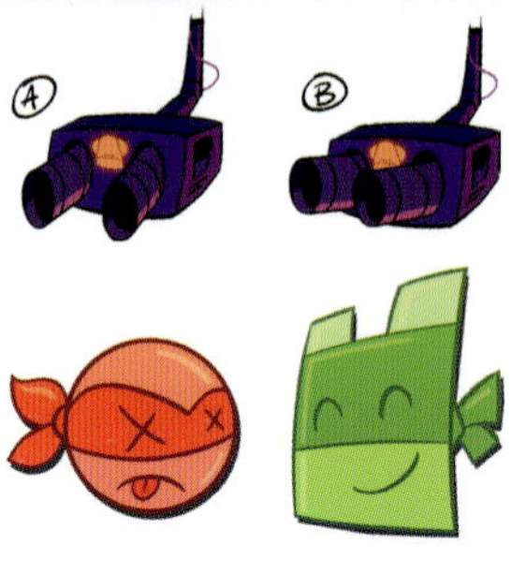

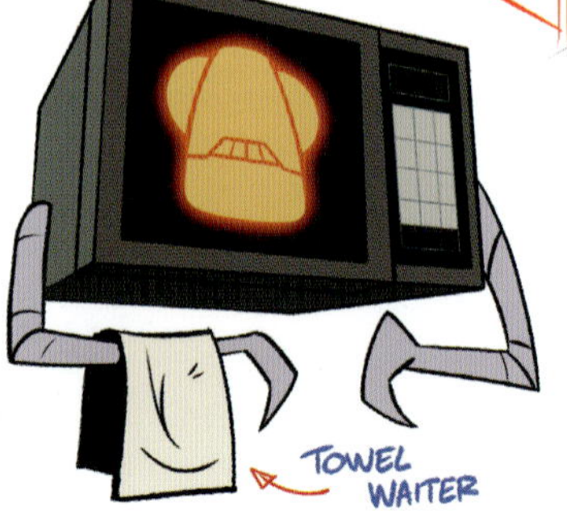

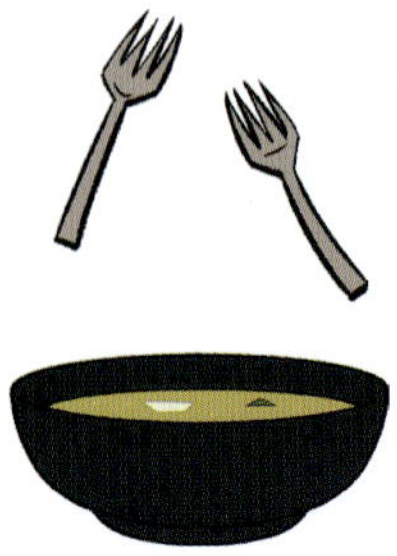

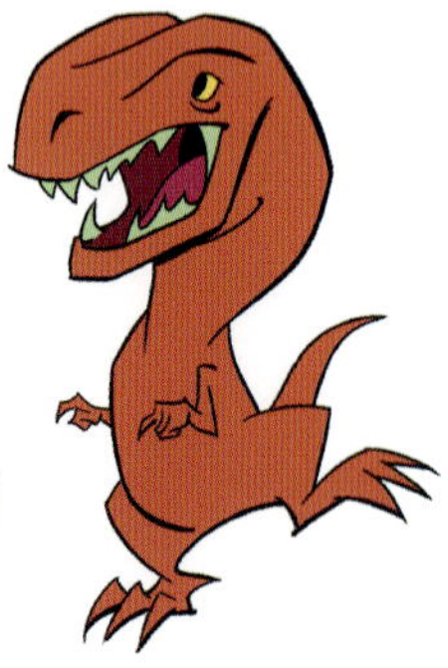

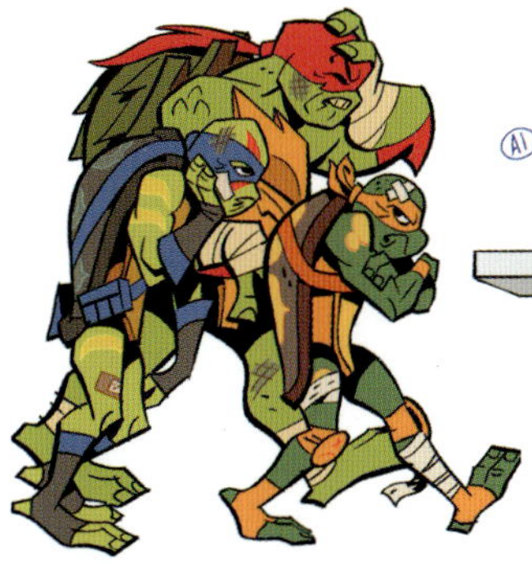

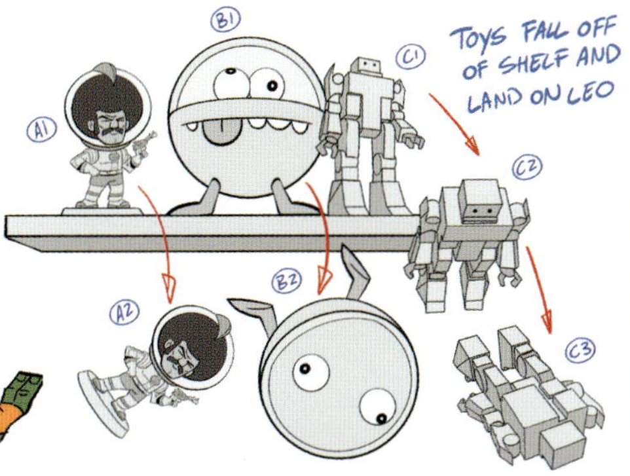

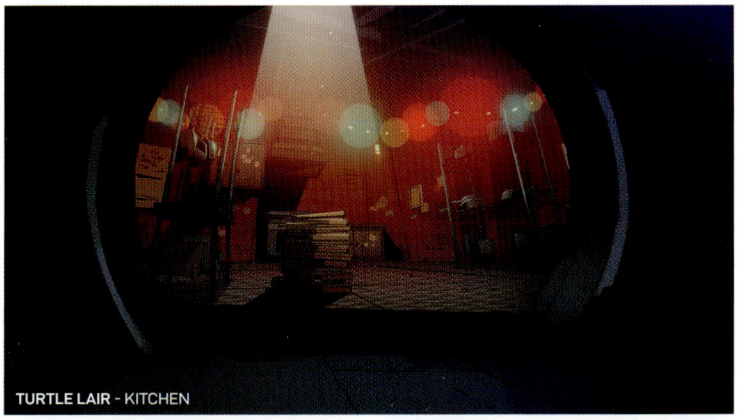

TURTLE LAIR - KITCHEN

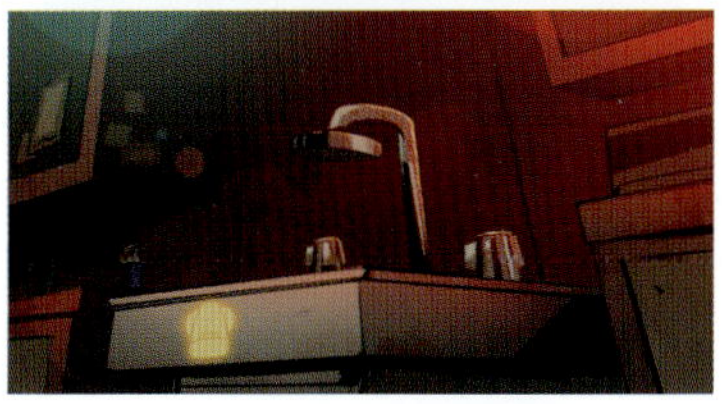

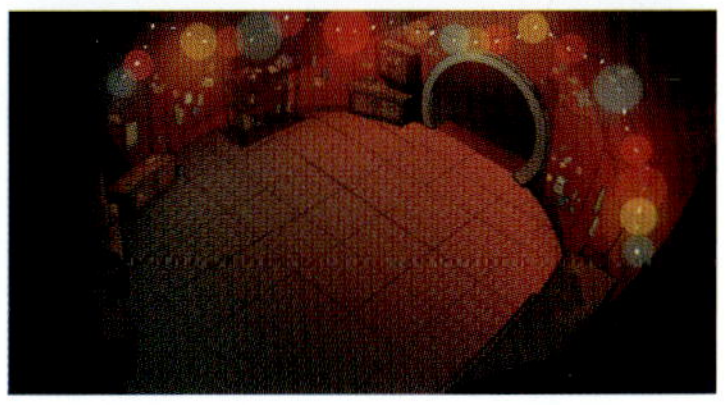

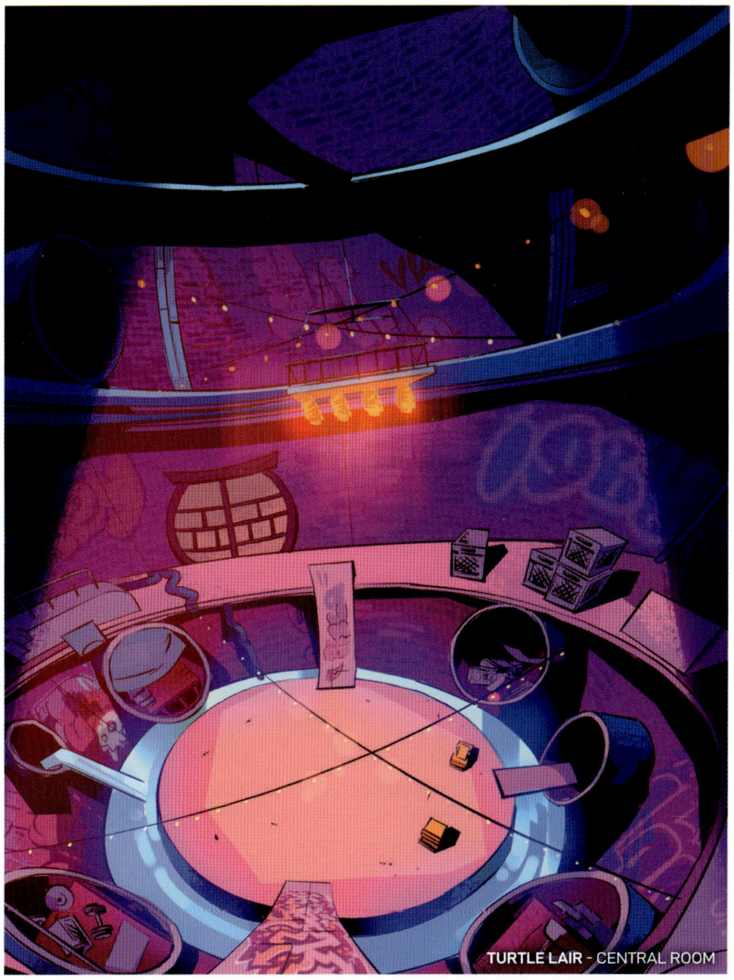

TURTLE LAIR - CENTRAL ROOM

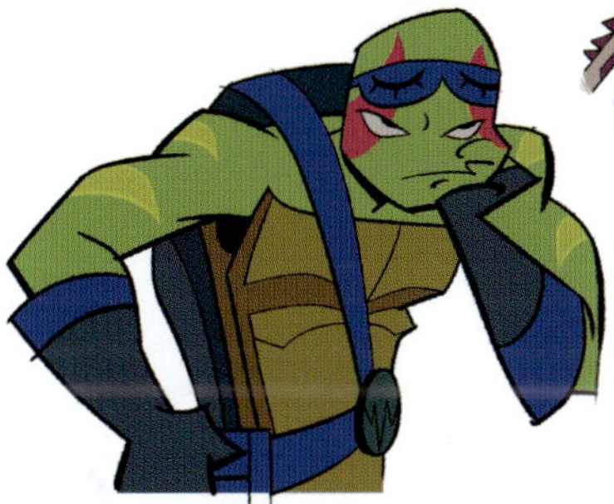

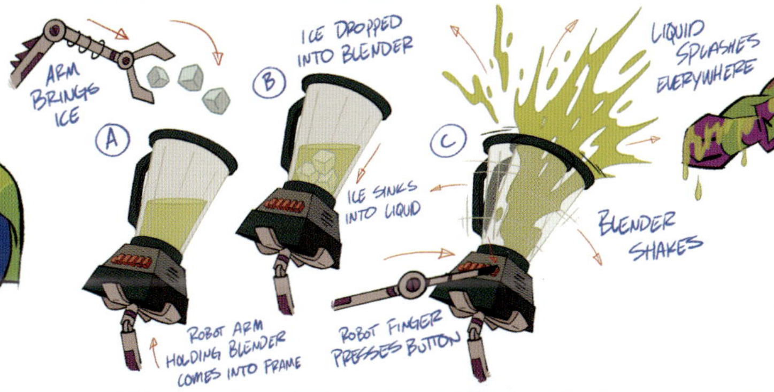

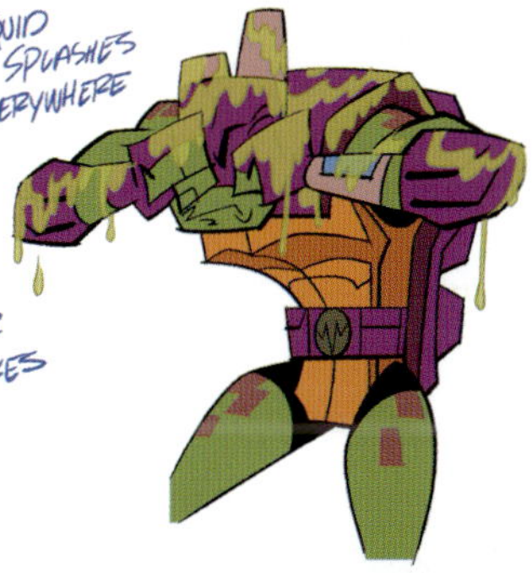

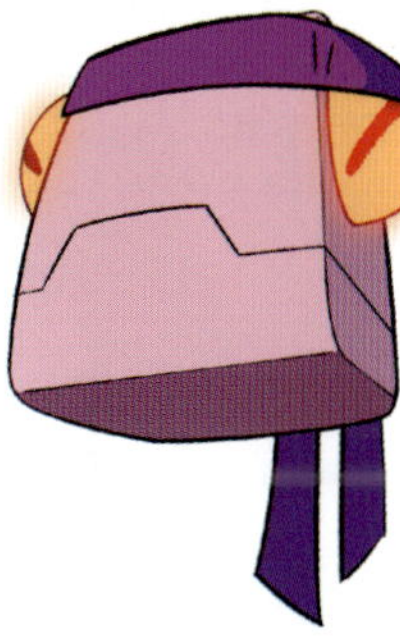

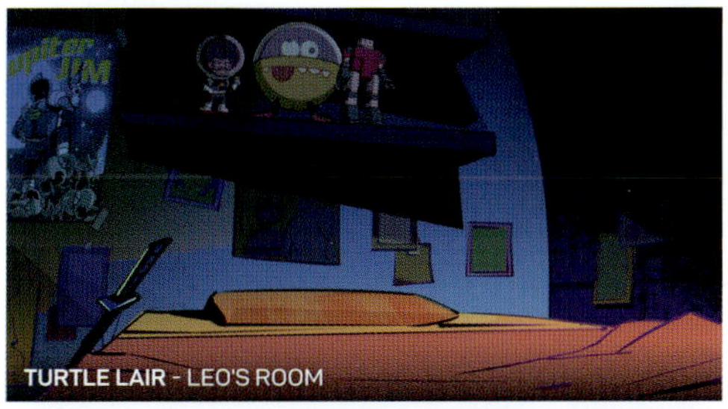

TURTLE LAIR - LEO'S ROOM

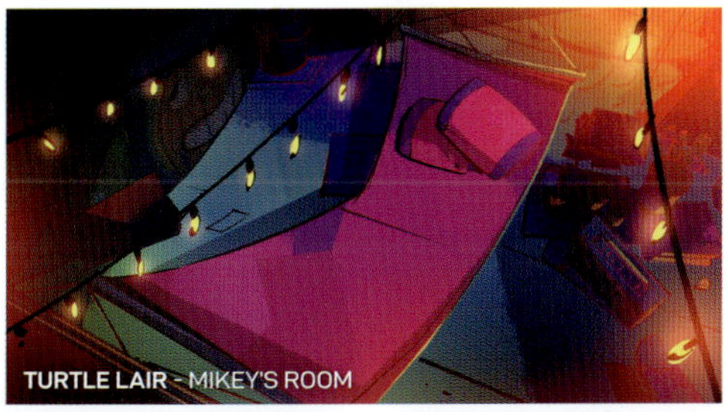

TURTLE LAIR - MIKEY'S ROOM

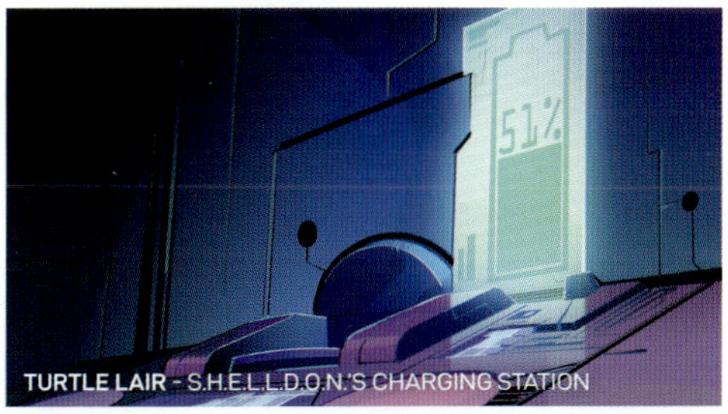

TURTLE LAIR - S.H.E.L.L.D.O.N.'S CHARGING STATION

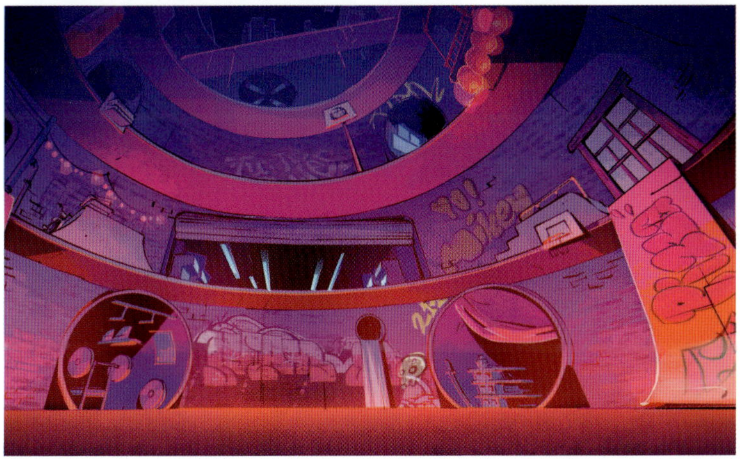

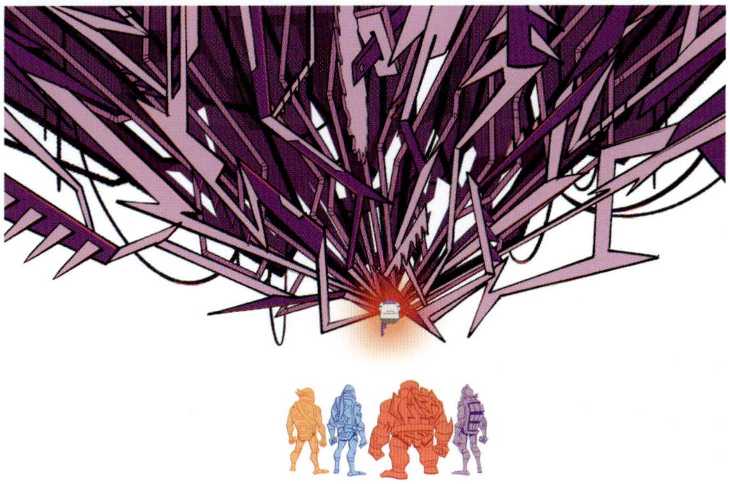

HOT SOUP: THE GAME

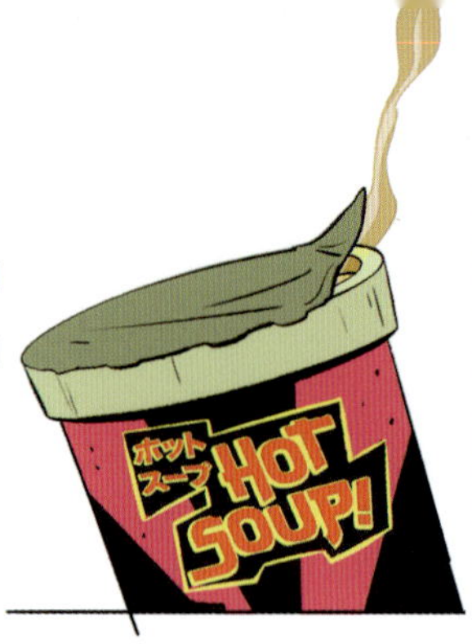

ORIGINAL AIR DATE: FEBRUARY 16, 2019
PRODUCTION CODE: 024

WRITTEN BY **RUSS CARNEY & RON CORCILLO**
STORYBOARDS BY **ALICIA CHAN, CHRISTINA "KIKI" MANRIQUE**
DIRECTED BY **ABE AUDISH**

RUSS CARNEY: This episode was essentially meant to be one big *Pink Panther*–esque Clouseau vs. Cato fight, but it also had a great character story. Young Mikey wants to prove himself, as does the Foot Recruit, and older Raph struggles with his natural instinct to protect his little bro, as does the Foot Brute.

RON CORCILLO: It took us a few tries to nail the Foot Recruit's character. Initially, we wrote her as a teacher's-pet type, but that approach nearly got the episode scrapped. When we made her wildly unpredictable, she became an instant hit! Zelda Williams was our first and only choice for the role—she brought incredible energy. At one point during the record, she took a breath and asked, *"So you just want me to shout all of these lines?" Yes. Yes, please!*

RUSS CARNEY: Jokes aside, voice actors take a lot of punishment to their vocal cords, and we wanted to be sensitive to that, but once she understood the character, she seemed quickly on board with all the shouting! We're sorry, Zelda!

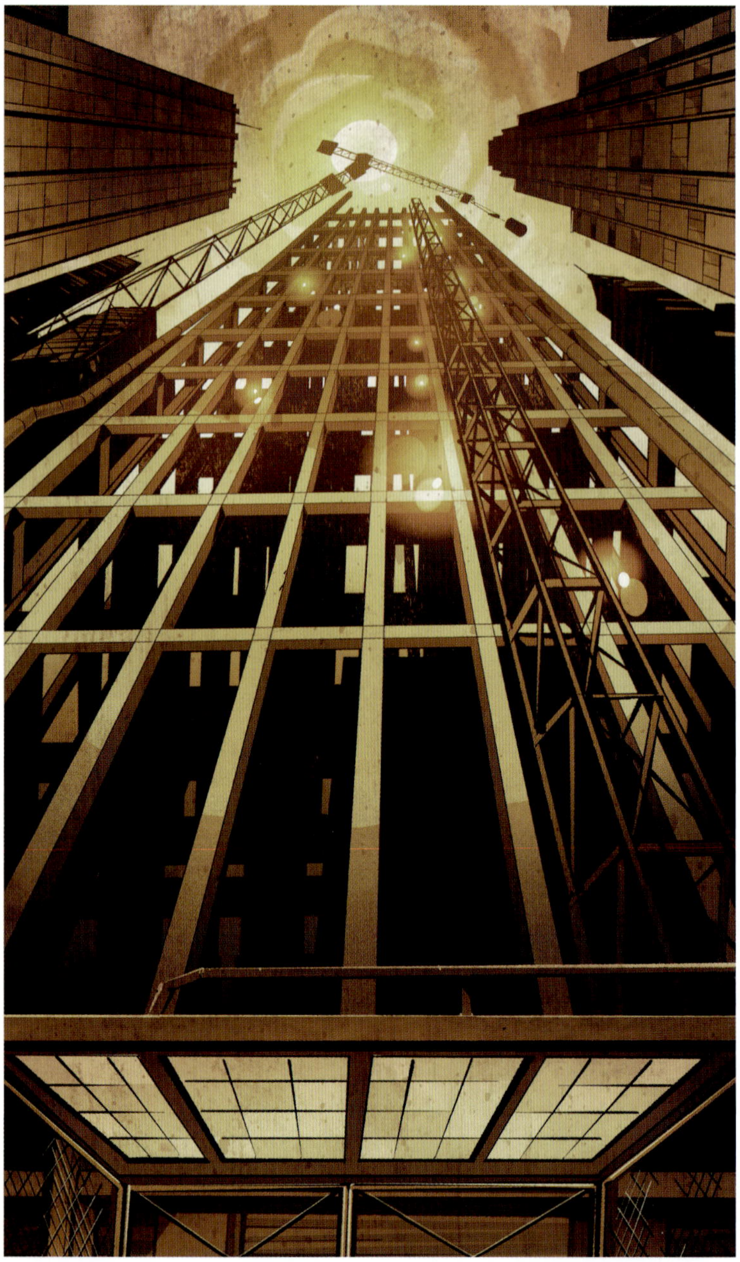

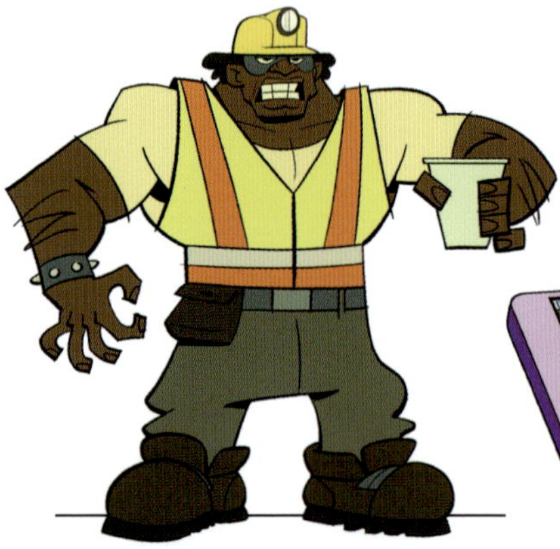

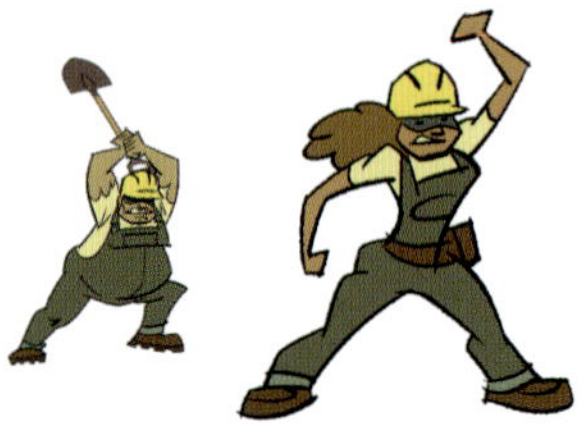

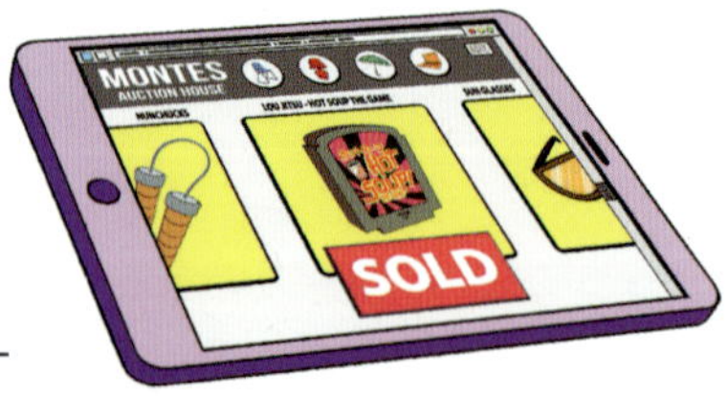

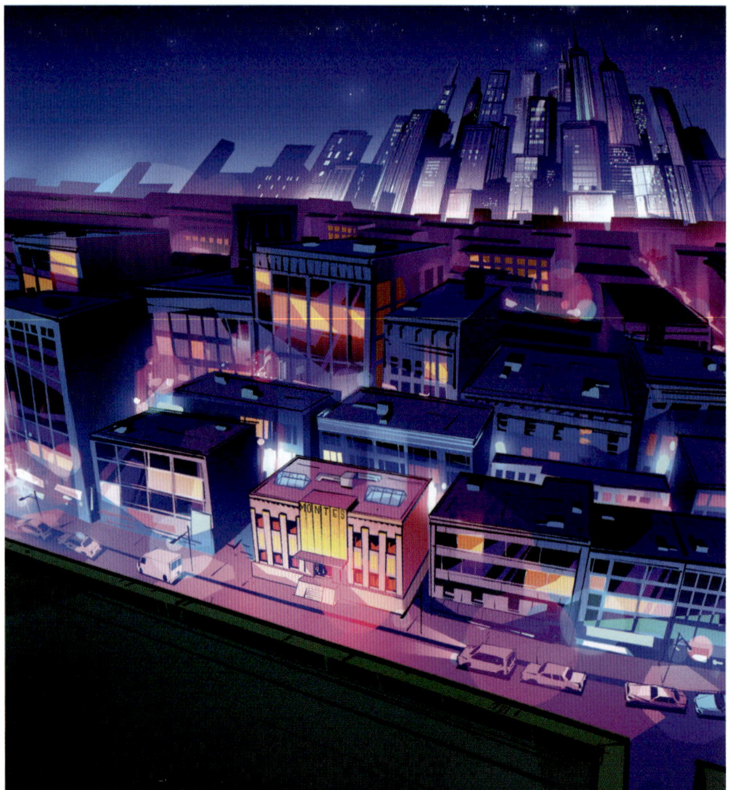

MONTES AUCTION HOUSE

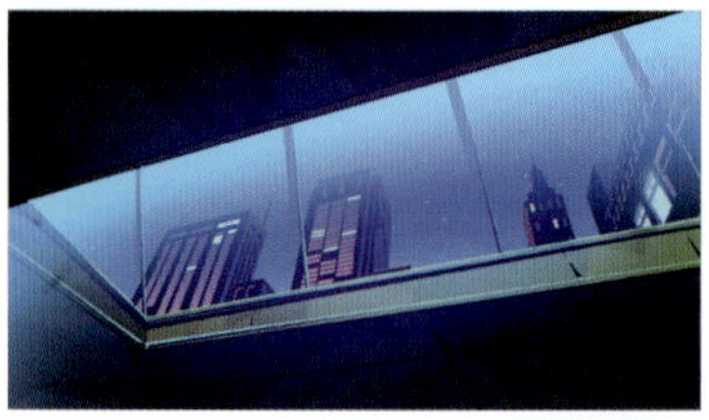

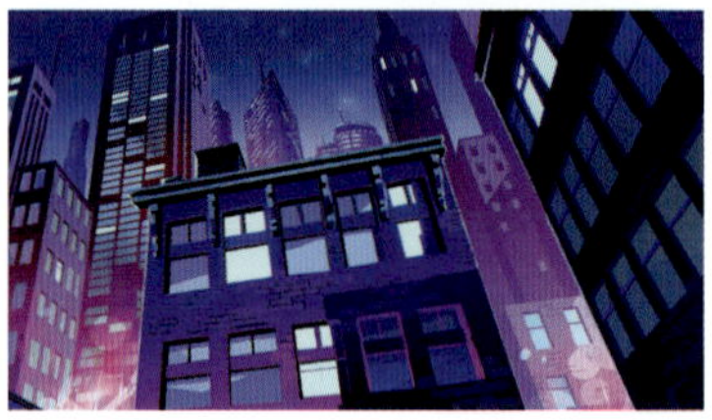

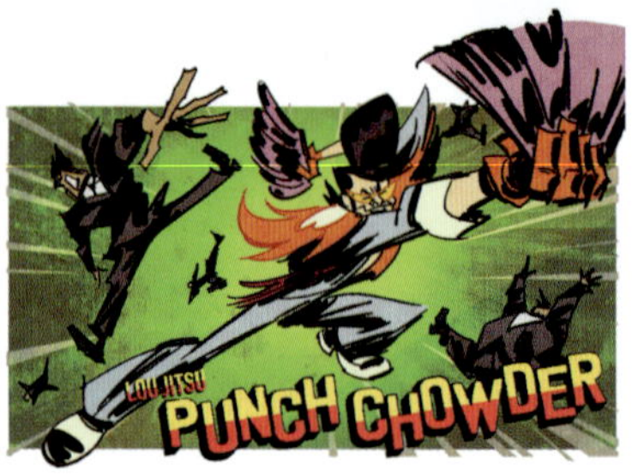

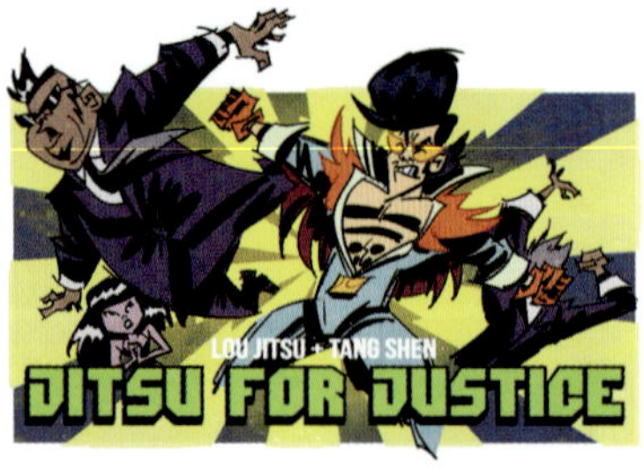

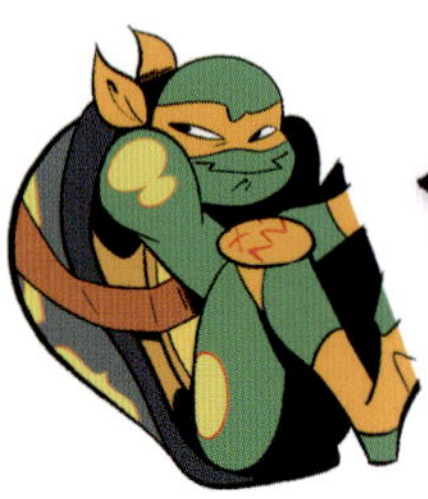

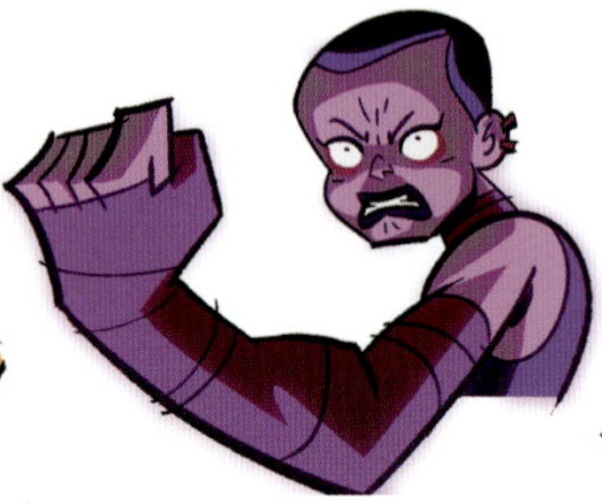

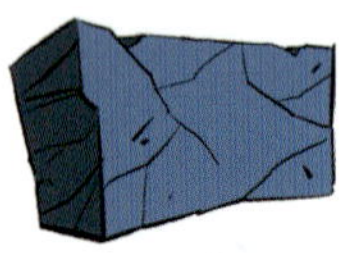

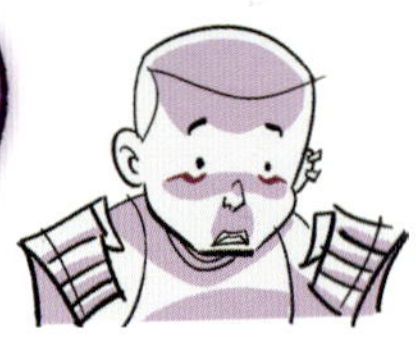

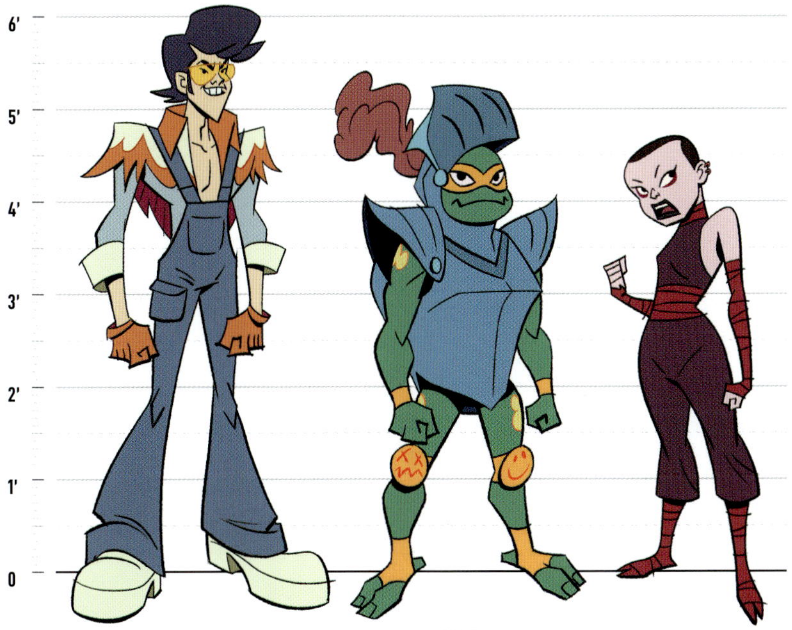

LOU JITSU
HOT SOUP: THE GAME

MIKEY
KNIGHT ARMOR

FOOT RECRUIT

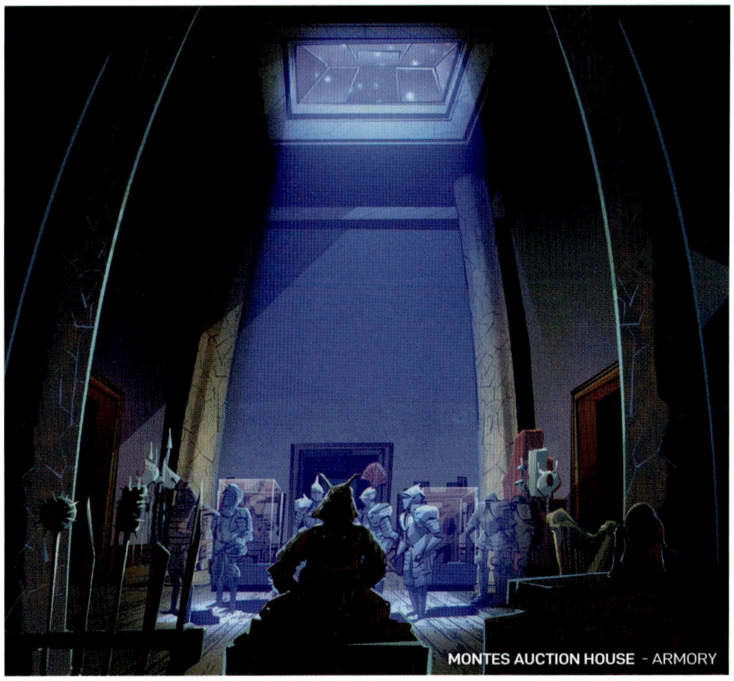

MONTES AUCTION HOUSE - ARMORY

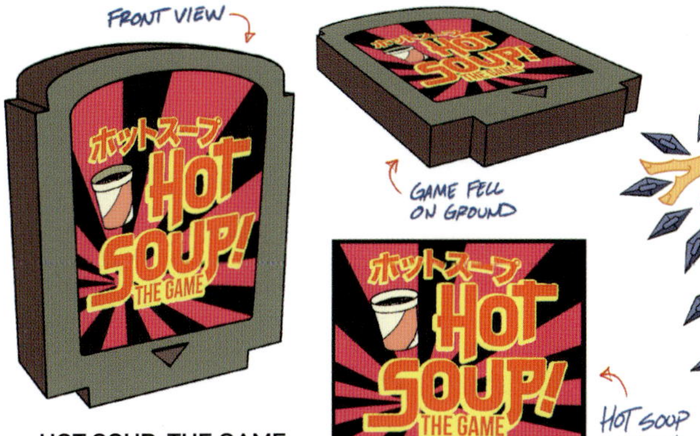

HOT SOUP: THE GAME CARTRIDGE

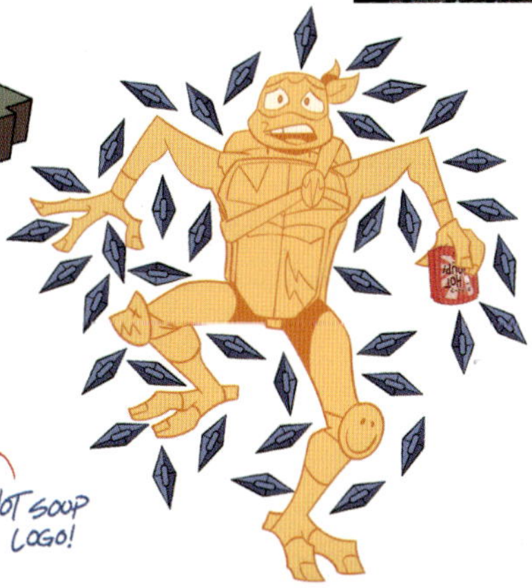

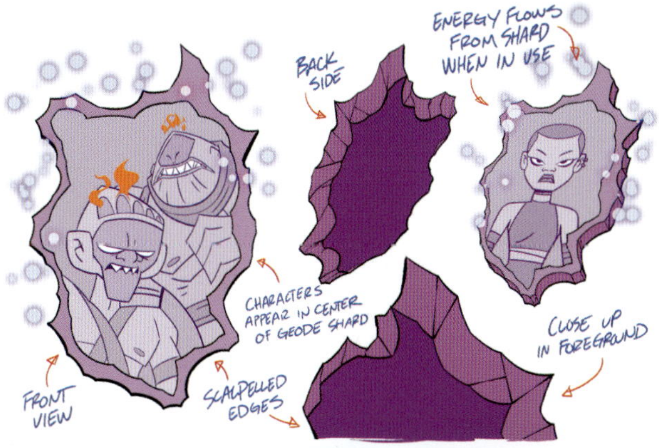

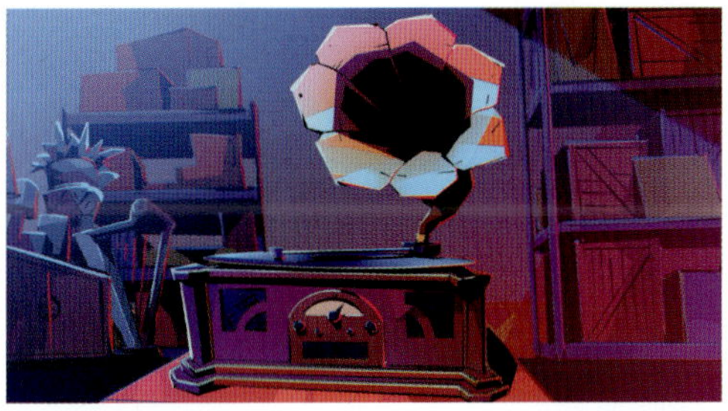

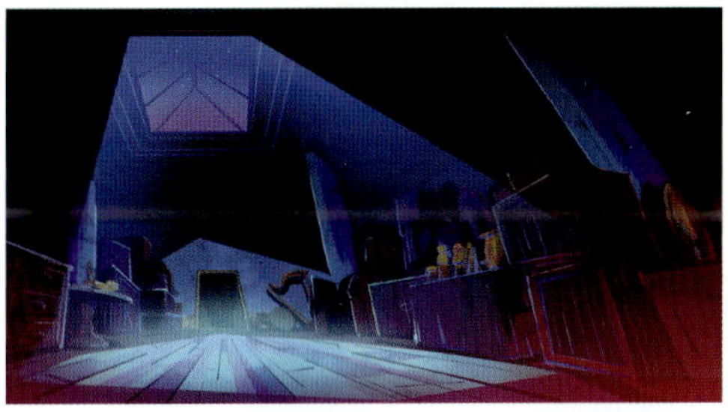

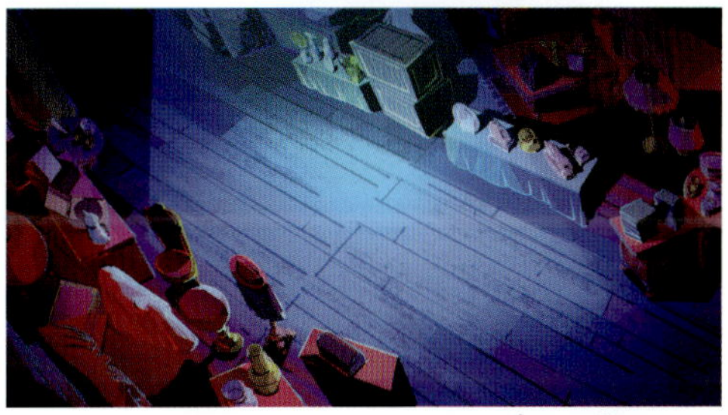

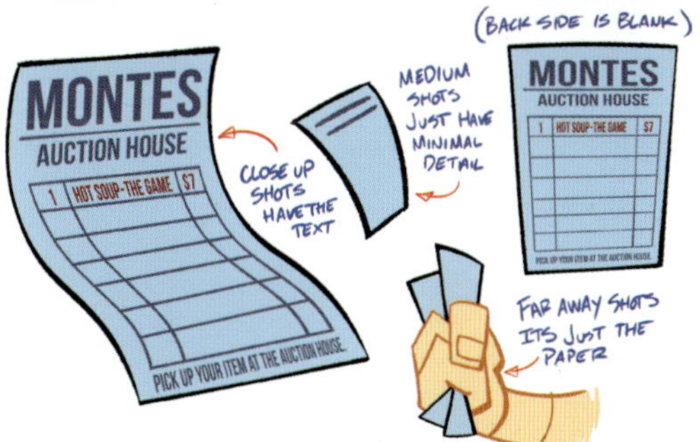

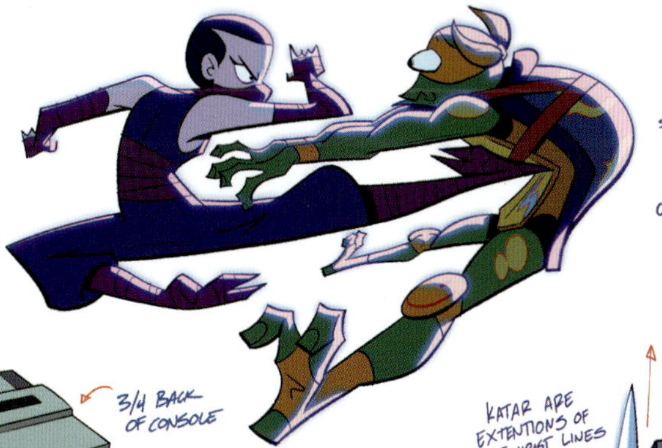

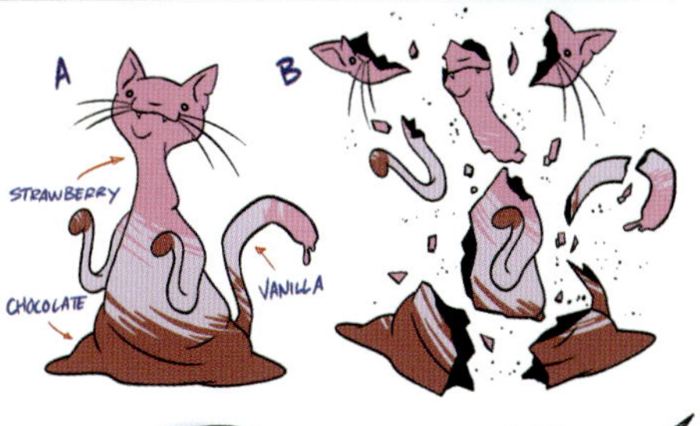

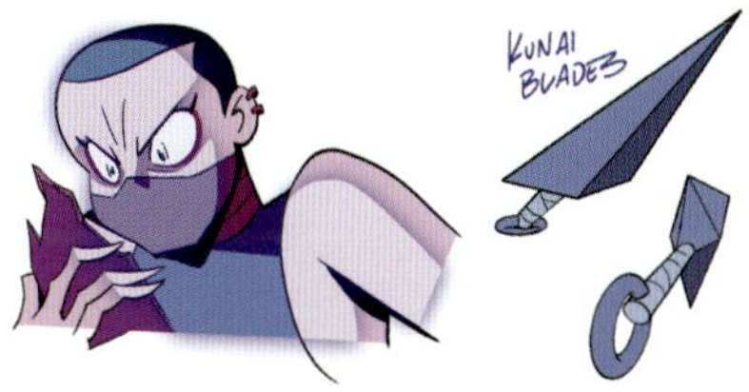

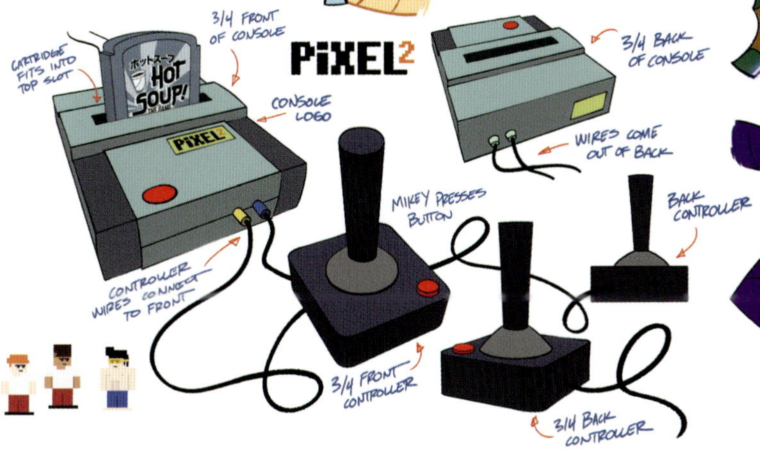

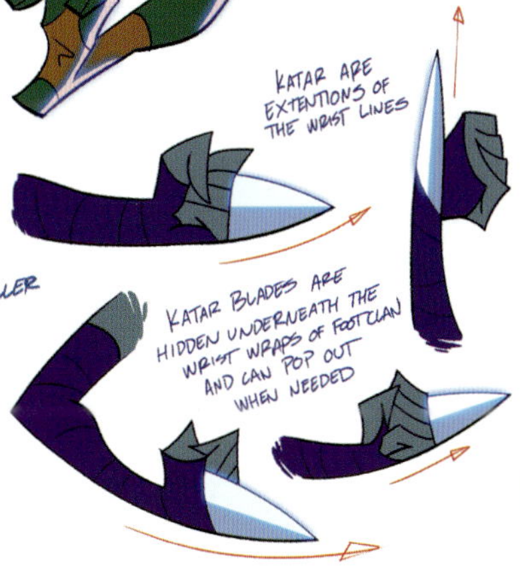

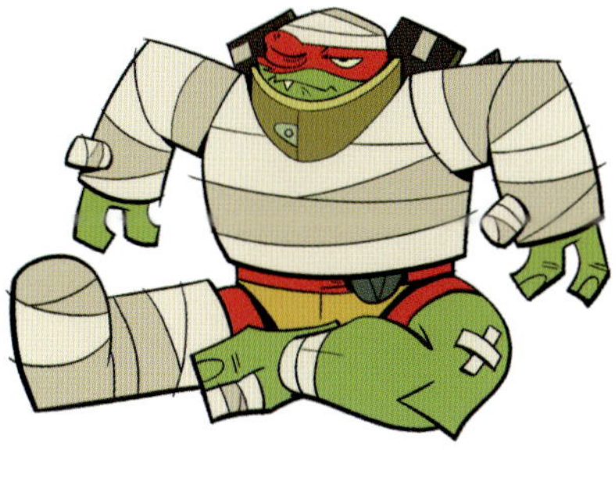

THE EVIL LEAGUE OF MUTANTS

ORIGINAL AIR DATE: JANUARY 19, 2019
PRODUCTION CODE: 025-026

WRITTEN BY **JESSE GORDON**
STORYBOARDS BY **JULIA BRAID, KAI LYNN JIANG, KEVIN MOLINA-ORTIZ**
DIRECTED BY **SEBASTIAN MONTES**

JESSE GORDON: This was one of the most fun experiences I had on the show. Since it was a two-parter I had the room to stuff it full of extra story we'd been plotting out. The basic idea was for the mutants to band together to take on the Turtles. We also needed to get the story of Lou Jitsu's connection to the Turtles, which was a lot of exposition, and I thought it would be really fun to do it in the form of a musical number. The team was shockingly on board with it!

JJ CONWAY: "Todd's Lemonade" is our villain-defining song, so I took major inspiration from Disney classics "Poor Unfortunate Souls" (*The Little Mermaid*, 1989) and "Hellfire" (*The Hunchback of Notre Dame*, 1996) while storyboarding it. For Draxum's performance I took cues from iconic Tim Curry roles like Dr. Frank-N-Furter (*The Rocky Horror Picture Show*, 1975), the Lord of Darkness (*Legend*, 1985), and Hexxus (*FernGully: The Last Rainforest*, 1992).

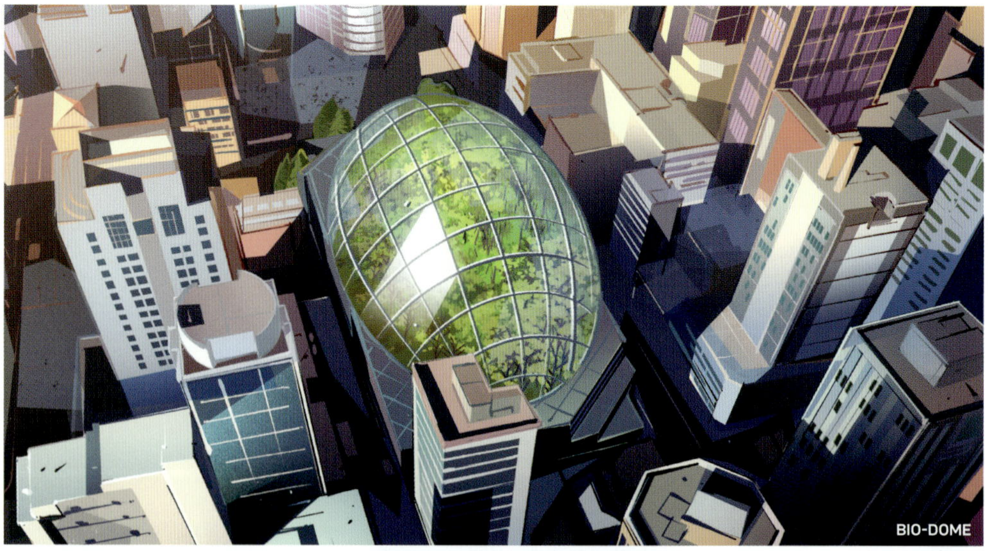
BIO-DOME

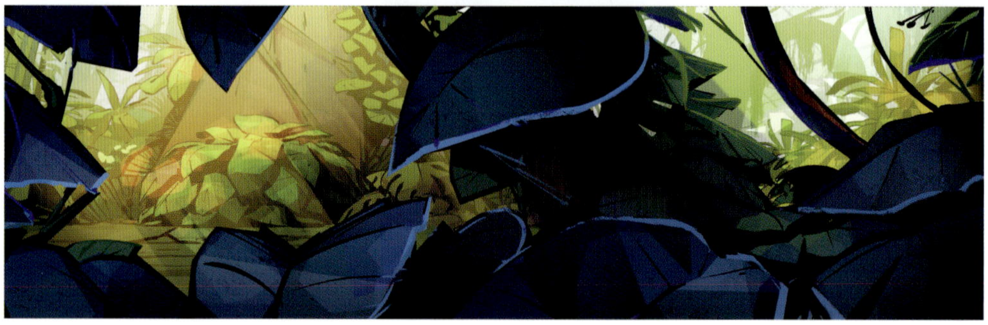

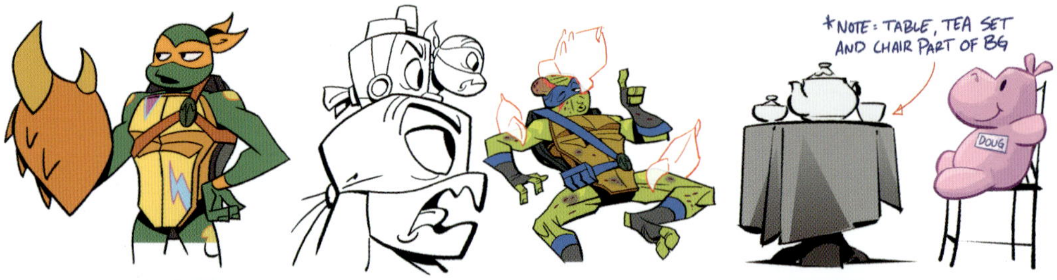

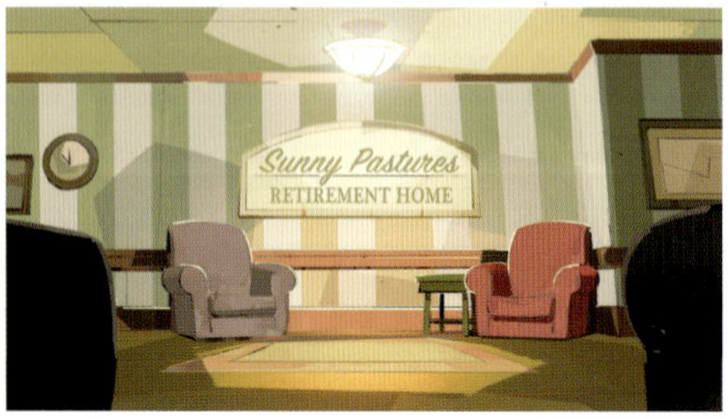

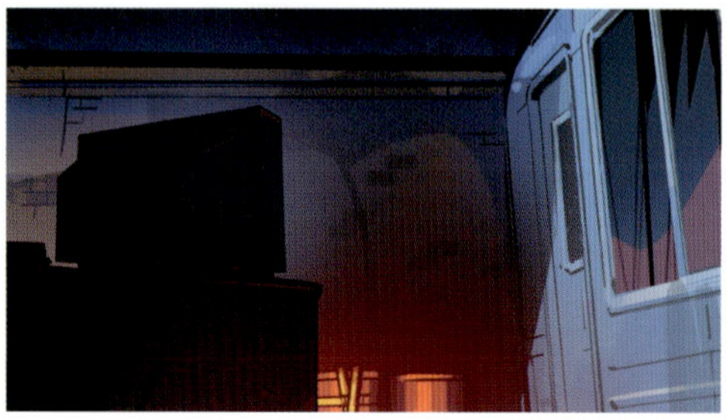

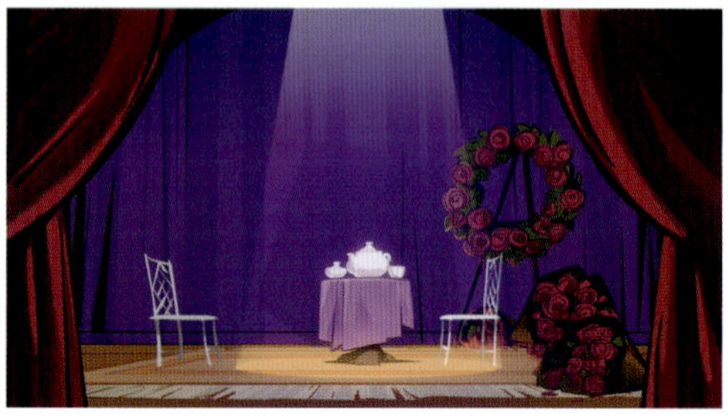

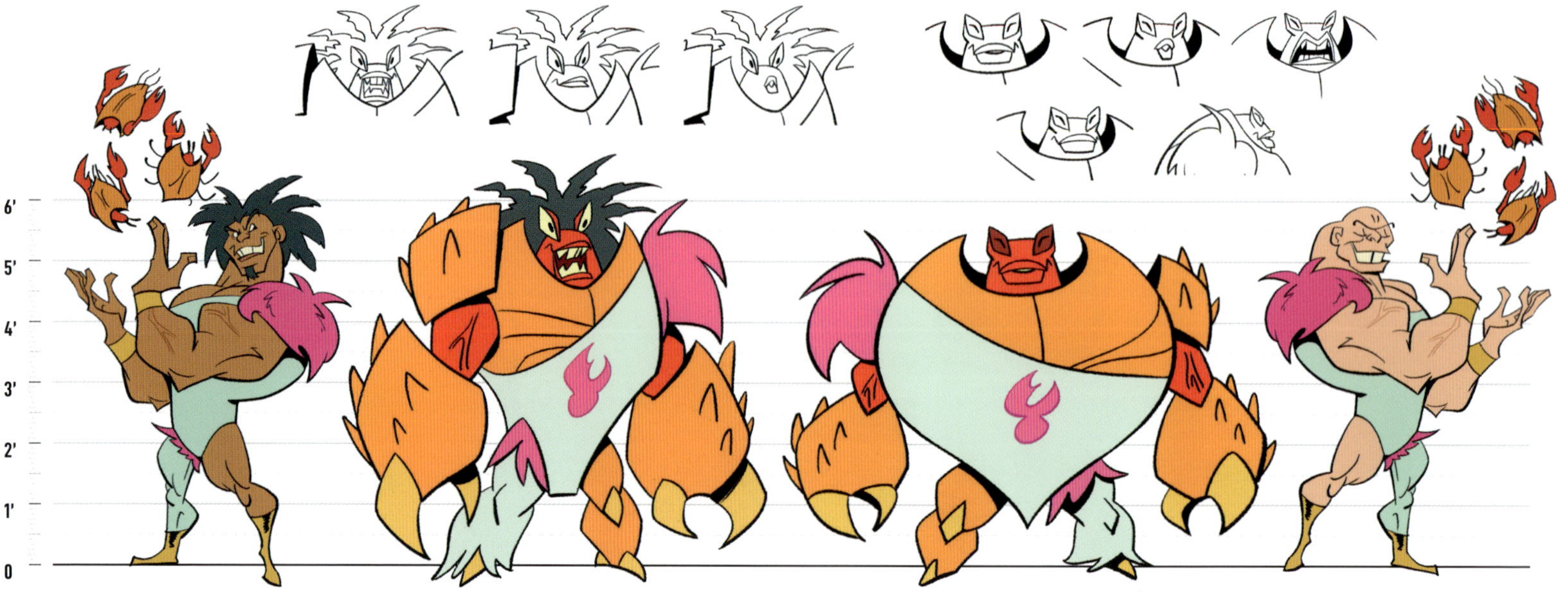

BEN SANDOS HUMAN FORM | **BEN SANDOS** MUTANT FORM | **CARL SANDOS** MUTANT FORM | **CARL SANDOS** HUMAN FORM

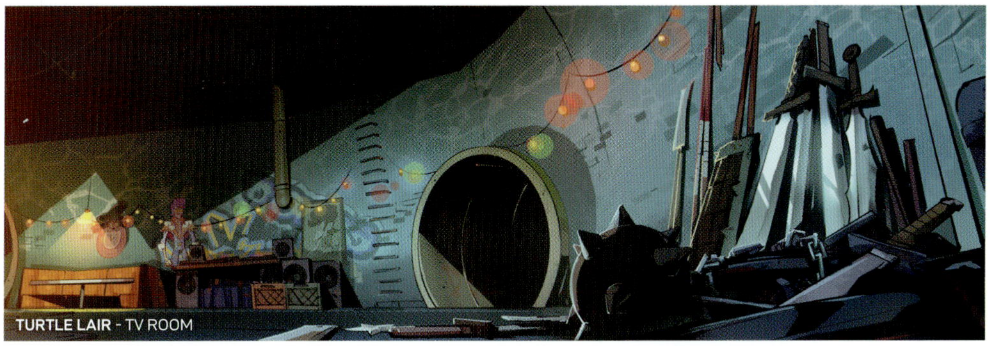

TURTLE LAIR - TV ROOM

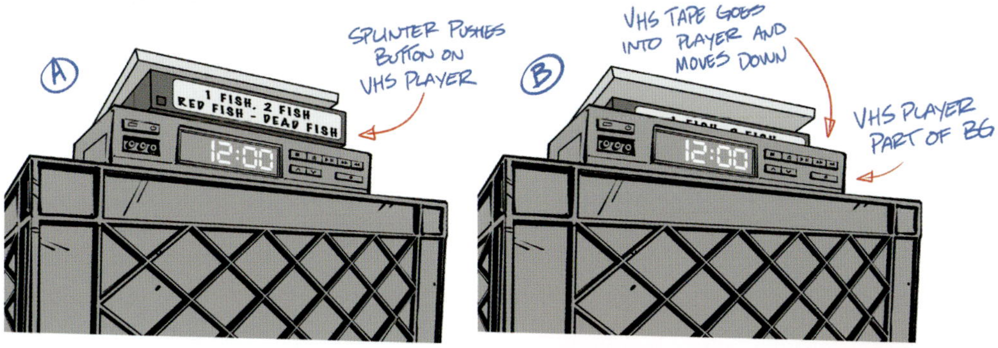

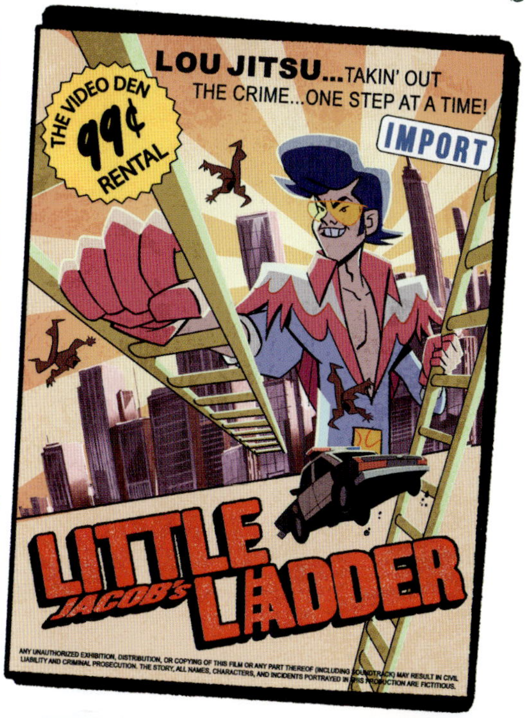

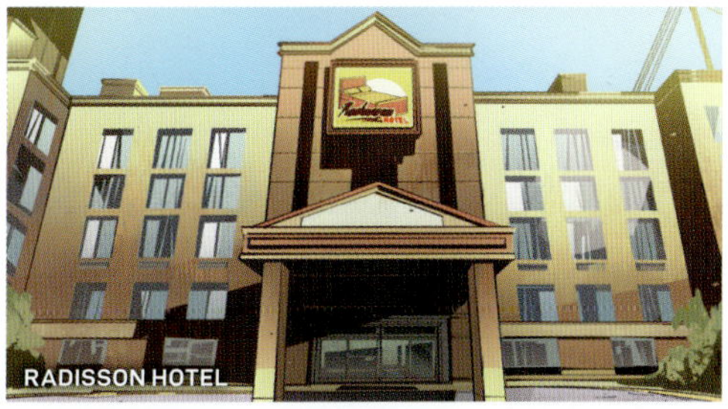

RADISSON HOTEL

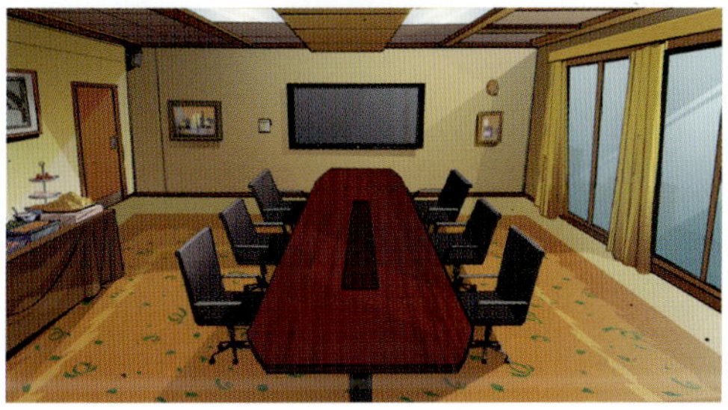

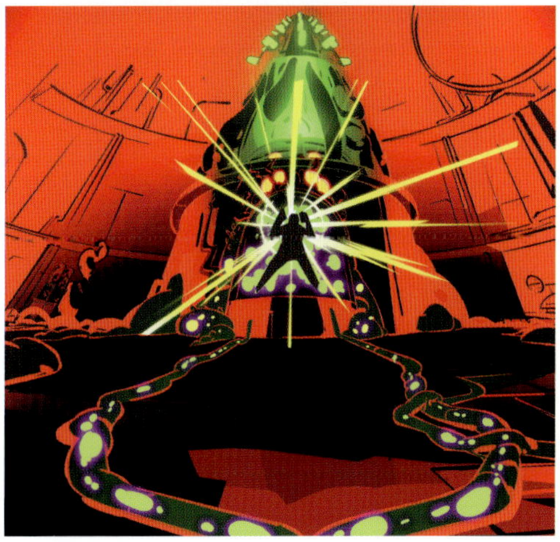

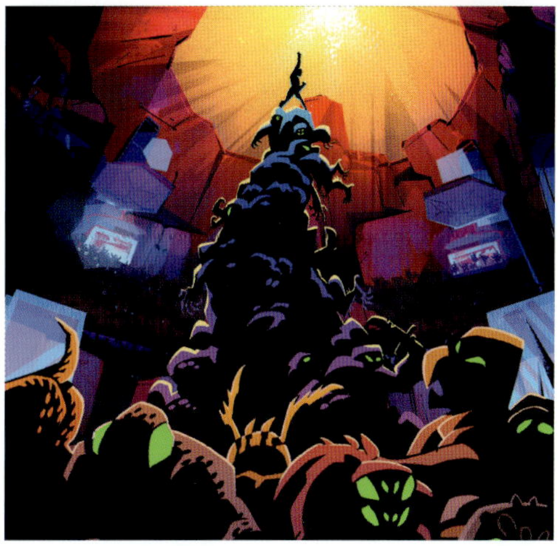

CARL BEU: Blink and you miss it—there are actually six pods on the transformation chamber. I wasn't sure if we were going to see other Turtles down the road, so I quietly added more pods to Lou Jitsu's tank just in case!

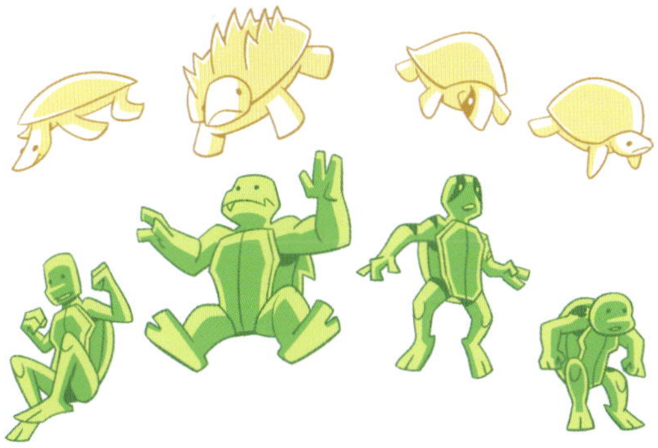

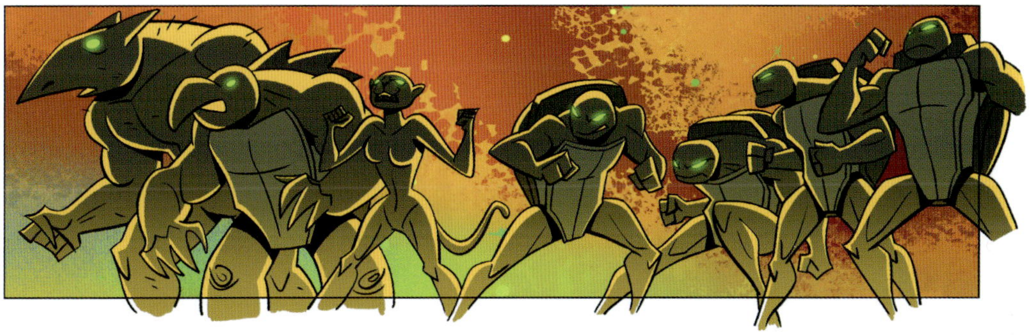

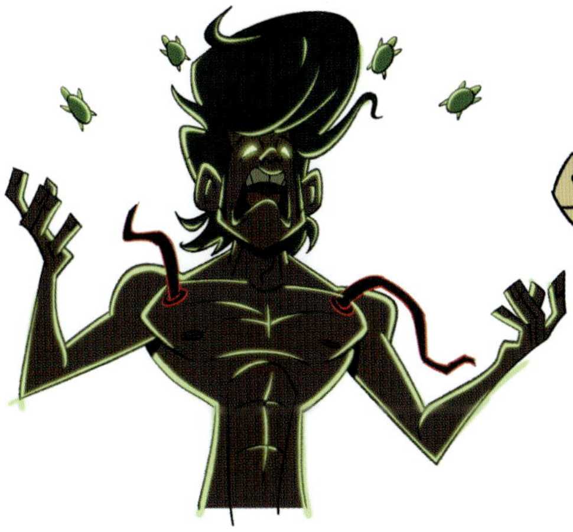

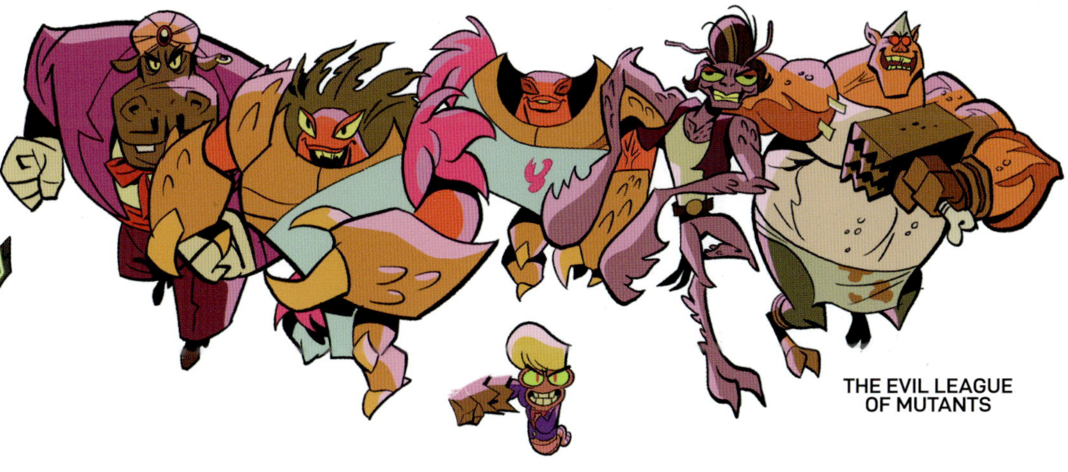

THE EVIL LEAGUE OF MUTANTS

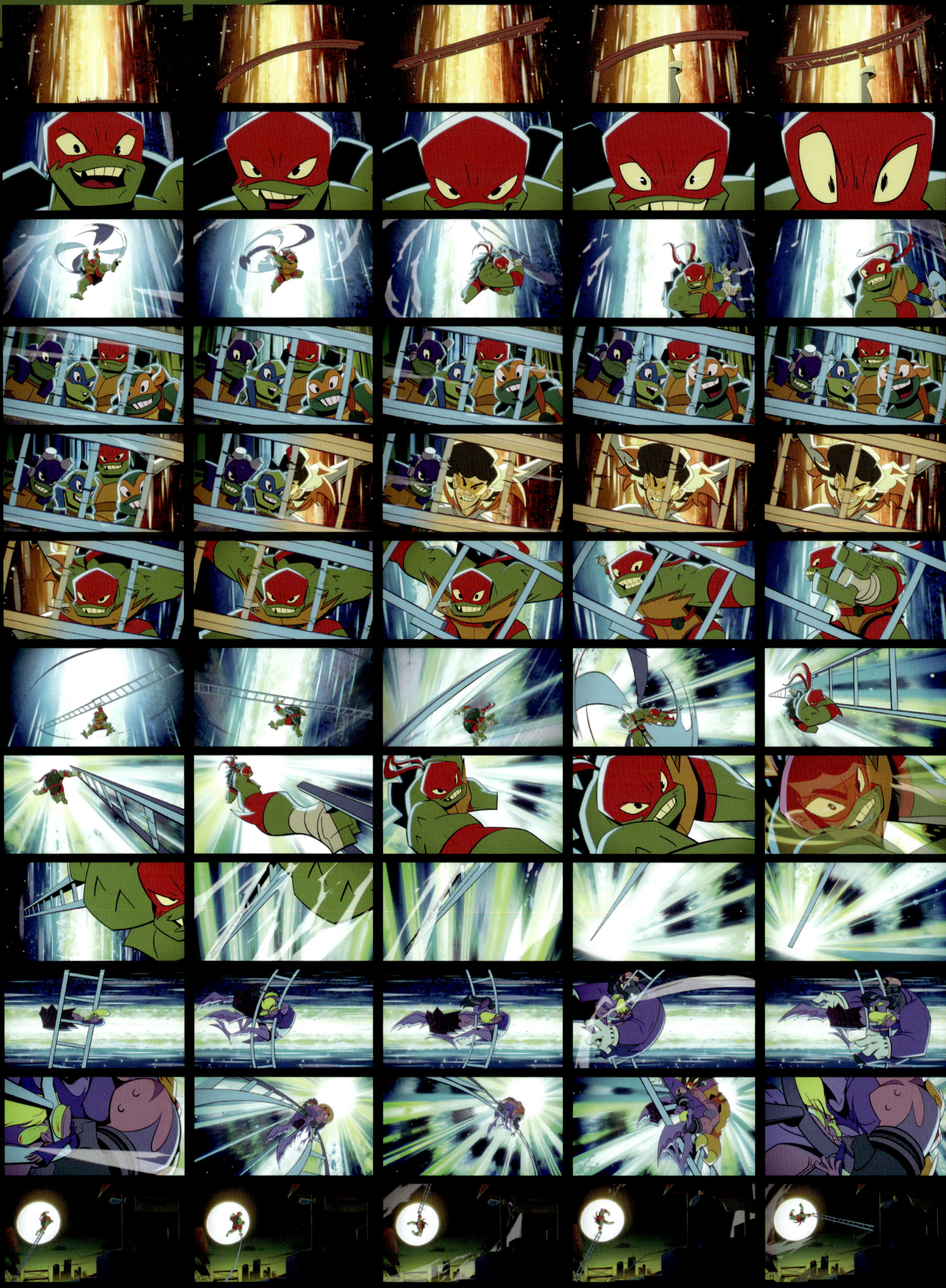

STORYBOARD ARTIST: **KEVIN MOLINA-ORTIZ**

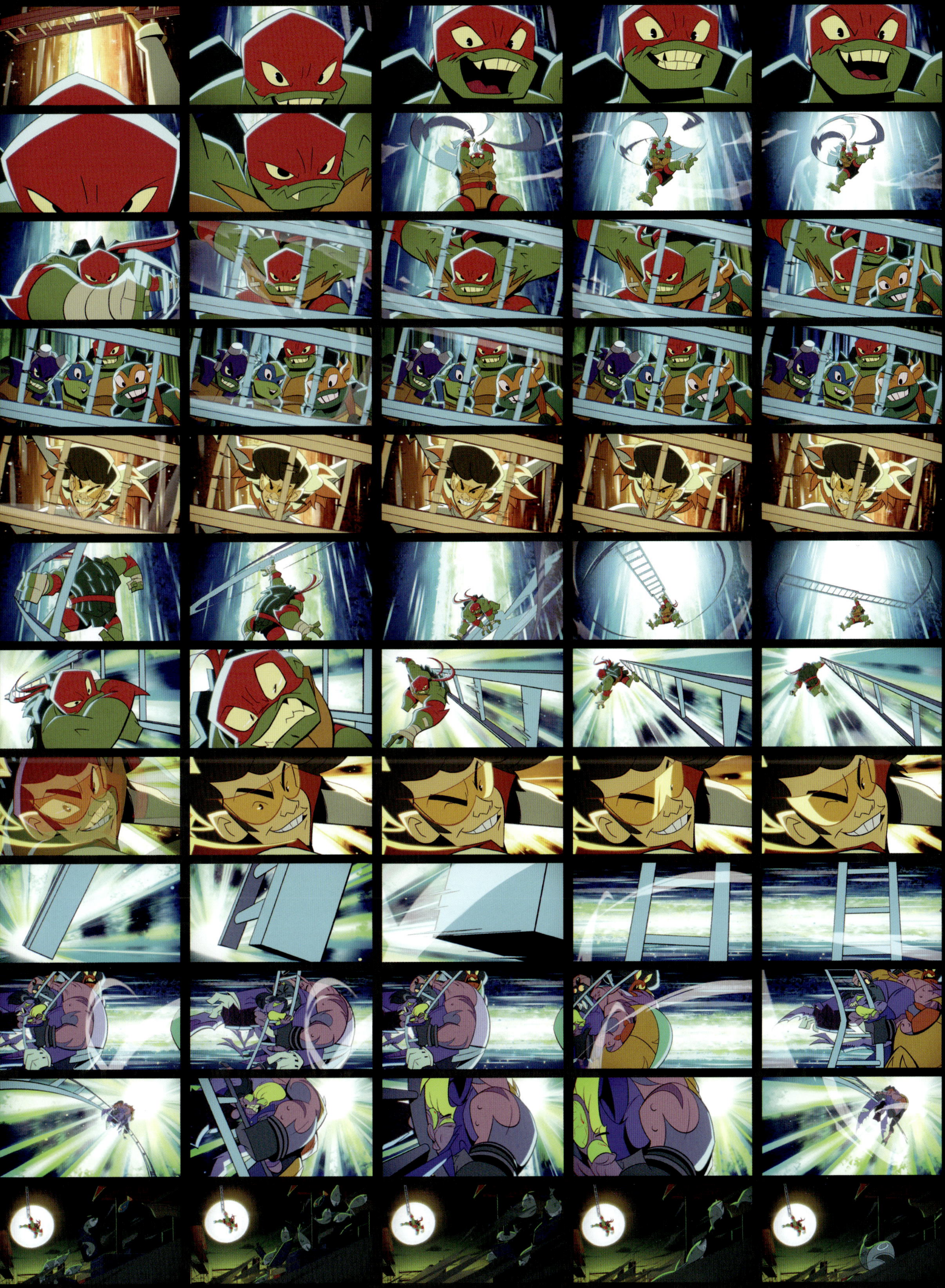

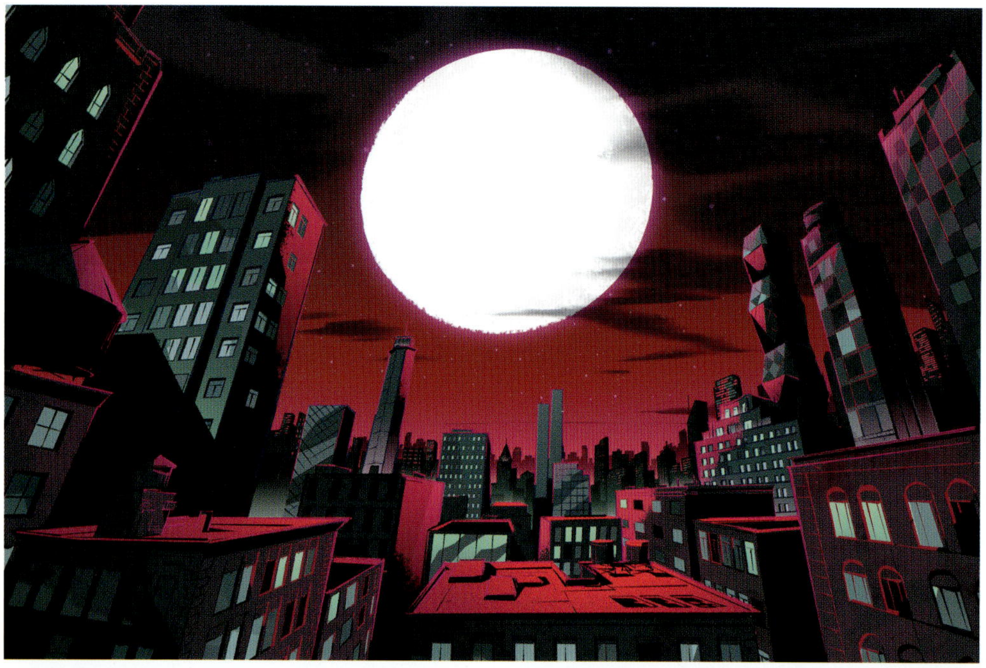

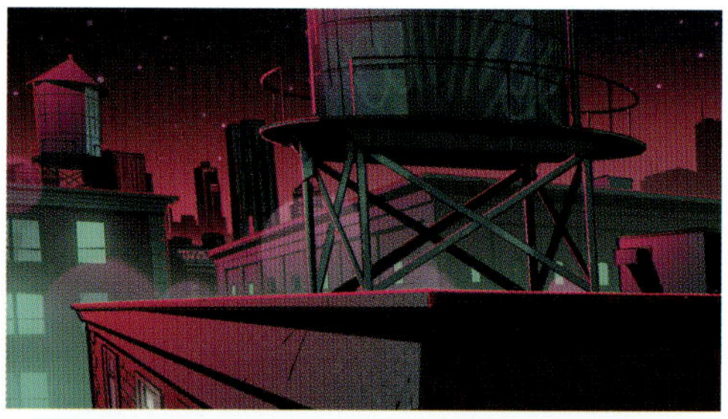

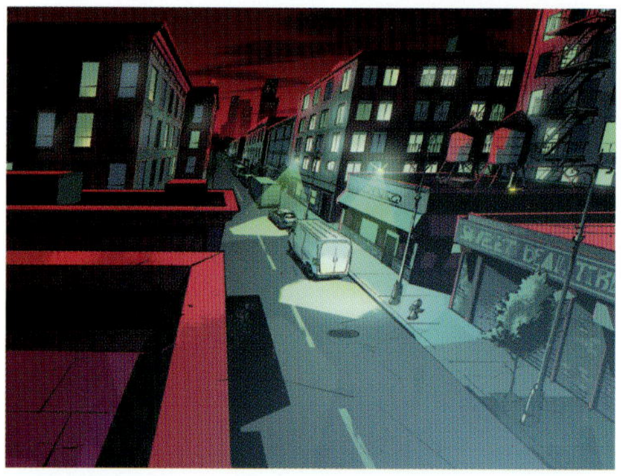

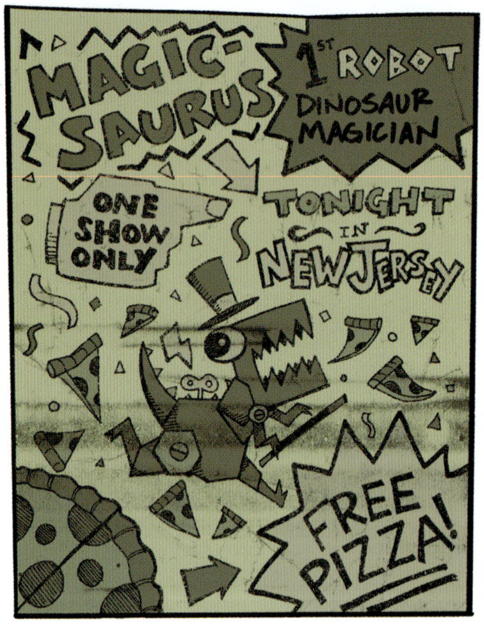
MAGIC-SAURUS
1st ROBOT DINOSAUR MAGICIAN
ONE SHOW ONLY
TONIGHT IN NEW JERSEY
FREE PIZZA!

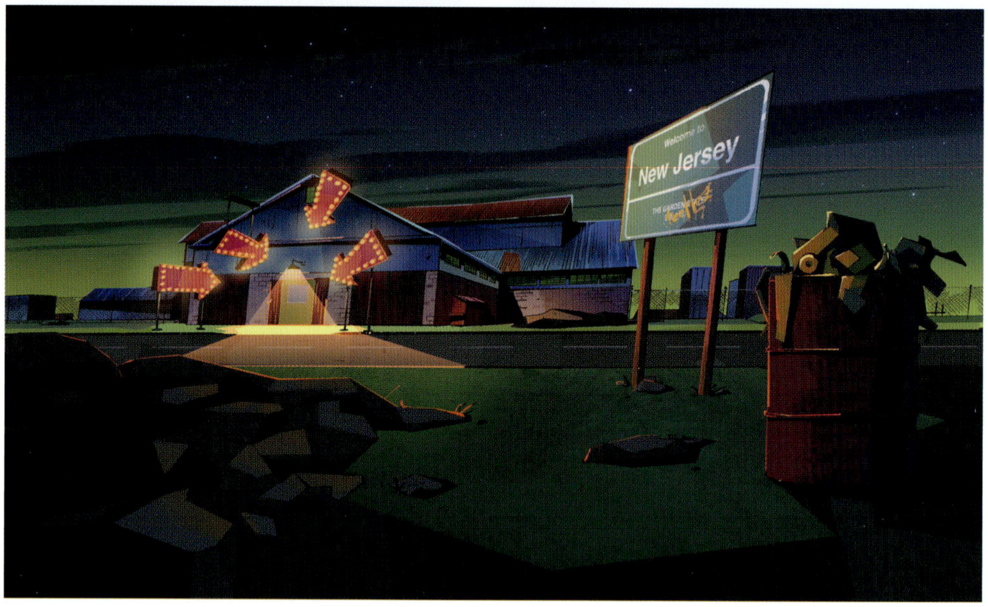
Welcome to
New Jersey

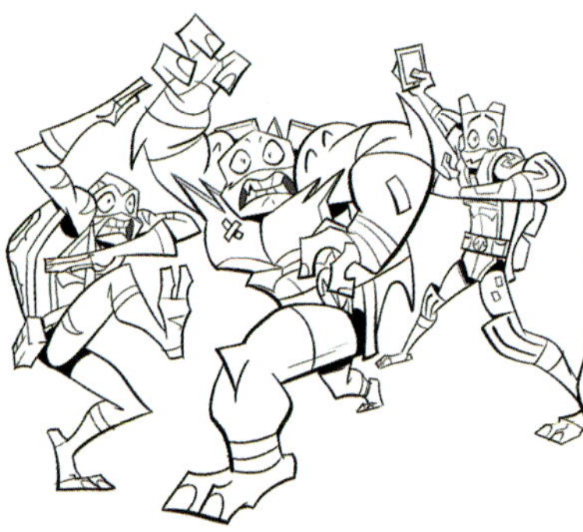

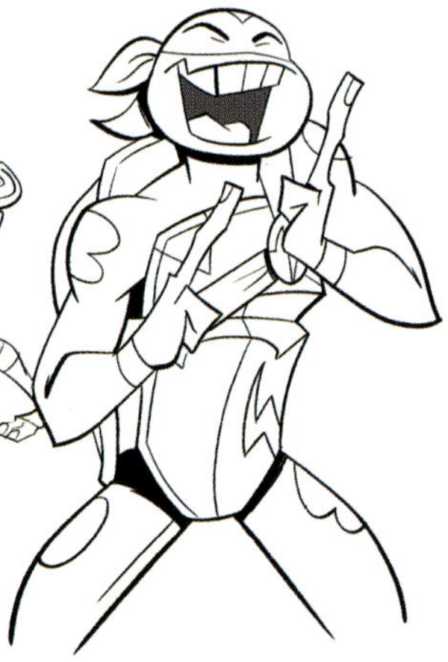

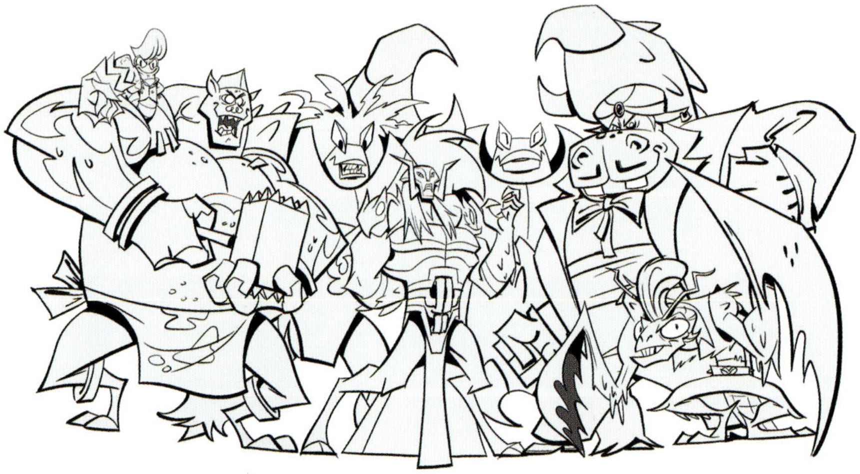

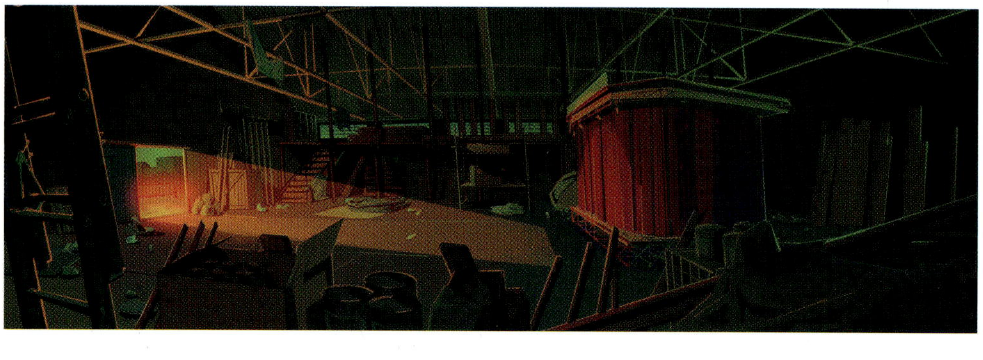

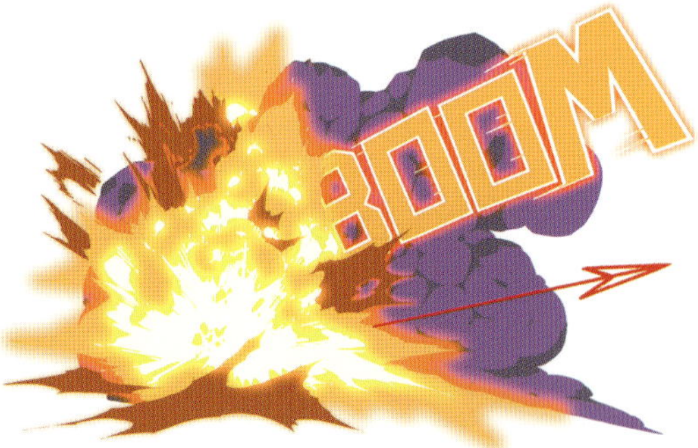
BOOM

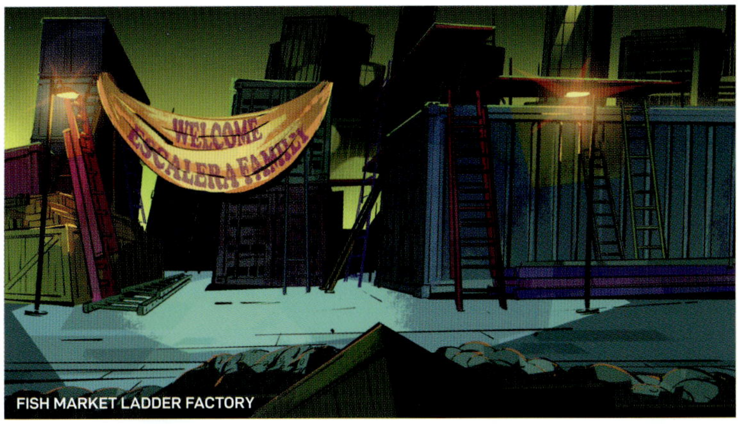

FISH MARKET LADDER FACTORY

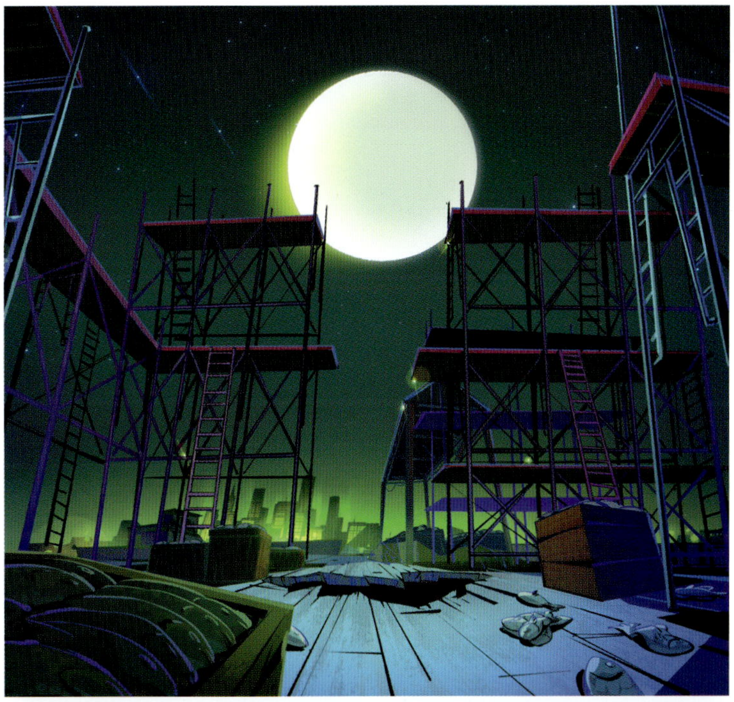

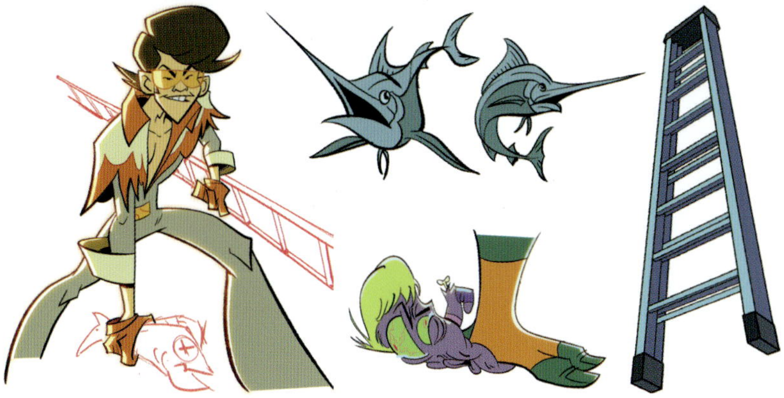

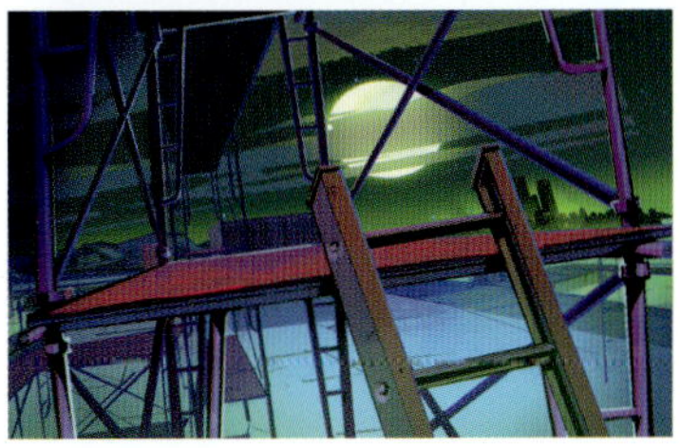

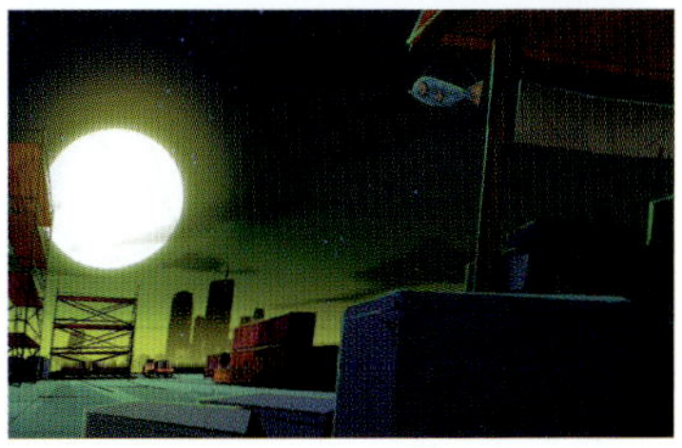

JESSE GORDON: Lou Jitsu is a throwback to martial artist performers like Jackie Chan. If you ever see him fight with ladders, those fights are amazing! At the top of the show they say, *"What are the odds we're ever going to fight in a fish market or ladder factory?"* and, of course, that's what happens!

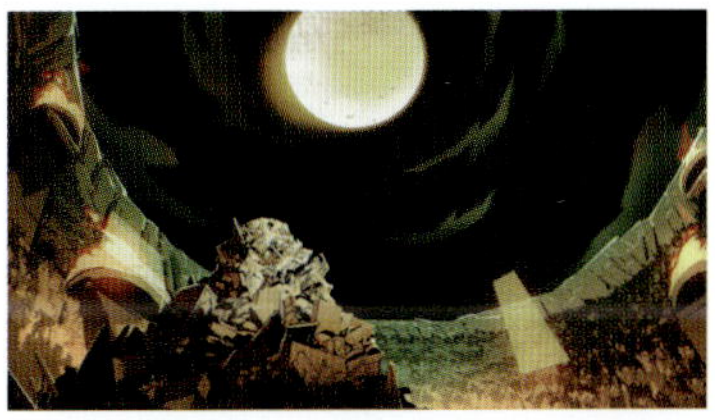

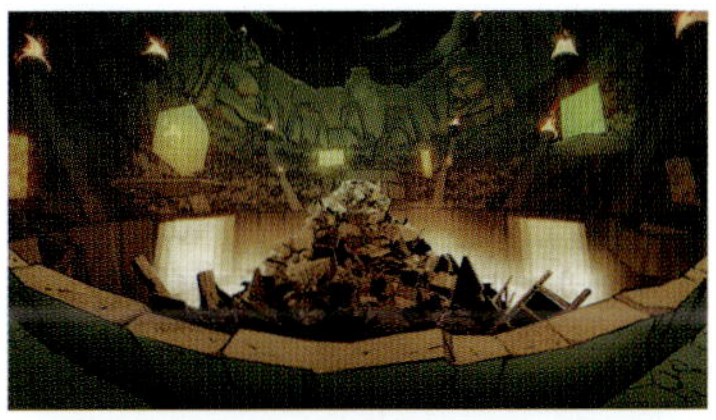

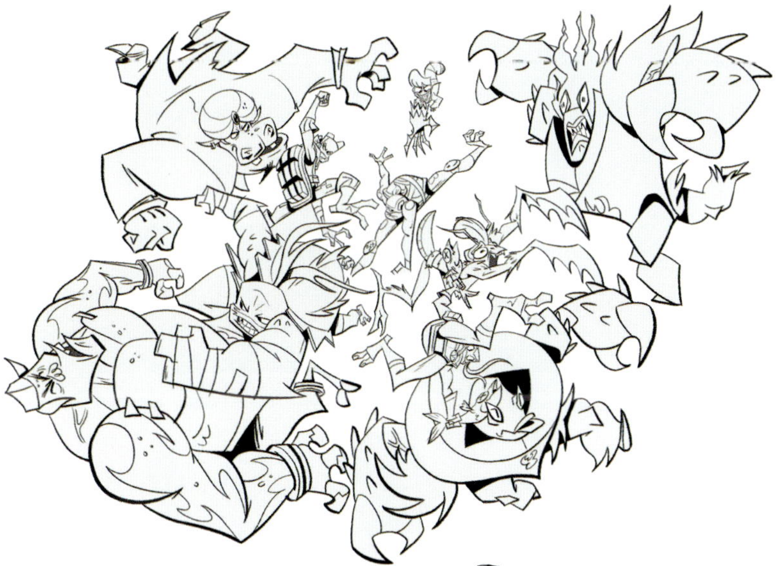

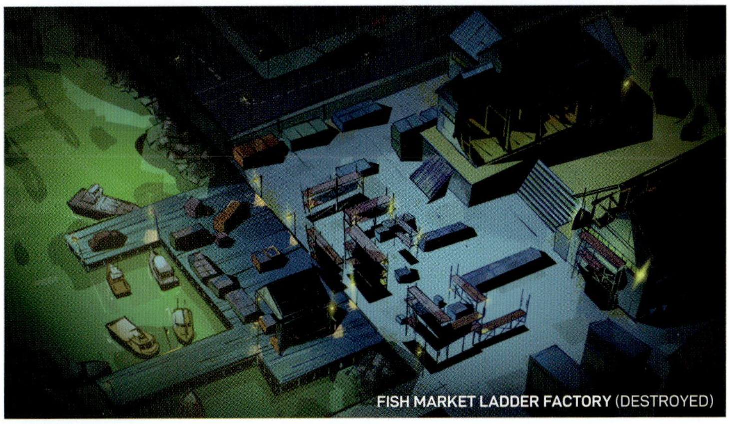
FISH MARKET LADDER FACTORY (DESTROYED)

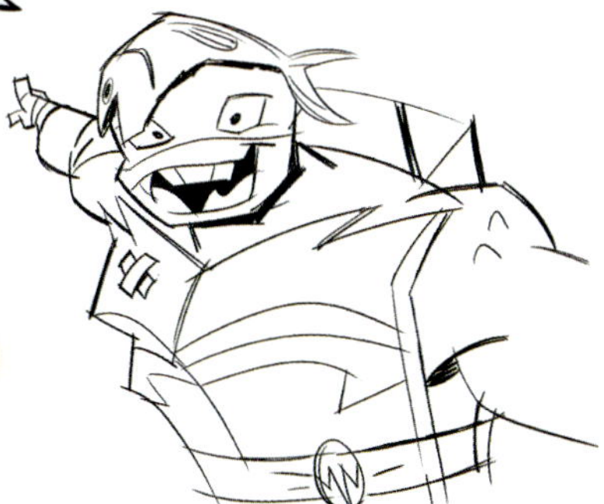

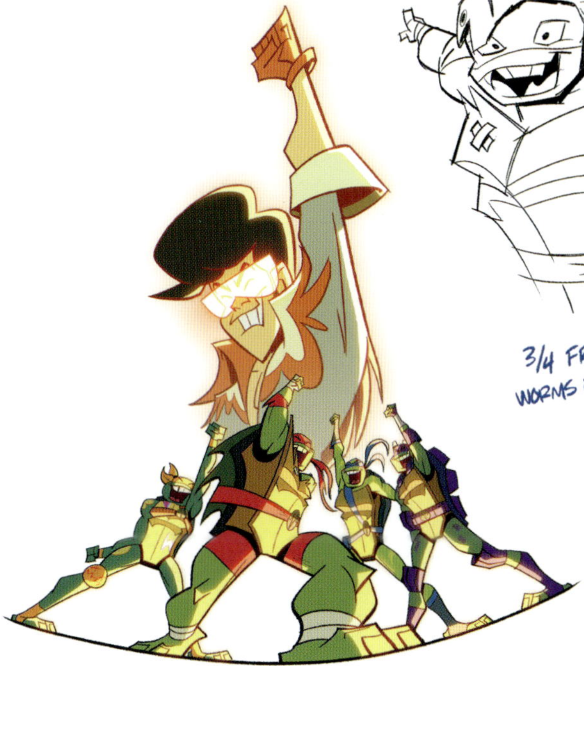

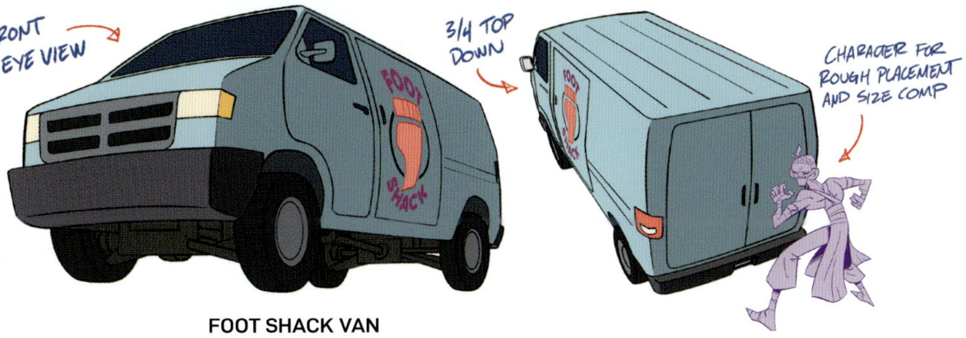

FOOT SHACK VAN

LATE FEE

ORIGINAL AIR DATE: FEBRUARY 23, 2019
PRODUCTION CODE: 027

WRITTEN BY **DALE MALINOWSKI**
STORYBOARDS BY **CHRISTOPHER LUC**
DIRECTED BY **ABE AUDISH**

DALE MALINOWSKI: I remember wanting to use New York City as a character and Ian lending me his DVD of Martin Scorsese's *After Hours* (1985) for inspiration. It worked! While working on the story in L.A., I listened to a lot of hip-hop and rap by New York artists, and songs about the city, which helped me stay in a "New York State of Mind." Previously, I was never able to concentrate on writing while listening to music with lyrics, and this experience broke that barrier in me, which I am extremely grateful for. My favorite part of this episode is what the Turtles are really working for: affection (a hug) from their dad. Splinter is a good father, but we reveal later in the series that he had a complicated relationship with his parents, so showing affection doesn't come naturally to Splinter.

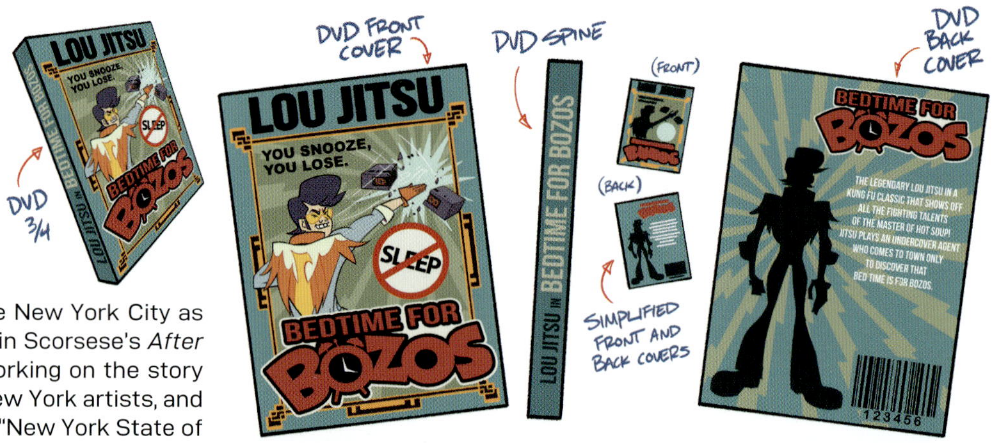

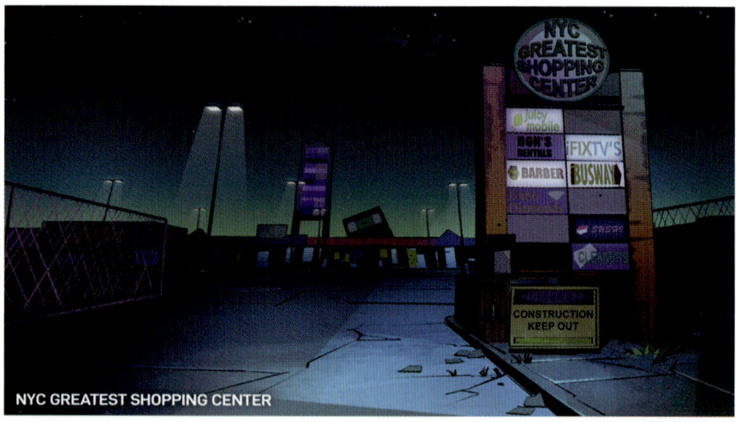

NYC GREATEST SHOPPING CENTER

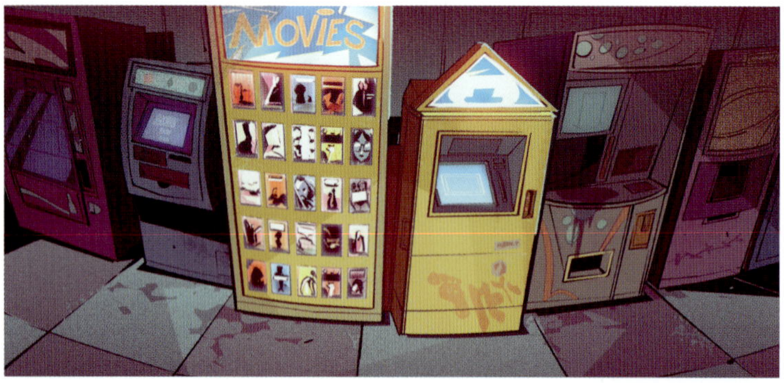

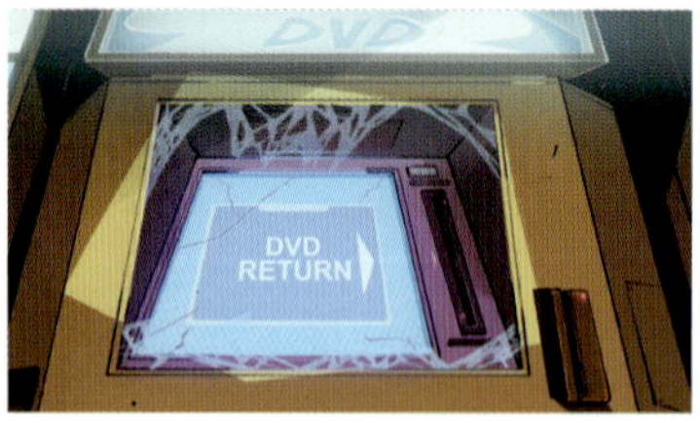

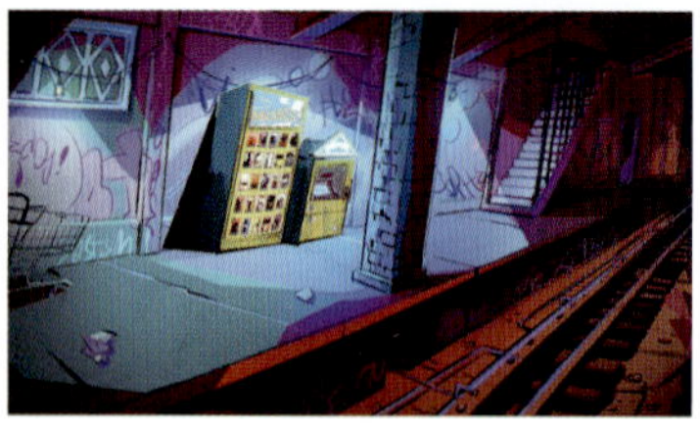

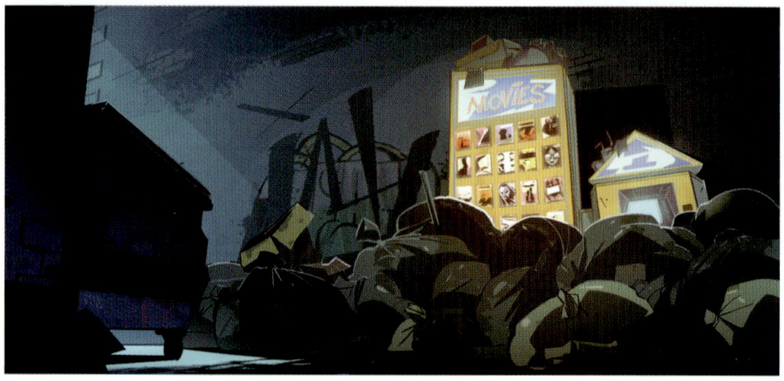

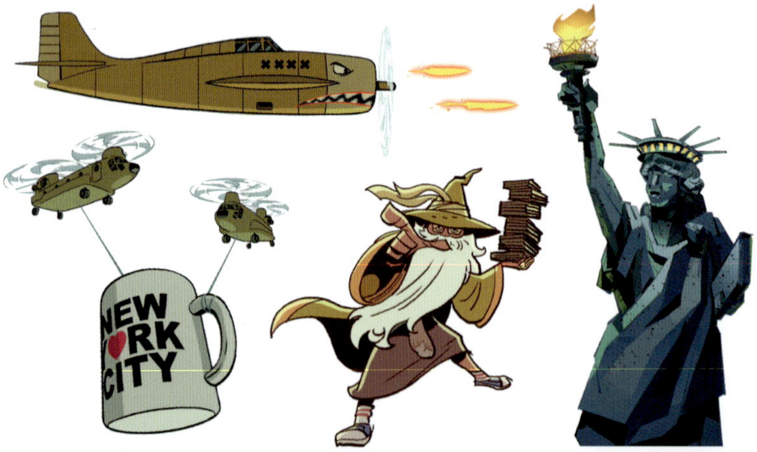

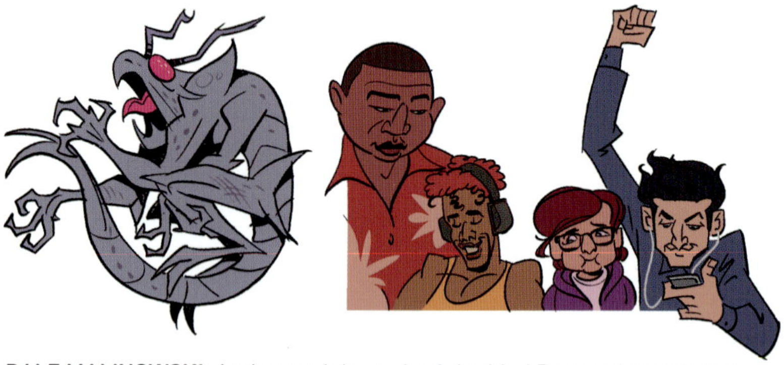

DALE MALINOWSKI: Andy snuck in each of the Mad Dogs voice actors in the subway scene. From left to right: Omar Benson Miller (Raph), Brandon Mychal Smith (Mikey), Josh Brener (Donnie), Ben Schwartz (Leo).

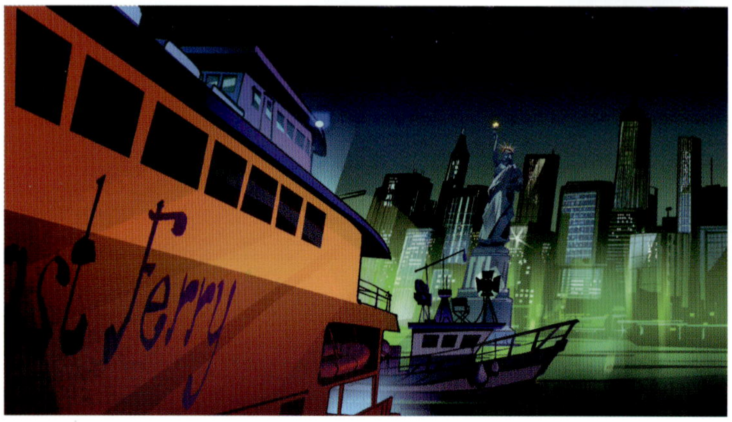

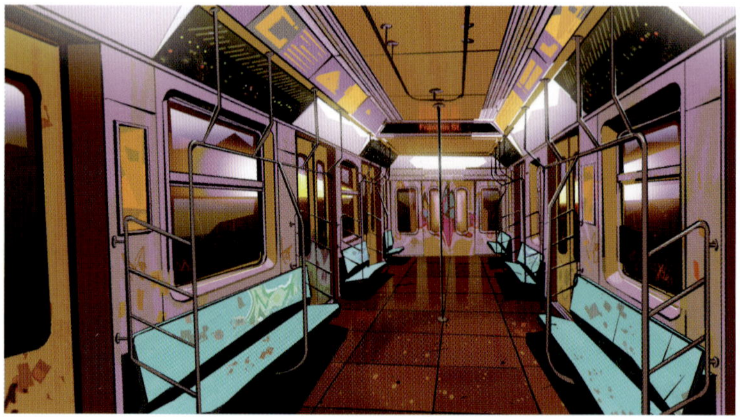

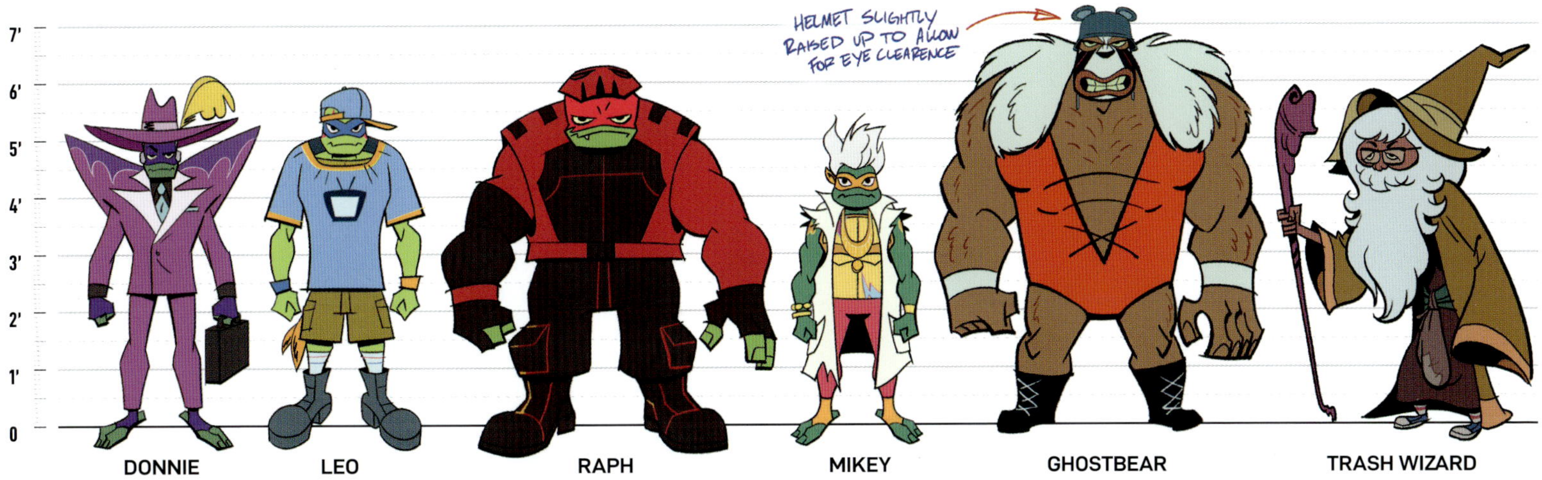

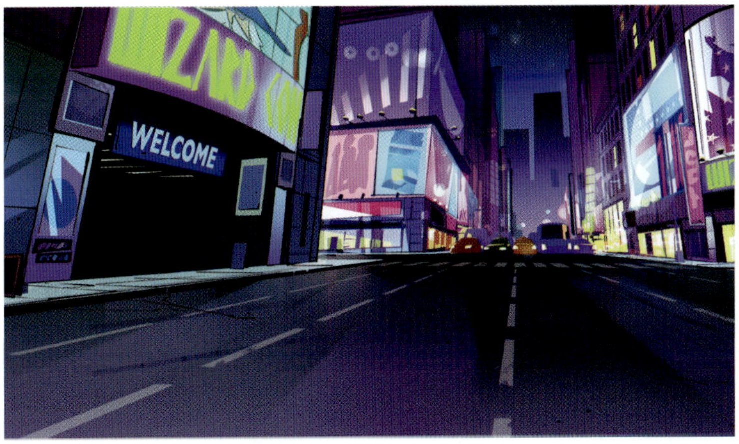

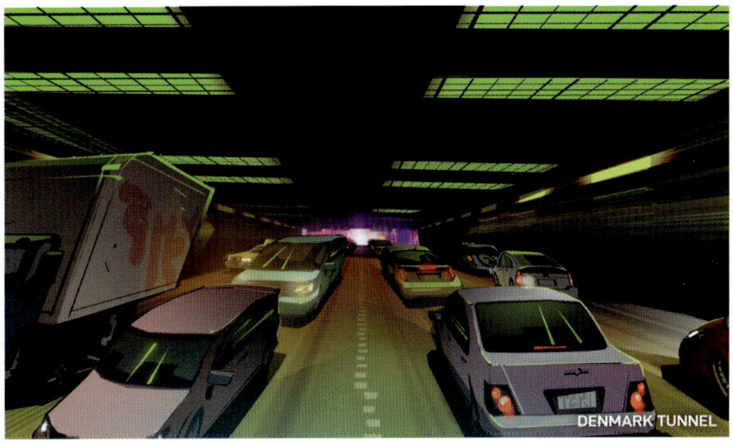

DENMARK TUNNEL

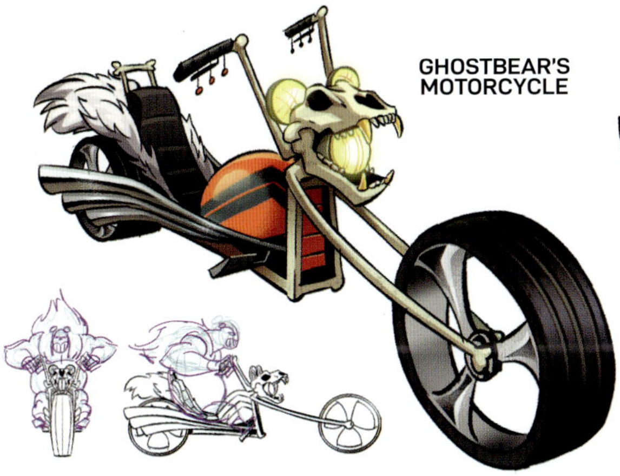

GHOSTBEAR'S MOTORCYCLE

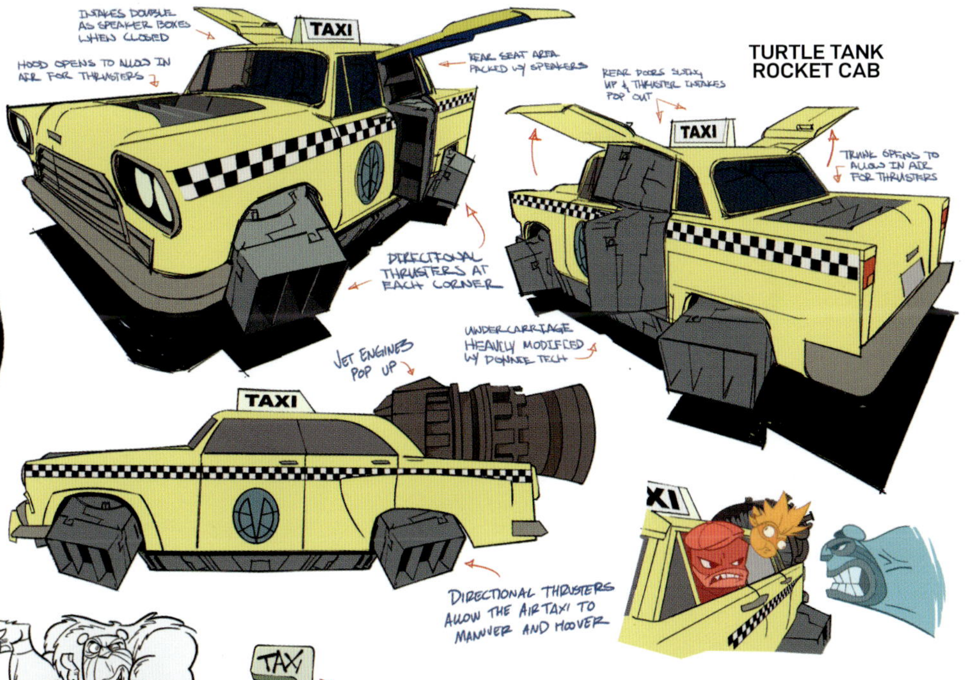

TURTLE TANK ROCKET CAB

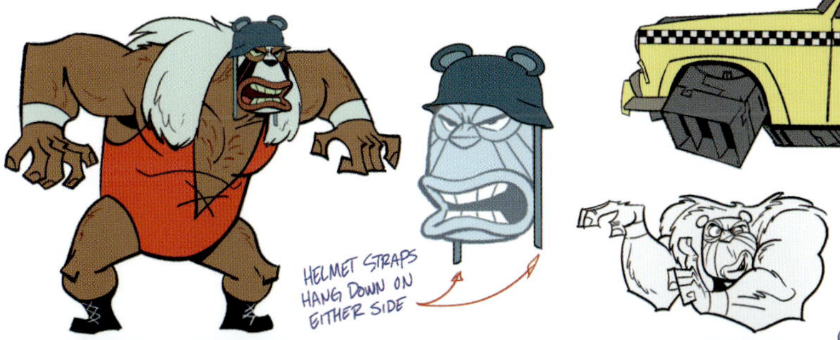

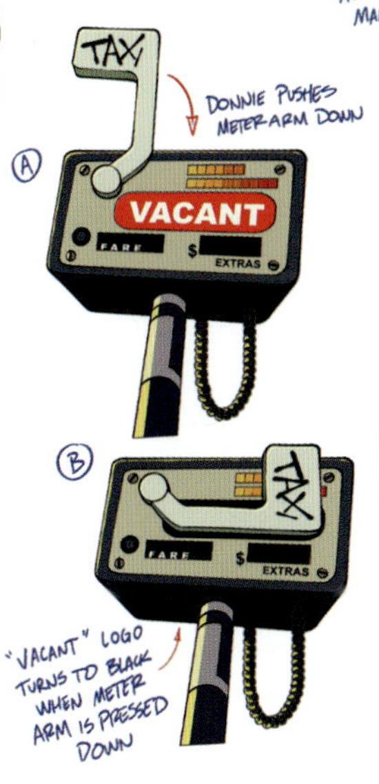

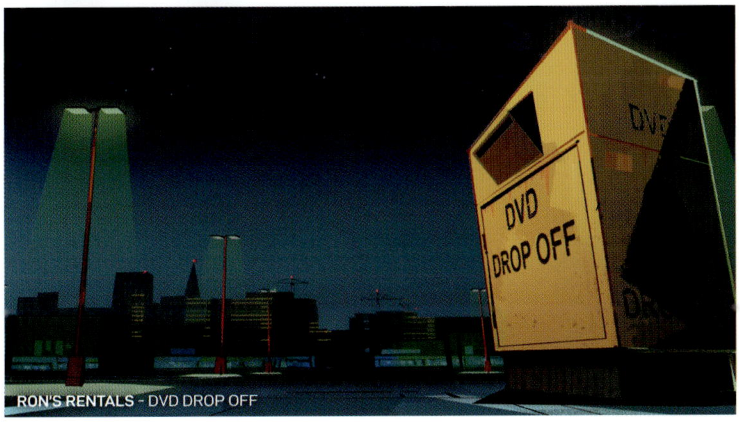

RON'S RENTALS - DVD DROP OFF

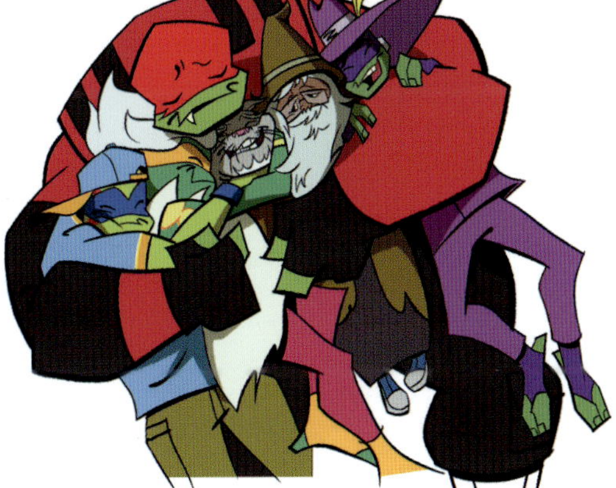

BULLHOP

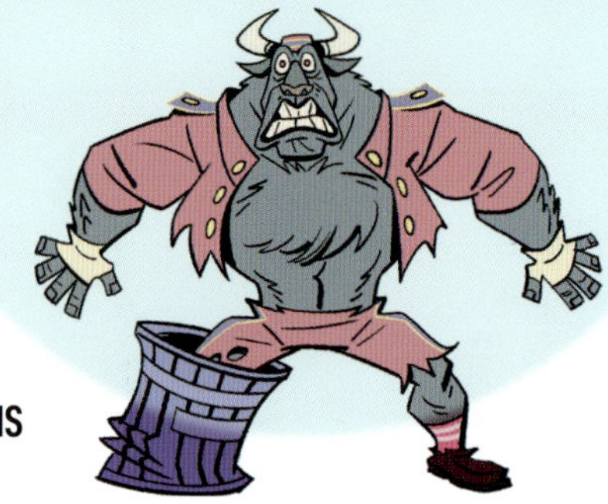

ORIGINAL AIR DATE: MARCH 2, 2019
PRODUCTION CODE: 028

WRITTEN BY **RUSS CARNEY & RON CORCILLO**
STORYBOARDS BY **GLADYFAITH ABCEDE, MAX COLLINS**
DIRECTED BY **SEBASTIAN MONTES**

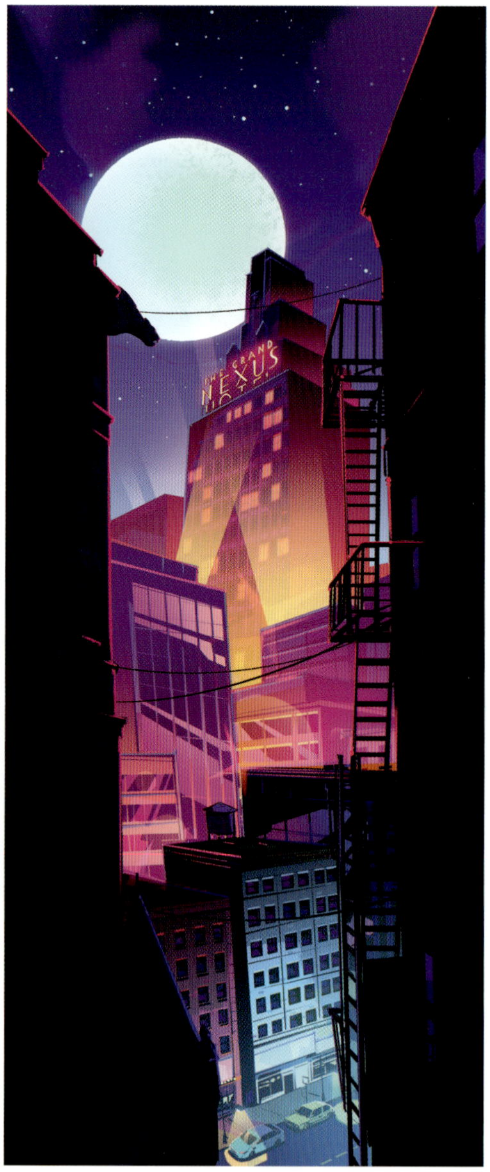

RON CORCILLO: We thought it would be fun to start the episode with Donnie spying on Bullhop while narrating what he sees in a David Attenborough–esque way. Josh Brener thought that was funny, which was flattering, and it turns out that he can do a wide range of accents.

RUSS CARNEY: This is the episode that originated Mikey's "Dr. Delicate Touch" persona. Let's face it, we all wish we could be as brutally honest as he is. It's unbridled rage that comes from a warm cuddly place of love!

RON CORCILLO: Bullhop's voice actor, Dave Foley, is from Etobicoke, Canada, so naturally we made Etobicoke Bullhop's hometown. At one point, Andy was eager to have us write a story featuring Monty Moose, an obscure action figure from the 1988 TMNT toy line. We thought that maybe Monty Moose could be an over-the-top Canadian mounted police officer in pursuit of Bullhop, but none of the writers could ever figure out a Monty story that knocked our socks off.

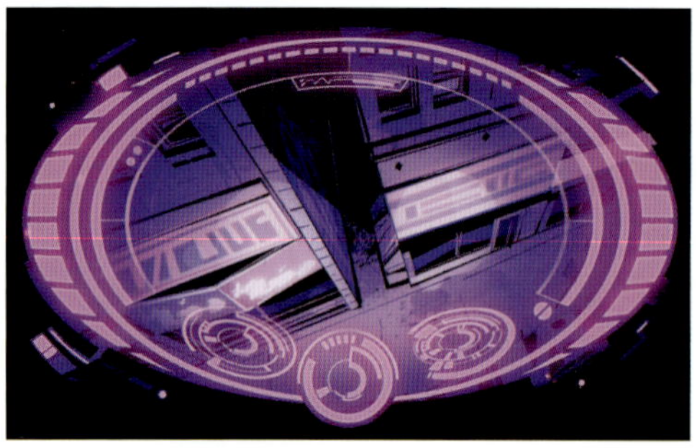

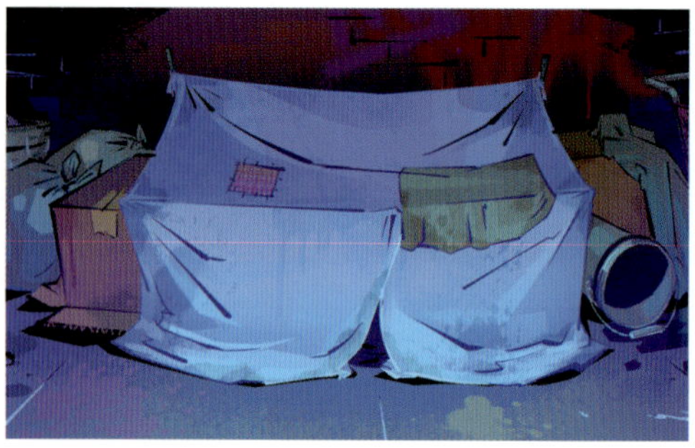

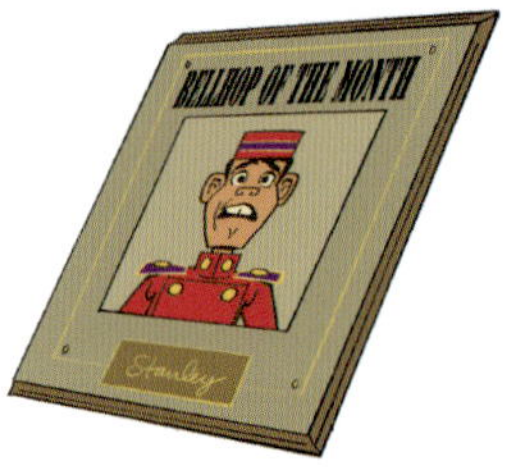

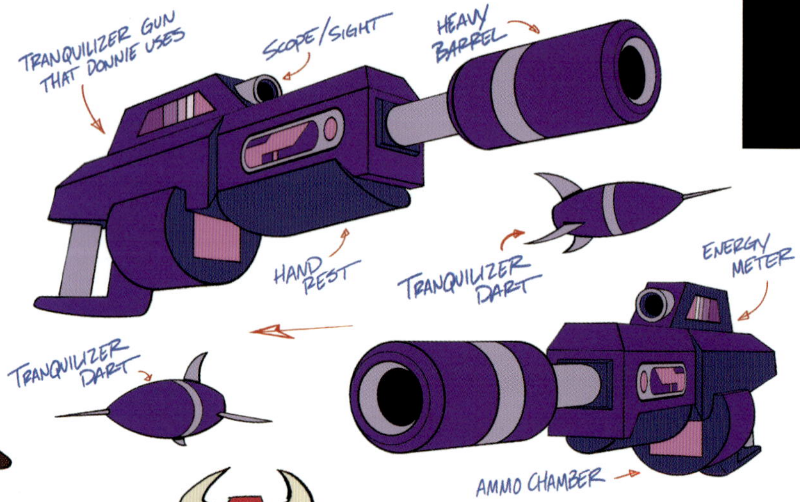

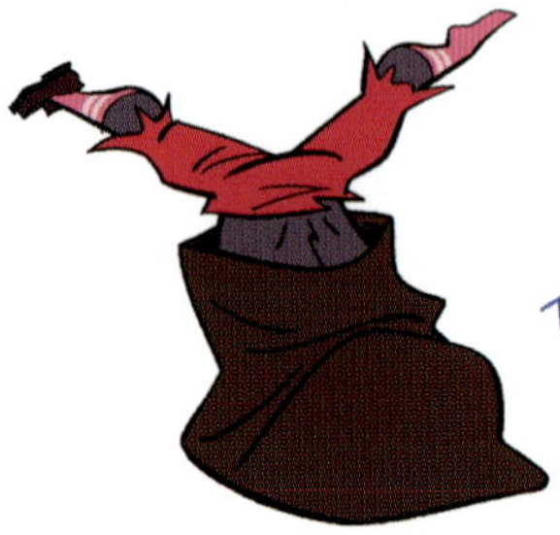

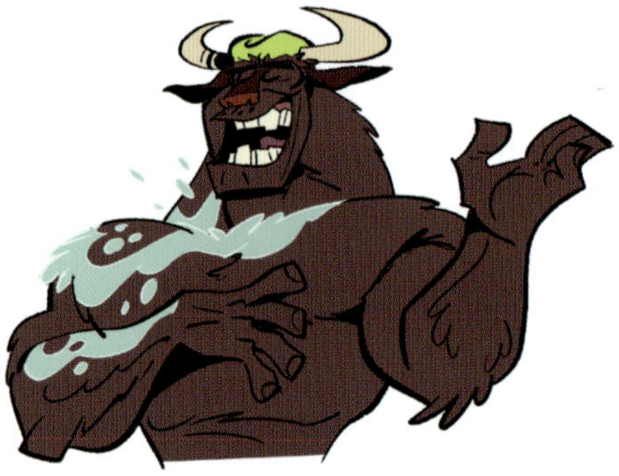

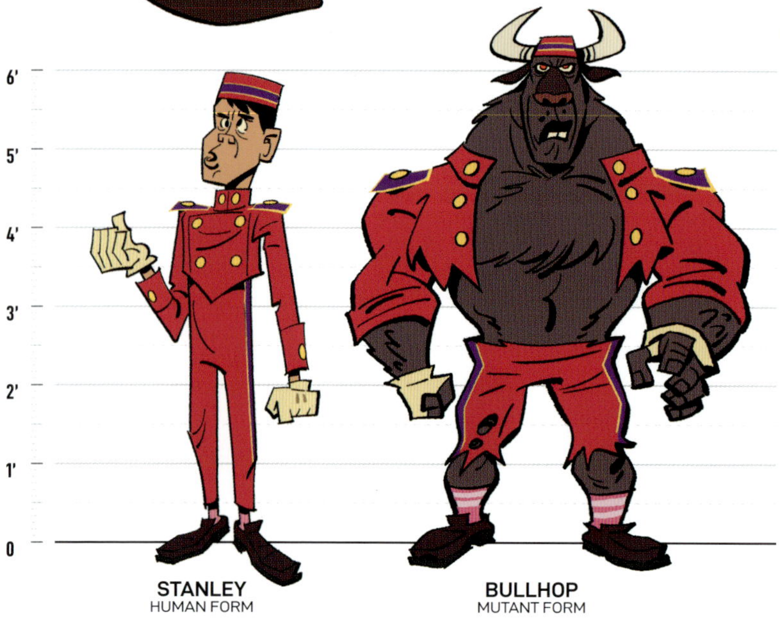

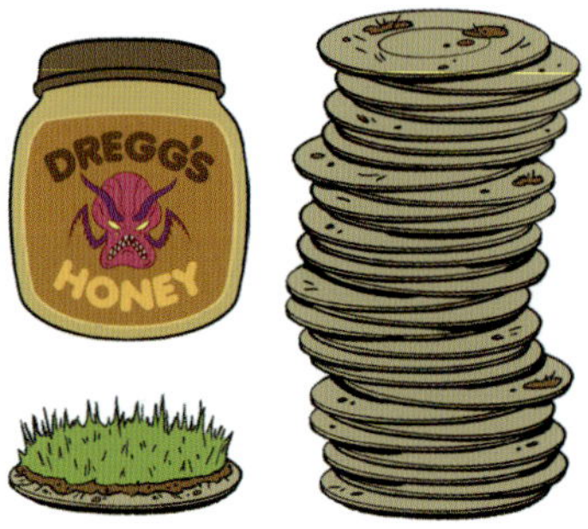

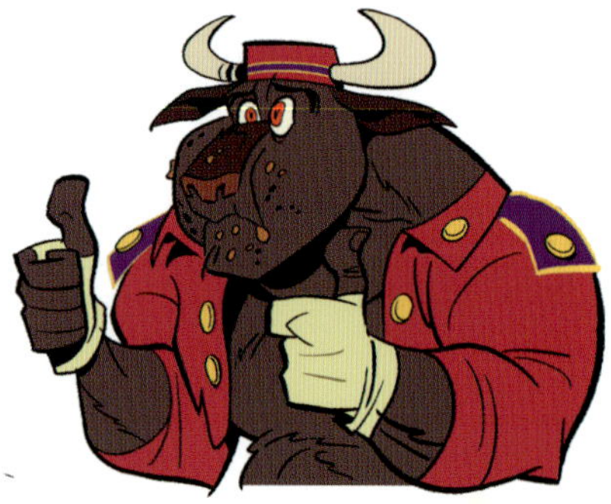

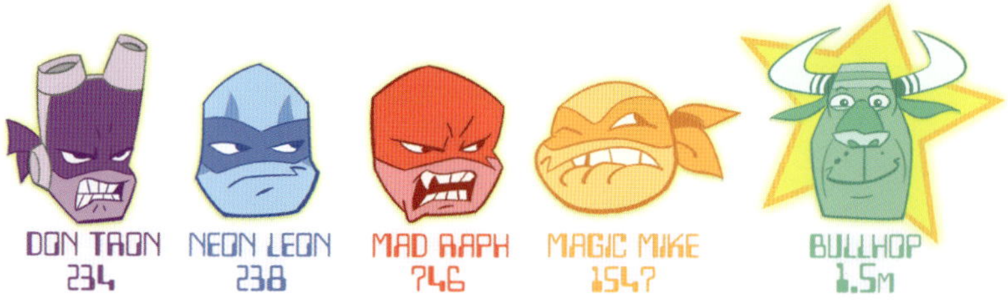

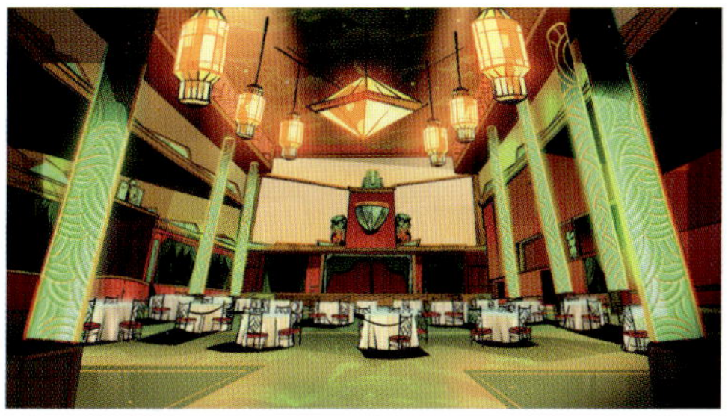

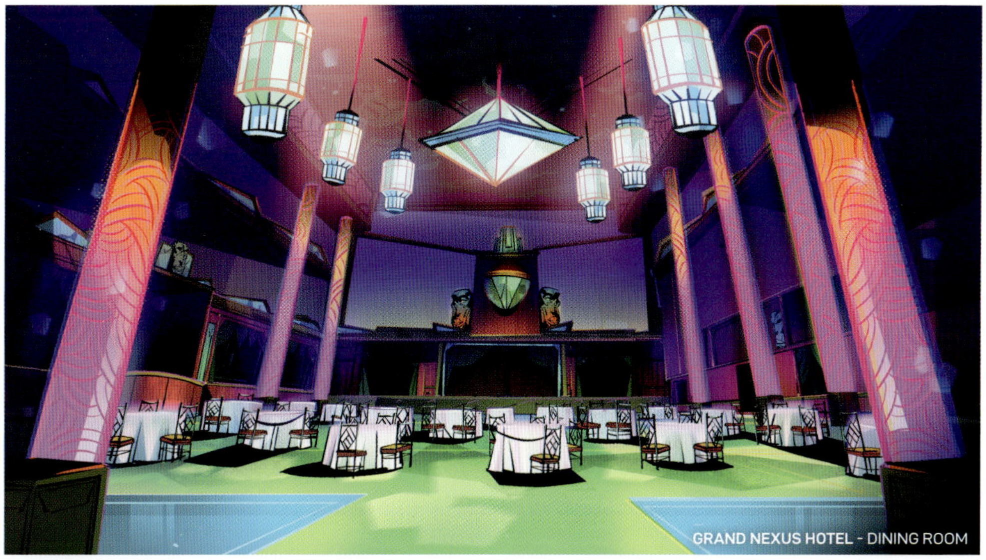

GRAND NEXUS HOTEL - DINING ROOM

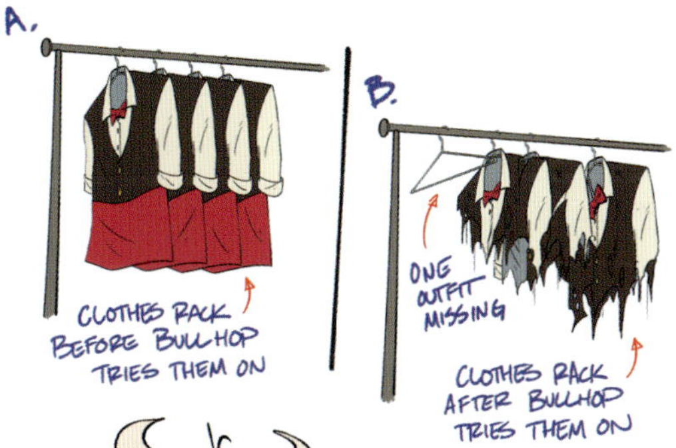

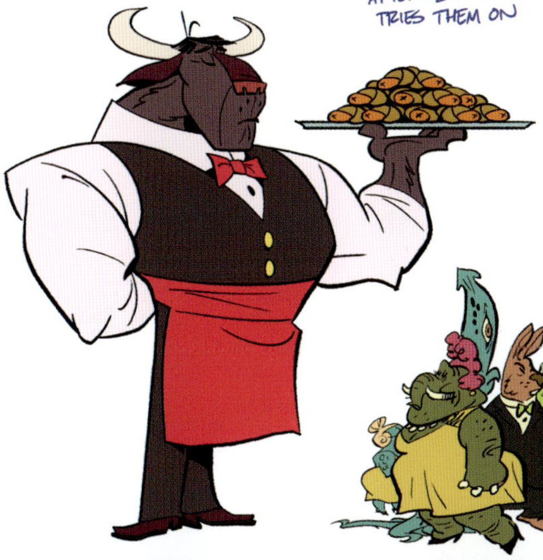

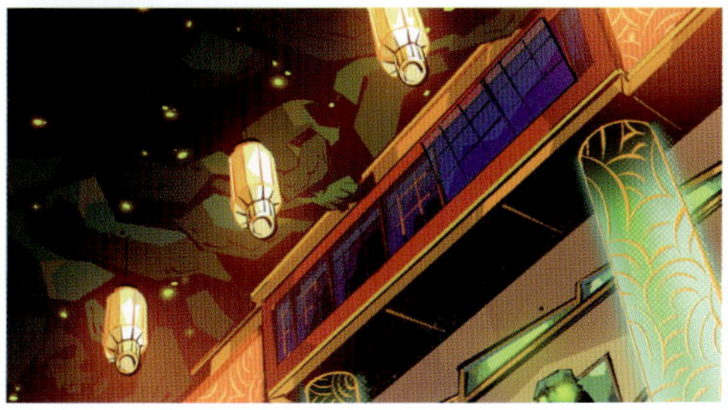

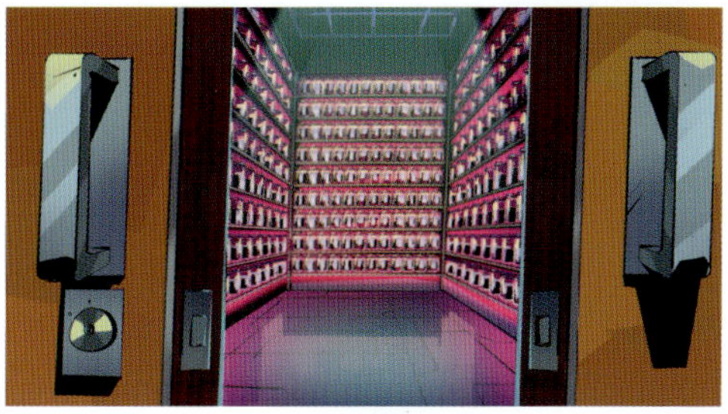

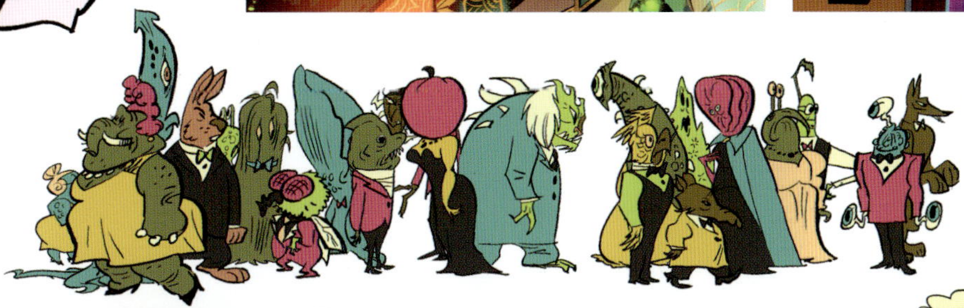

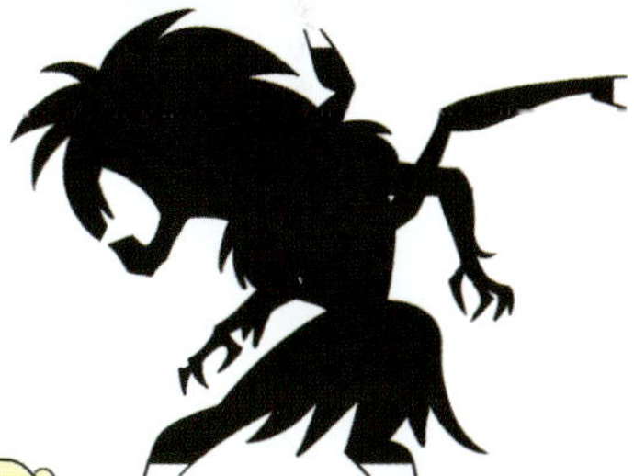

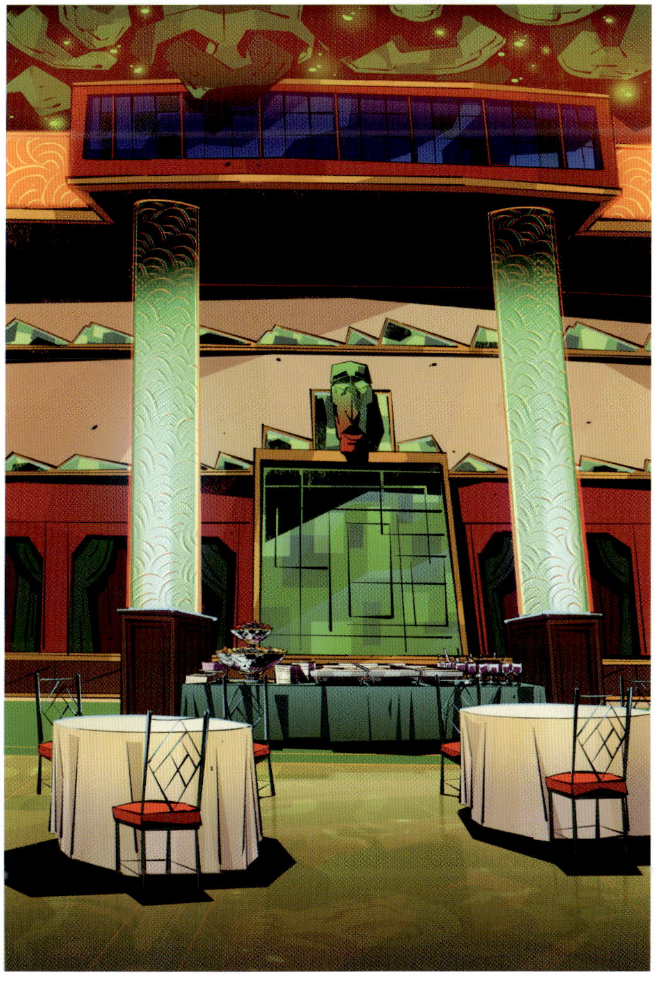

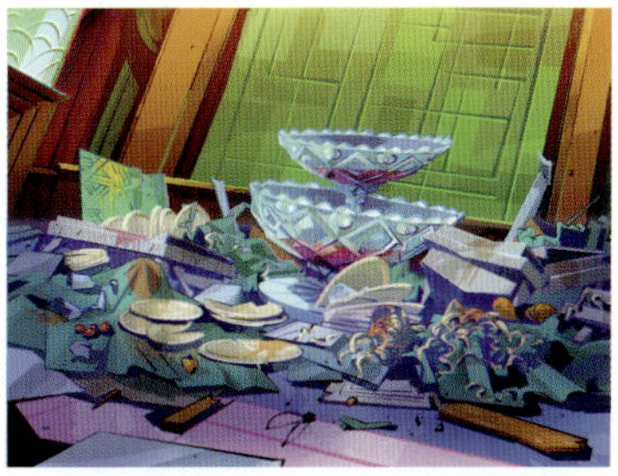

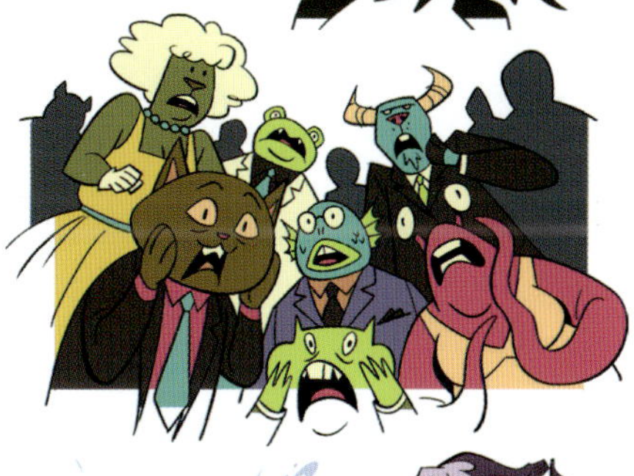

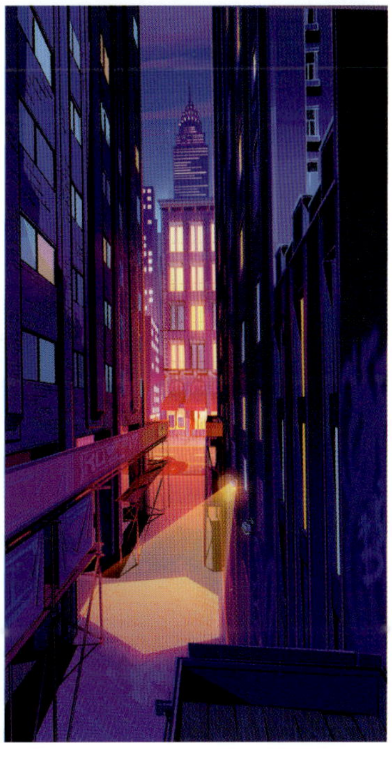

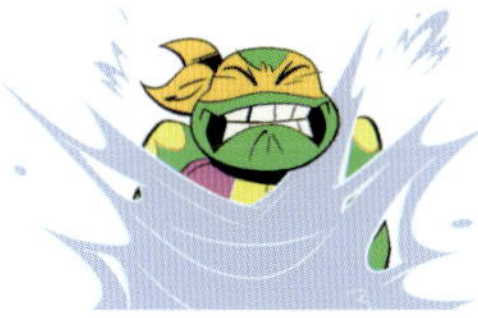

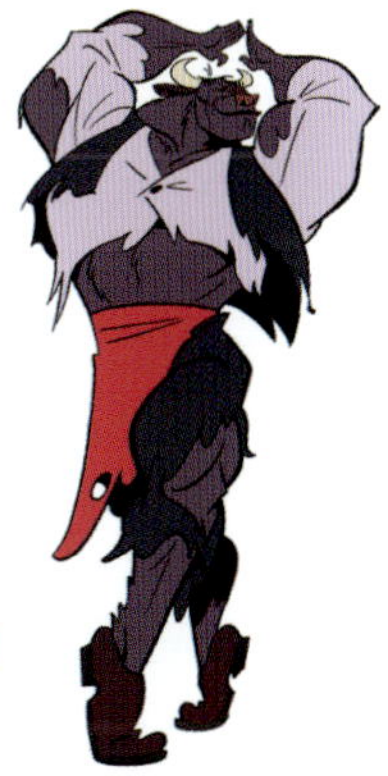

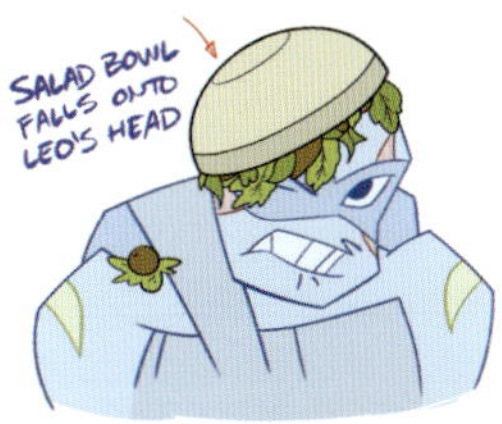

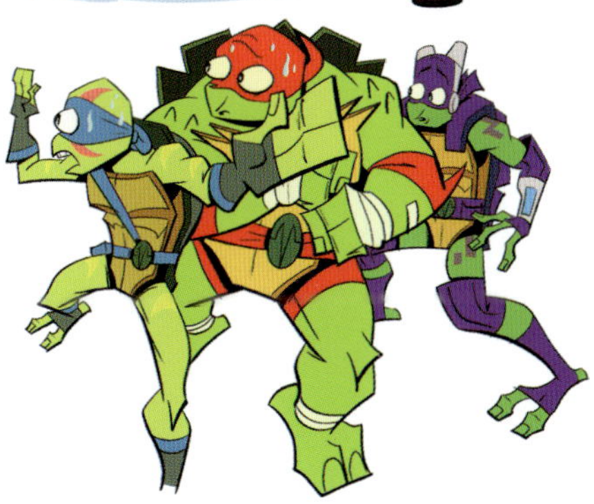

NOTHING BUT TRUFFLE

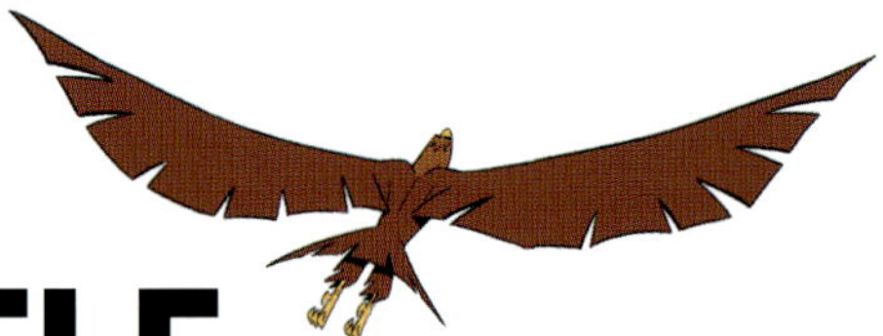

ORIGINAL AIR DATE: MARCH 16, 2019
PRODUCTION CODE: 029

WRITTEN BY **RUSS CARNEY & RON CORCILLO**
STORYBOARDS BY **CHRISTINE LIU**
DIRECTED BY **ALAN WAN**

RON CORCILLO: We think that a story about Mikey becoming best friends with his hero might have been some wishful projection by Russ at becoming BFFs with John Lydon, but only Russ' therapist knows for sure.

After rewatching the episode, it was pretty striking how poorly Mikey treated Todd, but fortunately he learned a lesson. We loved the performances Thurop Van Orman (Todd) and John delivered. John has an iconic rolled *R* that he uses in songs, and we would often have fun asking him to go overboard with it here and there. In this ep, right before he assimilates Todd's power, Meat Sweats shouts *"Give me your powerrrrrr!"* with a very impressive rolled *R*.

RUSS CARNEY: At the end of the episode, we weren't sure that we'd get to keep Meat Sweats' euphemistic *"Oh shallots"* line, as there was some Standards pushback when we wrote the episode, but eventually it was approved.

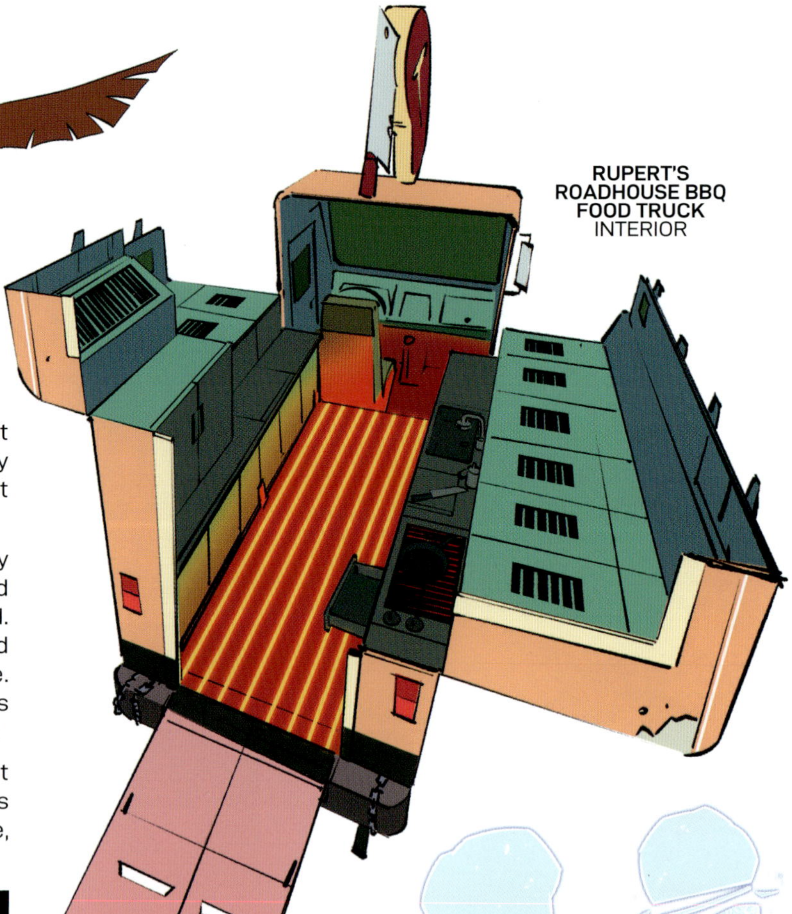

RUPERT'S ROADHOUSE BBQ FOOD TRUCK INTERIOR

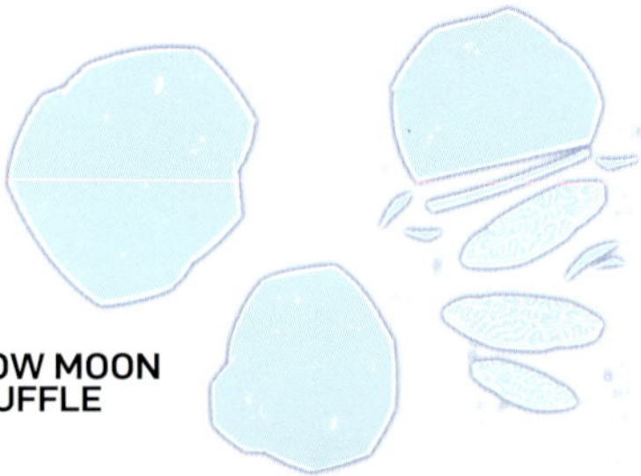

SHADOW MOON TRUFFLE

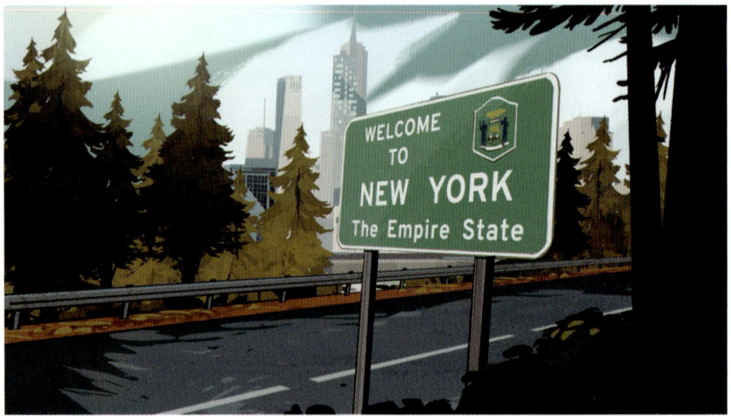

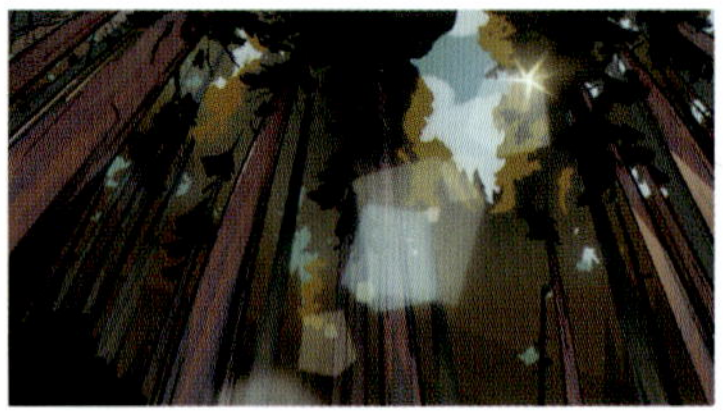

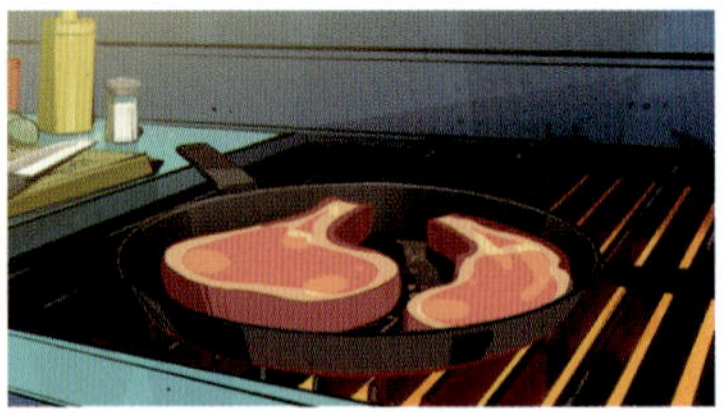

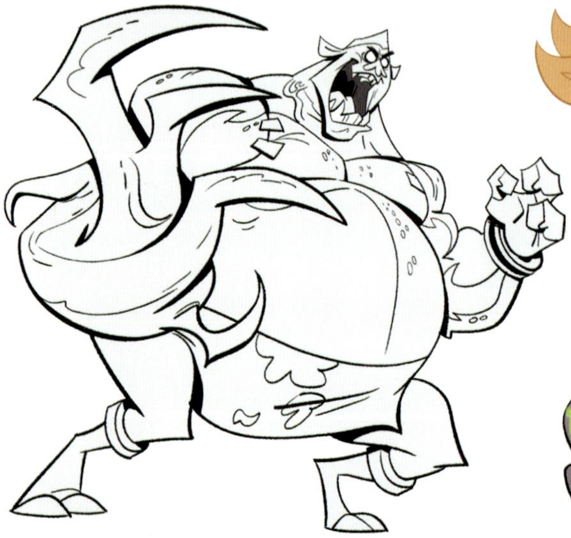

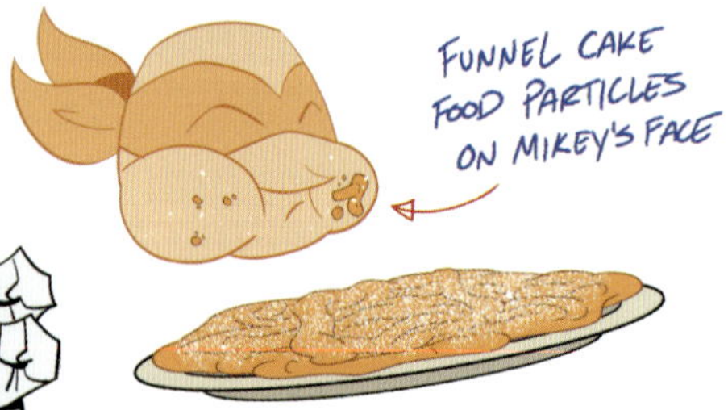

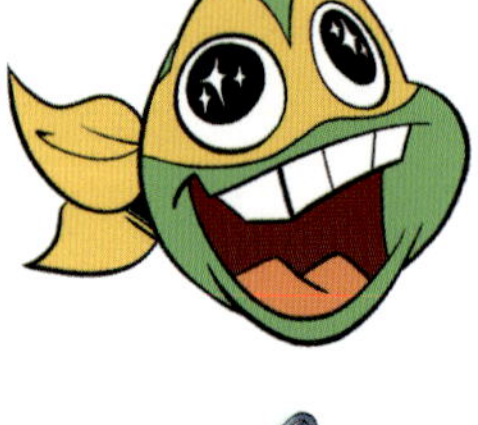

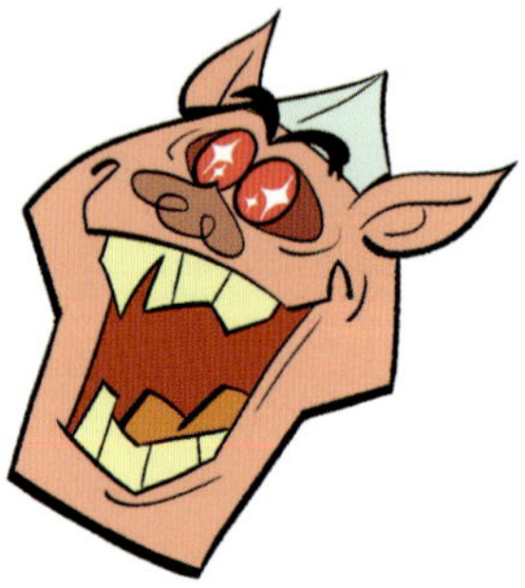

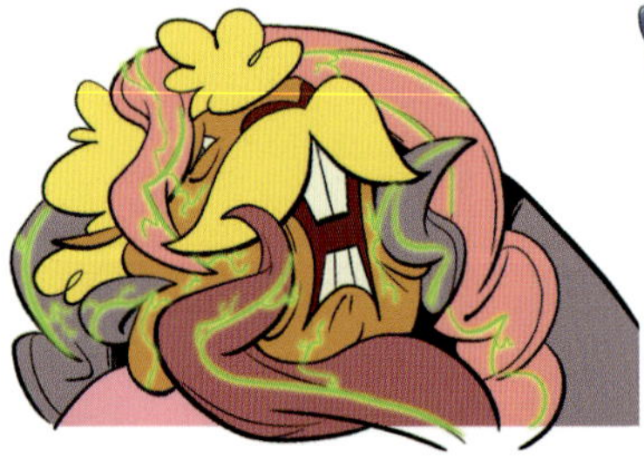

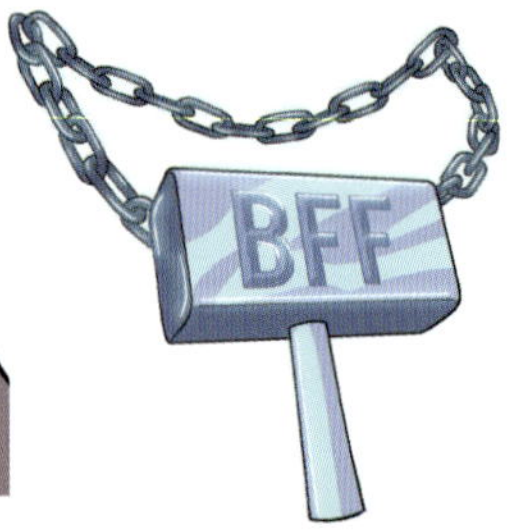

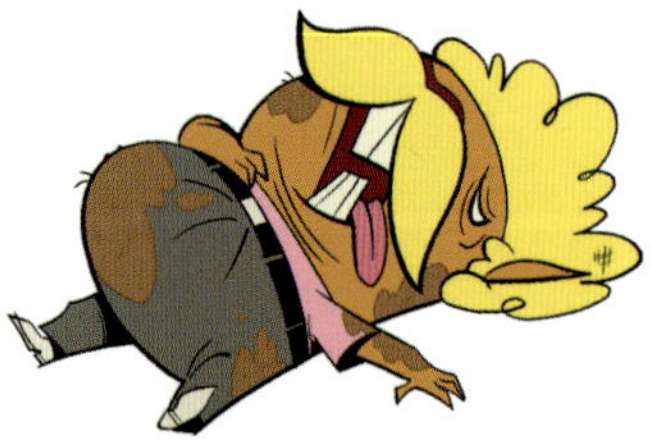

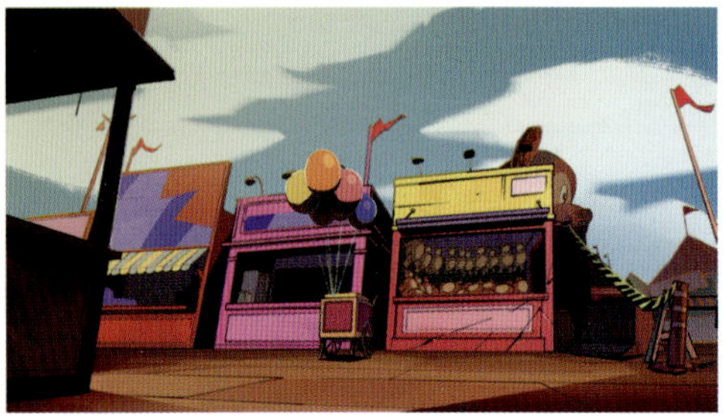

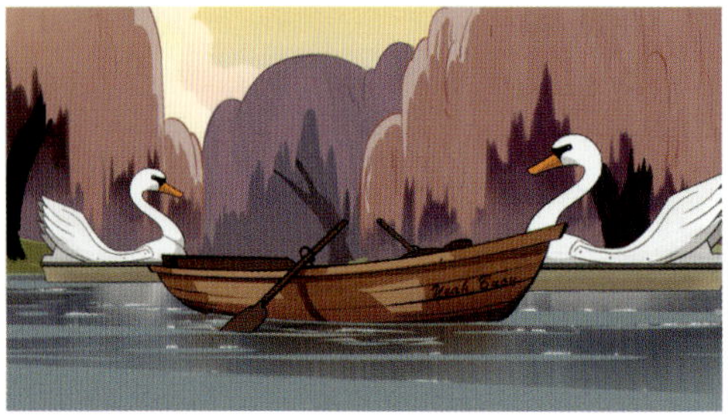

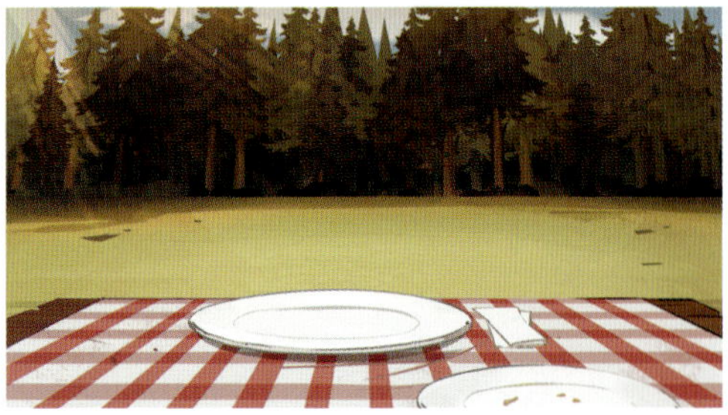

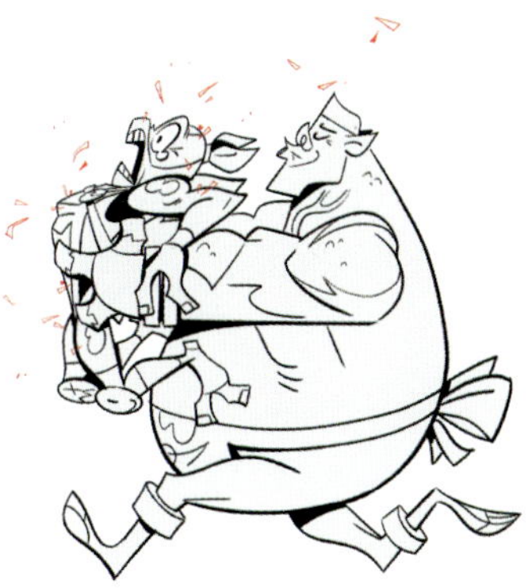

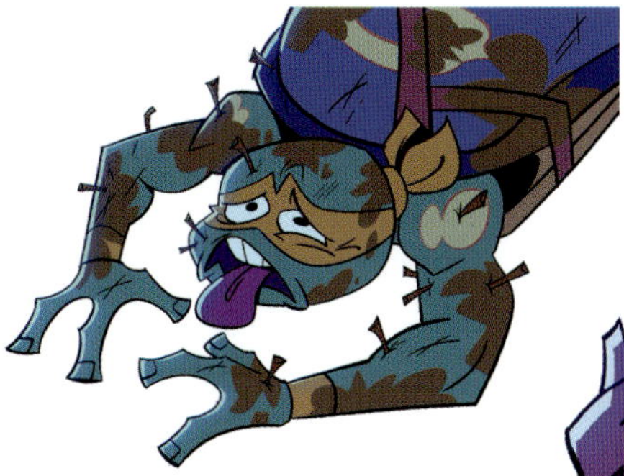

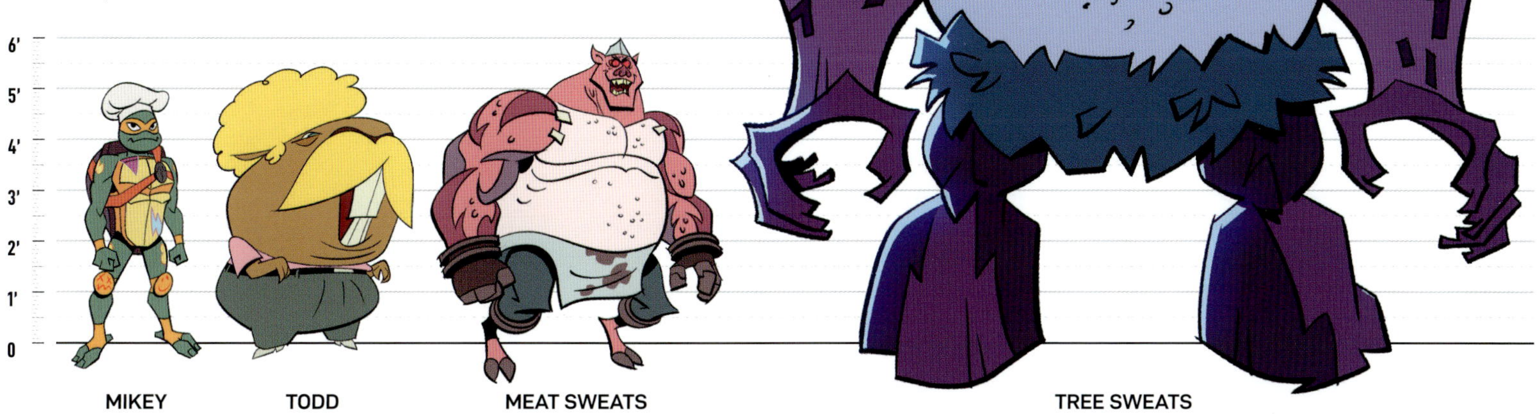

MIKEY TODD MEAT SWEATS TREE SWEATS

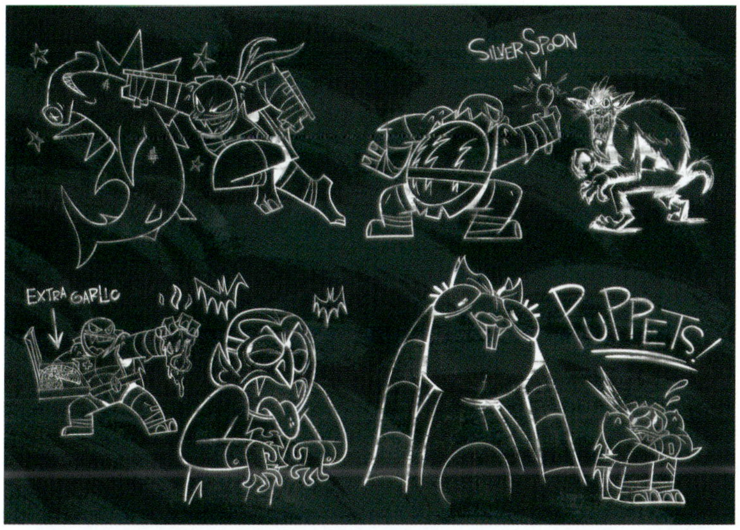

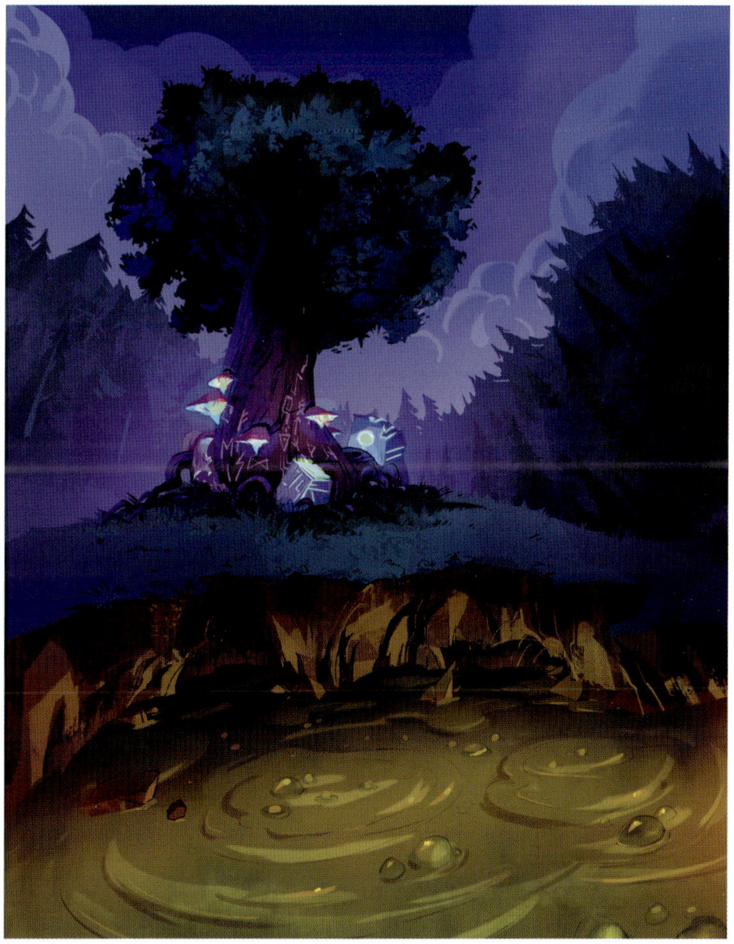

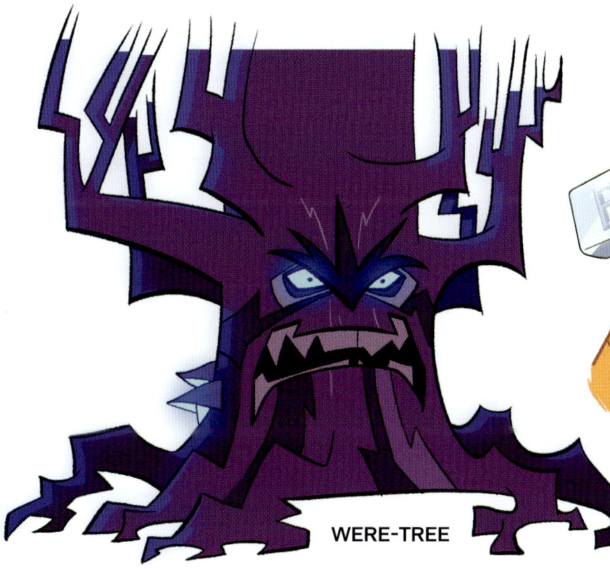

WERE-TREE

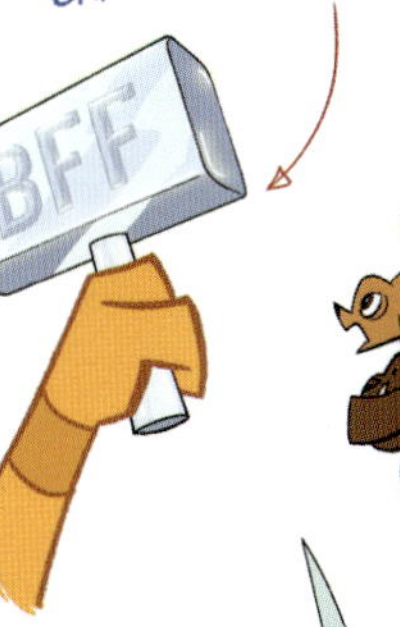

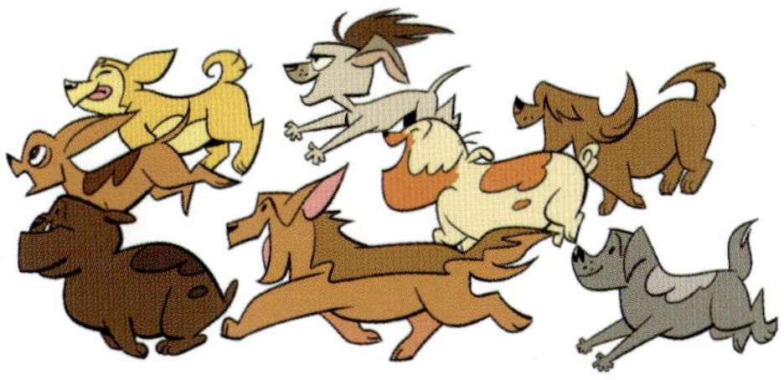

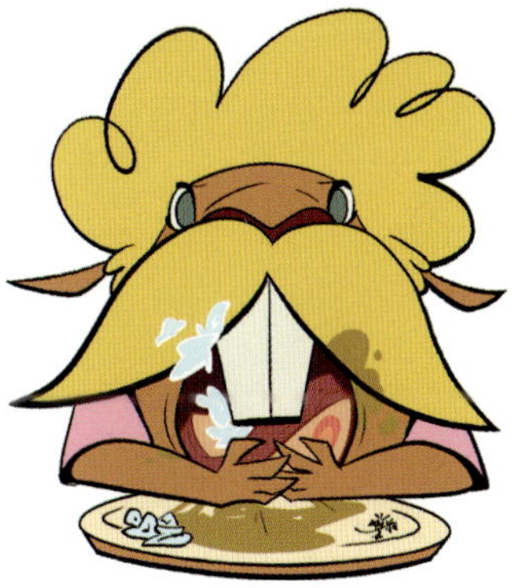

TURTLE-DEGA NIGHTS: THE BALLAD OF RAT MAN

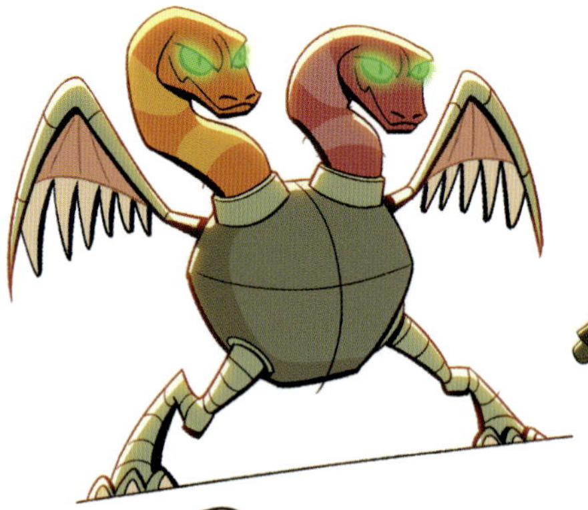

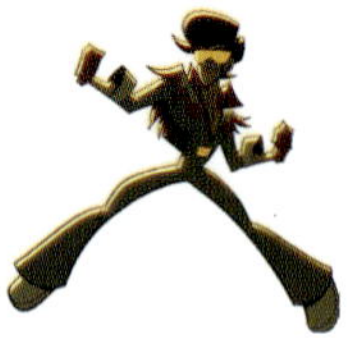

ORIGINAL AIR DATE: OCTOBER 26, 2019
PRODUCTION CODE: 030

WRITTEN BY **JESSE GORDON**
STORYBOARDS BY **ALICIA CHAN**
DIRECTED BY **ABE AUDISH**

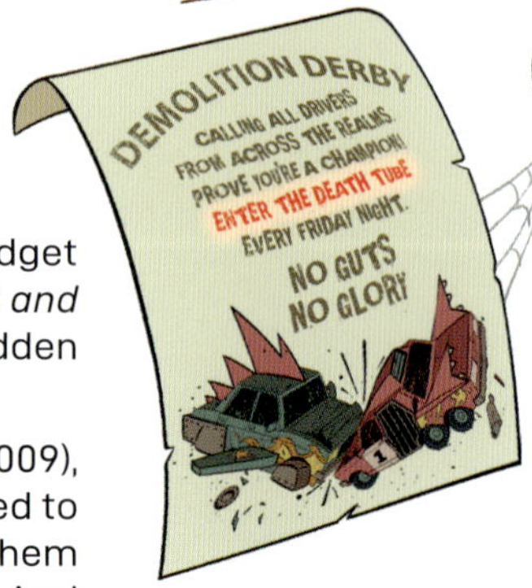

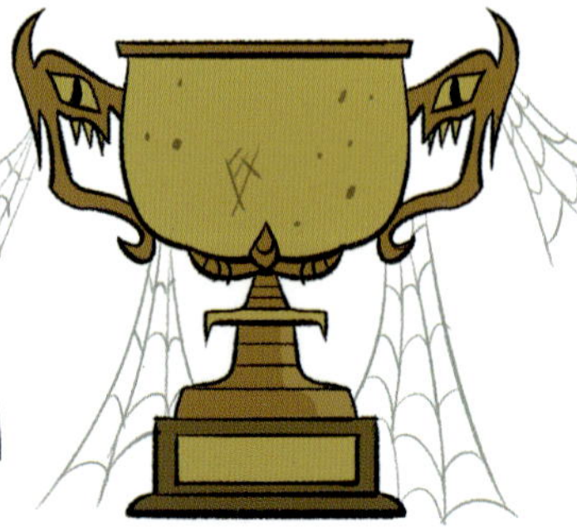

JESSE GORDON: Rise provided such a great platform to try to do huge, big-budget movies in an 11-minute format. This wasn't just doing *Mad Max* and *The Fast and the Furious* car-racing battle stuff—it was just another way to open up the Hidden City. We just kept pushing the limits to see if a show could pull it off.

So many people on staff like Alan Wan told me to watch this anime, *Redline* (2009), which I wasn't familiar with before working on this show, but I felt they wanted to do something like that. Sometimes you would hear from the board what got them excited, so I would try to do a story for it, and this one was born out of that. And then at the end of the story was my homage to the movie *Armageddon* (1998); the ending is incredibly poignant and sad when Ben Affleck thinks he's going to die and then Bruce Willis trades places with him, and I was just trying to do a comedy version of that.

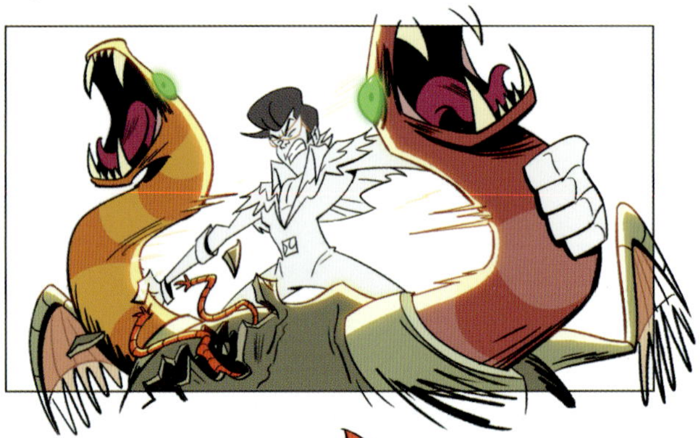

I'm biased, obviously, but I think we created such fun mutants, so it's like a sort of *Hanna-Barbera Wacky Races* (1968), getting to see all the crazy cars battle together with such variety. We had Big Mama behind it all, and expanding the lore of the Hidden City, it was a blast getting to play in a sandbox of different genres, being able to create these big action movies in a finite amount of time.

I think the show is always incredibly ambitious and I think I didn't appreciate that at the time, but looking back, we packed so much story, so much comedy, so much action into these tiny little chunks, and it was always a ton of fun.

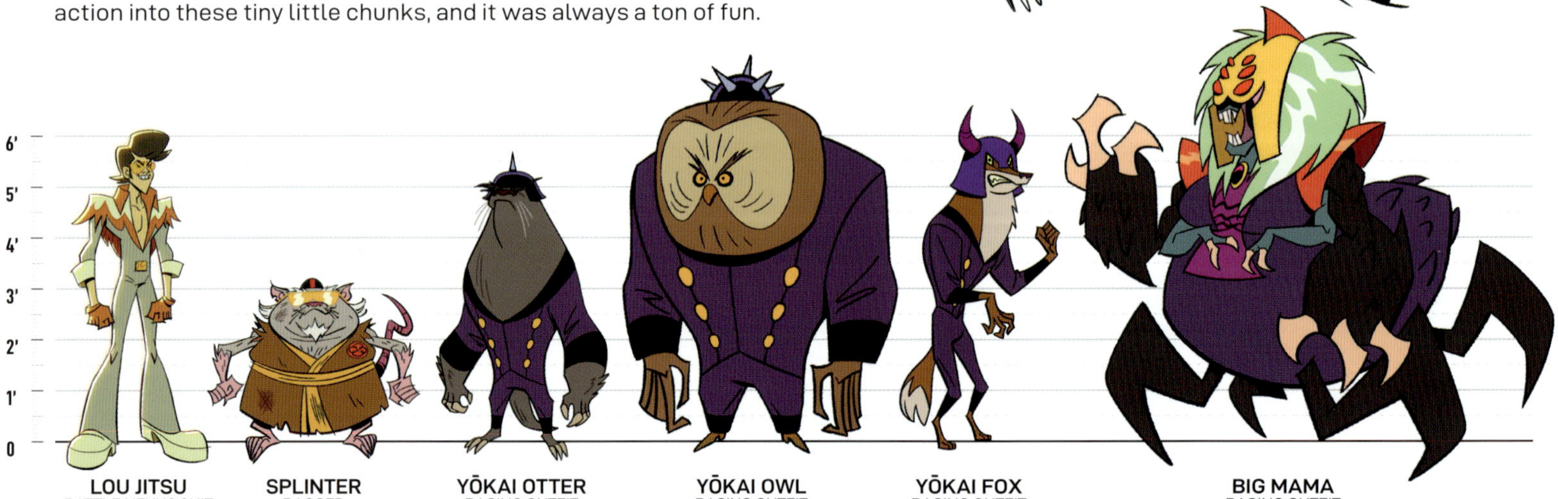

LOU JITSU BATTLE NEXUS SUIT | **SPLINTER** RAGGED | **YŌKAI OTTER** RACING OUTFIT | **YŌKAI OWL** RACING OUTFIT | **YŌKAI FOX** RACING OUTFIT | **BIG MAMA** RACING OUTFIT

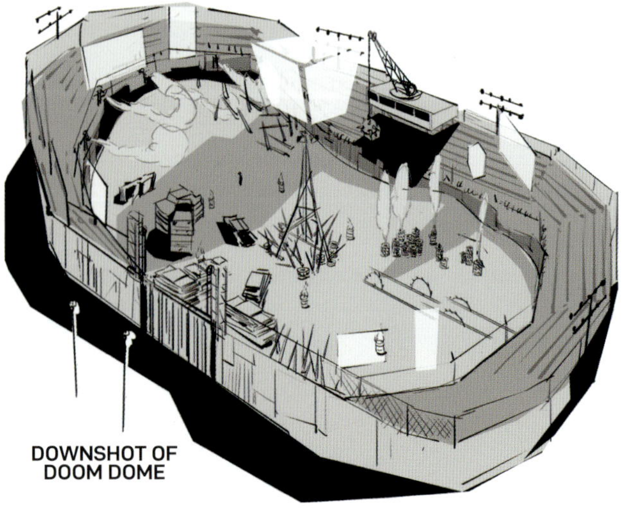

DOWNSHOT OF DOOM DOME

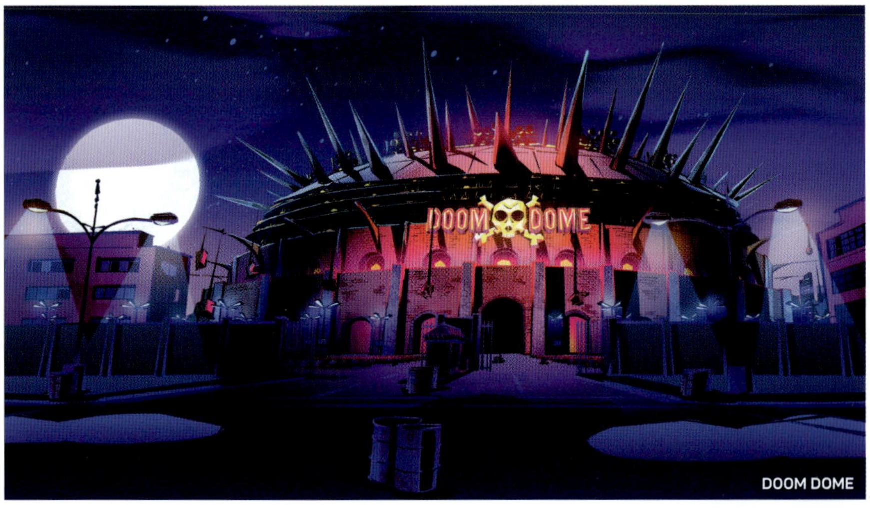

DOOM DOME

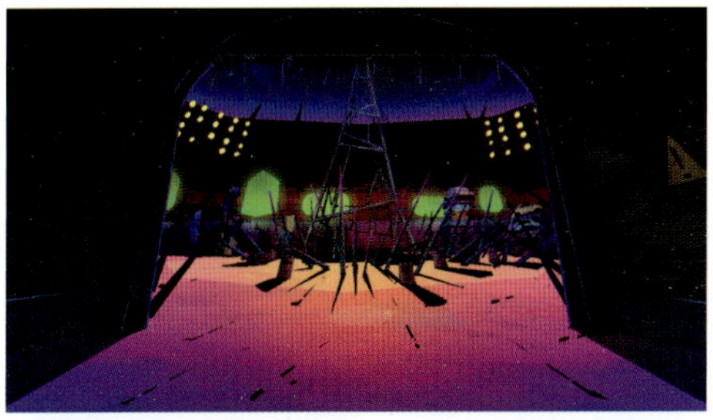

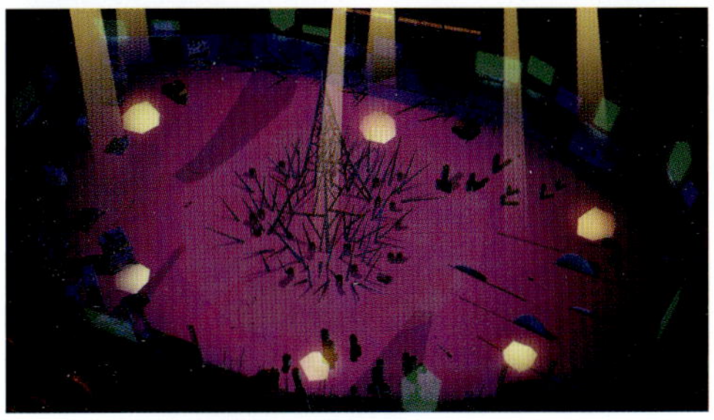

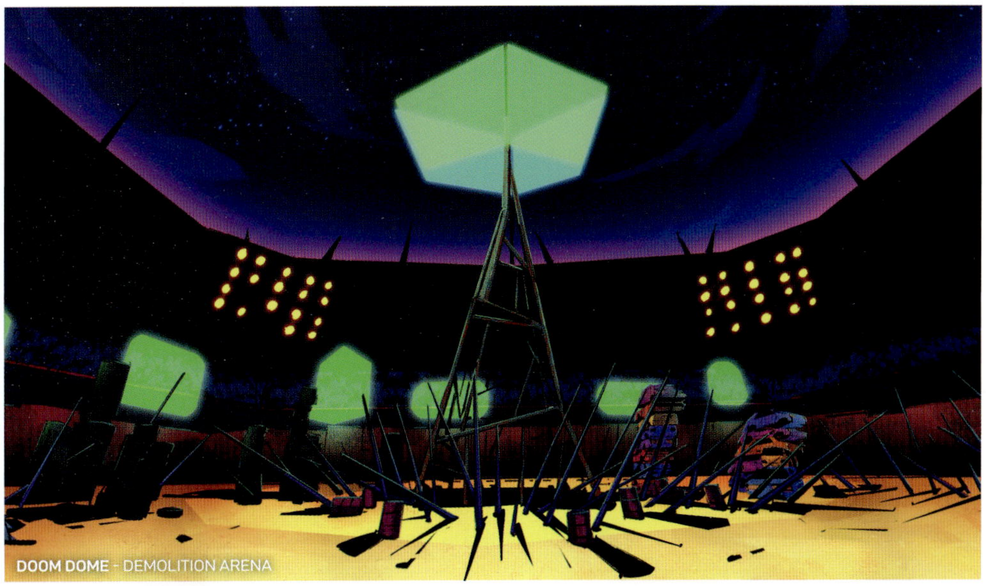

DOOM DOME - DEMOLITION ARENA

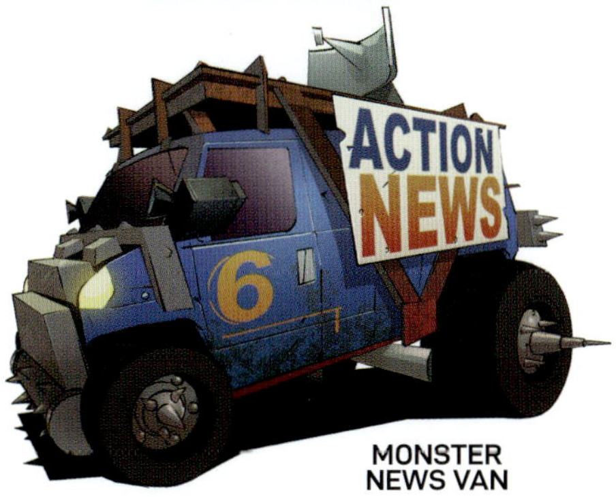

MONSTER NEWS VAN

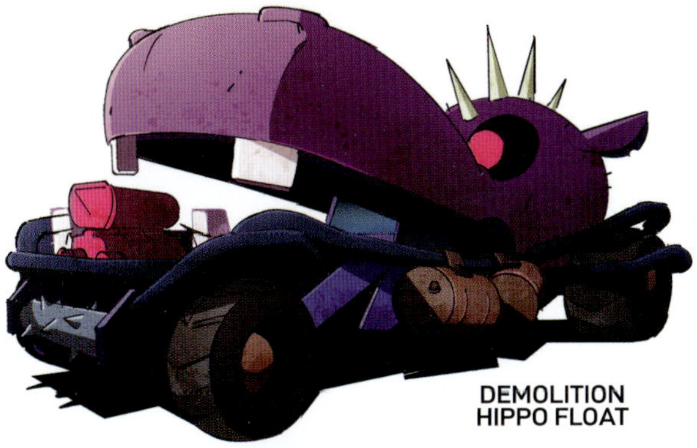

DEMOLITION HIPPO FLOAT

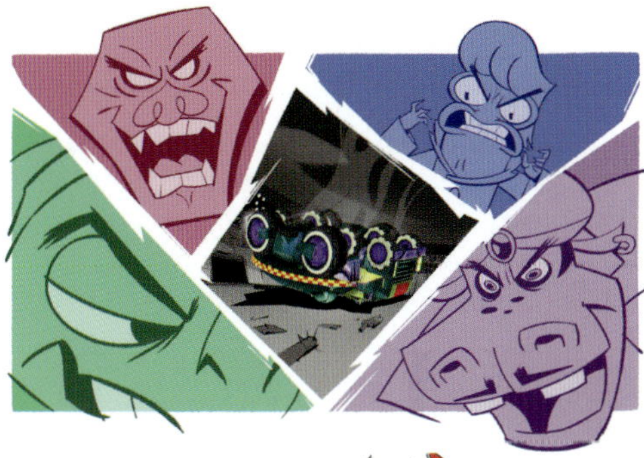

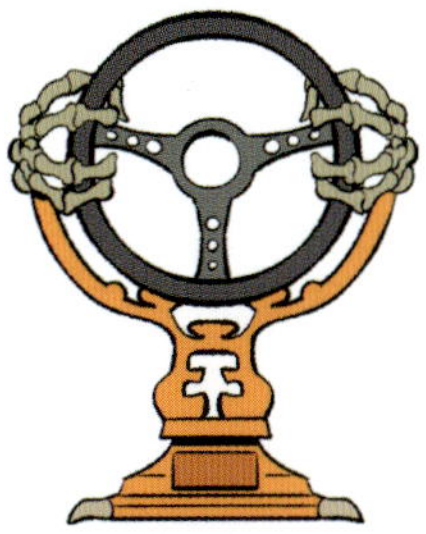

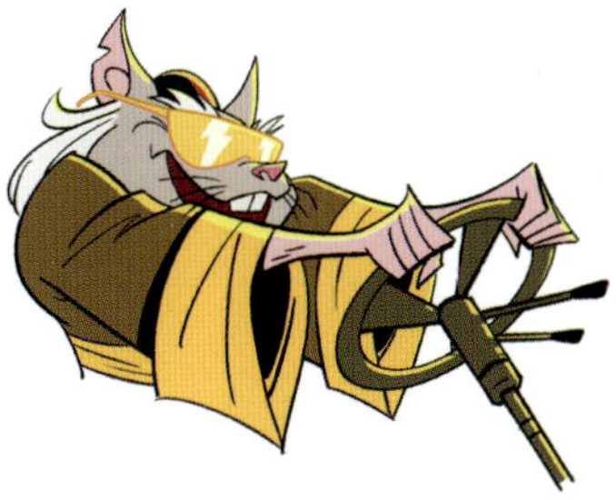

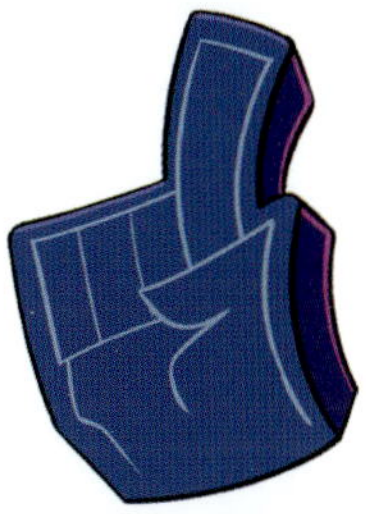

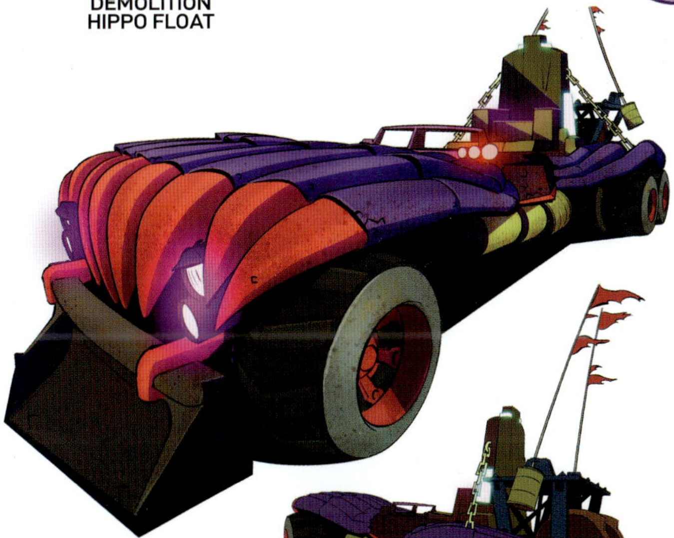

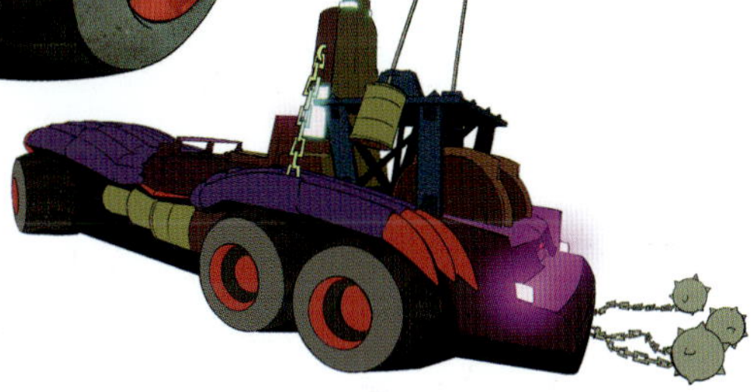

BIG MAMA'S CHARIOT

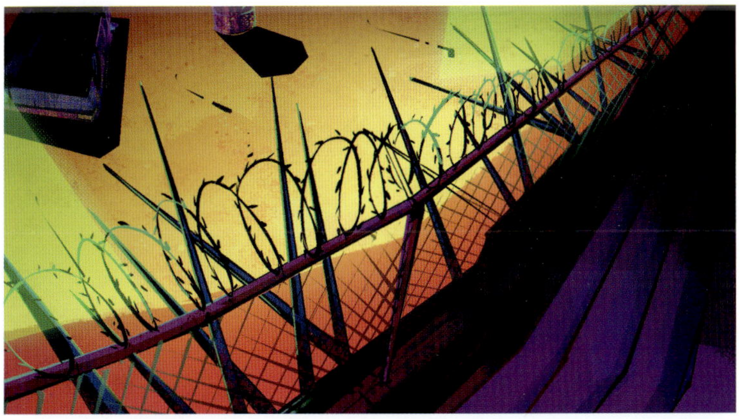

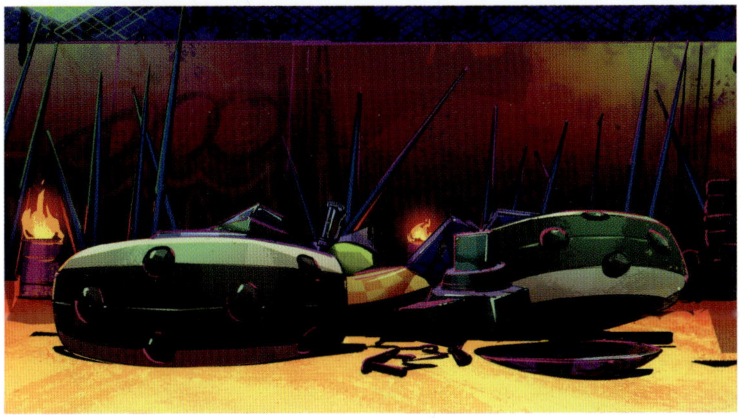

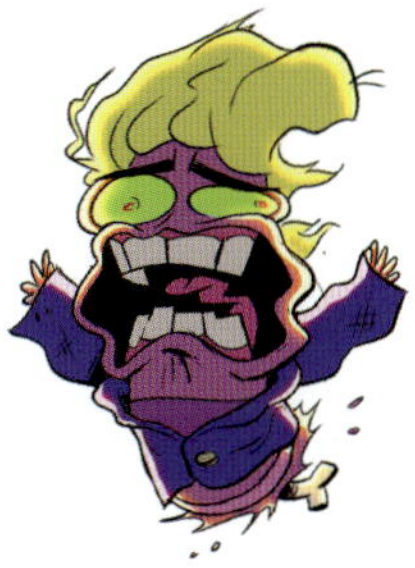

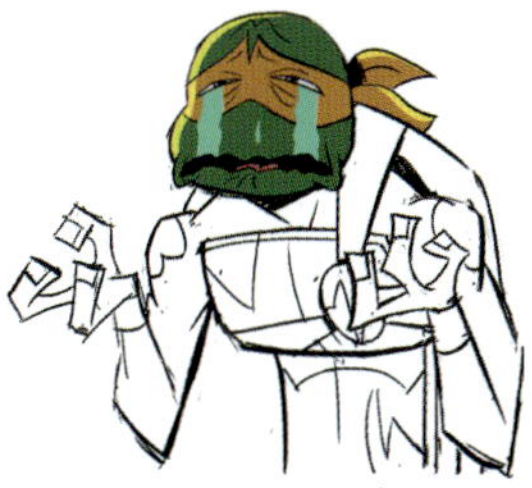

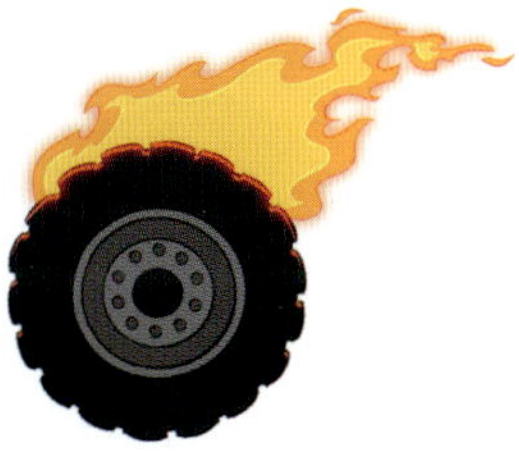

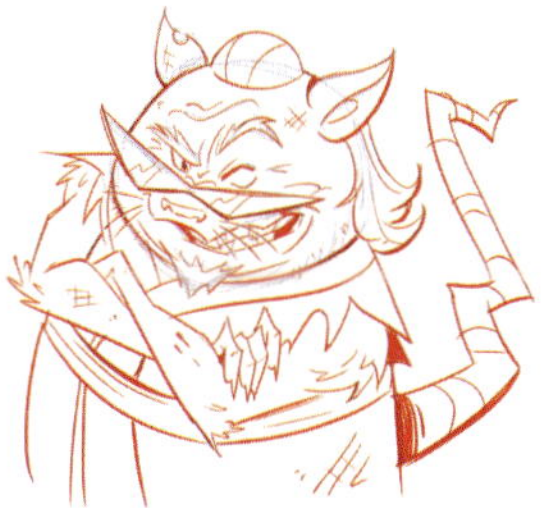

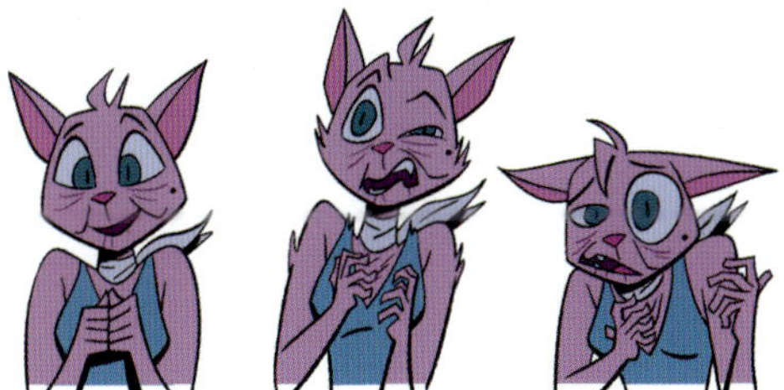

SHADOW OF EVIL

ORIGINAL AIR DATE: APRIL 20, 2019
PRODUCTION CODE: 031-032

WRITTEN BY **IAN BUSCH**
STORYBOARDS BY **JULIA BRAID, JJ CONWAY, KEVIN MOLINA-ORTIZ**
DIRECTED BY **JJ CONWAY & ALAN WAN**

IAN BUSCH: One of the origins of the story came about because we wanted to find a way where the boys could fight Splinter. After a long stretch of selling Splinter as a lazy dad and couch potato, this is the first time we see shades of who Splinter used to be, and the fight he still has inside of him. Before we aired, fans seemed to be up in arms about Splinter's character design and persona, but we always knew he was, and is, one of the most epic heroes of all time.

JJ CONWAY: The fight between the Turtles and Splinter is one of the most important scenes I storyboarded on the show. On a story level it was about Splinter realizing that his sons are actually capable warriors, something he learns by underestimating them. It's also the first time we see Splinter fight, so I gave him the resourcefulness of Jackie Chan mixed with the agility of Yoda.

JJ CONWAY: The *Rise* version of Splinter was controversial at first, but I feel the subway sequence is when we finally show our cards and expose the true depth of the character. Storyboarding it was a juicy challenge because of how many high-stakes reveals needed to land in a short period of time, and because of how emotionally charged it was for Splinter.

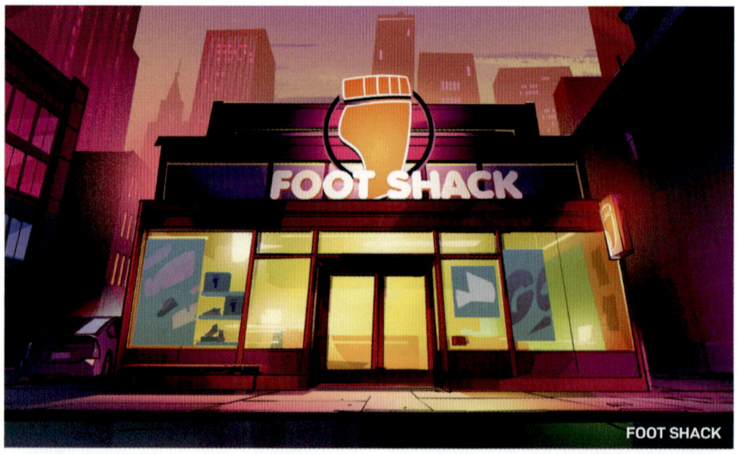

FOOT SHACK

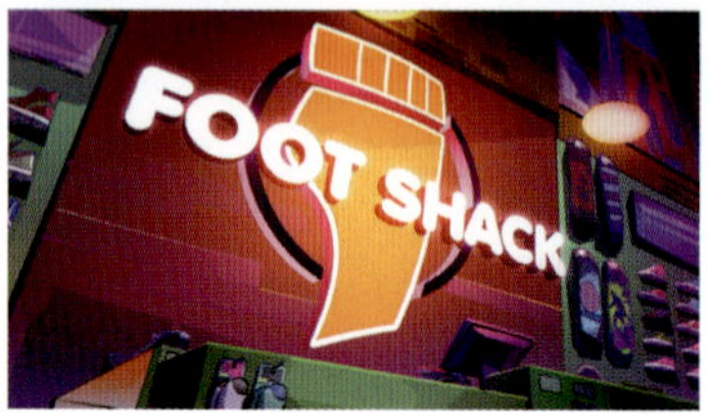

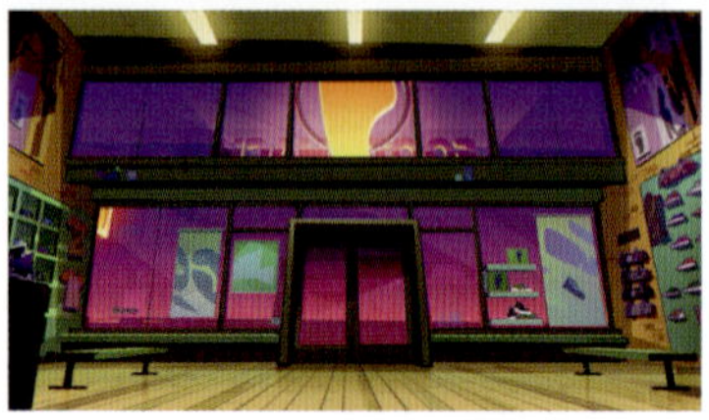

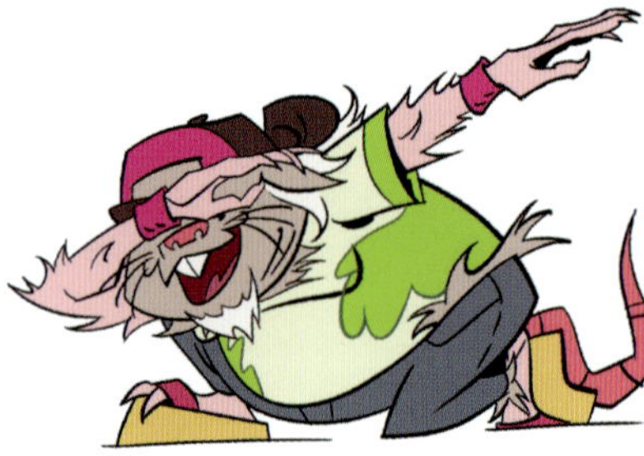

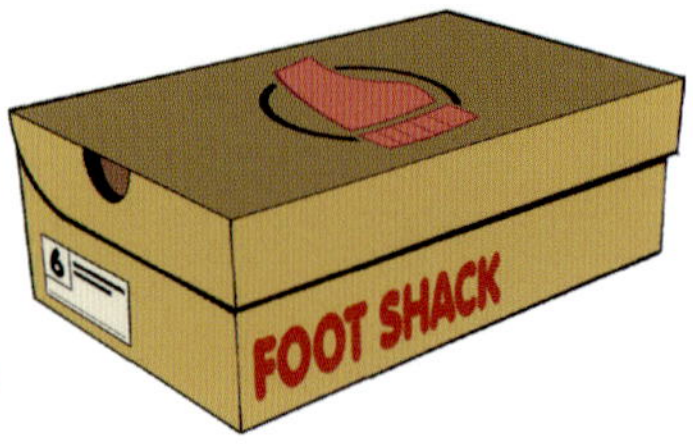

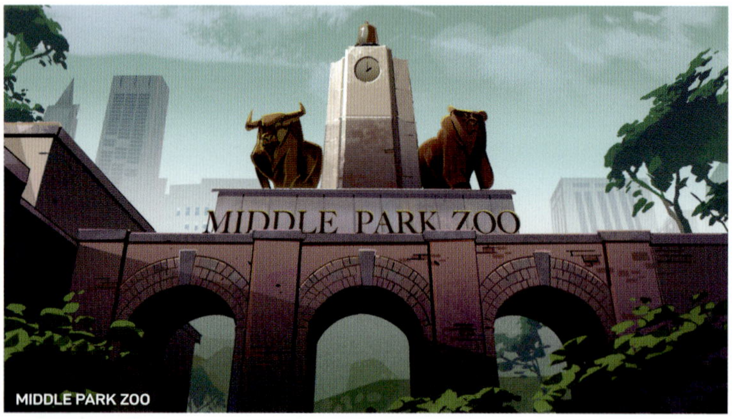

MIDDLE PARK ZOO

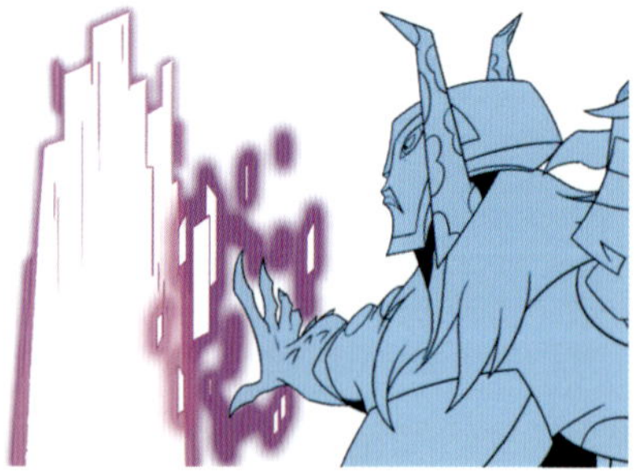

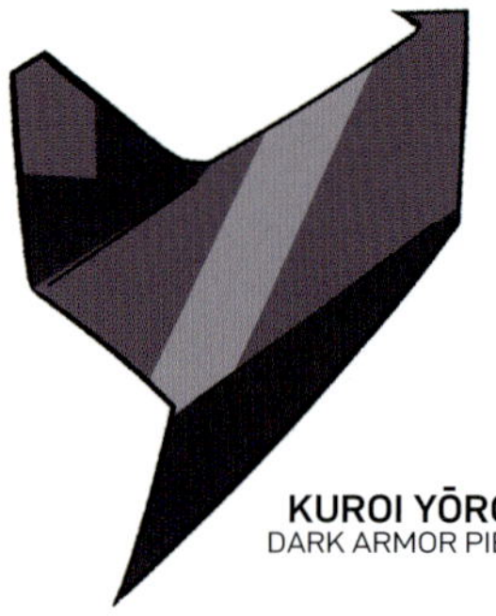
KUROI YŌROI
DARK ARMOR PIECE

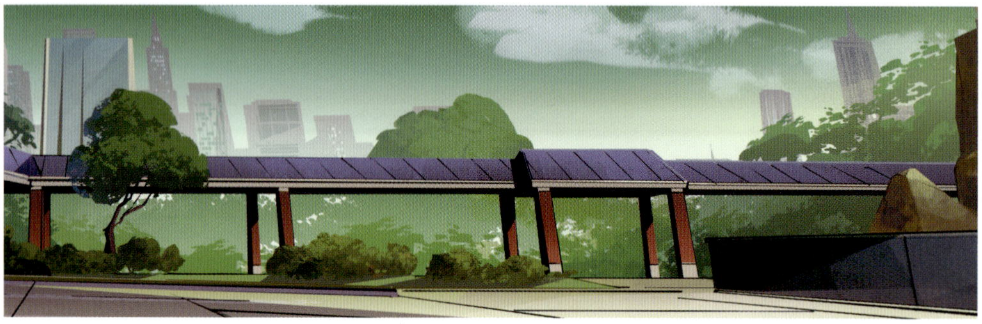

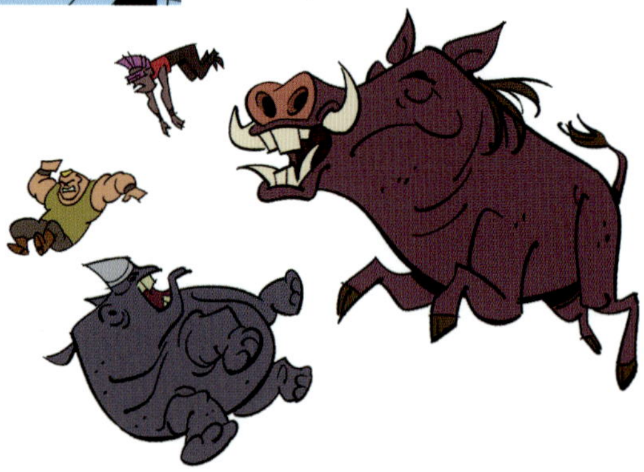

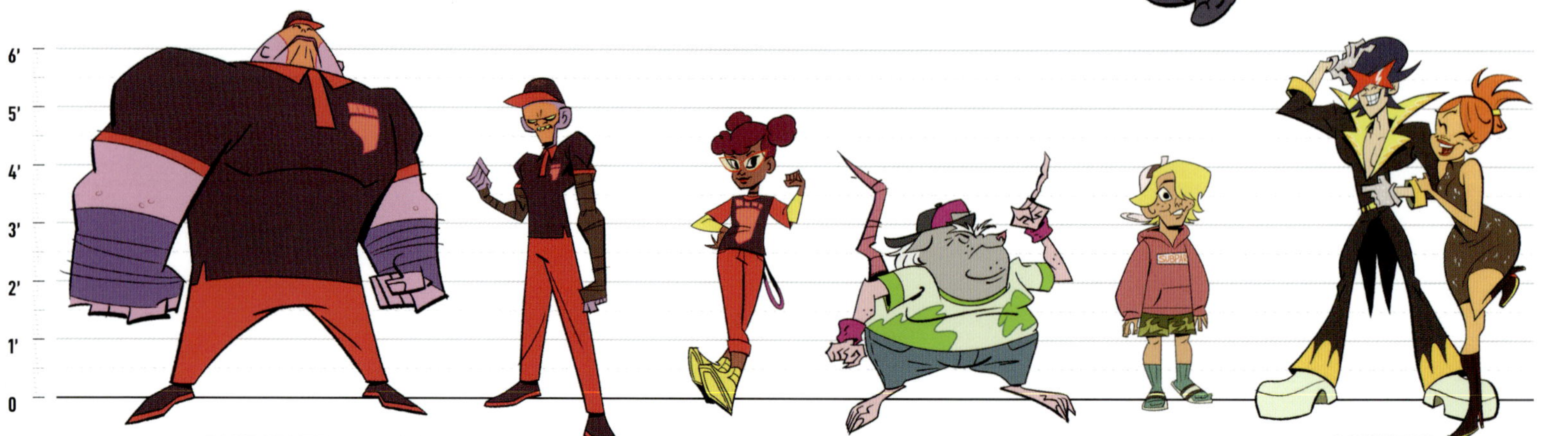

FOOT BRUTE
FOOT SHACK UNIFORM

FOOT LIEUTENANT
FOOT SHACK UNIFORM

APRIL O'NEIL
FOOT SHACK UNIFORM

RANDALL
SPLINTER

TEEN CUSTOMER

LOU JITSU
AND KRYSTAL YISTAL

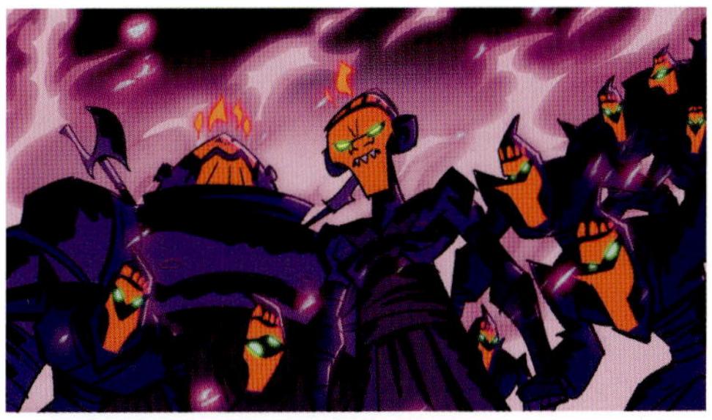
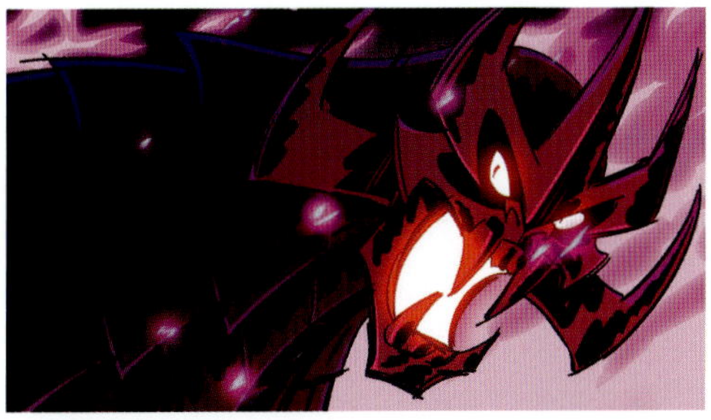
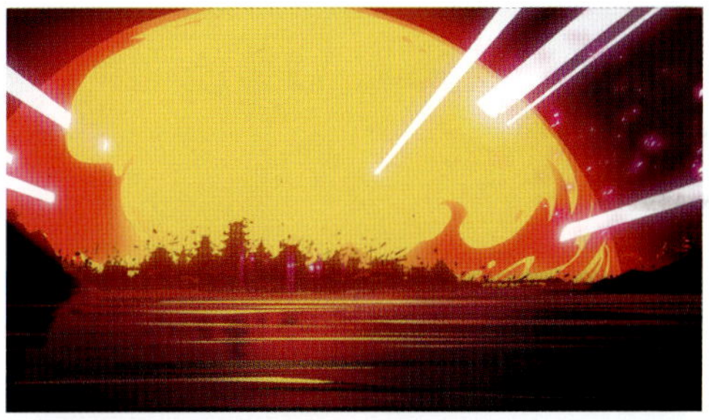
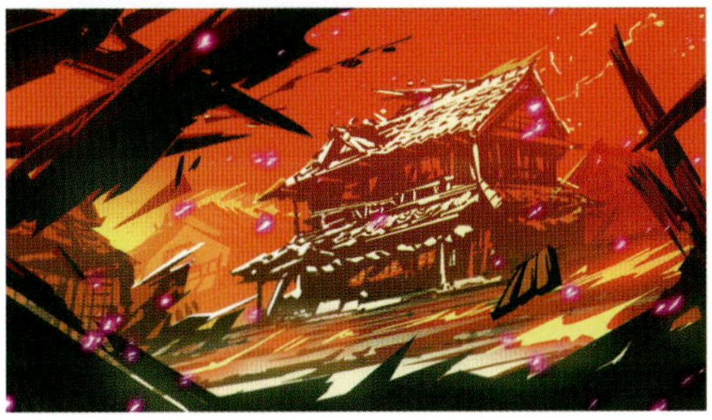
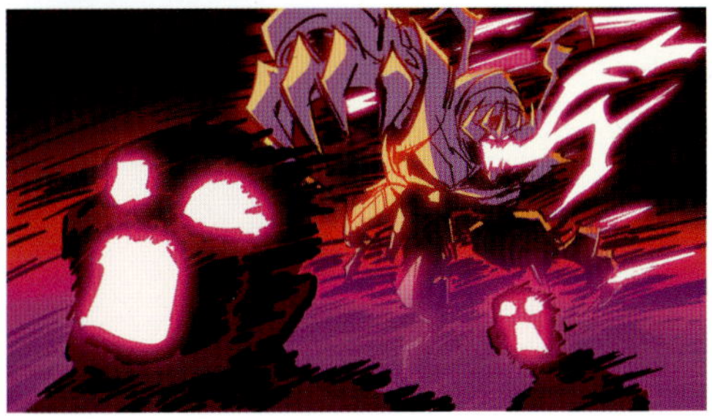
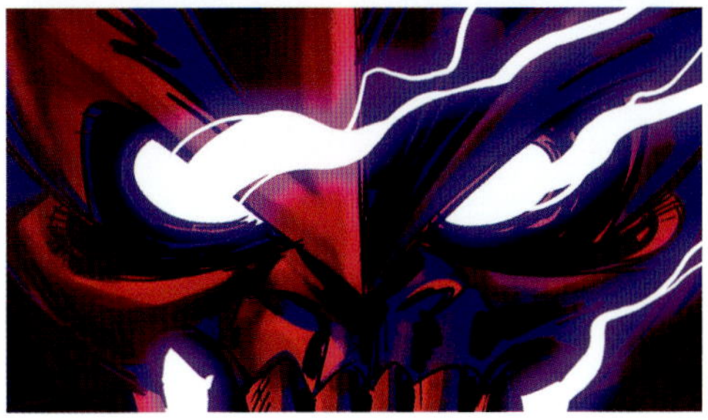
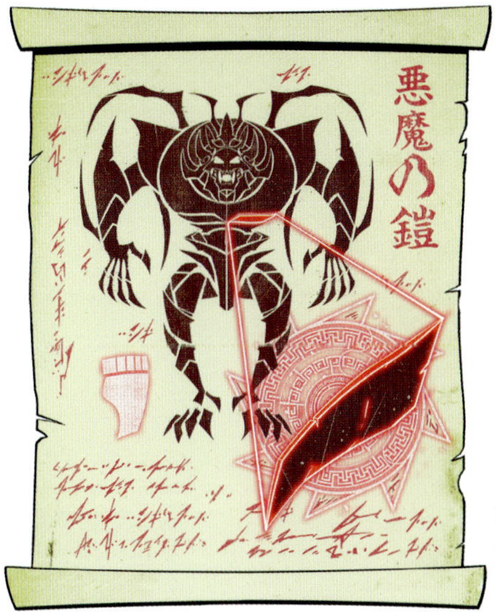
悪魔の鎧
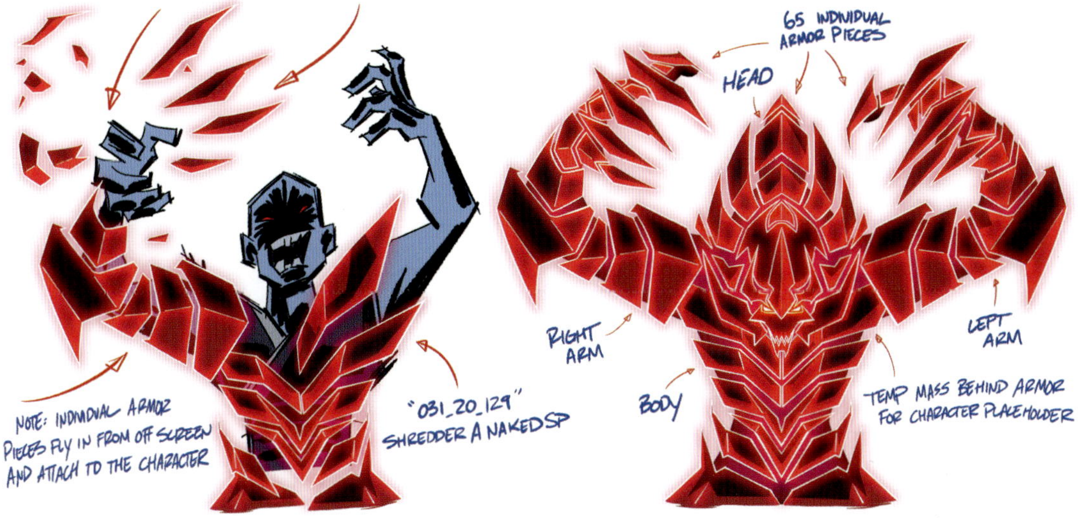
NOTE: INDIVIDUAL ARMOR PIECES FLY IN FROM OFF SCREEN AND ATTACH TO THE CHARACTER
"031_20_129" SHREDDER A NAKED SP
65 INDIVIDUAL ARMOR PIECES
HEAD
RIGHT ARM
LEFT ARM
BODY
TEMP MASS BEHIND ARMOR FOR CHARACTER PLACEHOLDER
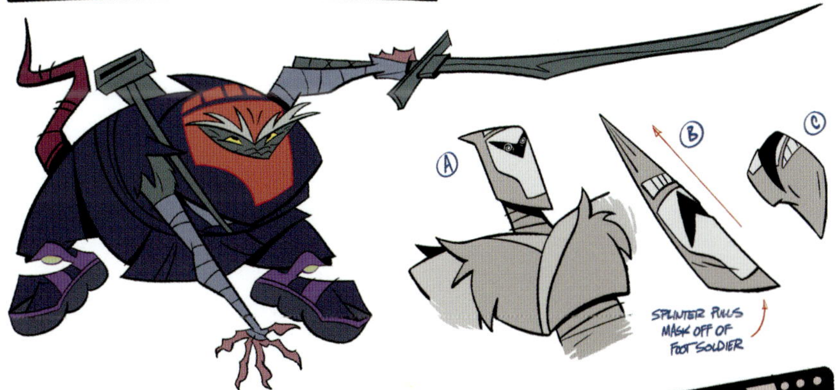
A
B
C
SPLINTER PULLS MASK OFF OF FOOT SOLDIER
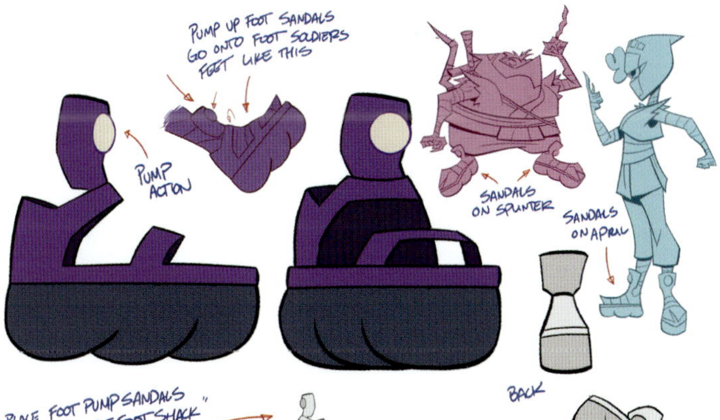
PUMP UP FOOT SANDALS GO ONTO FOOT SOLDIERS FEET LIKE THIS
PUMP ACTION
SANDALS ON SPLINTER
SANDALS ON APRIL
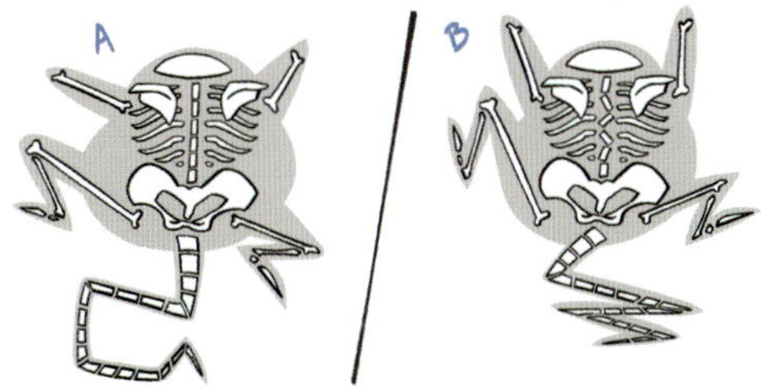
A
B
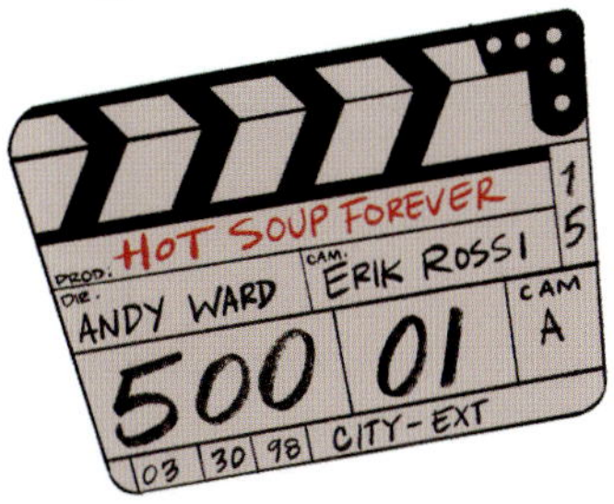
HOT SOUP FOREVER
PROD. DIR.
ANDY WARD
CAM.
ERIK ROSSI
1 5
CAM A
500
01
03 30 98
CITY-EXT
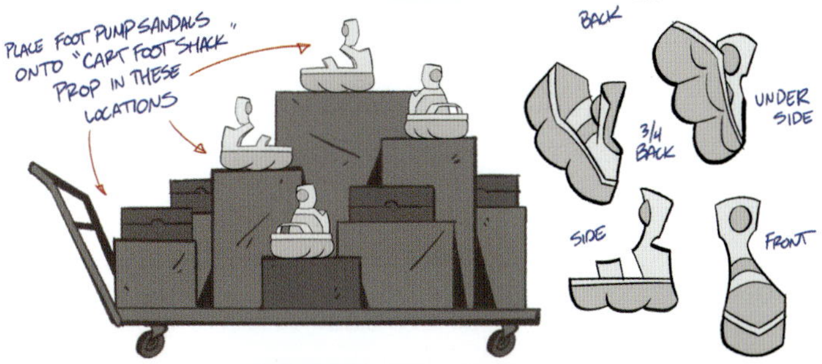
PLACE FOOT PUMP SANDALS ONTO "CART FOOT SHACK" PROP IN THESE LOCATIONS
BACK
UNDER SIDE
3/4 BACK
SIDE
FRONT
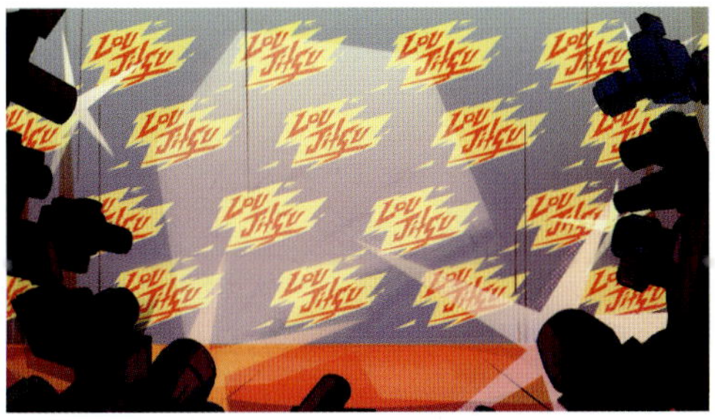
LOU JITSU
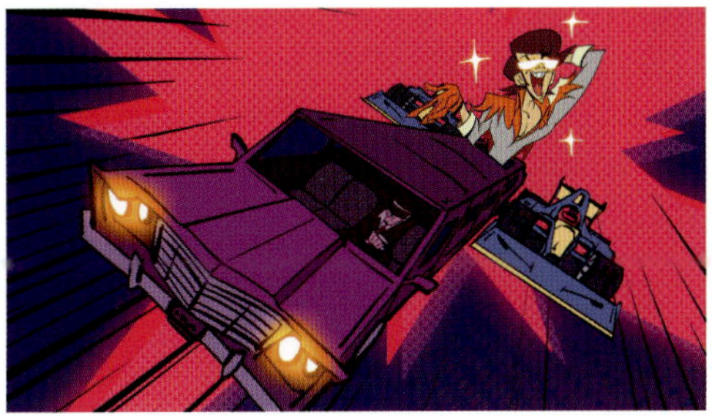
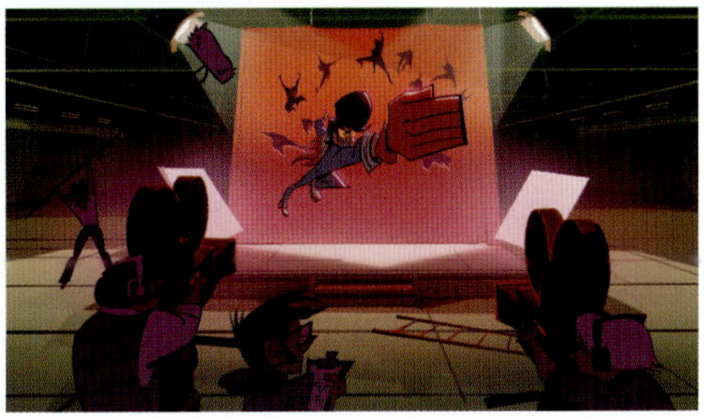

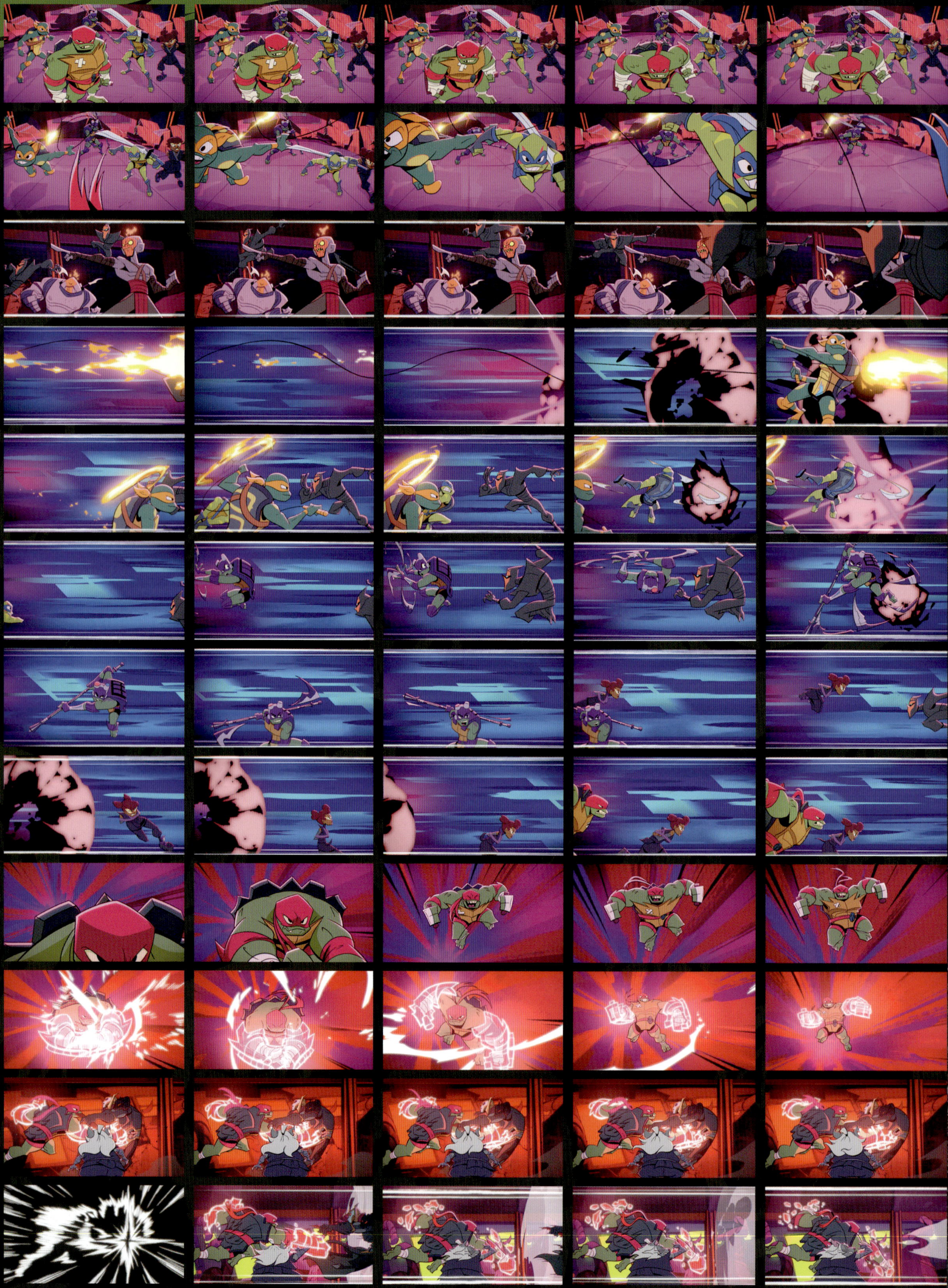

STORYBOARD ARTIST: **JJ CONWAY**

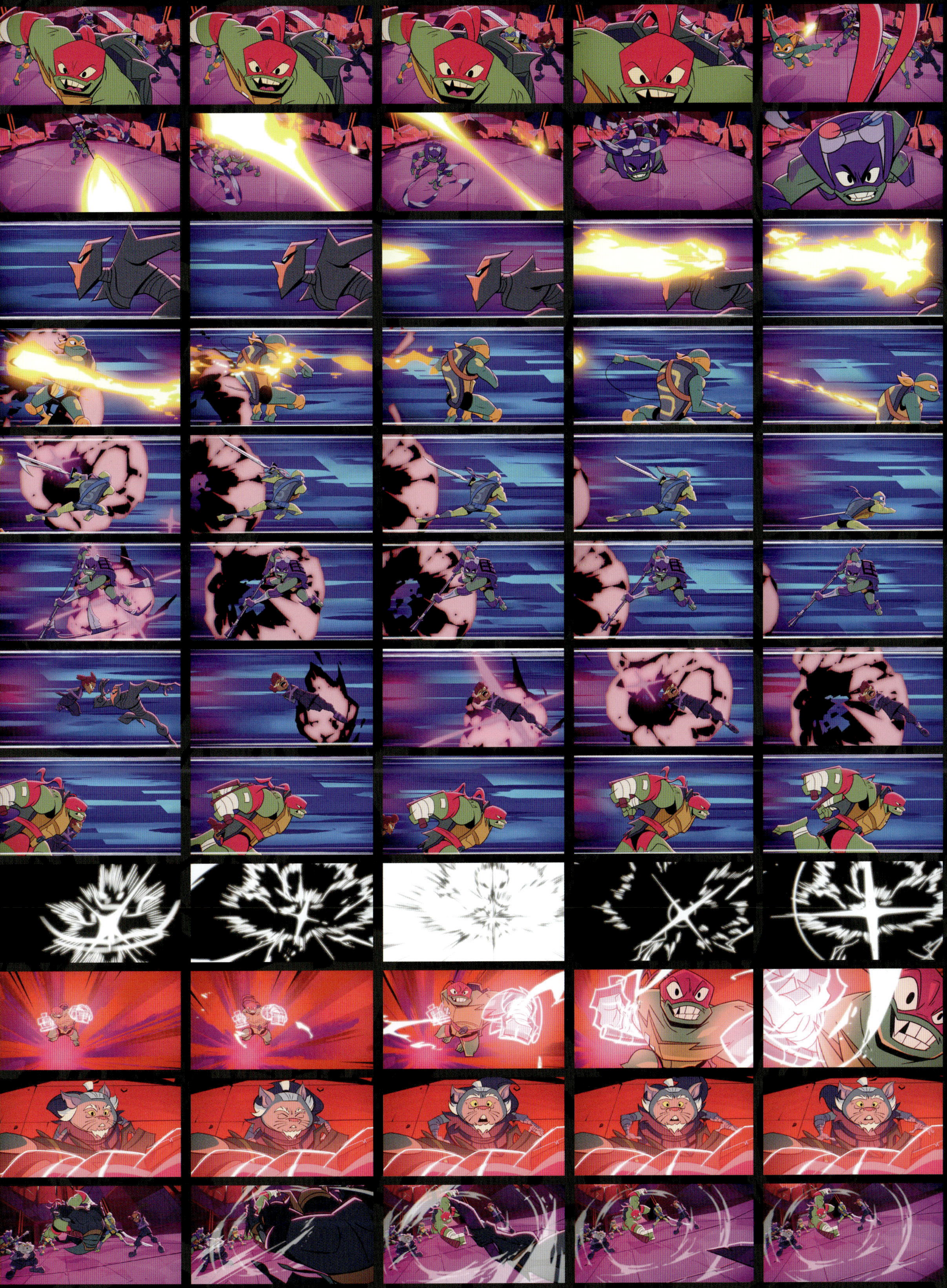

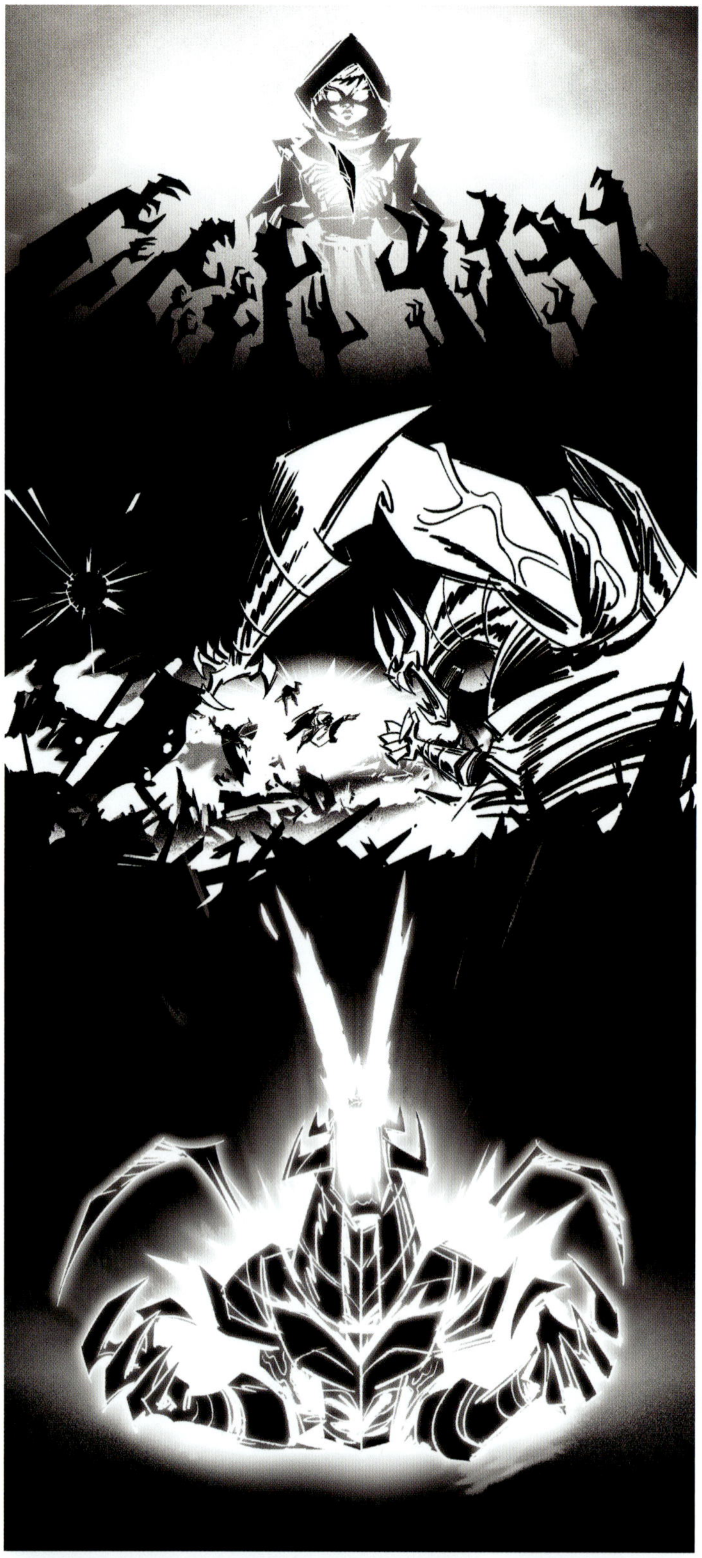

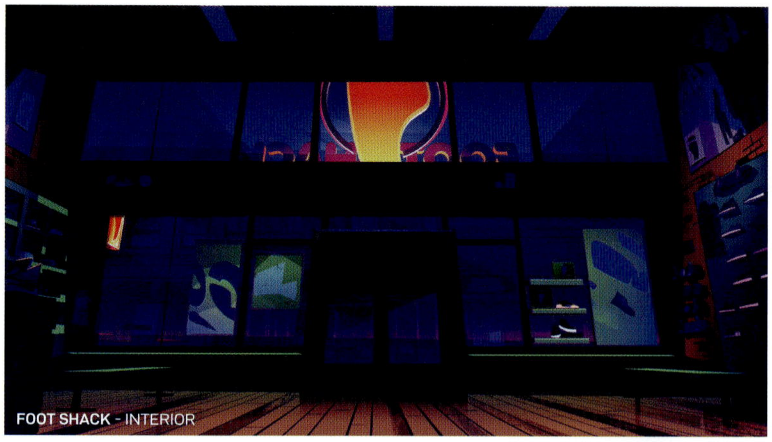
FOOT SHACK - INTERIOR

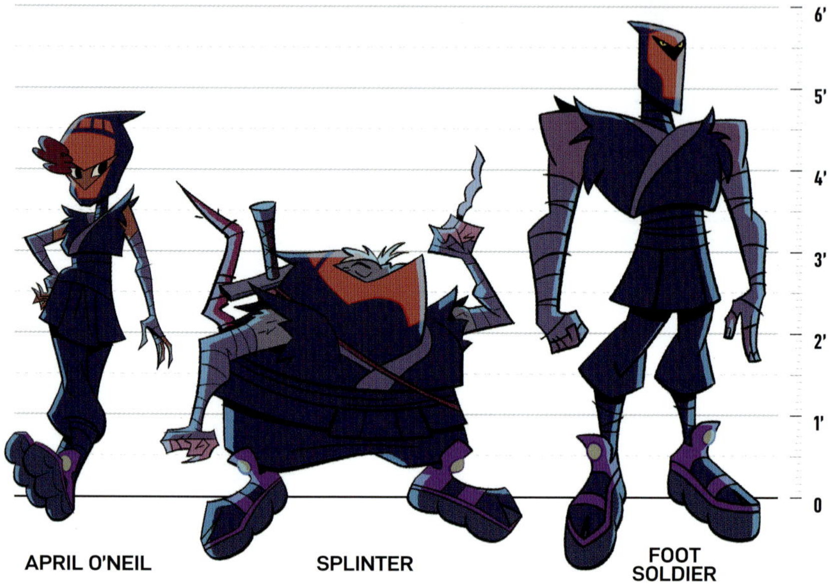

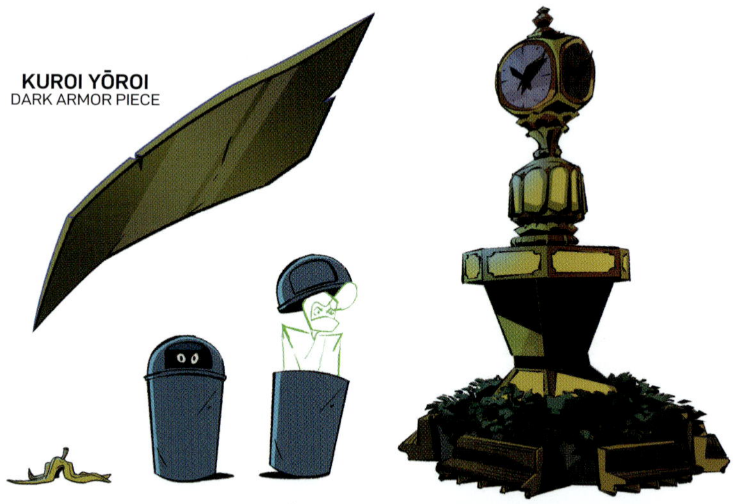

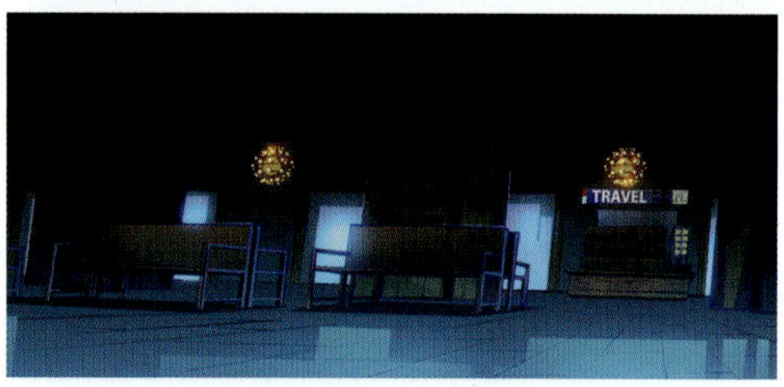

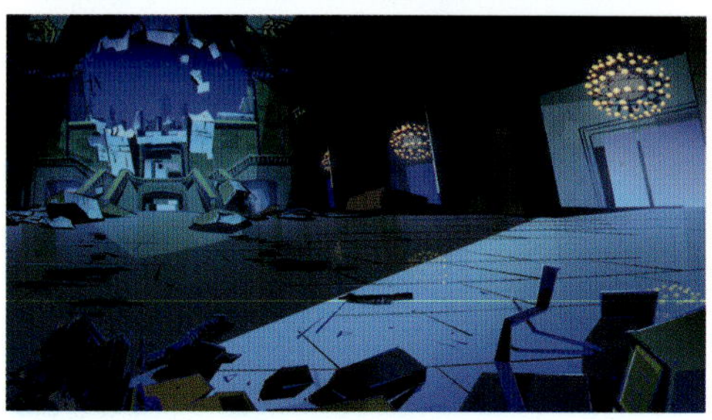

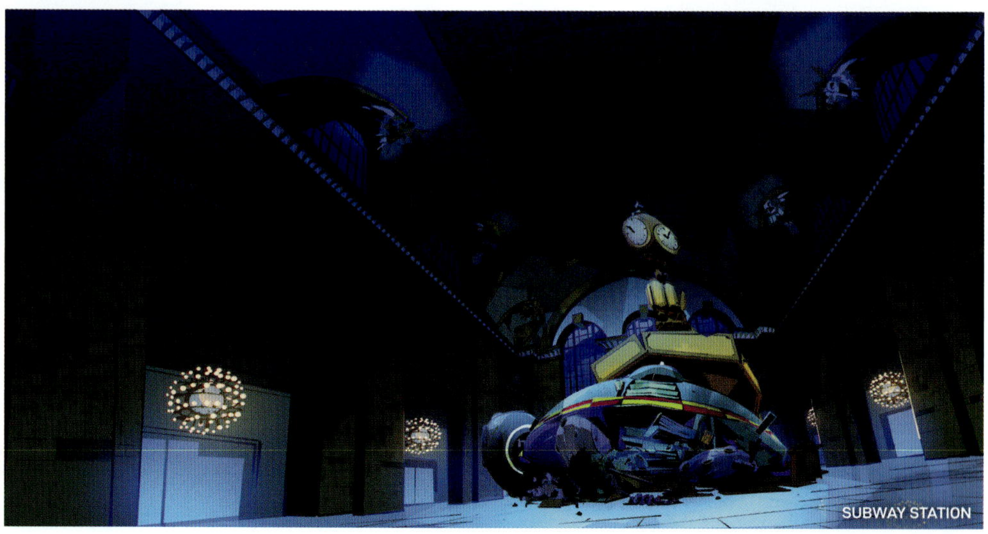
SUBWAY STATION

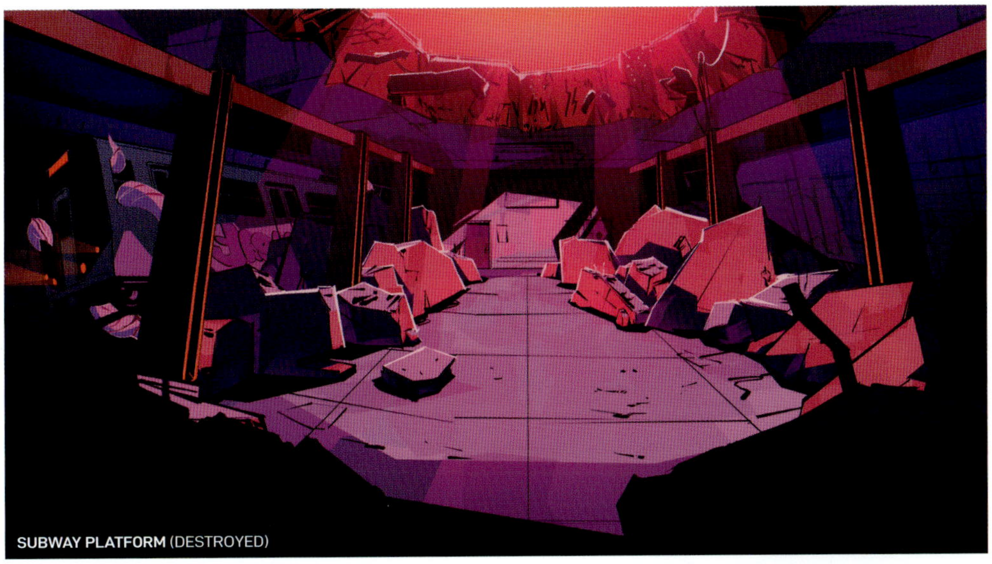
SUBWAY PLATFORM (DESTROYED)

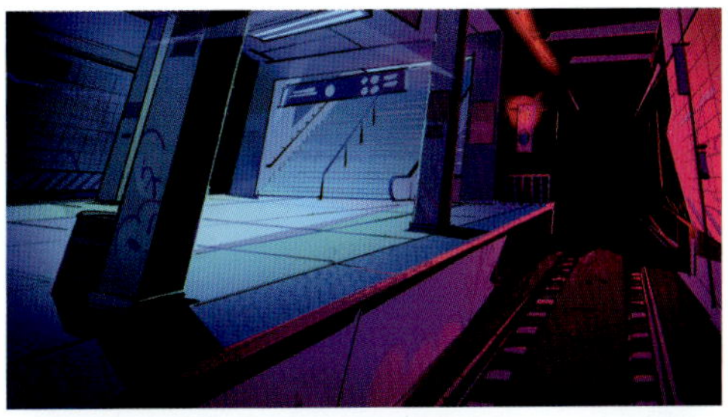

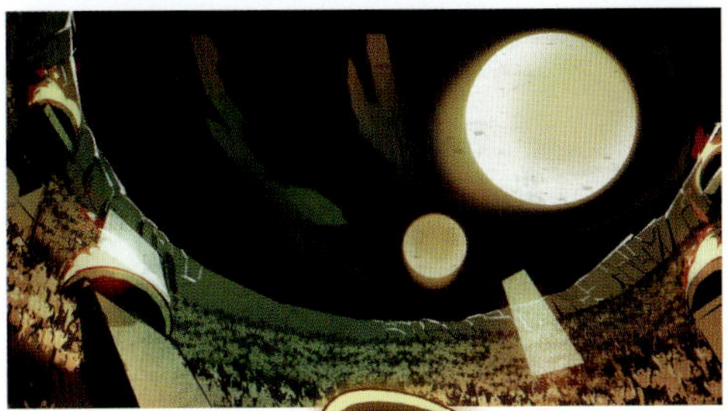

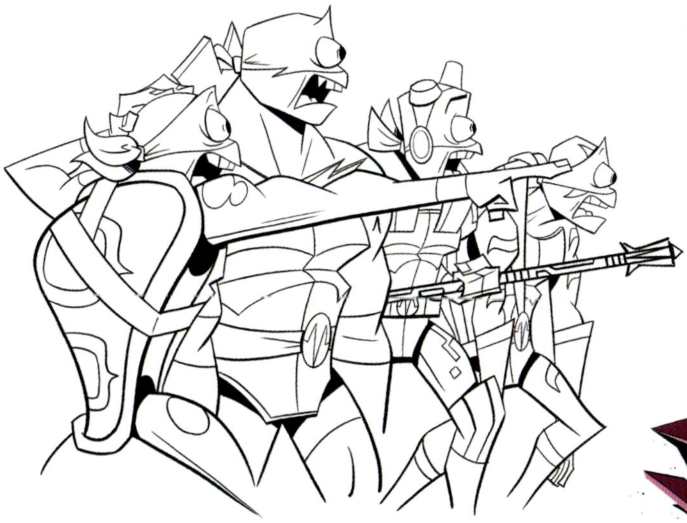

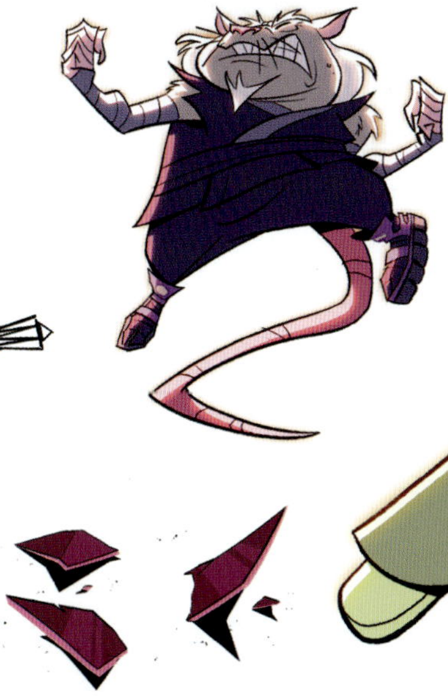

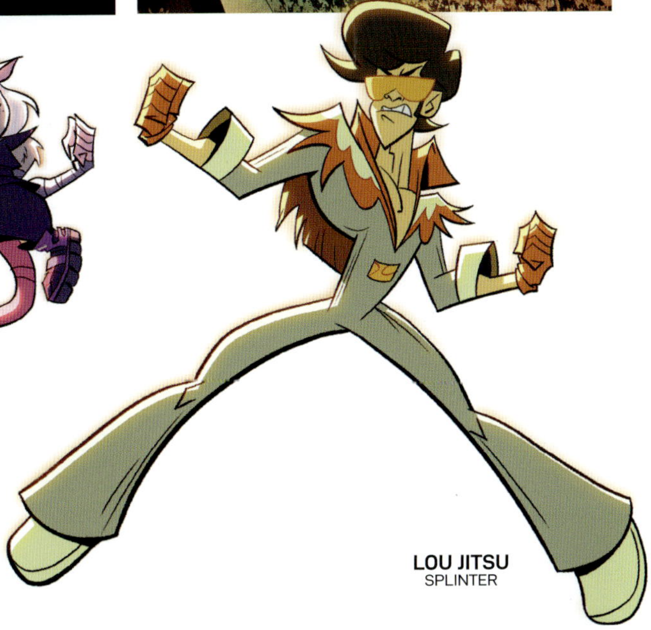
LOU JITSU
SPLINTER

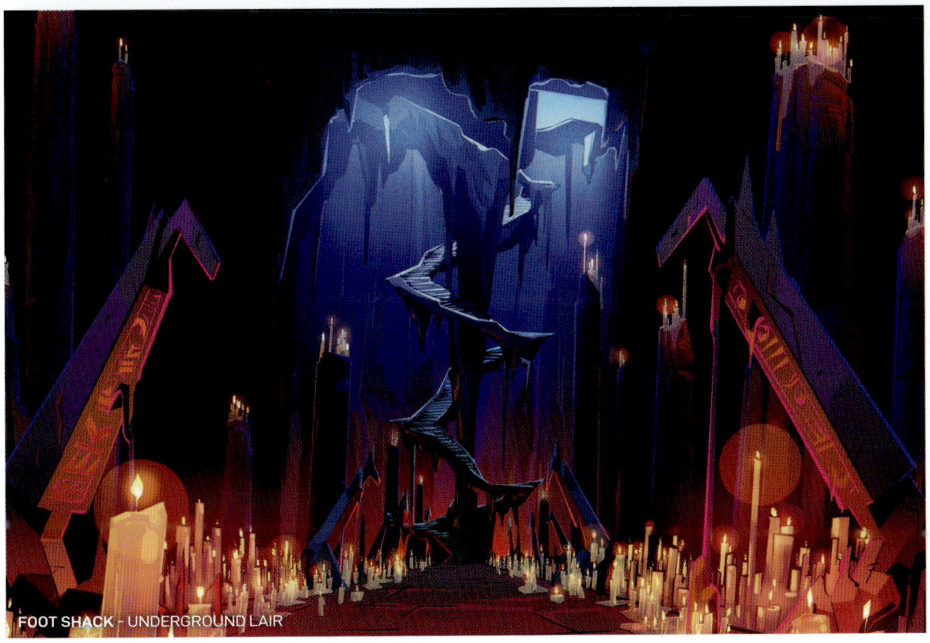
FOOT SHACK - UNDERGROUND LAIR

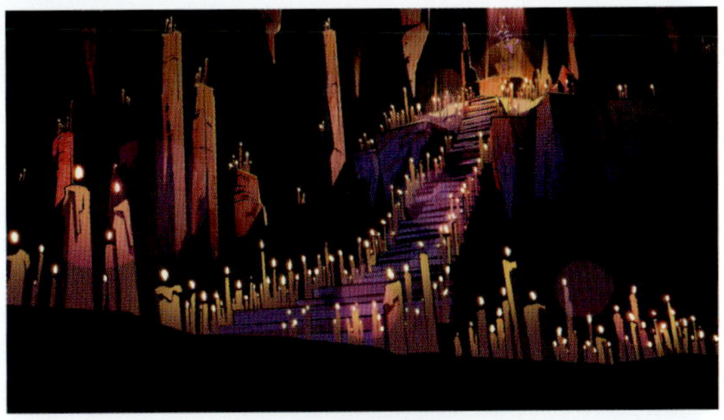

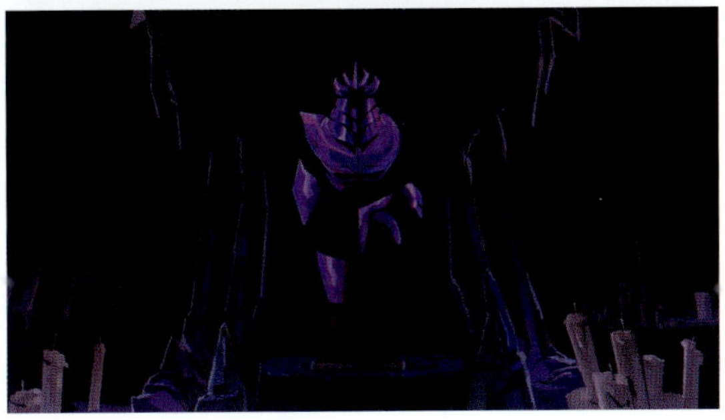

MIND MELD

ORIGINAL AIR DATE: MARCH 9, 2019
PRODUCTION CODE: 033

WRITTEN BY **JESSE GORDON**
STORYBOARDS BY **CHRISTOPHER LUC**
DIRECTED BY **ABE AUDISH**

JESSE GORDON: I truly don't remember why Donnie is afraid of beach balls.

This episode was born out of a very simple premise: Donnie finding deficiency in his brothers and meddling with what he thought was wrong only to realize that they're perfect as they are. Josh's Donnie always has this hilariously condescending attitude towards his brothers, and this was a great opportunity to turn that around on him. Brandon, Omar, and Ben doing their own smart Donnie impressions was really funny.

There's a line where S.H.E.L.L.D.O.N. asks if he should "ready the disposal unit," revealing a ridiculously huge arsenal and showing us just how unhinged a scientist Donnie truly is. Only someone as fervent as he is would have a protocol to get rid of his brothers prepped and ready to go. (But he would never!)

Pizza Pigeon was an homage to the internet-famous celebrity at the time Pizza Rat. The "Dragon's Tooth" is a MacGuffin homage to the "Rabbit's Foot" from J.J. Abrams' *Mission: Impossible III* (2006).

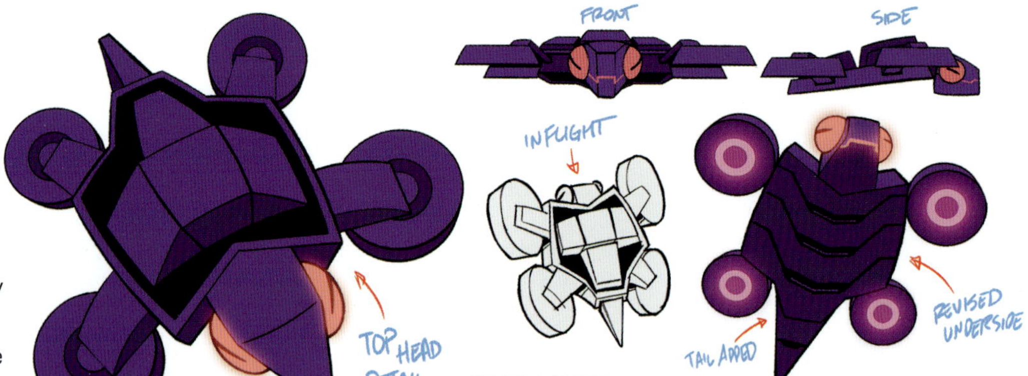

S.H.E.L.L.D.O.N.
VERSION 2.0

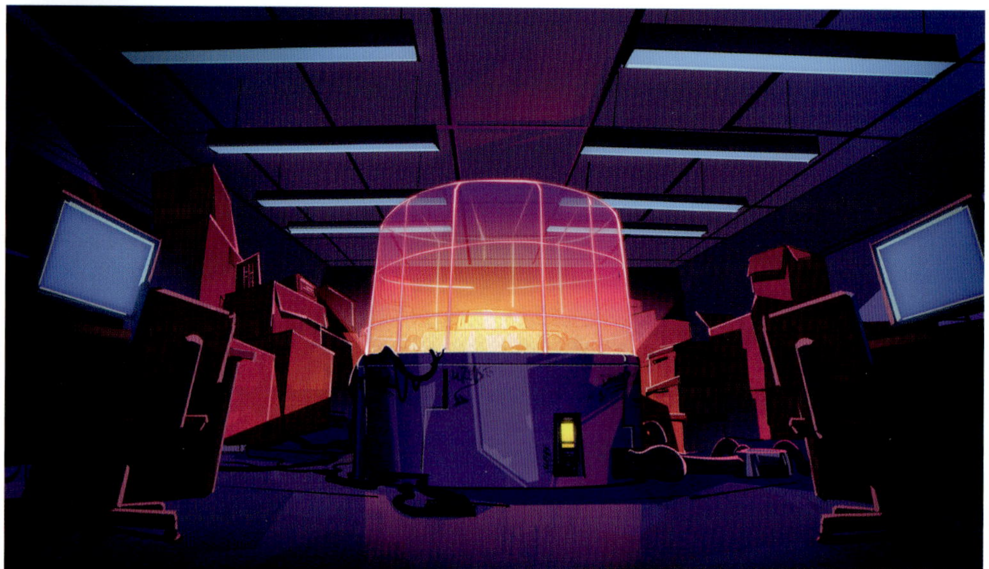

WASHINGTON IRVING HIGH SCHOOL - COMPUTER LAB

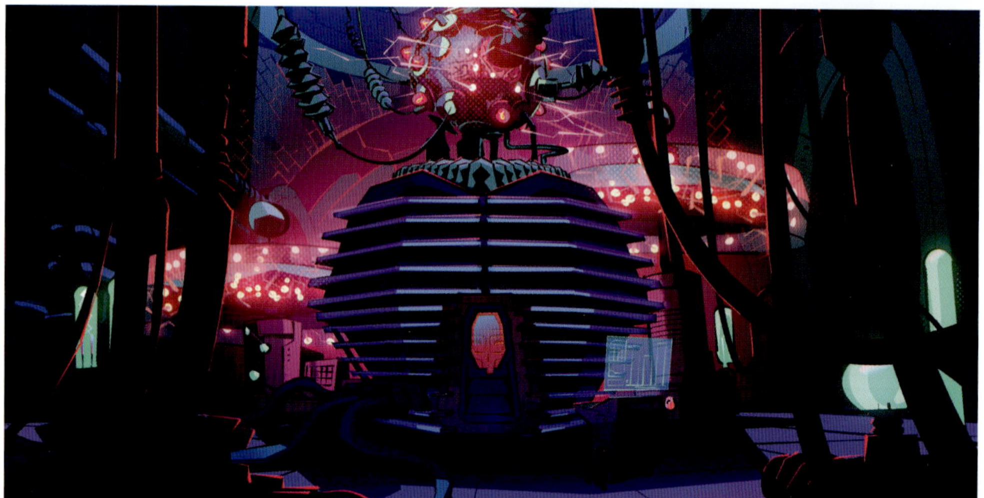

MENTAL INTELLIGENCE REPROGRAMULATOR

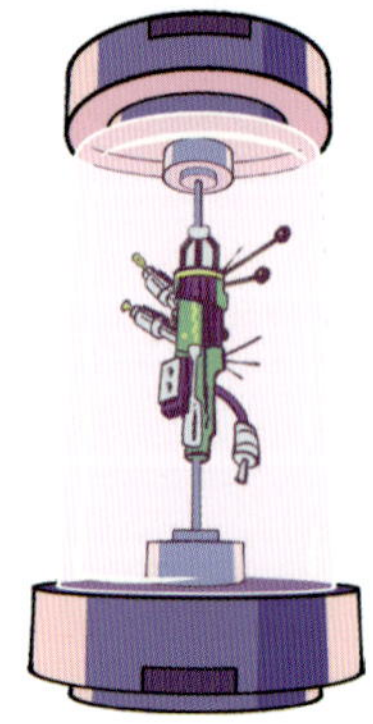

DRAGON'S TOOTH COMPUTER CHIP

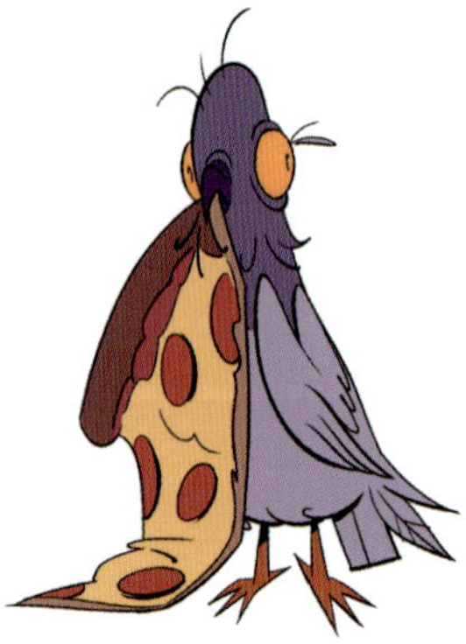

PIZZA PIGEON

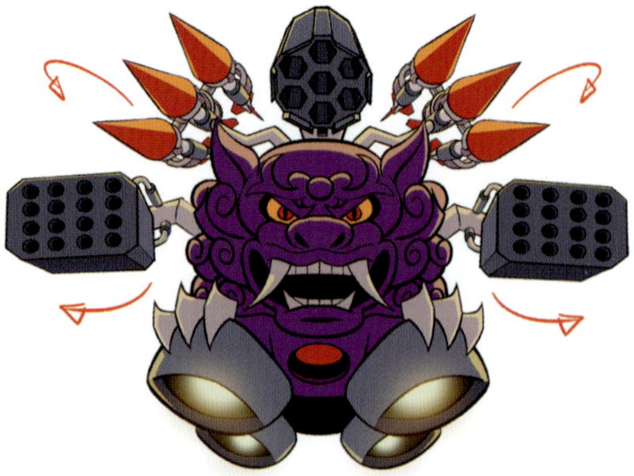

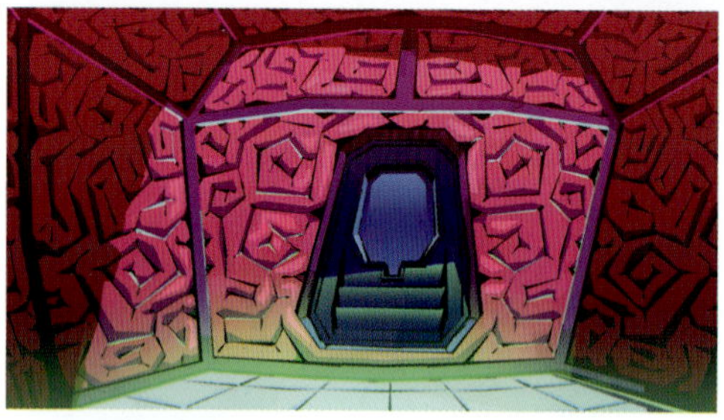

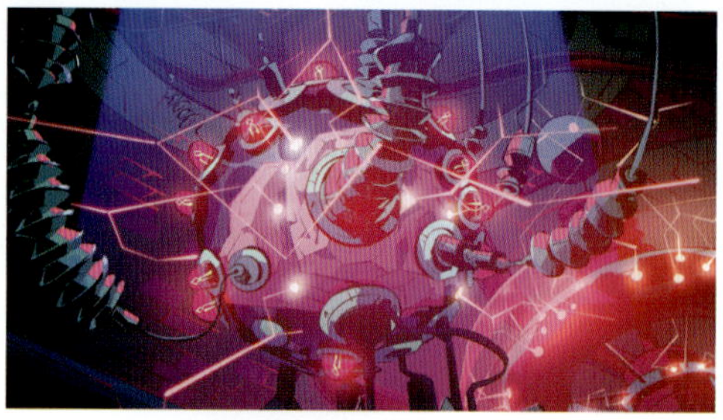

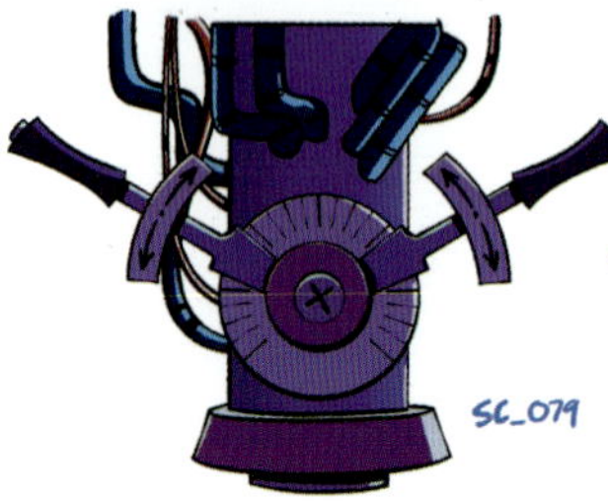

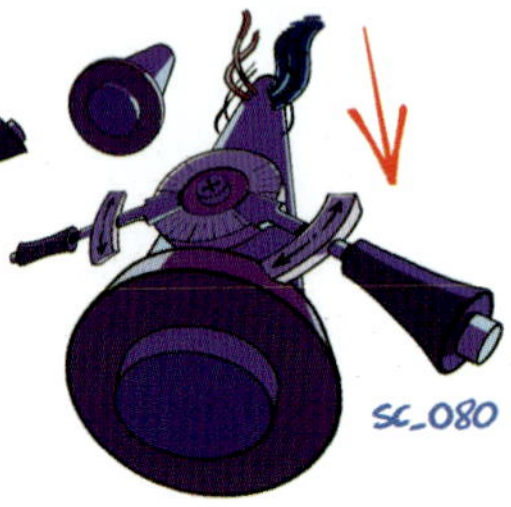

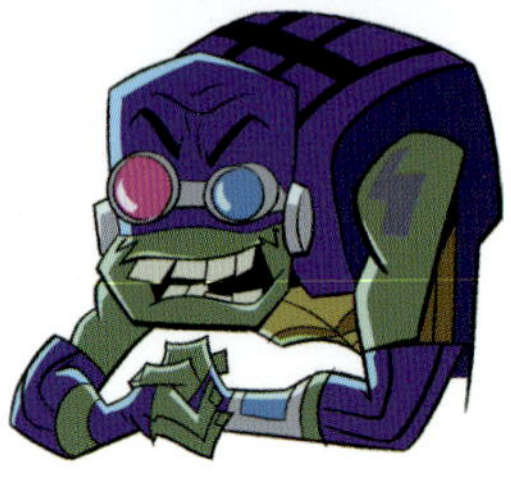

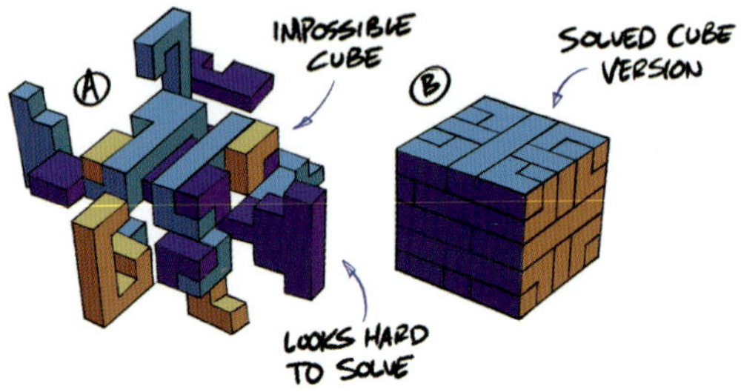

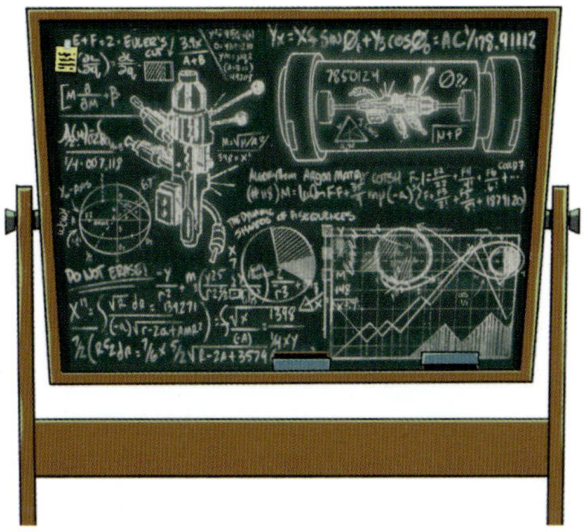

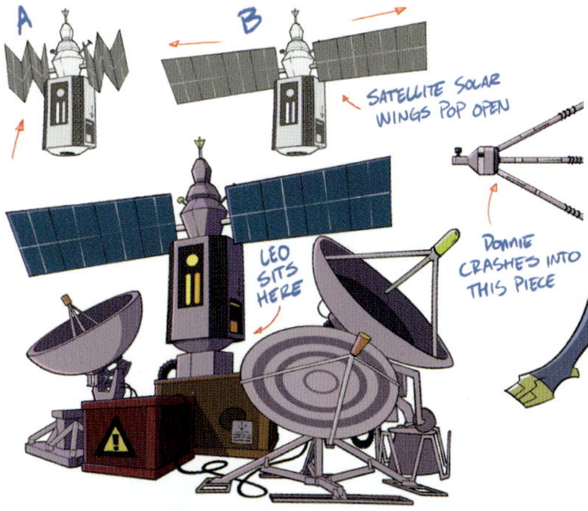

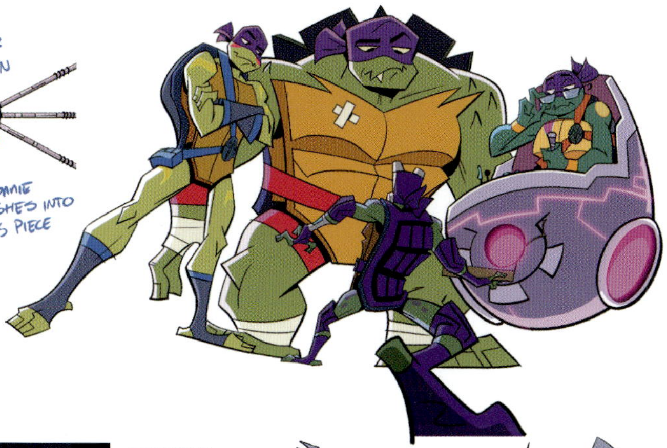

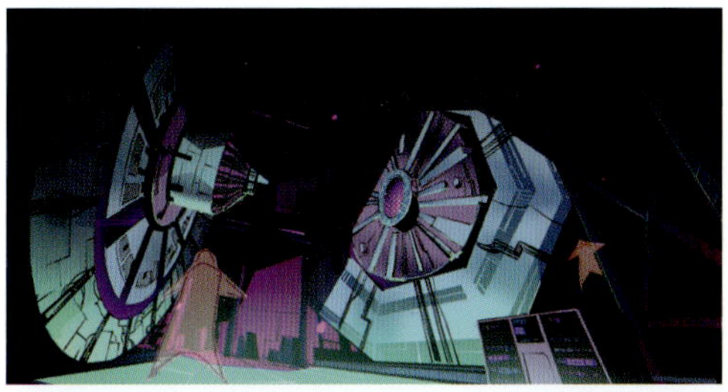

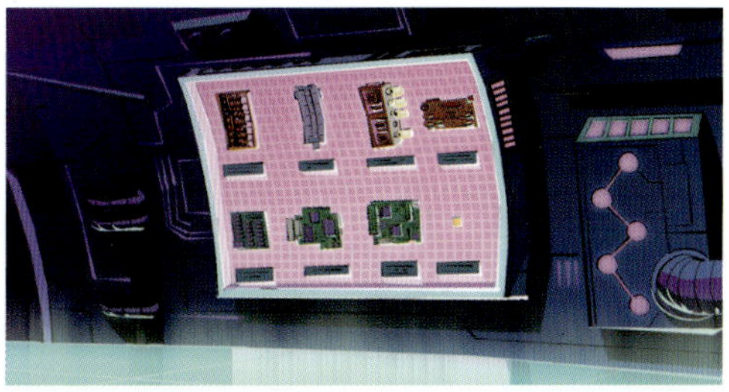

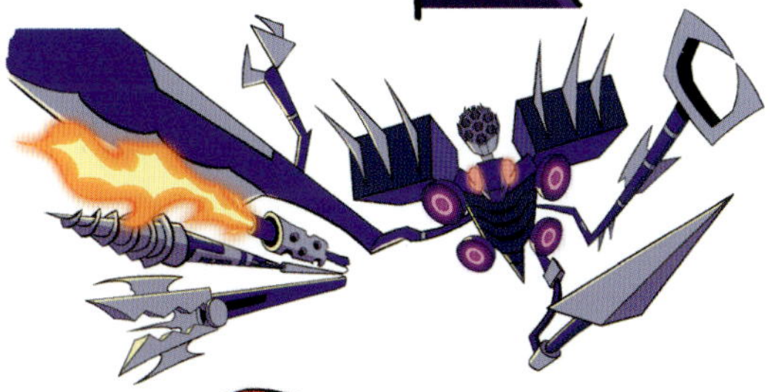

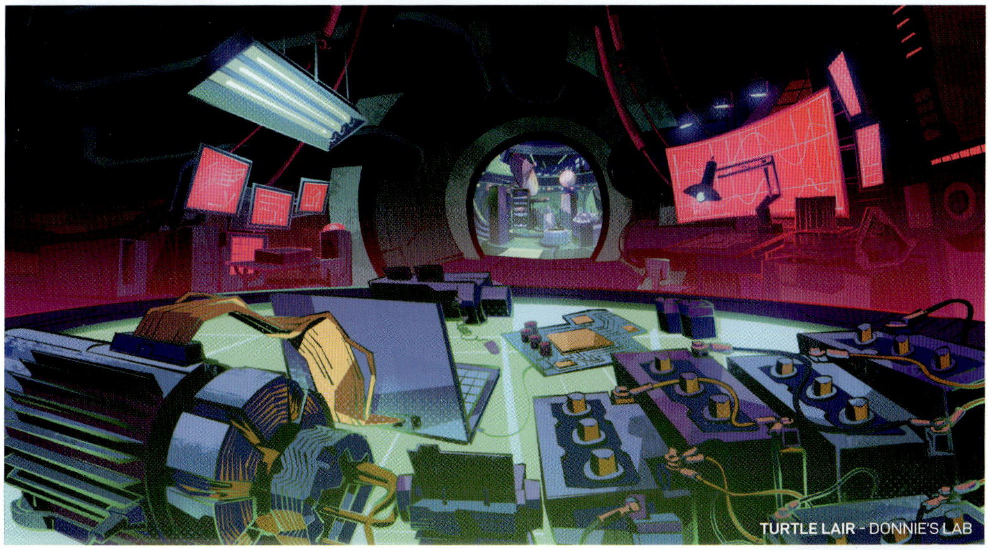
TURTLE LAIR - DONNIE'S LAB

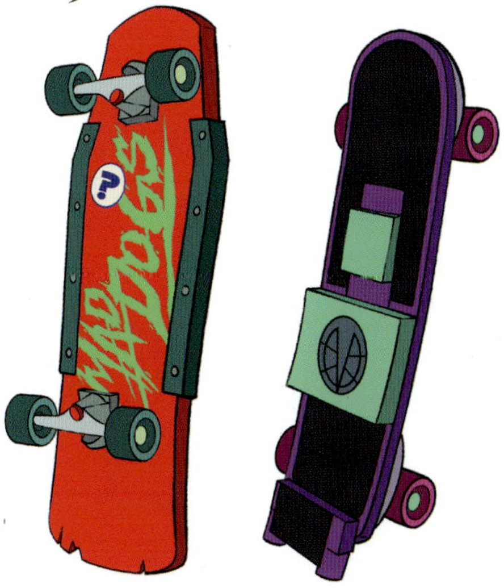

RAPH'S SKATEBOARD

DONNIE'S SKATEBOARD

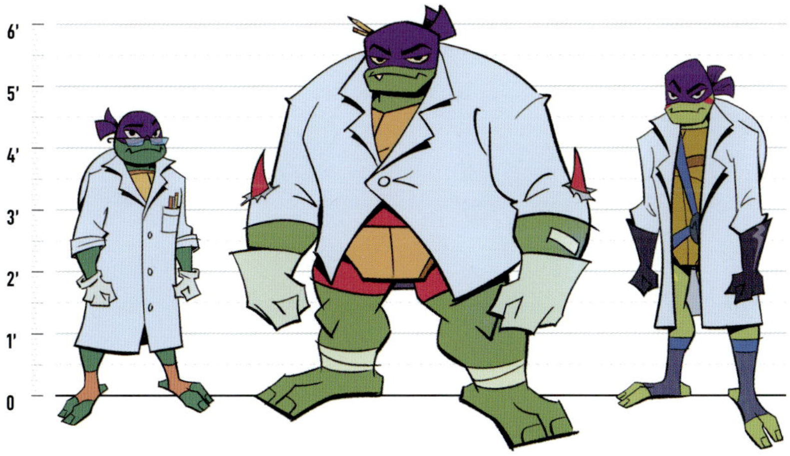

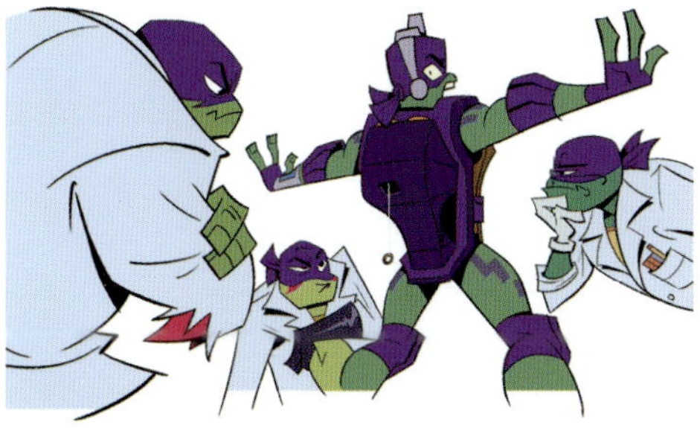

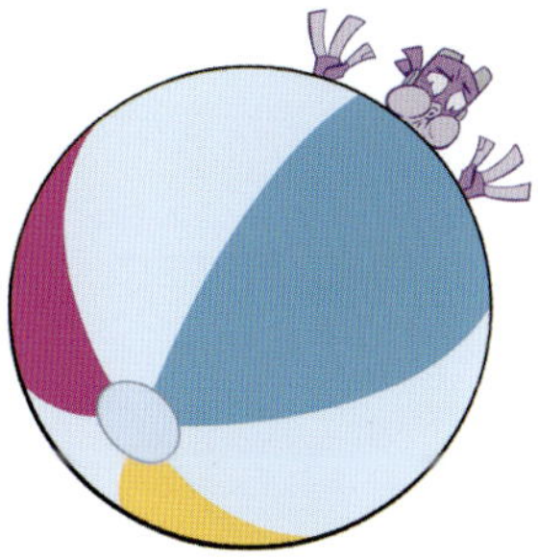

IAN BUSCH: We never explained what caused Donnie's fear of beach balls, but it runs deep and he mentions it several times throughout the series.

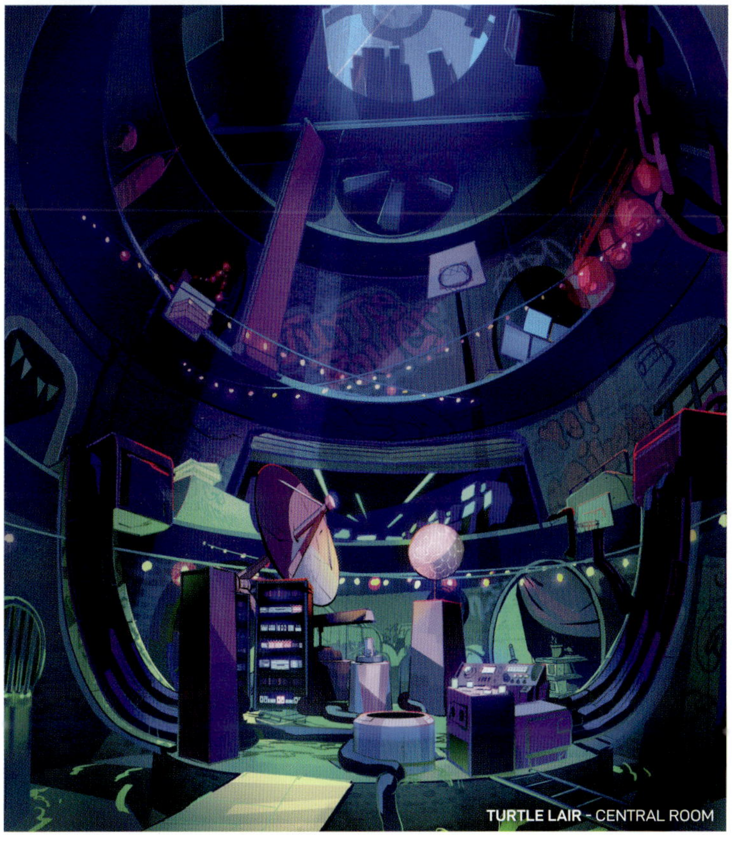
TURTLE LAIR - CENTRAL ROOM

PORTAL JACKED!

ORIGINAL AIR DATE: APRIL 6, 2019
PRODUCTION CODE: 034

WRITTEN BY **RUSS CARNEY & RON CORCILLO**
STORYBOARDS BY **MAX COLLINS, ZANE YARBROUGH**
DIRECTED BY **SEBASTIAN MONTES**

RON CORCILLO: We really loved developing the frenemy relationship between Señor Hueso and Leo. Why did we have Hueso call Leo *"pepino"* all the time? It dates back to when we were writing "Repo Mantis." As we were trying to crack what Repo's personality would be like, we knew he had to be a tough New Yorker, so we thought maybe he'd use Italian American slang insults, like *"mamaluke"* (dumb, fool) and *"cidrule"* (pronounced "jadrool," meaning fool or loser), a corruption of the Italian word for cucumber, *cetriolo*. Andy wasn't on board with *"cidrule,"* but we still thought that calling Leo a cucumber was funny, so we had Señor Hueso use the Spanish word, *pepino*.

RUSS CARNEY: Director Sebastian Montes asked us to write a silly song that the pirates are singing when Leo and Hueso first arrive at the docks. In the background, you can hear our genius lyrics: *"Yar har, yar har / The greatest pirates by far, far / We takes your portal / It makes us chortle! / Blah blah, blah, blah / We're pirates, not lyricists."* We spent a solid five minutes on it.

RON CORCILLO: This episode made it clear that despite his cavalier attitude, Leo really does love his brothers. Ben delivered a truly sincere moment of Leo sadness when Leo gives up on trying to pressure Hueso to help him.

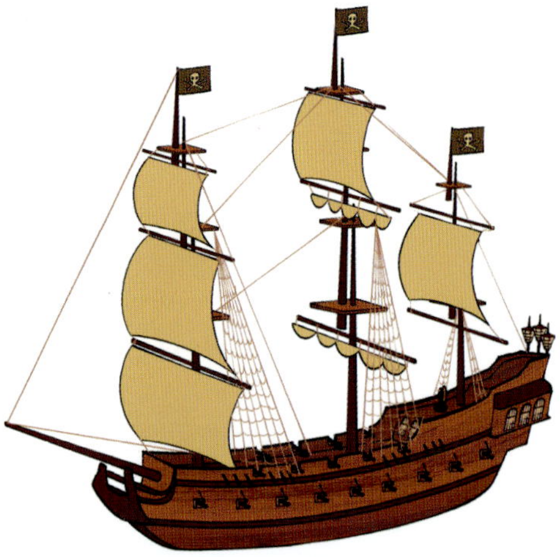

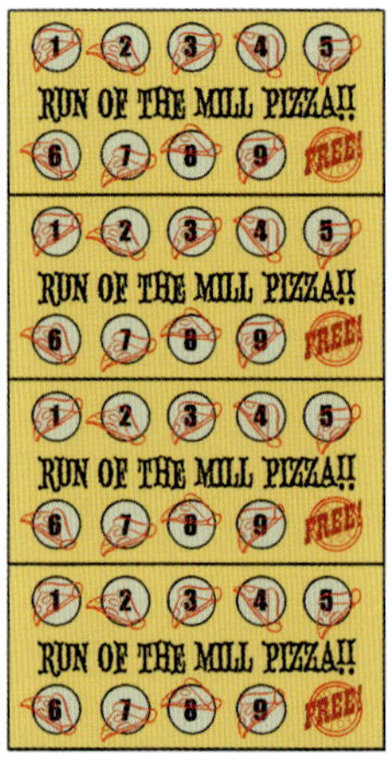

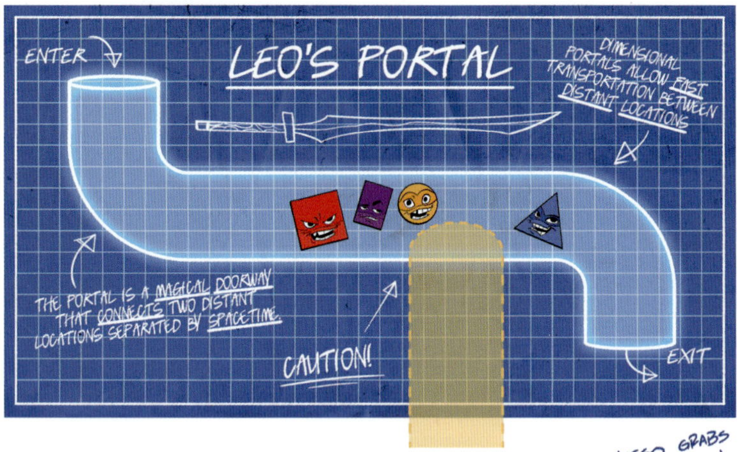

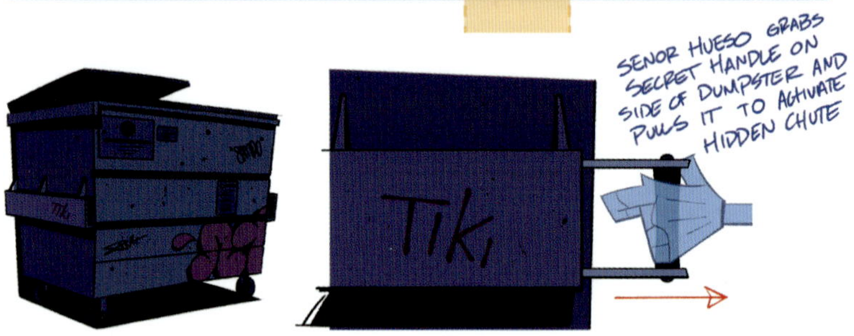

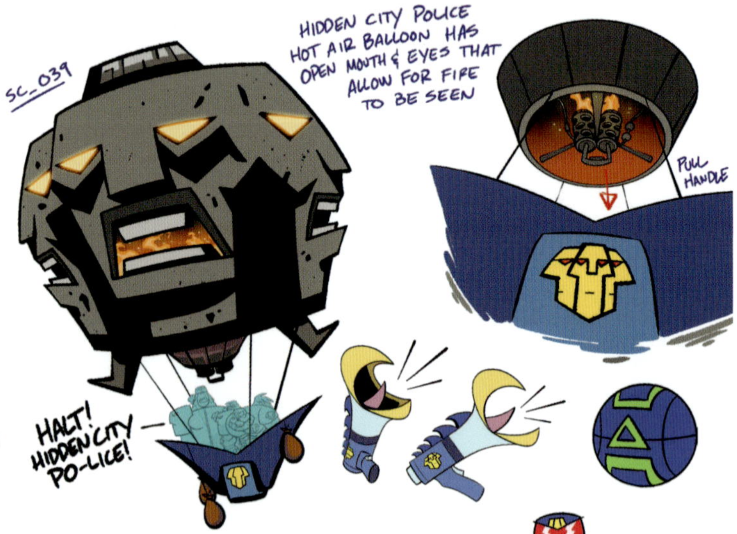

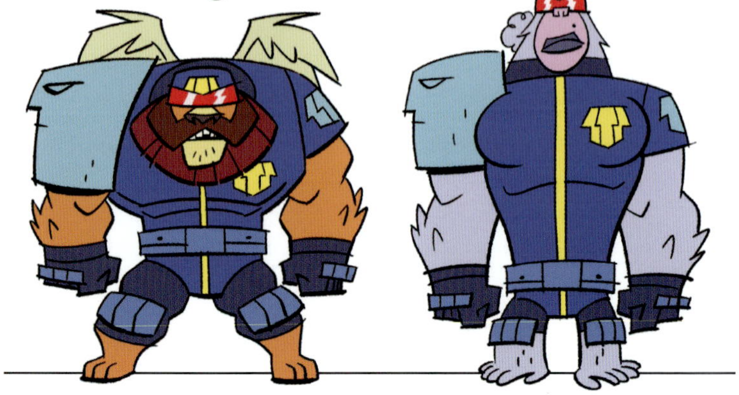

HIDDEN CITY POLICE OFFICERS

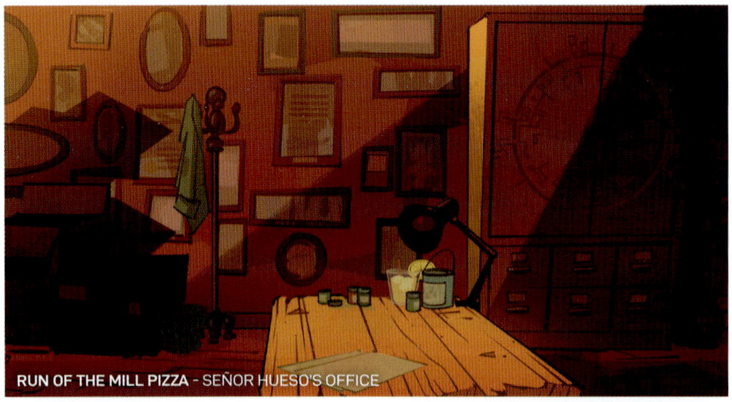

RUN OF THE MILL PIZZA - SEÑOR HUESO'S OFFICE

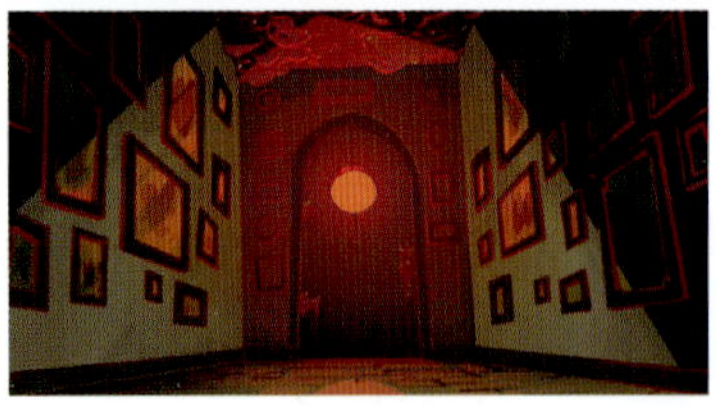

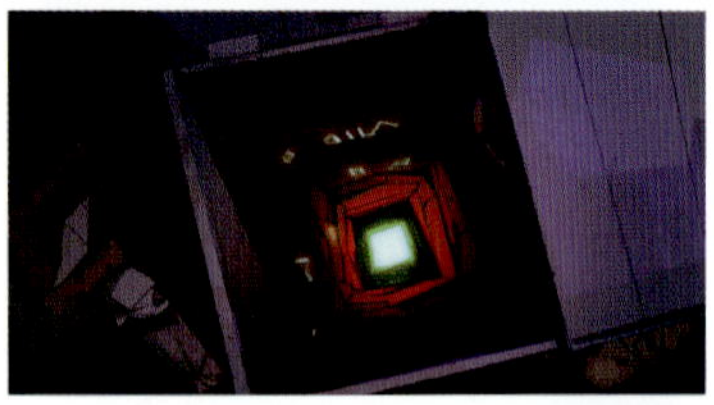

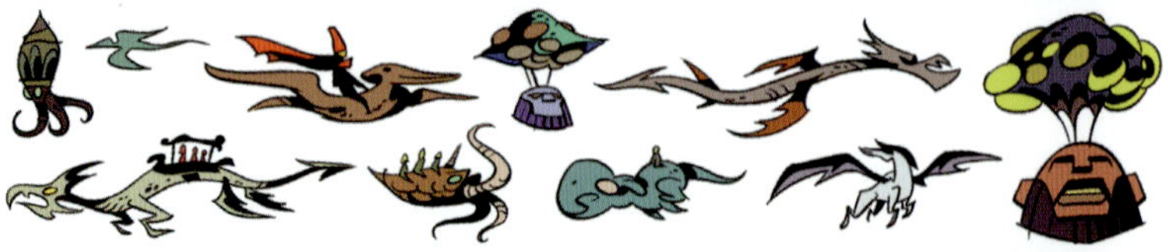

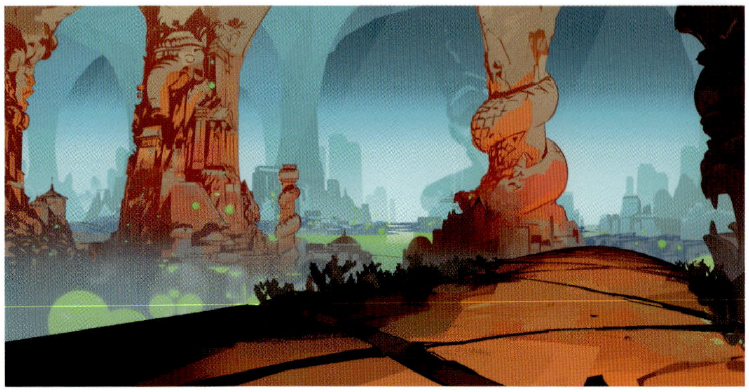

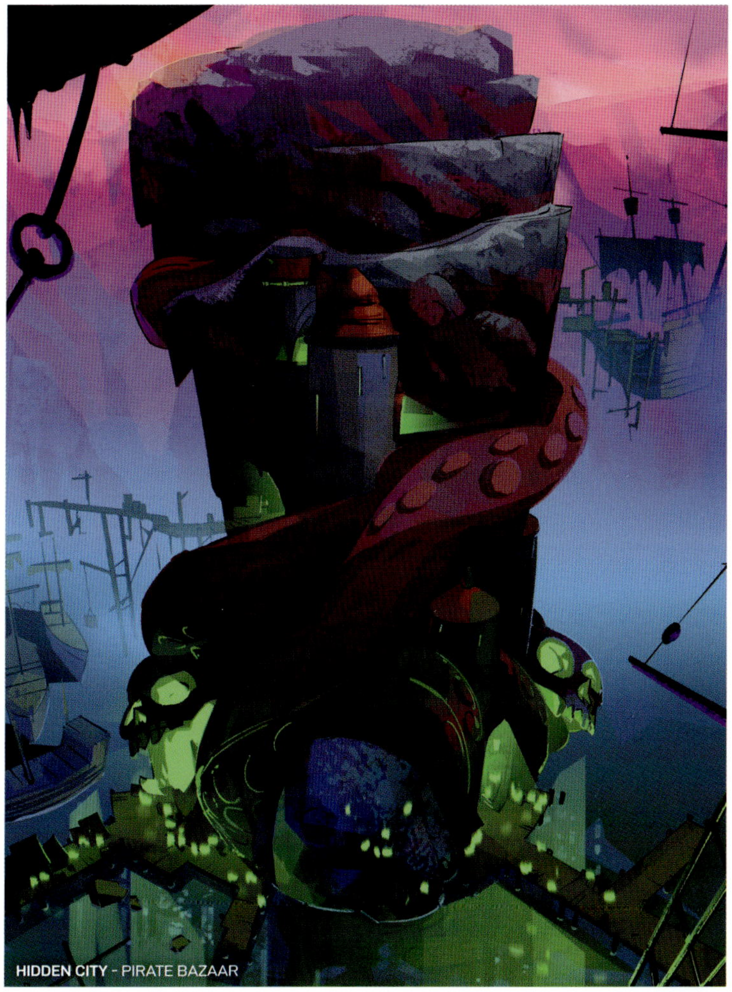

HIDDEN CITY - PIRATE BAZAAR

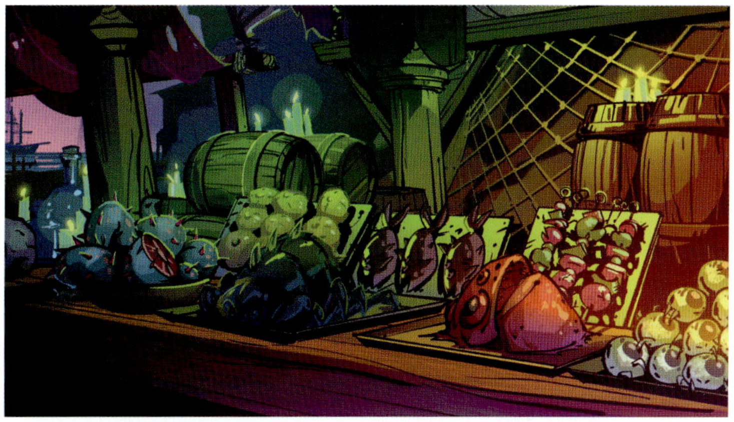

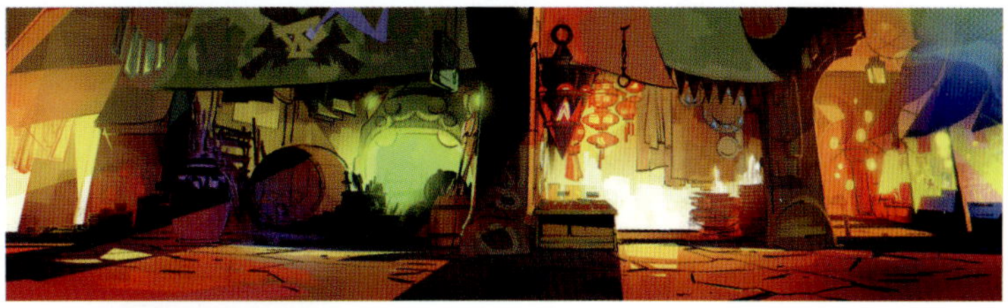

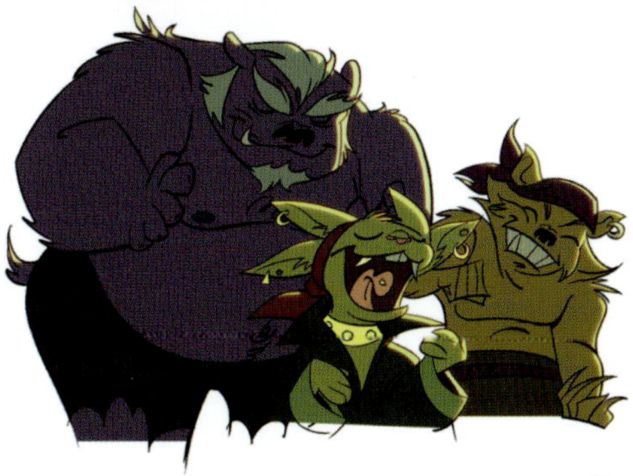

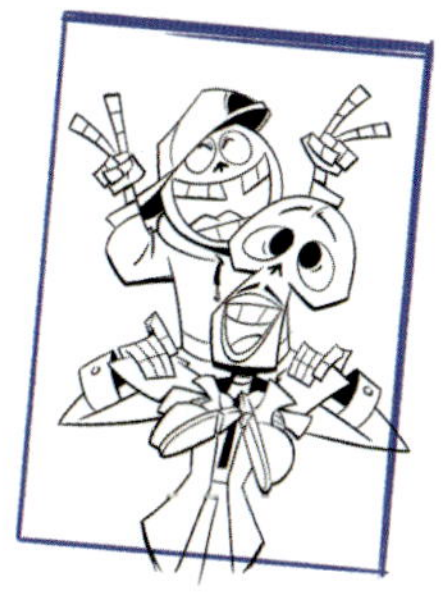

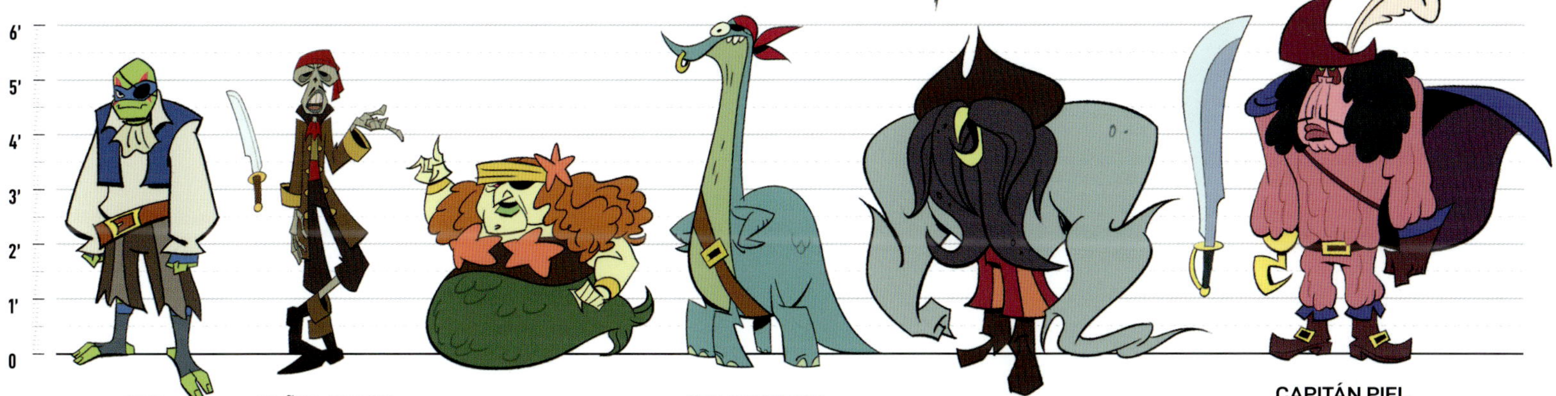

LEO
CAPTAIN BLUE MASK

SEÑOR HUESO
JOLLY ROGER

MERMAID PIRATE

SEA SERPENT PIRATE

KRAKEN PIRATE

CAPITÁN PIEL
CAPTAIN OF THE S.S. *QUEEN ALEXIS*
100% MADE OF SKIN

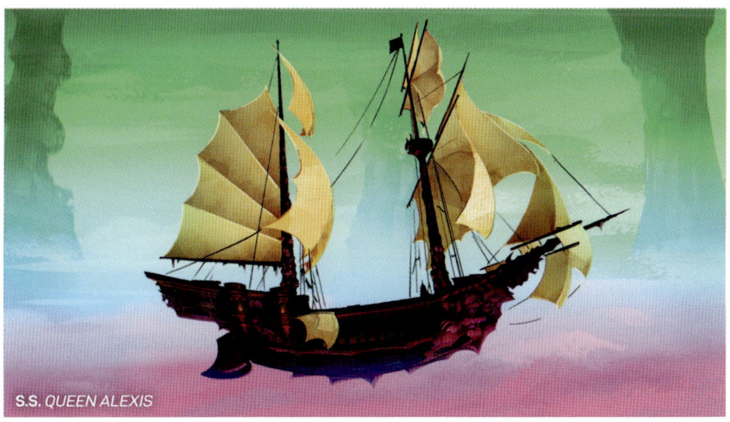

S.S. *QUEEN ALEXIS*

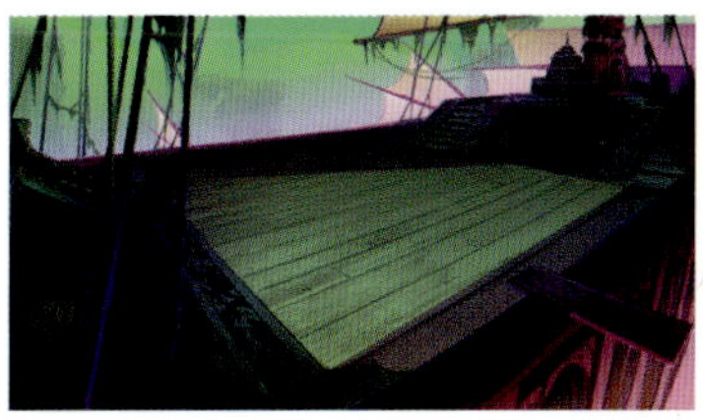

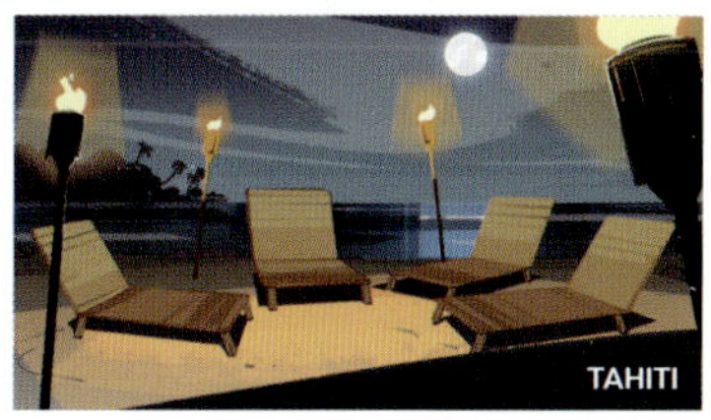

TAHITI

RUSS CARNEY: Capitán Piel's ship, the S.S. *Queen Alexis*, was named after one of our talented character designers, Alexis Page.

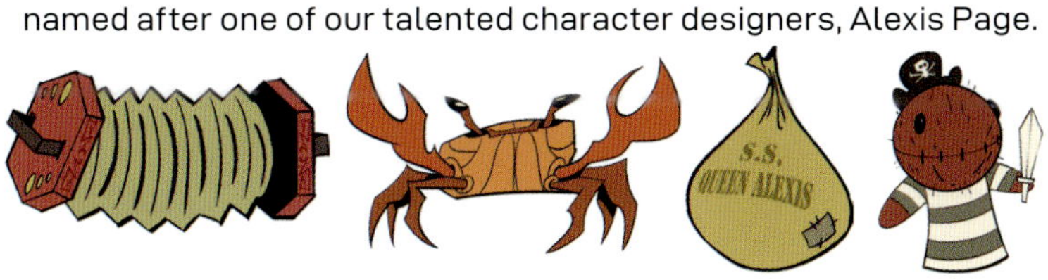

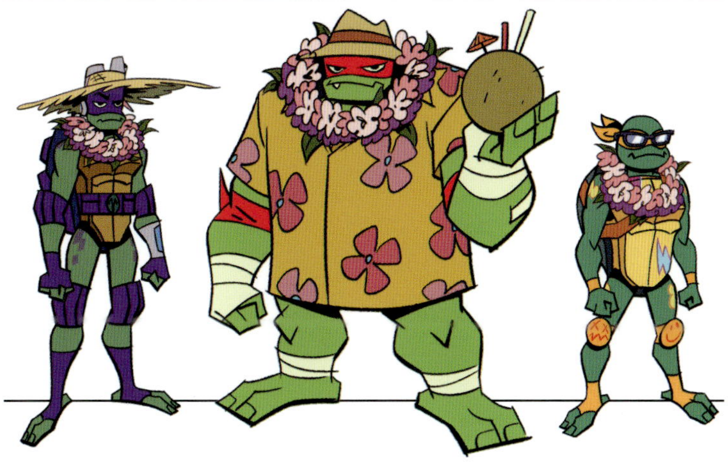

WARREN & HYPNO, SITTING IN A TREE

ORIGINAL AIR DATE: MAY 7, 2019
PRODUCTION CODE: 035

WRITTEN BY **JESSE GORDON**
STORYBOARDS BY **CHRISTINE LIU**
DIRECTED BY **JJ CONWAY**

JJ CONWAY: This is one of the first times we see Draxum in action, so to help make his fighting style distinct from the other characters, I looked to Earthbenders and Waterbenders from *Avatar: The Last Airbender* (2005) for inspiration.

The original concept for this episode is that the Turtles had forgotten April's birthday, but it just wasn't clicking. In a review we were discussing how to fix it, and our story editor Tony mused about a friend of his who was convinced his birthday was cursed. Immediately the pieces fell into place, giving us the through line about April's cursed birthdays.

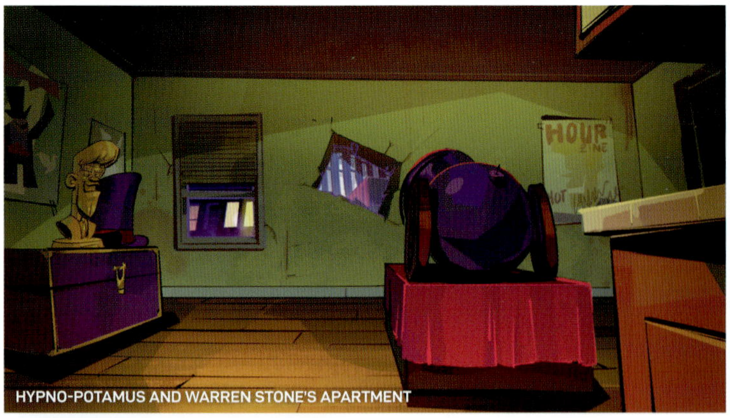

HYPNO-POTAMUS AND WARREN STONE'S APARTMENT

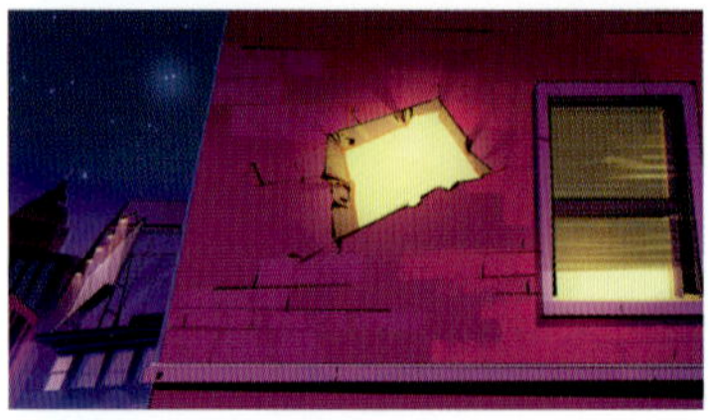

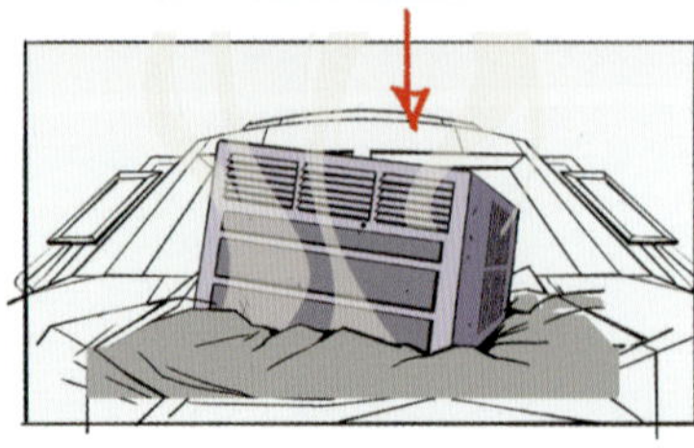

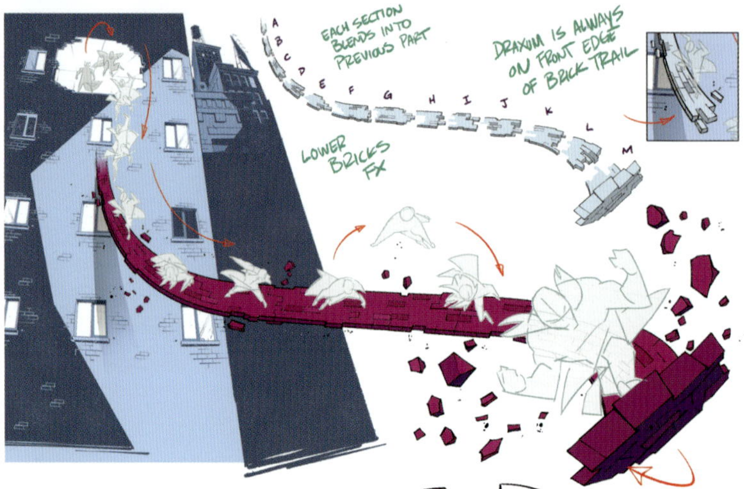

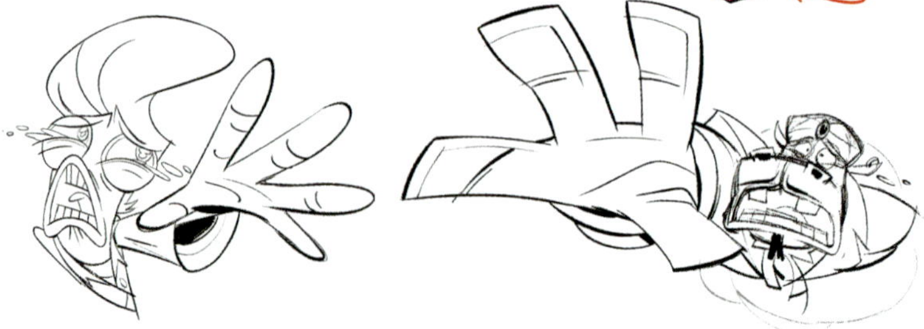

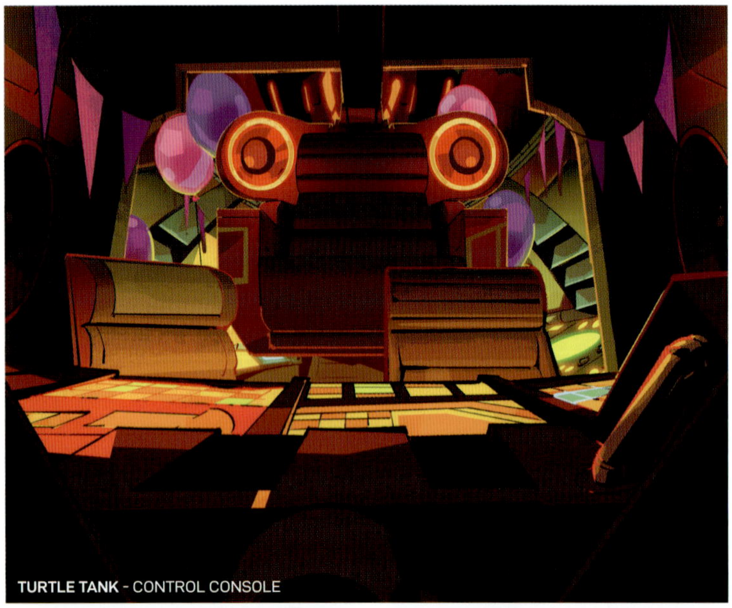

TURTLE TANK - CONTROL CONSOLE

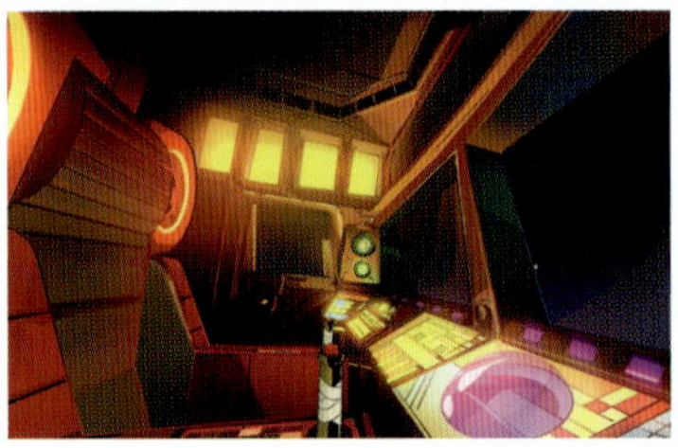

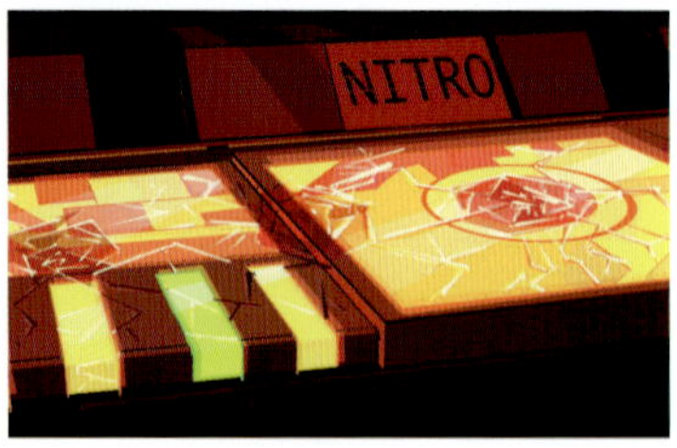

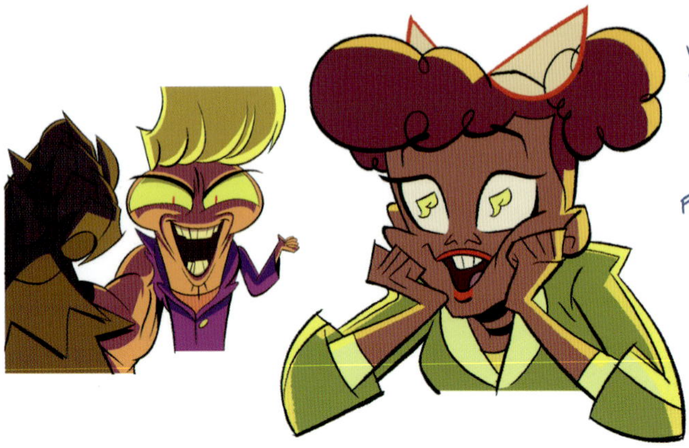

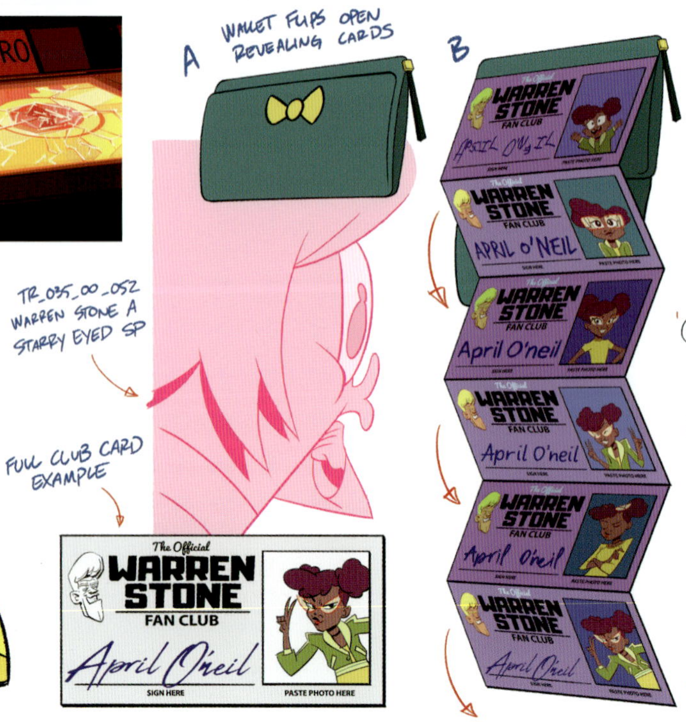

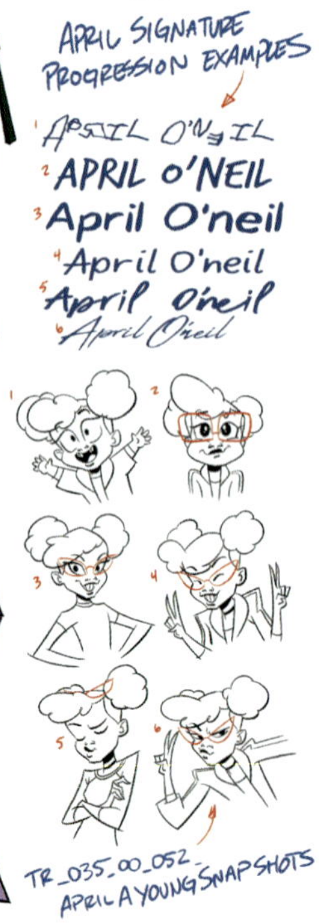

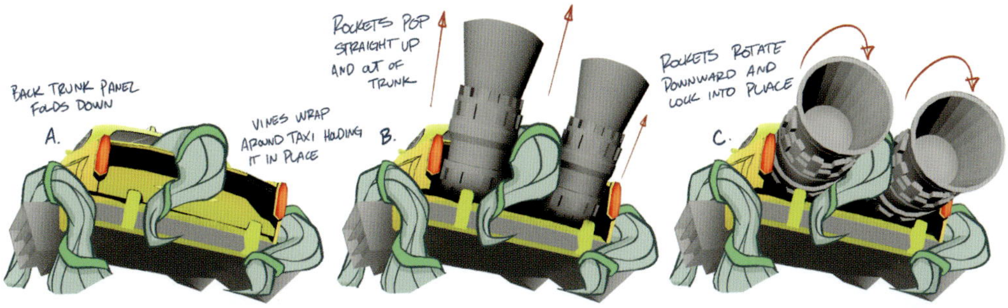

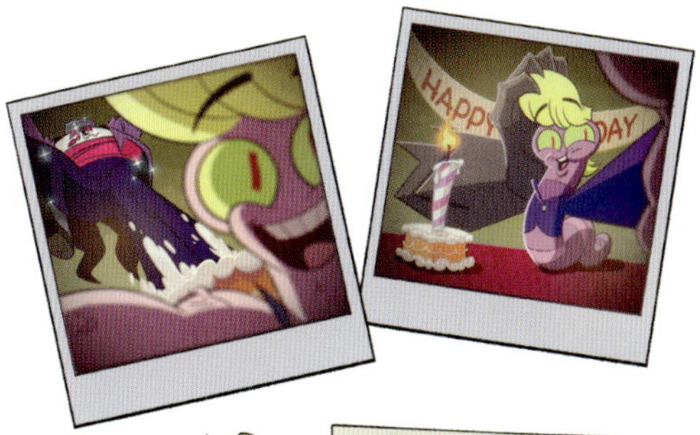

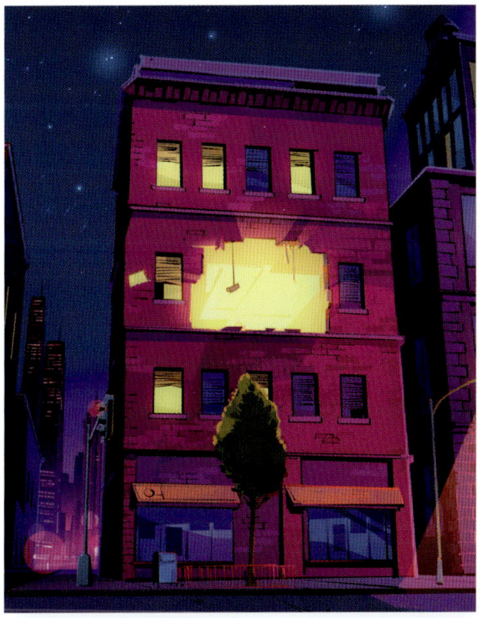

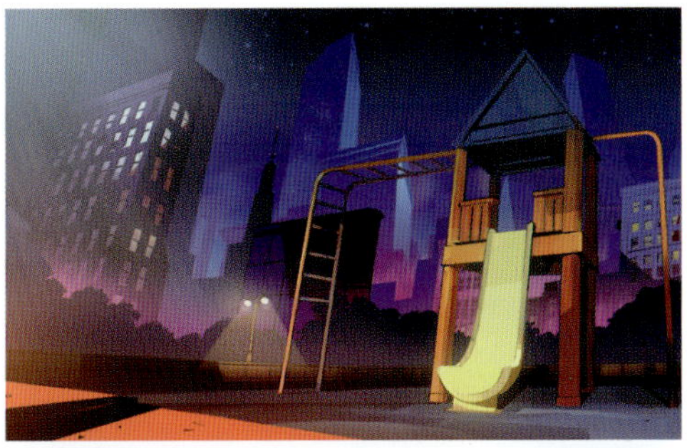

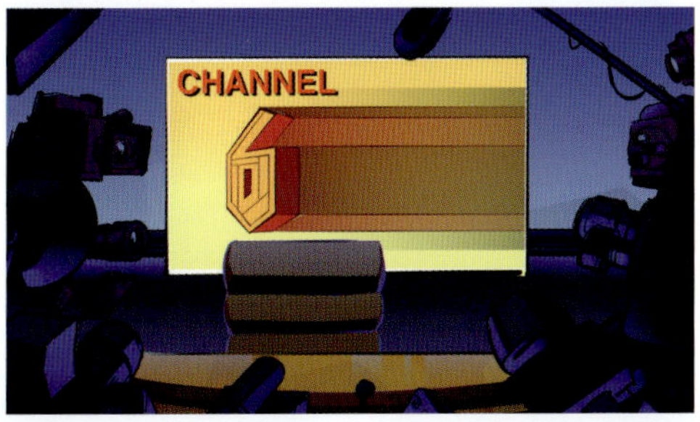

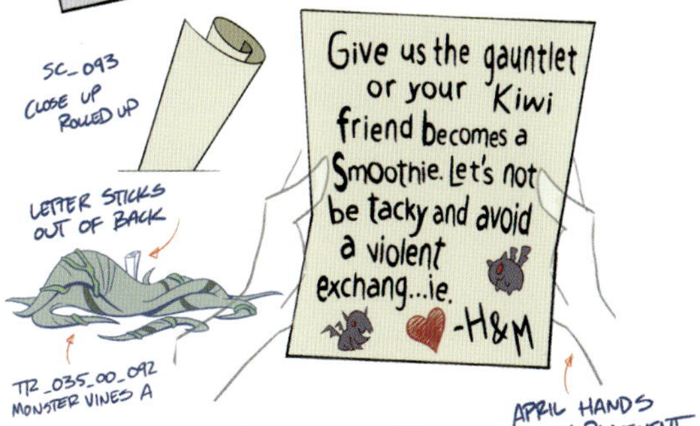

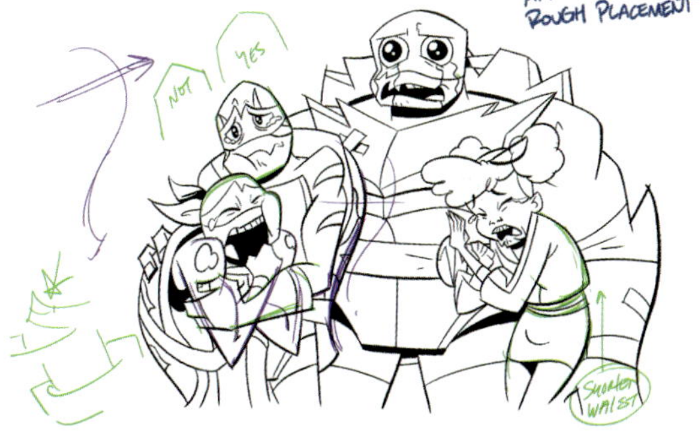

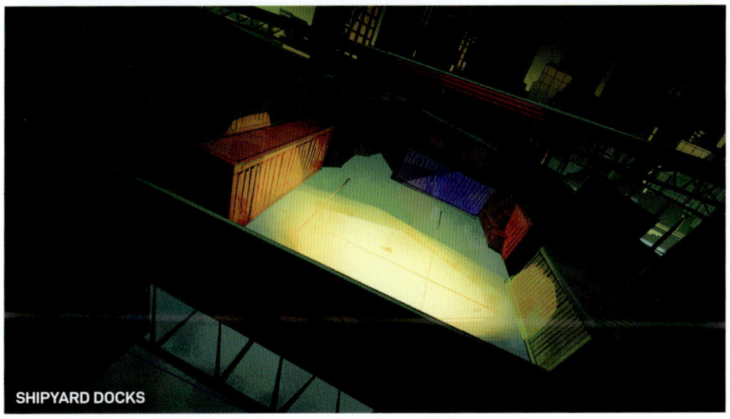
SHIPYARD DOCKS

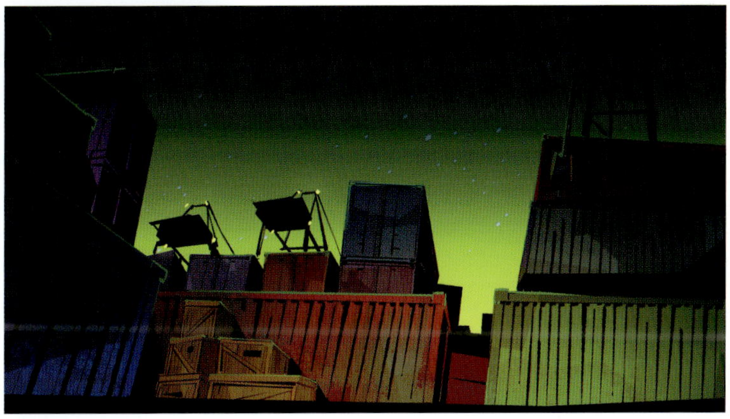

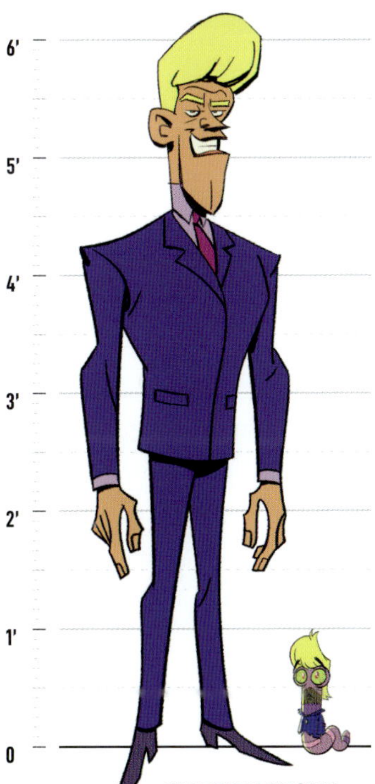

WARREN STONE
HUMAN FORM

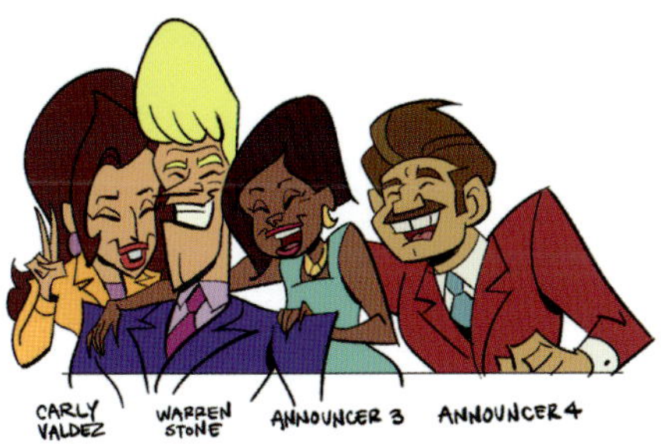

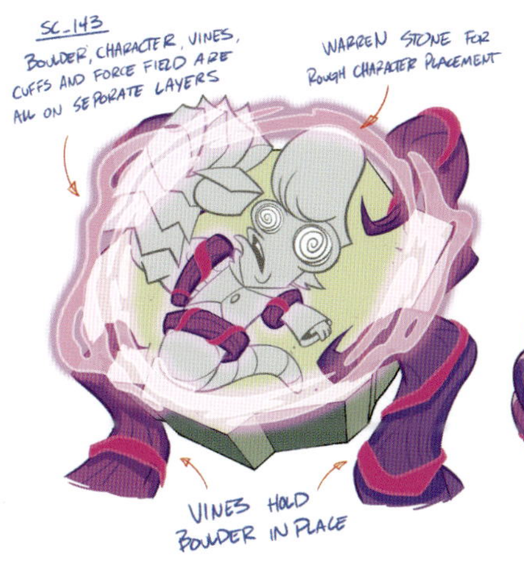

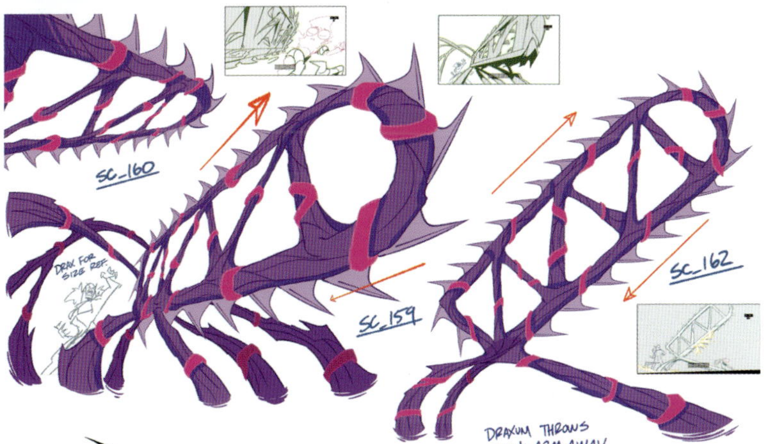

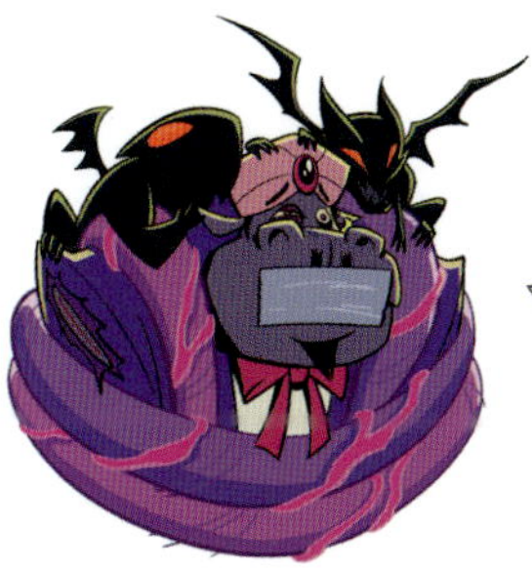

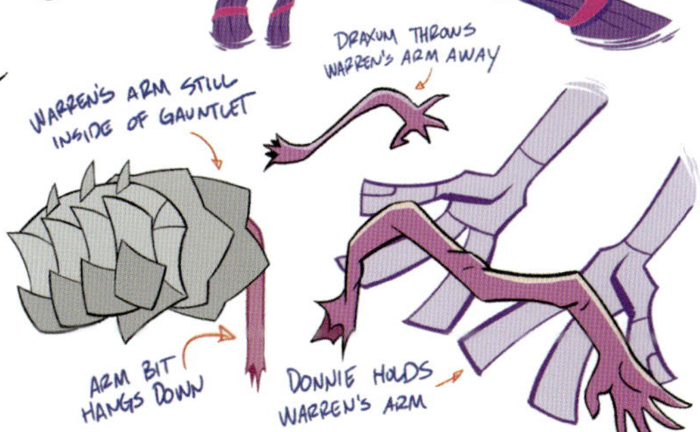

WARREN STONE'S ARM

SPARRING PARTNER

ORIGINAL AIR DATE: APRIL 13, 2019
PRODUCTION CODE: 036

WRITTEN BY **IAN BUSCH**
STORYBOARDS BY **ALICIA CHAN**
DIRECTED BY **ABE AUDISH**

IAN BUSCH: With the core of our show being the relationship between the brothers, I felt it would be fun to find something that gets in the way of their bond. Enter the paper ninja sparring partner. With Raph as the strongest of all the brothers, it just felt right that one problem he could have with his brothers is that they just weren't enough of a challenge in hand-to-hand combat. And then, along the way of writing and producing the episode, it was so easy to fall in love with Frankenstein's monster-esque sweetness of the sparring partner.

Zelda Williams also made our job so easy to write for her Foot Clan Recruit because she brought so much verve to the role. And that comes across hugely in this episode.

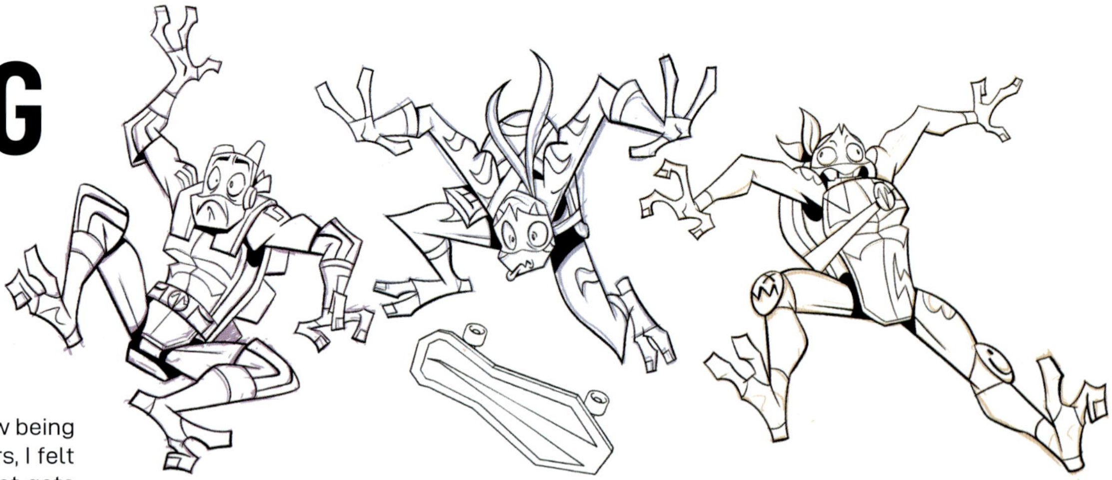

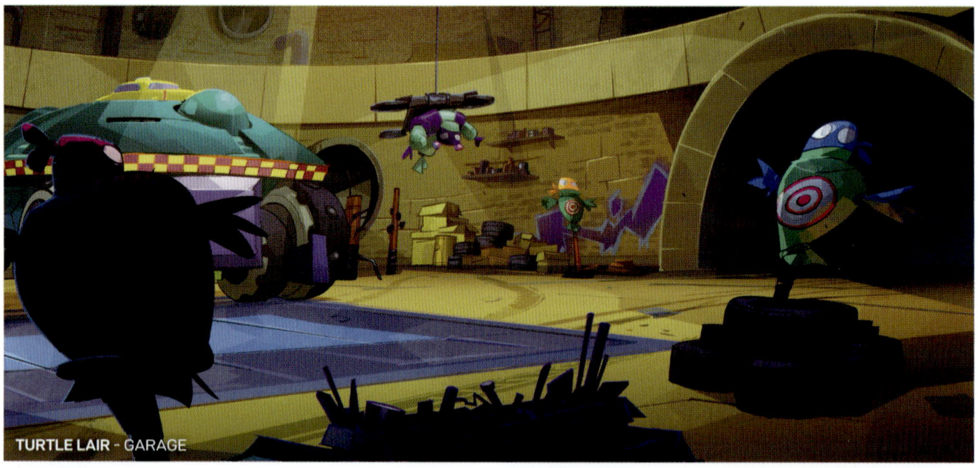

TURTLE LAIR - GARAGE

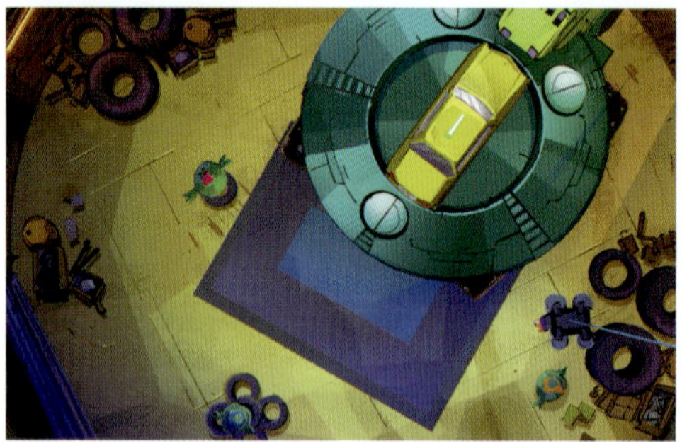

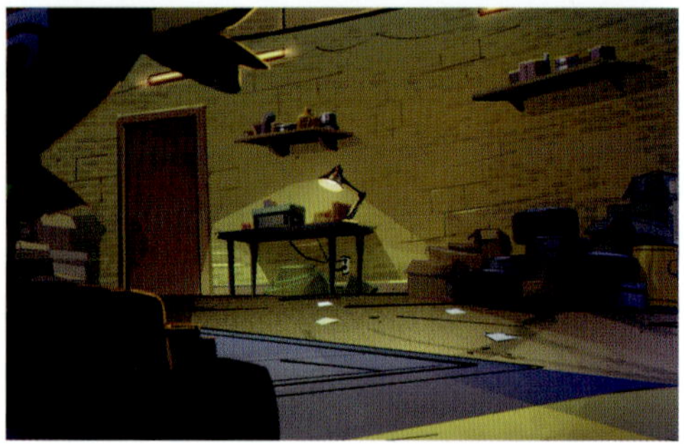

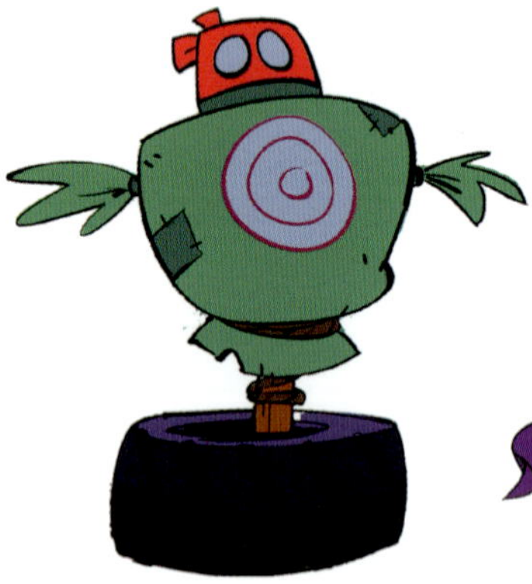

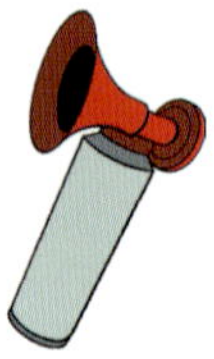

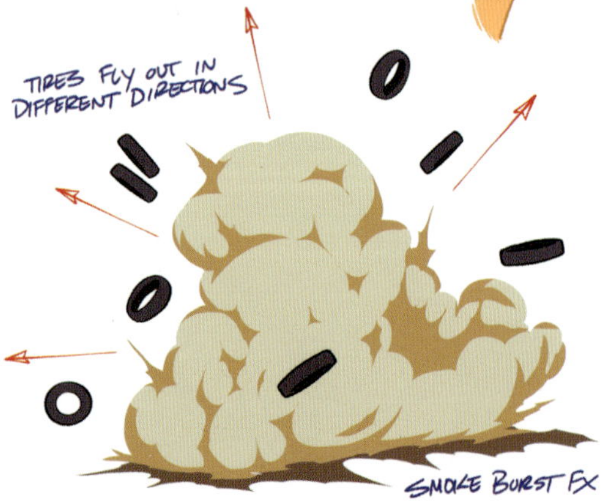

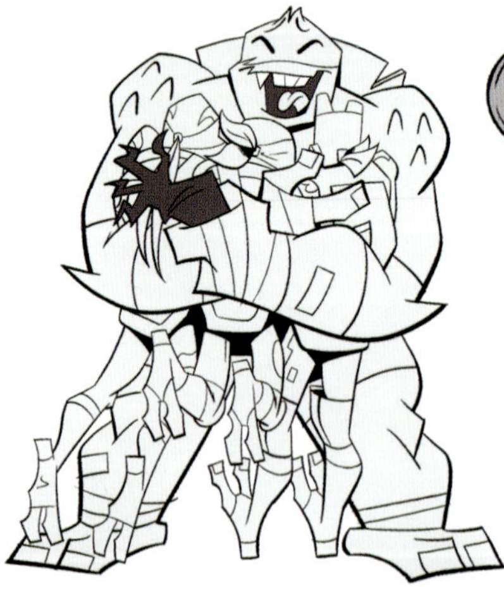

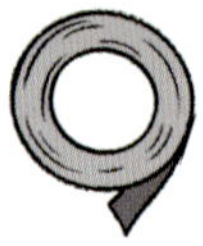

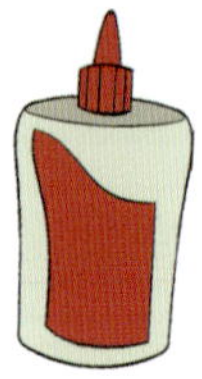

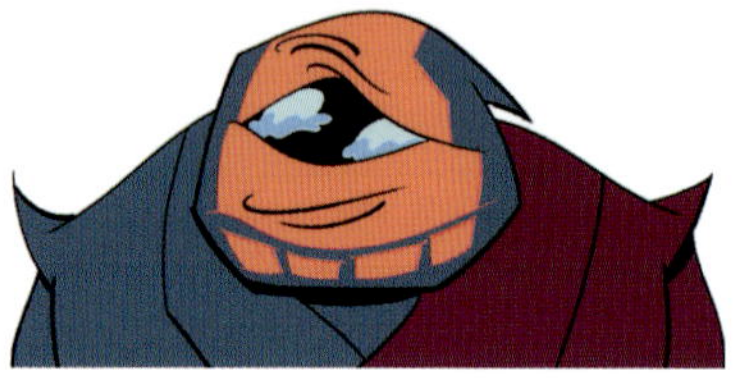

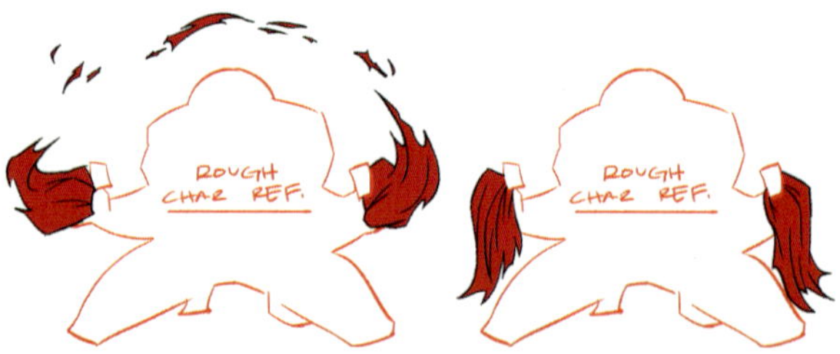

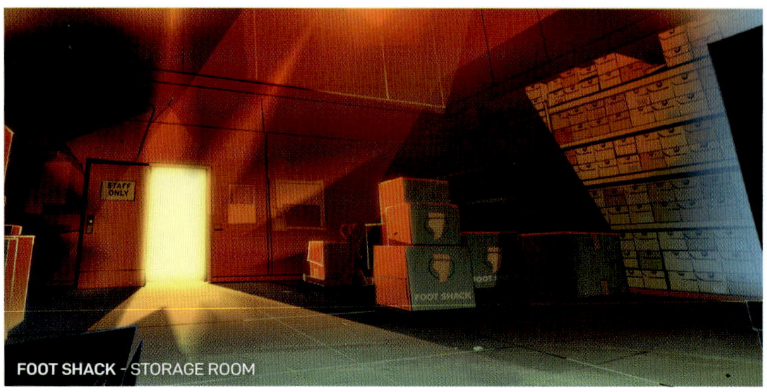

FOOT SHACK - STORAGE ROOM

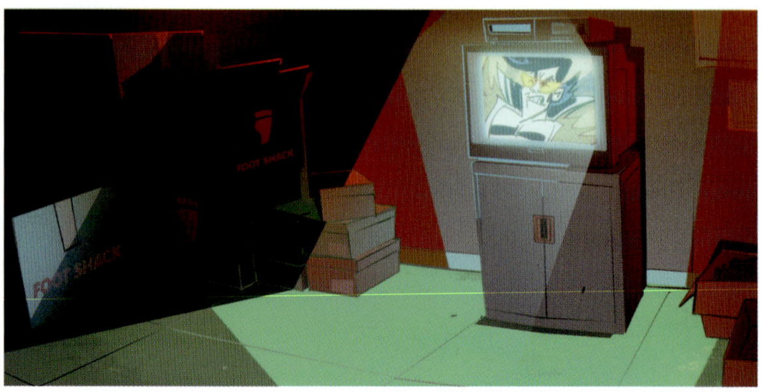

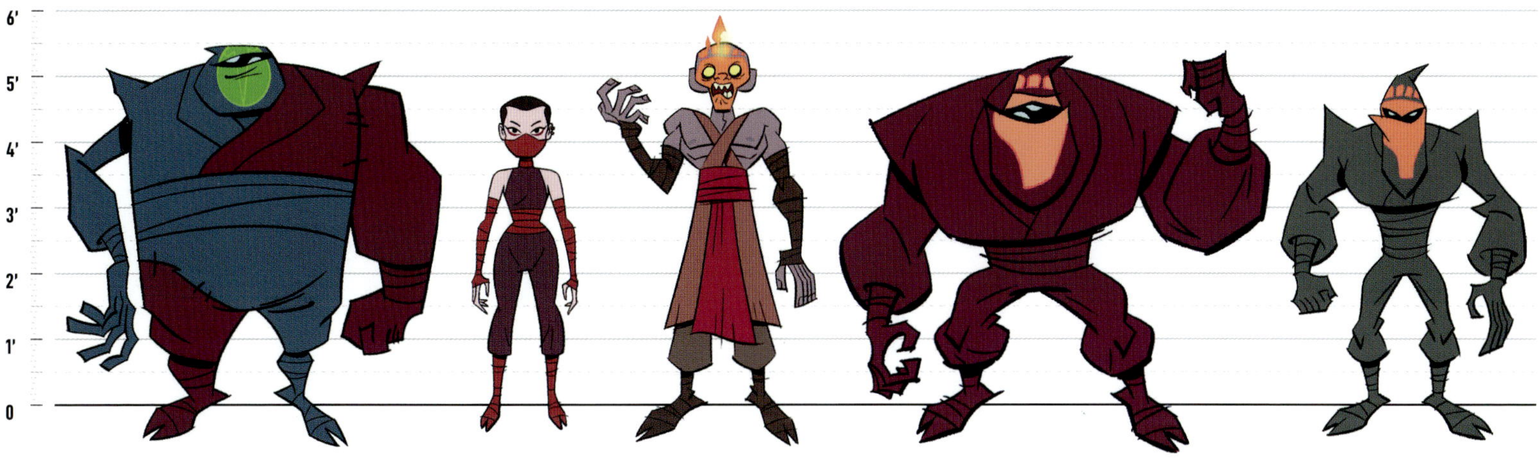

FRANKEN-FOOT FOOT RECRUIT FOOT LIEUTENANT ORIGAMI NINJAS

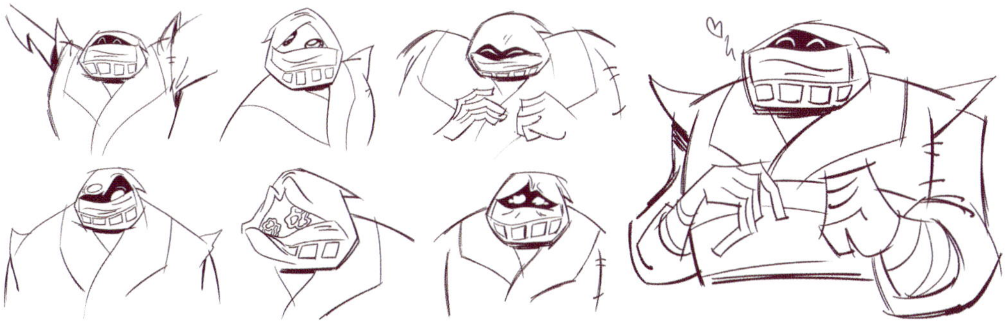

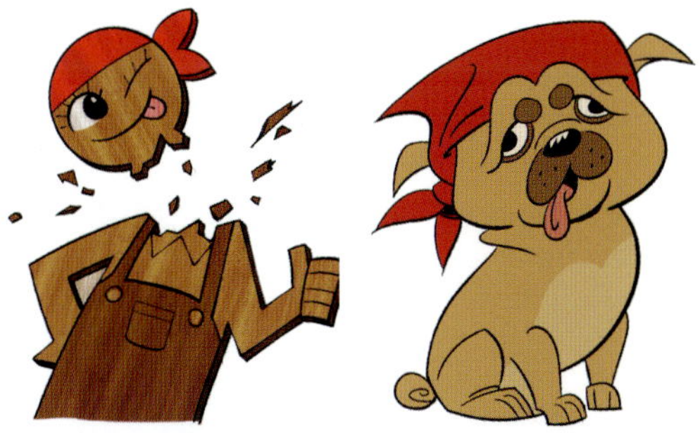

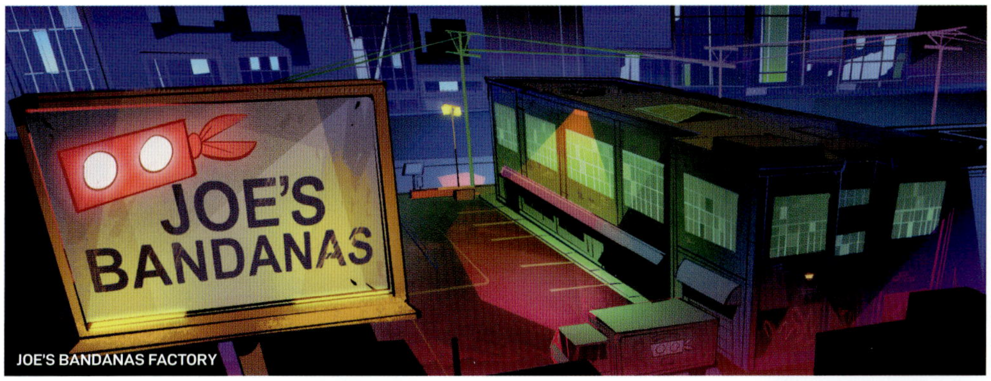

JOE'S BANDANAS FACTORY

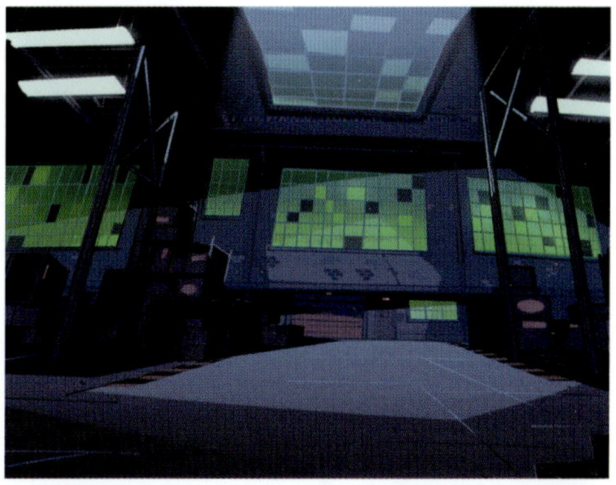

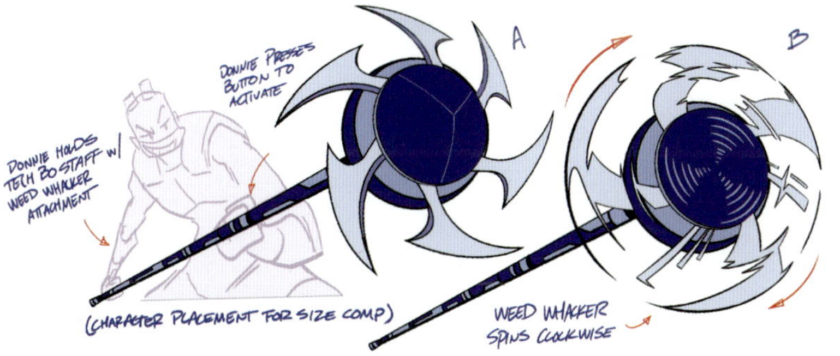

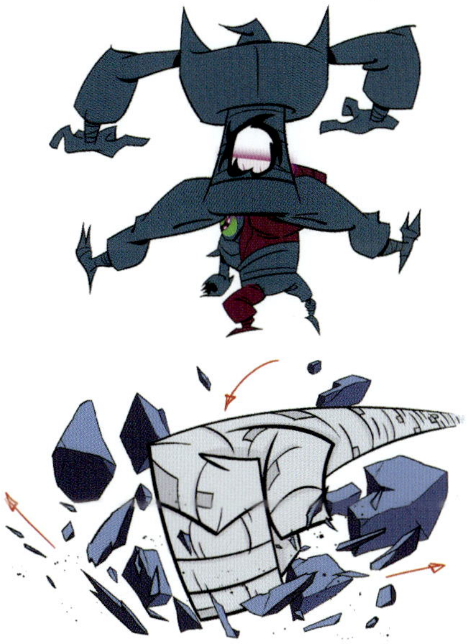

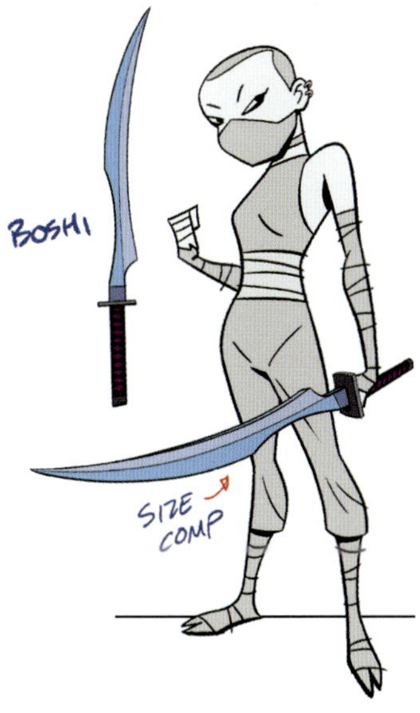

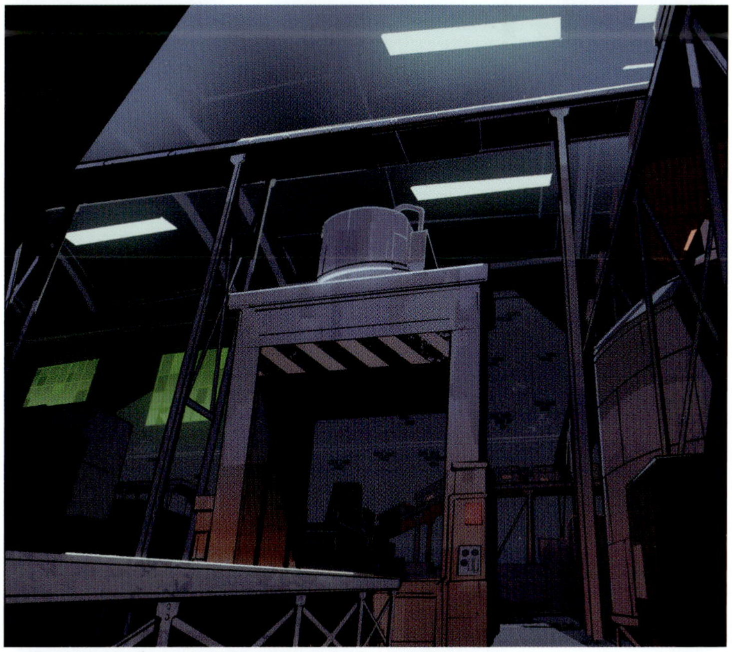

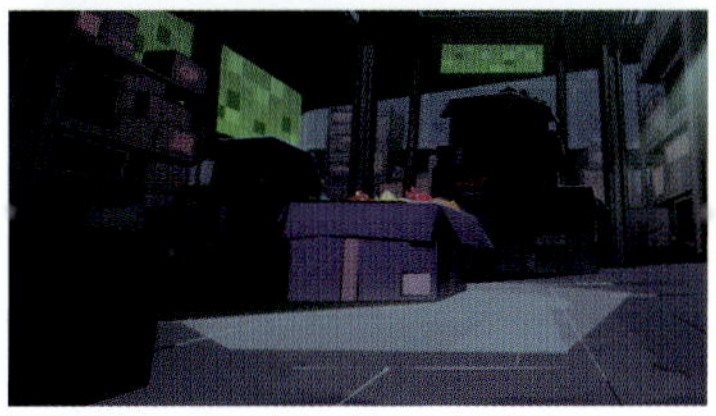

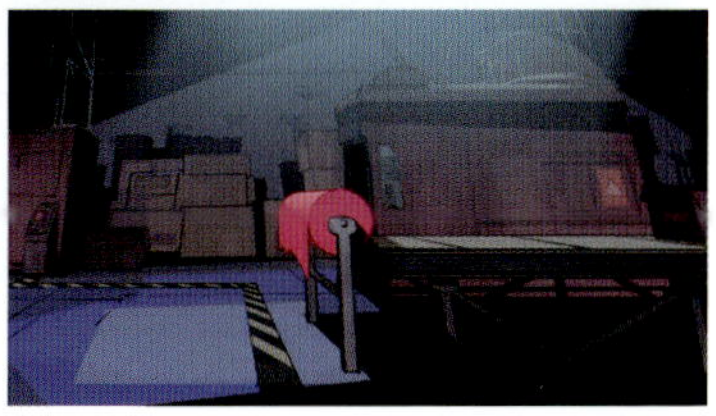

MYSTIC LIBRARY

ORIGINAL AIR DATE: JUNE 29, 2019
PRODUCTION CODE: 037

WRITTEN BY **RUSS CARNEY & RON CORCILLO**
STORYBOARDS BY **KEVIN MOLINA-ORTIZ**
DIRECTED BY **SEBASTIAN MONTES**

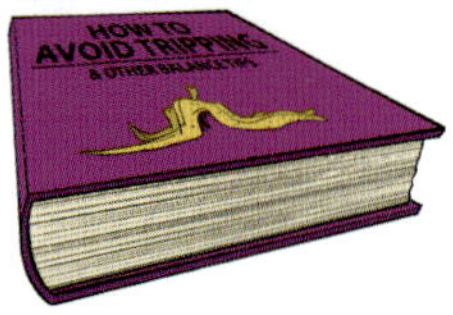

JERMAINE JOSE (BACKGROUND PAINTER): The library is massive and has this M.C. Escher–esque quality to it—I didn't want the color to get in the way. I also knew that Raph had this crazy sequence where he'd be tearing through it, so simplifying the palette felt like the way to go. I just looked at print colors and settled on CMYK: cyan, magenta, yellow, and key (black). Clear enough to visualize the eclectic floors and where they might lead, yet weird enough to feel like the Hidden City.

CARL BEU: Big credit to Jermaine Jose for really pushing the sense of scale on these with his colors while still keeping the style graphic and bold—it really complements the crazy vibe of the episode. You can see his influence and distinct style all over the show and movie.

RUSS CARNEY: We thought that the Mystic Library would be a frequent setting for our heroes. Since they know nothing about Hidden City mysticism, it would make sense that they'd occasionally need to look up spells that counteract spells and curses that were put upon them, but alas, we only went there once.

RON CORCILLO: Donnie's rap that he uses to navigate the library is set to the rhythm of the rap breakdown from the 2012 *Teenage Mutant Ninja Turtles* theme song. We did that mainly to avoid copyright violations. The ibis tapestry Donnie mentions is a reference to one of the symbols of the *Harvard Lampoon*, a humor magazine that I somehow wrote for in college. Apparently, their standards were low.

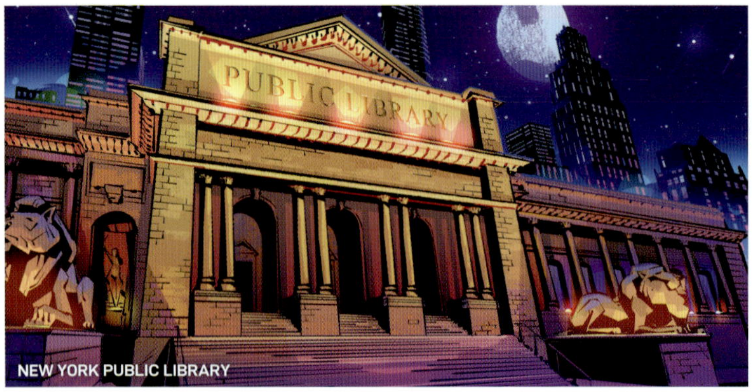

NEW YORK PUBLIC LIBRARY

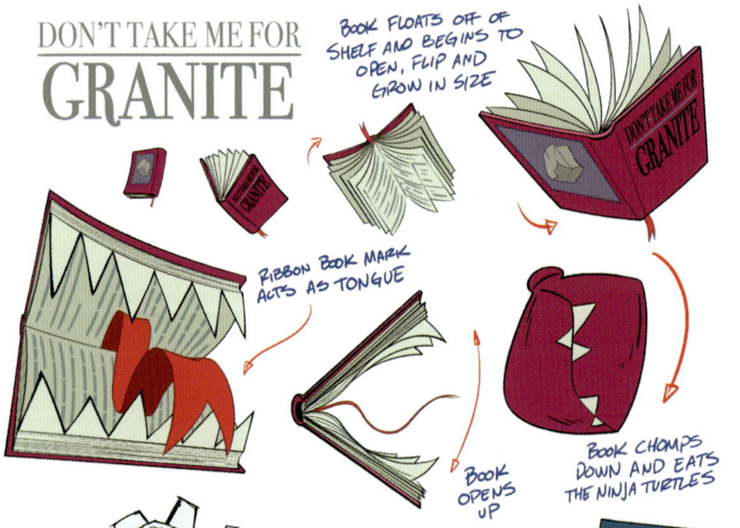

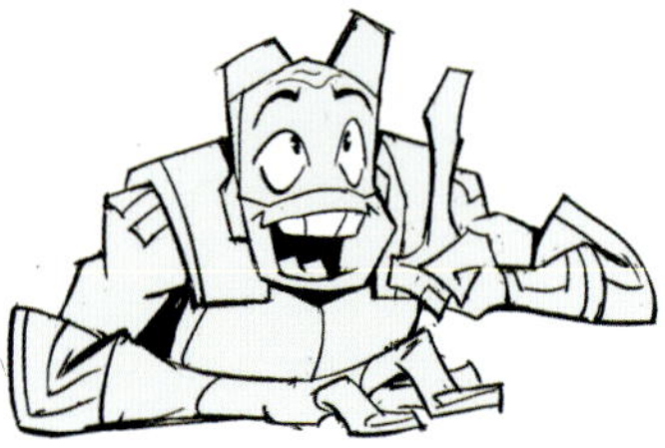

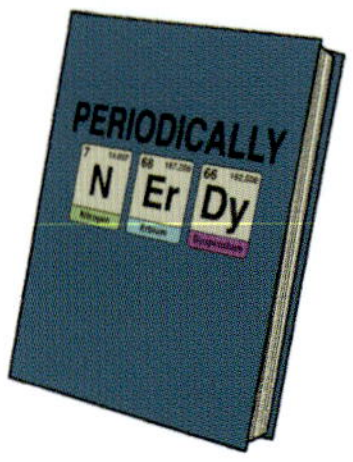

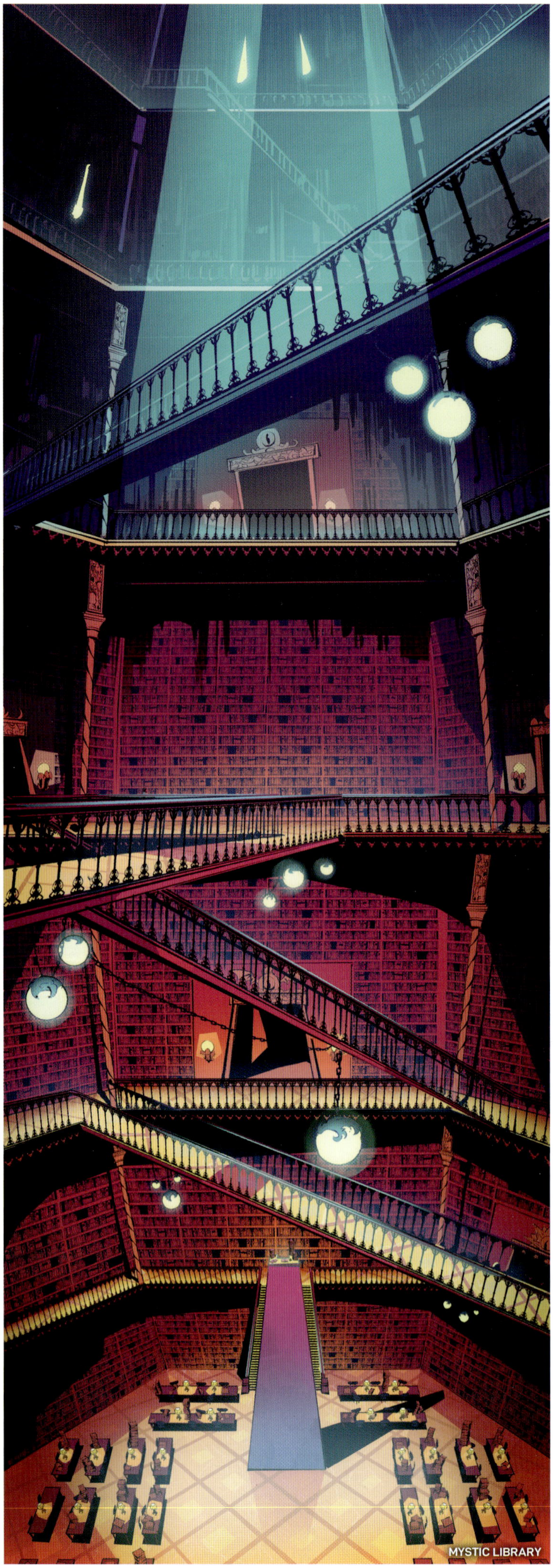
MYSTIC LIBRARY

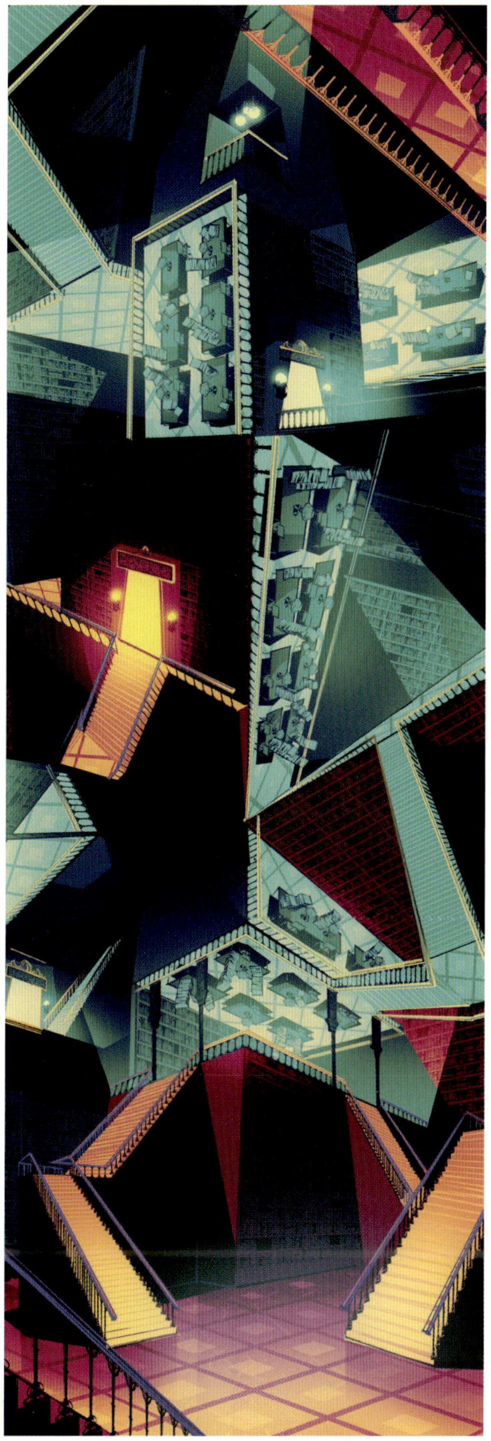

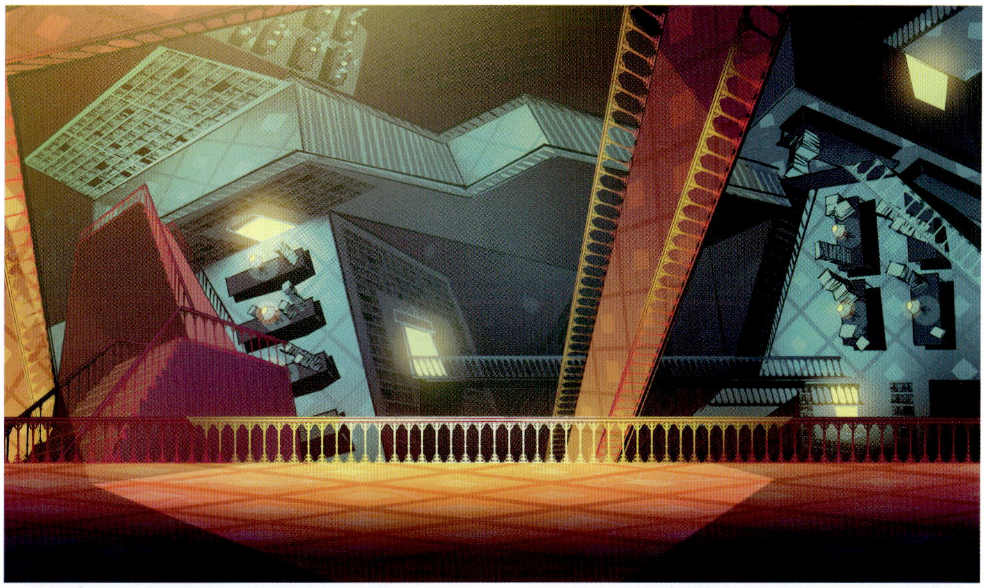

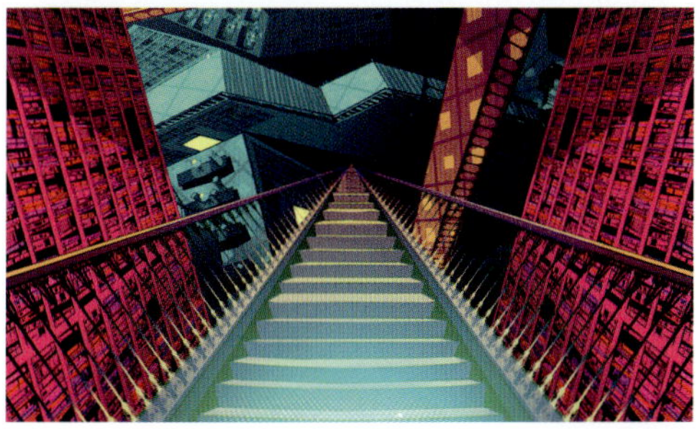

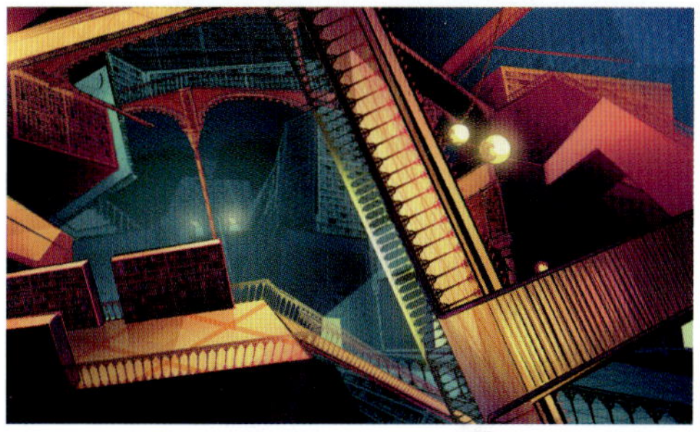

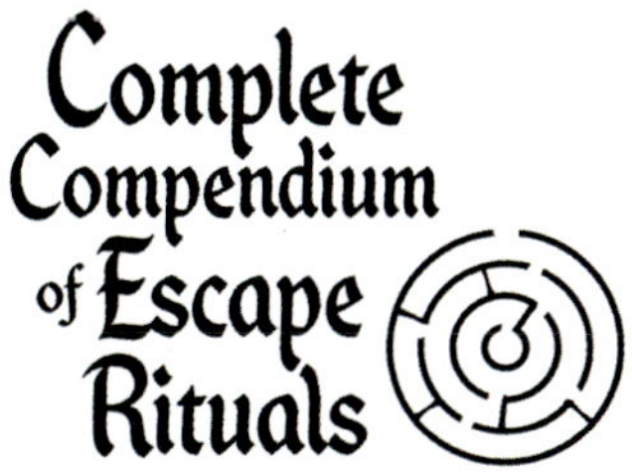

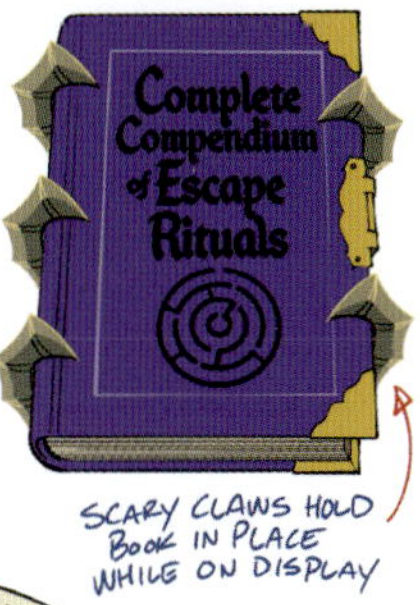

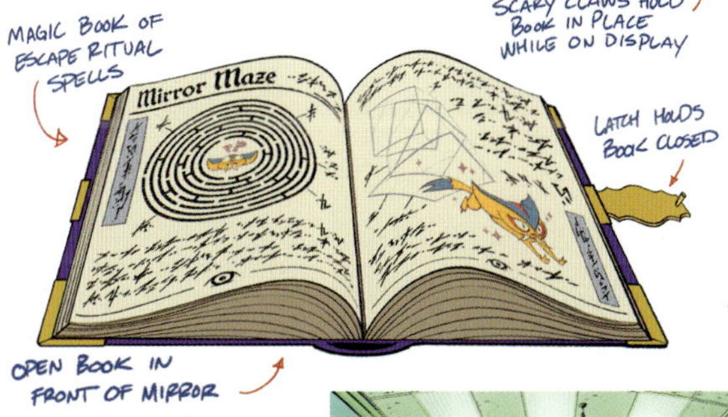

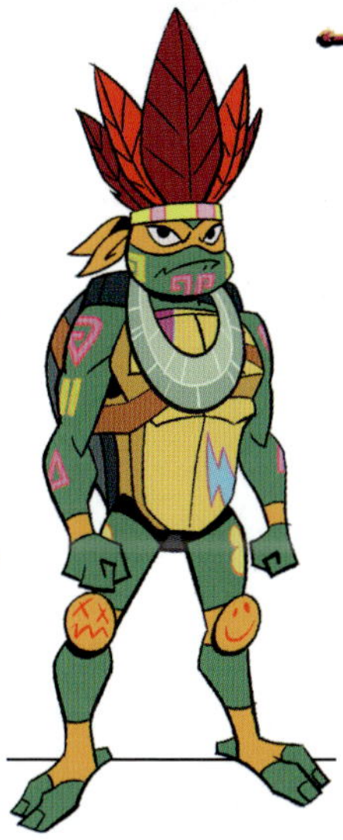

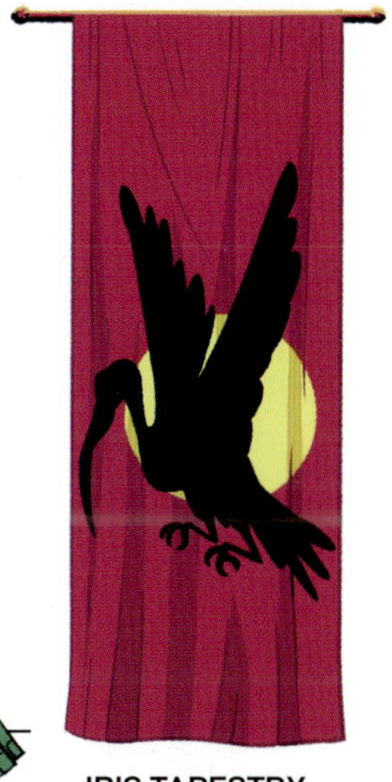

IBIS TAPESTRY

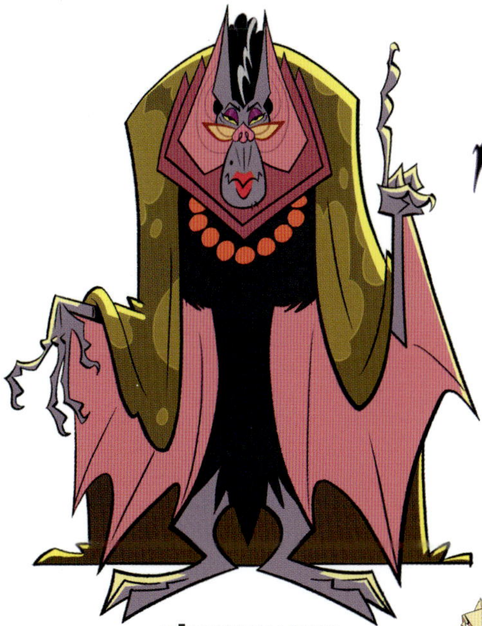

YŌKAI LIBRARIAN

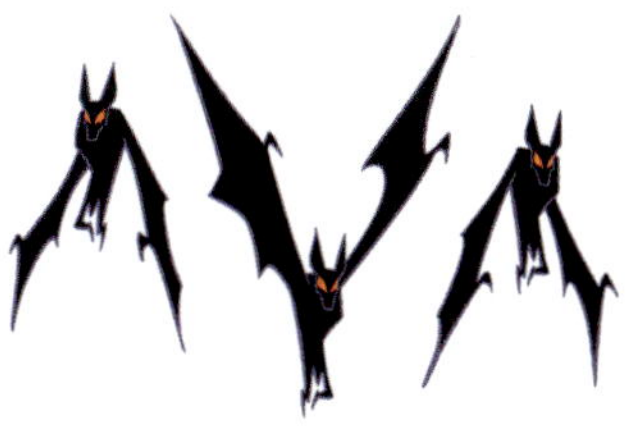

HUSH BATS

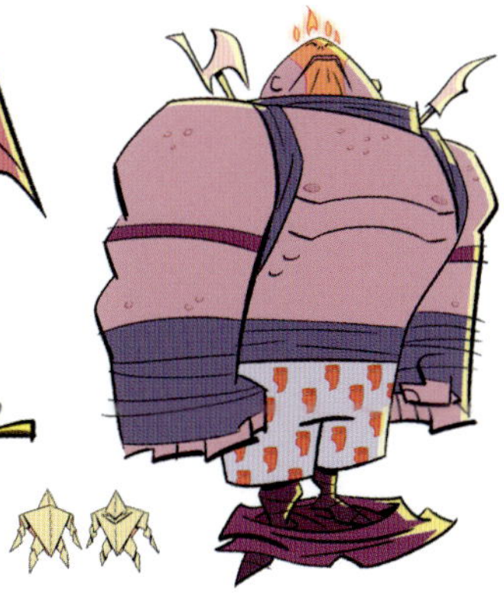

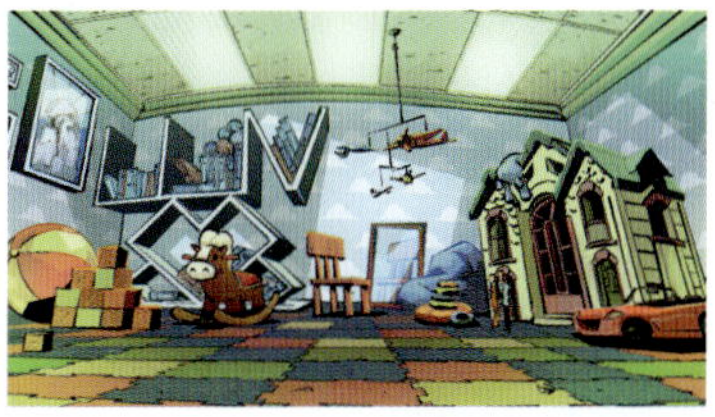

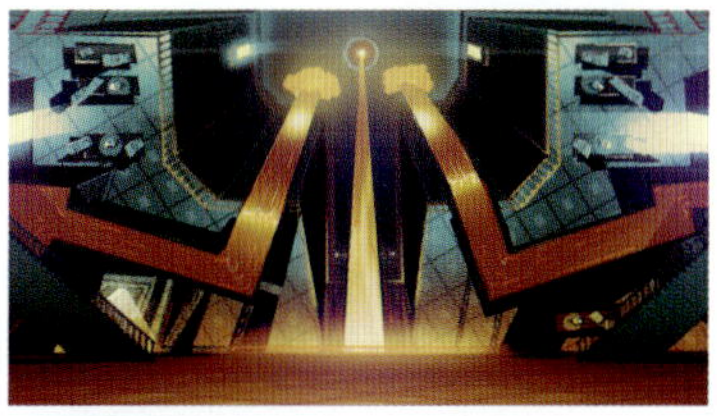

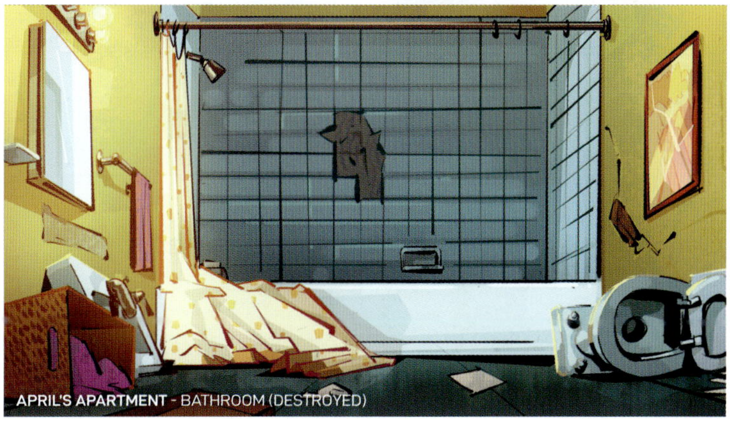

APRIL'S APARTMENT - BATHROOM (DESTROYED)

OPERATION: NORMAL

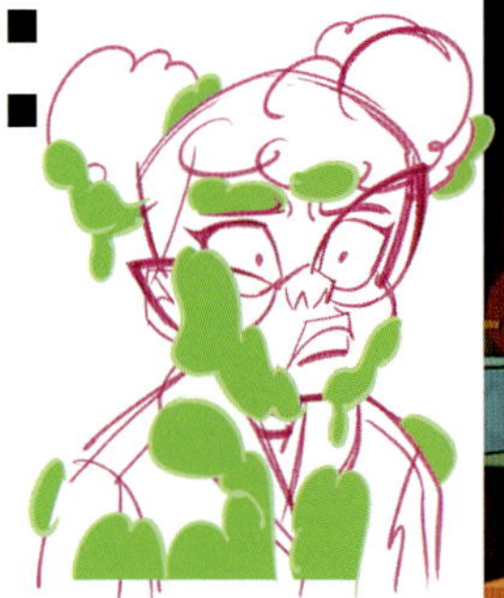

ORIGINAL AIR DATE: JUNE 8, 2019
PRODUCTION CODE: 038

WRITTEN BY **LAURA SREEBNY**
STORYBOARDS BY **JULIA BRAID**
DIRECTED BY **ALAN WAN**

RUSS CARNEY: Freelance writer Laura Sreebny named Sunita after an acquaintance of hers, and that choice led to the casting of the energetic and talented Kody Kavitha! Go, Kody! We'll always remember the amazed look on Kody's face when she saw her character animated for the first time.

Ian pitched the species name "Googlyschmootz." It was a from-the-hip pitch that nobody ever countered, because *Rise* was supposed to be goofy, and so the species name stuck. It was a good lesson for us to learn, that something as simple as a choice of name has the power to inspire and bring joy to others.

KODY KAVITHA (SUNITA): Working on *Rise* was such an honor. The first time I saw Sunita in action, I cried. Knowing that a whole generation of brown girls would grow up with her meant so much to me. Recording with Kat Graham (April O'Neil) for "Operation: Normal" is my favorite memory. Kat's kindness and generosity gave me the confidence boost I needed to bring Sunita to life.

Another joy is the fan art! The talent of TMNT fans blows me away. At the beginning of this adventure, Rob Paulsen told me to brace myself. He explained that TMNT fans are the most dedicated group he's ever known and that this booking would forever be a career highlight. He was right. I got to create awesome memories and make some great friends (hi, Ron and Russ!). I'll forever be grateful to Ant and Andy for including me and the TMNT fans for embracing me. Aloha!

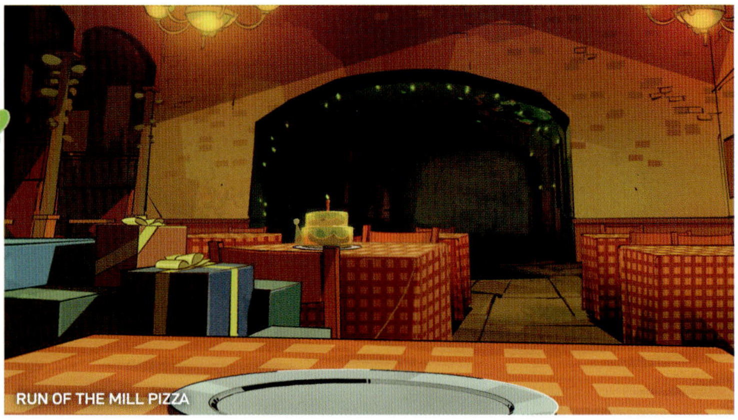

RUN OF THE MILL PIZZA

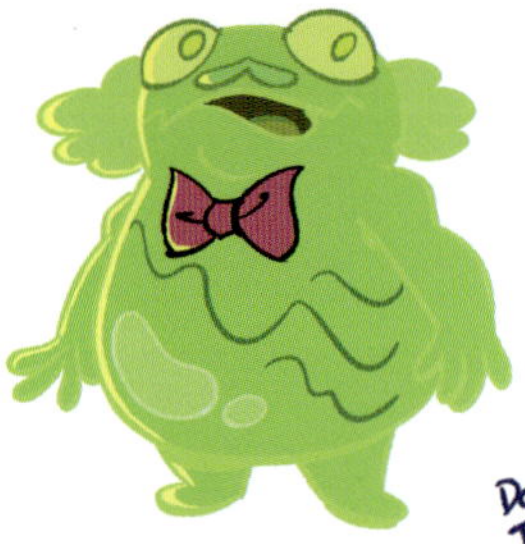

EXPLODING FRANKIE

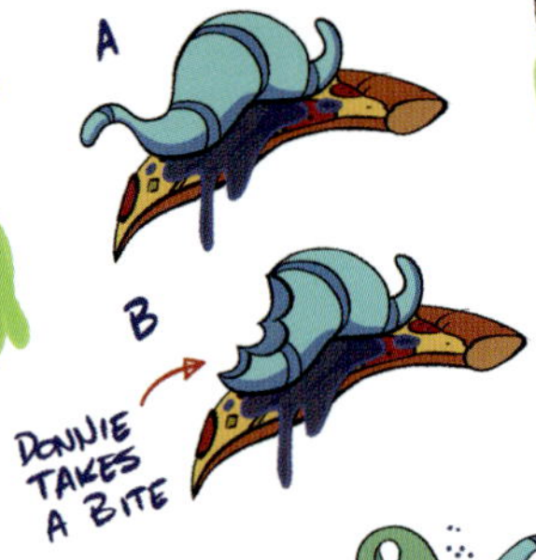

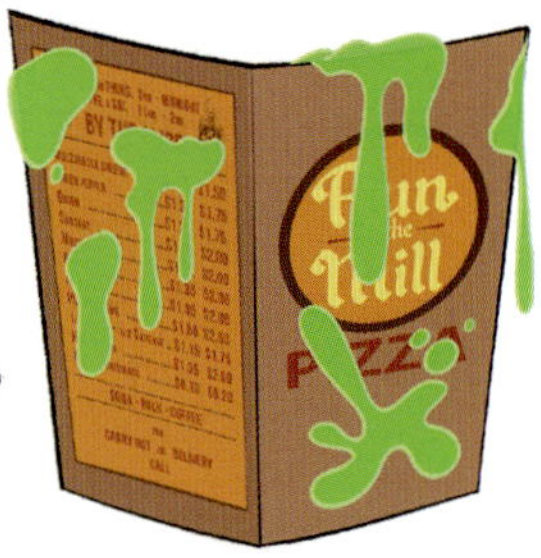

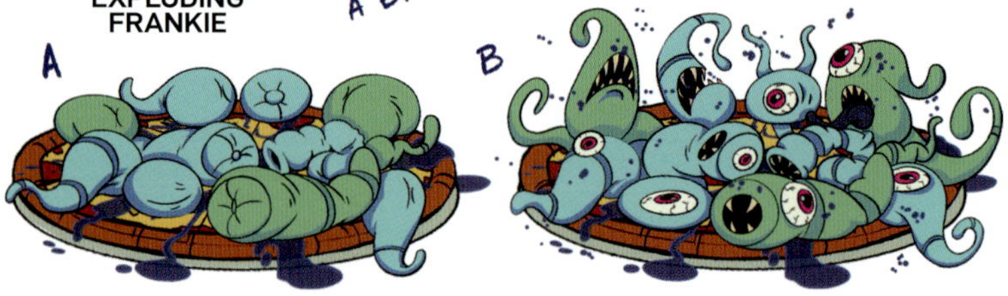

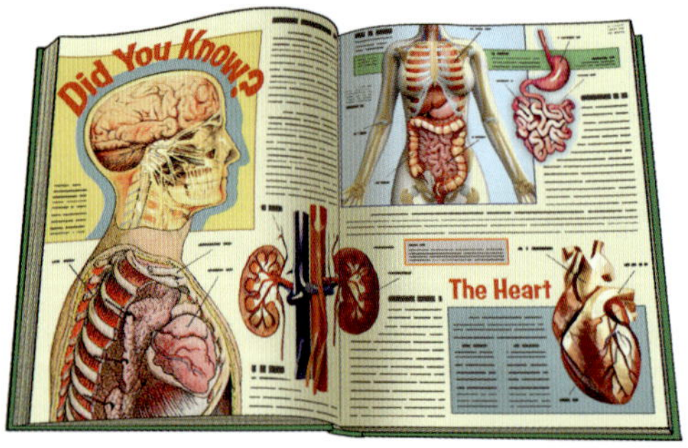

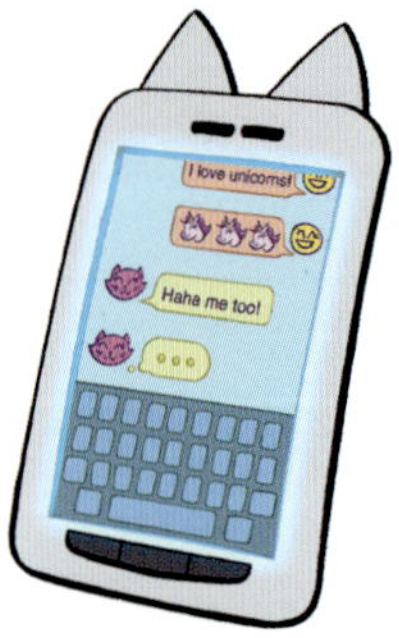

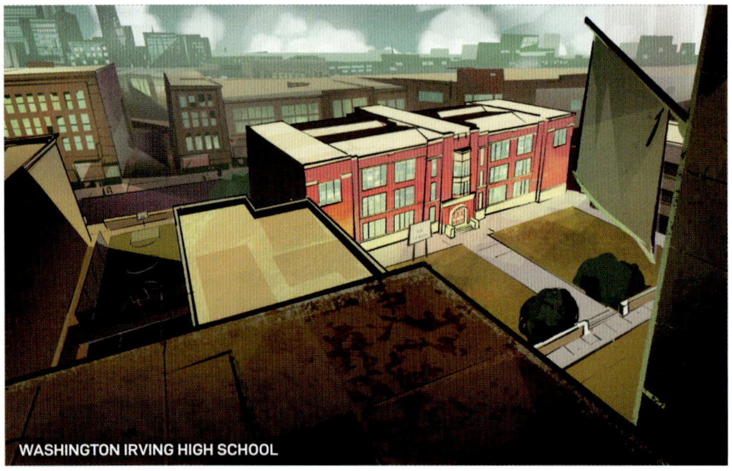

WASHINGTON IRVING HIGH SCHOOL

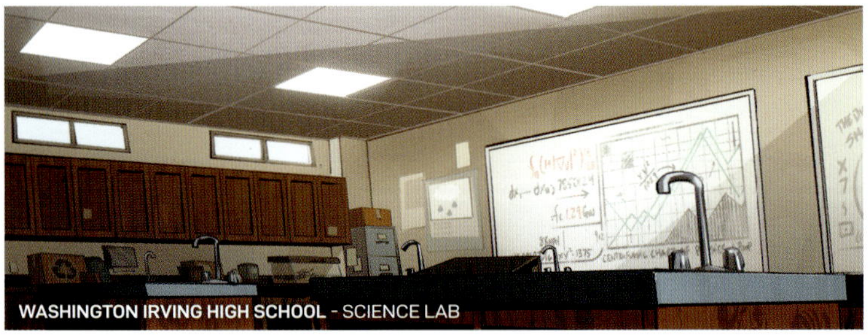

WASHINGTON IRVING HIGH SCHOOL - SCIENCE LAB

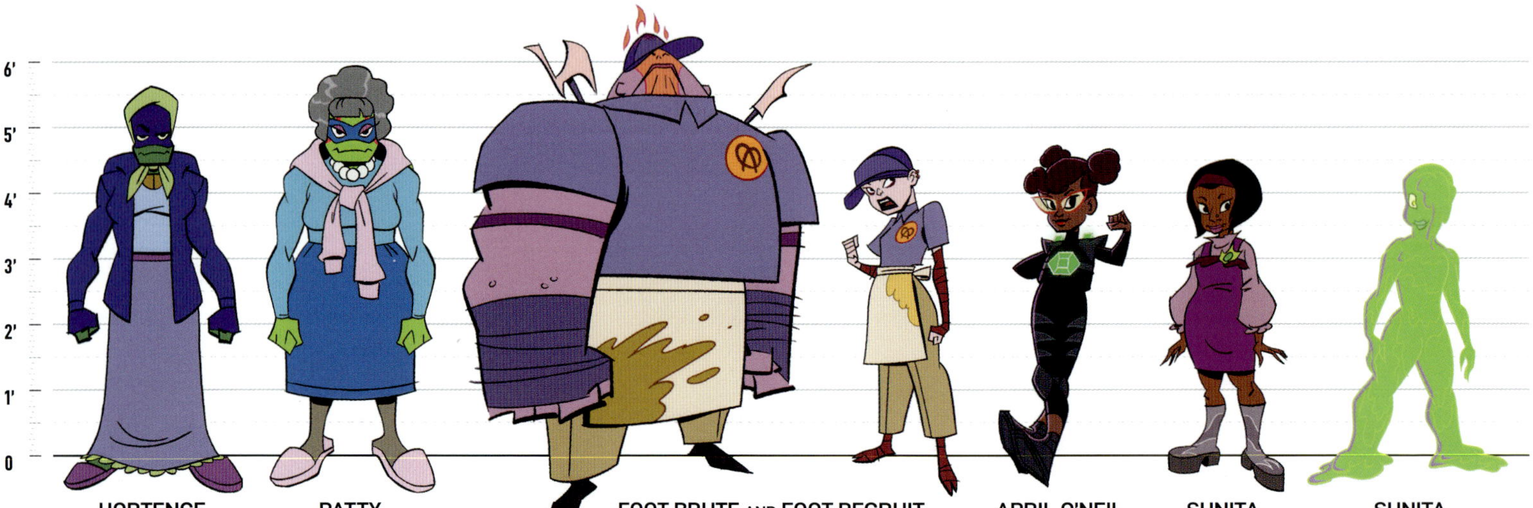

HORTENCE
DONNIE

PATTY
LEO

FOOT BRUTE AND FOOT RECRUIT
PRETZEL VENDOR UNIFORM

APRIL O'NEIL
LASER TAG UNIFORM

SUNITA
CLOAKED FORM

SUNITA
YŌKAI FORM

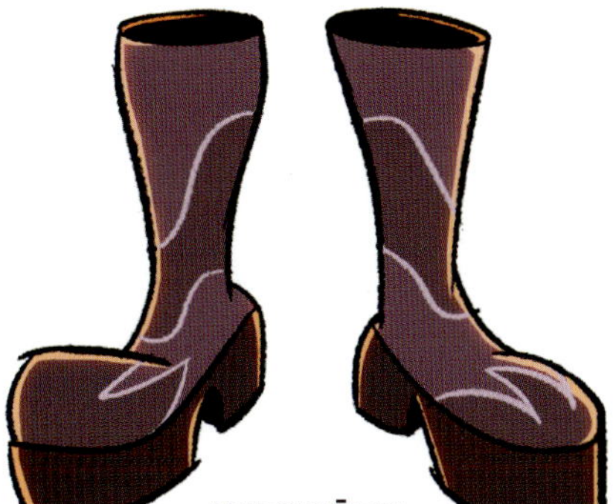

KUROI YŌROI
BOOTS

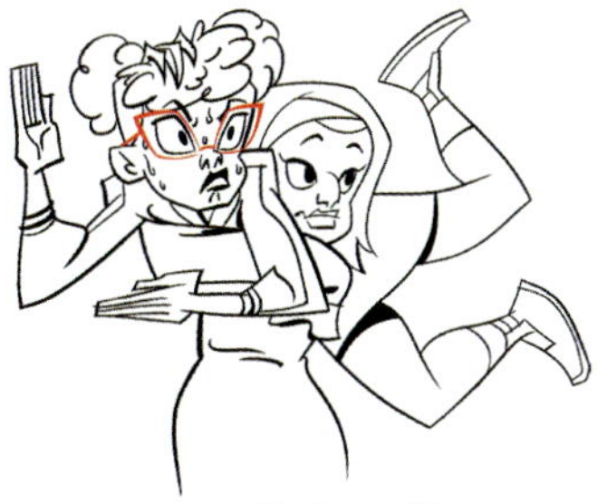

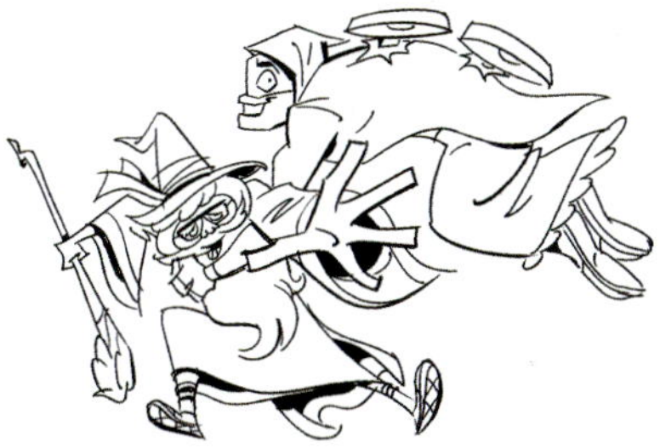

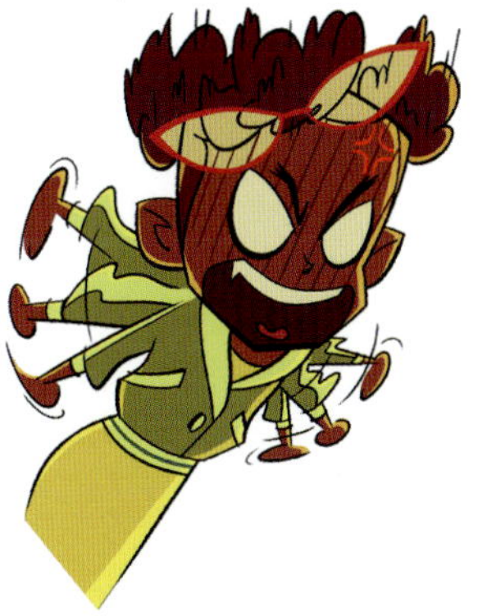

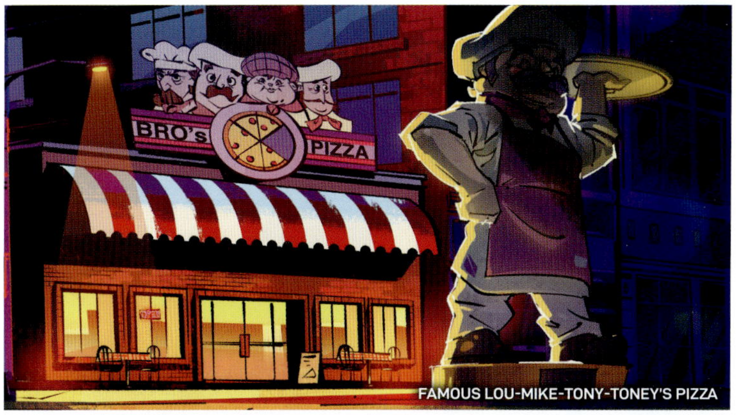

FAMOUS LOU-MIKE-TONY-TONEY'S PIZZA

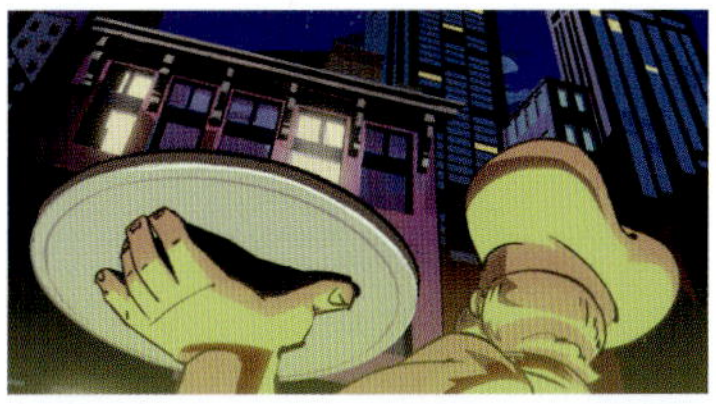

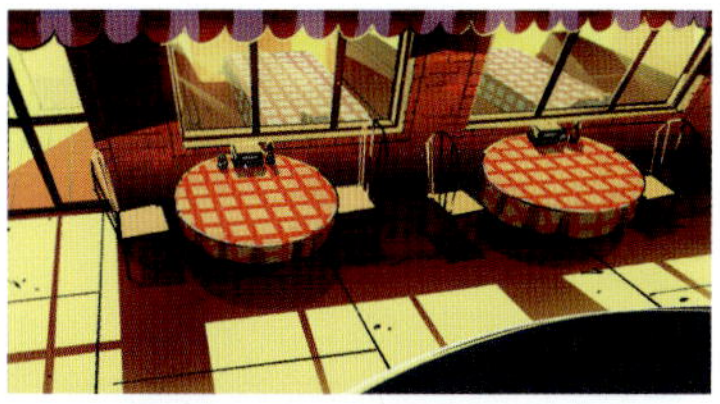

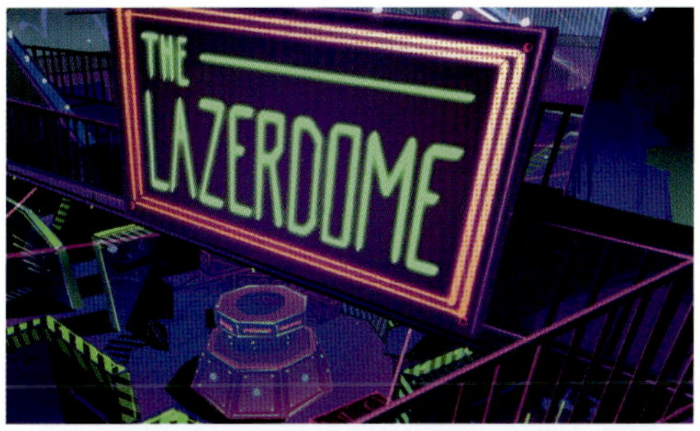

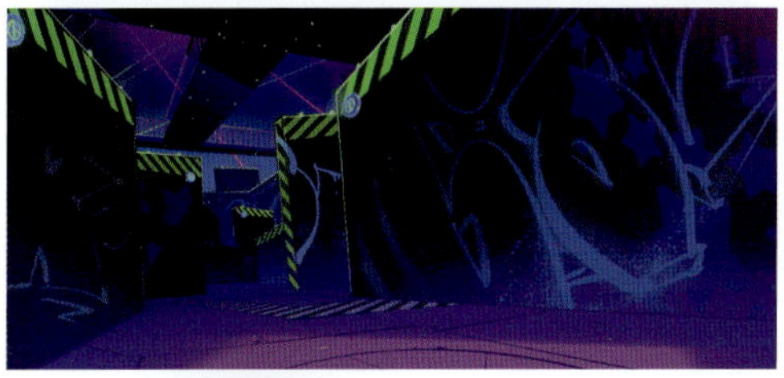

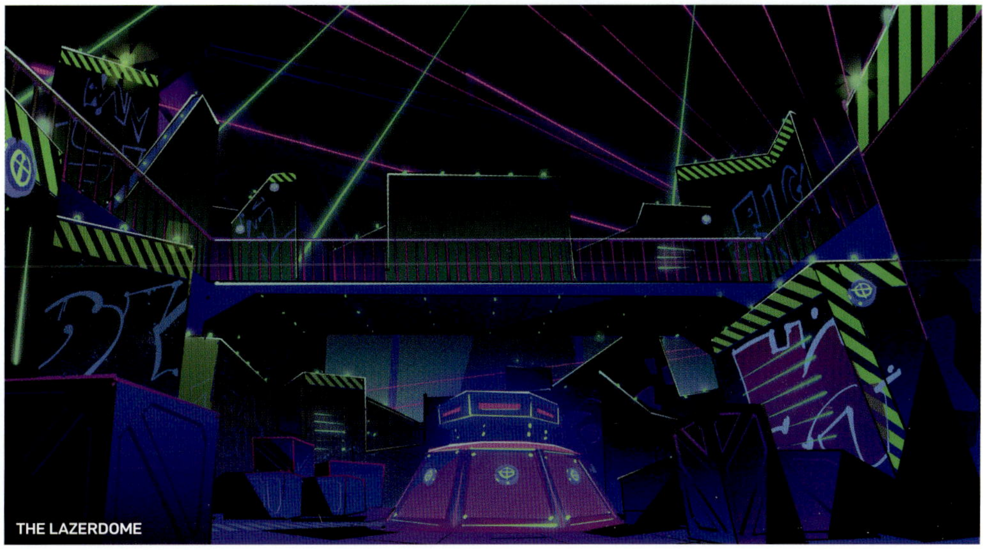

THE LAZERDOME

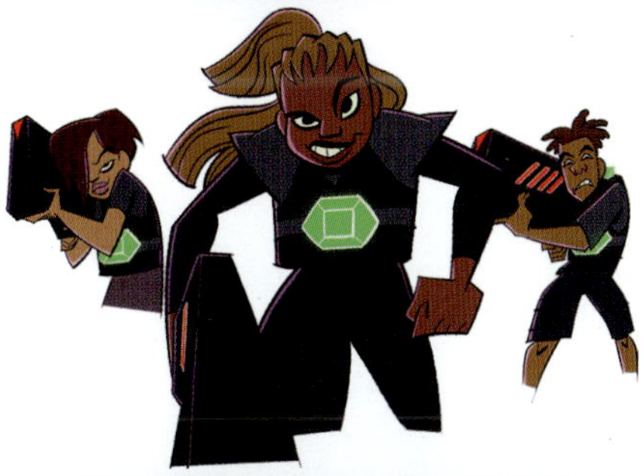

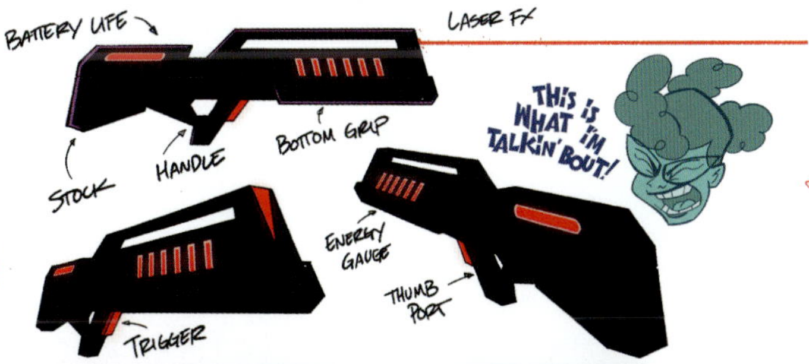

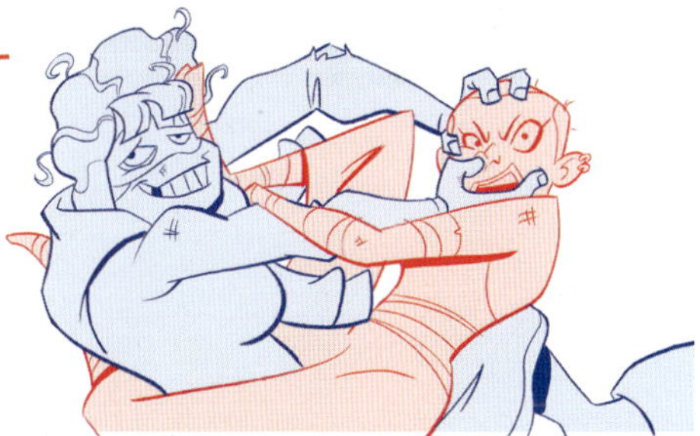

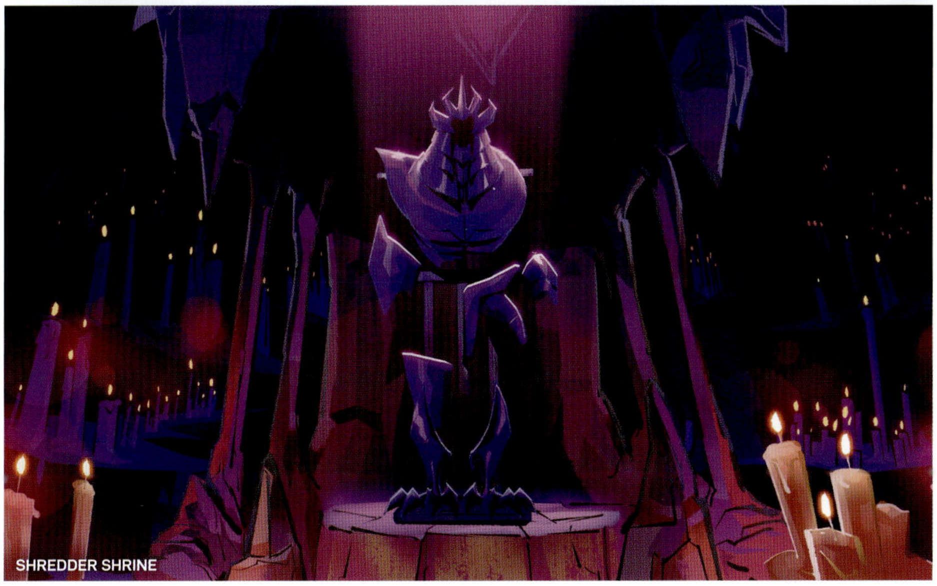

SHREDDER SHRINE

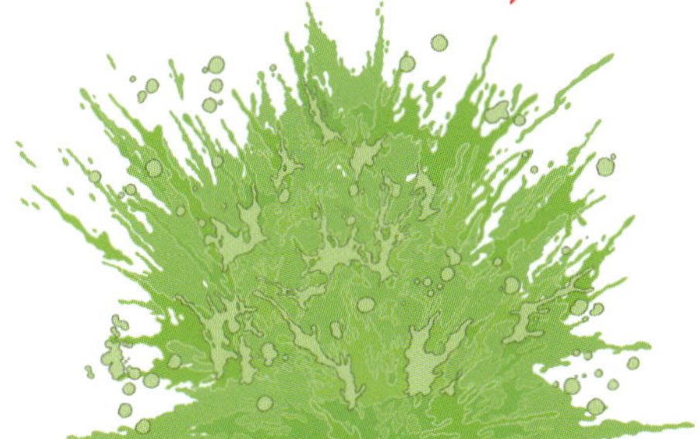

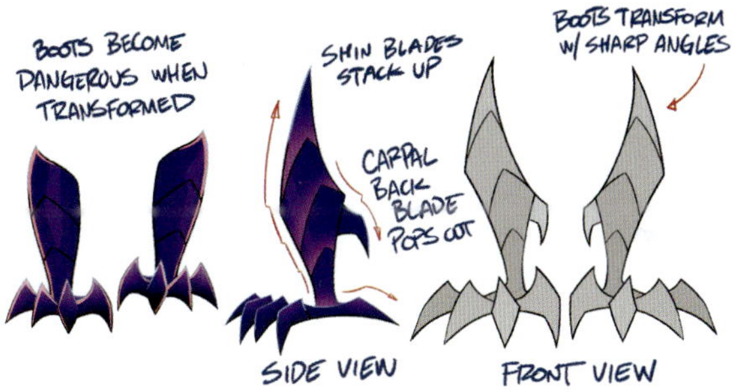

HOW TO MAKE ENEMIES AND BEND PEOPLE TO YOUR WILL

ORIGINAL AIR DATE: JUNE 22, 2019
PRODUCTION CODE: 039

WRITTEN BY **RUSS CARNEY & RON CORCILLO**
STORYBOARDS BY **CHRISTOPHER LUC**
DIRECTED BY **ABE AUDISH**

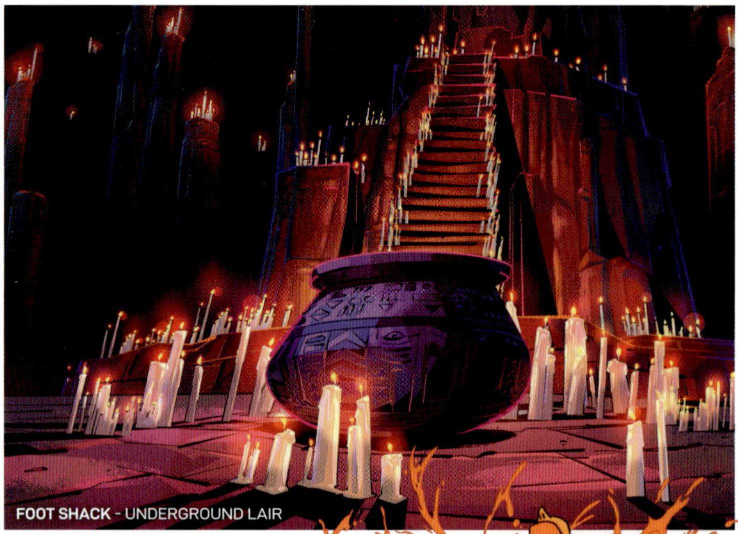
FOOT SHACK - UNDERGROUND LAIR

RON CORCILLO: Every few years at the Huntington Library in San Marino, California, a corpse flower (*Amorphophallus titanum*) blooms. It is so named because it smells like rotting flesh. So naturally, four goofball turtle teens would tempt each other into huffing the deep stank of the corpse flower.

The hypervigilant gardener, Harold, was heavily inspired by Huell Howser, a television journalist from Tennessee who moved to California and produced a number of beloved educational programs on the Los Angeles public broadcasting station, KCET, including *California's Gold* (1991). Howser was well liked for his wide-eyed, enthusiastic Southern personality, and he taught millions of Californians about the history and treasures that surround them. Russ was a devoted fan of his. Huell's first name was a portmanteau of his parents' names, Harold and Jewell. So when gardener Harold was mutated with the DNA of the corpse flower Jewel, might he have become Huell? Seeeecrets!

RUSS CARNEY: We pitched stand-up comic James Adomian as the voice of Harold because years earlier, he did a couple of shorts on YouTube where he lampooned Howser's unbridled enthusiasm at the most mundane stuff, such as a water spigot in someone's backyard.

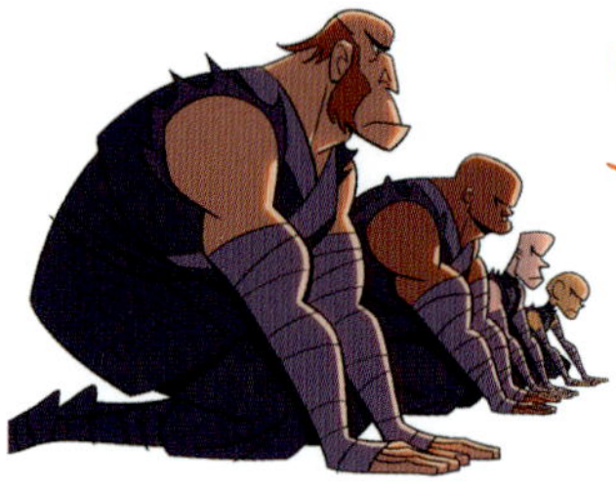

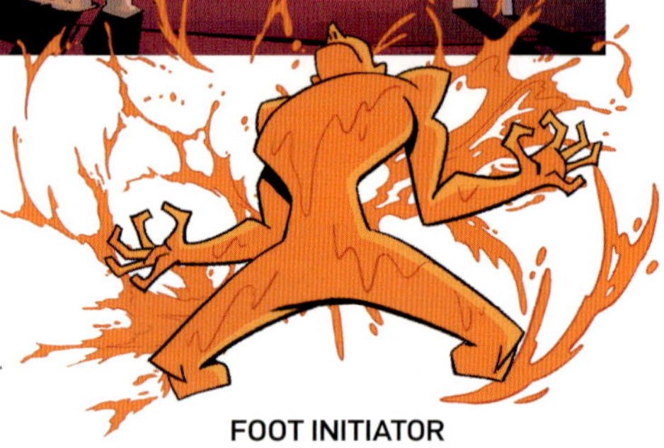
FOOT INITIATOR

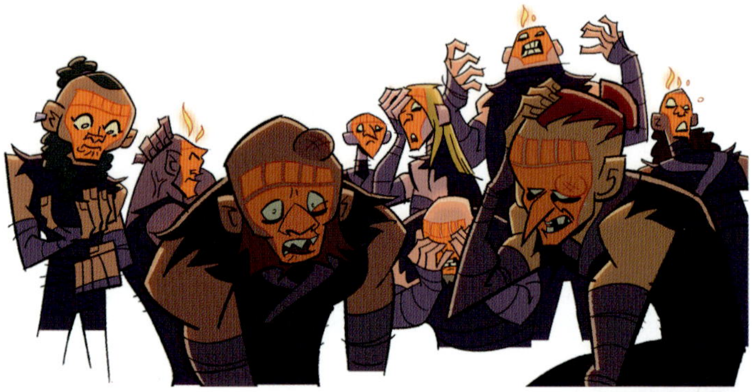

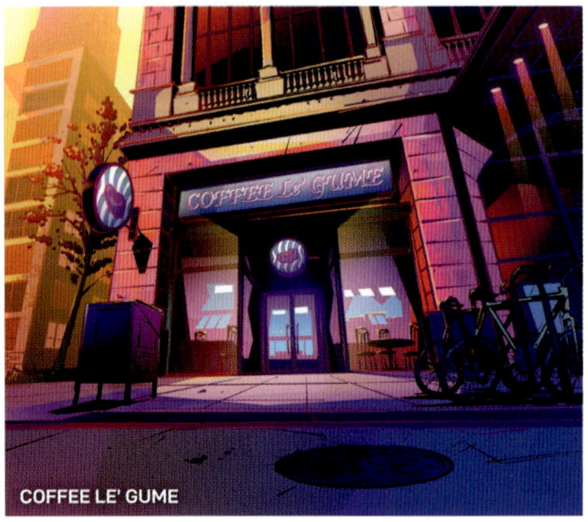

COFFEE LE' GUME

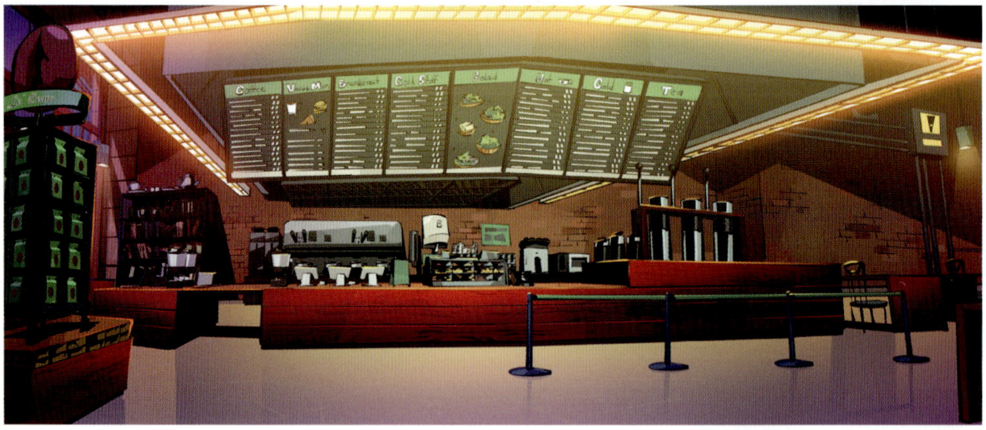

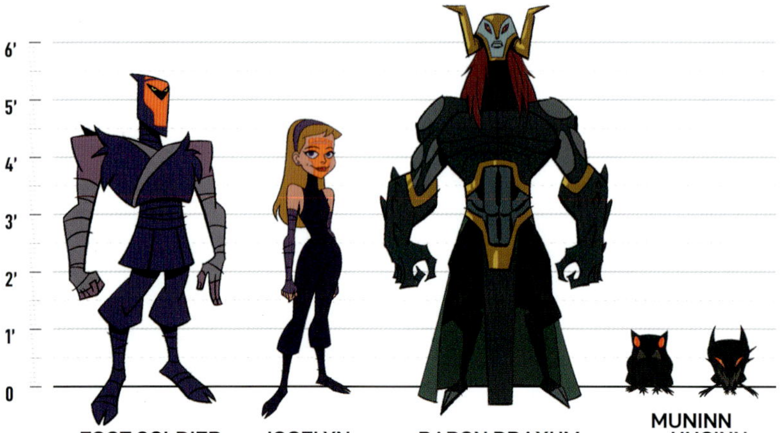

FOOT SOLDIER JOCELYN BARON DRAXUM MUNINN AND HUGINN

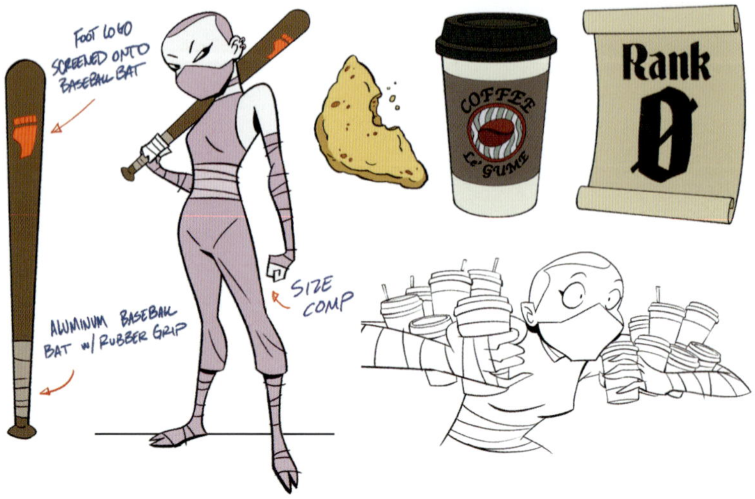

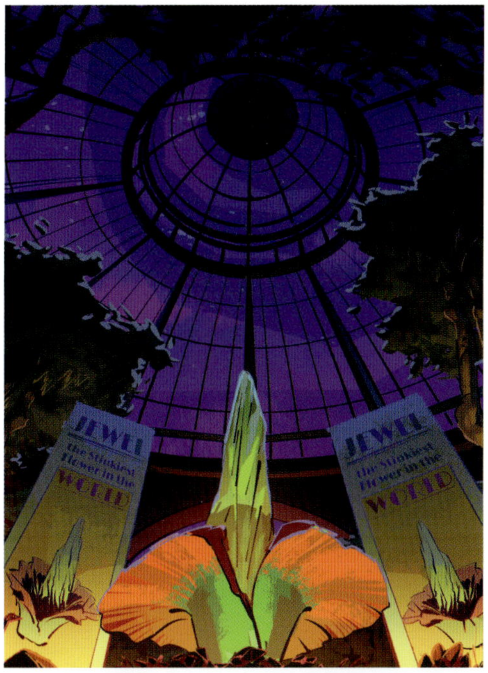

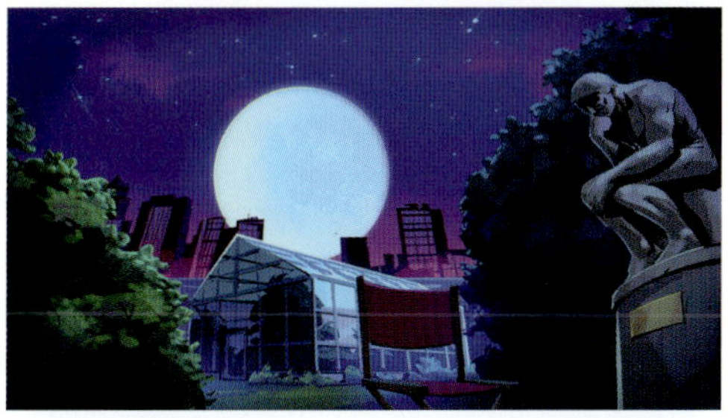

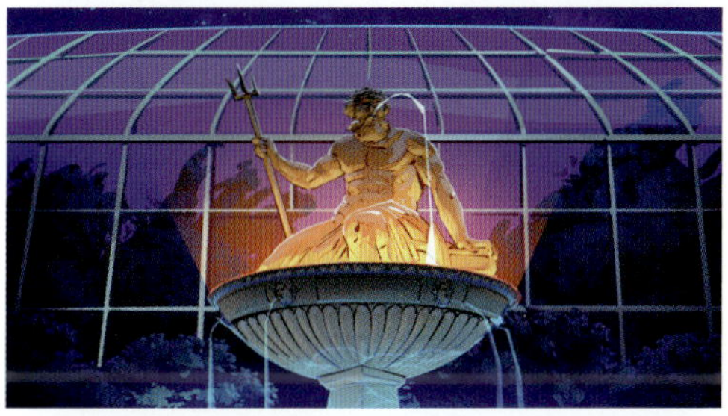

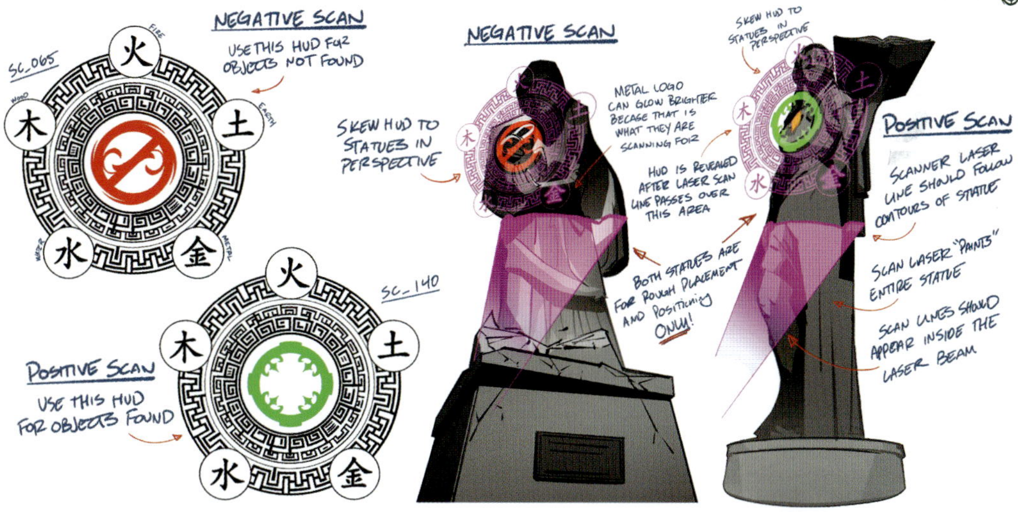

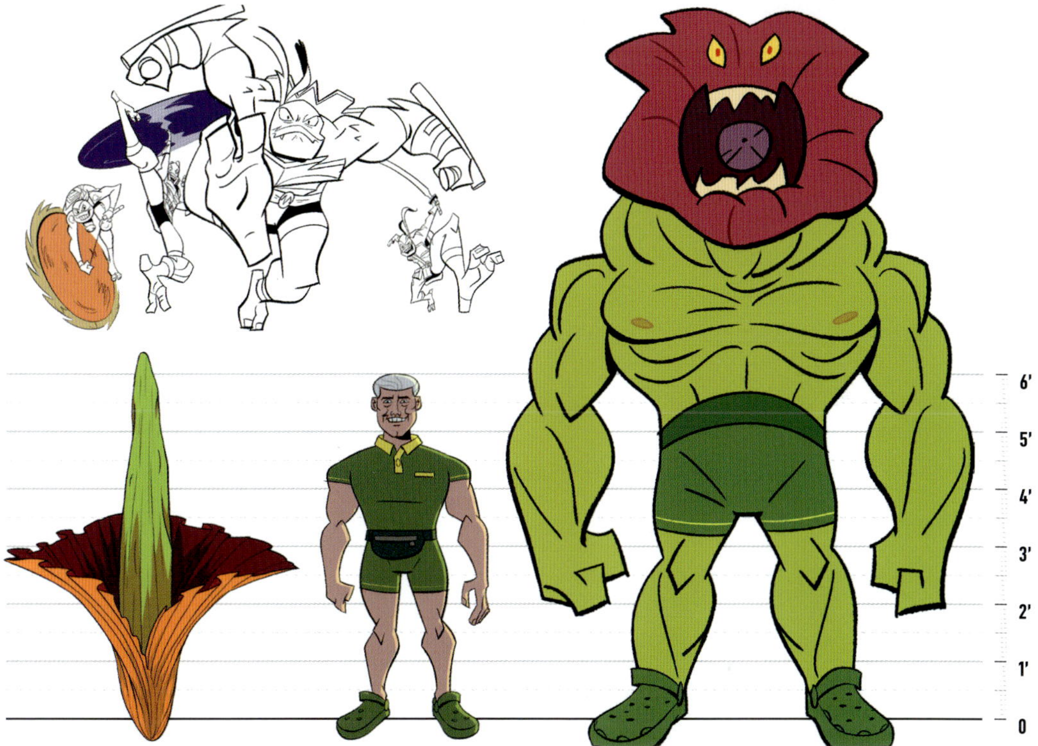

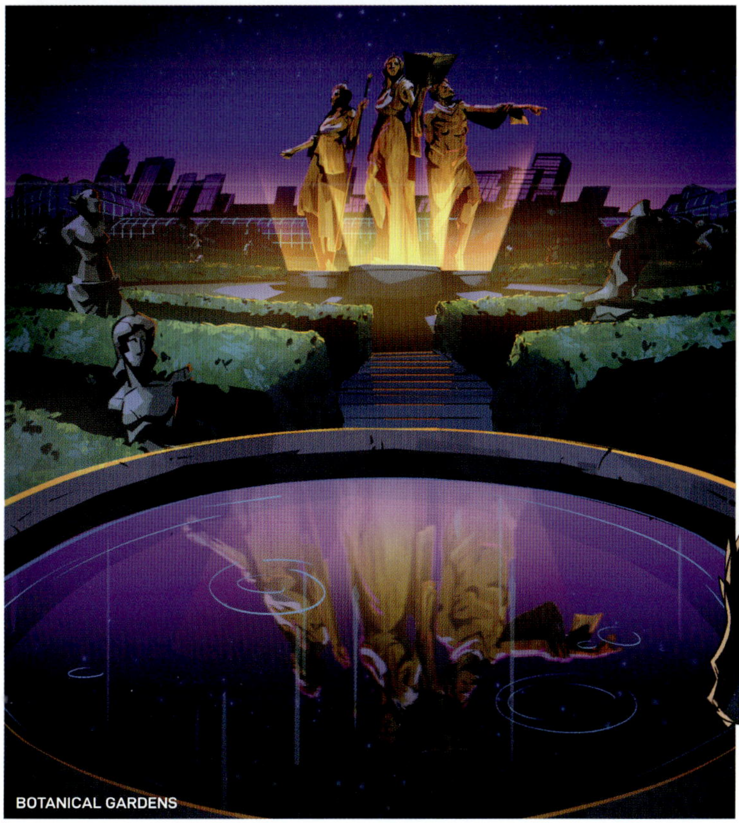
BOTANICAL GARDENS

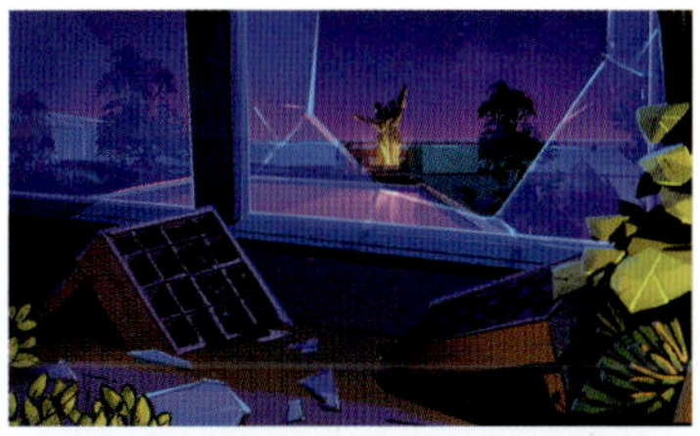

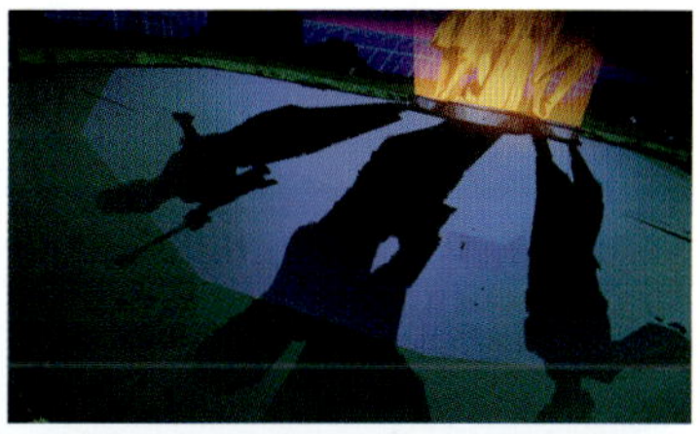

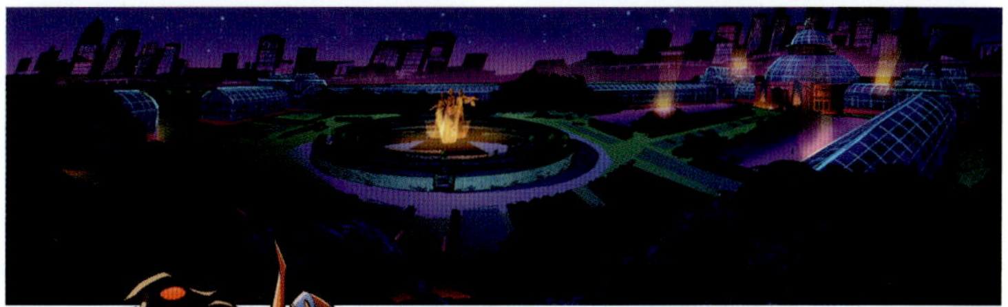

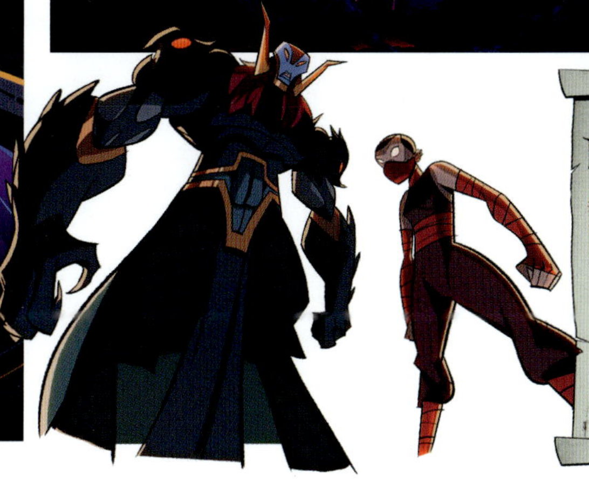

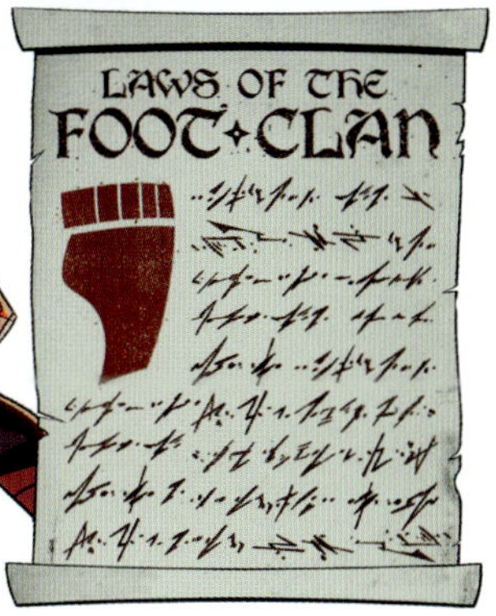

YOU GOT SERVED

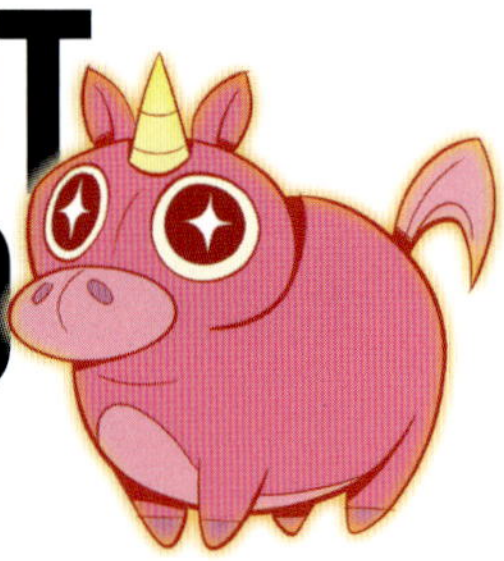

ORIGINAL AIR DATE: JUNE 15, 2019
PRODUCTION CODE: 040

WRITTEN BY **IAN BUSCH**
STORYBOARDS BY **MAX COLLINS, POLYNA KIM**
DIRECTED BY **SEBASTIAN MONTES**

IAN BUSCH: It was always fun to pit the boys against one another, and that's exactly where this story idea started. For the sake of both story and animation assets, it was imperative to often pair our heroes up so the story wouldn't be too overwhelmed with too many characters on the screen at once. It took us a bit to figure out what the fun currency would be that the boys are vying for, but we couldn't have been happier to land at those cute little unicorns.

SEBASTIAN MONTES: One fun note about this episode was that the designs for the Masters of Barbarianism henchmen were based off Bruce Lee and Jet Li.

This was also Max Collins' first time storyboarding on a show and he *cooked.* He picked up *Rise's* story rhythm quickly, which made for a crazy dynamic kitchen battle between Mikey and Leo.

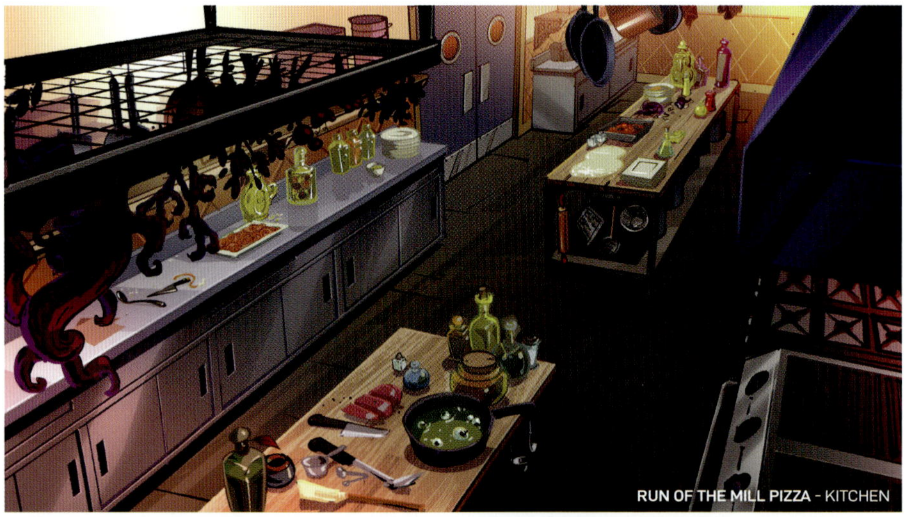

RUN OF THE MILL PIZZA - KITCHEN

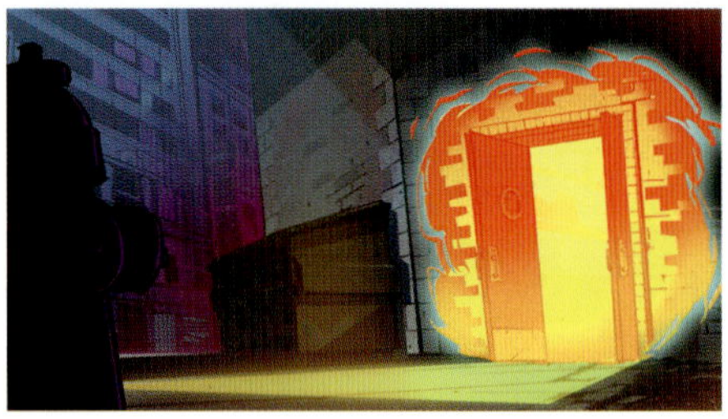

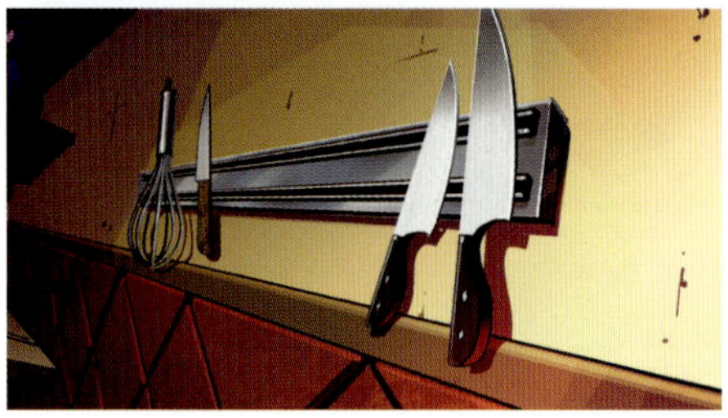

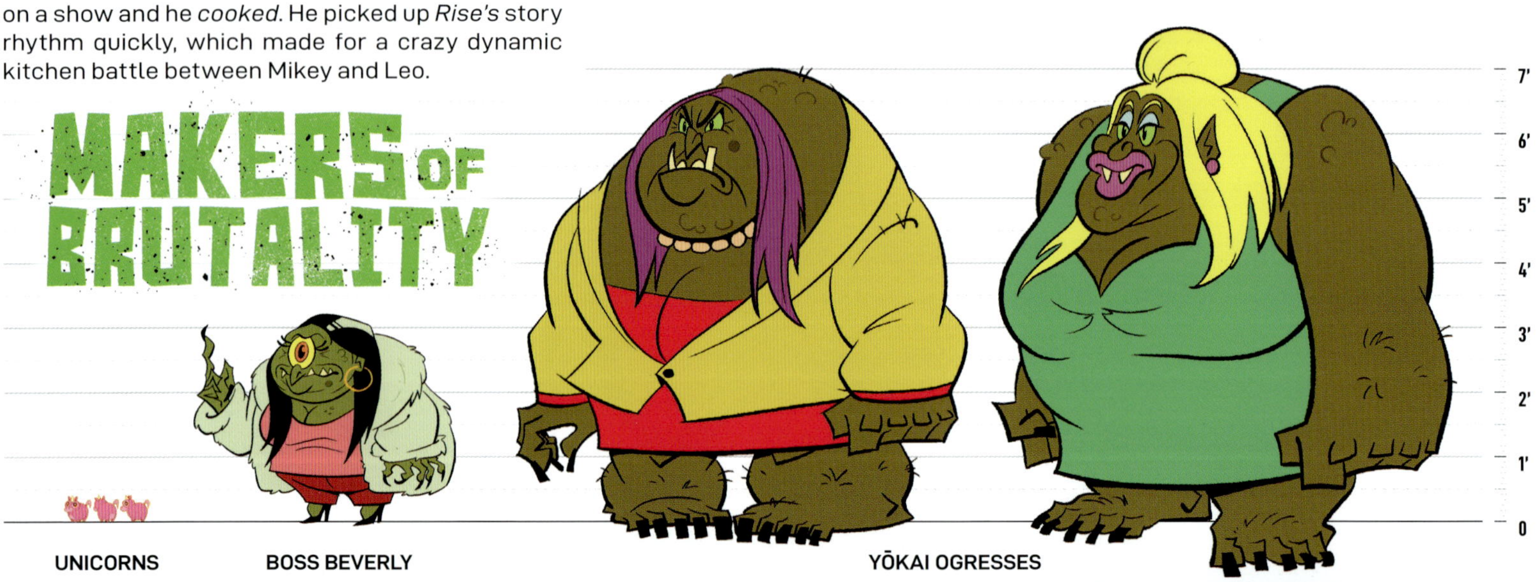

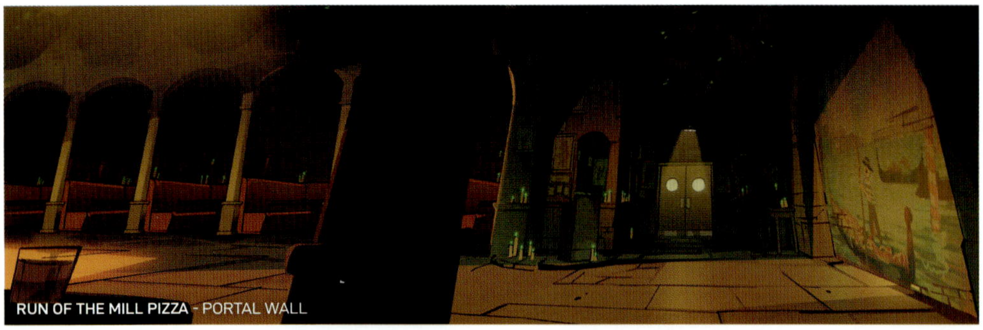

RUN OF THE MILL PIZZA - PORTAL WALL

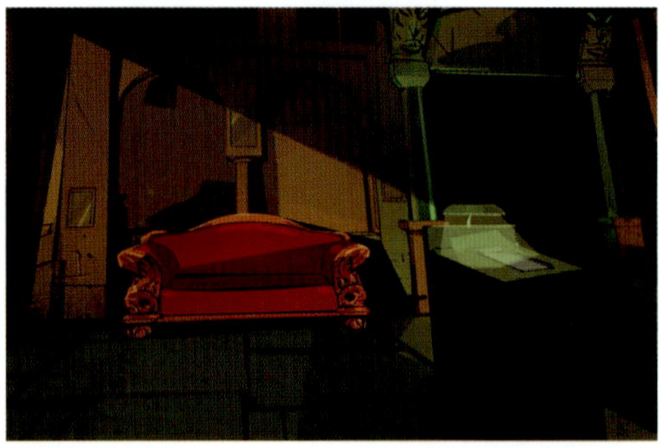

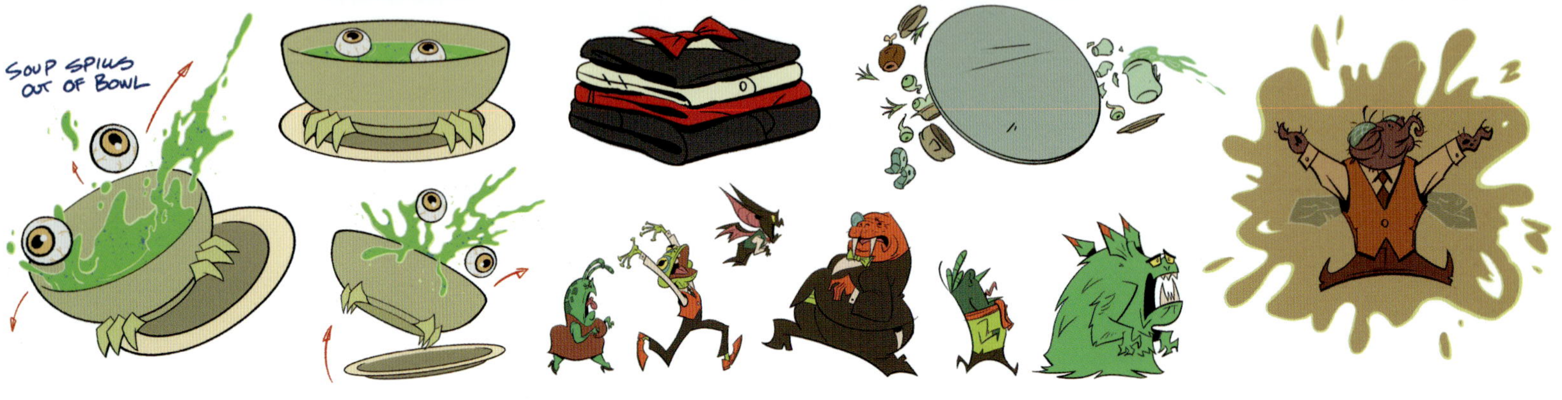

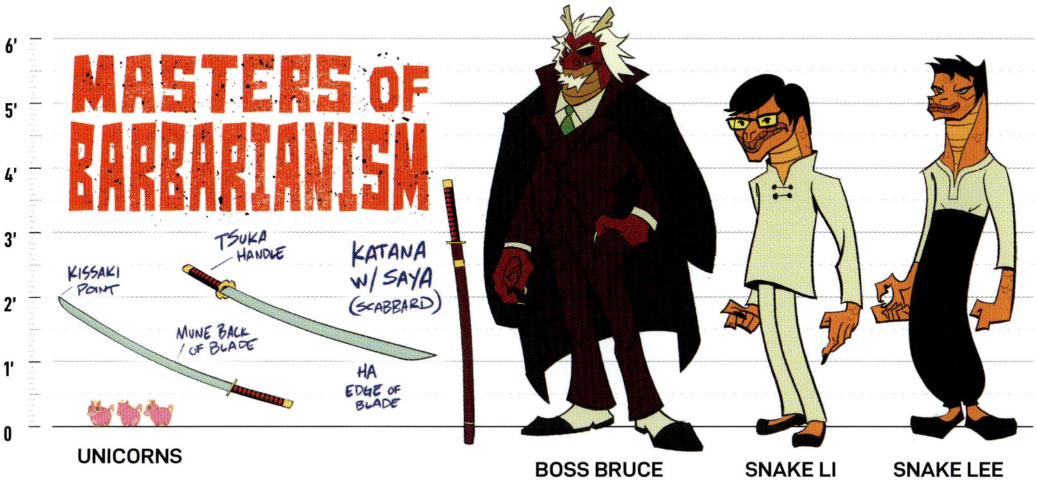
MASTERS OF BARBARIANISM
6'
5'
4'
3'
2'
1'
0
TSUKA HANDLE
KISSAKI POINT
KATANA W/ SAYA (SCABBARD)
MUNE BACK OF BLADE
HA EDGE OF BLADE
UNICORNS
BOSS BRUCE
SNAKE LI
SNAKE LEE

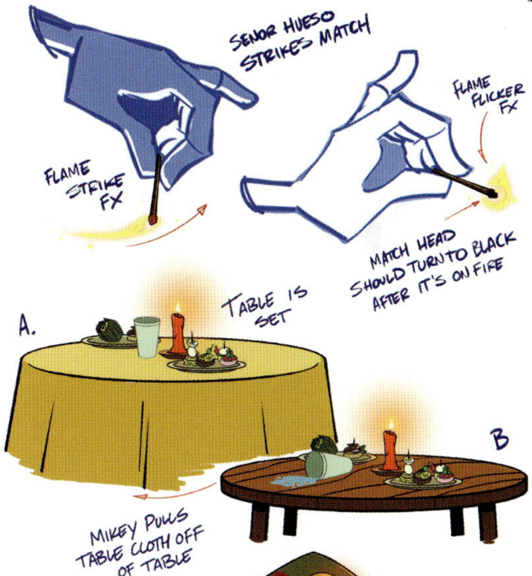
SENOR HUESO STRIKES MATCH
FLAME STRIKE FX
FLAME FLICKER FX
MATCH HEAD SHOULD TURN TO BLACK AFTER IT'S ON FIRE
A.
TABLE IS SET
B
MIKEY PULLS TABLE CLOTH OFF OF TABLE

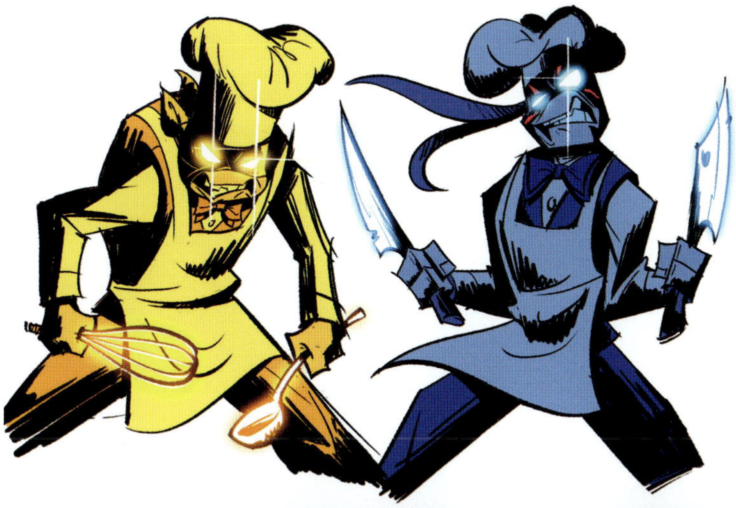

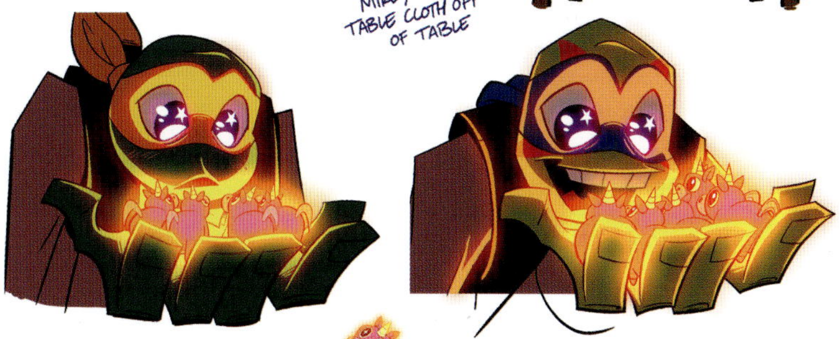

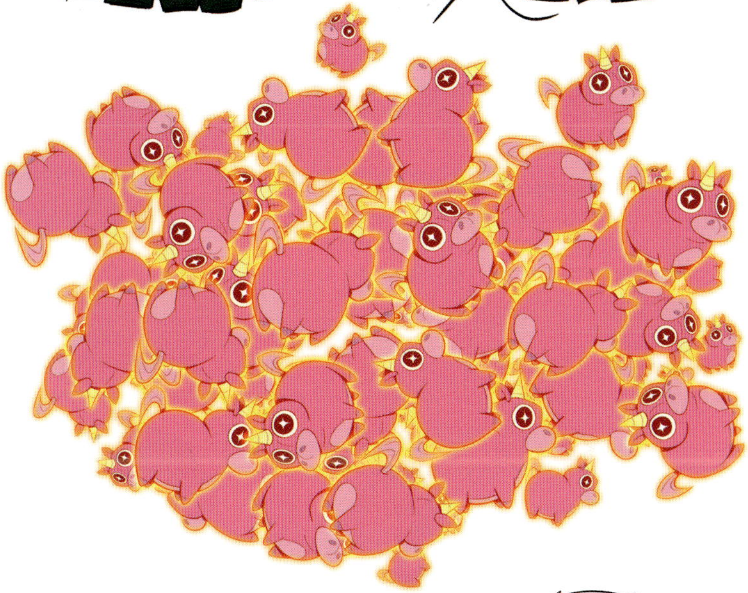

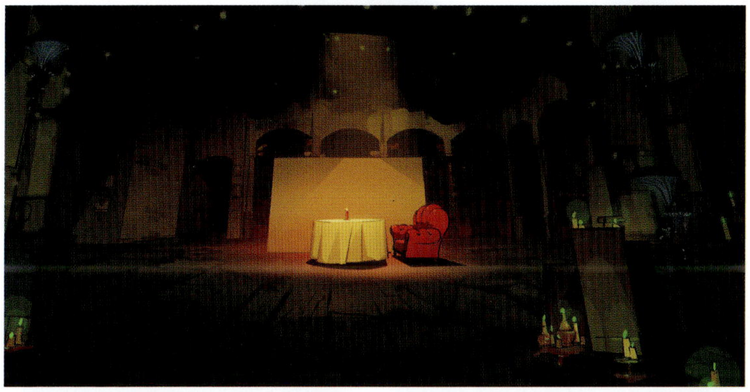

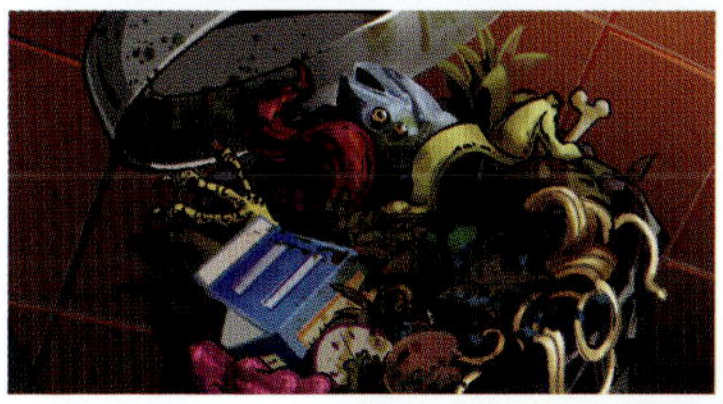

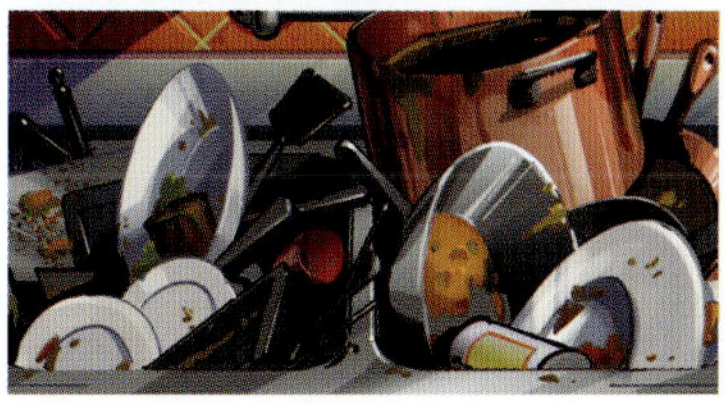

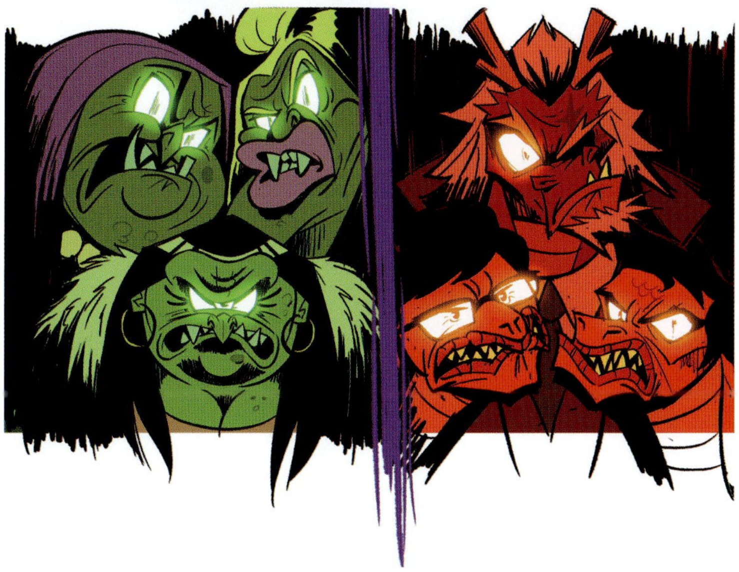

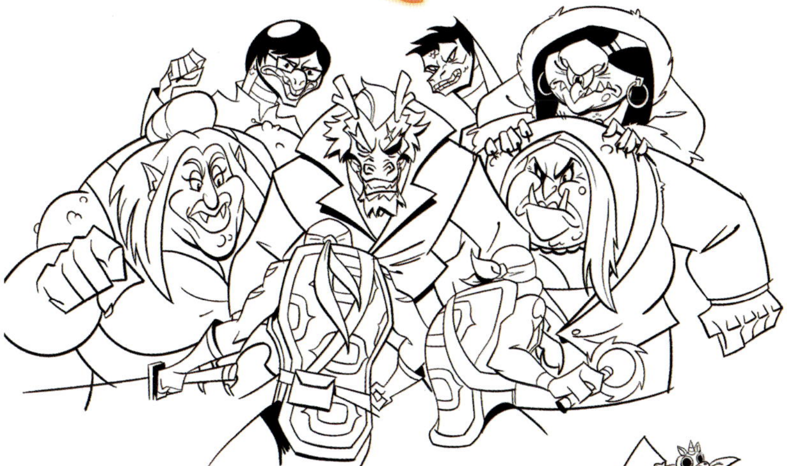

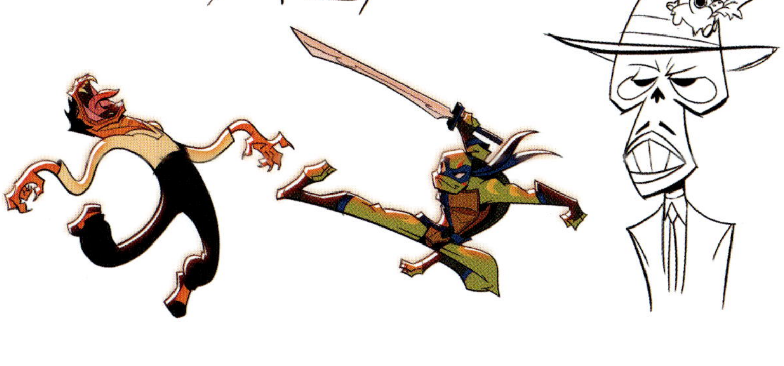

THE PURPLE GAME

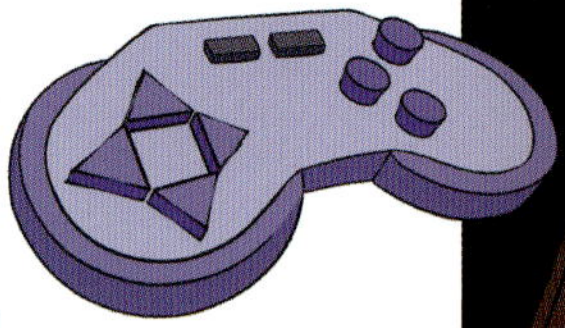

ORIGINAL AIR DATE: JULY 6, 2019
PRODUCTION CODE: 041

WRITTEN BY **JESSE GORDON**
STORYBOARDS BY **CHRISTINE LIU**
DIRECTED BY **ALAN WAN**

JESSE GORDON: I grew up watching *The Last Starfighter* (1984), and this was my version of it. I thought the mech would be about 20 feet tall, but when the boards came back with it being 200, I thought it was the funniest thing! There was a lot of discussion about whether it was too big, but Alan Wan was like, *"It's going to be awesome! People are gonna love it!"*

As someone who plays video games and finds microtransactions, as everyone does, incredibly annoying, this was sort of a fun parody of them. This was also a classic after-school special about addiction, and we used a video game as the vehicle. It was also playing into Donnie's addiction to technology and anything purple, which is just so Donnie. RE-GOM still makes me laugh every time.

The crew love dressing the Turtles up, and coming up with reasons for them to have outfits is always a lot of fun. Lumberjack Donnie just might be my favorite Donnie costume.

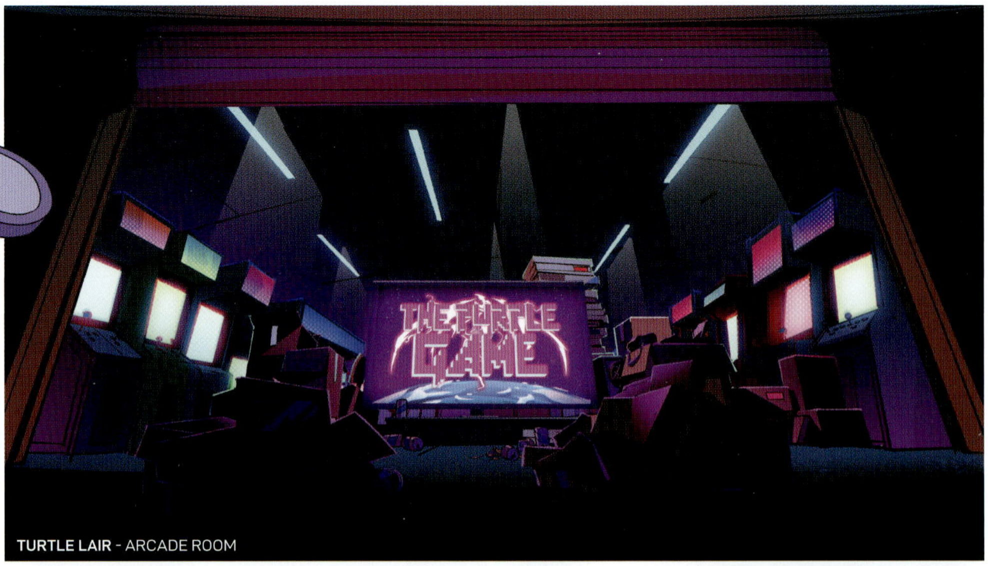

TURTLE LAIR - ARCADE ROOM

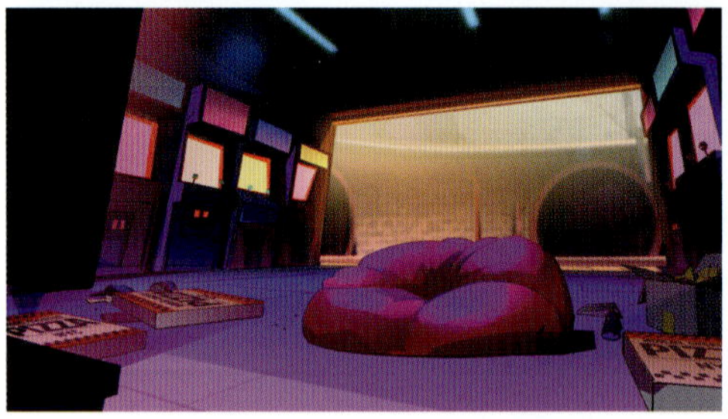

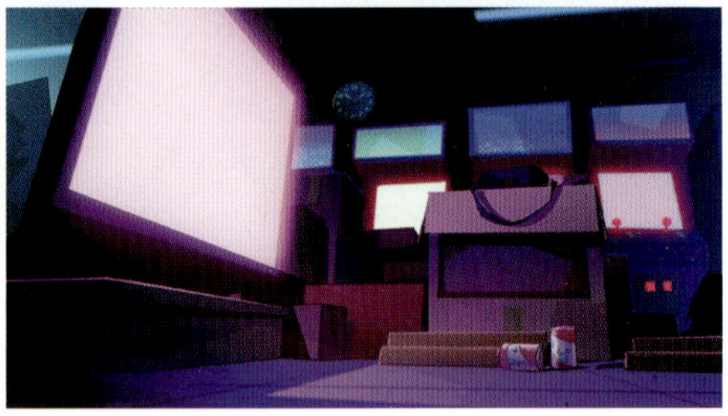

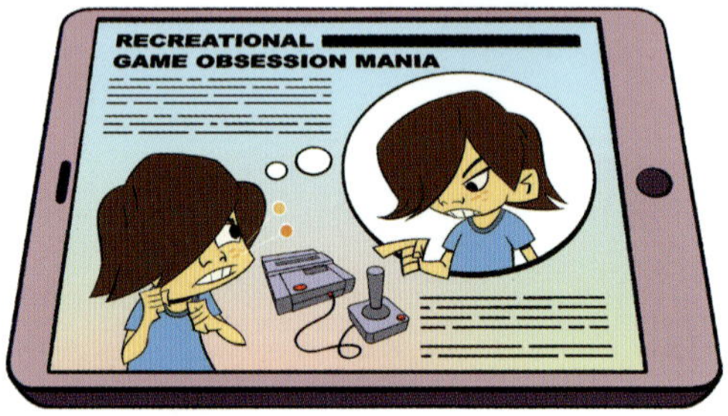

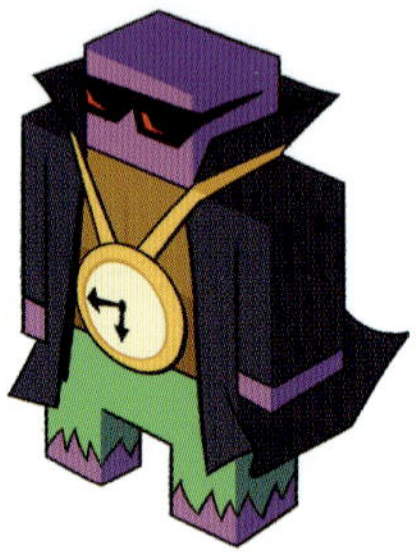

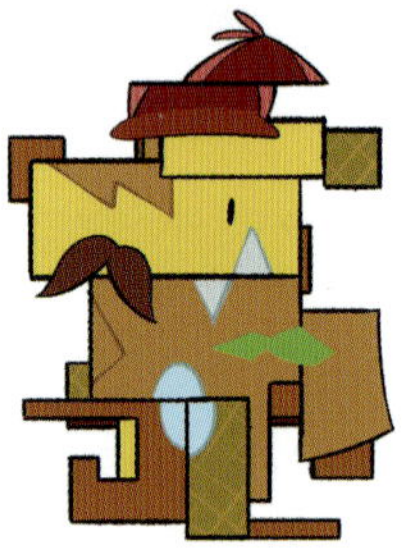

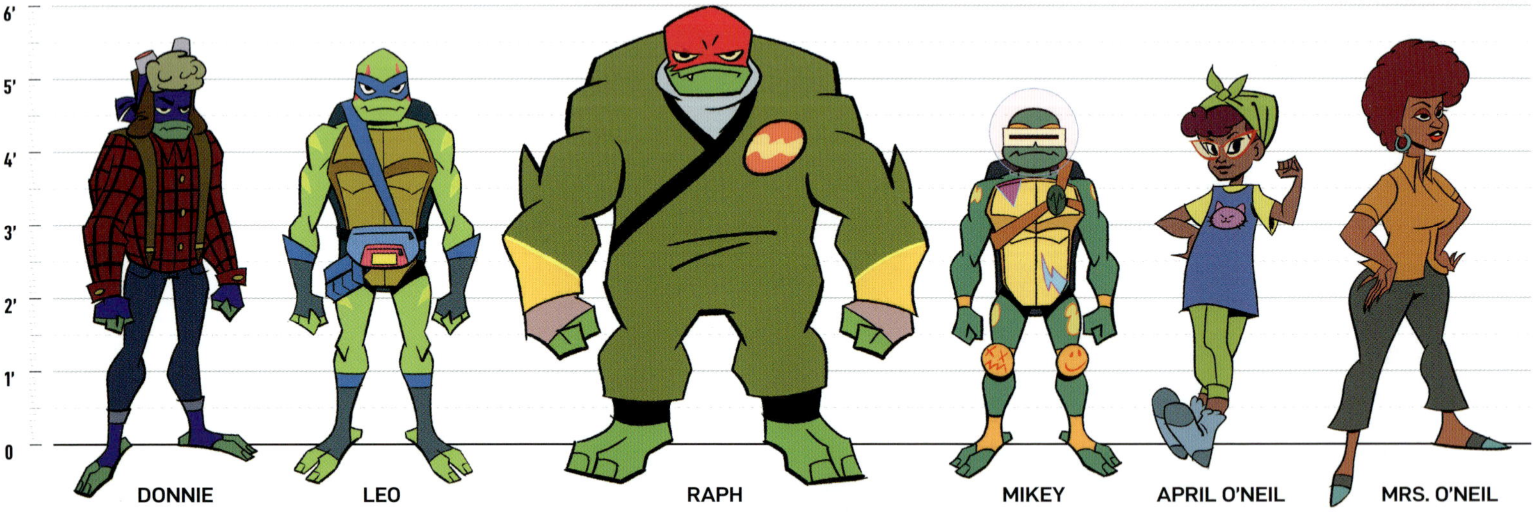

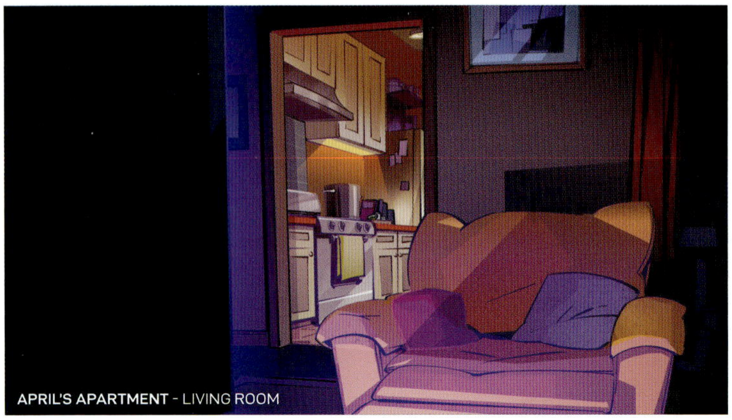

APRIL'S APARTMENT - LIVING ROOM

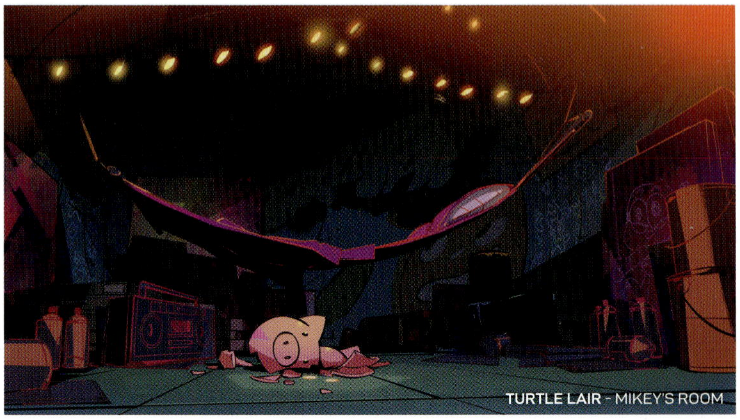

TURTLE LAIR - MIKEY'S ROOM

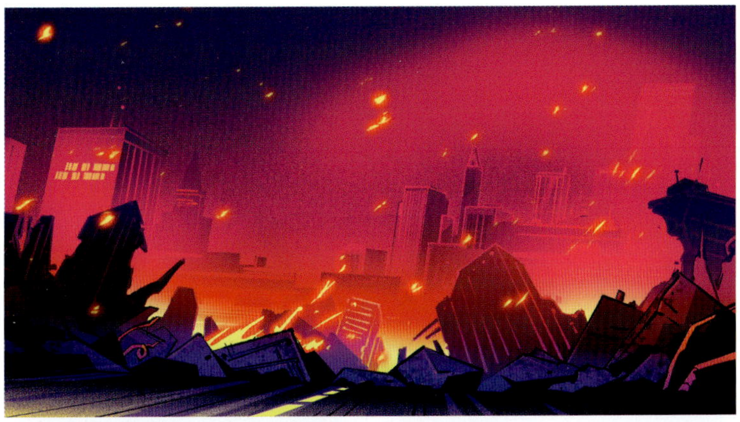

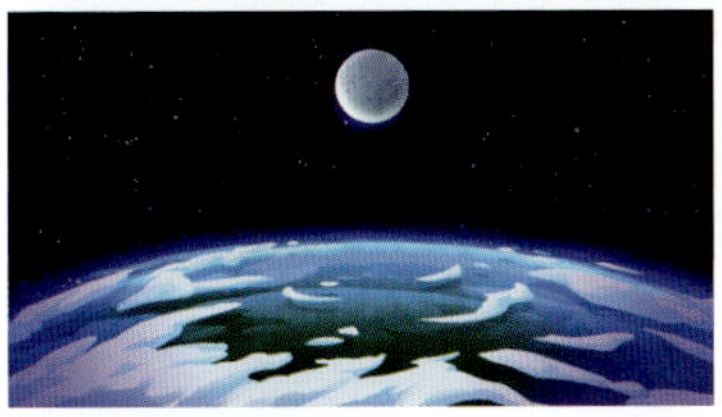

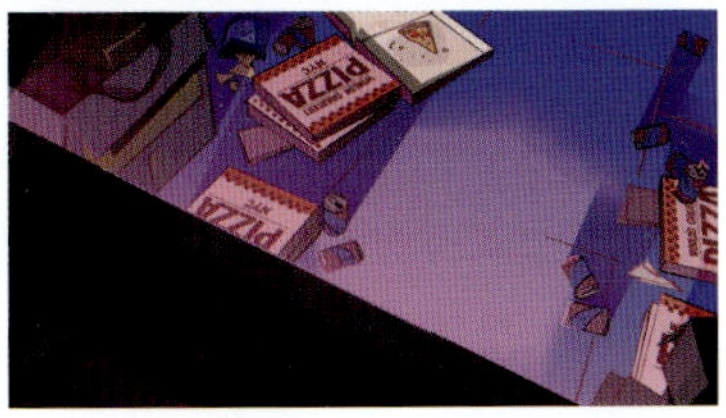

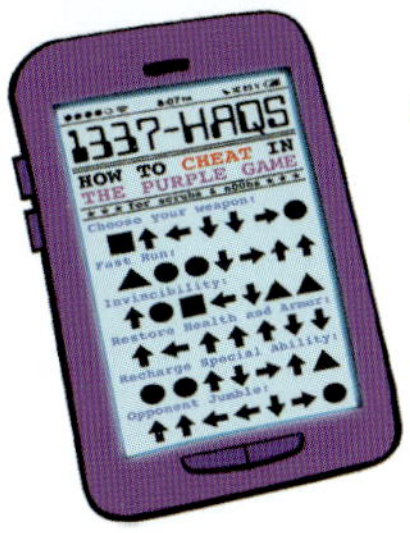

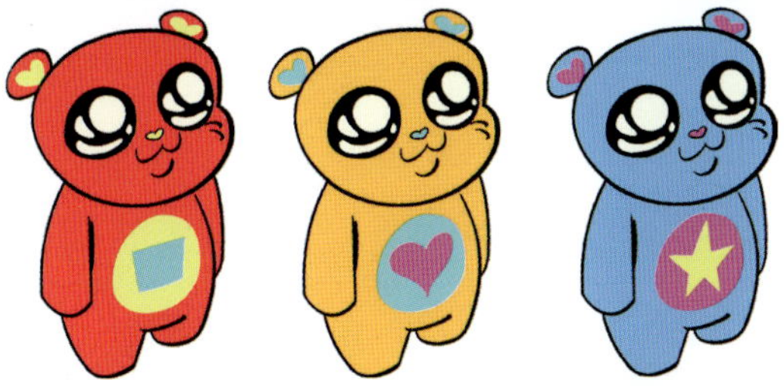

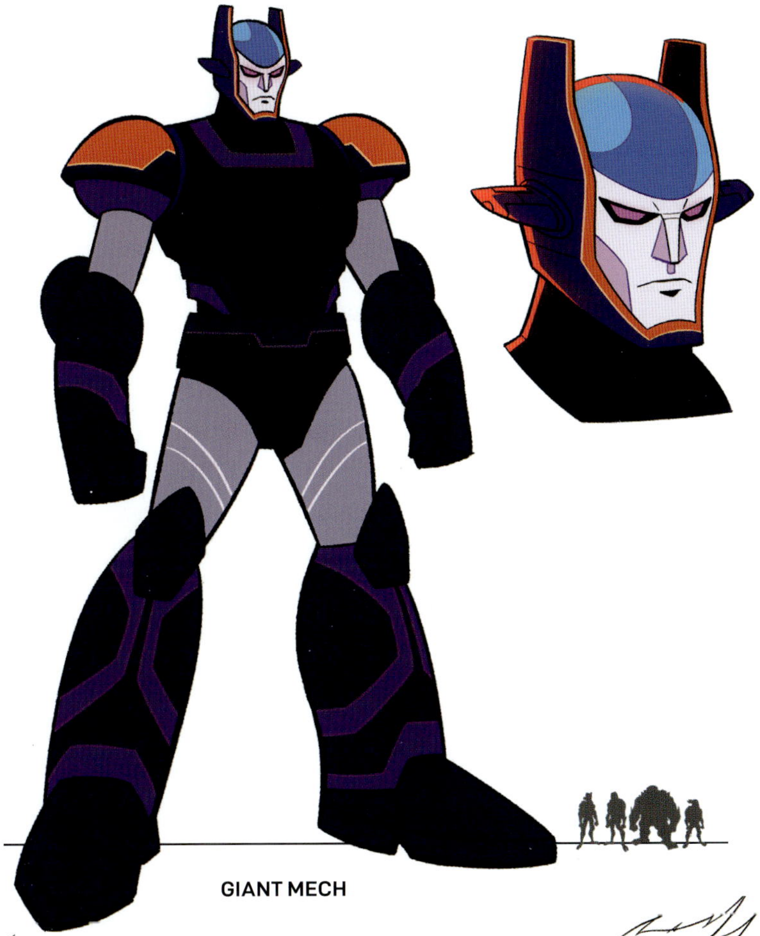

GIANT MECH

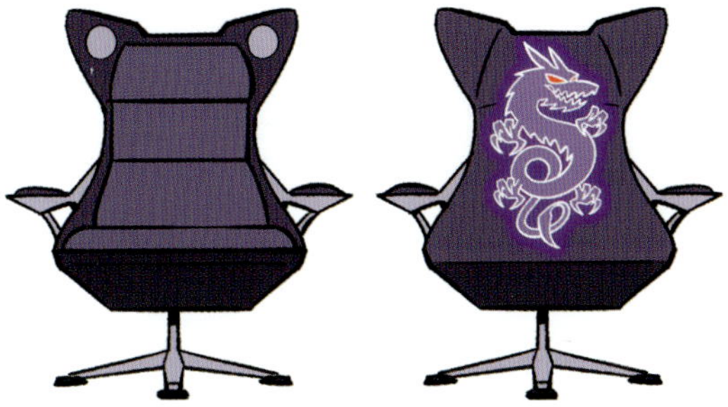

PURPLE DRAGONS CHAIR

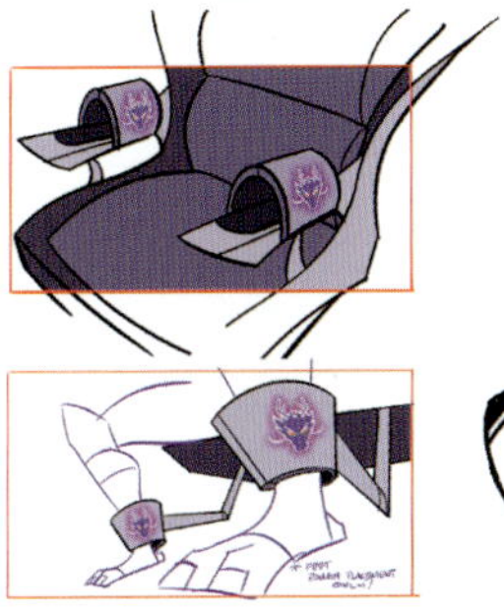

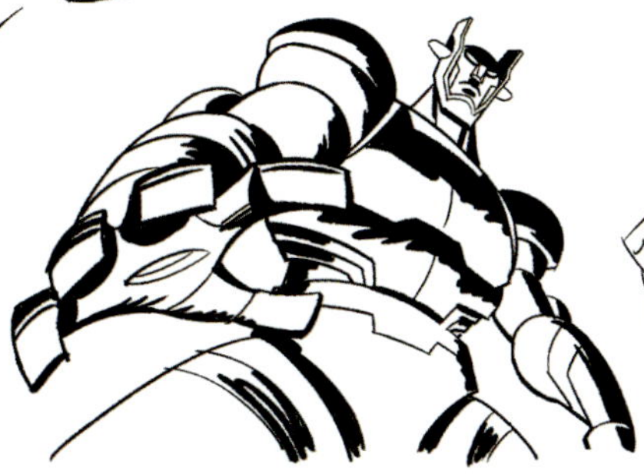

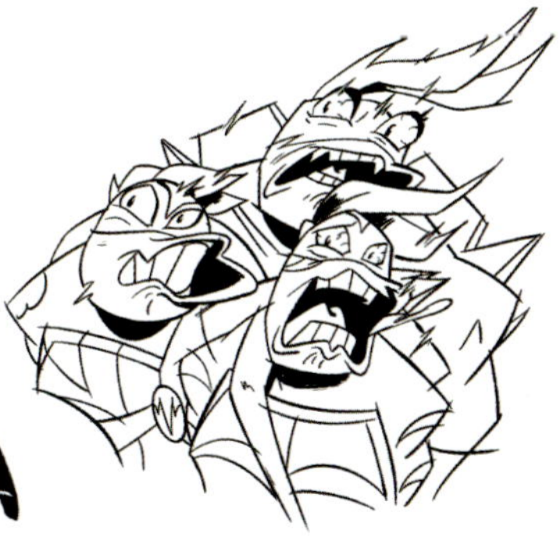

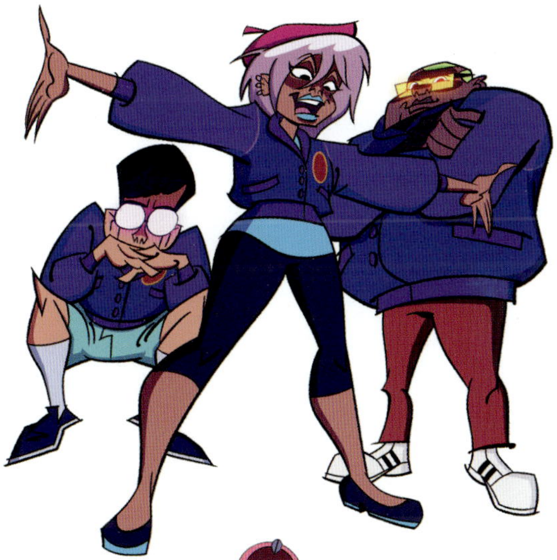

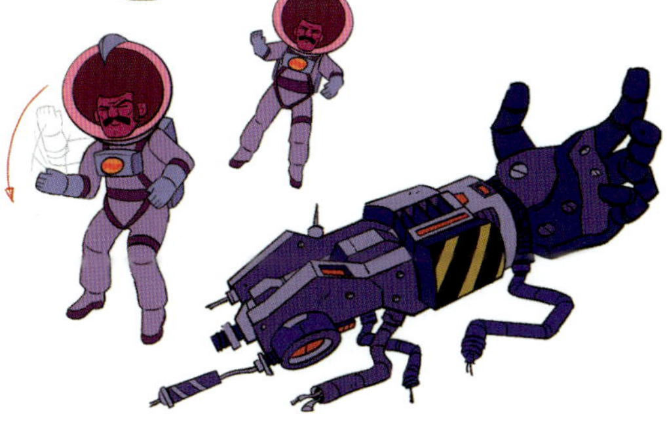

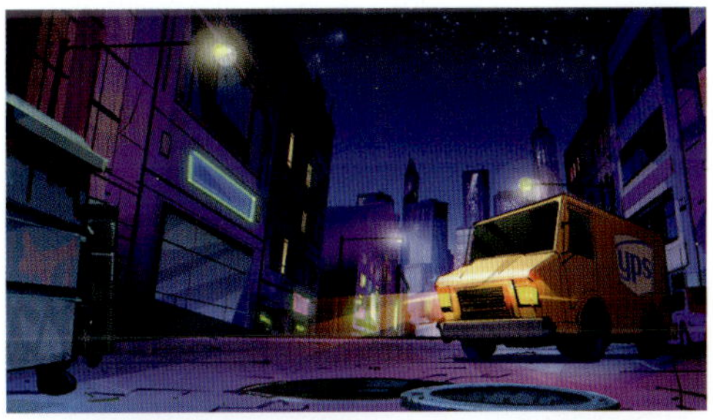

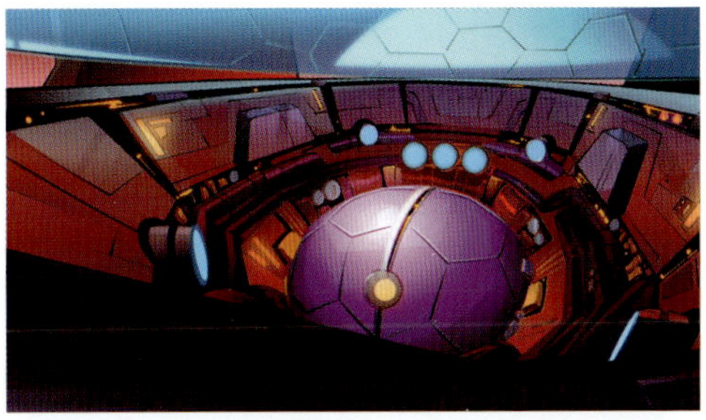

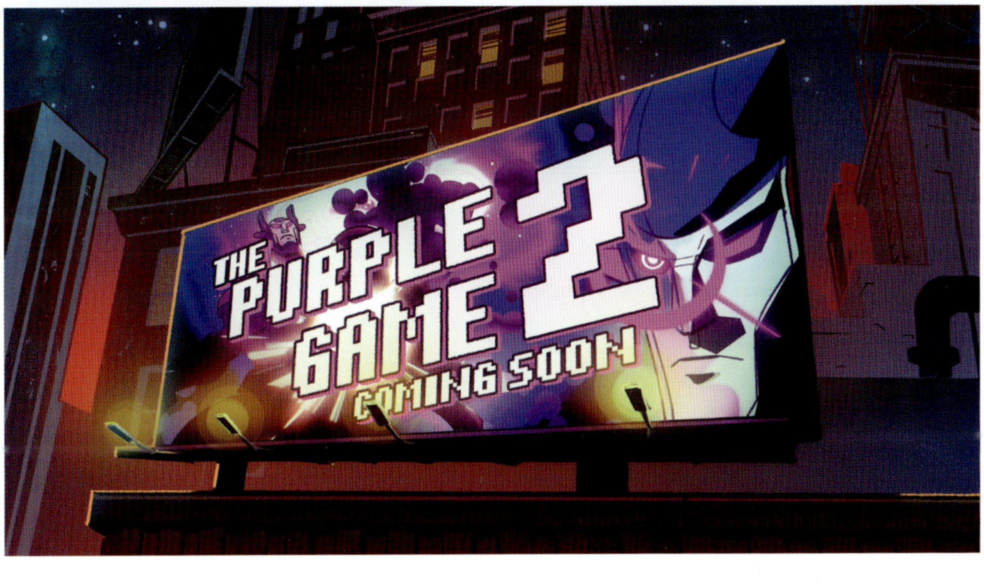

MAN VS. SEWER

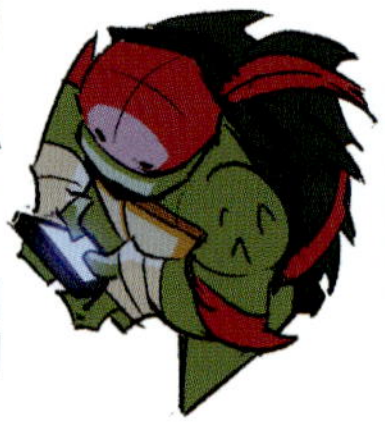

ORIGINAL AIR DATE: OCTOBER 19, 2019
PRODUCTION CODE: 042

WRITTEN BY **DALE MALINOWSKI**
STORYBOARDS BY **ALICIA CHAN**
DIRECTED BY **ABE AUDISH**

DALE MALINOWSKI: I love Bear Grylls and his shows, so I wanted to do something with the Turtles in a survival scenario. In my outline, while searching for Raph, the brothers encountered TV survival expert Flair Thrills, who was filming his new series in the sewers. He joined their mission and taught the Turtles some valuable search-and-rescue techniques. In the third act, Flair fell ill and revealed he was concealing a small bug bite he didn't think much of but turned out to be from an oozesquito, so he changed into a beaver mutant. That was all fun and weird, but it required a ton of setup that robbed the Turtles of precious screen time, so we scrapped it and plugged in the mutant crabs, whose hatred for the Turtles was already known to the audience. I remember Abe being an absolute champion of a director on this because showing characters interacting with water is extremely difficult to animate well, so Abe ended up revising loads of scenes to cleverly hide or minimize contact points. Thanks, Abe!

Raph's one-handed catch was inspired by Odell Beckham Jr.'s famous one-handed catch that scored the New York Giants a touchdown in 2014, and I loved the idea that Raph is a fan of his hometown football team. Lace Face was inspired by Wilson from the movie *Castaway* (2000). Donnie's meta line about Leo selling the least action figures was something we came up with during the record with Josh.

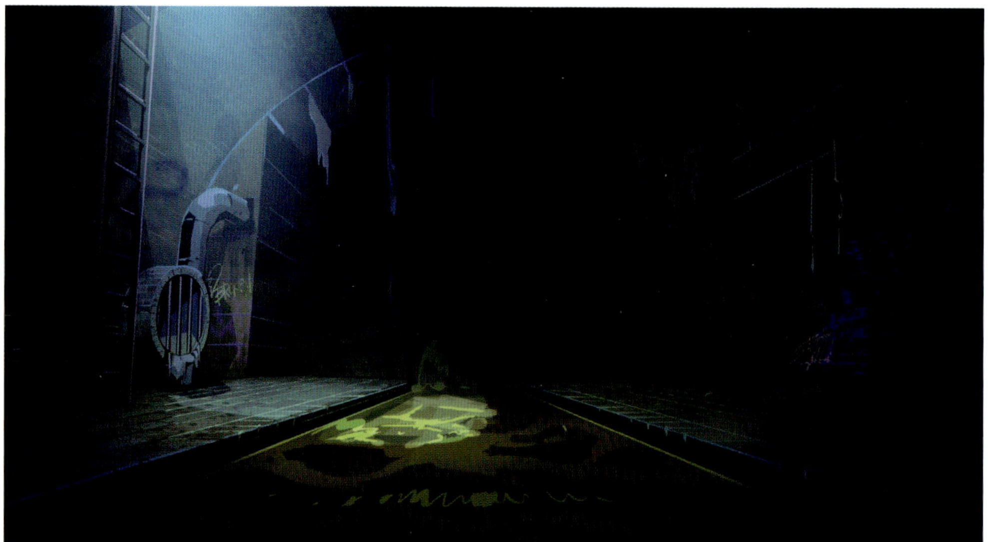

SEWER WATERWAY

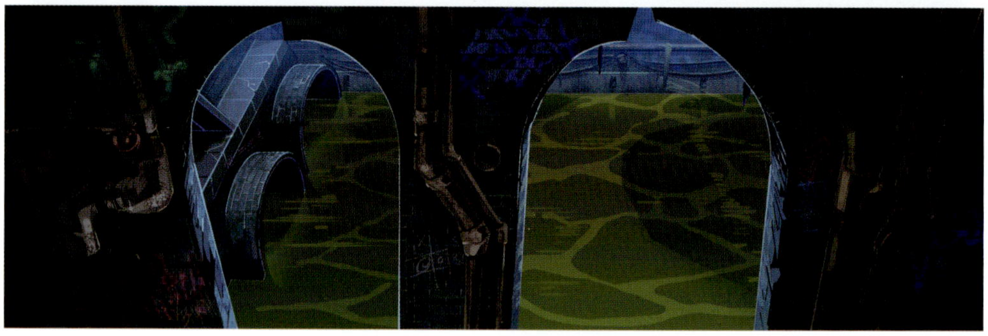

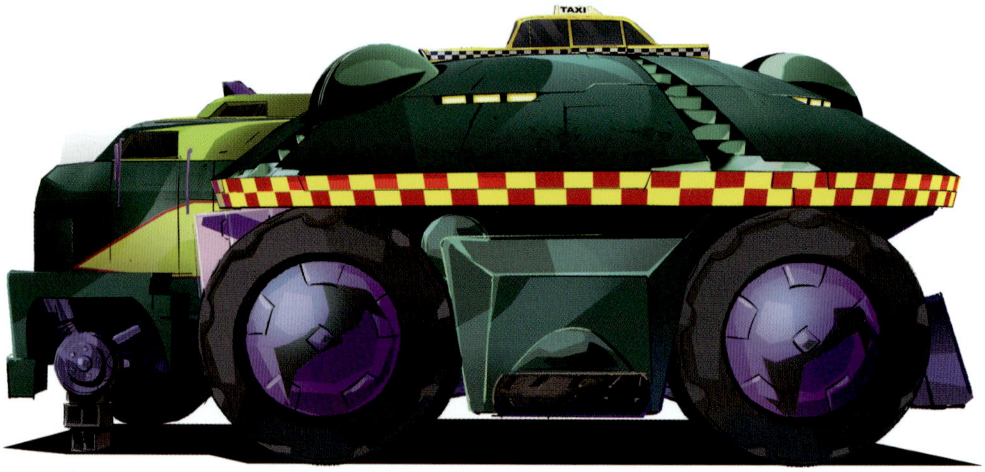

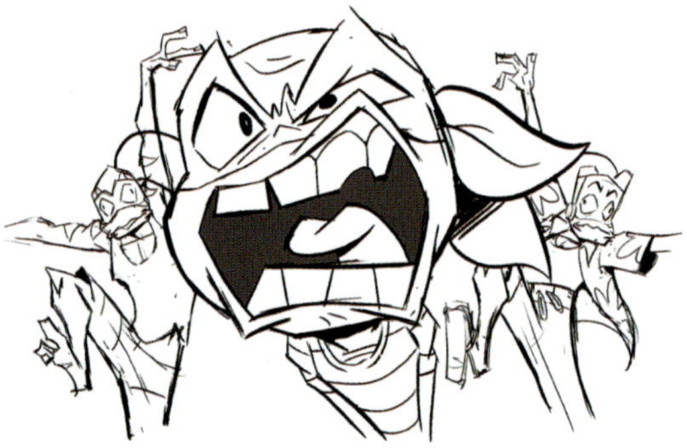

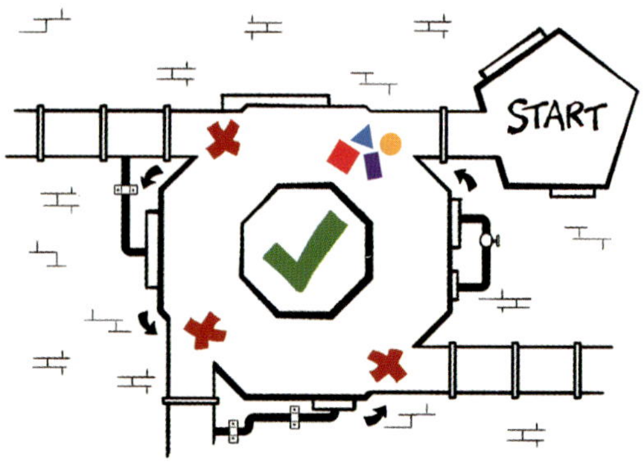

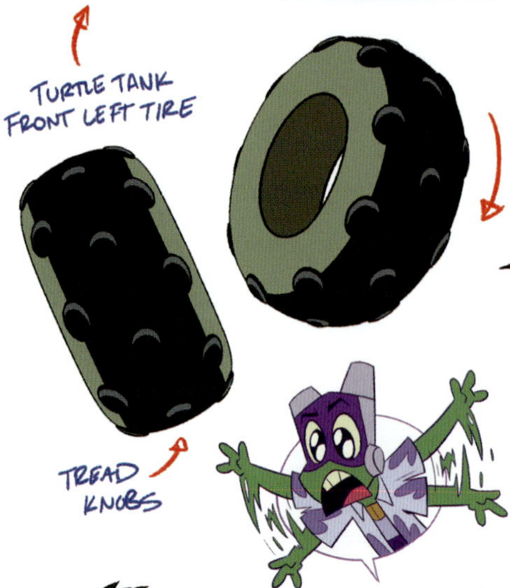

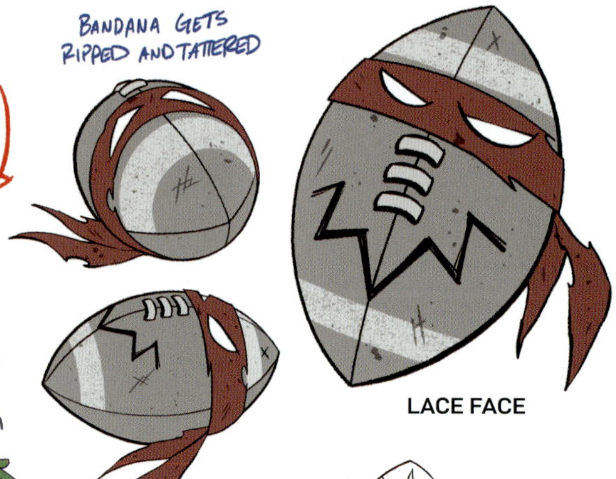

LACE FACE

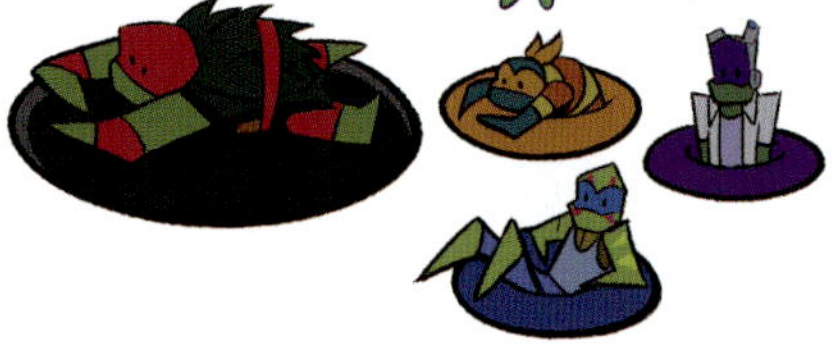

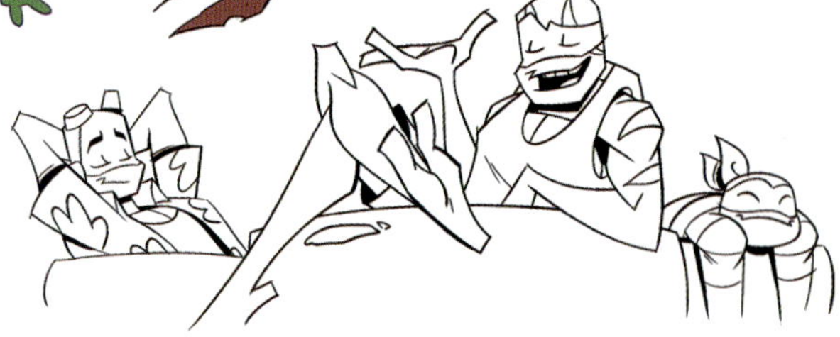

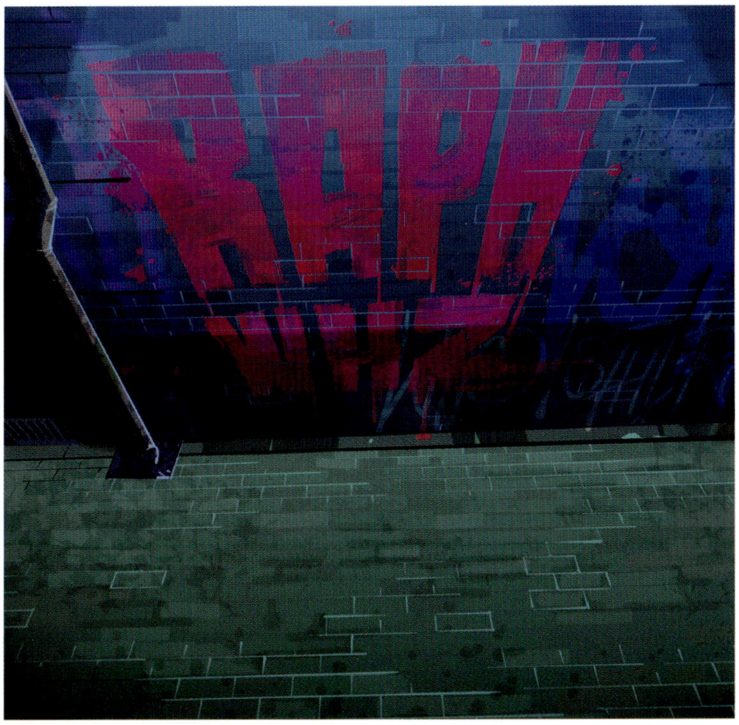

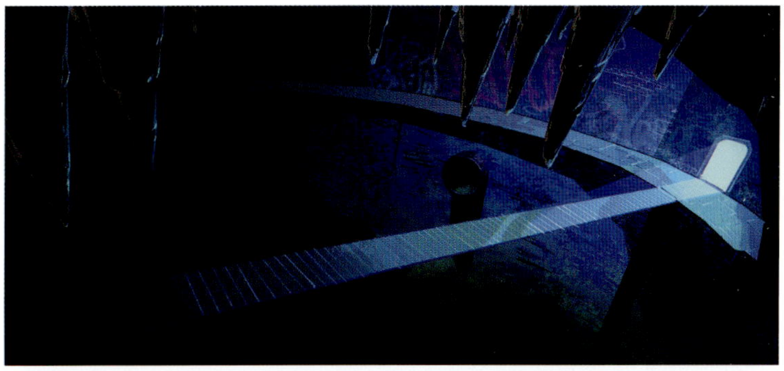

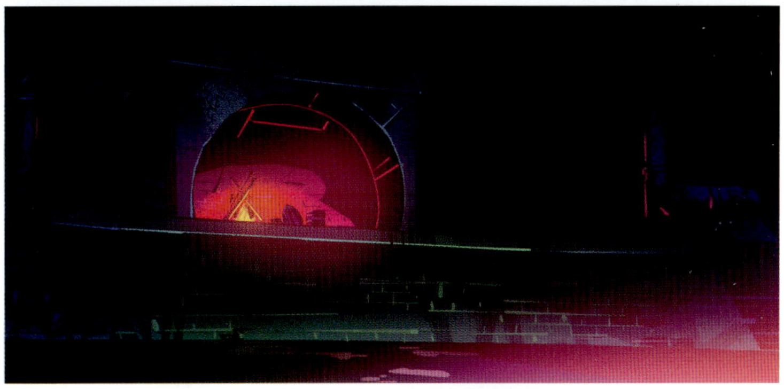

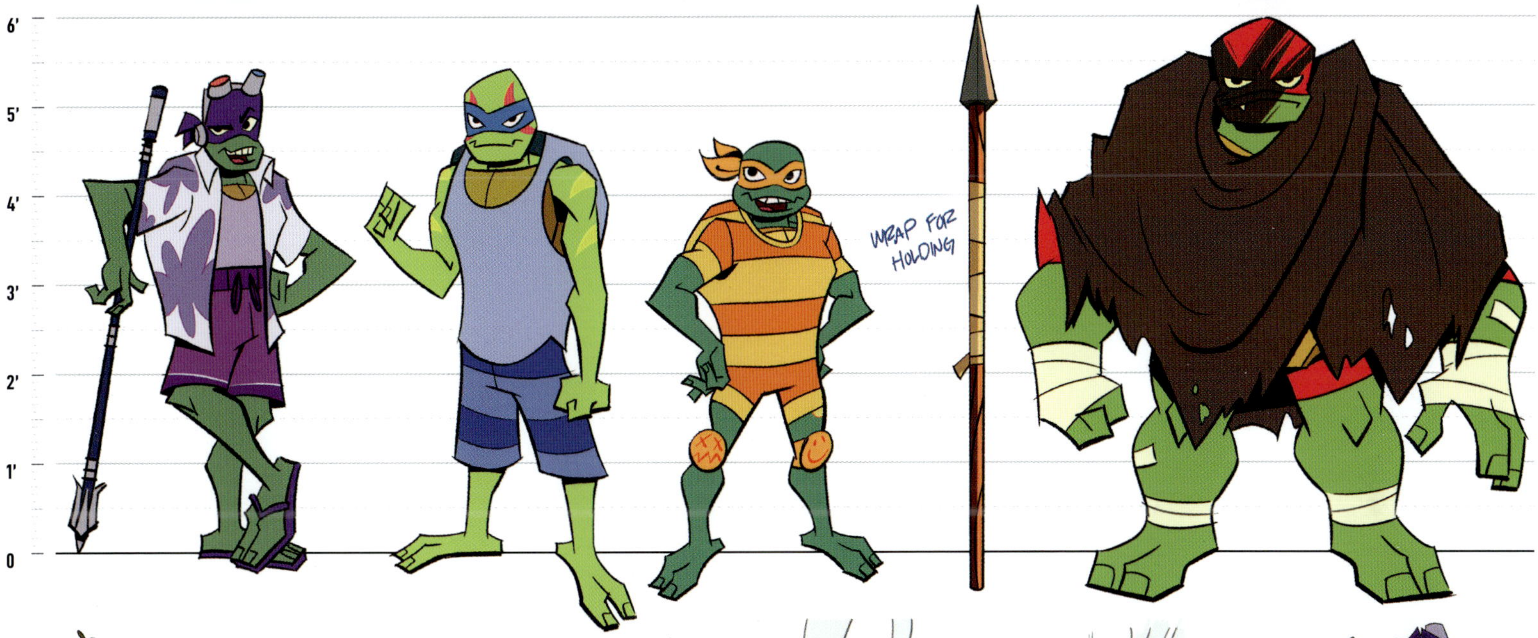

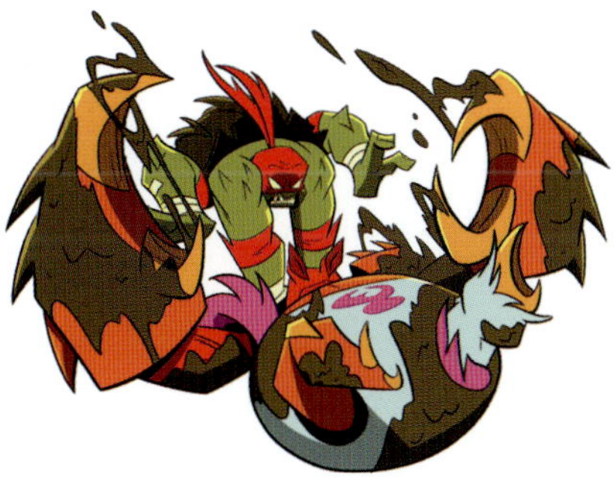

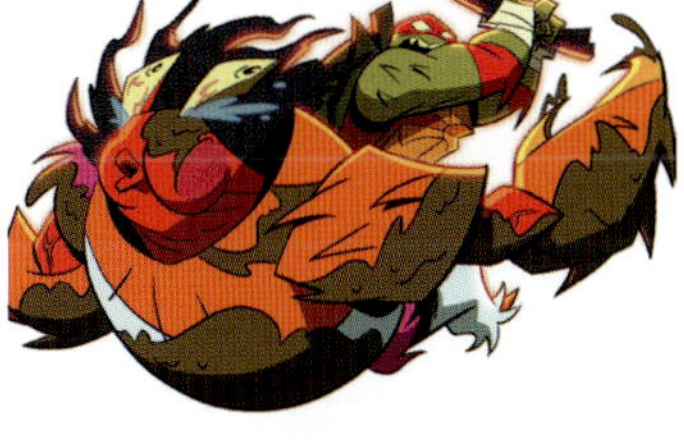

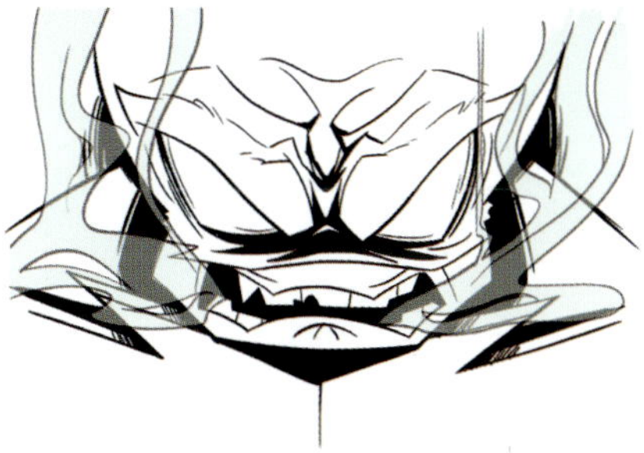

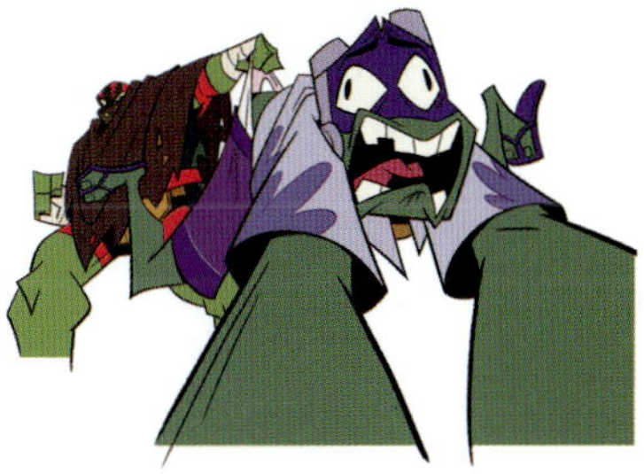

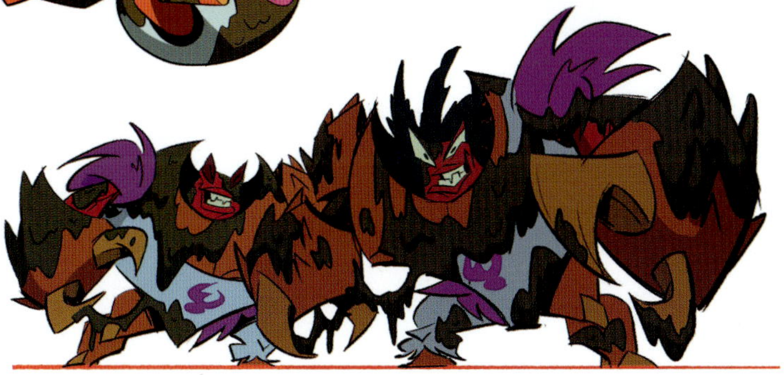

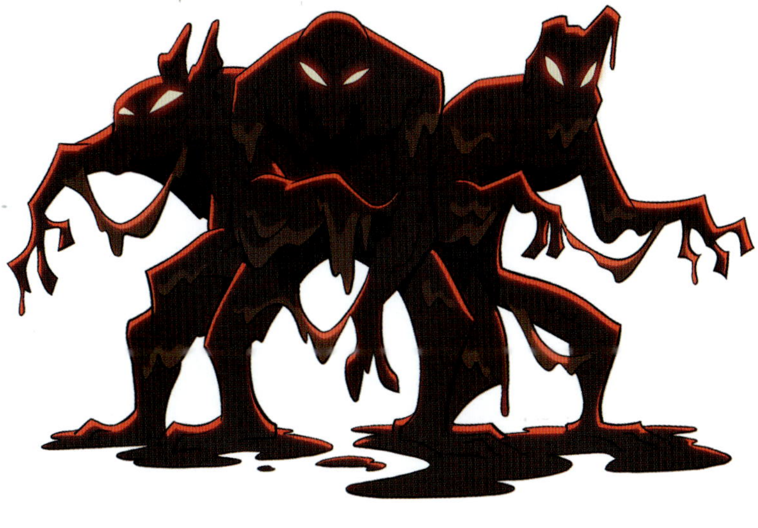

DALE MALINOWSKI: The crab mutant Carl Sando's sign-off line, "So long, jerks!" is a spin on voice actor Jason Mantzoukas' famous way of greeting the crowd at live recordings of *How Did This Get Made?*—the podcast that he co-hosts with Paul Scheer, who coincidentally voices the other crab mutant, Ben Sando.

THE ANCIENT ART OF NINJA HIDE AND SEEK

ORIGINAL AIR DATE: OCTOBER 26, 2019
PRODUCTION CODE: 043

WRITTEN BY **IAN BUSCH**
STORYBOARDS BY **KEVIN MOLINA-ORTIZ**
DIRECTED BY **SEBASTIAN MONTES**

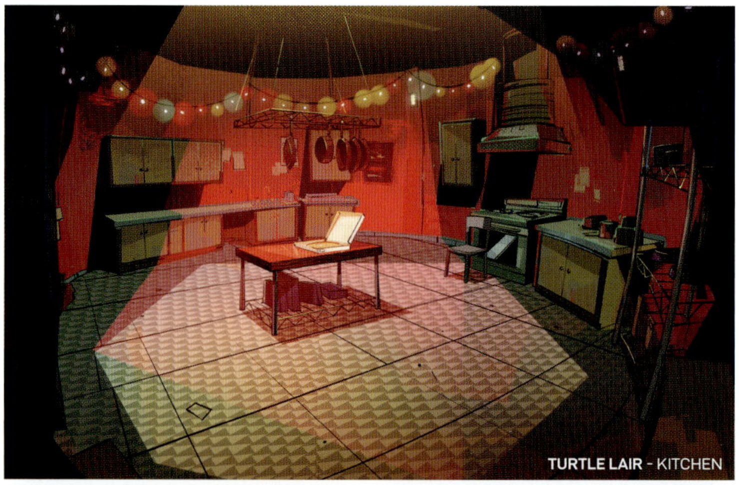
TURTLE LAIR - KITCHEN

IAN BUSCH: In so many iterations of Turtles, there are scenes of Splinter training the boys, and it was so fun to jump into this episode to show everyone what *Rise's* version of this kind of scene is. Since Splinter was a loving father first and foremost, I felt it would be key for him to also be working on his parenting skills while simultaneously teaching the boys what he knows. Him disguising himself as one of the Turtles still gets me every time I watch it. He's a great dad who feels sincerely awful that he may have forced them into something they weren't ready for...but just like any good parent, he lets them figure their way out of it on their own.

SEBASTIAN MONTES: This is the episode where we find out that Splinter and Big Mama had a history. The crew was just as shocked and giddy about it as the viewers were.

The hallmark of this episode for me is Kevin Molina-Ortiz's storyboarding creativity. He really dug deep into anime special effects for Splinter's hide-and-seek abilities. It was both hilarious and brilliant.

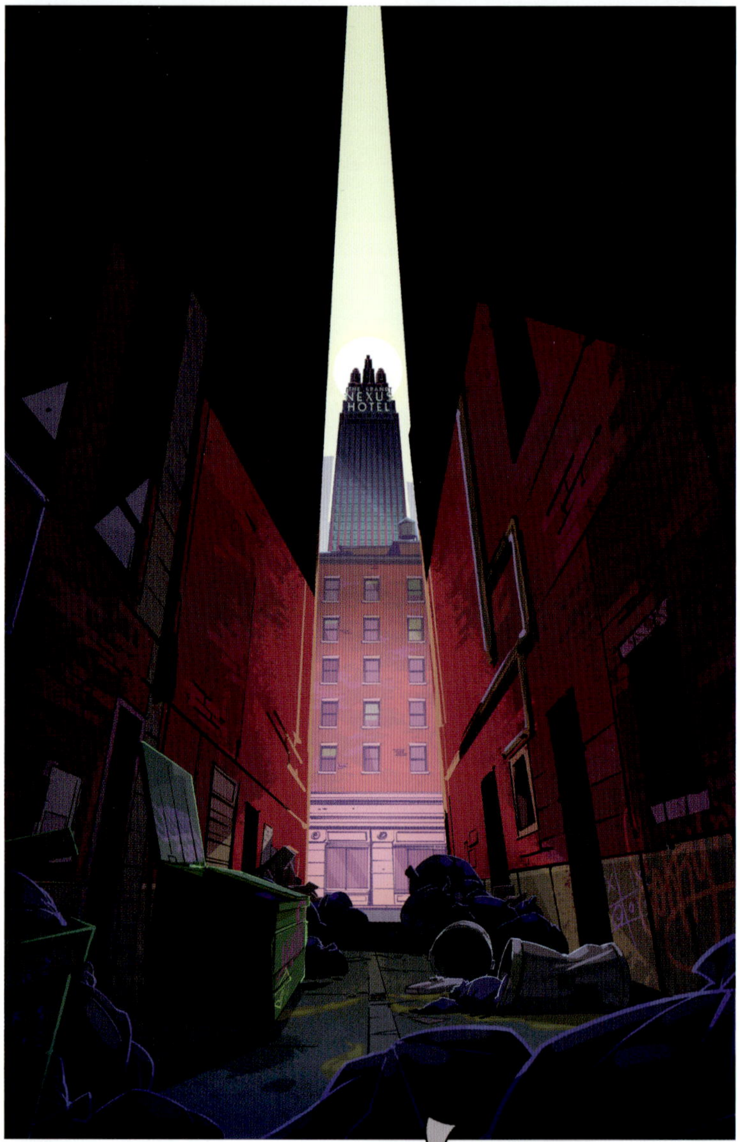

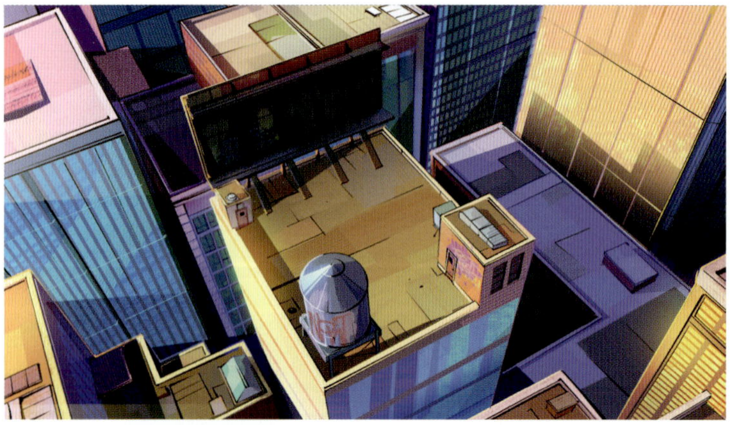

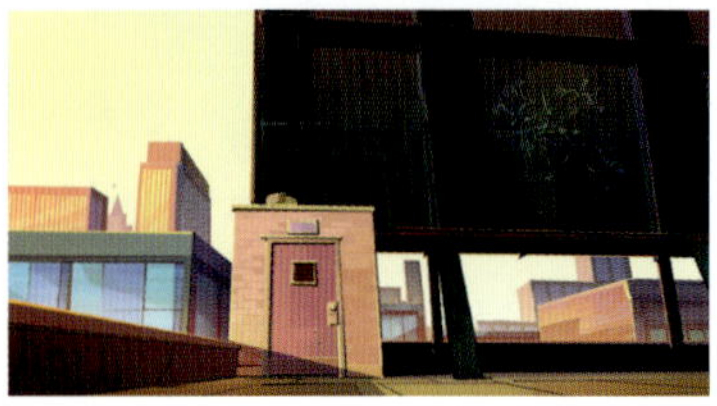

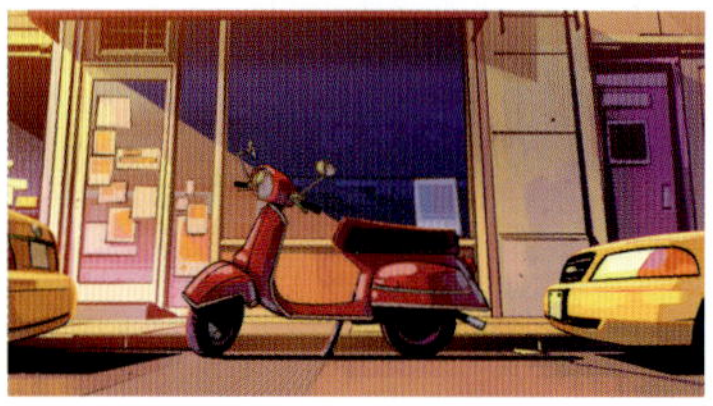

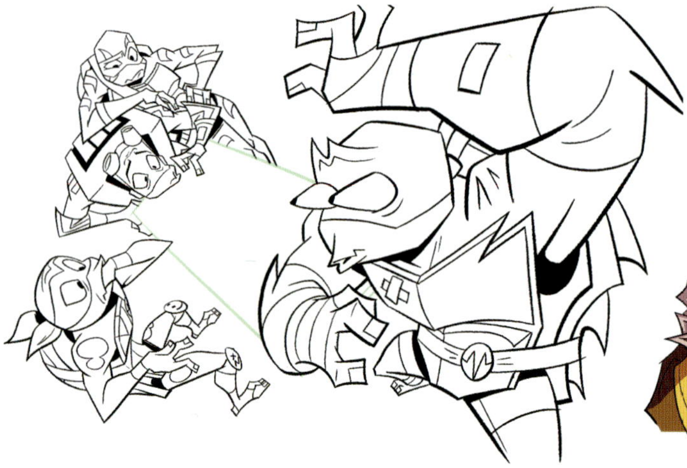

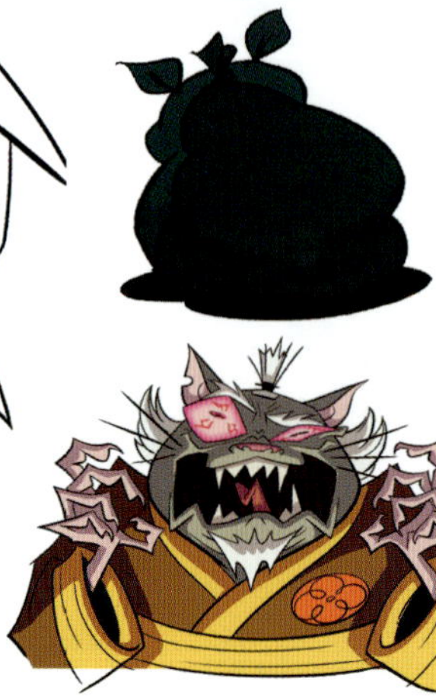

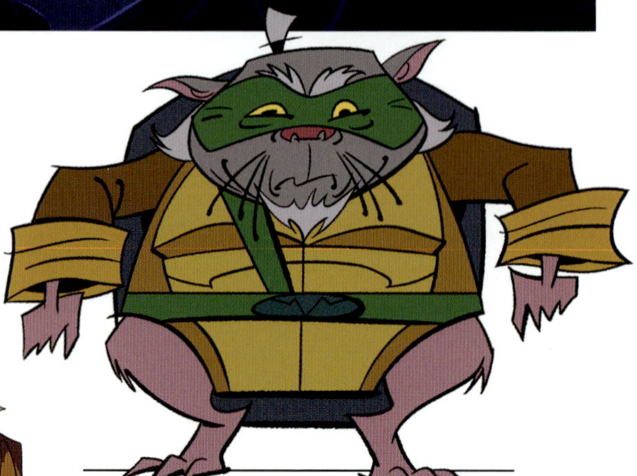
TINIEST BROTHER

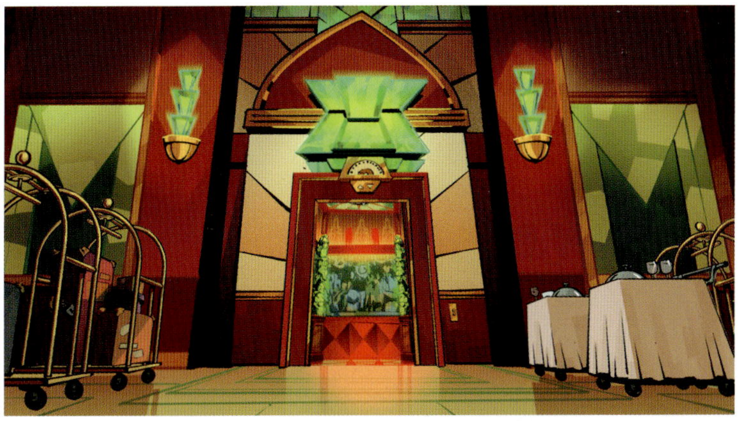

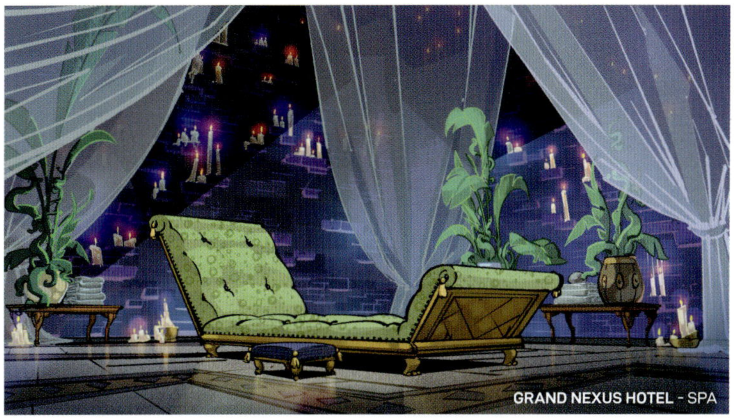

GRAND NEXUS HOTEL - SPA

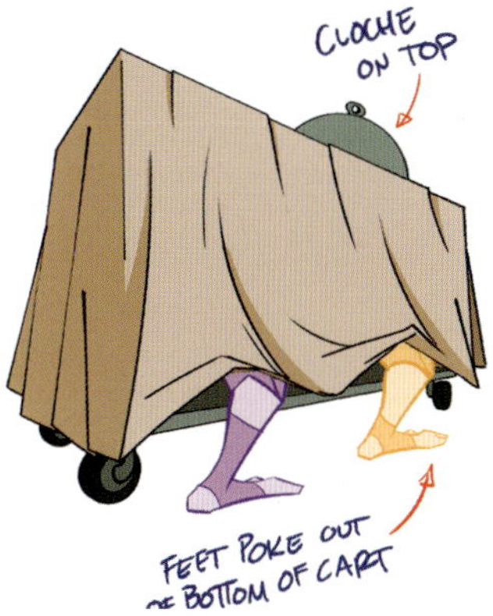

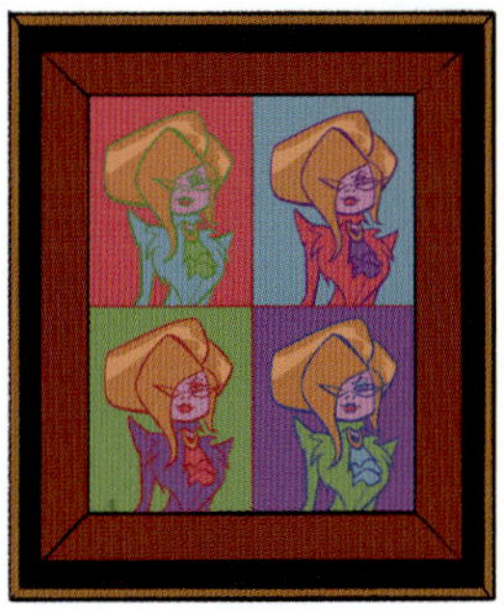

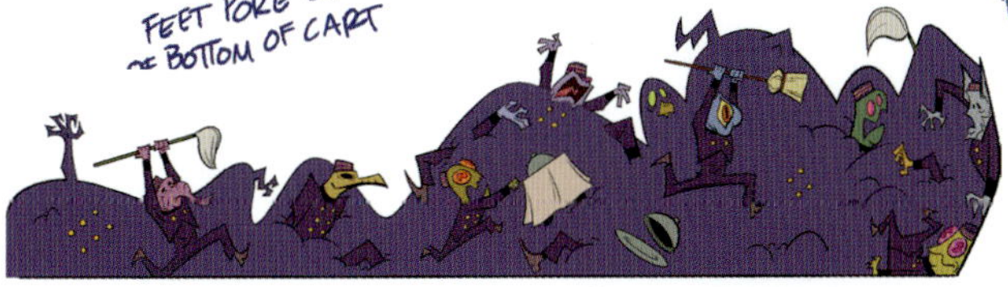

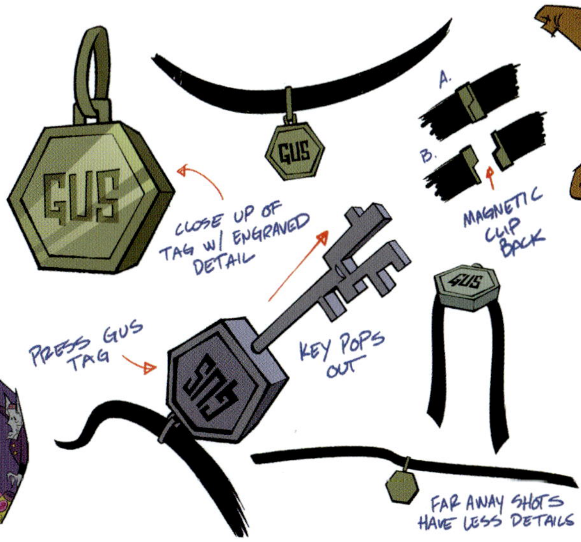

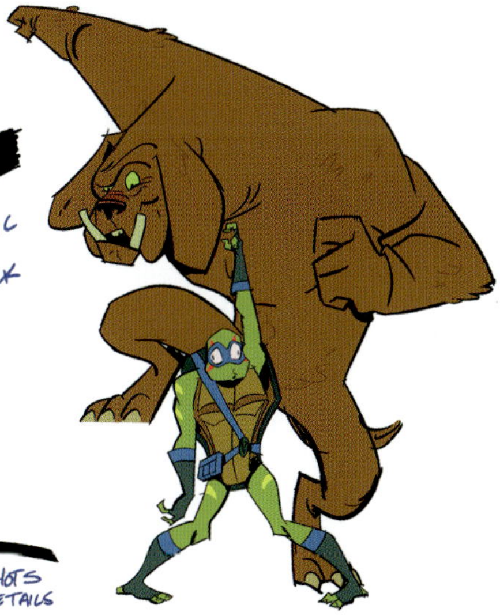

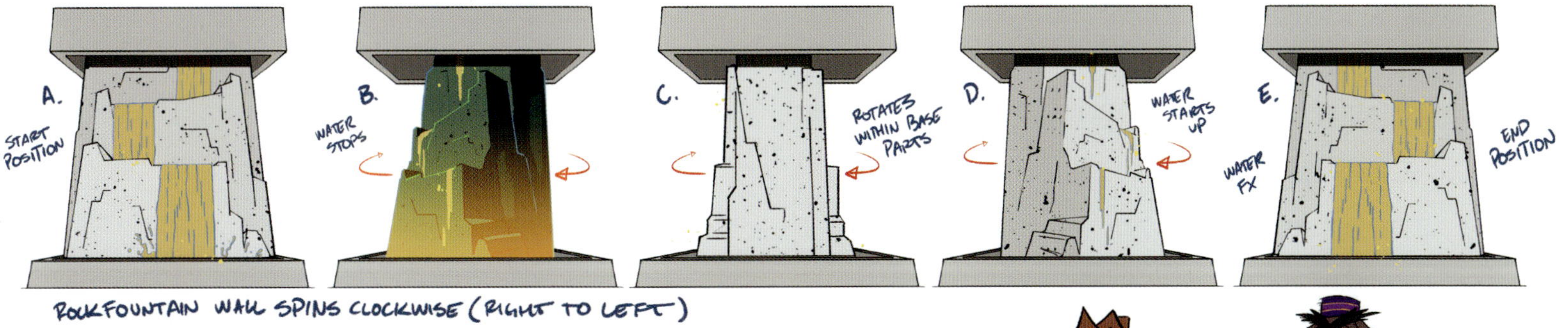

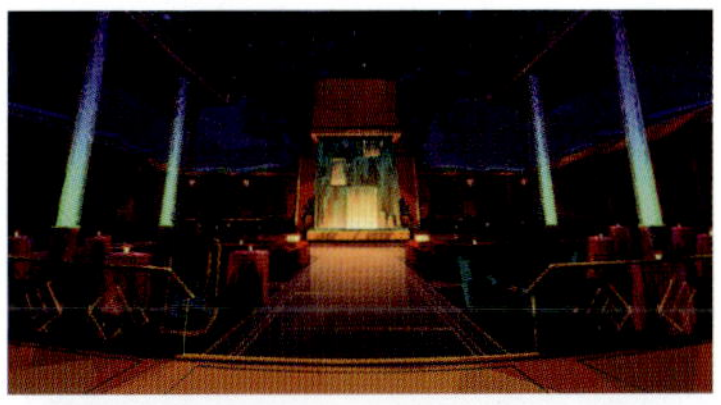

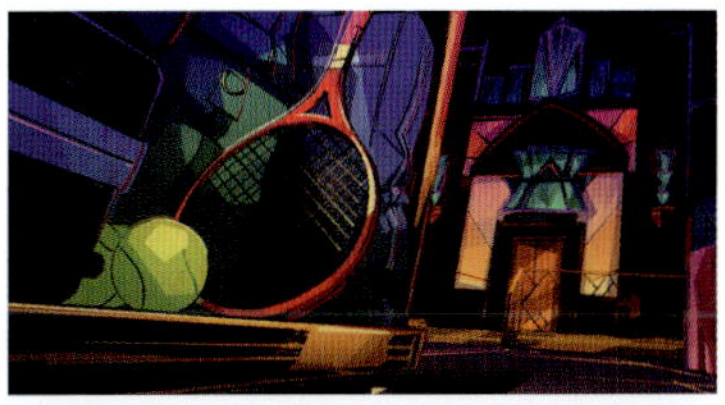

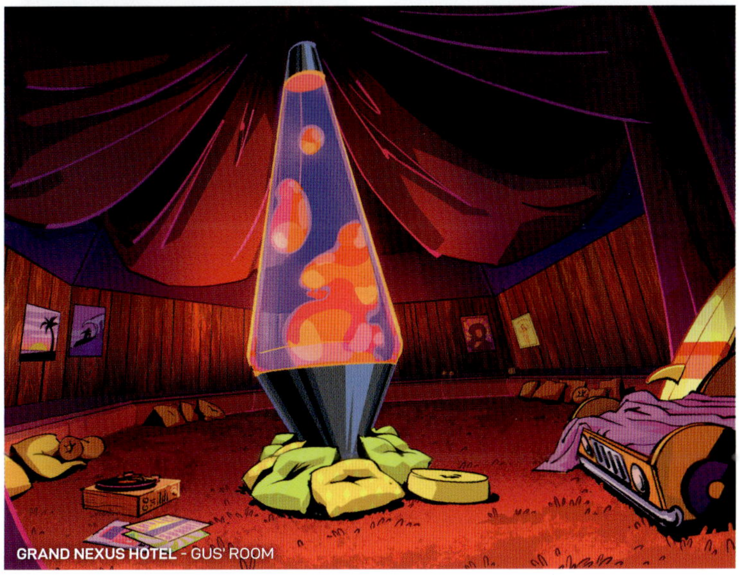

GRAND NEXUS HOTEL - GUS' ROOM

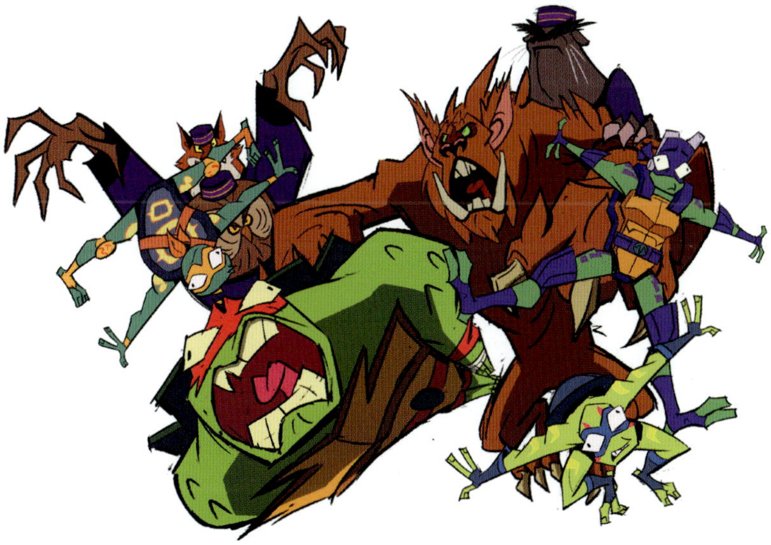

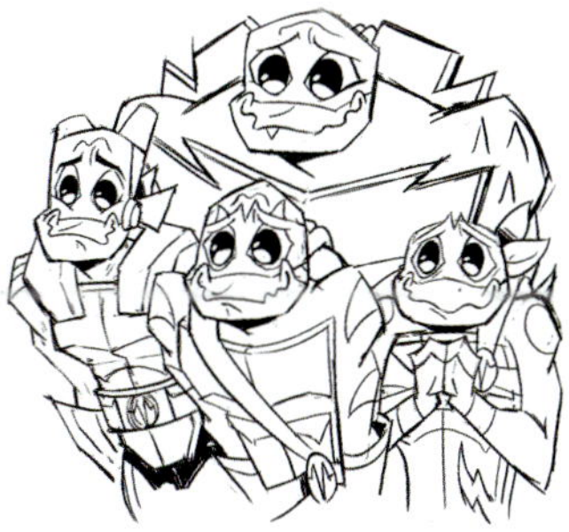

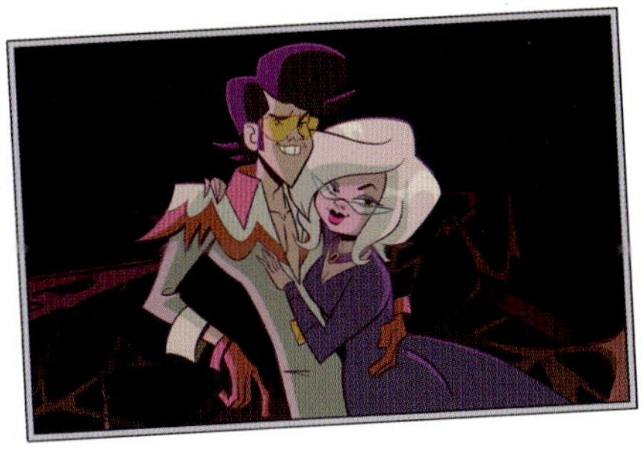

THE MUTANT MENACE

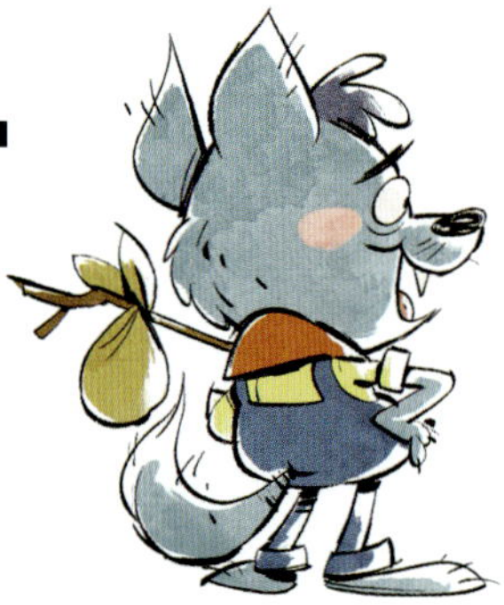

ORIGINAL AIR DATE: OCTOBER 19, 2019
PRODUCTION CODE: 044

WRITTEN BY **RUSS CARNEY & RON CORCILLO**
STORYBOARDS BY **JULIA BRAID, JAKE CASTORENA, MATTHEW HUMPHREYS**
DIRECTED BY **JJ CONWAY**

JJ CONWAY: We worked extensively with Flying Bark to ensure our episodes were producible for the animation team, but to allow for the occasional animation-intensive episode, we would balance that with more economic episodes that were easier for the animation teams. "The Mutant Menace" was one of those. To achieve that, we heavily reused Turtle Tank and city street backgrounds from previous episodes, and we even tried to reuse animation where we could. My rule of thumb for these economic episodes was to never sacrifice the integrity of the story, but any time reuse wouldn't hurt, go with the reuse.

RON CORCILLO: One of the best things about writing is going to voice-record sessions and getting to know the actors' individual personalities. Brandon Mychal Smith is super enthusiastic and huggy in real life, so our version of Mikey started to reflect that. Josh Brener, on the other hand, is a bit more germ-averse, and so Donnie does most of his hugging with his robot arms. Since Ben Schwartz is one of those comedians who's always on (in a good way), we gave Leo a personality to match.

RUSS CARNEY: Similarly, after working with Omar for a while, we became more in sync with his phenomenal acting style, and we started writing lines that we knew he'd slay. In this episode Raph rallies the troops with *"Yeah, we're good-doers! And what do good-doers do? They good-do, and they good-do it well!"* It's always a great feeling when you can write in the voice of the actor.

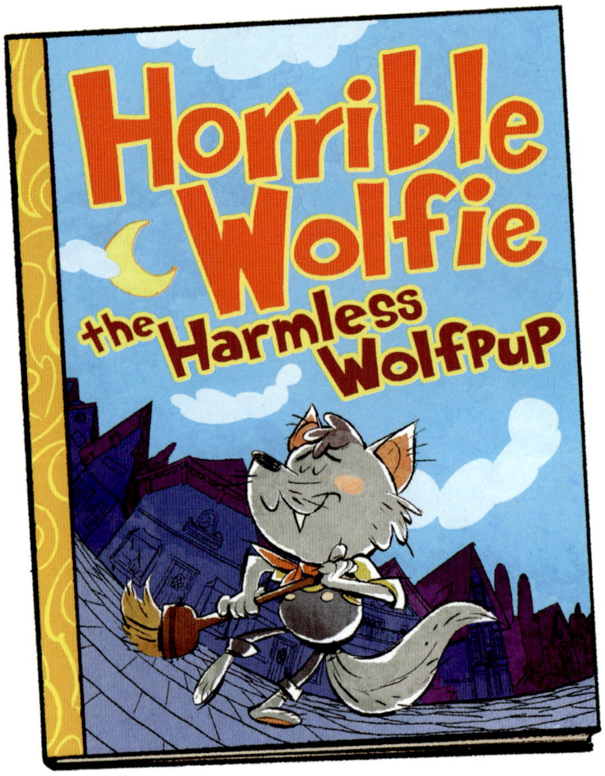

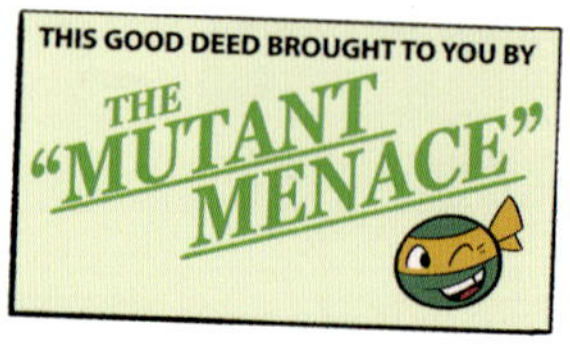

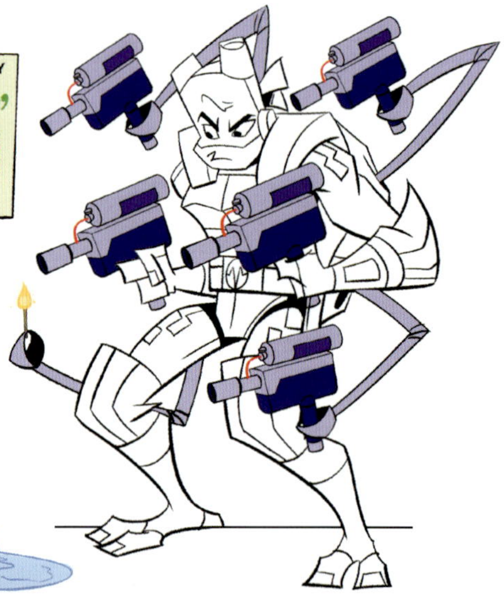

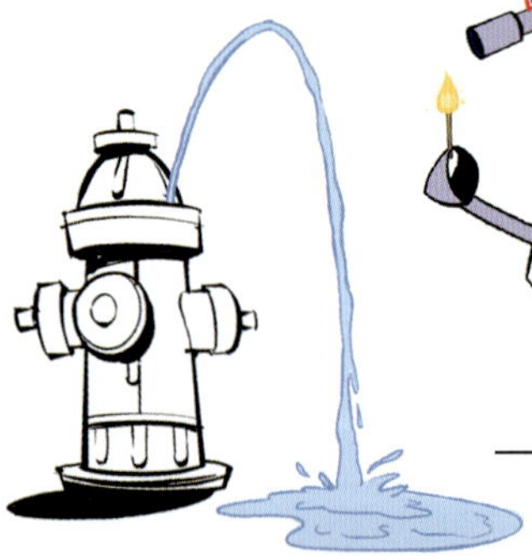

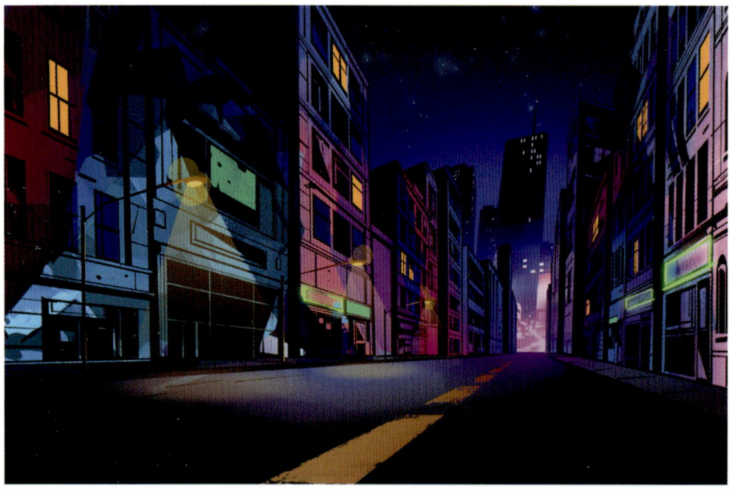

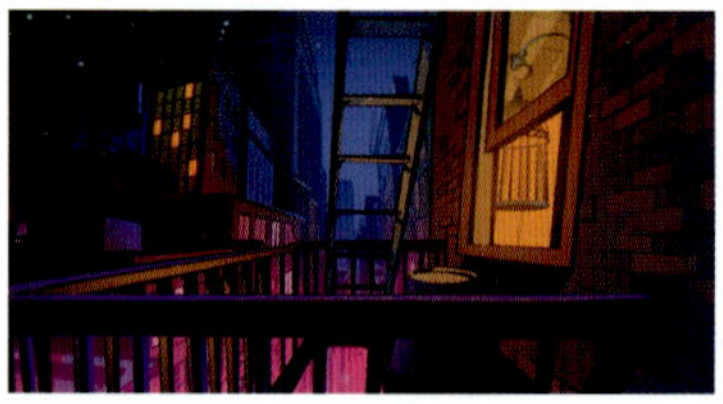

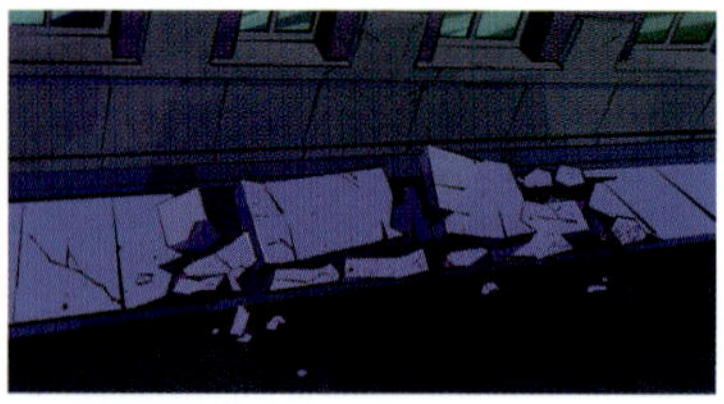

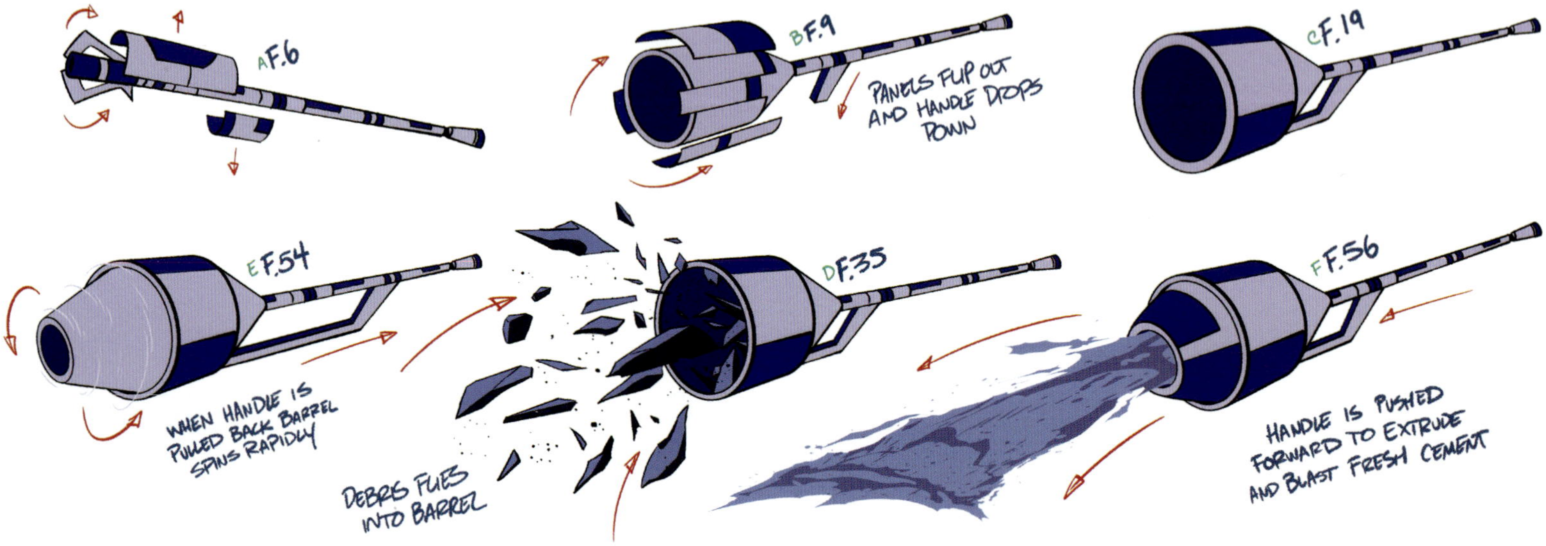

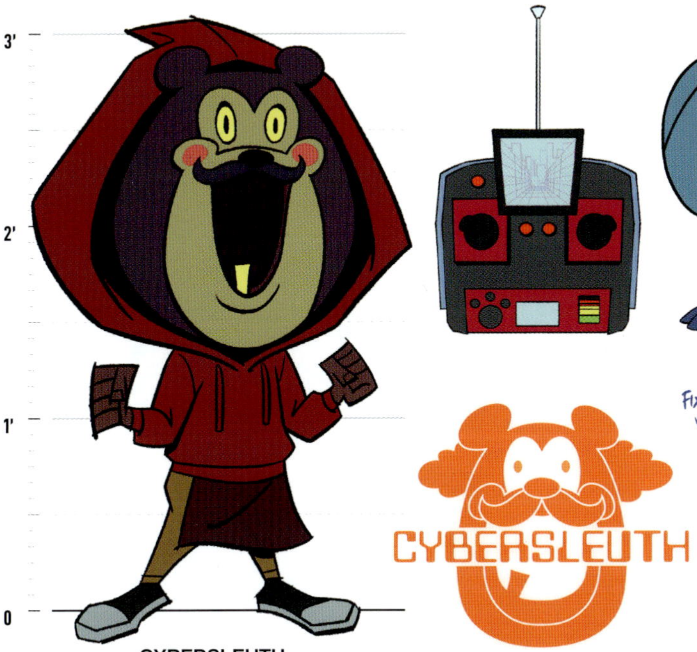

CYBERSLEUTH
BAXTER STOCKBOY

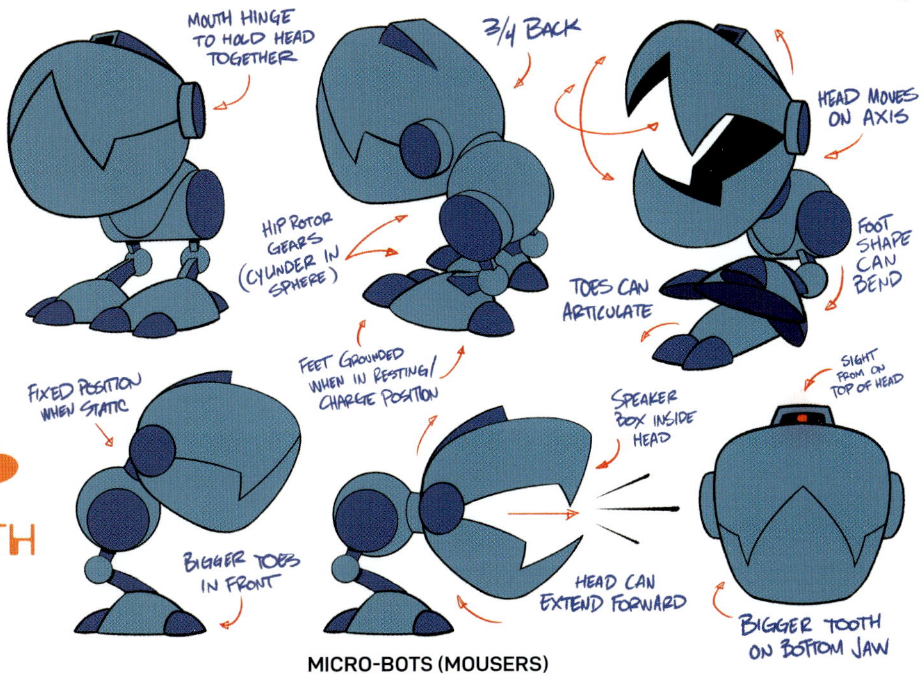

MICRO-BOTS (MOUSERS)

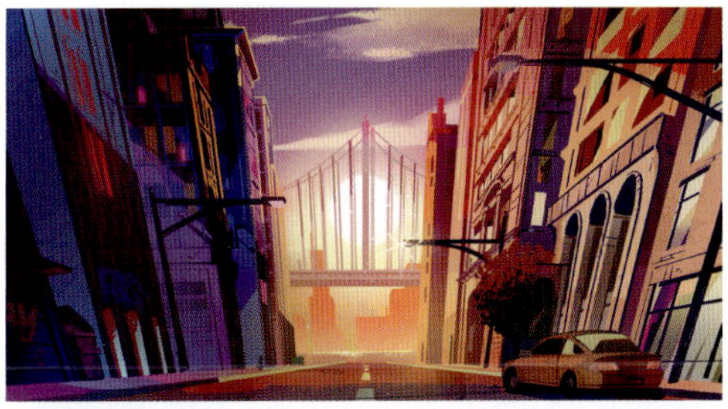

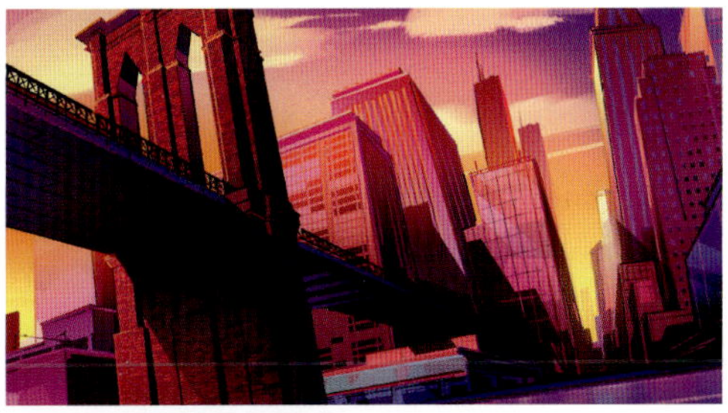

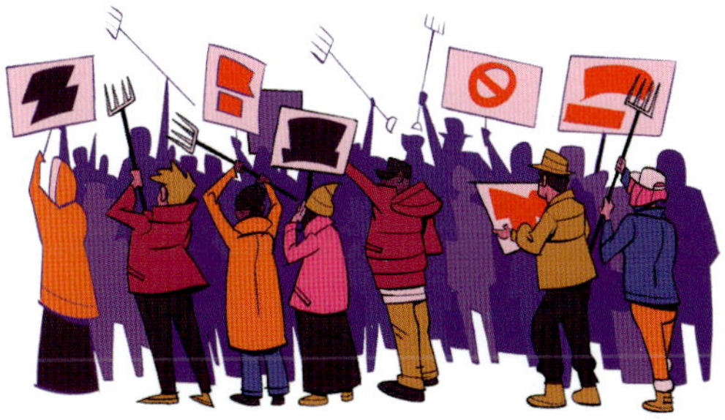

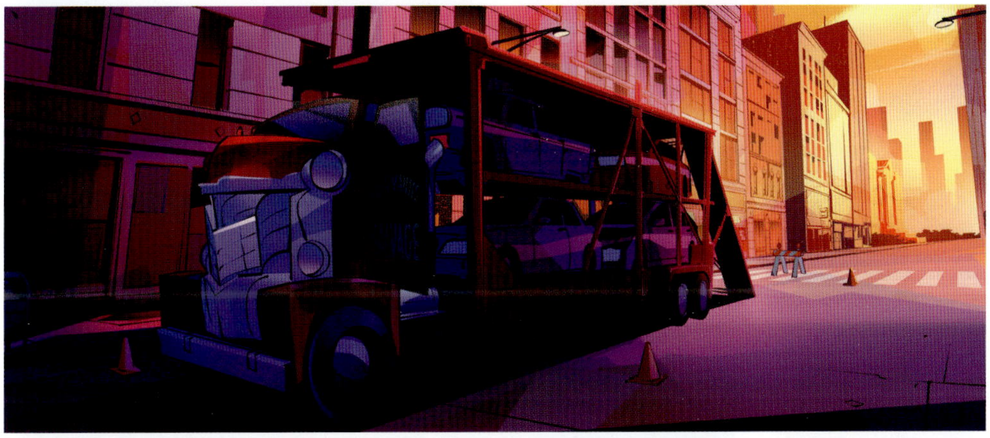

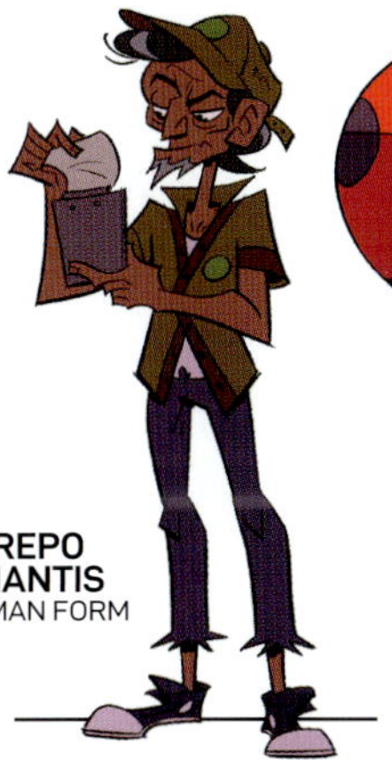

REPO
MANTIS
HUMAN FORM

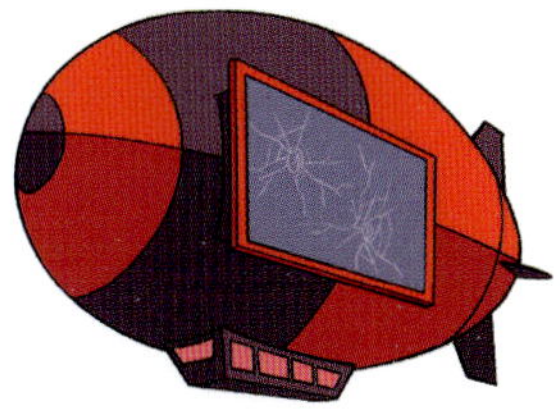

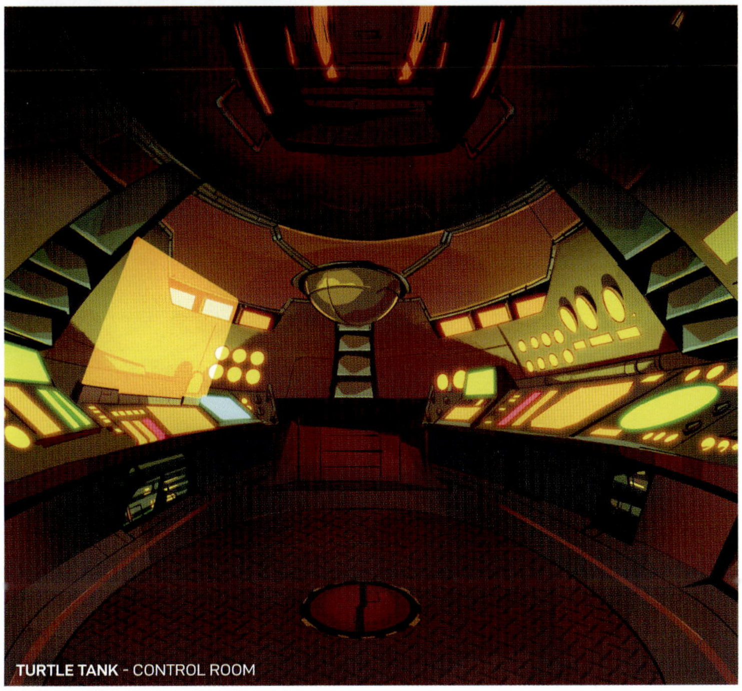

TURTLE TANK - CONTROL ROOM

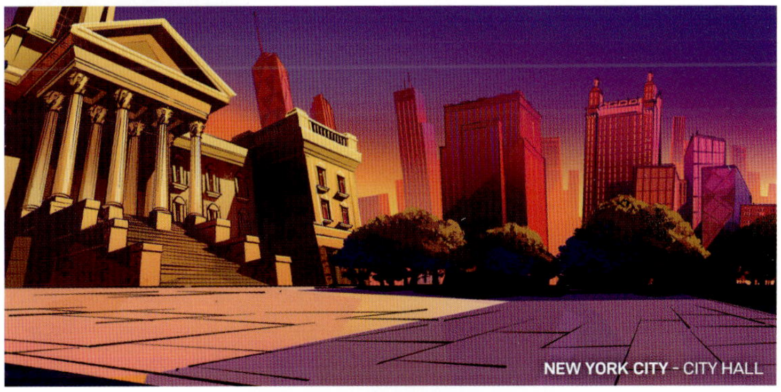

NEW YORK CITY - CITY HALL

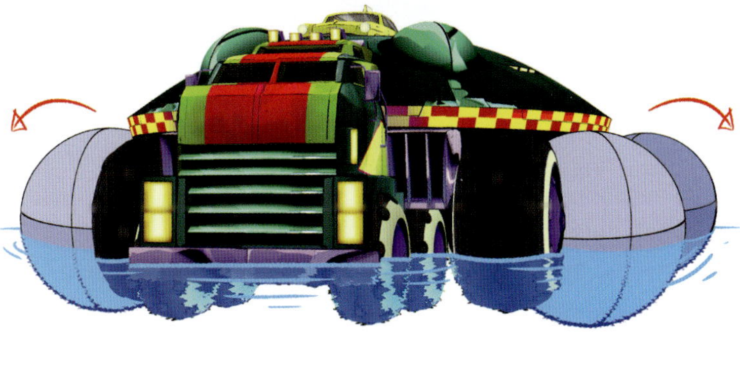

ONE MAN'S JUNK

ORIGINAL AIR DATE: NOVEMBER 2, 2019
PRODUCTION CODE: 045

WRITTEN BY **RUSS CARNEY & RON CORCILLO**
STORYBOARDS BY **CHRISTOPHER LUC**
DIRECTED BY **ABE AUDISH**

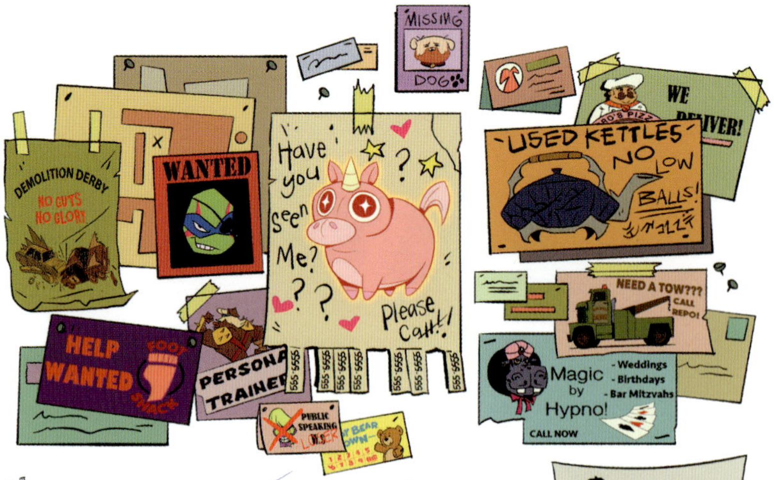

RUSS CARNEY: Since our season 1 arc was largely focused on the acquisition of Shredder armor, we needed a few episodes that furthered that goal, and pairing Donnie and Mikey to lead the mission seemed fun.

[Some backstory: When Russ and Ron worked on *Fanboy & Chum Chum* (2009), Russ made Ron laugh so hard that he passed out, hit his head on a doorjamb, and slammed unconscious onto the floor. Russ did a victory lap around the office, fist-pumping and celebrating himself for having near-deadly comedy chops, but it turned out that Ron, a pescatarian, had an iron deficiency that contributed to the event, and the doctor determined that Russ wasn't funny at all. That whole event was the inspiration for Raph passing out while lifting the school bus, and Leo asking him if he was getting enough iron. The pure sense of concern that Ben delivered that line with made it all the more hilarious.]

RON CORCILLO: Meanwhile, Russ is still trying to find a doctor willing to give a second opinion about his deadly wit.

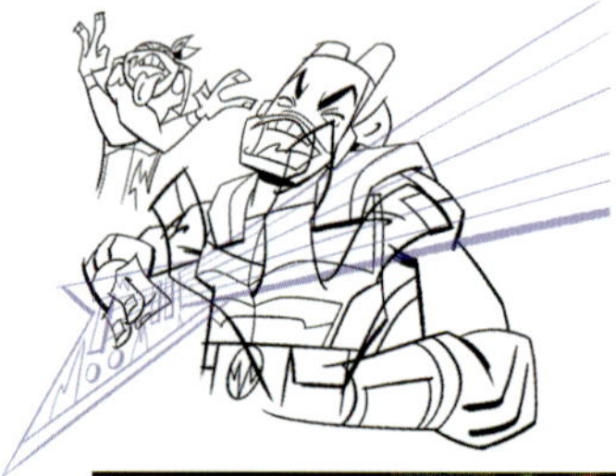

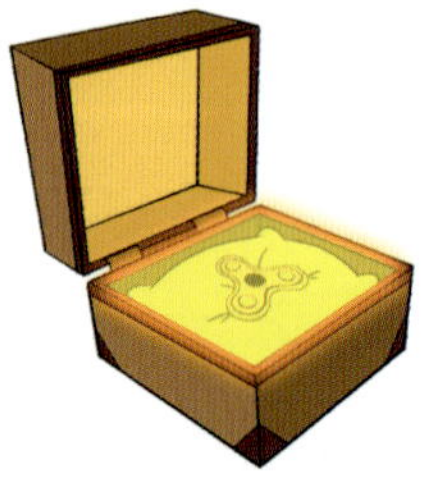

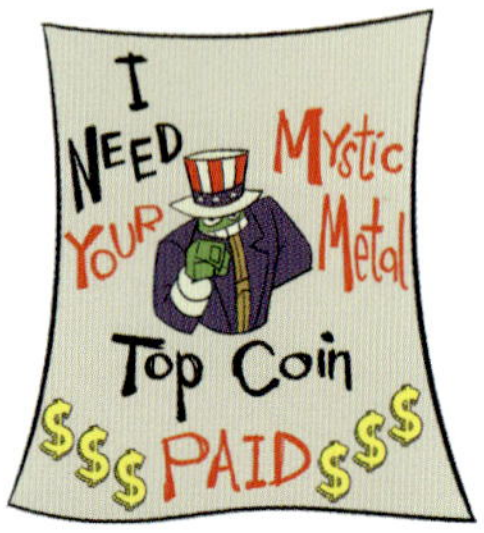

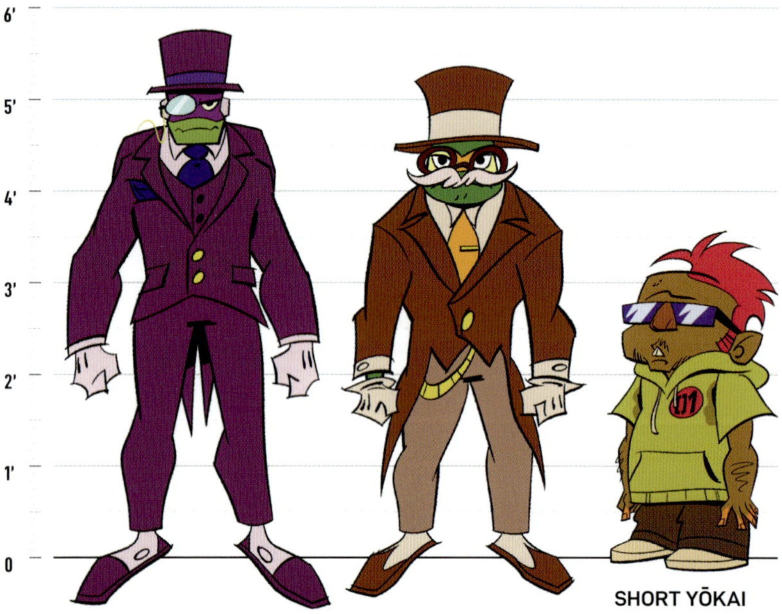

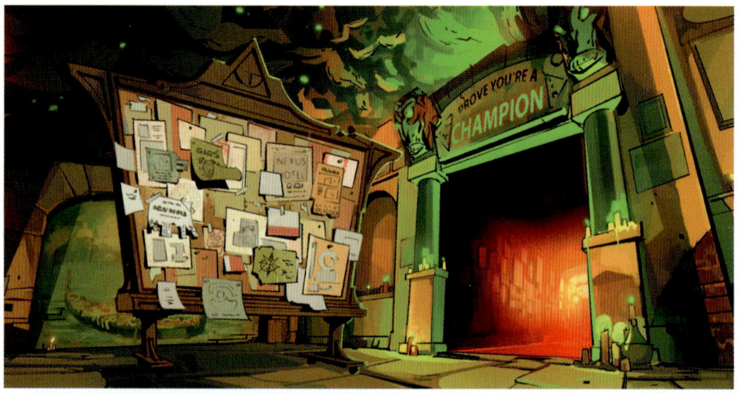

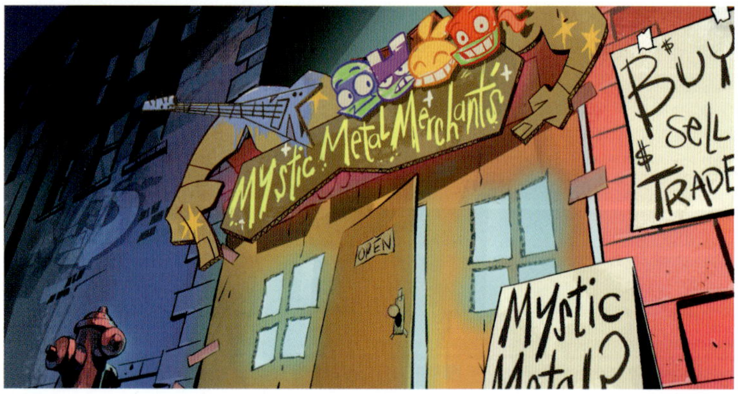

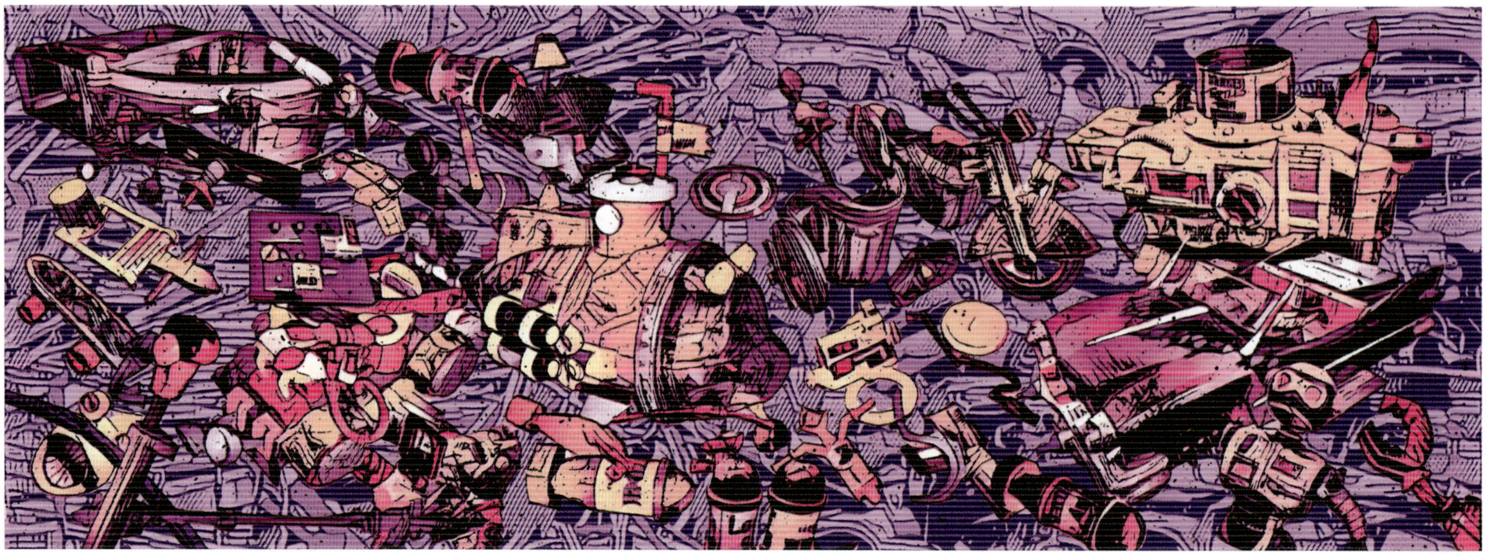

The junkyard scan is full of retro TMNT toys, such as the Sewer Sub, Turtlecycle, Pizza Thrower, Toilet Taxi, Foot Cruiser, Fugitoid, and various accessories.

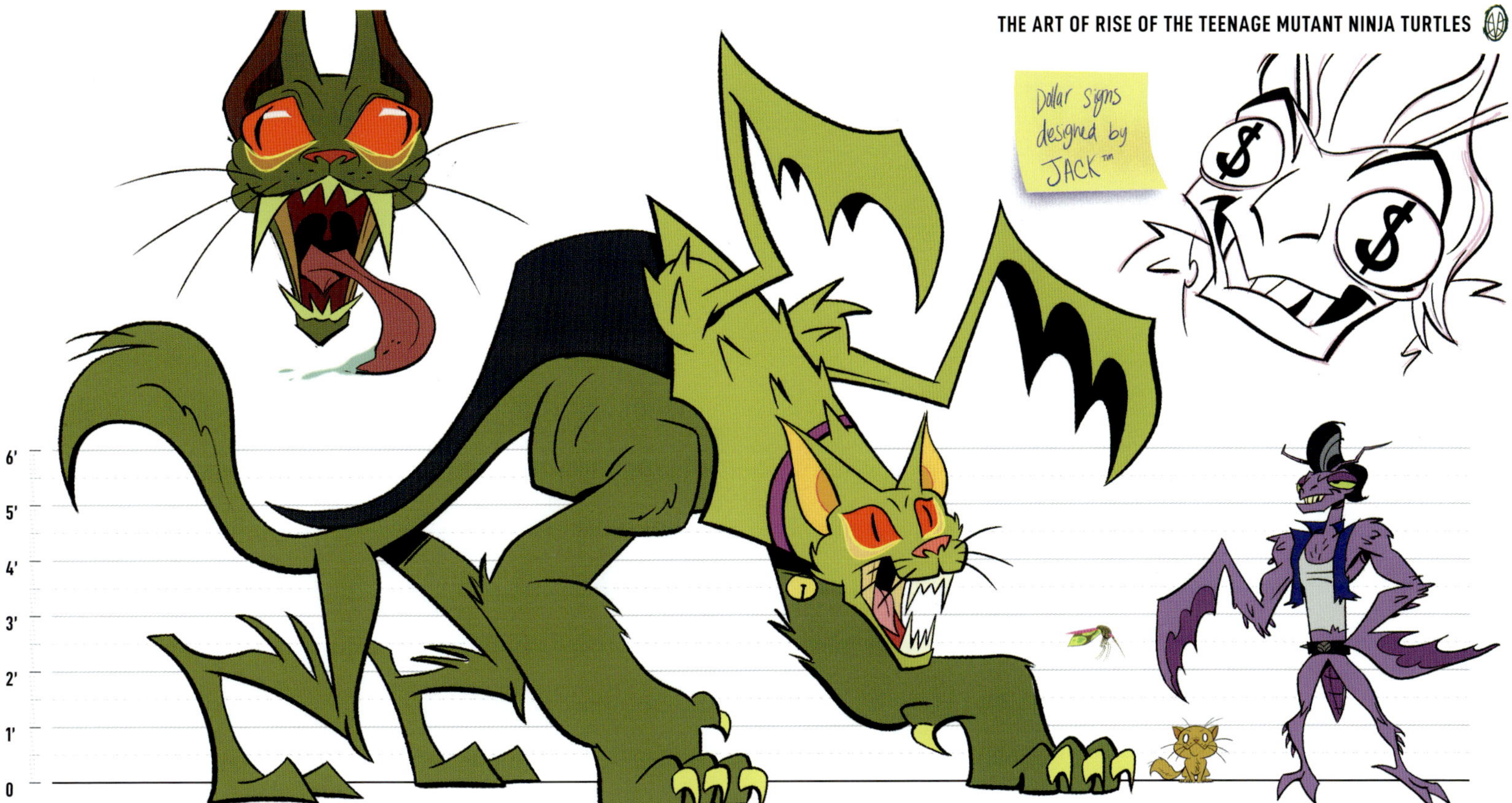

MRS. NUBBINS
MANTICAT

MRS. NUBBINS
UNMUTATED

REPO MANTIS

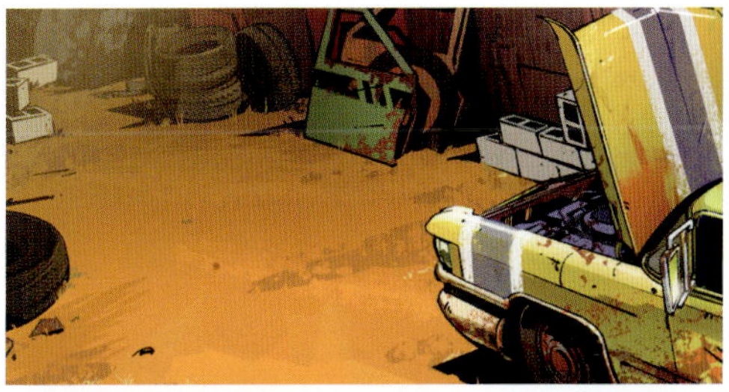

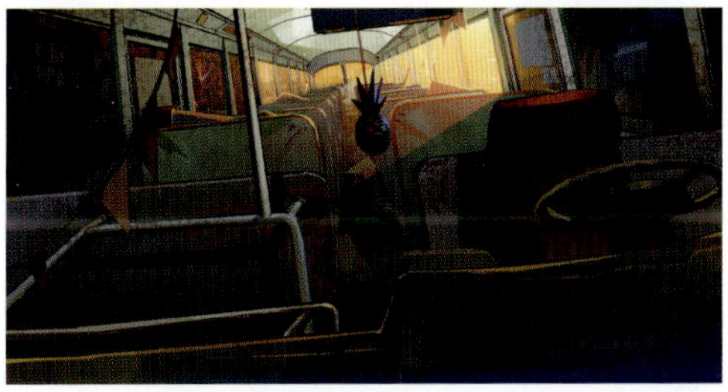

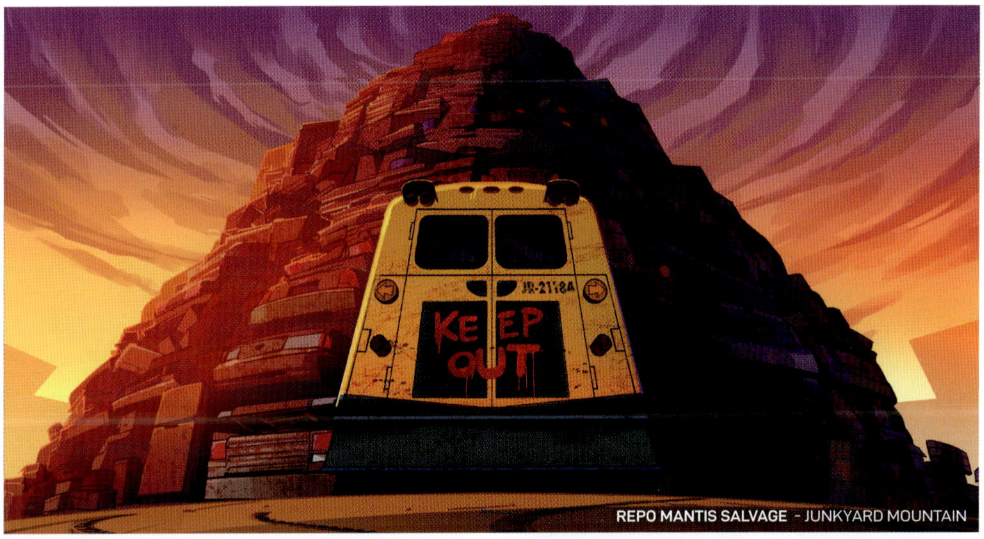

REPO MANTIS SALVAGE - JUNKYARD MOUNTAIN

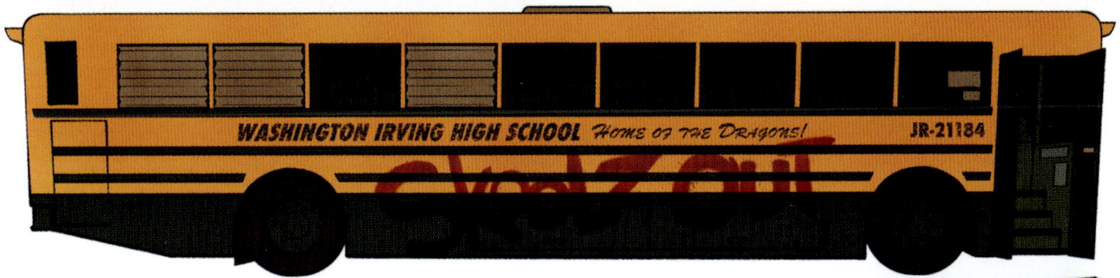

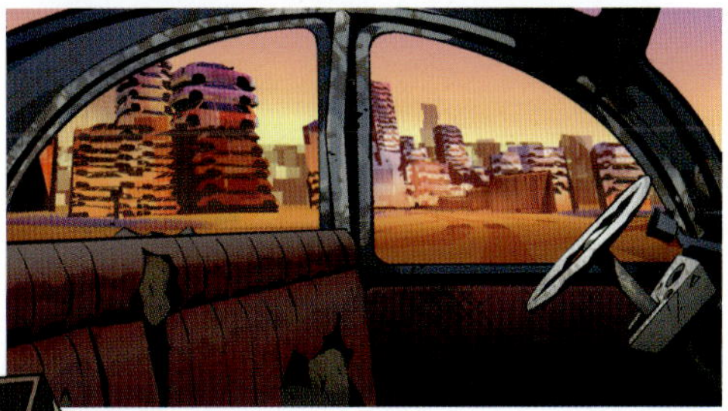

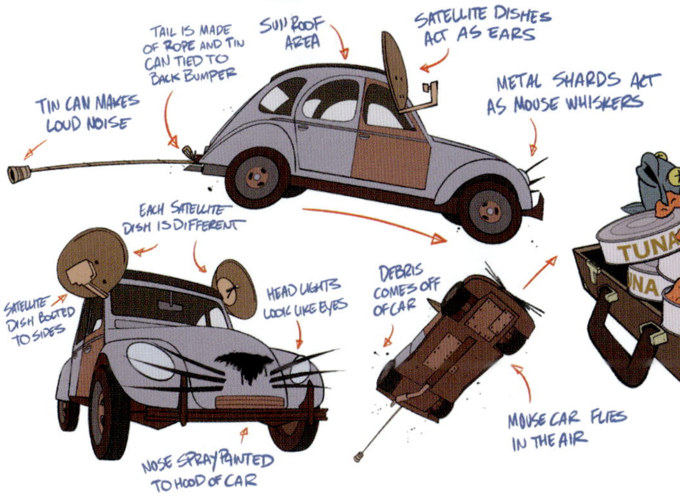

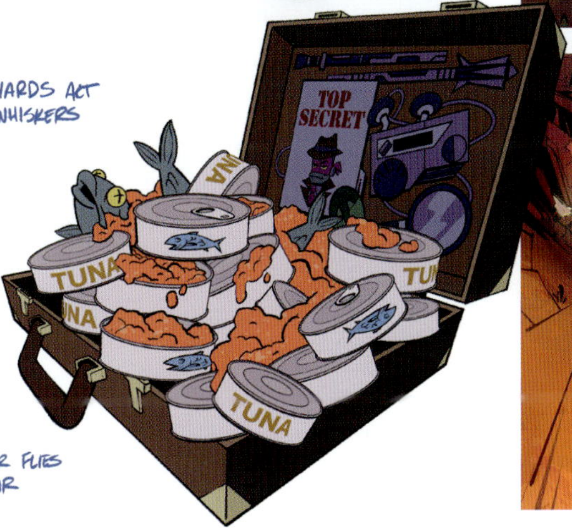

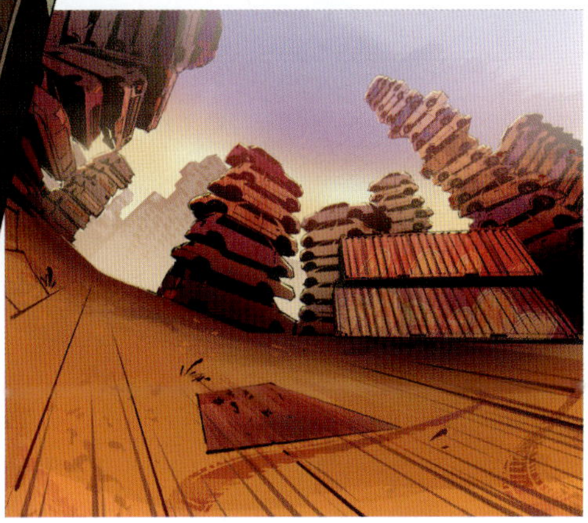

SNOW DAY

ORIGINAL AIR DATE: NOVEMBER 2, 2019
PRODUCTION CODE: 046

WRITTEN BY **DALE MALINOWSKI**
STORYBOARDS BY **MAX COLLINS, KAI LYNN JIANG**
DIRECTED BY **SEBASTIAN MONTES**

DALE MALINOWSKI: I grew up in Pennsylvania, and I loved how snow days off from school had a magical feel to them, so I wanted to tap into those feelings through the Turtles. I live in L.A. now, and animation takes a very long time to produce, so I wrote this winter wonderland episode in July 2017 during a brutal heat wave! I didn't have AC, but playing winter-themed movies in the background while I imagined a blizzard in my mind prevented my brain from frying. The story opens with a song—the first one I ever wrote—which was inspired by Danny Elfman's "What's This?" from *The Nightmare Before Christmas* (1993). Our series composer, Matt Mahaffey, loved the concept and made a scratch demo that was so good some of the crew complained that the song would get stuck in their head for days. Tony felt we were on to something good and helped me punch up Donnie's verse before the cast absolutely crushed recording their parts. Shout-out to the cast, who were always down to share their special talents with us. The last thing I'll share about this episode is Ant was cool with me mutating Ghostbear by this point in the series. He still liked the idea of the Turtles having a human adversary, but he's very collaborative and he fully supported my vision for the character's growth.

Two of the "illegal" snowballs that Mikey names, Pepper Poppers and Liberty Launchers, were named after my nieces.

Prop designer extraordinaire, Jack Rossi, told me the flag for *Pluto Vacation IV* was inspired by the original *Gremlins* (1984) theatrical poster.

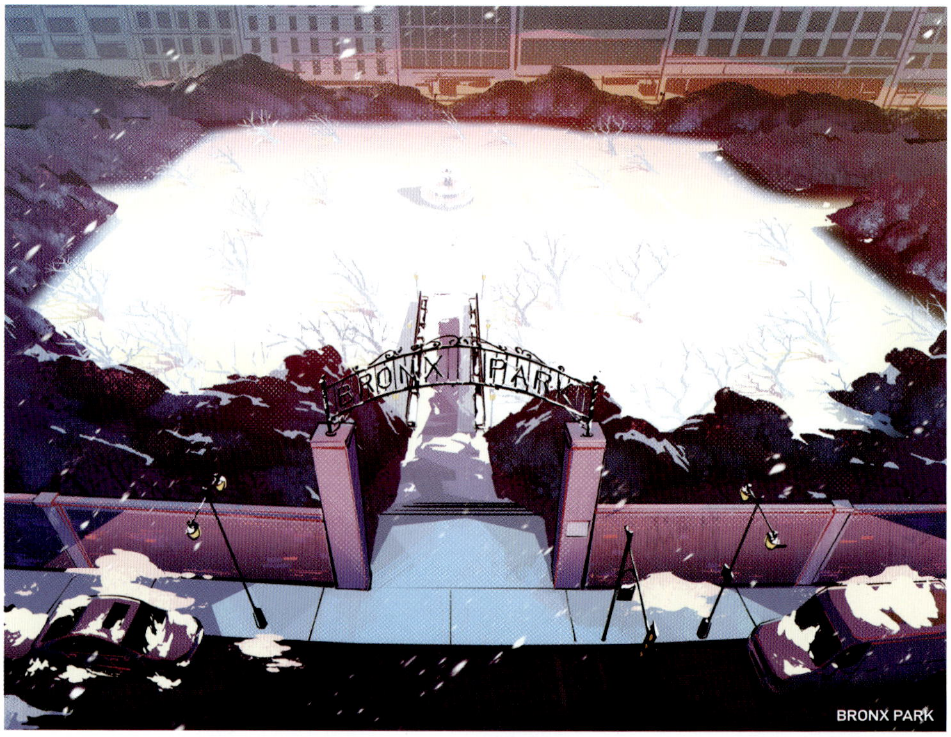

BRONX PARK

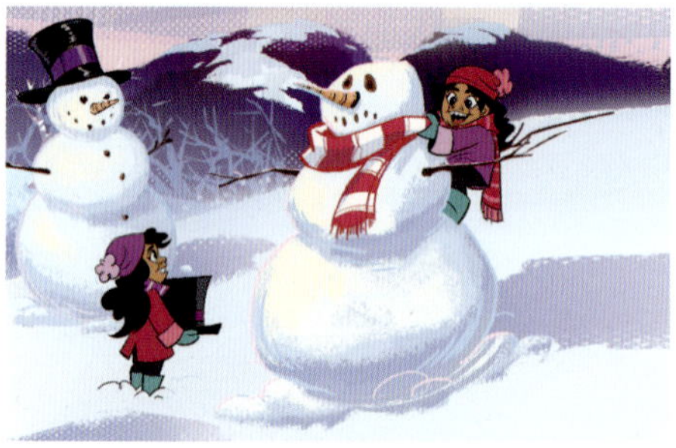

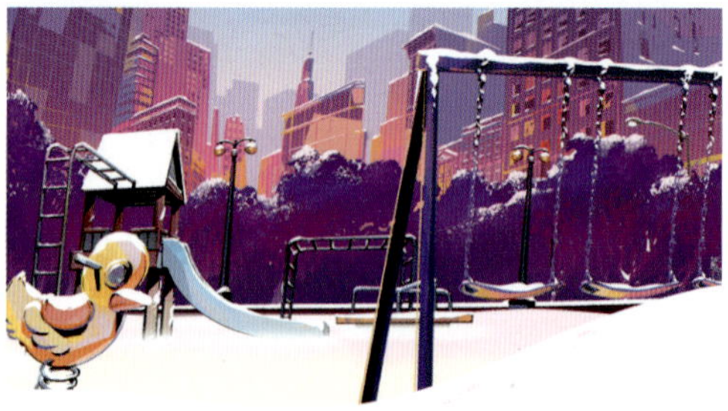

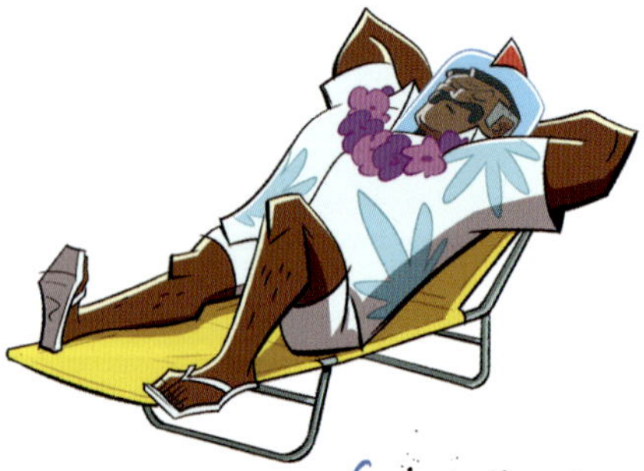

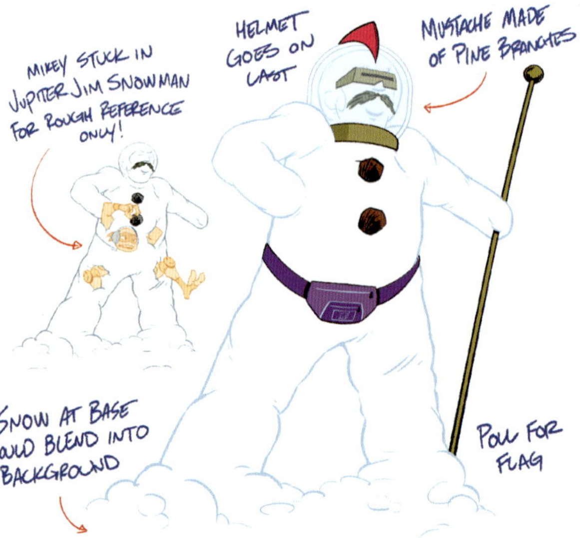

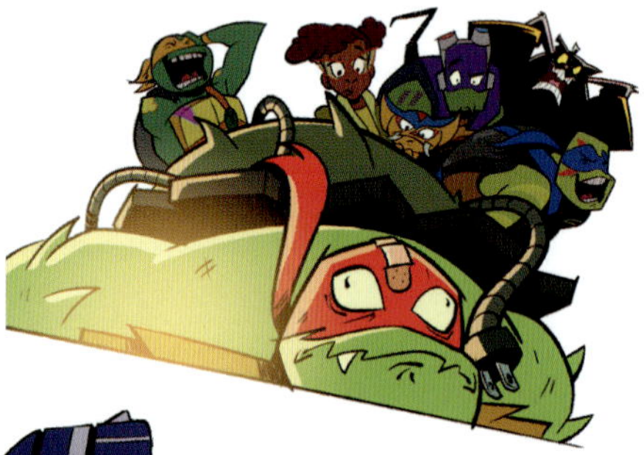

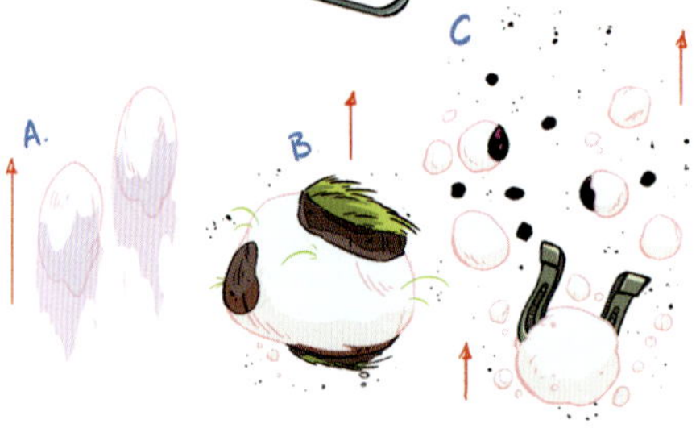

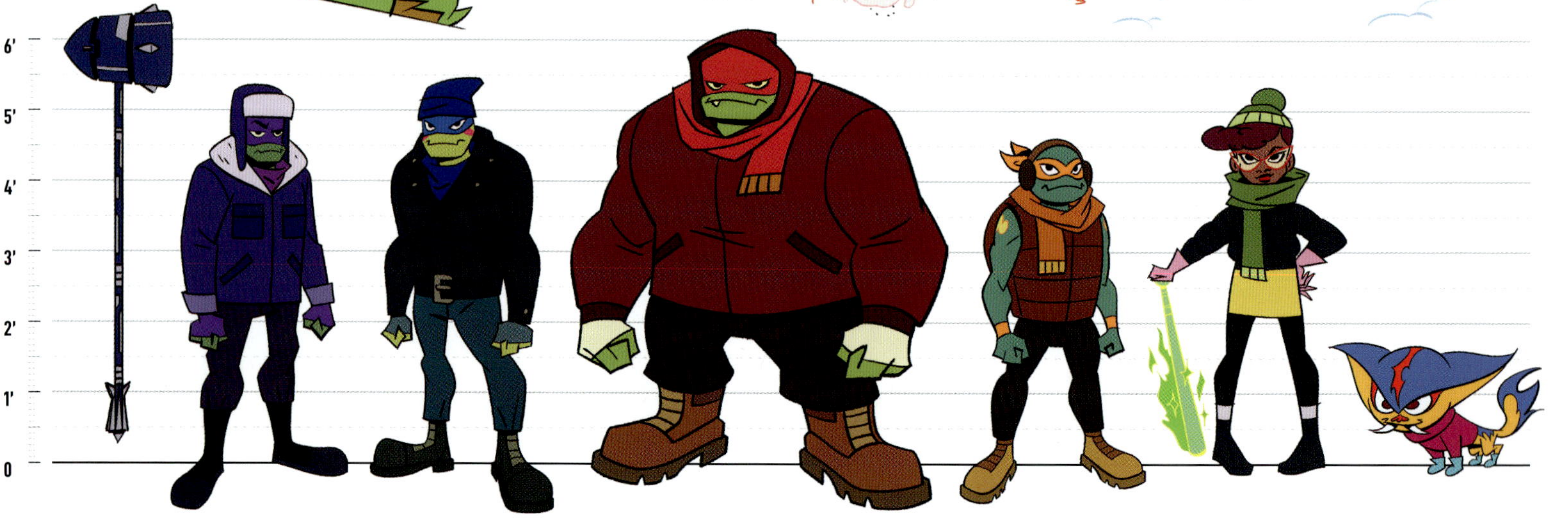

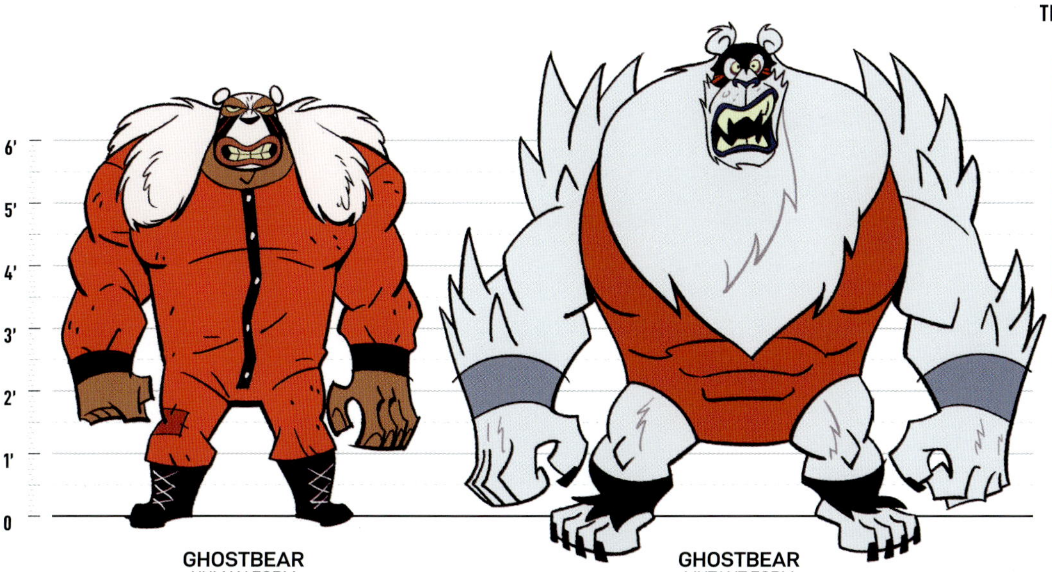

GHOSTBEAR
HUMAN FORM

GHOSTBEAR
MUTANT FORM

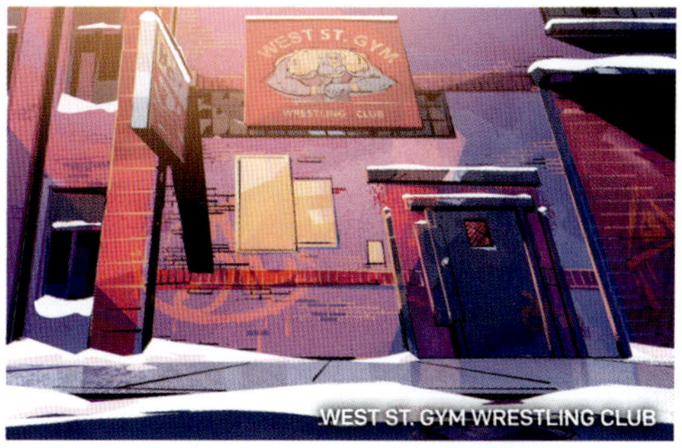

WEST ST. GYM WRESTLING CLUB

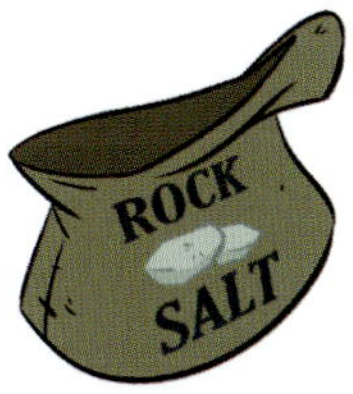

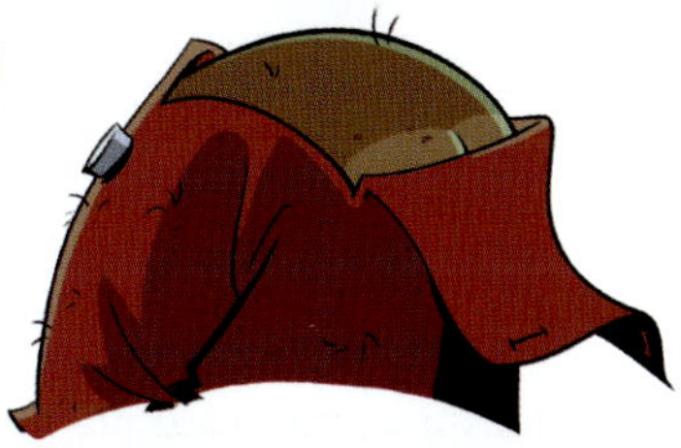

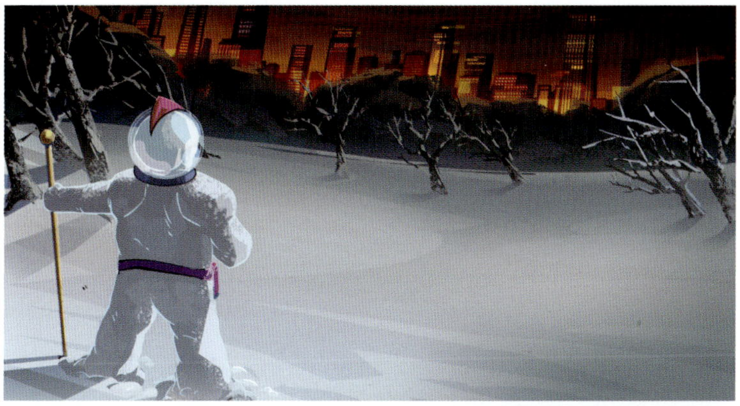

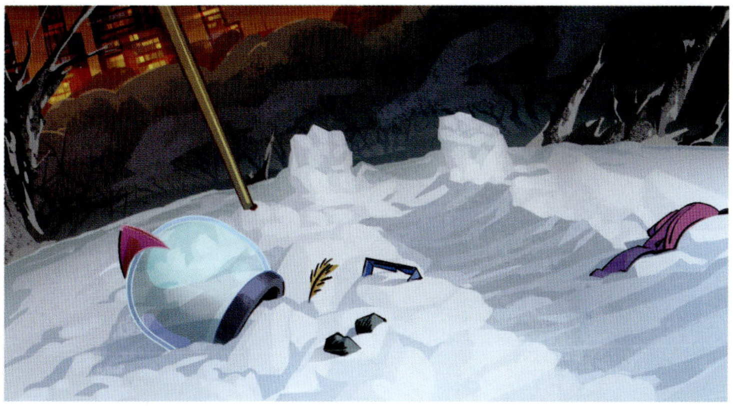

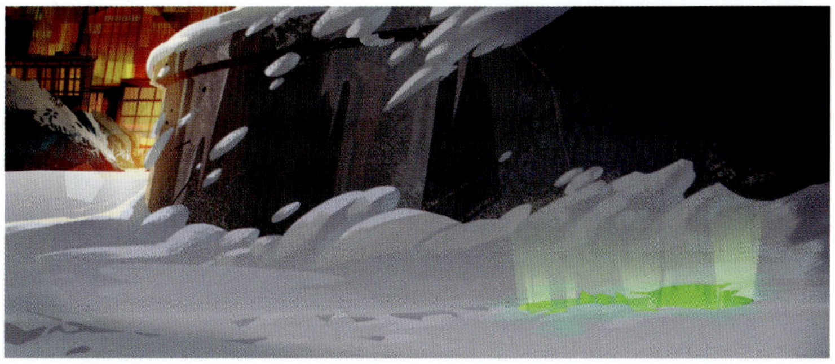

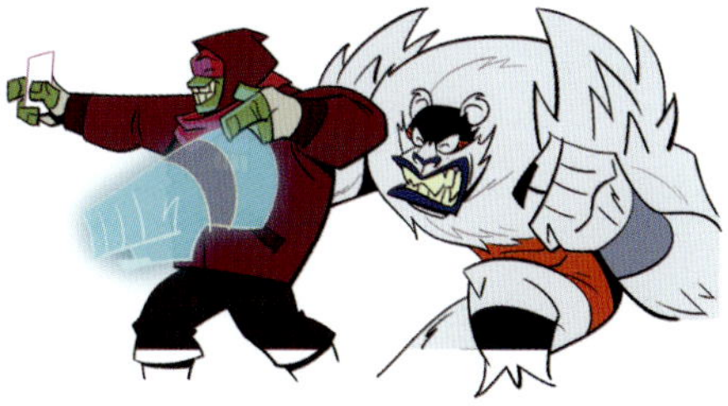

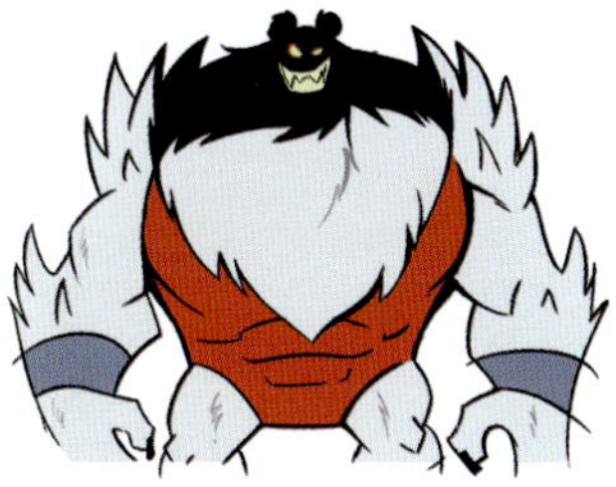

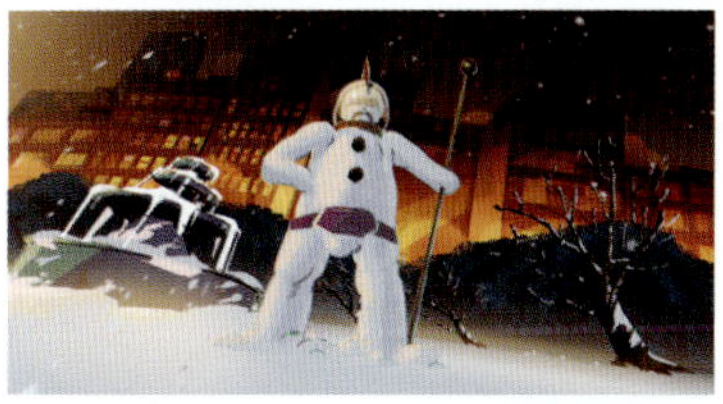

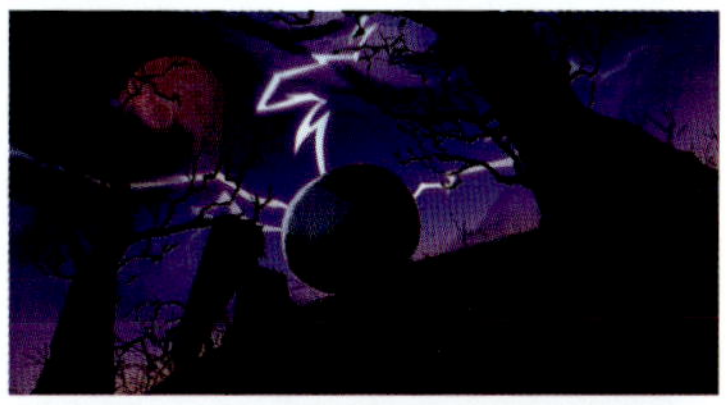

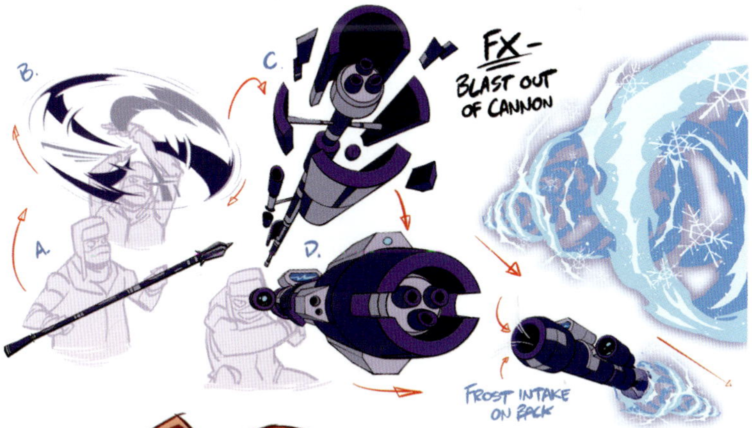

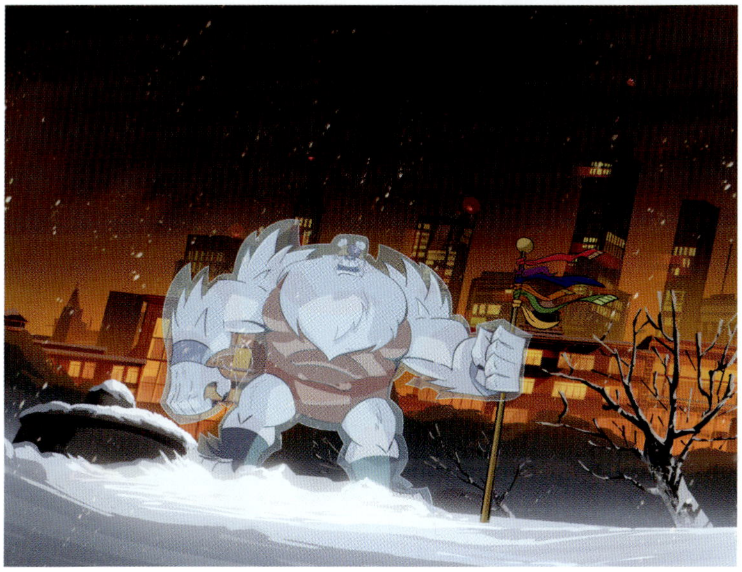

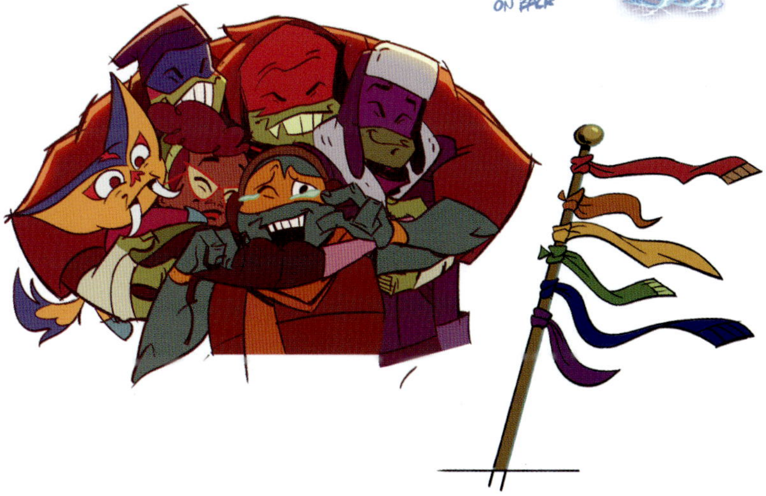

CLOAK AND SWAGGART

ORIGINAL AIR DATE: NOVEMBER 9, 2019
PRODUCTION CODE: 047

WRITTEN BY **JASON MEIER**
STORYBOARDS BY **CHRISTINE LIU**
DIRECTED BY **ALAN WAN**

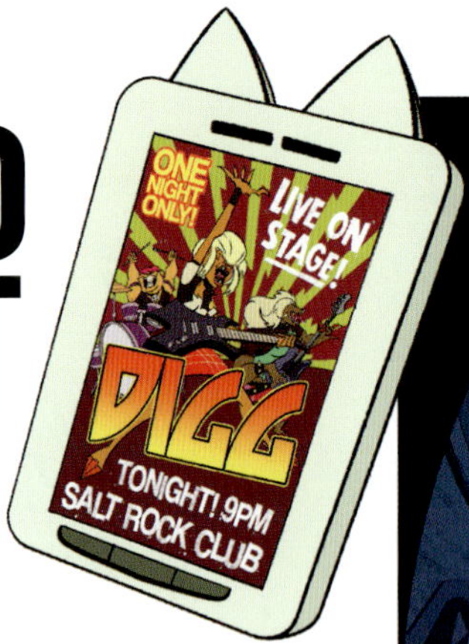

RON CORCILLO: I think we can all agree that Loose Lips Malinowski is one of the more important subordinate characters in entertainment history, and this episode marks his gravel-throated debut, portrayed by Russ. Russ also plays the second barbecue host who shouts *"That's some prime swine!,"* which is based on his obscure alter ego Clem Barnwank. We love Kat's delivery of "Too much hot sauce!" and the shot of her surfing on Sunita's goo. One of our favorite shots, boarded by Morgan Hillebrand, is when Splinter is freaking out inside the Turtle Tank, and he scrambles across the interior and claws right across the camera. That's a great sight gag!

When Rupert Swaggart (a.k.a. Meat Sweats) is describing his appearance, he uses the phrase "boat race," which is Cockney rhyming slang for "face."

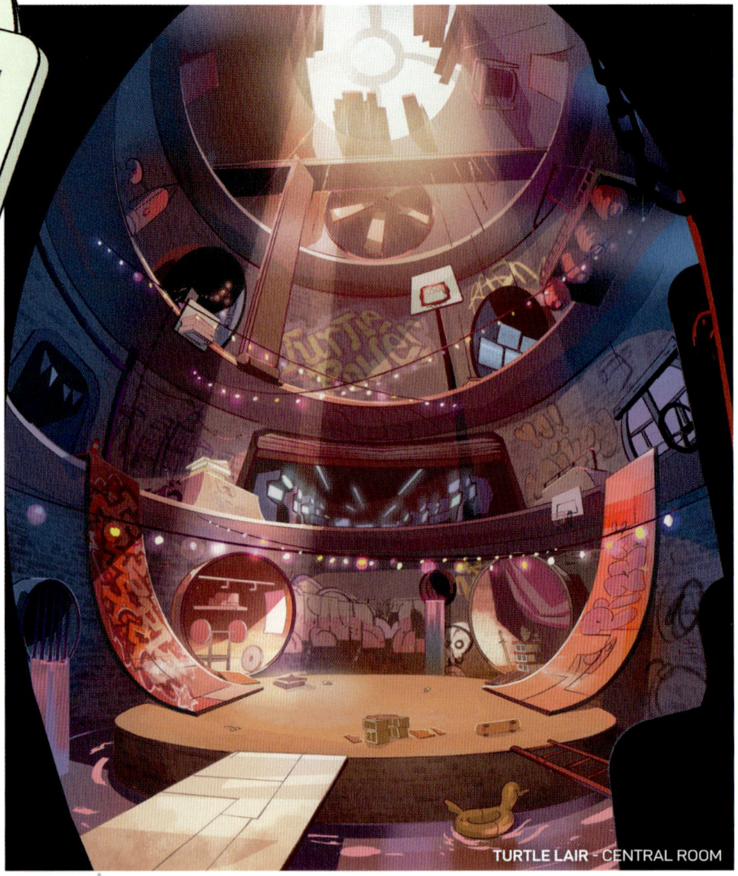
TURTLE LAIR - CENTRAL ROOM

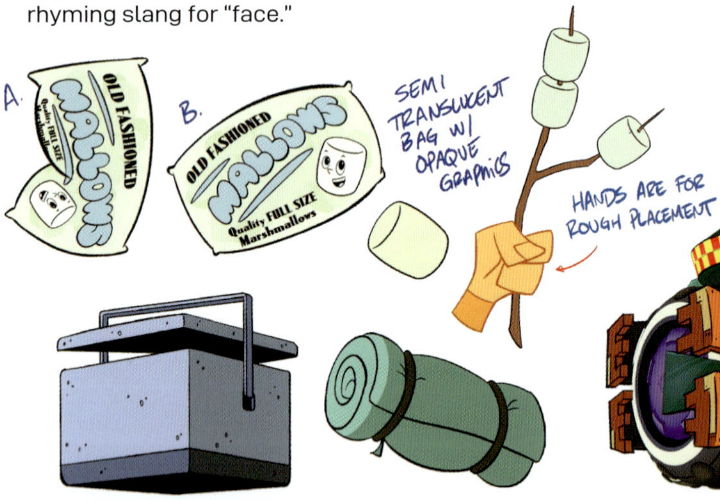

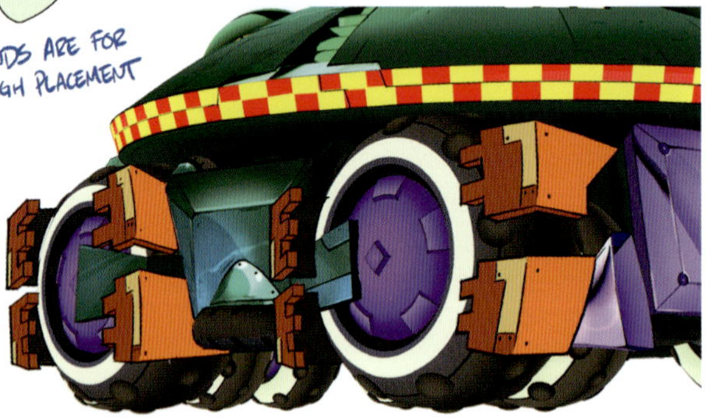

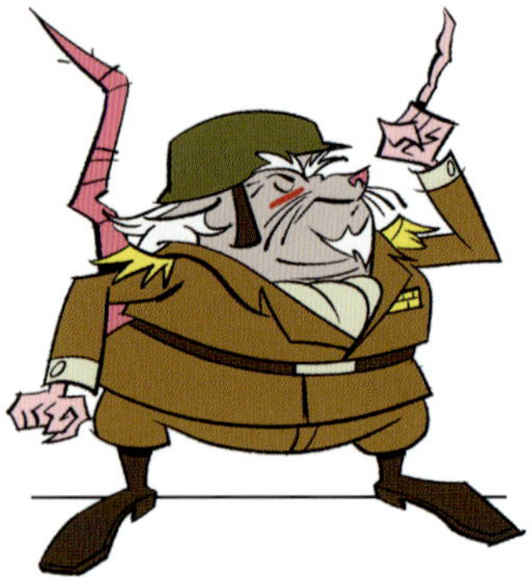

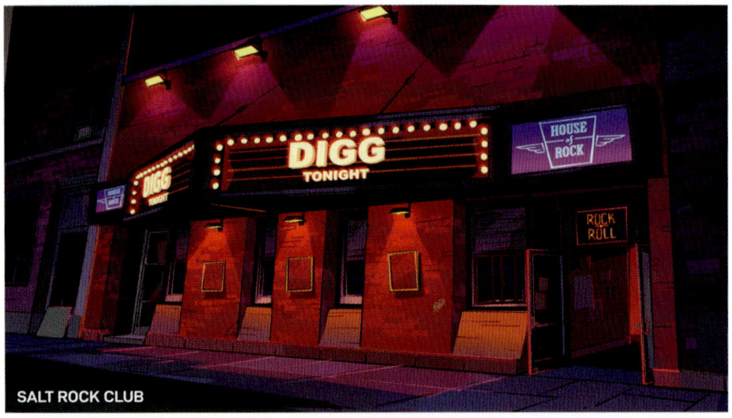

SALT ROCK CLUB

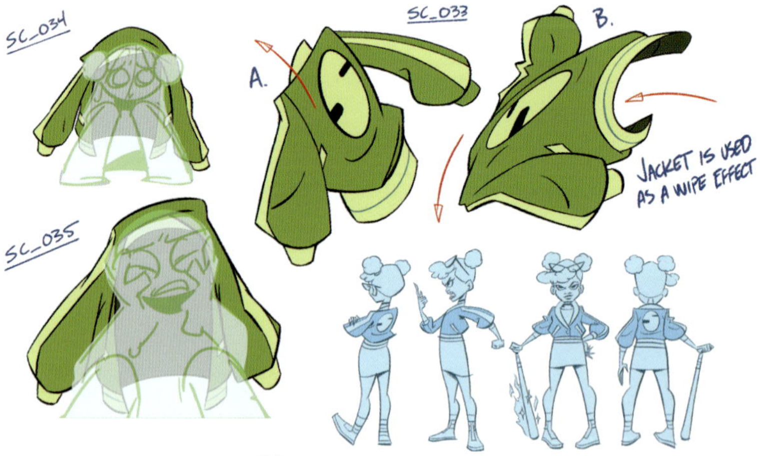

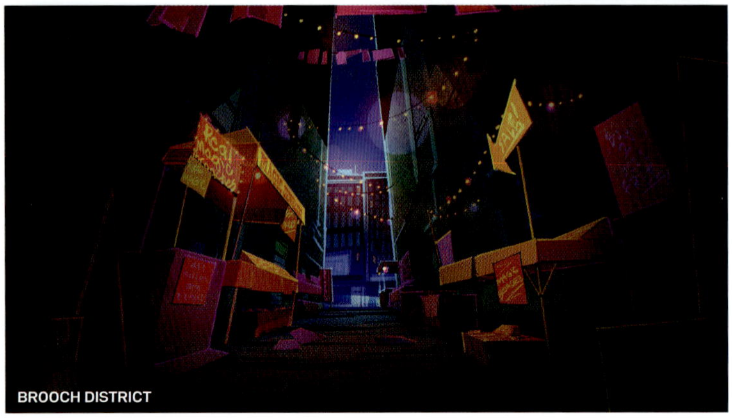
BROOCH DISTRICT

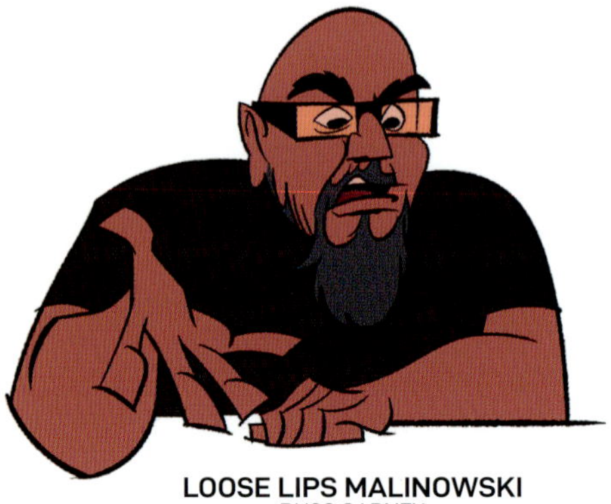
LOOSE LIPS MALINOWSKI
RUSS CARNEY

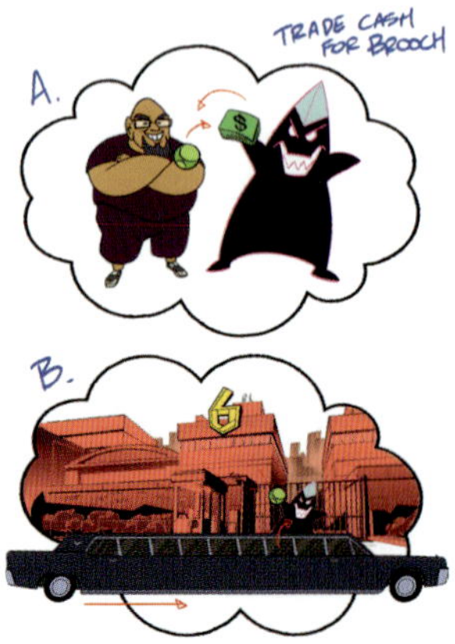

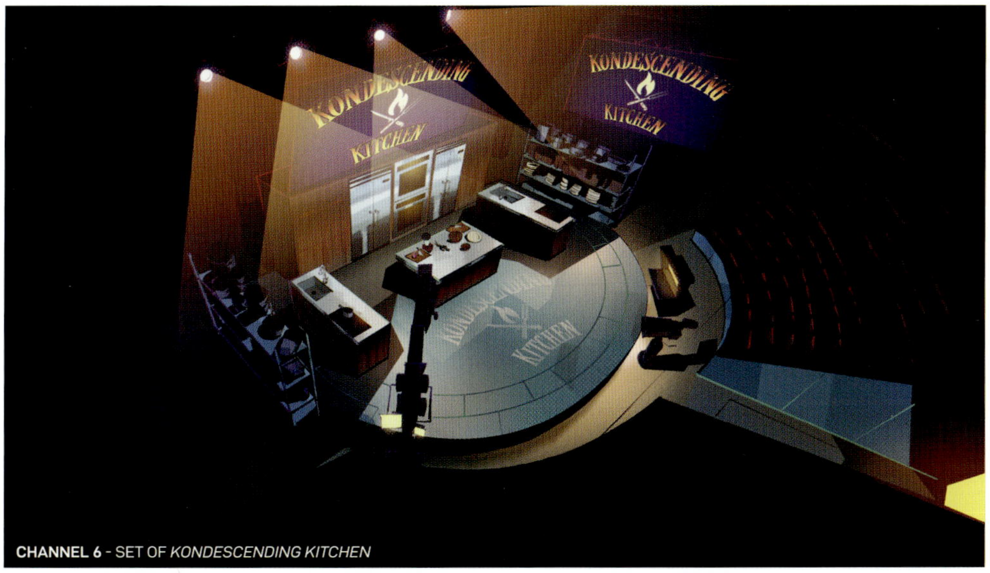

CHANNEL 6 - SET OF *KONDESCENDING KITCHEN*

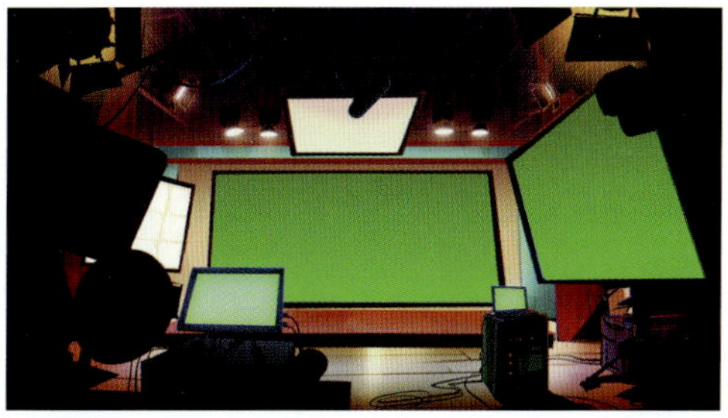

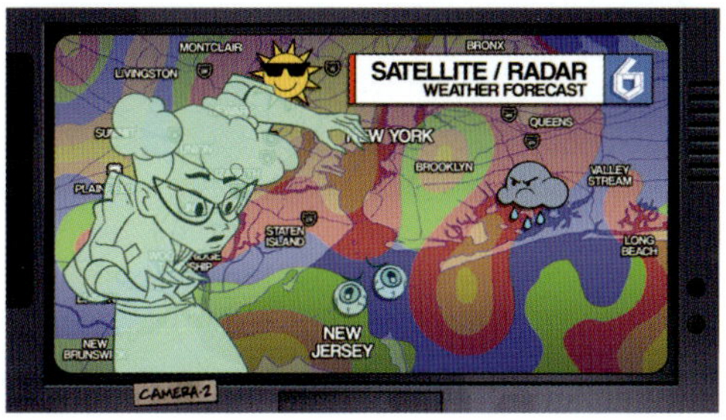

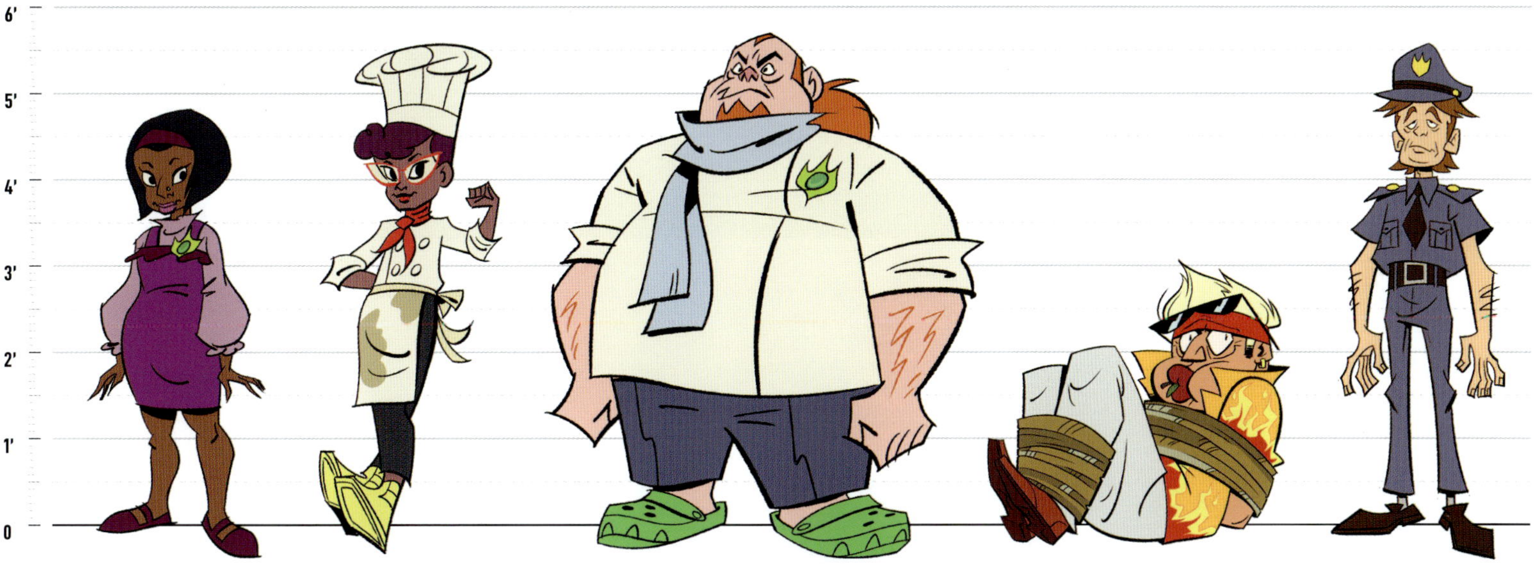

SUNITA
HUMAN FORM

APRIL O'NEIL

RUPERT SWAGGART
MEAT SWEATS

GUY FLAMBÉ

SECURITY GUARD

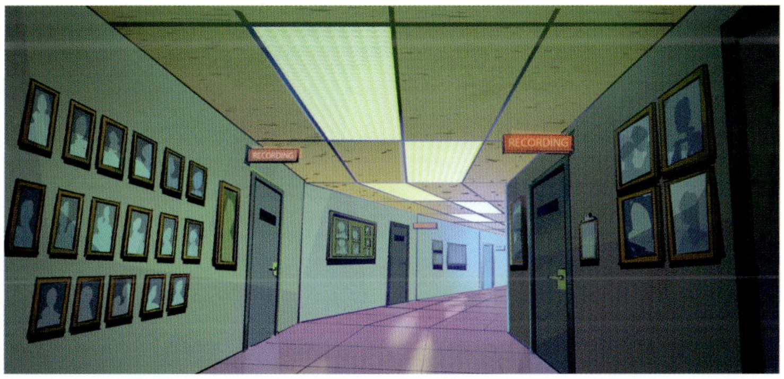

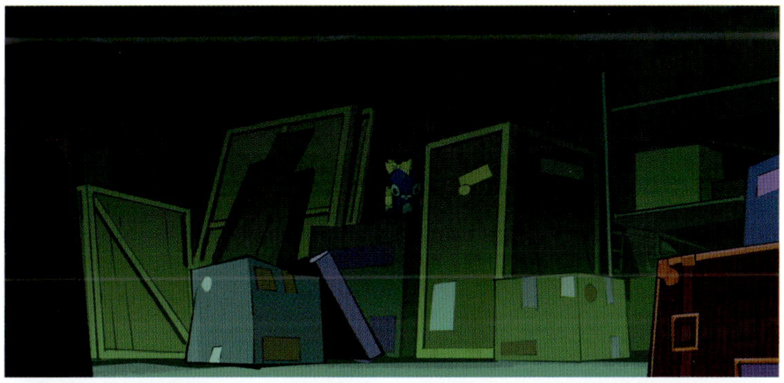

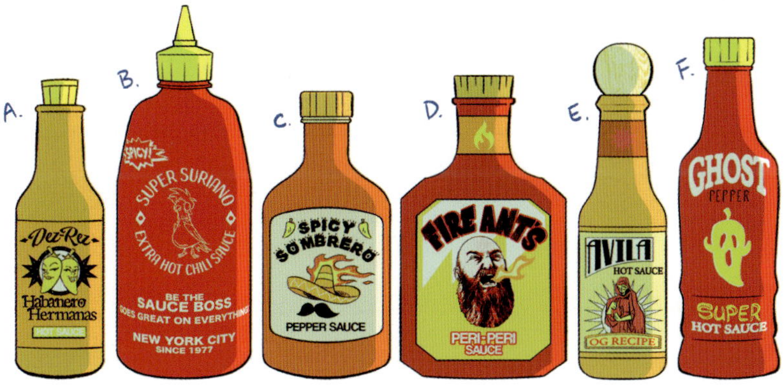

RUSS CARNEY: The hot sauce bottles were inspired by several crew members including art director Andy Suriano, co-creator Ant Ward, associate producer and color designer Tanya Melendez, and production coordinator Cindy Avila.

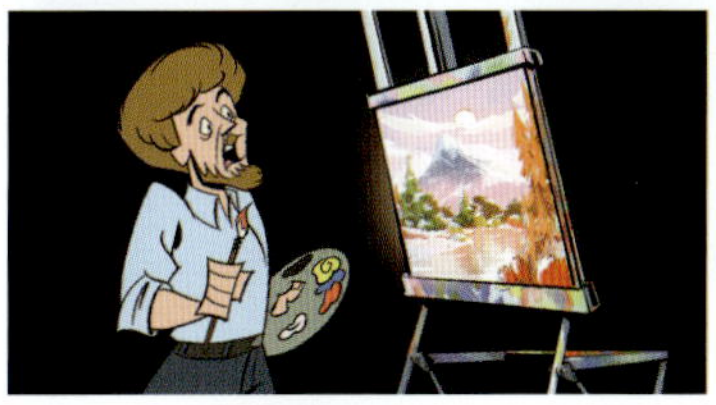

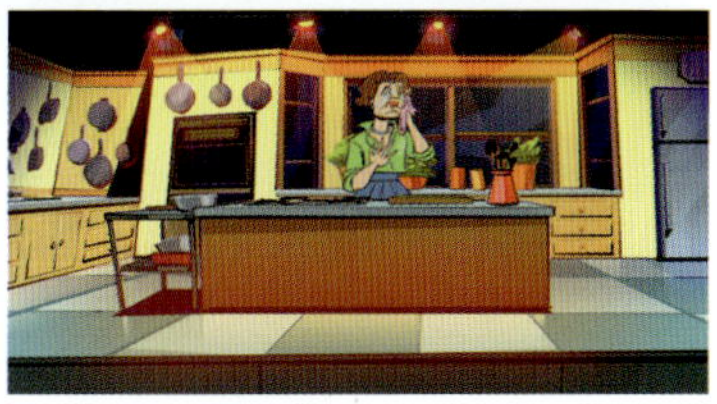

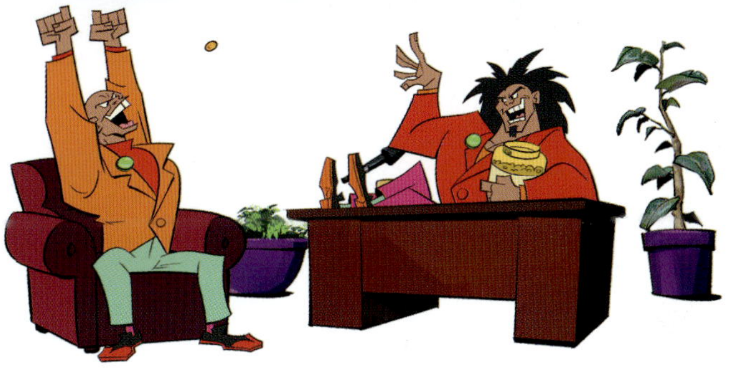

JUPITER JIM AHOY!

ORIGINAL AIR DATE: NOVEMBER 9, 2019
PRODUCTION CODE: 048

WRITTEN BY **IAN BUSCH**
STORYBOARDS BY **ALICIA CHAN**
DIRECTED BY **ABE AUDISH**

IAN BUSCH: The mantra the Turtles shout out in the pilot episode, "Mutant Mayhem," was *"Weapons ahoy!,"* which was inspired by the Jupiter Jim mantra *"Jupiter Jim ahoy!"* that we hear for the first time in this episode.

The actor who plays Jupiter Jim, Marcus Moncrief (voiced by Phil LaMarr), is named after two all-time great Milwaukee Bucks basketball players—Marques Johnson and Sidney Moncrief.

The Robot Vampires make their second appearance in the series. We see they are tied in to Jupiter Jim lore, explaining why they were Times Square mascot characters back in "Mascot Melee."

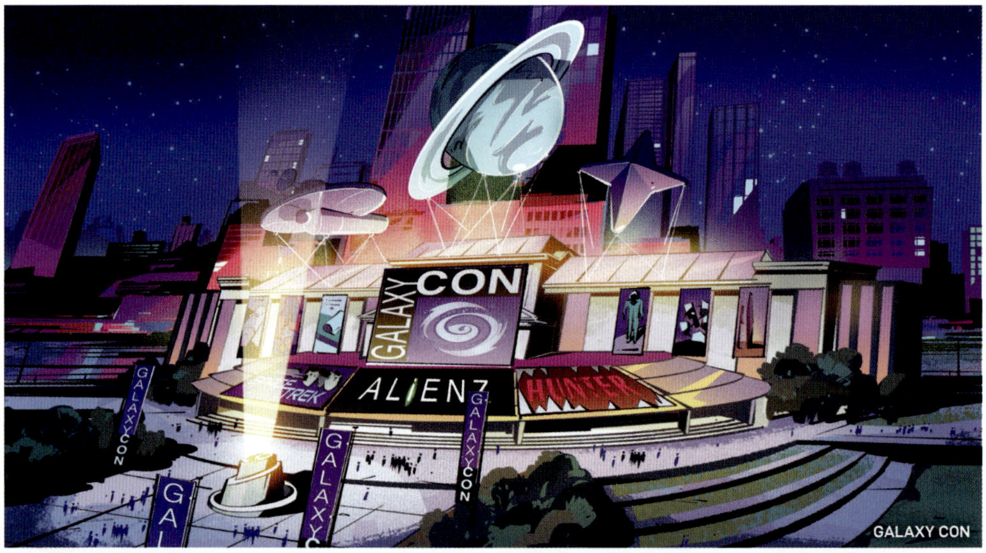

GALAXY CON

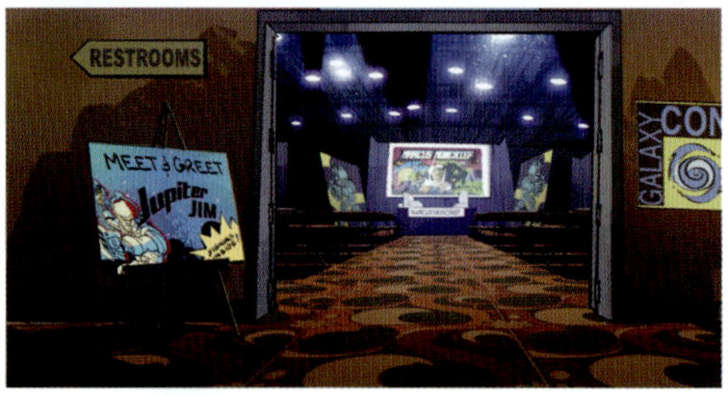

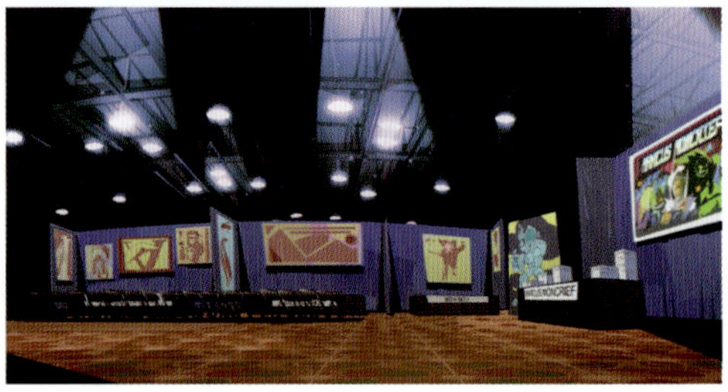

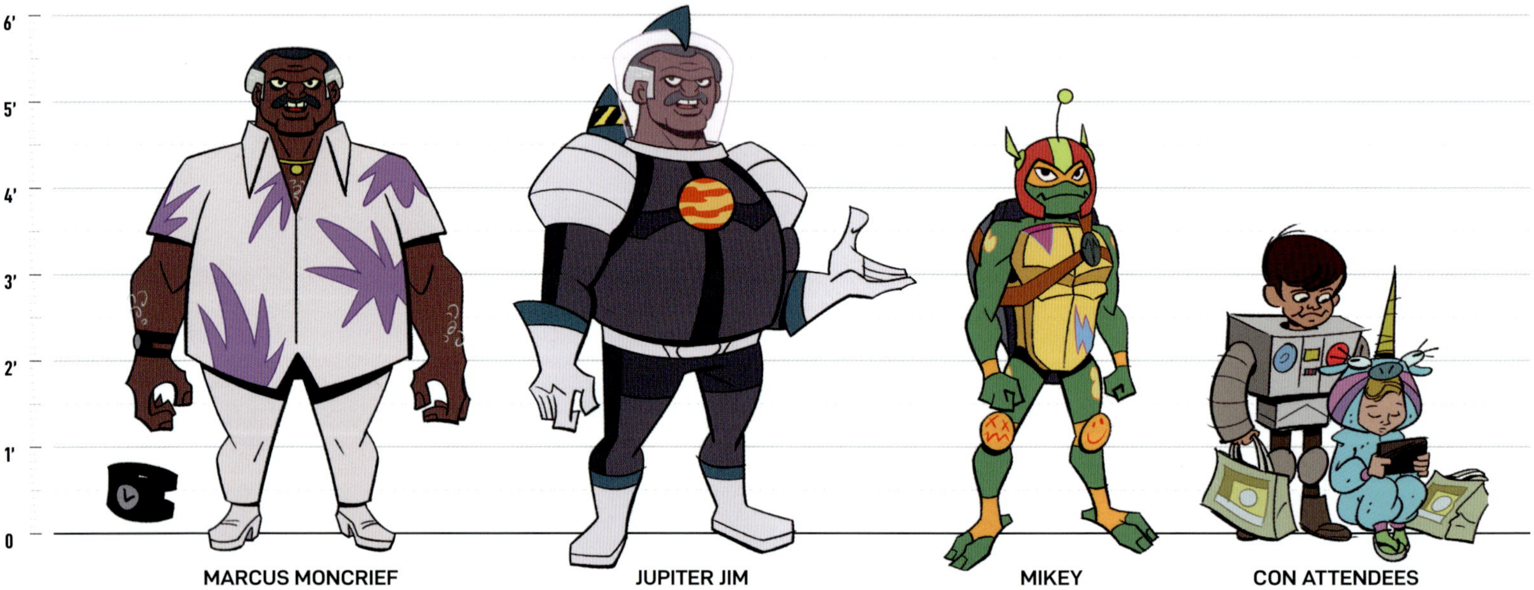

MARCUS MONCRIEF

JUPITER JIM

MIKEY

CON ATTENDEES

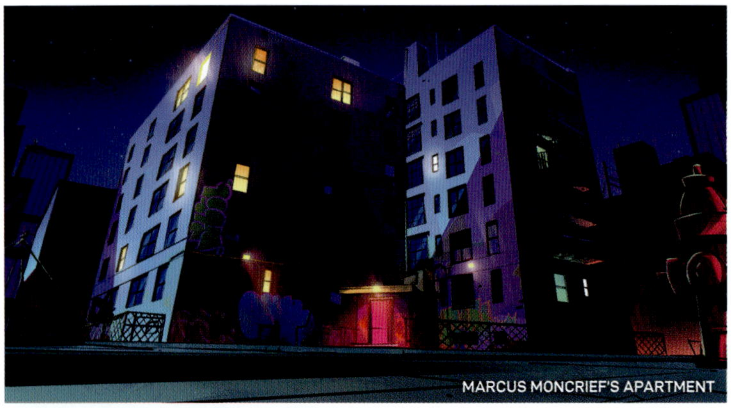

MARCUS MONCRIEF'S APARTMENT

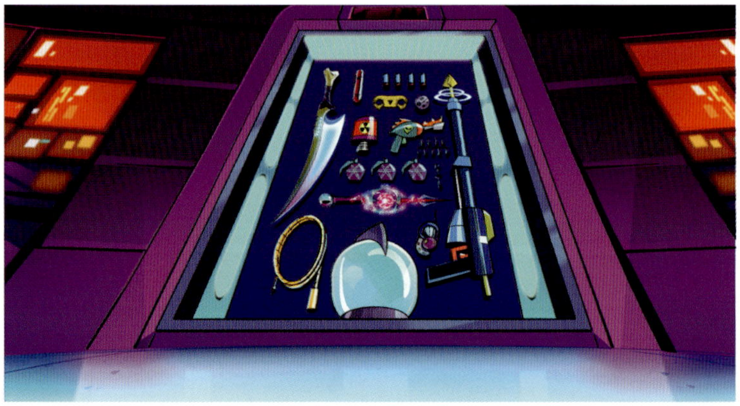

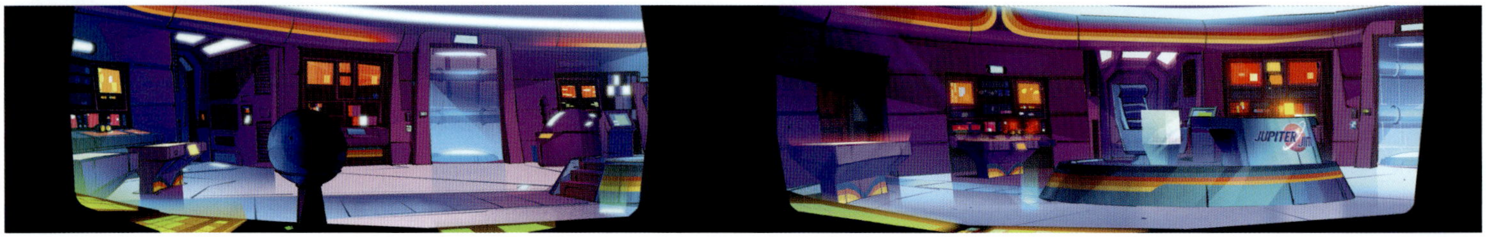

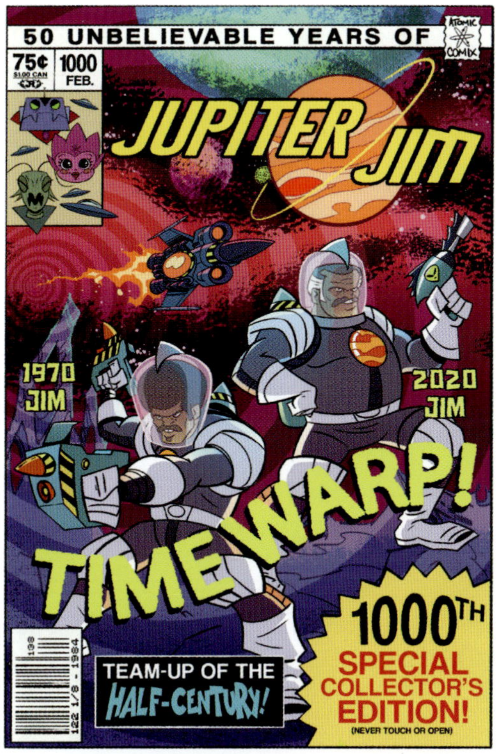

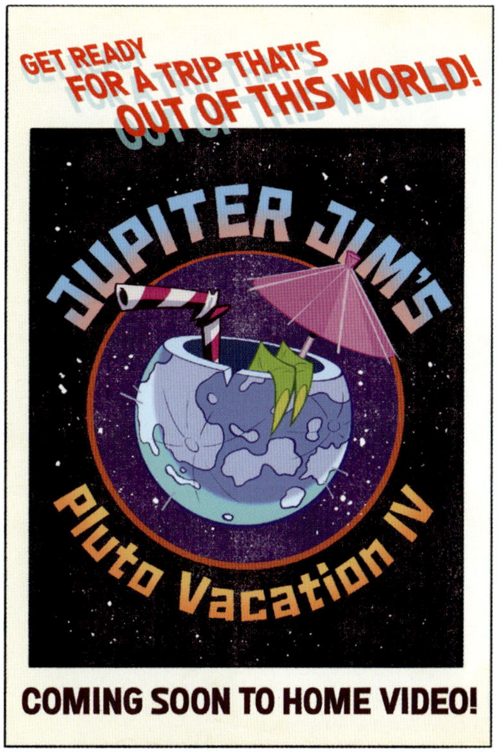

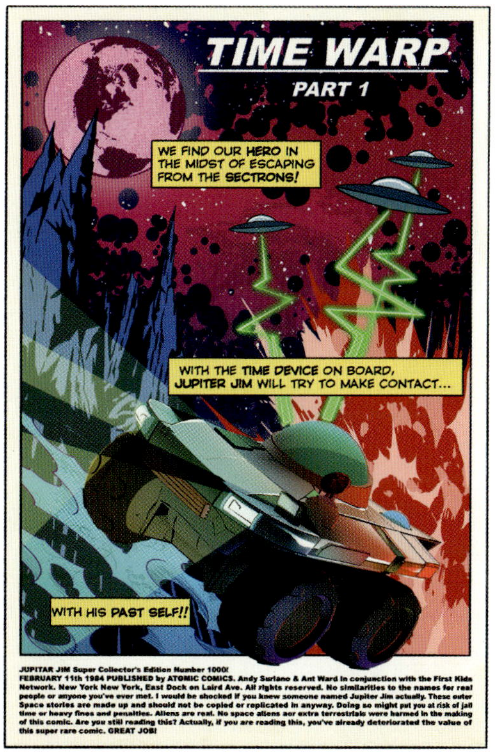

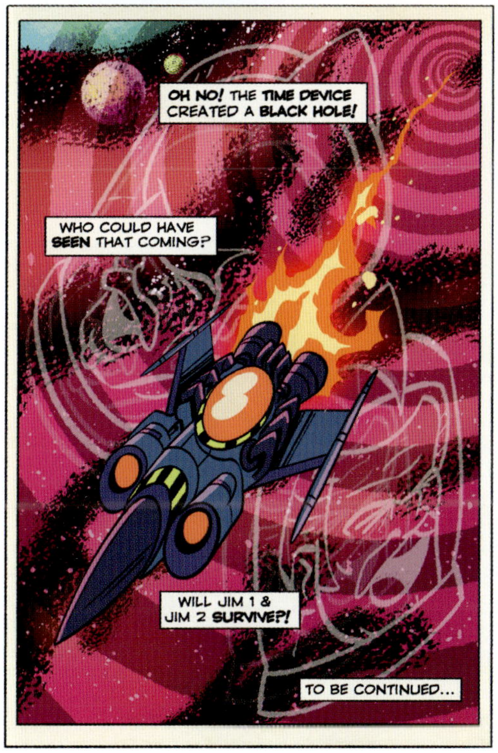

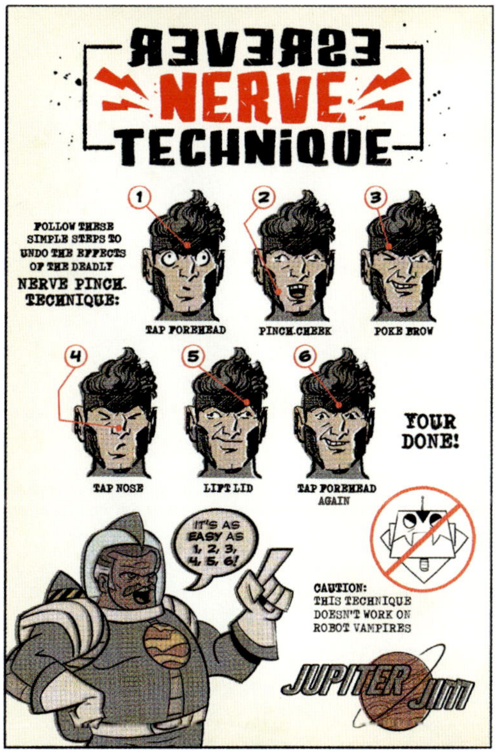

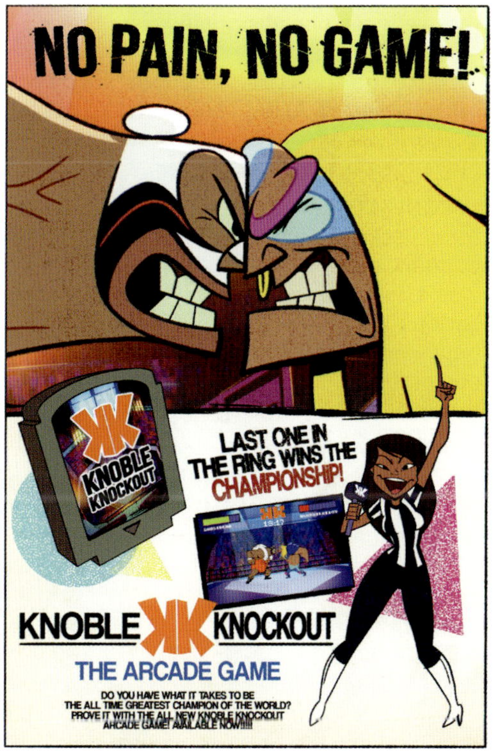

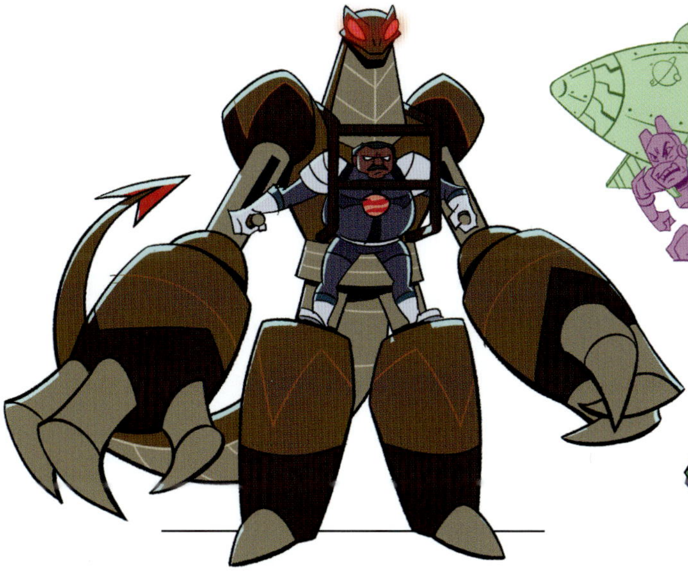
CRUSHASAURUS MECH

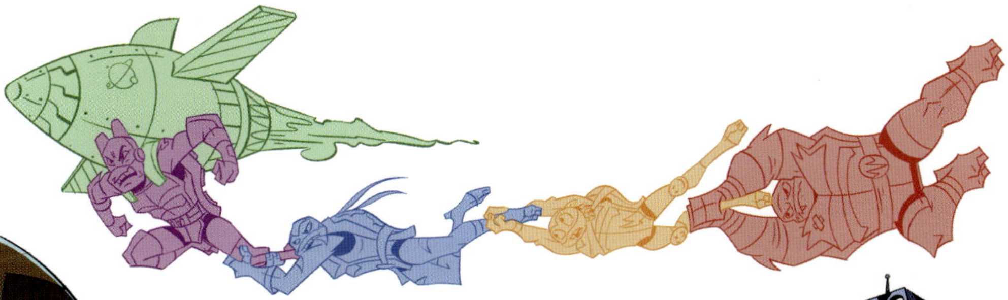

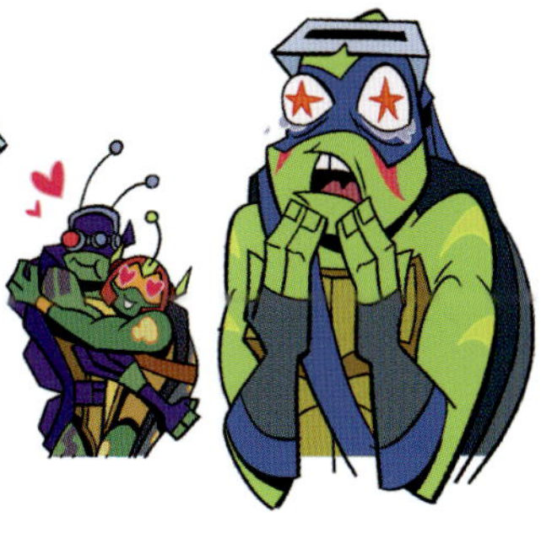

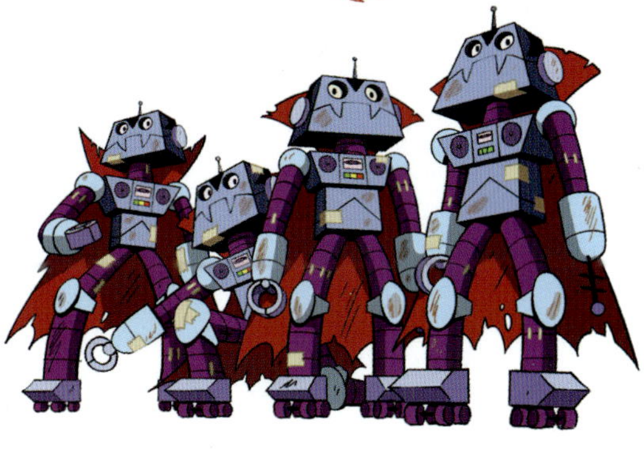

INSANE IN THE MAMA TRAIN

ORIGINAL AIR DATE: NOVEMBER 16, 2019
PRODUCTION CODE: 049-050

WRITTEN BY **JESSE GORDON**
STORYBOARDS BY **JAKE CASTORENA, JJ CONWAY, KEVIN MOLINA-ORTIZ, SAM MONTES**
DIRECTED BY **SEBASTIAN MONTES**

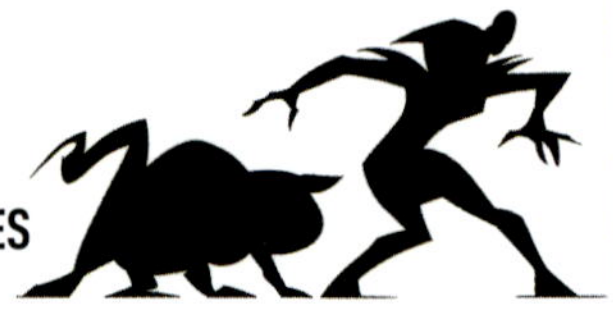

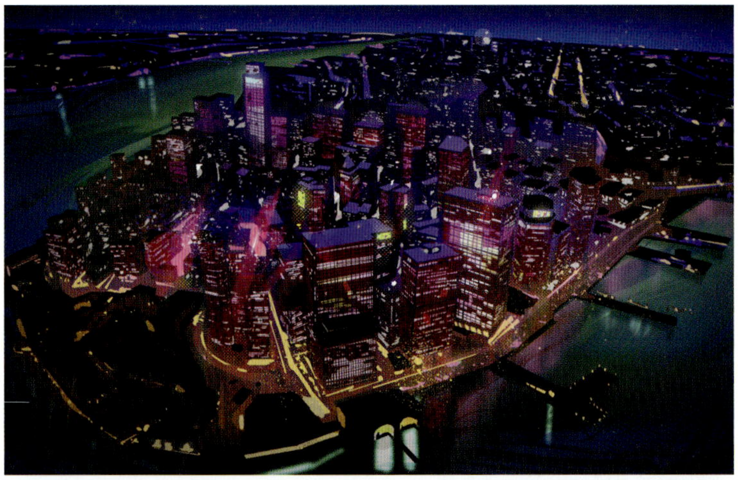

TONY GAMA-LOBO (STORY EDITOR): We knew we needed a massive season finale to the Dark Armor storyline, so we broke the last two double episodes as one big story. "Breaking a story" is a writing term that describes the effort of turning an idea into a full-fledged story. You have to figure out all of the story's comedy, action and drama beats, and character arcs and work out all of the logic problems, and it's the hardest part of writing a script.] It had to tie in all the things—the Hidden City, the Foot Clan, Splinter becoming the mentor and father everyone wanted, and of course the Turtles "rising." Jesse had this crazy idea for a while about a luxury *Snowpiercer*-esque train, so we decided that's how Draxum was moving the armor. The fight sequences were awesome—the train car portal-hopping was bananas—but what made this episode for me was the emotional story of the Turtles trying to prove to their dad they're serious, succeeding at being "real ninjas," but ultimately failing and getting caught. The Ancestor Spirit inside the ancient scroll was voiced by Hoon Lee, the actor who played Splinter in the 2012 series.

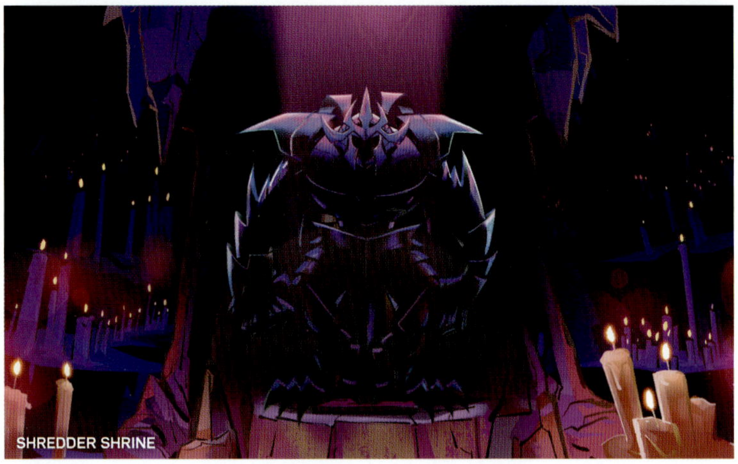

SHREDDER SHRINE

JJ CONWAY: It's easy for comedy and drama to undermine each other, so the montage where the Turtles shed their colorful bandanas and embrace their responsibility as Hamato warriors was a tough balancing act. We leaned into the Turtles being "so serious it's funny" because we never wanted to doubt that they believed in their change. To symbolically show that the Turtles had embraced this more serious side of themselves, I ended their training montage with a homage to the cover of Mirage's *TMNT* #1.

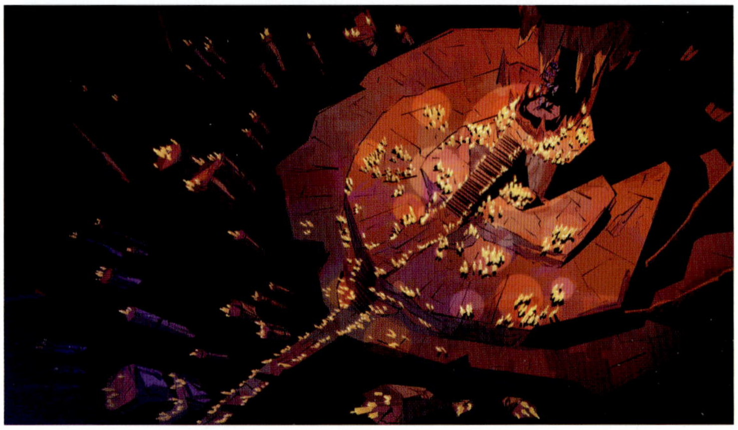

TONY GAMA-LOBO: The scene where Draxum pays Big Mama for the use of her Mystic Train was originally an homage to the briefcase in *Pulp Fiction* (1994). We were gonna have Draxum open this briefcase and never show the inside—just a gold glow. But then, as the episode was being finalized, we were working on the script for "Battle Nexus: New York" and had the idea that maybe the Mystic Orb was the thing Draxum gave Big Mama. So Andy had someone do a quick design for the orb and we inserted it into "Mama Train" at the last minute.

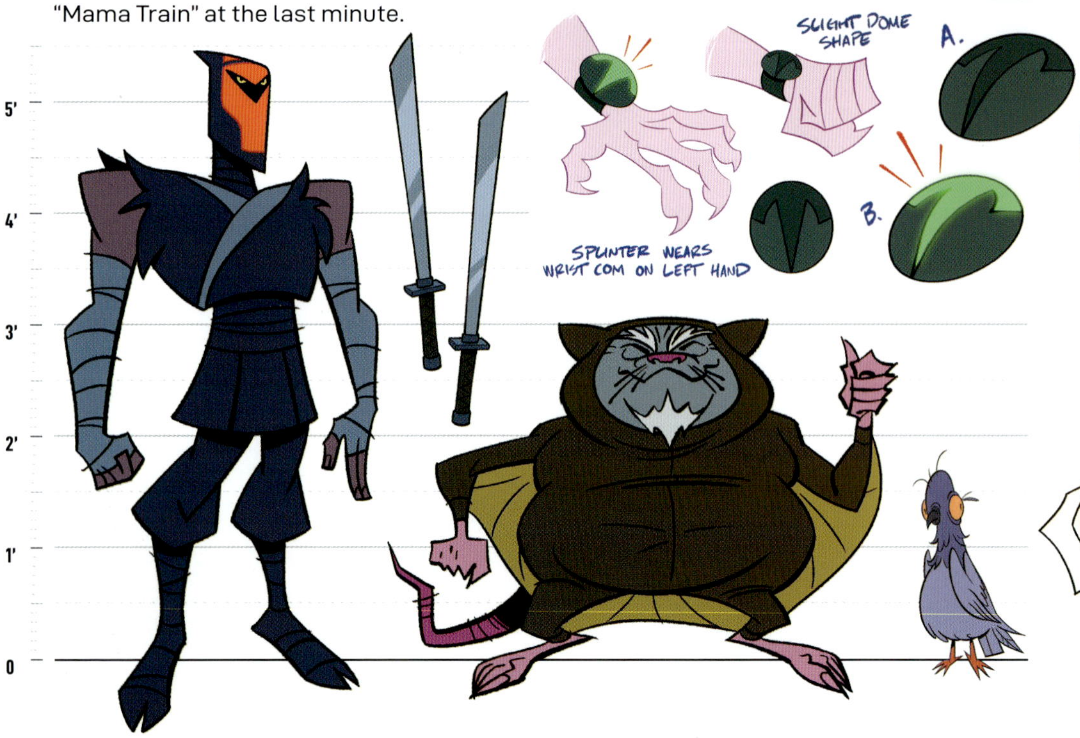

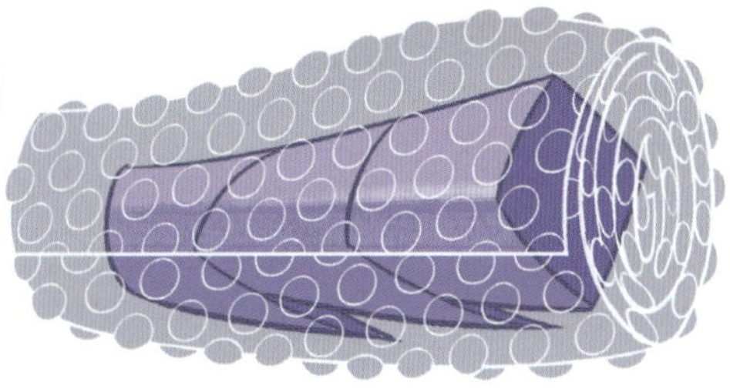

KUROI YŌROI
REREBRACE

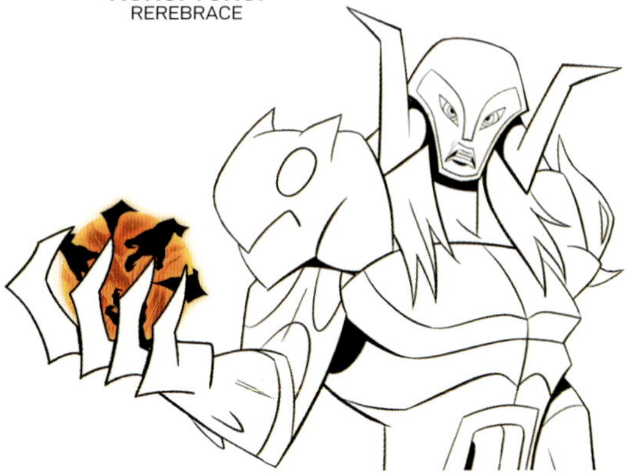

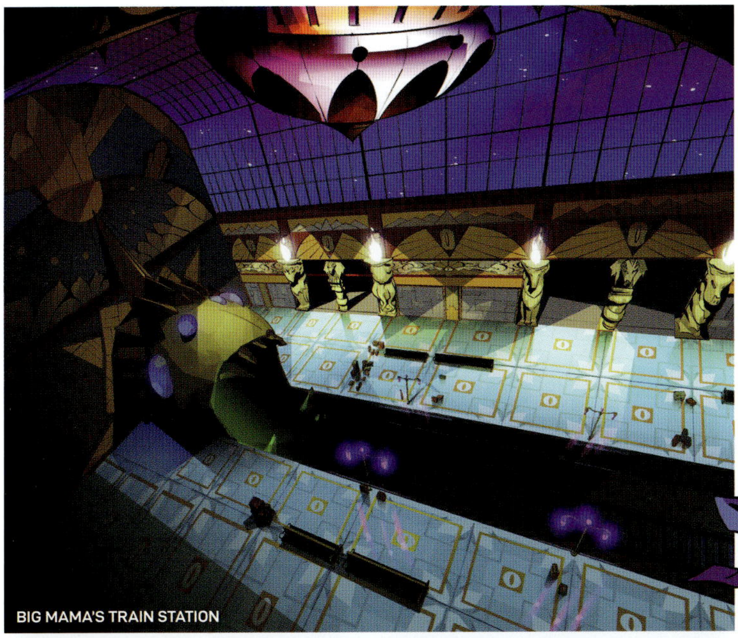

BIG MAMA'S TRAIN STATION

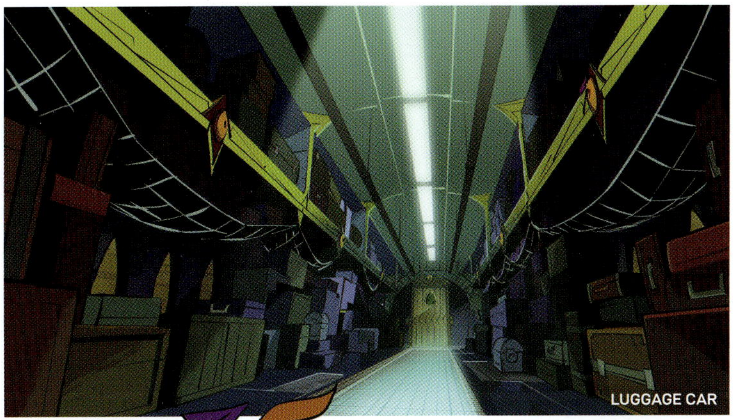

LUGGAGE CAR

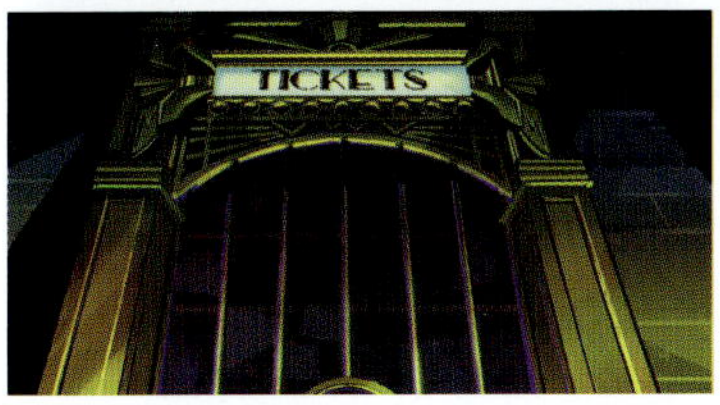

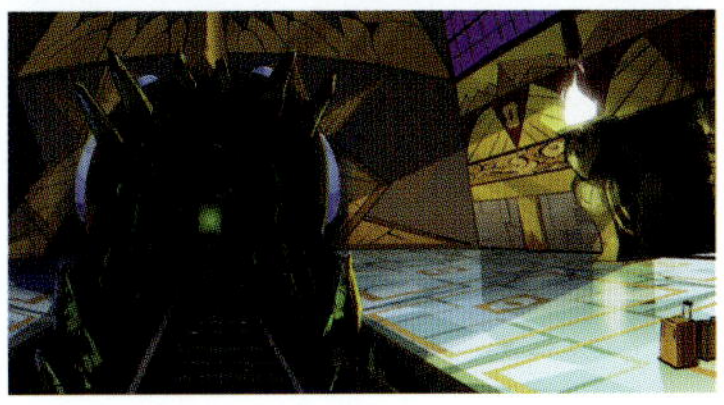

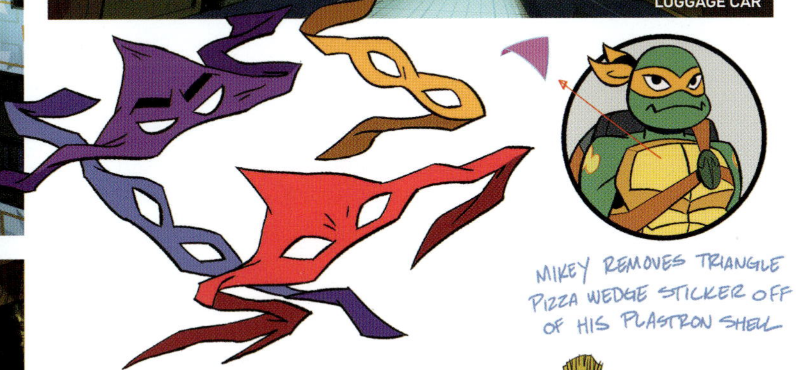

JESSE GORDON: This episode has so much going on. We had a lot of stuff to pay off, and I really wanted to do a train heist. The whole point of the show was that it was the start of the Turtles; at this point they were not experts with their weapons or being a team. The show was very comedy forward, which may be different than some other Turtle shows. I always loved that they were imperfect and not a great team. It was so much fun for comedy, and I loved that after a prank war, which was sort of an homage to *Neighbors* (2014), it was time to get serious.

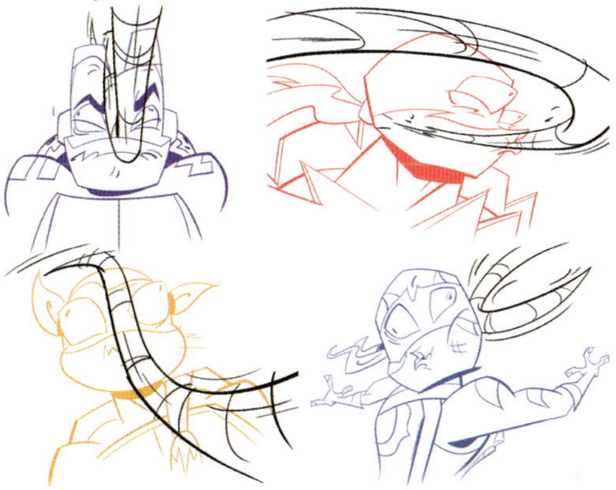

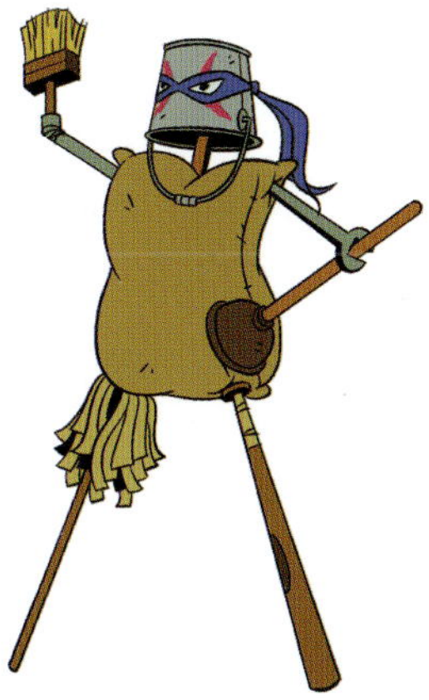

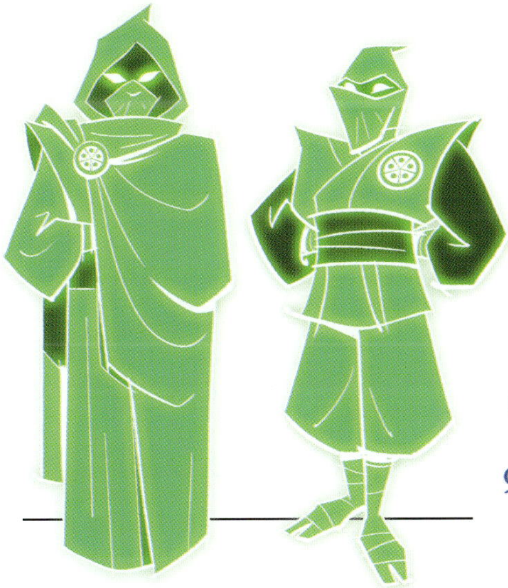

MYSTIC AURA

HAMATO CLAN ANCESTORS

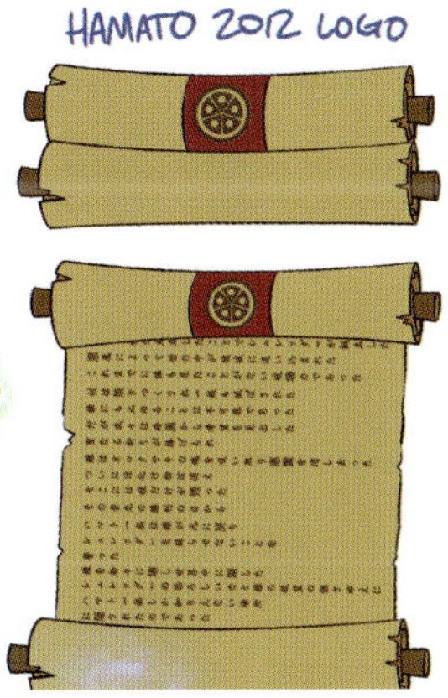

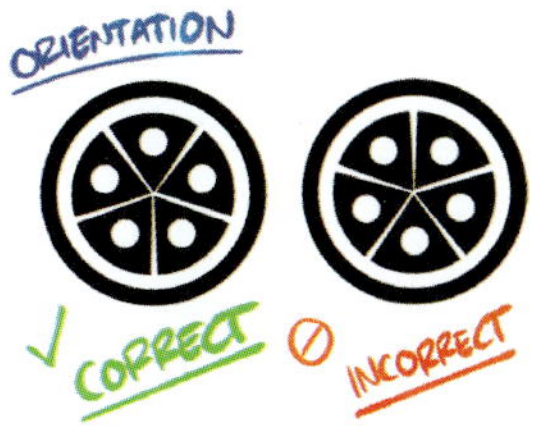

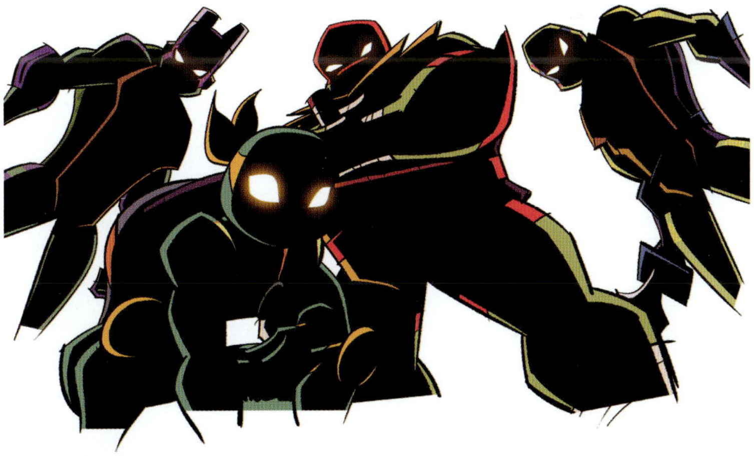

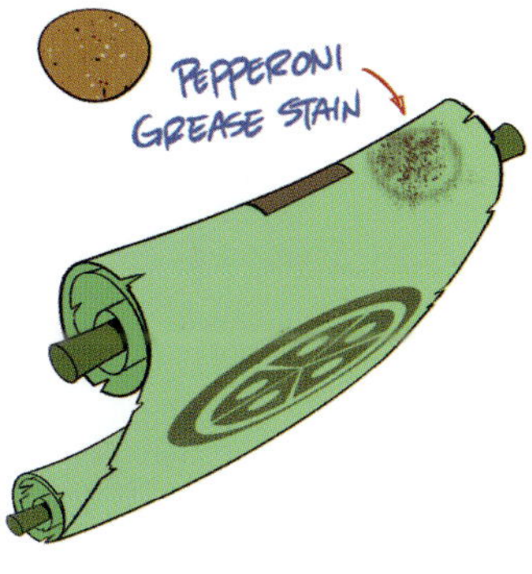

そして鍵が完成したことでシュレッダーが誕生した
悪魔によって世の中が破滅に追い込まれた
これまでに誰も見たことがない破壊力であった
村は焼きつくされ一族も滅ぼされた
誰にも止めることは不可能であった
だが我々は暗黒から希望を見出した
聖なる祈りが捧げられ
鍵はオロクサキの魂を吸い取り悪霊を消し去った
ついには化け物は消え
そこには鍵だけが残った
その栄光の勝利の日から
ハマト一族は鍵が元に戻り
シュレッダーを蘇らせないことを
誓った
鍵を粉々に壊し世界中に隠した
シュレッダーの恐ろしい力と鍵の欲望の強さゆえに
ハマト一族しか知りえない場所
に隠されたのであった
だが
もしまた鍵が元の形に戻りシュレッダーが蘇ることがあれば
地球を守るために
命をかけて闘うことがこの一族の使命である
鍵を隠すヒント

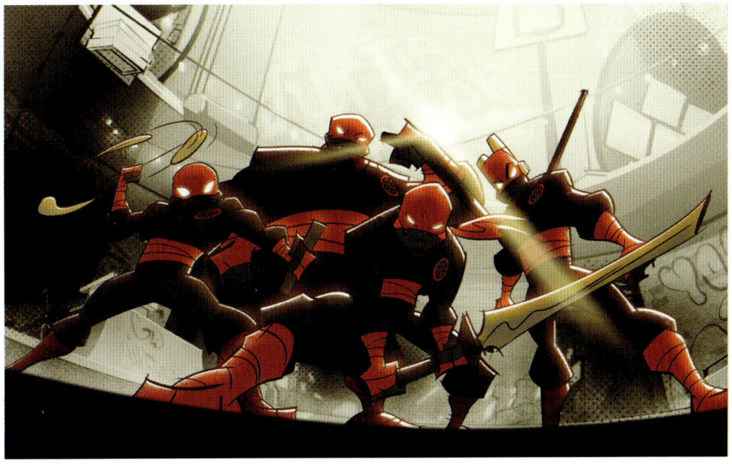

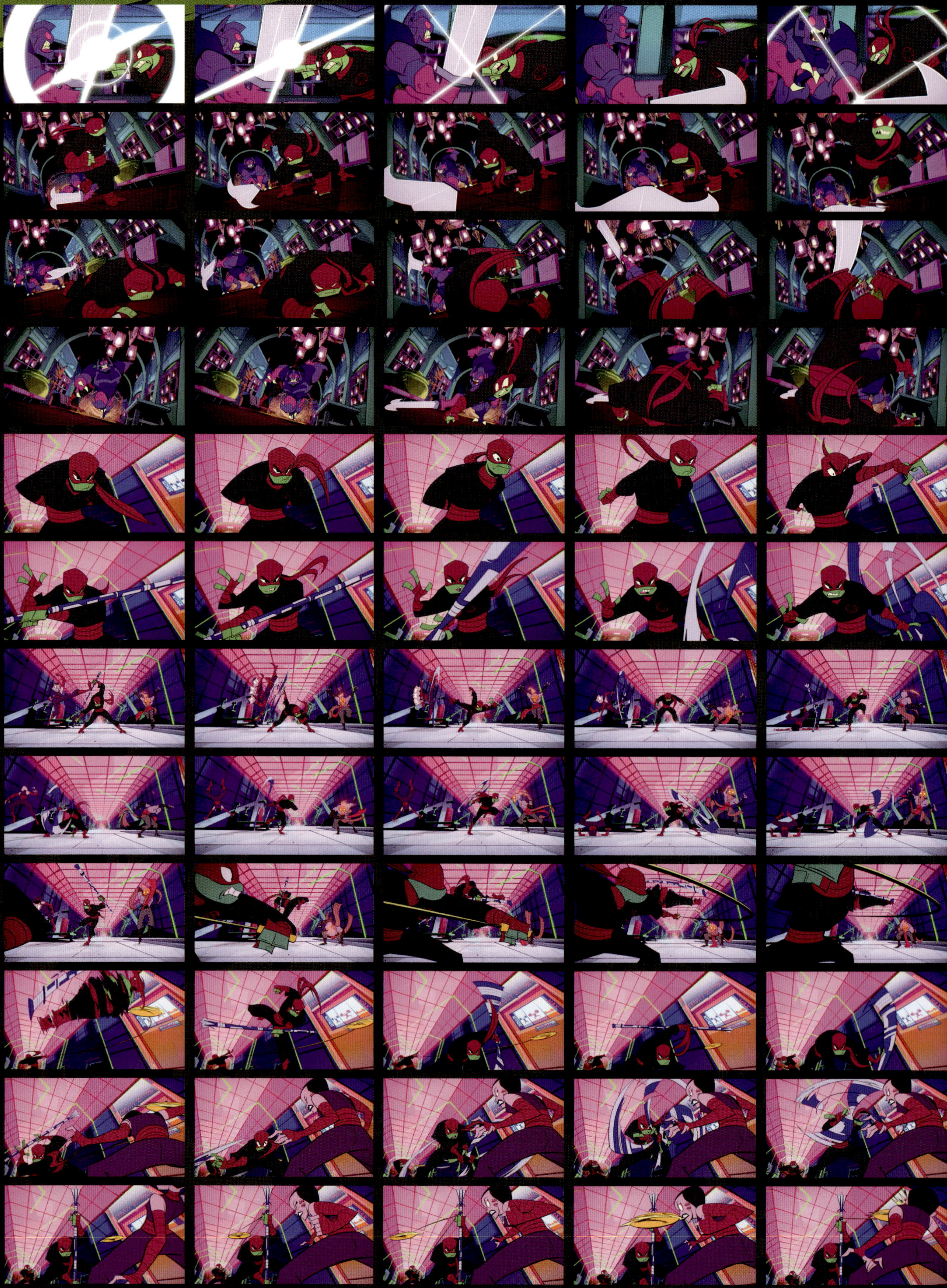

STORYBOARD ARTIST: **KEVIN MOLINA-ORTIZ**

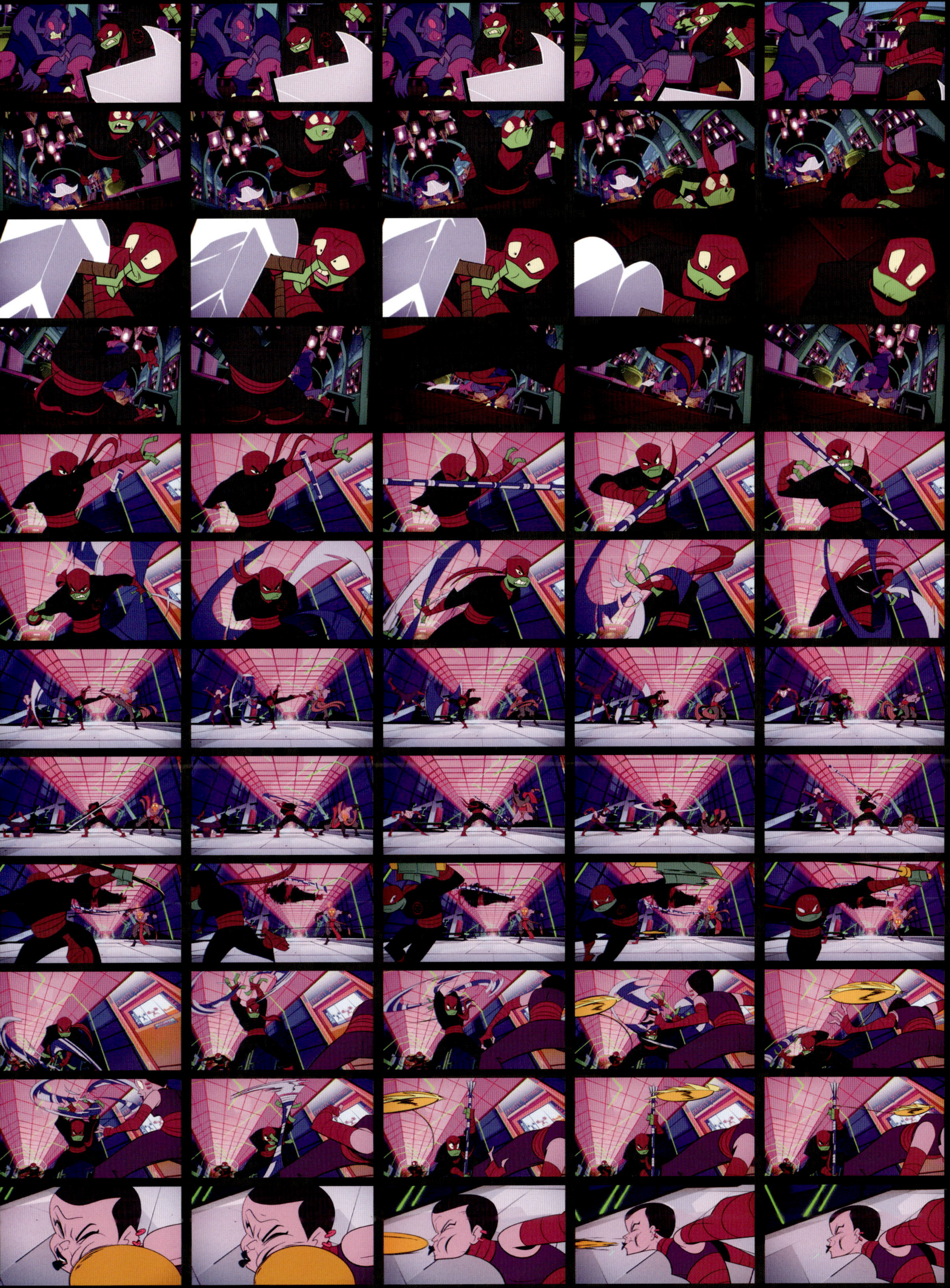

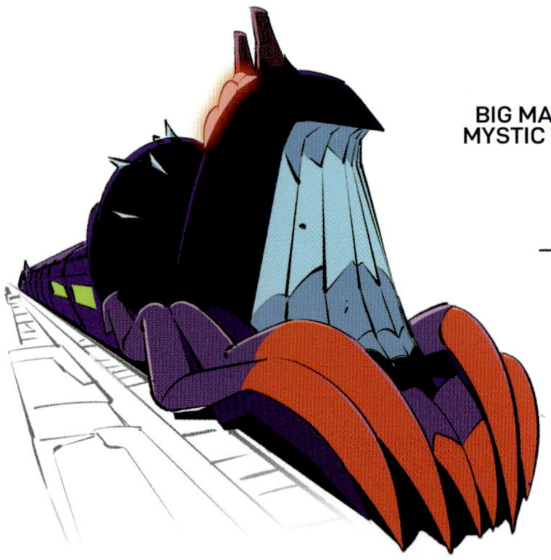

BIG MAMA'S MYSTIC TRAIN

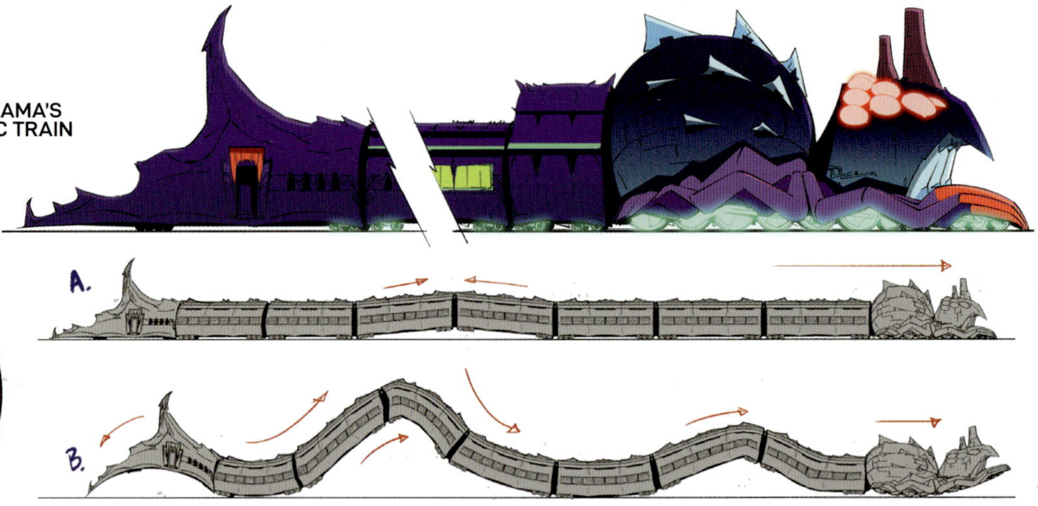

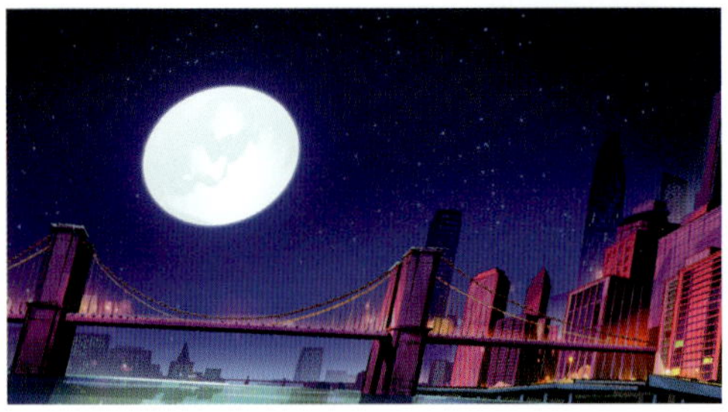

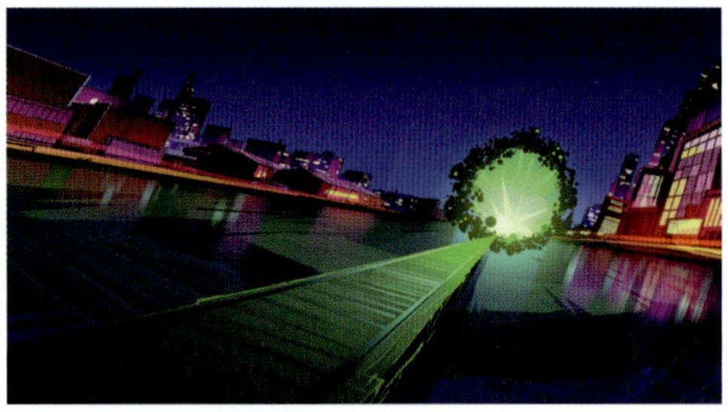

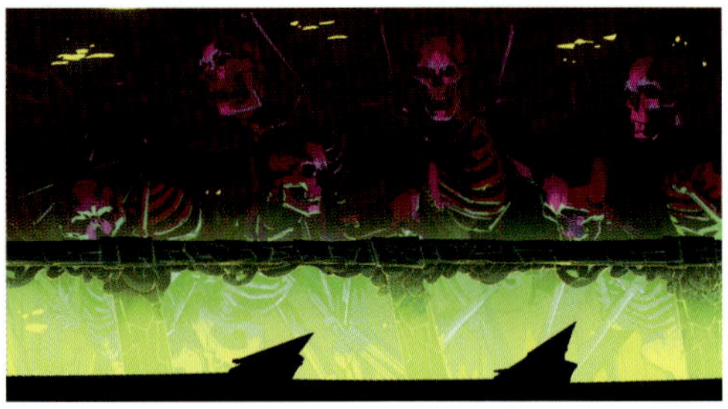

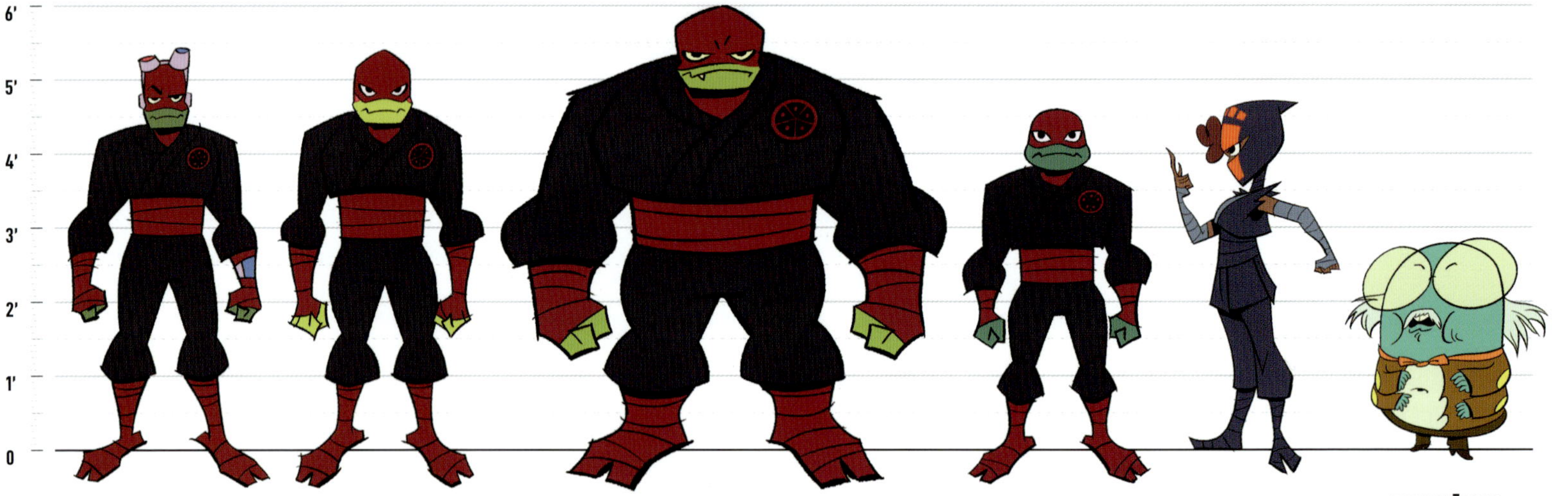

DONNIE
HAMATO CLAN

LEO
HAMATO CLAN

RAPH
HAMATO CLAN

MIKEY
HAMATO CLAN

APRIL O'NEIL
FOOT SOLDIER

TAX YŌKAI

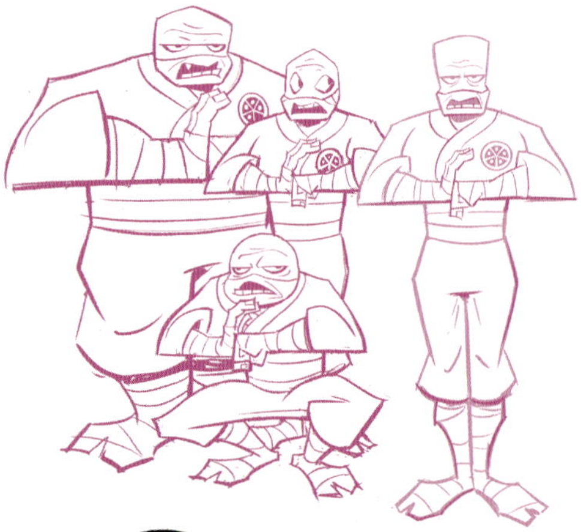

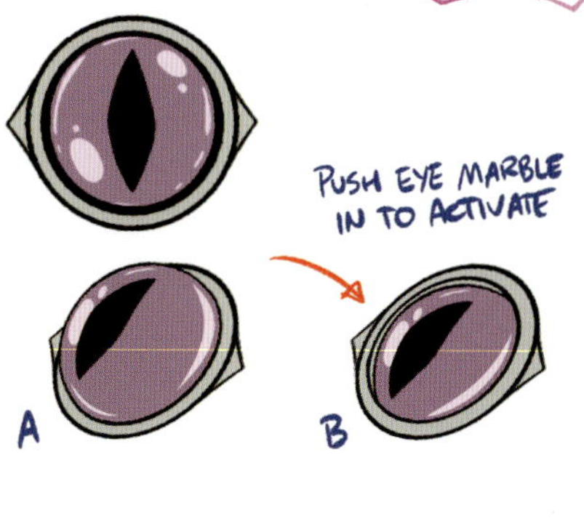

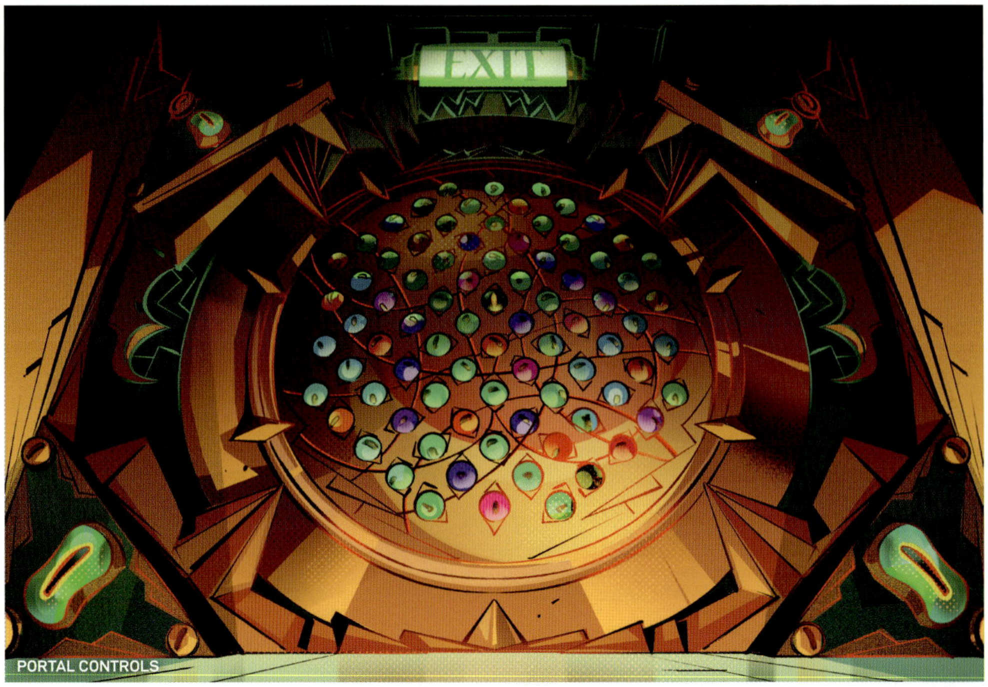

PORTAL CONTROLS

TONY GAMA-LOBO: Two full whiteboards in the writers room were needed to map the portal-jumping from car to car. And we still were confused when the animatic came back!

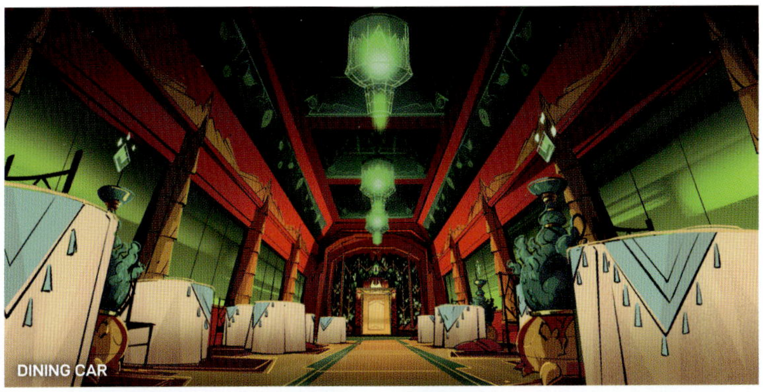
DINING CAR

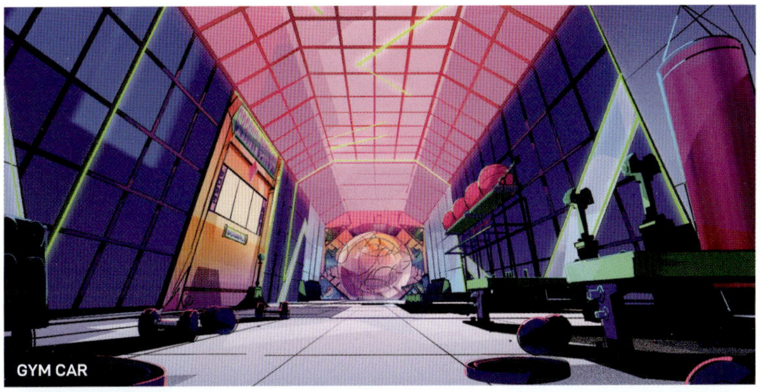
GYM CAR

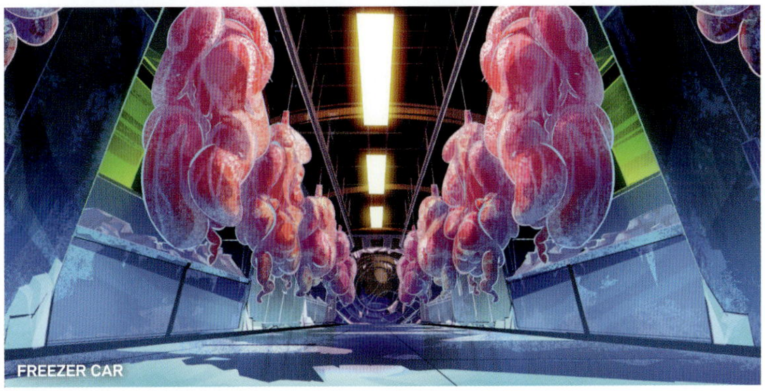
FREEZER CAR

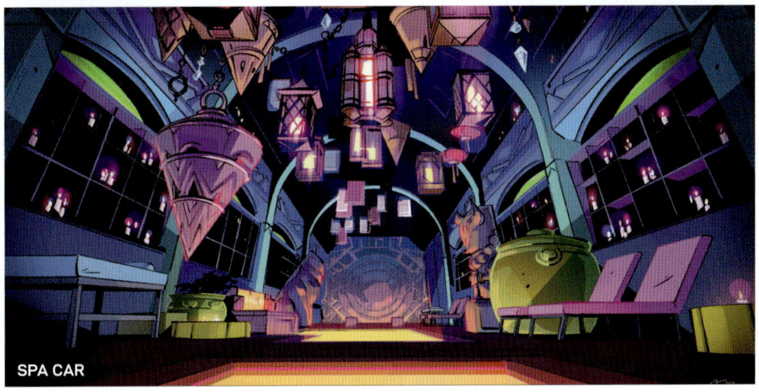
SPA CAR

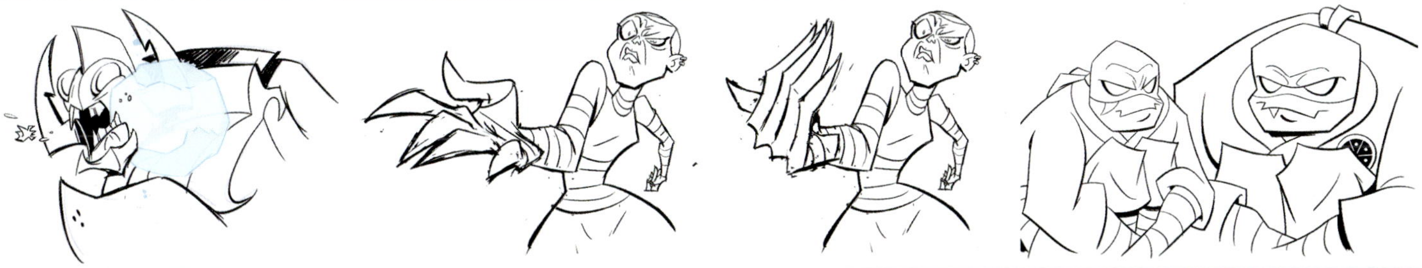

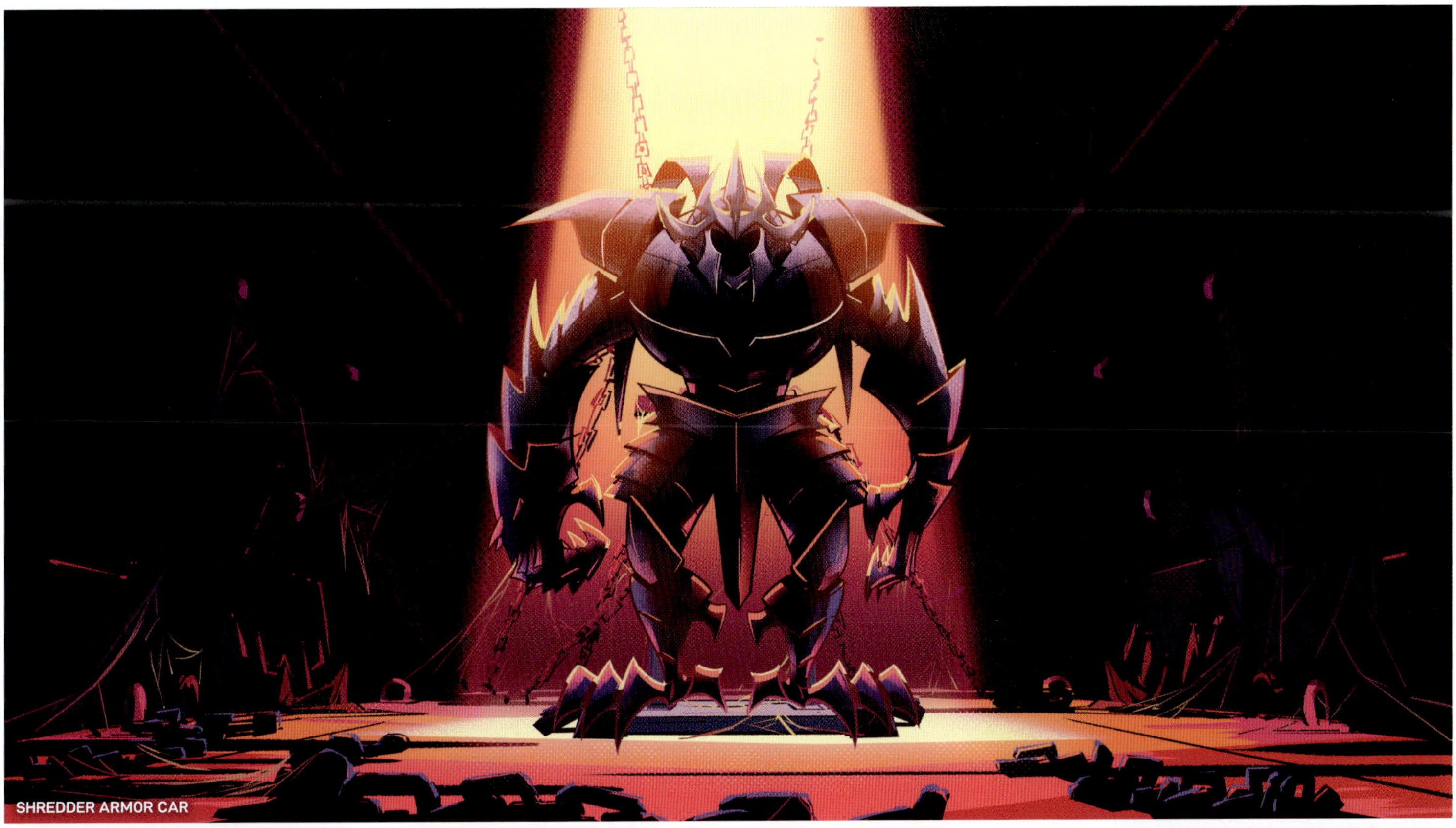
SHREDDER ARMOR CAR

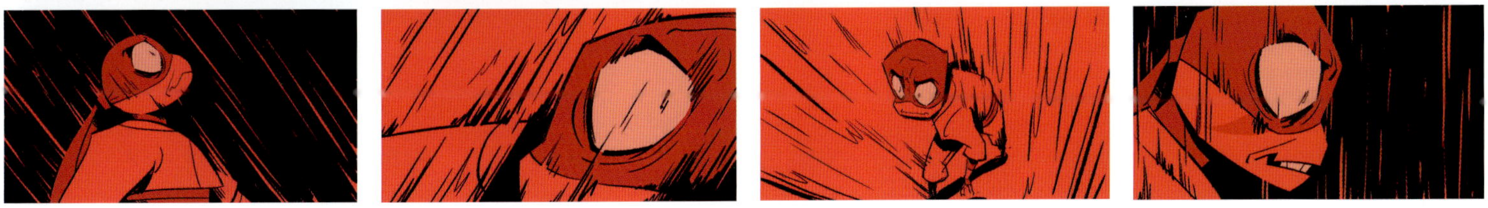

END GAME

ORIGINAL AIR DATE: NOVEMBER 16, 2019
PRODUCTION CODE: 051-052

WRITTEN BY **RUSS CARNEY & RON CORCILLO**
STORYBOARDS BY **JJ CONWAY, CHRISTOPHER LUC, SAM MONTES, SAM SZYMANSKI, SHELDON VELLA**
DIRECTED BY **ABE AUDISH**

TONY GAMA-LOBO: Ron and Russ were masters of finding the funniest way to tell an emotional character story. Once we landed on the journey the Turtles were on, Russ just nailed it with the iconic *"We be we, baby!"* By the end of the season we had all really fallen in love with our Turtles. And there seemed to be no more fitting lesson for them and Splinter to learn (and for us to teach our audience) than *"Being yourself is what makes you powerful."* Man, that was satisfying.

The hard part, however, was figuring out what to do with the whole Draxum/Dark Armor/Shredder thing. We worked on that forever. Not sure who pitched the idea, but it broke open once someone suggested the Foot having this ulterior motive and using Draxum this whole time to resurrect their deity—the Shredder! What a cliffhanger! (And I just have to mention, for all the writers in the room who were parents, putting Splinter in the impossible position of choosing between his boys and the fate of the world was devastatingly wonderful. Splinter in his super-fly Lou Jitsu jumpsuit and sunglasses making that heartbreaking decision made you both laugh and cry.)

RON CORCILLO: Splinter delivers the line *"Let's see how well they fare against my Macho Gazpacho kick!" Macho Gazpacho* was one of the titles we had on our list of soup-related Lou Jitsu films. Some others were *Bouillabasic Instinct, Udon but Not Forgotten,* and *Albondigas, Food and Lodging.*

JJ CONWAY: Originally there was no fight between Splinter and Draxum, but I felt like we had built the tension between those two to such a boil that we needed the catharsis of seeing them finally go face-to-face (especially knowing that season 2 would be about them reconciling). So, at the storyboard launch, I pitched the idea and how I saw the fight unfolding, how even though Splinter won the battle, Draxum won the war because Splinter would sacrifice the world for his sons. I got the thumbs-up with the caveat "If this doesn't work, you broke it, so you get to fix it."

Once the armor is assembled, I wanted to watch Draxum's triumph turn to face-melting horror, like when the ark is opened at the end of *Raiders of the Lost Ark* (1981). For the actual transformation, one major influence was the horror of Venom's birth in *Spider-Man 3* (2007). It was all about watching Draxum realize that he was losing himself to the power of this uncontrollable force, ending with him screaming as the mask closed over his face, leaving us with the lingering image of someone who is now someone else.

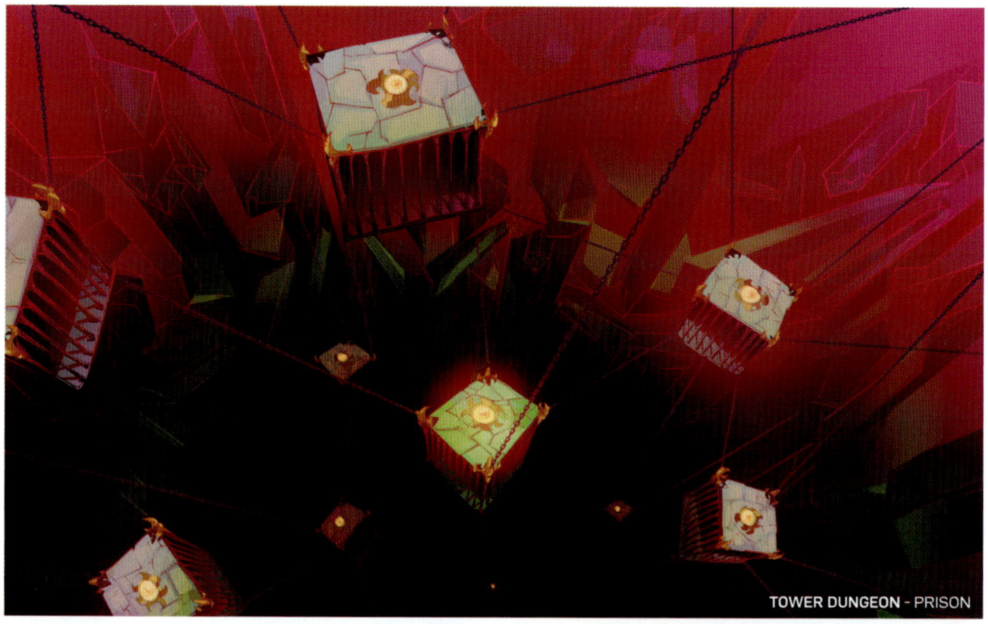
TOWER DUNGEON - PRISON

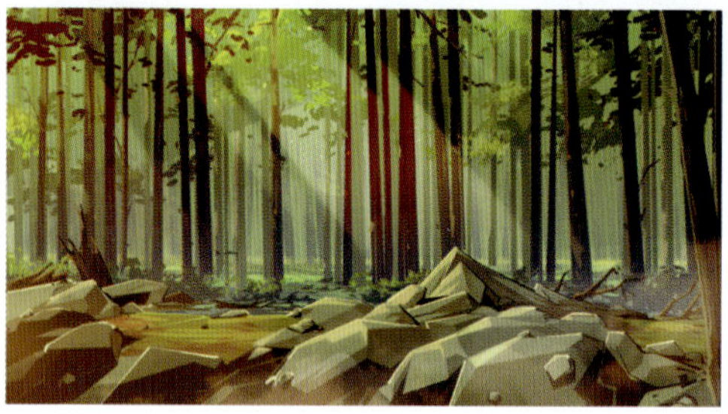

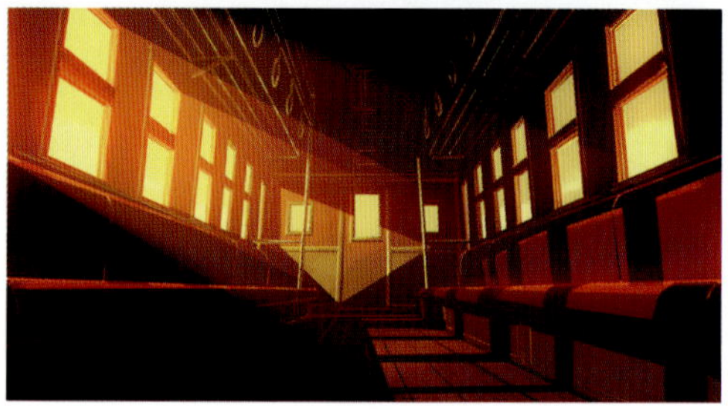

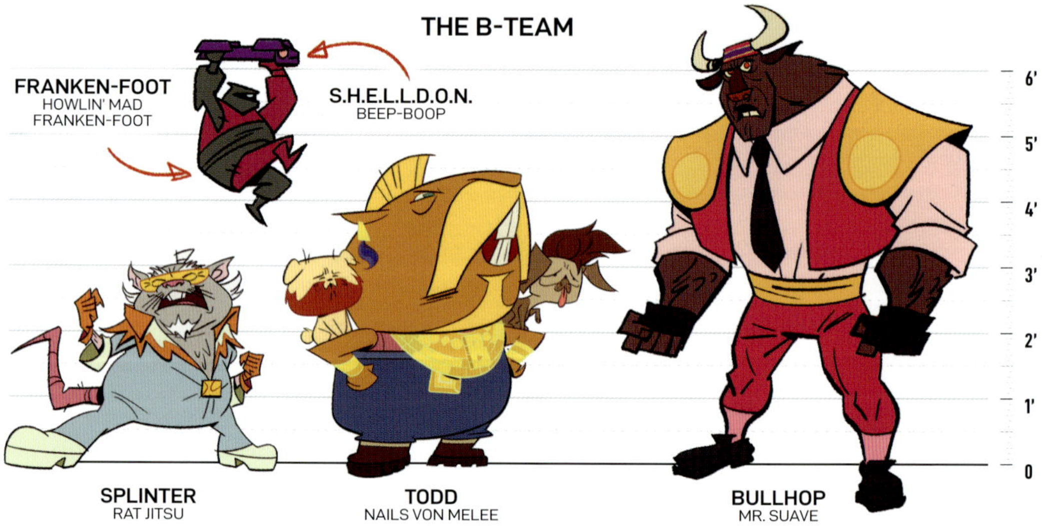

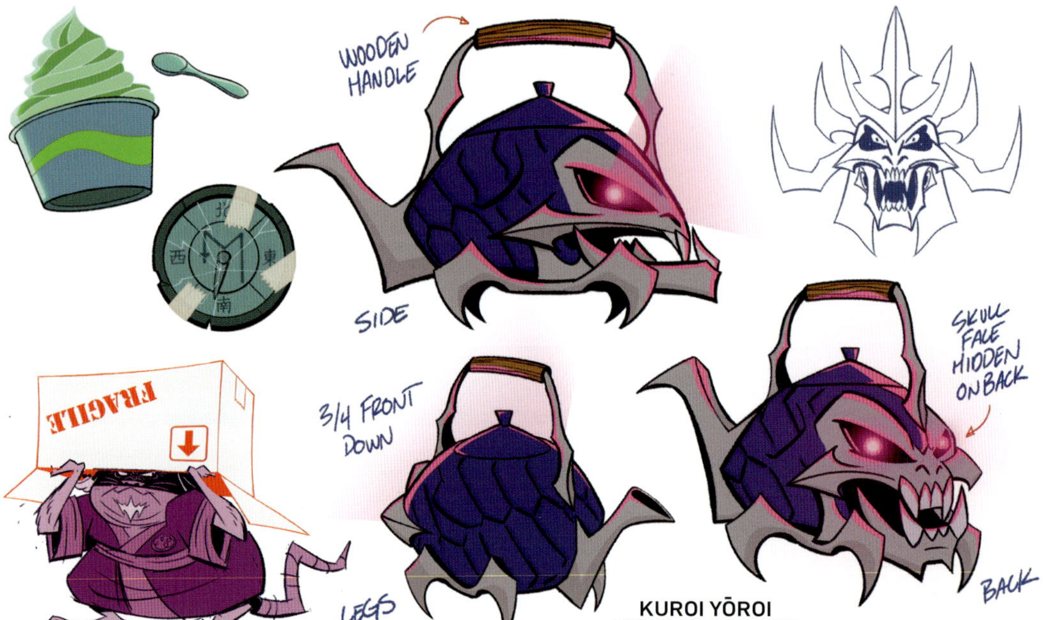

KUROI YŌROI
FACEPLATE / "SKULLY"

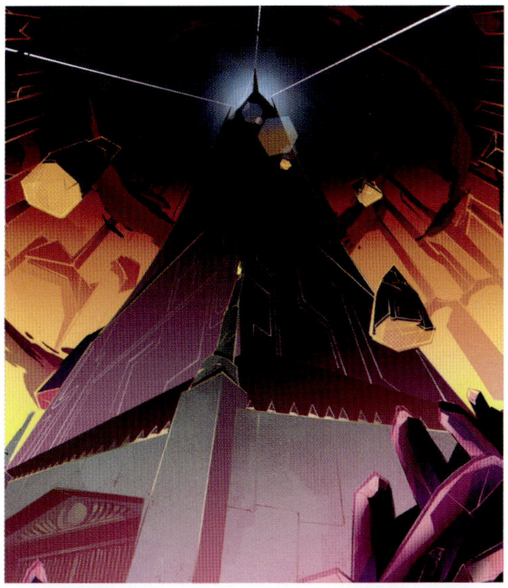

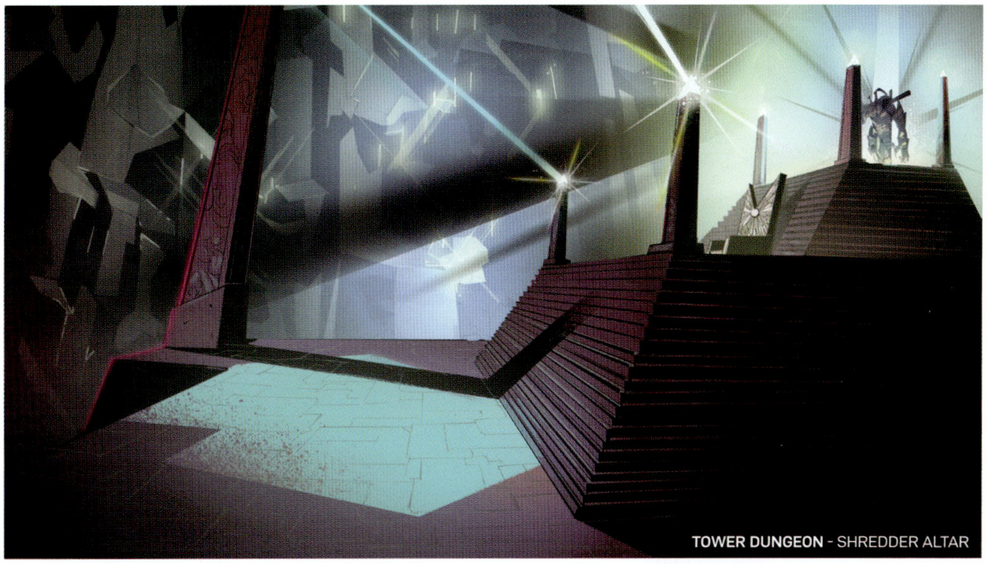

TOWER DUNGEON - SHREDDER ALTAR

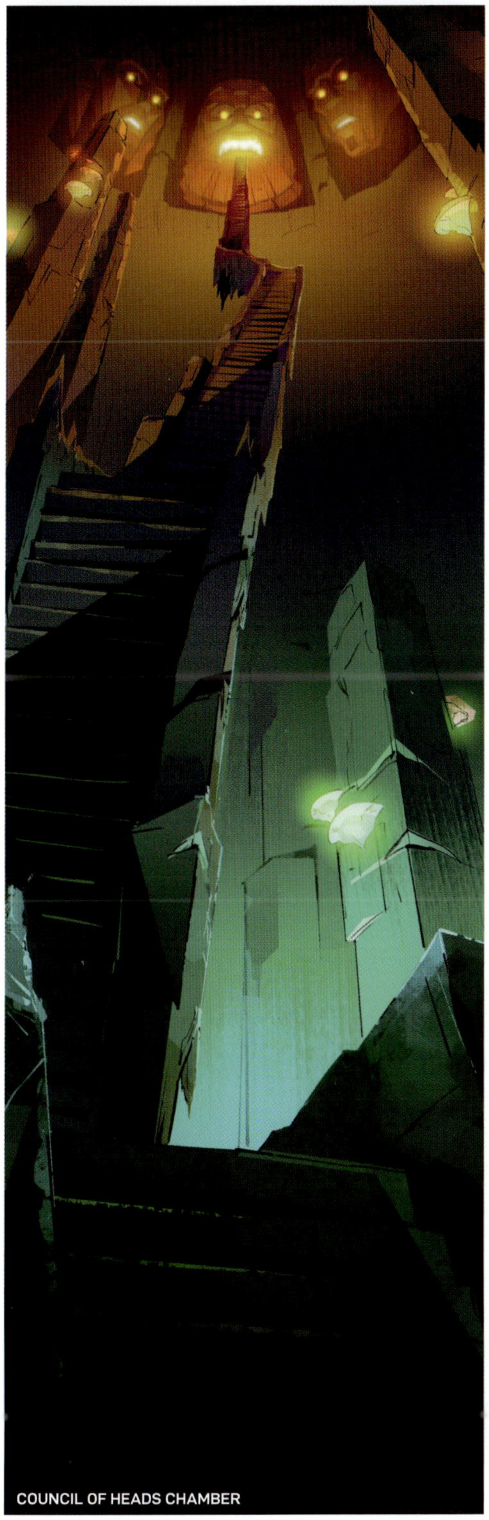

COUNCIL OF HEADS CHAMBER

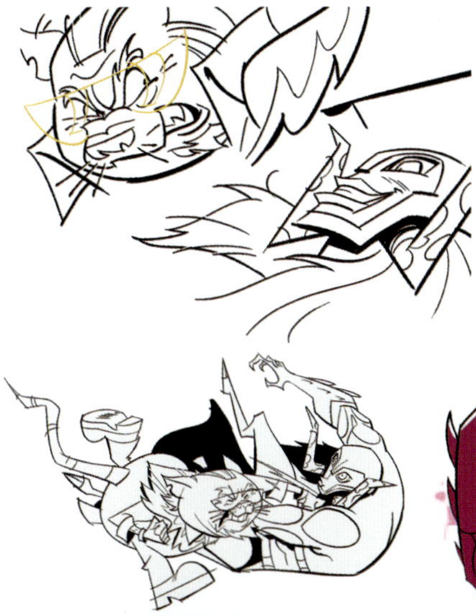

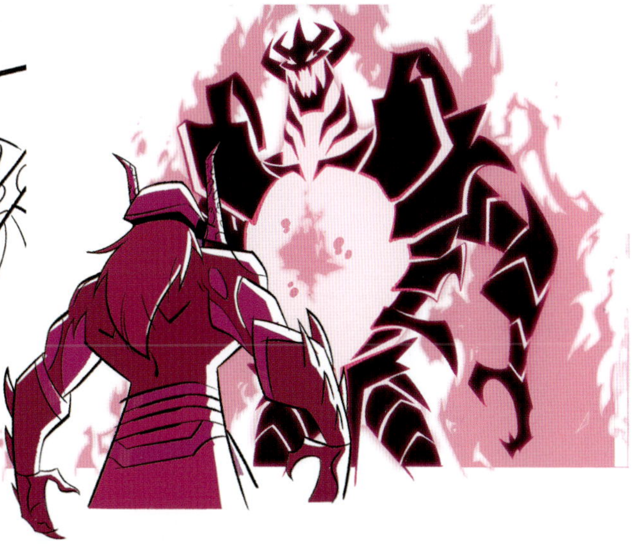

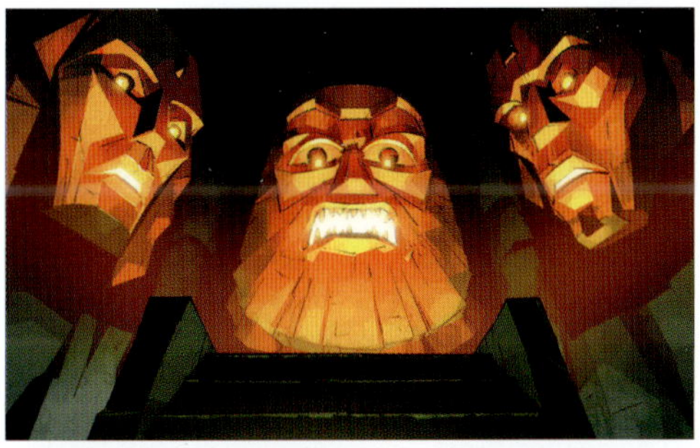

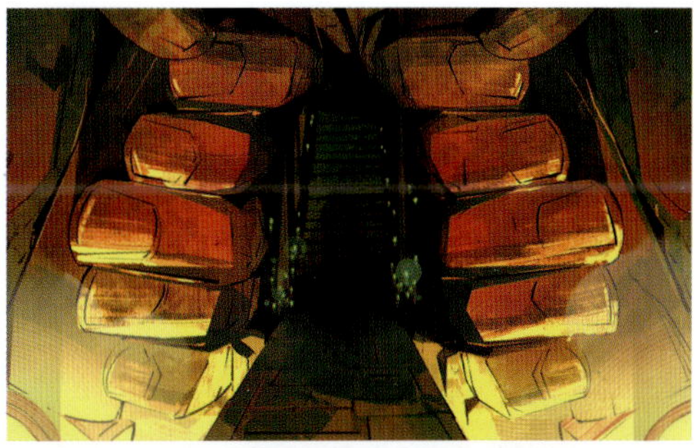

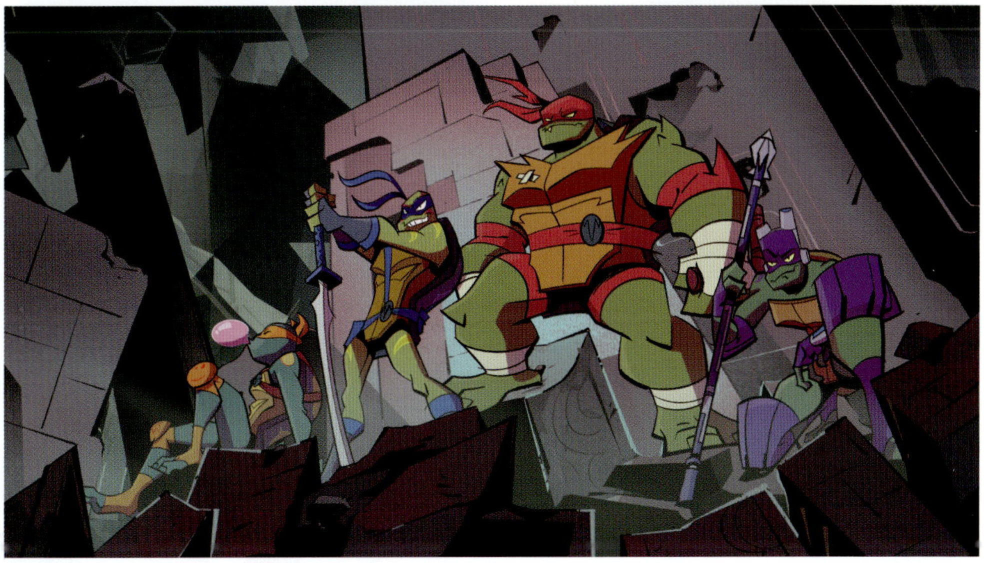

TONY GAMA-LOBO: *"I love it when no plan comes together"* is based off a famous catchphrase from the '80s show *The A-Team*, whose opening title sequence was parodied earlier in the episode when April rounds up the "B-Team."

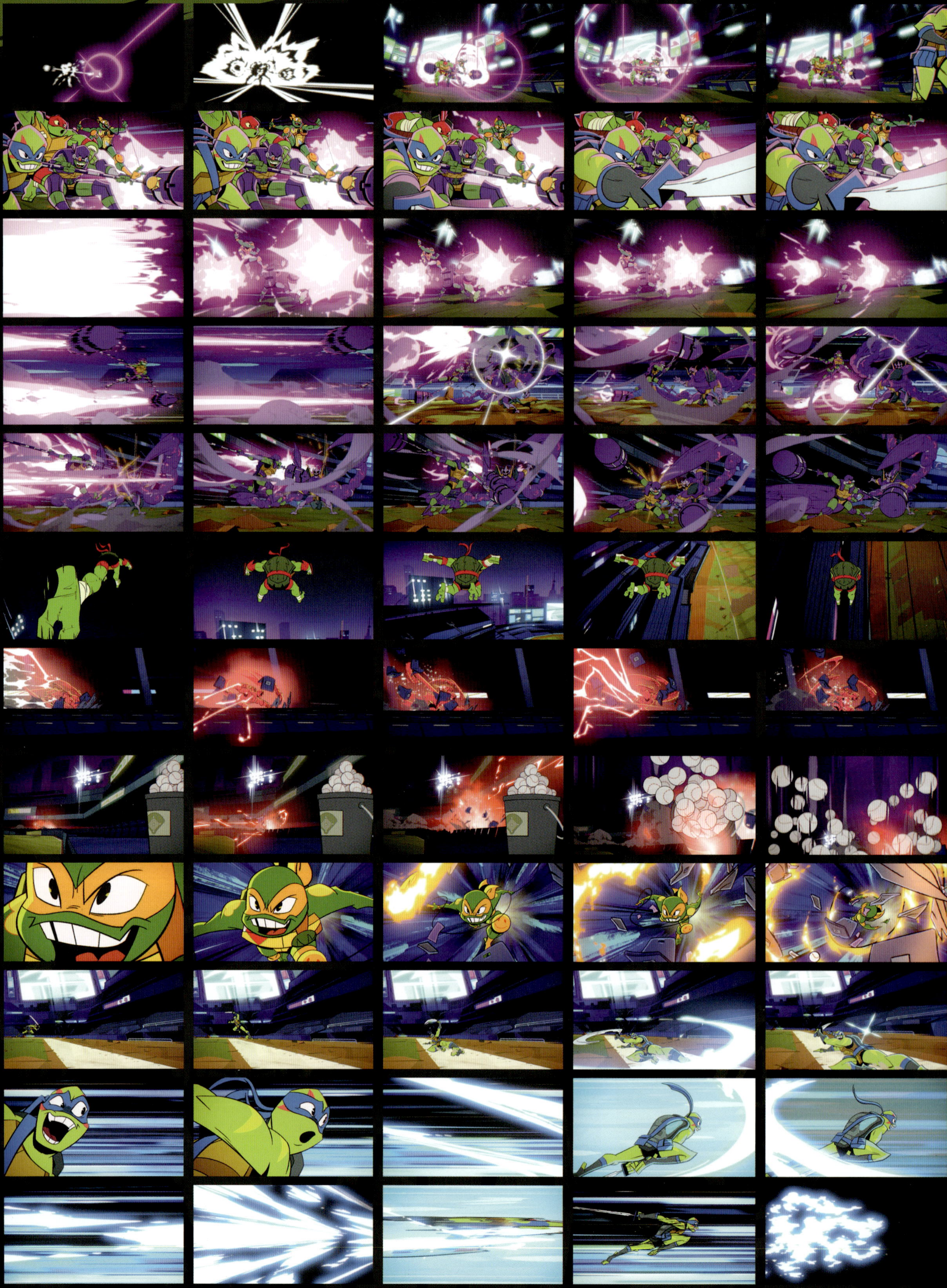

STORYBOARD ARTIST: **SHELDON VELLA**

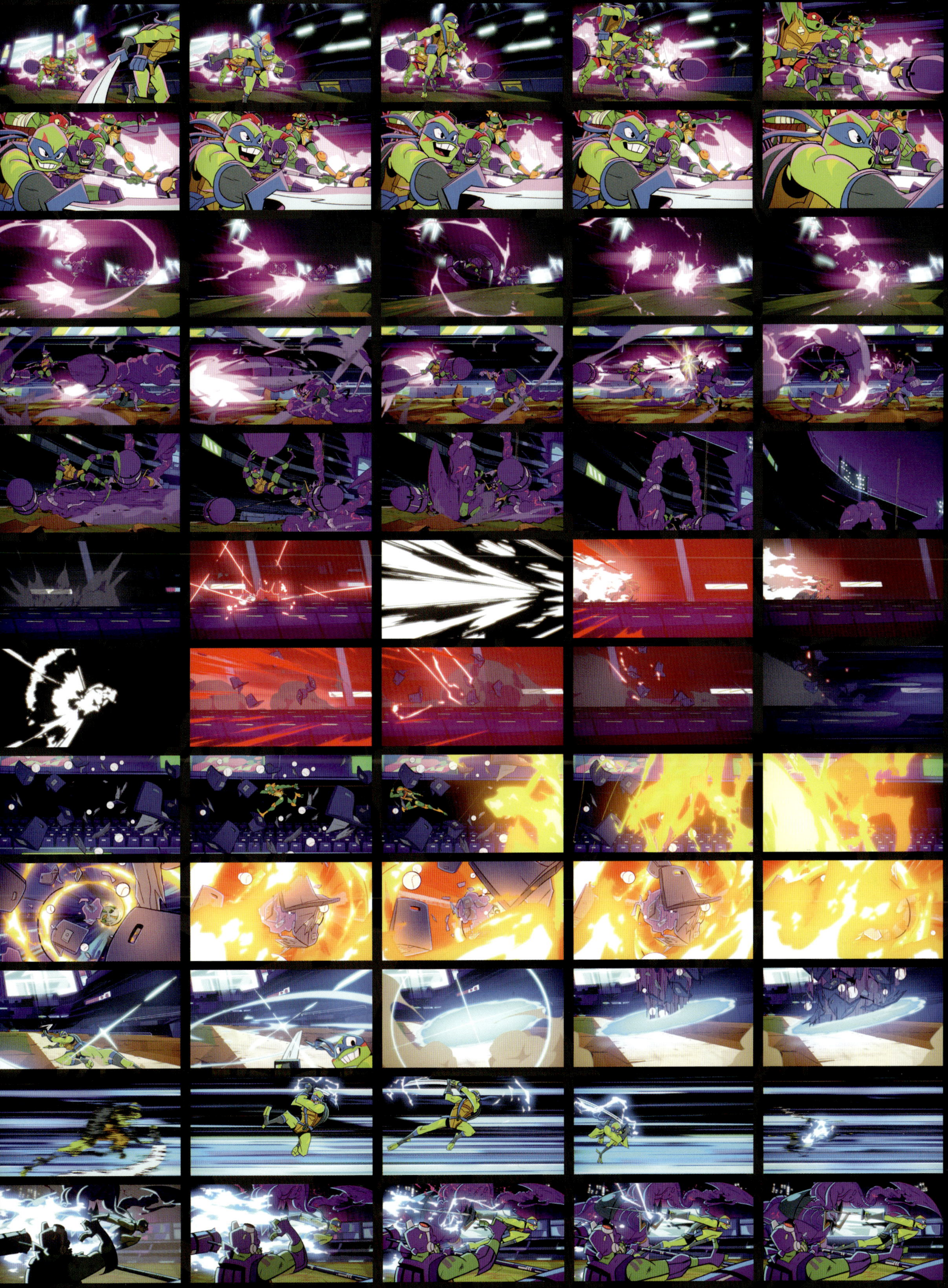

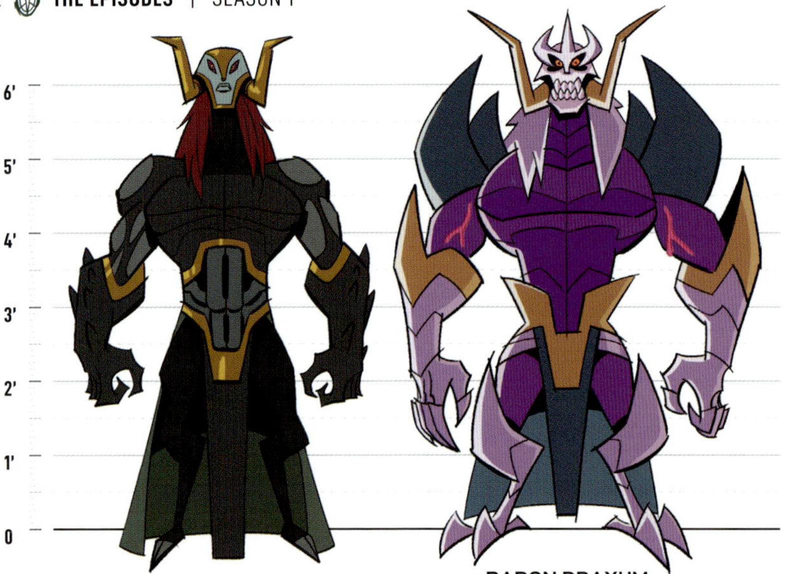

BARON DRAXUM

BARON DRAXUM
DARK ARMOR

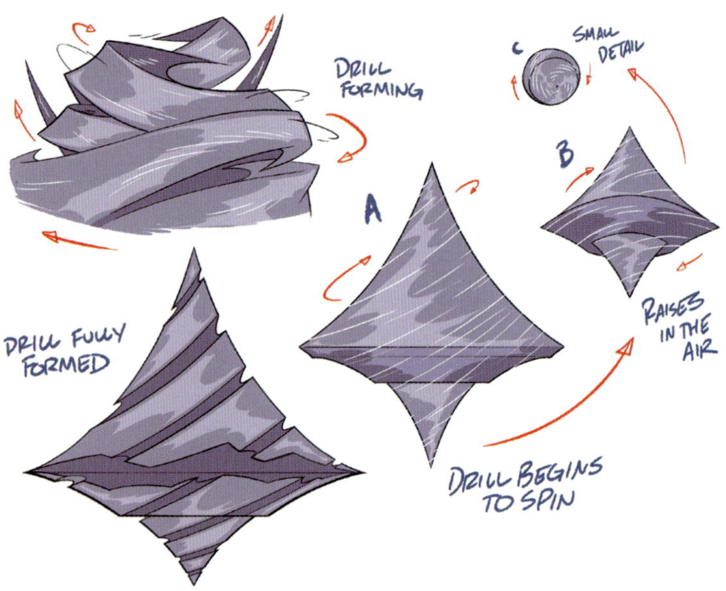

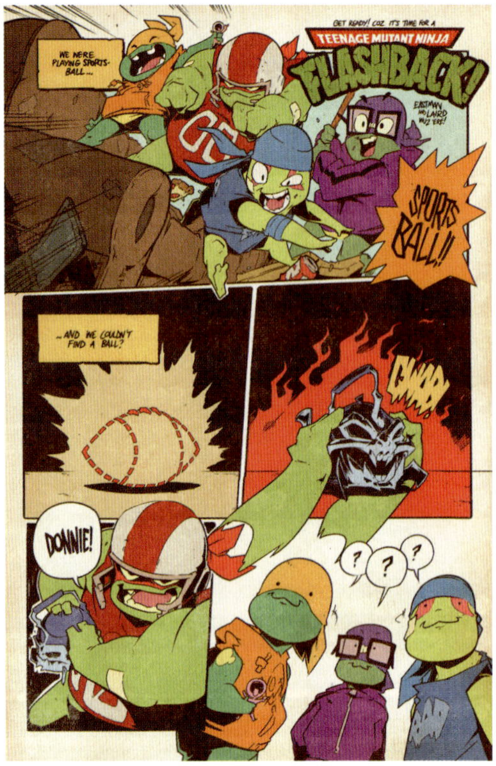

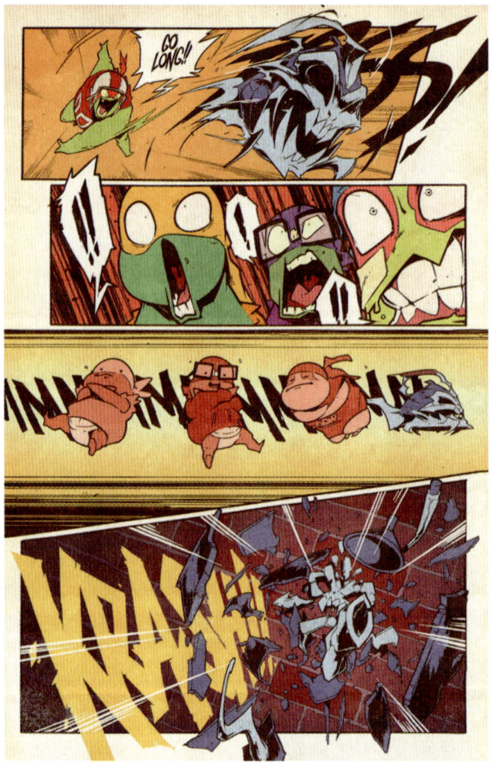

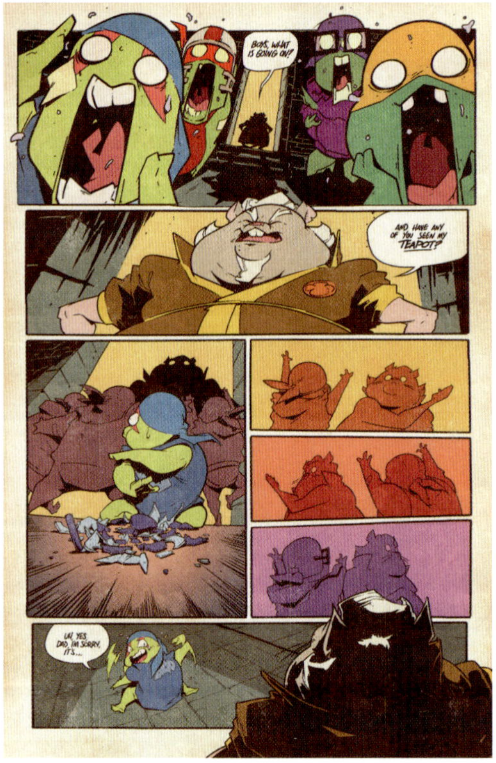

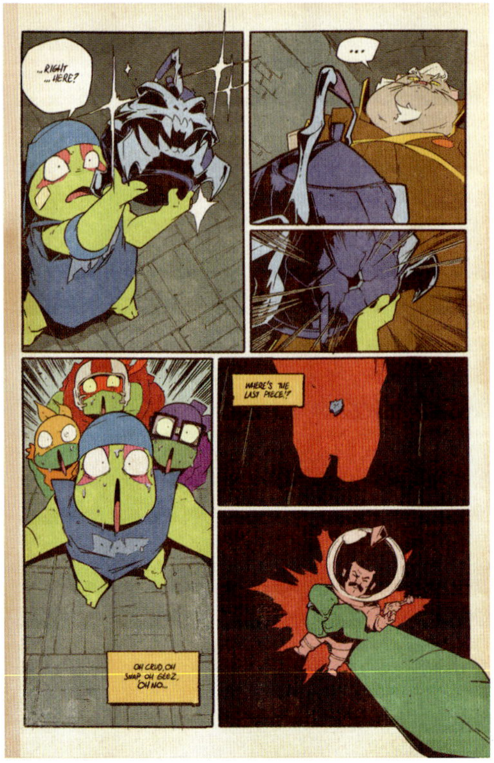

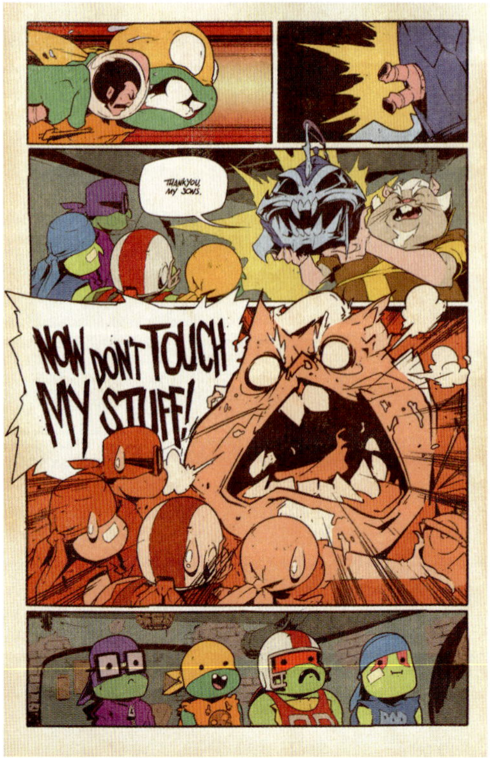

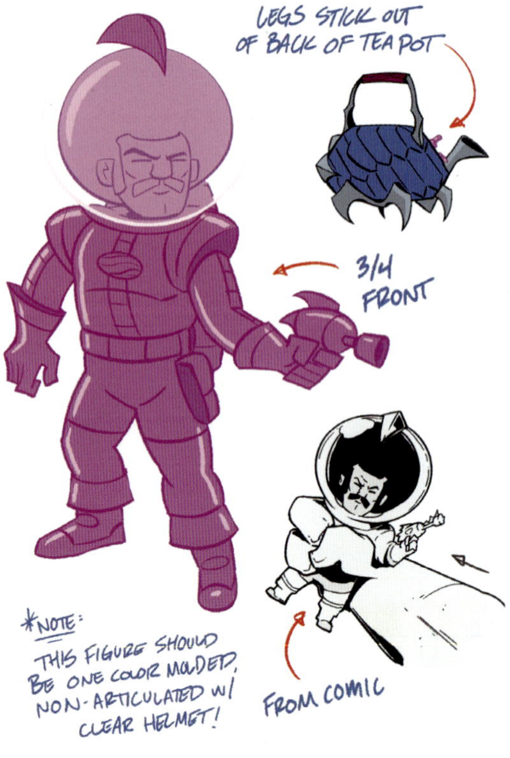

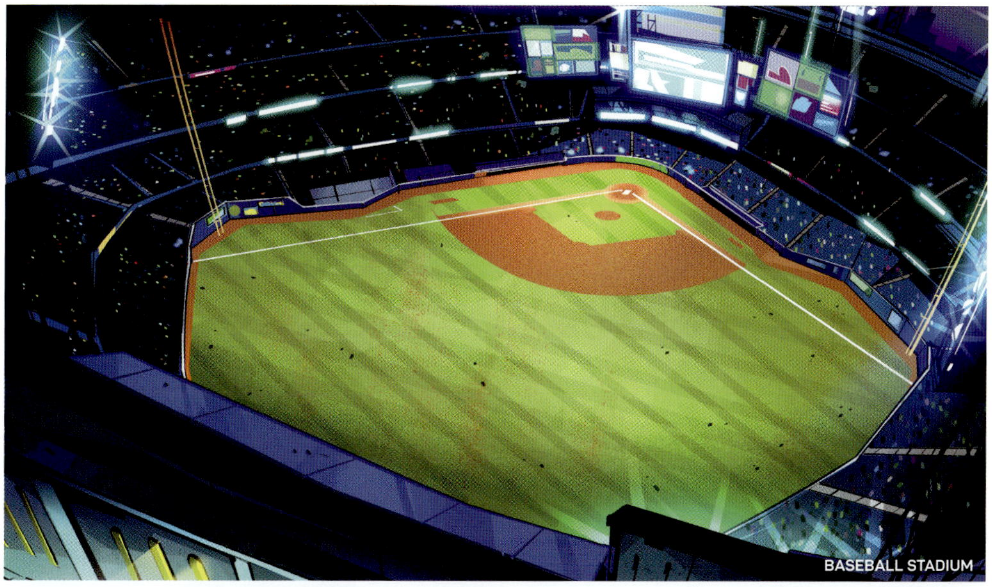
BASEBALL STADIUM

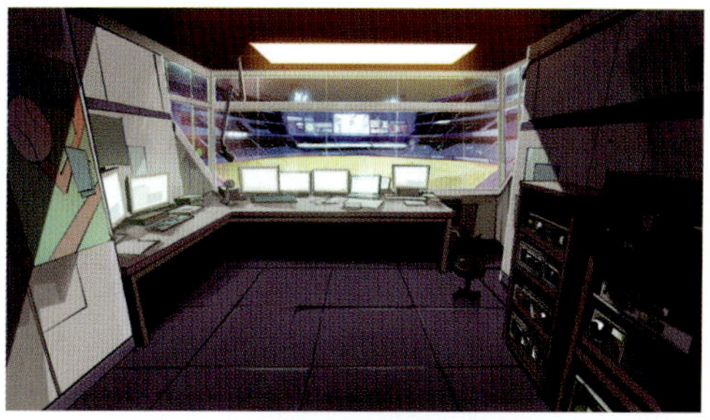

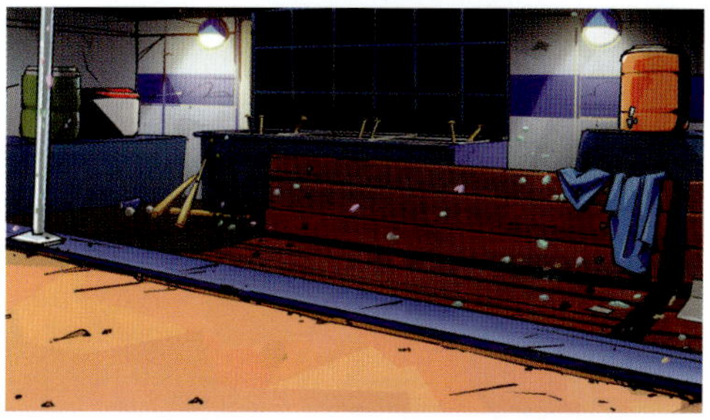

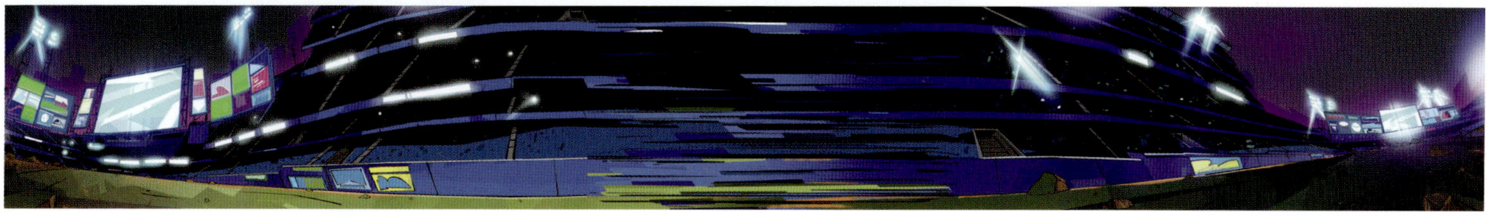

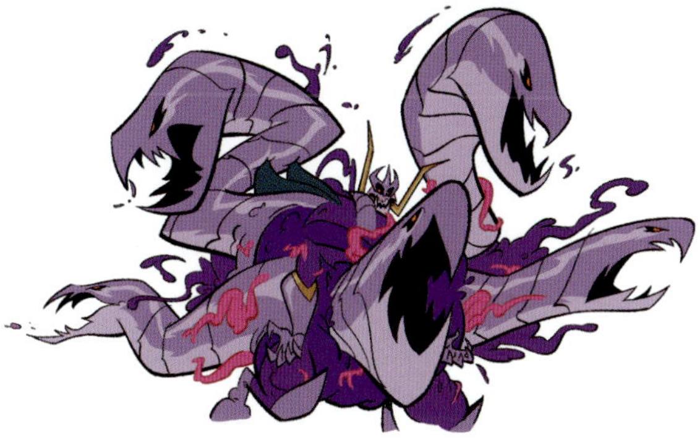

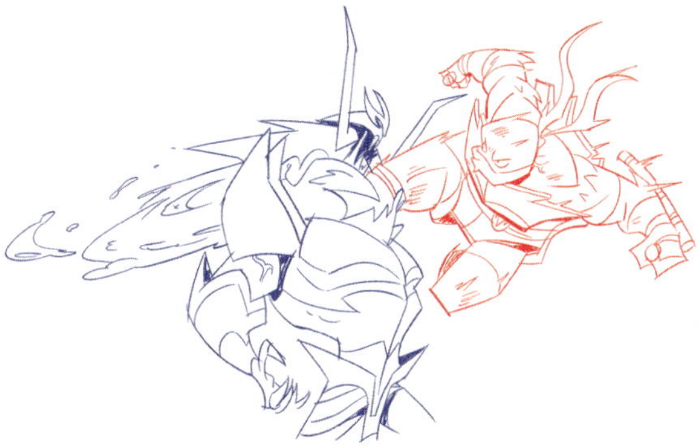

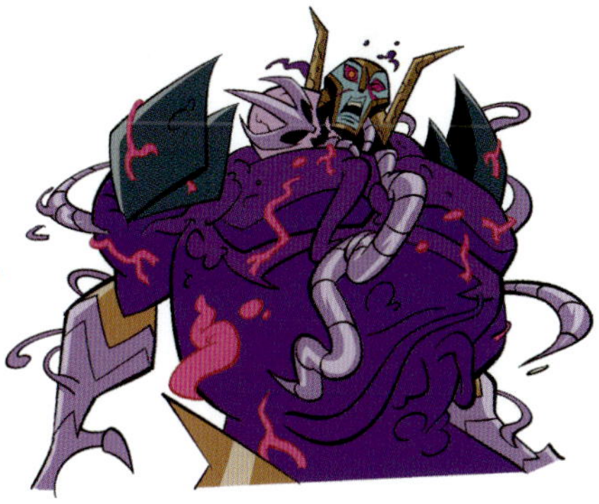

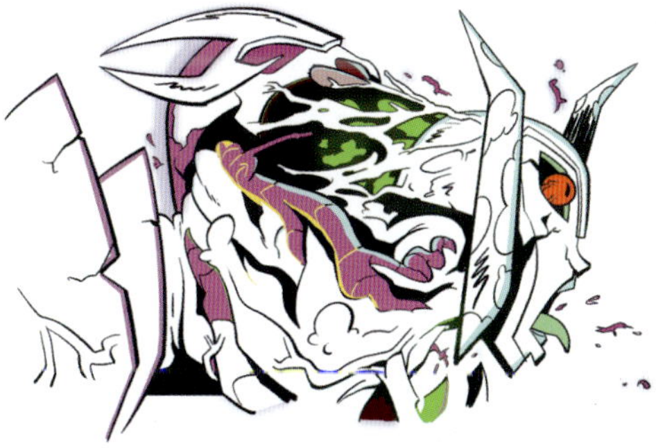

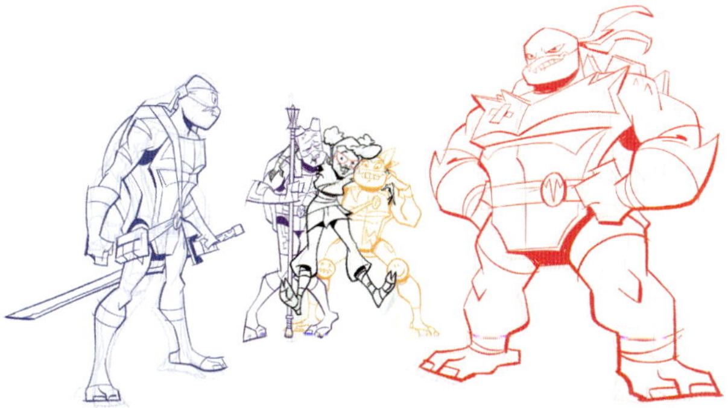

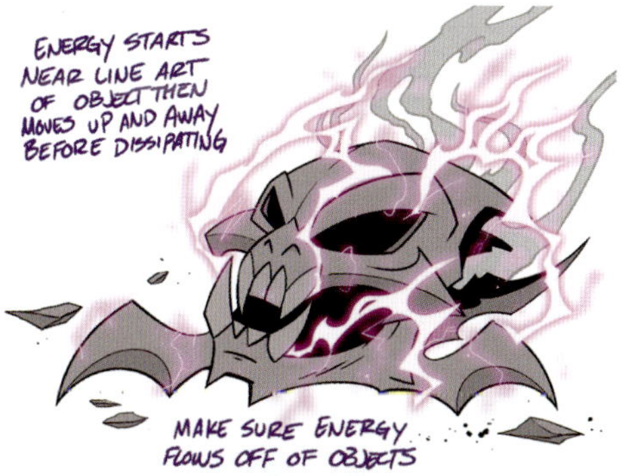

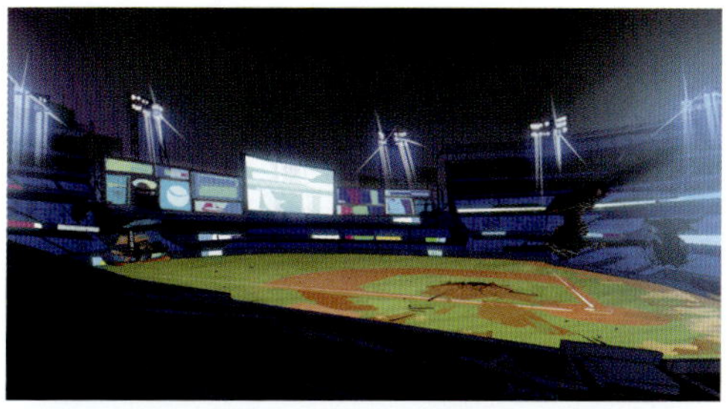

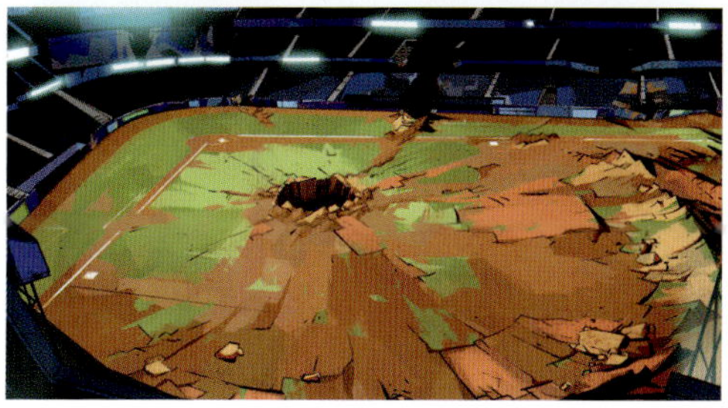

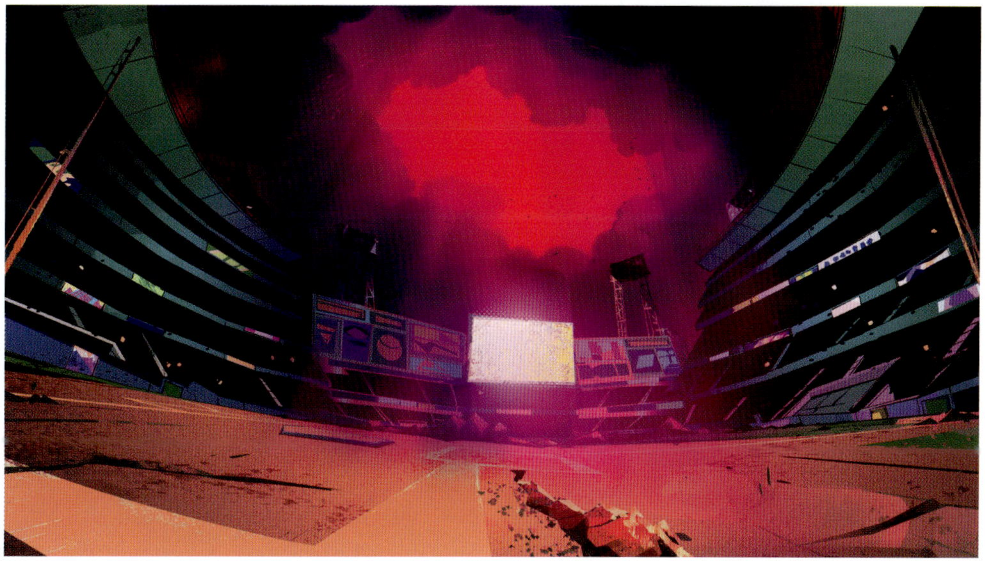

MANY UNHAPPY RETURNS

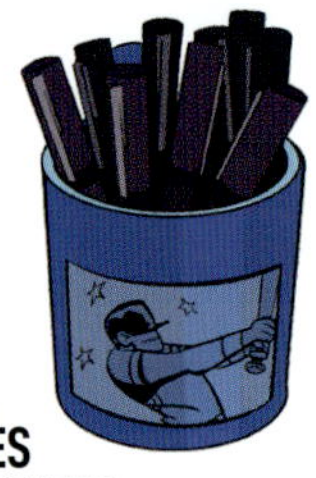

ORIGINAL AIR DATE: NOVEMBER 23, 2019
PRODUCTION CODE: 057-058

WRITTEN BY **IAN BUSCH**
STORYBOARDS BY **JAKE CASTORENA, ALICIA CHAN, ASHE JACOBSON, KEVIN MOLINA-ORTIZ, SAM MONTES**
DIRECTED BY **KEVIN MOLINA-ORTIZ & SEBASTIAN MONTES**

TONY GAMA-LOBO: One of the biggest issues we had in the entire series was what to do with Shredder once he came back. Andy designed this incredible version of Shredder that was different from anything that had ever been done. He was so badass and powerful and evil—and that was the problem. From a storytelling perspective, once a villain like that is on the loose, how can our heroes focus on anything else? How do we do fun stories or other villain stories? So we needed to bring Shredder back, have some fun, and then put him on a shelf. That's why we give him to Big Mama at the end of the episode.

Ian and I were big *Battlestar Galactica* (2004) fans and loved the episode where the Cylons kept popping in every 33 minutes. The relentless attacks, the energy, the hopelessness. So we thought maybe Shredder keeps popping up at regular intervals and causing mindless mayhem. How do we stop it? That's why we send Leo and Splinter to Big Mama for help.

This was a huge Leo story. Until now we had trouble really pinning down Leo as a character. We had always said he was Bill Murray in *Ghostbusters*. Confident, a little bit of a jerk, not serious. When we zeroed in on his *"I got this"* attitude for this episode, we knew we had him locked in. Under all the jokes and hilarious Leo attitude, this is a touching story about a kid thinking his dad and brothers don't believe in him. And the audience thinks they're right! That's exactly what makes the moment Leo asks his family (and us) to trust him work so well.

Breaking this story was tricky. Leo's whole thing is essentially a big con. We had to figure out how to keep Splinter (and the audience) worried that Leo was continually screwing up while also planting seeds that we could call back later in the big solution.

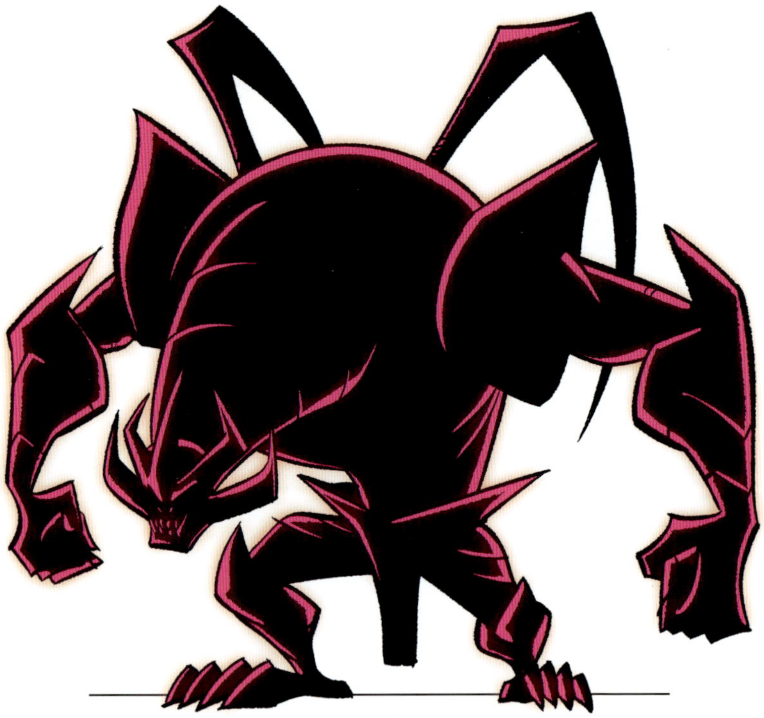

THE SHREDDER
DARK ARMOR

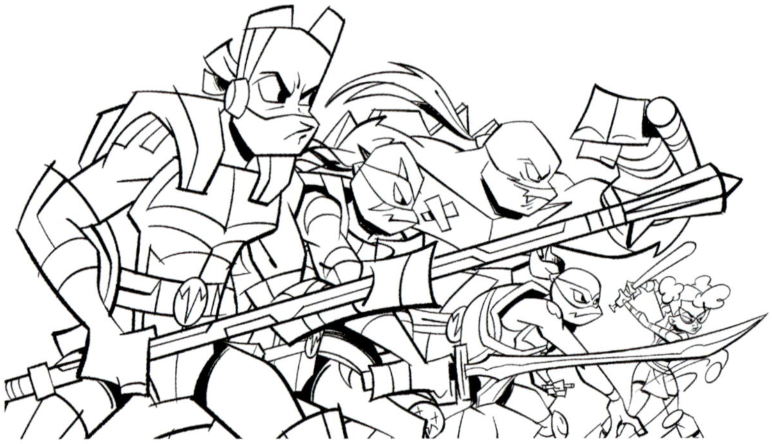

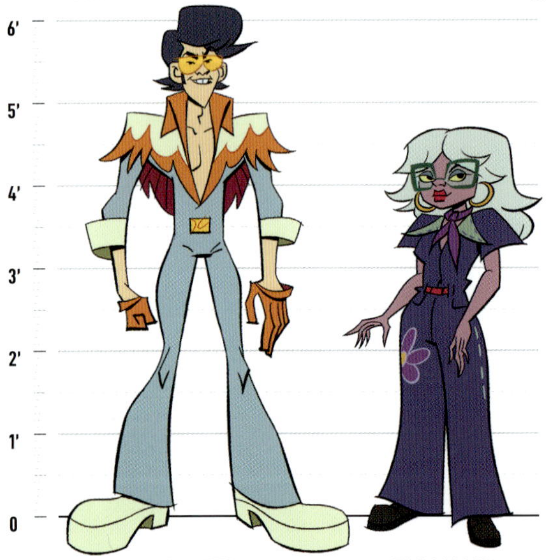

LOU JITSU
FLASHBACK

BIG MAMA
FLASHBACK

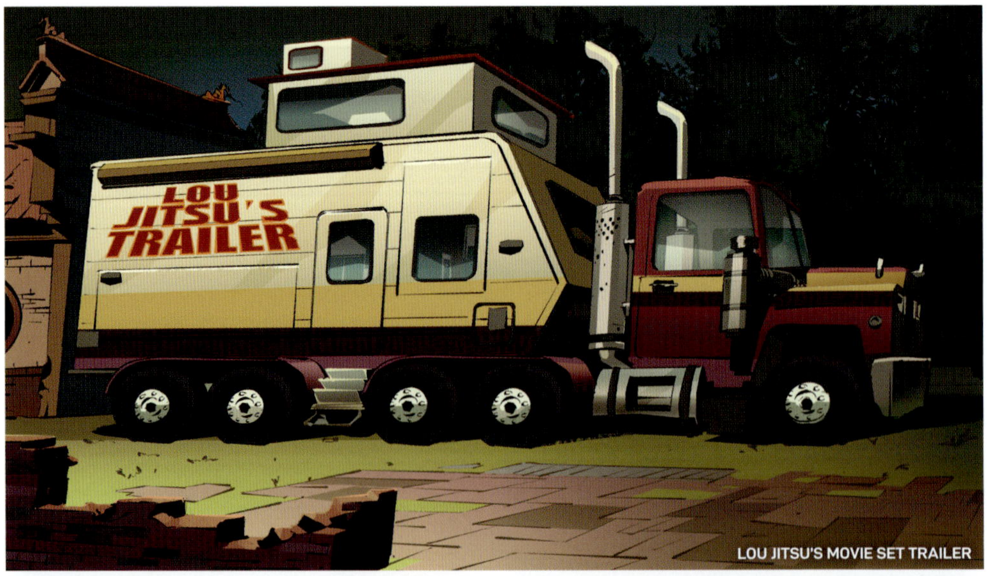

LOU JITSU'S MOVIE SET TRAILER

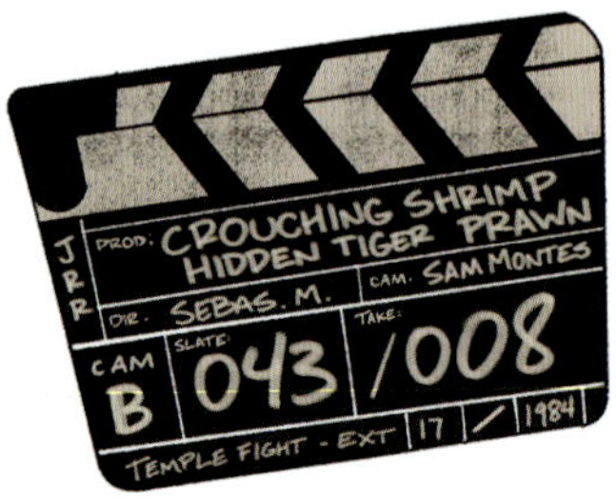

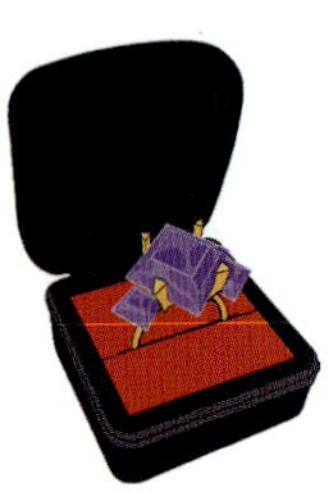

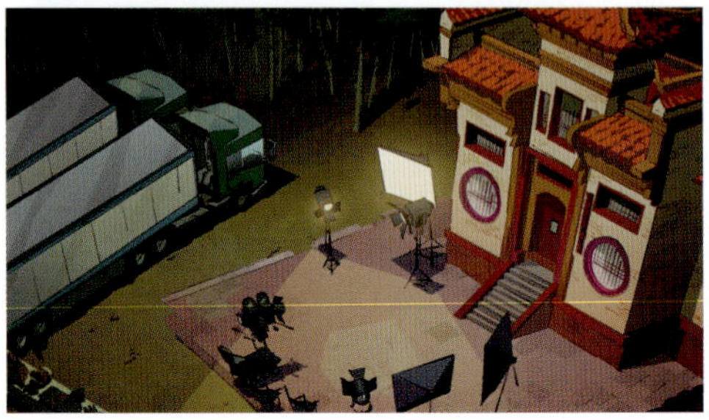

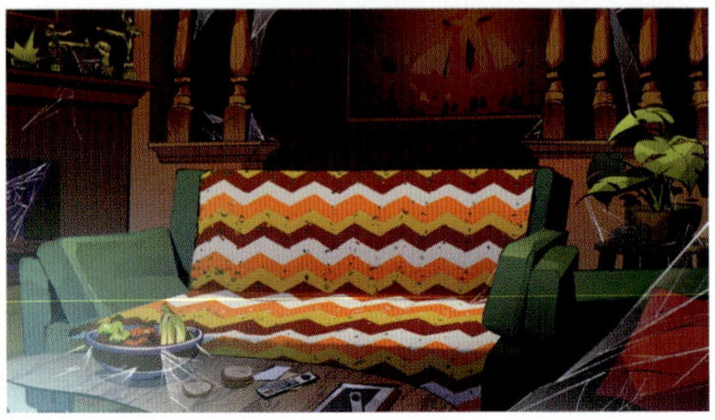

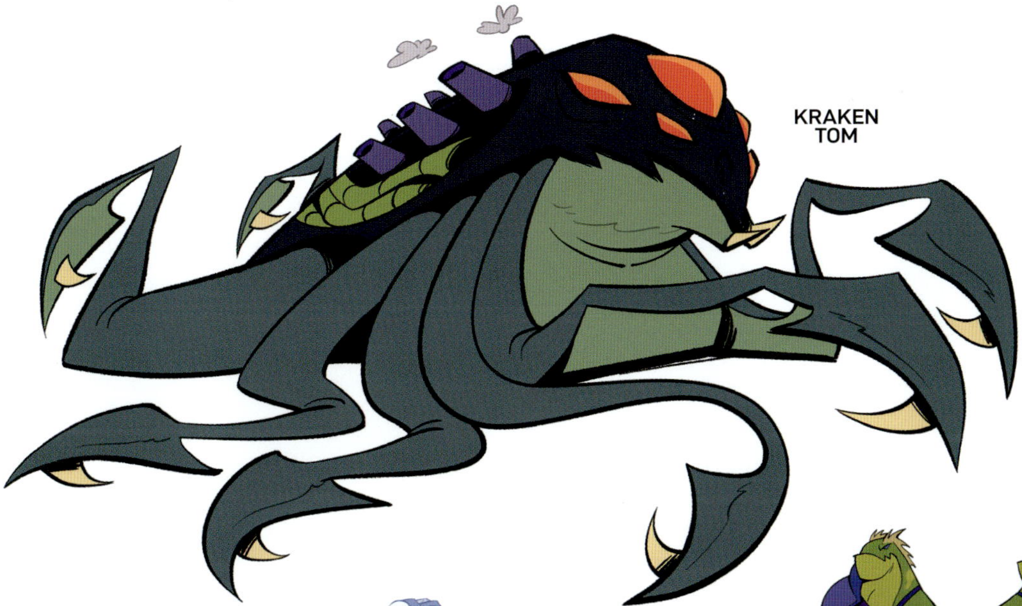

KRAKEN TOM

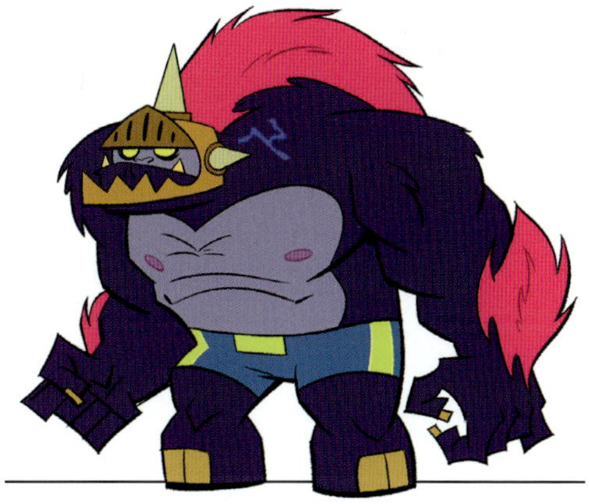

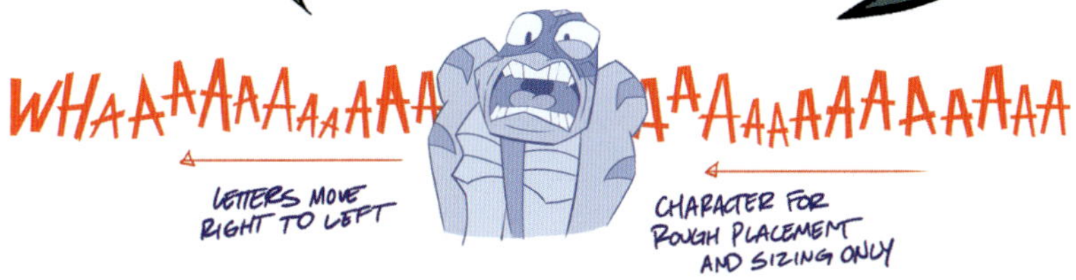

EVIL SIX

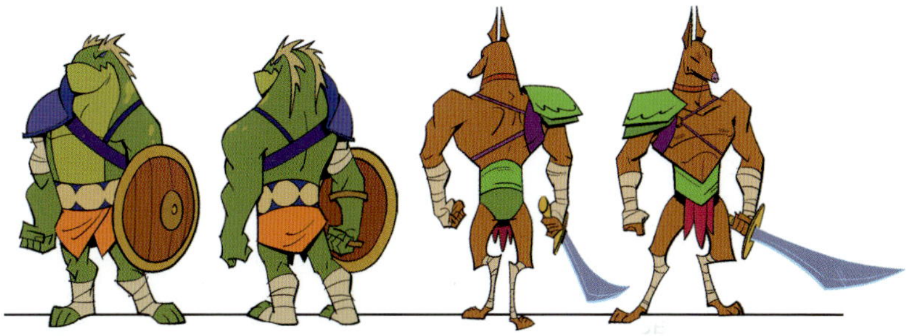

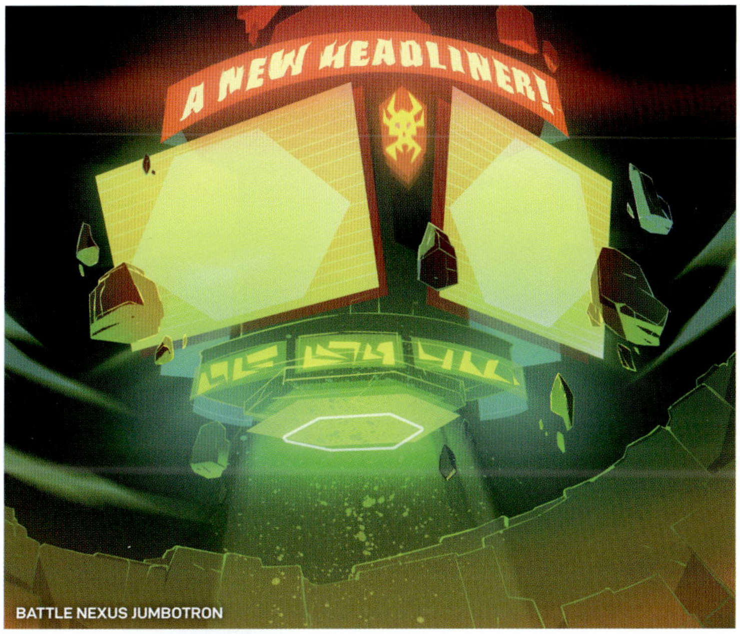

BATTLE NEXUS JUMBOTRON

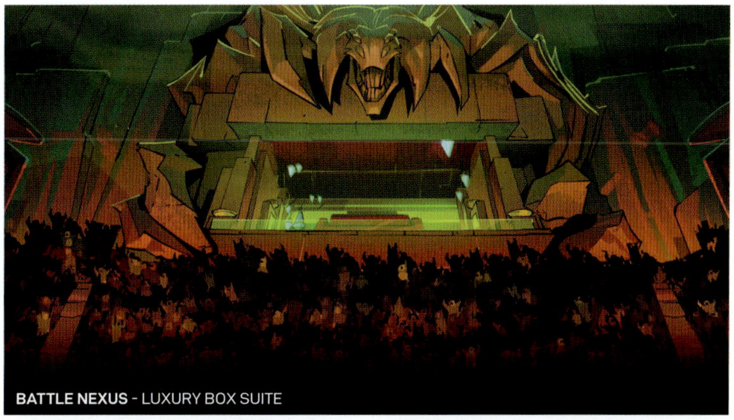

BATTLE NEXUS - LUXURY BOX SUITE

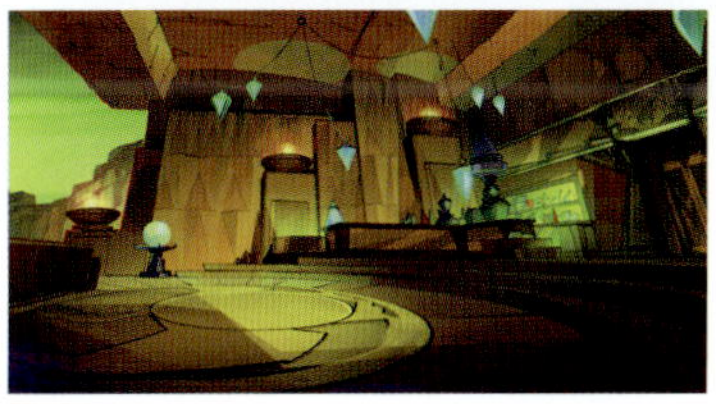

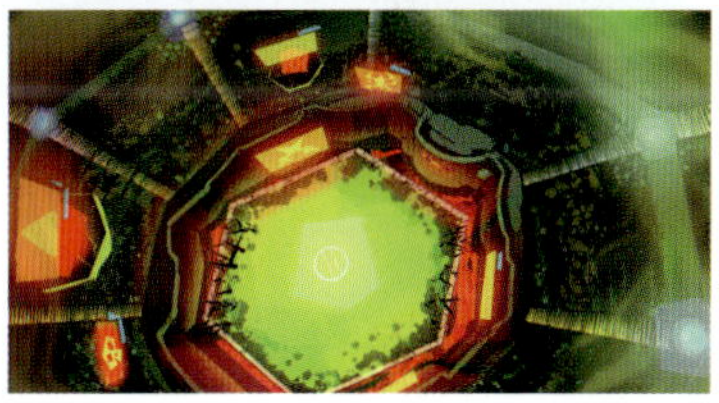

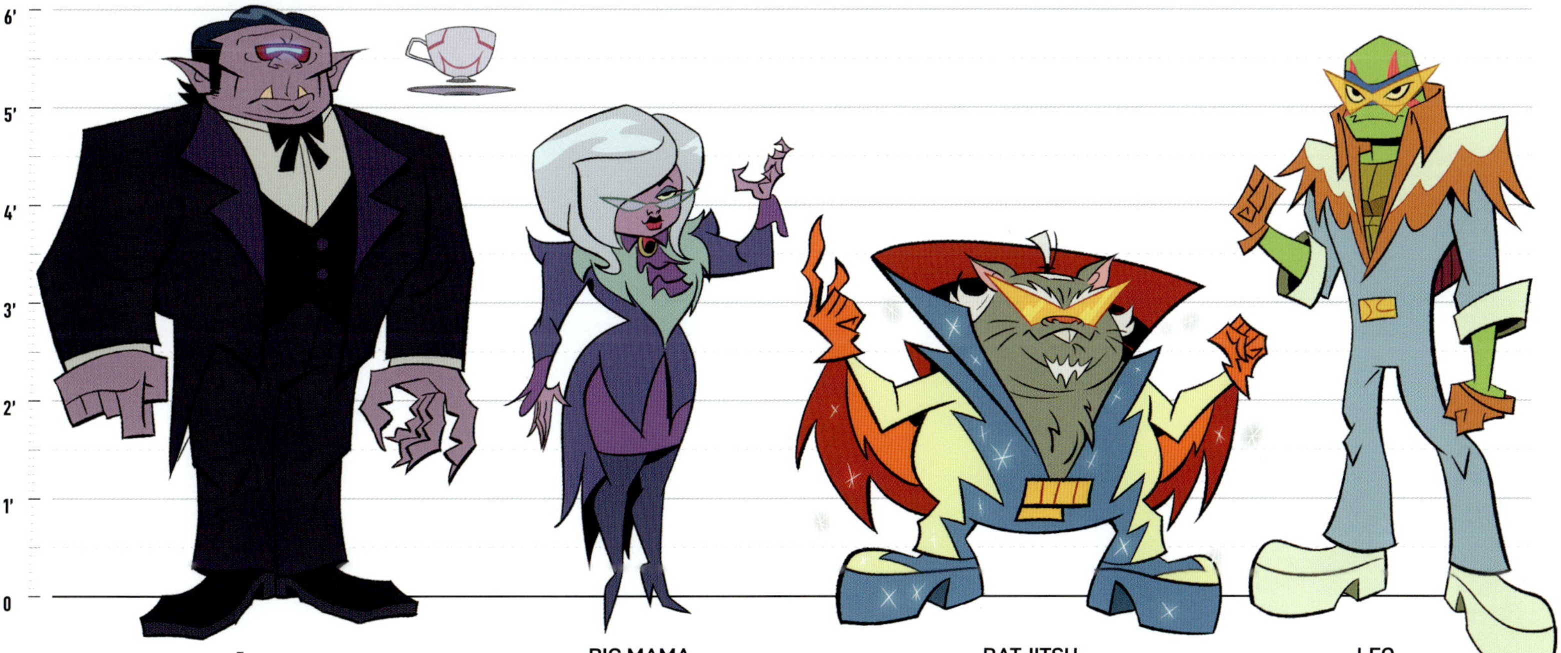

YŌKAI BUTLER

BIG MAMA
HUMAN FORM

RAT JITSU
BATTLE NEXUS CHAMPION

LEO
LOU JITSU UNIFORM

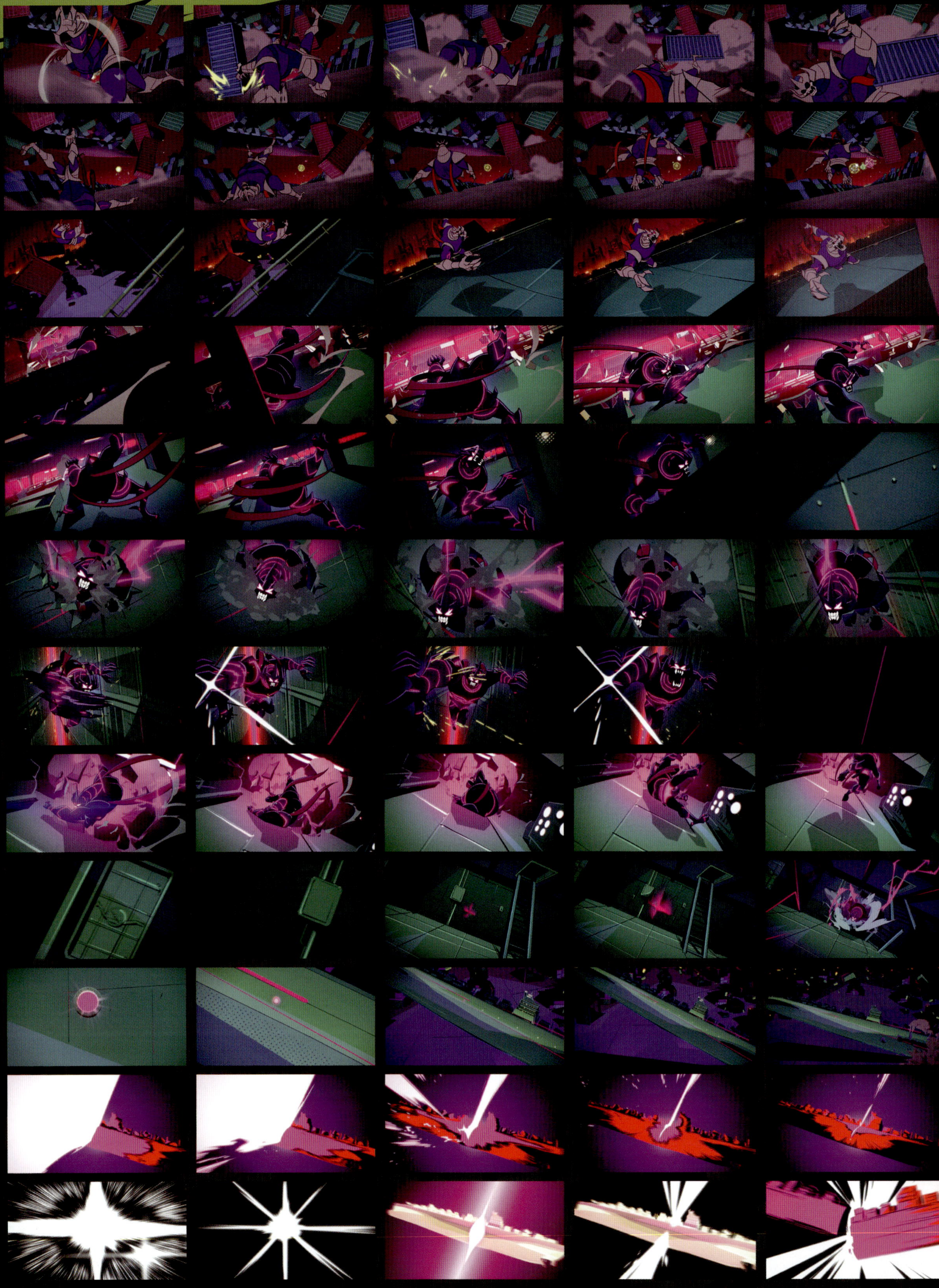

STORYBOARD ARTIST: **KEVIN MOLINA-ORTIZ**

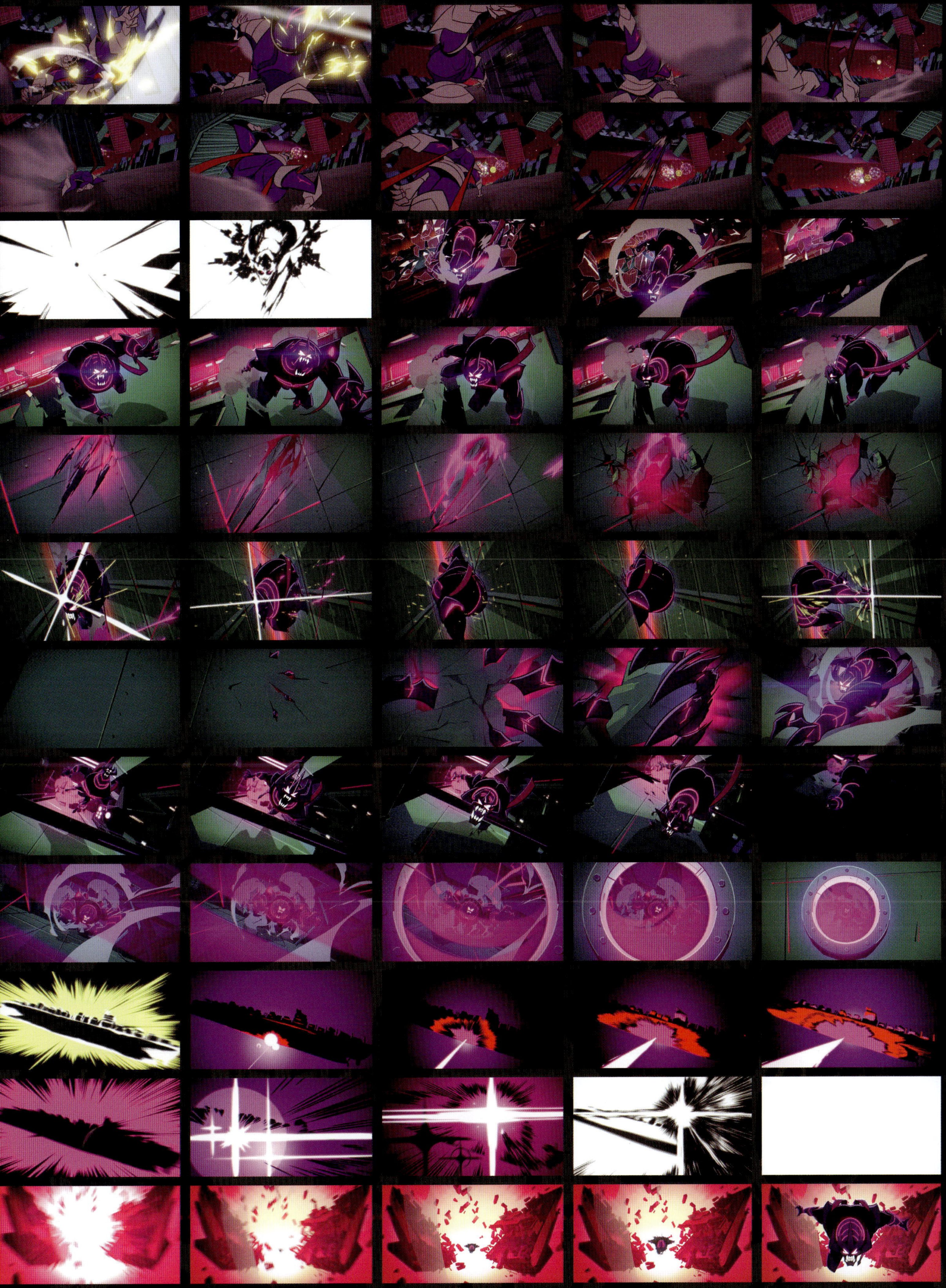

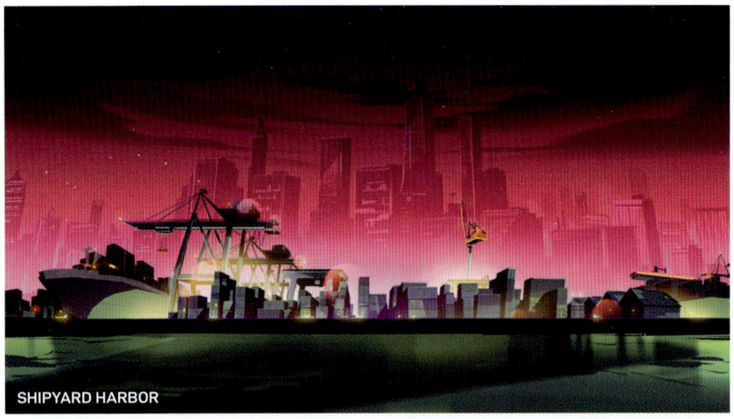
SHIPYARD HARBOR

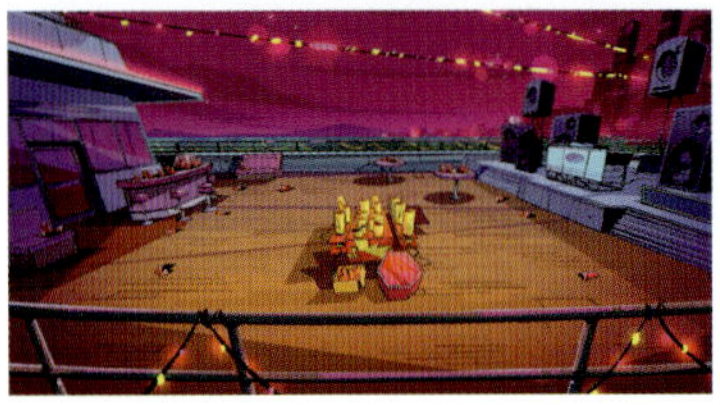

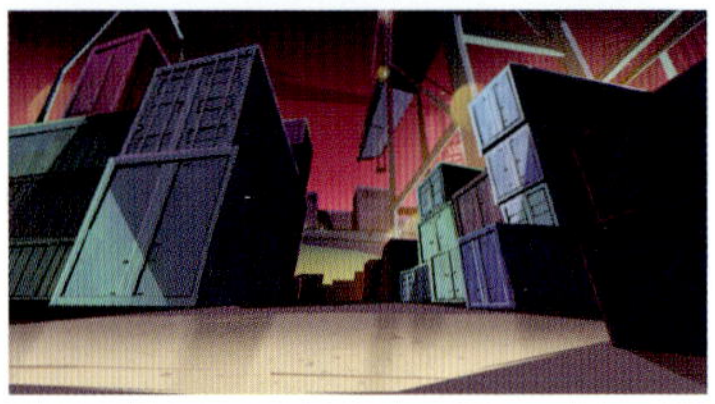

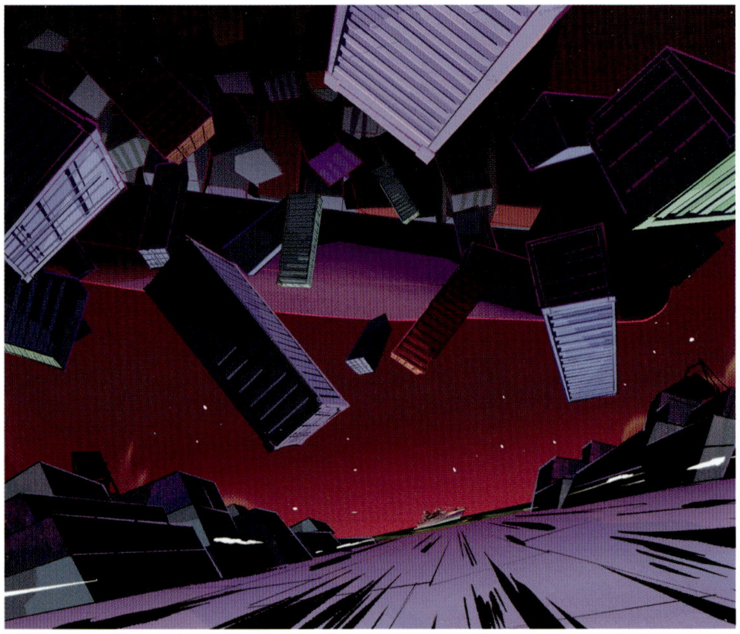

TONY GAMA-LOBO: April having a crane license was a memorable laugh in the writers room. Kevin Molina-Ortiz's storyboard sequence with Shredder slicing through the cargo ship was stunning! It was a perfect, terrifyingly clear illustration of Shredder's raw, unstoppable power and a clear reason why our heroes needed Leo to come through with the save.

JERMAINE JOSE: For the Shredder rampage sequence where he annihilates a cargo ship, we faced another situation needing simplified visual clarity. Shredder: purple. Turtles: green. The solution? Stylize the sequence with Shredder tearing straight through that green boat—reducing it to splinters. A clear visual nod to the audience that the Turtles might have finally met their match.

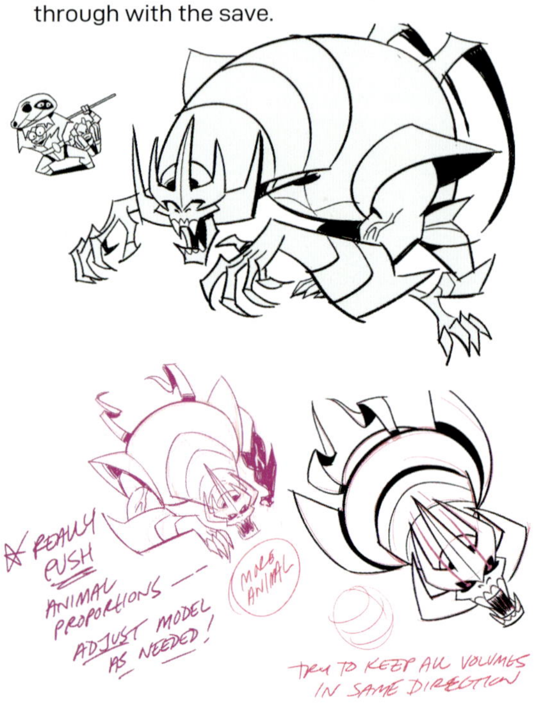

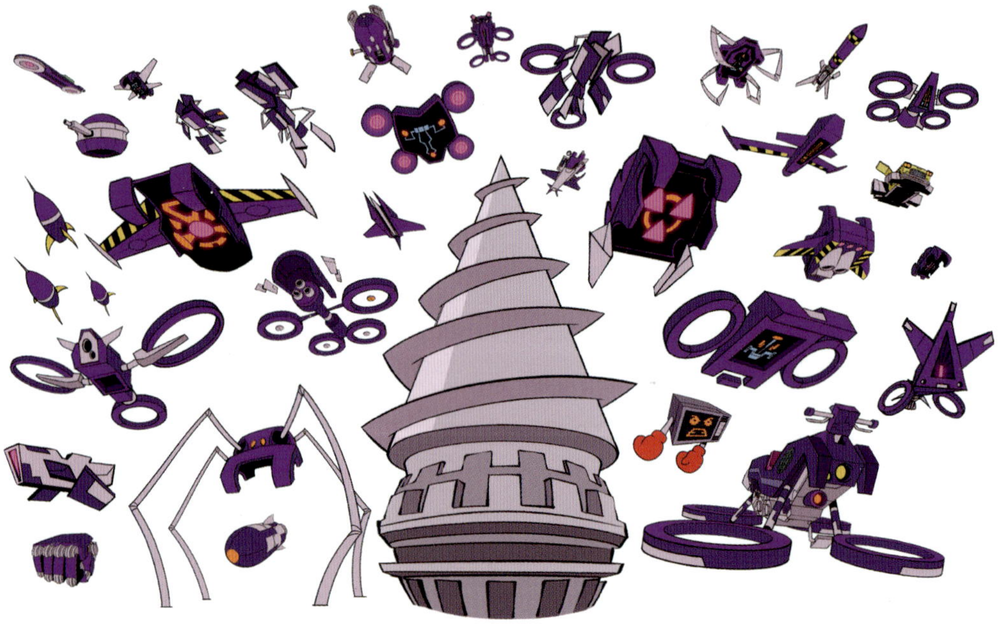

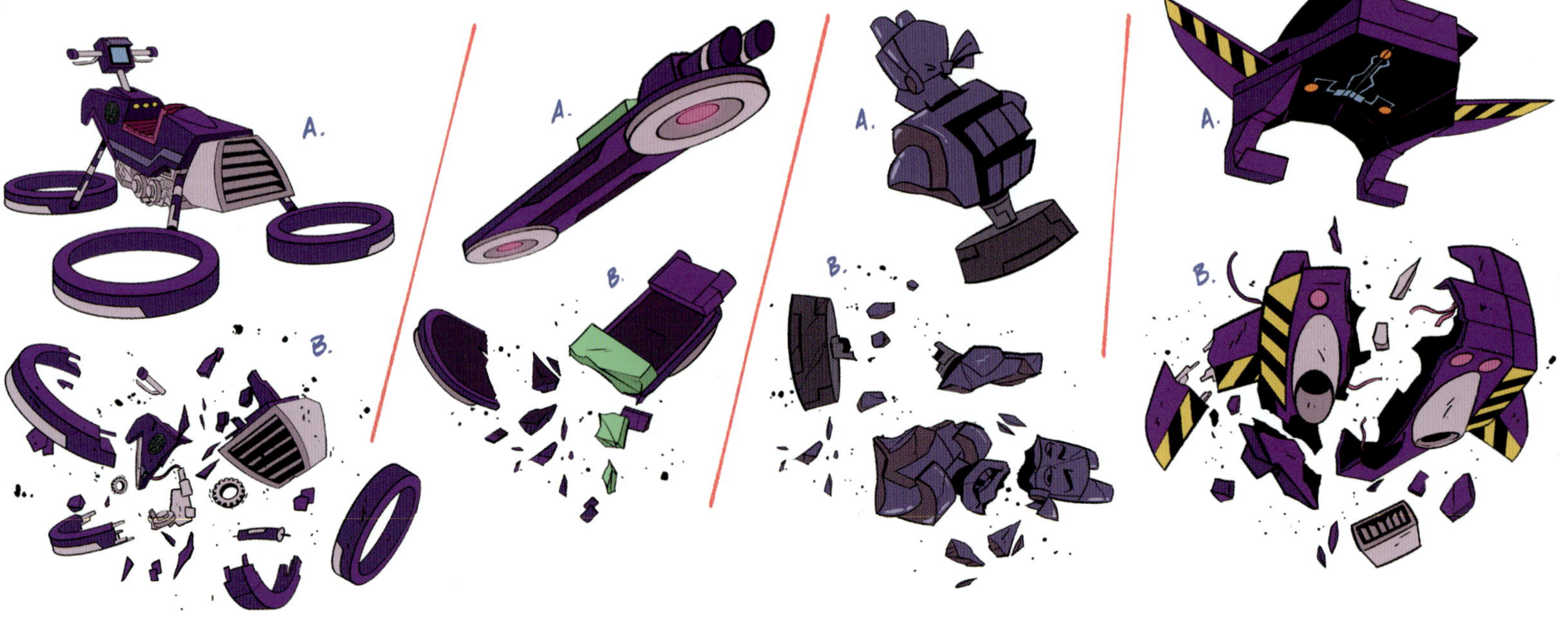

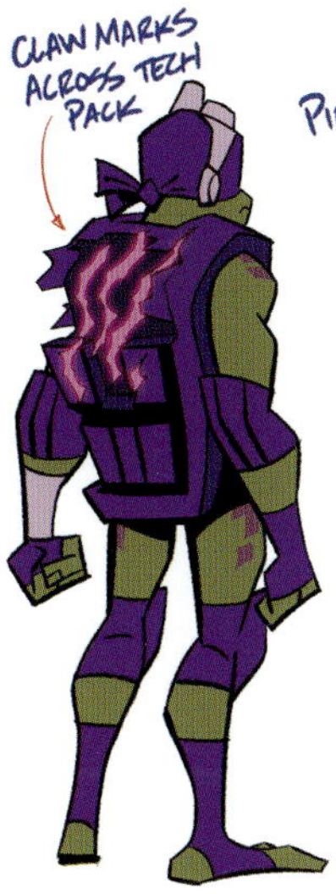

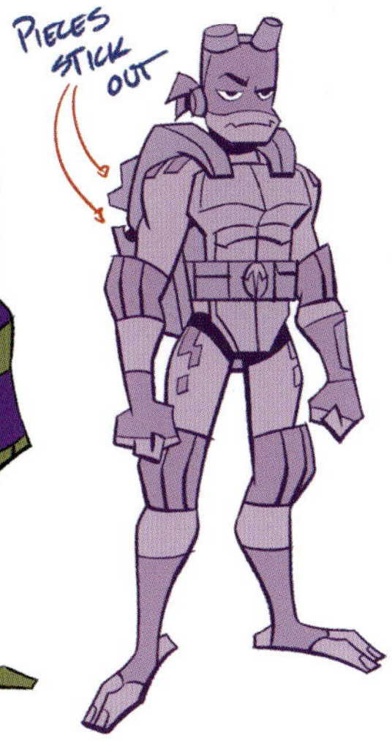

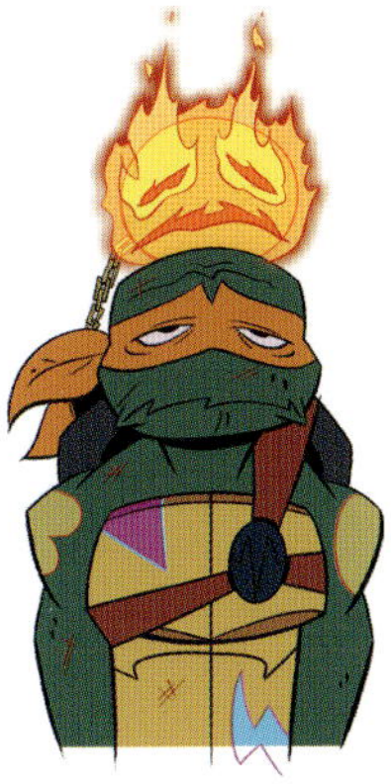

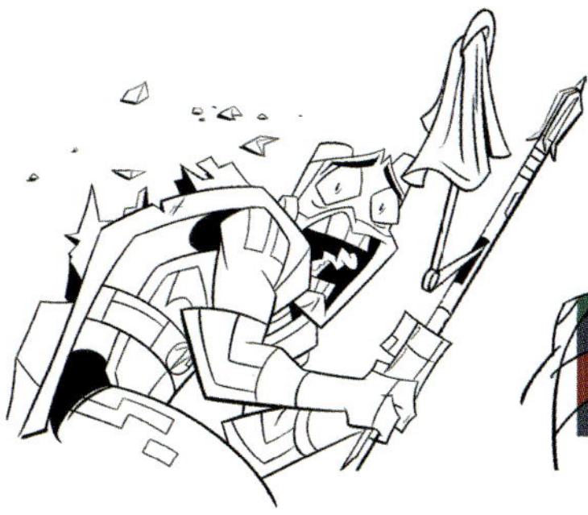

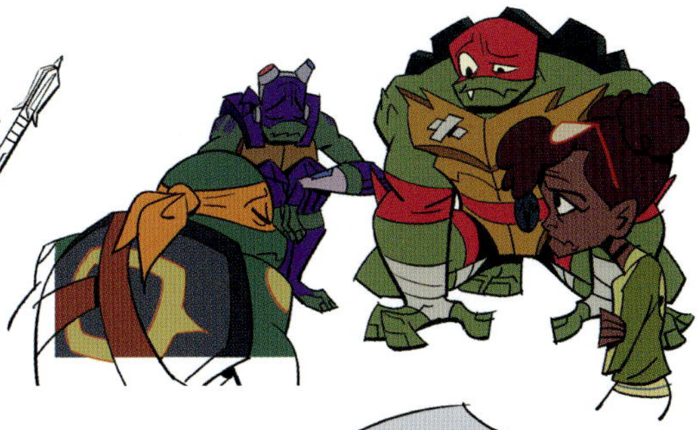

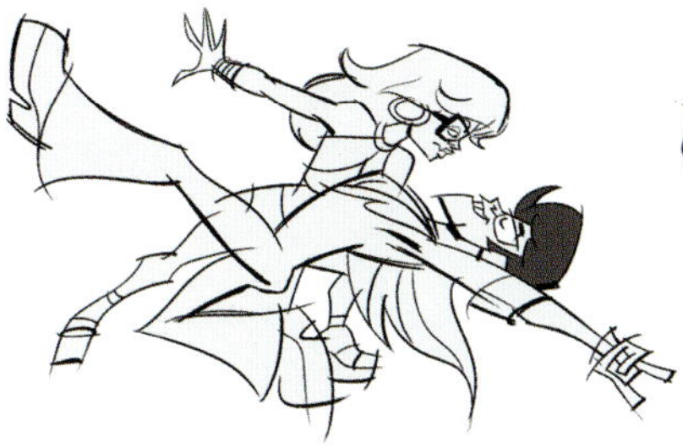

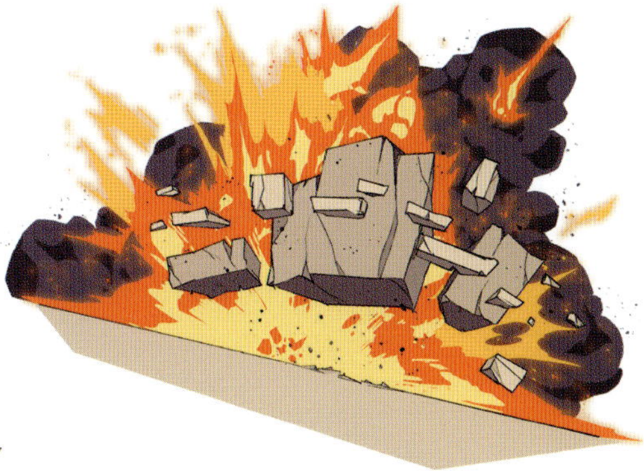

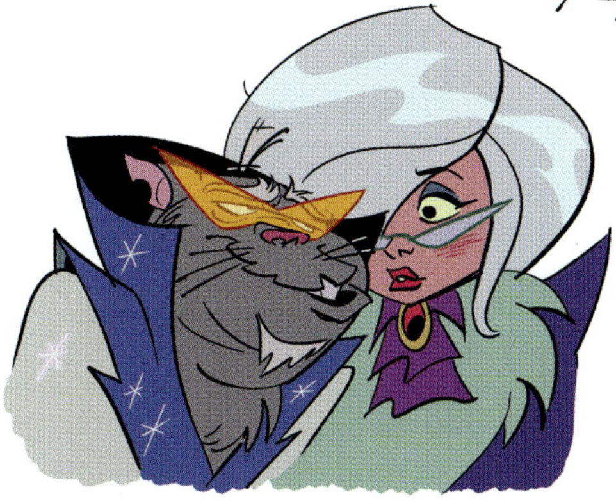

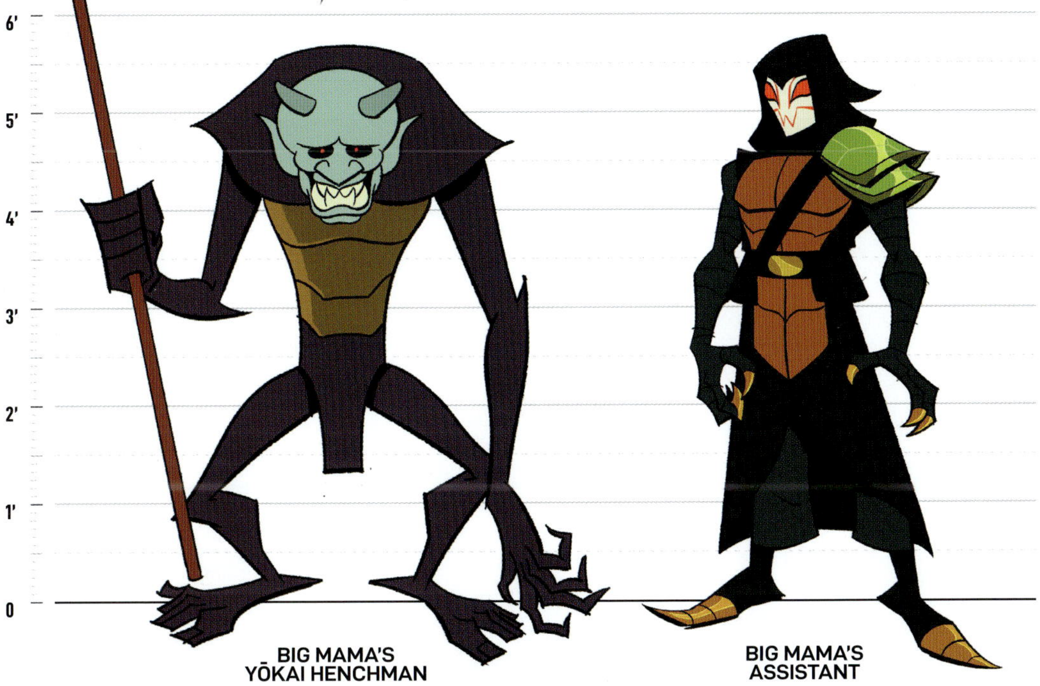

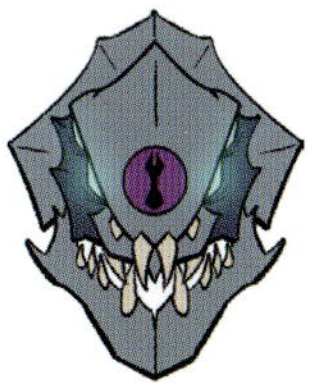

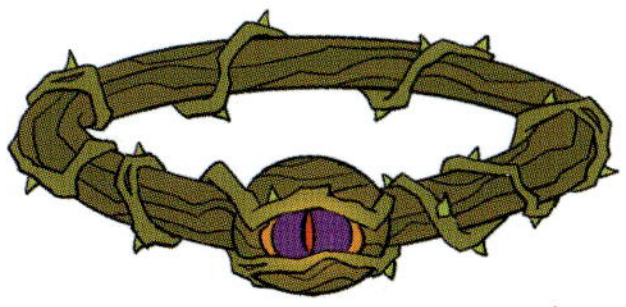

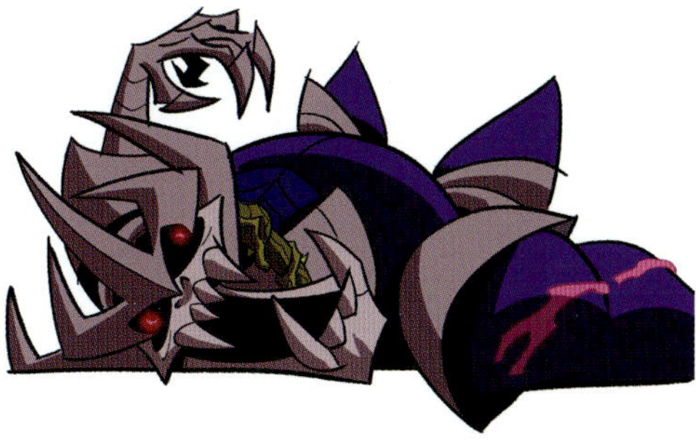

TONY GAMA-LOBO: We ultimately didn't have time to explore this before the cancellation, but the plan was that Big Mama used a mind-controlled Shredder to be her big-money champion in the Battle Nexus. We alluded to the champion Shadow Fiend a few times but never really got to discover it properly.

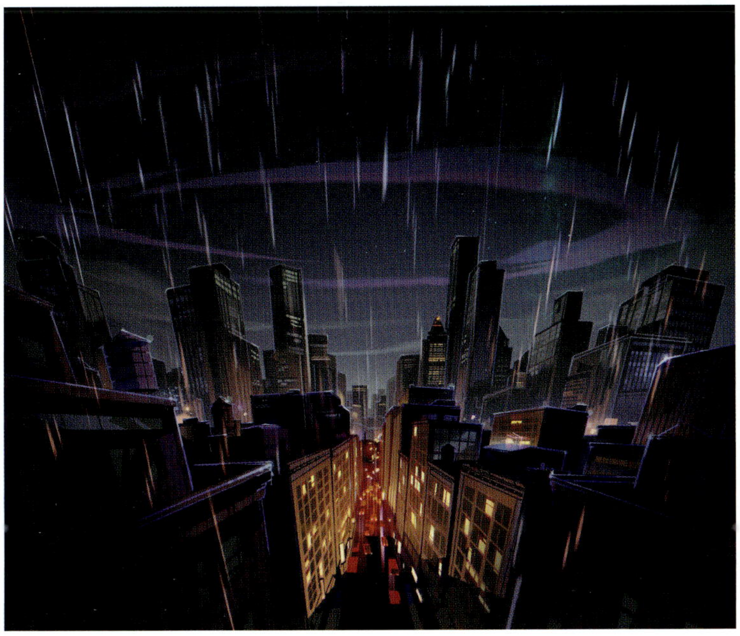

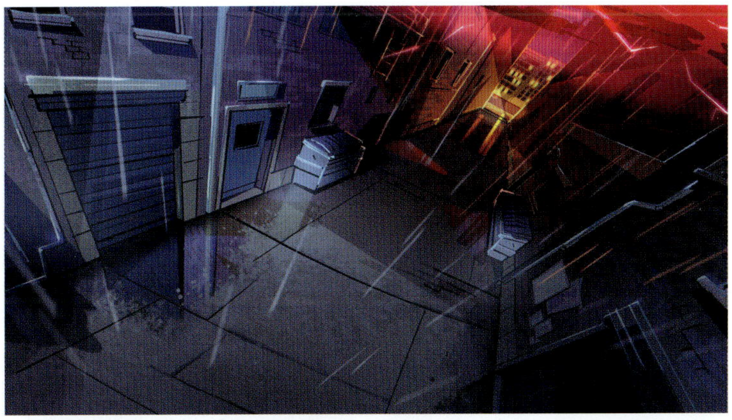

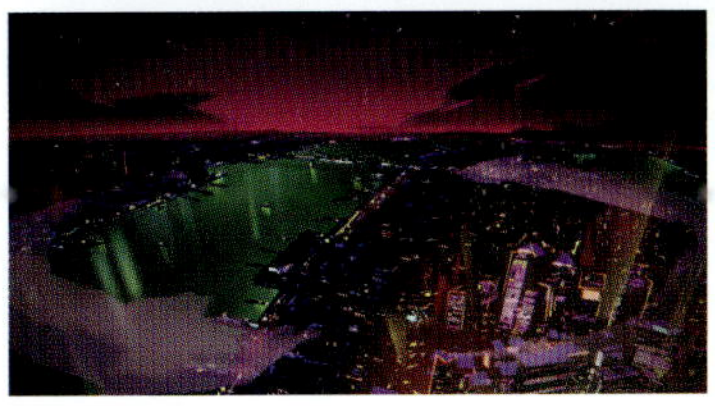

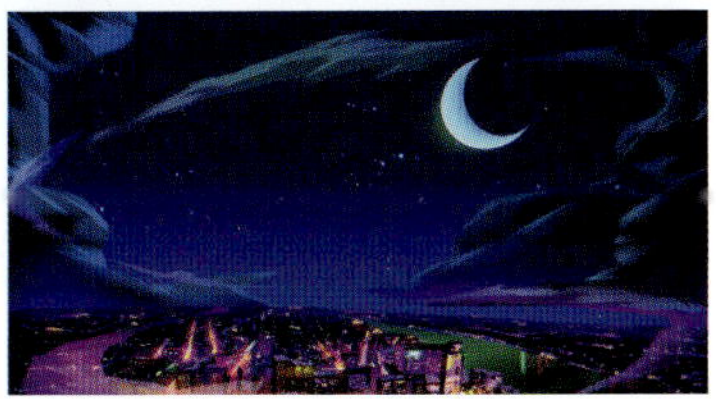

TODD SCOUTS

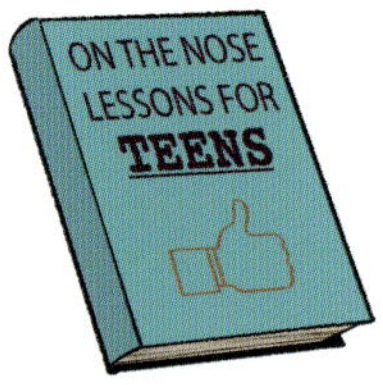

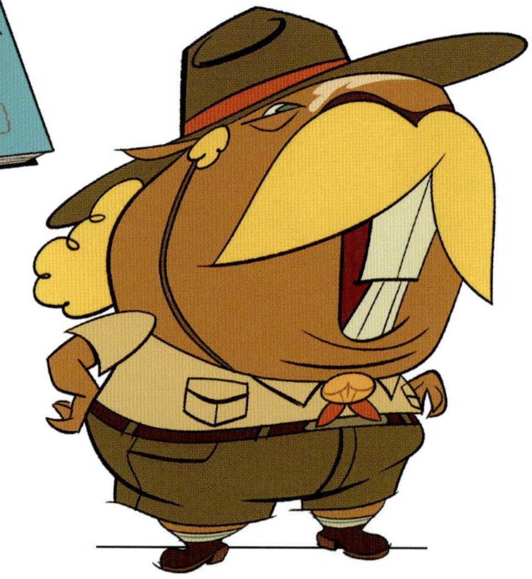

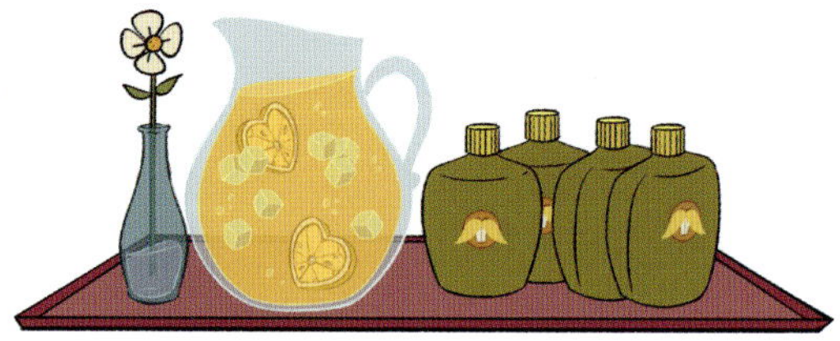

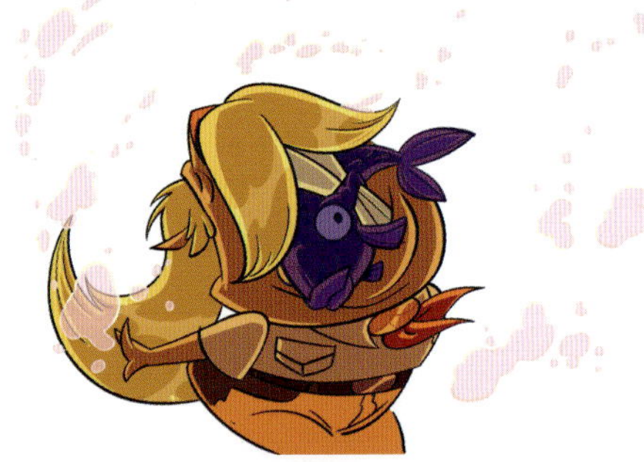

ORIGINAL AIR DATE: NOVEMBER 30, 2019
PRODUCTION CODE: 053

WRITTEN BY **JESSE GORDON**
STORYBOARDS BY **JULES BRIDGERS, JAKE CASTORENA, MORGAN HILLEBRAND, WILL RUZICKA**
DIRECTED BY **JJ CONWAY**

JESSE GORDON: By this point, we'd all fallen so hard for Todd that we were constantly inventing reasons to bring him back. The concept was simple: Strand our tech-dependent Turtles in the wilderness and force them to survive without their gadgets. I still don't know exactly how all the elements came together so perfectly, but they just did.

JJ Conway absolutely crushed this episode—the whole team did! They took that script and elevated it into one of my personal favorites. We originally had even more bonkers stuff planned for Donnie's squirrel-powered treehouse before trimming it for time. Honestly, this could have easily carried a full 22-minute episode.

You never know what you'll get when you write "giant animal stampede" on a TV budget, but holy crap did they deliver. And Todd's Super Saiyan moment? Whatever I imagined while writing it, the final version blew my expectations out of the water. The entire episode kills me—it's just so damn funny.

One of the best parts of working on this show was having not only an incredible main cast but also landing dream guest stars. As a huge *Arrested Development* (2003) and *Veep* (2012) fan, getting Tony Hale to voice Dr. Alex Noe was genuinely special for me.

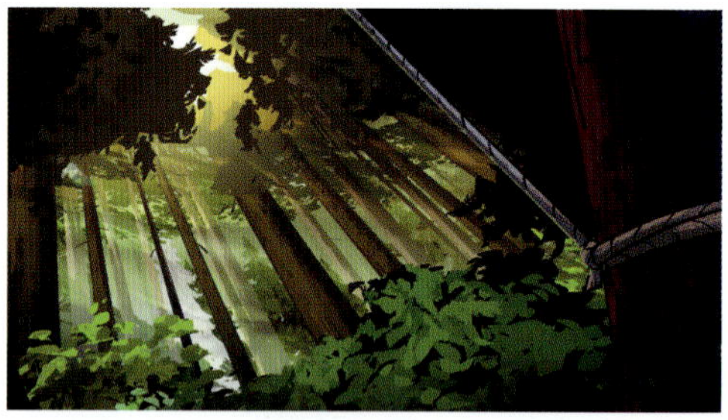

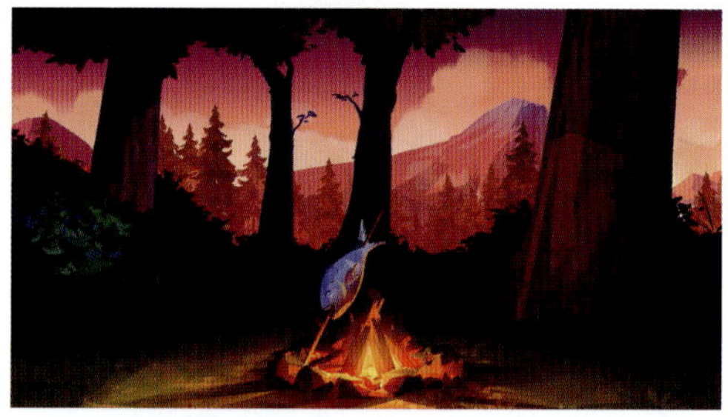

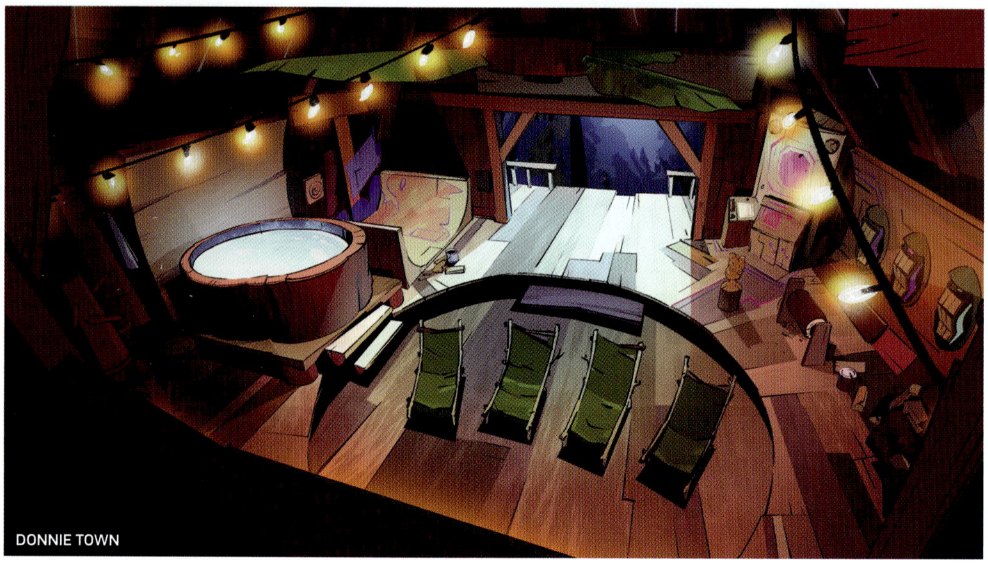
DONNIE TOWN

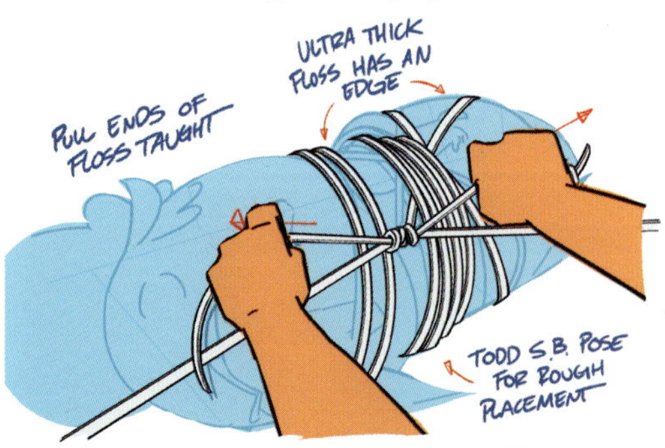

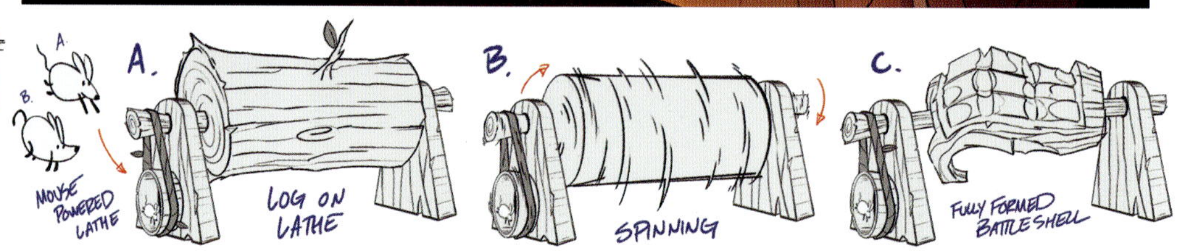

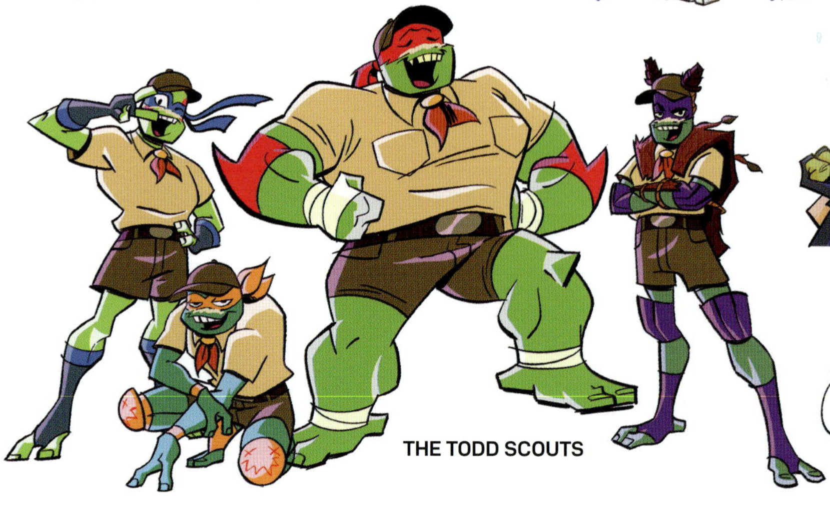
THE TODD SCOUTS

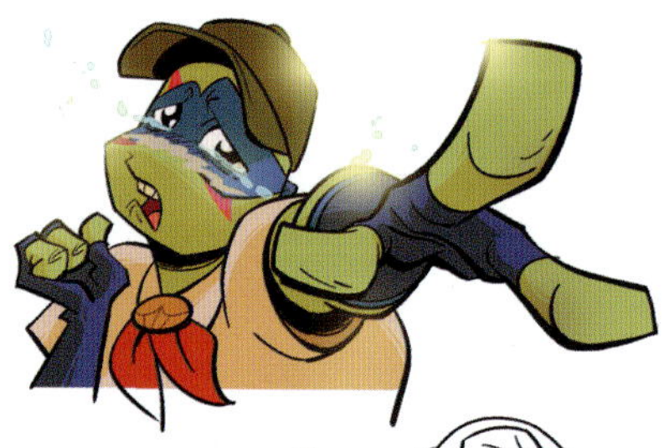

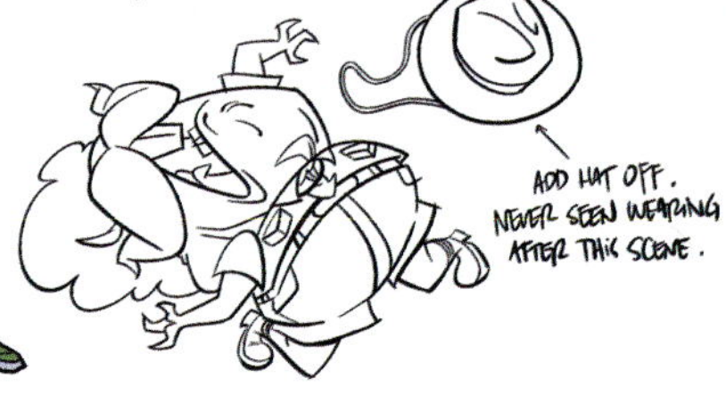

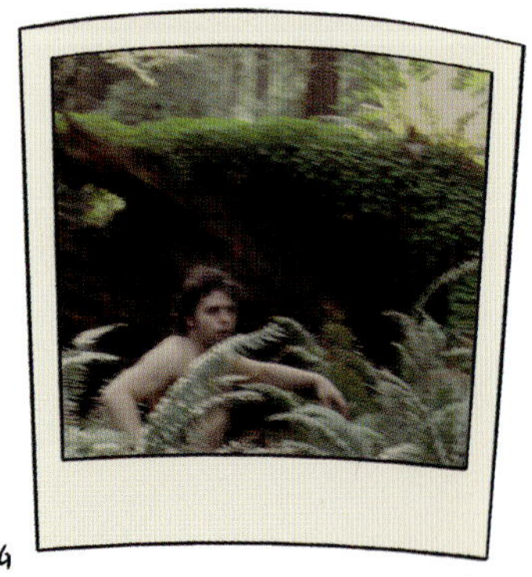
Art director Andy Suriano cameos as the Sasquatch

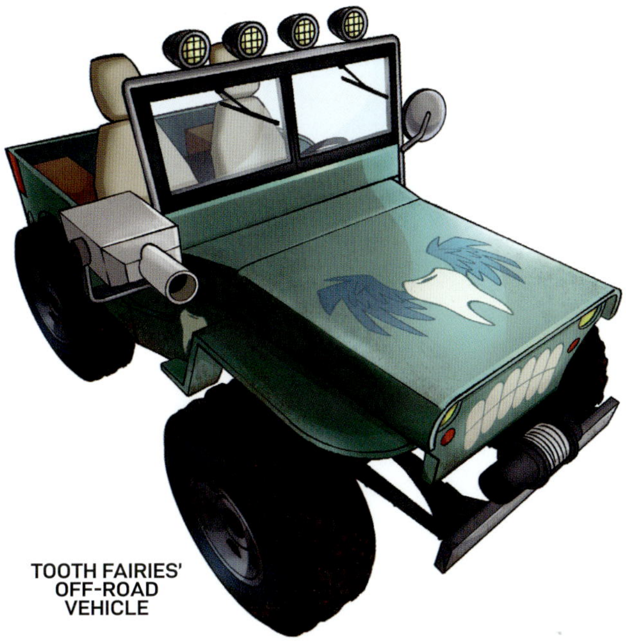

TOOTH FAIRIES' OFF-ROAD VEHICLE

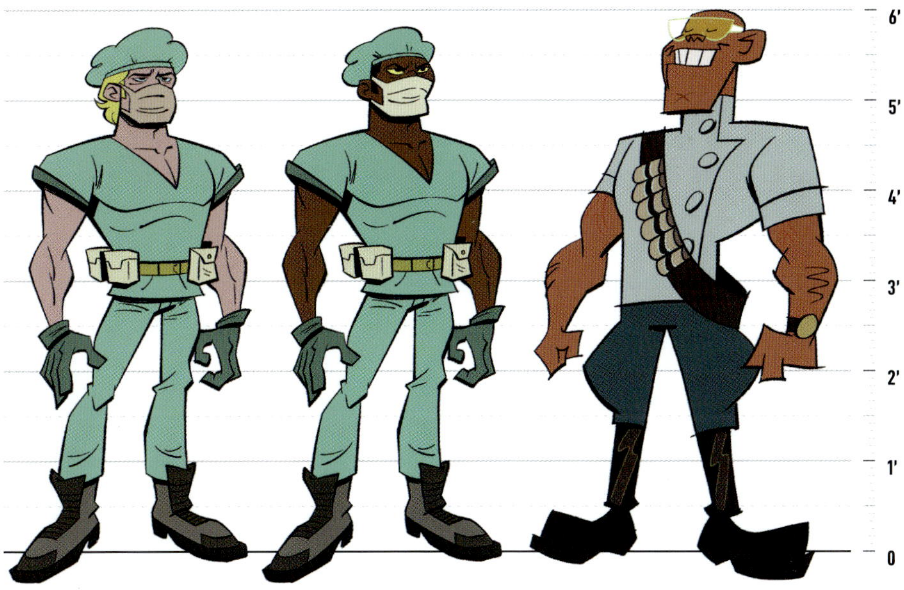

TOOTH FAIRIES HUNTERS

DR. ALEX NOE

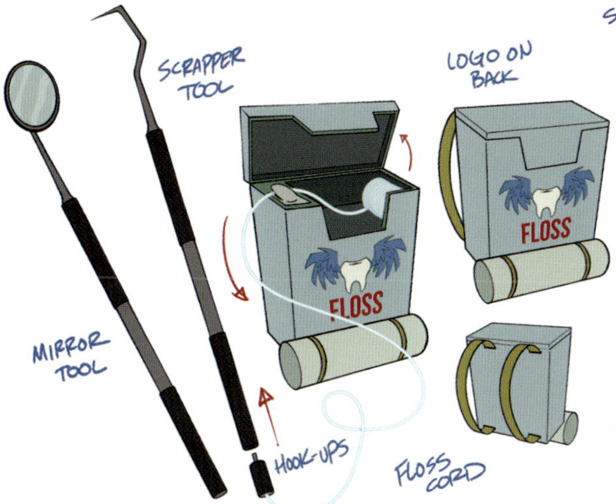

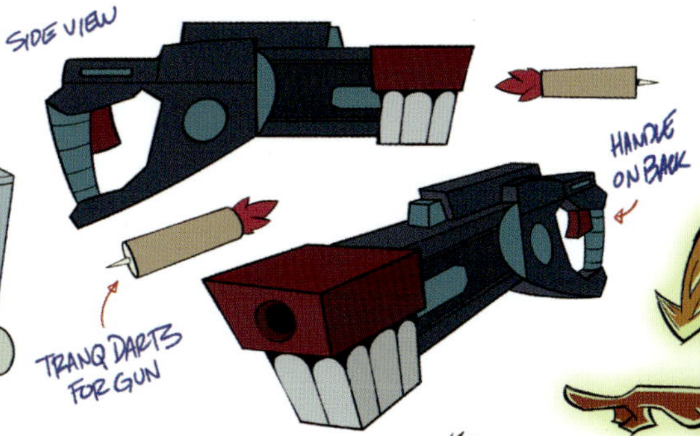

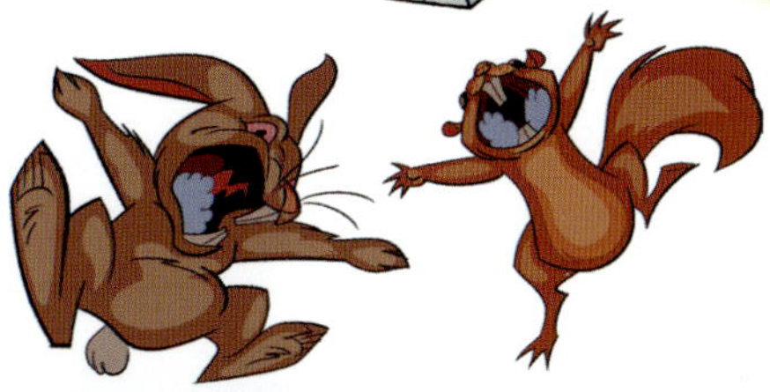

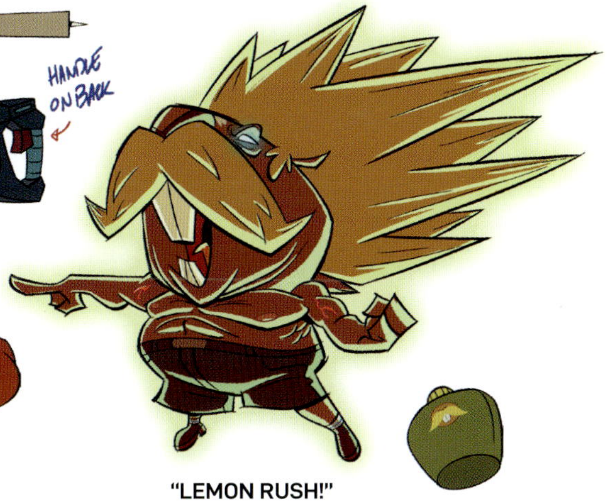

"LEMON RUSH!"

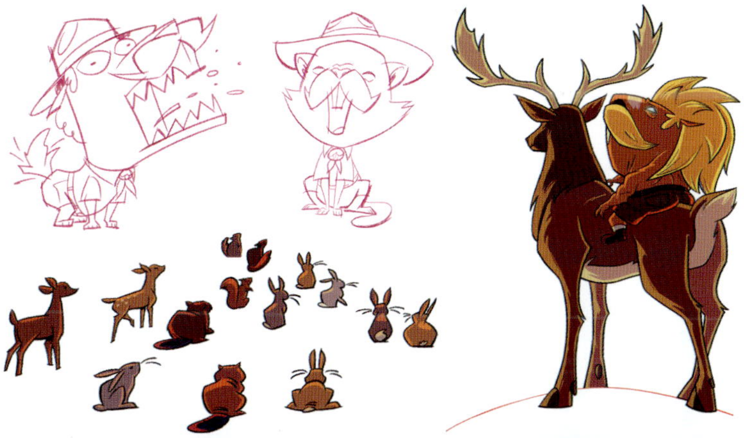

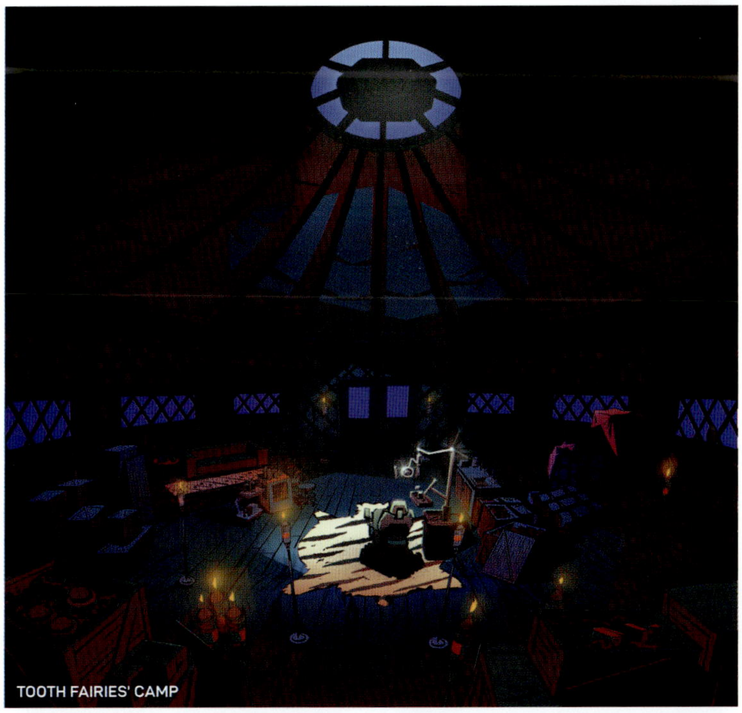

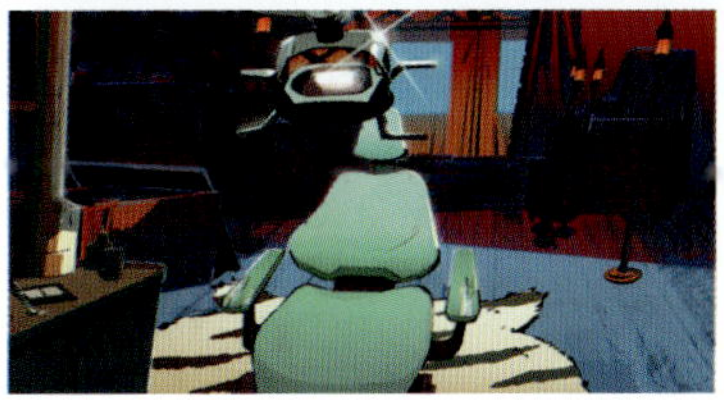

TOOTH FAIRIES' CAMP

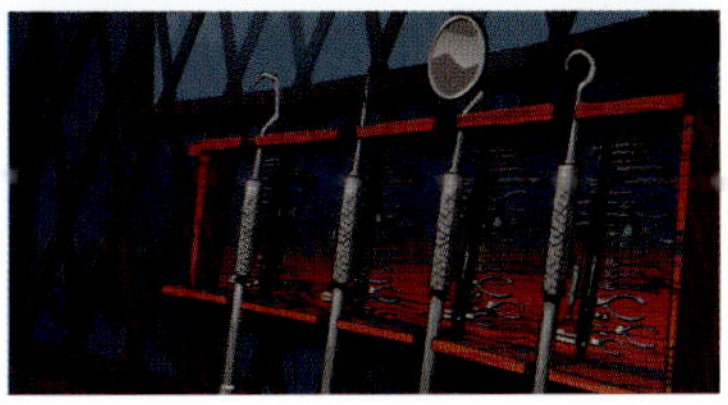

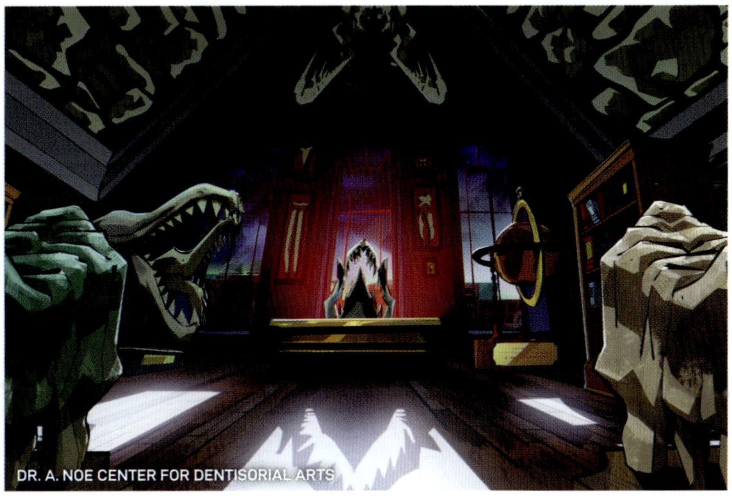

DR. A. NOE CENTER FOR DENTISORIAL ARTS

GOYLES, GOYLES, GOYLES

ORIGINAL AIR DATE: NOVEMBER 30, 2019
PRODUCTION CODE: 054

WRITTEN BY **RUSS CARNEY & RON CORCILLO**
STORYBOARDS BY **MAX COLLINS, MATTHEW HUMPHREYS, ANDREW KIM**
DIRECTED BY **ABE AUDISH**

RON CORCILLO: We thought it would be fun to tell the origin story of Splinter and the Turtles through the point of view of two minor, and unreliable, characters. We thought that paying homage to the old Terrytoons cartoon *Heckle and Jeckle* would be fun as well, so we leaned heavily into a silly story that saw two underdogs clawing for a slightly better life. When the two goyles are relaxing in the dog bed, they call each other *"old chum"* and *"old bean,"* which Heckle and Jeckle frequently called each other.

RUSS CARNEY: Josh Brener, who hails from Texas, winds up at the Battle Nexus (rhyme time!), where he plays the good-ol'-boy guard who Huginn and Muninn have to impress, yet again demonstrating his proficiency for accents. We also love Sam Richardson's delivery of *"Check out these walnuts!"* It cracked up everybody in the record session.

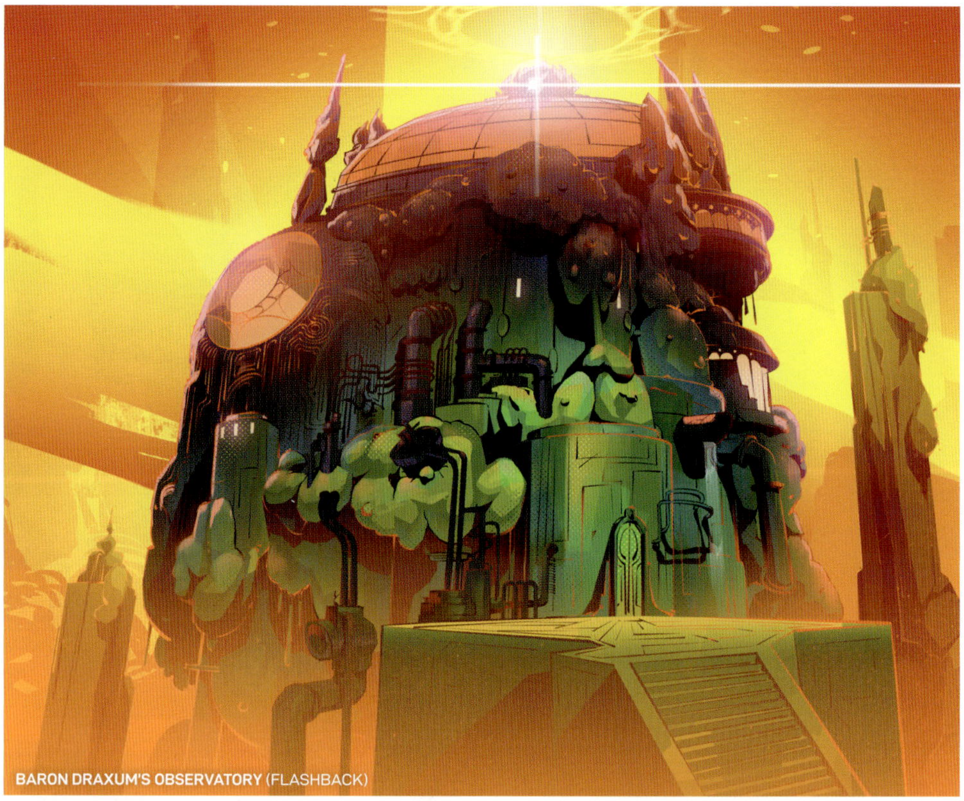
BARON DRAXUM'S OBSERVATORY (FLASHBACK)

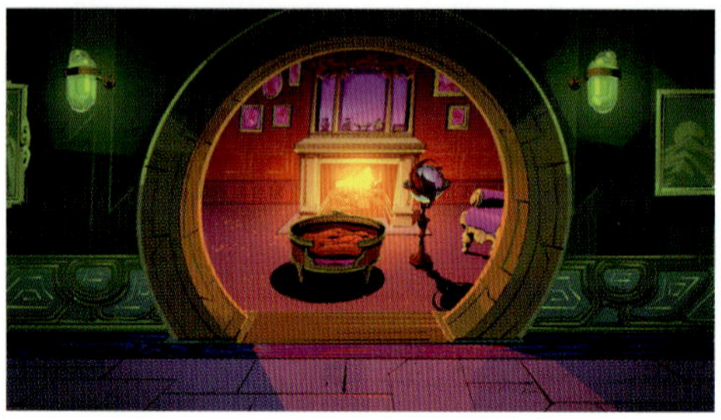

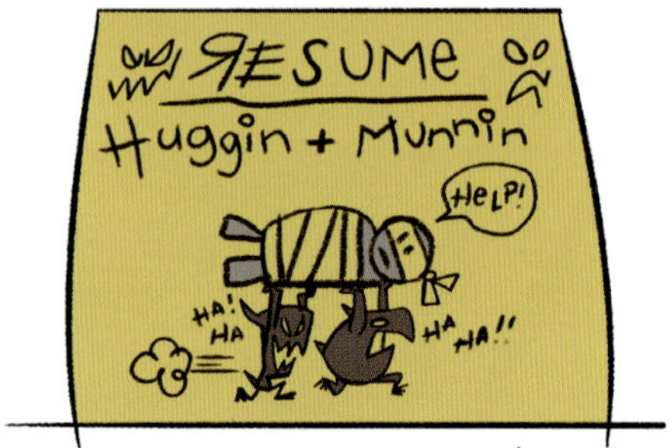

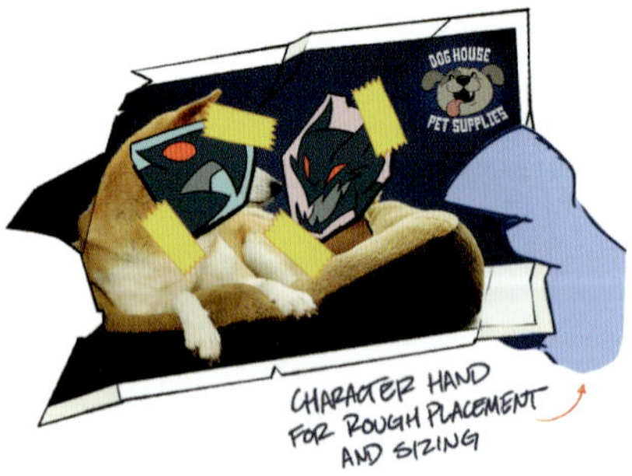

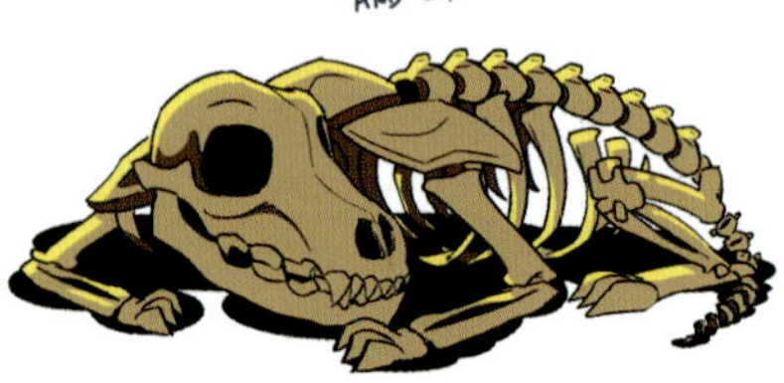

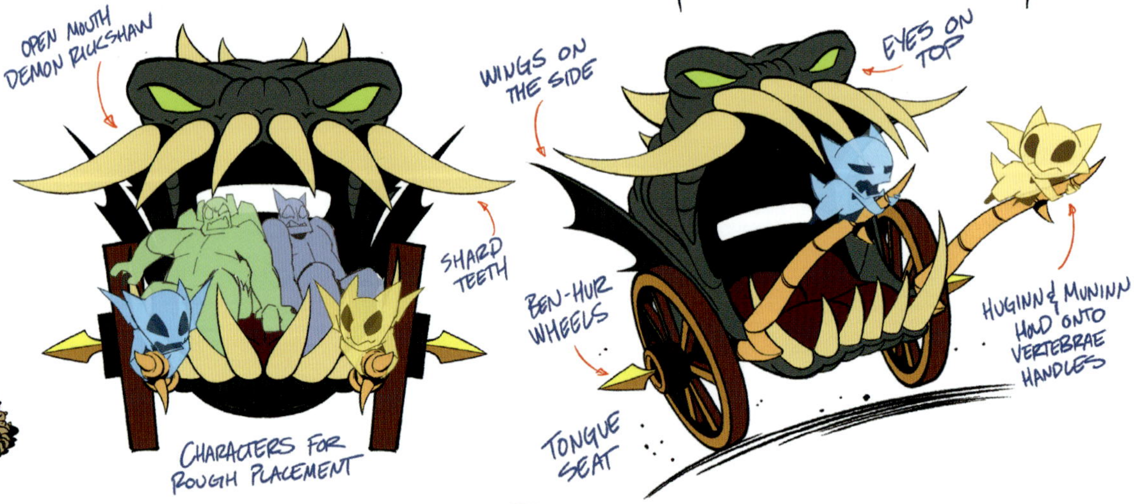

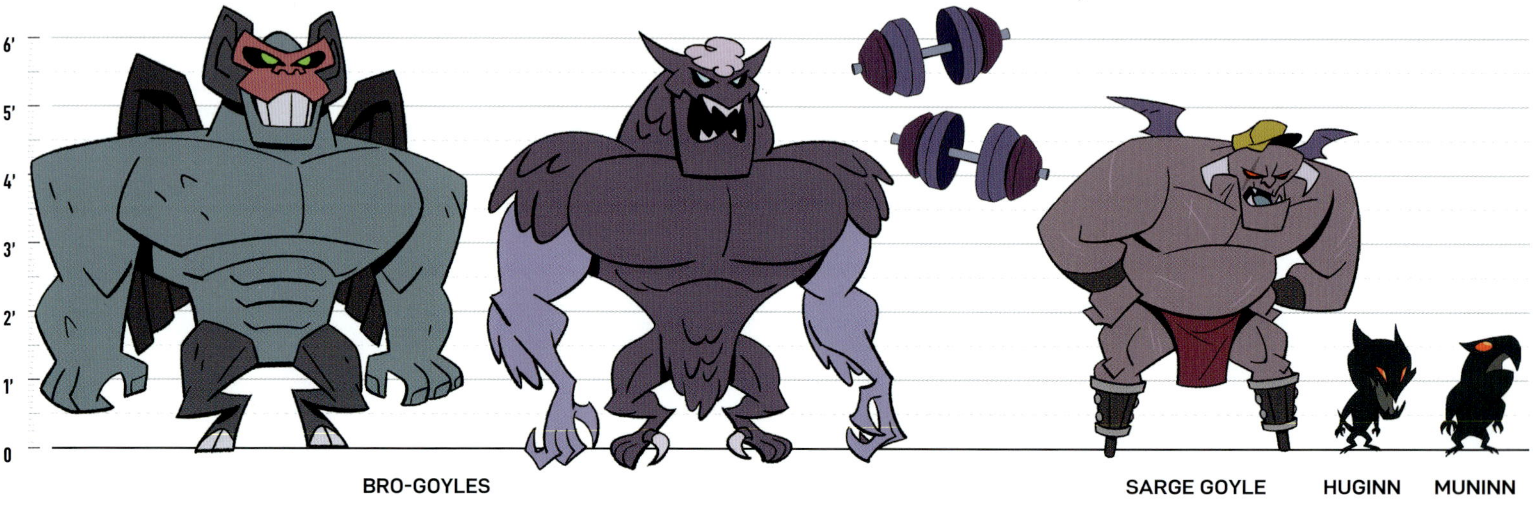

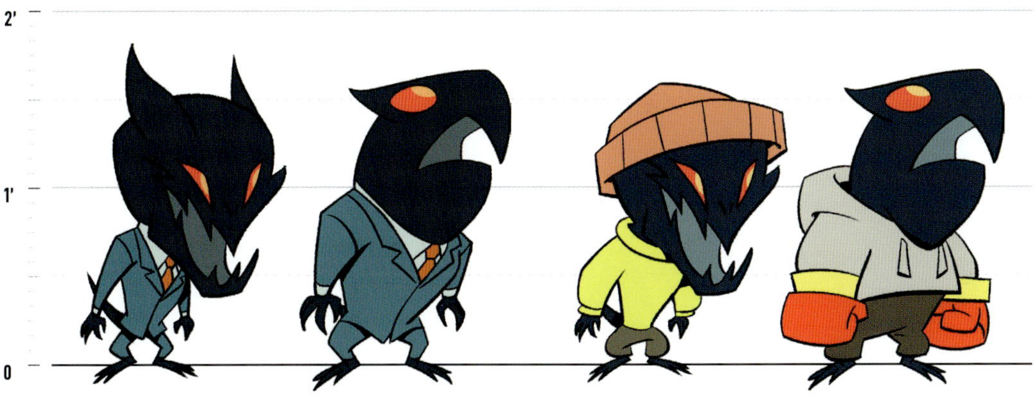

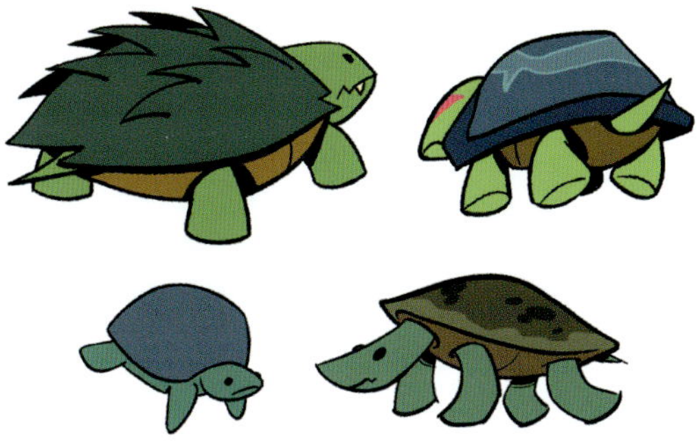

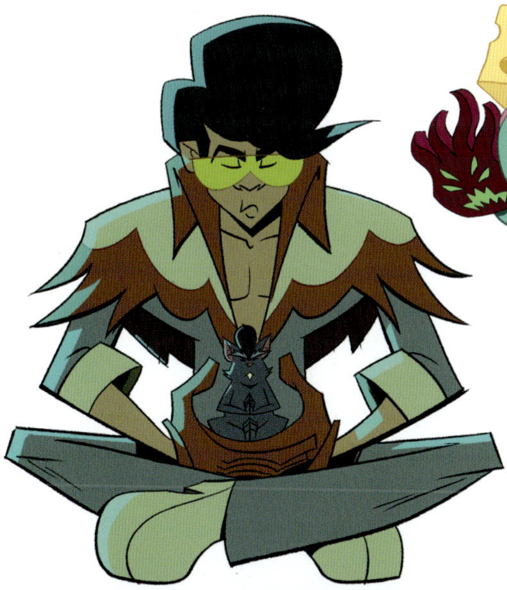

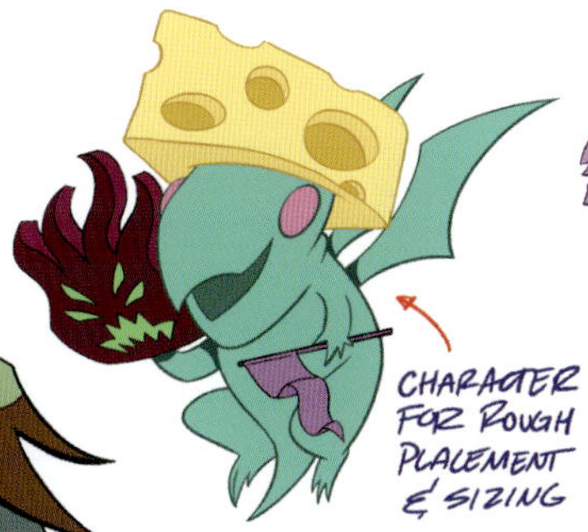

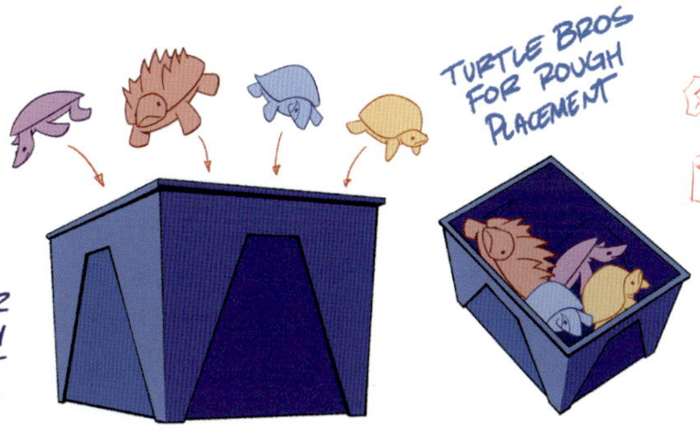

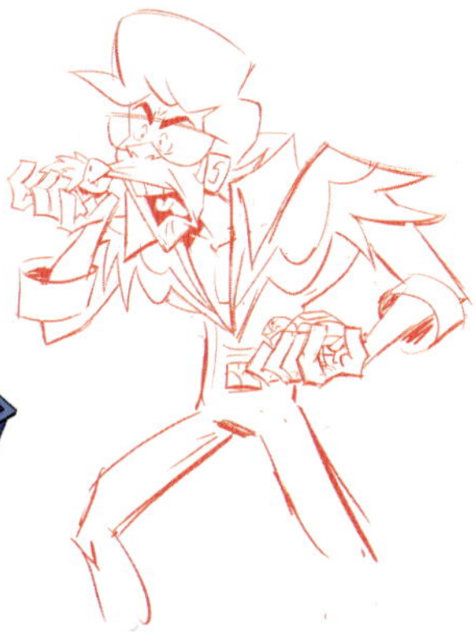

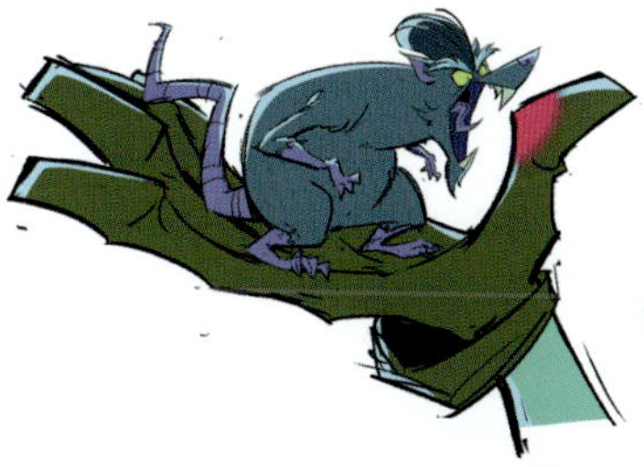

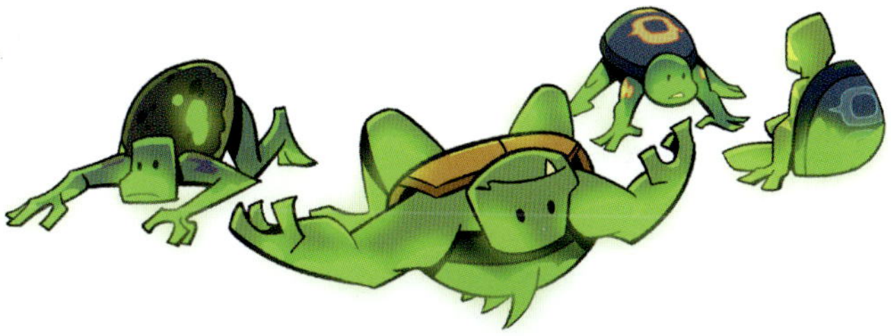

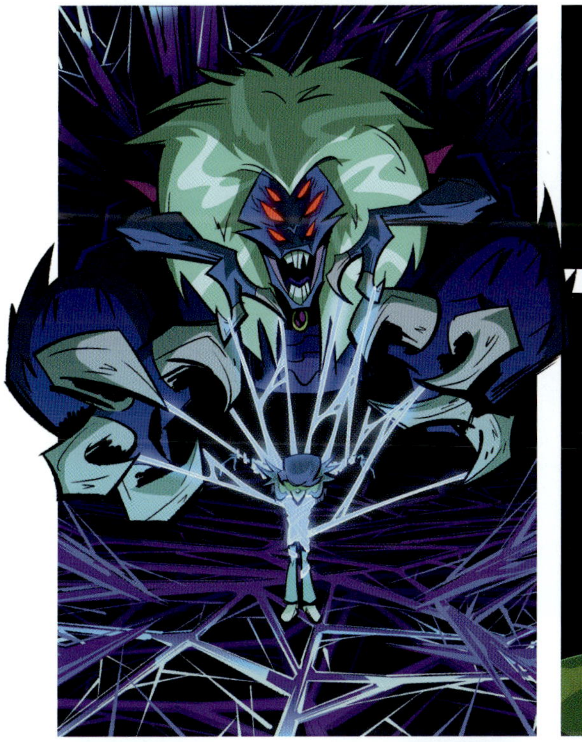

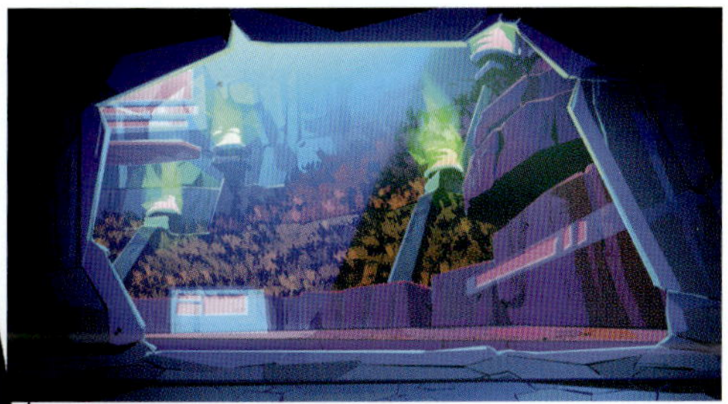

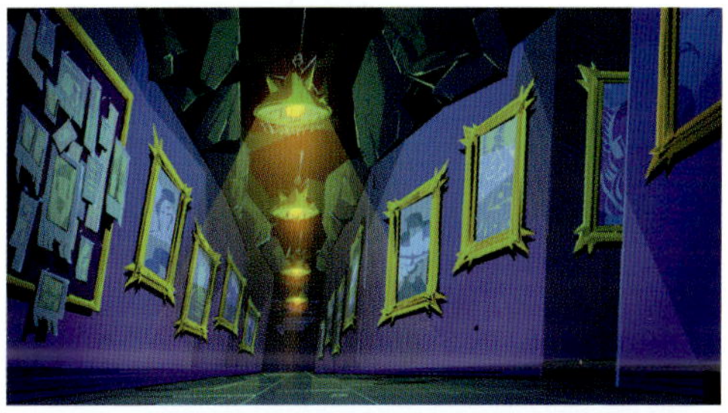

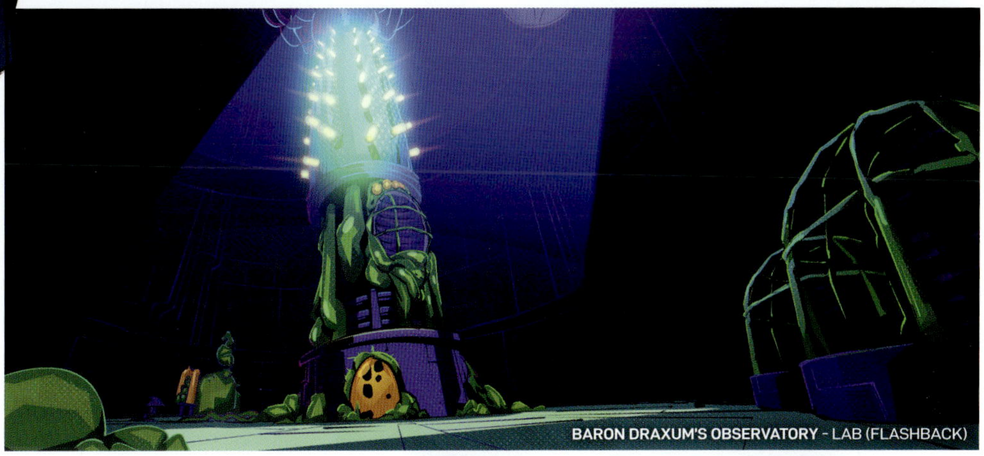
BARON DRAXUM'S OBSERVATORY - LAB (FLASHBACK)

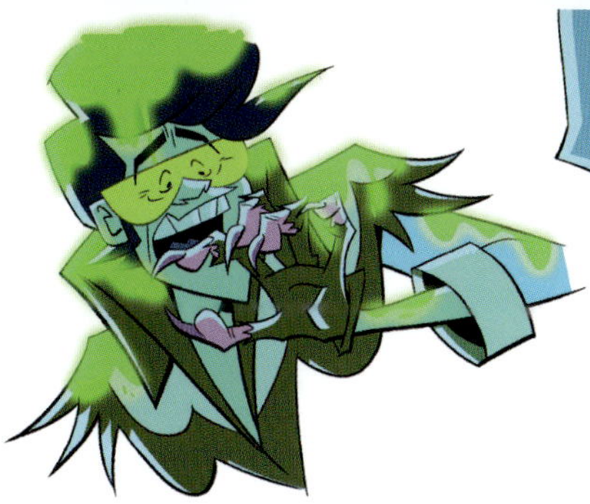

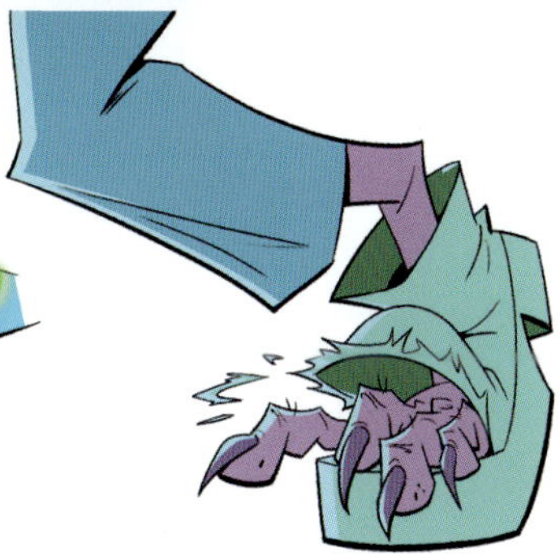

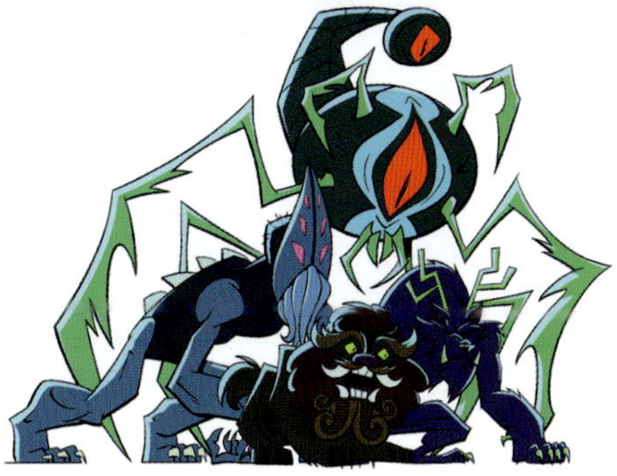

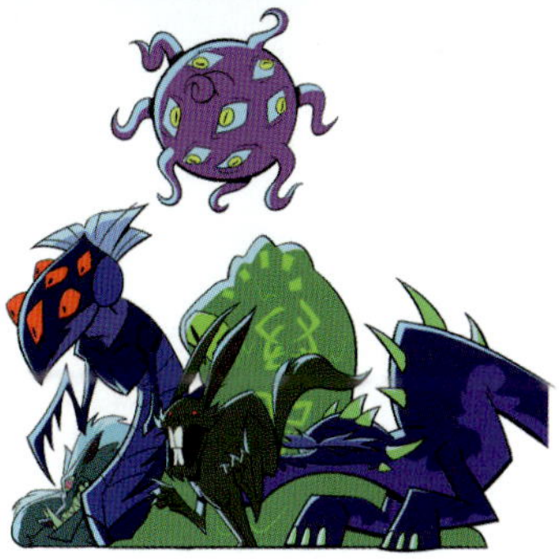

FLUSHED, BUT NEVER FORGOTTEN

ORIGINAL AIR DATE: OCTOBER 12, 2019
PRODUCTION CODE: 055

WRITTEN BY **DALE MALINOWSKI**
STORYBOARDS BY **KEVIN MOLINA-ORTIZ**
DIRECTED BY **ALAN WAN**

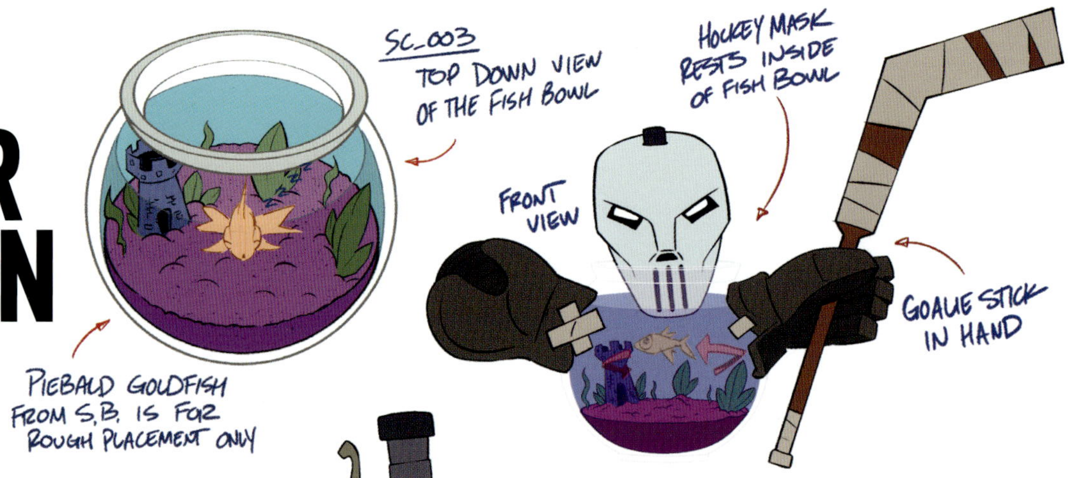

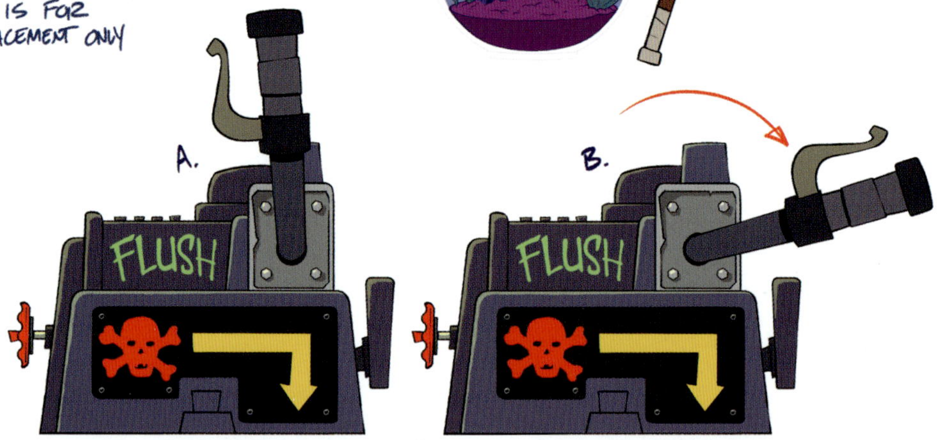

DALE MALINOWSKI: I had an idea for a new character before I had a story in mind. I shared my goldfish mutant concept with Jesse, and he pointed out how lots of kids have a goldfish as their first pet, suggesting that the Turtles are no different. We quickly worked out how the episode could play like a revenge tale and drew inspiration from *I Know What You Did Last Summer* (1997).

The whole story takes place in the lair, so figuring out how to incorporate Splinter in a meaningful way was a fun challenge. I think it was Jesse who suggested looking at the hilarious *"that's why you always leave a note"* bit from *Arrested Development*, wherein a father recruits a friend's help to stage a ridiculously over-the-top and traumatic scenario just to teach his kids a very simple lesson. That got us to the goldfish being Splinter's beloved pet, making the Turtles collectively culpable for her demise. Keeping a shared secret gave the Turtles an emotional conflict to work through beyond their primal will to survive. I think Russ pitched giving Raph dental headgear to show our young viewers the Turtles deal with regular kid stuff, too.

I remember Omar incorporating Raph's headgear into his performance by recording all of Raph's dialogue with a slight lisp. During the session, we tweaked a few lines to add more *S*'s because Omar's deliveries were so funny!

My mom pitched the name Piebald, and the word means *"having irregular patches of two colors,"* which applies to some breeds of goldfish. A multicolored blotchy pattern reminded me of camouflage, so that became Piebald's mutant power, and that worked well with the story's plot and genre.

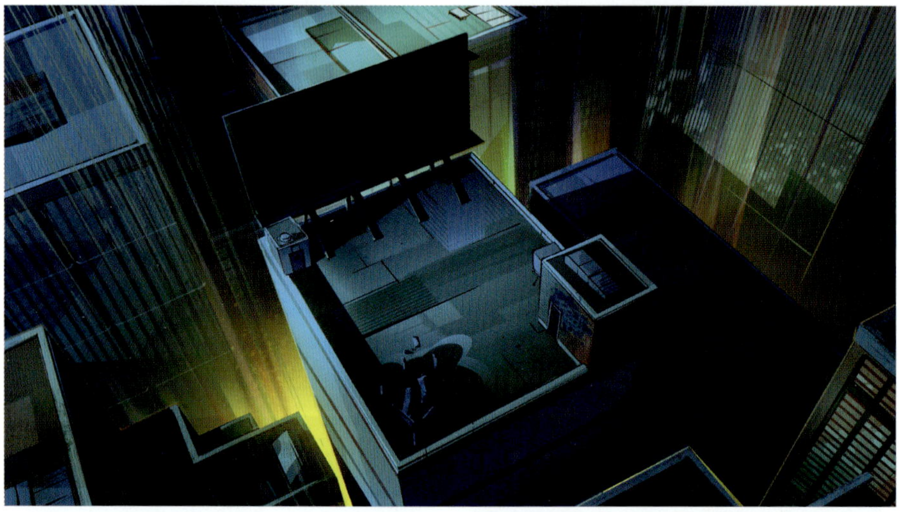

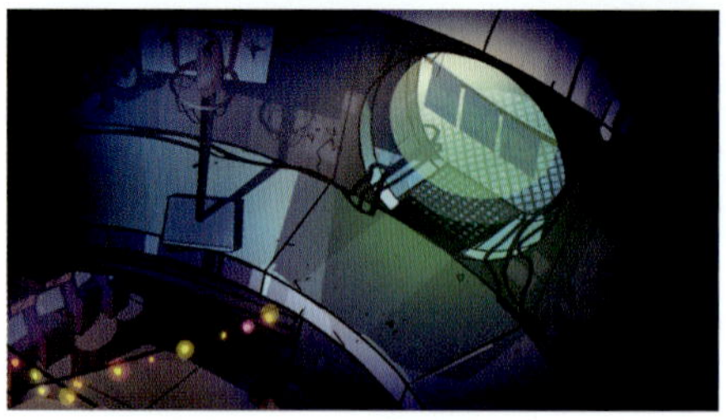

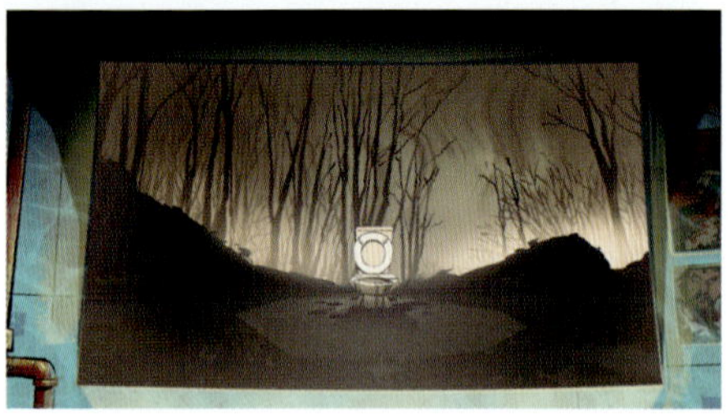

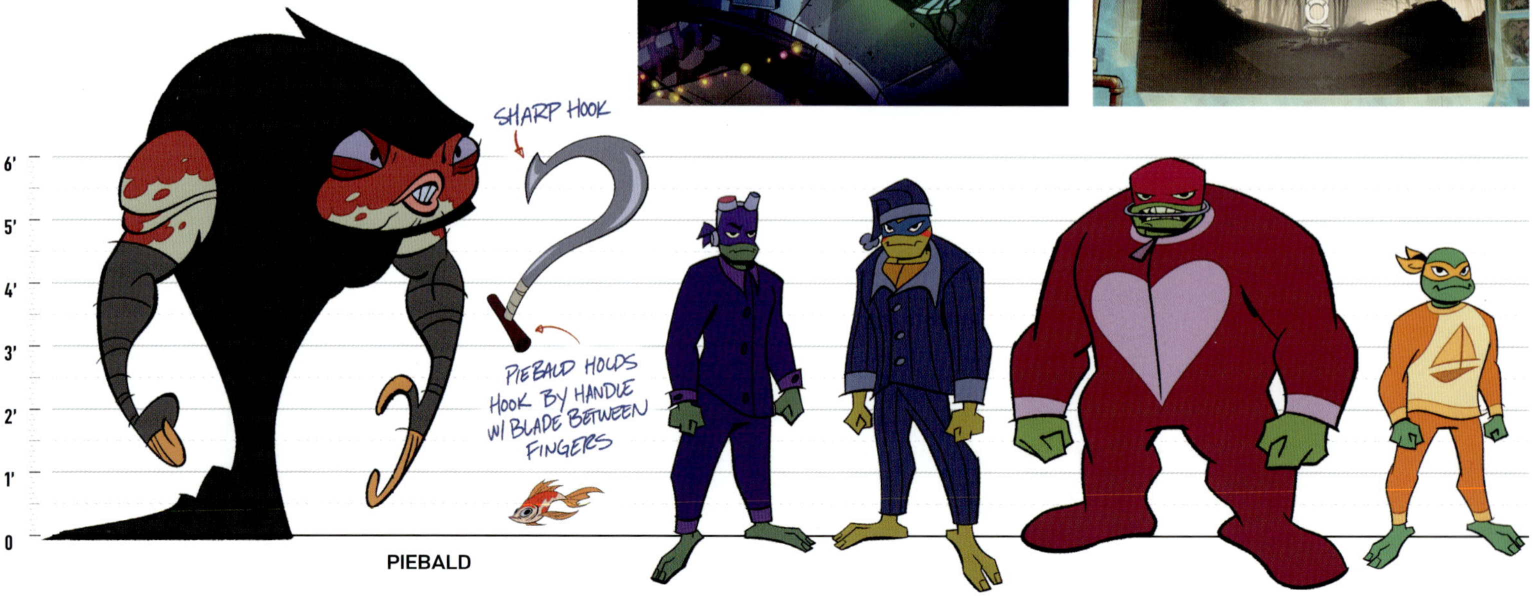

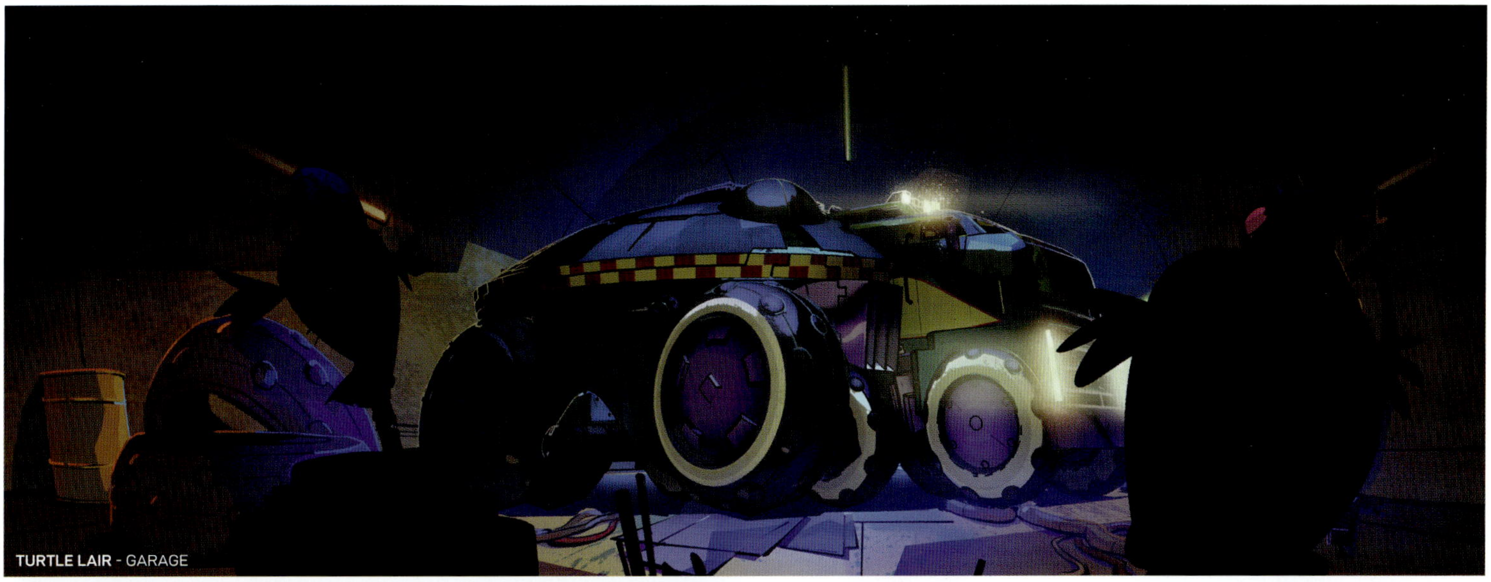

TURTLE LAIR - GARAGE

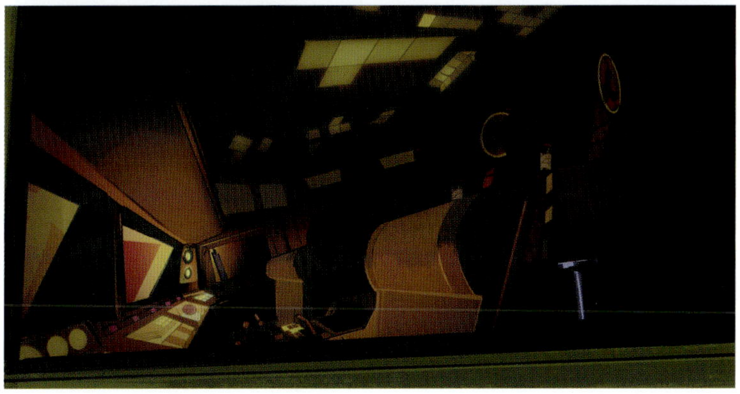

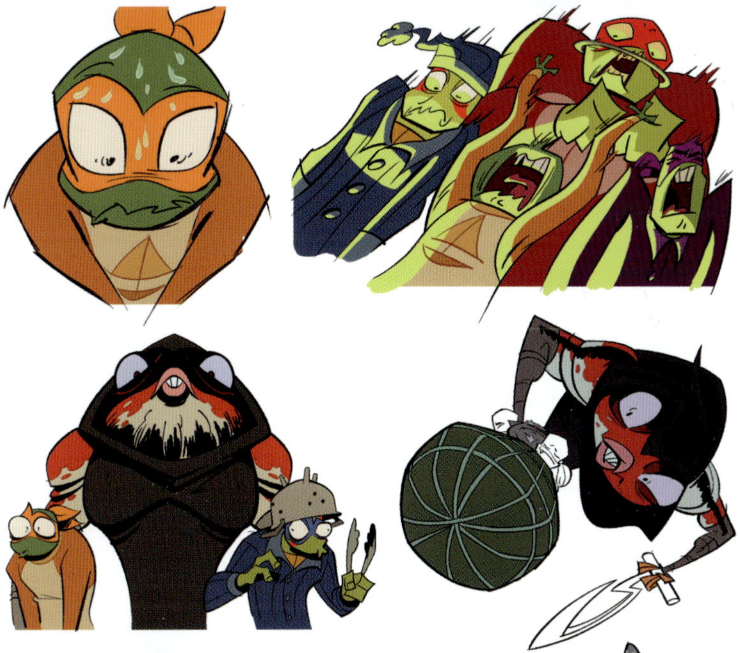

DALE MALINOWSKI: Tony pitched Bishop's demise in *Aliens* (1986) as inspiration for Franken-Foot's demise in the garage. Kevin's first pass of boards was incredible, but Standards and Practices asked us to tone it down.

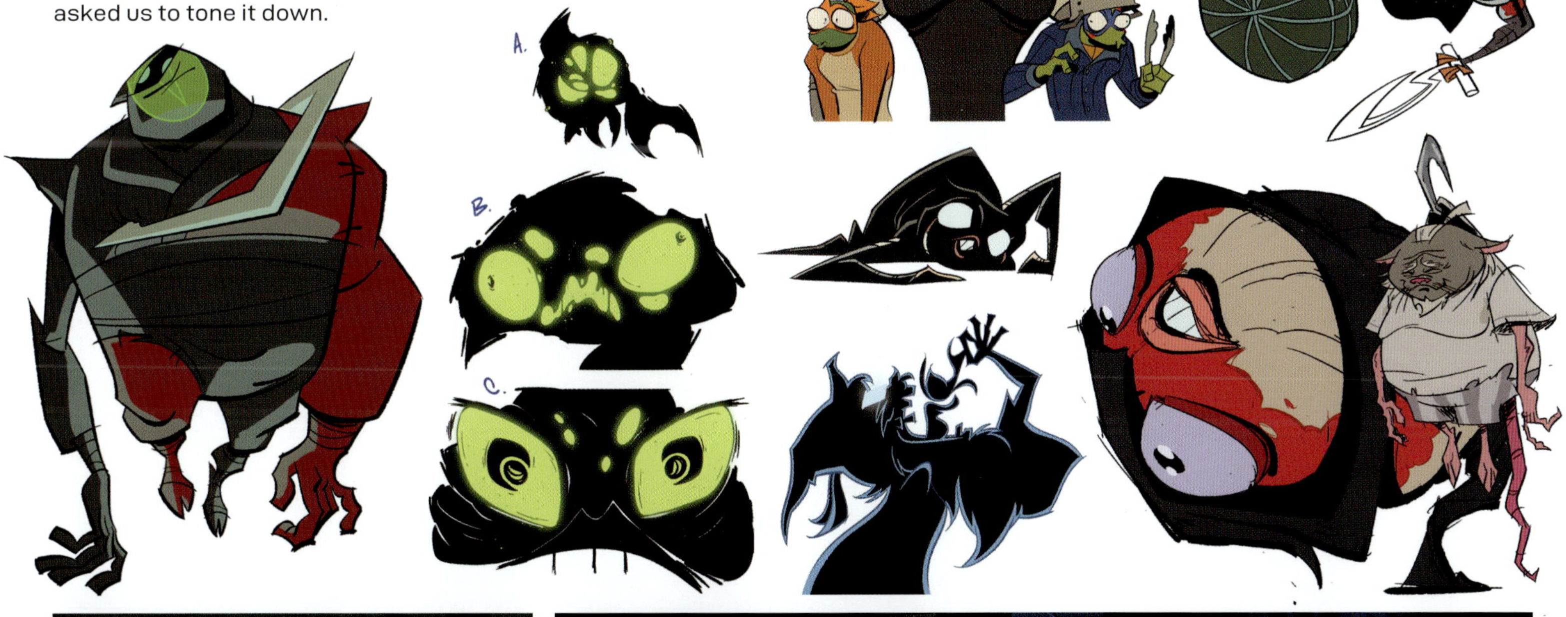

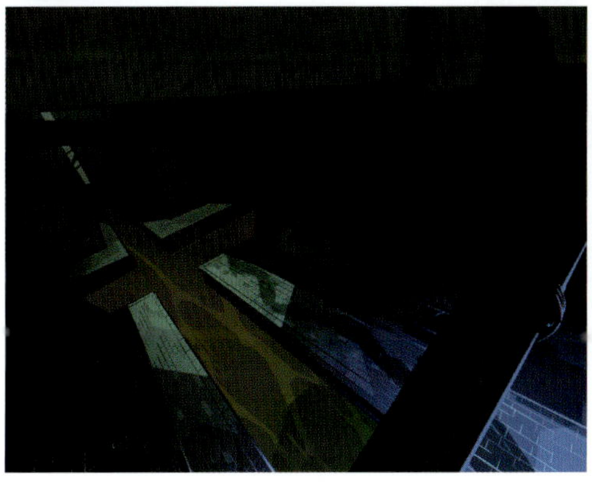

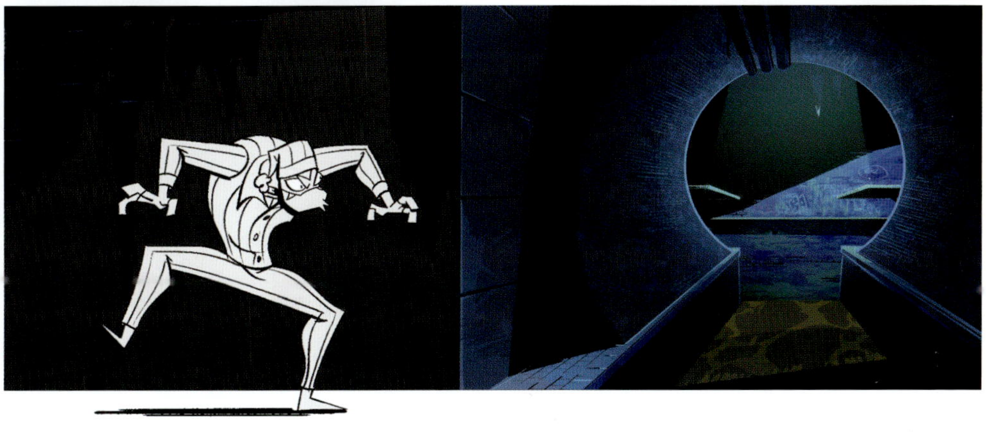

LAIR GAMES

ORIGINAL AIR DATE: OCTOBER 12, 2019
PRODUCTION CODE: 056

WRITTEN BY **JESSE GORDON**
STORYBOARDS BY **SHELDON VELLA**
DIRECTED BY **JJ CONWAY**

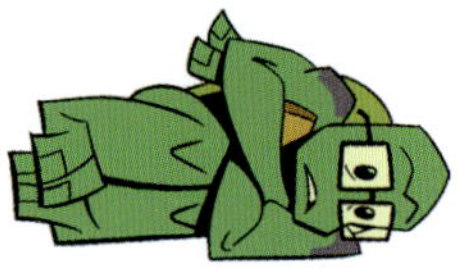

JESSE GORDON: You know, doing a documentary-style episode is such a classic TV move—like what *The Office* (2005) or *Community* (2009) would do. I ended up setting a bunch of episodes in the lair, partly to make production easier but also because it's fun to just play with the Turtles hanging out in their own space.

The whole thing came from those dumb games my friends and I used to play, like trying to toss a Hula-Hoop onto someone or catch hats. I was definitely thinking about that "Office Olympics" episode from *The Office*, plus this British show *Taskmaster* (2015) where they do ridiculous challenges.

The real MVP was this board artist Sheldon Vella. Never met the guy, but he was legendary. Everyone knew if Sheldon was on your episode, the boards would be next-level. He did this *"Pipe Goop Chicken"* bit with these crazy exaggerated facial expressions—so over-the-top they actually had to tone it down, but it was still hilarious.

Oh man, and the *"Slippery Whippery Woo!"* gag almost got us in trouble with Standards. Apparently having Splinter both greased up and in revealing underwear was too much? They said pick one, so obviously we went with a greased-up naked rat. Way funnier that way.

Those April O'Neil production cards killed me. The little chyrons with everyone's names and those snarky captions—no idea who came up with them, but they were perfect. It's those small touches that really make an episode special, you know? Like when you're watching and suddenly there's this little detail that just cracks you up. That's the good stuff!

JJ CONWAY: Jesse's script was written as a documentary, so I leaned into that at every angle, from amateur title cards to treating every shot as if it had been filmed by a camera. We did a lot of this by cheating whip pans and having the camera autofocus when it whipped to a new subject, making it feel like a person was actively moving the camera around. We then put the other cameras in the background of shots, really making the camera folks active and integrated into the scenes.

We rarely got major notes from Standards and Practices, but this one really pushed the boundaries of what we could get away with. I told my team that you never know where the line is until you cross it, so let's just go as far as we wanted then back up to the line if necessary. Needless to say, a shaved, oiled Splinter in a gold thong (that comes off at the end) was about as far as we could go, but I'm glad we pushed to see if we could get it that far, 'cause boy is that an unforgettable scene! Truly some of the most cursed stuff Sheldon has ever drawn.

I think "Lair Games" is the most cursed thing I'll ever do in my career. We got away with *almost* everything we wanted for Splinter.

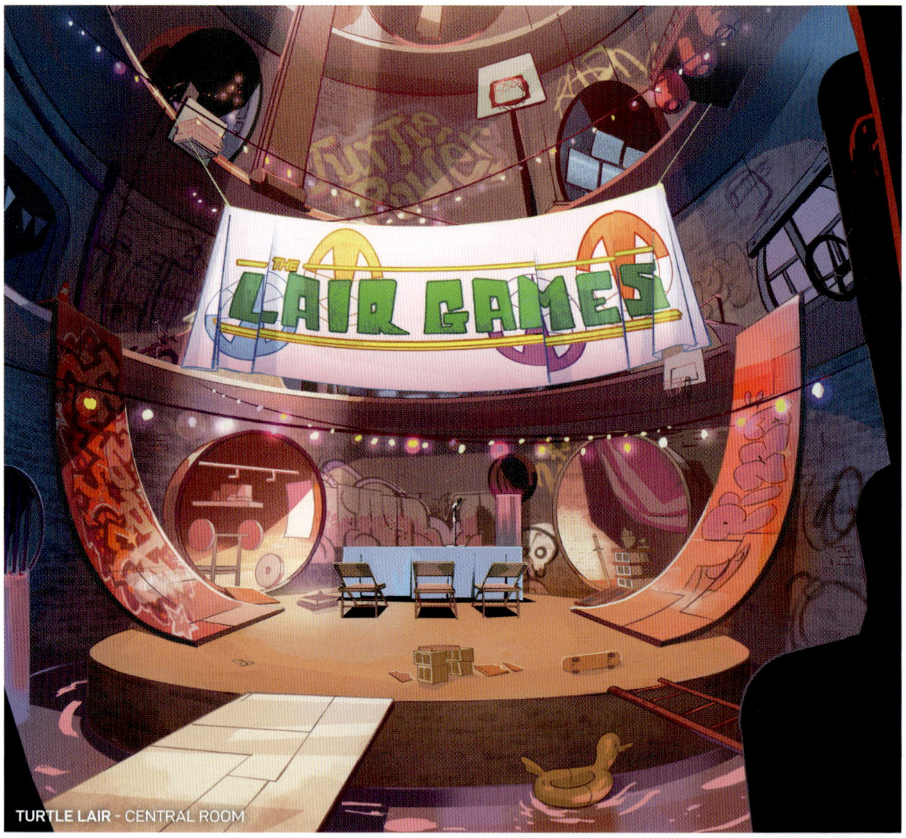

TURTLE LAIR - CENTRAL ROOM

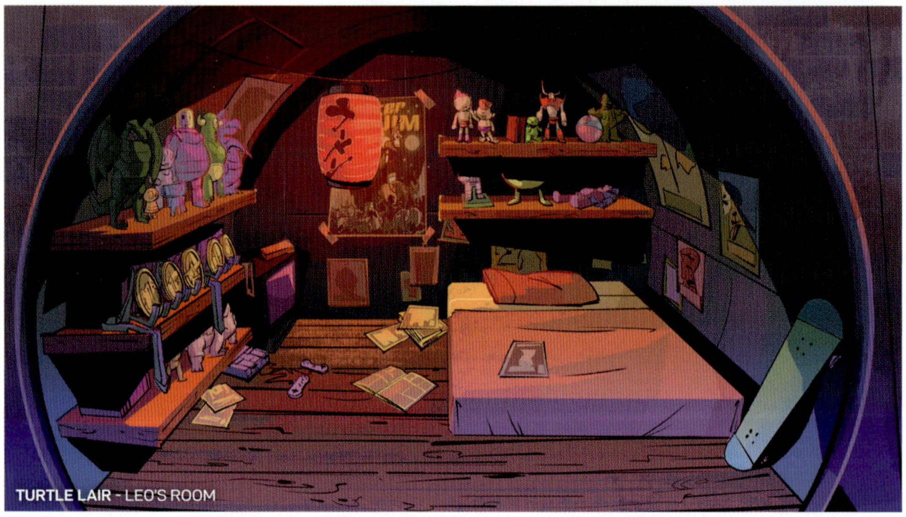
TURTLE LAIR - LEO'S ROOM

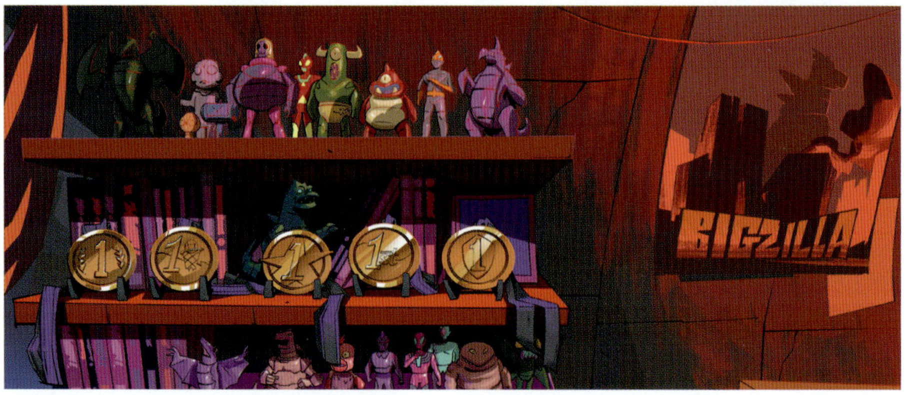

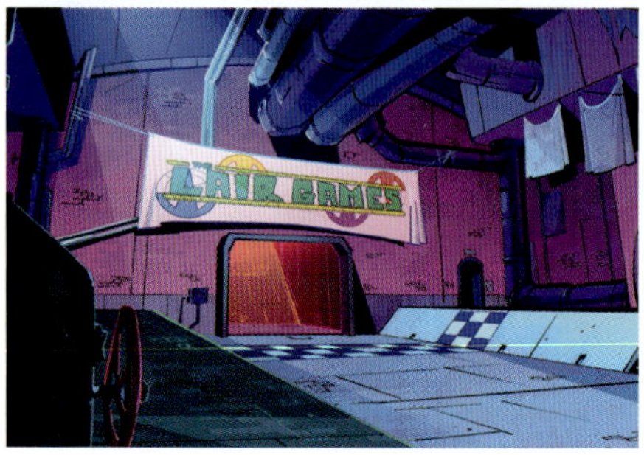

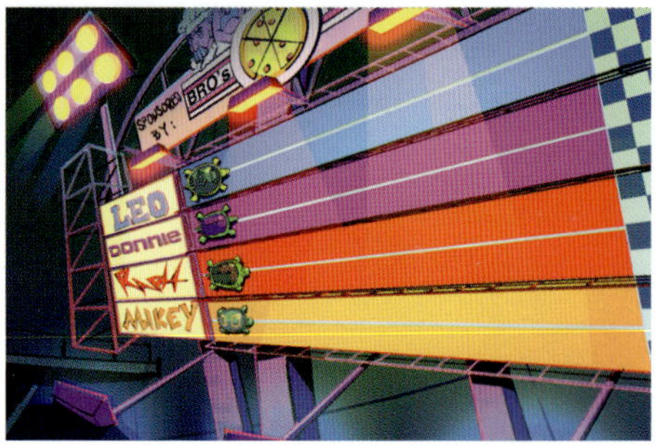

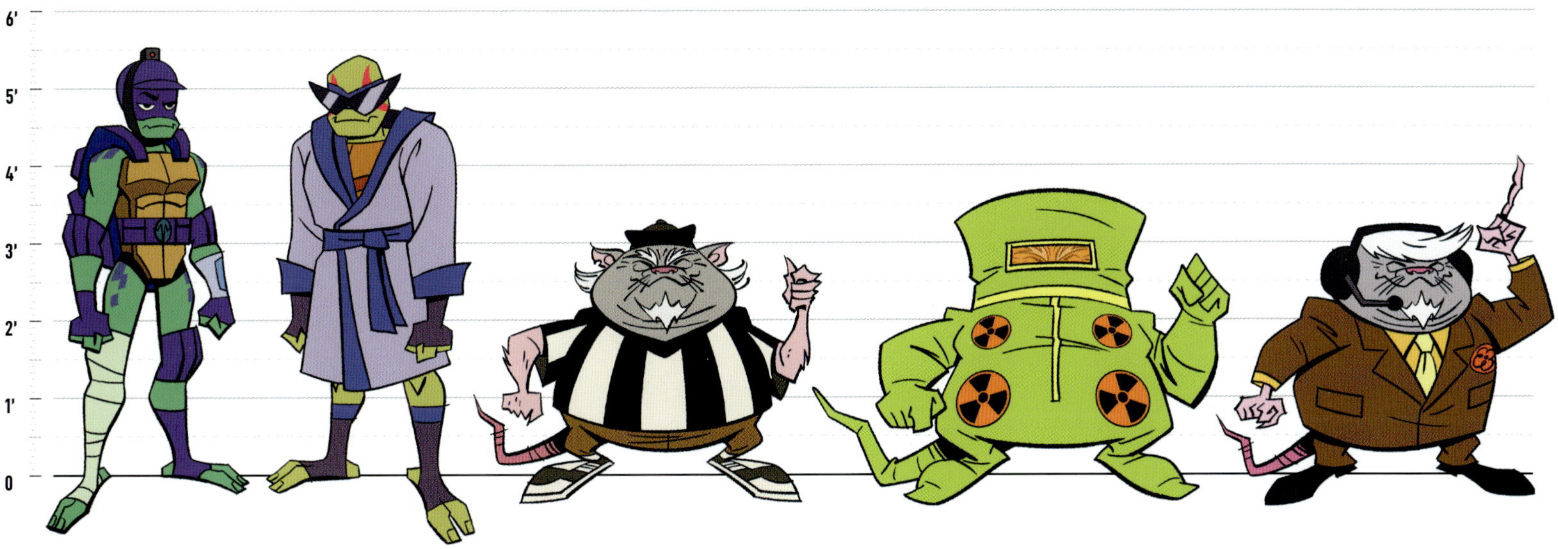

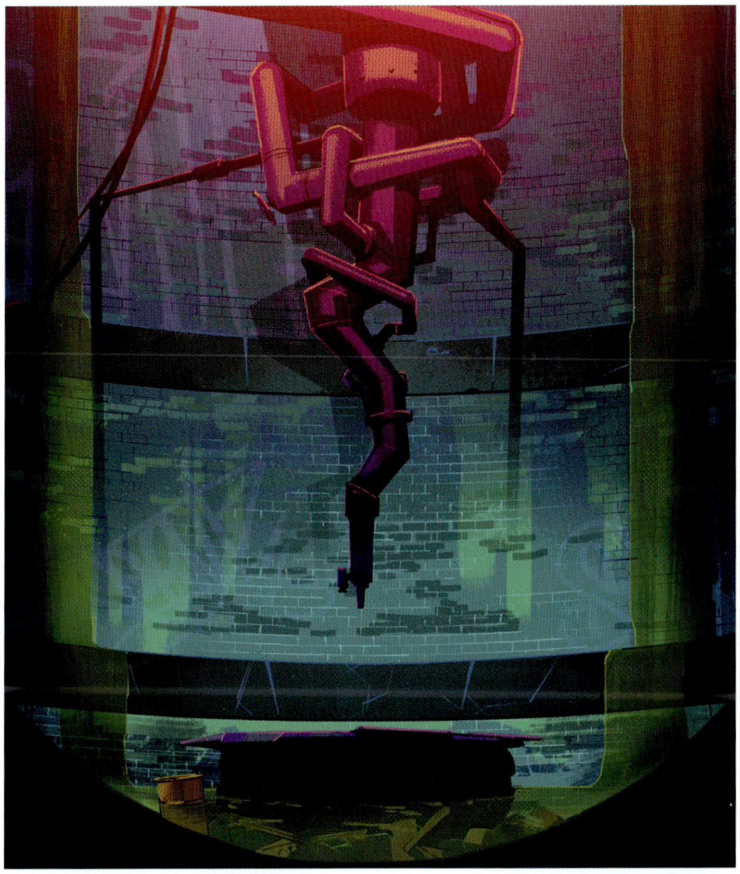

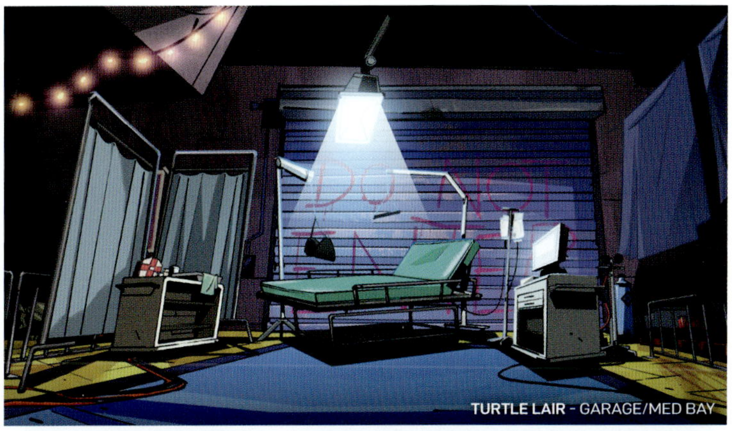

TURTLE LAIR - GARAGE/MED BAY

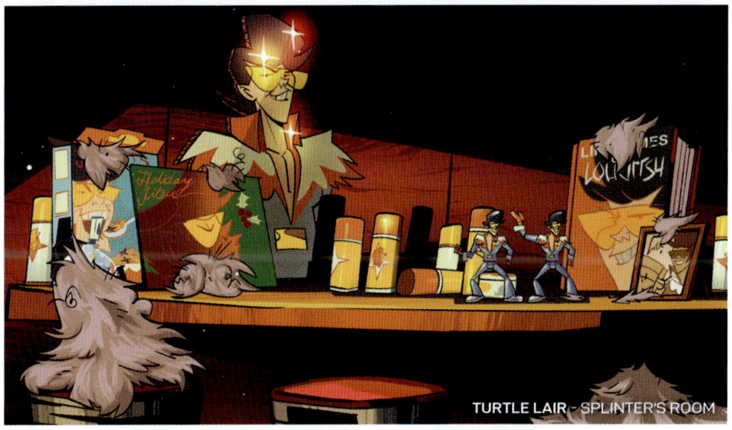

TURTLE LAIR - SPLINTER'S ROOM

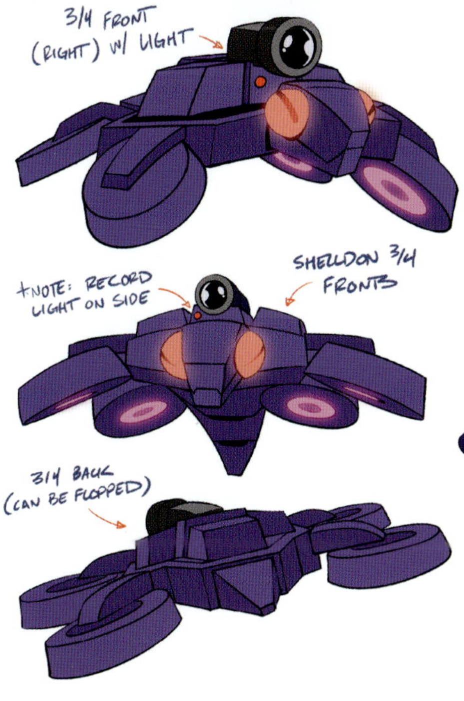

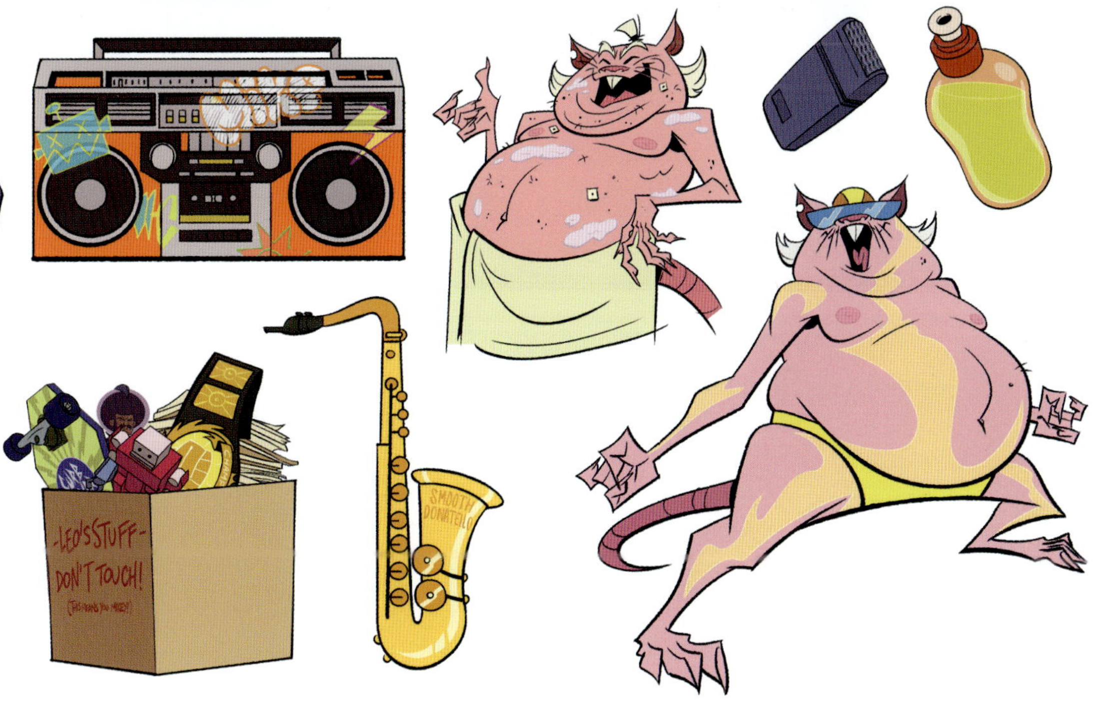

BREAKING PURPLE

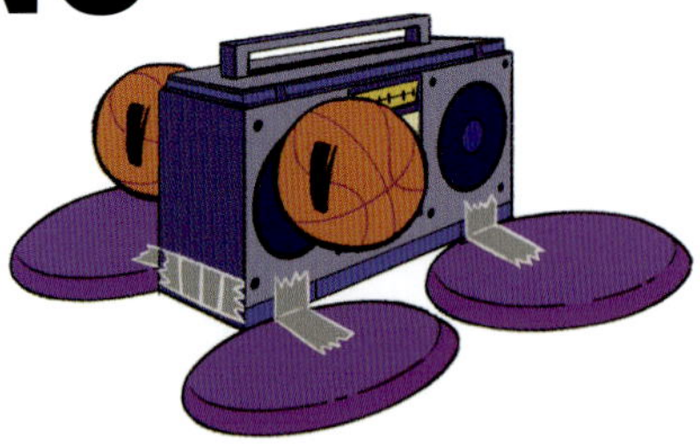

ORIGINAL AIR DATE: APRIL 24, 2020
PRODUCTION CODE: 059

WRITTEN BY **JOSH RILEY BROWN**
STORYBOARDS BY **CHRISTINE LIU**
DIRECTED BY **JJ CONWAY**

JOSH RILEY BROWN: After several months on *Rise* as a junior writer from the Nickelodeon Writing Program, I was thrilled when Tony offered me the chance to pitch an episode. One of my last ideas on my big list of pitches was a story about S.H.E.L.L.D.O.N. getting a "version 13" upgrade that made him act like a teenager. In retrospect, I can see why that idea worked for Tony and the series. First and foremost, it was funny to play with Donnie as a dad and S.H.E.L.L.D.O.N. as a rebellious teen who *"talks back in binary."* Secondly, it pushed Donnie on a character level. *Rise* Donnie (my absolute favorite iteration of Donnie) isn't exactly a people person. He's more interested in science and technology than empathizing with other people. It was fun to put him in a position where he had to learn some interpersonal skills to connect with his wayward drone son. At some point in the process, someone pitched Donnie having a fear of becoming his father, Splinter, and we were off to the (drone) races.

We also see Baxter Stockboy return as one of the drone racers along with Loose Lips Malinowski. Billionaire Guy Eccentric was originally a literal billionaire until someone pitched the joke that he changed his first name to Billionaire to draw attention away from his overwhelming debt.

The revelation that Jase and Kendra are stepsiblings was added by one of the writers late in the process as a joke. *"I wish my dad never married your mom"* cracks me up every time.

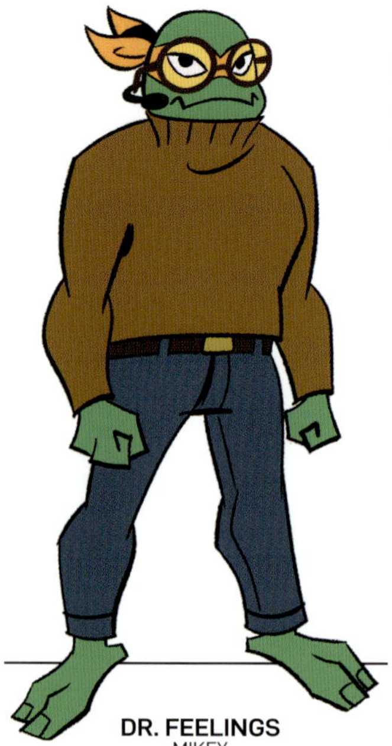

DR. FEELINGS
MIKEY

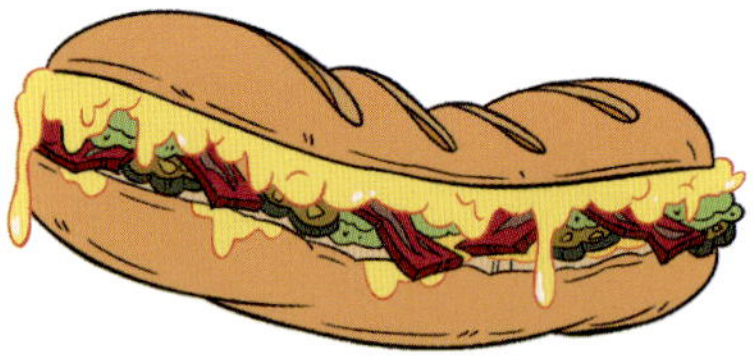

TOASTED AVOCADO BACO-BAGEL-RITO WITH CHEESE

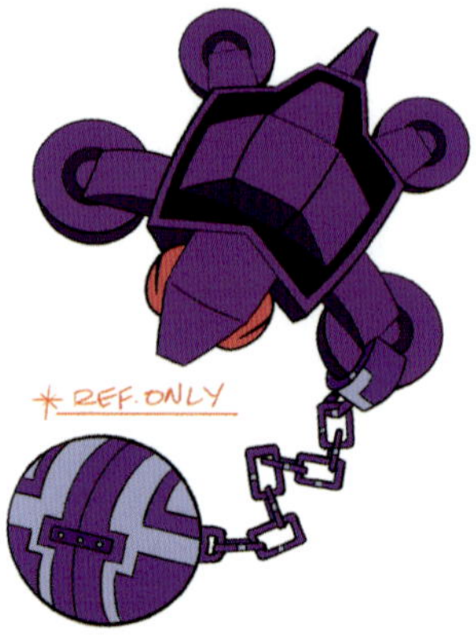

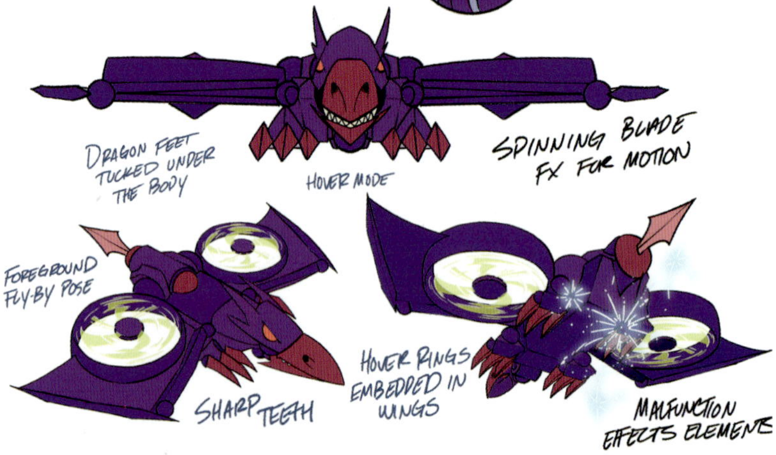

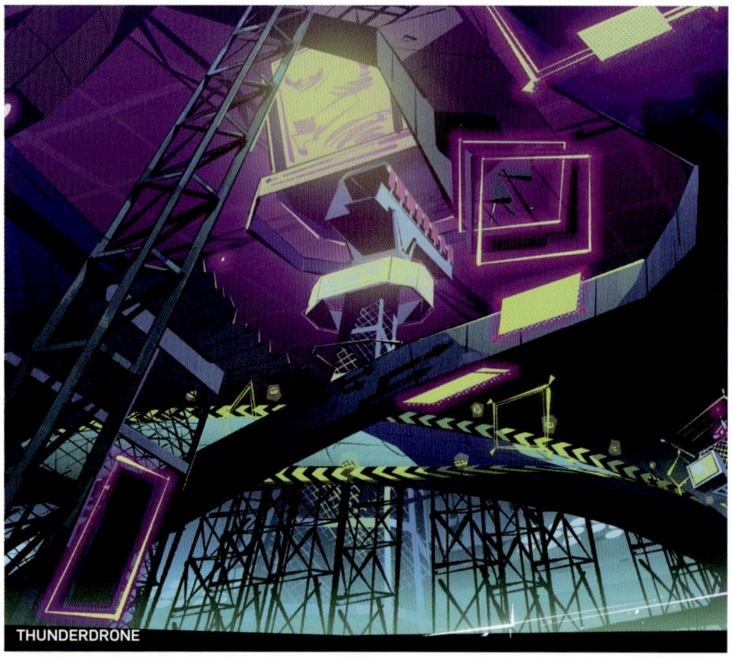

THUNDERDRONE

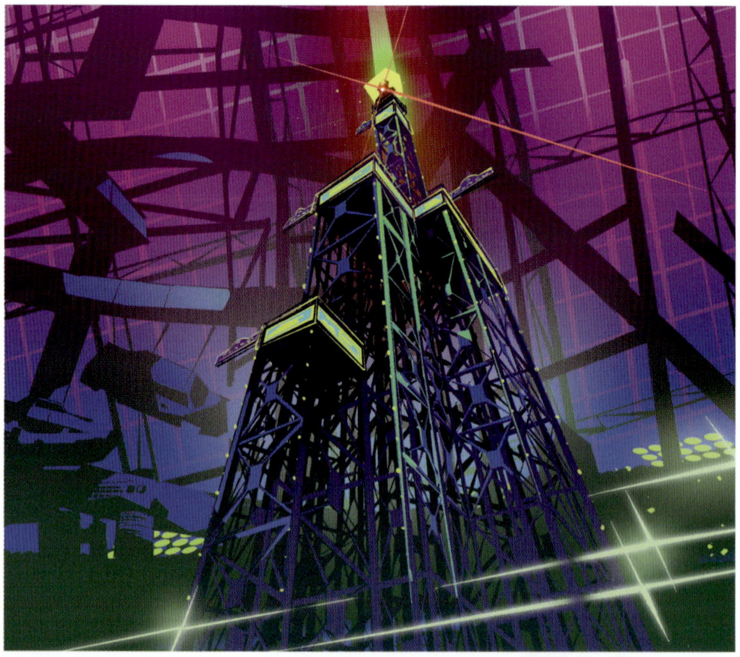

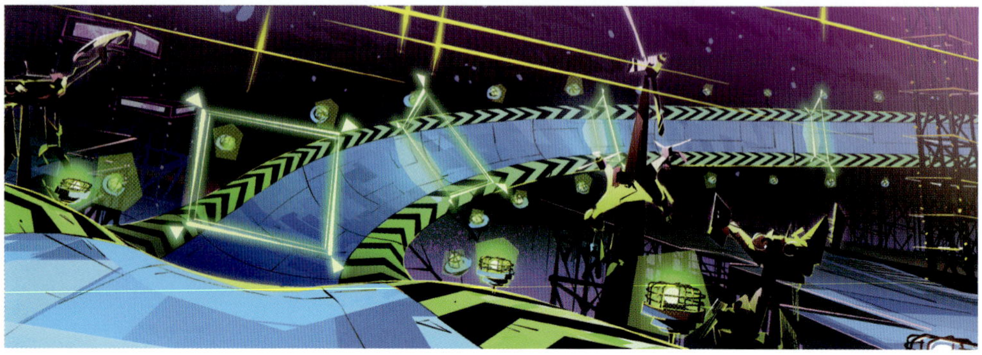

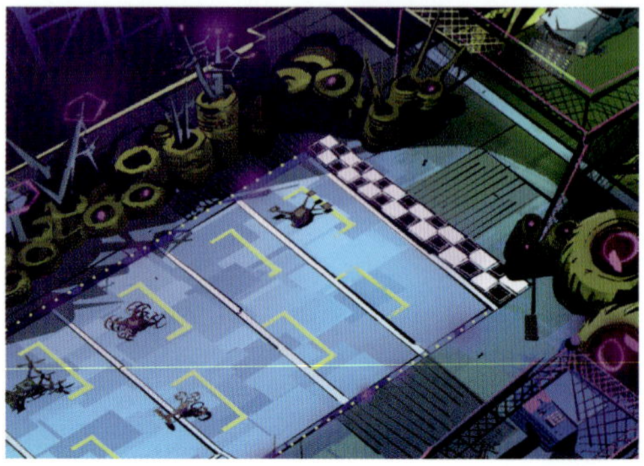

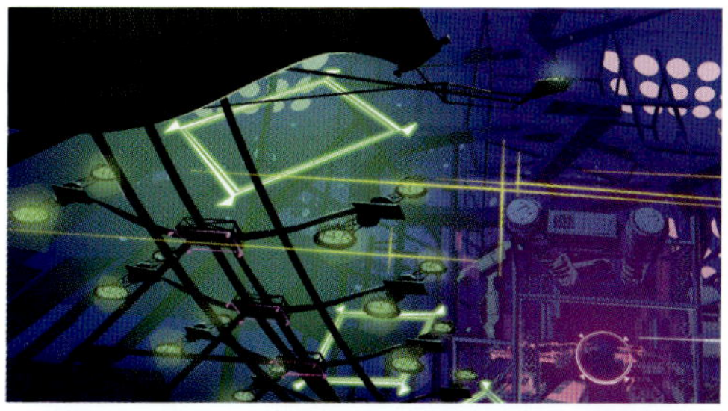

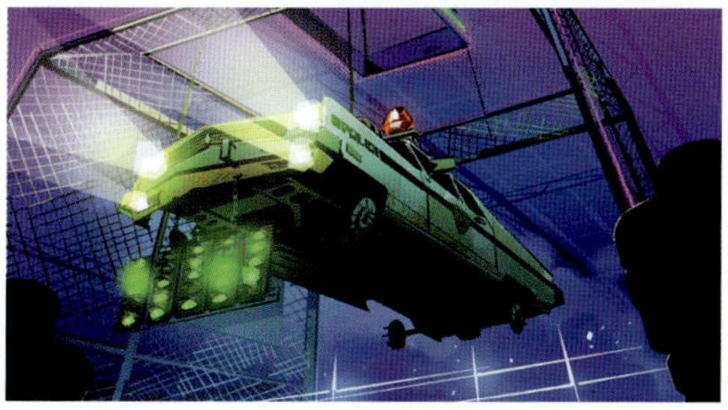

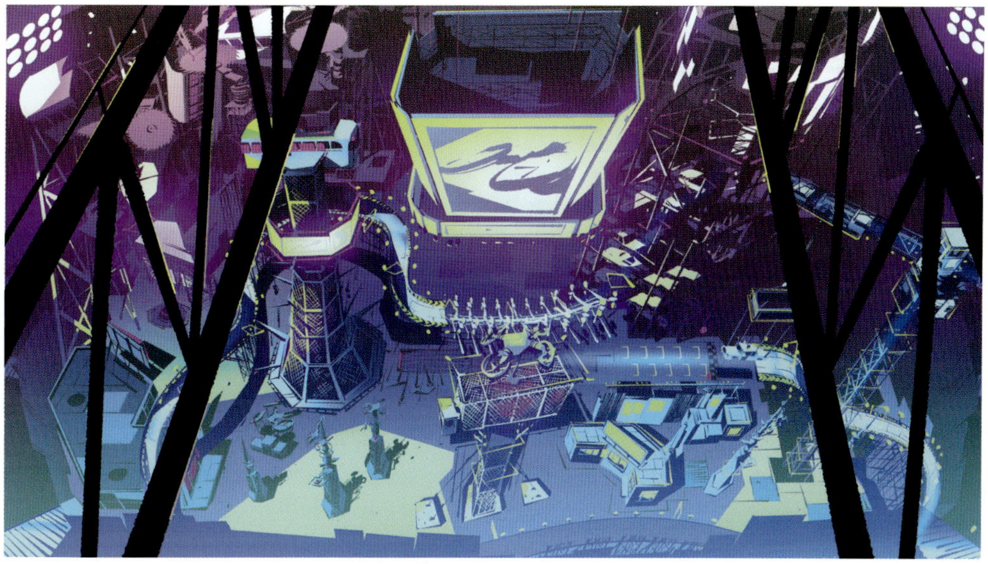

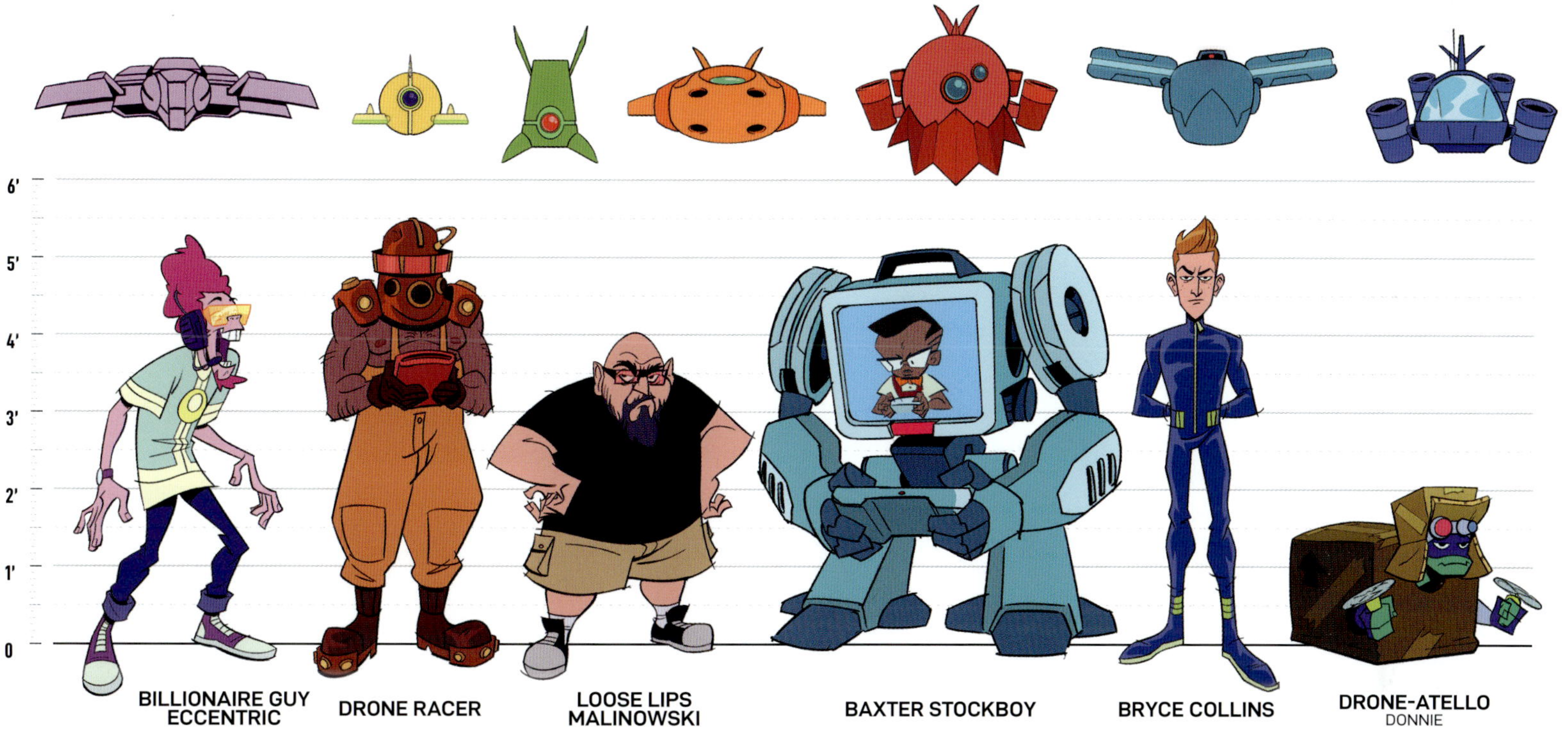
6'
5'
4'
3'
2'
1'
0
BILLIONAIRE GUY ECCENTRIC
DRONE RACER
LOOSE LIPS MALINOWSKI
BAXTER STOCKBOY
BRYCE COLLINS
DRONE-ATELLO
DONNIE

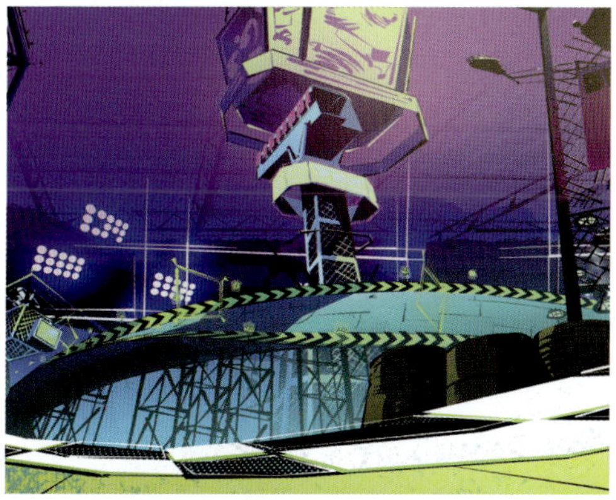

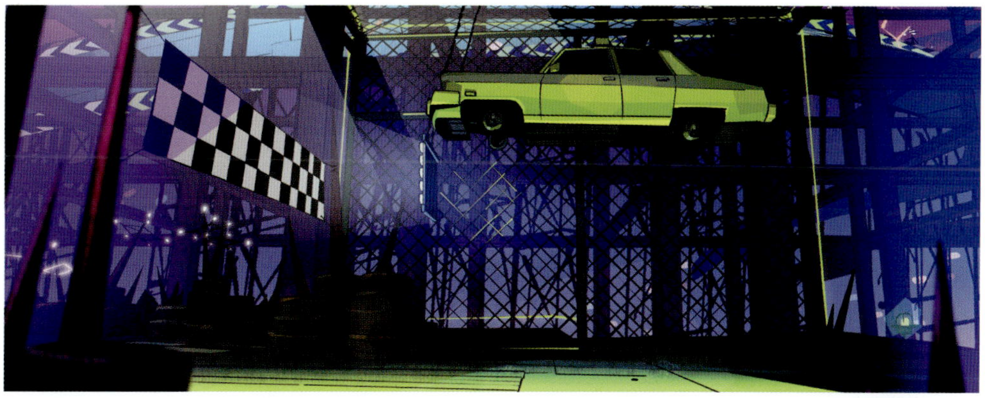

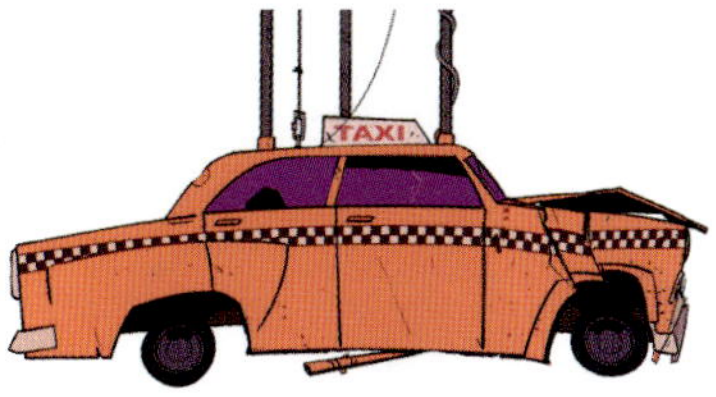
TAXI

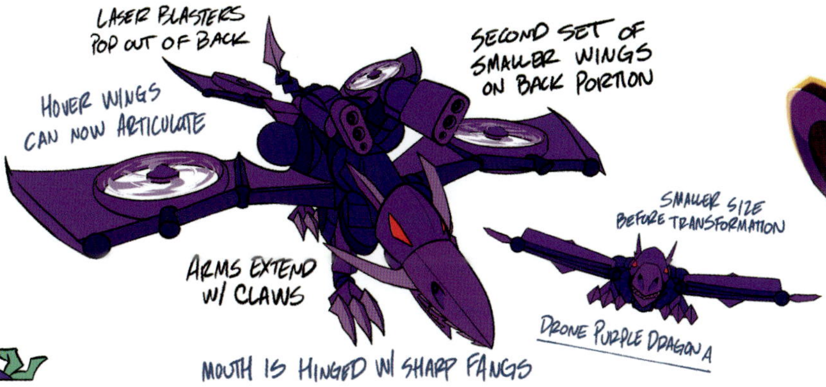
LASER BLASTERS POP OUT OF BACK
SECOND SET OF SMALLER WINGS ON BACK PORTION
HOVER WINGS CAN NOW ARTICULATE
SMALLER SIZE BEFORE TRANSFORMATION
ARMS EXTEND W/ CLAWS
DRONE PURPLE DRAGON A
MOUTH IS HINGED W/ SHARP FANGS

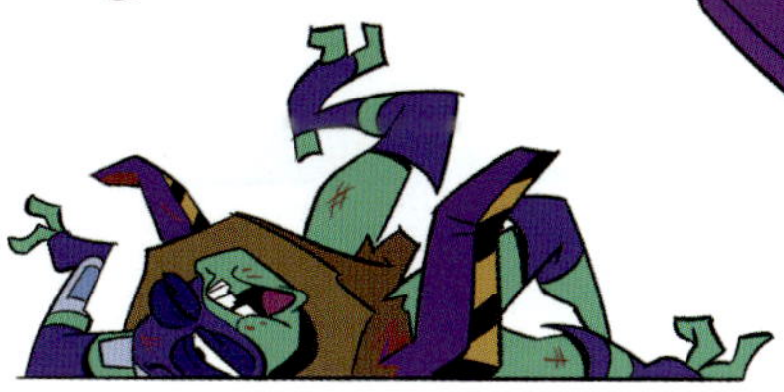

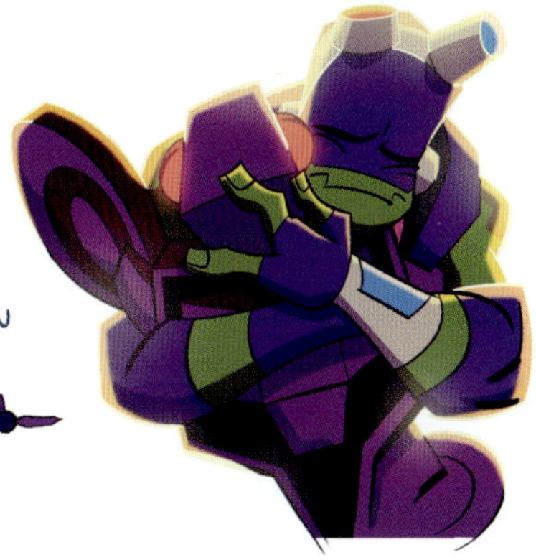

REPAIRIN' THE BARON

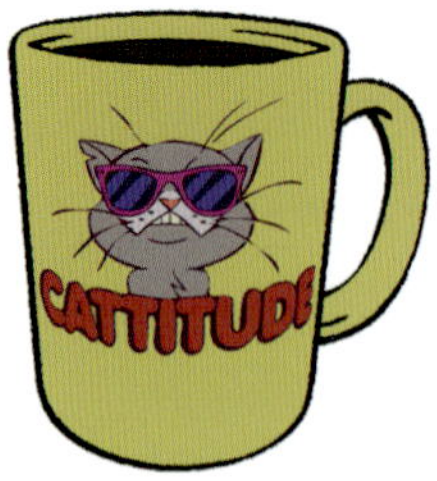

ORIGINAL AIR DATE: APRIL 24, 2020
PRODUCTION CODE: 060

WRITTEN BY **RUSS CARNEY & RON CORCILLO**
STORYBOARDS BY **ALICIA CHAN, MAX COLLINS**
DIRECTED BY **ALAN WAN**

TONY GAMA-LOBO: At the season 2 writers retreat, we were talking about how cool Baron Draxum was and how bummed we were that he was essentially going to die when the Shredder returned. So there was this bulletin board where we were slapping up cards of the cool stuff we wanted to do and Andy wrote this card and put it up: DRAXUM THE WHITE. And we were like, cool, yes, let's make Draxum a hero!

So that was the goal for season 2—by the end, he would join the team. It was a lot of work considering he was responsible for turning Splinter into a rat, creating the Turtles, and the whole "plot to destroy the human race" thing. This was perfectly illustrated in the totally awkward and hilarious dinner scene in "Repairin' the Baron." When breaking the story, we had all the setup moments with Mikey discovering Draxum and the fun character conflict scenes, but the episode didn't have a story engine yet. We stayed really late one night (ordered pizza, of course) and finally Ron had the brainstorm of adding in the bounty hunters looking for Draxum. It gave the whole story tension and structure and also the perfect moment at the end where Draxum proves to the Turtles he has it in him to change. A great reminder in storytelling that you need more than just a bunch of great scenes—you need an engine to drive you to a satisfying conclusion. And the ending! Oh man, I wish I remembered who pitched Draxum as becoming the weird lunch lady. Still makes me laugh!

After season 1, John Cena, who voiced Baron Draxum, told the studio that due to scheduling conflicts he was not able to continue with the character. So we ended up with the incomparable Roger Craig Smith, best known for his work on *Regular Show* (2010) and as the voice of Sonic in the video games. The man is a wizard with his voice. Roger did more than just a perfect John Cena imitation—he was able to add an emotional complexity and warmth, which was crucial to Draxum's redemption arc.

RUSS CARNEY: One day when we were all pitching ideas on new mutants that might appear in the series (the half-bat, half-rabbi Bat Mitzvah comes to mind), one of the other writers pitched a giant corn mutant named King Corn. It went over like a lead balloon with Ant and Andy, but as a gag, we referenced King Corn in Splinter's dinner-table freakout. We love Alan Wan's pacing of this scene. The tense silence and awkward conversation at the beginning creates a great setup for Splinter's freakout.

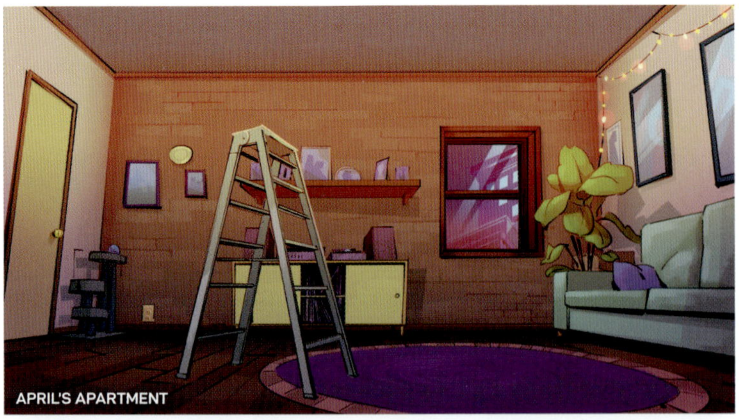
APRIL'S APARTMENT

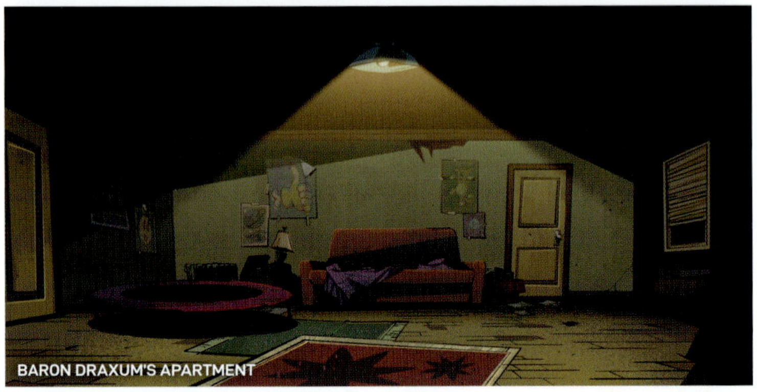
BARON DRAXUM'S APARTMENT

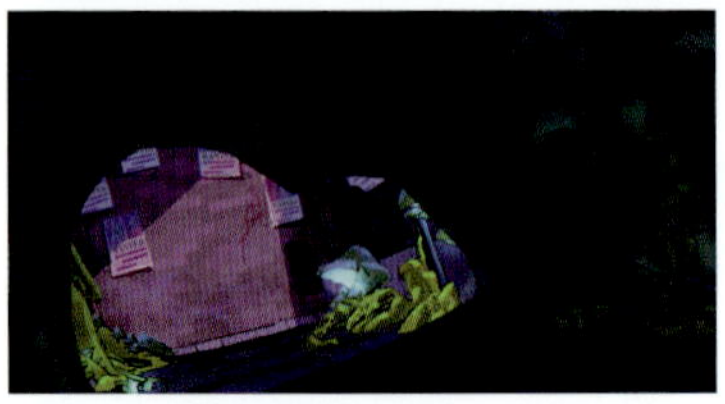

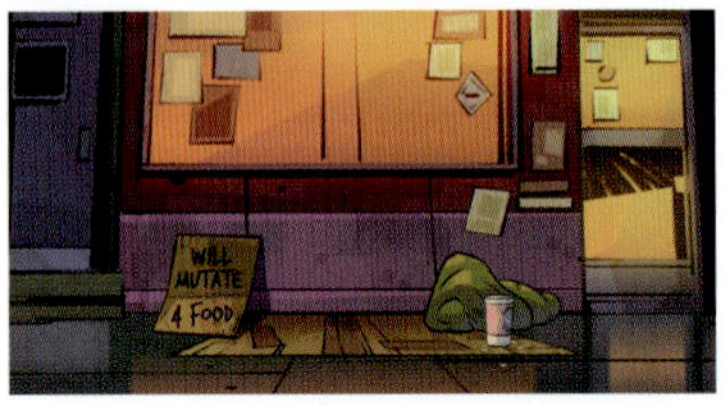

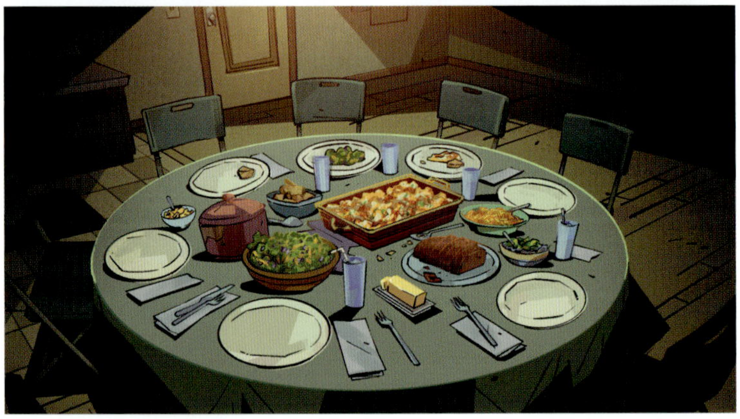

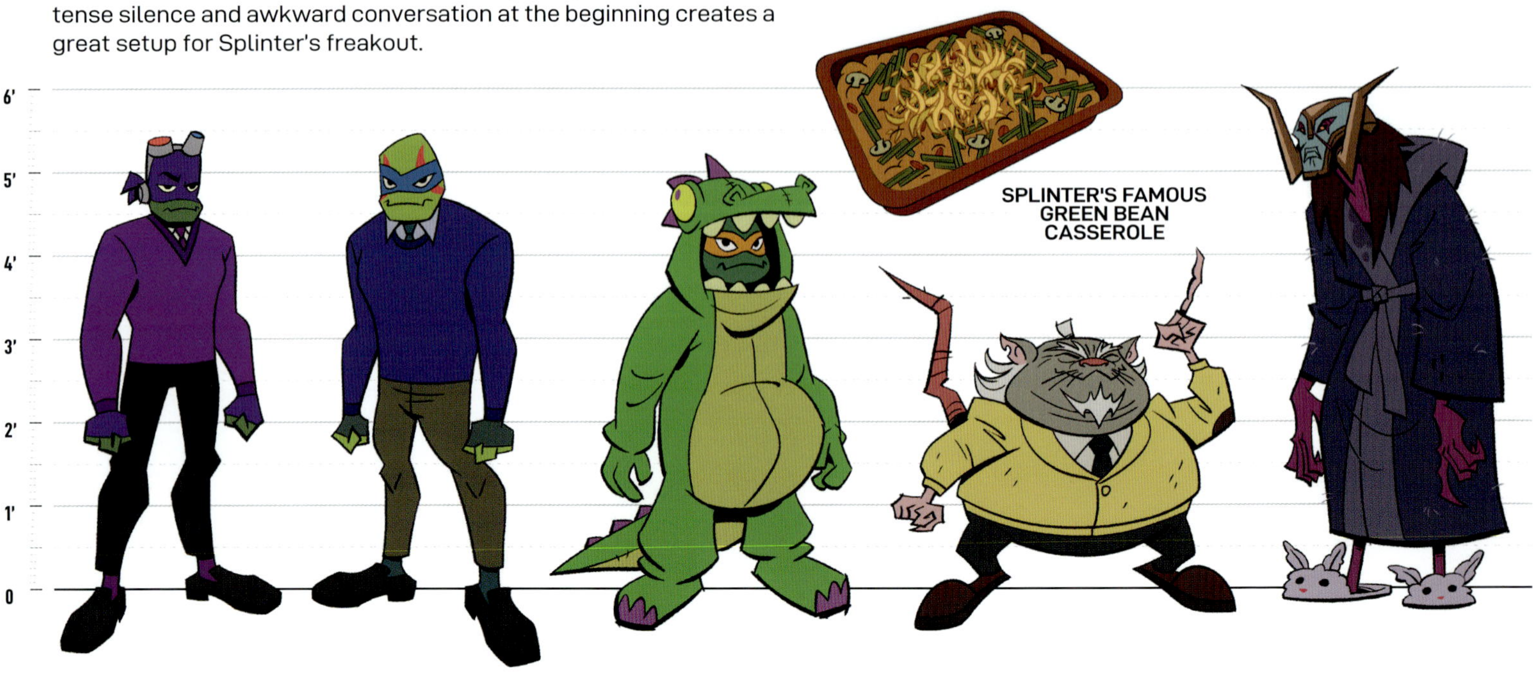

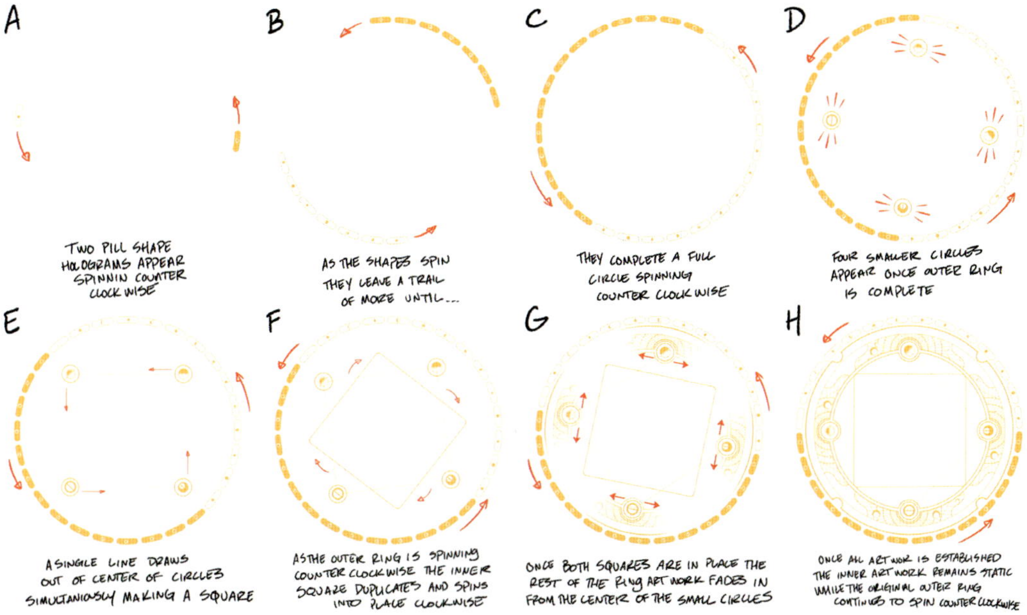

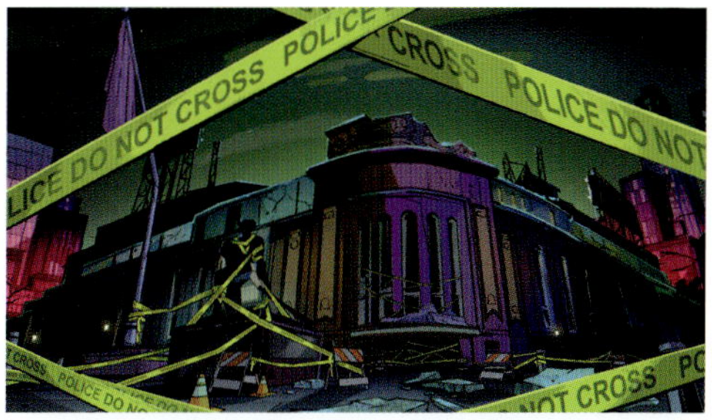

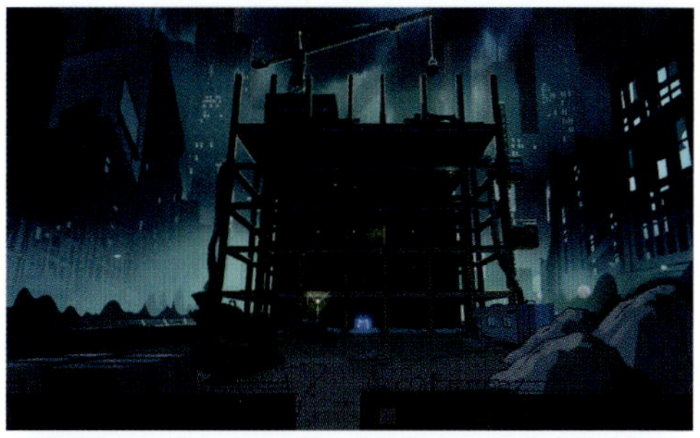

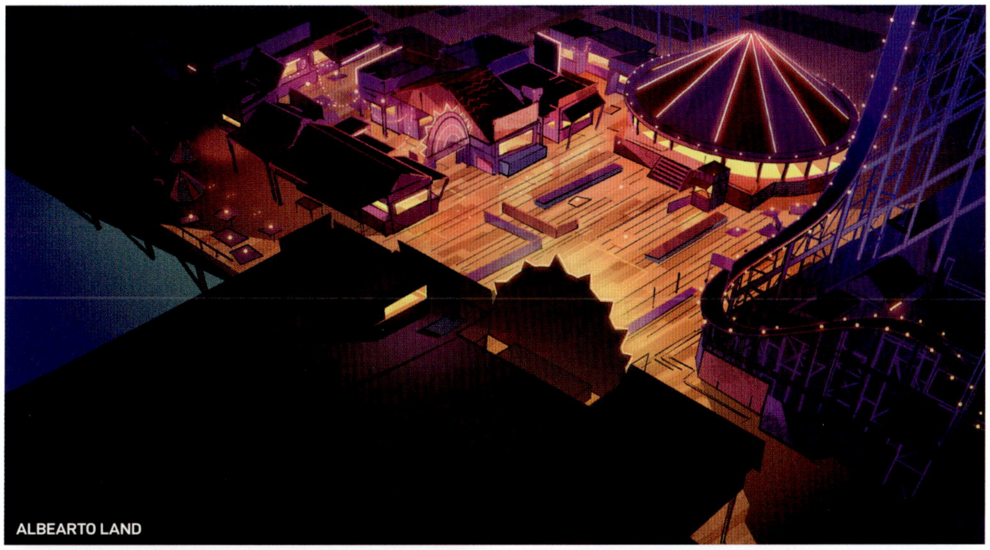
ALBEARTO LAND

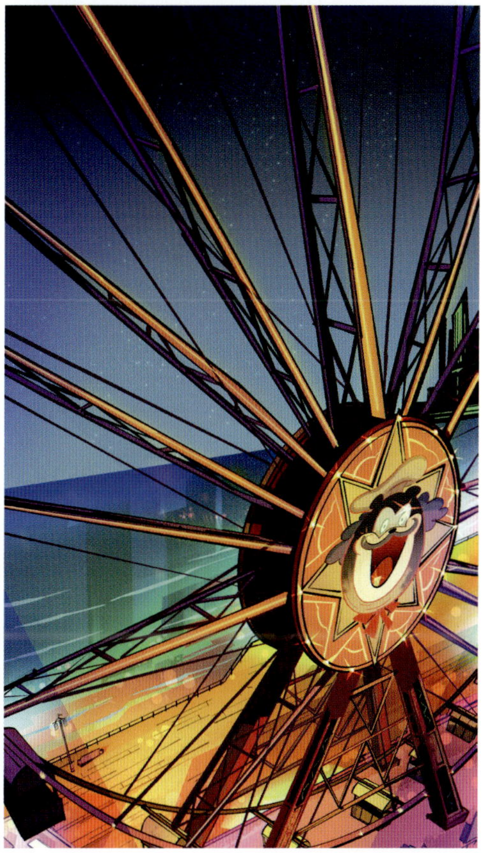

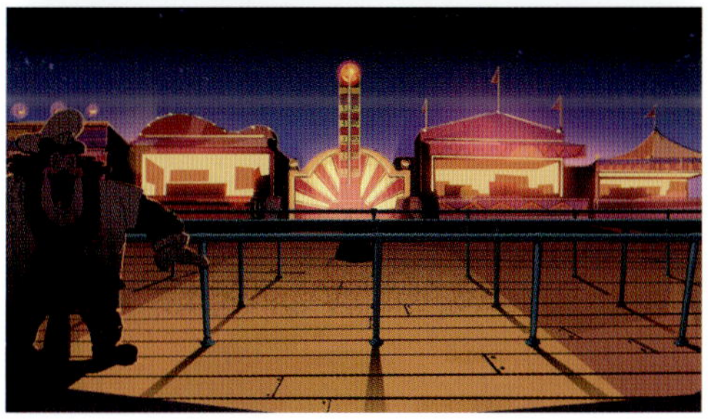

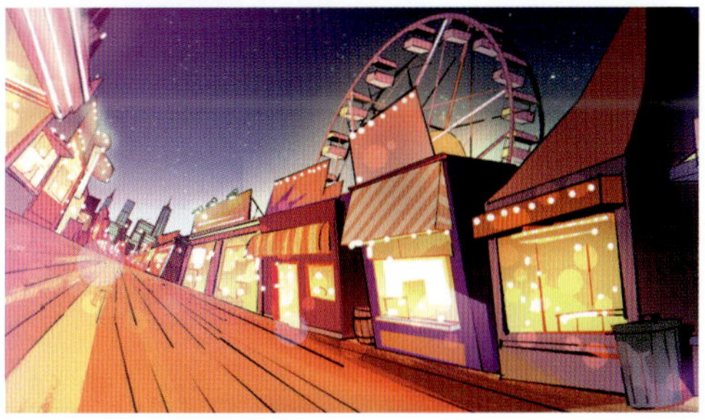

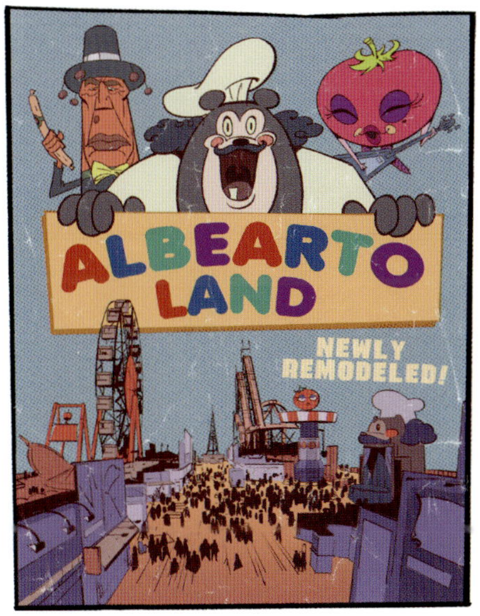

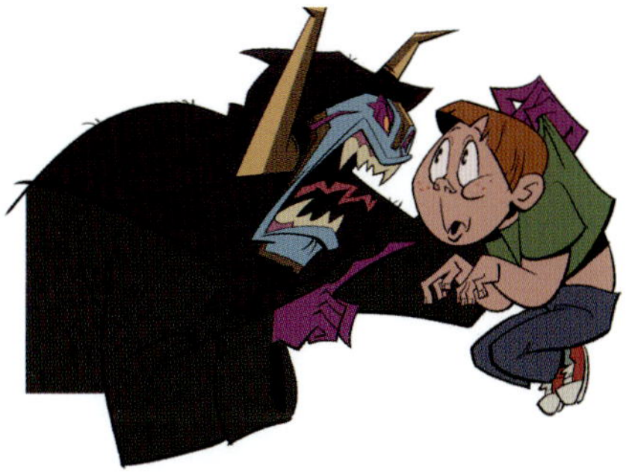

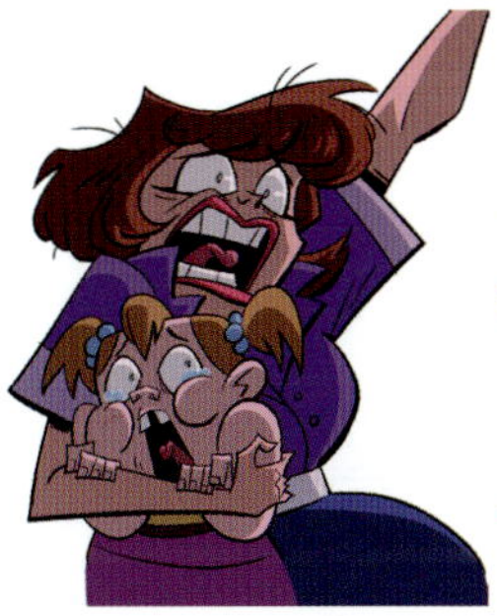

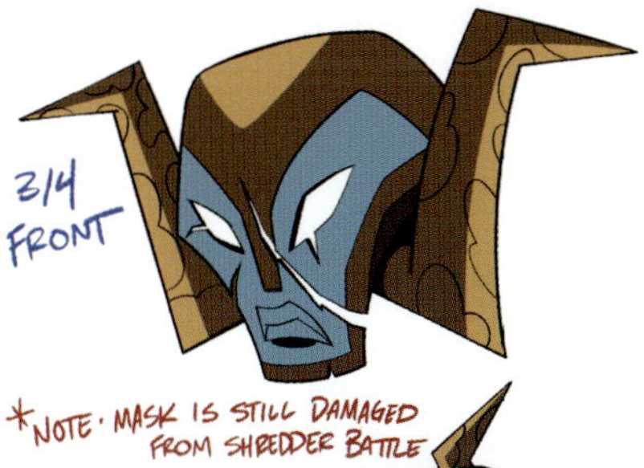

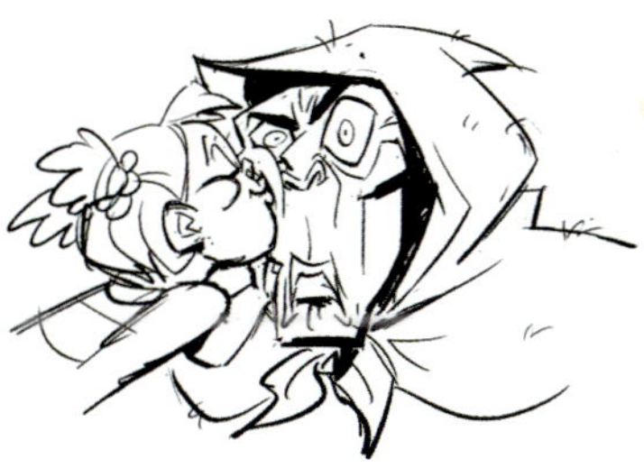

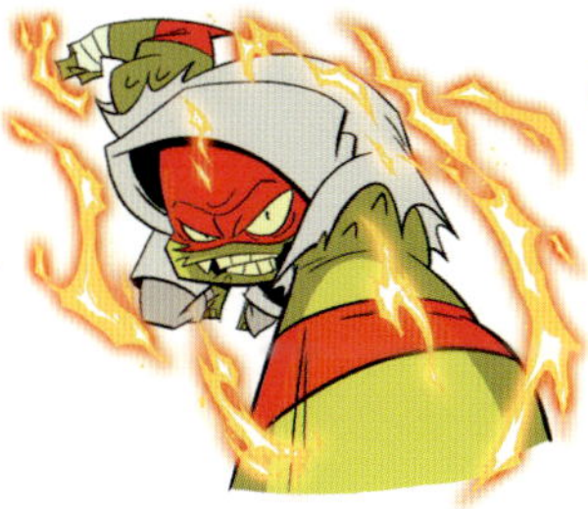

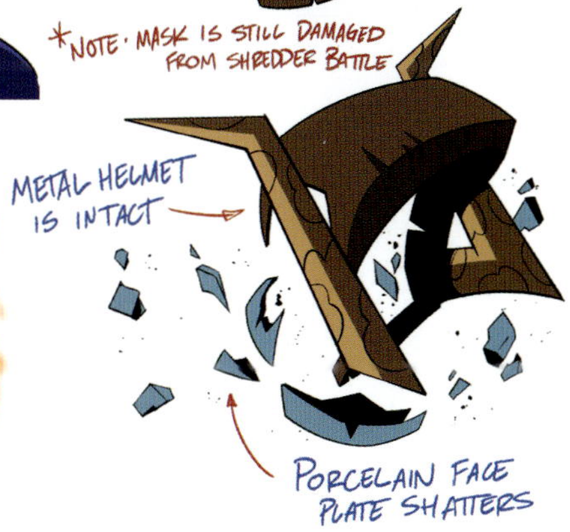

AIR TURTLE

ORIGINAL AIR DATE: APRIL 24, 2020
PRODUCTION CODE: 061

WRITTEN BY **JESSE GORDON**
STORYBOARDS BY **SHELDON VELLA**
DIRECTED BY **SEBASTIAN MONTES**

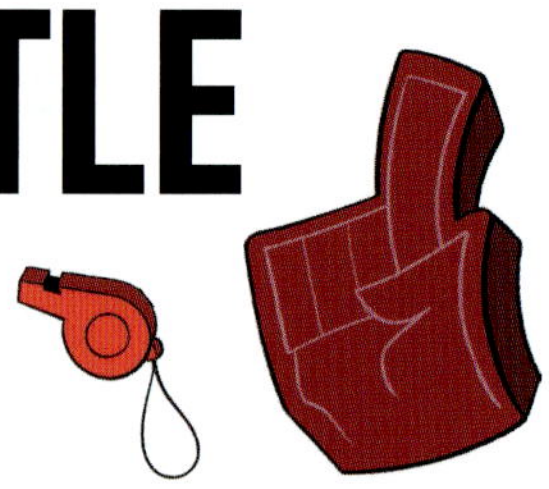

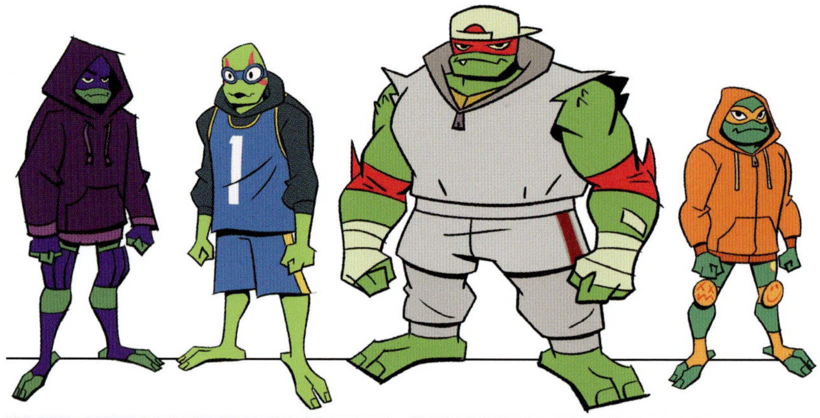

TONY GAMA-LOBO: Jesse is a huge NBA fan (*Chicago Bulls*) and pitched a fun supernatural basketball episode in the vein of *Shaolin Soccer* (2001). He thought the way in could be Leo becoming the mascot for a fringe New York team. We knew it was a Leo story, we knew where we wanted to end up with the action, and we had this great character in Dunkman. The trick was figuring out what Leo's arc was. Once Jesse pitched Leo's win-at-all cost attitude (*"Sorry, Don-ton, gotta win—tried losing once, it wasn't for me"*), we knew we had a good story that Ben Schwartz could really eat up.

Dave, the fan and winner of the contest who names the team the New York Daves, was modeled after, and voiced by, one of our incredible designers, Jack Rossi. Daves player wearing #67 is modeled after writer Jesse Gordon.

Donnie's line *"Game, blouses"* references the classic *Chappelle's Show* sketch, "Charlie Murphy's True Hollywood Stories," where he describes getting schooled by Prince in a pickup game of basketball.

I still really love how we build to the classic feel-good sports movie ending where we expect Leo to learn his lesson and let Donnie make the final shot...and then totally undercut it. (*Leo: "Just because I became a team player doesn't mean that Donnie is magically good at basketball!"*)

Josh Brener (Donnie) is a huge sports fan, so it was always funny to me that Donnie was such a sports dummy. I think Josh actually improved the line "sportsball."

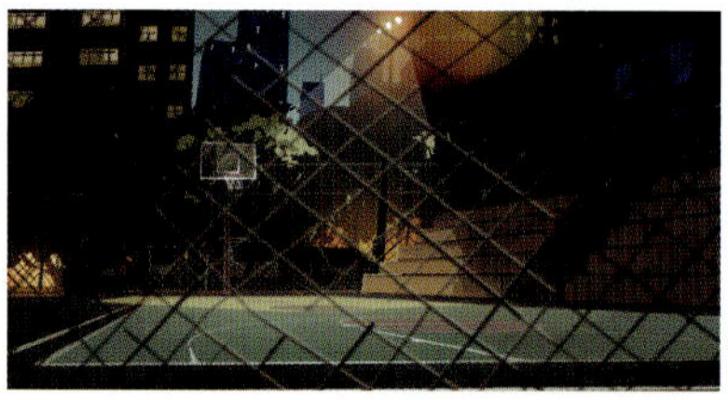

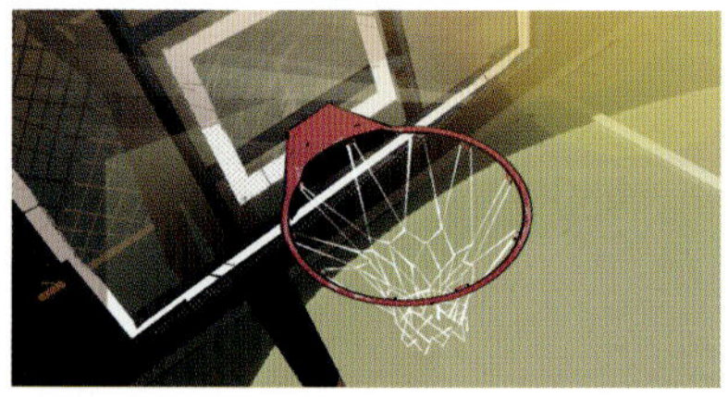

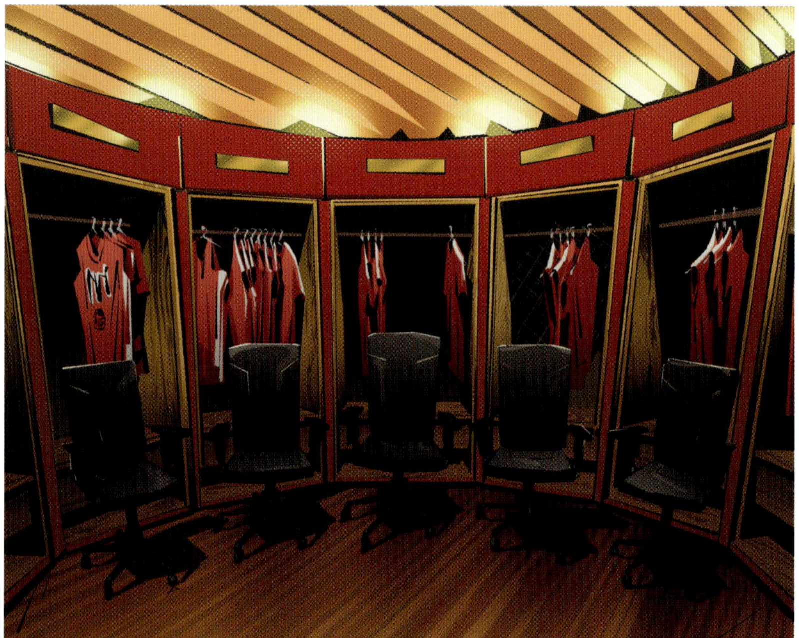

DAVES LOCKER ROOM

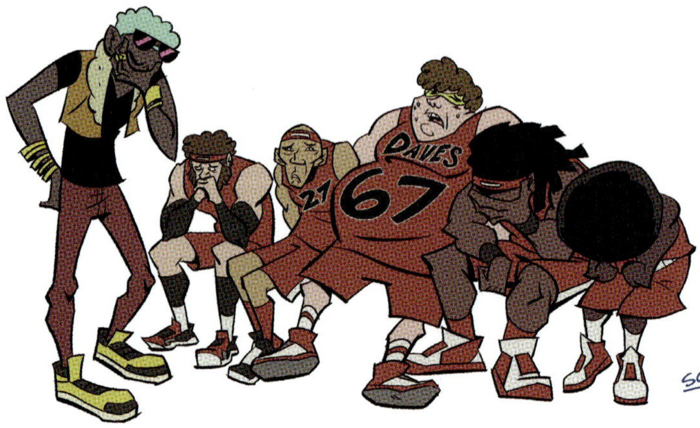

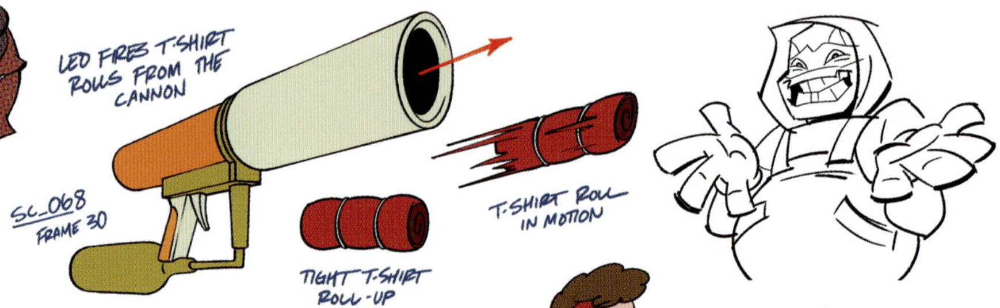

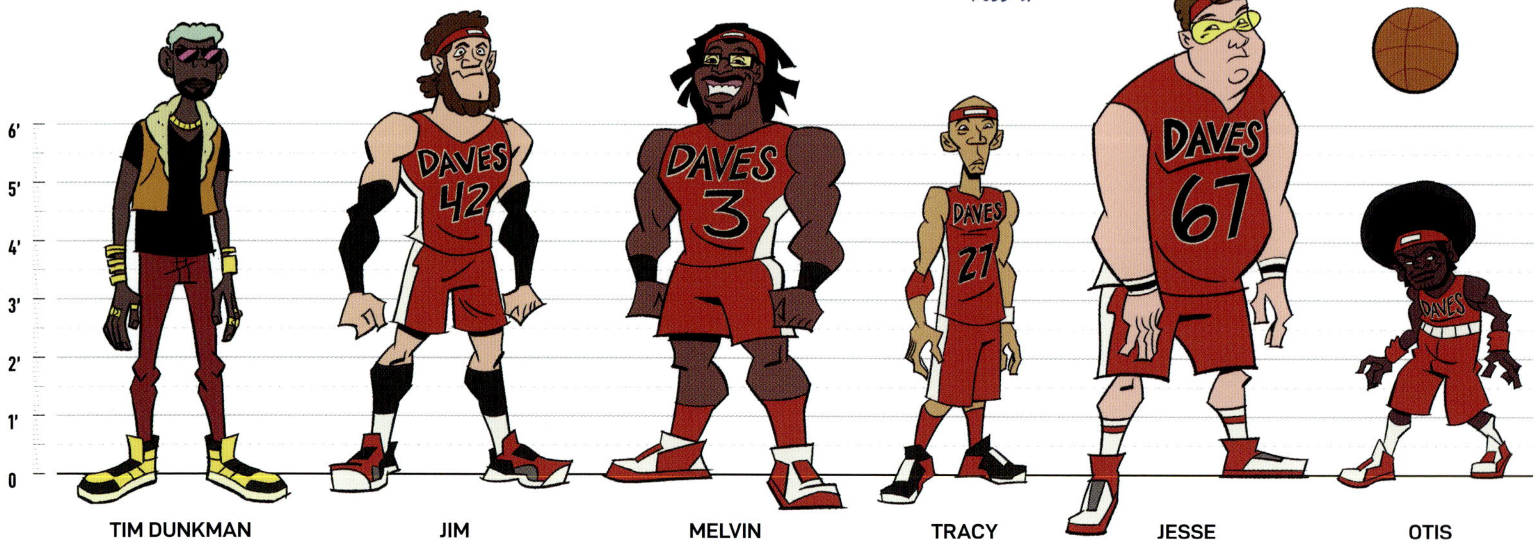

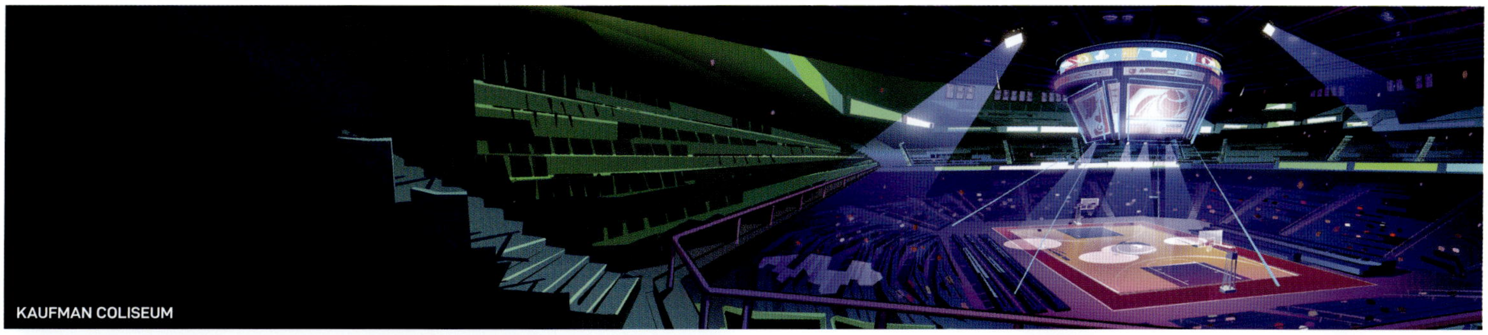
KAUFMAN COLISEUM

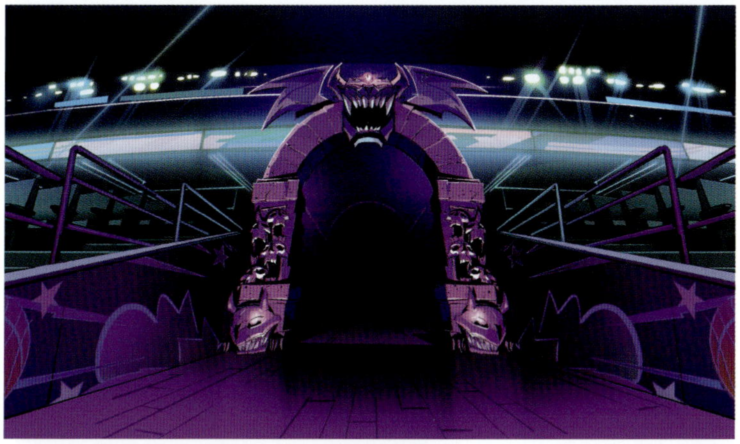

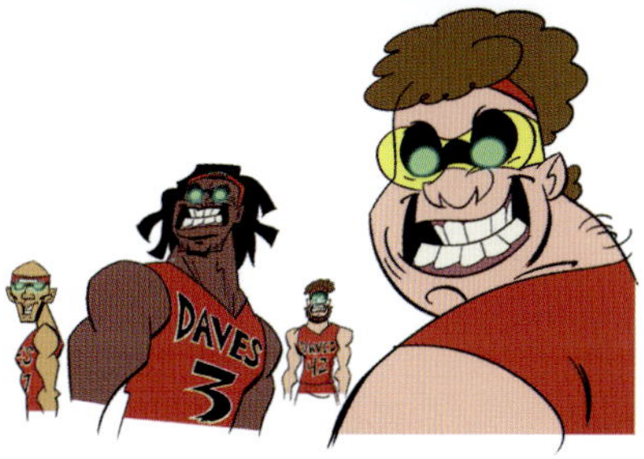

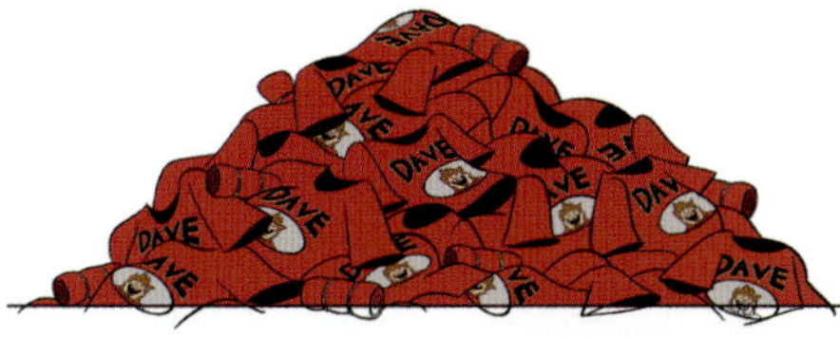

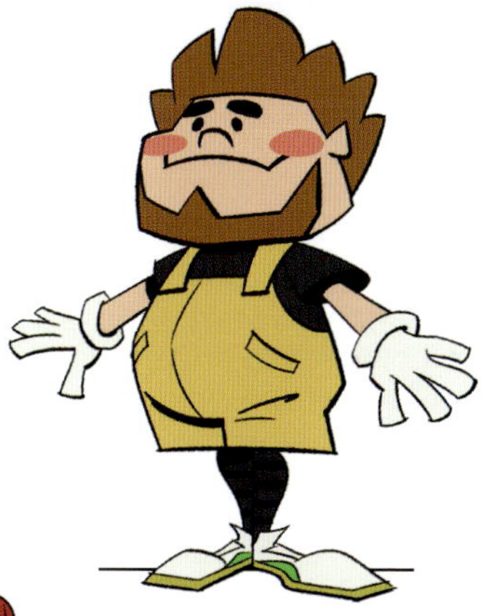
DAVES MASCOT

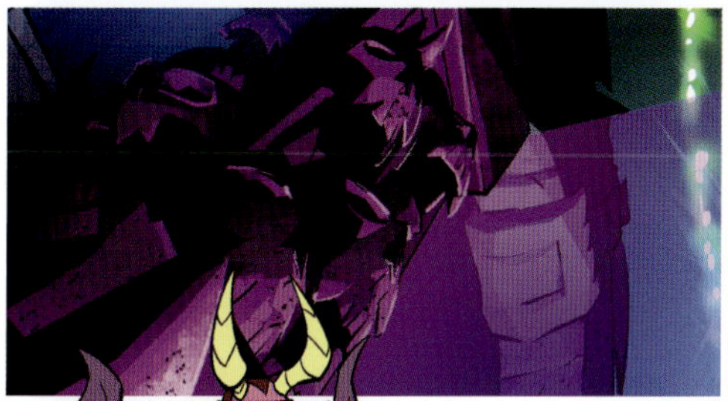

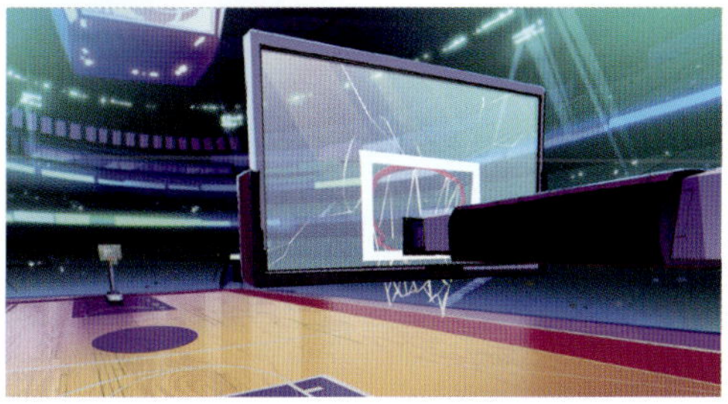

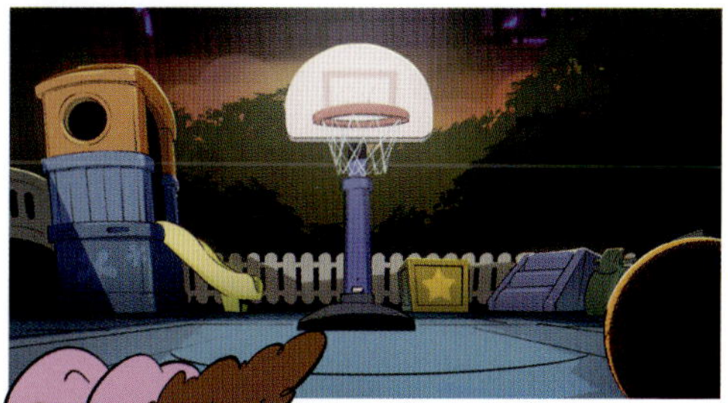

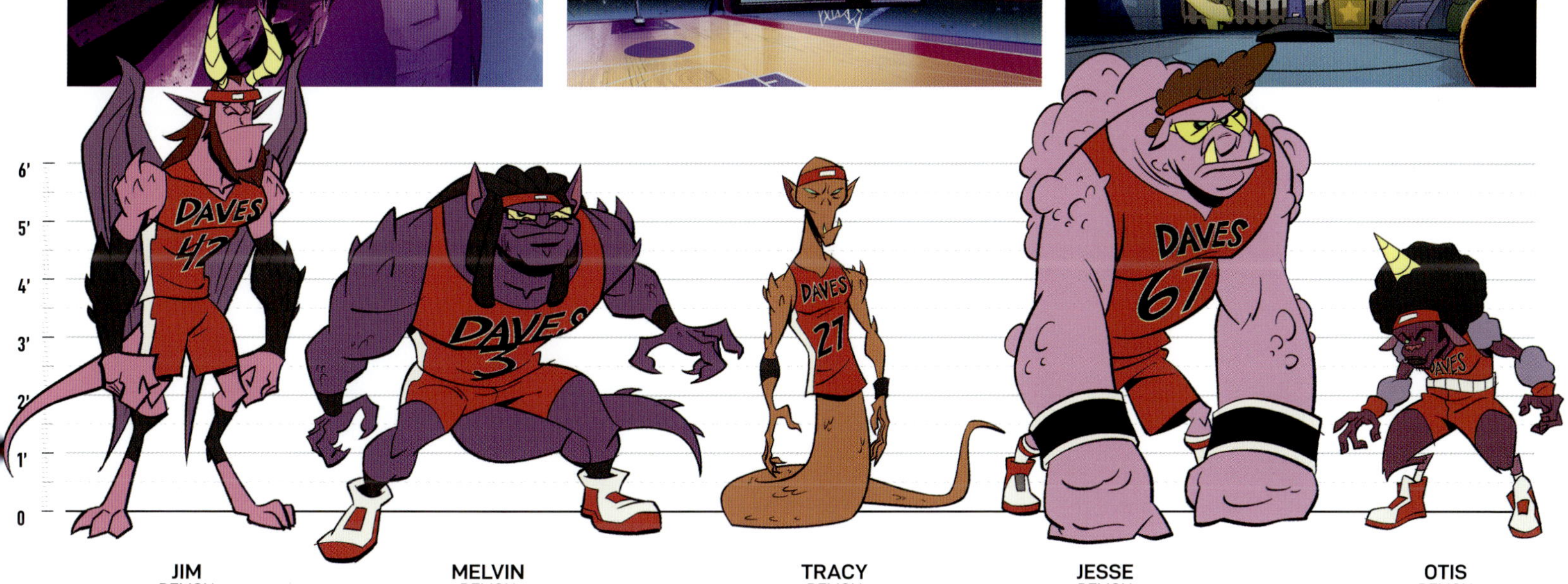

JIM
DEMON

MELVIN
DEMON

TRACY
DEMON

JESSE
DEMON

OTIS
DEMON

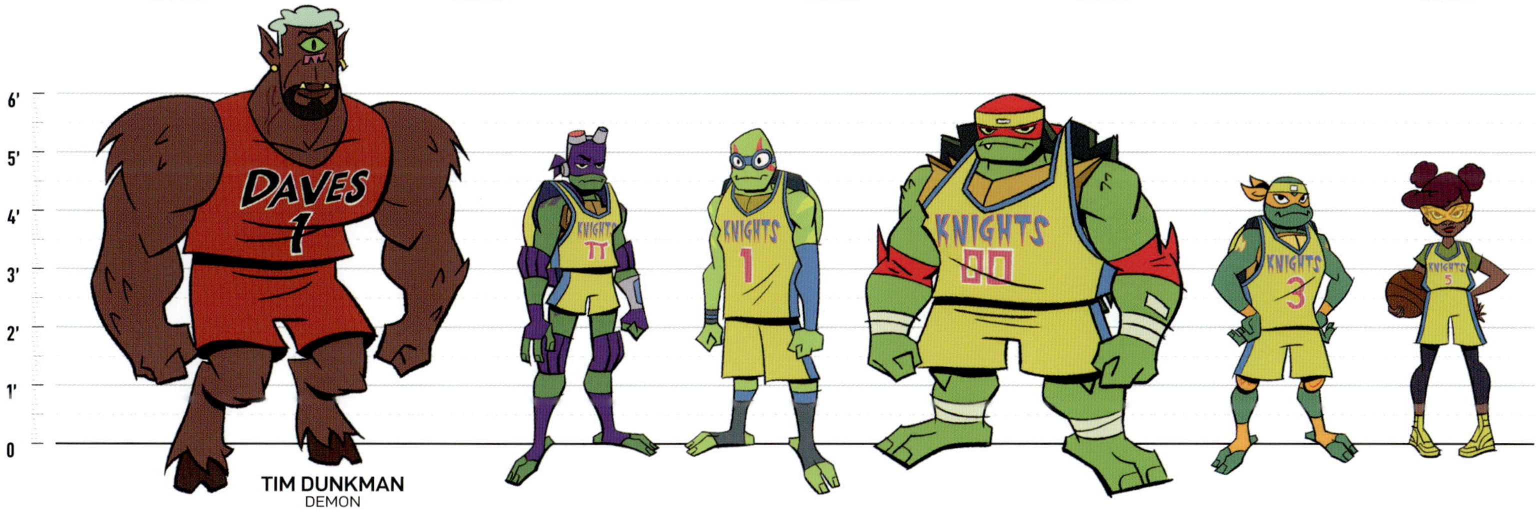

TIM DUNKMAN
DEMON

PIZZA PUFFS

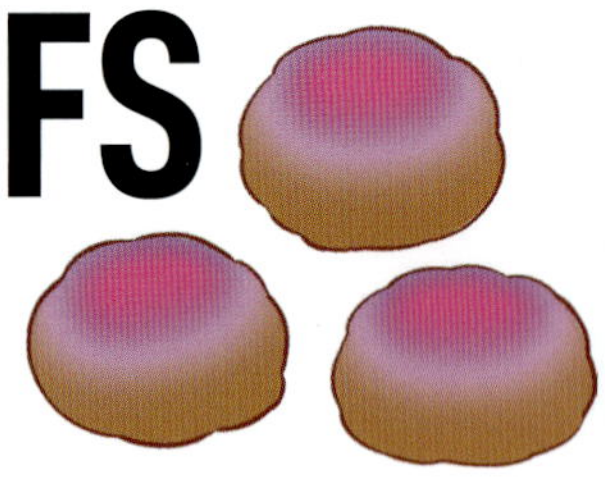

ORIGINAL AIR DATE: APRIL 24, 2020
PRODUCTION CODE: 062

WRITTEN BY **RUSS CARNEY & RON CORCILLO**
STORYBOARDS BY **MIRA ONGCHUA**
DIRECTED BY **JJ CONWAY**

TONY GAMA-LOBO: Standards and Practices was a little nervous with us having the Turtles eat poison. *"We can't encourage children to eat something that could potentially hurt them!"* Our solution? Call it *mystic poison!*

Our next big tentpole double episode was "Battle Nexus: New York"—Big Mama was going to force the Turtles to fight monsters on the streets of New York. And that's about all we had figured out. At some point Dale had the idea that each Turtle be teamed up with one of our villains. Cool! And then we thought maybe it would be a fun mystery for the audience to see a dark force kidnap the villains at the end of previous episodes. "Pizza Puffs" was already in production when we had this brainstorm, so we added Meat Sweats being kidnapped late in the game.

RUSS CARNEY: This episode is one of our favorites, and we often use it as a writing sample. We racked up the goofy with Tummytello, Mikey's jelly bones, Donnie's Smell-U-Lator, and a hint that Raph might be struggling with his own version of Mind Raph. We are big fans of Ben Schwartz's improv comic chops. In his record session, while confronting the Swedish Baker, Ben did one take as scripted, then we pitched that he put the script aside and do another take from memory, so it would seem like more of a struggle for feverish Leo to do his spiel. The result was pure delirious Leo perfection. If there's one lesson to take away from this episode, it's *"Don't. Eat. The poison!"*

TONY GAMA-LOBO: I have never seen a room of writers laugh harder than when someone pitched Tummytello having the big moment of the episode: *"Believe in yourselves!"* So funny! The problem is in all our fun we inadvertently created a sentient being in Tummytello that we were about to kill off at the end! At least we gave him that classic war buddy/dying parent sendoff: *"I will always be with you."*

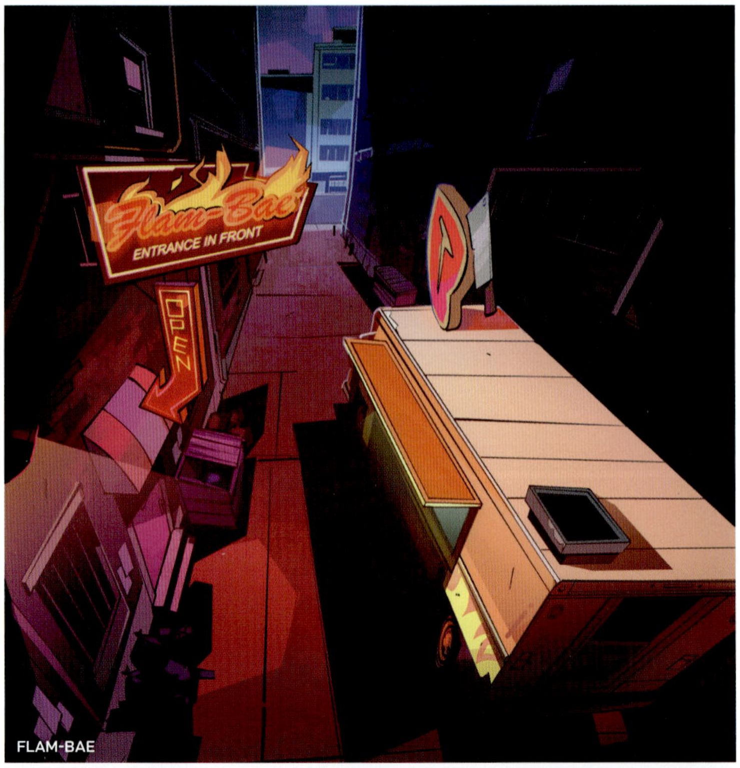

FLAM-BAE

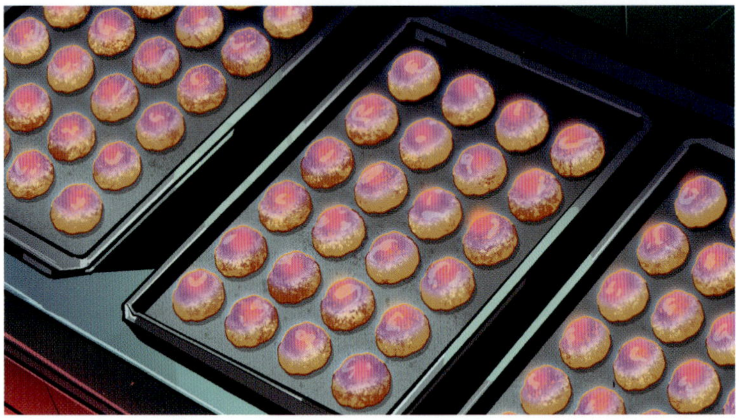

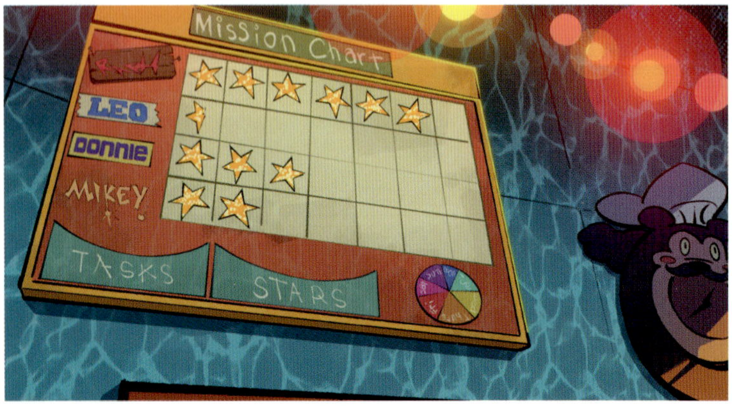

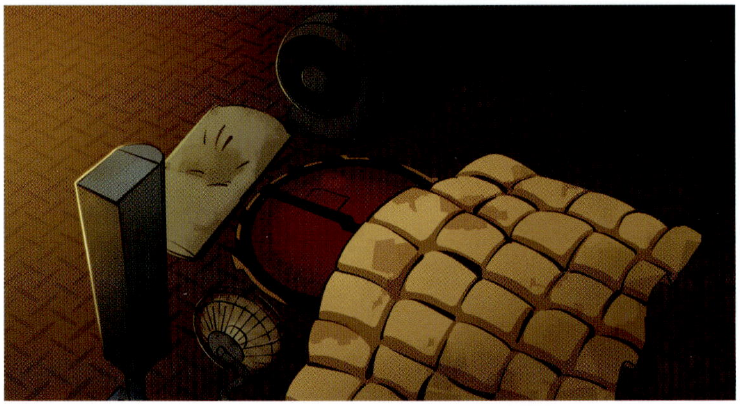

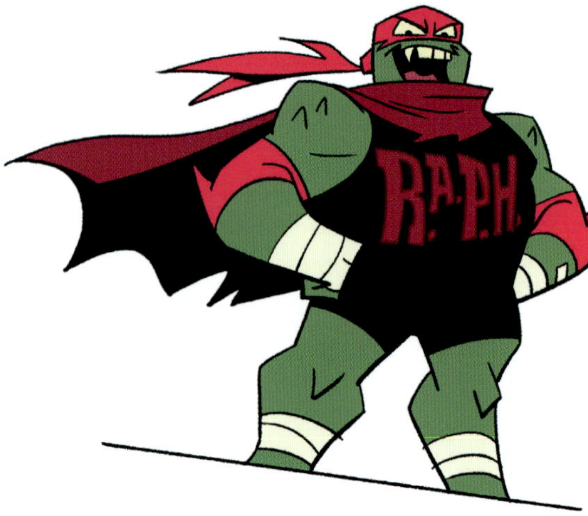

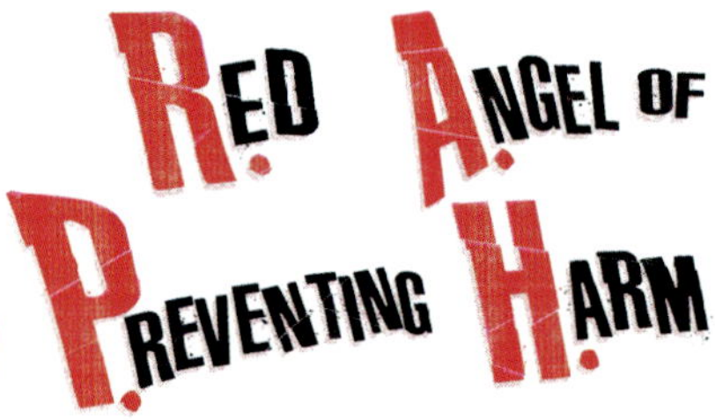

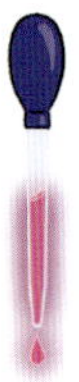

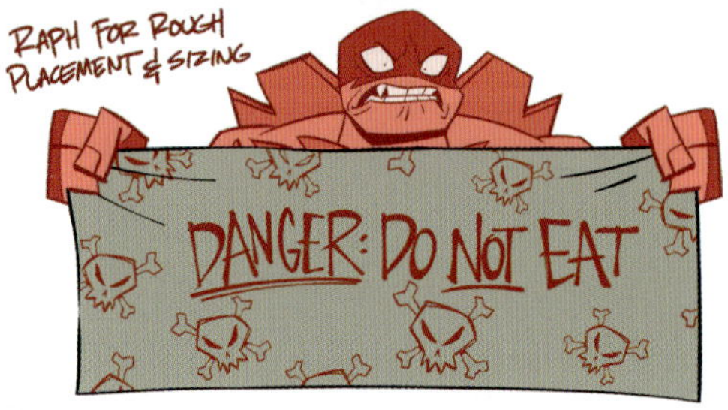

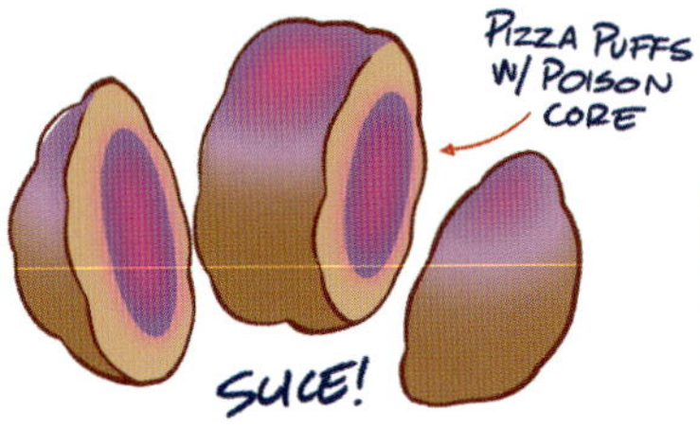

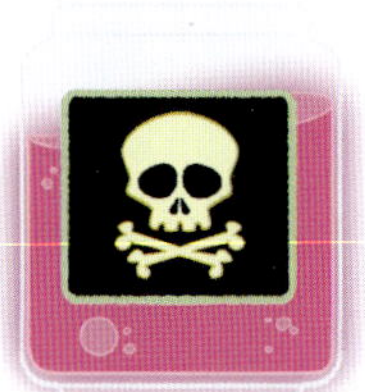

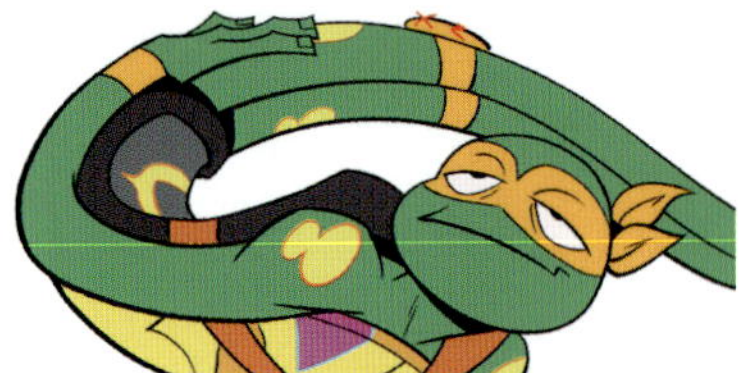

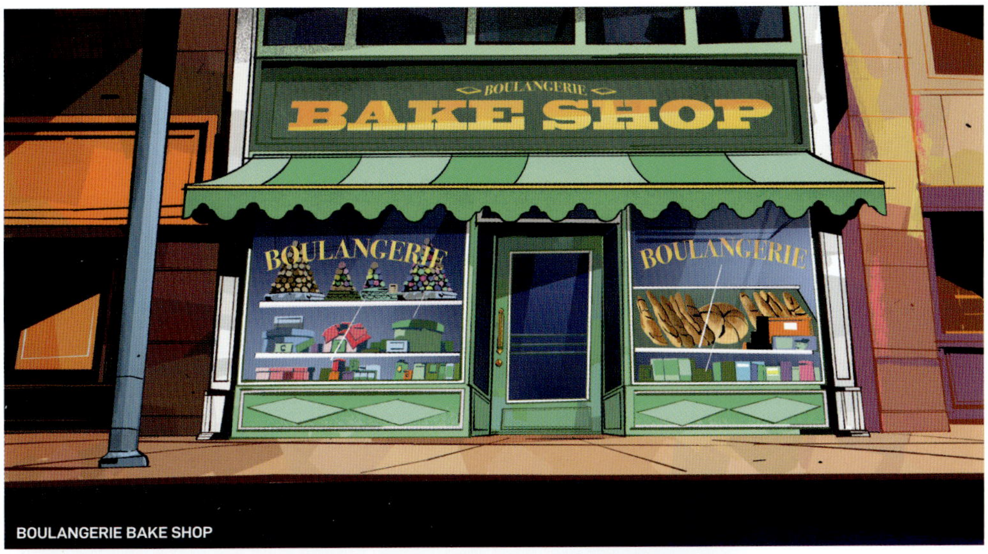

BOULANGERIE BAKE SHOP

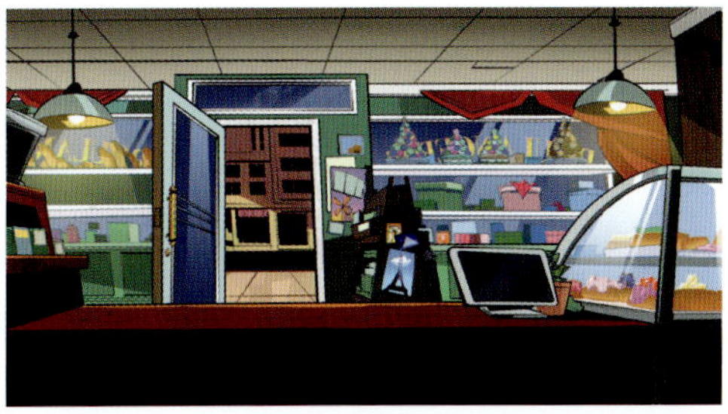

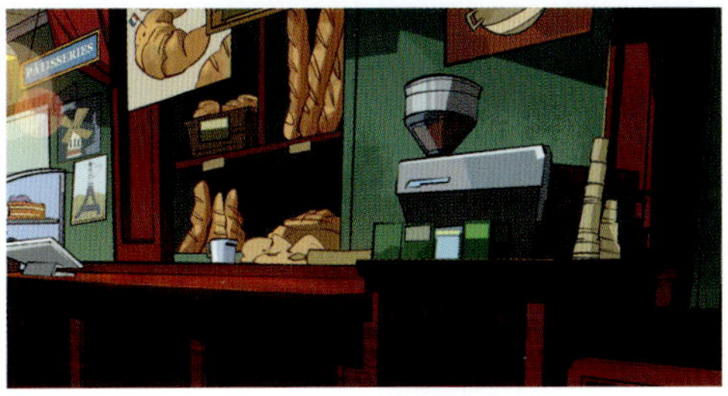

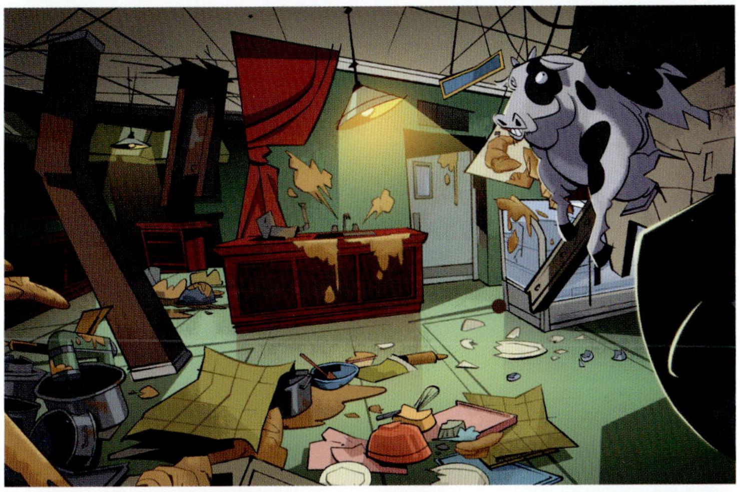

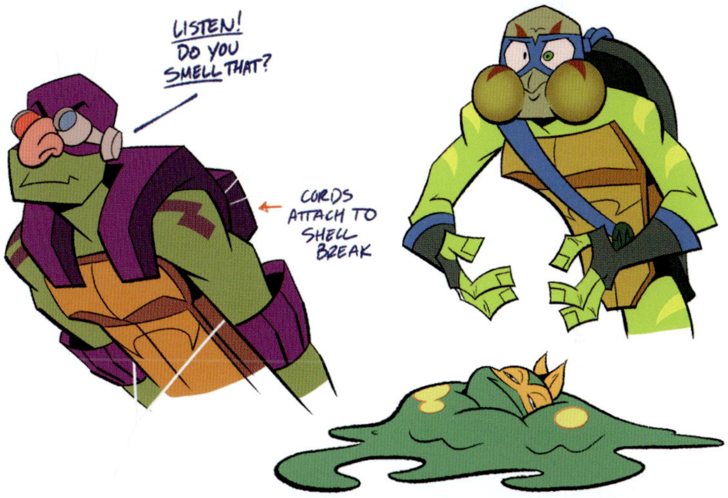

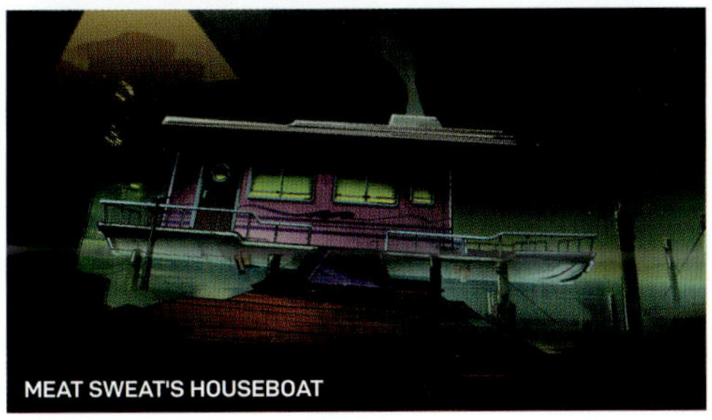

MEAT SWEAT'S HOUSEBOAT

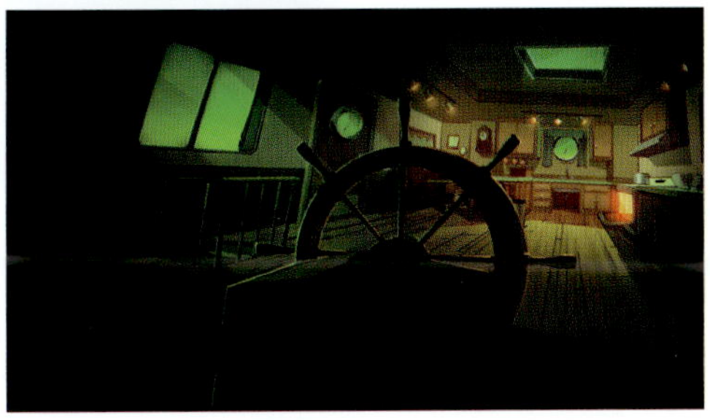

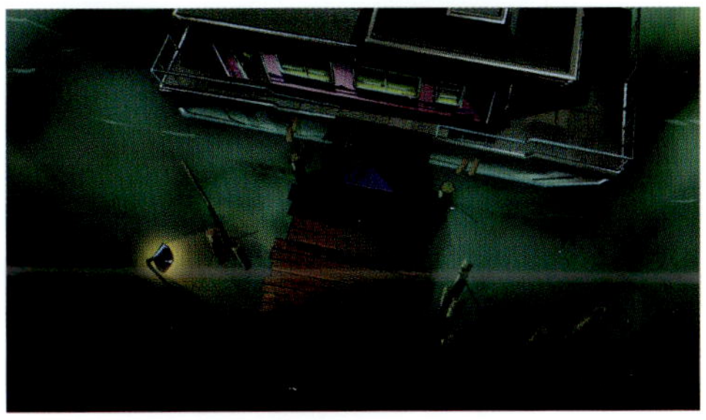

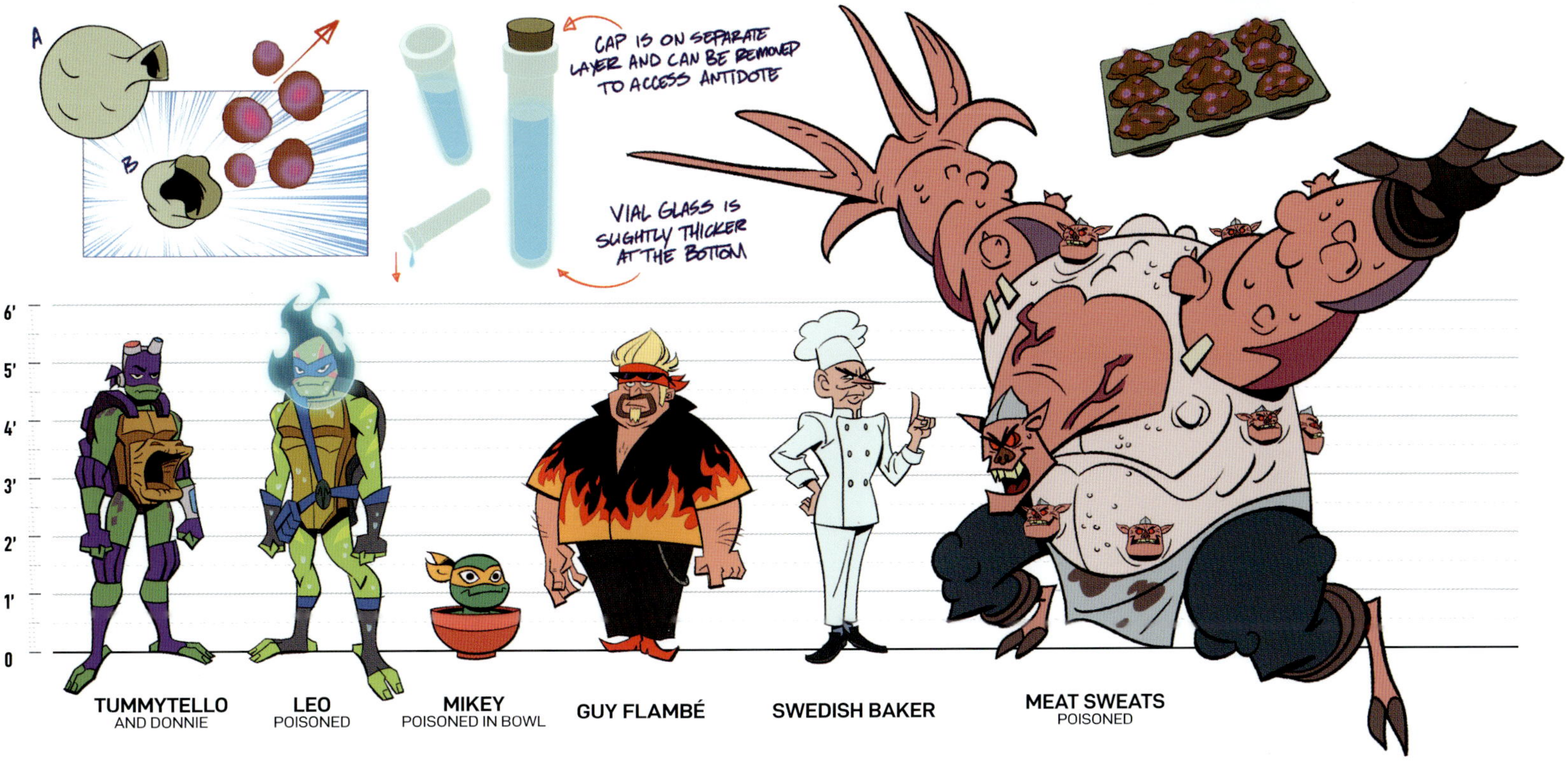

SIDEKICK AHOY!

ORIGINAL AIR DATE: MAY 15, 2020
PRODUCTION CODE: 063

WRITTEN BY **IAN "BLAST-OFF" BUSCH**
STORYBOARDS BY **JUPITER JAKE CASTORENA**
DIRECTED BY **JUPITER JAKE CASTORENA**

IAN BUSCH: The most fun we had in making this episode was in coming up with the bomb threat and making things as hard as possible for the boys to get out of at the end. Phil LaMarr is an amazing pro at every role he's ever taken on, and it was such a pleasure watching him bring Jupiter Jim to life again.

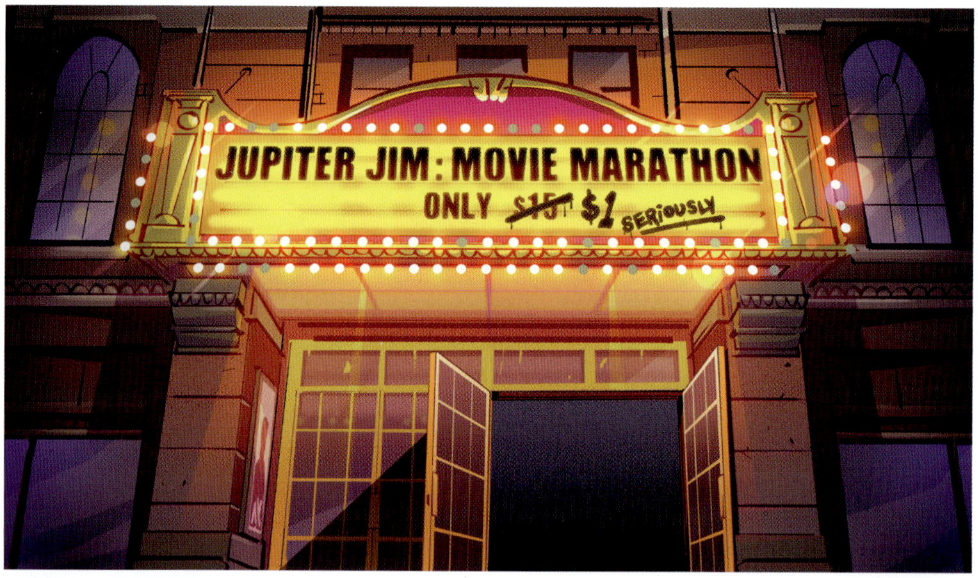

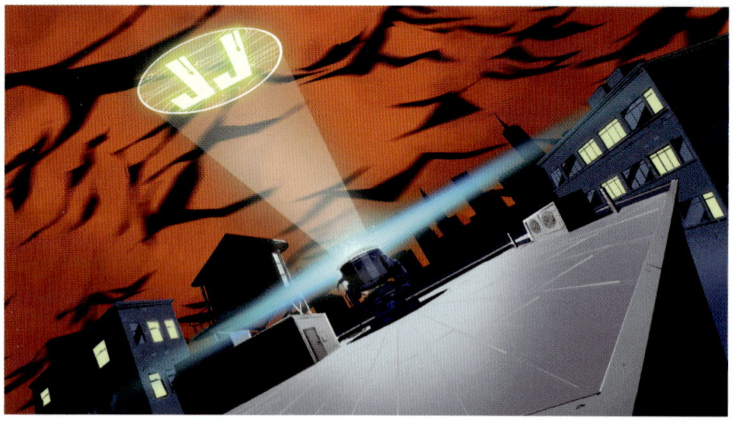

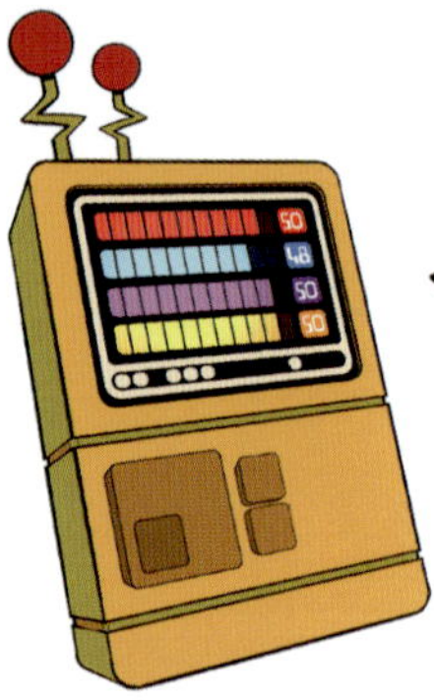

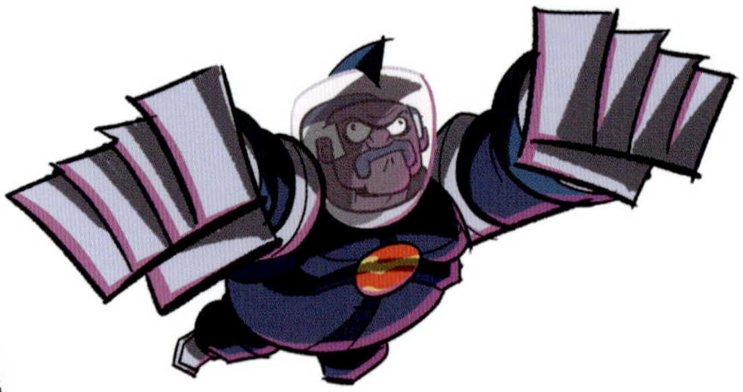

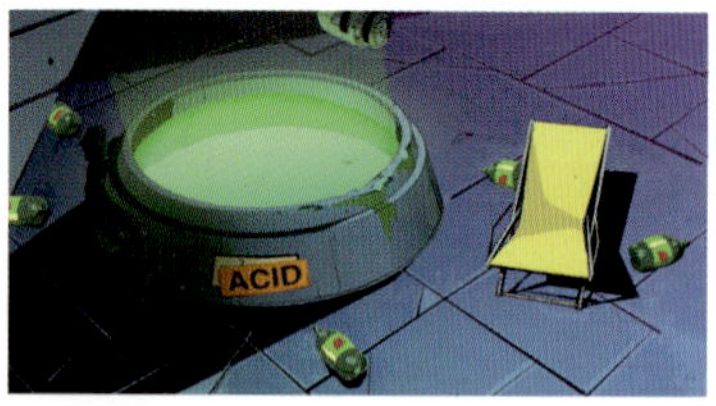

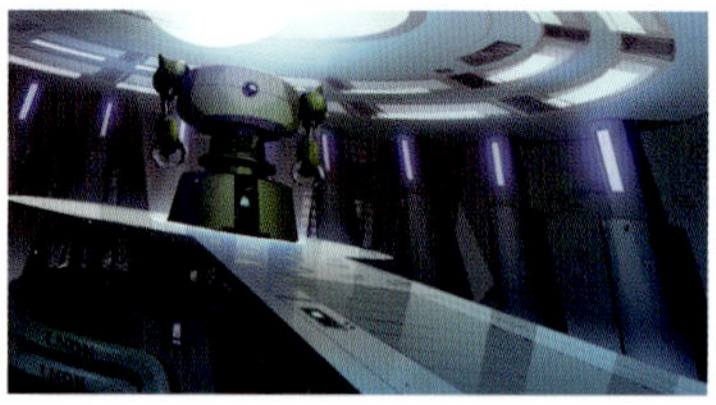

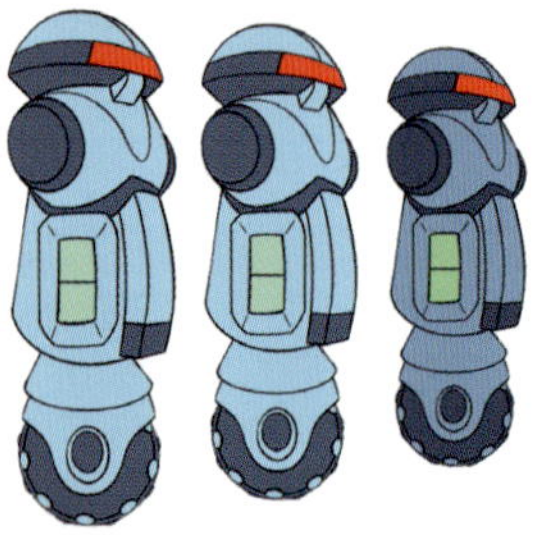

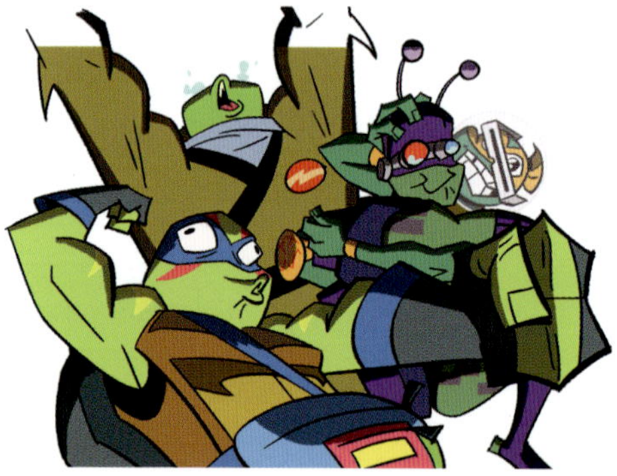

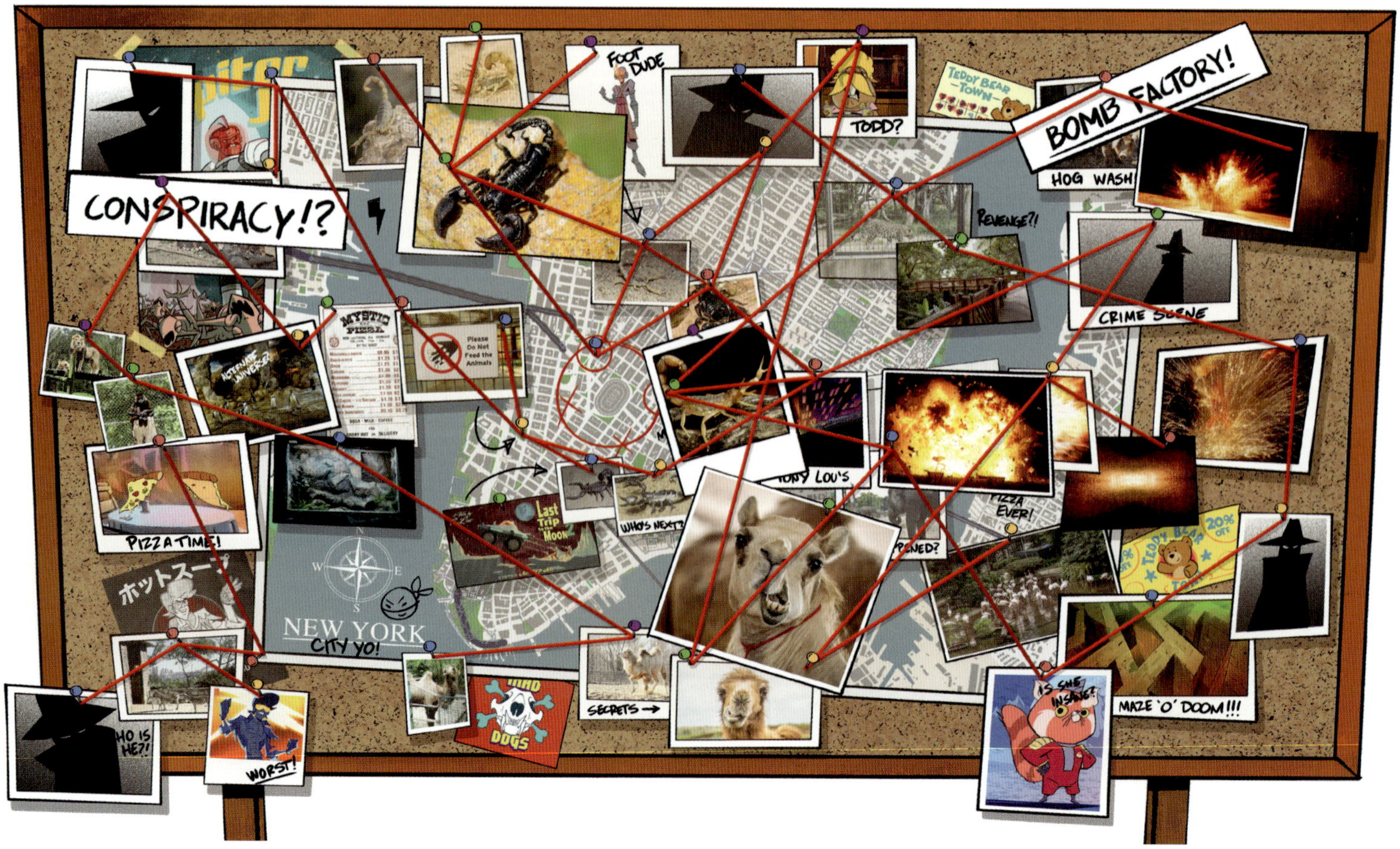

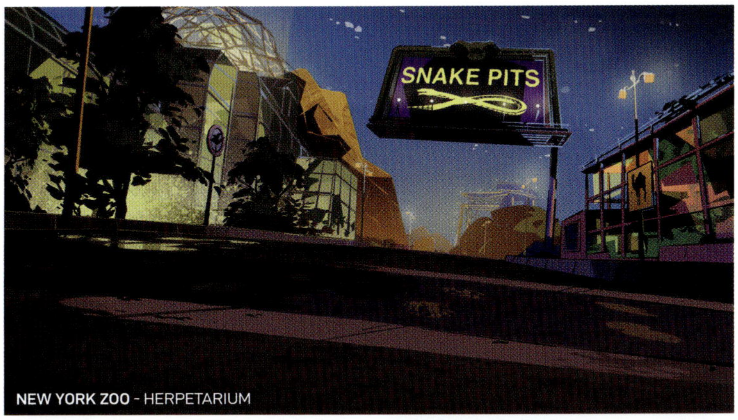

NEW YORK ZOO - HERPETARIUM

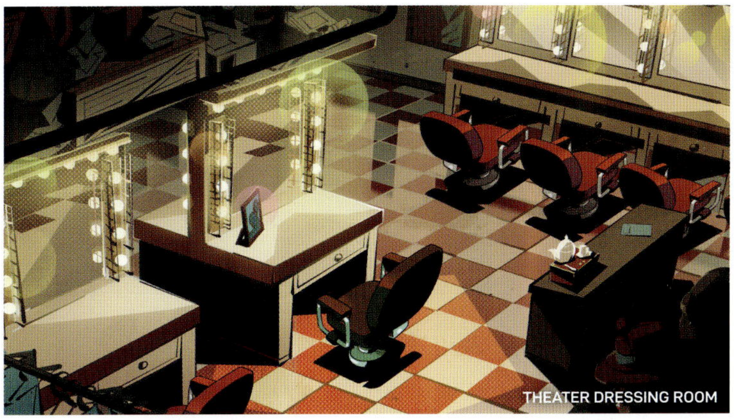
THEATER DRESSING ROOM

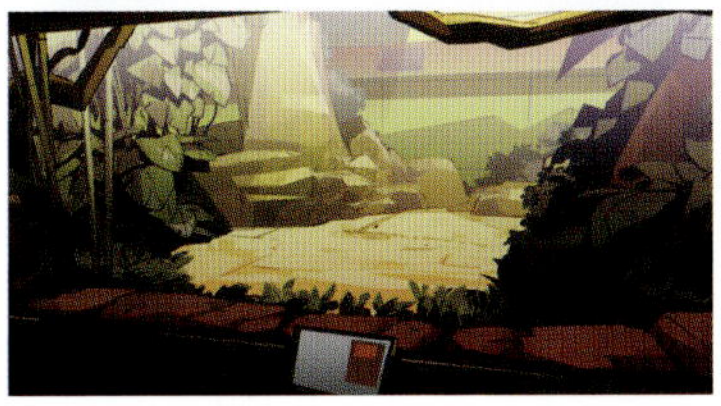

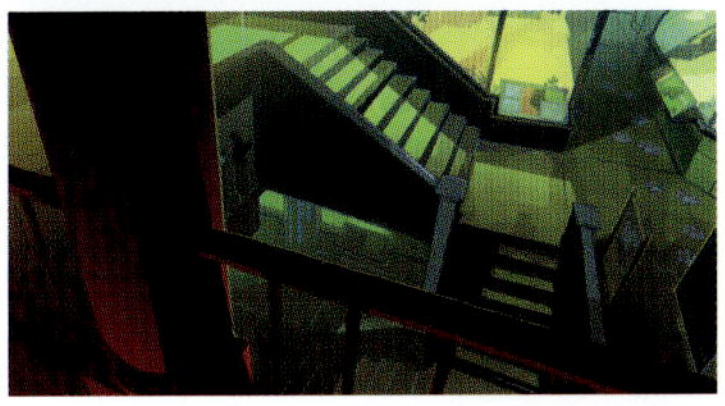

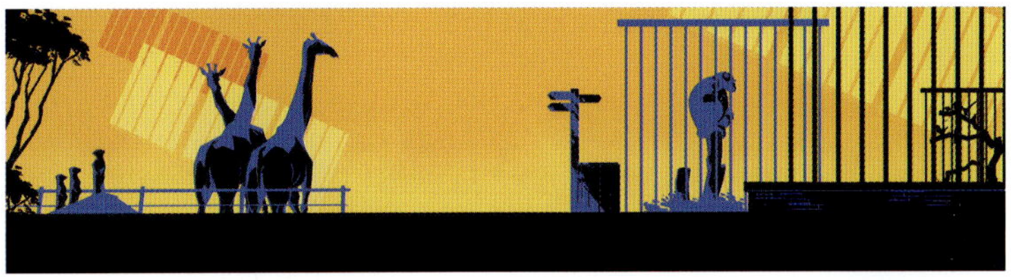

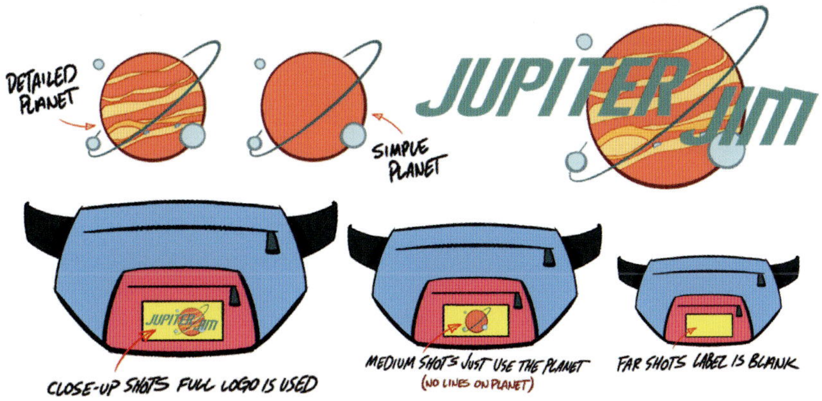

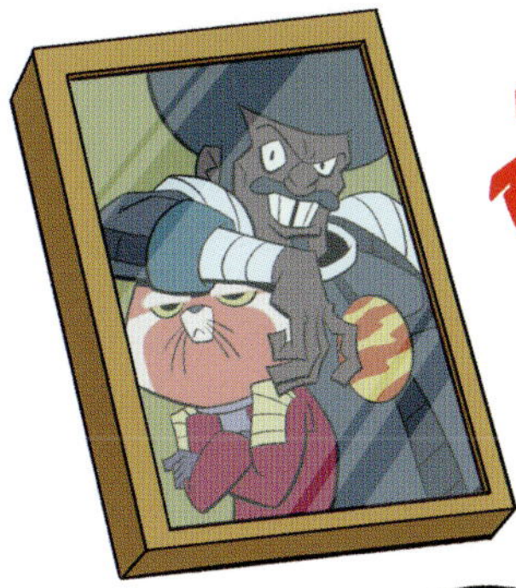

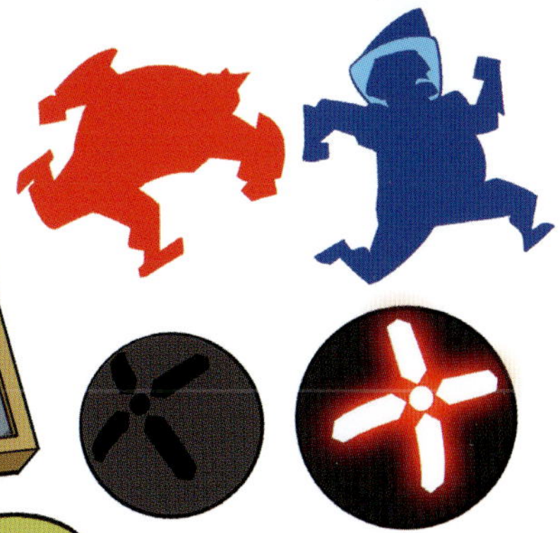
STINGER BOMBS

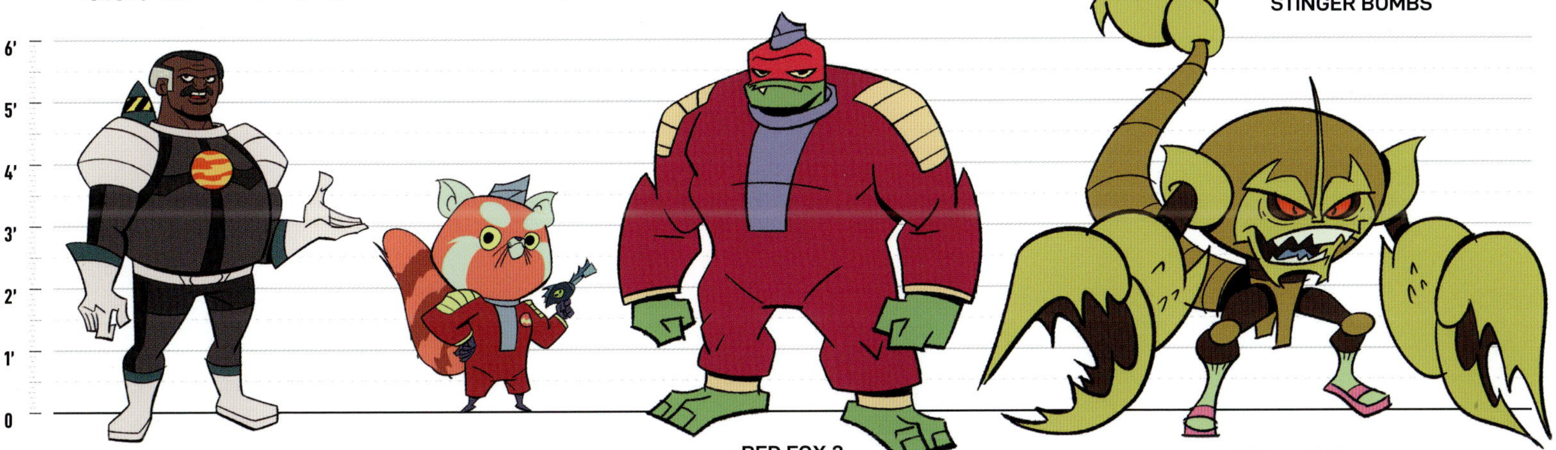

JUPITER JIM

RED FOX

RED FOX 2
RAPH

SCOR-PION

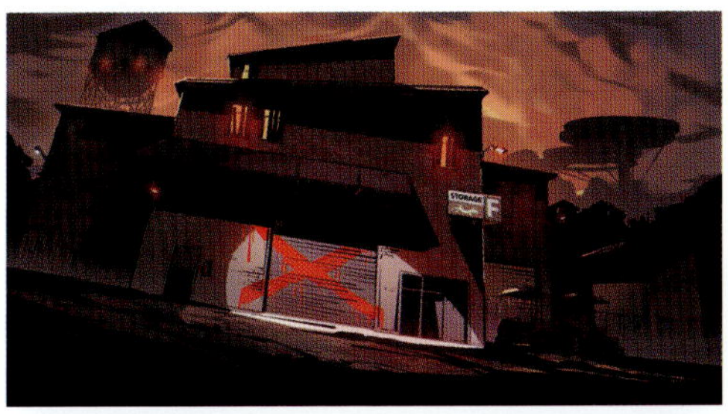

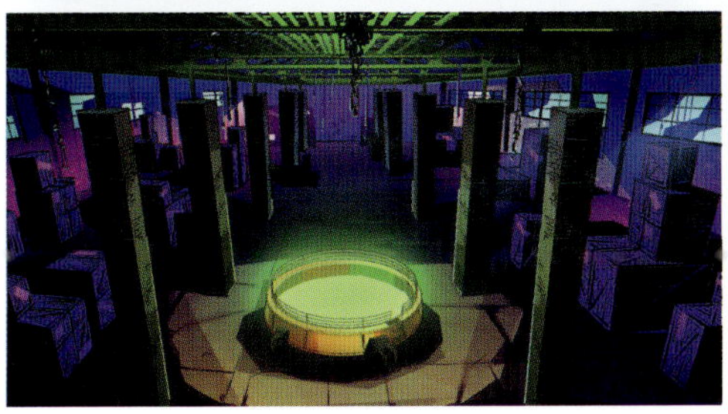

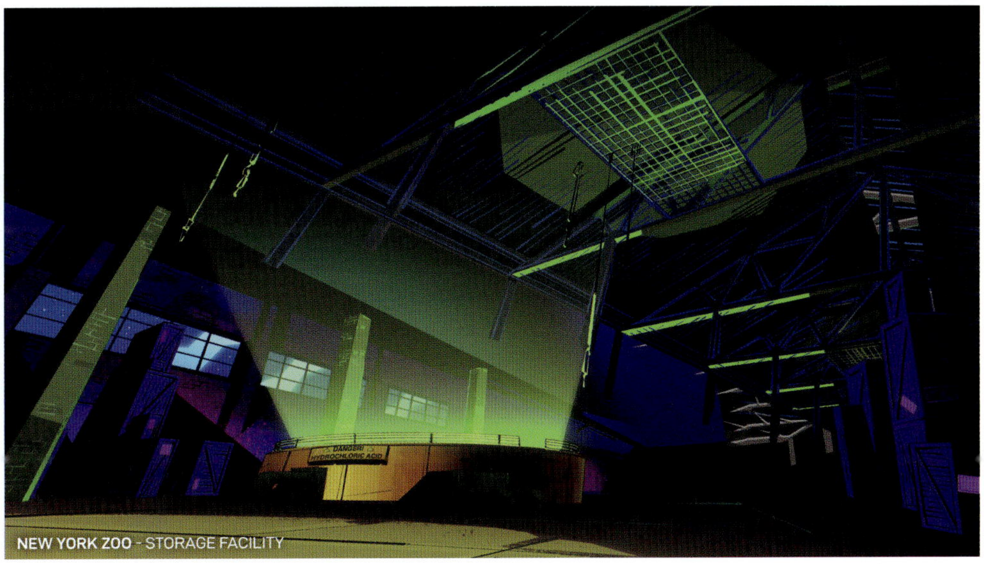
NEW YORK ZOO - STORAGE FACILITY

THE HIDDEN CITY JOB

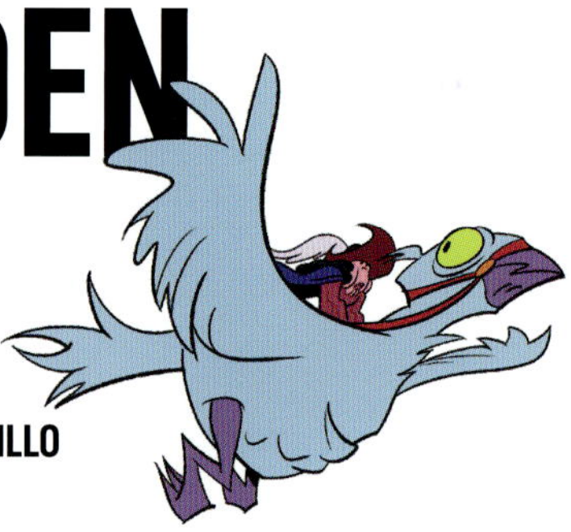

ORIGINAL AIR DATE: MAY 15, 2020
PRODUCTION CODE: 064

WRITTEN BY **RUSS CARNEY & RON CORCILLO**
STORYBOARDS BY **MAX COLLINS**
DIRECTED BY **SEBASTIAN MONTES**

RUSS CARNEY: We really loved the dynamic between Leo and Señor Hueso in "Portal Jacked," so we thought it would be fun to do another team-up, this time in the form of a heist with heart. I envisioned that the bird would look something like the 1980s Italian pop singer Nocera, who has a cute birdlike quality, but either I forgot to mention this to Andy or nobody was listening to me when I brought it up (most likely). I think Dale Malinowski pitched the idea of the joey pouch.

RON CORCILLO: The "battle" with Big Mama and her henchmen is delightfully silly. We thought it would be awesome for Hueso and Piel to combine into a singular person in an ultimate example of fraternal unity. And what if that person was the visual antithesis of a creepy bone man and a floppy skin dude? We wanted Don Suave to resemble a young Ricardo Montalbán (*"Khaaaan!"*), a very handsome leading actor with great natural swagger. His lines are performed by both voice actors (the amazingly talented Messrs. Eric Bauza and Christian Lanz), and our brilliant dialogue editor John Deligiannis (easily the best employee at Nickelodeon) blended them together seamlessly. Max Collins did a great job boarding this episode, and the Hueso/Piel union was a lot of fun to see.

We regret using the word "machismo" for Don Suave, because it has a negative connotation, but we meant it in the 1970s–'80s "macho man" sense.

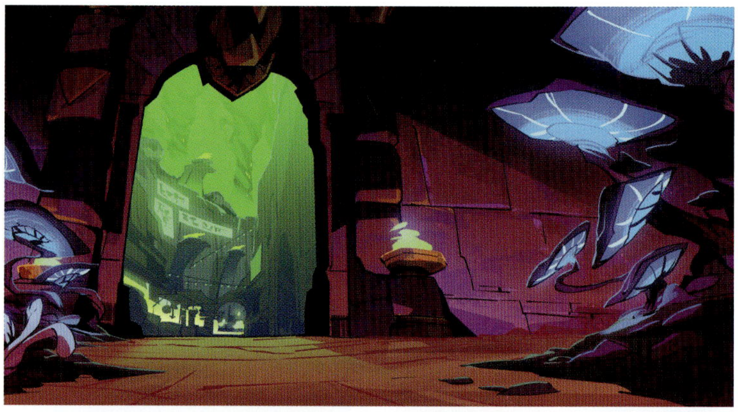

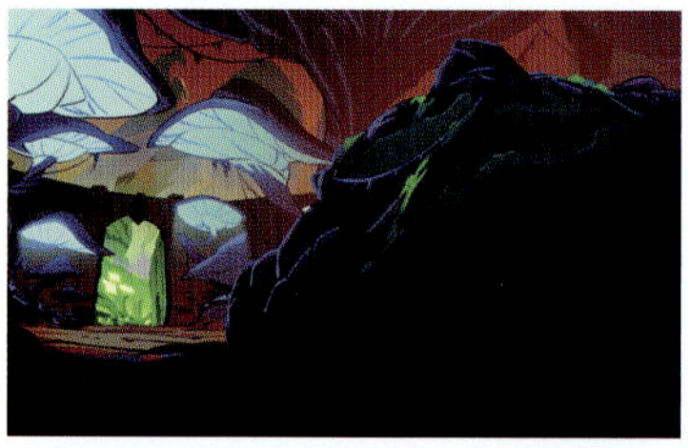

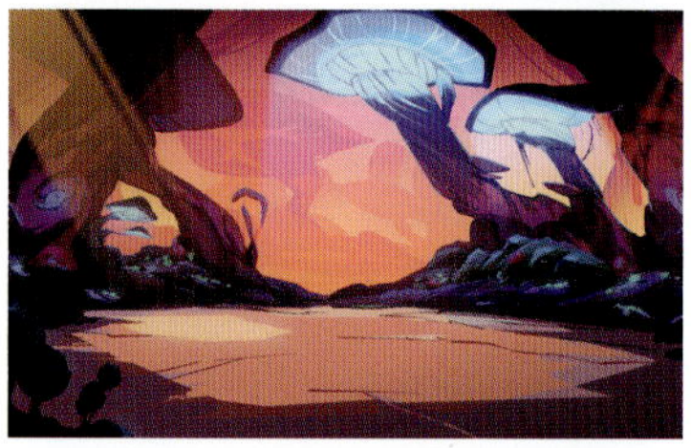

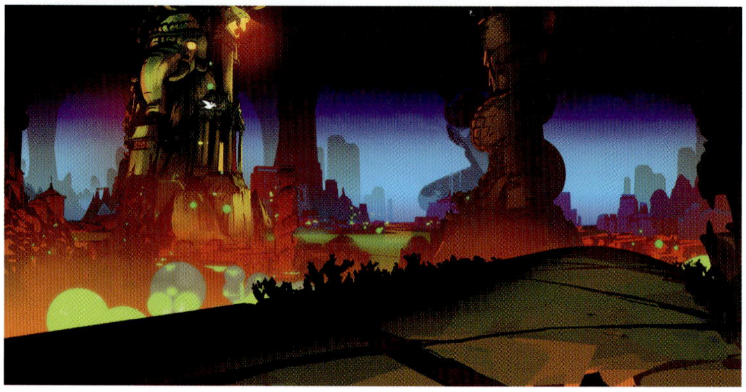

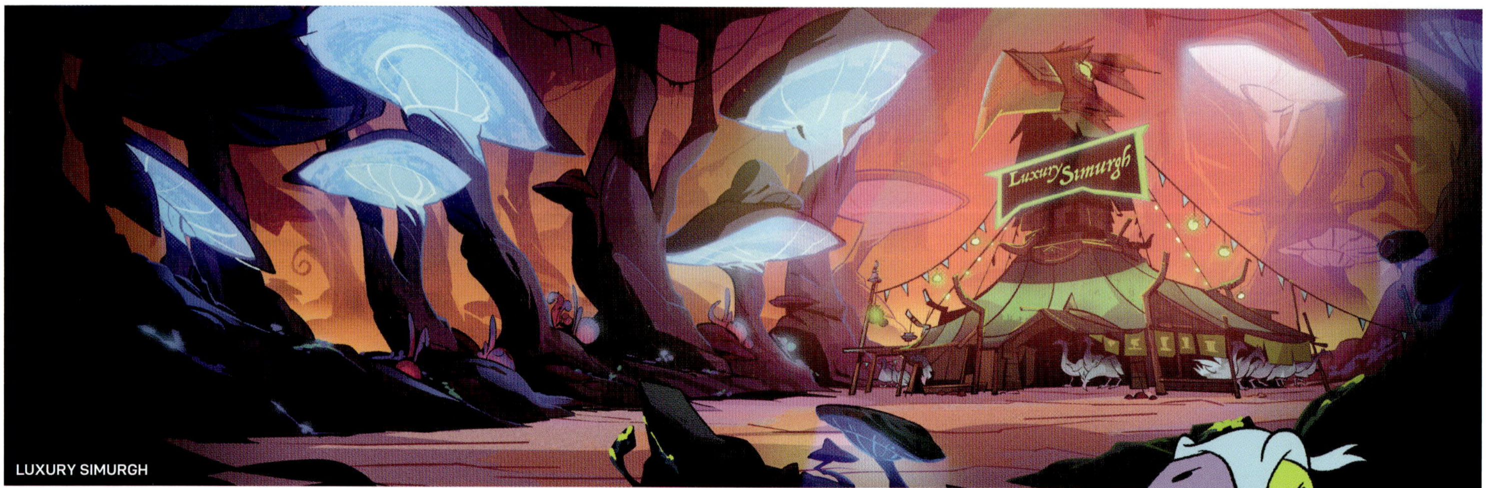

LUXURY SIMURGH

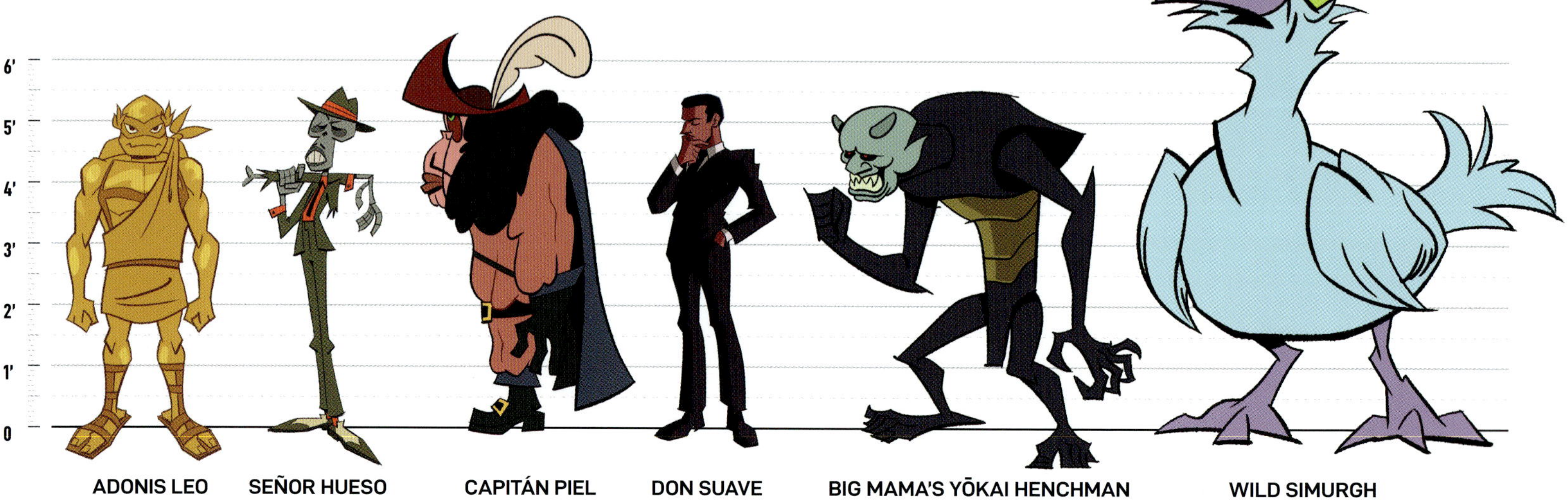

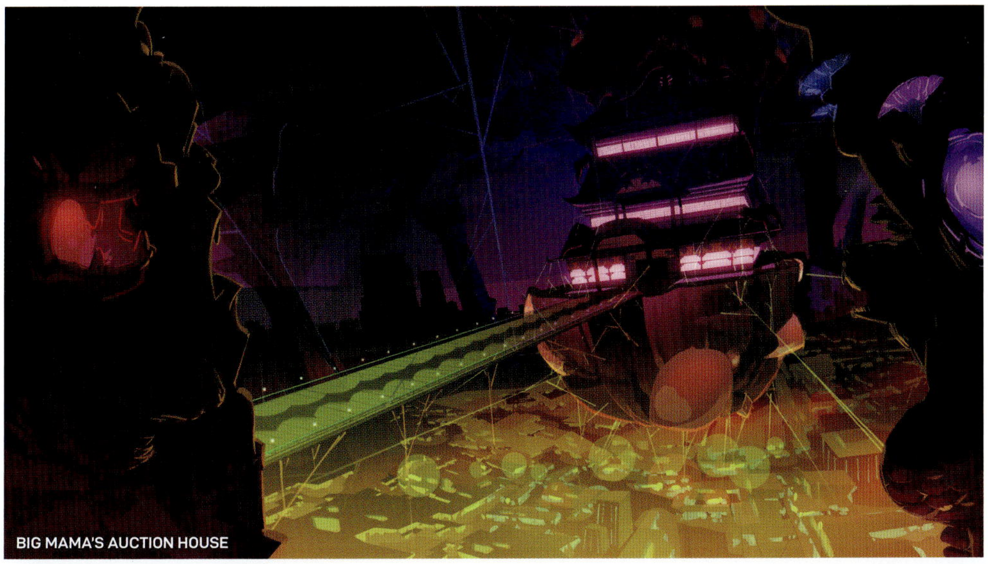
BIG MAMA'S AUCTION HOUSE

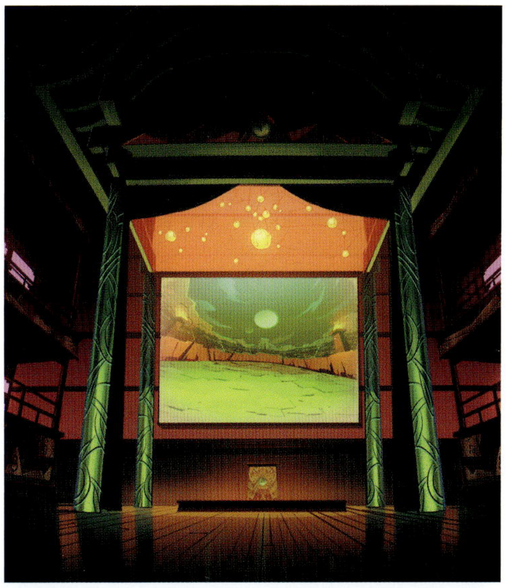

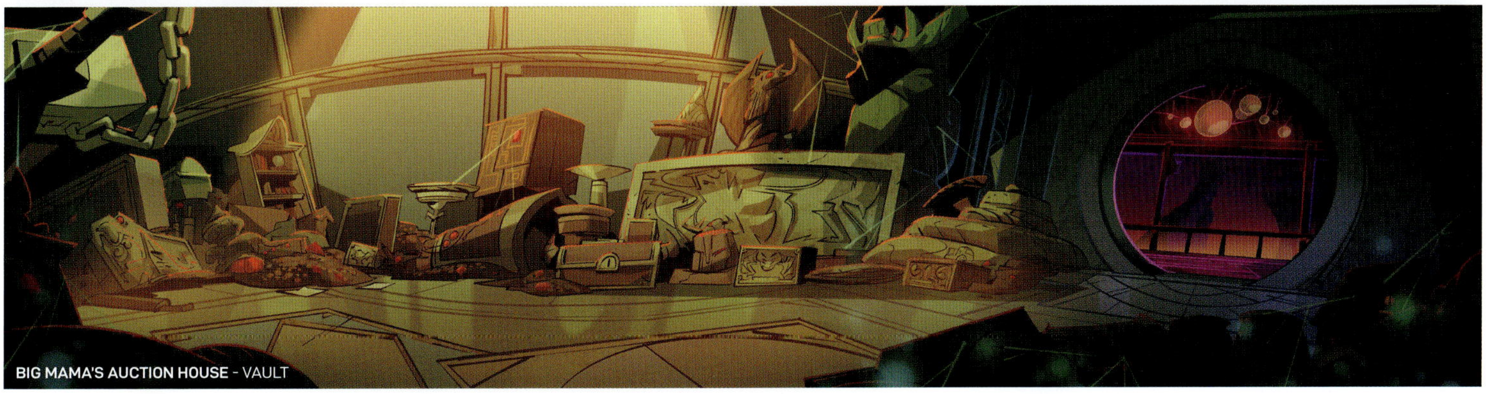
BIG MAMA'S AUCTION HOUSE - VAULT

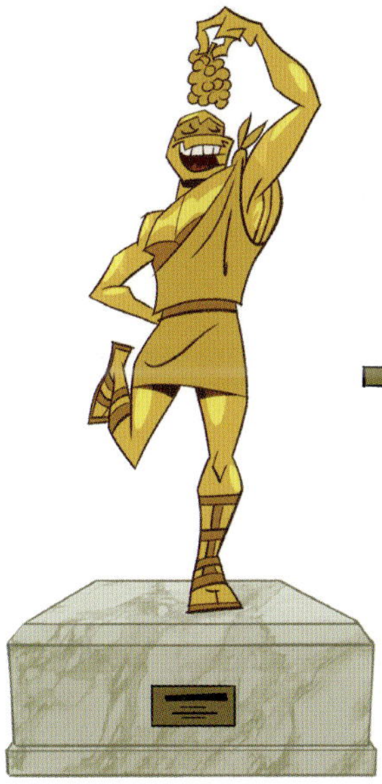

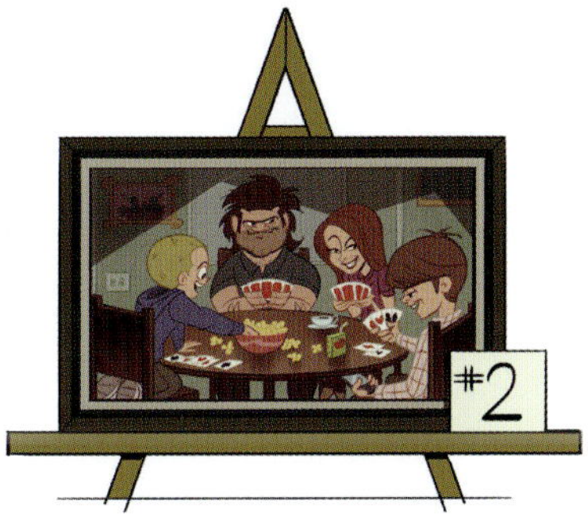

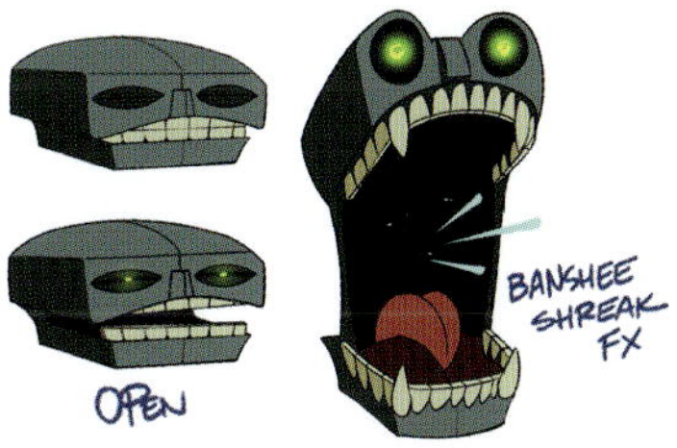

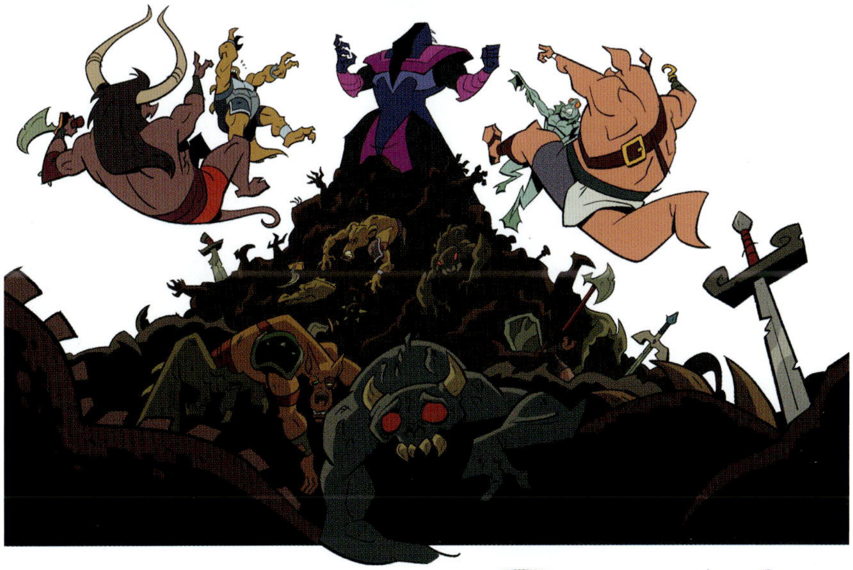

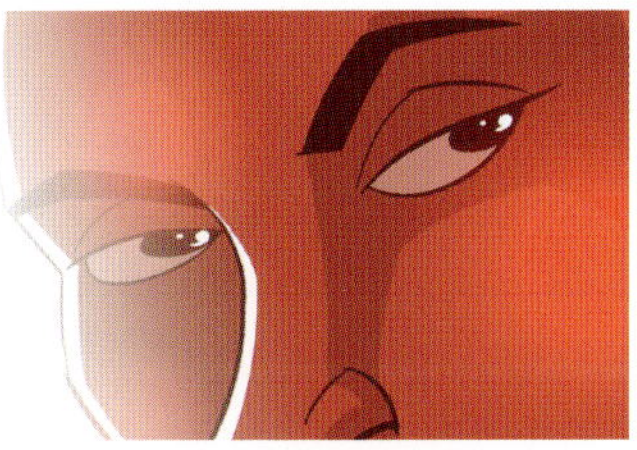

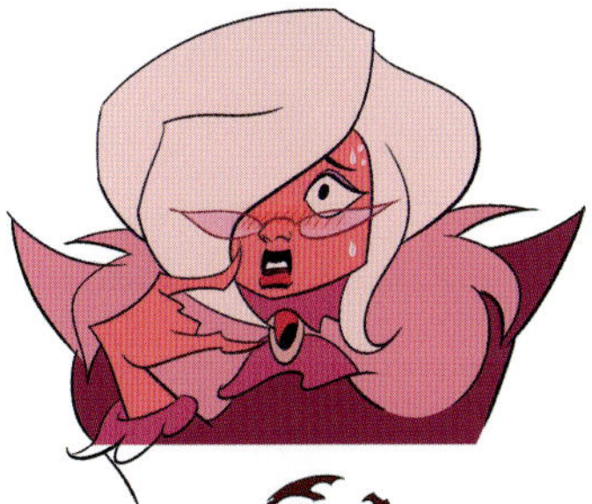

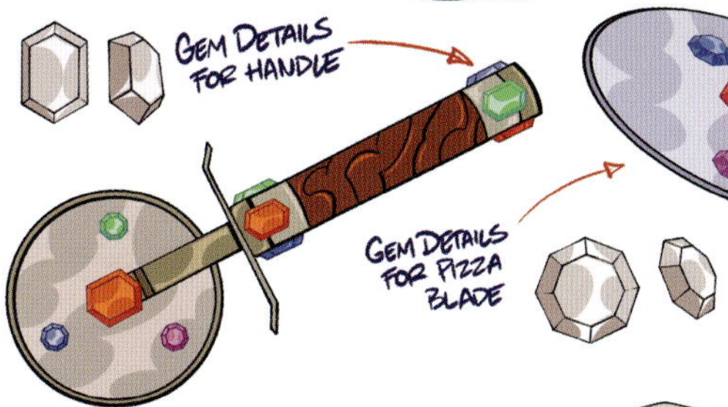

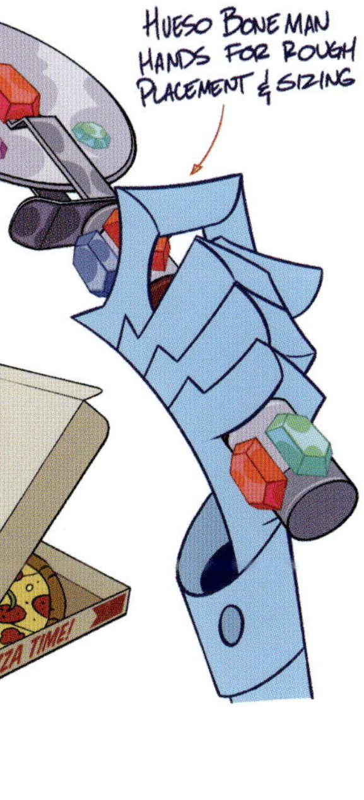

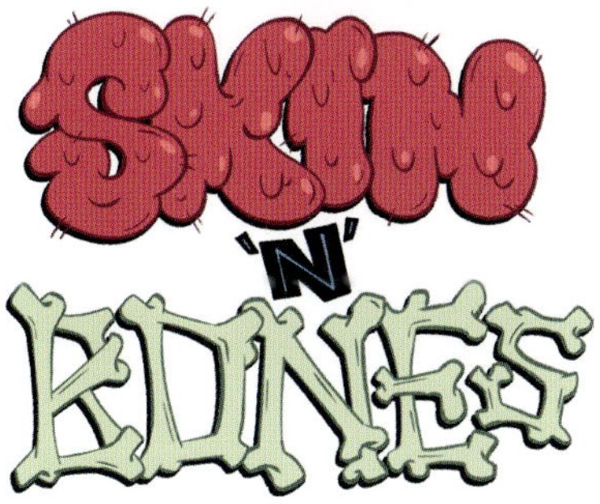

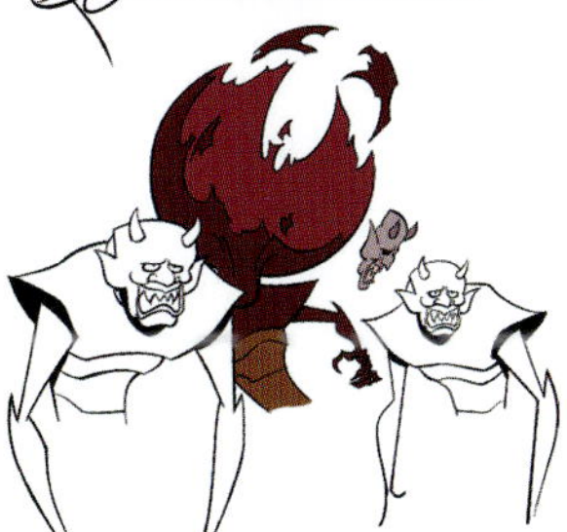

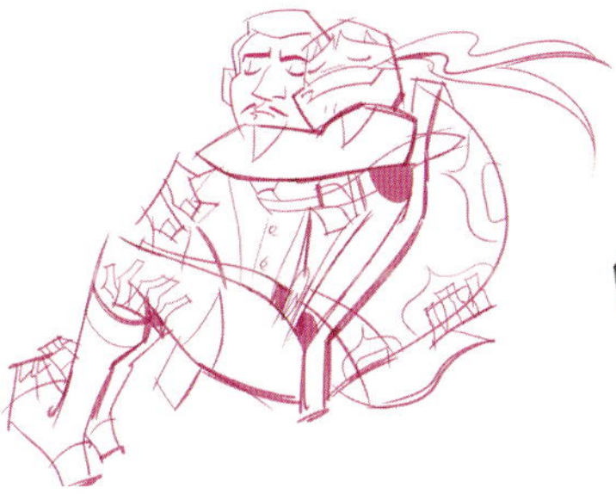

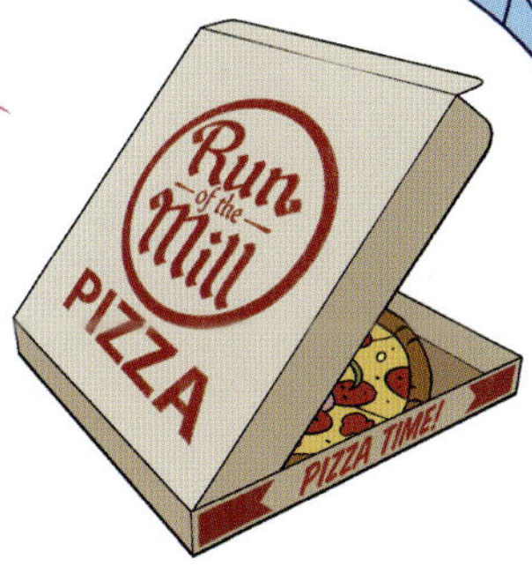

ALWAYS BE BROWNIES

ORIGINAL AIR DATE: MAY 15, 2020
PRODUCTION CODE: 065

WRITTEN BY **JESSE GORDON**
STORYBOARDS BY **CHRISTINE LIU**
DIRECTED BY **JJ CONWAY**

TONY GAMA-LOBO: When you're planning out a season of episodes for any show, it's important to make sure every character has several strong stories. Otherwise you end up with certain characters just not ever being that developed. That's why *Rise* has maybe the best April O'Neil of any iteration of Turtles. We really took time to develop her character: what makes her cool, what makes her funny, what are her strengths, what are her weaknesses. And we always made sure to give her agency.

At the heart of our April was this endless enthusiasm. We loved that no matter how many times she failed, she just kept trying. Well, that begged the question of "What happens when she fails one too many times and stops believing in herself?" Jesse had this idea to tackle that story inside a hilarious idea of Foot Recruit heading up a diabolical Girl Scouts–esque group trying to take over the world through selling brownies. And a Splinter/April team-up was always so fun and funny. Splinter as a mentor/father figure was always so sweet. My favorite part of the episode is that final inspirational speech Splinter gives to Foot Recruit while we watch April be the badass she didn't realize she was...and then Foot Recruit takes the wrong lesson!

This episode plants the seed for the Splinter connection to Foot Recruit in the series finale. We kidnapped Foot Recruit at the end of this episode for "Battle Nexus: New York" before we knew what her role would be.

The title of the episode is a reference to a *Glengarry Glen Ross* (1992) line: *"Always. Be. Closing."*

JESSE GORDON: This Splinter/April team-up episode let us explore new dynamics after season 1's events. The concept of Splinter having '70s/'80s infomercials for his business ventures was hilarious to our staff. I loved creating the villainous Brownie troop—their spiked bat weapons and the tall/short leader dynamic were perfect *Rise* absurdity. The episode balances April's badass fight sequences with genuine emotion, particularly in Splinter's speech to Foot Recruit that intercuts with April's actions. That final moment where April realizes her own worth without needing validation was exactly the character growth we wanted.

JJ CONWAY: This is my favorite episode that Jesse wrote. Originally there was a B plot involving the TMNT stealing honey from bees, but the A plot between April, Foot Recruit, and Splinter was so strong and special that we lobbied our network exec Dana Vasquez-Eberhardt (DVE), asking if we could cut the Turtles from the episode so we could fully realize April and Recruit's story. Dana supported us, got approval from way up the ladder, and we were able to make an episode of *Rise* without any of the actual Turtles.

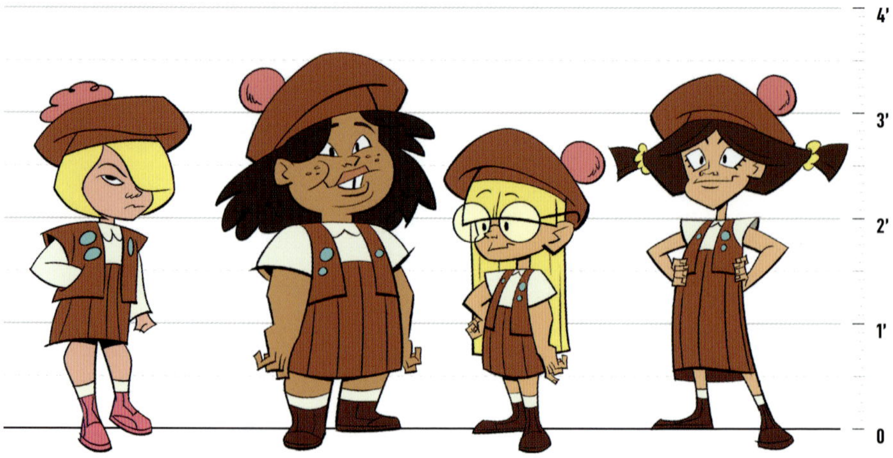

JULIA GRANDMA CJ'S BROWNIE GIRLS

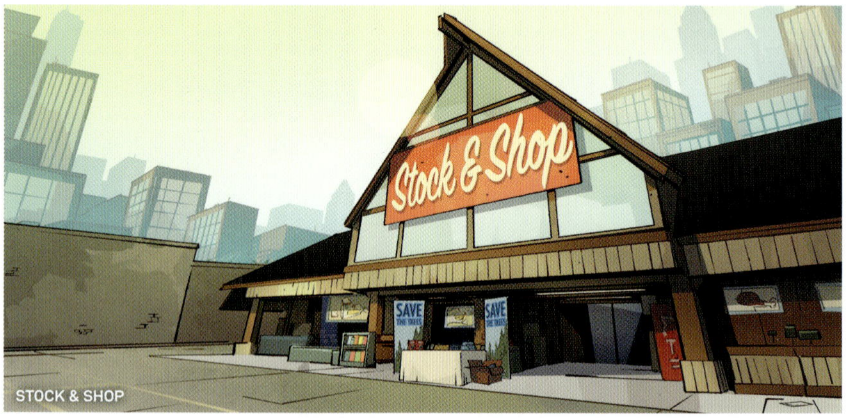

STOCK & SHOP

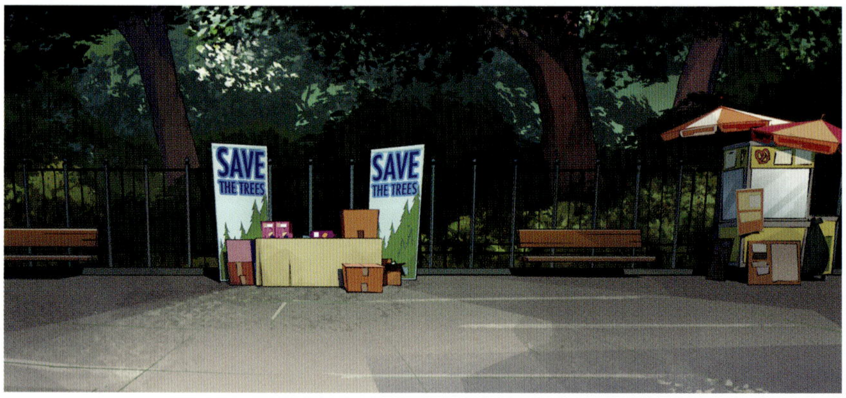

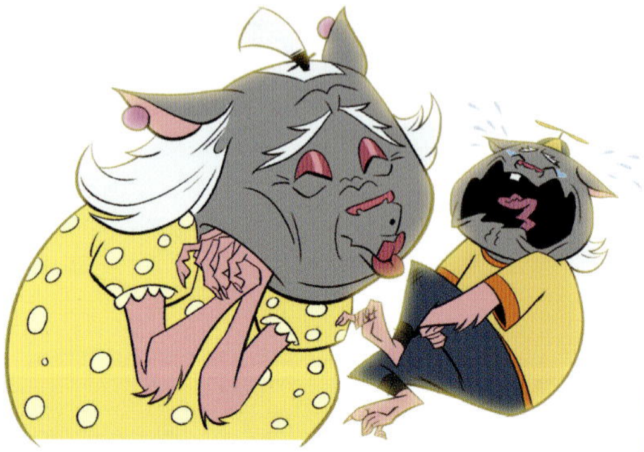

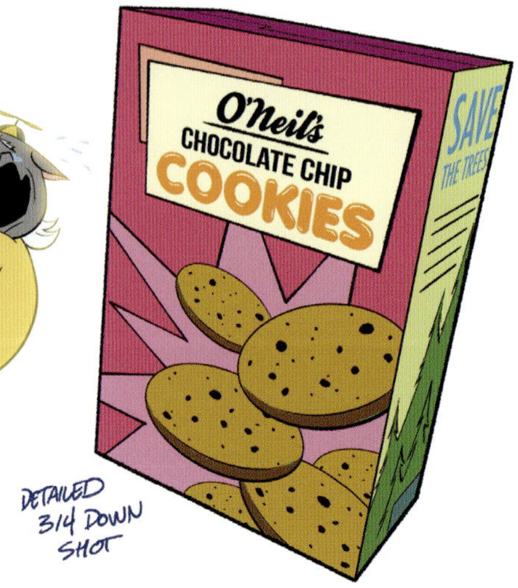

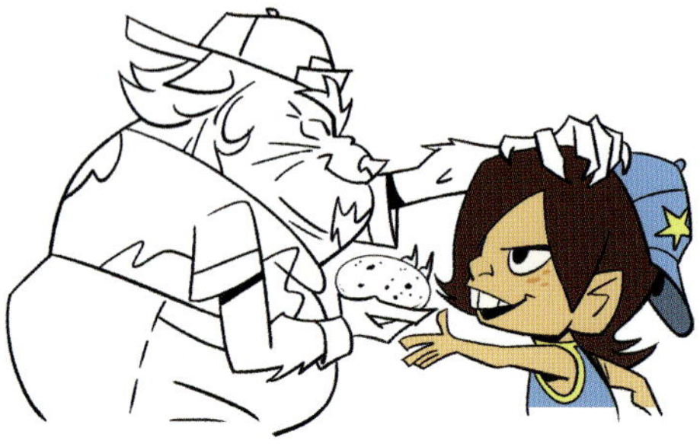

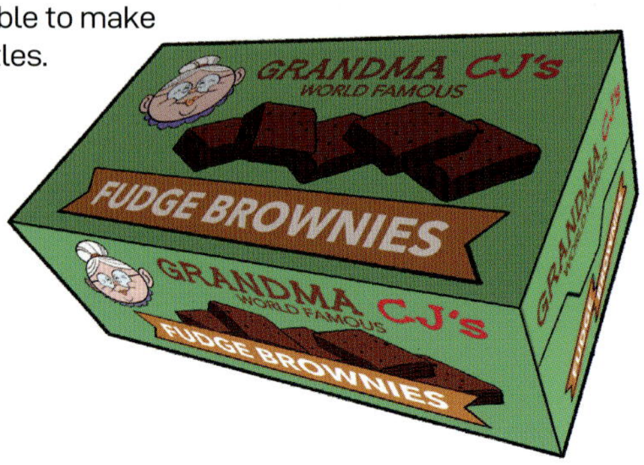

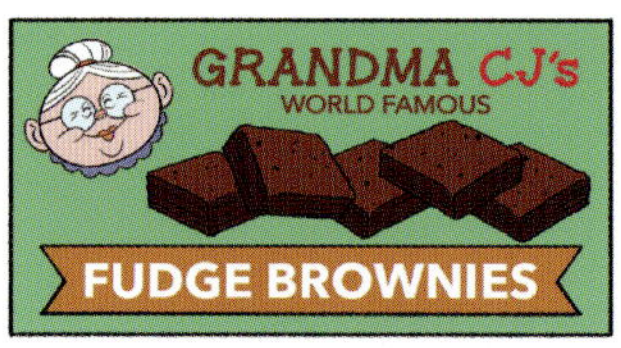

BOX TOP FLAT

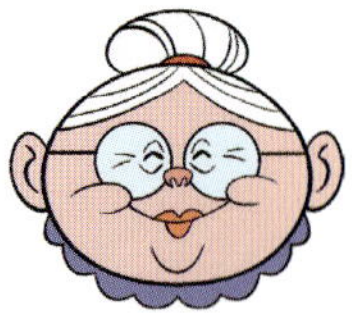

CHARACTER LOGO

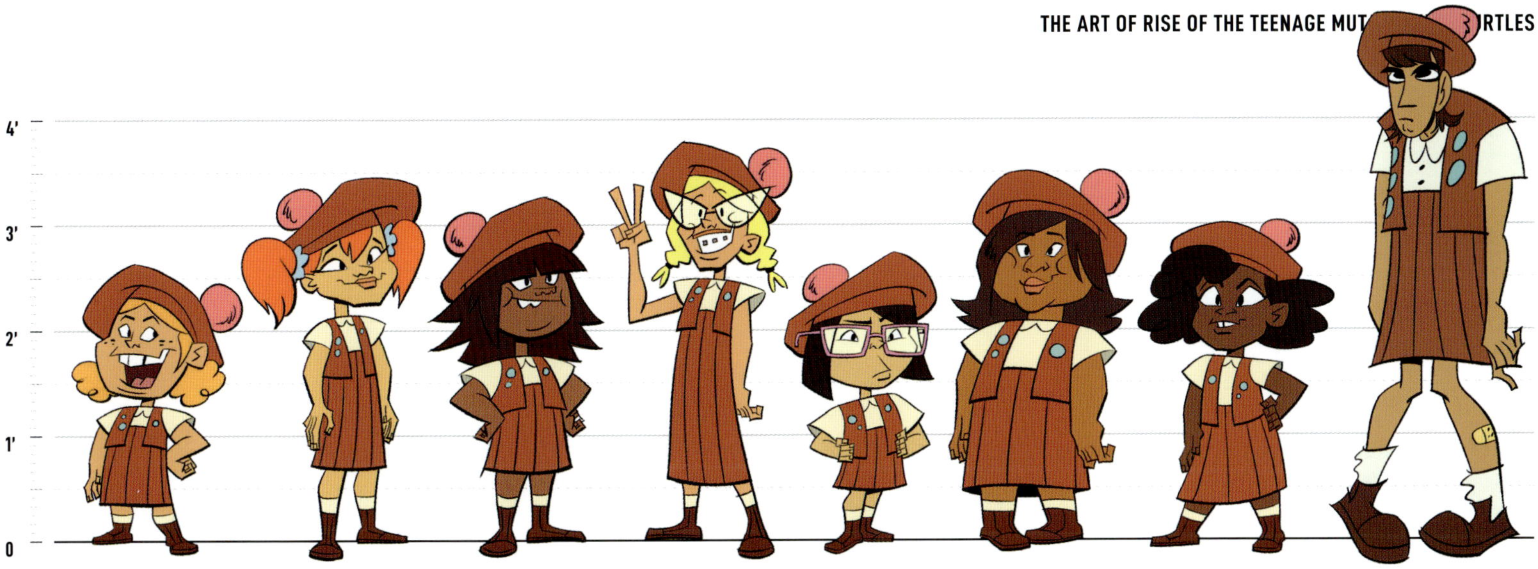

GRANDMA CJ'S BROWNIE GIRLS

CJ GIRL

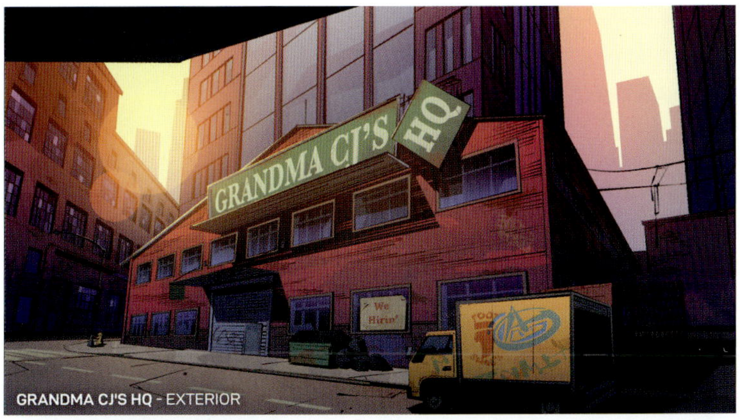

GRANDMA CJ'S HQ - EXTERIOR

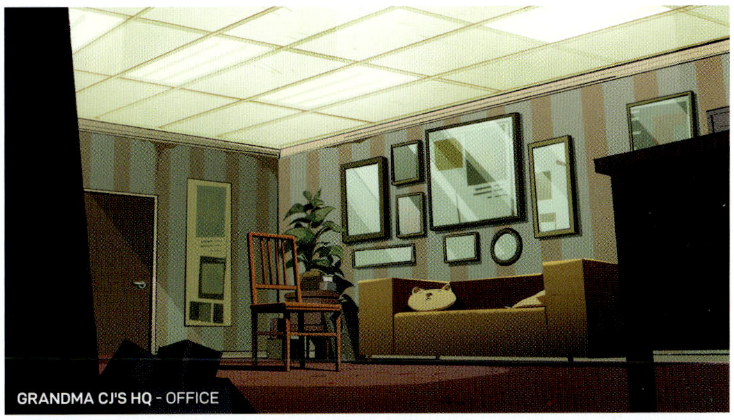

GRANDMA CJ'S HQ - OFFICE

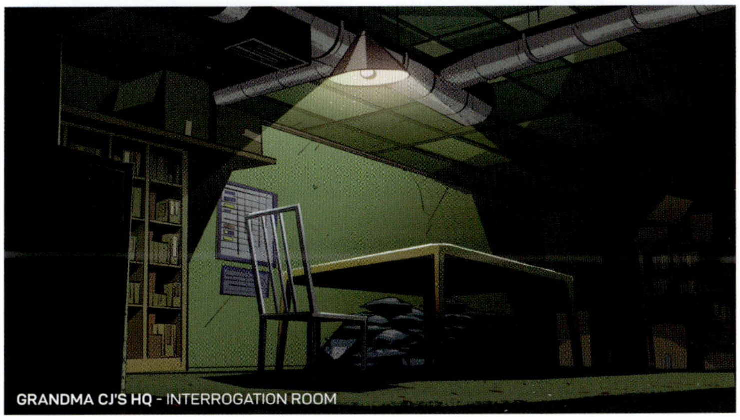

GRANDMA CJ'S HQ - INTERROGATION ROOM

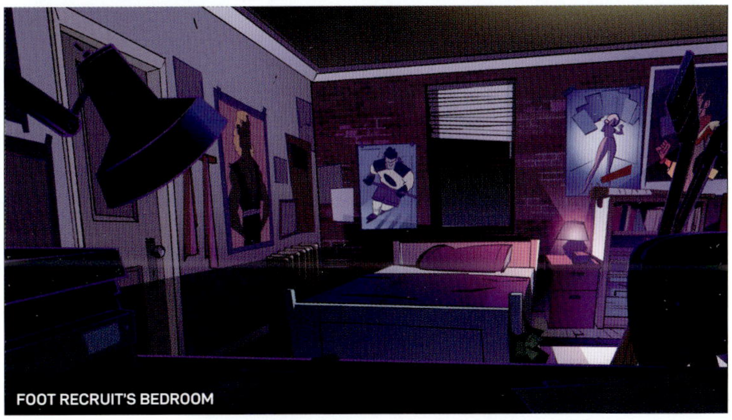

FOOT RECRUIT'S BEDROOM

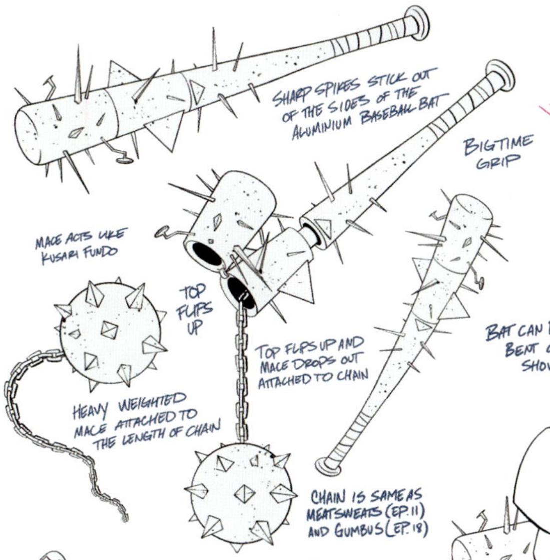

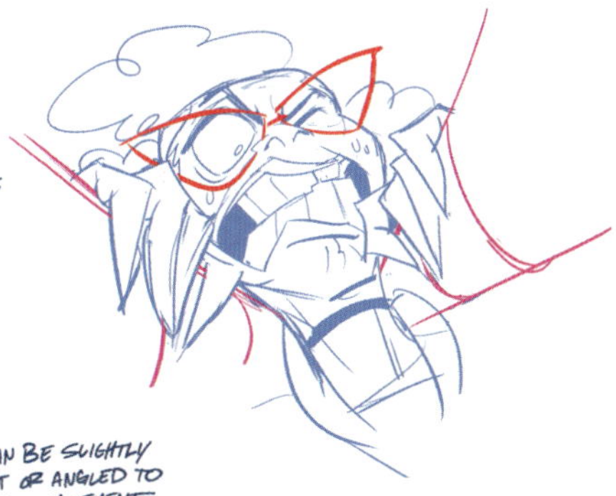

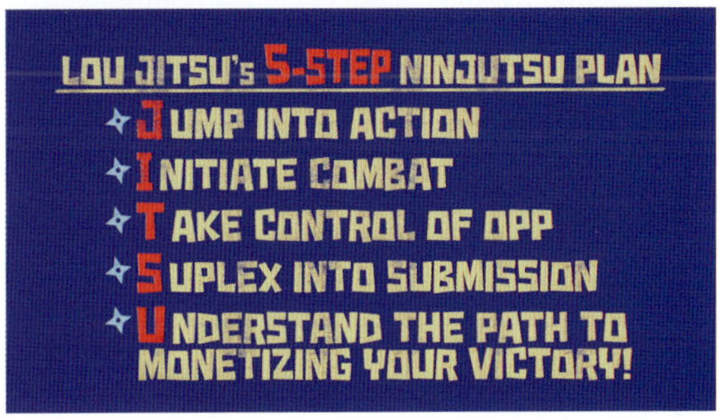

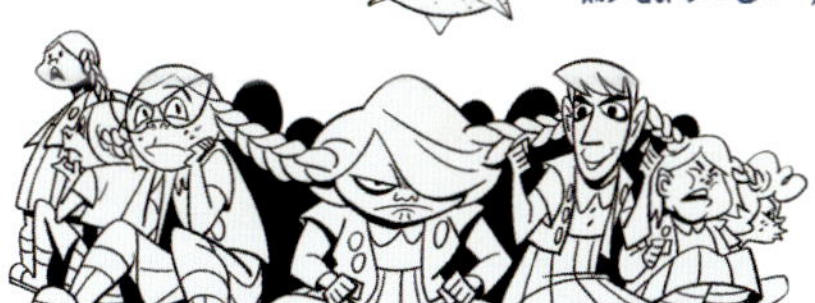

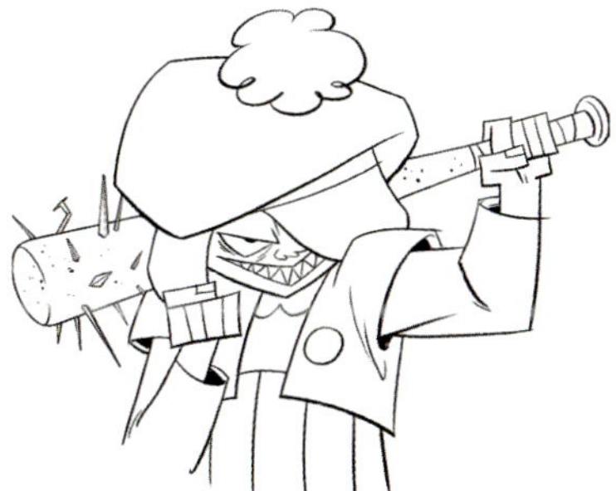

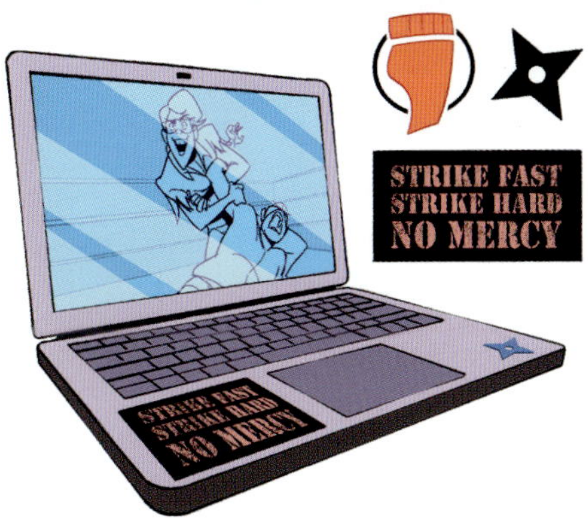

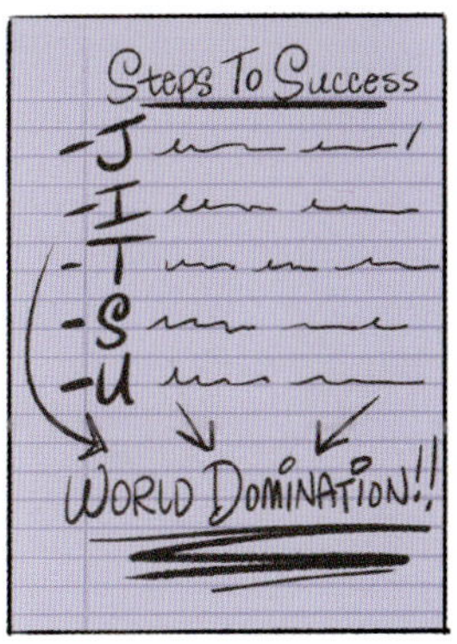

MYSTERY MEAT

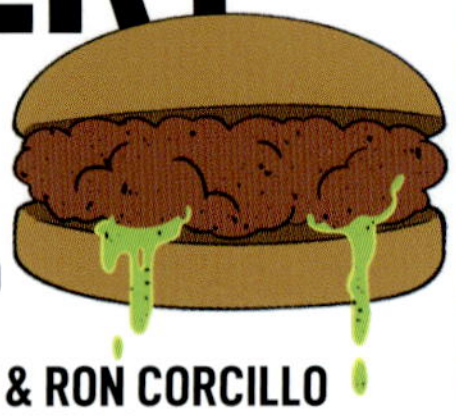

ORIGINAL AIR DATE: MAY 15, 2020
PRODUCTION CODE: 067

WRITTEN BY **RUSS CARNEY & RON CORCILLO**
STORYBOARDS BY **SHELDON VELLA**
DIRECTED BY **SEBASTIAN MONTES**

RON CORCILLO: With Draxum now working as a lunch lady in April's school cafeteria, it seemed like a good opportunity for a wackadoodle April and Draxum team-up. Amy Sedaris is a hilarious comedic actor with a great voice, and we thought she'd be perfect as Vivian Slopworth. Unfortunately, her record session was done remotely, so we never got to meet her.

RUSS CARNEY: What should have been a simple *Three's Company*–type farce, where most of what we're doing is trying to keep Mr. Furley from seeing what's actually going on, the episode really went delightfully off the rails with the madcap board artistry. There were multiple board artists on this episode, and everybody really went all out on their sections, which resulted in a thumbnail pitch that was double the length of a standard 11-minute episode. It made for some really tough choices about what had to be cut.

RON CORCILLO: The original ending, as written, had Draxum deciding to be himself and use his mystic powers to defeat Sloppy Joseph. It would have set up a moment of relief for Draxum when the cafeteria workers accept him despite his magic, because they know how tough the job is, and so *"what happens in the lunchroom stays in the lunchroom."*

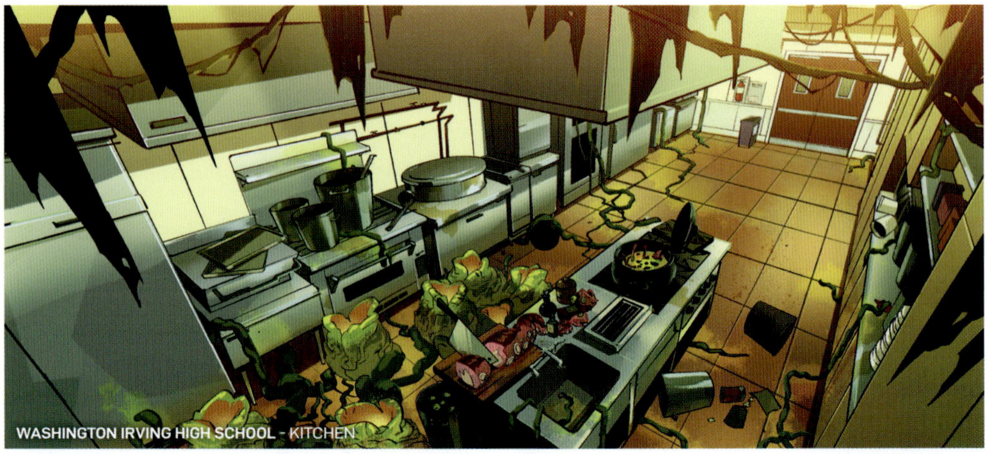

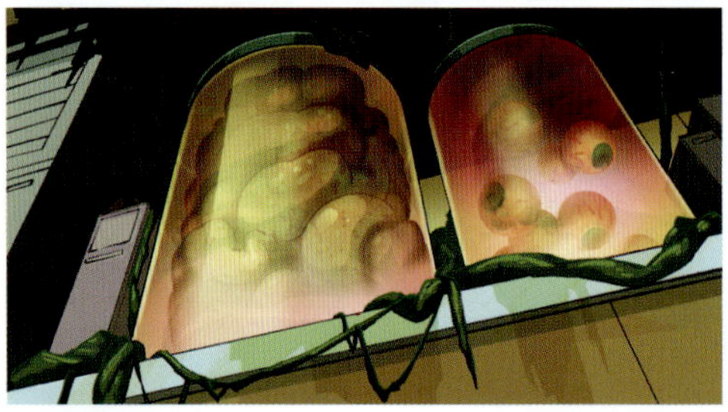

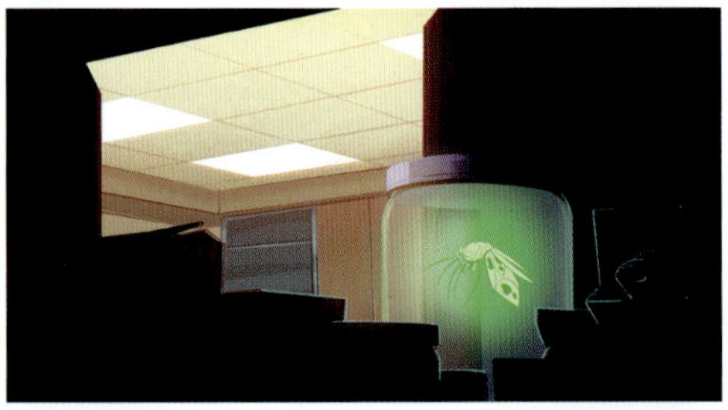

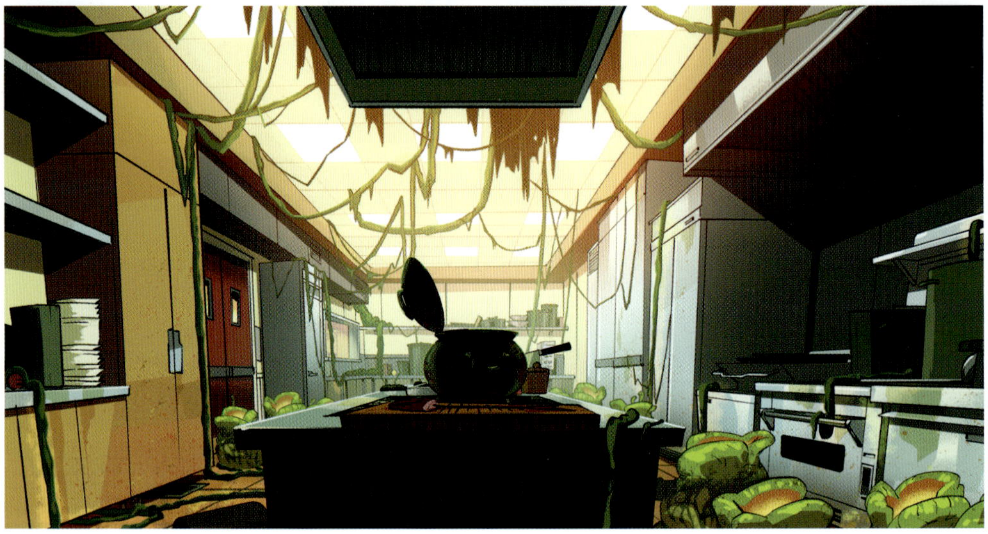

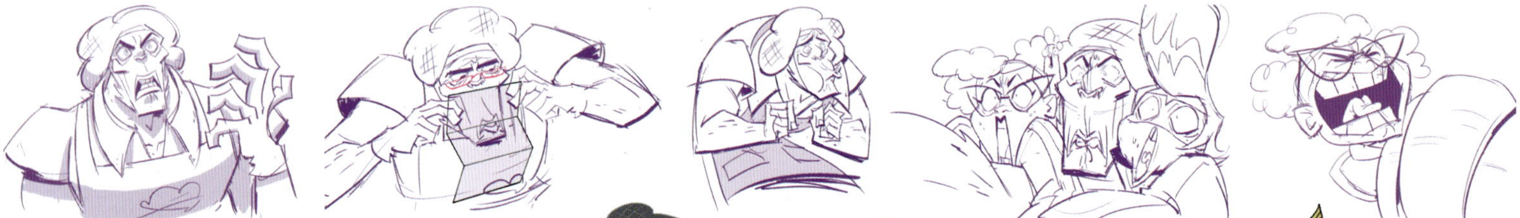

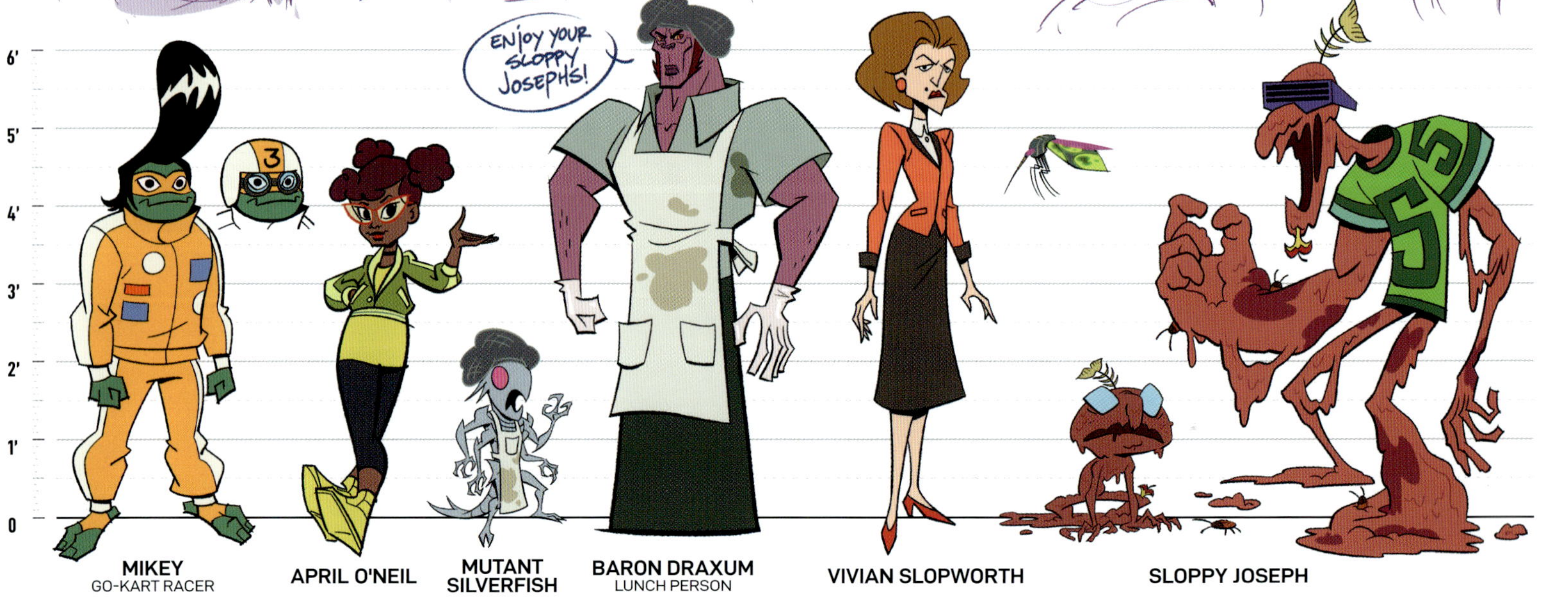

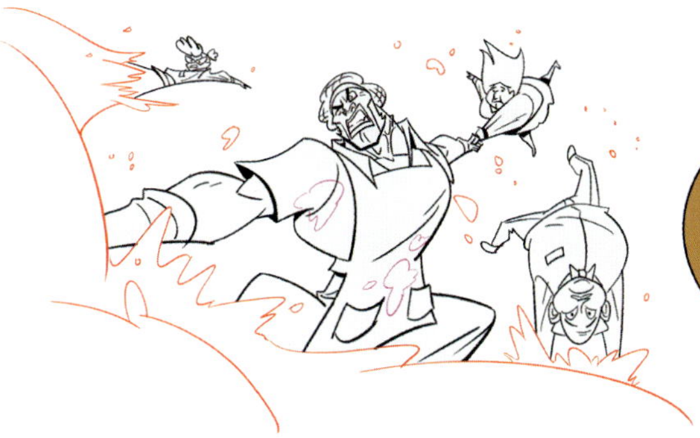

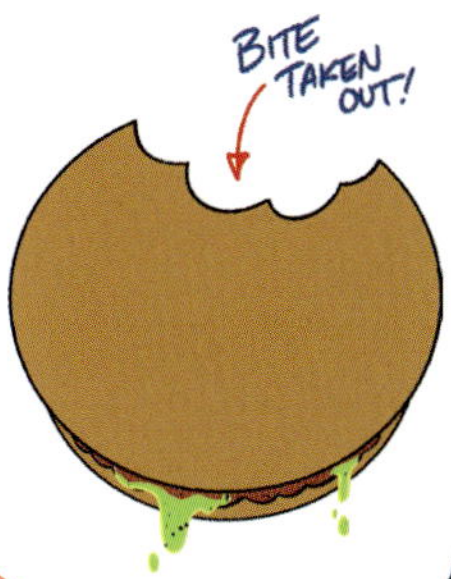

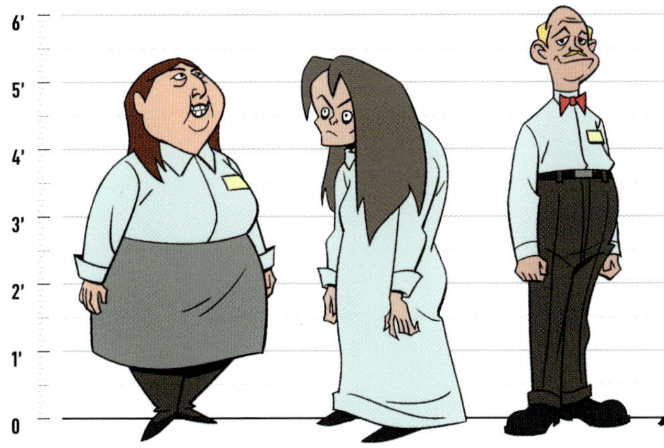

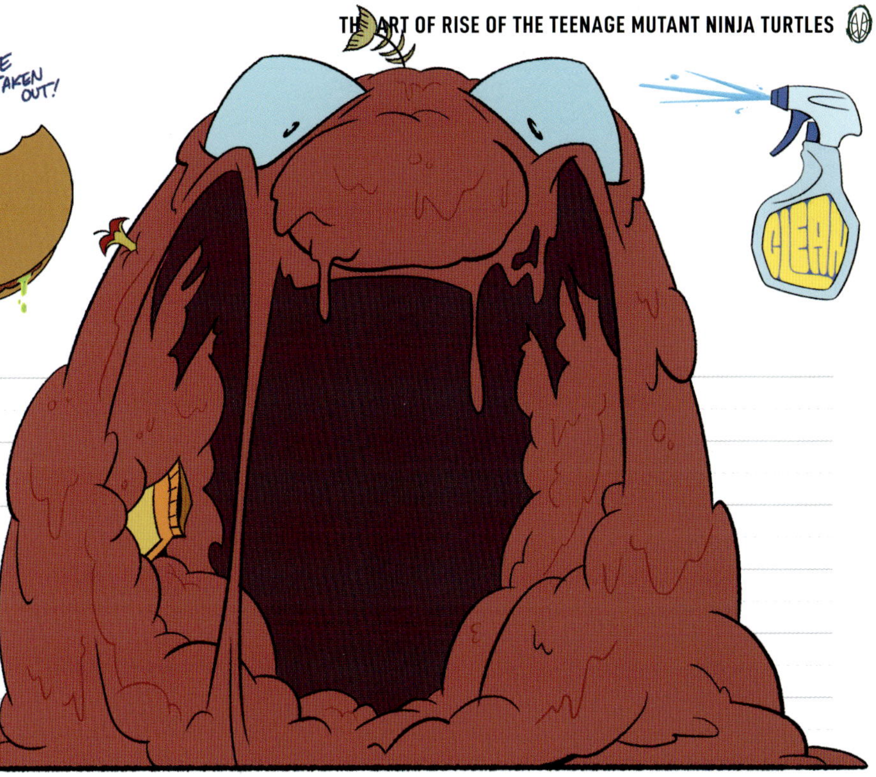

LUNCH LADY EDNA

LUNCH LADY GLADYS

LUNCH MAN STAN

SLOPPY JOSEPH

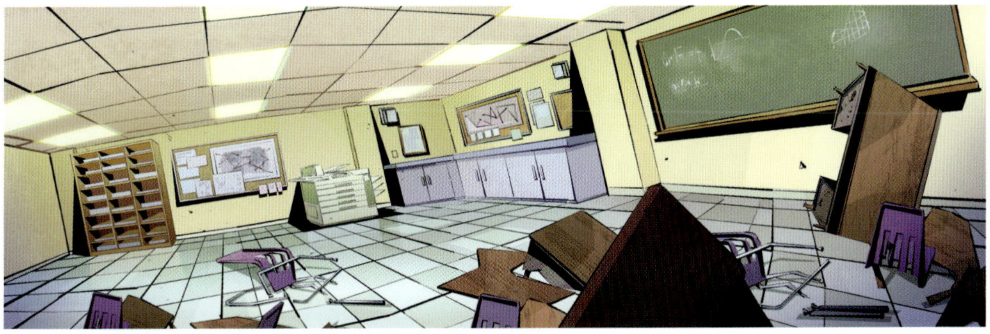

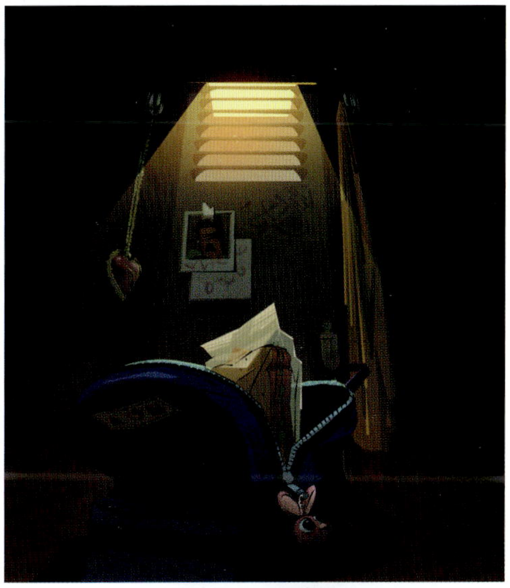

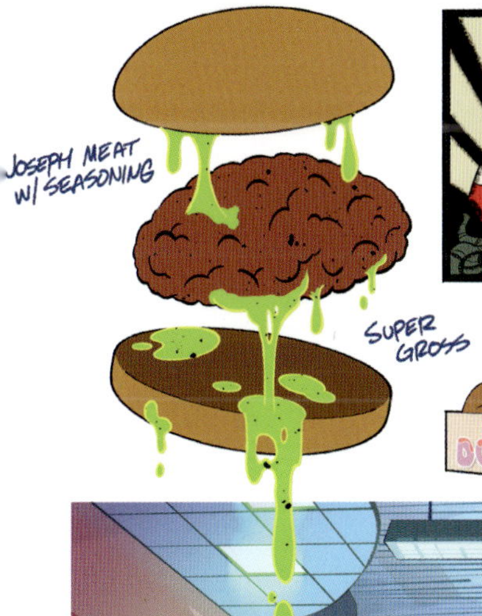

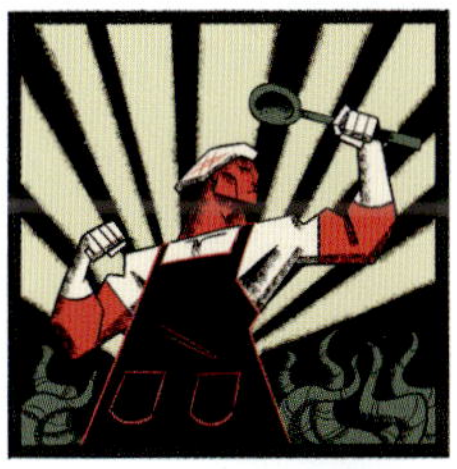

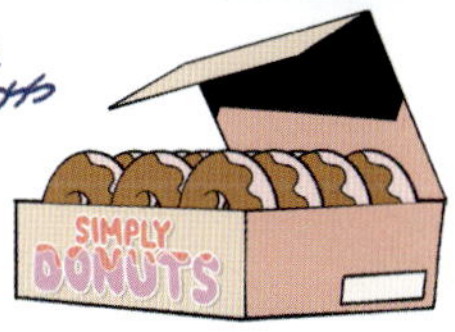

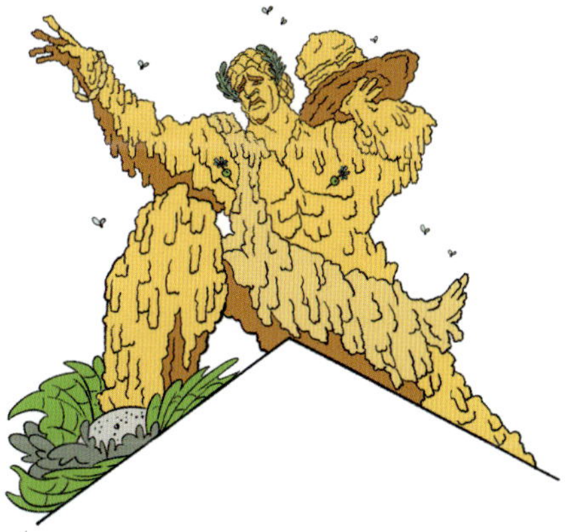

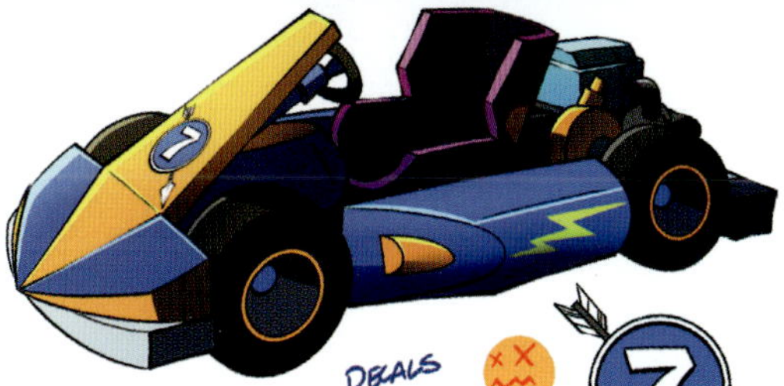

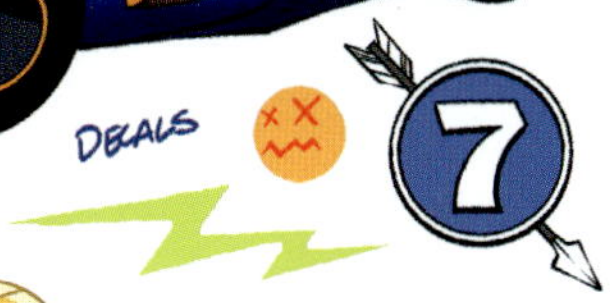

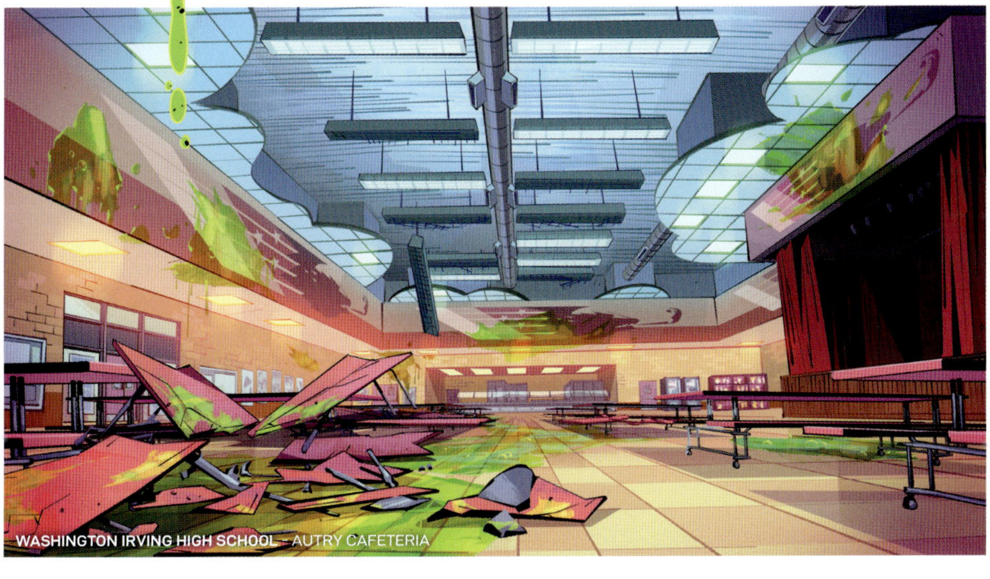

WASHINGTON IRVING HIGH SCHOOL – AUTRY CAFETERIA

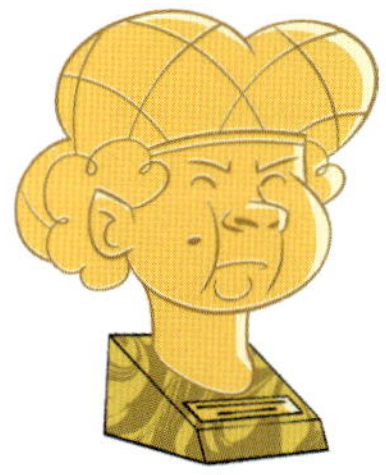

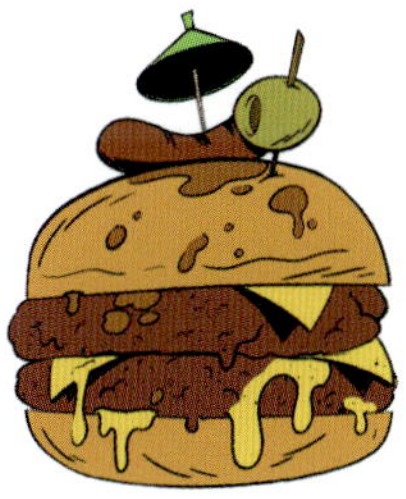

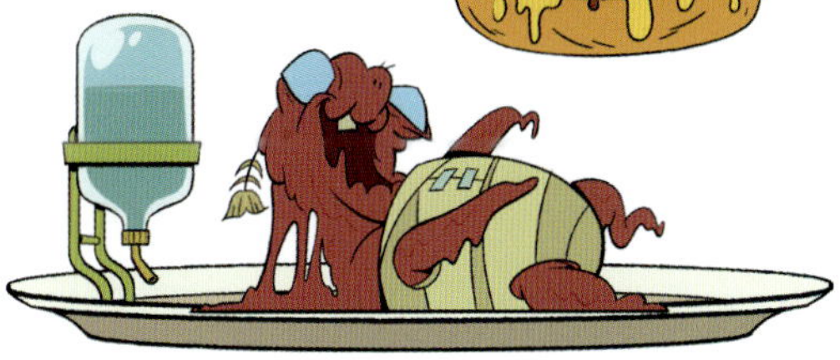

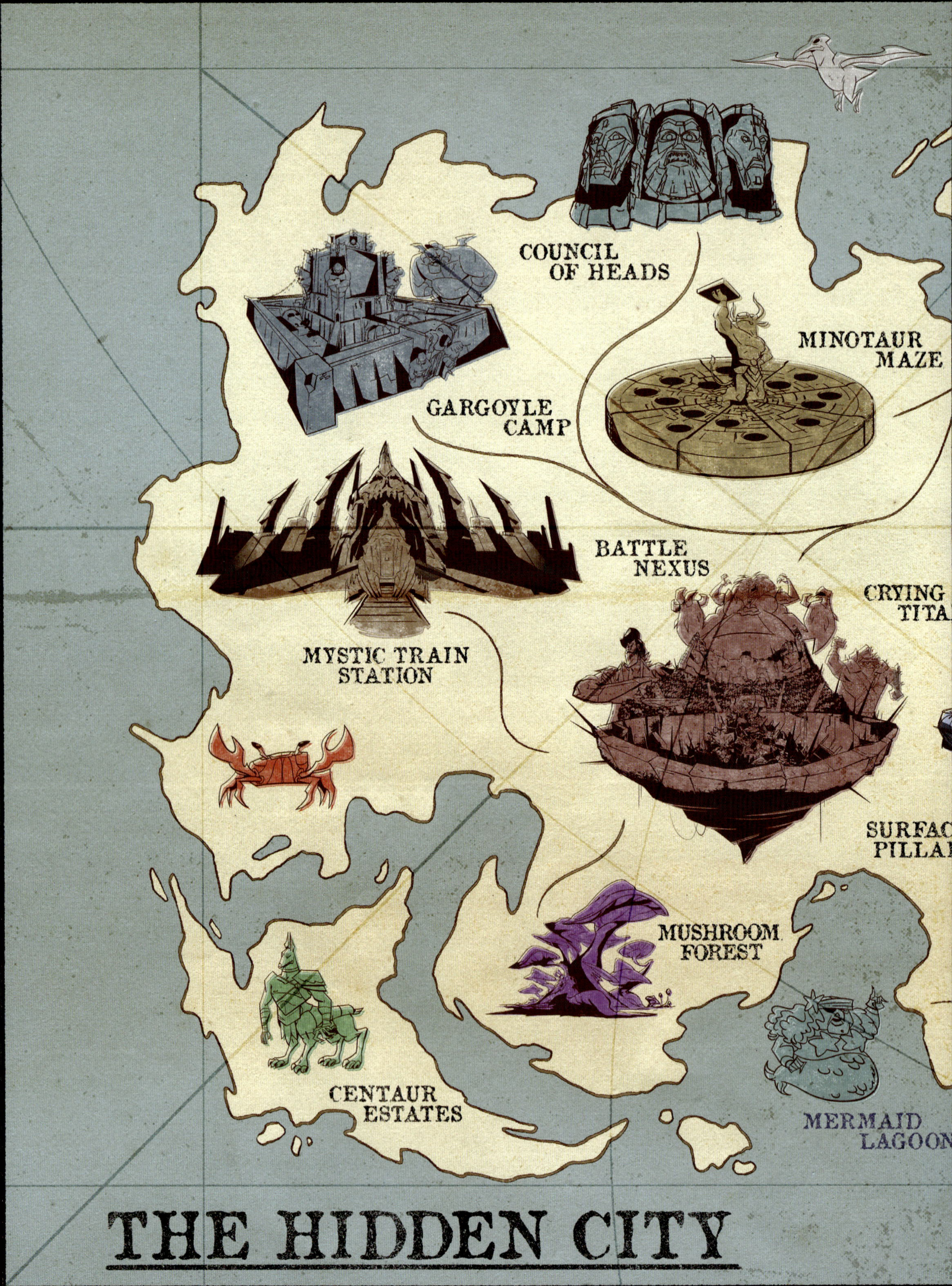
COUNCIL OF HEADS
MINOTAUR MAZE
GARGOYLE CAMP
BATTLE NEXUS
CRYING
MYSTIC TRAIN STATION
MUSHROOM FOREST
CENTAUR ESTATES
MERMAID
THE HIDDEN CITY

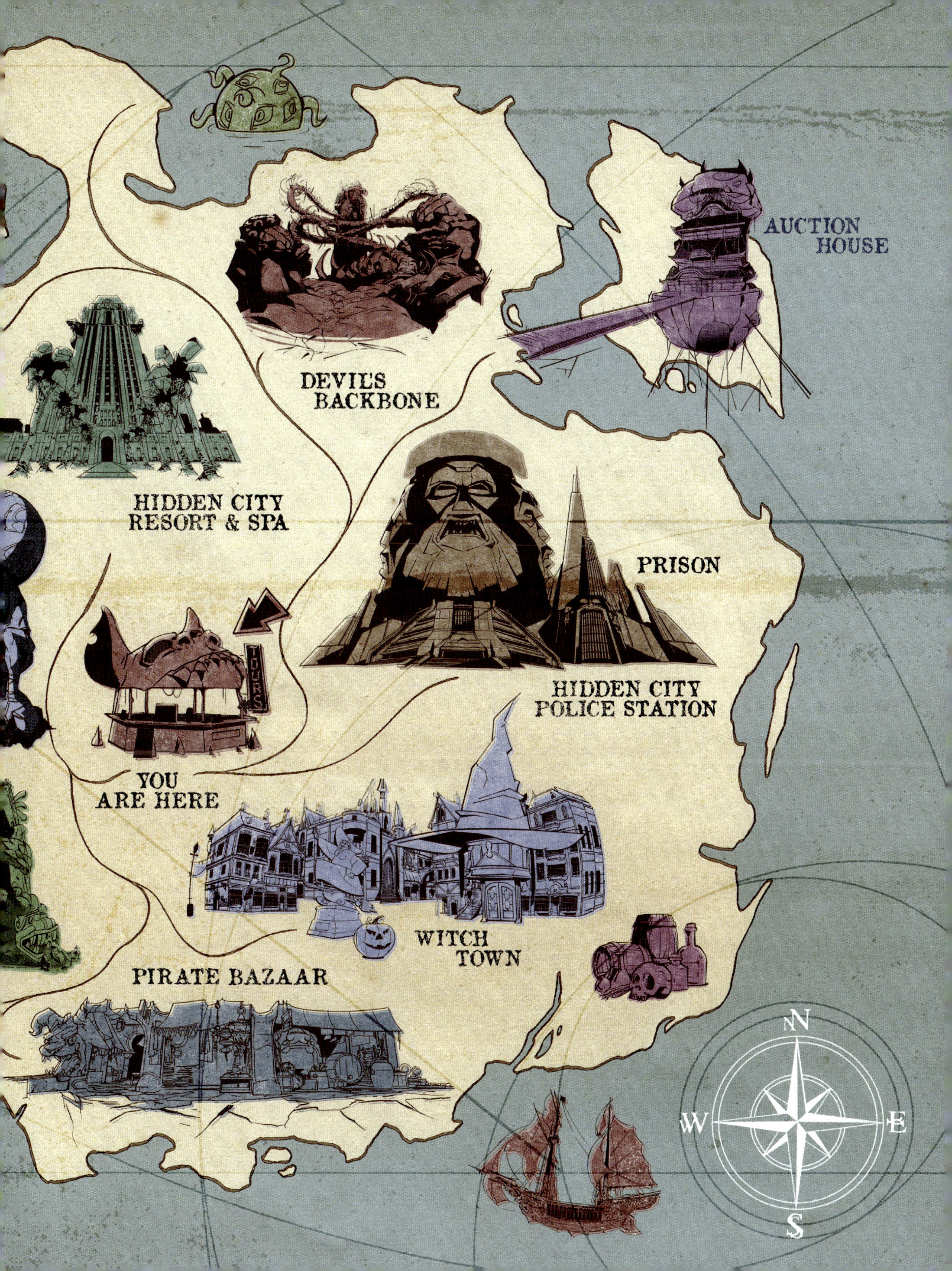
AUCTION HOUSE
DEVIL'S BACKBONE
HIDDEN CITY RESORT & SPA
PRISON
TOURS
HIDDEN CITY POLICE STATION
YOU ARE HERE
WITCH TOWN
PIRATE BAZAAR
N
W
E
S

TALES OF THE HIDDEN CITY, PART 1: DONNIE VS. WITCH TOWN

ORIGINAL AIR DATE: JUNE 19, 2020
PRODUCTION CODE: 066

WRITTEN BY **IAN BUSCH**
STORYBOARDS BY **ALICIA CHAN**
DIRECTED BY **ABE AUDISH**

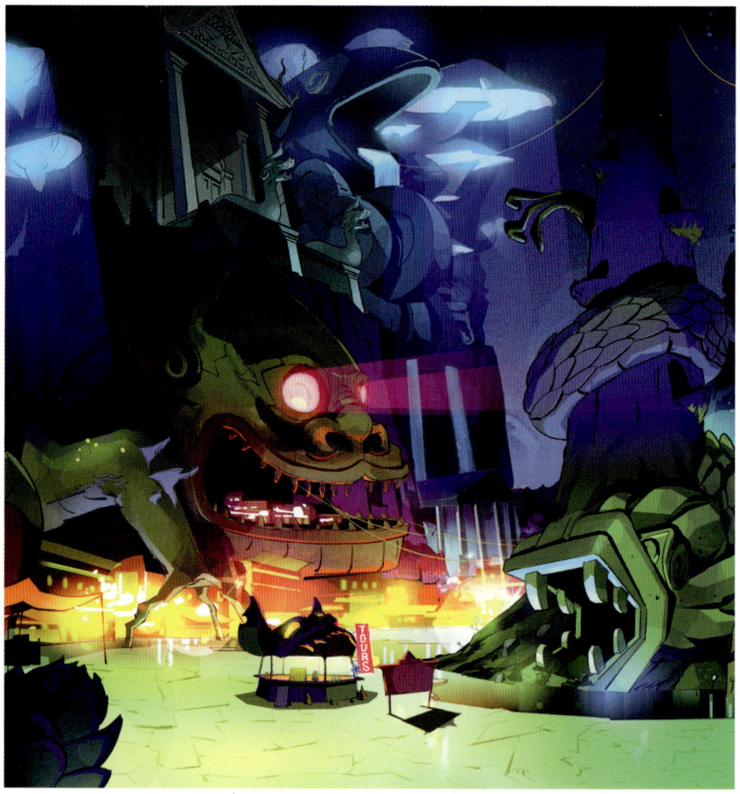

TONY GAMA-LOBO: One of the coolest additions to the Turtleverse that Ant and Andy brought was the Hidden City. Super fun to have this mystic world of Yōkai and magic just underneath the surface of New York. But at a certain point we realized we hadn't explored it enough, so I had this idea of doing a four-part series where we have the Turtles split up and simultaneously have an adventure in the Hidden City. The writers crushed it! Such inventive, hilarious, and touching stories. And [the Turtles] all ended up in jail! The rest of the *Rise* crew knocked it out of the park with the most inspiring designs and boards. It took all of us working closely to nail these. It really was the perfect synergy of story influencing design, which influenced story.

After all four episodes were written and being boarded, we had this idea to create fun moments where our stories would cross over. Sounded easy enough, but it was a huge pain coordinating with all the different writers, board teams, directors, and designers. But everyone really rose to the challenge. And now fans will see these incredible little spots where the other Turtle stories pop in. The weirdest (and my favorite) is when Mind Raph shows up to give Leo advice.

Ian had this hilarious idea of putting Donnie's ego and love of science to the test vs. witches. Honestly, it's gotta be the Donnie-est version of Donnie in the whole series. So funny! But to me what makes it a great episode is how we uncover that little bit of insecurity underneath all his tech and arrogance. Deep down he's afraid he's not needed. That's why I think *Rise* was so exceptional—regardless of the amazing action, cool mythology, or hilarious jokes, the writers always found a way to explore the depth of these characters and their relationships in an emotional and satisfying way. No story was wasted.

All the Turtles had these cool mystic weapons and April didn't. She had a bat, which is what shipped with her action figure for a reason no one fully understood. So we wanted to power up April and figured this could be a good spot to do it. Hence the special callout in the dialogue: "Aprilllllll O'Neilllll!!!... And bat!"

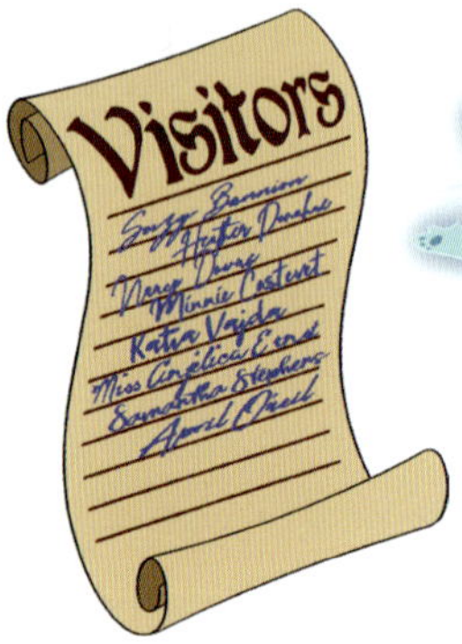

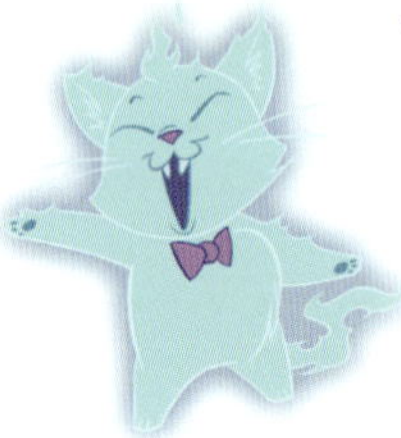

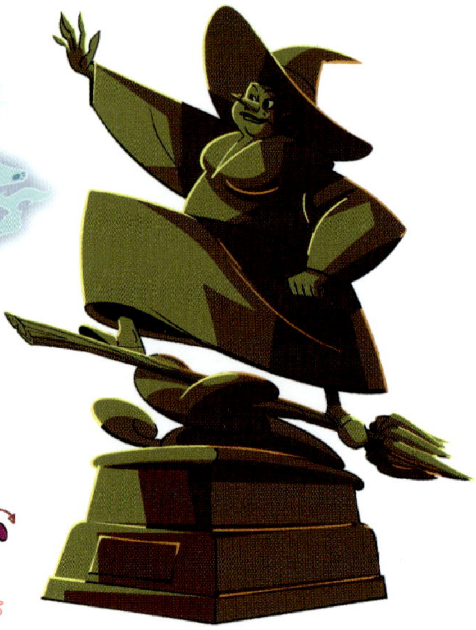

ABIGAIL THE GOOD

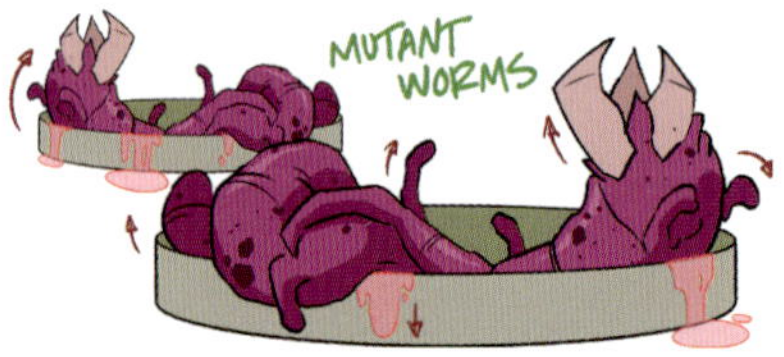

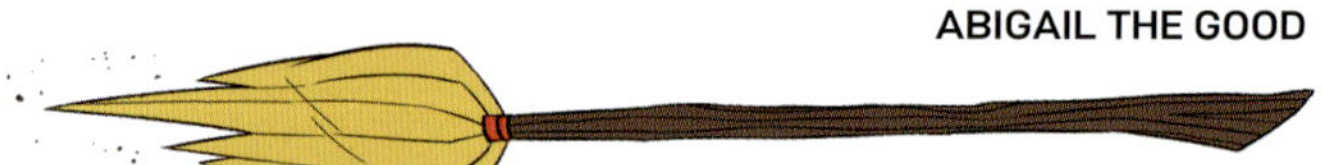

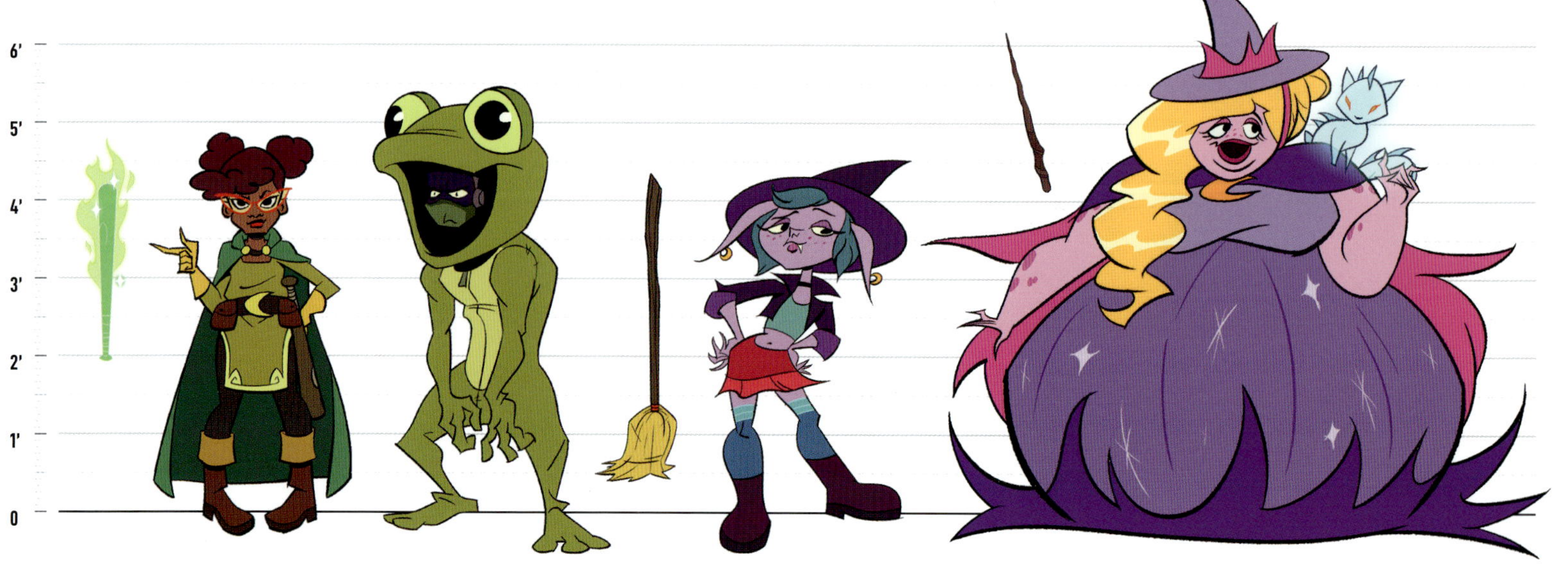

APRIL O'NEIL
WITCH TOWN OUTFIT

DONNIE
FROG SUIT

GENTRY

MAYOR MIRA

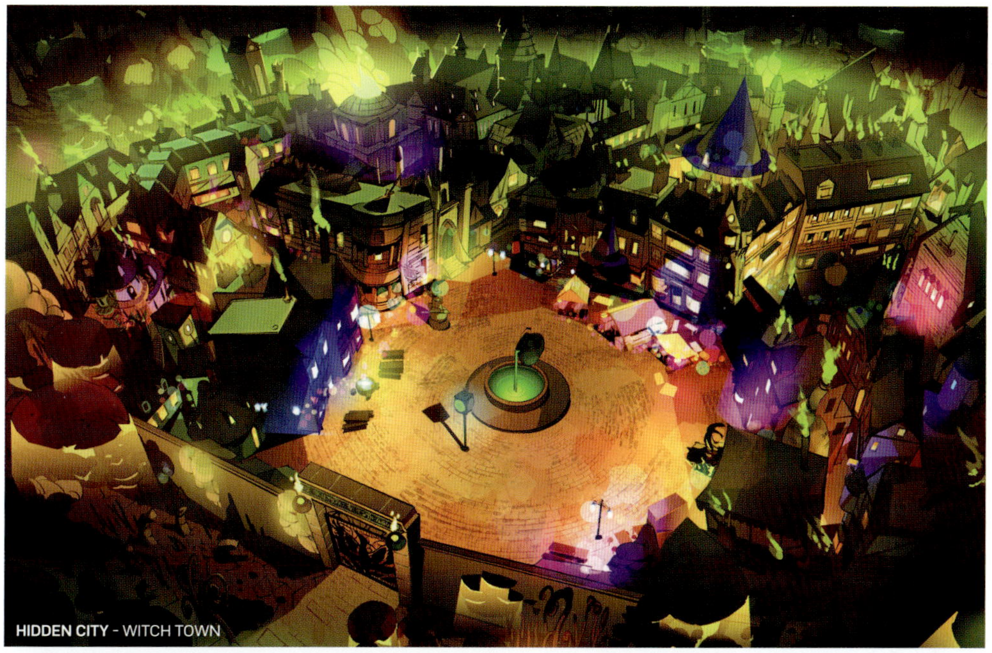

HIDDEN CITY - WITCH TOWN

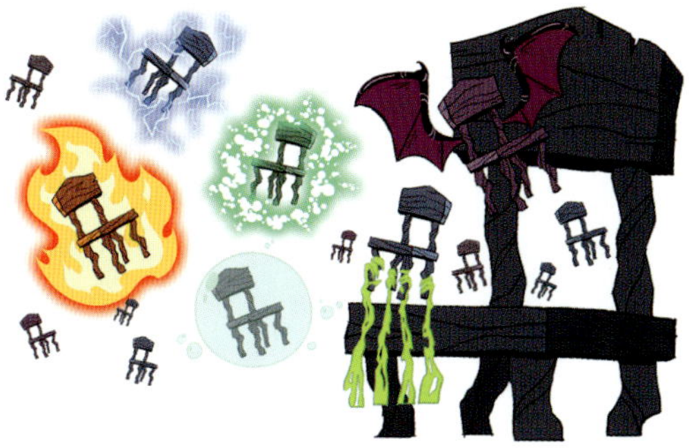

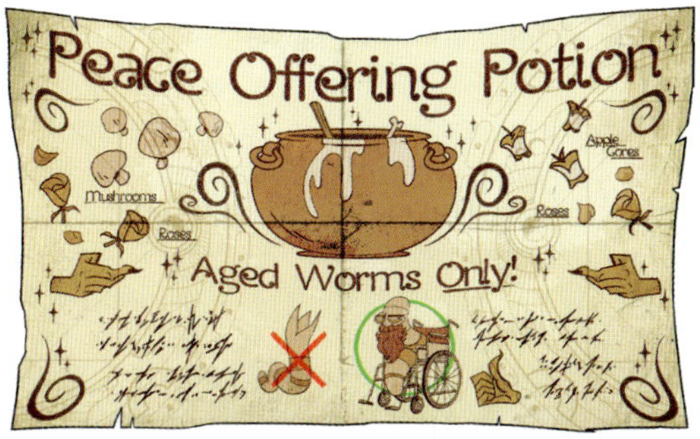

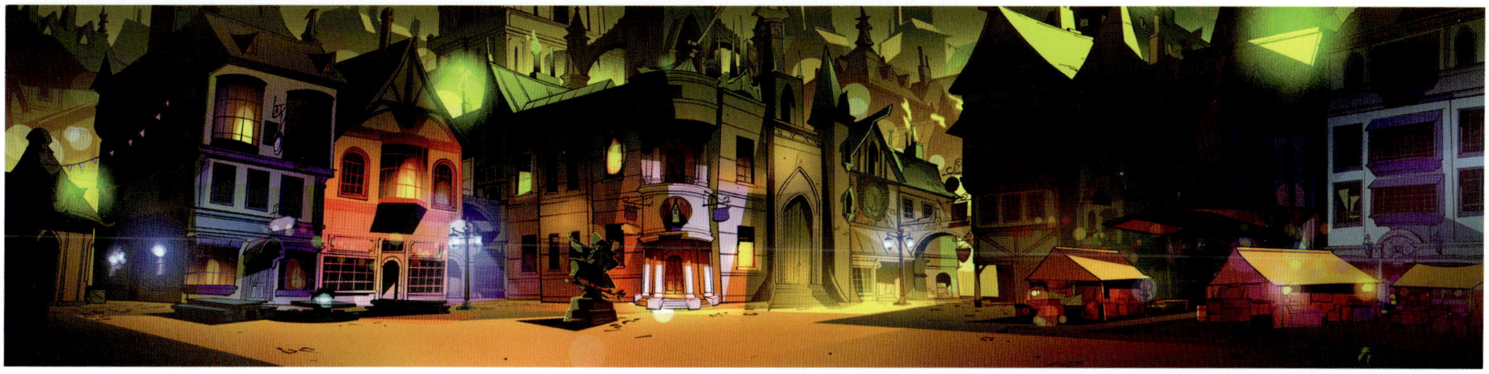

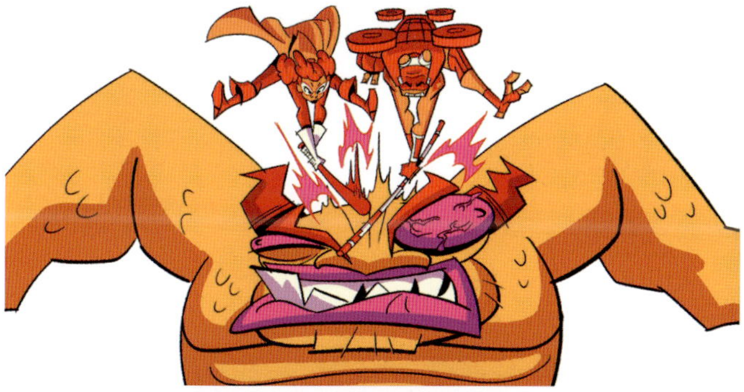

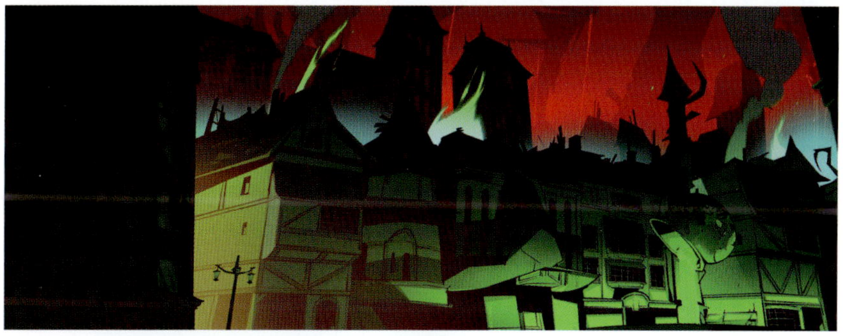

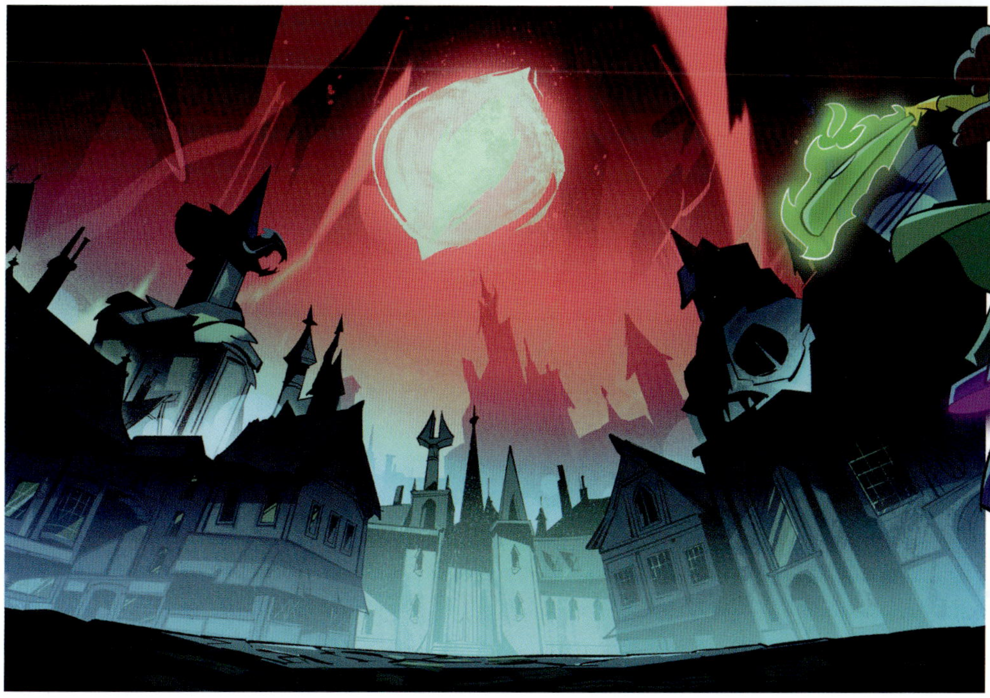

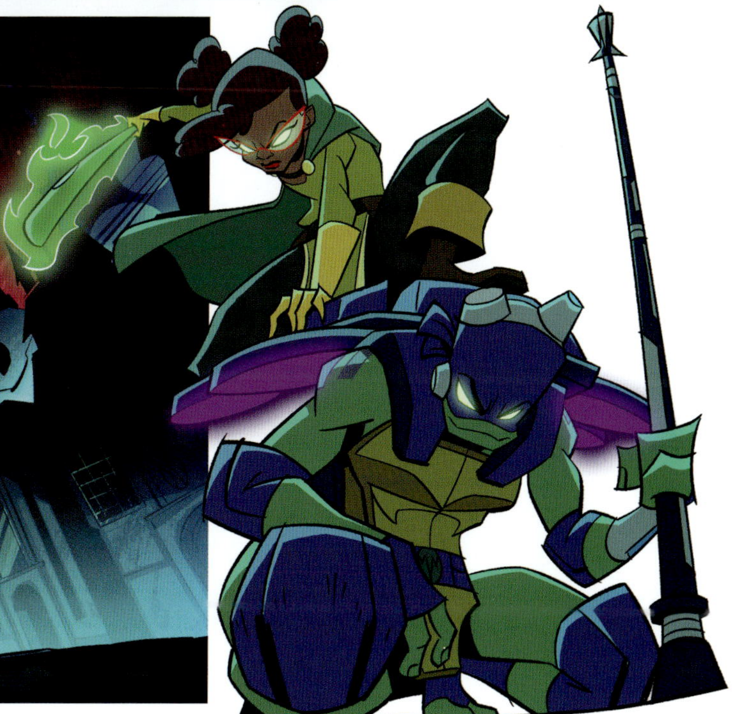

TALES OF THE HIDDEN CITY, PART 2: RAPH'S RIDE-ALONG

ORIGINAL AIR DATE: JUNE 19, 2020
PRODUCTION CODE: 068

WRITTEN BY **RUSS CARNEY & RON CORCILLO**
STORYBOARDS BY **MIRA ONGCHUA**
DIRECTED BY **JJ CONWAY**

TONY GAMA-LOBO: When we first floated this fun mistaken-identity story where Raph becomes the unwitting leader of a gang of criminals, the studio pushed back. They were hypervigilant about making sure our Turtles always acted like heroes. Sometimes in storytelling you have to lean into the obstacles, which in this case ended up creating the entire comedic engine of the story: Raph pretending to be this criminal mastermind while actually being a hero.

We always have Turtle fans in mind, so when Ron and Russ had the idea to make Raph an unwitting member of a new gang, someone suggested we cast the voice actors of the 2012 *TMNT* series. Donatello's Rob Paulsen was *Dastardly Danny* (wearing purple), Michelangelo's Greg Cipes was *Malicious Mickey* (in orange), and Leonardo's Seth Green was *Loathsome Leonard* (dressed in blue). And of course they were called the *Mud Dogs*.

When *Rise* first came out, there was a lot of pushback from fans about us making Raph the leader over Leo. We had a little wink to that "controversy" with a couple of *Loathsome Leonard's* lines: *"Blue guy is always the leader!"* and *"At first I thought you were put in charge just for change, which actually hurt my feelings."*

We knew the next big tentpole episode was going to be "Battle Nexus: New York," so we wanted to drop in a quick tease where Big Mama is looking at the Mystic Orb she got from Draxum at the end of season 1.

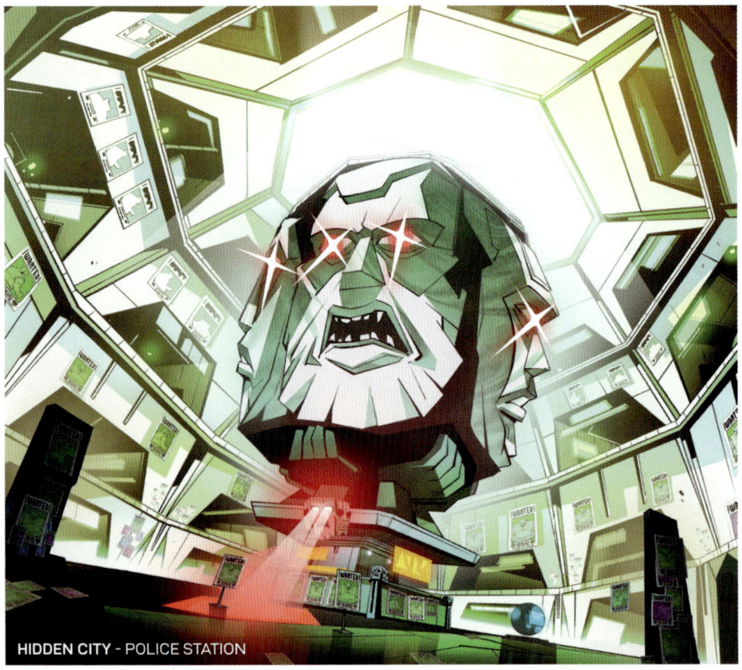
HIDDEN CITY - POLICE STATION

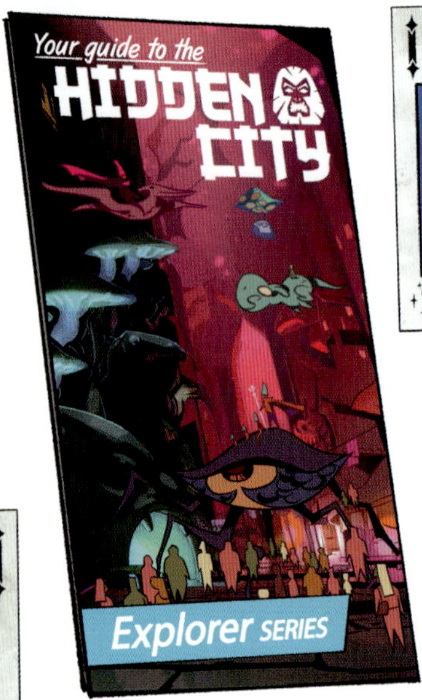

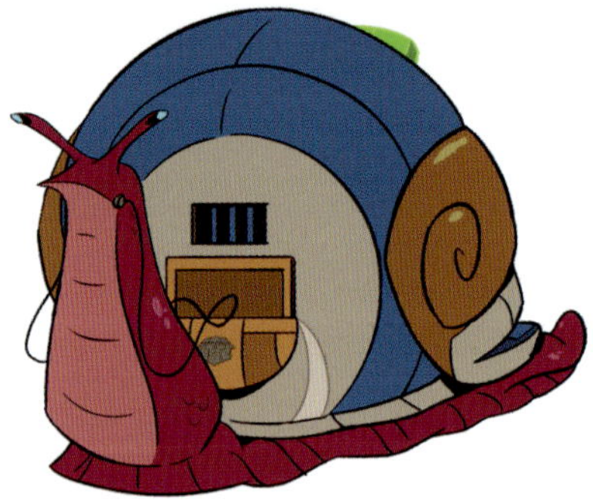

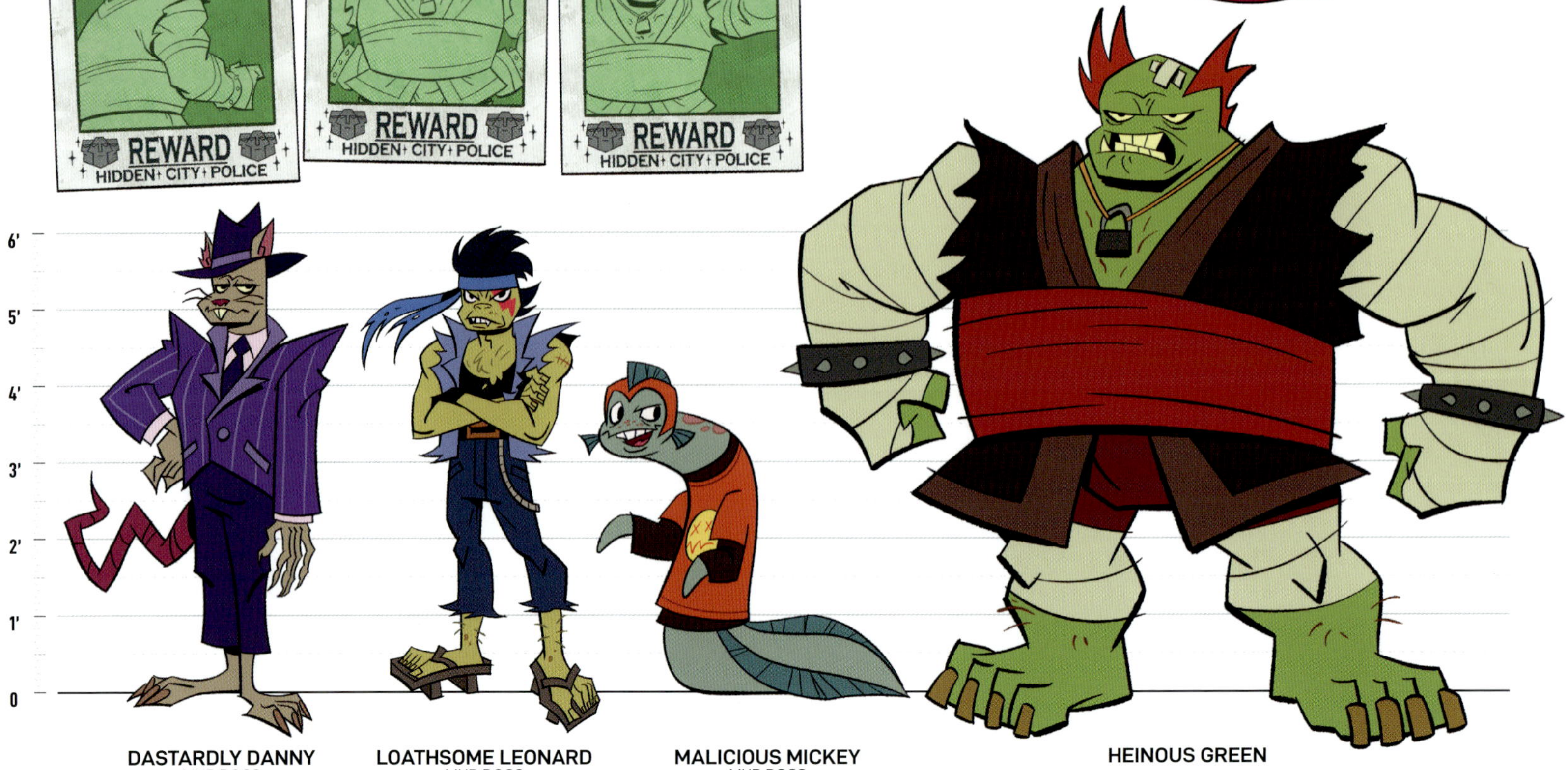

DASTARDLY DANNY
MUD DOGS

LOATHSOME LEONARD
MUD DOGS

MALICIOUS MICKEY
MUD DOGS

HEINOUS GREEN

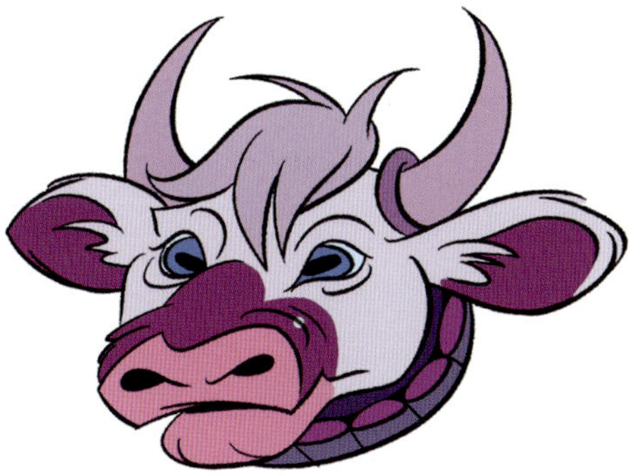

CUDLEY THE COWLICK

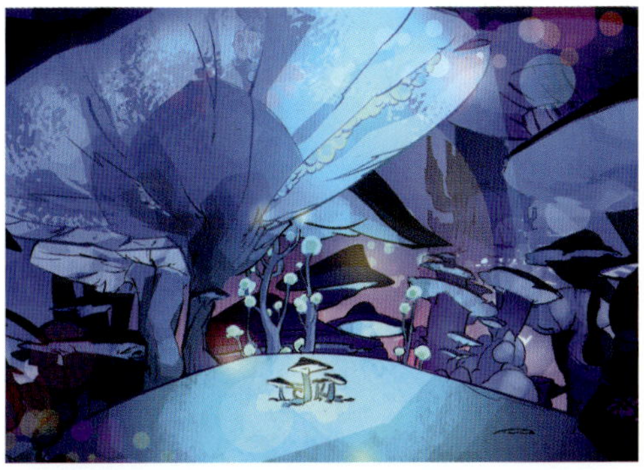

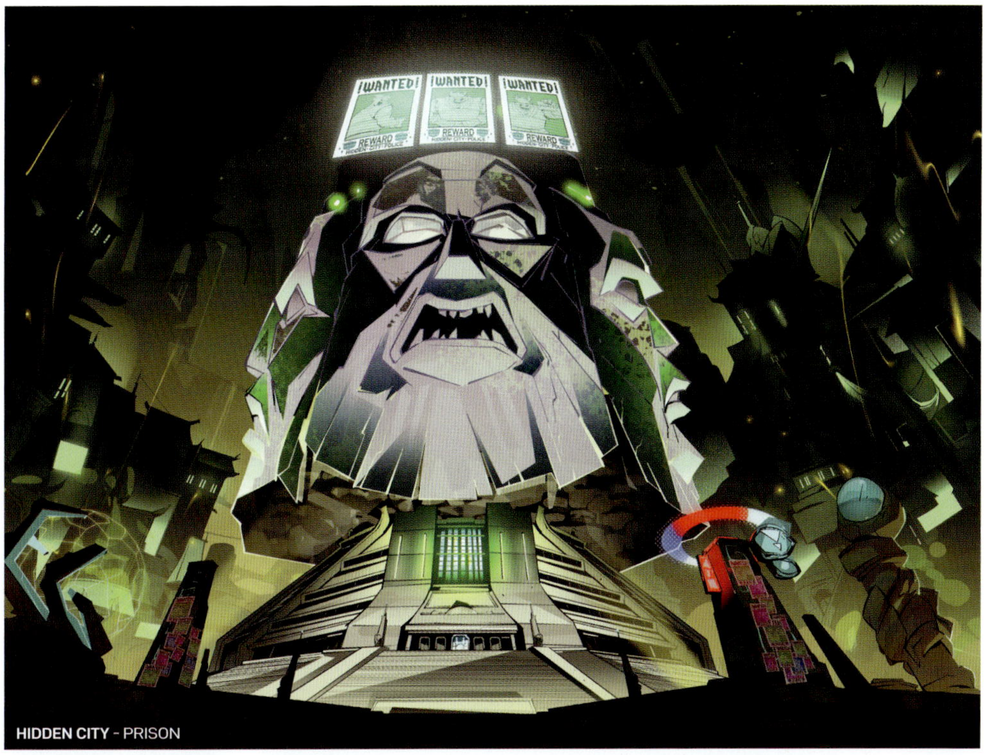

HIDDEN CITY - PRISON

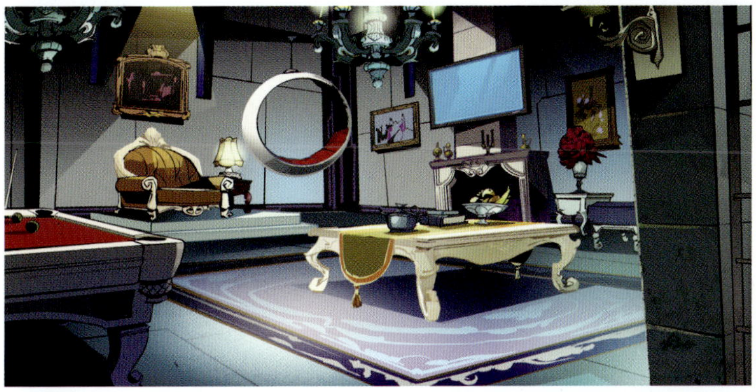

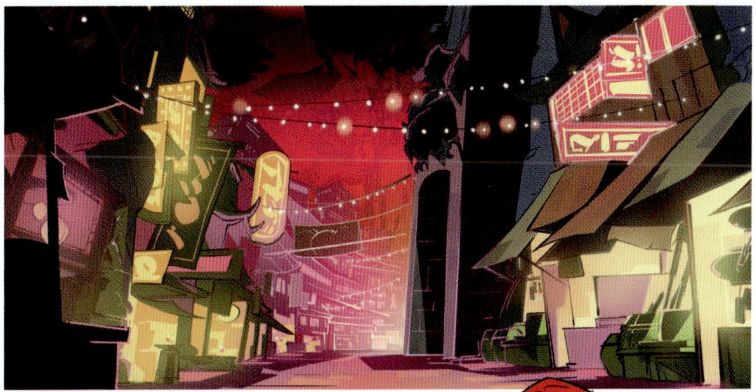

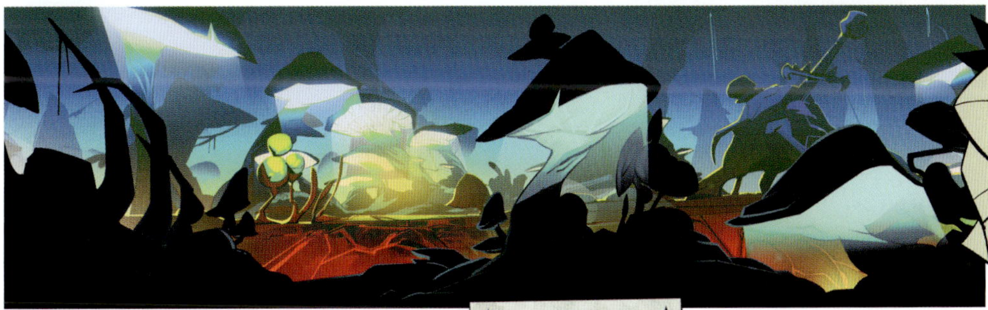

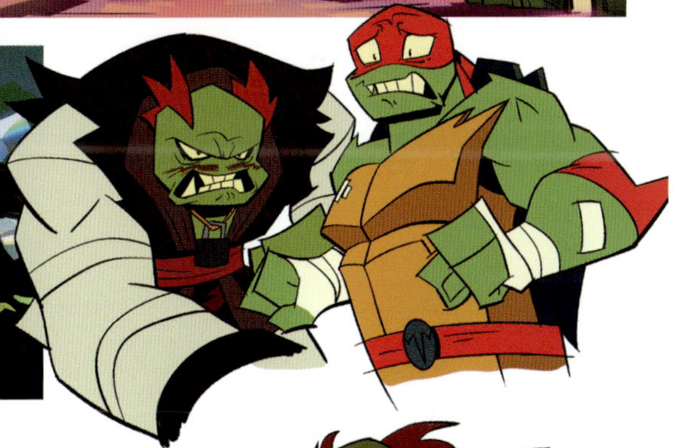

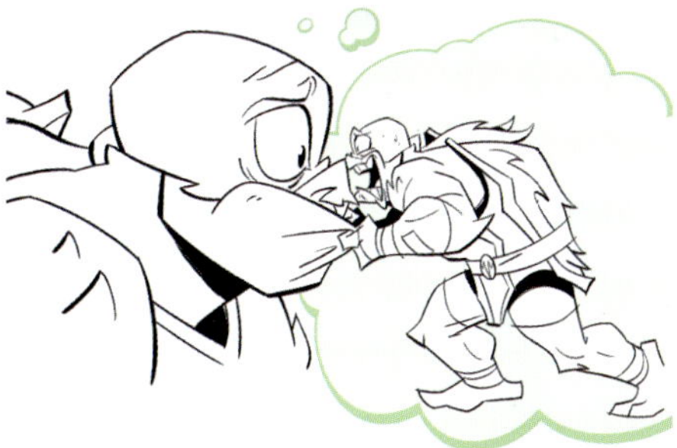

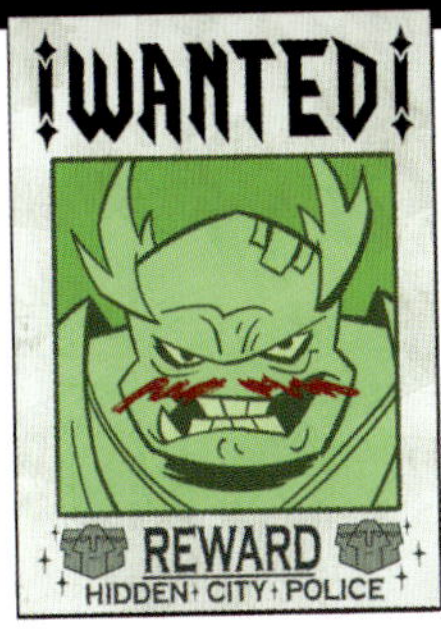

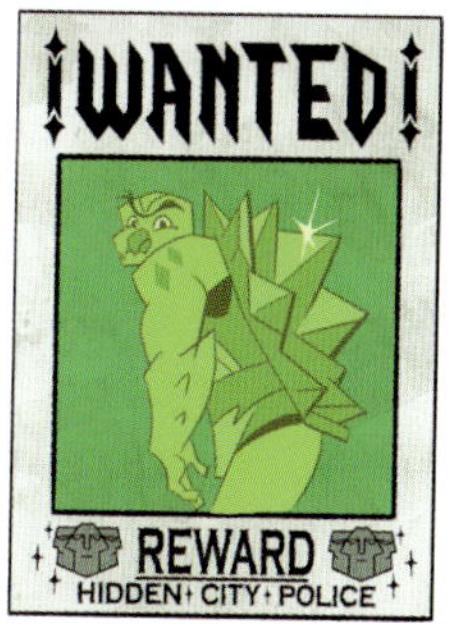

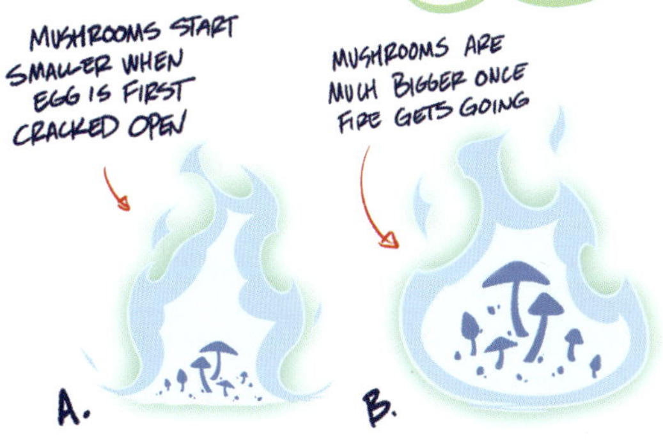

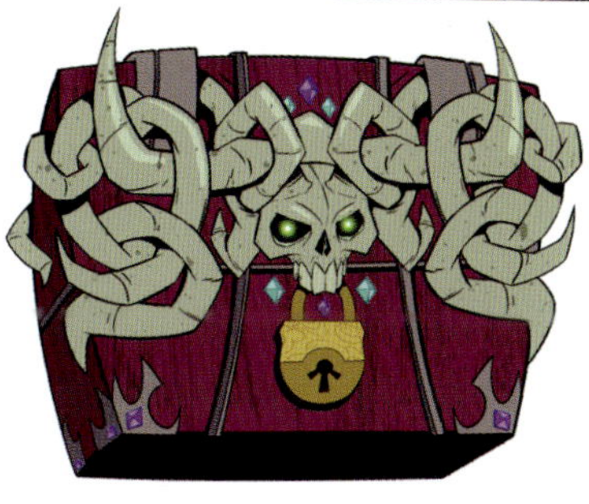

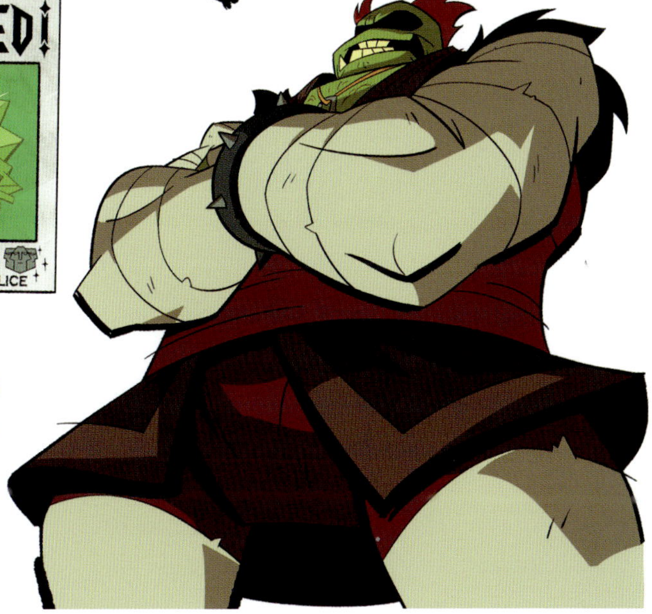

TALES OF THE HIDDEN CITY, PART 3: HIDDEN CITY'S MOST WANTED

ORIGINAL AIR DATE: JUNE 19, 2020
PRODUCTION CODE: 069

WRITTEN BY **JESSE GORDON**
STORYBOARDS BY **CHRISTINE LIU**
DIRECTED BY **JAKE CASTORENA**

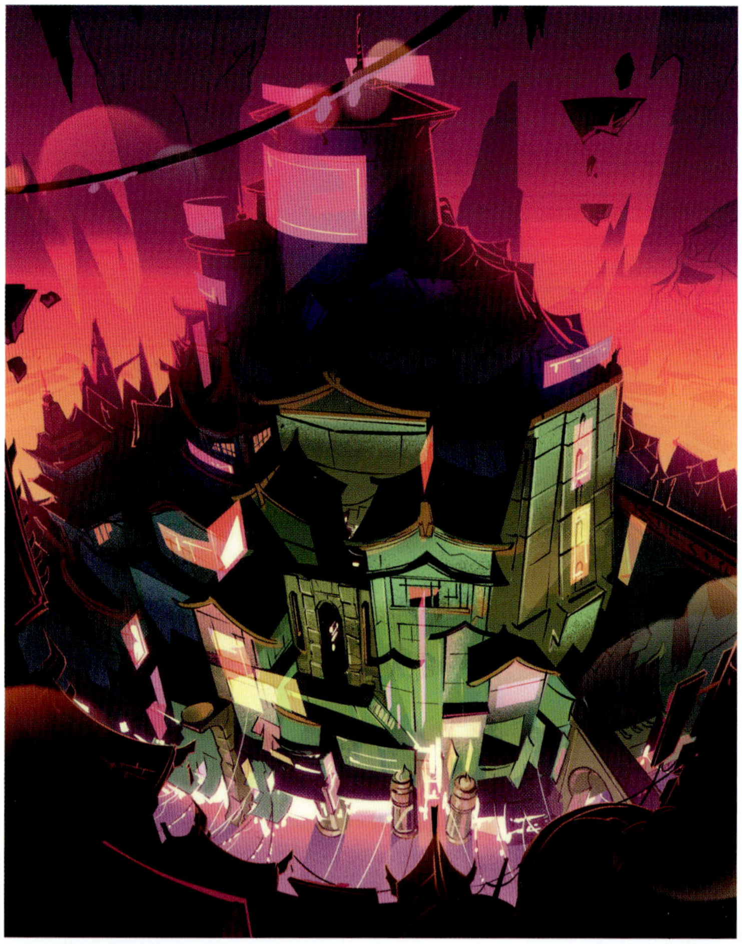

TONY GAMA-LOBO: The Splinter/Draxum dynamic in "Repairin' the Baron" was so hilarious we couldn't wait to play with it again. So when we were trying to figure out a Splinter and Mikey adventure in the Hidden City, Jesse had this great idea to bring Draxum along in disguise. Yes, this was a really funny episode, but it was also a *huge* milestone in transitioning Draxum into a hero. And when we started breaking the story, it became clear it was going to be one of our most emotional. That Splinter line in the dumpster—*"Thank you for turning me into...me"*—was everything. All the bitterness and anger and regret Splinter felt about how his life turned out because of Draxum turning him into a rat just melted away. And that flashback to New York in the rain with rat Lou Jitsu and his baby turtles was the greatest! Here we set out to do a story about Draxum becoming more of a hero and we ended up doing a story about a father realizing he should let go of the past and embrace his family.

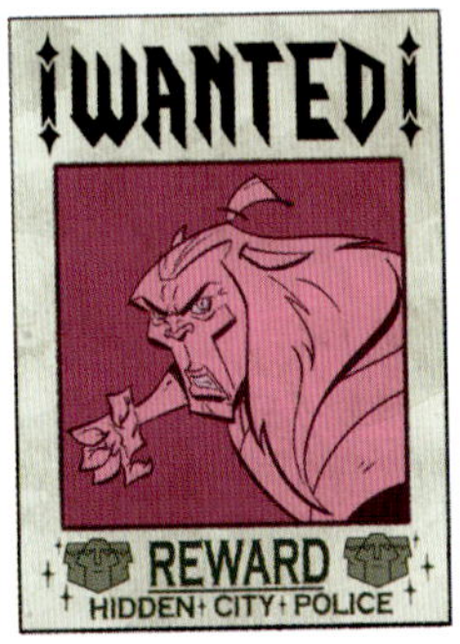

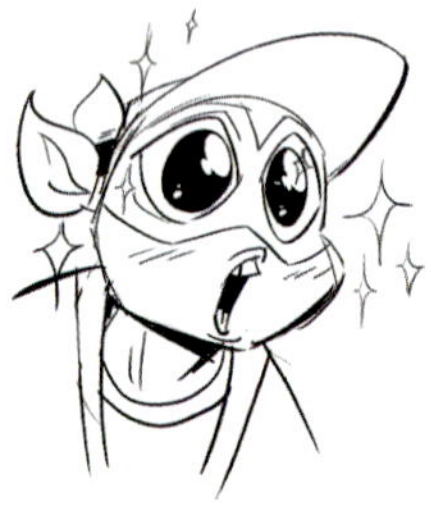

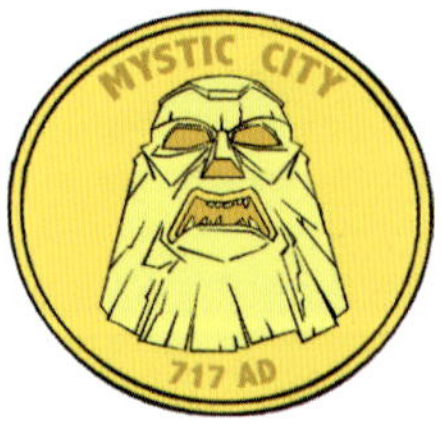

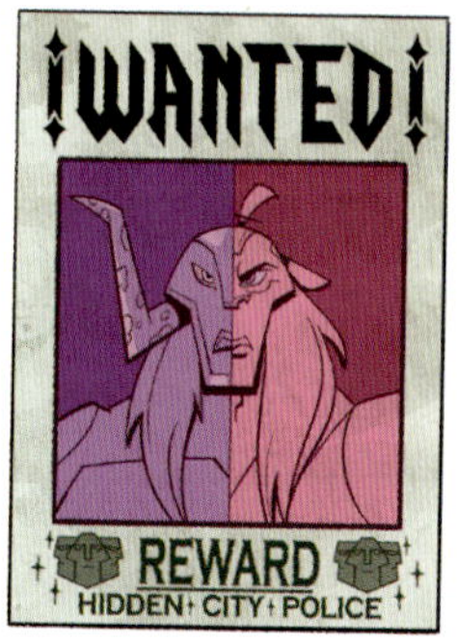

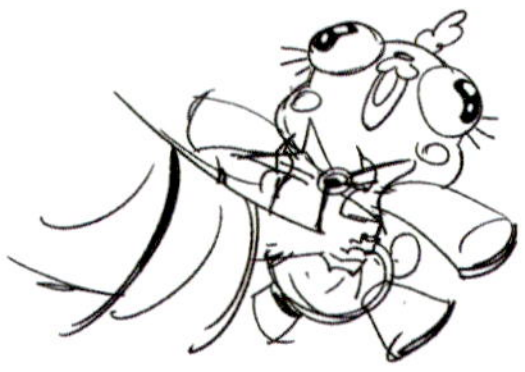

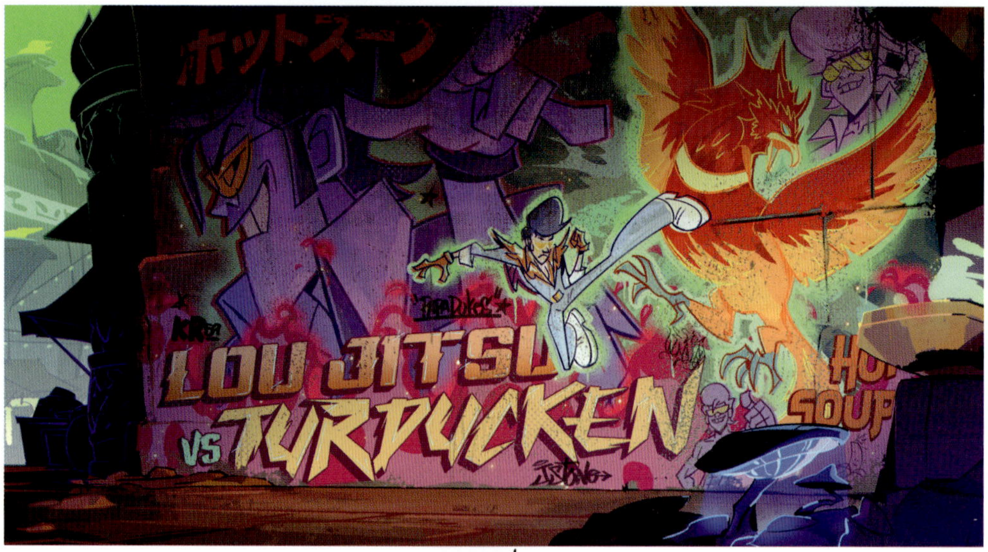

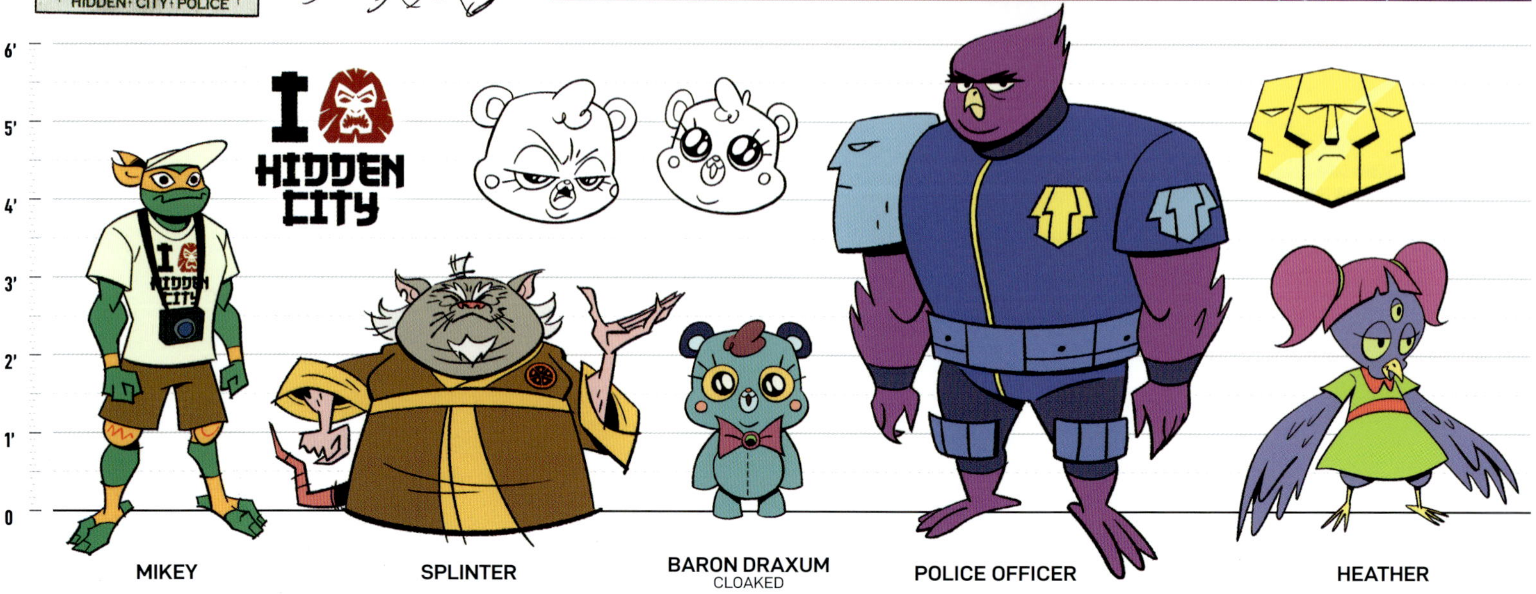

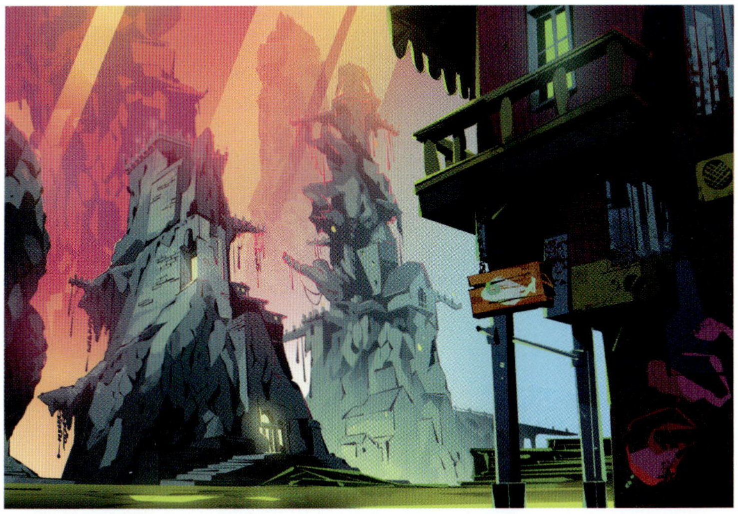

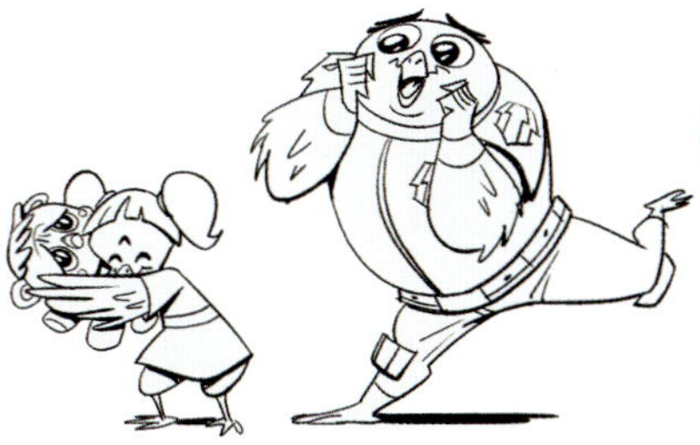

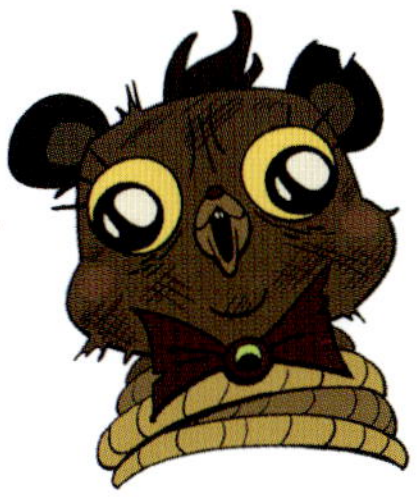

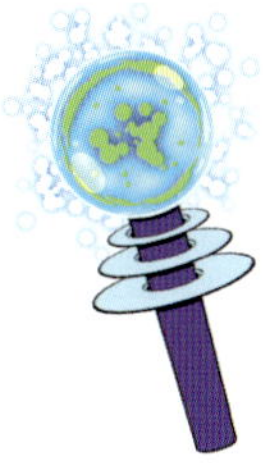

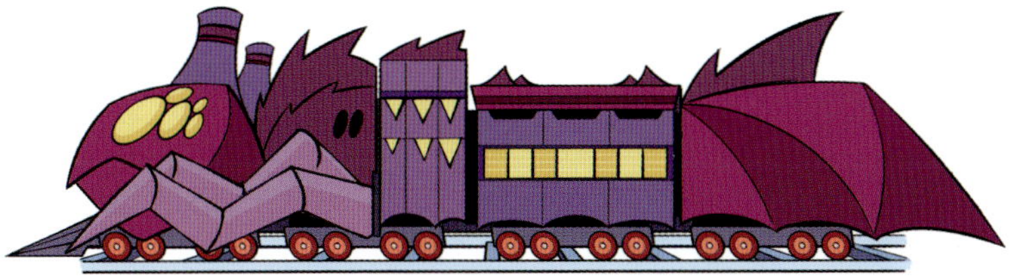

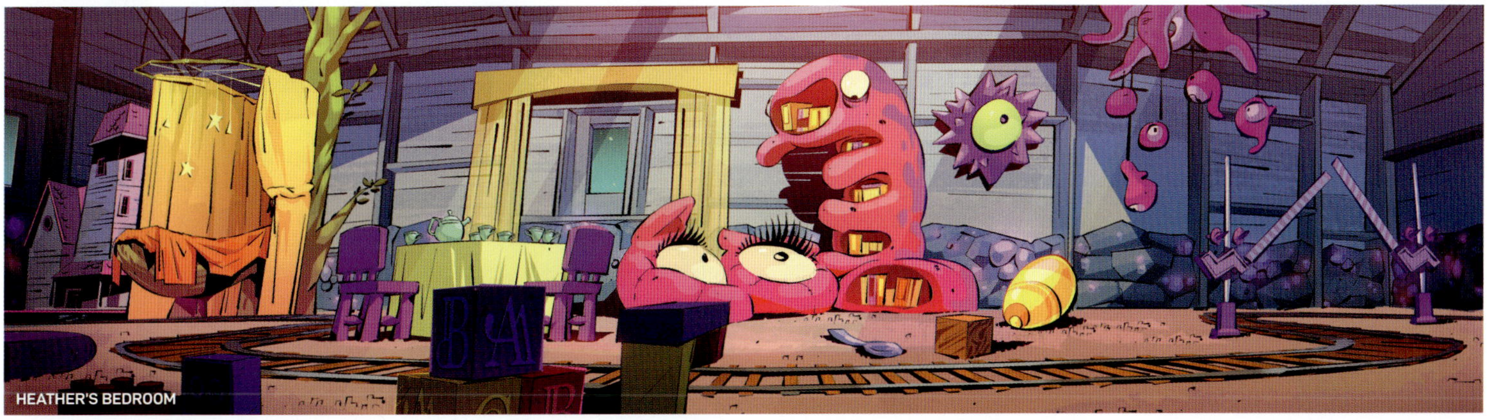
HEATHER'S BEDROOM

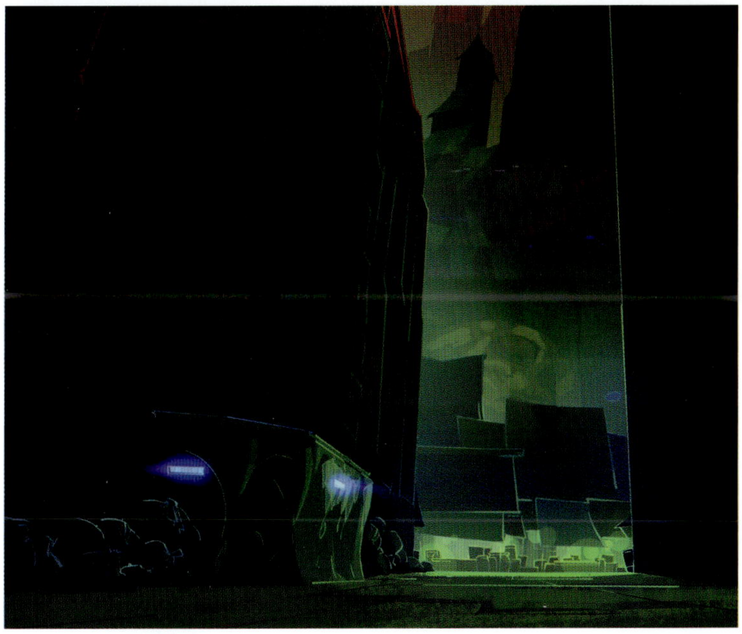

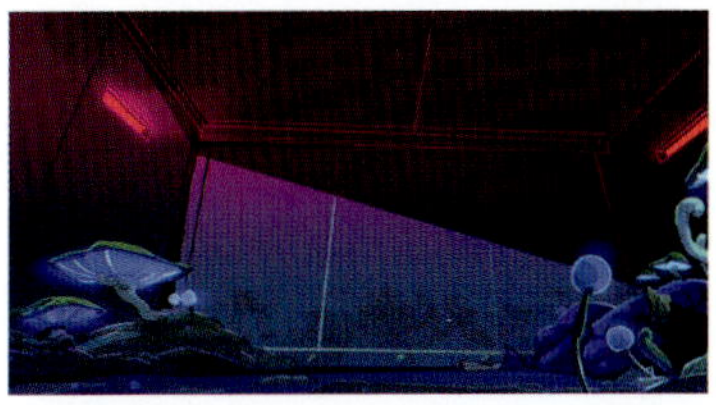

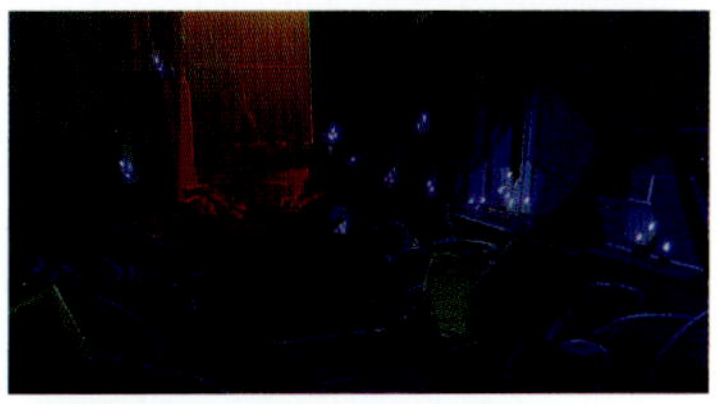

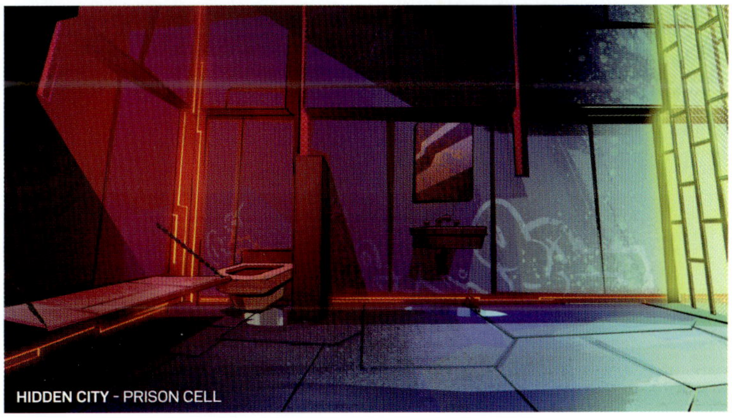
HIDDEN CITY - PRISON CELL

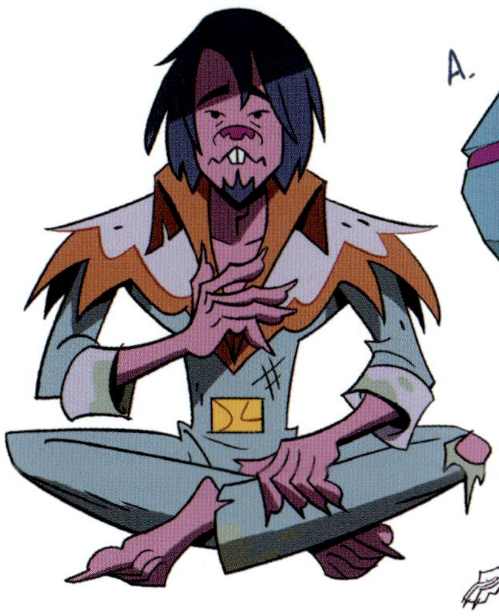

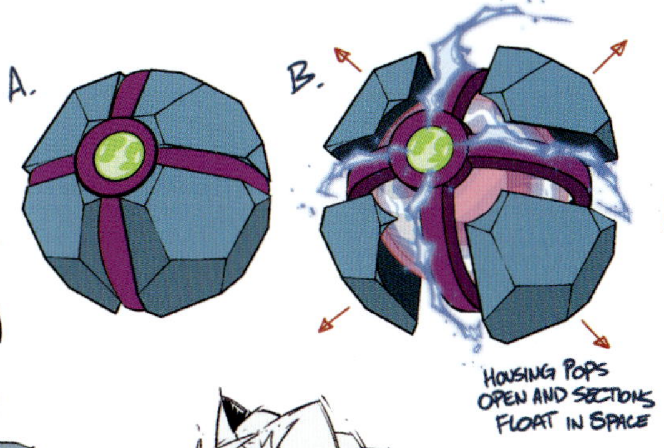

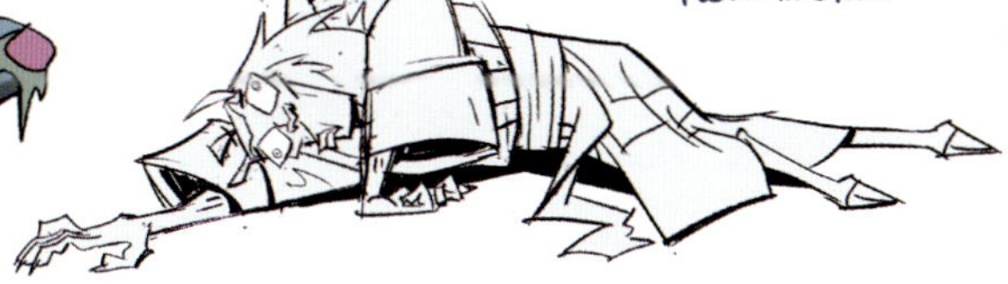

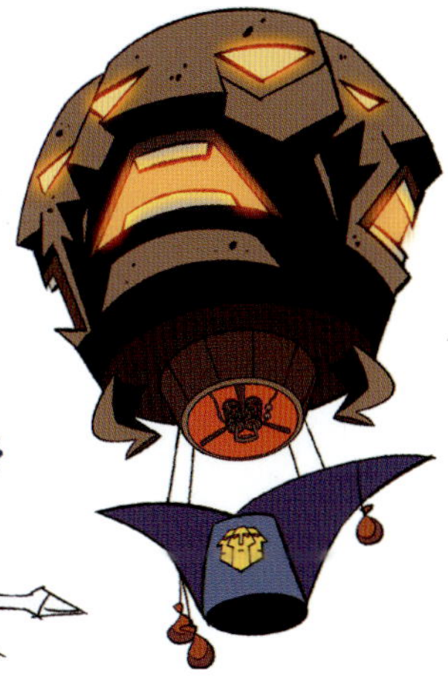

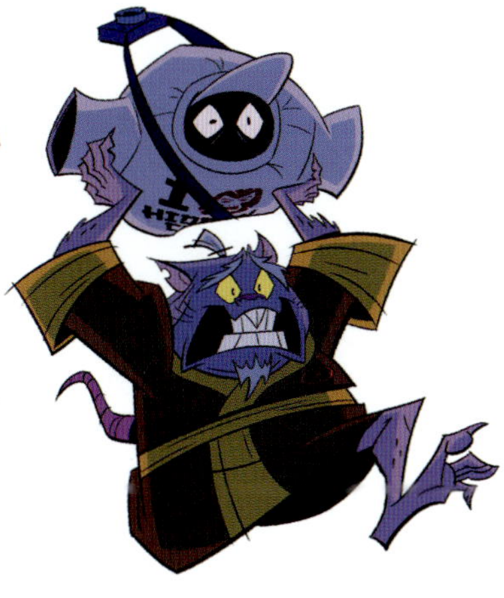

TALES OF THE HIDDEN CITY, PART 4: BAD HAIR DAY

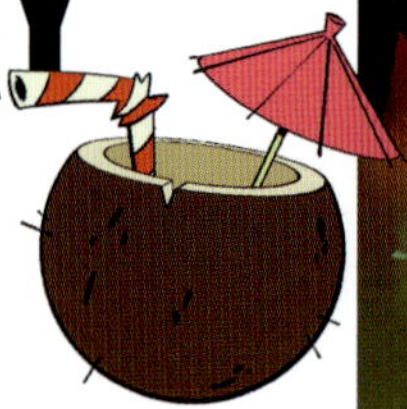

ORIGINAL AIR DATE: JUNE 19, 2020
PRODUCTION CODE: 070

WRITTEN BY **RUSS CARNEY & RON CORCILLO**
STORYBOARDS BY **GLADYFAITH ABCEDE, MAX COLLINS**
DIRECTED BY **SEBASTIAN MONTES**

TONY GAMA-LOBO: Ron and Russ are the masters of a hilarious setup. I remember them calling me into the writers room and saying all Leo wants to do is relax at this fancy resort, but they won't let him in because he's...bald! So of course Leo grows a lush head of hair—evil hair! Made me laugh so hard. But then we had to figure out what the story was once he was in. Heists and mysteries are always a bear to break. But we got there! My favorite part was that we always did a big action set piece in every episode. We'd ask every story, "What's the action going to be?" This one—a full-on fight between Leo and his hair—was just inspired. And of course we needed Leo thrown in jail with everyone else, so him solving the case and still getting blamed because he's bald again was the perfect circle.

RON CORCILLO: The Tales of the Hidden City episodes were very challenging, because we wanted there to be intersections with our various characters' stories over the four episodes. The directors and board artists did a great job ensuring that these intersections would make sense when watching all four episodes. For instance, in one "Bad Hair Day" shot, Splinter swipes Leo's ōdachi so he can use it in "Hidden City's Most Wanted," and if you watch the latter episode, you'll see that Splinter spent a little more time with sleeping Leo than we saw in "Bad Hair Day." Fun!

RUSS CARNEY: Mikey's "shmoo-shmoo" at the end came from a line that Ben improvised early on in the series, so we had a few characters say it, including Mikey in this episode. Leo's hair was modeled after '70s disco icon Barry Gibb of the Bee Gees, and the "masseur" who scams Leo was inspired by Elton John, who was known for his garish sunglasses.

TONY GAMA-LOBO: Originally we had *everyone* end up in jail and figured by the time we got to the fourth episode we'd have a great idea for how they could escape. We did not. So at some point after the animatics we made the switch to having Mikey and Splinter evade the police and ultimately being the ones to break everyone else out.

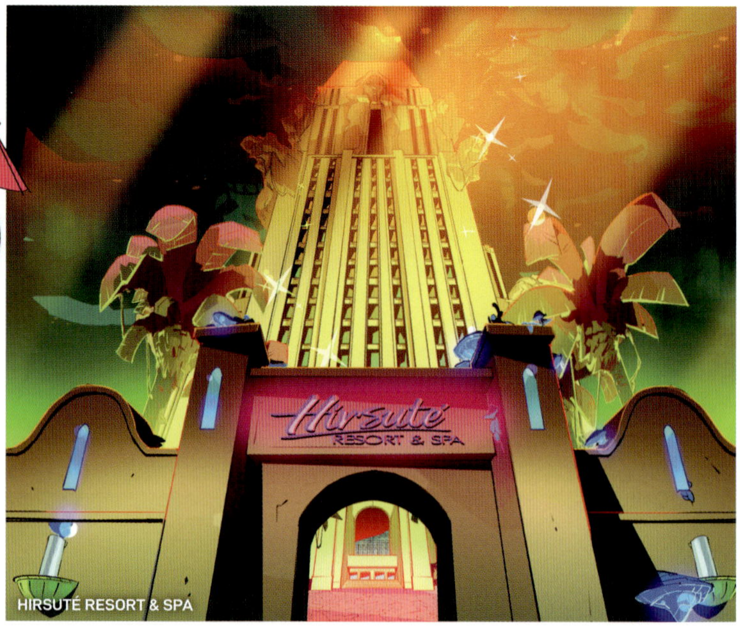

HIRSUTÉ RESORT & SPA

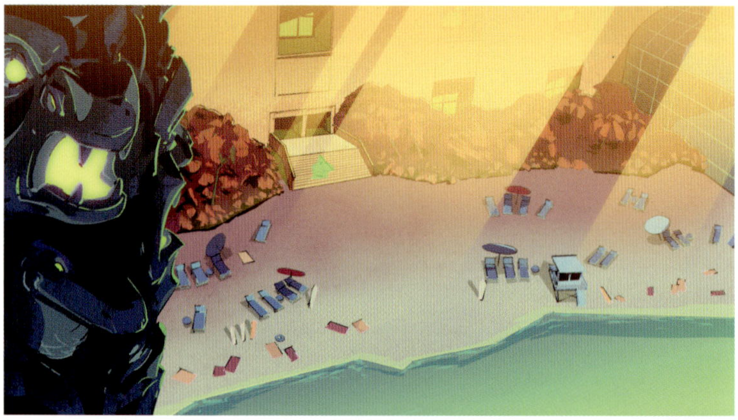

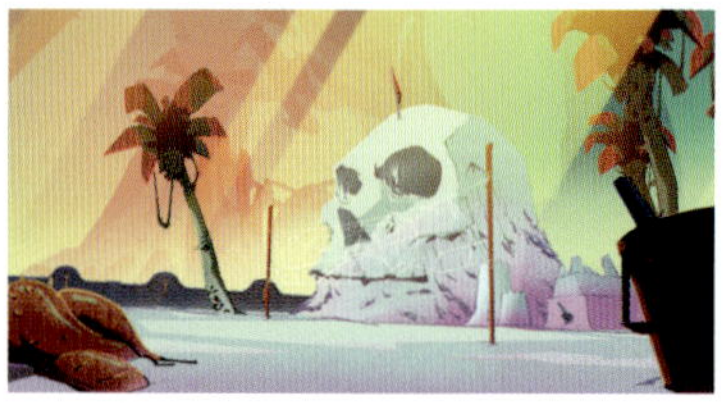

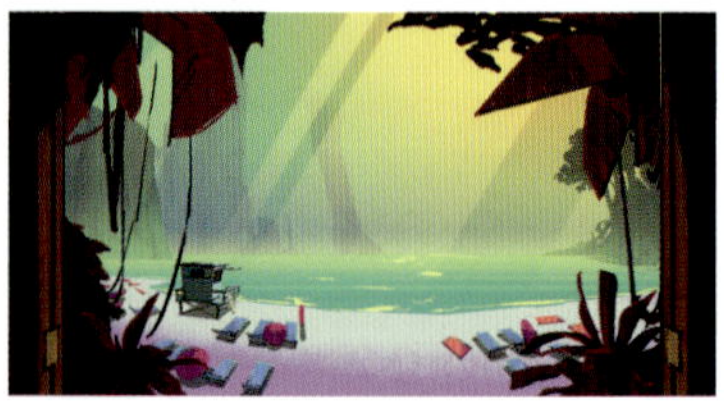

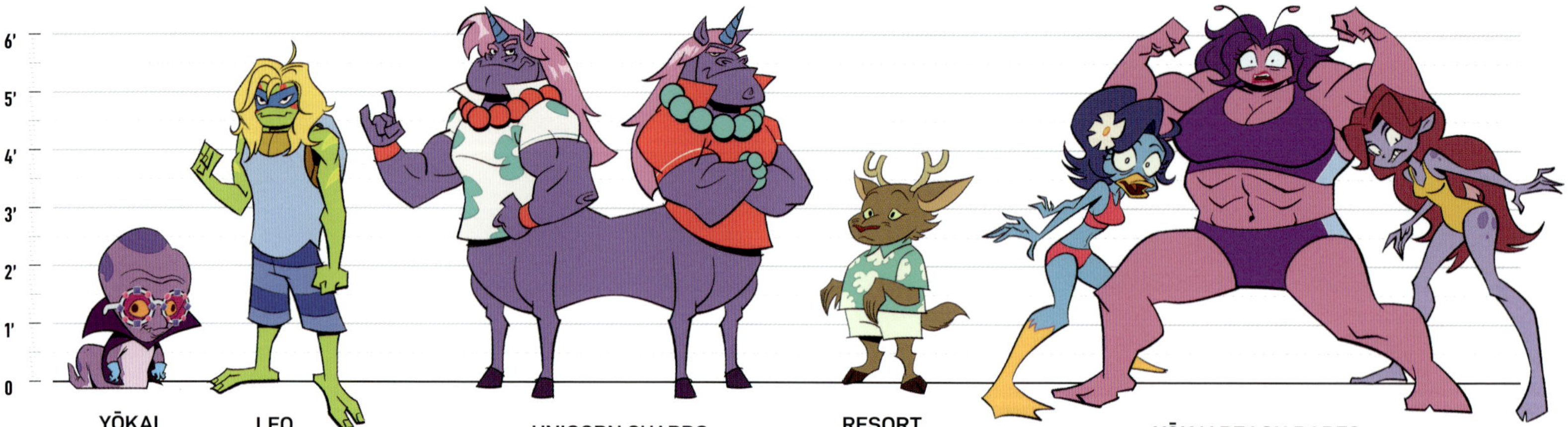

YŌKAI MASSEUR
LEO WITH HAIR
UNICORN GUARDS
RESORT GREETER
YŌKAI BEACH BABES

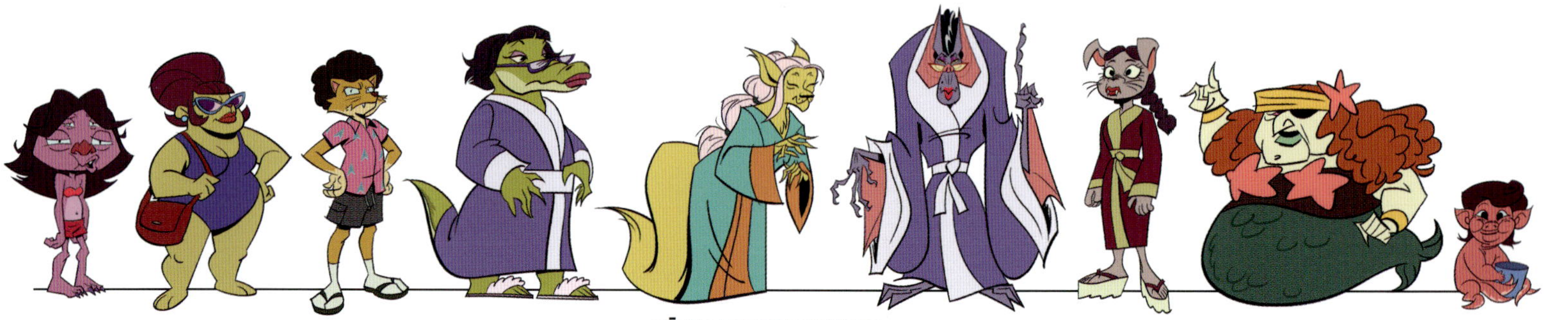
YŌKAI RESORT GUESTS

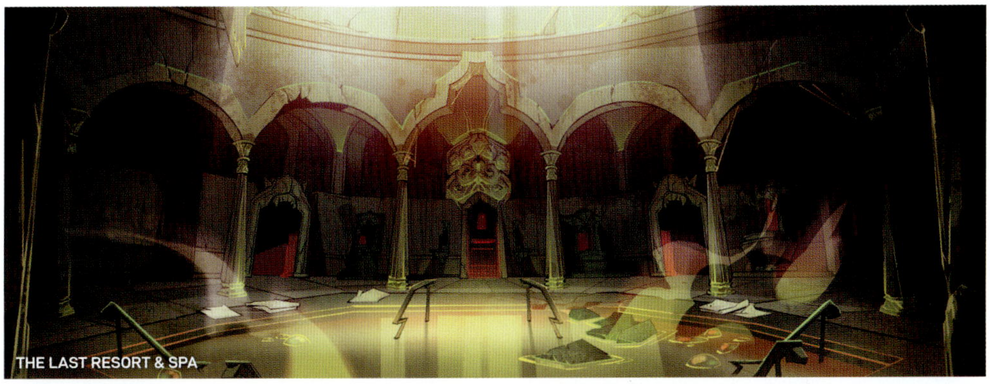
THE LAST RESORT & SPA

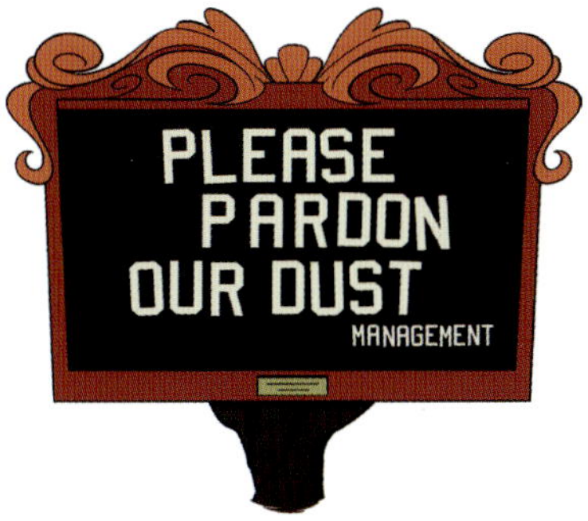

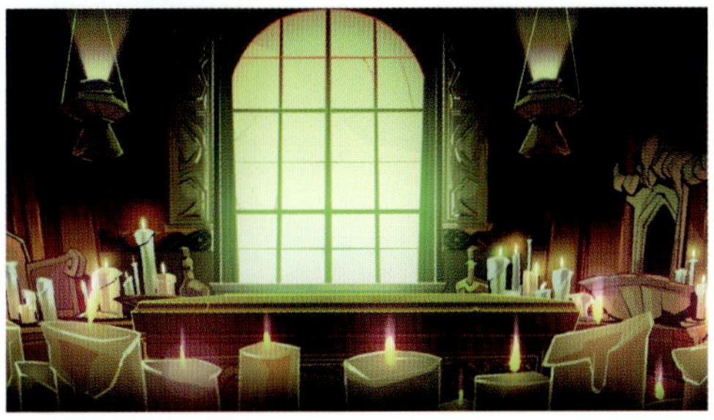

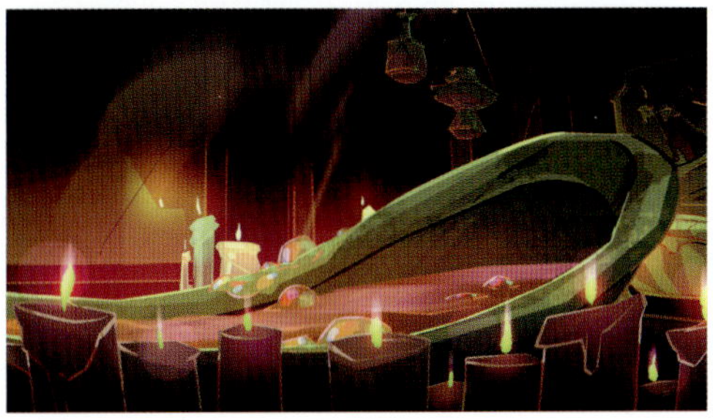

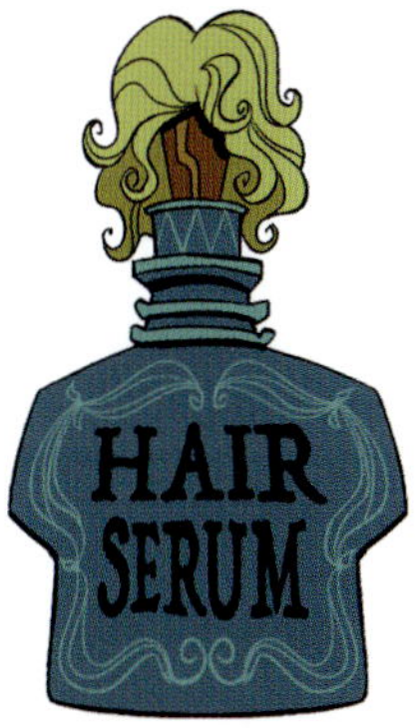

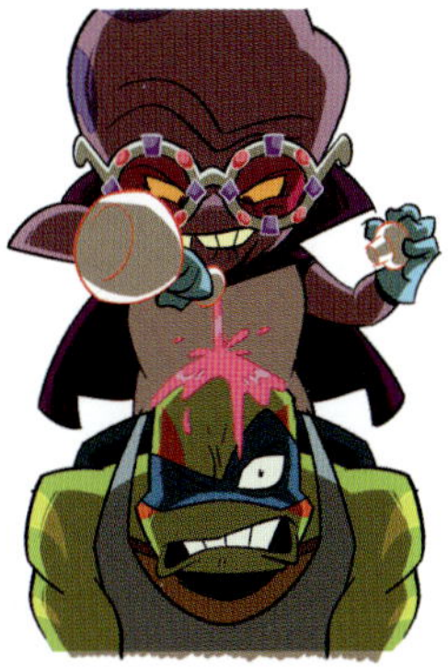

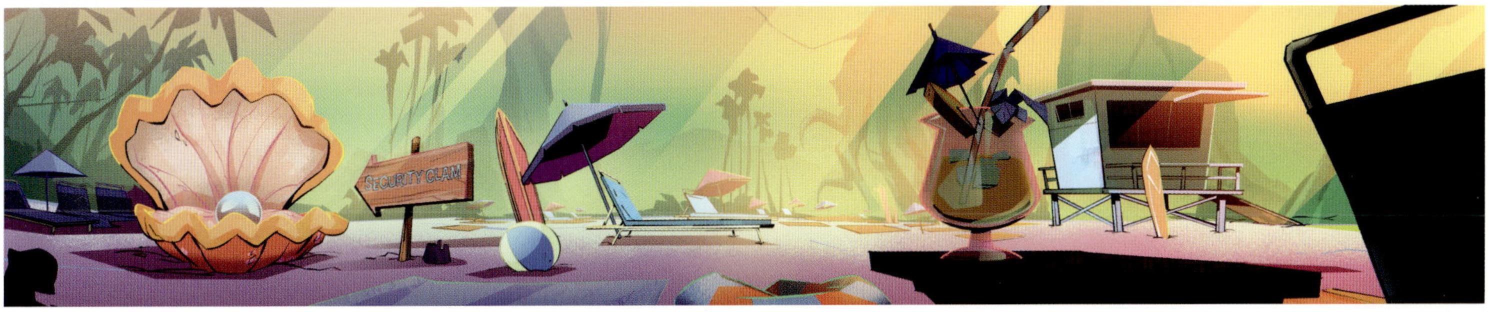

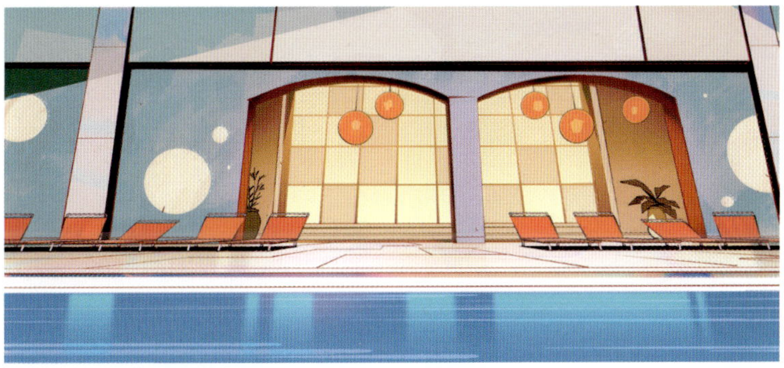

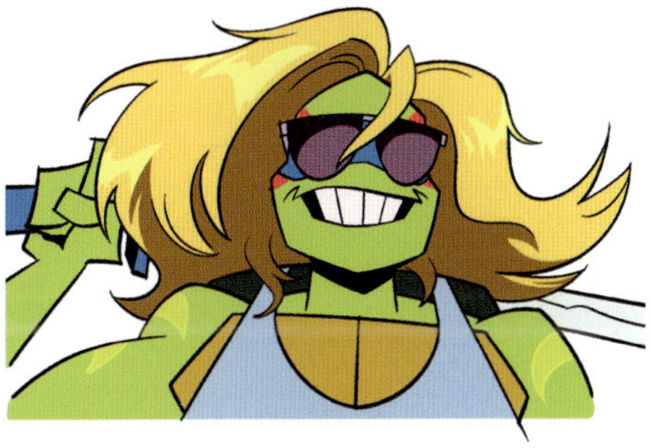

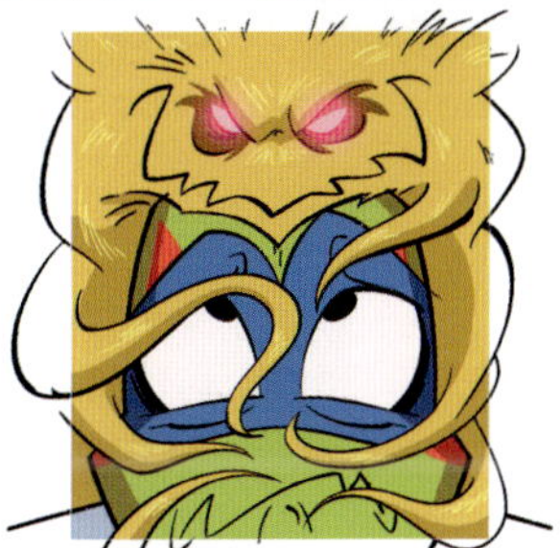

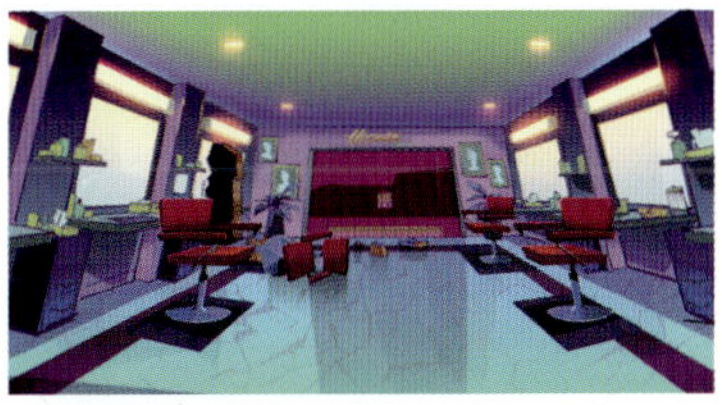

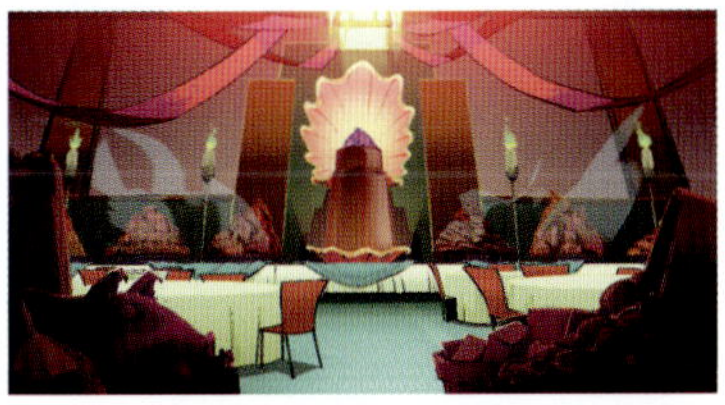

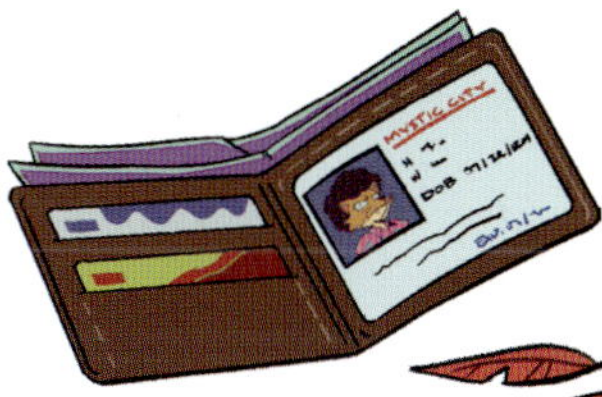

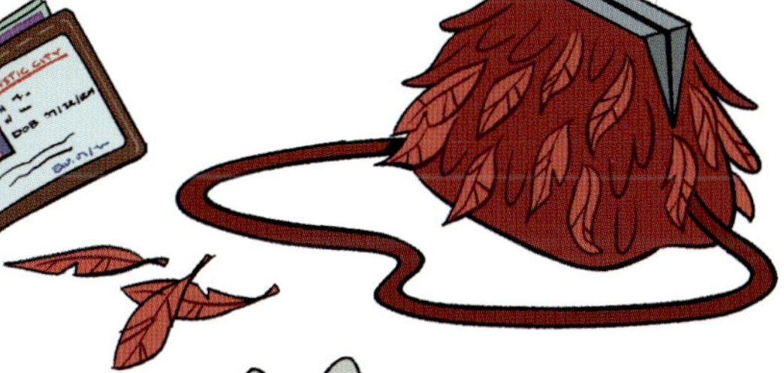

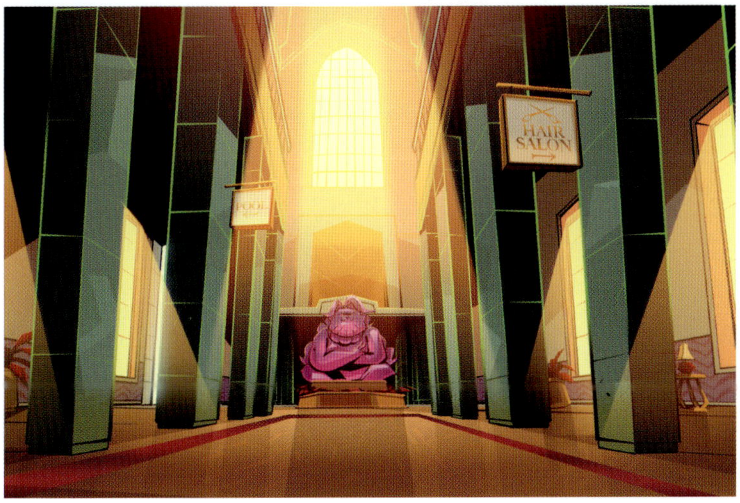

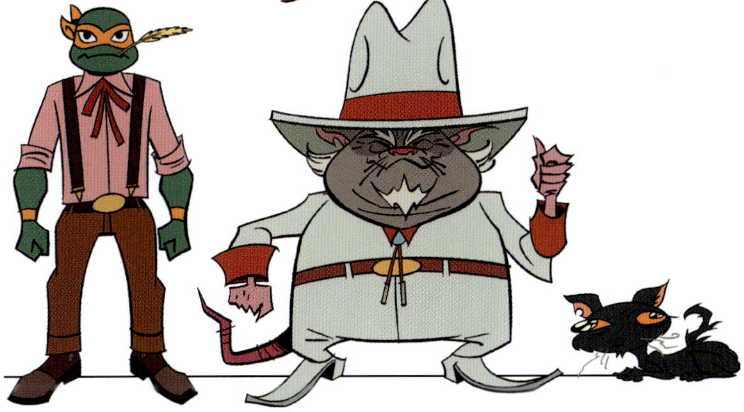

TONY GAMA-LOBO: For some reason, one of our amazing board artists Kevin Molina-Ortiz was obsessed with drawing this random cat in the background all over the place.

FISTS OF FURRY

ORIGINAL AIR DATE: JULY 17, 2020
PRODUCTION CODE: 071

WRITTEN BY **IAN BUSCH**
STORYBOARDS BY **MORGAN HILLEBRAND**
DIRECTED BY **JJ CONWAY**

IAN BUSCH: JJ did an amazing job in upping the threat of the villain as the episode went along. He becomes a truly grotesque and legitimate foe for the Turtles to go up against when he goes through his mutation. Due to the cost of having too many animated people in crowd scenes, we erred towards making the fight competition a smaller-attended event...which plays out perfectly because we really feel the boys are there to support their bestie, April. The most challenging thing in the voice recording was to get all of the various takes of the kids from the competing dojo to match up together, but when we finally got them all in sync I think that joke plays very well.

JJ CONWAY: When you're making 11-minute episodes, there's a constant battle between what you want to do and how much screen time you have to pull it off, so distilling *The Karate Kid* into 11 minutes was challenging. On top of that, we had to be mindful of animation complexity, given how many characters were in the episode. We had to be creative about reusing animation and implying action instead of showing it (especially with the training), so a lot of the Bradford kids reuse the same animation with different lip sync, and we leaned into cheats like having characters "blur" off screen instead of walking.

We generally got away with a lot on the series, but the beat where Frank breaks his hand really gave us a lot of trouble with the S&P department. They really felt it was too grotesque and upsetting, so instead of pulling it back we pushed it farther until it was so inflamed and broken that it didn't look realistic anymore. Problem solved!

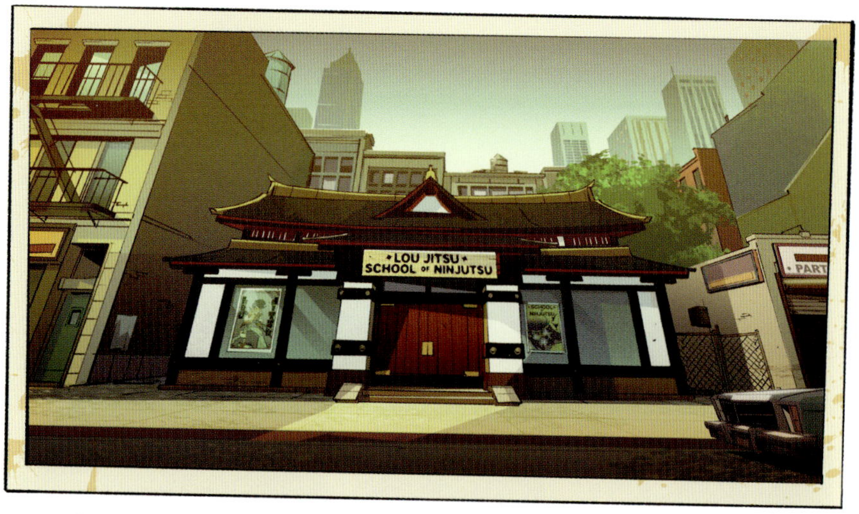

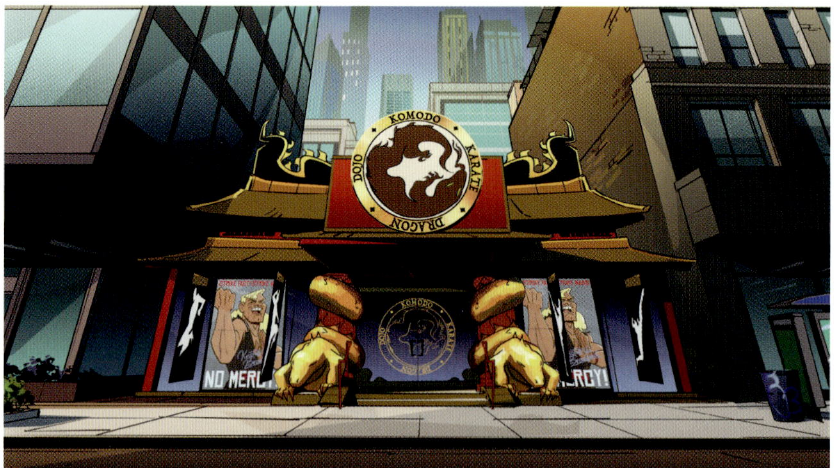

KOMODO DRAGON KARATE DOJO

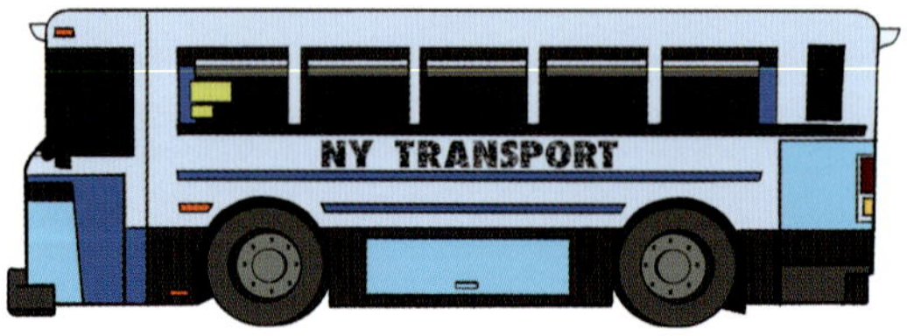

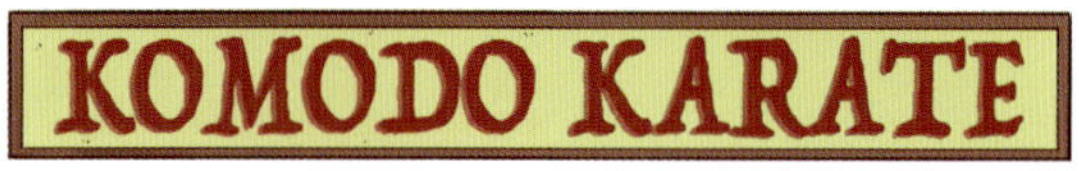

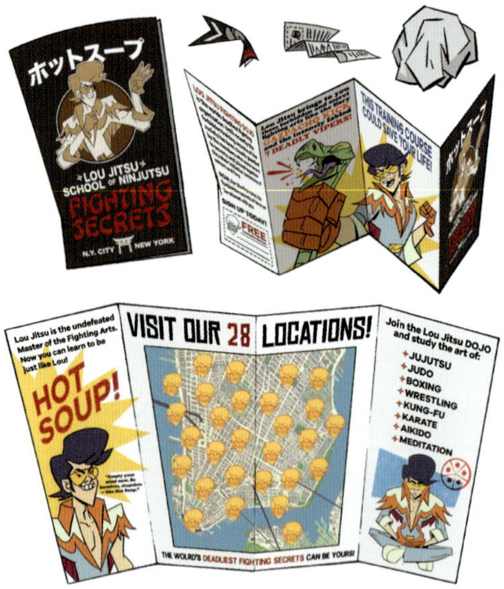

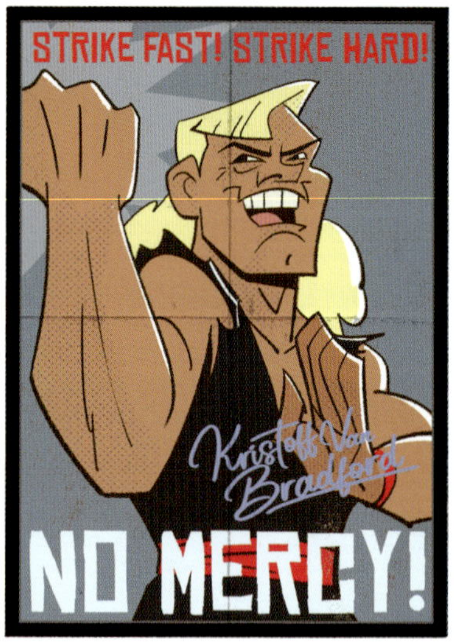

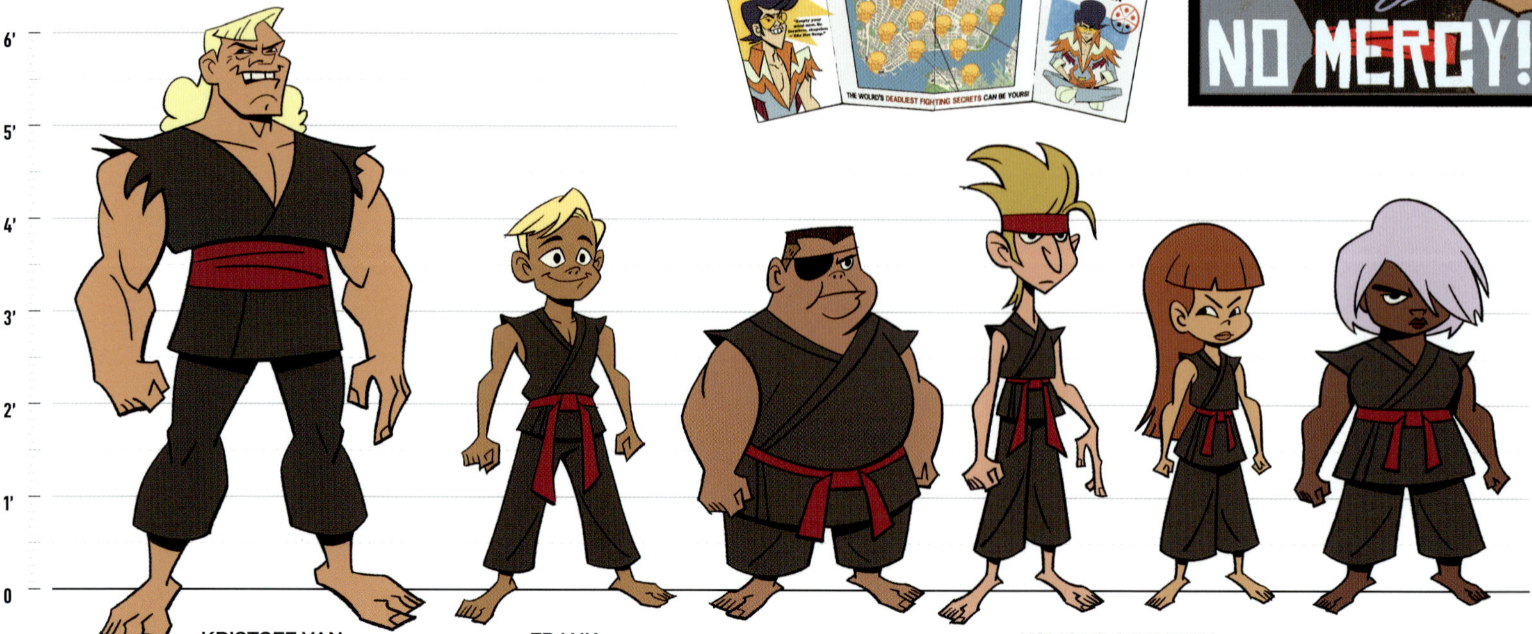

KRISTOFF VAN BRADFORD | FRANK | KOMODO STUDENTS

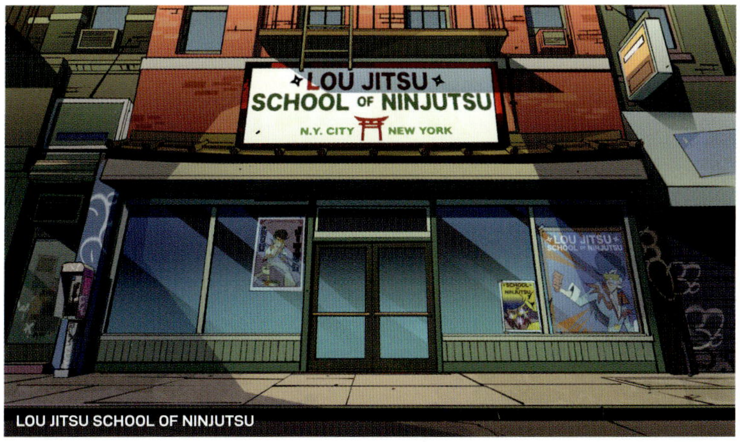

LOU JITSU SCHOOL OF NINJUTSU

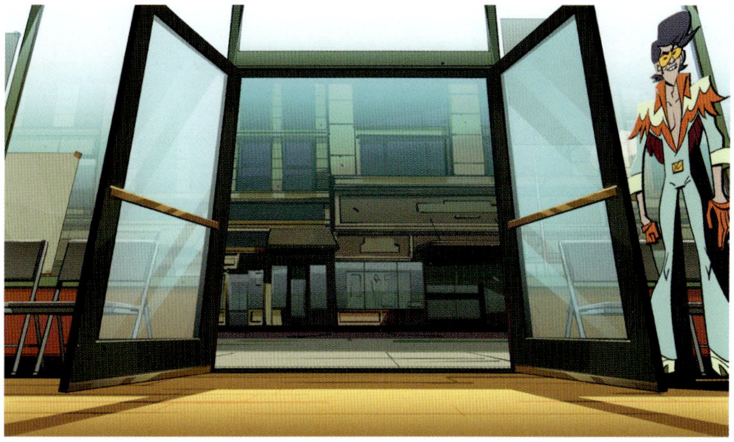

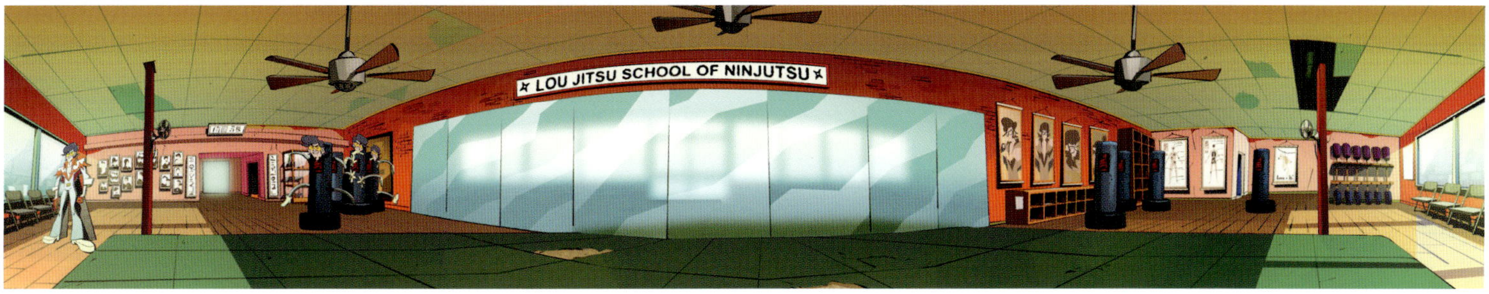

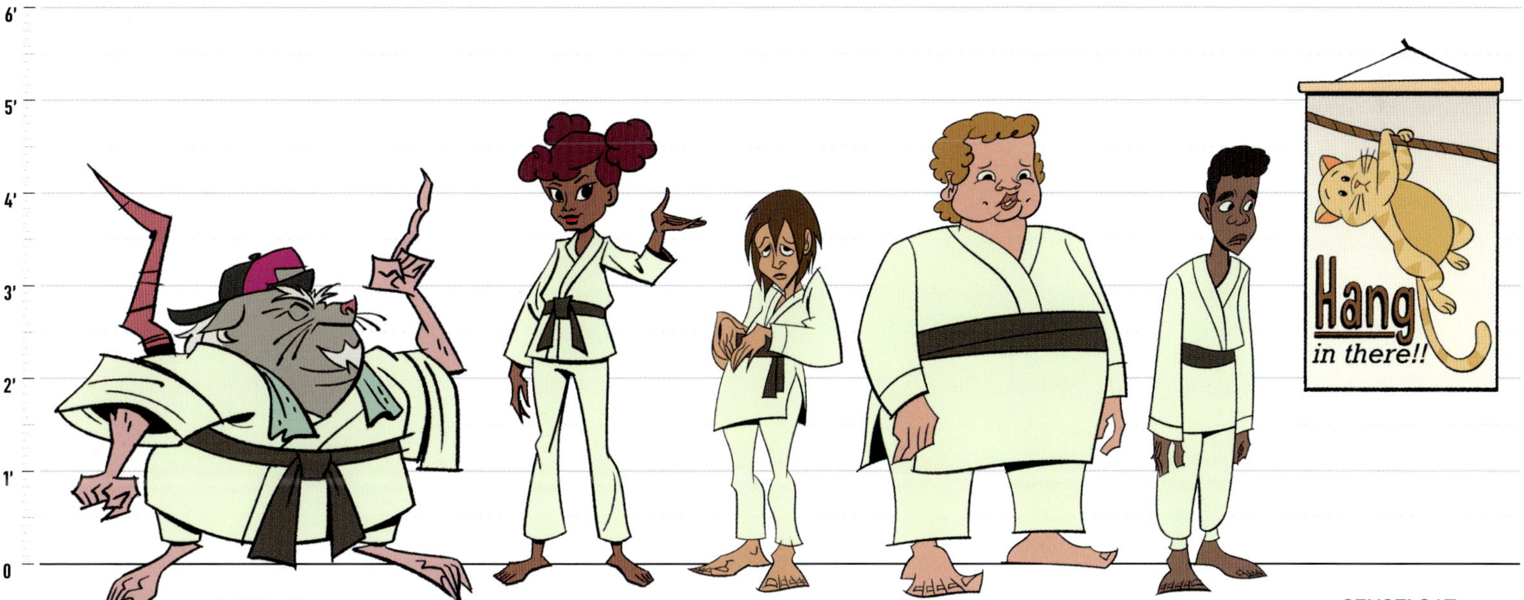

RANDALL
SPLINTER

APRIL O'NEIL

LOU JITSU STUDENTS

SENSEI CAT
POSTER

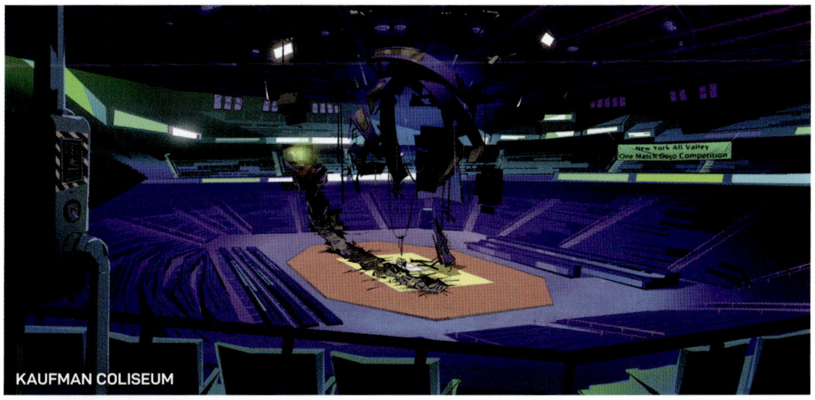
KAUFMAN COLISEUM

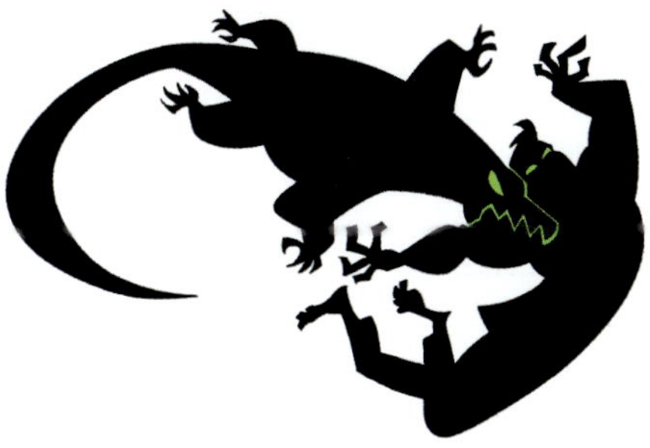

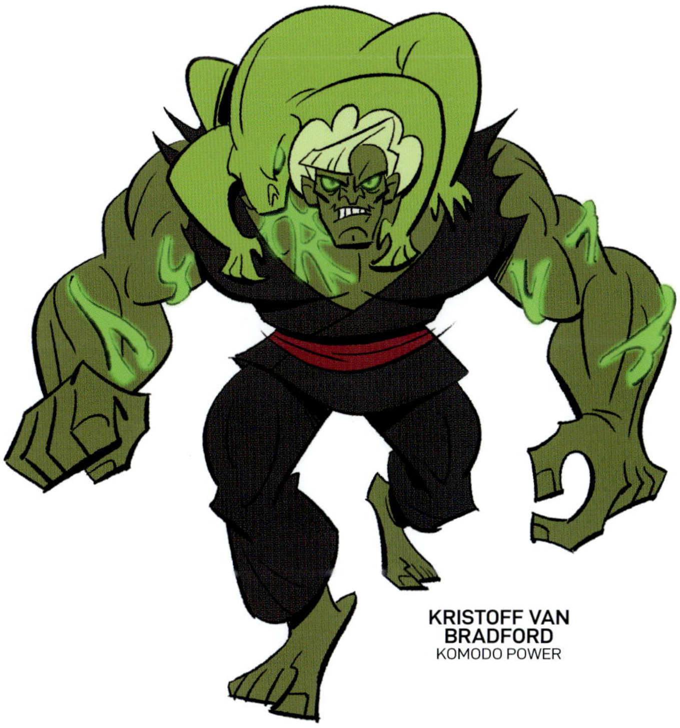
KRISTOFF VAN
BRADFORD
KOMODO POWER

THE CLOTHES DON'T MAKE THE TURTLE

ORIGINAL AIR DATE: JULY 17, 2020
PRODUCTION CODE: 072

WRITTEN BY **JESSE GORDON**
STORYBOARDS BY **ALICIA CHAN**
DIRECTED BY **JAKE CASTORENA**

JESSE GORDON: This was the last episode I wrote for the show, and it might be the silliest idea I ever got through. I don't even remember exactly how it came about—probably during one of those late-night writers room sessions where someone mentioned '80s movies and it just clicked. The concept of doing an entire episode as one continuous '80s training montage was so stupid it circled back to brilliant.

What really makes it work is watching the Turtles trapped in this endless cycle of changing outfits and hyping each other up. That magical New York townhouse setting we created became the perfect backdrop for the madness. The fact that fans connected with it so deeply—even creating their own animated versions—still blows me away! That kind of response is why we do this.

People often overlook how strong the action sequences were in our show. We always prioritized comedy in the writing because we had such incredible board artists who could take simple descriptions and turn them into spectacular fight scenes. They never missed!

Looking back, this script really distills everything I loved about working on the series: that perfect combination of ridiculous humor and genuine heart. There's something special about my final contribution being something this unapologetically goofy yet heartfelt. Not a bad way to wrap up my time with these characters.

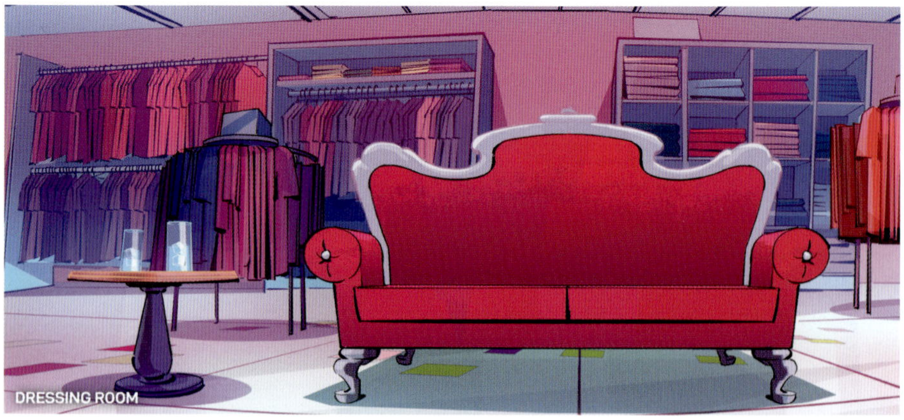
DRESSING ROOM

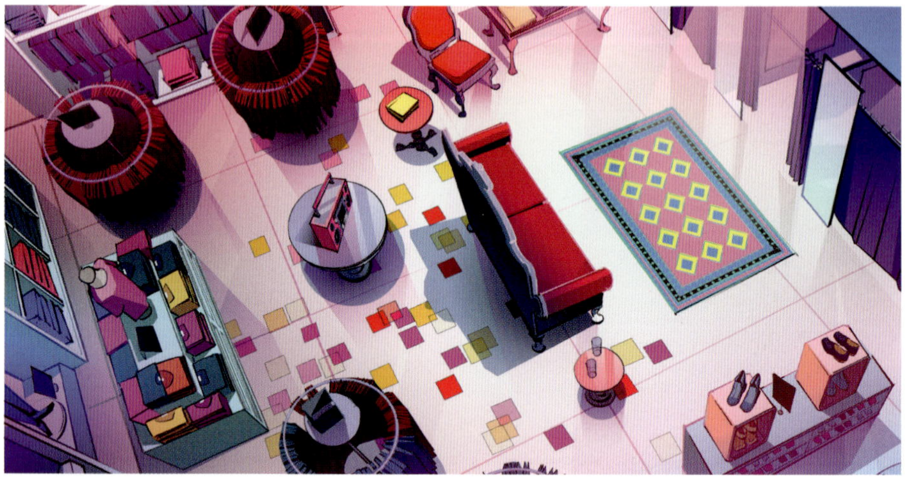

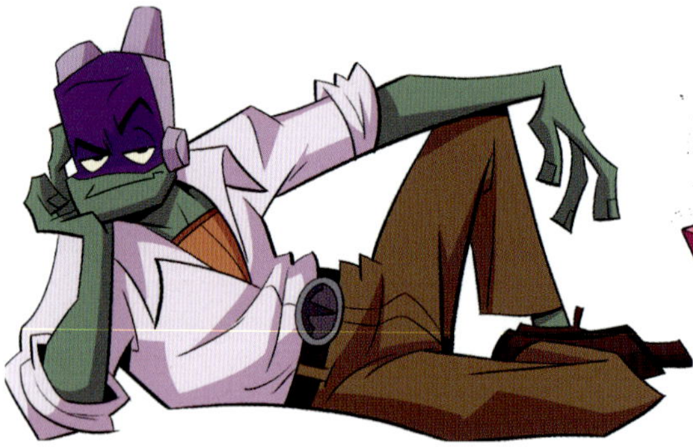

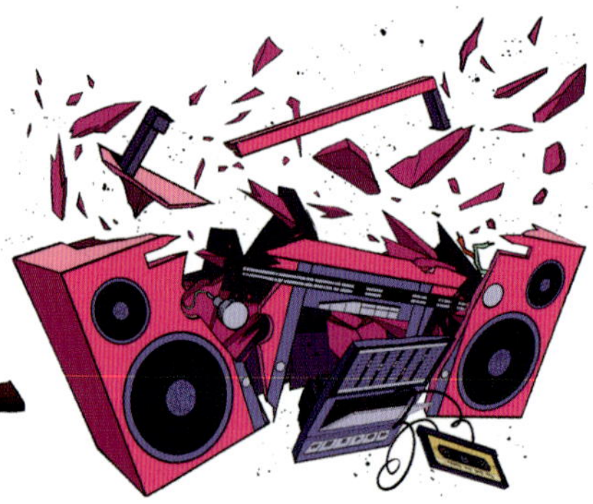

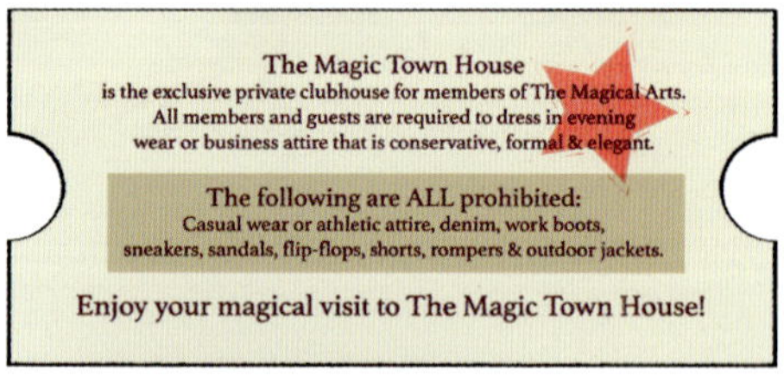

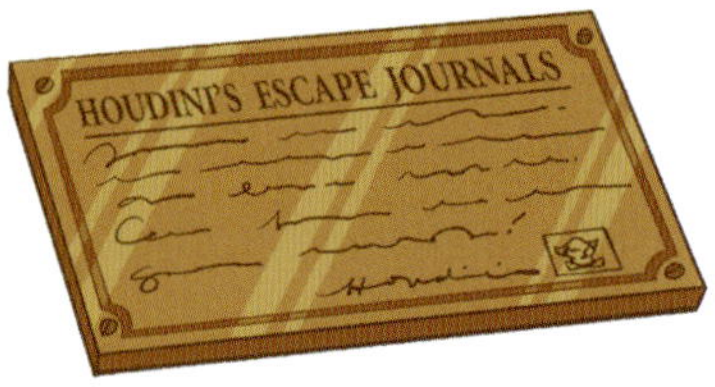

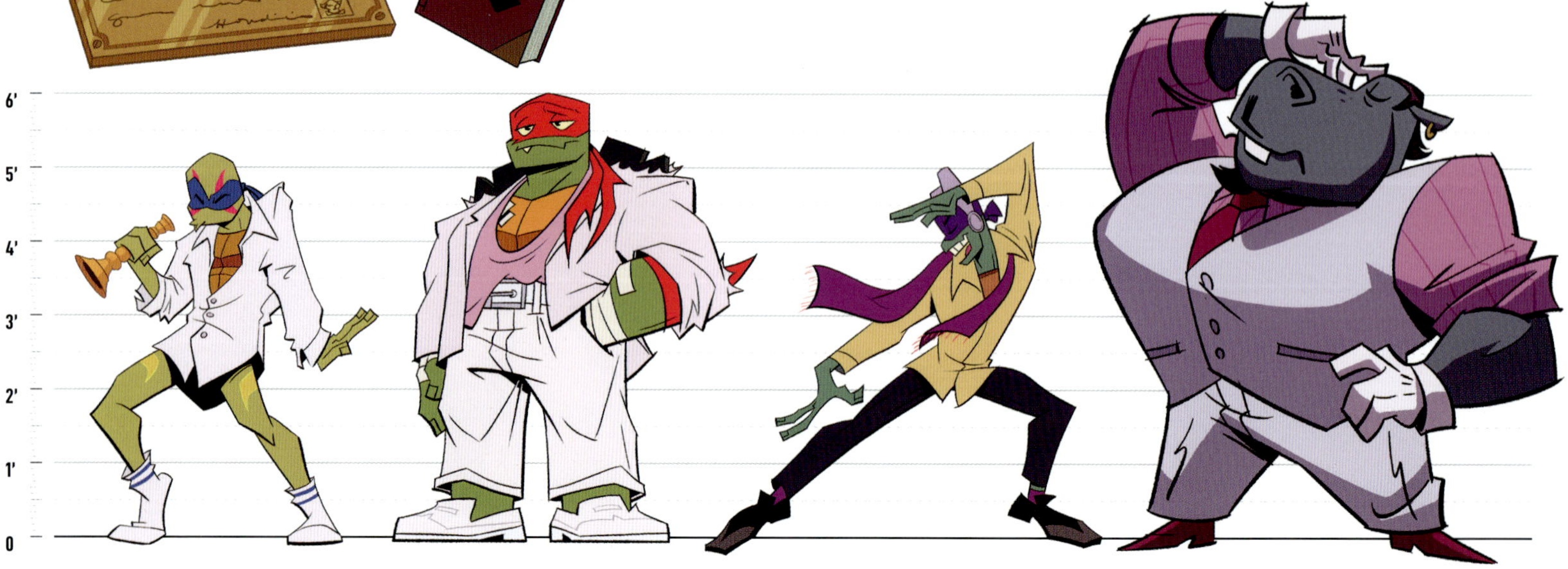

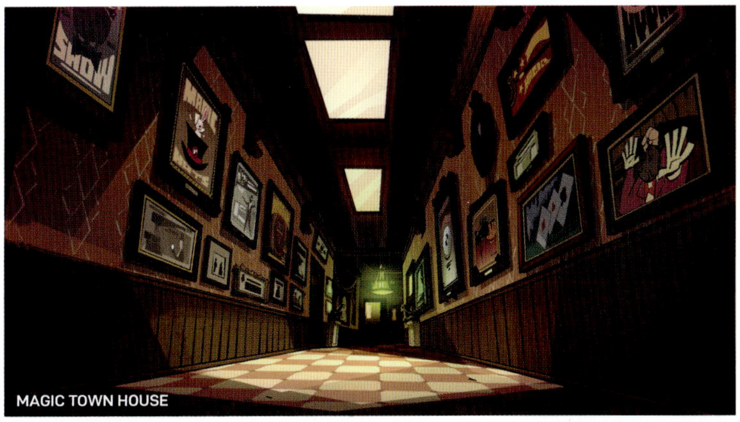

MAGIC TOWN HOUSE

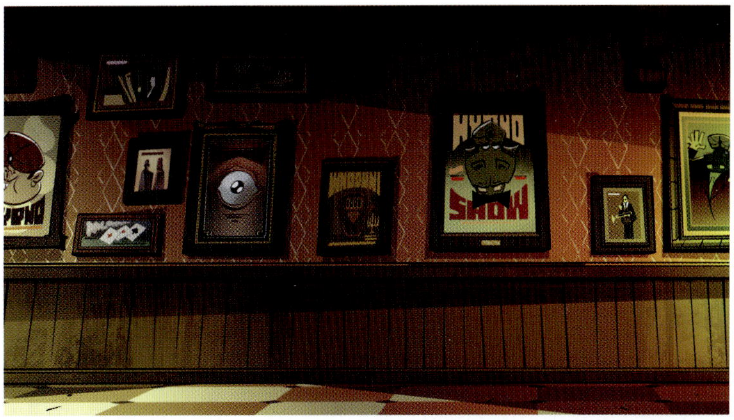

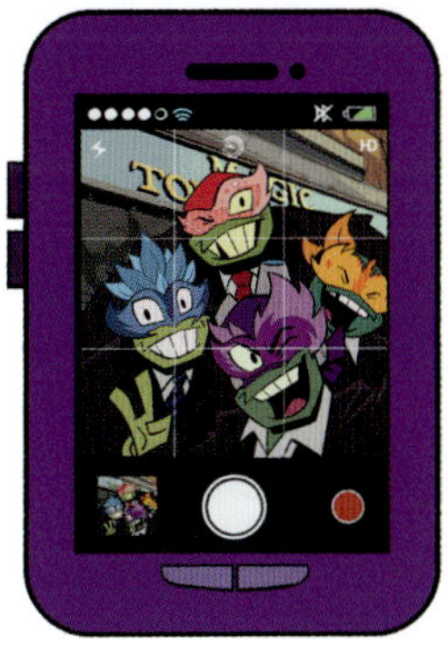

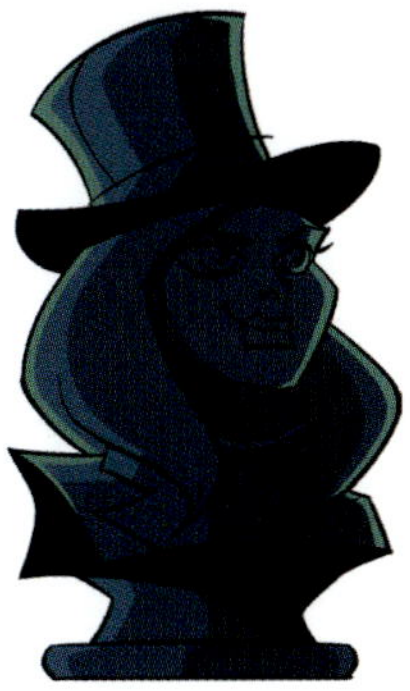

VENUS DE MAGIC

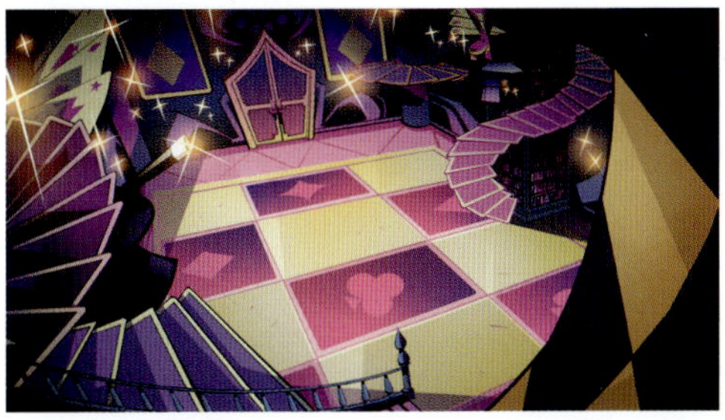

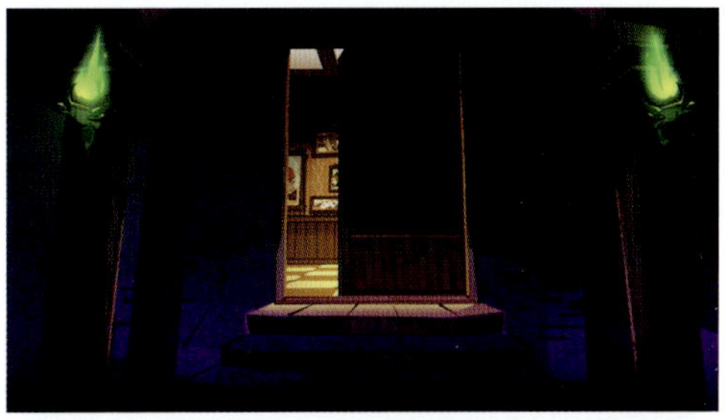

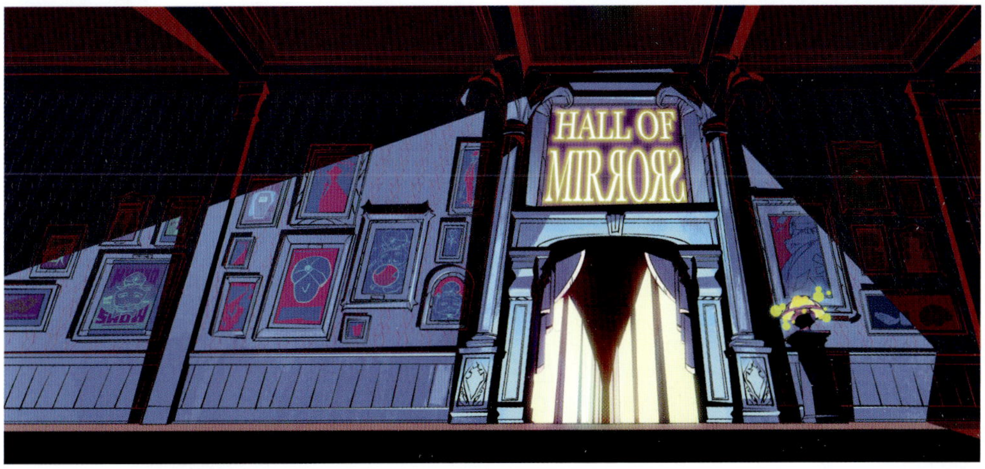

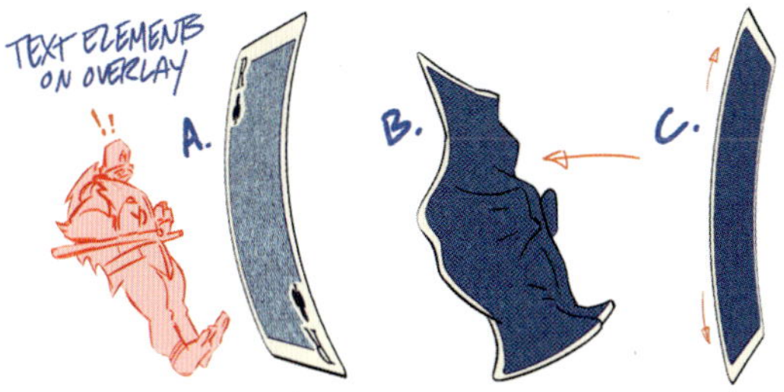

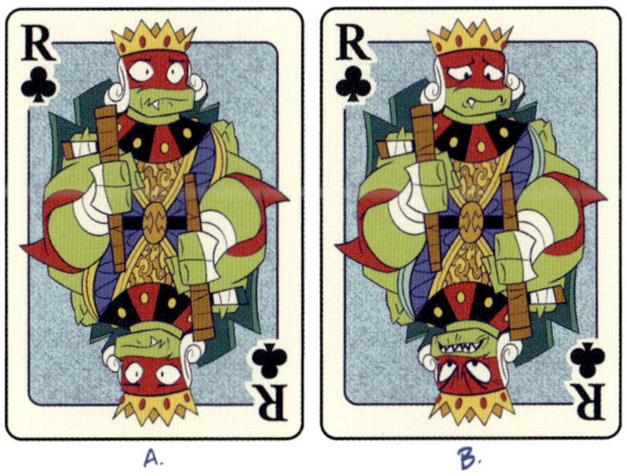

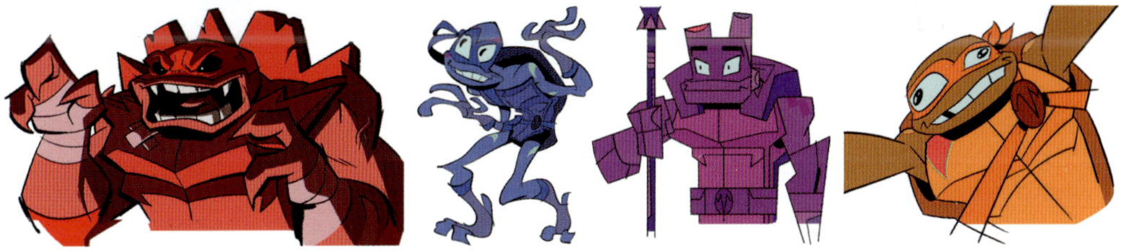

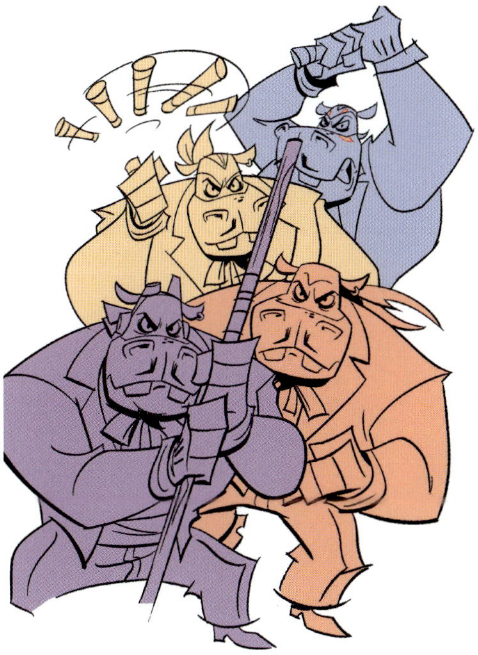

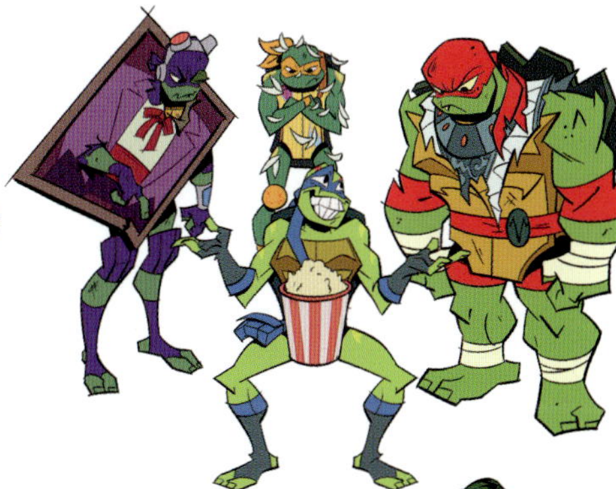

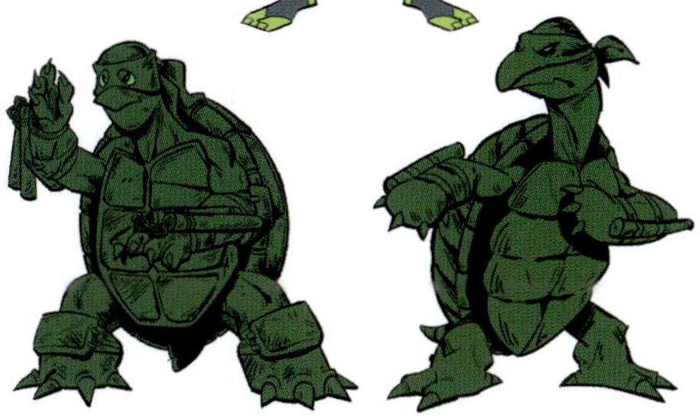

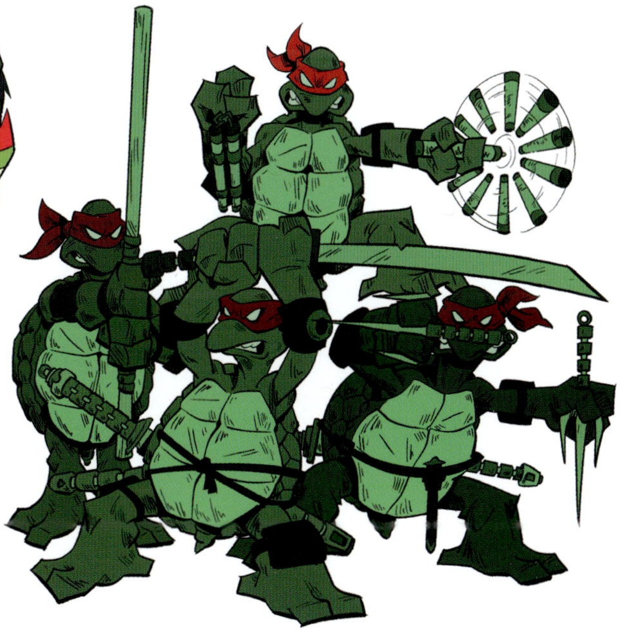

KEVIN EASTMAN AND PETER LAIRD'S ORIGINAL TURTLE SKETCHES

BATTLE NEXUS: NEW YORK

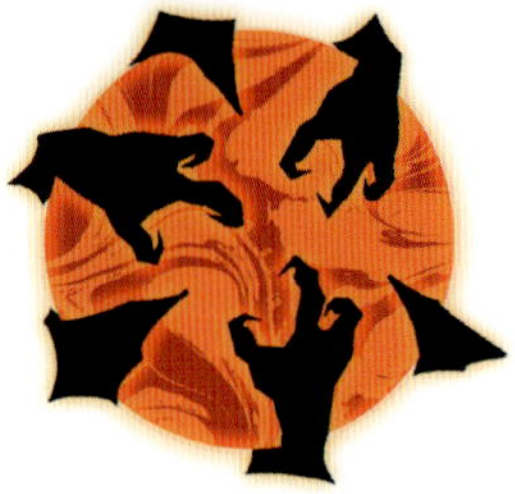

ORIGINAL AIR DATE: JULY 17, 2020
PRODUCTION CODE: 075-076

WRITTEN BY **DALE MALINOWSKI**
STORYBOARDS BY **MAX COLLINS, CHRISTINE LIU**
DIRECTED BY **KEVIN MOLINA-ORTIZ, ALAN WAN**

TONY GAMA-LOBO: "Battle Nexus: New York" was one of the first ideas we put up on the board during our writers retreat. But it wasn't even an idea—it was just a title. Someone said it. Everyone was like "cooooooool." And that's how we ended up with the index card stuck to the writers room wall the whole year staring at us, daring us to come up with an actual story. Dale and Jesse finally did—Turtle/villain team-up on the streets of New York. But it was far from figured out.

DALE MALINOWSKI: I inherited this premise when a staff writer had to say goodbye to the show to go work on a movie at a different studio. Ant and Andy promoted me to staff writer around this time, too. I love those guys!

Speaking of people I love, this was the first time I had the opportunity to write about many of my favorite heroes and villains. Hypno was the first character I created for the series, but Jesse developed and used him first and most frequently. I was thrilled to contribute to the character's incredible legacy that Jesse started. In my opinion, Todd is the unsung hero of this adventure. If he didn't serve his world-class lemonade to Draxum, then Draxum's memories wouldn't have been triggered, and he and his crew may never have escaped Big Mama's mystic trap to go on and help the Turtles survive the final fight—probably subconsciously inspired by the rat in *Avengers: Endgame* (2019), which was still in theaters at the time. Foot Recruit's temptation and turn, revealing Shadow Fiend's secret identity, and Splinter extending an olive branch to his ex-flame even after all she's done were milestones that we knew we wanted to hit in this two-part spectacle. I even left one page of the script open for action since we were an action show and all that special sauce needs screen time.

TONY GAMA-LOBO: When we got the bad news that the show was shutting down, we were ready to ship "Battle Nexus: New York" overseas to be animated. It was glorious...but it was standalone. It did not connect in any way to the Shredder storyline. We had a whole separate episode discovering Shredder was being mind-controlled by Big Mama to fight in the Hidden City. But now we needed to collapse the whole last half of the season into just a couple episodes. So we reopened a finished "Battle Nexus: New York" (something we never did), cut a bunch of really great stuff (there was a lot more Donnie and Hypno playing chess), and figured out a new ending that fed into the finale. You watch it now and it feels like it was meant to be.

RUSS CARNEY: We were normally going to have about eighteen 11-minute episodes (known as "carts" in the industry) to complete the season arc. That was reduced to four carts. So there were huge amounts of story that were cut.

RON CORCILLO: Originally, Shadow Fiend was going to be sucked down to the Hidden City at the end of "Battle Nexus: New York," with Foot Recruit being the only member of the Foot who knew he was there. Then we would spend several episodes with the Foot attempting to free Shredder from Big Mama's clutches. There was also a whole storyline about Big Mama gaining ultimate power in the Hidden City. The Turtles would also go through a number of steps to become powerful enough to face down the newly revived Shredder, which included liberating Karai from the prison dimension and spending several episodes training with her and becoming stronger. Ninety percent of that had to go.

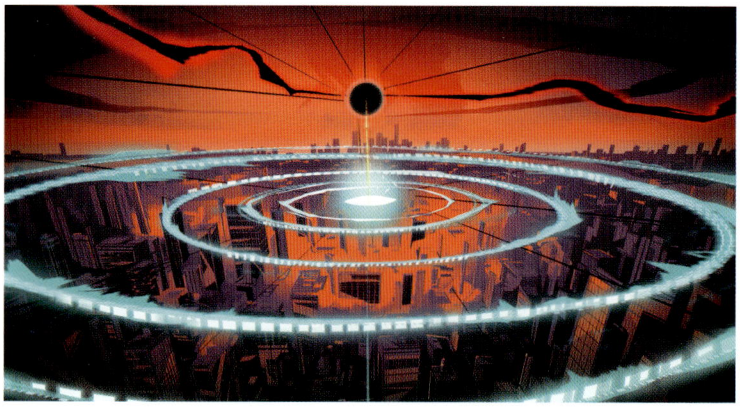

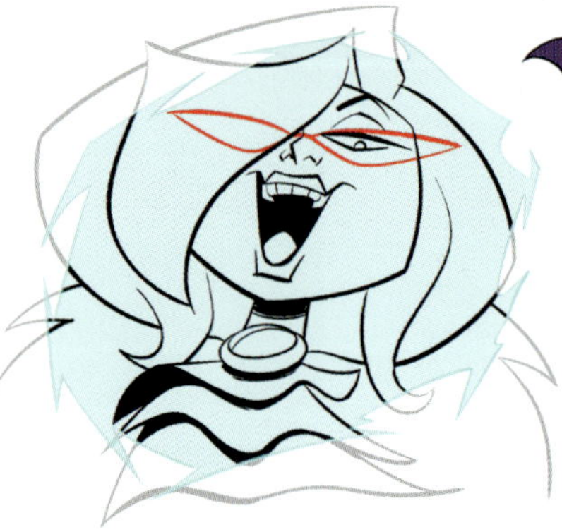

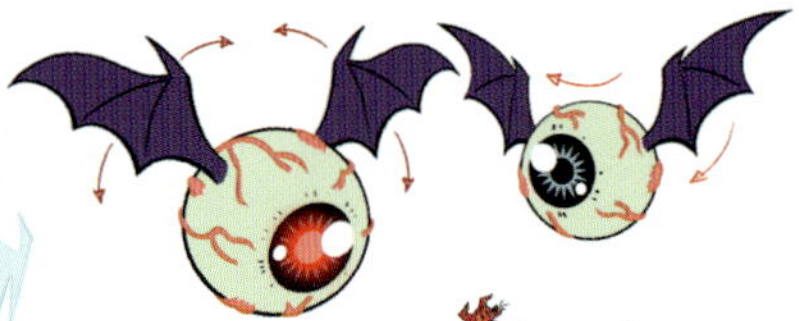

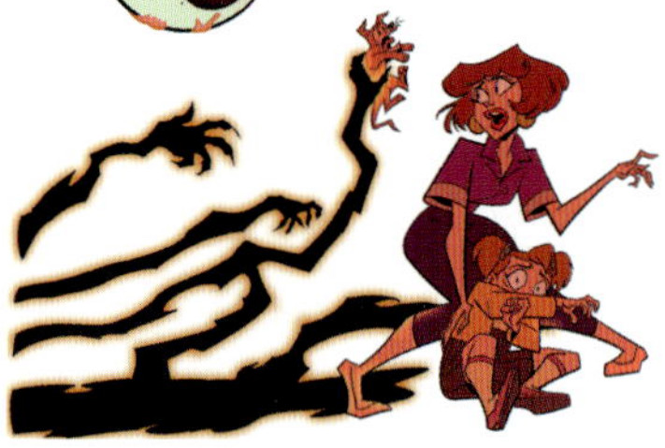

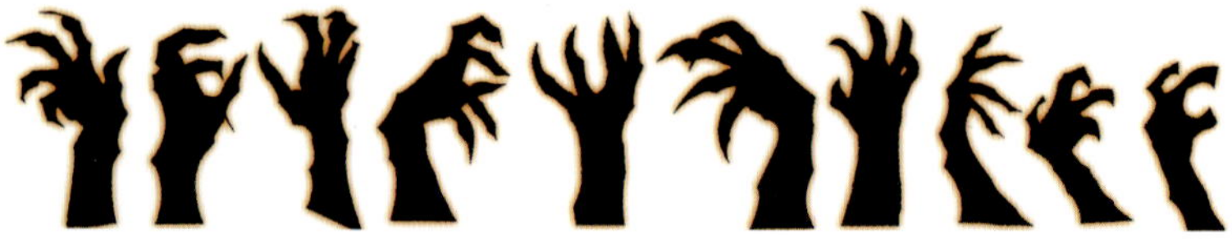

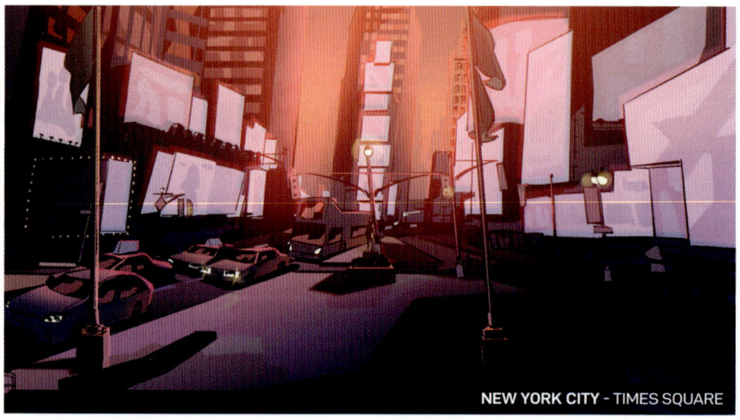

NEW YORK CITY - TIMES SQUARE

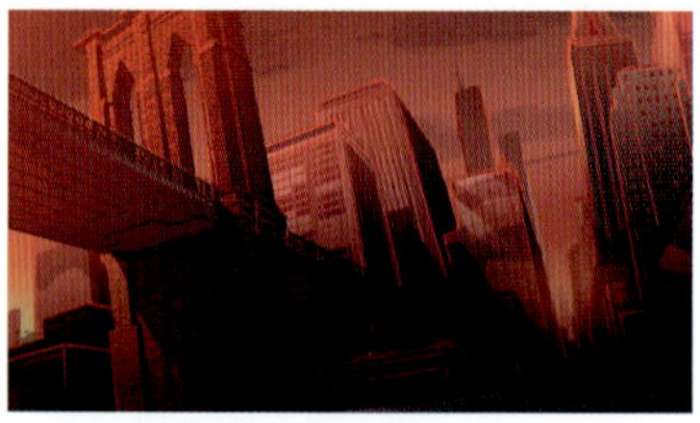

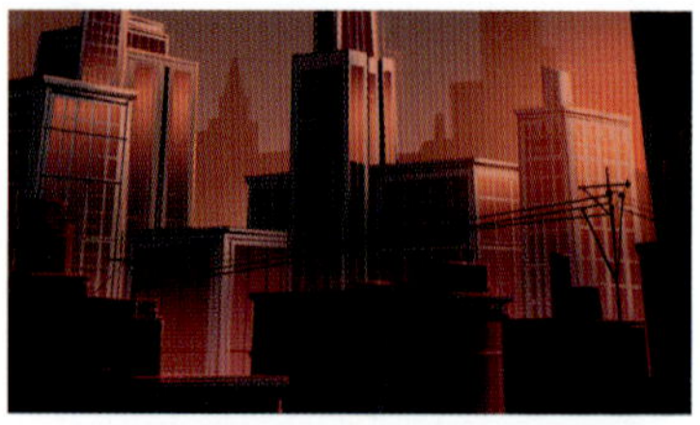

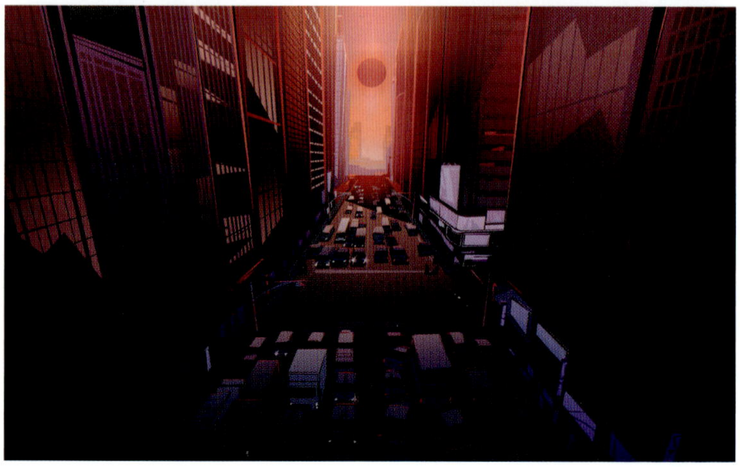

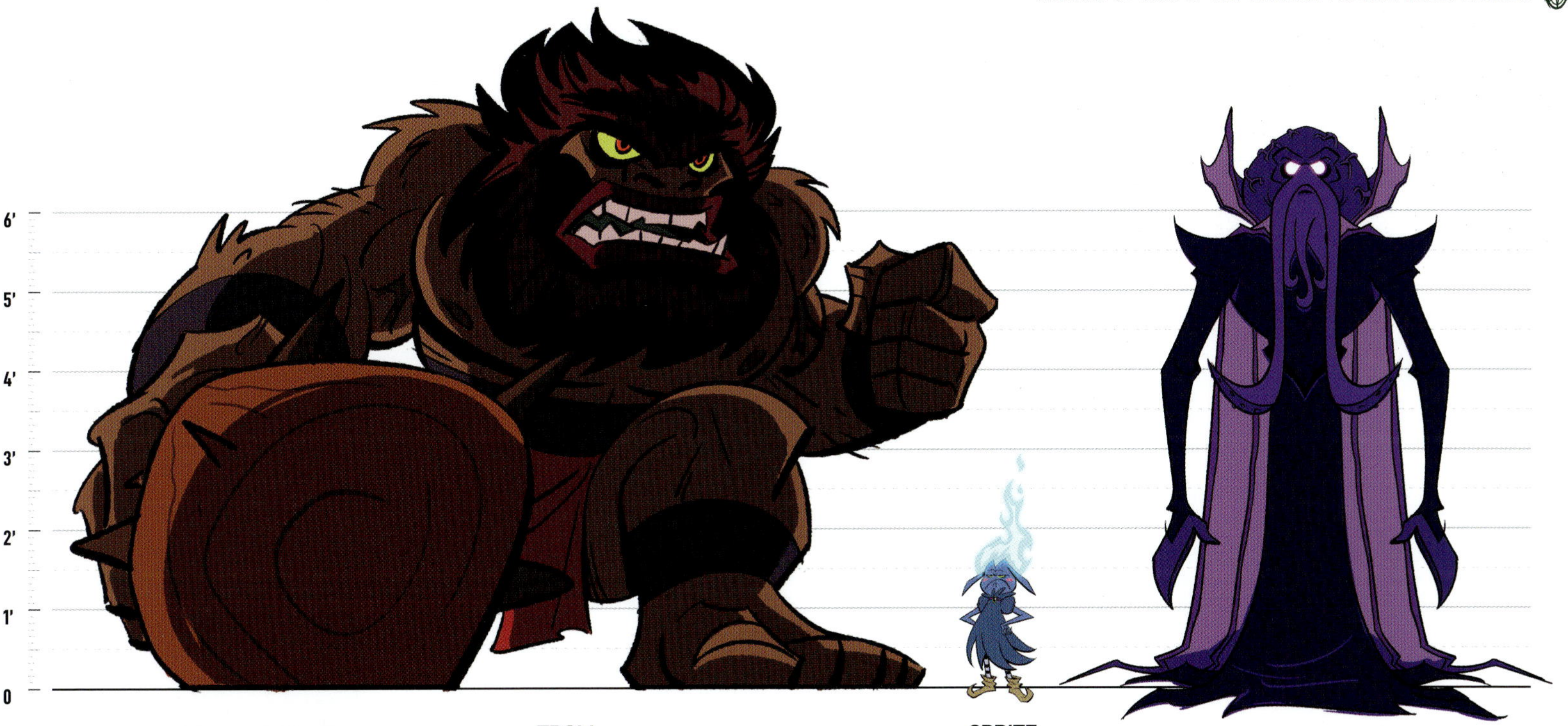

TROLL

SPRITE

CORTEX

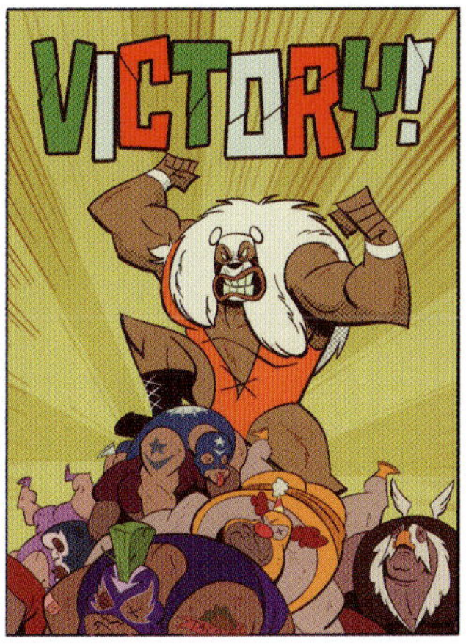

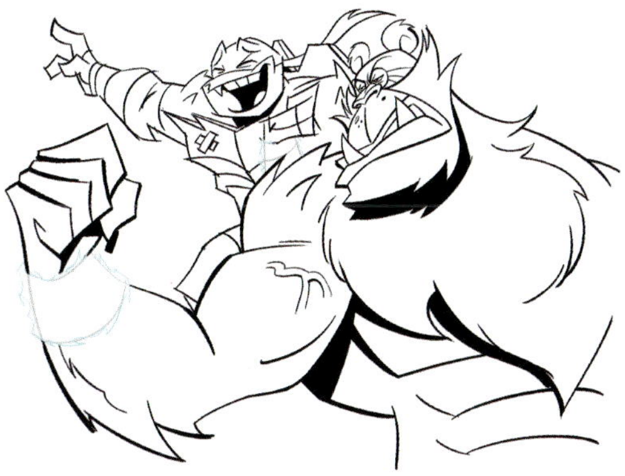

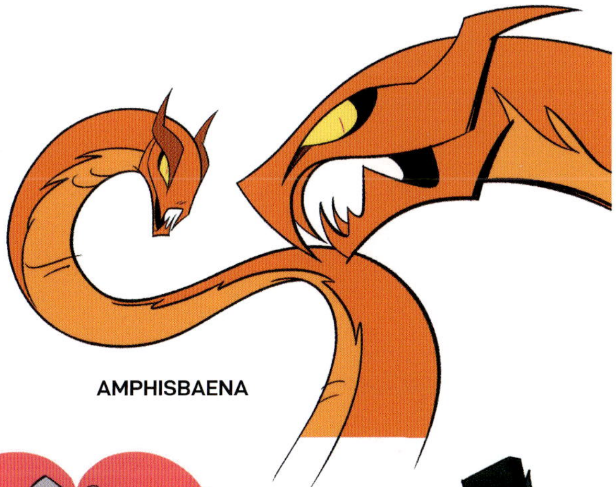

AMPHISBAENA

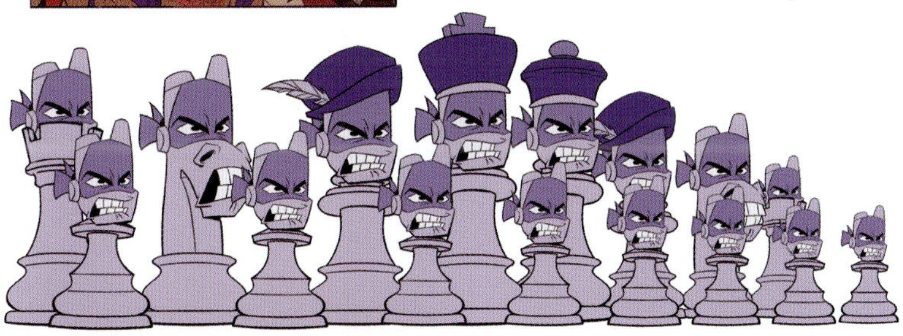

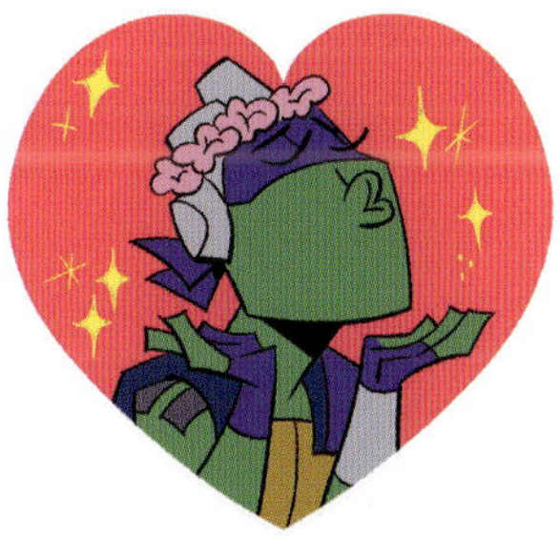

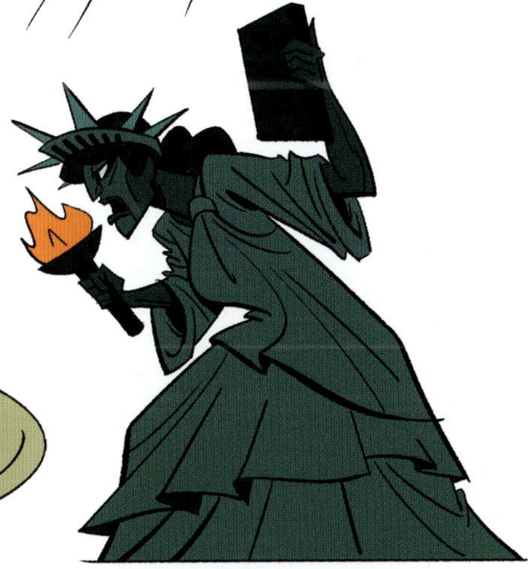

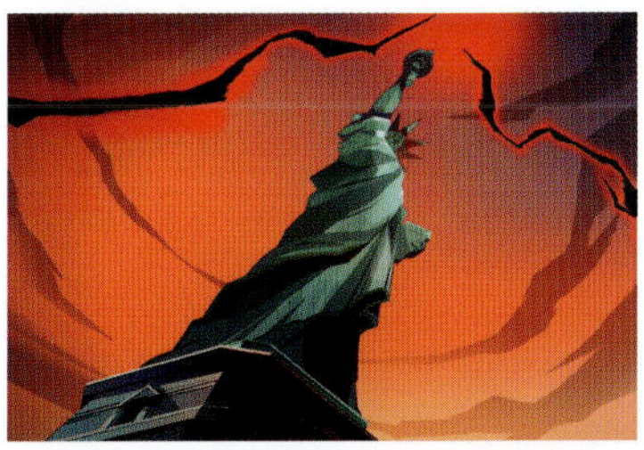

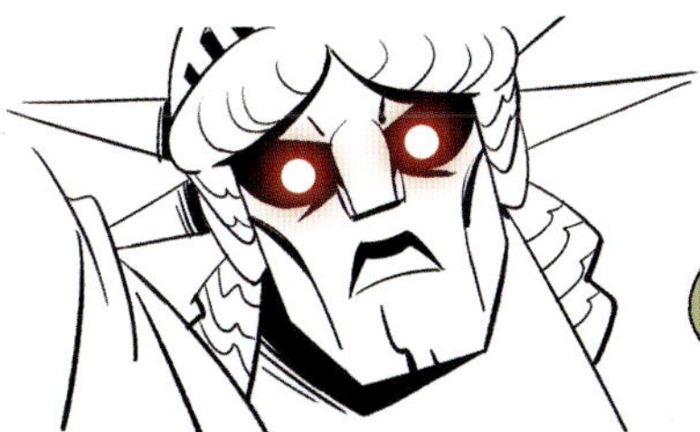

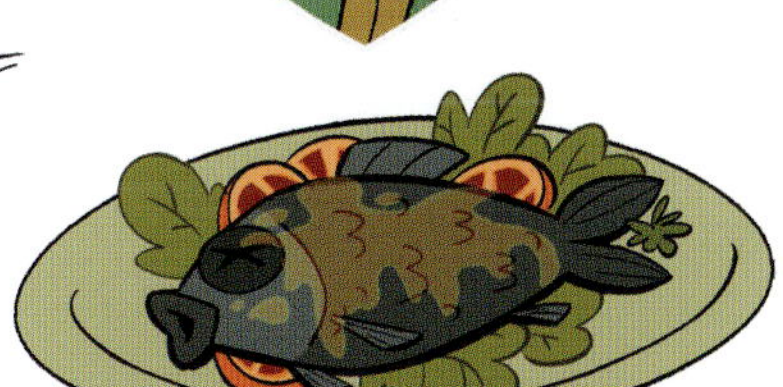

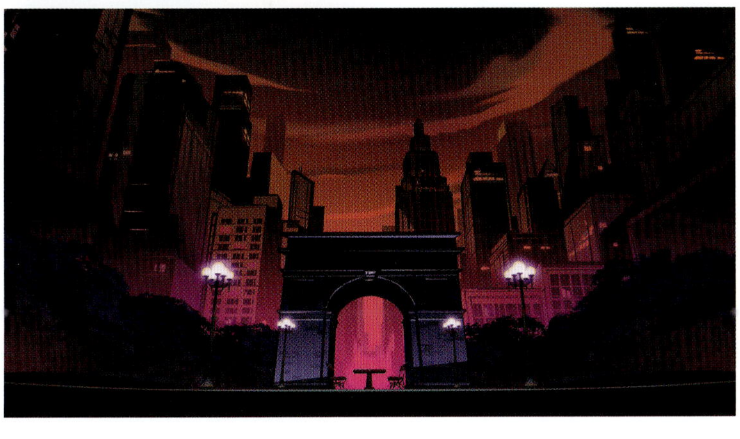

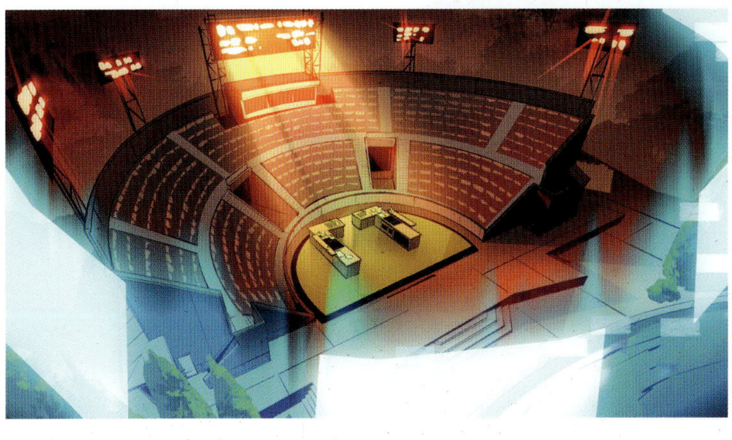

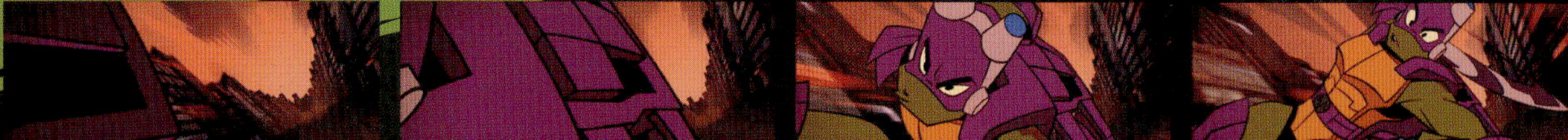

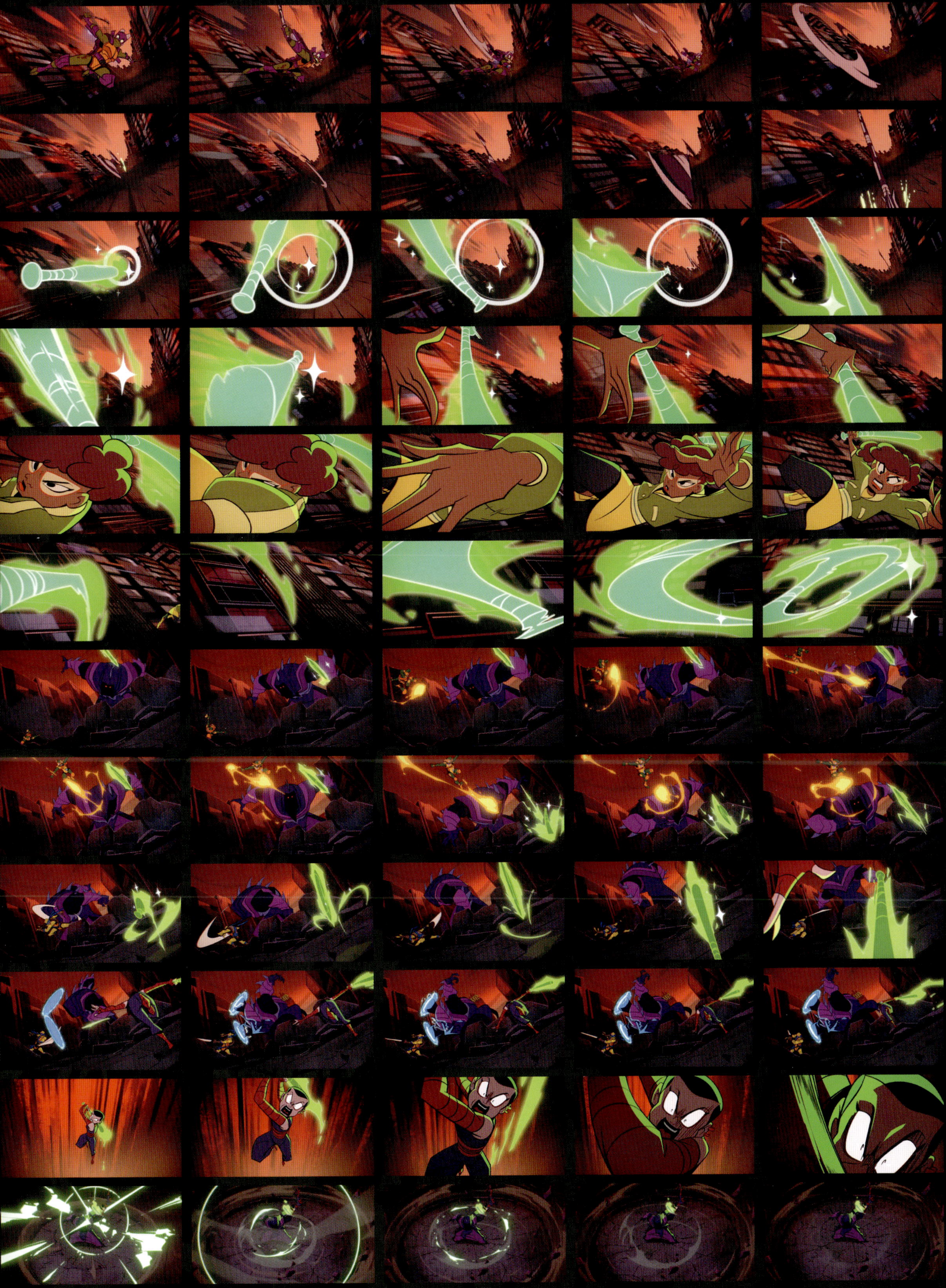

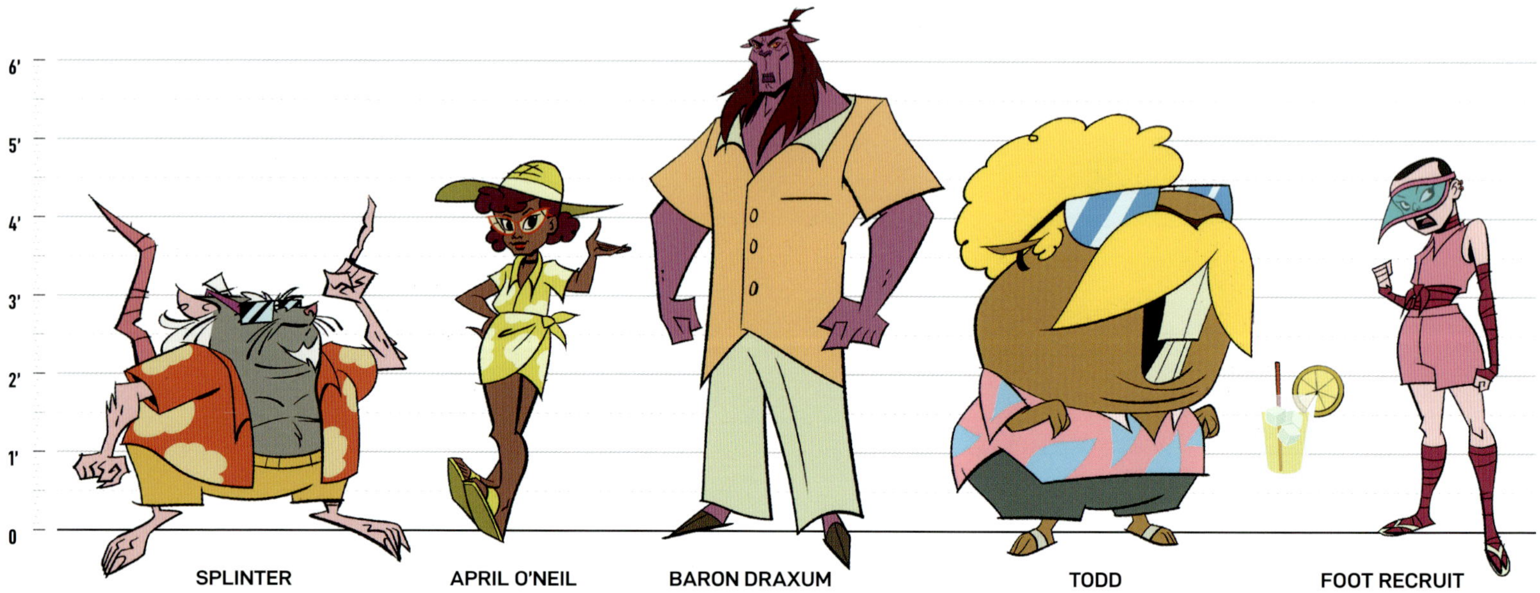
6'
5'
4'
3'
2'
1'
0
SPLINTER
APRIL O'NEIL
BARON DRAXUM
TODD
FOOT RECRUIT

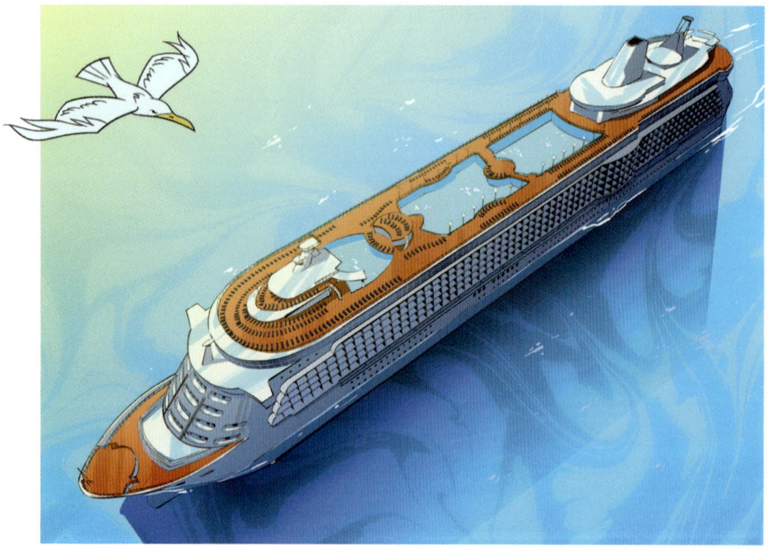

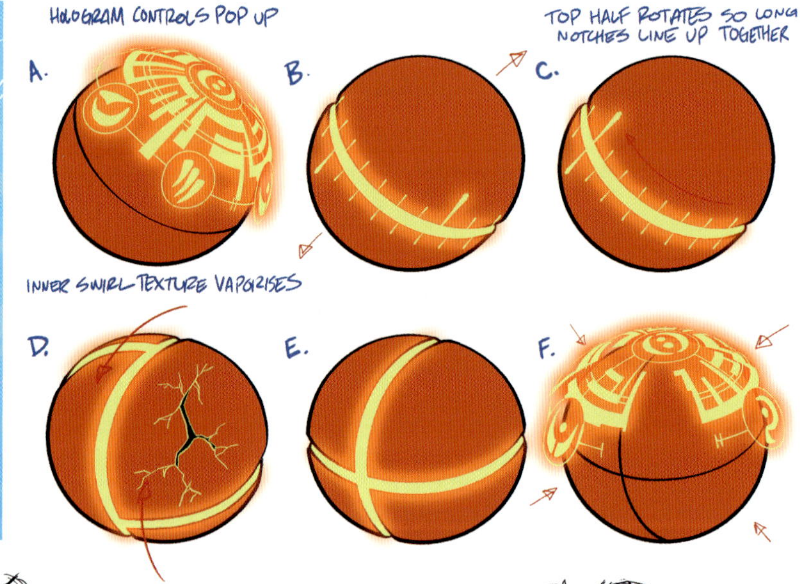
HOLOGRAM CONTROLS POP UP
TOP HALF ROTATES SO LONG NOTCHES LINE UP TOGETHER
A.
B.
C.
INNER SWIRL TEXTURE VAPORISES
D.
E.
F.

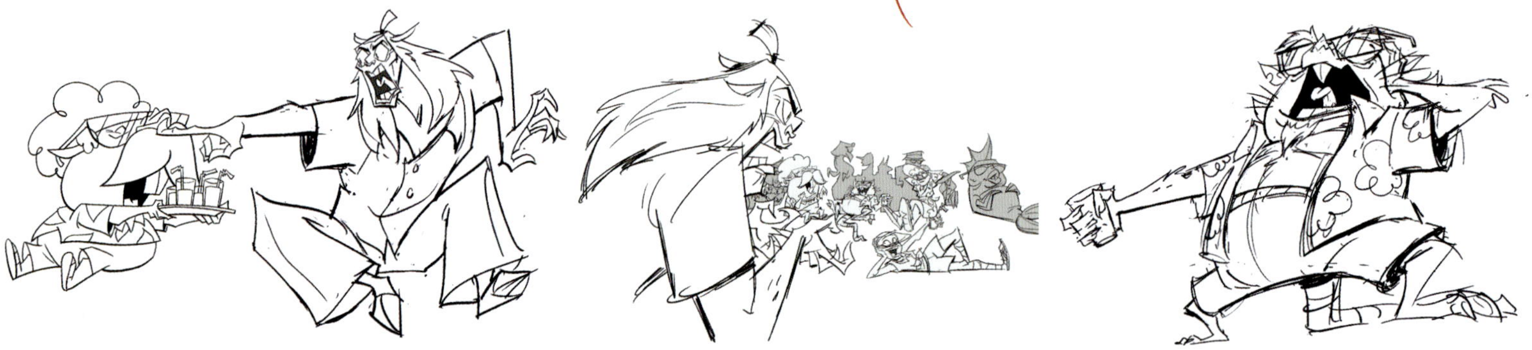

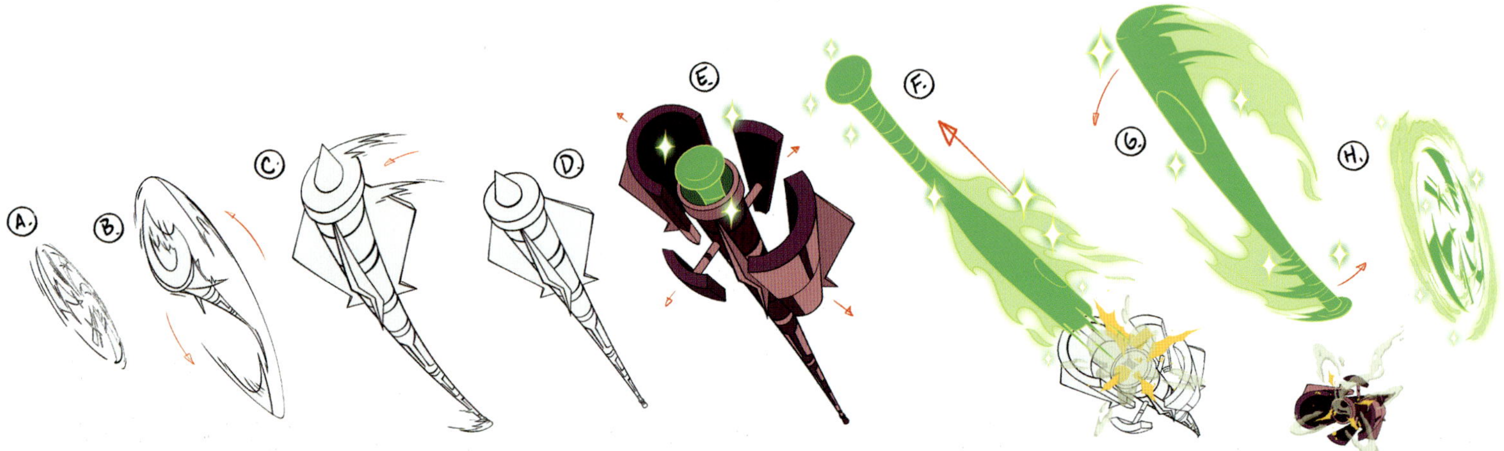
A.
B.
C.
D.
E.
F.
G.
H.

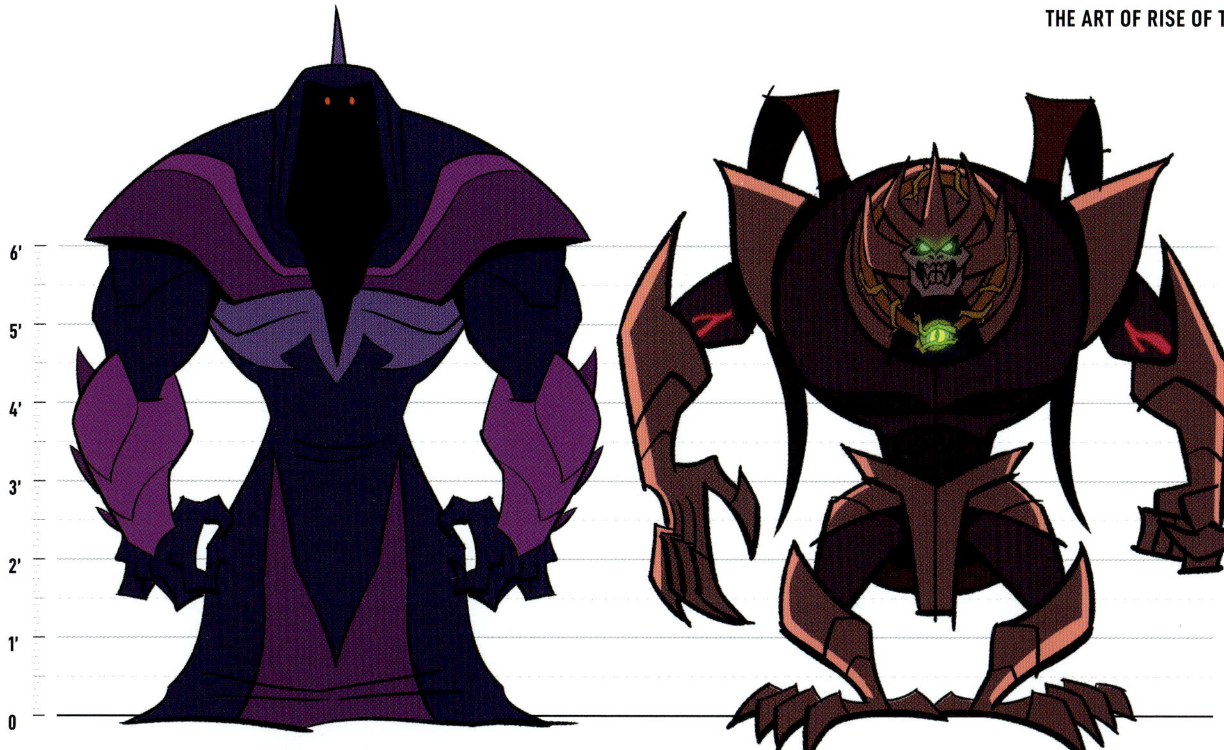

SHADOW FIEND

THE SHREDDER

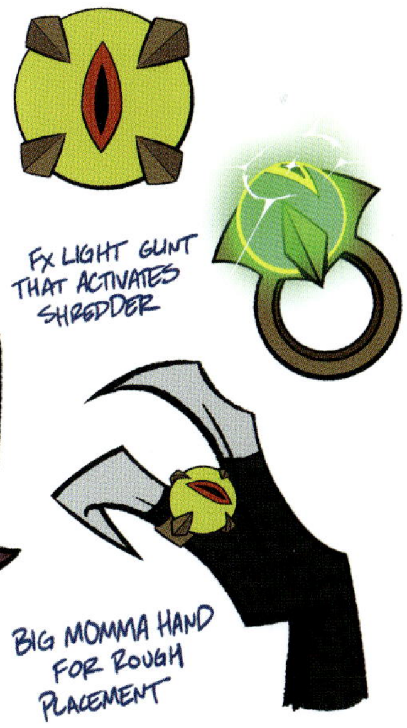

BIG MAMA'S MYSTIC RING

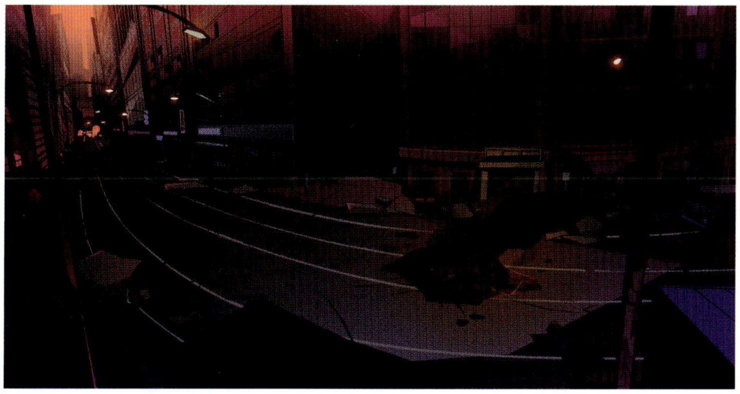

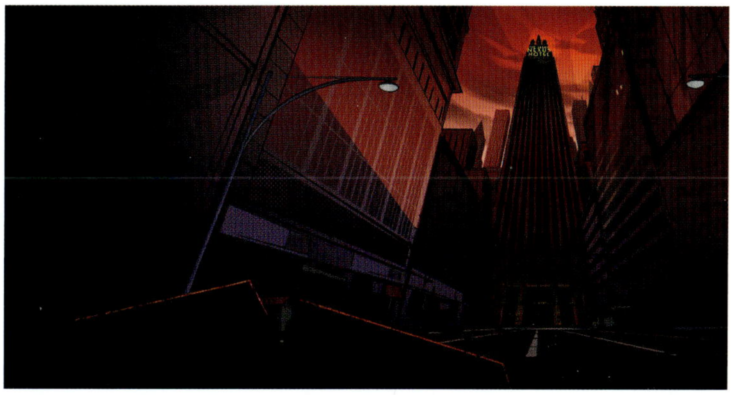

TONY GAMA-LOBO: We blew the budget on voice talent. Usually we were allotted one big villain guest star per episode. This time we had four! *Plus* Big Mama, plus Draxum, plus Foot Recruit, plus Todd! It was a cast of thousands. And they all needed something cool to do.

We started kidnapping villains from the end of episodes long before we figured out what the "Battle Nexus: New York" story was. Originally we were going to have Foot Recruit fight in the Battle Nexus, which is why we kidnapped her at the end of "Always Be Brownies." But then we decided against it. And we kidnapped Meat Sweats without knowing if Lydon was available to record! Really flew by the seat of our shells on this one.

I really loved the orb and the mystic kidnapping powers. I wish I knew what came first—the board artists kidnapping Meat Sweats with creepy shadow hands or Andy and the art team designing Orb with creepy shadow hands.

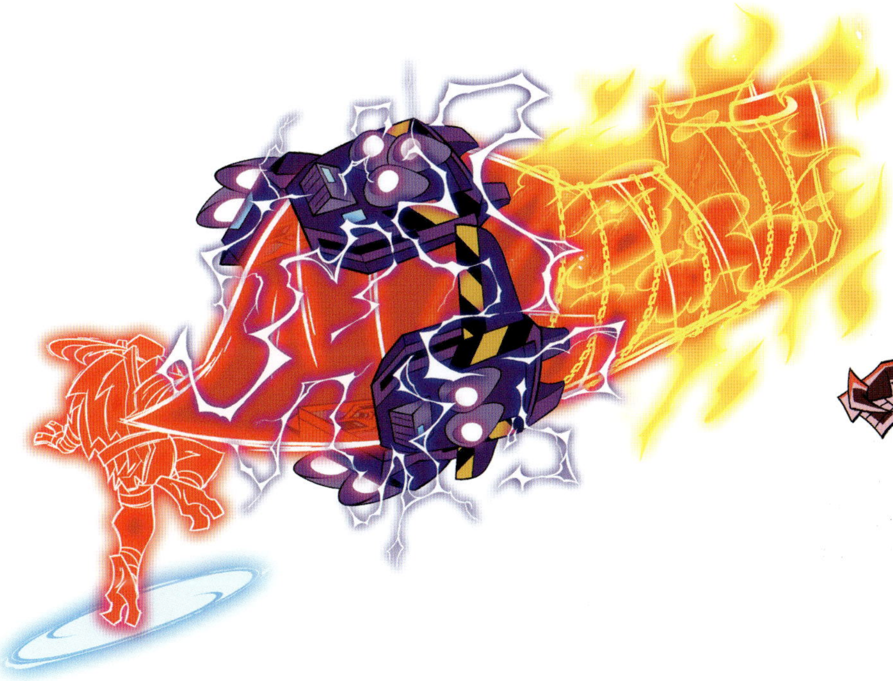

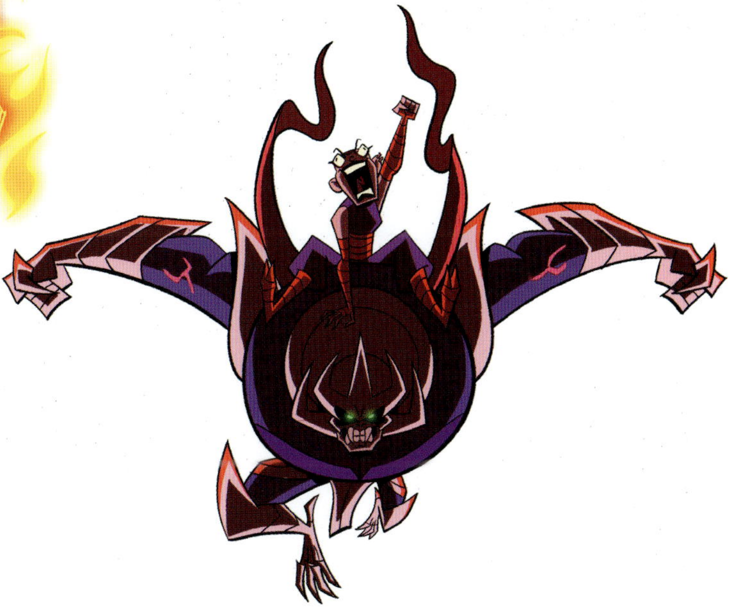

FINALE PART 1: E-TURTLE SUNSHINE OF THE SPOTLESS MIND

ORIGINAL AIR DATE: AUGUST 7, 2020
PRODUCTION CODE: 101

WRITTEN BY **JOSH RILEY BROWN**
STORYBOARDS BY **MAX COLLINS, SHELDON VELLA**
DIRECTED BY **SEBASTIAN MONTES**

JOSH RILEY BROWN: The big story with this episode was that we had an opportunity to end the show with an epic four-part finale but with a catch: We had to write each episode in one-fourth of the time of our normal schedule. We quickly fell behind, so to get us back on track (and prove I really wanted to write more *Rise* episodes), I pulled an all-nighter and wrote the first draft of "E-Turtle" in one night.

Luckily, a lot of the pieces of the story had been in the air for a while—including the concept of going inside Splinter's mind, which had been pitched originally as part of the season 1 finale. We also knew we wanted to explore Lou Jitsu's distant relationship to the Hamato Clan and why he didn't finish his training. Somewhere in the writing process (around 4:00 a.m. or so), the episode coalesced into the story of a young Hamato Yoshi turning his back on his clan because their sacred mission took his mother away from him. It was this one painful moment from his childhood that drove him away from his Hamato responsibilities. From there, the room took my fever dream of a rough draft and workshopped it into a proper start to our big finale.

I believe it was Dale who pitched the title "E-Turtle Sunshine of the Spotless Mind." I think he meant it as a joke, but we all loved it. The Turtles also reference another movie, *Inception* (2010), when they talk about Splinter's mind protecting itself *"like in that movie."*

TONY GAMA-LOBO: Shredder finally being resurrected still gives me chills. *"I am free!"* The voice actor, Hoon Lee, was the voice of Splinter in the 2012 series. Felt like a fun nod to the fans.

CARL BEU: I think we entered the finale as unprepared as our characters, yet just like them we defied the odds and rose to the challenge, riding the momentum of our incredible crew to what felt both like a finish line and a new starting point...because this story has always been about the rise, and this moment was only the end of the beginning!

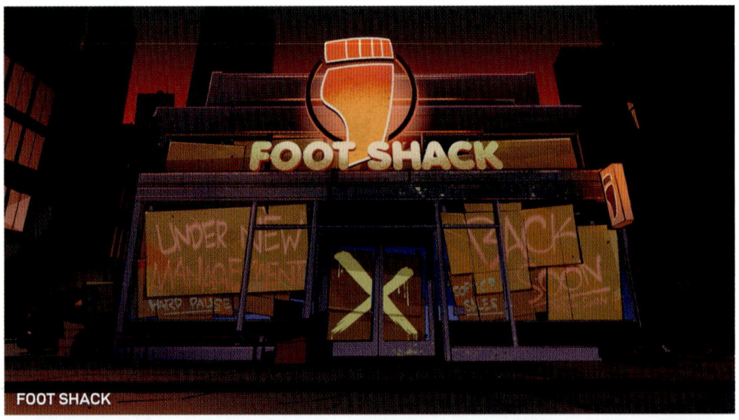

FOOT SHACK

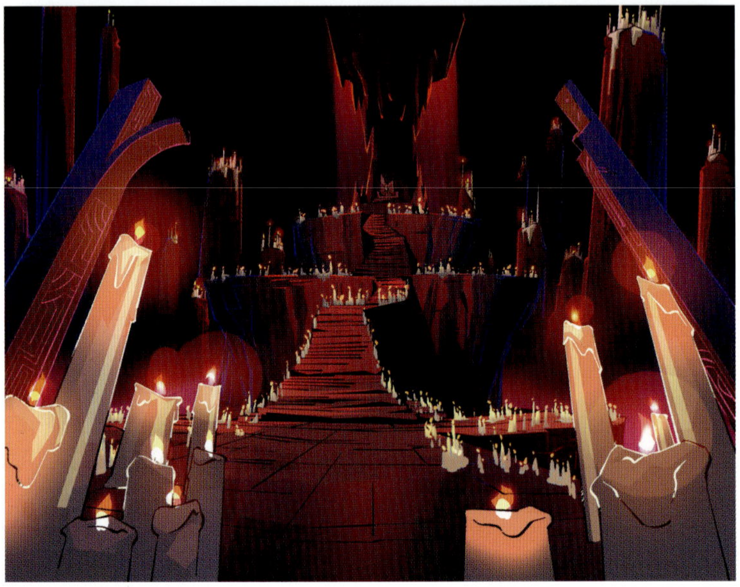

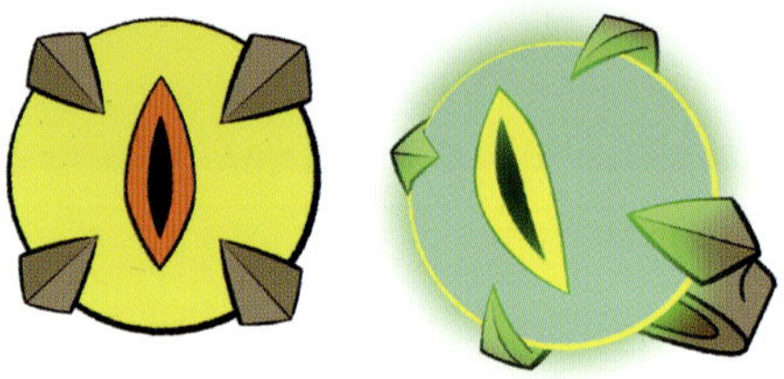

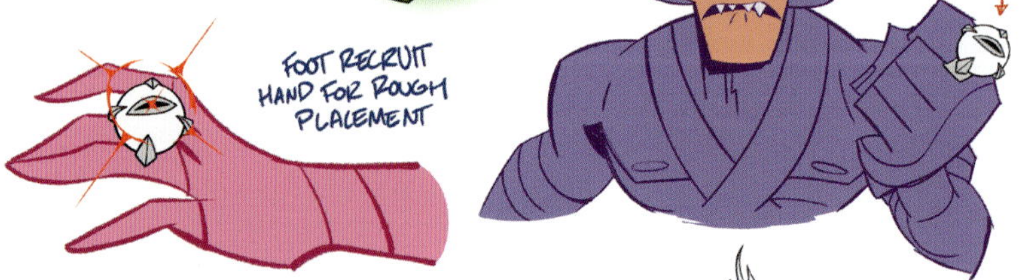

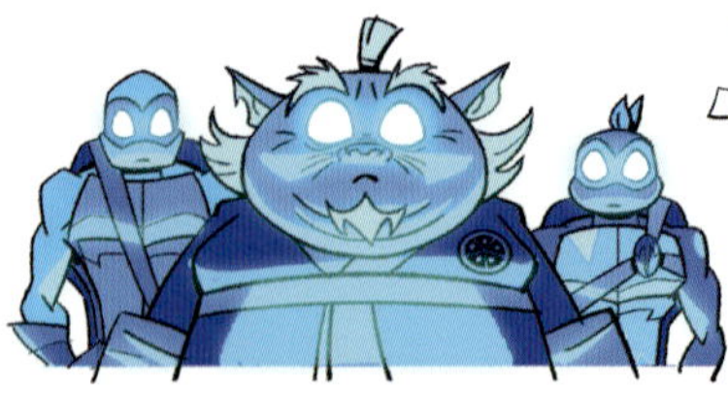

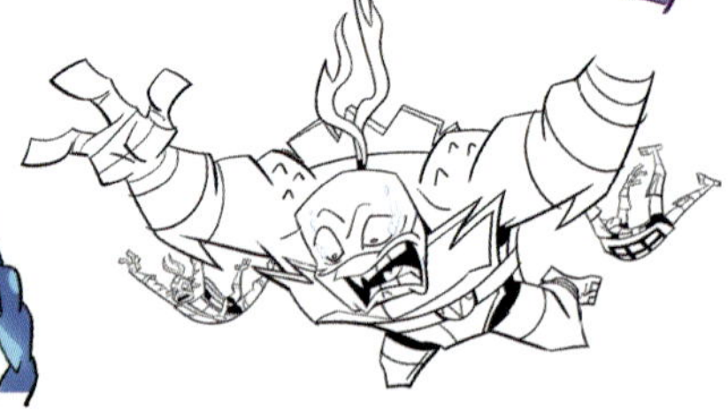

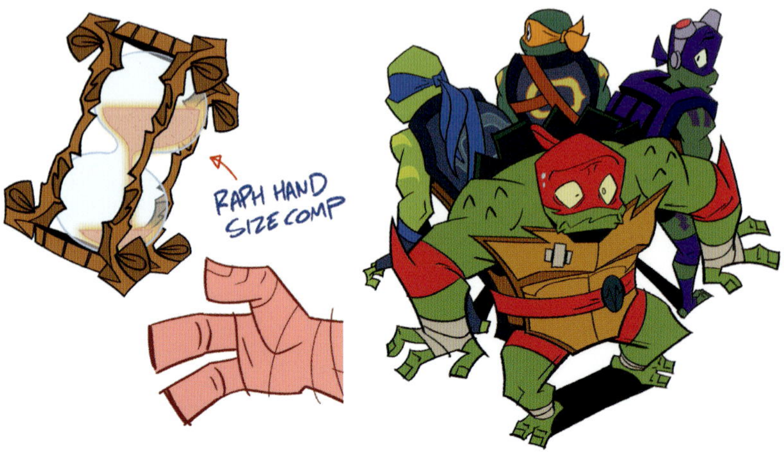

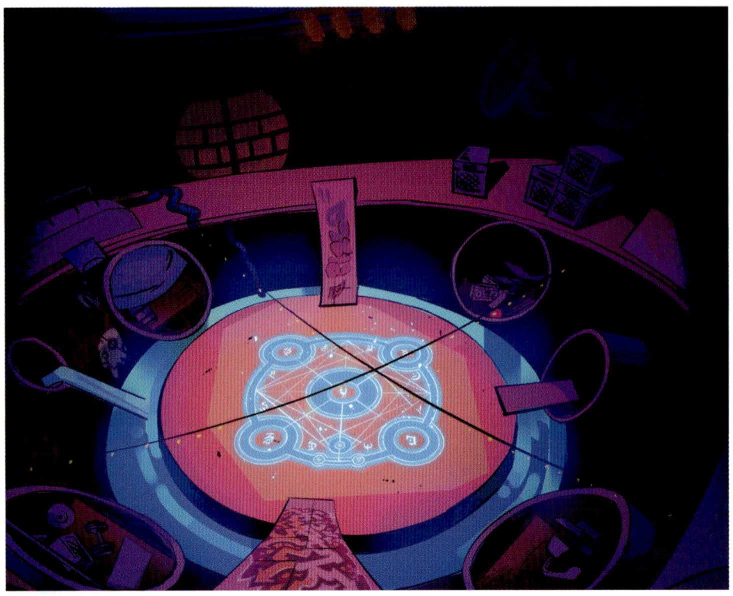

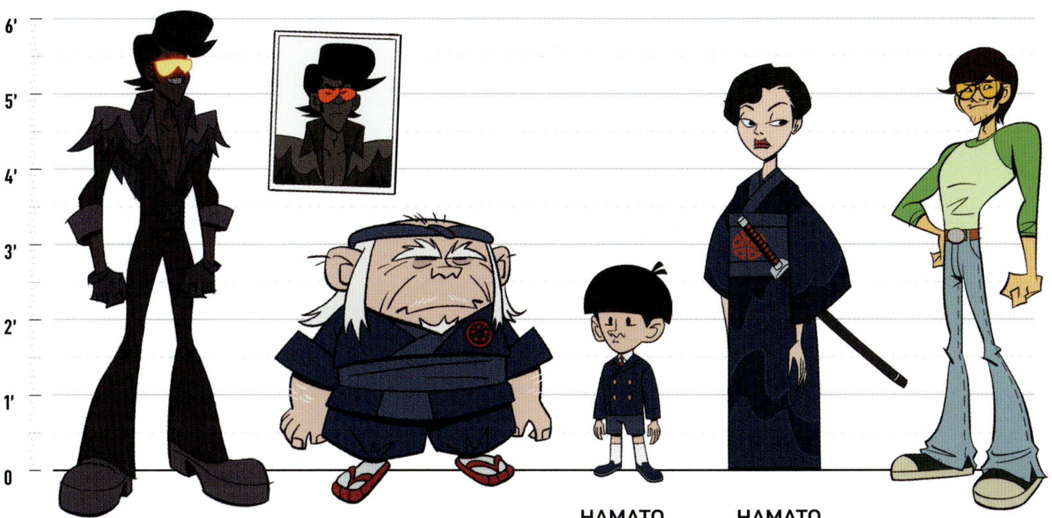

NEGA LOU JITSU

HAMATO SHO
YOSHI'S GRANDFATHER

HAMATO YOSHI
CHILD

HAMATO ATSUKO
YOSHI'S MOTHER

HAMATO YOSHI
TEEN

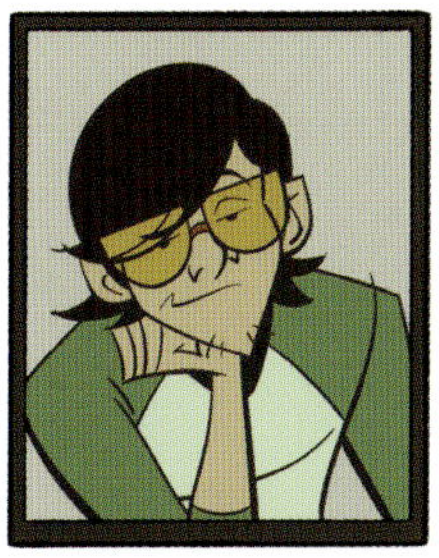

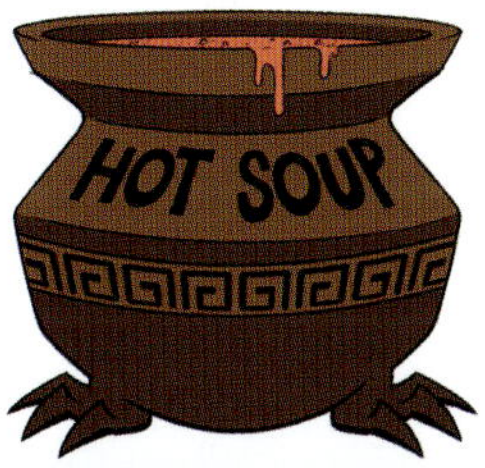

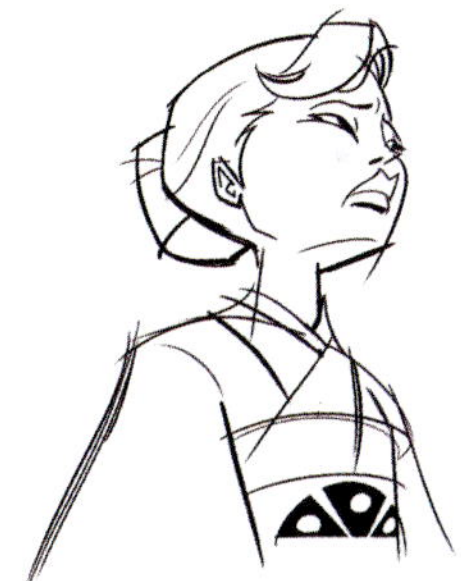

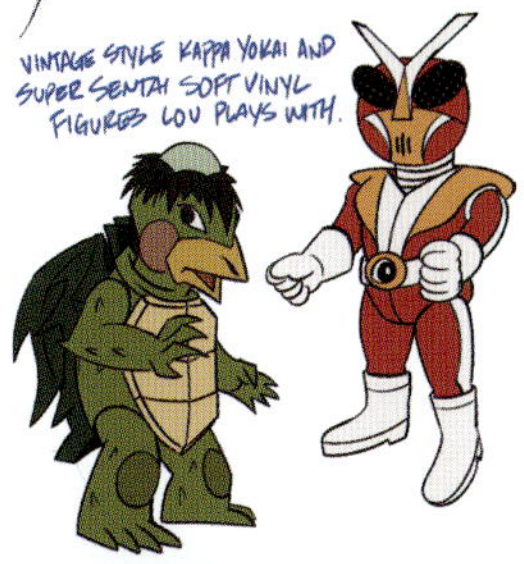

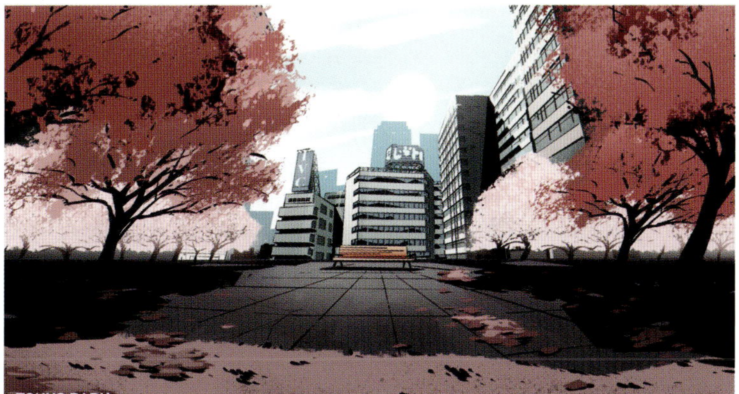
TOKYO PARK

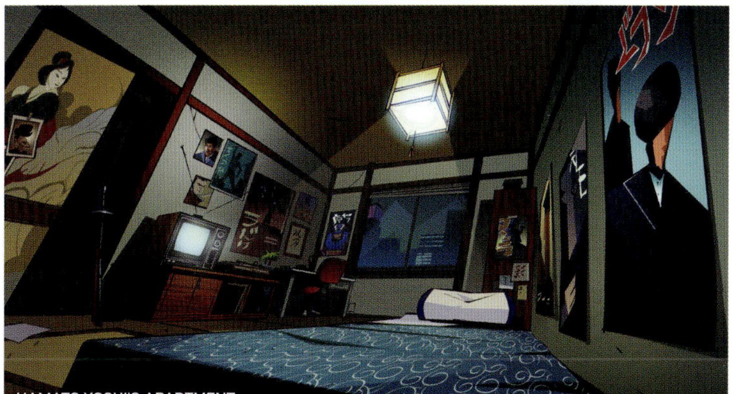
HAMATO YOSHI'S APARTMENT

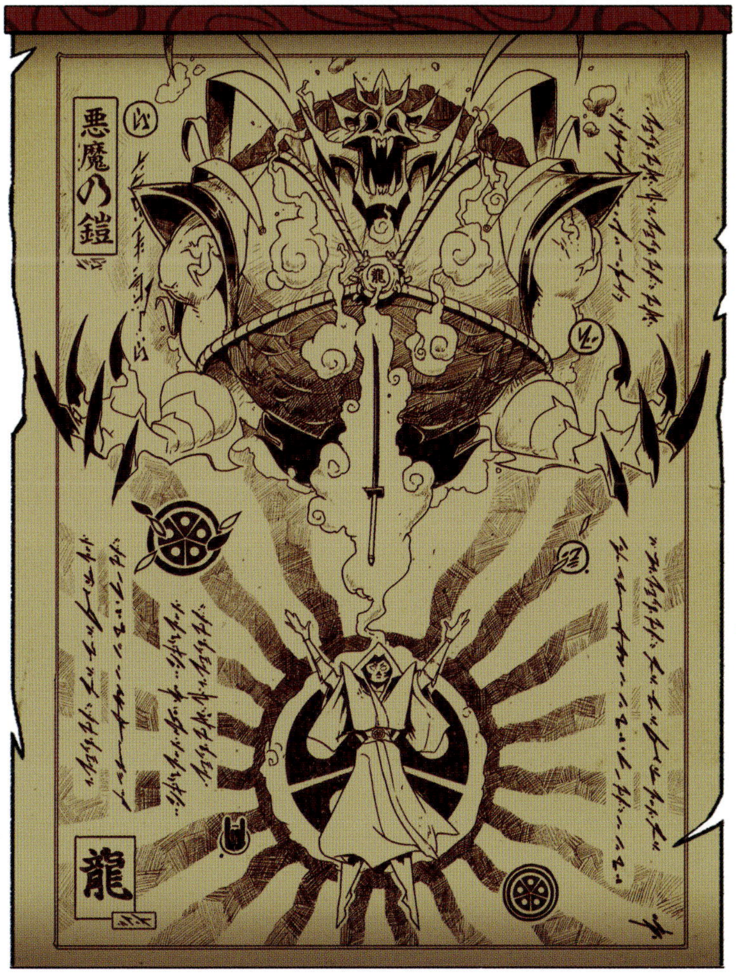

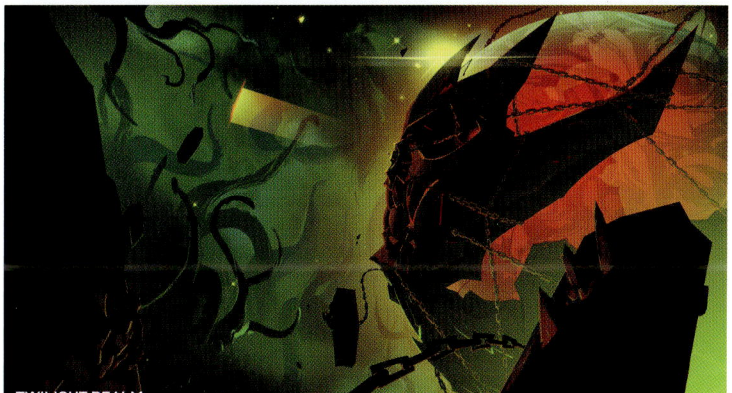
TWILIGHT REALM

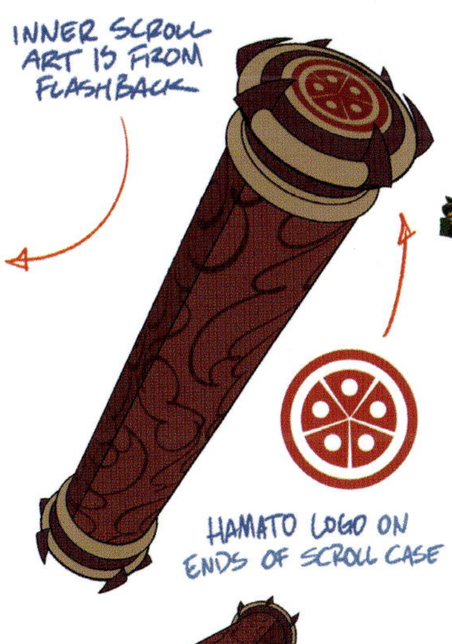

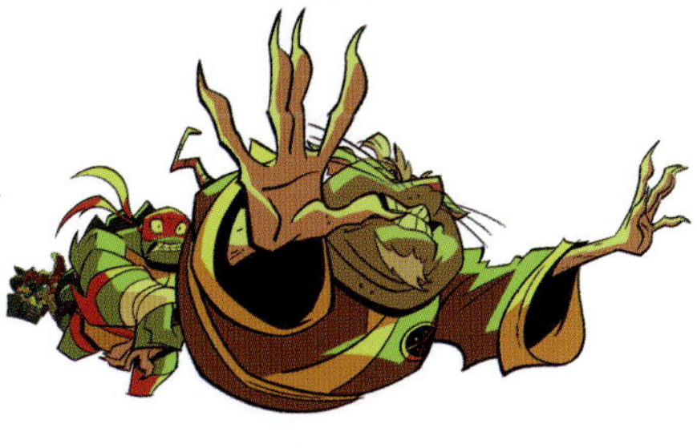

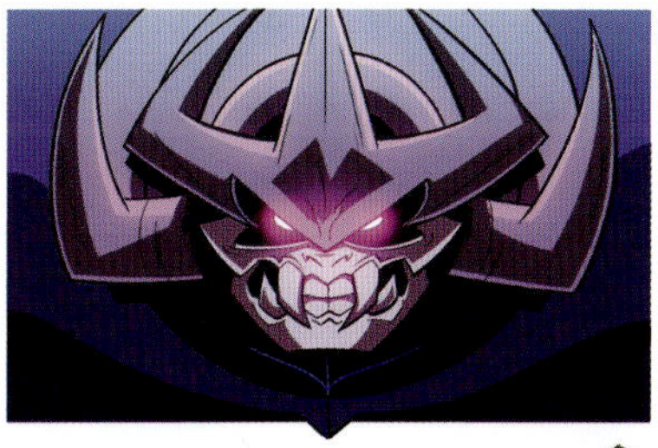

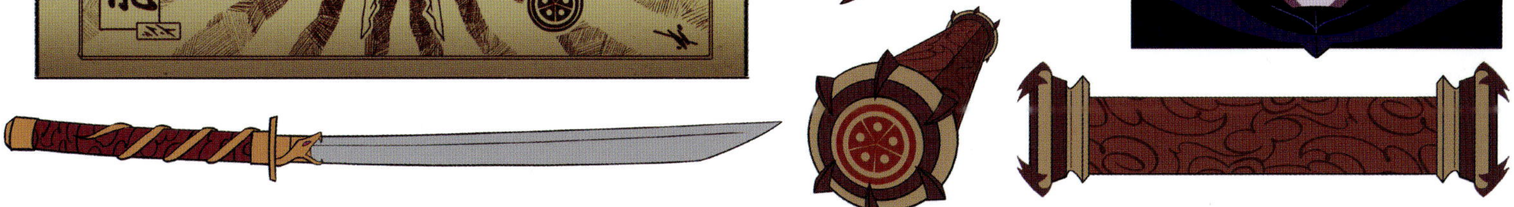

FINALE PART 2:
SHREDDY OR NOT

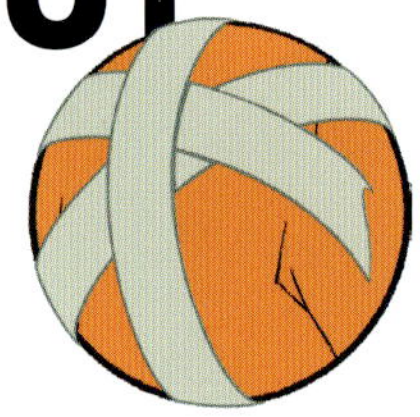

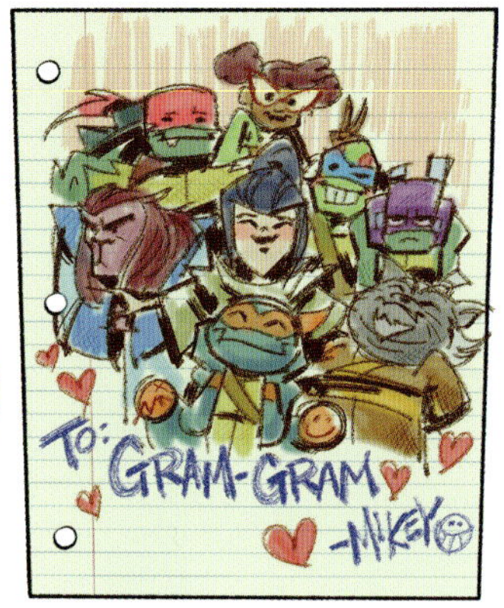

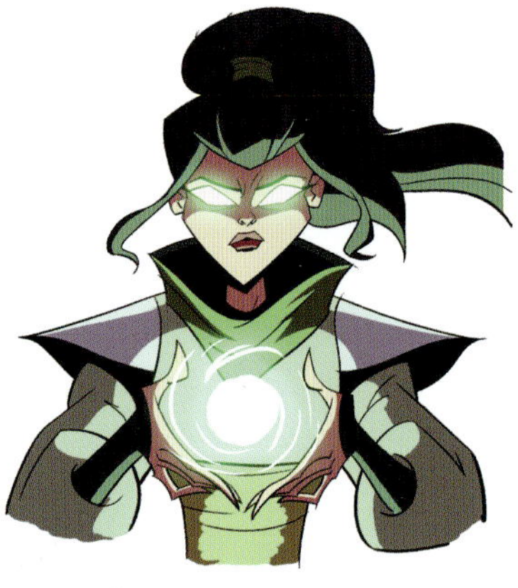

ORIGINAL AIR DATE: AUGUST 7, 2020
PRODUCTION CODE: 102

WRITTEN BY **JOSH RILEY BROWN**
STORYBOARDS BY **MAX COLLINS, MORGAN HILLEBRAND, CASSEY KUO, CHRISTINE LIU, SHELDON VELLA**
DIRECTED BY **JJ CONWAY**

JOSH RILEY BROWN: We were still moving at a breakneck pace when it was time to write part two of the finale, so I wrote the first draft of this one over a weekend. By that Monday, this episode was truly an "all hands on deck" situation, with everyone from the board artists to Ant pitching ideas and elements of the story.

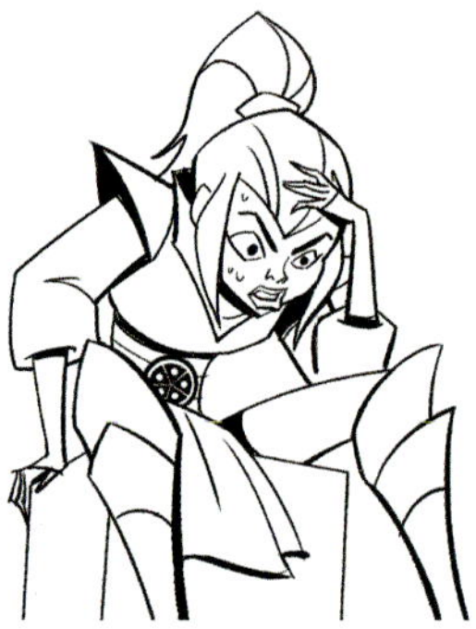

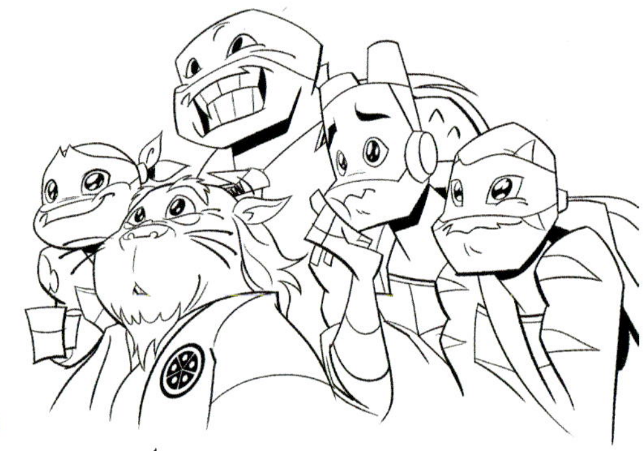

Initially, I wrote Karai as a much more severe character, but the episode really started to click when the room pitched the idea of her as the Turtles' beloved "Gram-Gram." The notion of the four brothers competing for the love of their long-lost maternal figure really made the story feel specific to the *Rise* Turtles. Beyond that, we knew we wanted this episode to be our *Empire Strikes Back* (1980) with Shredder finally at full power and the Turtles at their lowest point ever. It was the storyboard team who really pulled the final sequence together with the Turtles losing their weapons, their home, and their new mother figure.

In Karai's backstory, we learn that her father was granted the Dark Armor from what she believed to be a Japanese oni. It's clear that the creature is actually an alien Krang. After two seasons of keeping Shredder at bay in some form or another, it was so satisfying finally seeing him unleash his full strength and hear his true voice.

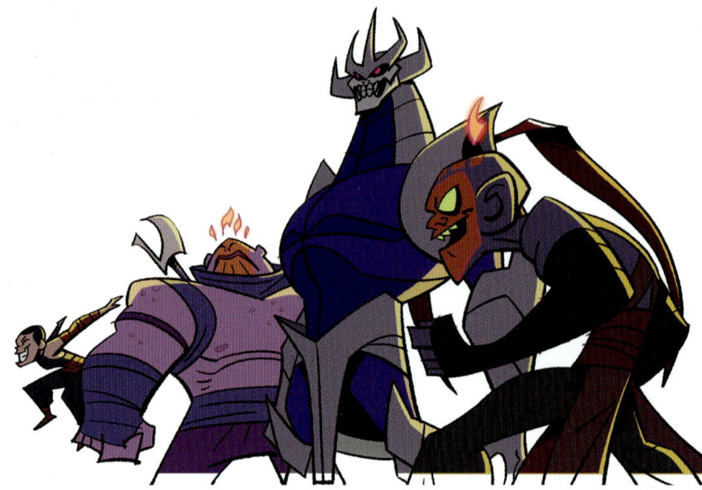

I'm 80 percent sure the concept of the leaking orb was an excuse for us to include Todd in the finale.

TONY GAMA-LOBO: S.H.E.L.L.D.O.N. taking the form of a robot turtle was our nod to Metalhead, a longtime TMNT character. Incredible idea by the director JJ Conway. I thought the direction of this episode was breathtaking—JJ Conway did some mind-bending action while never forgetting the emotional stakes of every single moment. Leo turning back to give his Gram-Gram one last hug before he portals into the heat of the battle makes me cry every time.

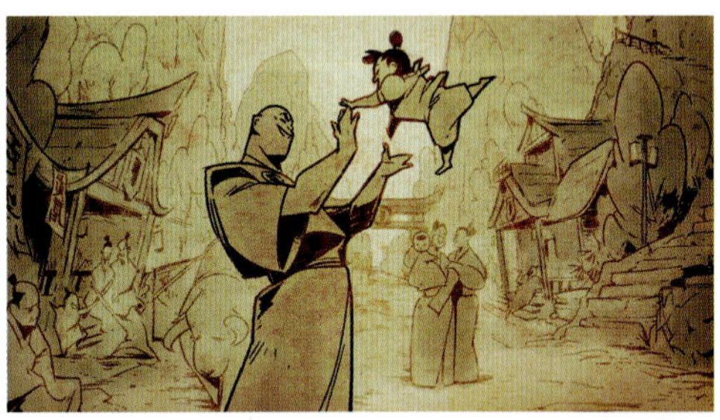

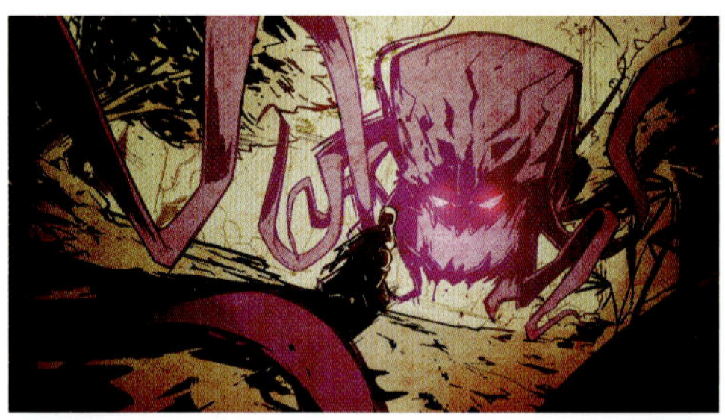

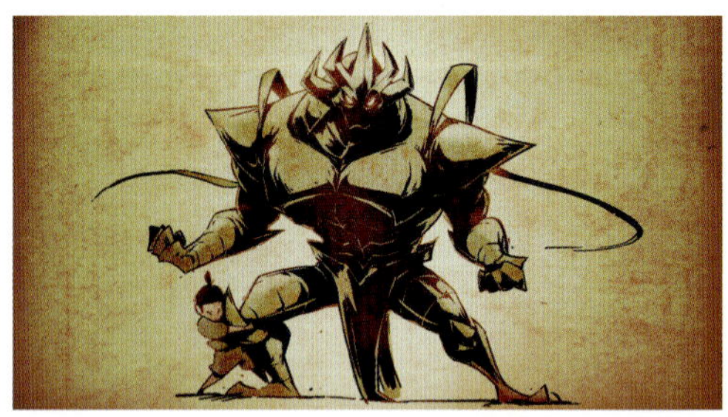

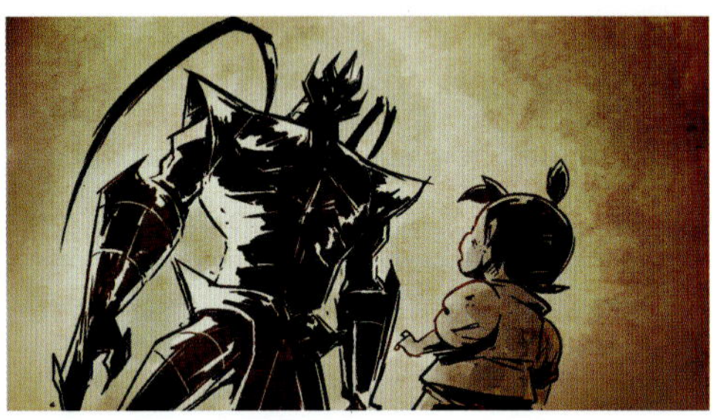

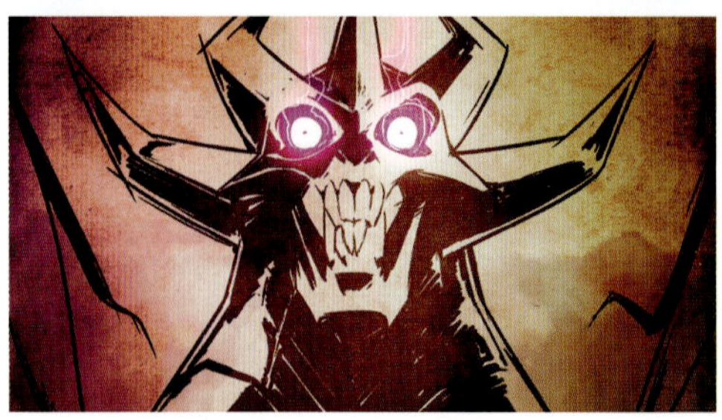

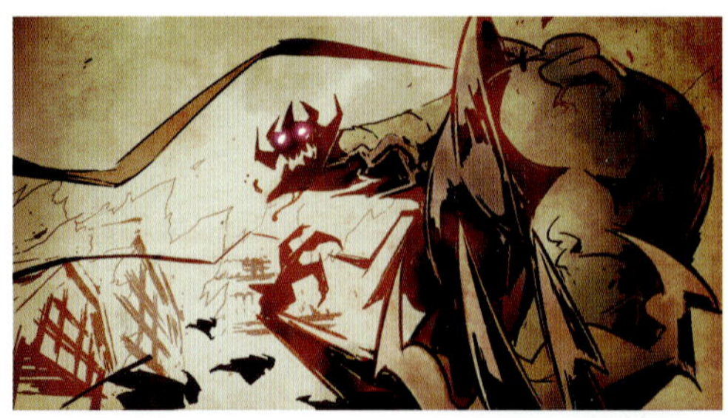

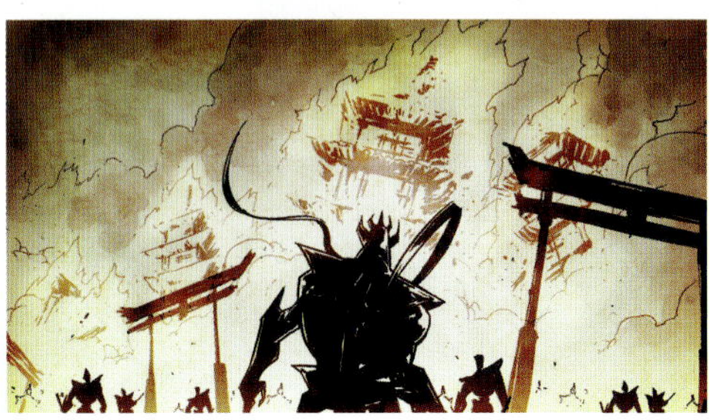

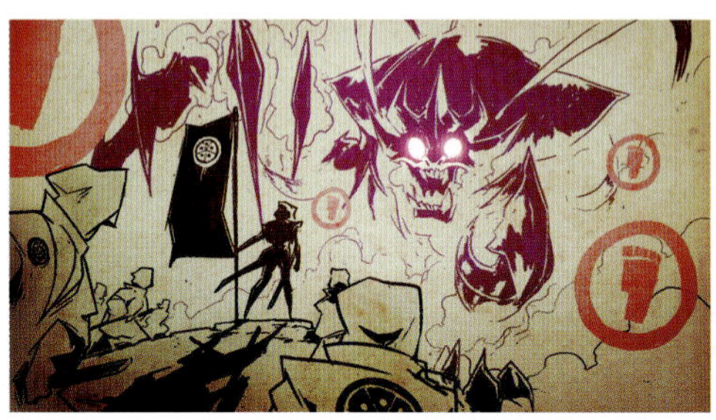

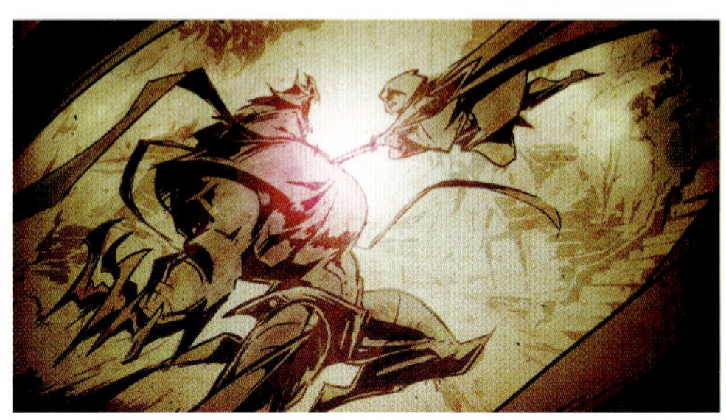

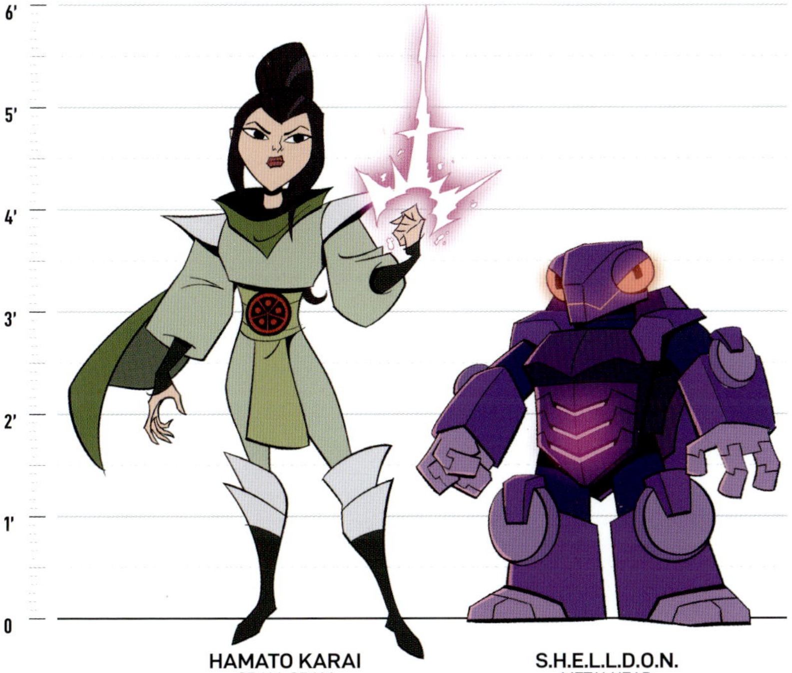

HAMATO KARAI
GRAM-GRAM

S.H.E.L.L.D.O.N.
METALHEAD

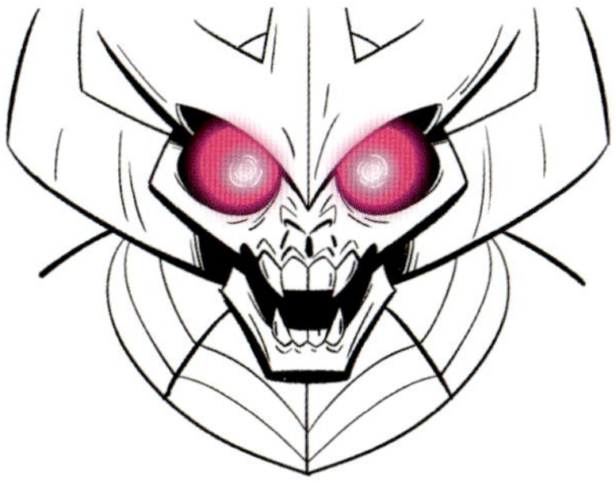

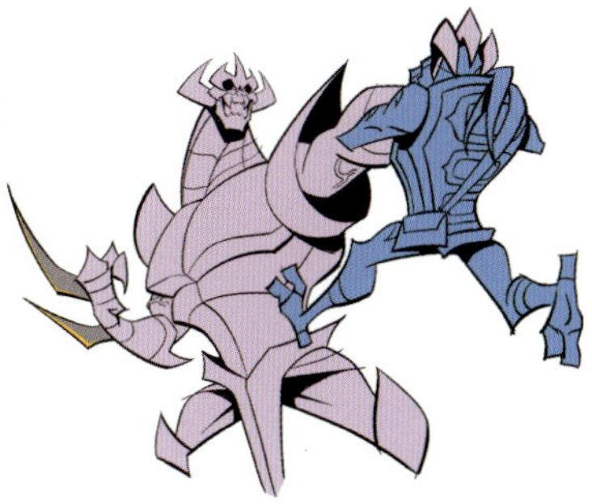

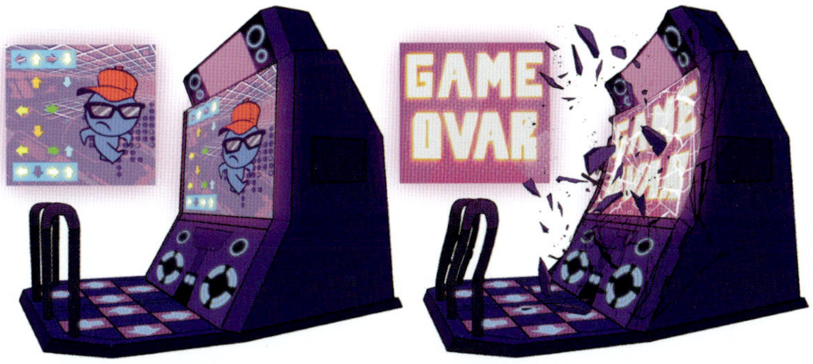

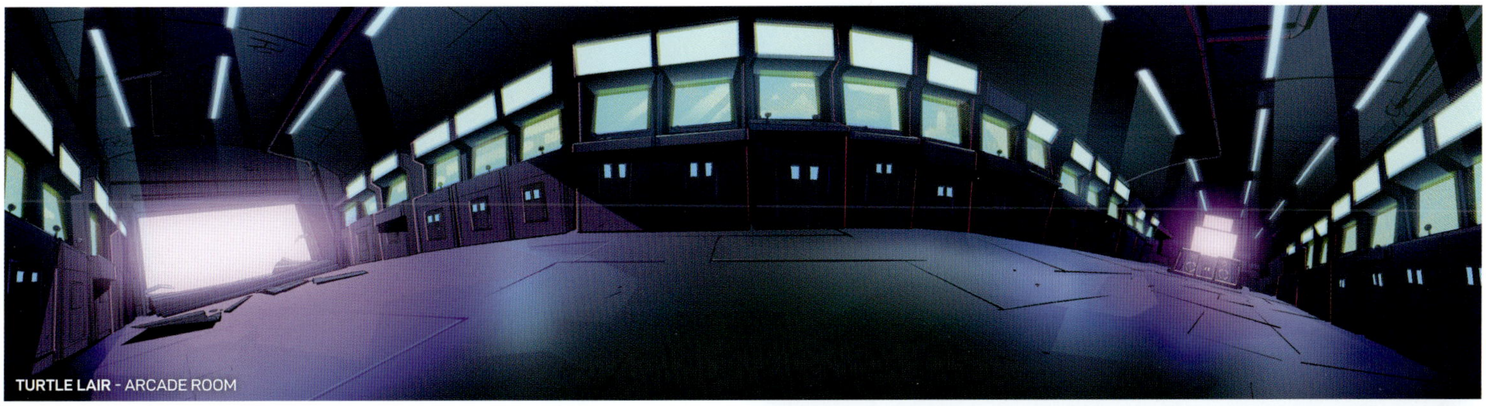

TURTLE LAIR - ARCADE ROOM

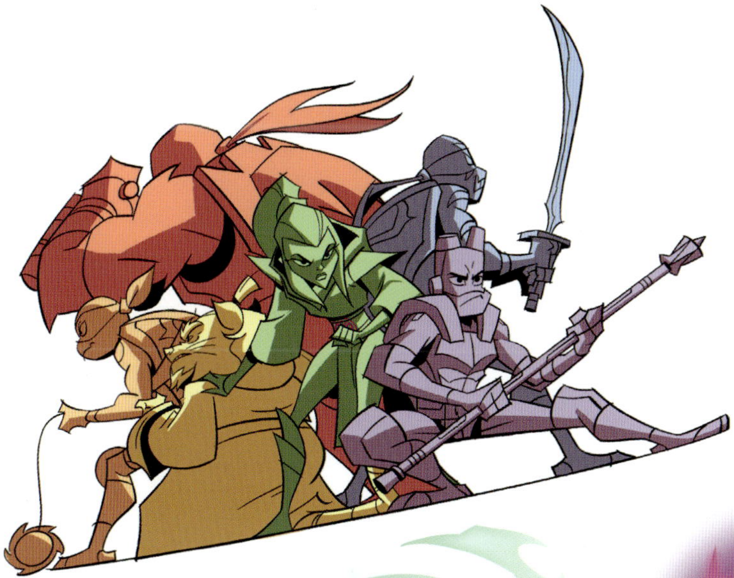

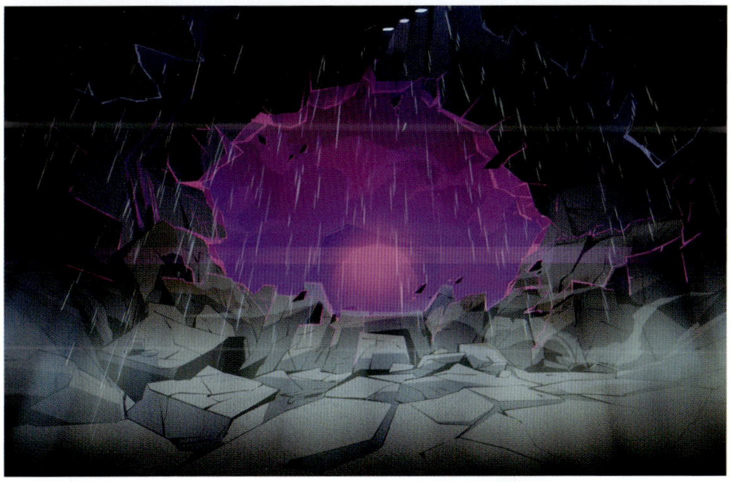

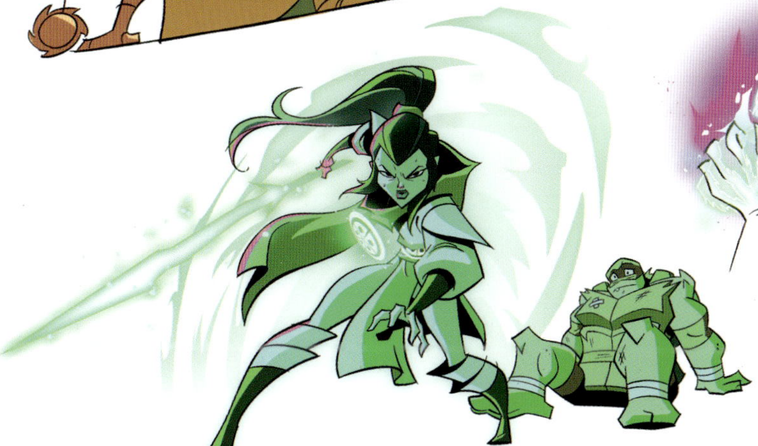

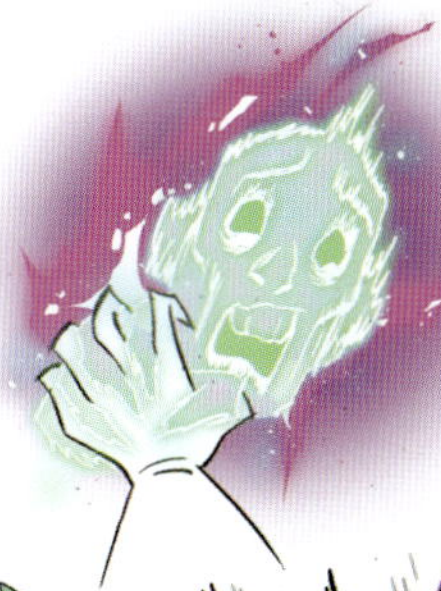

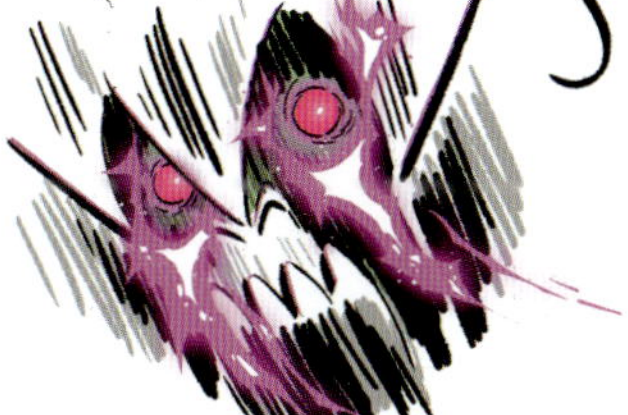

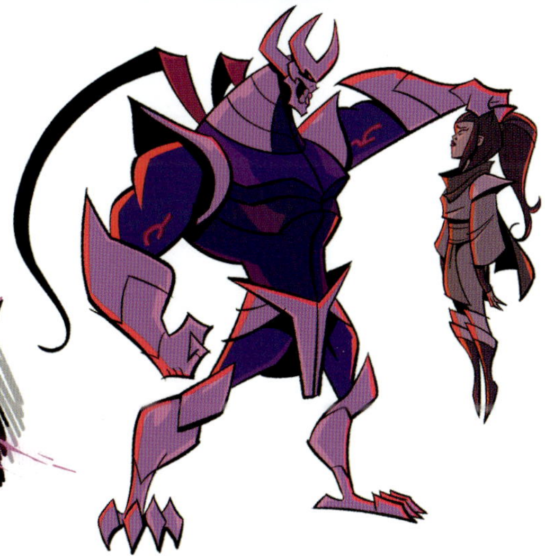

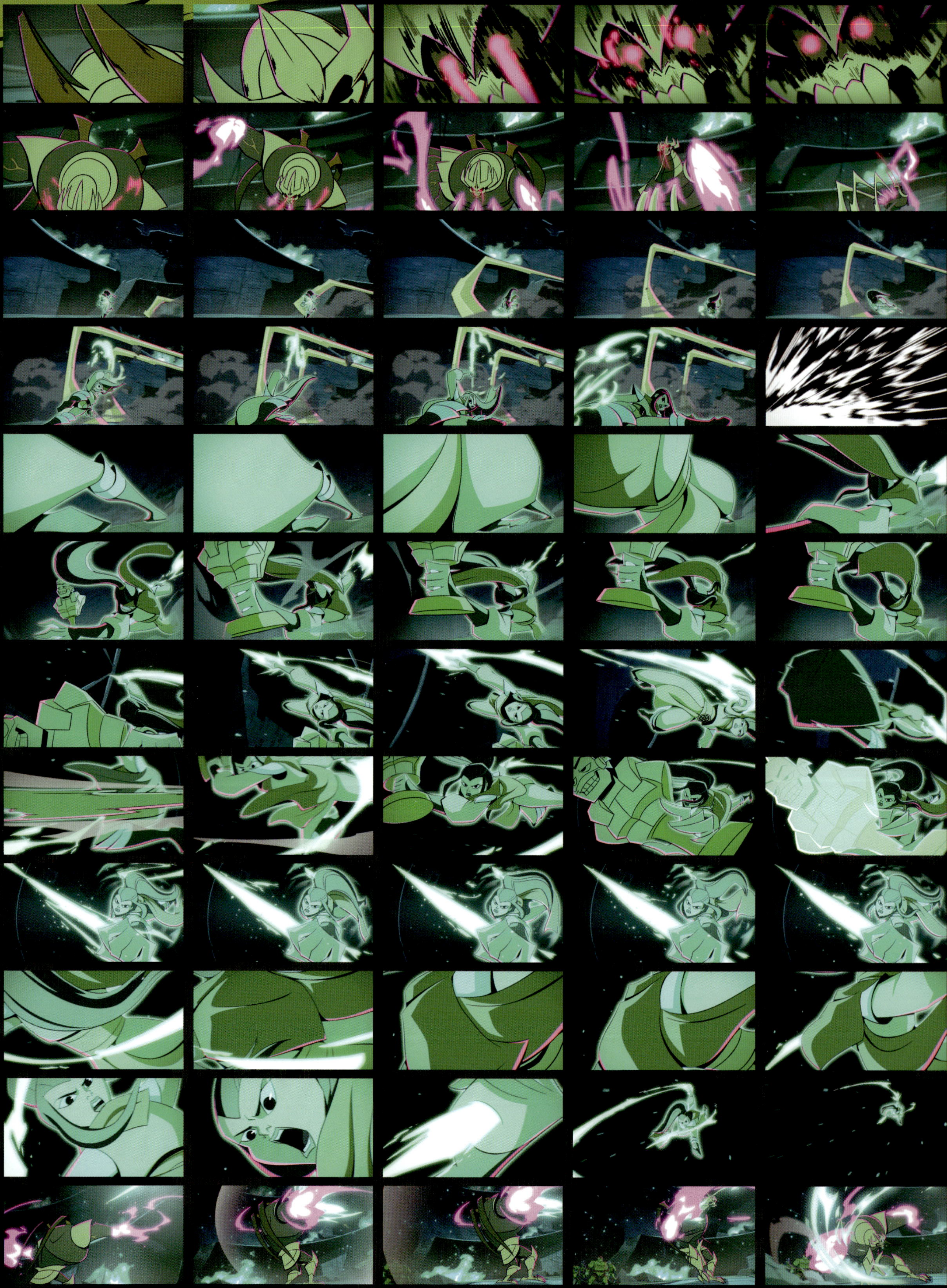

STORYBOARD ARTIST: **CHRISTOPHER LUC**

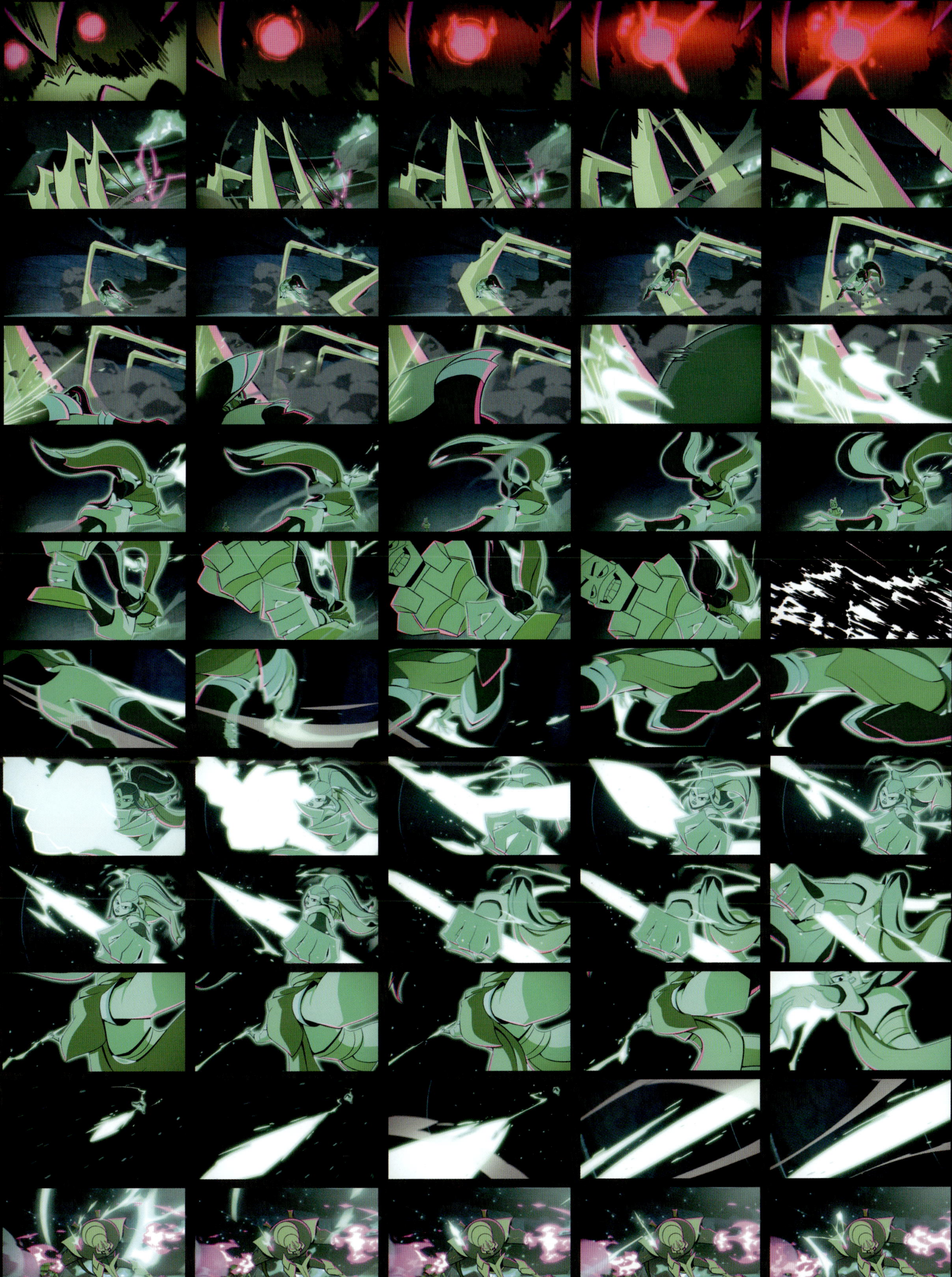

FINALE PART 3: ANATAWA HITORIJANAI

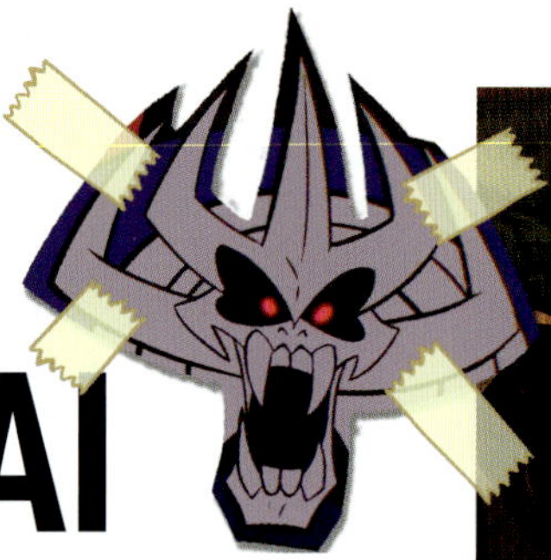

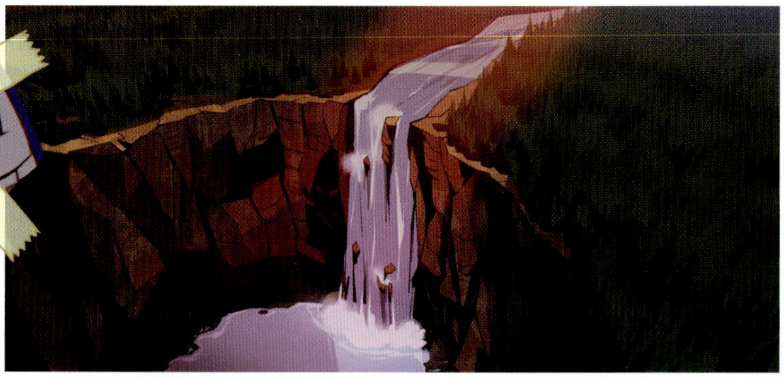

ORIGINAL AIR DATE: AUGUST 7, 2020
PRODUCTION CODE: 103

WRITTEN BY **RUSS CARNEY, RON CORCILLO, TONY GAMA-LOBO, DALE MALINOWSKI, JOSH RILEY BROWN & IAN BUSCH**
STORYBOARDS BY **JULES BRIDGERS, ALICIA CHAN, MORGAN HILLEBRAND, CASSEY KUO**
DIRECTED BY **JAKE CASTORENA**

TONY GAMA-LOBO: At the season 2 writers retreat—in what turned out to be bleak foreshadowing—Ant reminded us all that our version of Turtles wouldn't last forever. He wanted us to think about what we really wanted to say with *Rise*. So when the end came, we were prepared to say what the show was about: family. That was our North Star heading into the final four episodes. A lot of series don't get to make a final statement once they get canceled. We were lucky we could make ours.

When we were rewriting Josh's "E-Turtle," we needed something epic for Splinter's mom's last words to her son. Something he couldn't hear in his grief but would come to understand over his lifetime. When I pitched *"You are not alone,"* we knew we had our guiding principle for the entire finale. I thought it would be cool (and make the message more of a discovery) if we did it in Japanese. So we had a relative of one of our board artists translate it for us.

Throughout the entire series, everything has always rested on Raph's shoulders. It's all on him. And he finally cracks. It's so powerful, especially how Omar performed it. Raph doesn't have the answers. And then the show says he doesn't have to—that it's okay to ask for help, it's okay to rely on someone else. That's so relatable and such an important message for people to hear. Karai tells him, April tells him, and his brothers tell him: "You are not alone."

RON CORCILLO: After we submitted our premises that described the general shape of the finale episodes, the writers were approached by three board artists, Morgan Hillebrand, Alicia Chan, and Cassey Kuo, who were concerned that we would be killing off Karai so quickly because of the truncated schedule. They explained to us the concept of "fridging," or killing off a female character (Karai) to further the heroic goal of a male hero or heroes (the Turtles et al.), which was a great lesson for a room full of doofus men. We had been concerned about killing her off so quickly because it's not great storytelling, but we hadn't seen the sexist aspect of it, and we'll always be grateful to them for that lesson. Since it was always in the cards that Karai would sacrifice herself in the final battle with Shredder, Russ pitched a compromise: Karai dies, but her spirit is transferred into April's consciousness. This gave Karai the story she deserved, while also giving Kat an opportunity to channel two characters. And we think she turned out an amazing performance!

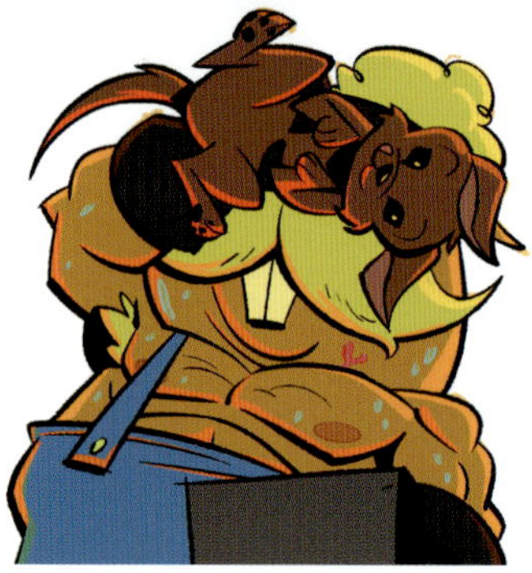

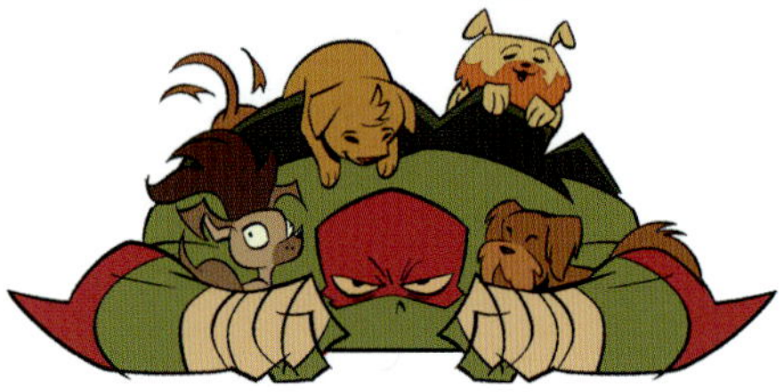

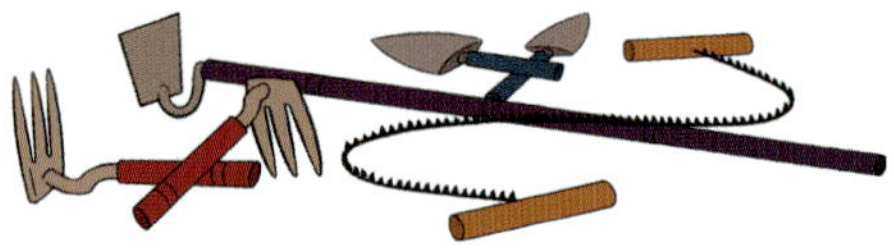

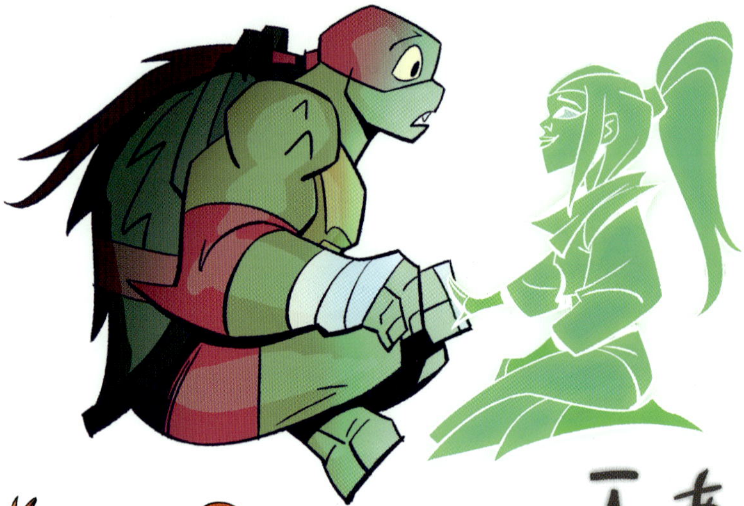

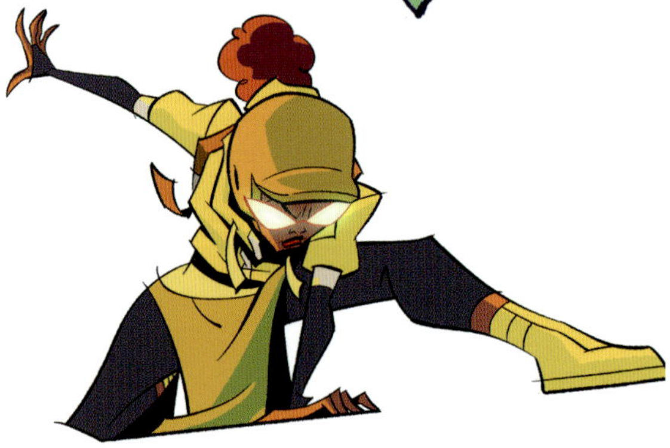

あなたは一人じゃない

"YOU ARE NOT ALONE"

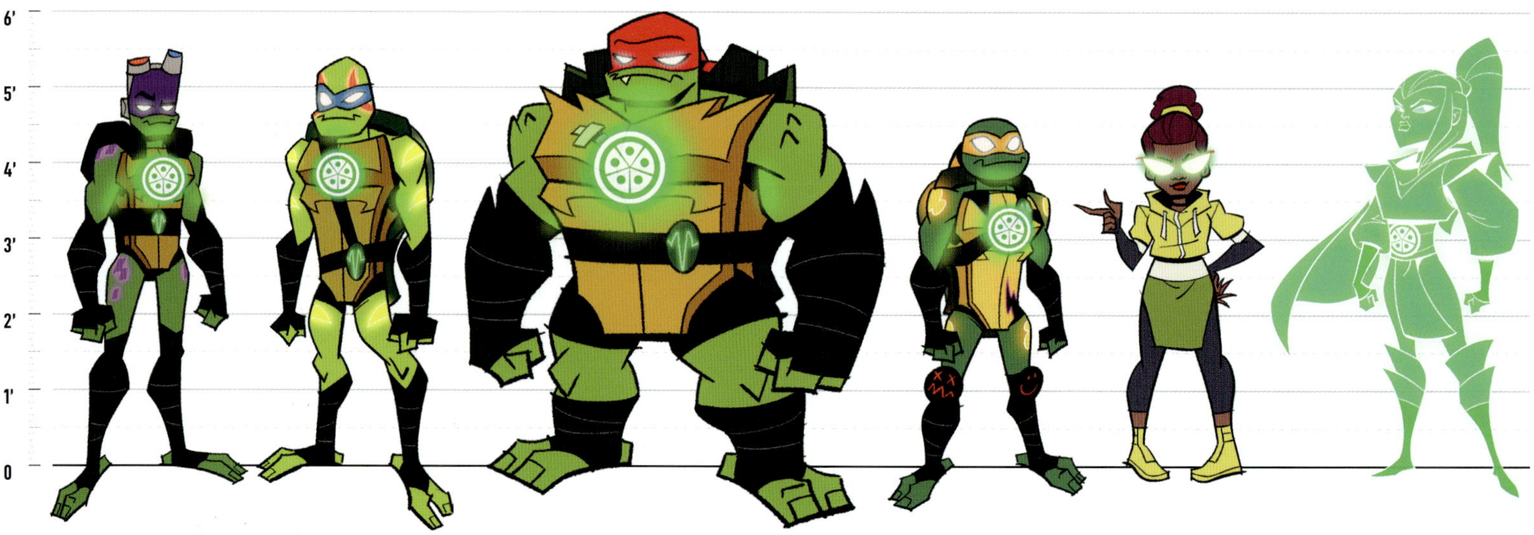

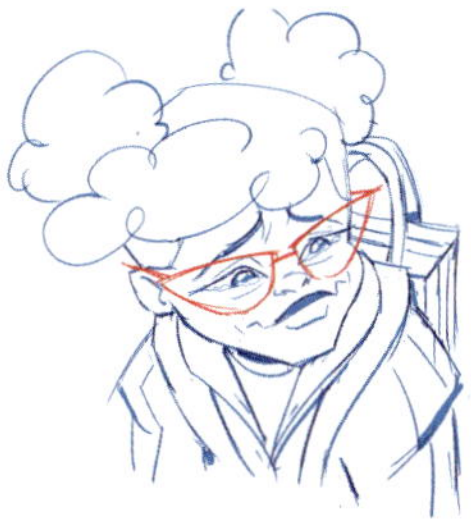

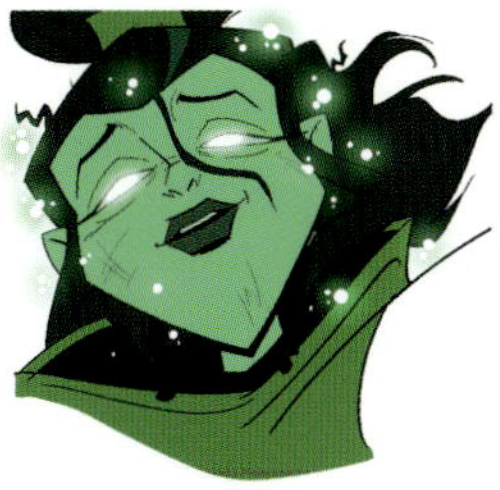

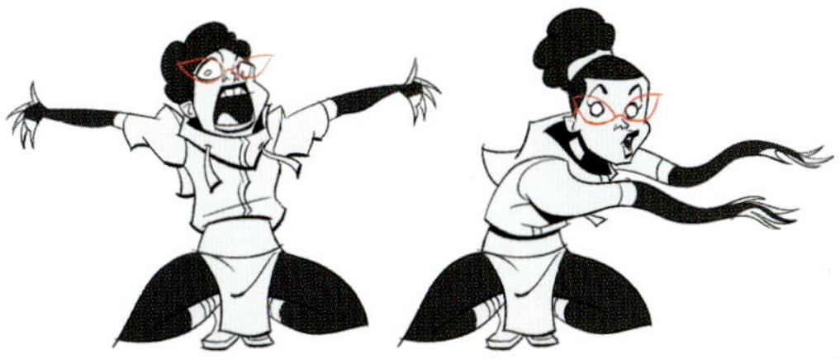

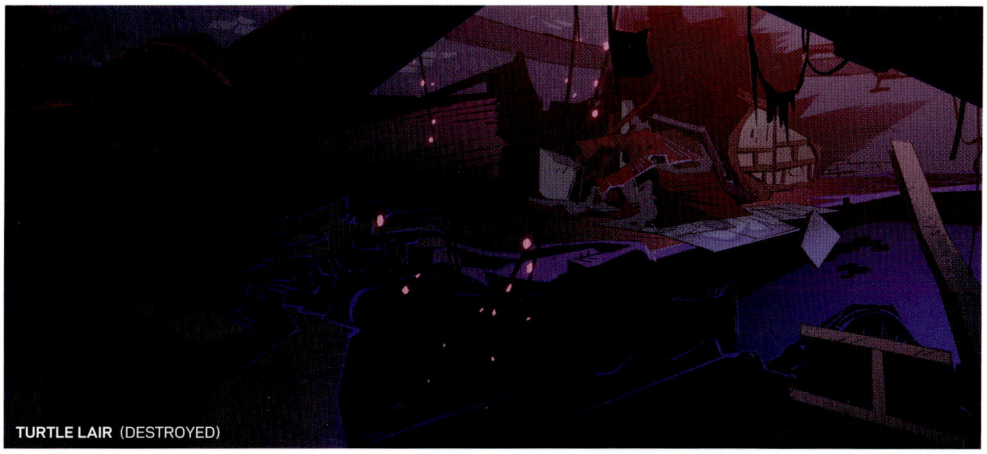

TURTLE LAIR (DESTROYED)

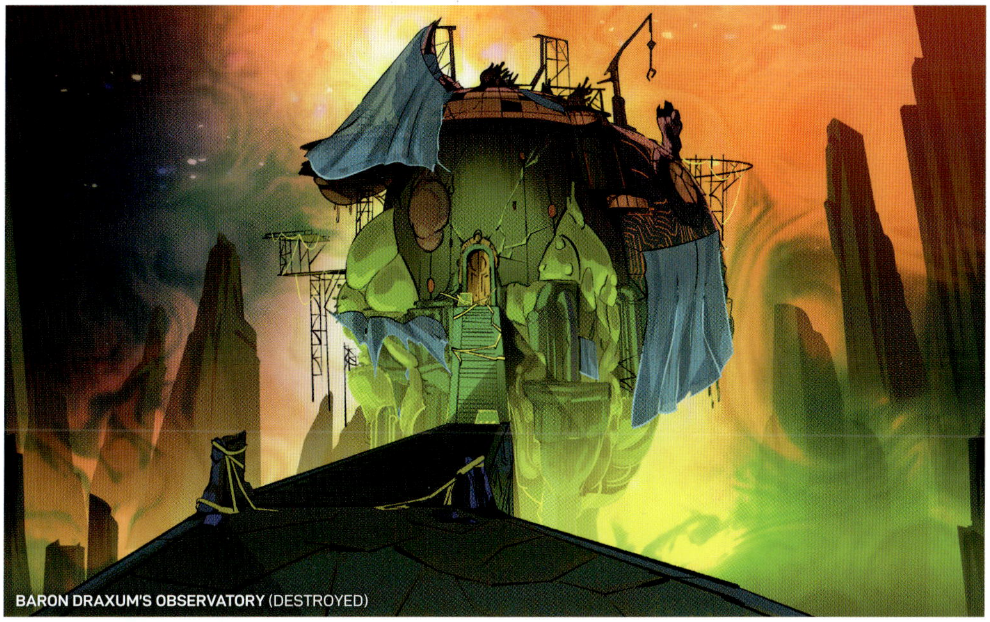

BARON DRAXUM'S OBSERVATORY (DESTROYED)

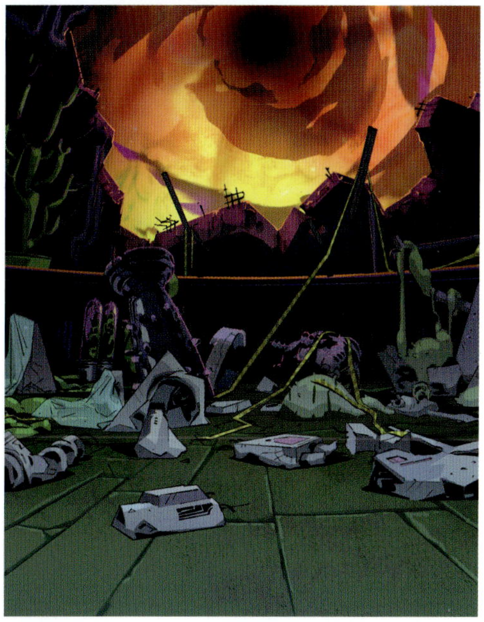

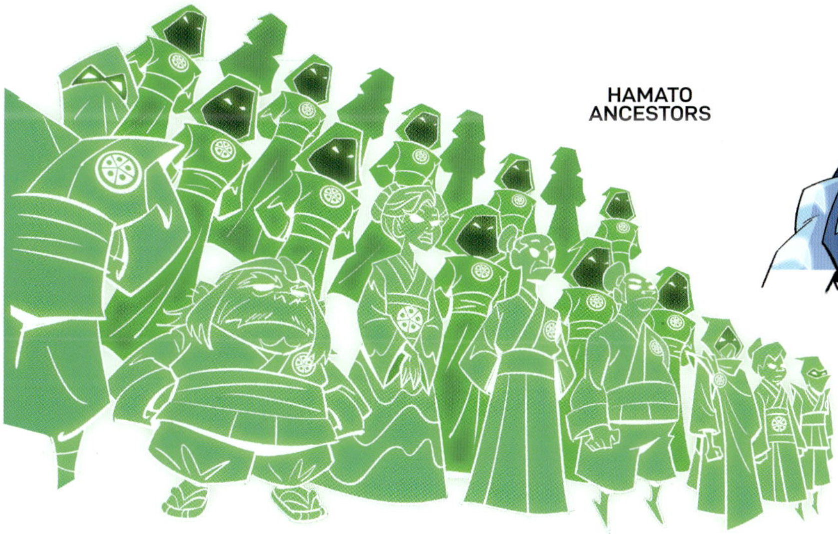

HAMATO ANCESTORS

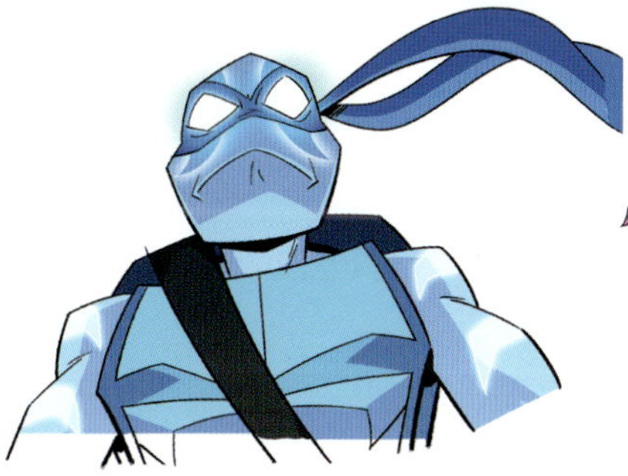

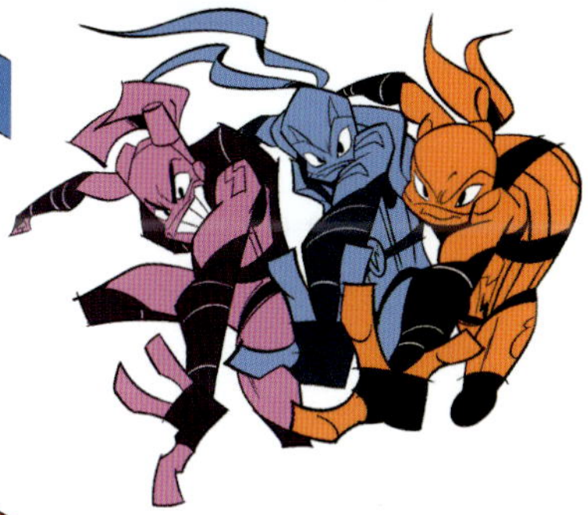

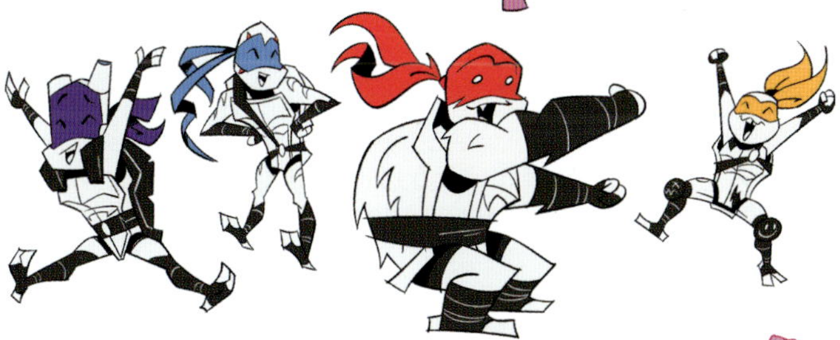

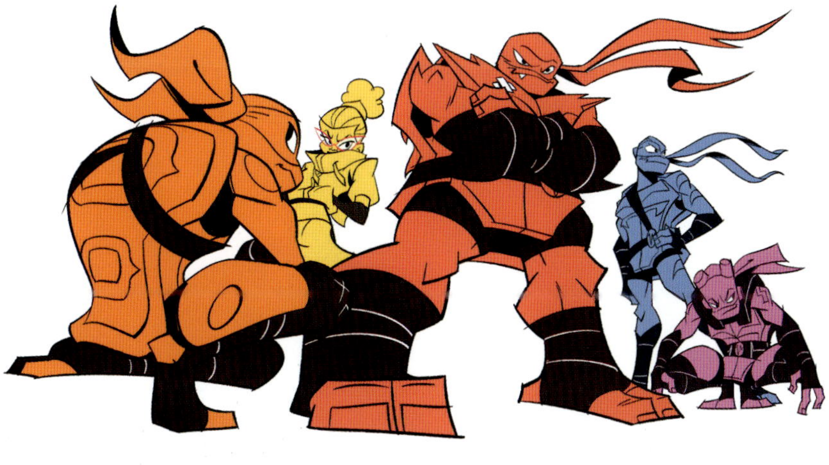

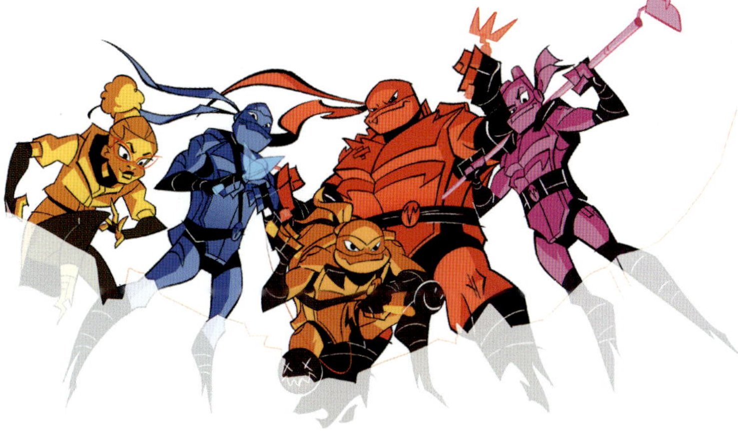

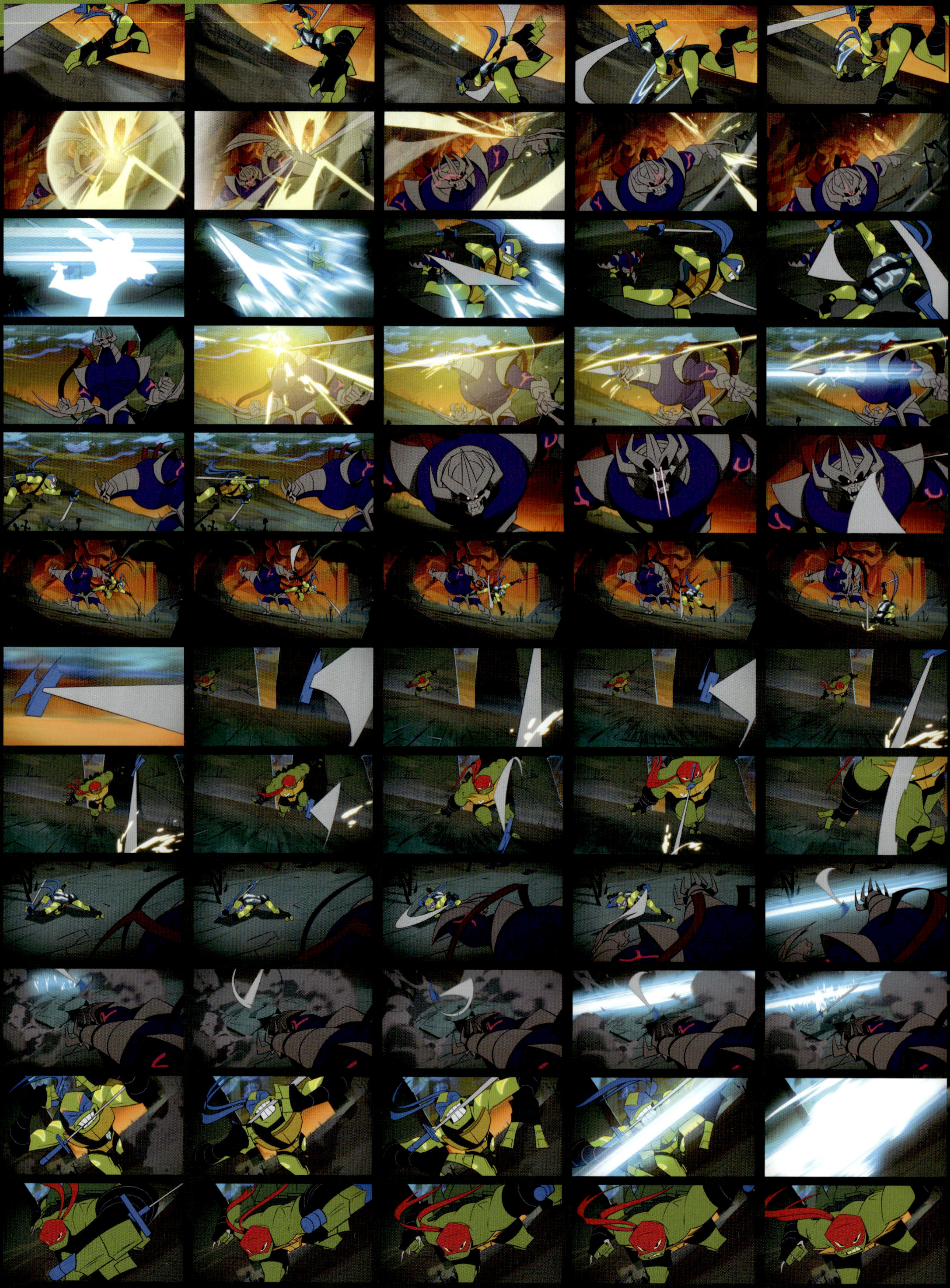

STORYBOARD ARTISTS: **KEVIN MOLINA-ORTIZ, JJ CONWAY, ASHE JACOBSON**

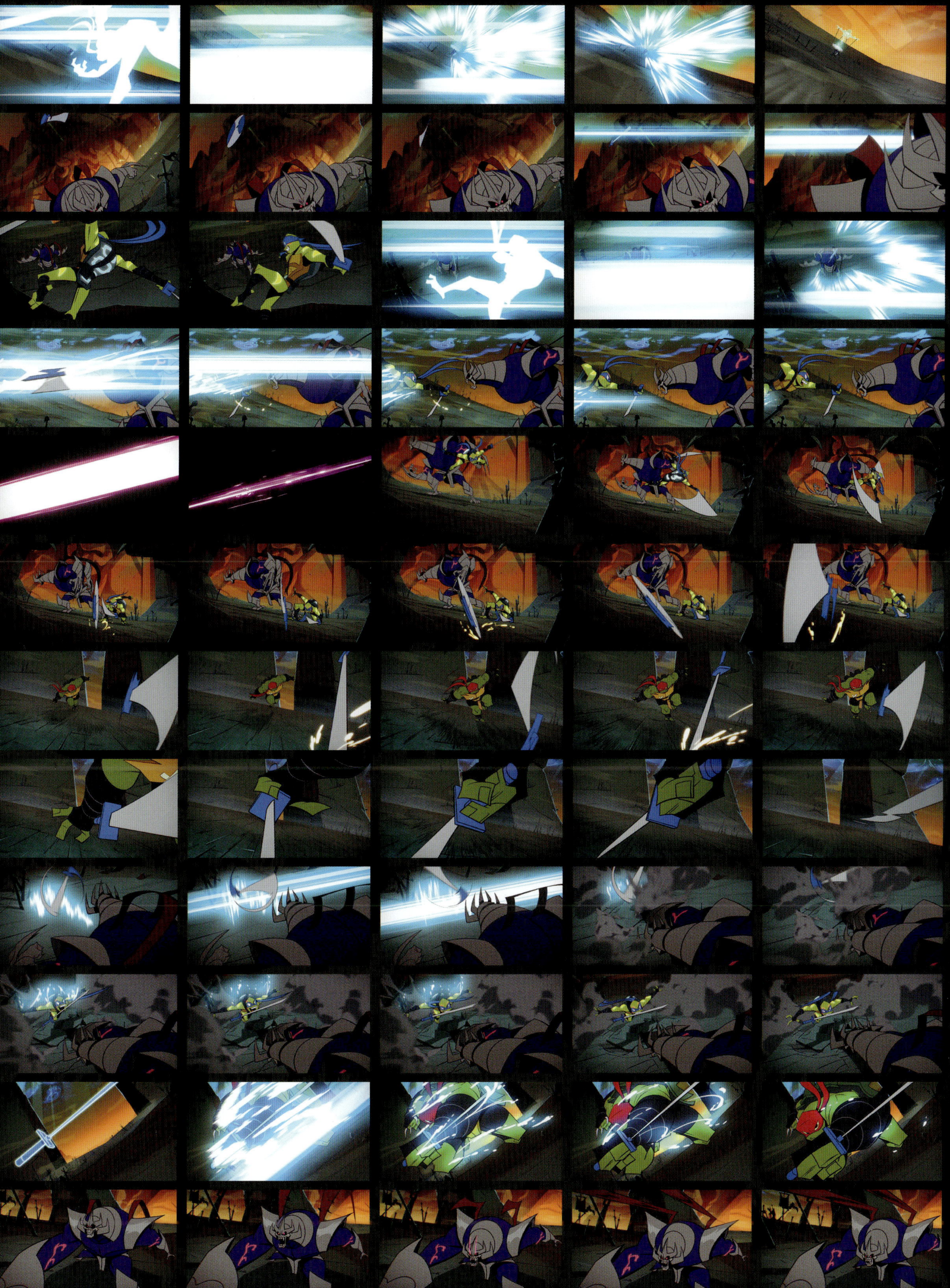

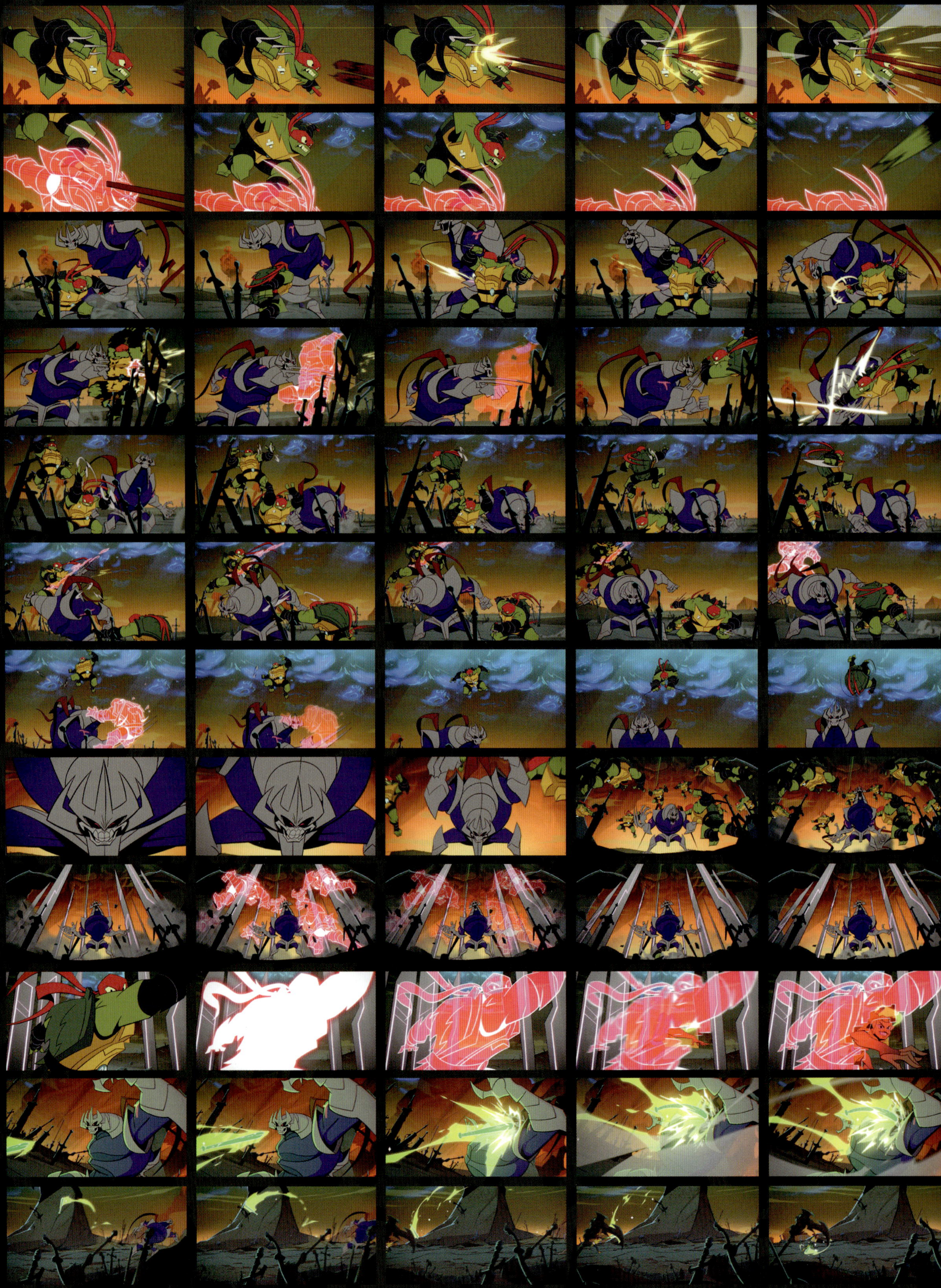

STORYBOARD ARTISTS: **KEVIN MOLINA-ORTIZ, JJ CONWAY, ASHE JACOBSON**

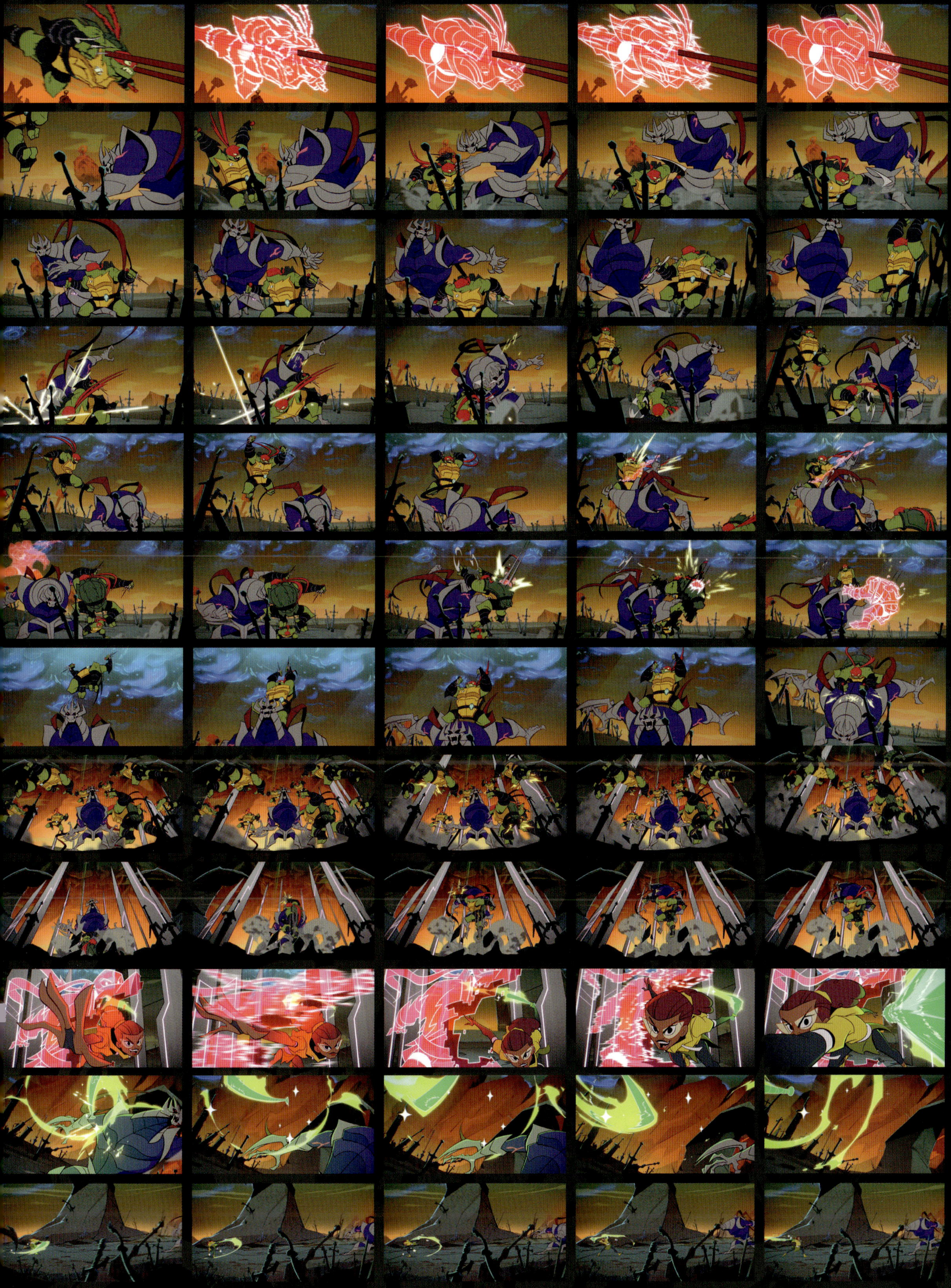

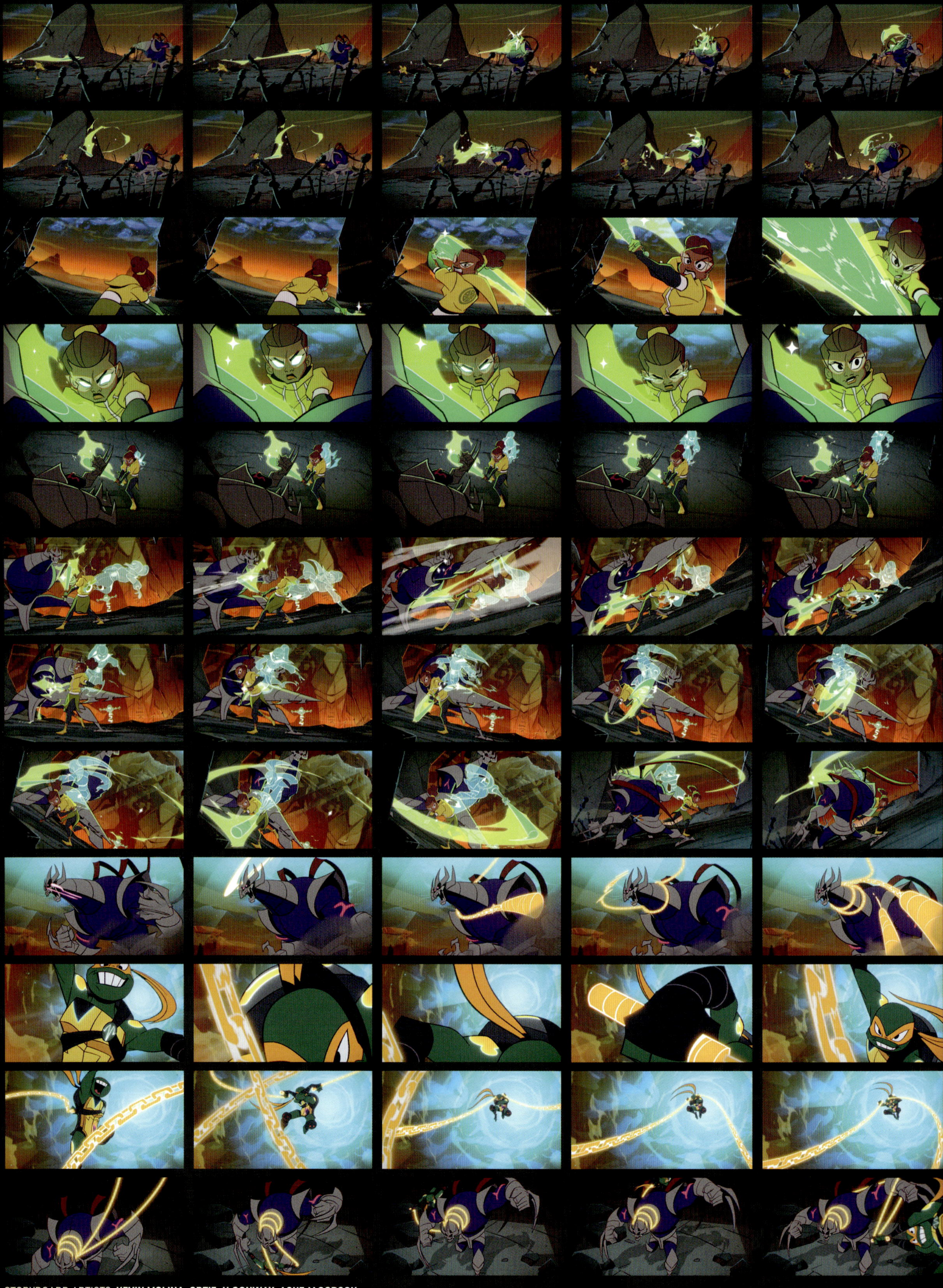

STORYBOARD ARTISTS: **KEVIN MOLINA-ORTIZ, JJ CONWAY, ASHE JACOBSON**

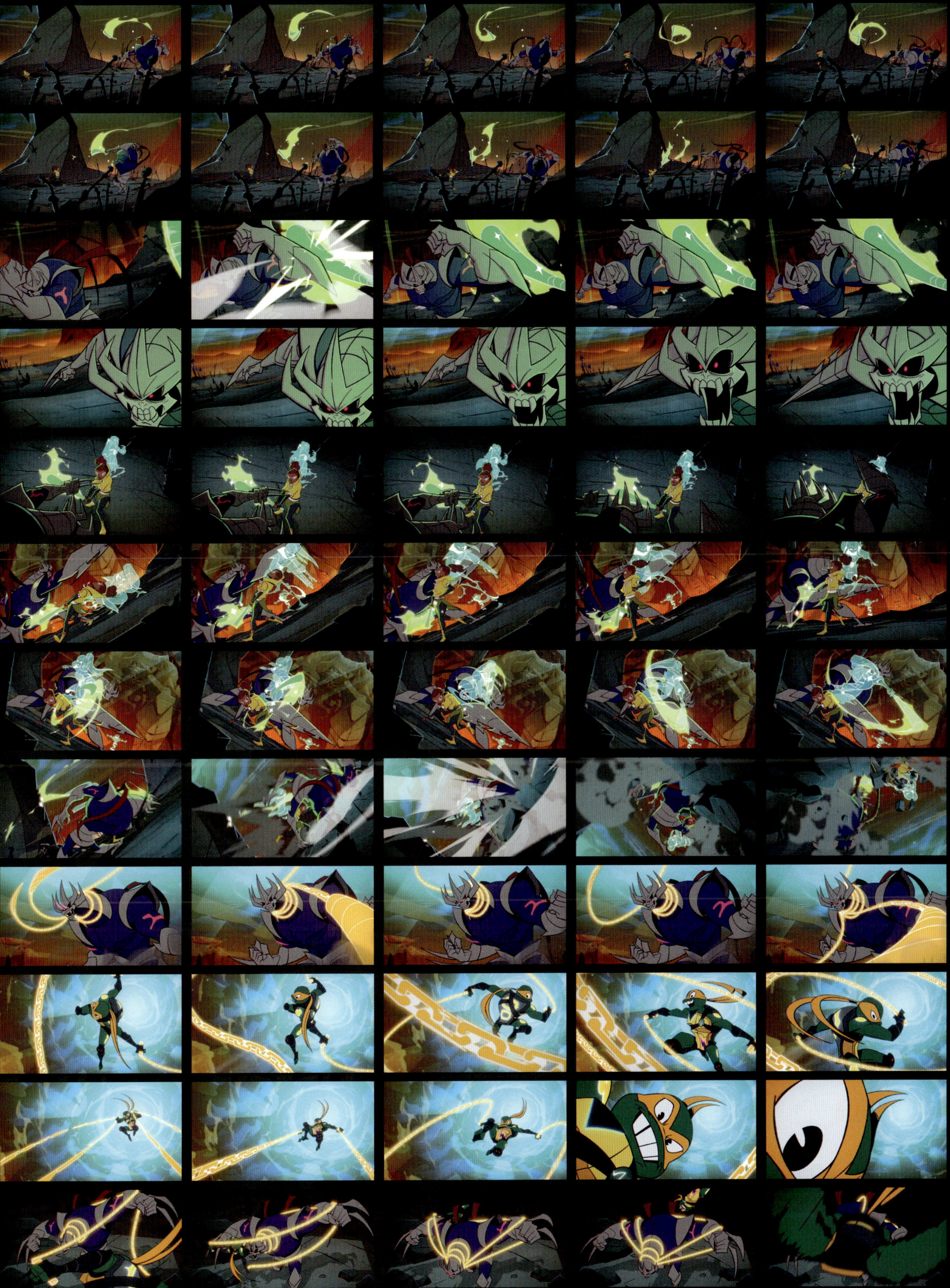

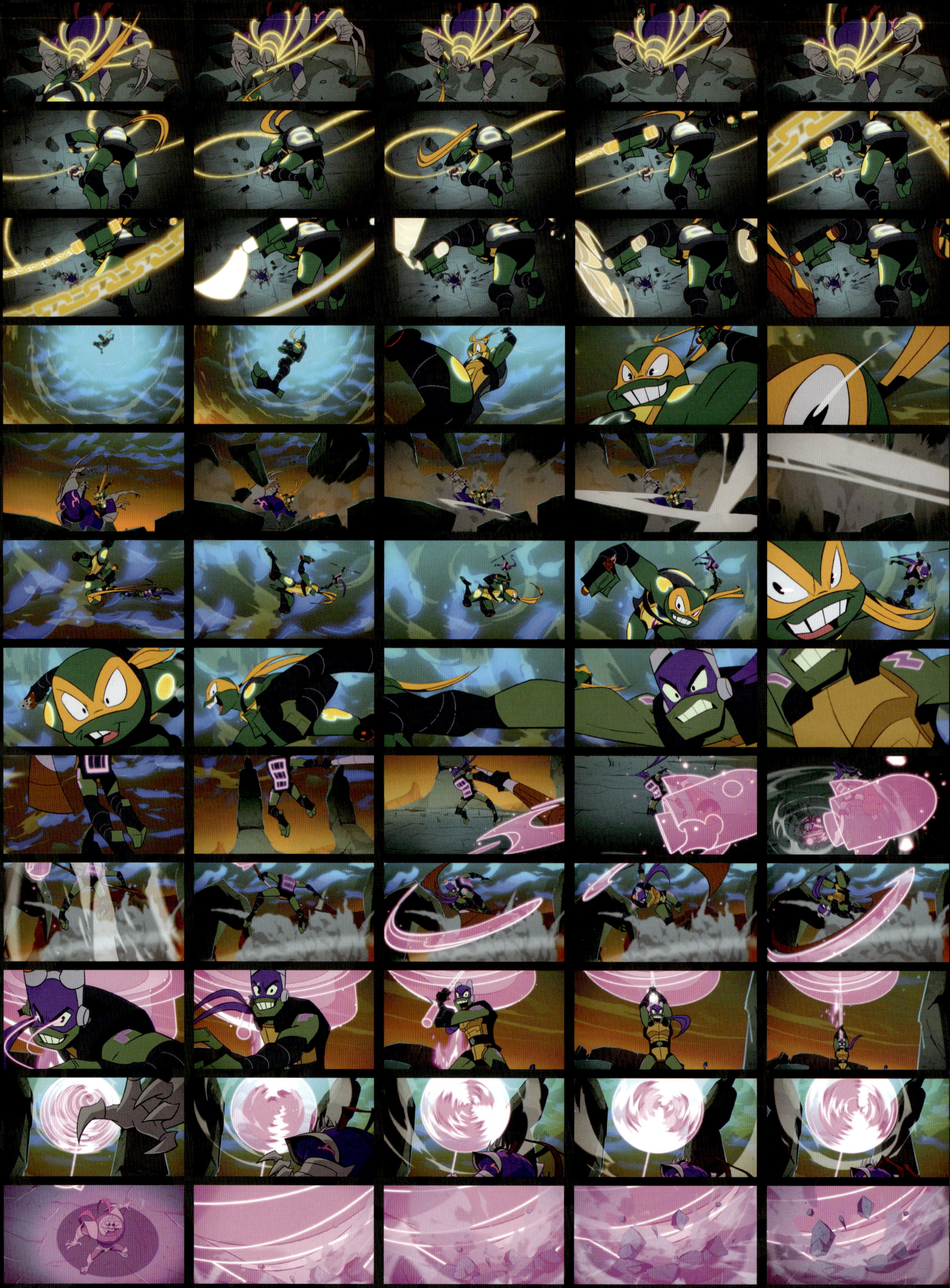

STORYBOARD ARTISTS: **KEVIN MOLINA-ORTIZ, JJ CONWAY, ASHE JACOBSON**

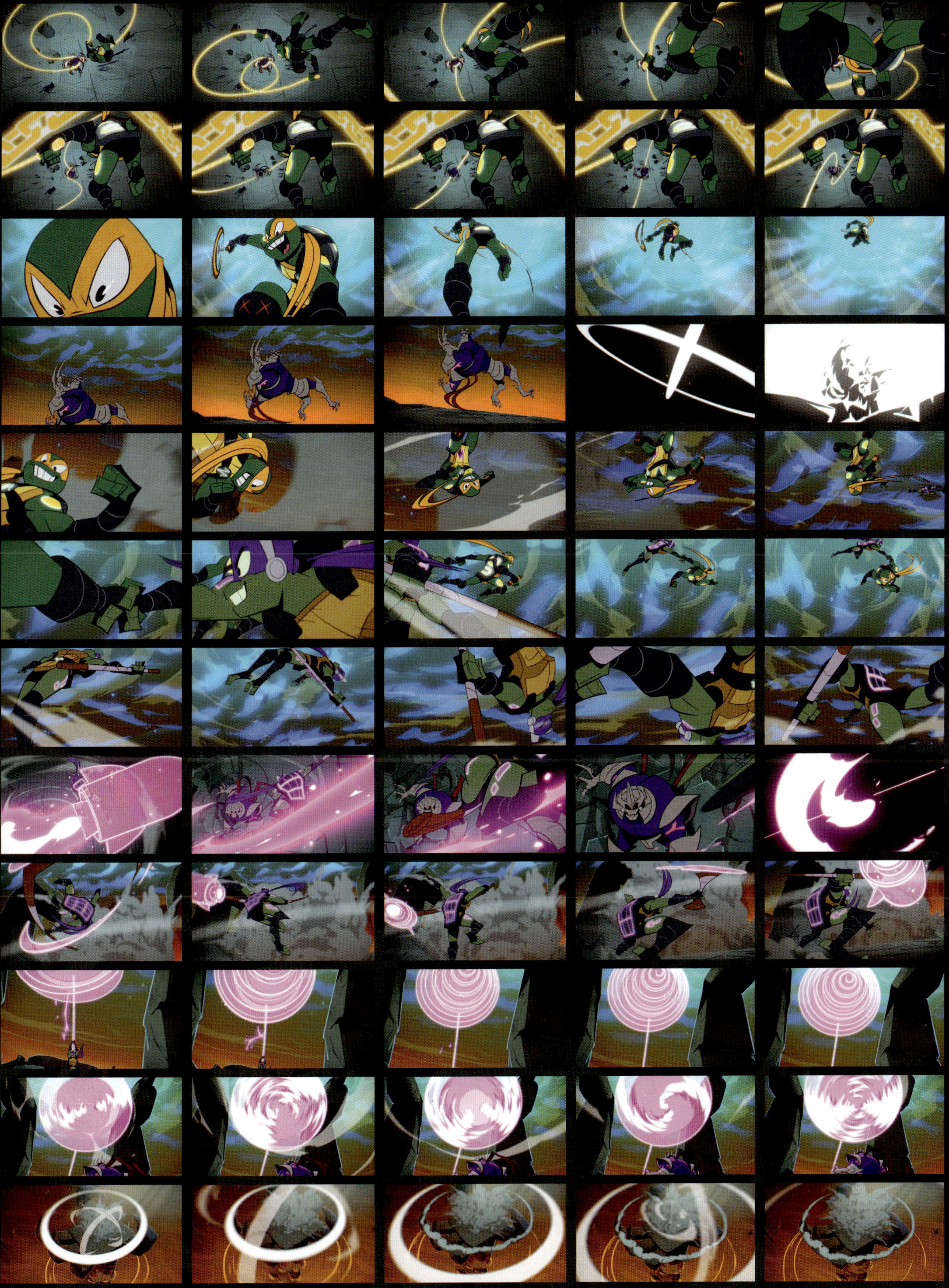

FINALE PART 4: RISE

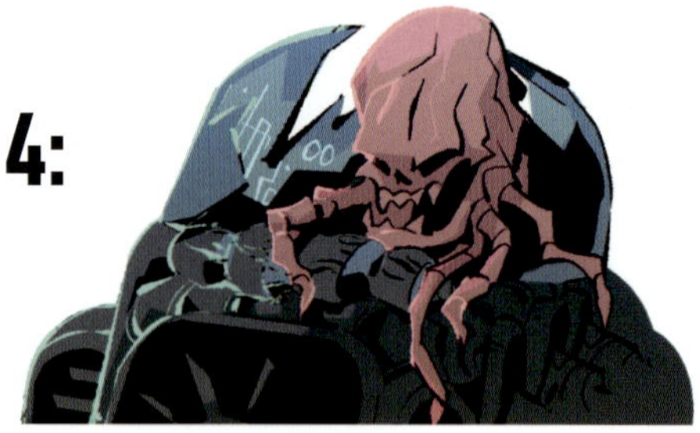

ORIGINAL AIR DATE: AUGUST 7, 2020
PRODUCTION CODE: 104

WRITTEN BY **JOSH RILEY BROWN, IAN BUSCH, RUSS CARNEY, RON CORCILLO, TONY GAMA-LOBO & DALE MALINOWSKI**
STORYBOARDS BY **JAKE CASTORENA, ALICIA CHAN, MAX COLLINS, JJ CONWAY, MORGAN HILLEBRAND, CASSEY KUO, SEBASTIAN MONTES**
DIRECTED BY **KEVIN MOLINA-ORTIZ**

TONY GAMA-LOBO: Bringing everything together in a satisfying final episode was a tall order. There were so many things! Powering up the Turtles and April, giving Draxum's prophecy story a conclusion, saving New York, tying in the mythology of the Hidden City, revealing Foot Recruit's true identity, and of course getting the drill out of beta.

I remember passing Ant in the hall one day early in the season and he says to me, "What if Foot Recruit's real name was Cassandra... Cassandra Jones?" Daaaaang, that would rock! So we started the process of moving her from the dark side to the light. The first step was having her bond with Splinter in "Always Be Brownies." Then we made her disillusioned with the Foot Clan. Unfortunately, before we got too far, the show got shut down. So we ended up needing to do a *lot* in these last couple episodes. One of our board artists, Ashe Jacobson, drew a truly inspired sequence for the big reveal, even giving Foot Recruit a hockey stick–esque weapon. It was awesome.

RON CORCILLO: Writing the finale was a major blur, and I think we were all operating on autopilot, fueled by buckets of coffee and a whole lot of free lunches that our esteemed exec, Dana Vasquez-Eberhardt, bought us to ease our pain. After it was announced that the series was ending, the studio allowed us to wrap everything up in four carts, but the hard part was that we only had six weeks to 1) conceive of a storyline, 2) get approval of said storyline, 3) break all four episodes, write all four episodes, punch them up, etc. For context, under normal circumstances, the production schedule from premise to record draft is usually afforded a time span of about 12 weeks.

RUSS CARNEY: To say that this process was hard is an understatement, but we were committed to doing good work for our fans, despite the impending unemployment. Ron remarked that after watching the finished finale, almost a full year later, he couldn't remember writing most of it and had to look back at the script to confirm that we had really done it. The finished product was a thing of beauty—a tribute to all the love and commitment that everyone on the cast and crew had to this show.

TONY GAMA-LOBO: By the time we were doing the last part of the finale, it was all hands on deck. Story and art were evolving at the same time. For example, we the writers knew we wanted the Turtles to have new mystic powers but had no idea what they could be. Alan Wan and the storyboard team came up with incredible power-ups as well as took Andy's vision for Shredder and showed us he could morph and transform like some kind of metal T-1000 (*Terminator 2: Judgment Day*, 1991). So we took that and rewrote the scenes showing Shredder drilling for Empyrean. It was this perfect back-and-forth in those few weeks—an artist grabbing me as I walked by to show me boards revealing Leo's new katanas, the writers pitching a great joke like bringing back the drill, Ant suggesting that inside the head of the Crying Titan was a Krang skeleton, and Andy designing the coolest Krang of all time. It was a creative hurricane at the end and I loved it.

The board teams created some images for this finale that will stay with me forever. Lou Jitsu's soul floating above Splinter's body, the Hamato ancestors joining the fight, Karai's father bursting from the burned-out remains of the Dark Armor, and our family standing above New York.

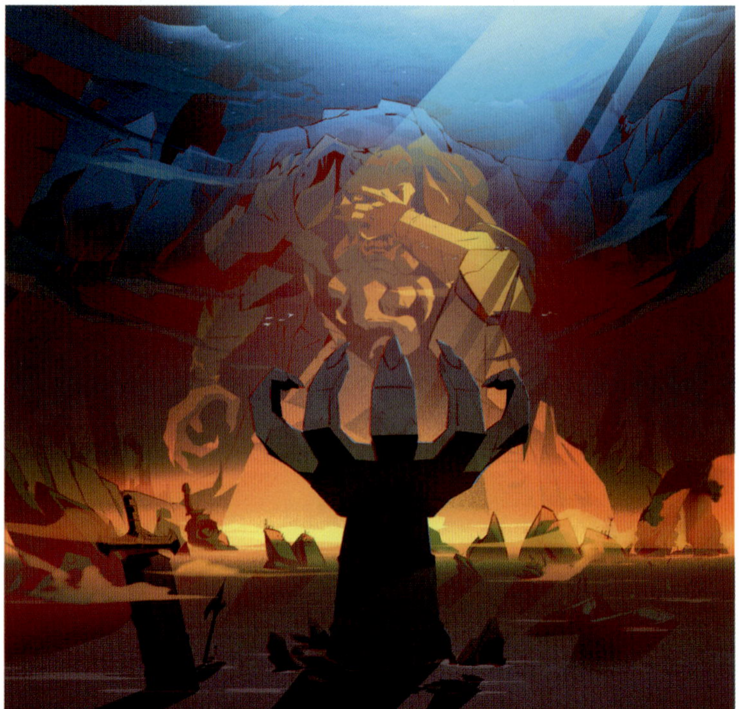

HIDDEN CITY - THE CRYING TITAN

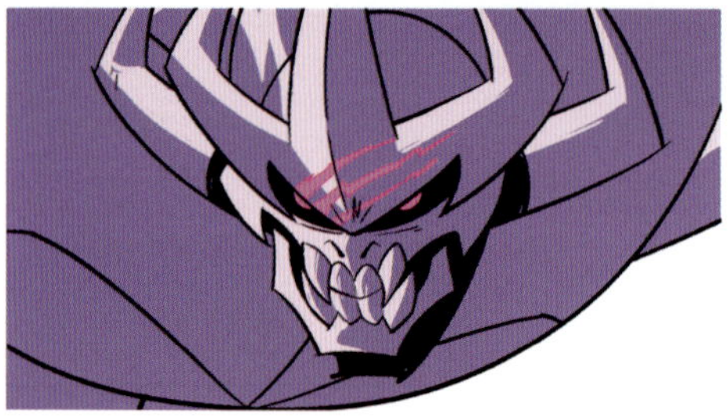

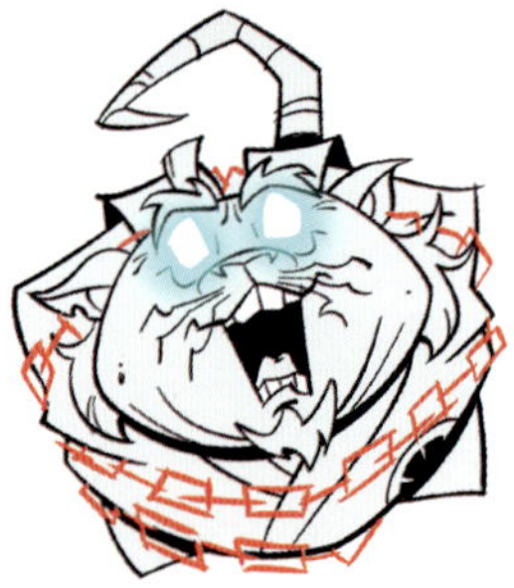

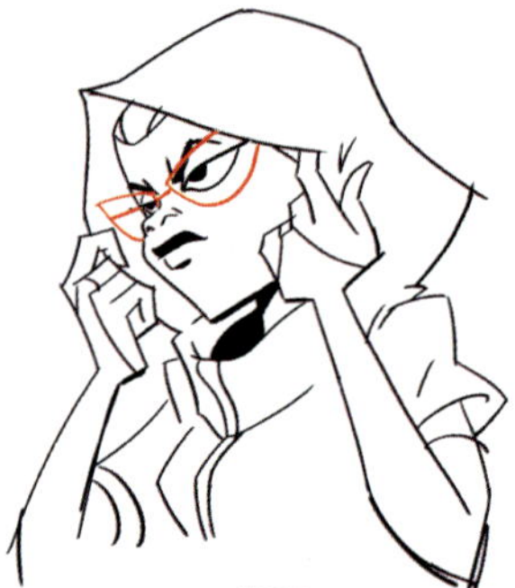

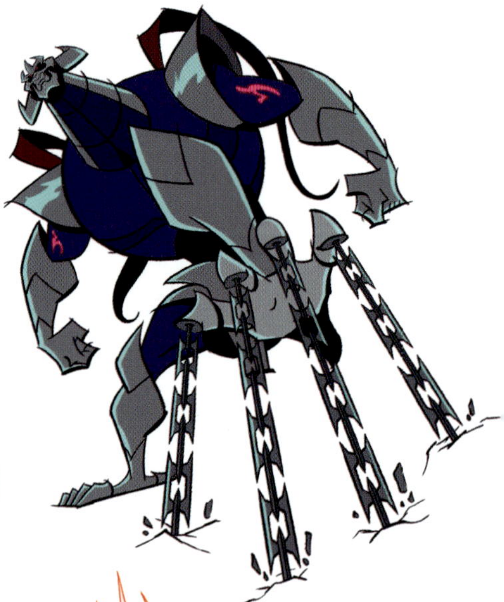

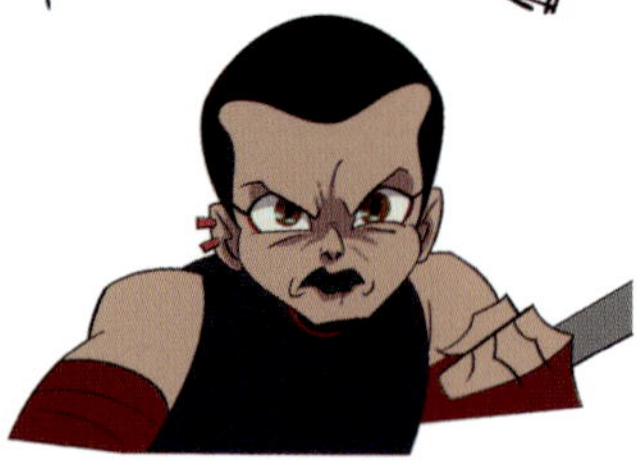

CASSANDRA "CASEY" JONES
EX-FOOT RECRUIT

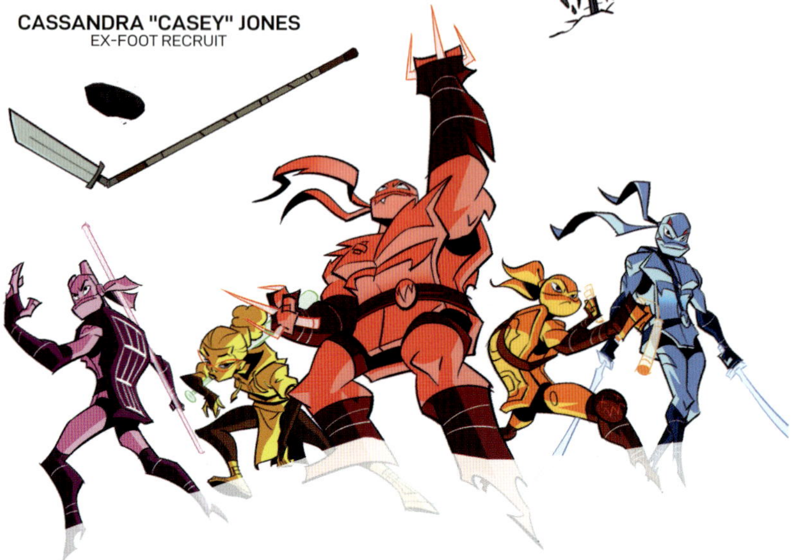

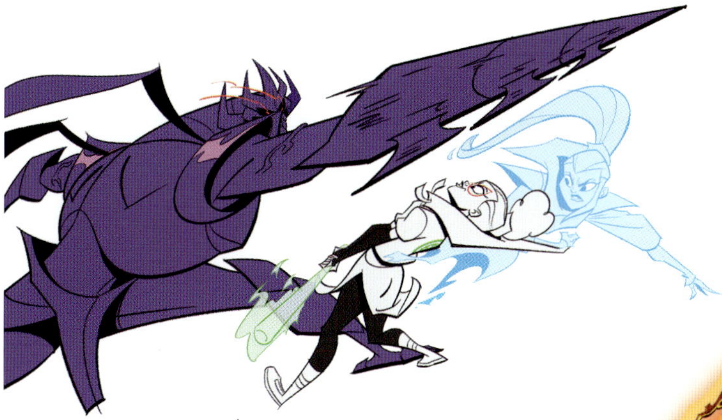

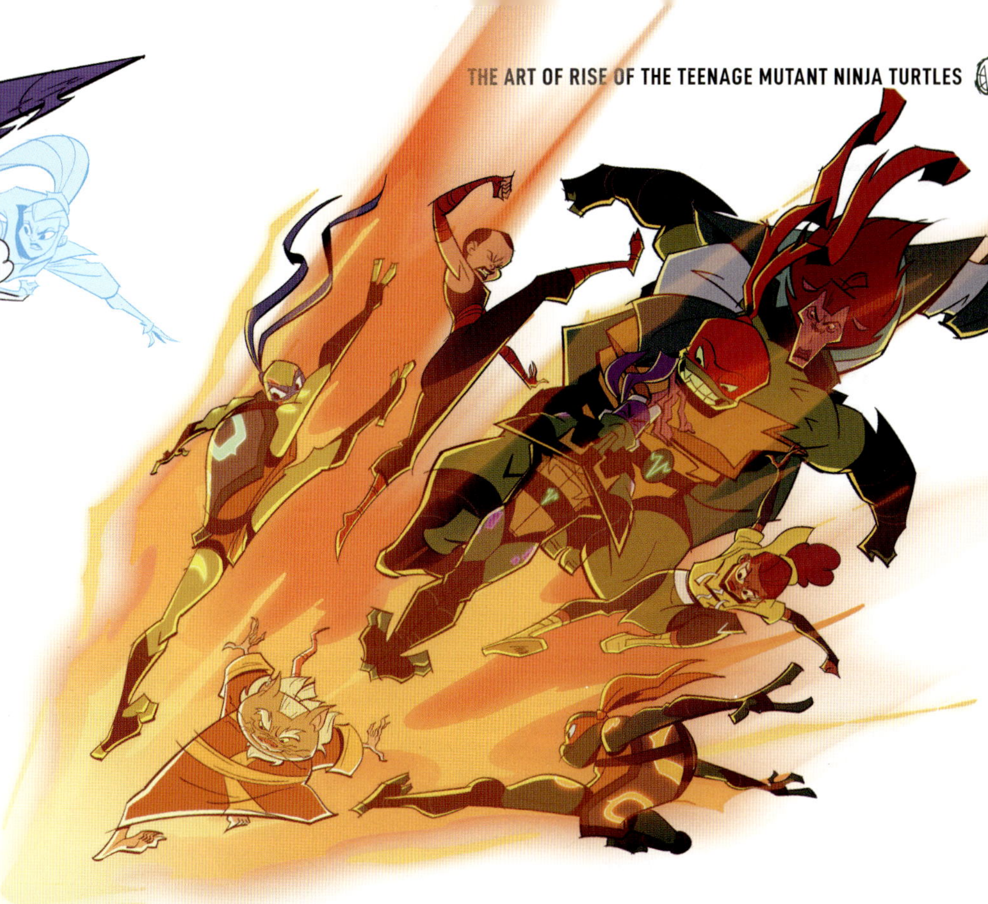

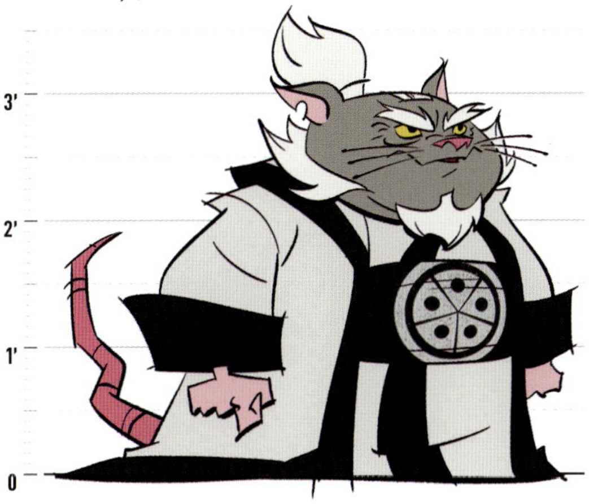

SPLINTER
HAMATO ROBES

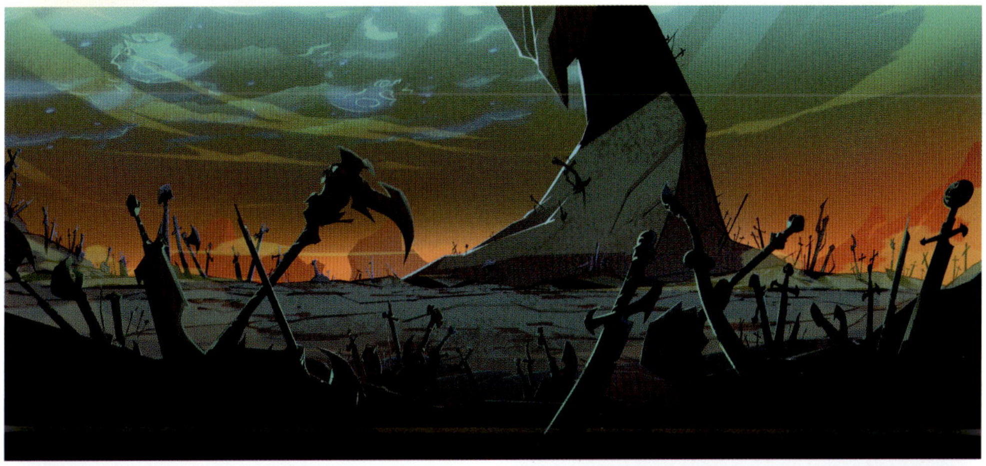

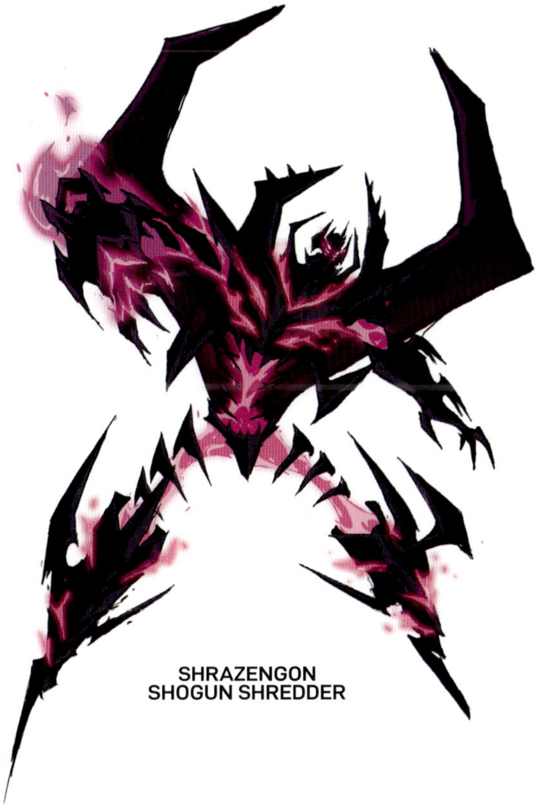

SHRAZENGON
SHOGUN SHREDDER

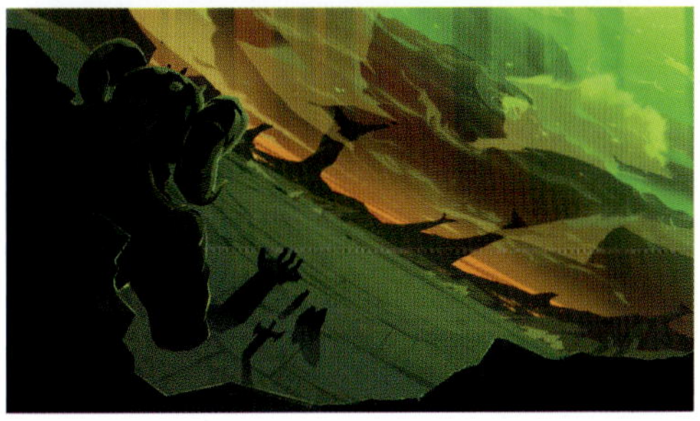

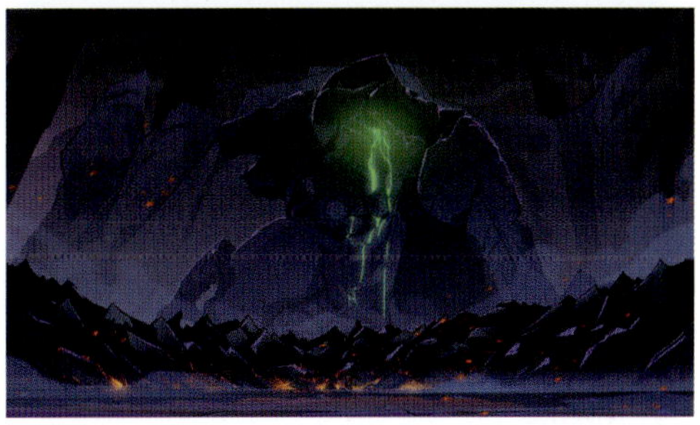

TONY GAMA-LOBO: I have a clear memory of sitting in the final edit with Ant and Andy and we all looked at each other and said, "Did we just do a series about the rise of Splinter?" Of course the boys were amazing and became incredible heroes, but Splinter's whole emotional journey ended up being the surprise heart of the series. Season 1 we got grief from the fan base about Andy's vision of Danny DeVito from *It's Always Sunny in Philadelphia* version of Splinter. *"He's not a father, he's not a mentor, he's not a hero!"* they said. But you need to start a character somewhere to show real growth. If we didn't start there, then when we reveal all the deep emotional reasons for Splinter's life choices, it wouldn't be nearly as impactful. Without the old Splinter and the old family dynamic and the adversity that Splinter has endured in his life, you would never have cried like I did when Splinter's sons remind him that he is not alone. That's the moment everyone *rises*.

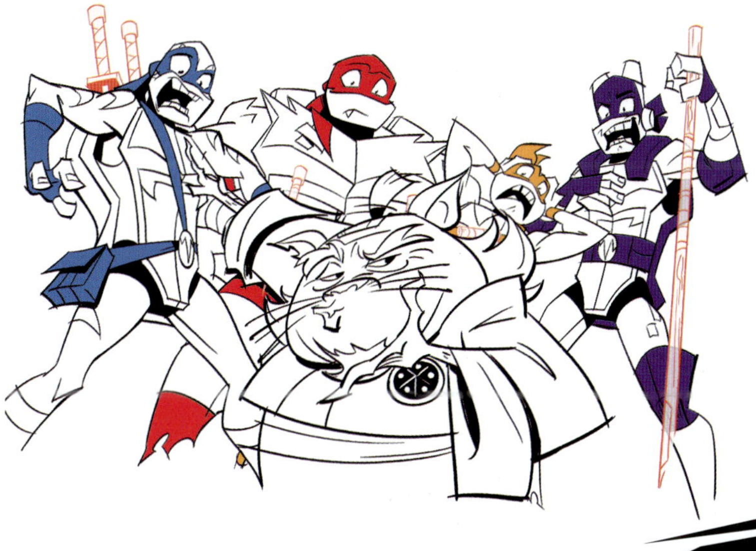

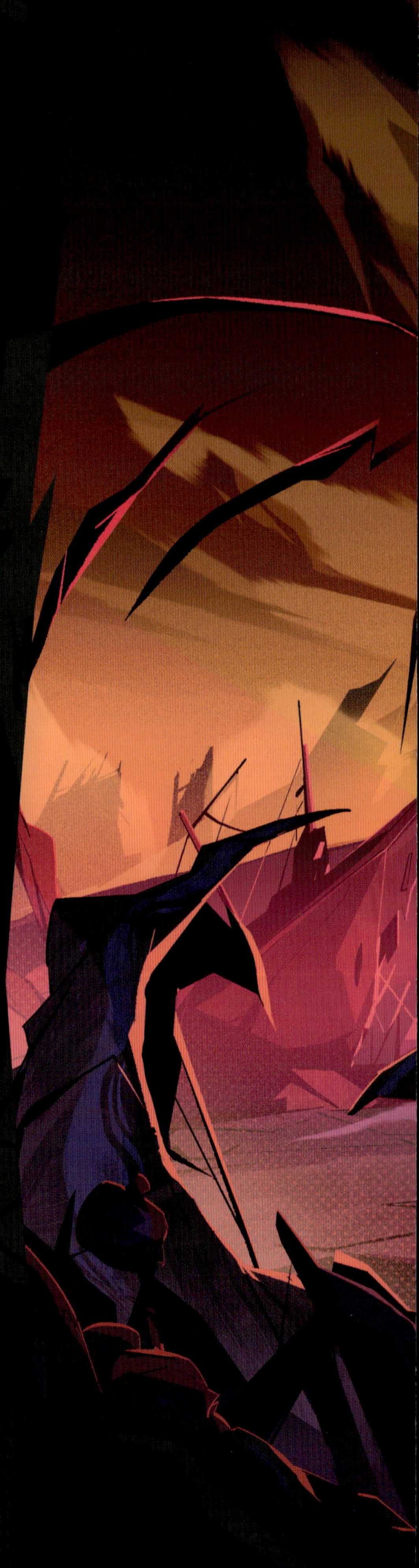

RISE OF THE TEENAGE MUTANT NINJA TURTLES THE MOVIE

RELEASE DATE: AUGUST 5, 2022

WRITTEN BY **TONY GAMA-LOBO, REBECCA MAY, ANT WARD & ANDY SURIANO**
DIRECTED BY **ANT WARD & ANDY SURIANO**

The series finale left fans hungry for more, and two years later, their patience was rewarded with Netflix's highly anticipated *Rise of the Teenage Mutant Ninja Turtles: The Movie*. This feature-length adventure introduced the Krang and Casey Jones—a longtime fan-favorite character who didn't appear in the series—into the *Rise* universe. Delivering a high-stakes, action-packed story that thrilled fans and newcomers alike, the movie expanded the Turtles' world in exciting and unexpected ways.

In a future where the alien faction known as the Krang has conquered Earth, the resistance is led by Master Leonardo. Desperate to save the planet, Leo sends his young pupil, Casey Jones, back in time to pre-invaded New York City. As a freedom fighter who has only known a world under alien rule, Casey must track down the Hamato Clan and prepare them for an enemy the likes of which they've never faced before. Leo, Raph, Donnie, Mikey, April, and Splinter must rise to the occasion and defend their home—or will the Krang's invasion succeed?

In this chapter, we'll dive into the development of the movie, exploring the creative decisions, challenges, and triumphs that brought this epic story to life. From the stunning animation to the emotional stakes and the explosive action sequences, this is your behind-the-scenes look at *Rise's* biggest adventure yet.

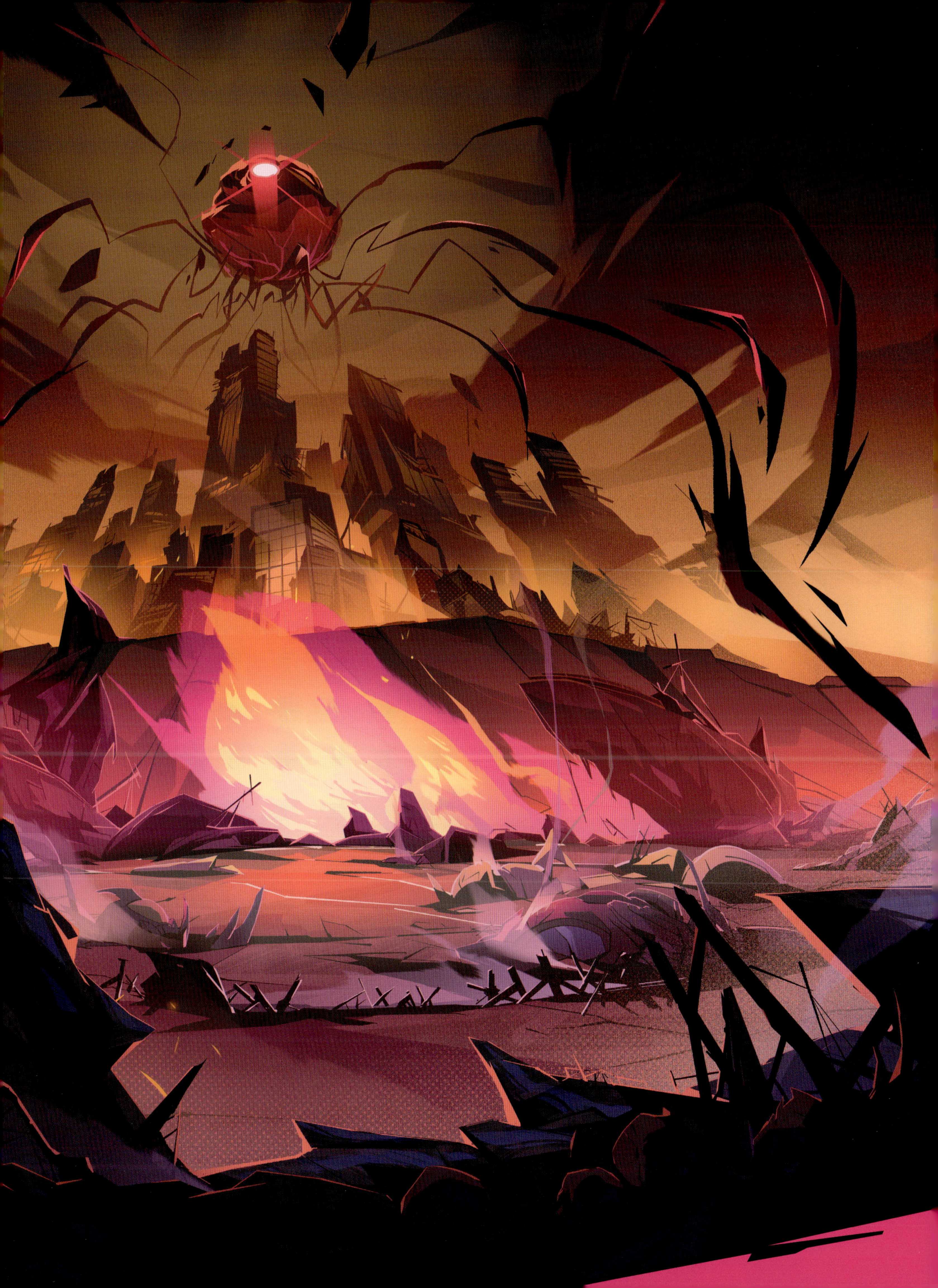

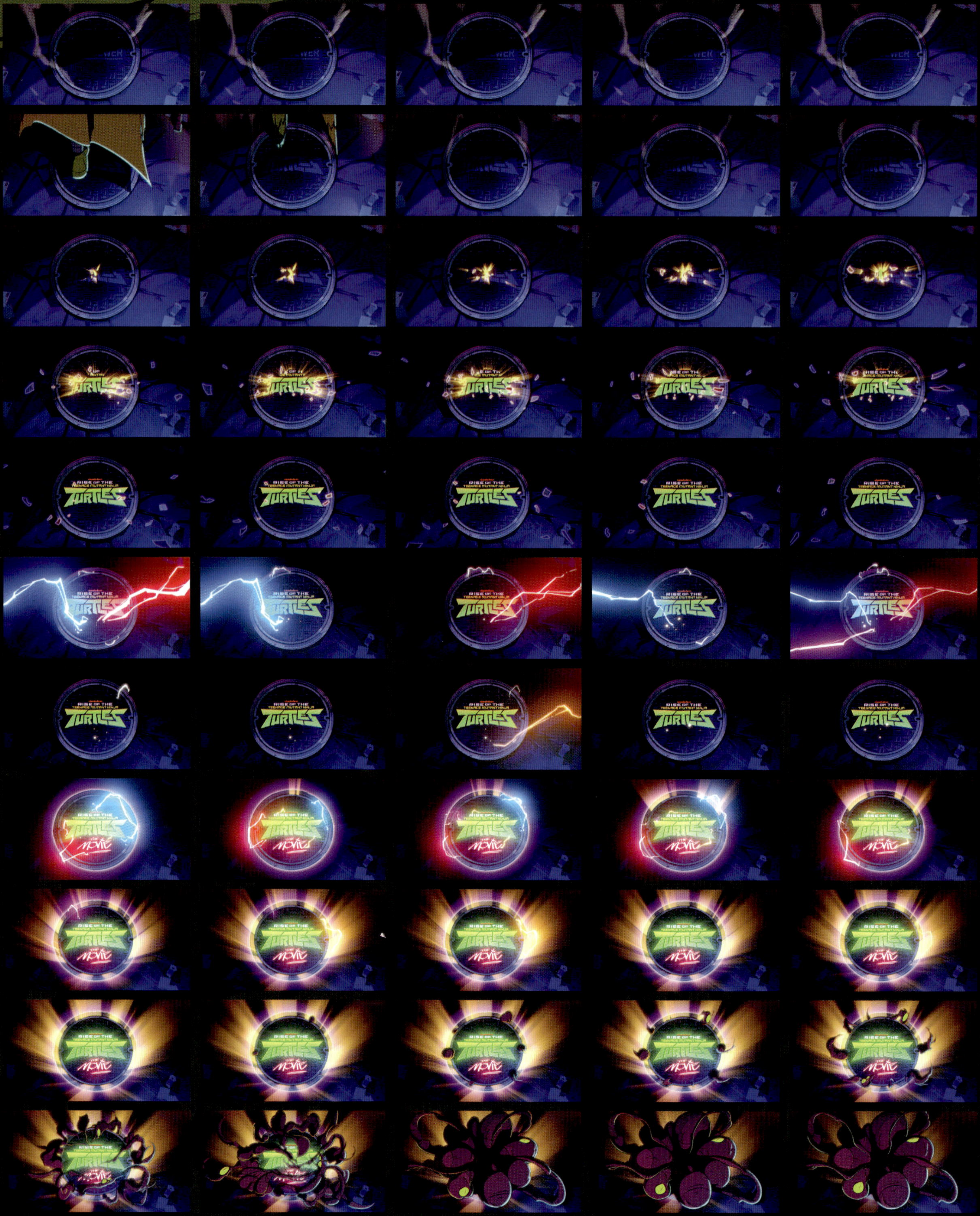

STORYBOARD ARTISTS: **CARL BEU, ANDY SURIANO, ANT WARD, JJ CONWAY, INDIA SWIFT, JERMAINE JOSE, JACK ROSSI**

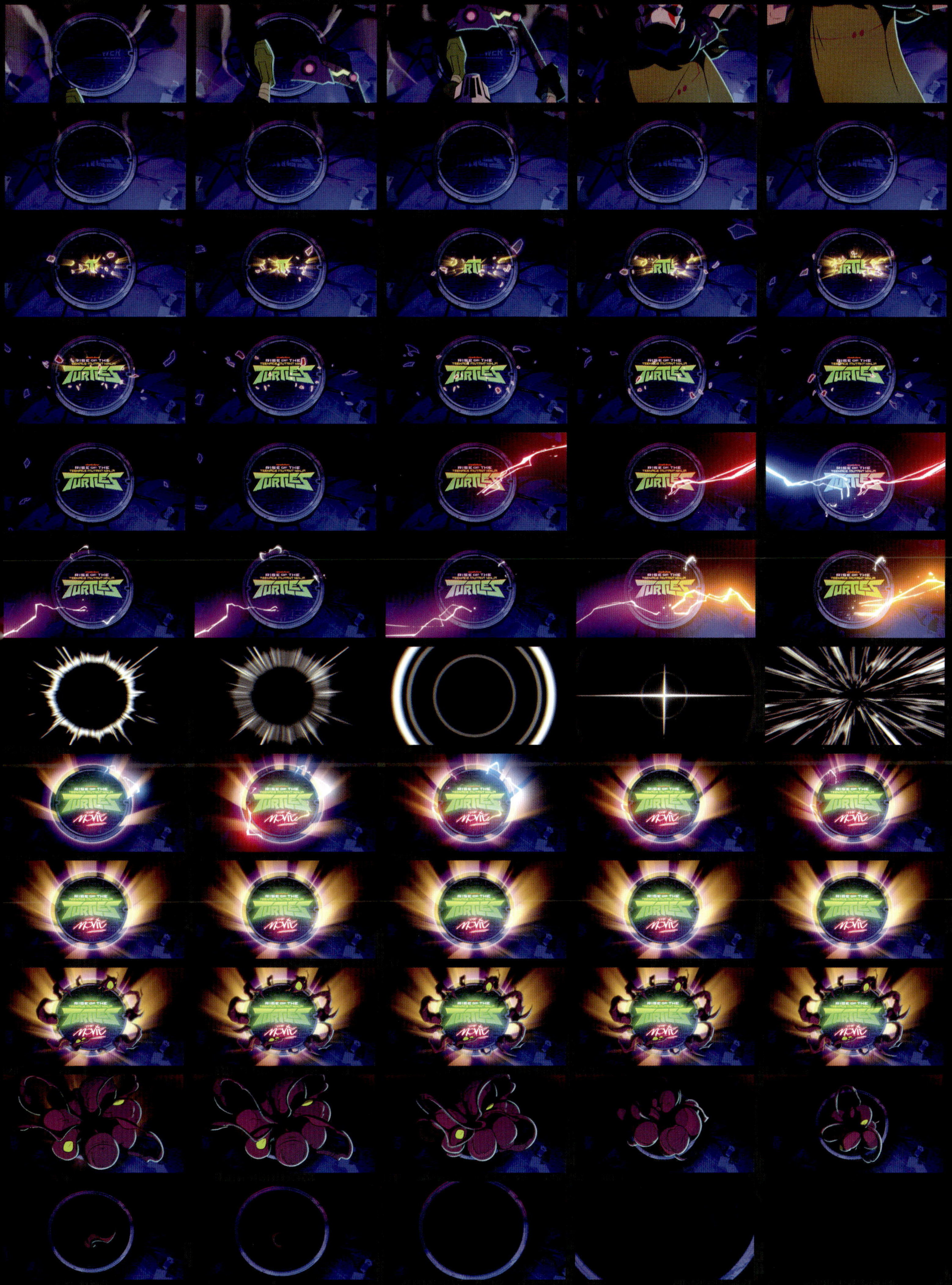

DEVELOPMENT

ANT WARD: During the early production of season 2, Dana Vasquez-Eberhardt called Andy and me on a Saturday morning and told us that the studio was showing interest in a *Rise* movie with one mandate: It had to incorporate recognizable elements from the TMNT franchise's legacy. We spent the weekend throwing around ideas that would be "classic" TMNT, still unique to *Rise*, and not step on anything we were planning for seasons 2 and 3 of the show. We pitched some ideas on the following Monday, one of which was a time-travel adventure with Casey Jones, Armaggon, and the Krang. Armaggon was the herald to the Krang, and Casey was a time-traveling space vigilante out to stop them. Netflix picked up the movie, with Andy and myself still attached as executive producers. We staffed the movie's creative team (director and writers), but unfortunately, it became very apparent within a few months that the team did not want to make a *Rise* movie but instead wanted to steer it in a traditional TMNT direction. By the time the first animatic of that iteration was complete, it was clear that things were not working out. Unfortunately, the show had been canceled by this point, but the studio still wanted to pursue the *Rise* movie. So, Andy and I took over directing and brought Tony and Becky on board for the writing side. The core of the story remained our original pitch, but we went back to square one with the writing.

ANDY SURIANO: We needed to hit the ground running on the production of the movie, which meant approaching it with a television production pipeline. We had no time or budget for mistakes, so we had to get it right the first time. This sort of rushed production is not common for typically more explorative movie preproduction, but we used the explosive, almost frenzied energy to our favor to create the exciting adventure that made it to screen. We brought back most of our crew from the series, relying on everyone's strengths and talents through trust and empowerment. Ant and I prided ourselves on promoting from within, having a philosophy of enabling and supporting our teams. Everyone had a stake in this, so everyone gave their absolute all.

TONY GAMA-LOBO: When Becky and I first read Ant and Andy's treatment about how Casey Jones comes back from the future to prevent the Krang from destroying the world, we were psyched! Time travel, postapocalyptic New York, a terrifying enemy, a battle to save humanity. So cool! But it got us thinking about what this meant for the Turtles. Whose story would we be telling in this epic movie? The answer seemed obvious—Leo. One of the key character questions the series didn't have a chance to answer was *"How does Leo become the leader?"* So this would be his story, his *Rise*.

To really showcase the horrifying power of the Krang and set the stakes for the movie, the story needed to start in the future. This setting was something not seen before in *Rise*—the reds and pinks were a contrast from the bright neon purples and greens of the series. Everything about Krang-conquered New York had an unworldly and infected feeling. A war had been fought and the good guys lost. The Krang had laid waste to the city. But what happened to the TMNT?

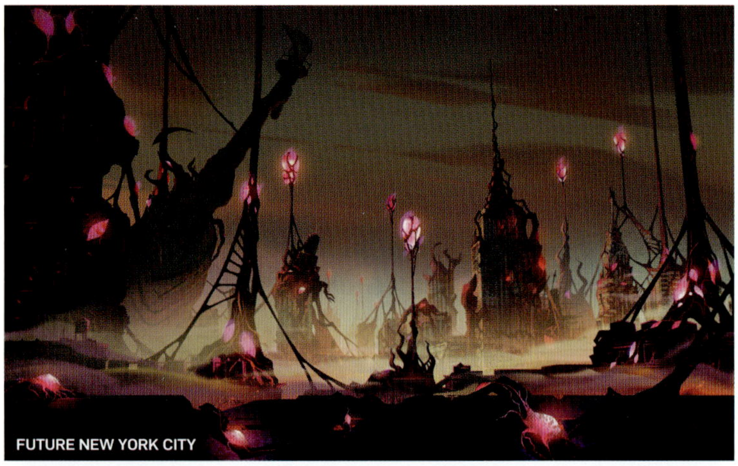

FUTURE NEW YORK CITY

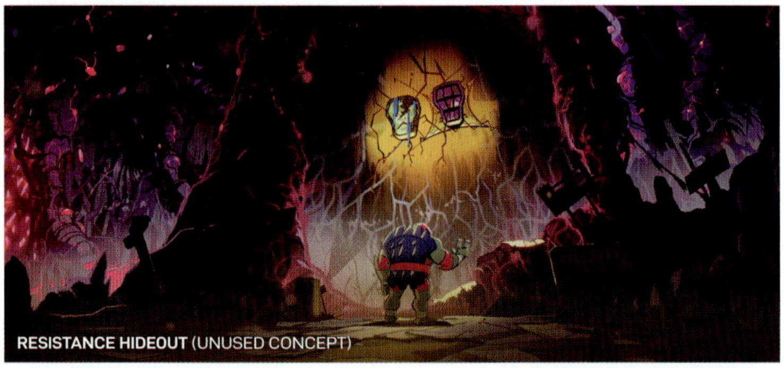

RESISTANCE HIDEOUT (UNUSED CONCEPT)

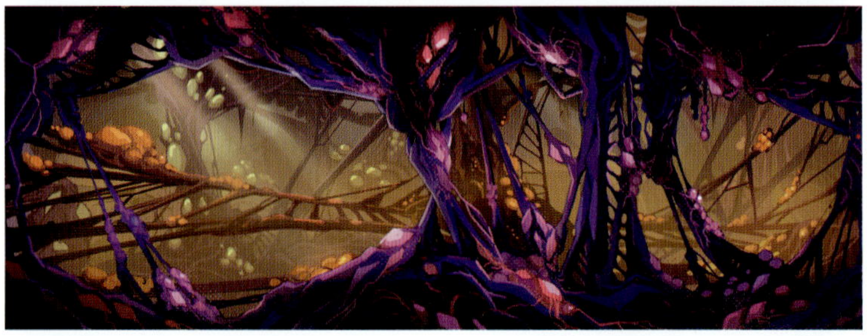

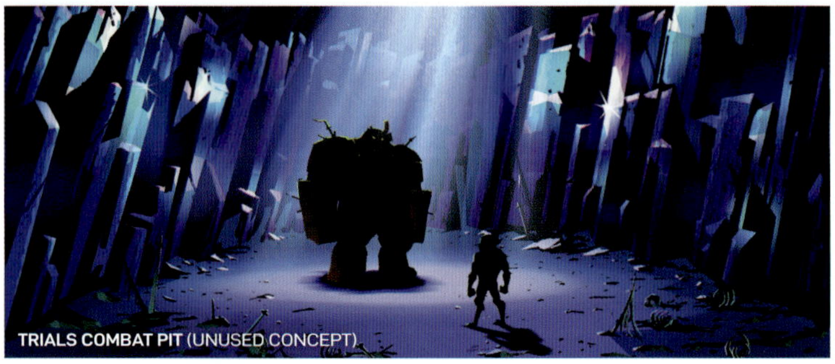

TRIALS COMBAT PIT (UNUSED CONCEPT)

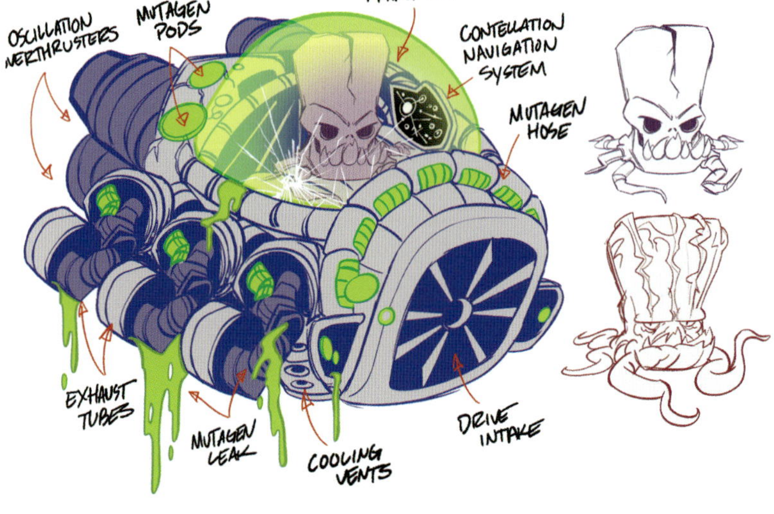

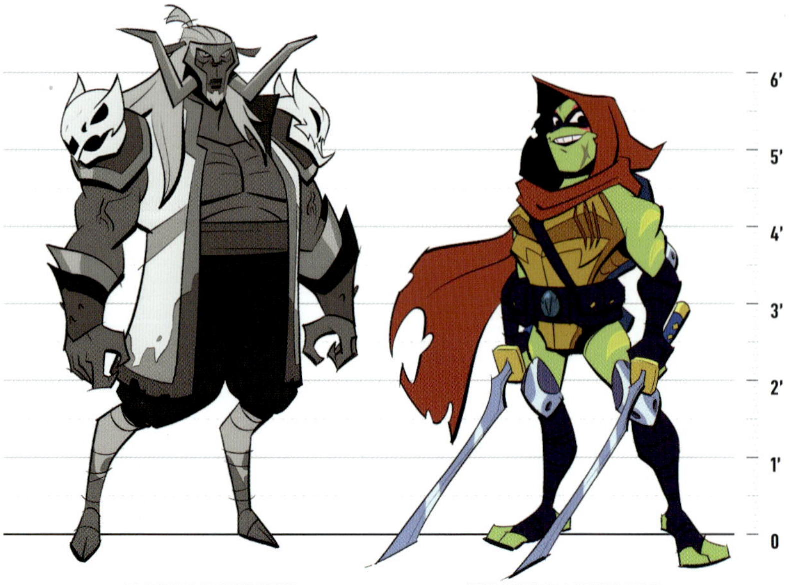

FUTURE DRAXUM
UNUSED CONCEPT

FUTURE LEONARDO
UNUSED CONCEPT

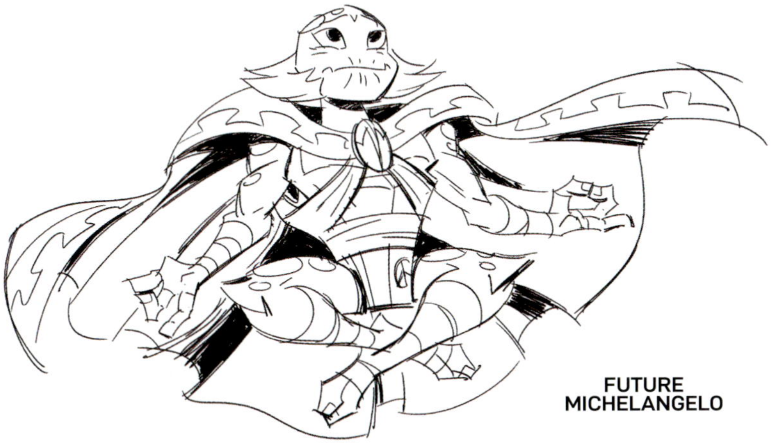

FUTURE MICHELANGELO

TONY GAMA-LOBO: While we were writing, Andy kept sending visual development of the world and characters. Mystic Mikey, Krangified New York, Casey Jones. Jaw-dropping. It was such a creative boost to see this world and these characters come to life as we were writing them. The design team was so detailed in the mythology of their designs that oftentimes art would drive the story.

As with most movies, many drafts and many storyboards were tried and discarded. The creative team behind *Rise* was not afraid to move on from things that were not serving the story. Ant and Andy, JJ and Kevin, Tony and Rebecca were tireless in finding the funniest, most exciting, and most emotionally fulfilling adventure they could. Considering the modest budget, time constraints, and challenges brought on by the pandemic, the results were nothing short of a miracle. The entire cast and crew put their heart and soul into the movie, and it really shows.

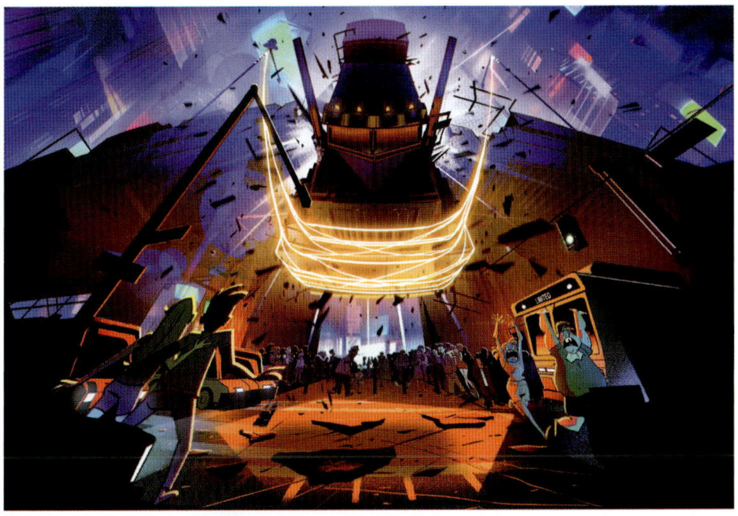

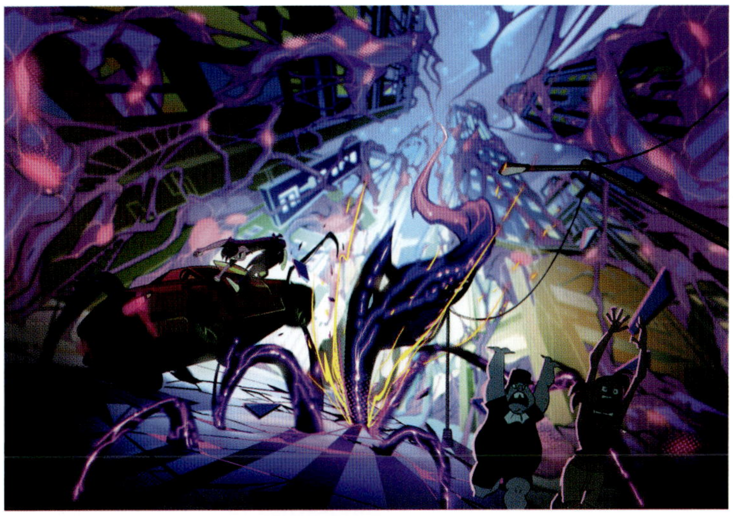

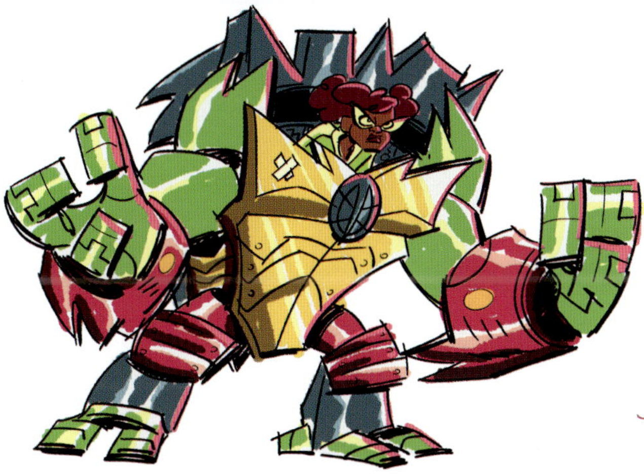

APRIL IN RAPH MECH
UNUSED CONCEPT

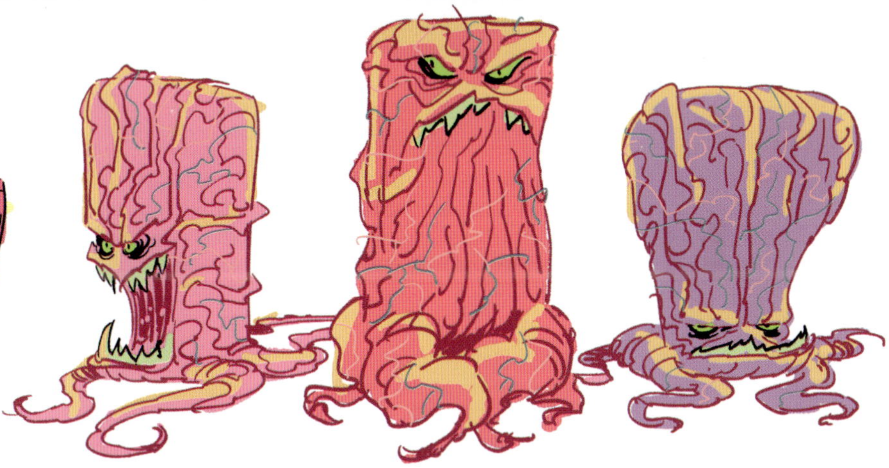

THE KRANG
EARLY CONCEPTS

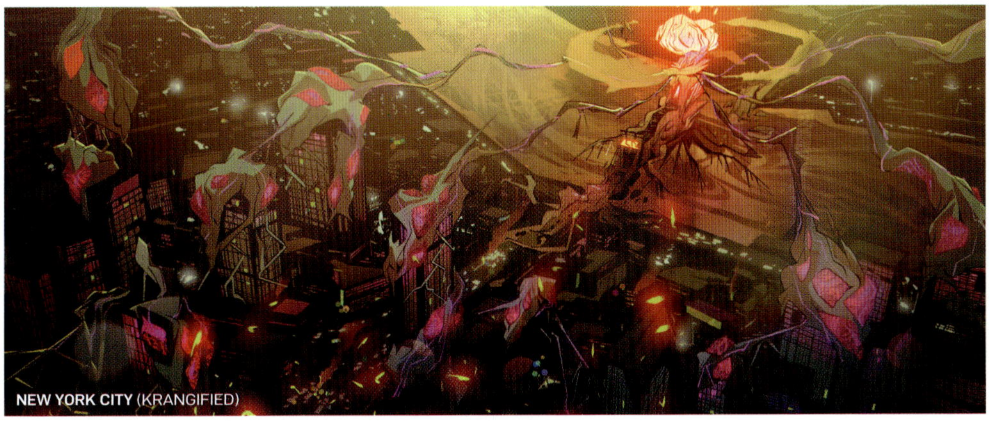

NEW YORK CITY (KRANGIFIED)

TONY GAMA-LOBO: One of the early concepts of the coming of the Krang was to already have them here. There was this creepy-cool version where the Krang's ship was buried deep beneath the Brooklyn Bridge centuries ago. Andy had the design team come up with these incredible visuals for the inside of the ship—gooey, organic, alive. Had a very *Aliens* (1986)/*Prometheus* (2012) vibe. The Turtles find out from Casey where the ship is and they go, accidentally waking up the Krang.

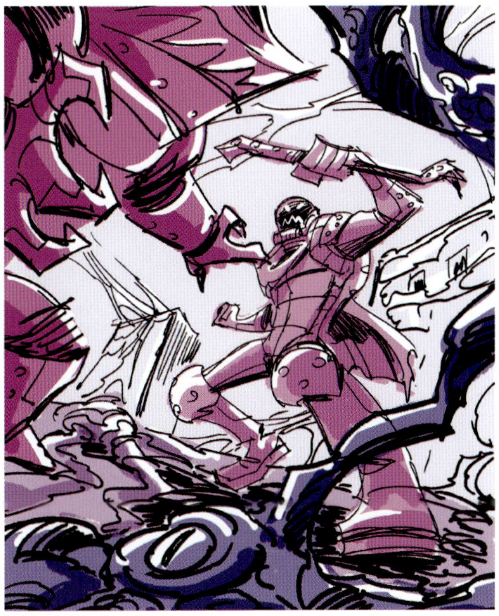

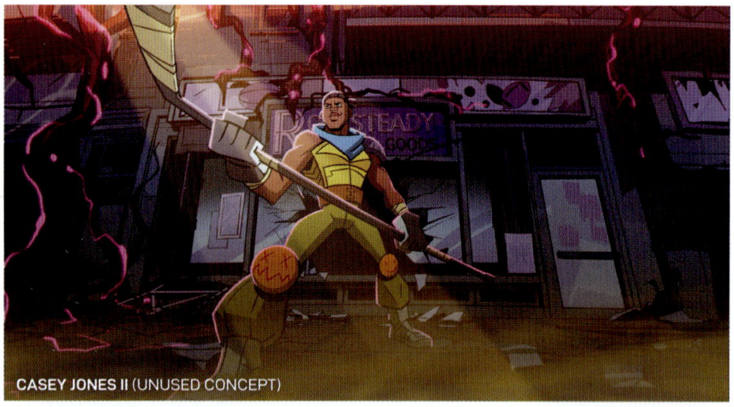
CASEY JONES II (UNUSED CONCEPT)

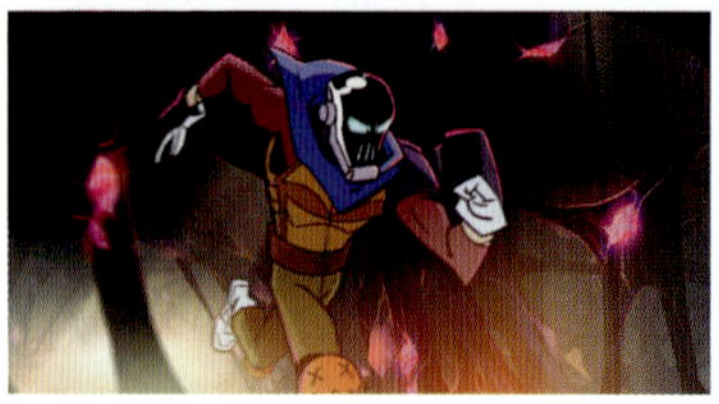

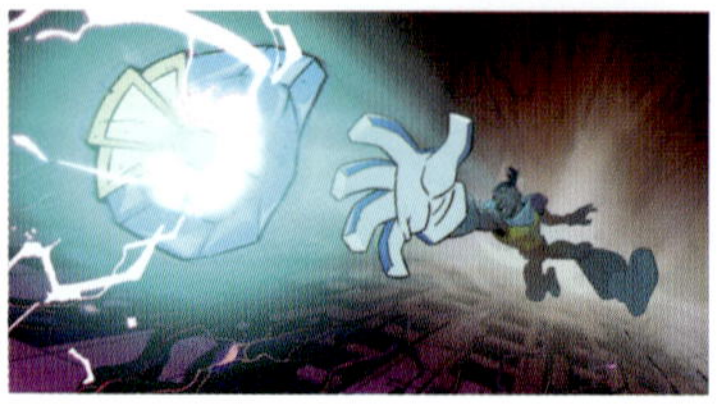

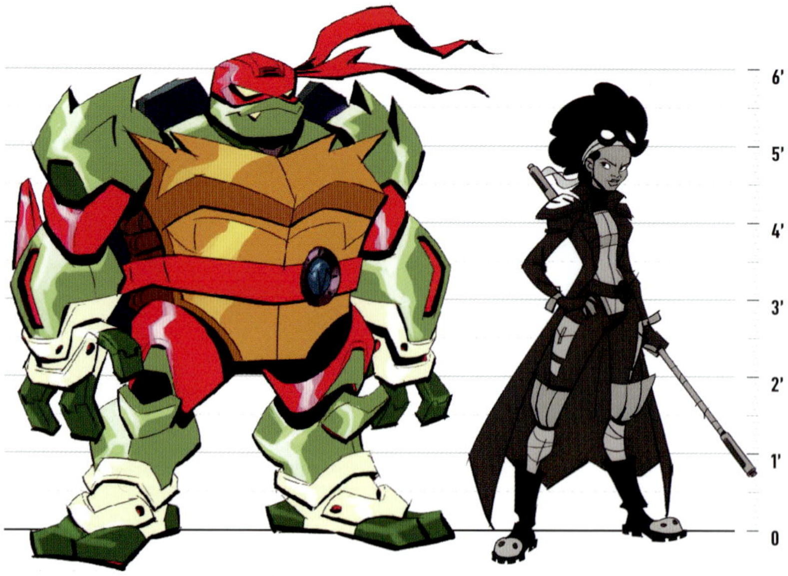

ROBO RAPH
UNUSED CONCEPT

COMMANDER O'NEIL
UNUSED CONCEPT

ANT WARD: As we were developing the movie, there were many different elements from TMNT lore that we wanted to use this opportunity to put our unique spin on. We were considering Armaggon to be the herald for the Krang, much like the Silver Surfer is to Galactus. Lord Simultaneous sending Mikey through time and having a bigger role. There was robotic Raph, a fun notion that Donnie had built robot versions of all his brothers (you never know...), which we found hilarious. April would end up piloting the suit and being a badass. It's actually Robo Raph's arm Leo has in the future sequence of the movie. There was a whole sequence in the future highlighting the villains and heroes from the show coming together to fight the Krang, led by Commander O'Neil. But at the end of the day, keeping the story as clear as possible...as Leo's journey became our North Star, a lot of these things ended up on the cutting-room floor as we found they were cool set pieces, but they started to make things too busy.

TONY GAMA-LOBO: One of the very first images we had was of future Leo at some hidden rebel base. He glances up at a wall honoring fallen soldiers and we see Raph's, Donnie's, and Mikey's empty shells! Gut punch! Immediately we're asking ourselves, "What happened? What mistakes did Leo make that led to his brothers dying?"

ANT WARD: We were able to carry a large part of the show's pipeline over to the movie. As the show was ending, we were able to roll a large amount of our art department onto the movie. The story department was tricky to staff up, as, at that time, most of our team had rolled onto other projects. Thankfully, we were able to bring Kevin and JJ onto the movie to oversee the storyboard department and ensure that new team members matched the show's style as closely as possible. With the sudden cancellation of the show, our animation studio, Flying Bark, had to move on to other projects, so we were tasked to bring a new studio, Top Draw, up to speed for the show style—which was initially very challenging, as the new studio's strength was in puppet (rigged 2D) animation, not hand-drawn. Thankfully, we were able to bring back Flying Bark for key moments of the movie, and with their help, particularly from the incredible Tom Barkel, we were able to bring Top Draw up to speed. Every team rose to the occasion.

CARL BEU: New talent joined development alongside veterans like Angelo Vilar, who had been with the show from the very beginning, and Kit Rigby contributing from Australia. We were extremely lucky to have a great mix of experience and new energy on the movie in every department.

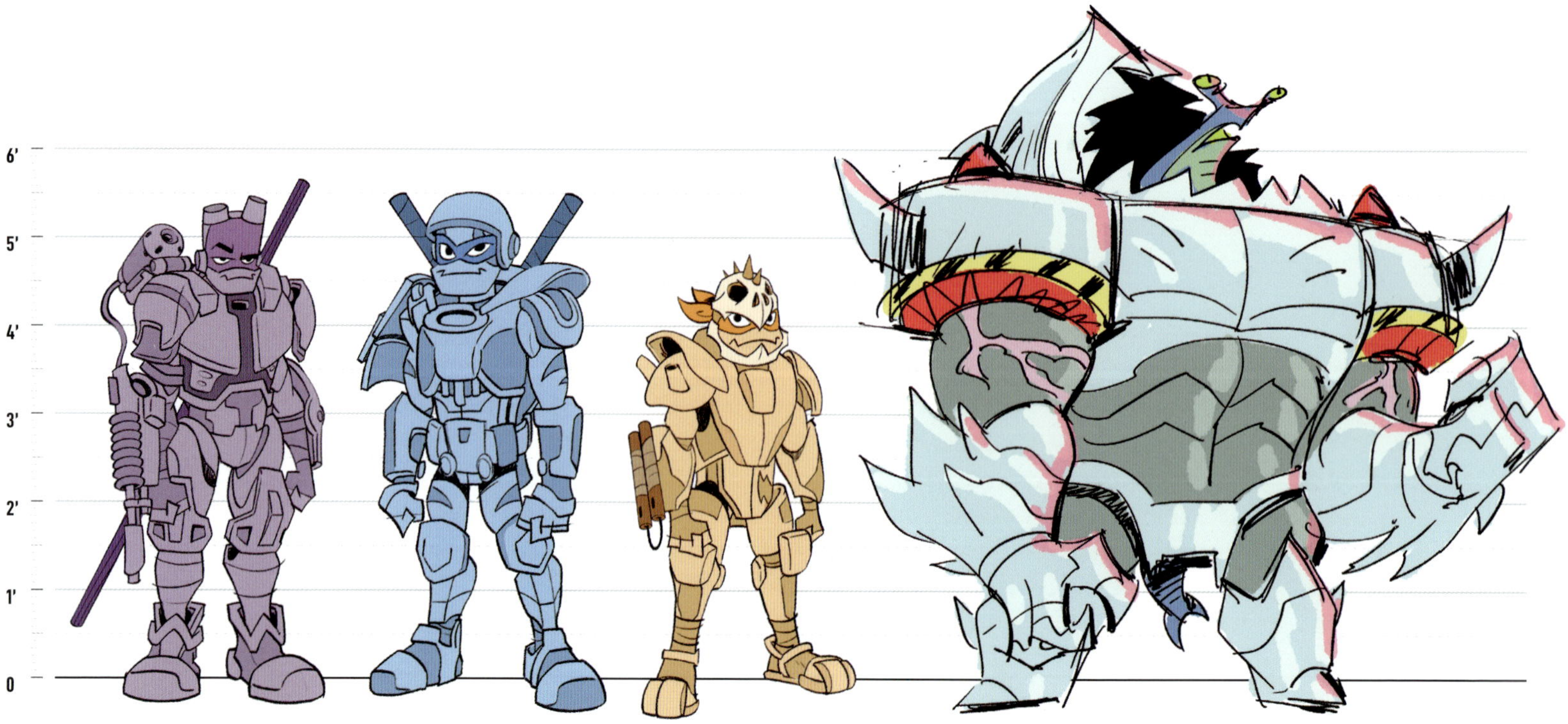

TURTLE TECH SUITS
UNUSED CONCEPTS

ARMAGGON
UNUSED CONCEPT

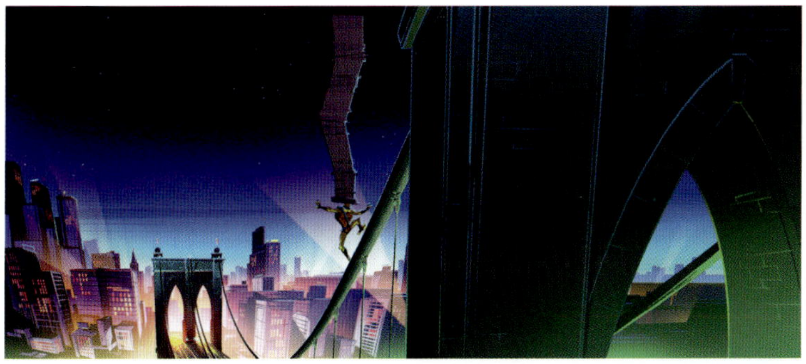

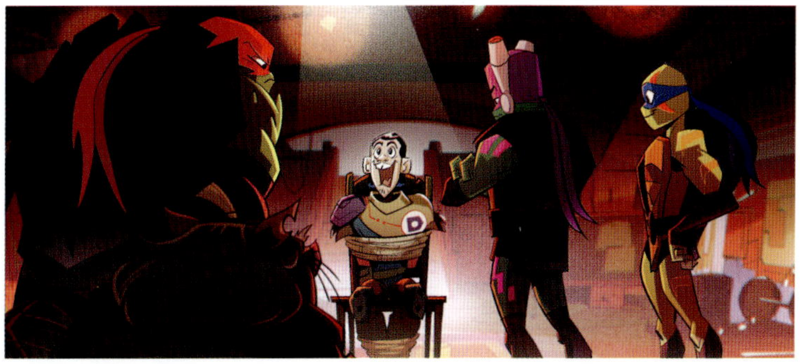

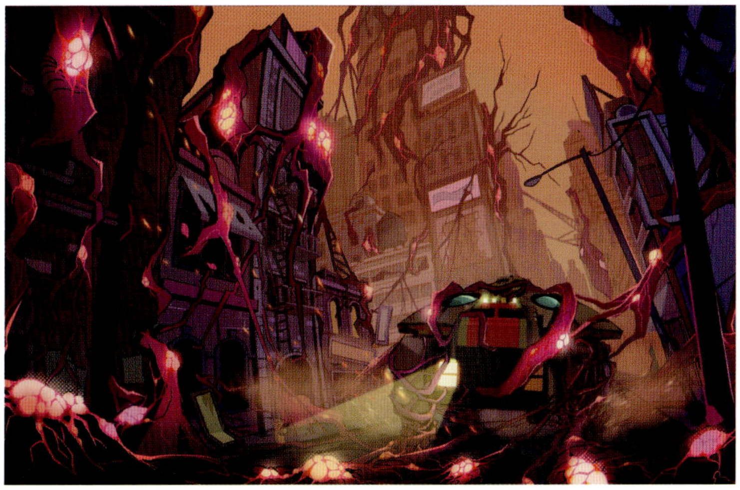

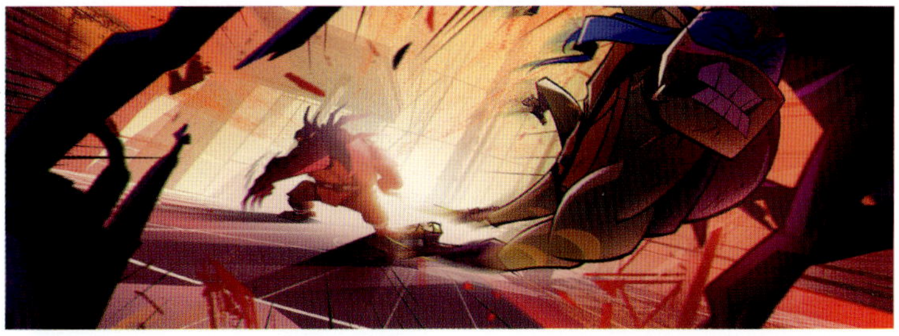

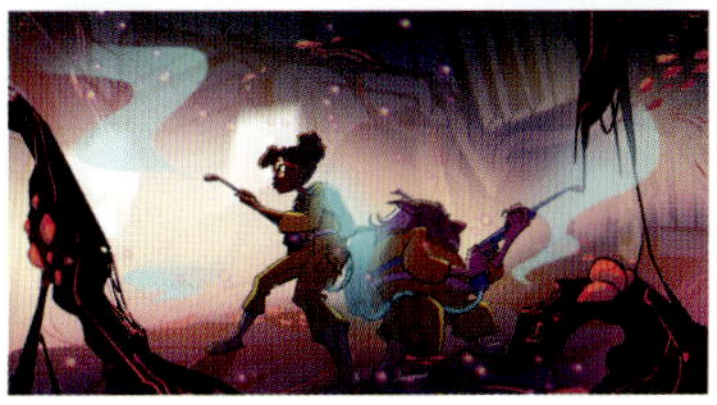

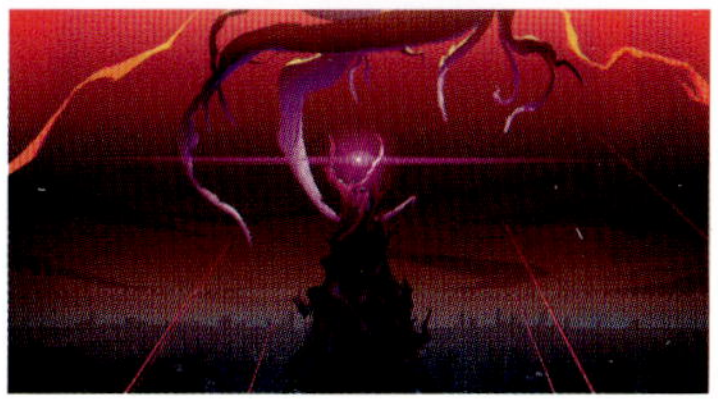

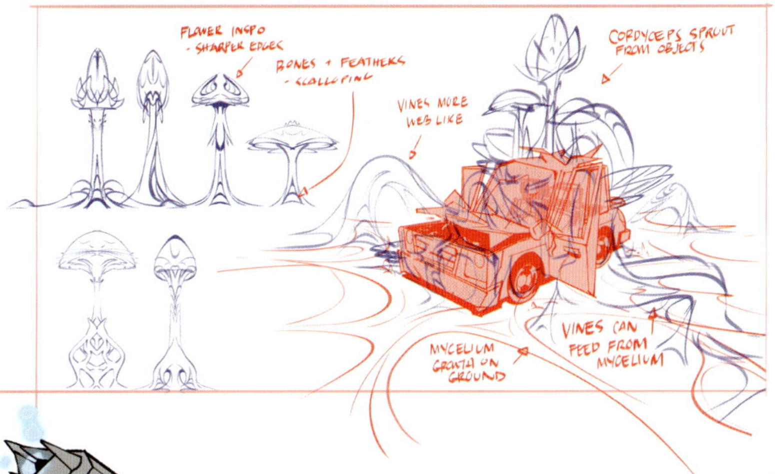

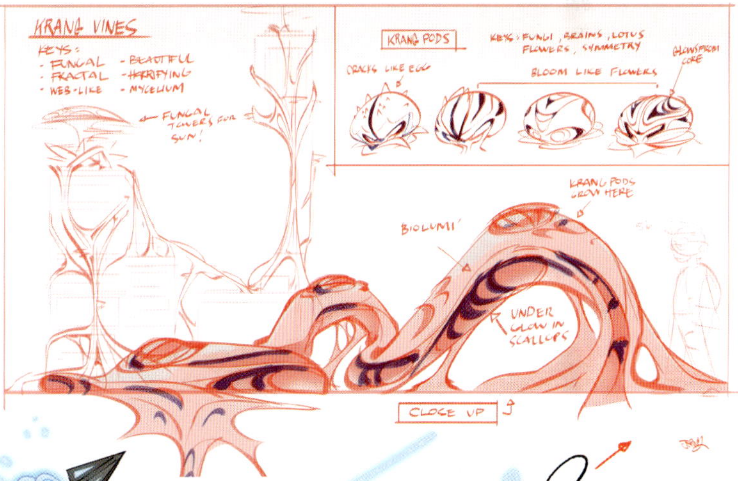

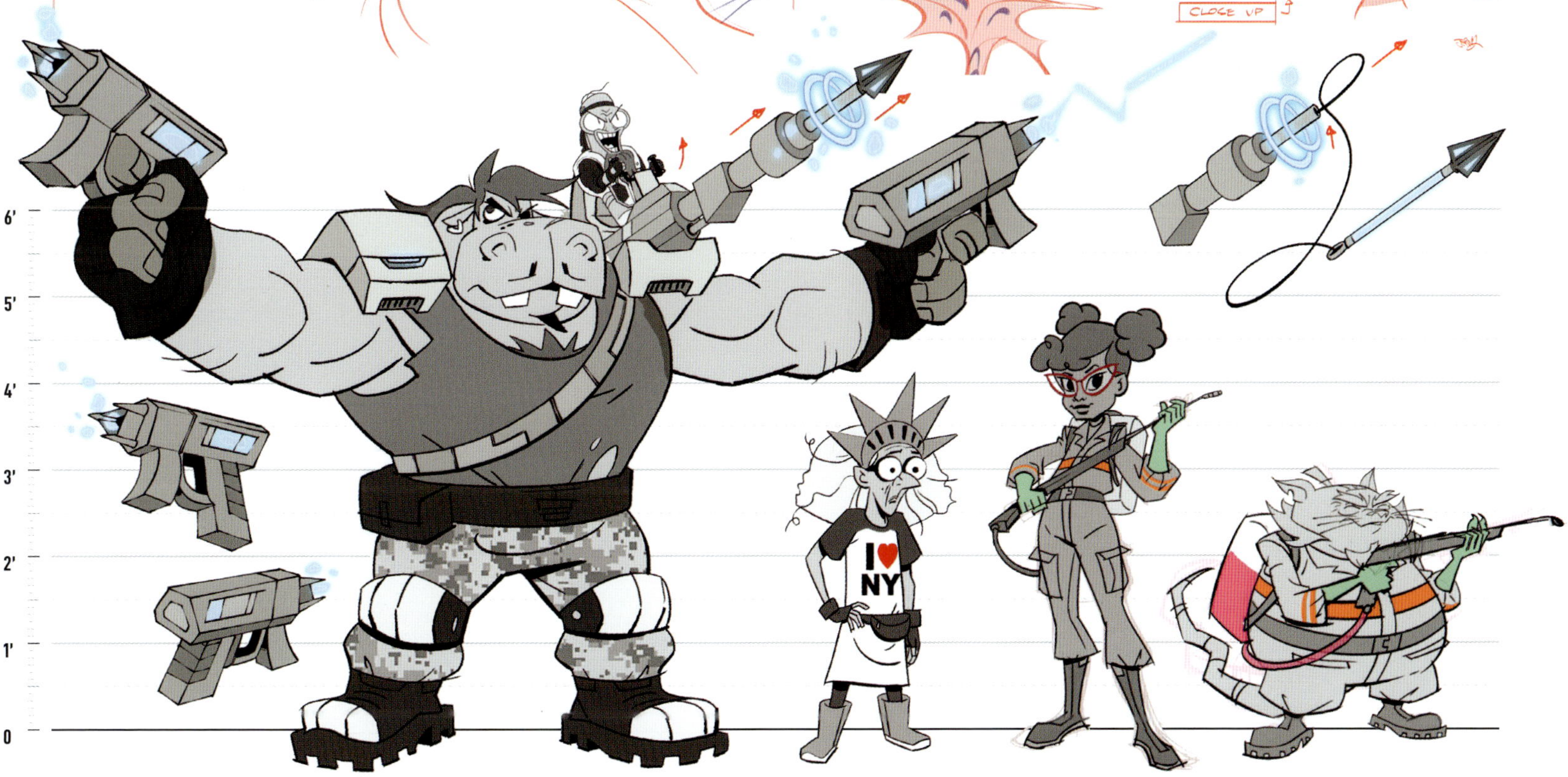

FUTURE HYPNO & WARREN STONE
UNUSED CONCEPTS

LORD SIMULTANEOUS
UNUSED CONCEPT

WEED KILLER SUITS
UNUSED CONCEPTS

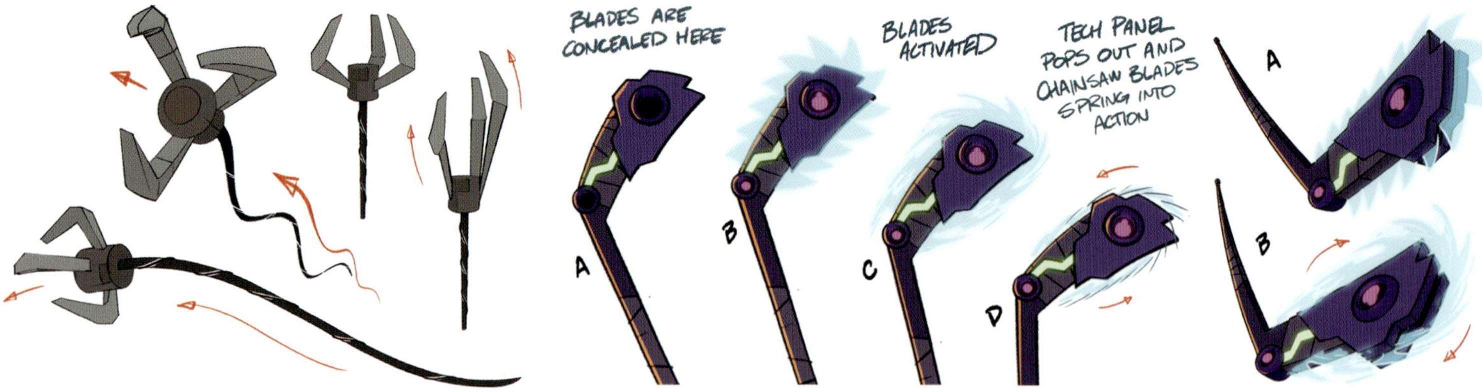

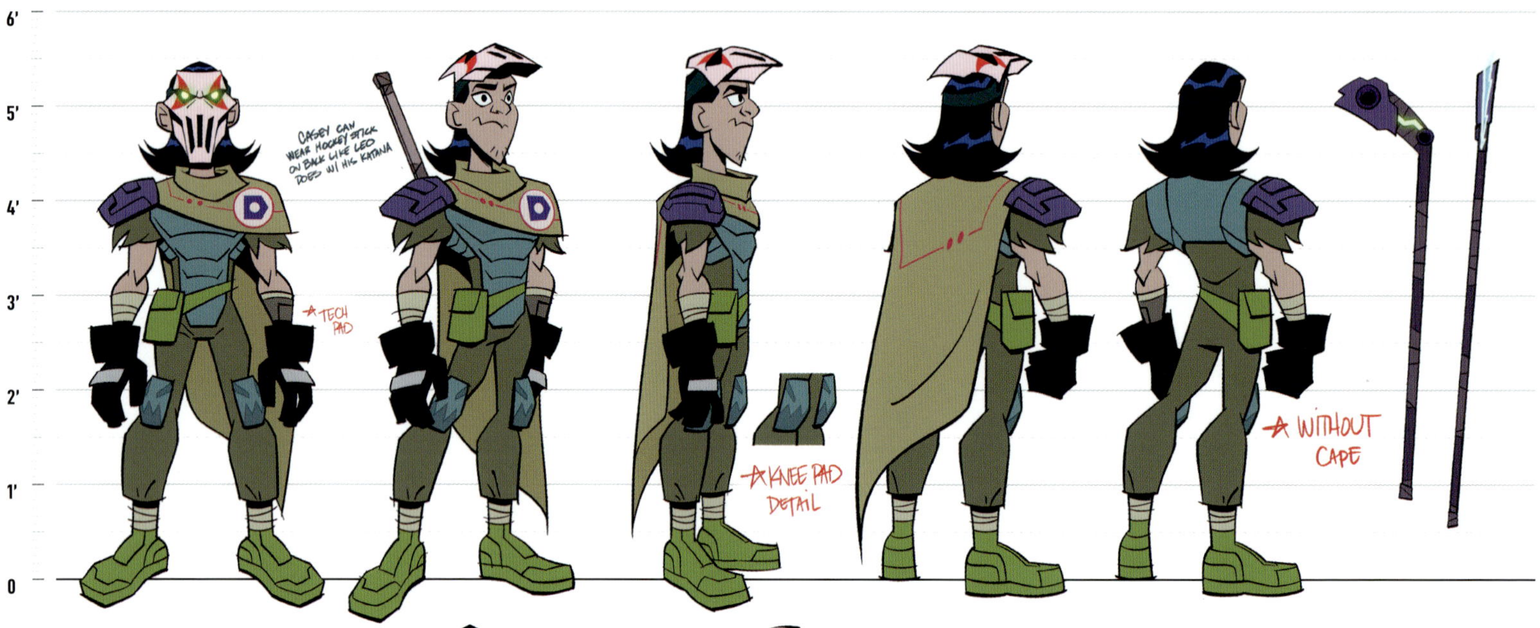

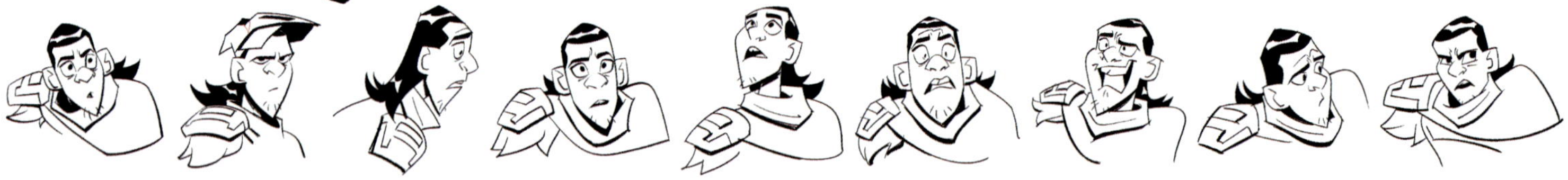

CASEY JONES II

VOICED BY HALEY JOEL OSMENT

SPECIES: HUMAN WEAPON: CHAINSAW ICE HOCKEY STICK

Casey Jones is the last human resistance fighter from a future where humans and mutants fight in an apocalyptic war against an alien race. Master Leonardo sends Casey back in time to stop their invasion before it begins, with only one mission: Find the key, stop the Krang.

ANT WARD: Cassandra Jones was always going to be the *Rise* Casey Jones. When we were approached to do the movie and the studio expressed interest in a more legacy Casey Jones being part of it, Andy and I used the time-travel trope to establish a more familiar Casey Jones while also not stepping on our canon for Cassandra. The future Casey would not have been in the show.

ANDY SURIANO: We really wanted to show the Foot Recruit in action as Casey, but we were given the mandate to have the movie be accessible and familiar to old and new fans, which meant "classic" version—but with our twist.

Casey Jones II (Haley Joel Osment) is the future son of Cassandra Jones and a student of the future Turtles. He comes from the year 2044, a dystopian future where the alien Krang have ruled Earth for over 20 years. As a young resistance fighter and the sole survivor of his faction, Casey was trained by Master Leonardo and sent back in time on a desperate mission: stop the Krang invasion before it starts.

Thrust into the past carrying the weight of a lost future, this Casey is the "classic" Casey Jones archetype. He's recognizable by his iconic white goaltender mask, now modified with Leonardo-inspired red stripes, and wields a customized chainsaw ice hockey stick.

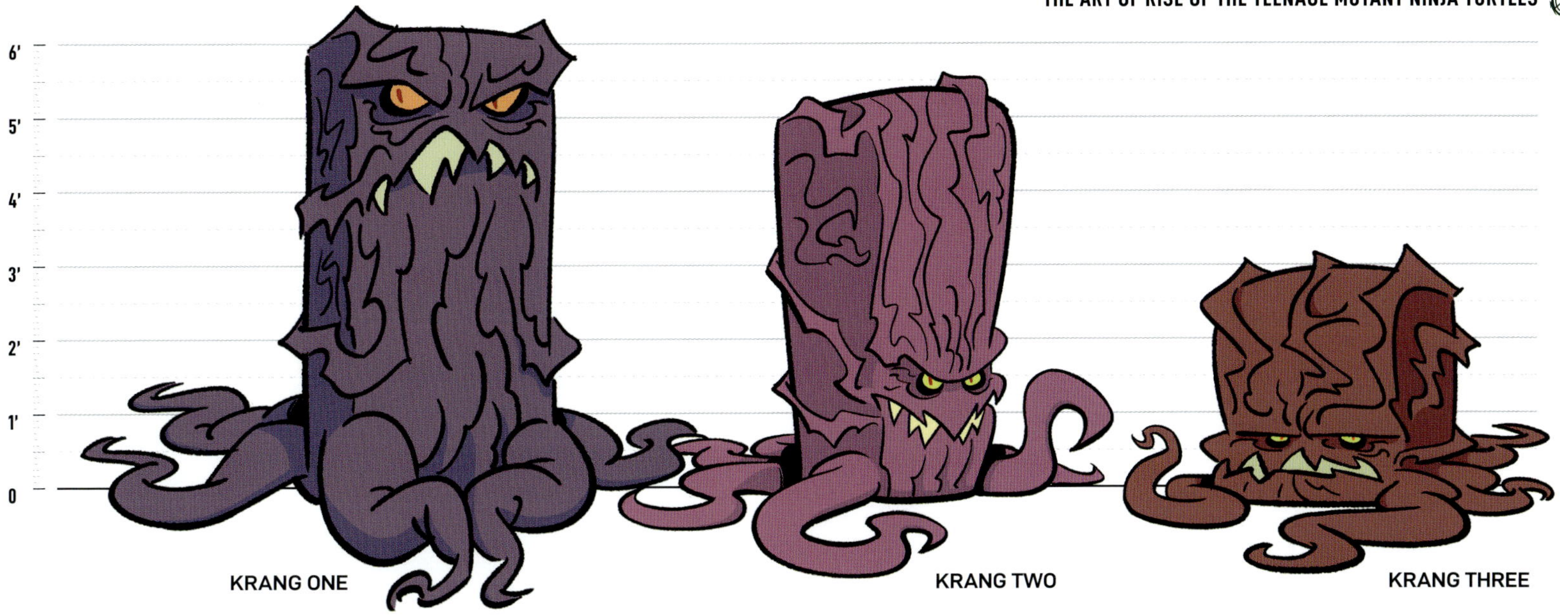

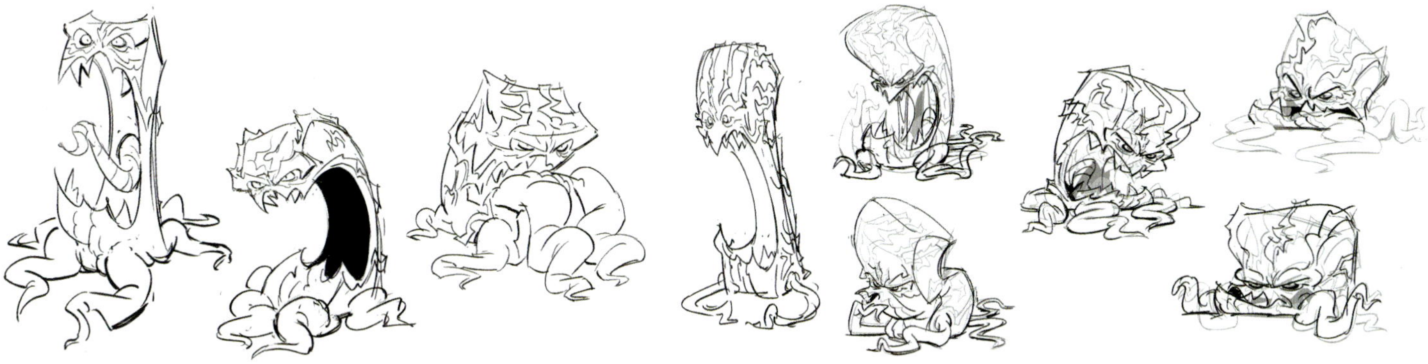

THE KRANG

VOICED BY JIM PIRRI AND TOKS OLAGUNDOYE

ABILITIES: MYSTIC POWER NULLIFICATION, TENTACLE-TO-HAND COMBAT, MIND READING, ENSLAVEMENT

The Krang are ancient alien conquerors who seek to enslave Earth. Trapped in Dimension X for a millennium, these powerful oni return to lay waste upon anyone who stands in their way. They corrupt living and nonliving matter, turning victims into Krangified zombies under their control. With the Technodrome, they reduce cities to wastelands, hunting survivors with enhanced brutality. To face them is to fight extinction itself.

ANT WARD: Originally, the Krang had a much larger role in the *Rise* canon. Not only were they the ones to give Shredder his dark suit, but they also were the source of the ooze that created all Yōkai under the Hidden City. This was all to be revealed and explored further in future seasons. We did adjust and pivot the canon slightly for clarity in the movie.

ANDY SURIANO: We had always planned on the Krang being the original creators of the Shredder armor; in fact, we had a whole premise where there was an enormous Krang craft housing thousands of set of armor, being seeded across multiple worlds—their own army.

JJ CONWAY: There have been many versions of the Krang, so early on we decided to set ours apart by making them terrifying and dangerous. Traditionally the Krang needed technology to be formidable, but we looked to the monster in John Carpenter's *The Thing* (1982) as inspiration for how our Krang could hold their own. This led us to the idea that they can infect, transform, and control the world around them. People, technology, the environment itself. And that's all before they summon their battle fortress, the Technodrome, and gain access to their battle suits.

Krang One (Pirri), the sinister supreme leader, embodies cunning arrogance. He spearheads the invasion, fixating on the Teenage Mutant Ninja Turtles as the sole obstacle to "to-tail victory." Unflinching in his ambition, he exploits a unique telepathic ability to violate minds and extract secrets, pursuing total control at any cost.

Alongside him stands Krang Two (Olagundoye), the faction's fearless military commander. A brash, hot-tempered tactician, she operates as the Krang's rogue warrior—agile, ferocious, and relentlessly destructive. Embodying the spirit of a "boots on the ground" general, she trudges through battlefields to eliminate all resistance, ensuring the Krang's triumph through sheer force.

Completing this lethal hierarchy is Krang Three, their soft-spoken yet catastrophic secret weapon. His mastery of invasive biotech renders him all-seeing and all-knowing, capable of spewing corruptive alien matter that transforms humans into mindless minions. This power makes him uniquely dangerous, as he terraforms cities and turns populations into extensions of the Krang hive mind.

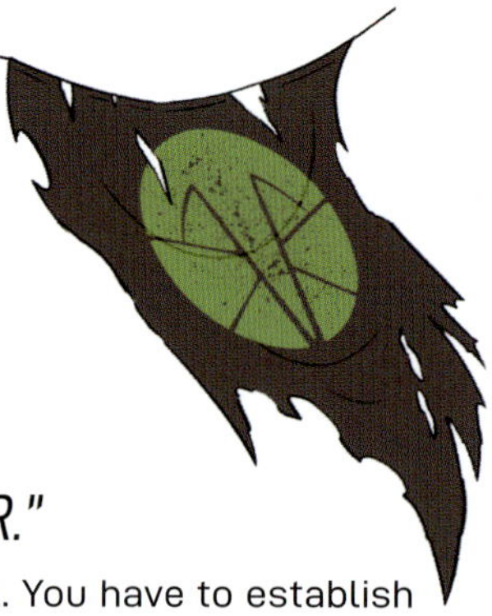

NEW YORK 2044

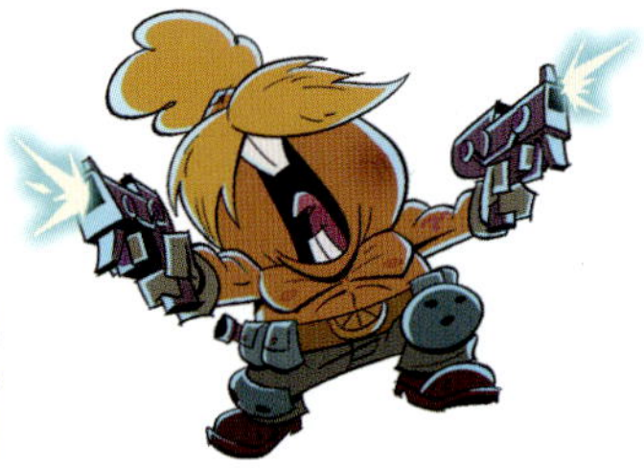

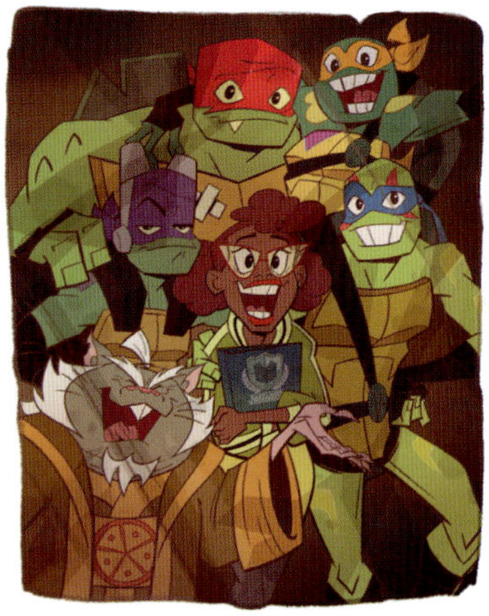

"THE KRANG WON, BUT IT ISN'T OVER."

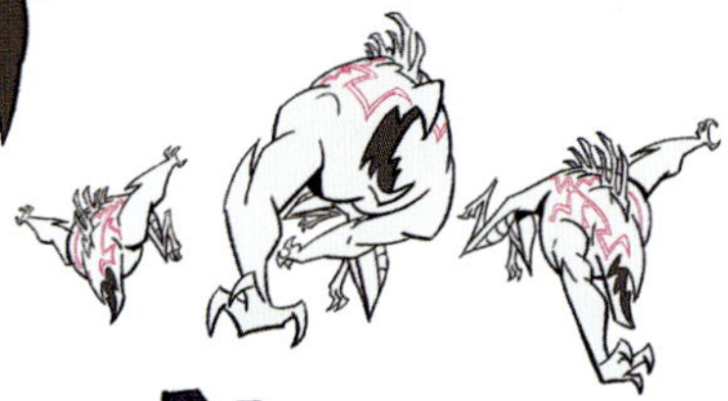

The opening scene of any movie is crucial. You have to establish characters, stakes, tone—and do it fast. The drumbeat from Ant and Andy and the studio was to elevate *Rise* the movie from *Rise* the series. Make it cinematic and grab the audience.

JJ CONWAY: We knew we wanted to start the film with a future prologue, but all our attempts were too big and too involved for the amount of screen time we had in the film. We seriously considered abandoning the prologue, but Tony said, "Wait, I have an idea—give me a day or two." And when he came back, he and Becky delivered a killer opening that was tight, lean, and packed a devastating punch.

TONY GAMA-LOBO: We had a *lot* of beginnings to the movie. There was Leo and Casey sneaking through a jungle Indiana Jones–style to steal a time-travel scepter from a mystic temple. Surprise, the jungle turns out to be postapocalyptic New York! Then they're hunted down by Armaggon, herald for the Krang, who ends up going back in time with Casey. Then there was the assault on the rebellion stronghold, where we got to see cool future warrior versions of April, Draxum, Warren, Hypno, and even Todd. Every version was amazing...and too convoluted. They took too long to establish the stakes, the rules, the characters and story. Sometimes you just have to strip out all the extra stuff and ask yourself what matters—it's hopeless, everyone we know and love is gone, but we have one last chance, boom you're in it. You do that *and* kill Leo and Mikey in the first five minutes and you got yourself a killer beginning.

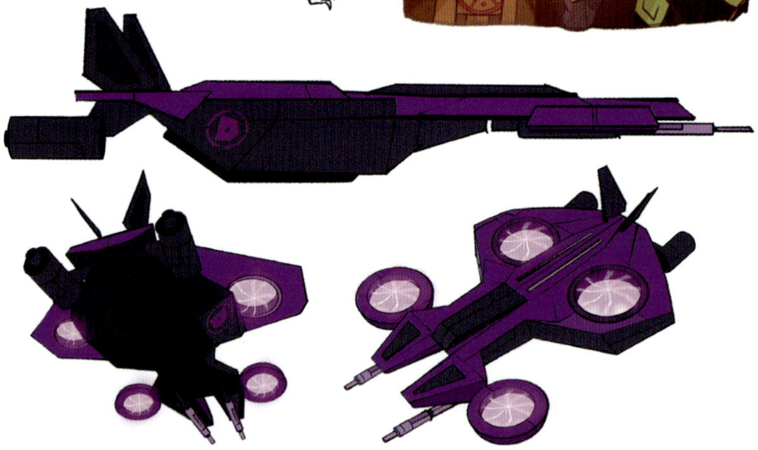

GENIUS BUILT MILITARY AIRCRAFT

JJ CONWAY: But now that we had an opening we liked on paper, the problem was that we were running out of schedule time. It needed to ship in, like, a week. To make it happen I did a quick thumbnail pass, then I got me, Kevin, and India Swift cleared for overtime, and together we boarded the entire prologue in one weekend. Monday it went to edit, Friday it was shipped to Flying Bark.

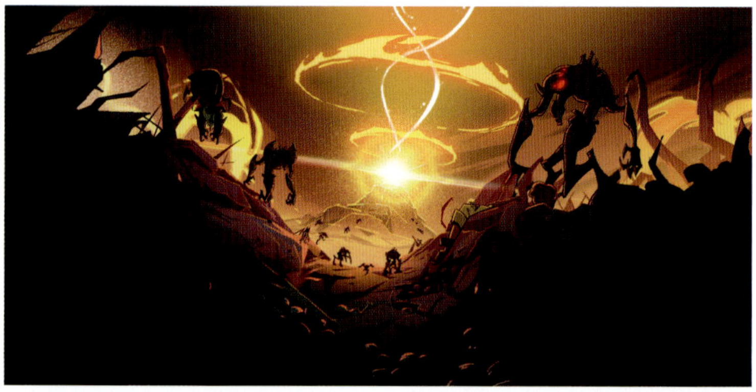

TONY GAMA-LOBO: Andy's design of Mystic Warrior Mikey and JJ's boards of him opening the portal took my breath away when I first saw them. And when Mikey explodes, heartbreak.

JJ CONWAY: When Ant and Andy got eyes on what had been boarded, their jaws were on the floor. Kevin's jaw-dropping battle in the opening shots set the tone for the film, and India broke our hearts with Mikey's and Leo's heroic sacrifices. It all sent a powerful warning: This future must be avoided at all costs.

JEFFRY CHOZON (BACKGROUND PAINTER): We had to figure out how to take a show, which was already dialed to 11, and crank it up even higher. One of my favorite parts is the cold opening of the film. The future where Casey Jones came from had to feel very different from what we had seen in the series thus far. It needed to feel like a war zone, but at the same time bleak with no possible [restitution] in sight. There were a multitude of iterations for how the colors could feel, and what we ultimately landed on definitely conveyed that idea the best.

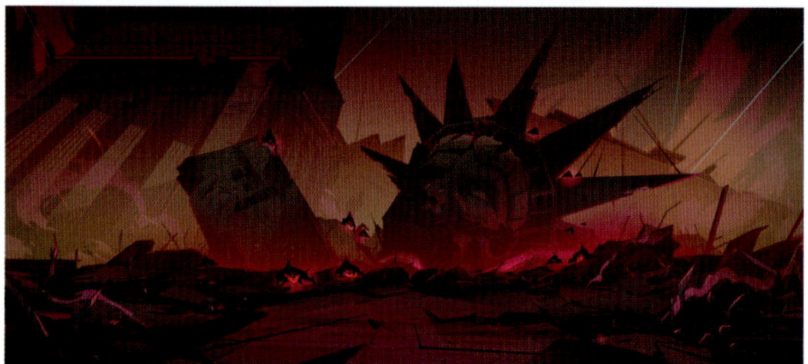

RESISTANCE BASE - EXTERIOR

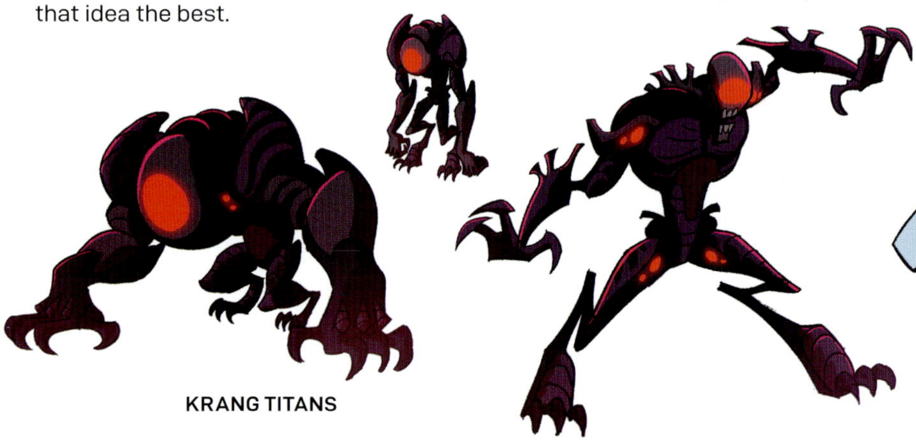

KRANG TITANS

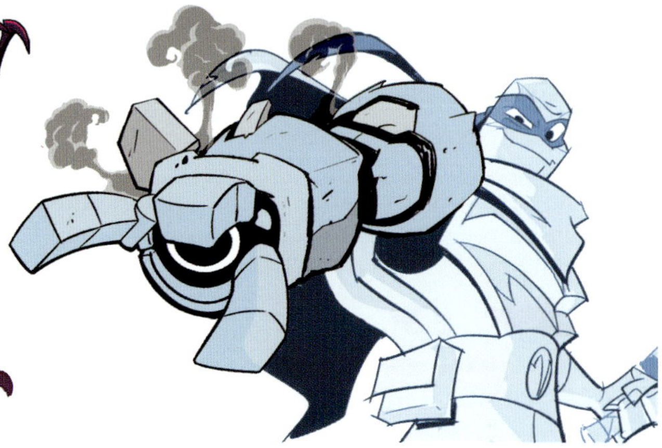

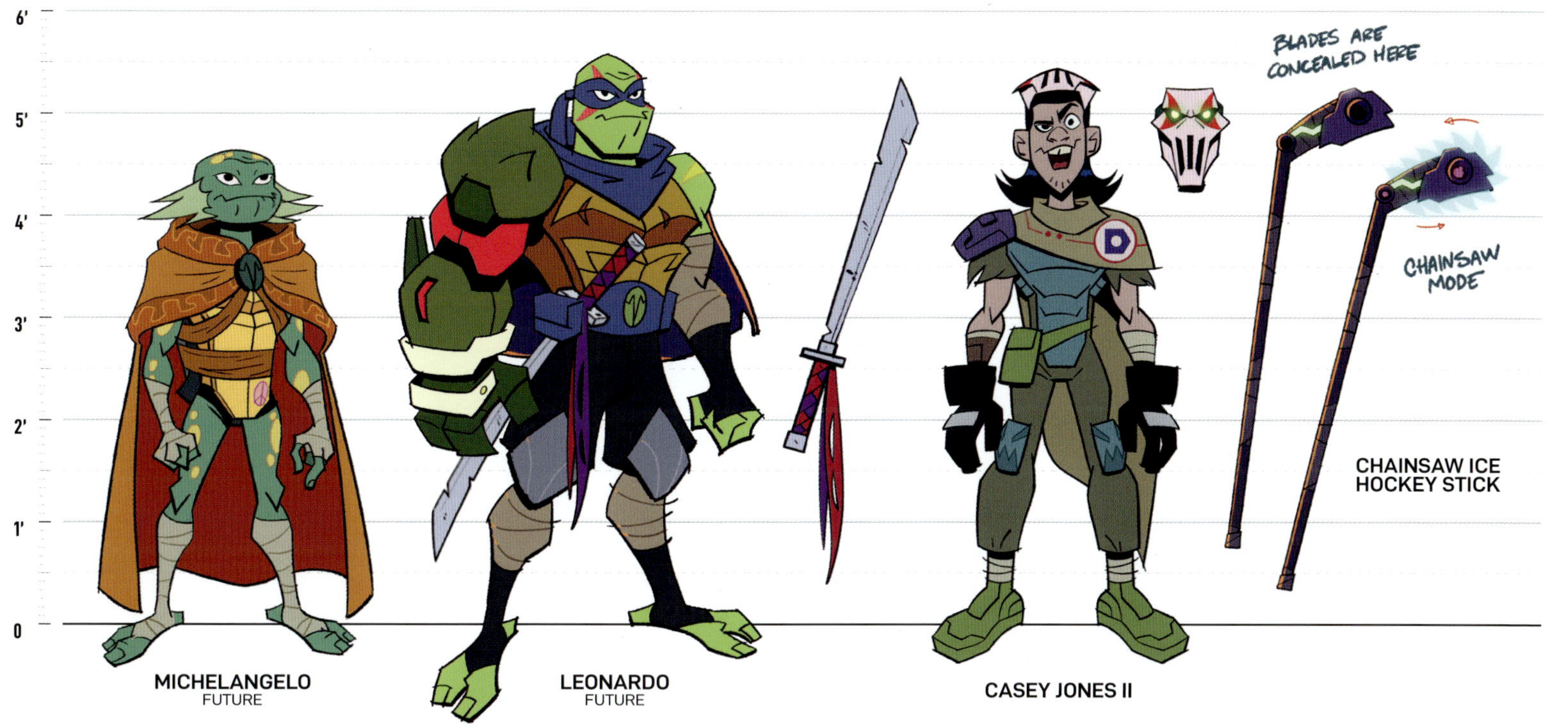
6'
5'
4'
3'
2'
1'
0
BLADES ARE CONCEALED HERE
CHAINSAW MODE
CHAINSAW ICE HOCKEY STICK
MICHELANGELO
FUTURE
LEONARDO
FUTURE
CASEY JONES II

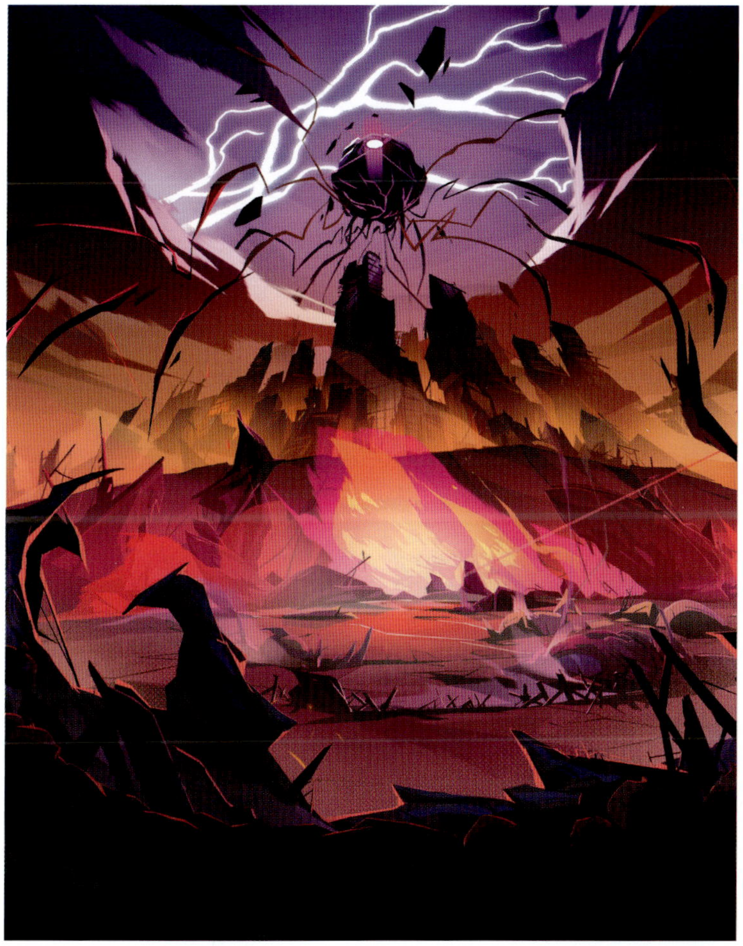

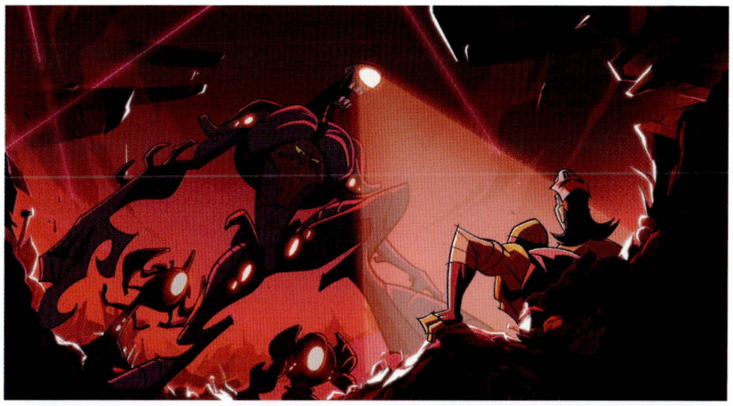

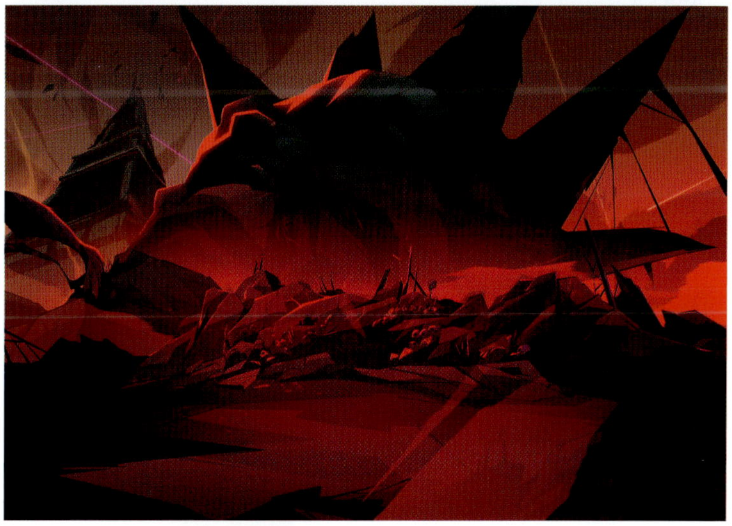

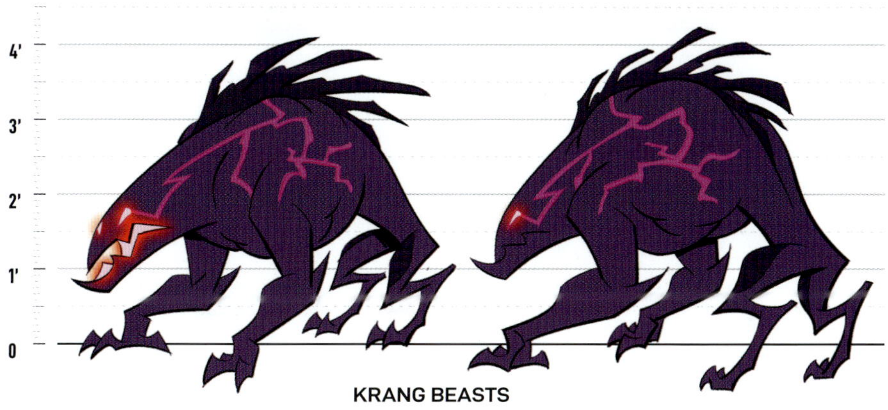
4'
3'
2'
1'
0
KRANG BEASTS

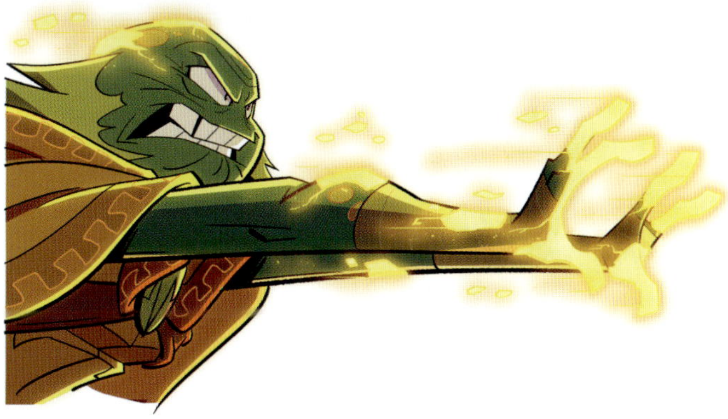

PRESENT DAY

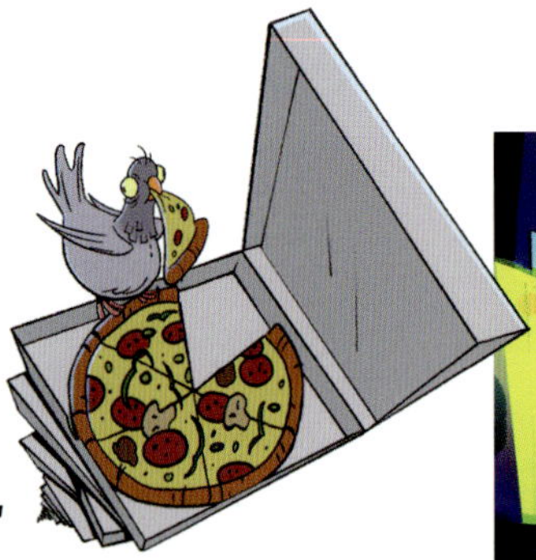

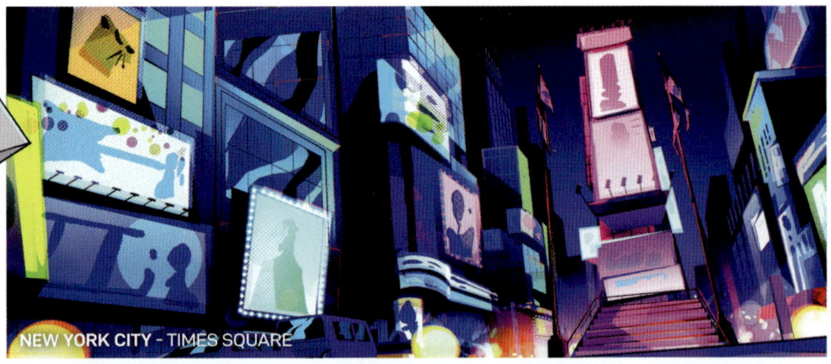

"FIND THE KEY, STOP THE KRANG."

The movie team had the herculean task of giving the fans of the series the continuous adventures of the Turtles they knew and loved while also introducing *Rise* to a whole new potential audience. Introducing present-day Raph, Leo, Donnie, and Mikey properly was key. The Turtles had grown, having defeated the Shredder and become heroes. *But* they also still needed to be goof-around teens who needed to learn something from this new adventure.

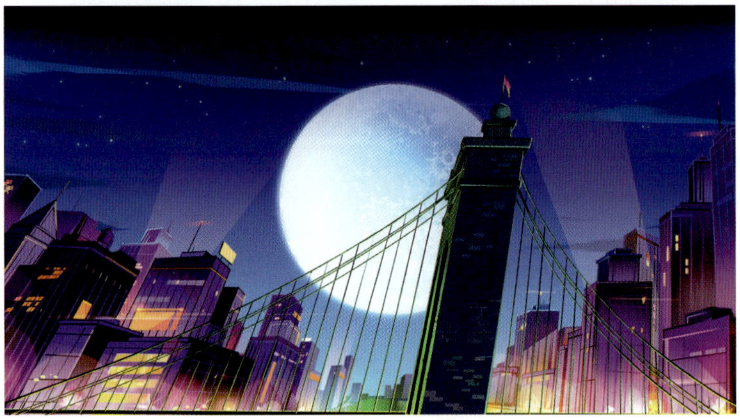

JJ CONWAY: There was a lot of groundwork to lay here. We went into this movie assuming that nobody in the audience had seen the show, so we needed to carefully and concisely introduce all of our main players, their powers, and the world they inhabit, while also making sure that all functioned as the foundation for the specific story and arcs we wanted to tell in the movie.

When we sat down to break the story on the film, we began with the assumption that Raph was our main character. The problem we had is that, by the end of the series, Raph is a great leader. Giving Raph an arc in the movie either felt forced or felt like we were retconning the journey he'd already been on. Then it hit us: This isn't Raph's story, it's Leo's. Suddenly it all fell into place, and we had the story of how Leo grows into the leader we recognize from the franchise lore.

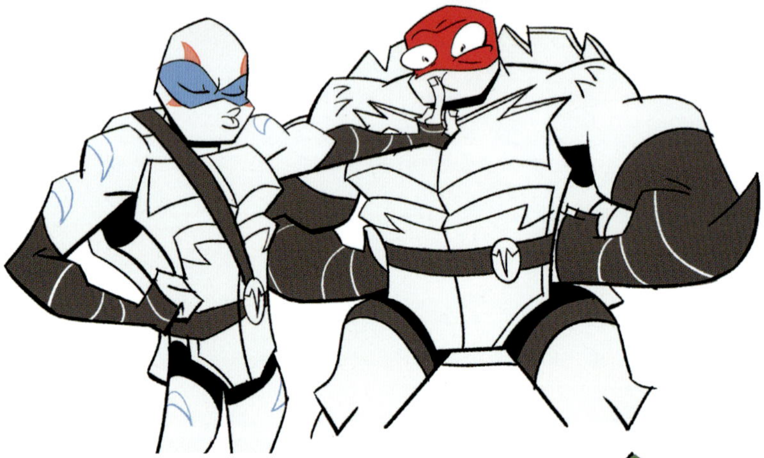

JERMAINE JOSE: I was tasked with painting the background for the movie logo. I scribbled in "The Movie" text below it, thinking it would just serve as a placeholder. I didn't realize it would be the final!

TONY GAMA-LOBO: The intro scene is one of my favorites. It needed to be funny, super cool, and quickly get across every character's POV. Our son had just had this competition at school where they stacked as many pizza boxes as a fourth grader could carry, and they would race. We thought, let's do that…but on the Brooklyn Bridge! It turned out to be the perfect way to start the cocky and overconfident Leo story. And Kevin nailed the boards—a visually epic and hilarious intro to the boys.

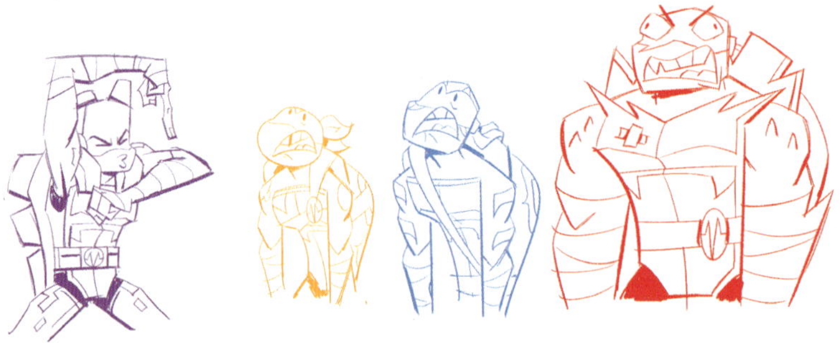

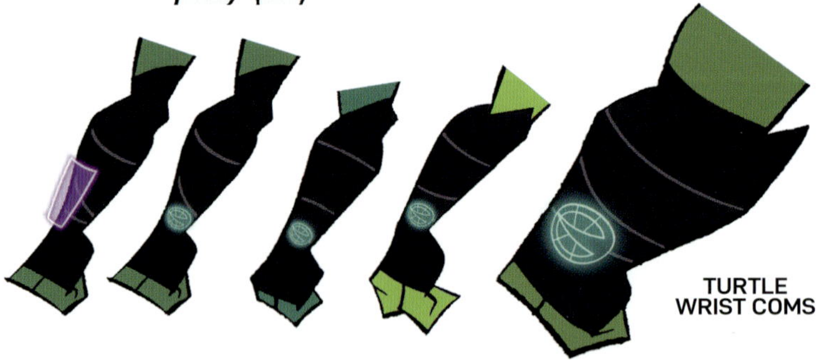

TURTLE WRIST COMS

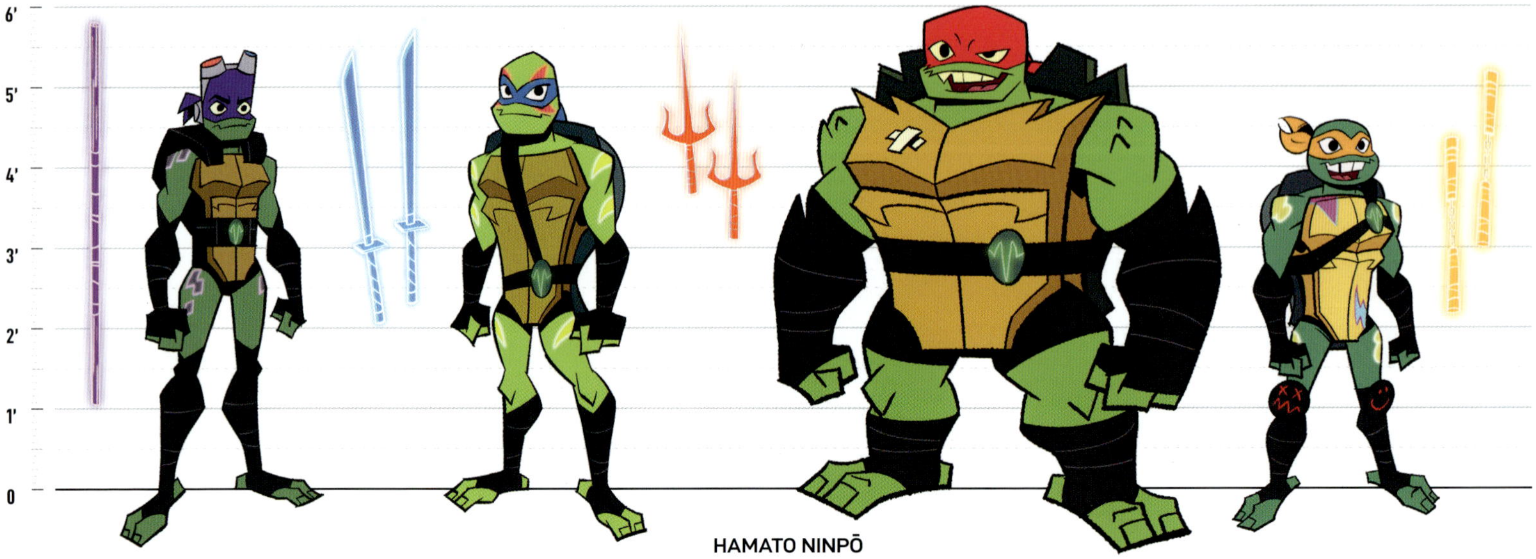

HAMATO NINPŌ

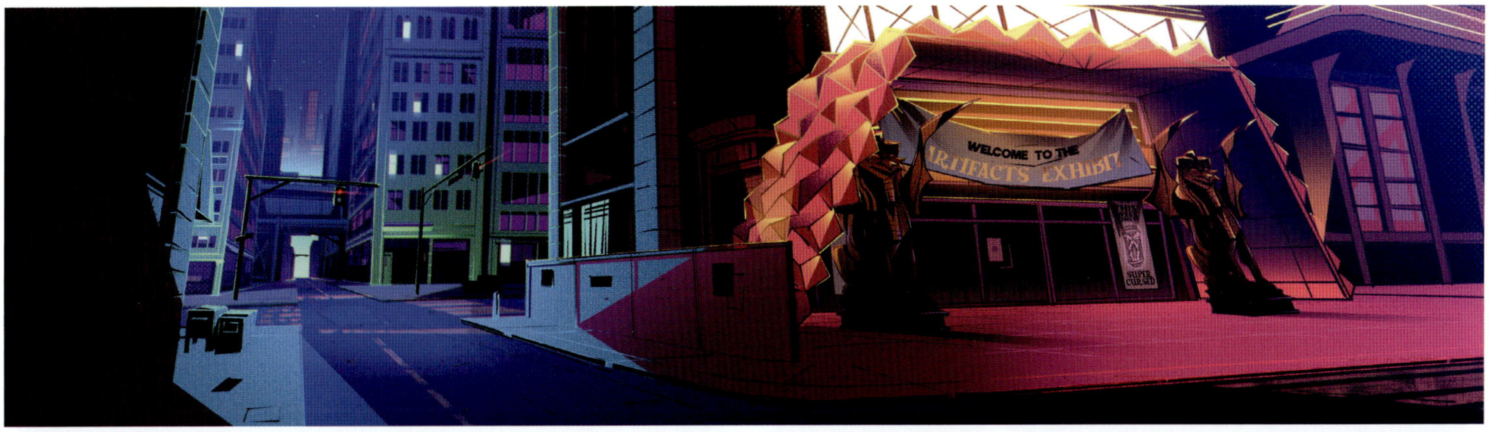

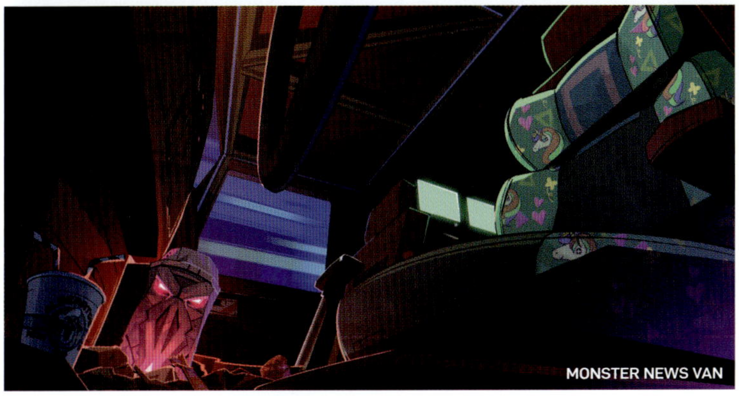
MONSTER NEWS VAN

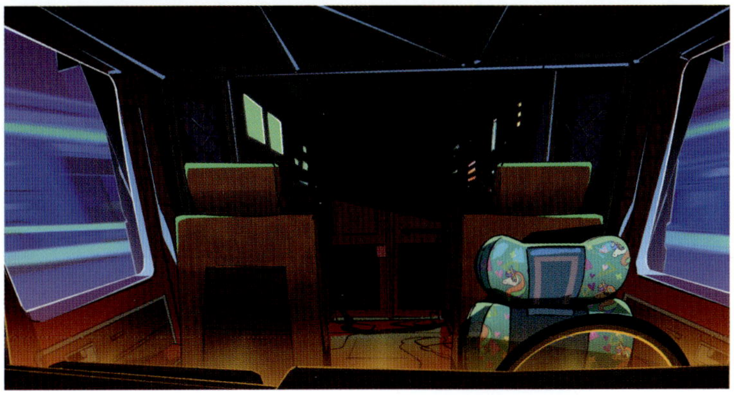

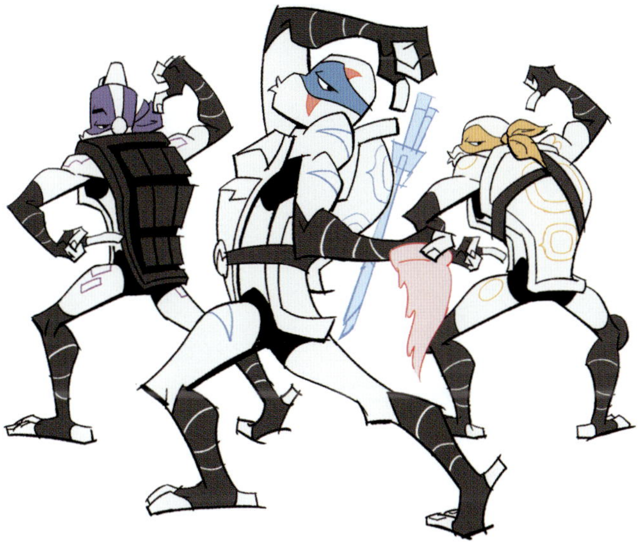

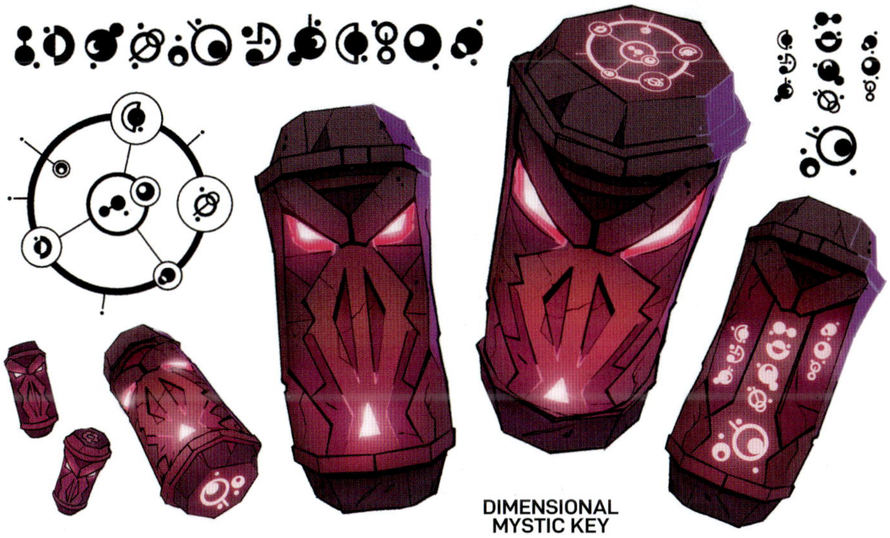
DIMENSIONAL MYSTIC KEY

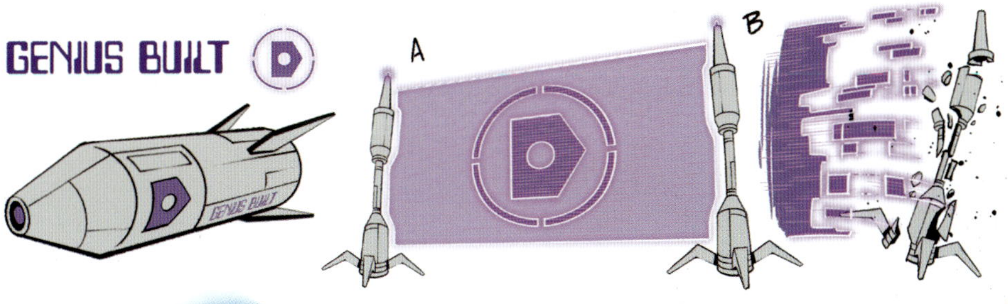

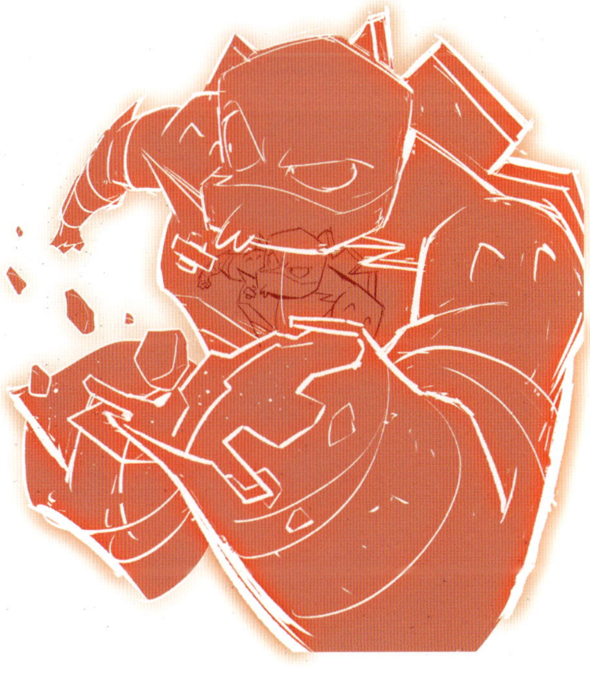

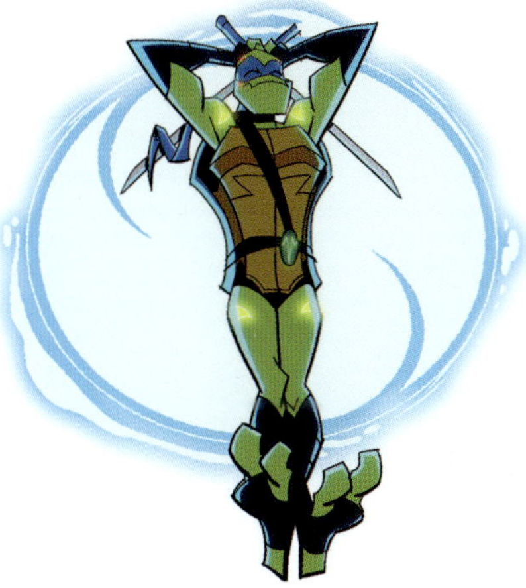

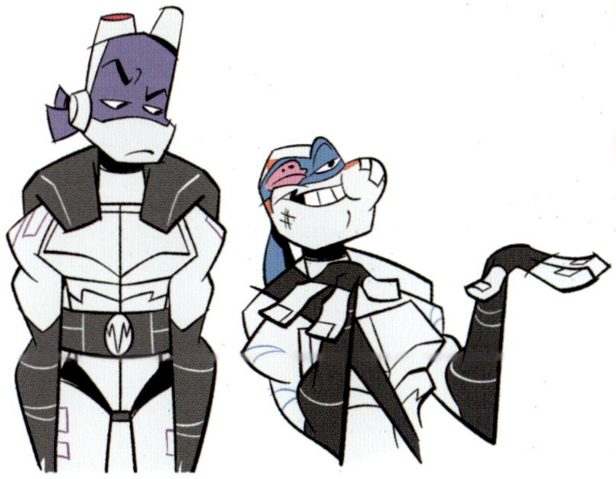

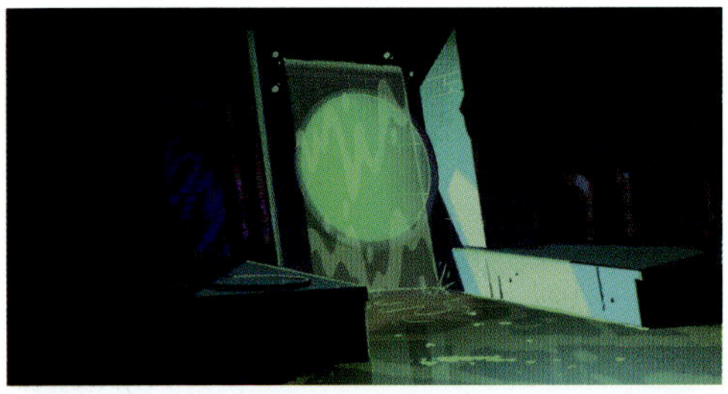

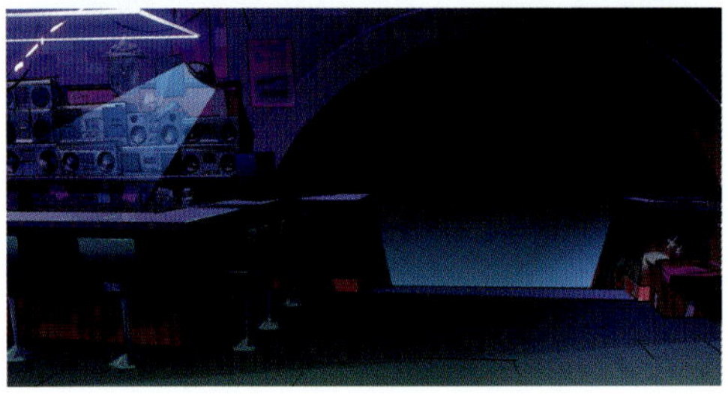

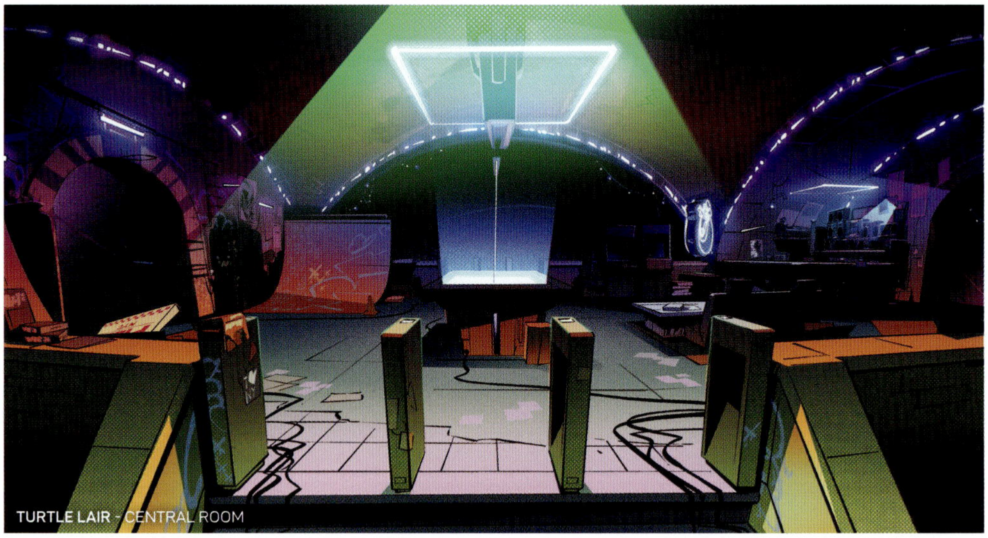

TURTLE LAIR - CENTRAL ROOM

JERMAINE JOSE: In the series we rarely got to use the color green, since, y'know, turtles. They'd blend right in. So we looked for an opportunity and decided that pinks and purples would represent the Krang and danger, so green could represent the Turtles and safety. In the new lair, there's a scene in the beginning: After Leo botches the mission, Raph scolds him. Raph, Donnie, and Mikey have a green light above them symbolizing a "cone of safety," which Leo walks away from. You'll see in key moments throughout the film where the Turtles feel safe or are in power that green will be a key part of the scene's palette.

JEFFRY CHOZON: One of my most memorable contributions to the film was color scripting the argument between Raph and Leo post-mission in the first act. I remember that production was expected to save a bit of time because all the backgrounds were already figured out since the entire scene was taking place in the Turtle lair.

When I saw the boards, I thought the staging was done so well that I felt we needed to support the conflict between Raph and Leo even further with color and light. I quickly painted a script for the sequences to pitch my idea to Carl, Ant, and Andy. It was a bit of an overhaul and the BGs needed to be repainted, but with the help of the team we were able to accommodate, and it turned out so great. It was subtle, but it helped add so much more depth to the character conflict between Leo and Raph. I still remember texting Andy apologizing for setting the schedule back, but in the end the work was worth the time, and he understood the importance.

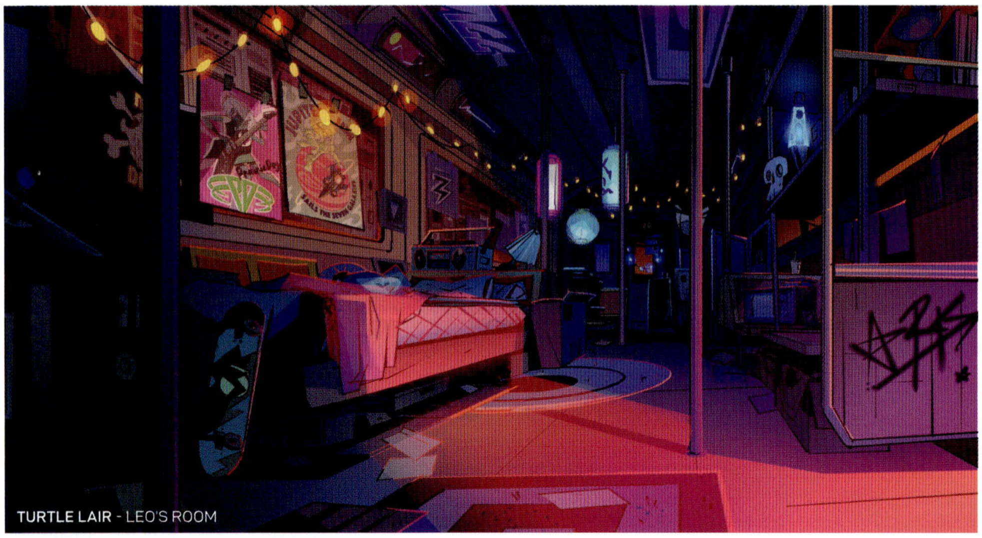

TURTLE LAIR - LEO'S ROOM

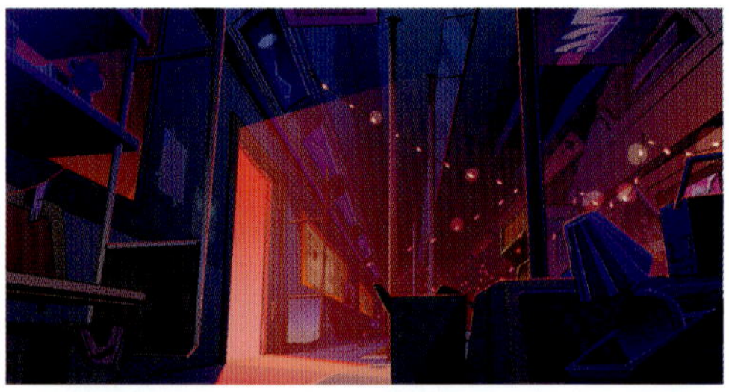

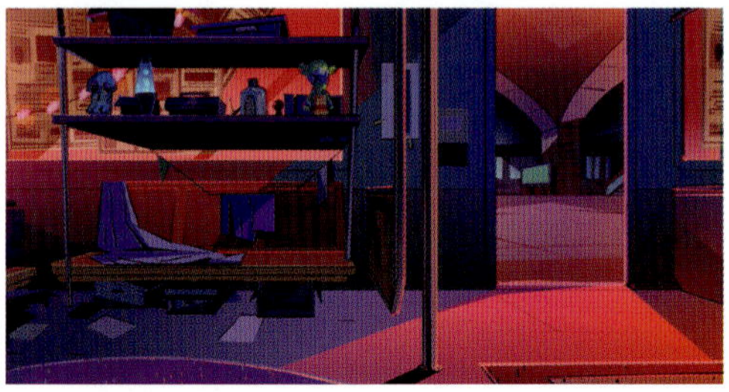

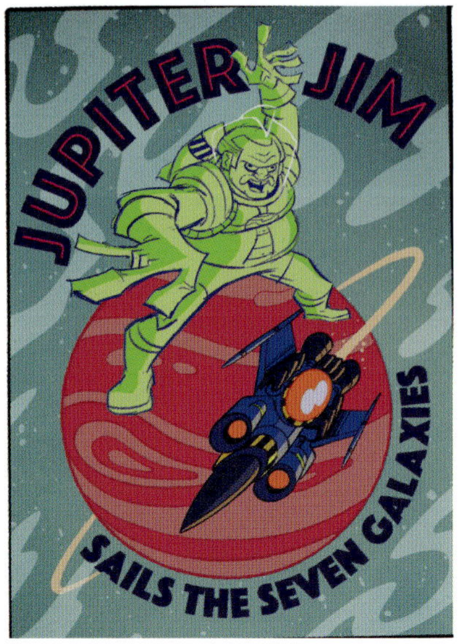

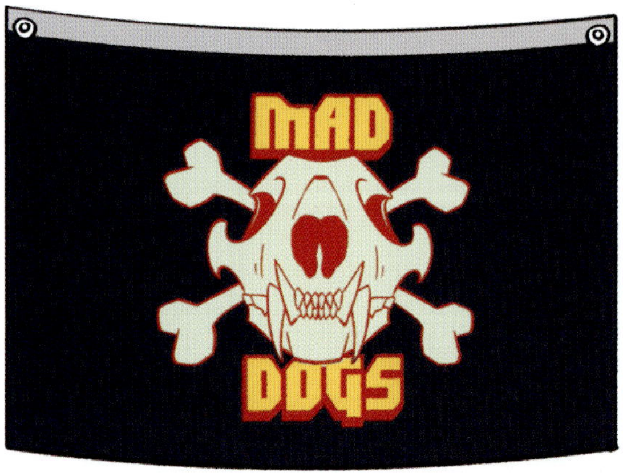

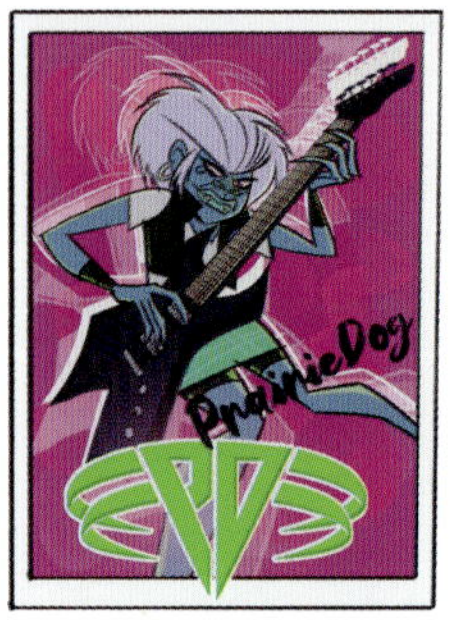

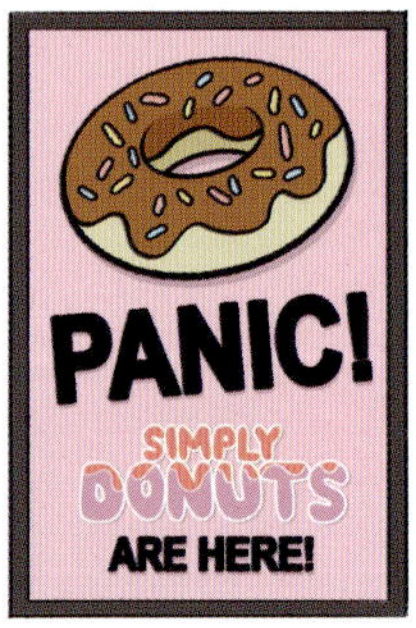

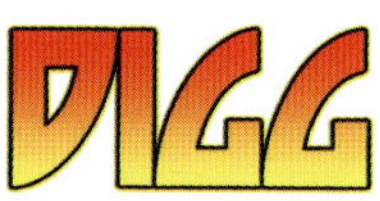

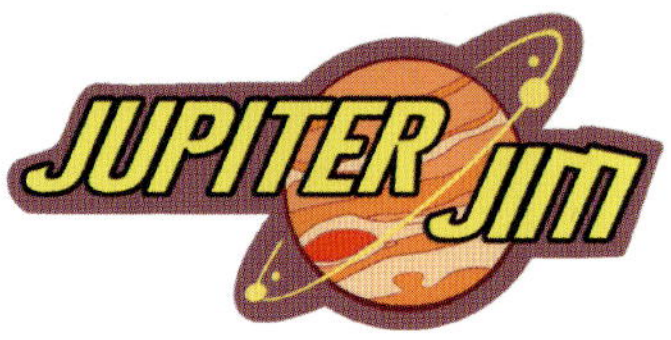

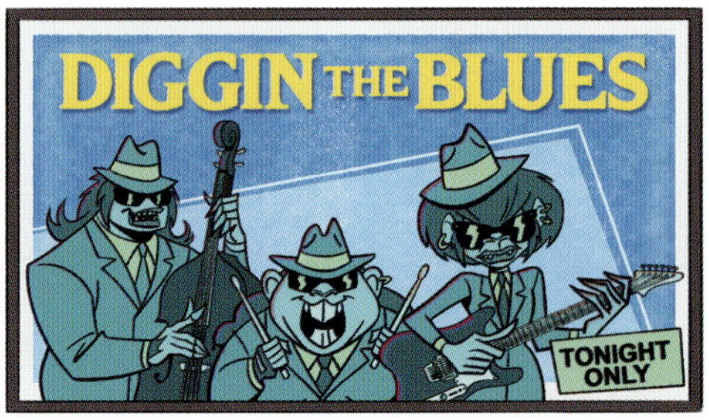

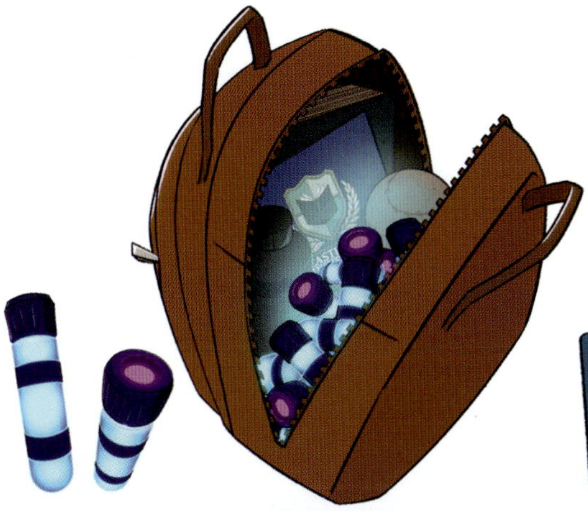

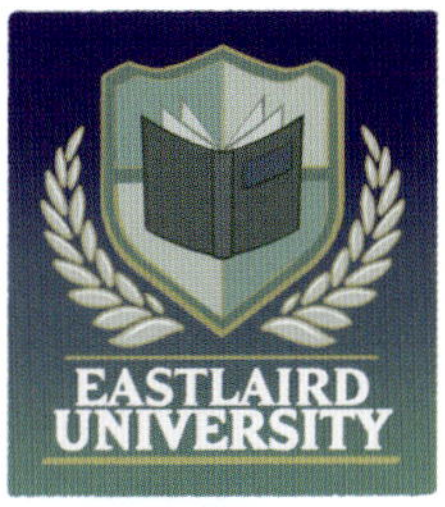

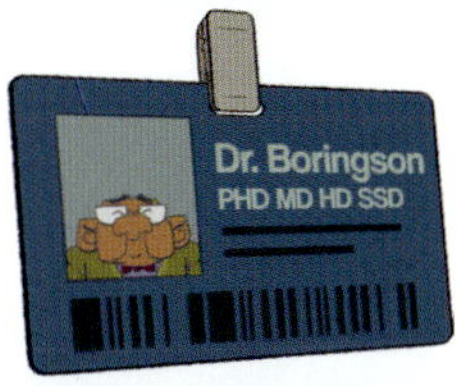

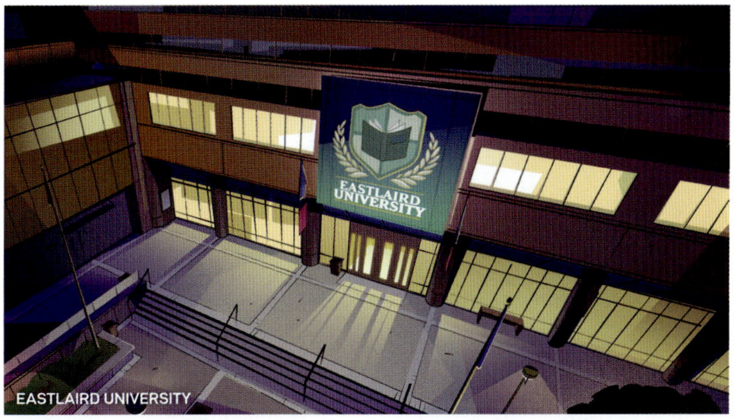

EASTLAIRD UNIVERSITY

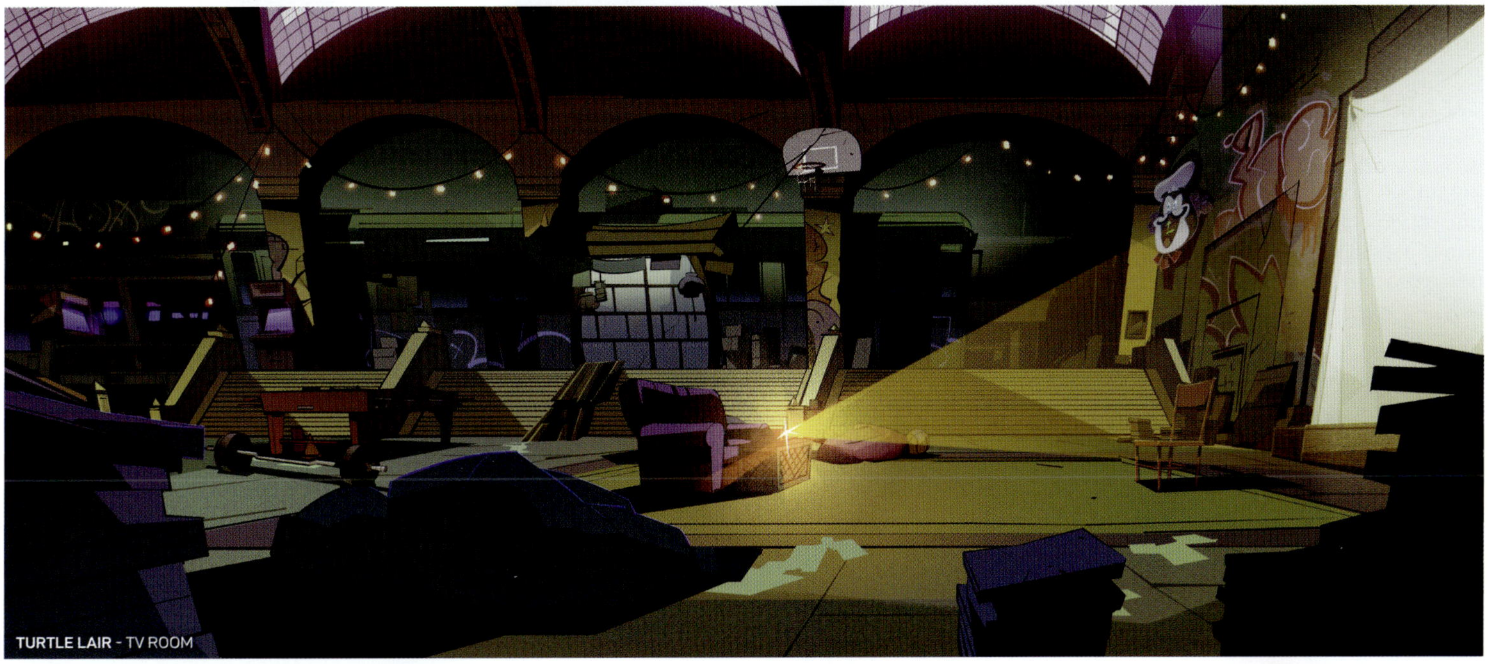
TURTLE LAIR - TV ROOM

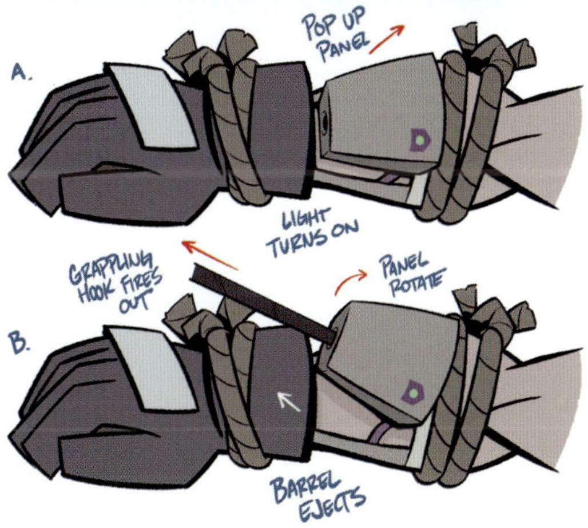

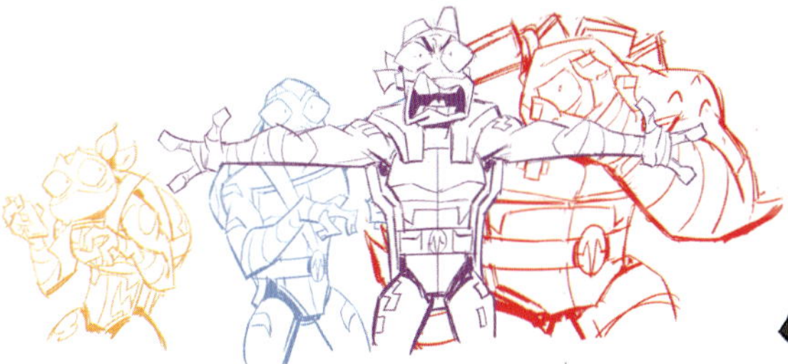

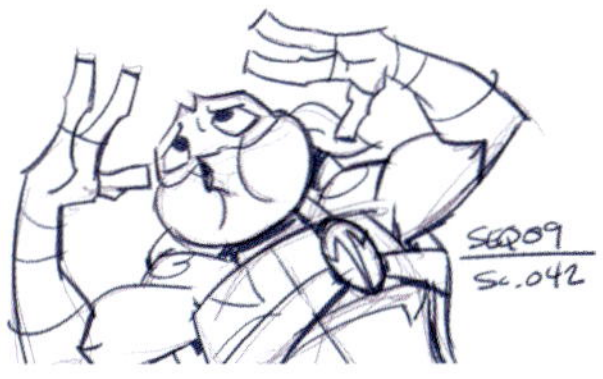

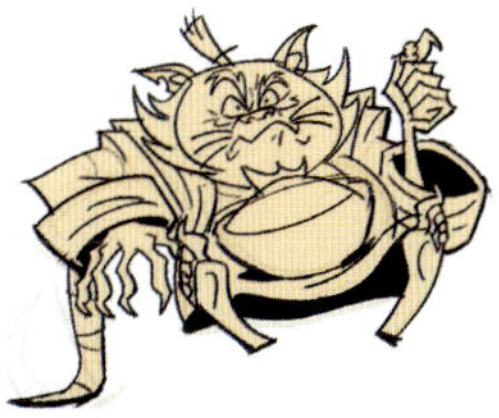

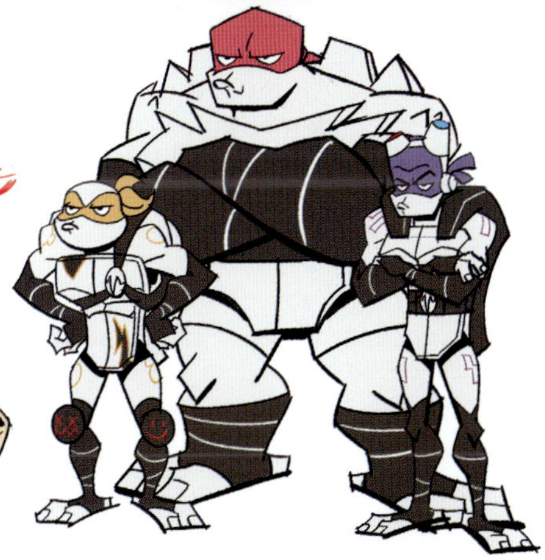

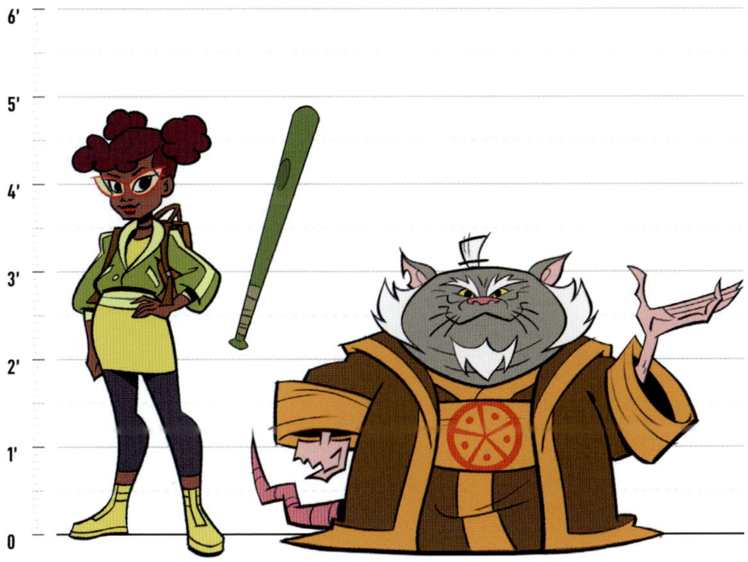

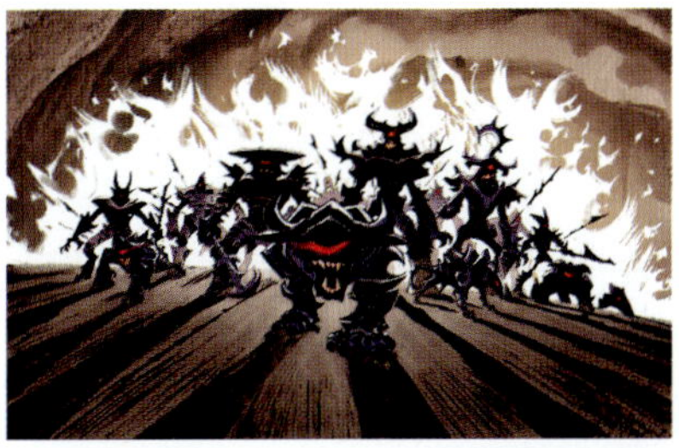

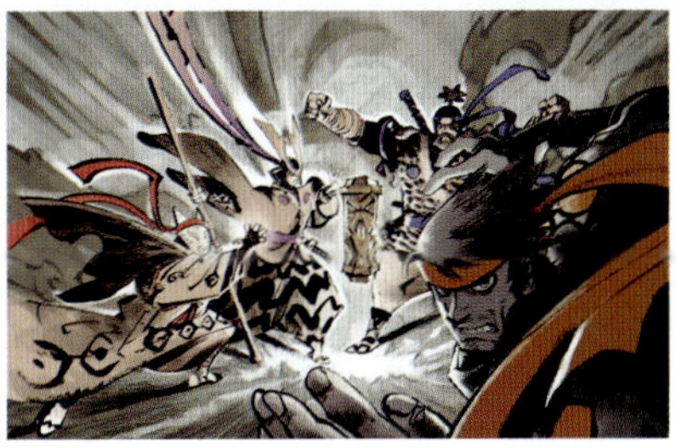

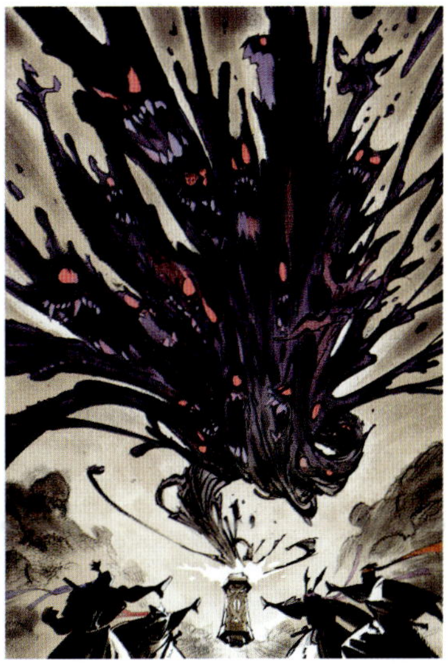

ENTER THE KRANG

"OH NO... THEY'RE HERE!"

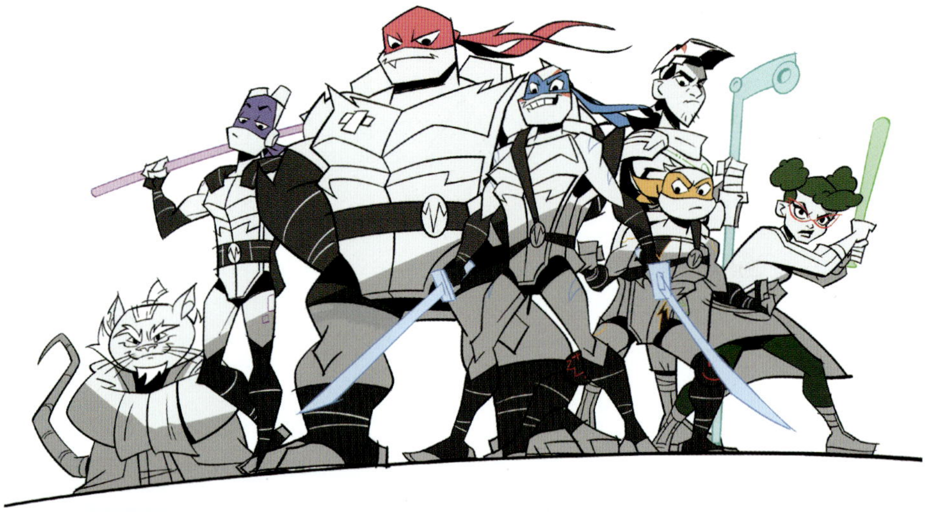

JJ CONWAY: The Krang's arrival was a massive undertaking. On a character level, we really needed Raph and Leo's tension to come to a boil, and for Leo's arrogance to make everything go to hell. But it was a fine line to walk, because we couldn't have the audience turning against Leo. Leo might be making the wrong decisions, but he had to believe in his heart that they were the correct ones.

CARL BEU: Productions this big and ambitious depend on many unsung heroes—from Tanya Melendez's color design work to production staff working tirelessly and animators and board artists whose countless revisions and roughs go unseen. Even the best art books can only show a fraction of the hundreds of layers, scrapped designs, and hidden work that made it all possible.

TONY GAMA-LOBO: I always loved the moment Hypno and Warren realize they are in *way* over their heads and they just slowly fade into the darkness like Homer into the hedge.

This sequence was a masterpiece. I love everything about it. The jokes, the energy, the mind-blowing choreography, and the heartbreaking end. The story moment was clear from the early days of the script—Leo makes what seems like the heroic choice, but he's wrong, and it costs him everything. But without a brilliant board team, you're nowhere. JJ Conway's boards were next level. Just think about everything that has to happen: We have to explain to the audience what the Foot Clan are doing and why, introduce the Krang in a dynamic and impactful way, quickly establish the Krang's personalities, hint at their backstory and motivation, demonstrate their power, choreograph a satisfying fight with ebbs and flows, track a dozen different characters and their individual goals, service the Leo/Raph tension, design a turning point where our heroes are forced into a bleak enough position that we buy that Raph sounds a retreat, but also leave enough space for the audience to believe what Leo believes—he can still save the day. And make it all look cool as hell.

The first time I saw the boards of the moment where Raph saves Leo took my breath away. And the look on Leo's face when he gets out of his escape pod back in the lair is truly devastating.

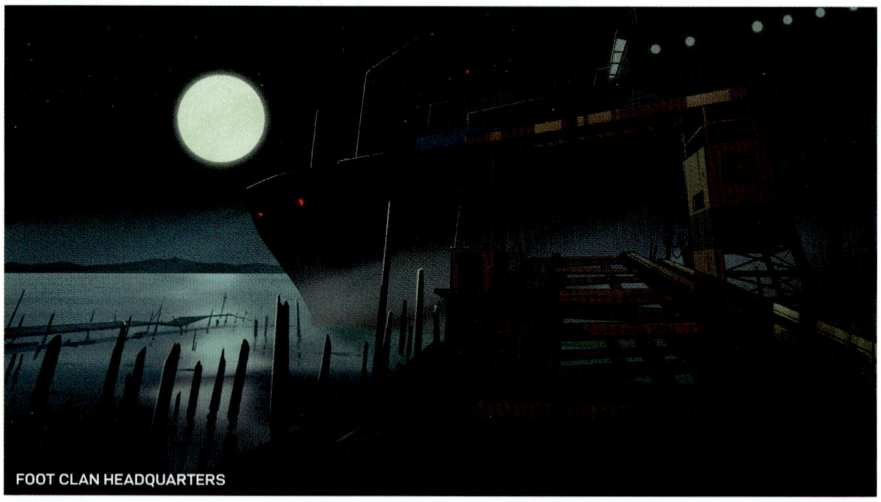

FOOT CLAN HEADQUARTERS

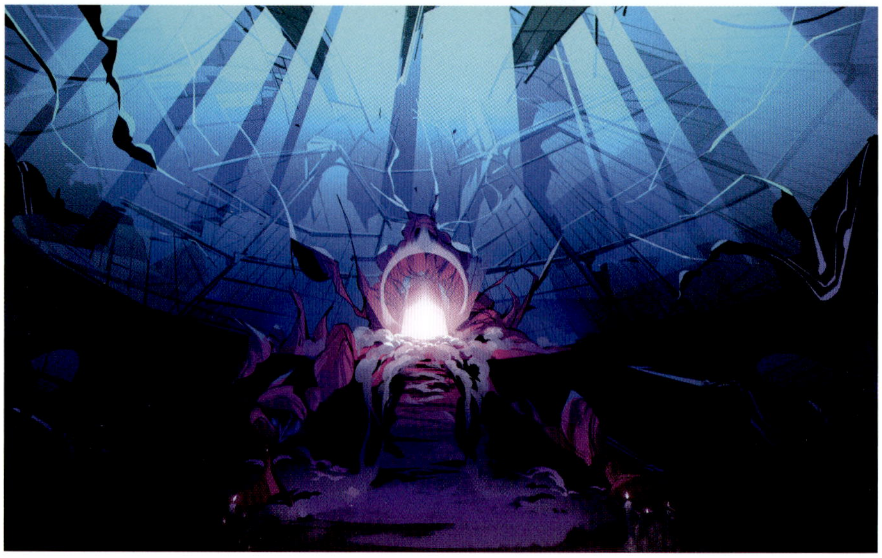

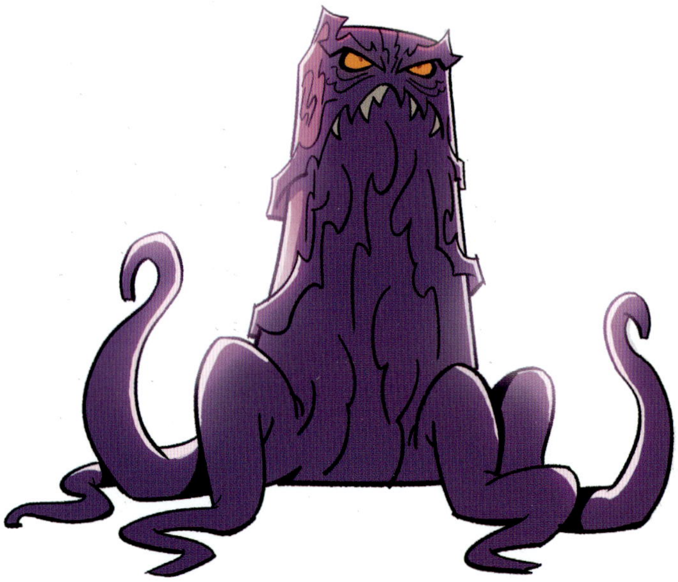

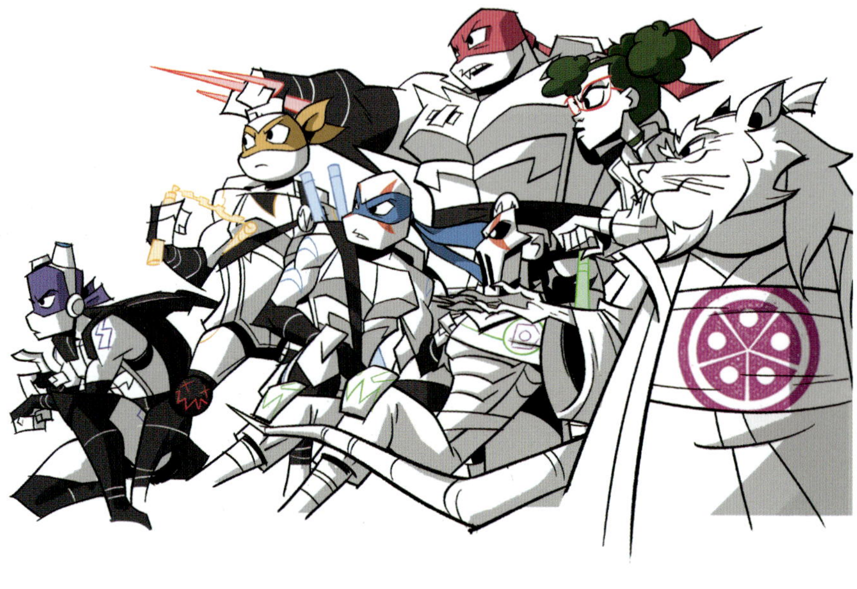

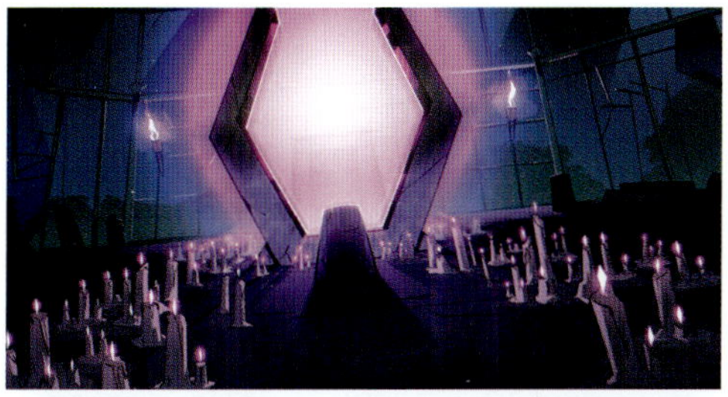

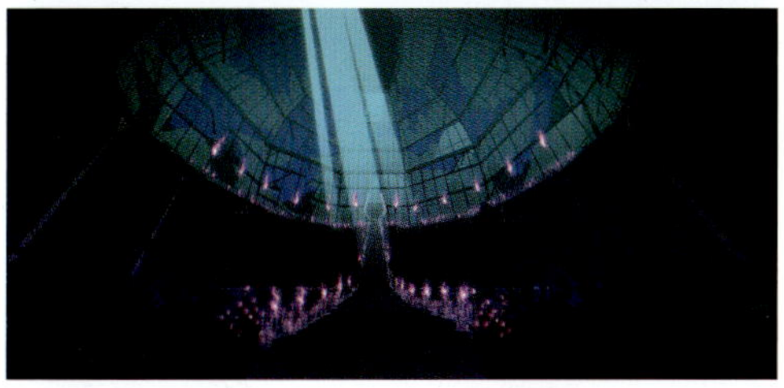

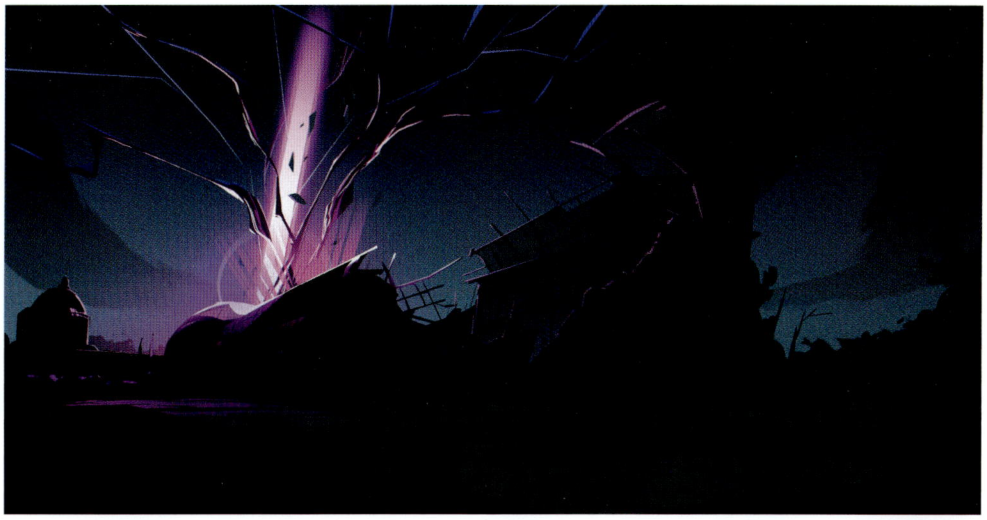

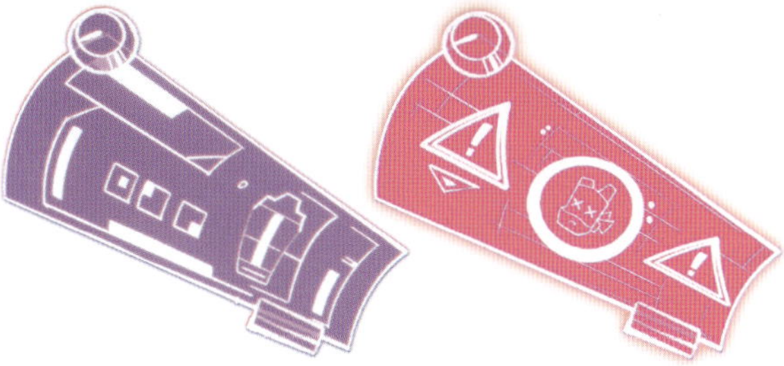

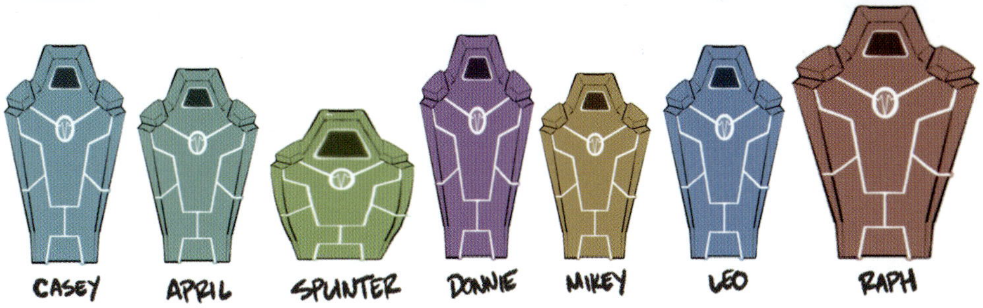

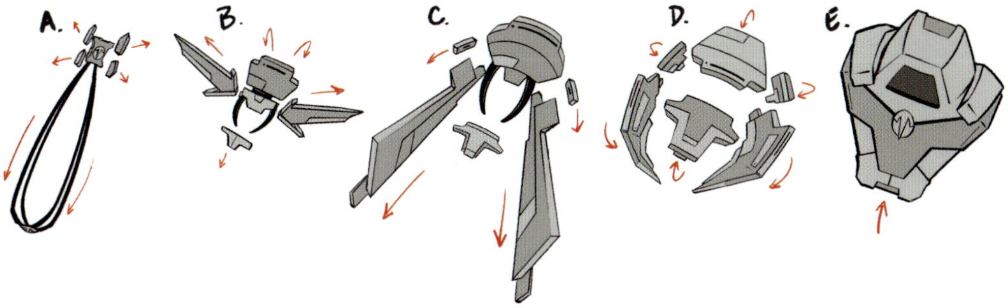

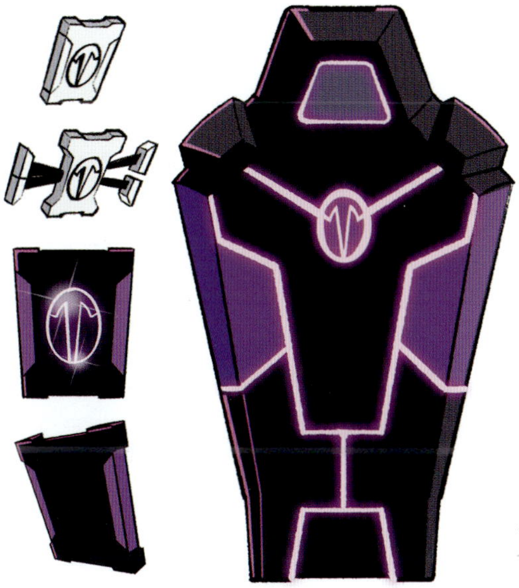

DONNIE PODS

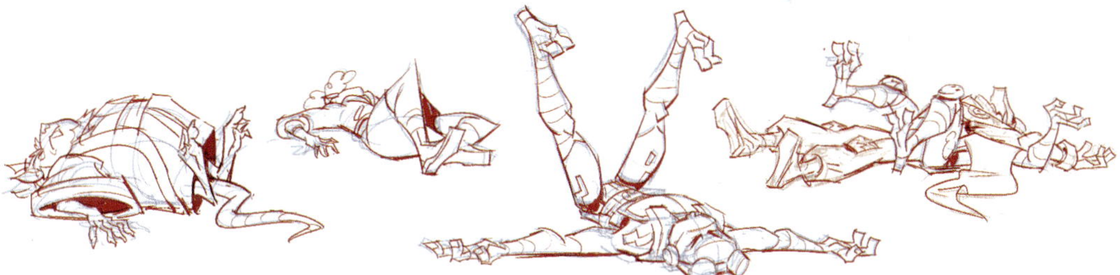

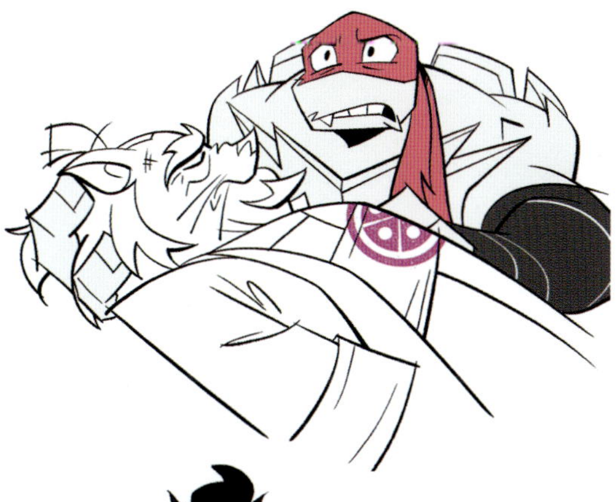

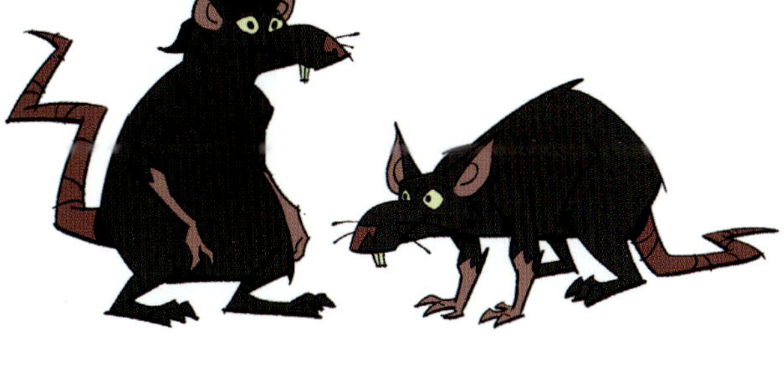

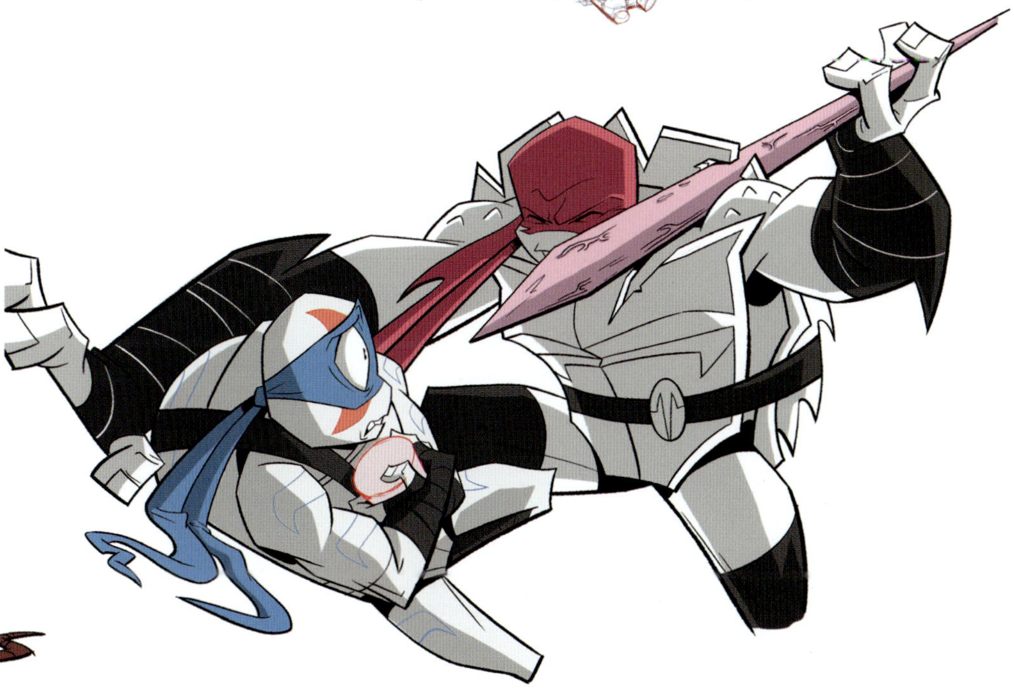

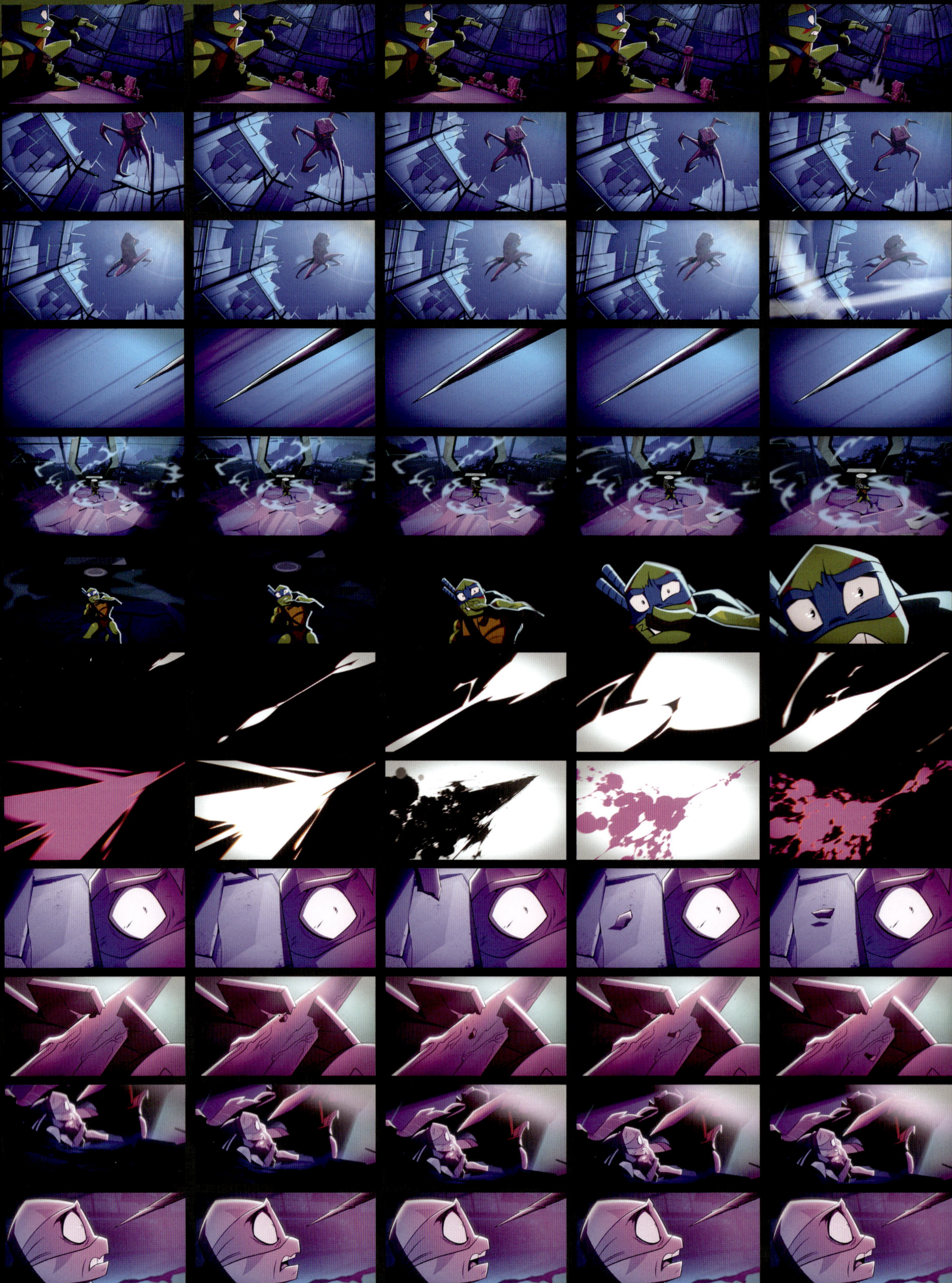

STORYBOARD ARTIST: **KEVIN MOLINA-ORTIZ**

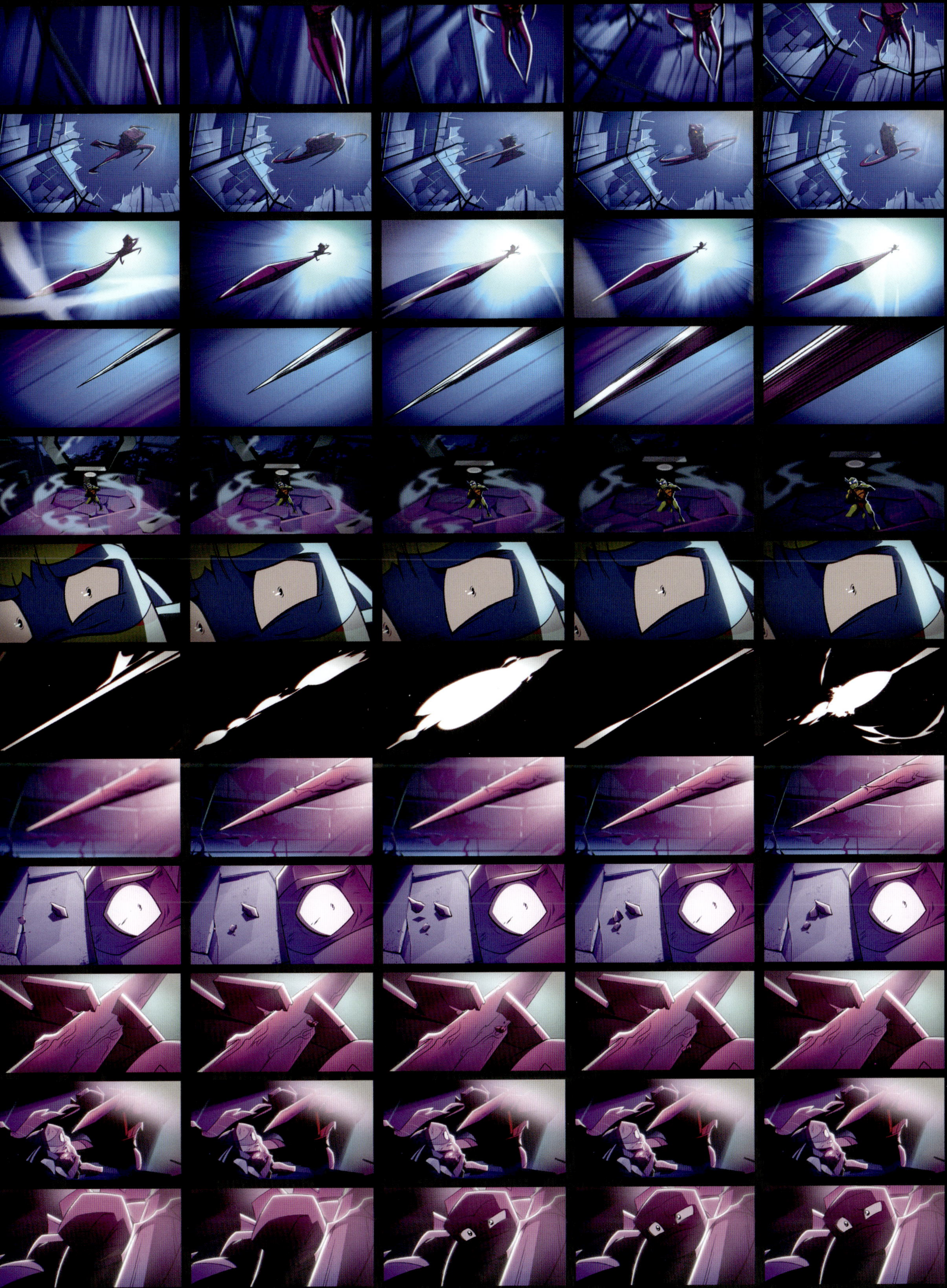

INVASION

"THE STRONG WILL DEVOUR THE WEAK."

TONY GAMA-LOBO: The Raph interrogation was a crucial scene to establish the warring philosophies at play in this story. The Krang view their power as permission to dominate weaker species. The Turtles view their power as a responsibility to protect those who are weaker. Heroes vs. villains.

JJ CONWAY: There was a lot to cover in this section of the film. On one level we had to sell that our Krang were uniquely dangerous, so we leaned into ideas of control and dehumanization. Matt Humphreys storyboarded the Foot Clan being Krangified, and Julia Braid storyboarded the Krang invading Metro Tower. For both sequences, we wanted to go as far as we could in showing the Krang stripping people of their humanity, leaving them mindless monsters under complete Krang control.

But on a story level, this part of the film needed to be about how Leo's failure as a leader brings his team to their lowest, most divided point. Leo knows this is all his fault and becomes fixated on setting things right, refusing to hear input from his team. This all leads to the ambush beneath Metro Tower, storyboarded by David Maximo and Piero Piluso. They went nuts with this sequence, going absolutely gonzo when they're attacked by the Krang growth and even a living subway train! This needed to be the team's lowest point, so we physically separated everyone to represent how Leo had fractured his family, and we had the floor physically fall out from below Leo to literally put him at his lowest point.

As soon as we discussed the scene when Casey tears into Leo after the ambush, I knew I wanted Zane Yarbrough to storyboard it. Leo's entire arc hinges on this moment, and we need to believe that hitting rock bottom had shaken Leo into confronting himself, and that this humbling had allowed him to start slowly, brick by brick, rebuilding himself into the hero the world needs.

But that kind of change isn't a light switch, it's the first step on a journey. And for the rest of the film we'd need to see Leo doing the legwork to mend the team that he'd fractured so they could rescue Raph and save the world.

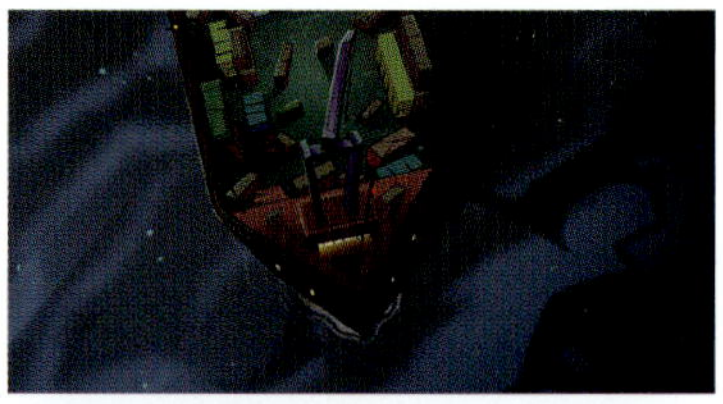

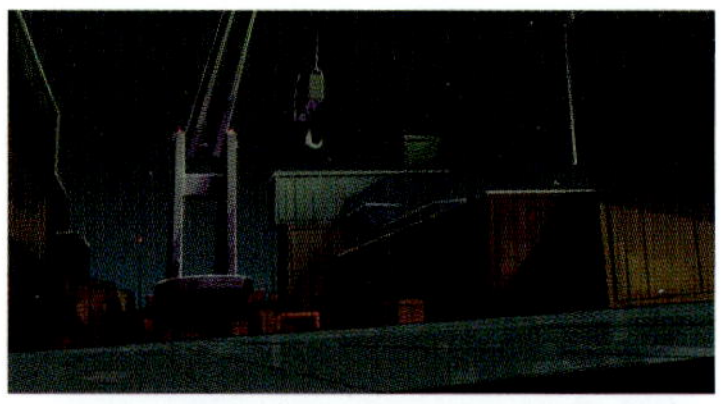

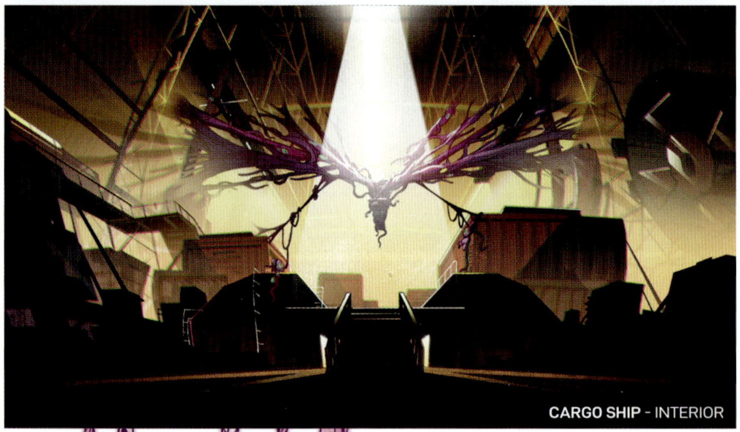

CARGO SHIP - INTERIOR

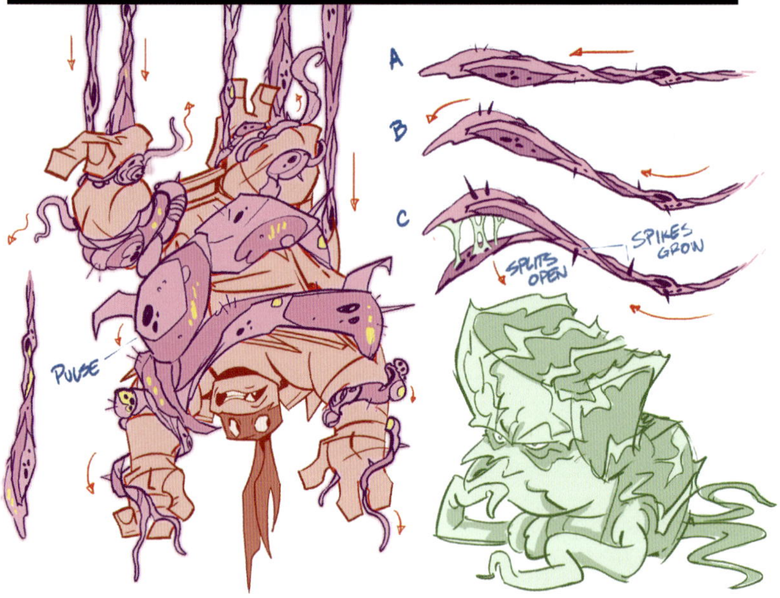

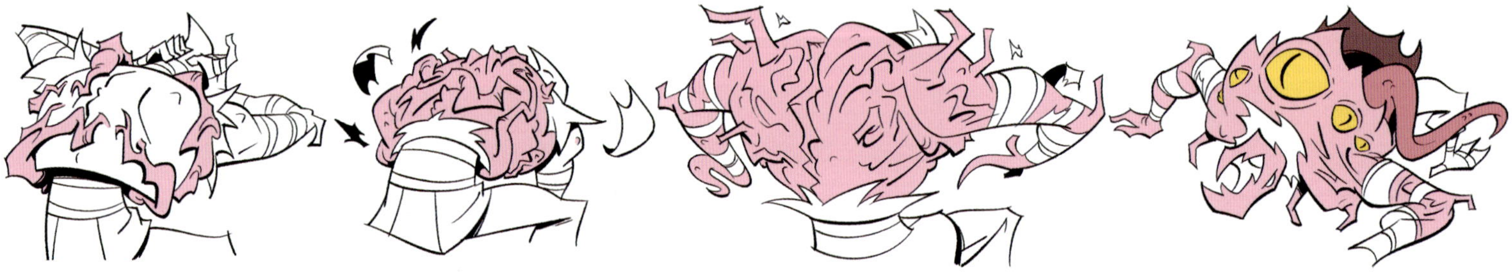

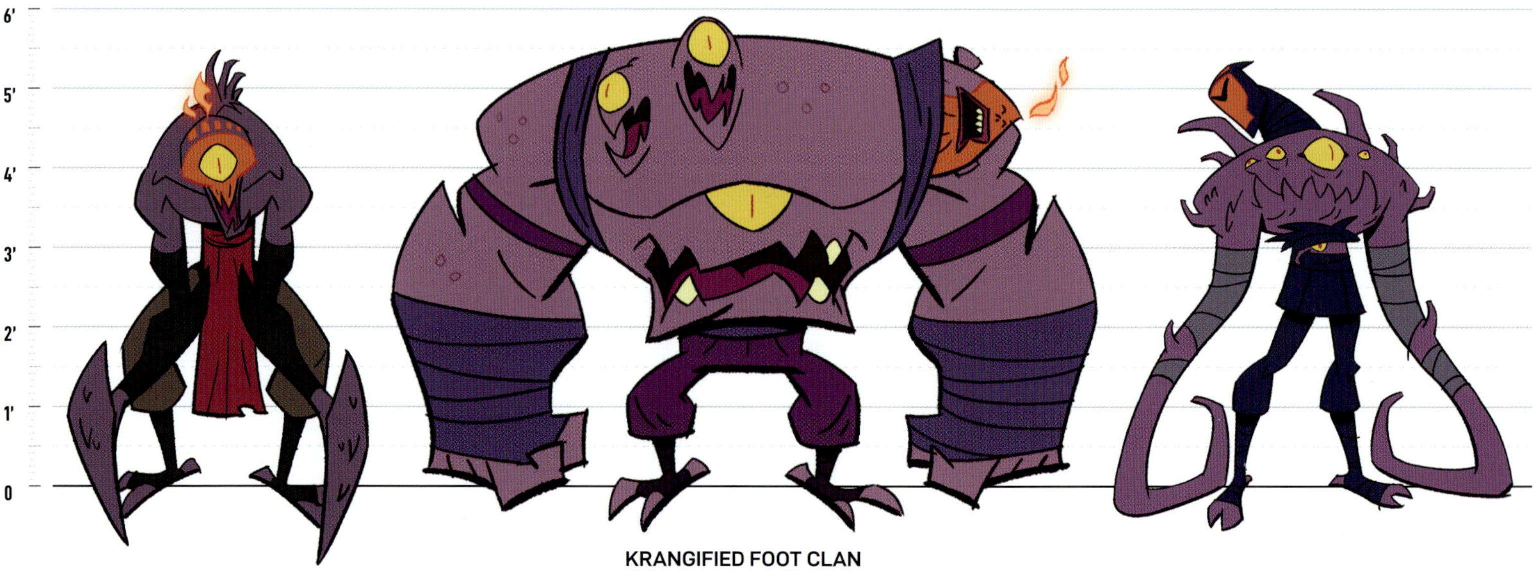

KRANGIFIED FOOT CLAN

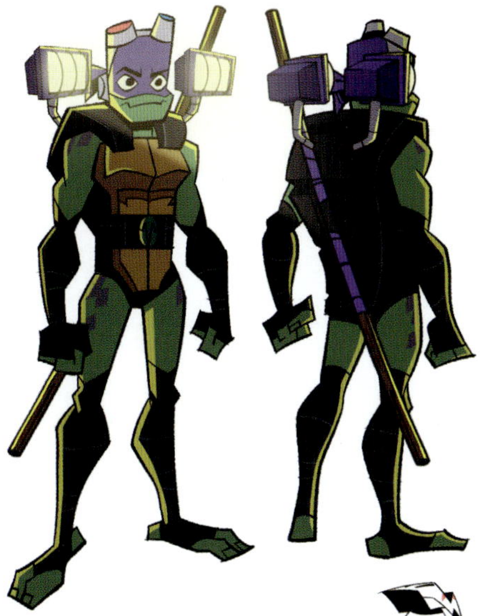

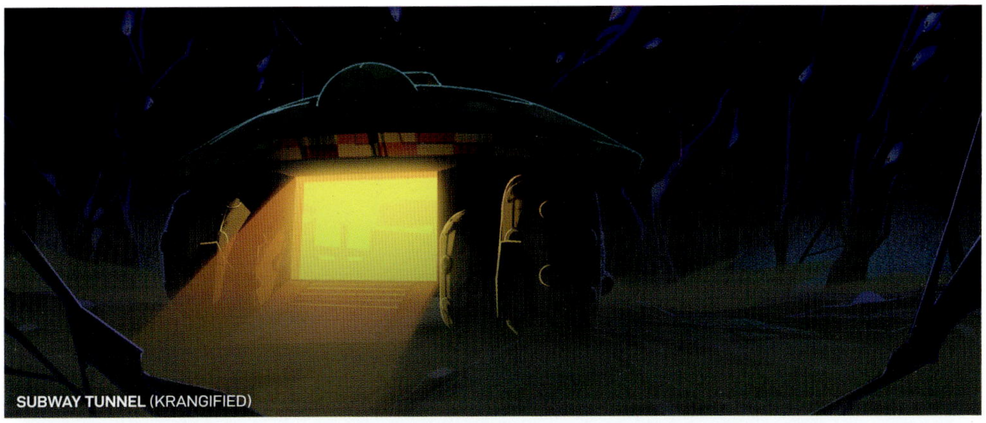

SUBWAY TUNNEL (KRANGIFIED)

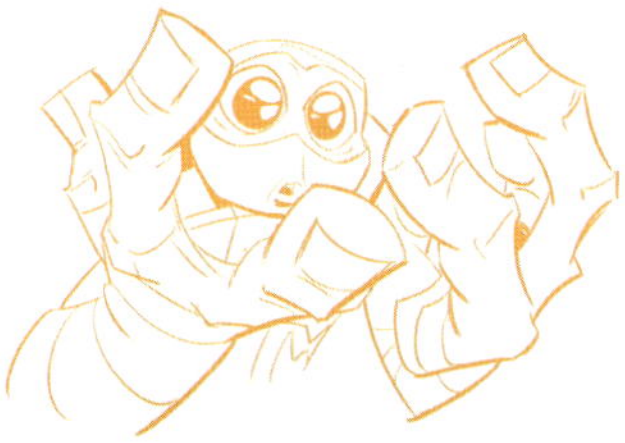

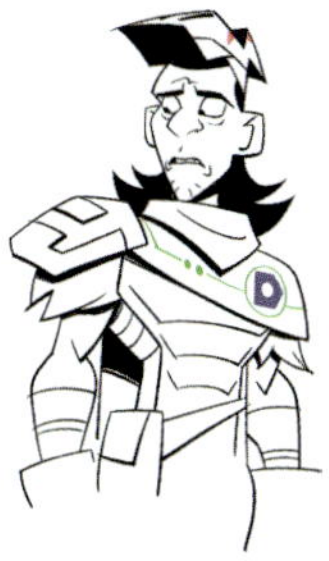

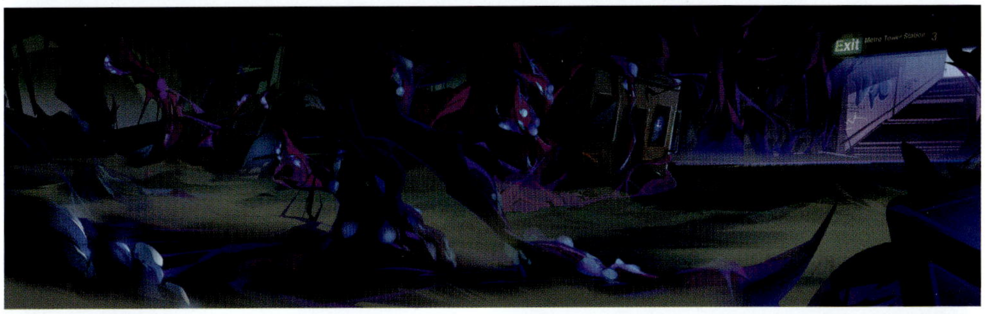

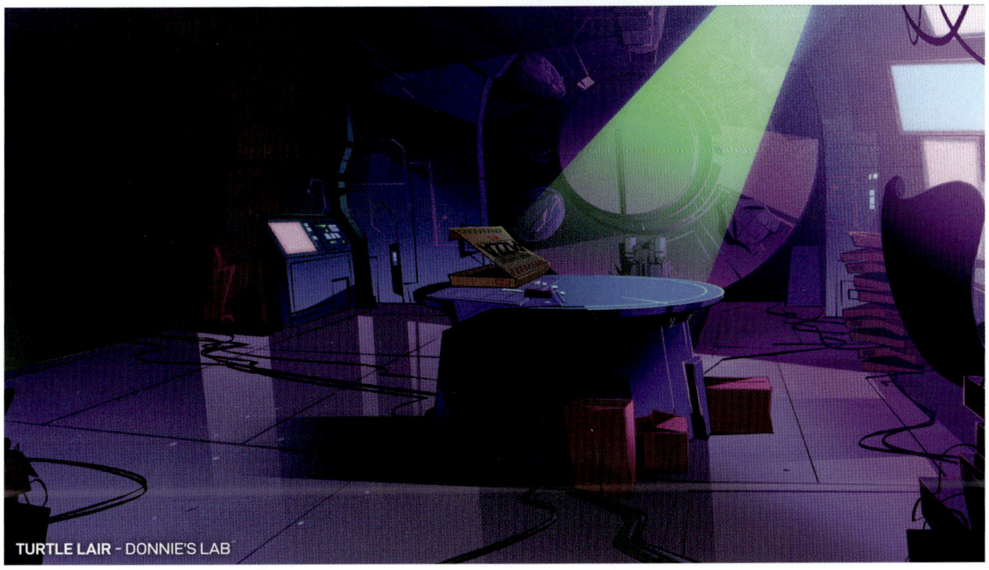

TURTLE LAIR - DONNIE'S LAB

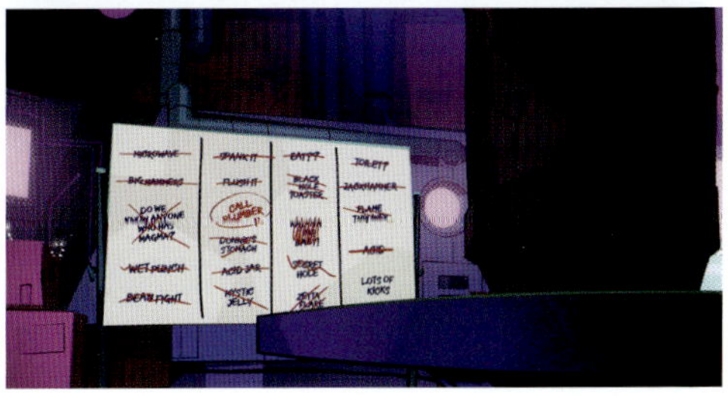

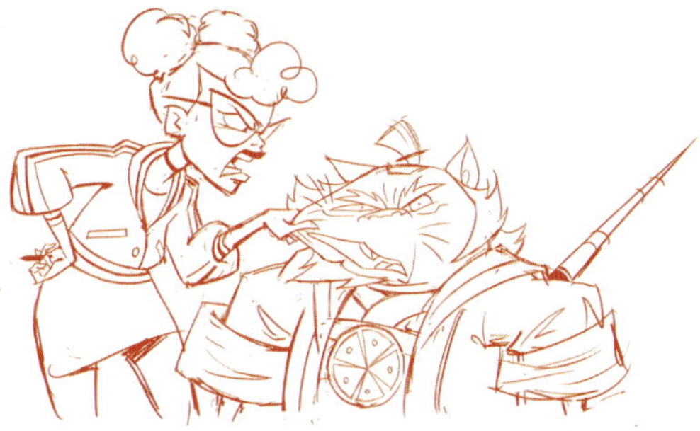

TONY GAMA-LOBO: A huge breakthrough in the story came early on when we all started to riff off of Andy's designs for the Krang. They were more than just brains inside protective suits—they were these formidable organic creatures. And their power sprang from that organic nature. The Krang's "tech" was organic, their fighting was organic, and their plan was organic: Krangify the people of Earth to remake them in their image. And that led us to the horrifying reveal at the midpoint of Krangified Raph.

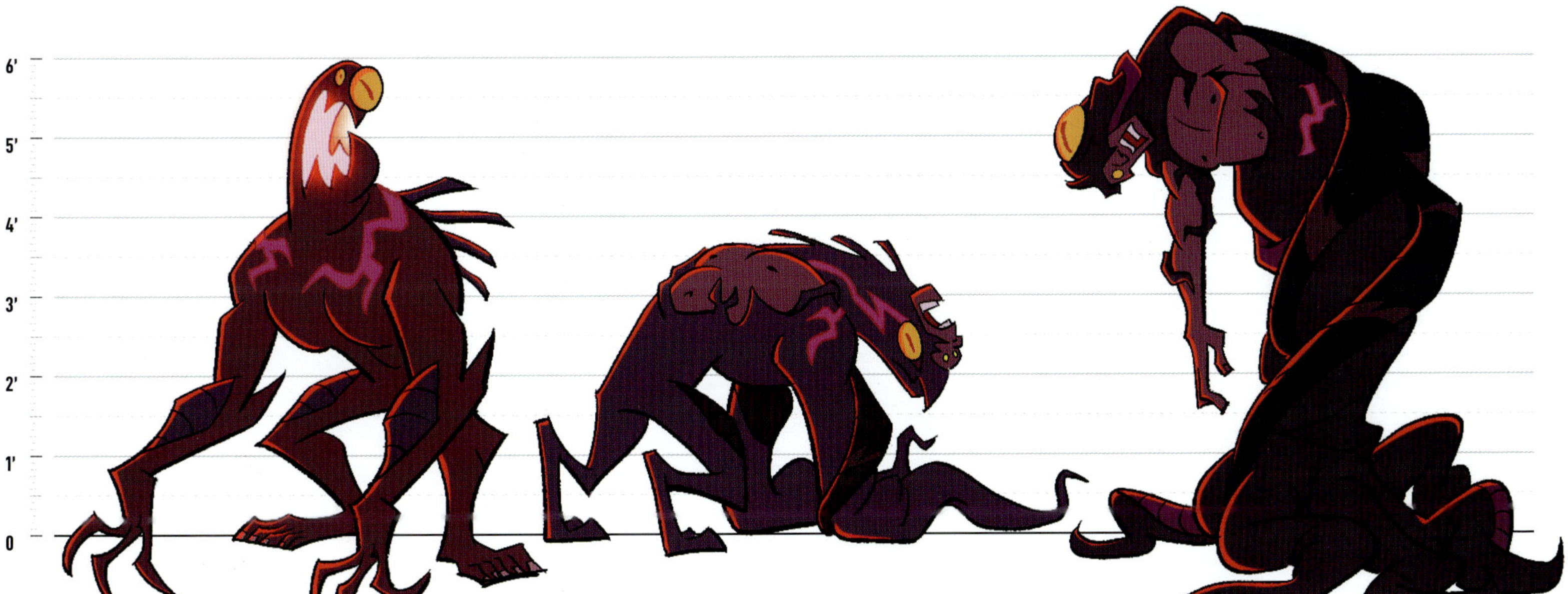

KRANG BEASTS

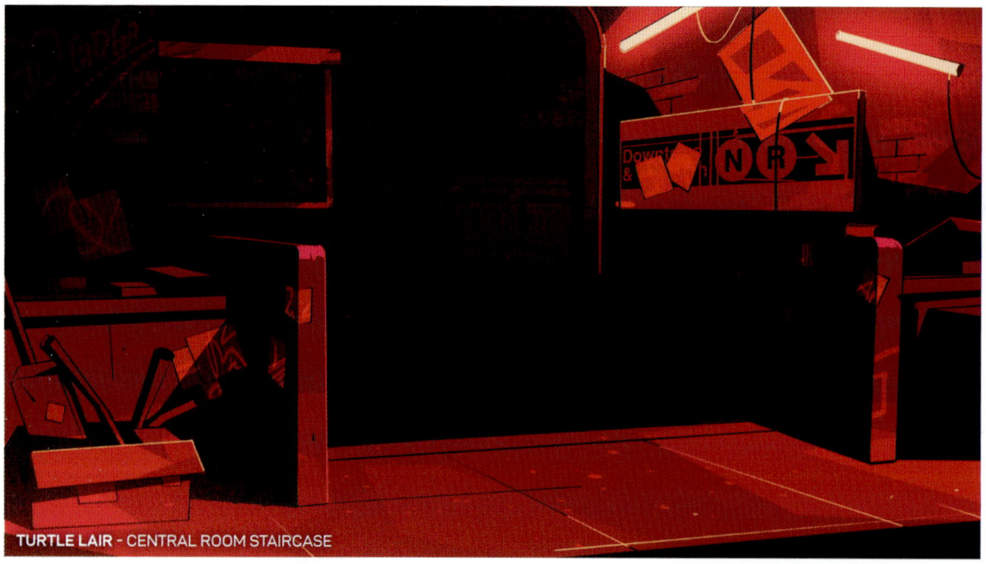

TURTLE LAIR - CENTRAL ROOM STAIRCASE

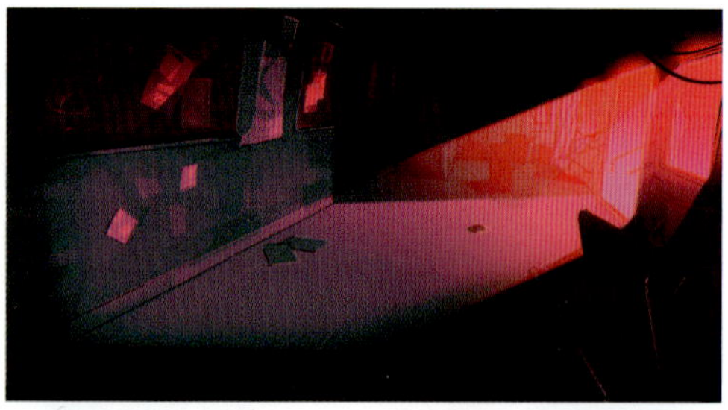

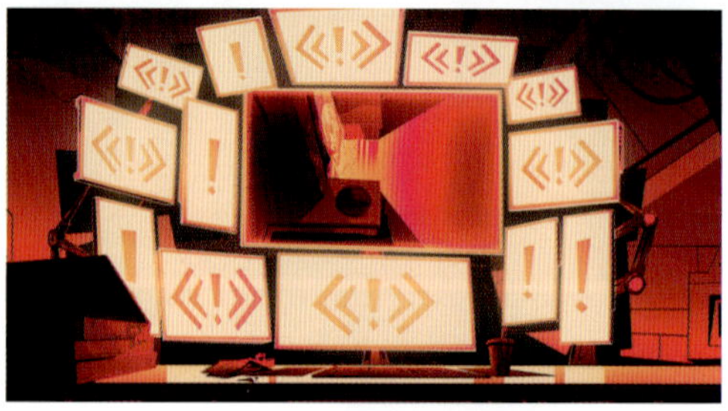

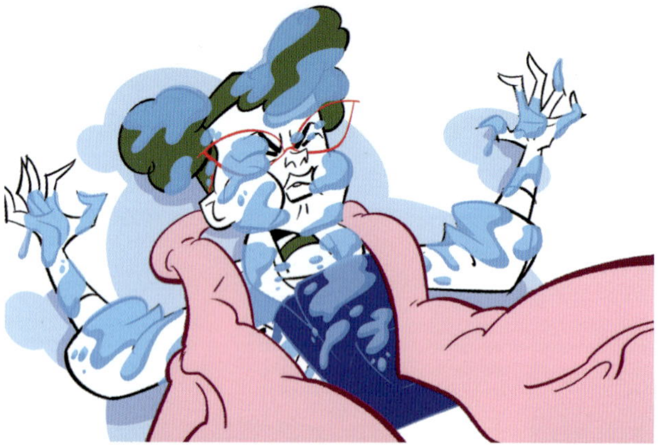

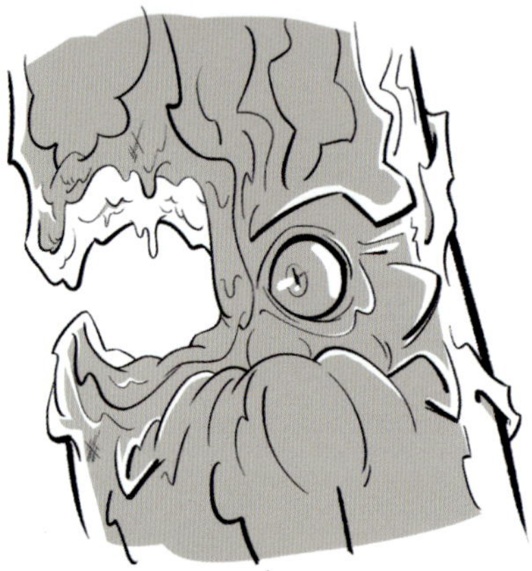

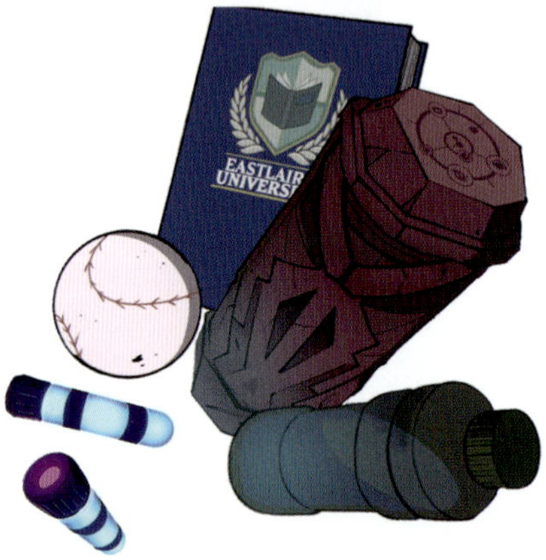

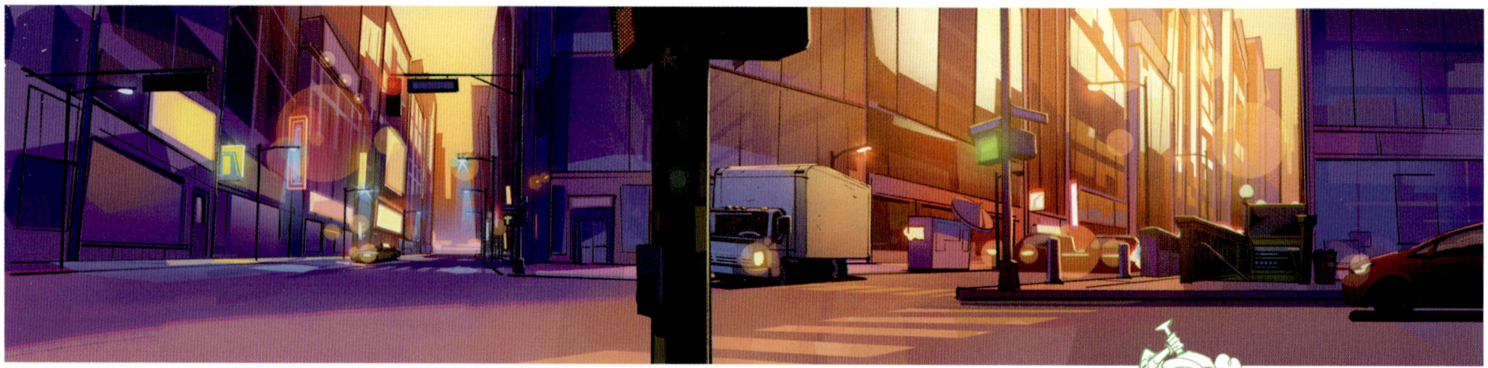

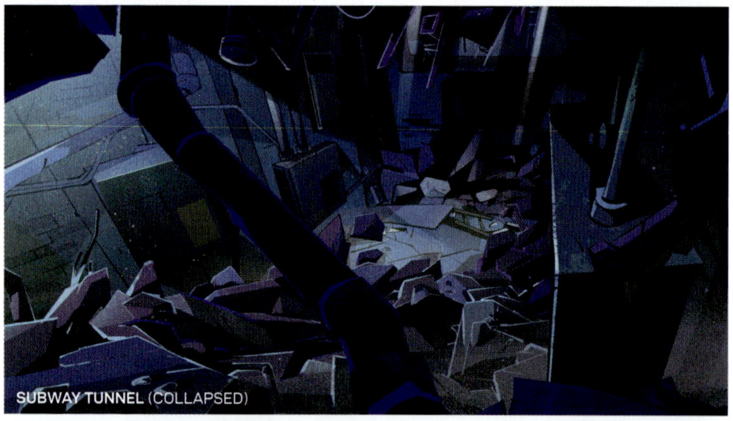

SUBWAY TUNNEL (COLLAPSED)

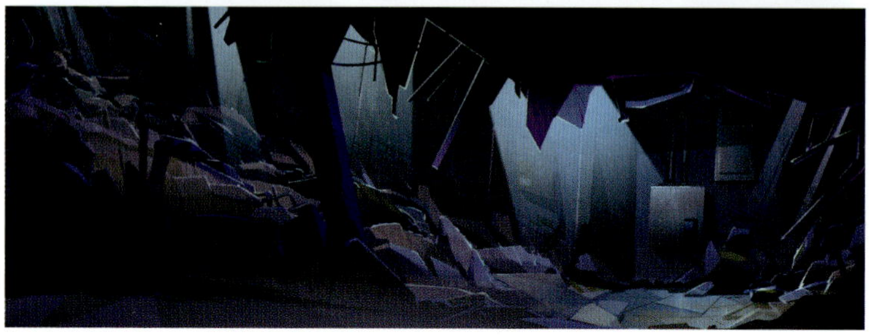

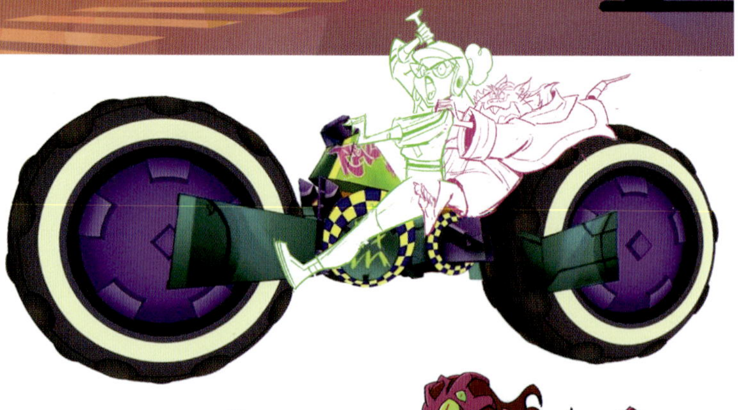

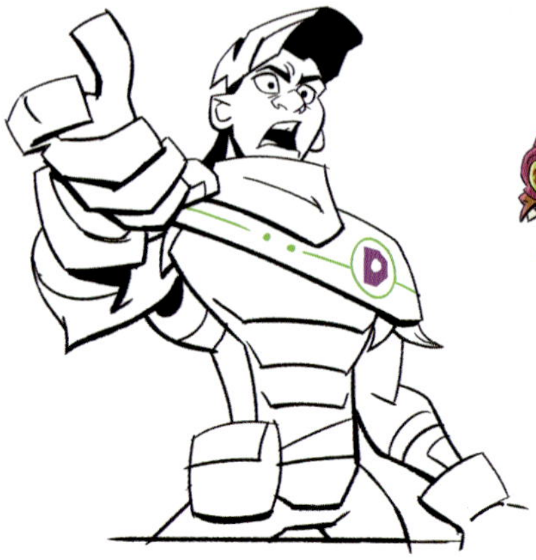

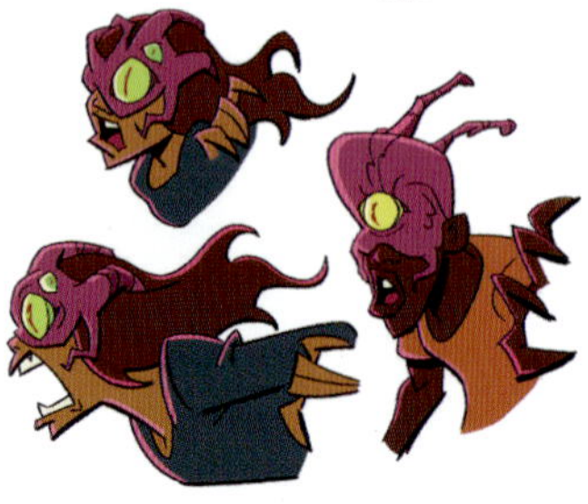

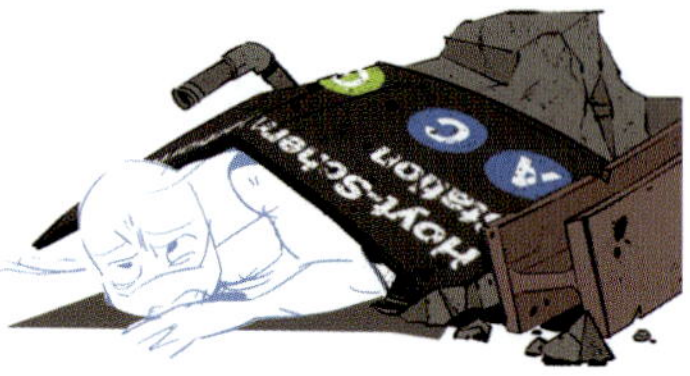

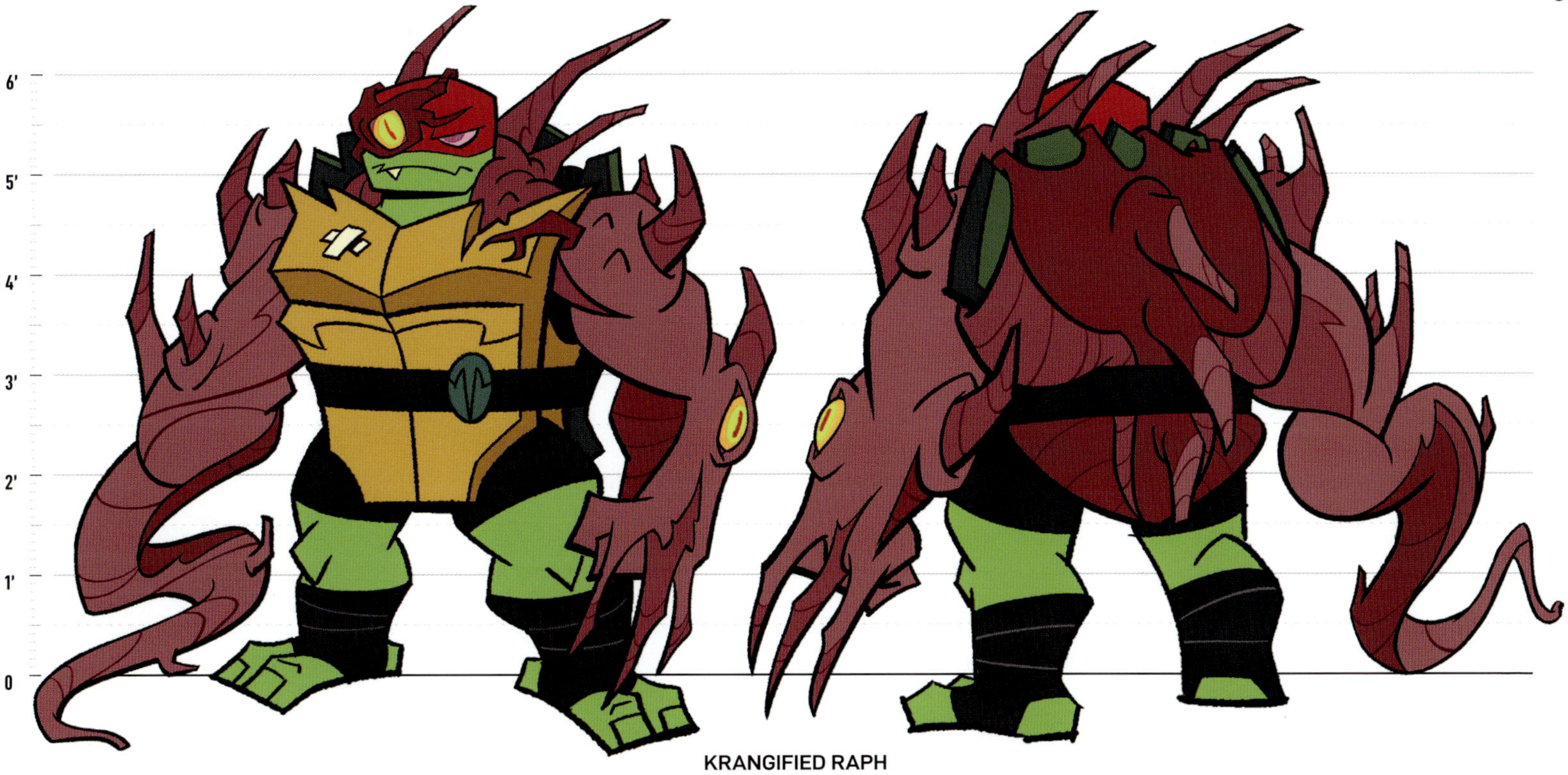

KRANGIFIED RAPH

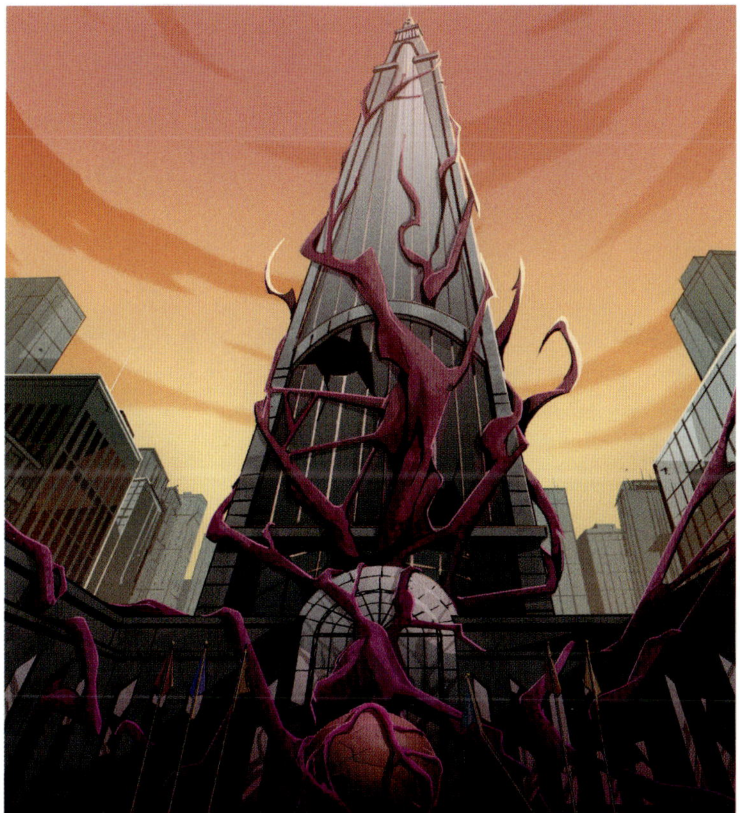

METRO TOWER (KRANGIFIED)

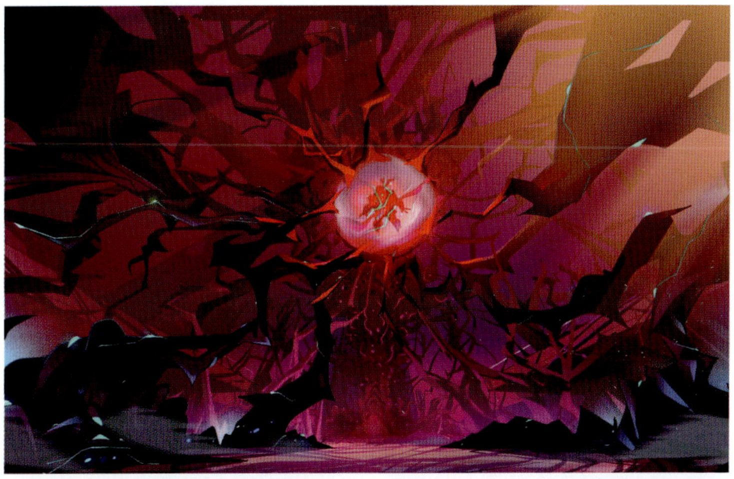

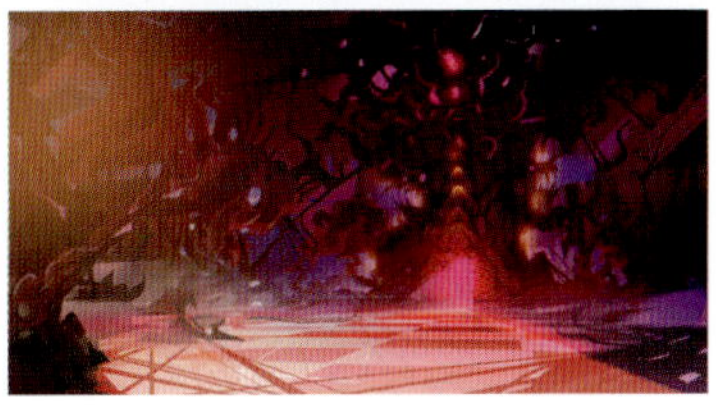

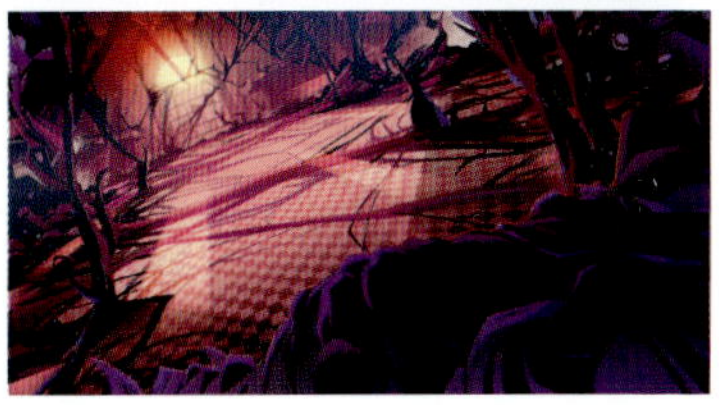

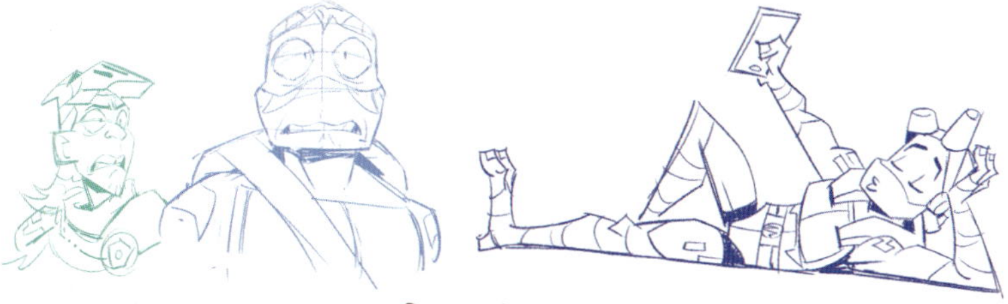

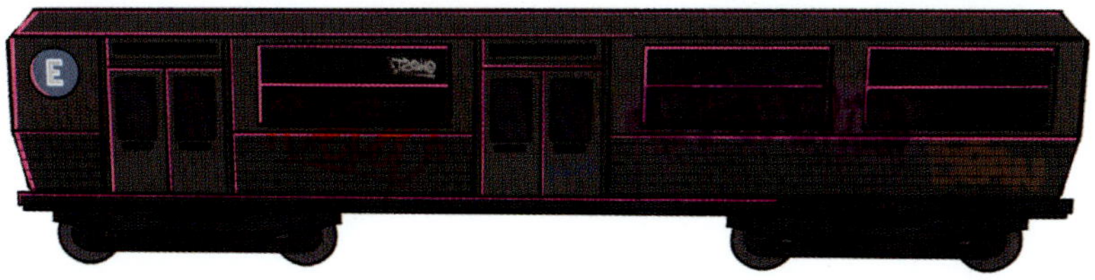

CARL BEU: Prop designer Jack Rossi brings deep knowledge of the Turtleverse and meticulous detail to every piece, from the dimensional key to the Krangified subway monster. We were so glad we were able to keep his expertise for the movie!

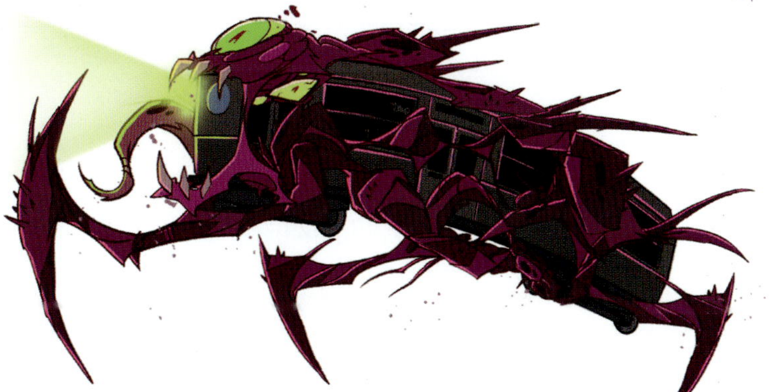

KRANGIFIED SUBWAY CAR

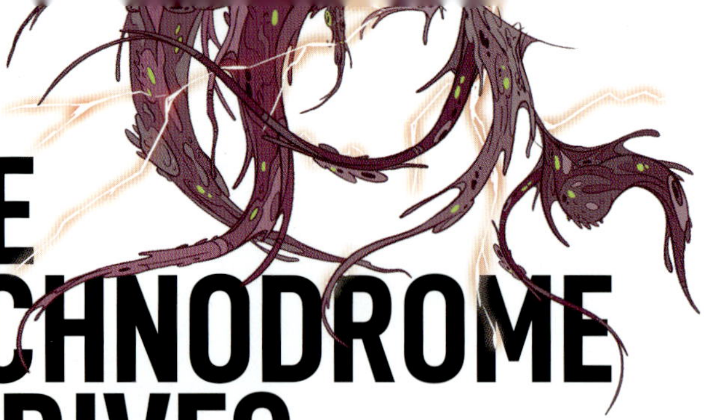

THE TECHNODROME ARRIVES

"IT'S POINTLESS TO RESIST KRANG."

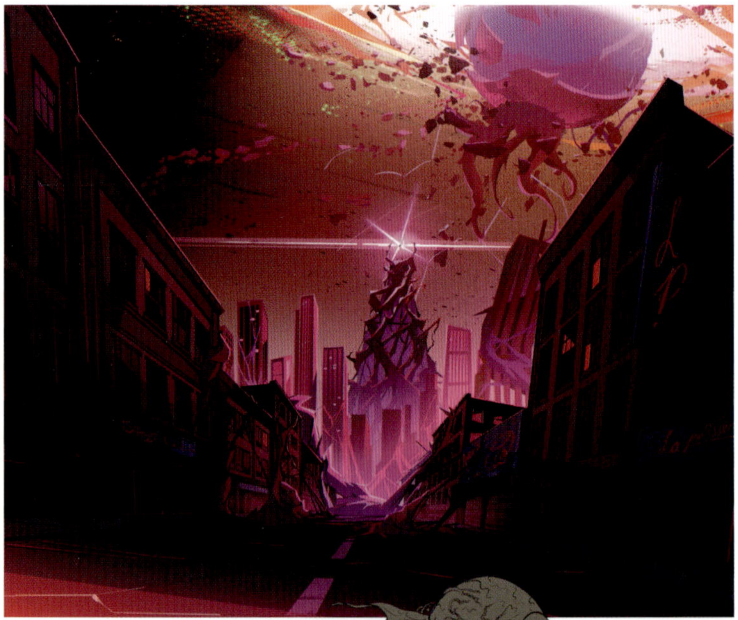

JJ CONWAY: The most important thing we wanted to achieve was scale. We wanted to feel like the entire city was facing an insurmountable foe, and to do so we tapped series superstars Christopher Luc and Max Collins to help Kevin storyboard the Technodrome's assault on the city. *Evangelion* was a major point of reference for how to visually achieve the scale and scope we were looking for.

Nas Pasha and Allison Smith handled the Turtles actually breaking into the Technodrome. We were always on the lookout for time cuts, but one thing Andy refused to touch was Allison's sequence when Donnie realizes he needs to get up to his elbows in the Krang guts and almost vomits. It was one of his absolute favorite parts of the film.

CHRISTOPHER LUC (STORYBOARD ARTIST): In this particular scene, we wanted to capture the utter futility of humanity's attempt at even having a chance of slowing the Technodrome's ascent. As a last-ditch effort, they unleash their entire military stock at the alien target in desperation.

I remember being holed up in my room working remotely, as was much of the crew at the time, while receiving direction for this sequence from Kevin. We wanted to draw inspiration and vibes from our favorite invasion scenes from films such as *Transformers: Dark of the Moon* (2011), *Evangelion* (1995), "Second Renaissance" from *The Animatrix* (2003), and maybe even a bit of *Independence Day* (1996). This scene took me a very long time to churn out and felt like an endless grind due to the amount of toning and moving objects I needed to coordinate and time out. I was really struggling to capture the scale of the battle going on, what type of lensing to use for each shot to best capture what was happening on screen, how to block out shots to make one missile barrage flow to the next, etc. We wanted the scene to be chaotic, but at the same time a beautifully destructive spectacle.

We envisioned the Krang to have a swift, efficient, and supremely devastating counter to humanity's missile and artillery spam, so what better response than a giant alien eye laser wiping out humanity's cute rocks? Back on the ground level we have the Krang dropping a bunch of alien doo-doo that horrifically assimilates animate and inanimate objects, overwhelming the population... Again, all of this was difficult to coordinate and even more difficult to draw, but thanks to everybody involved that was able to use, edit, and splice what I could to provide a thrilling and coherent invasion scene!

TECHNODROME CONCEPT

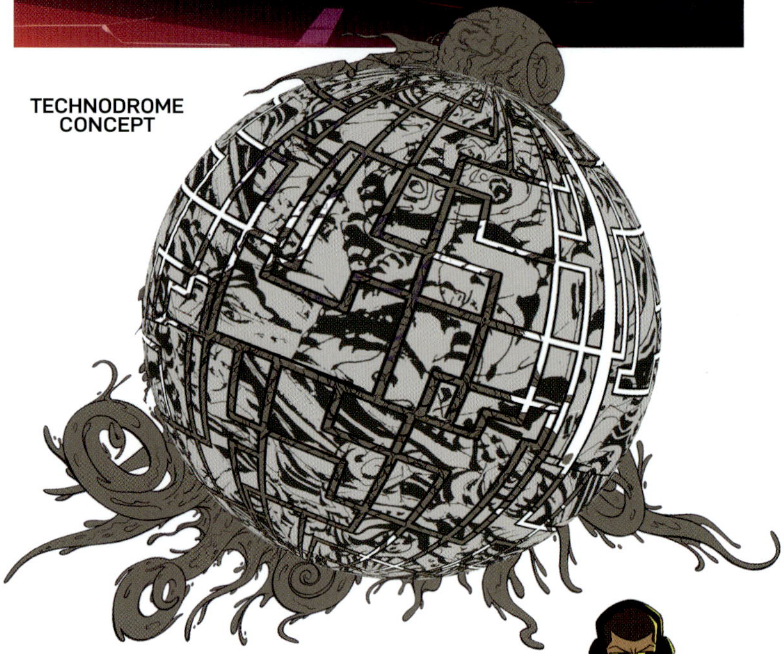

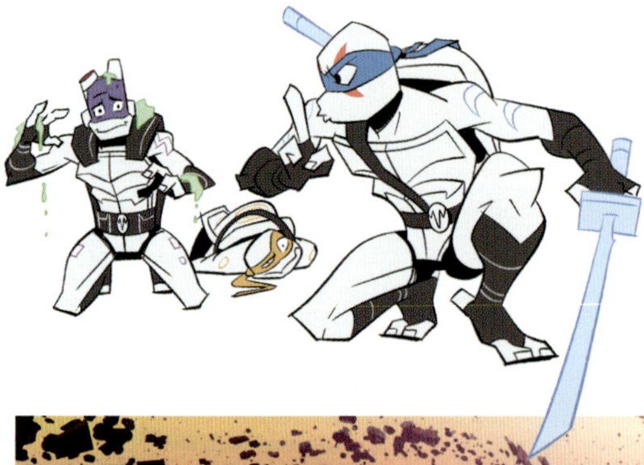

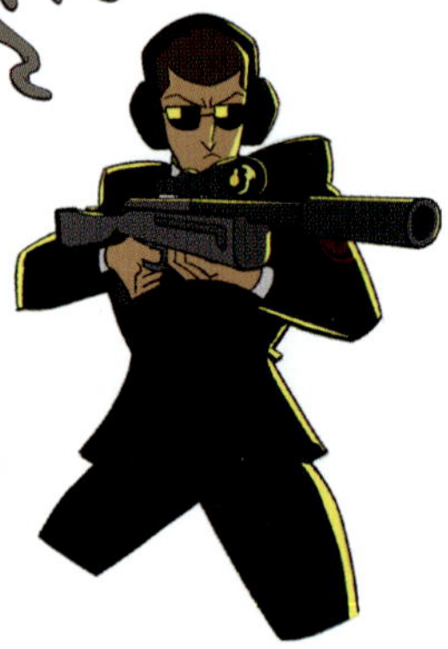

EARTH PROTECTION FORCE AGENT

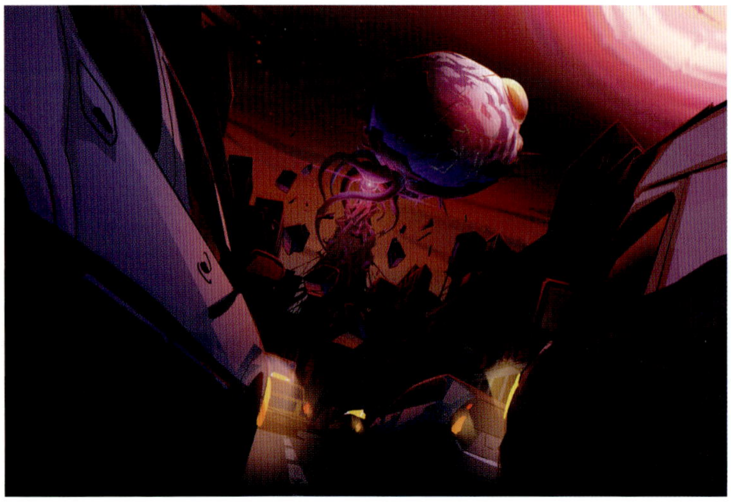

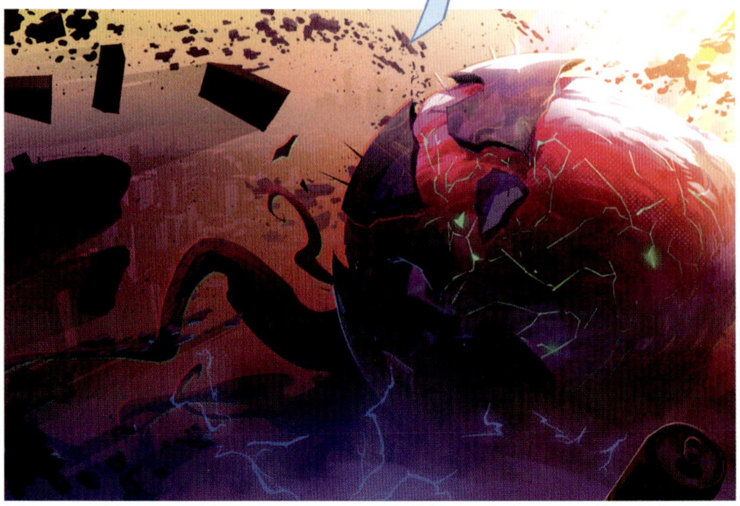

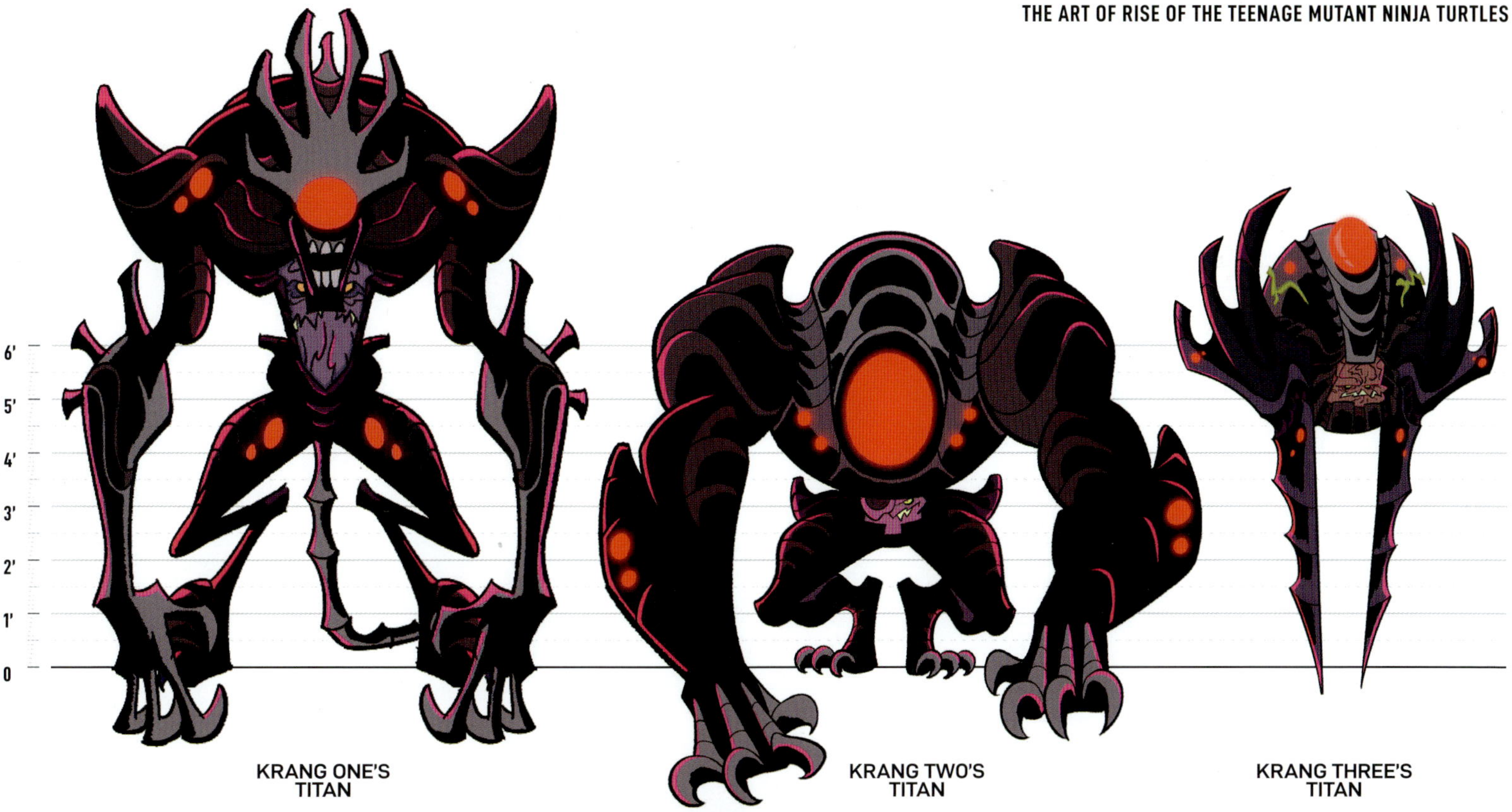

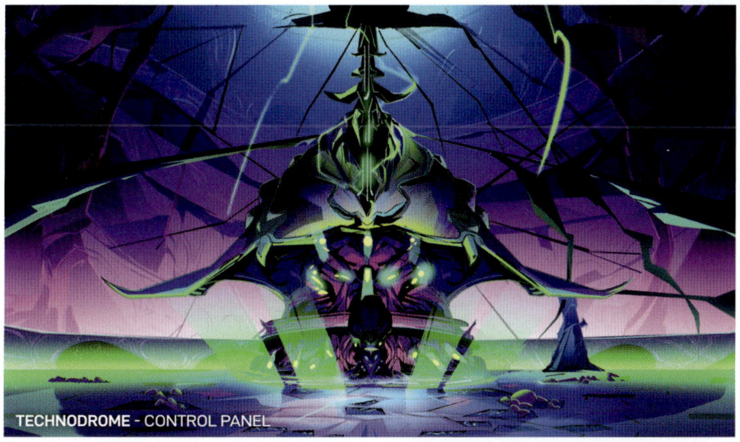
TECHNODROME - CONTROL PANEL

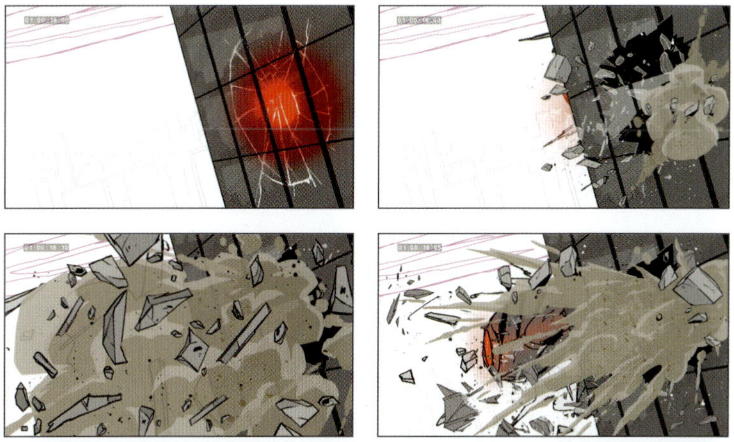

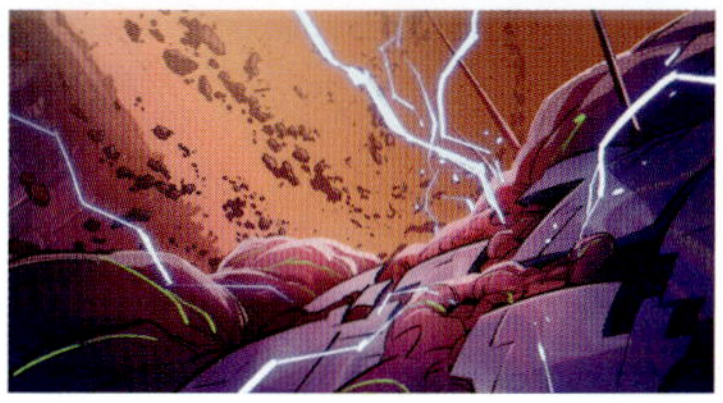

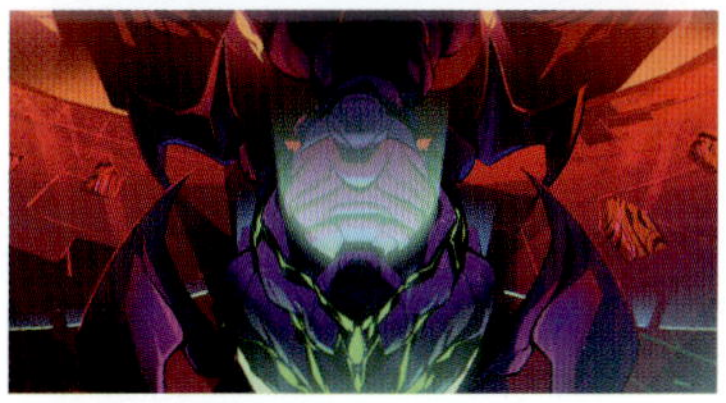

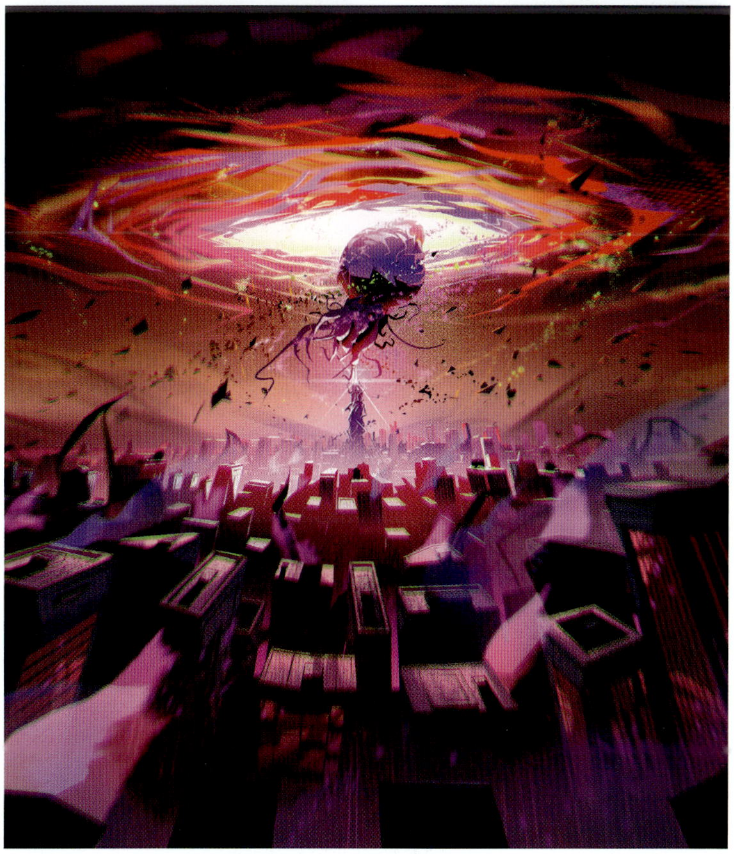

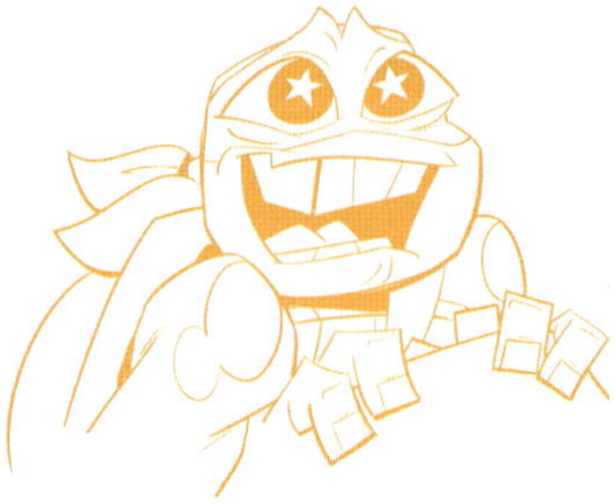

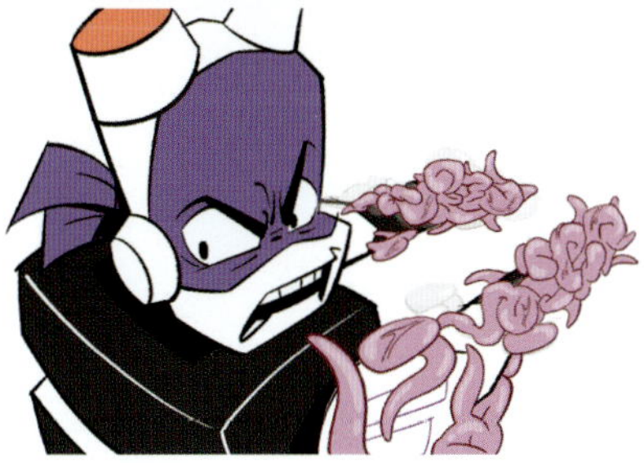

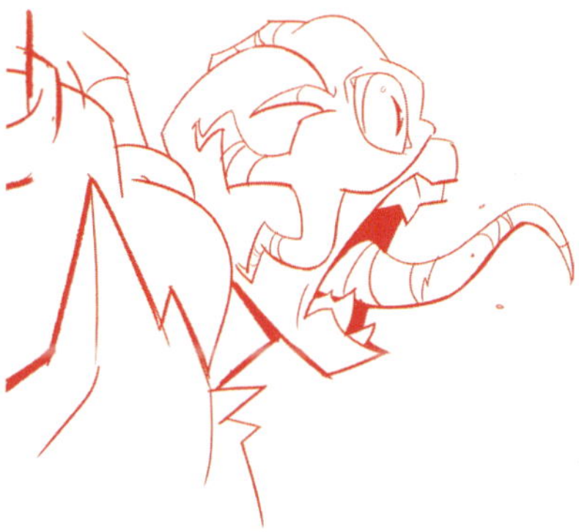

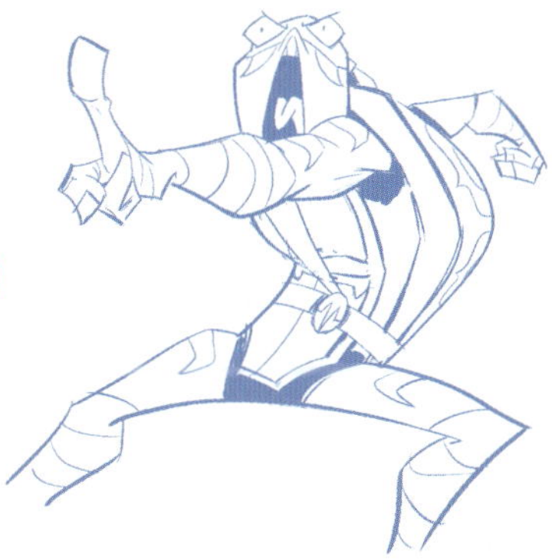

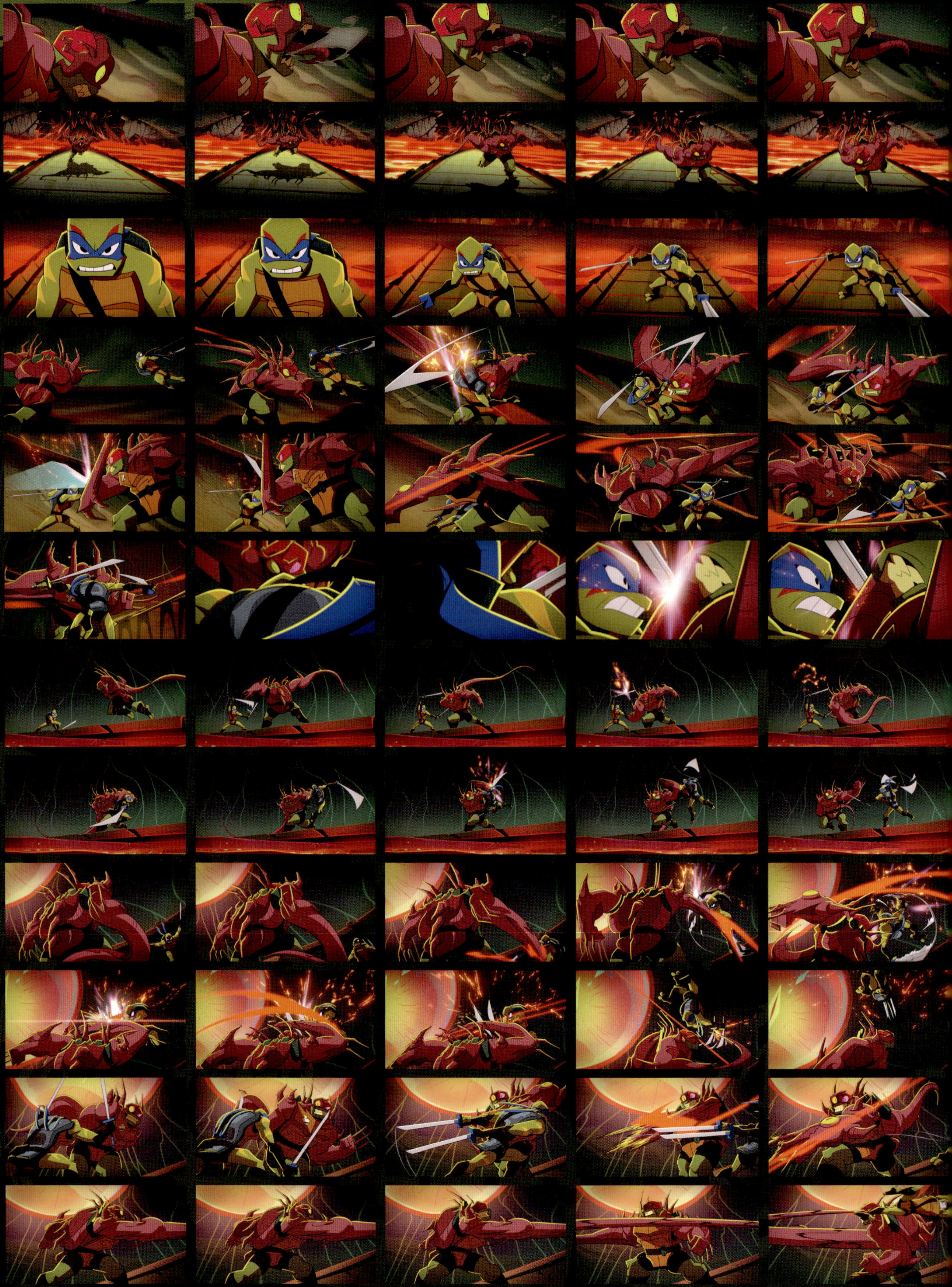

STORYBOARD ARTIST: **JJ CONWAY**

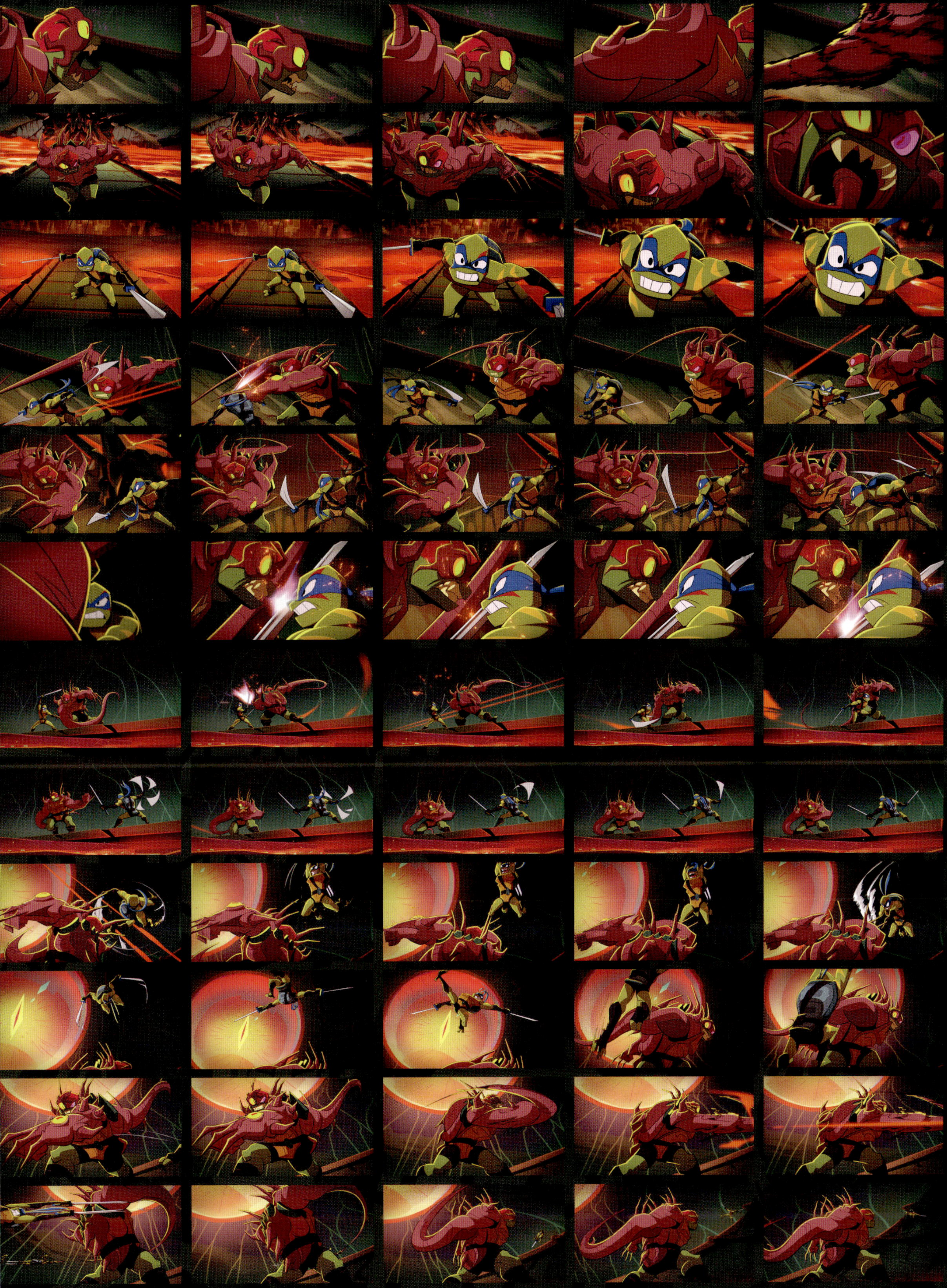

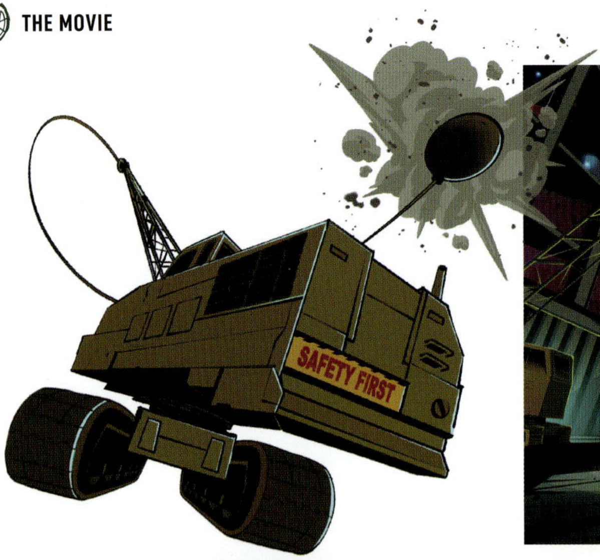

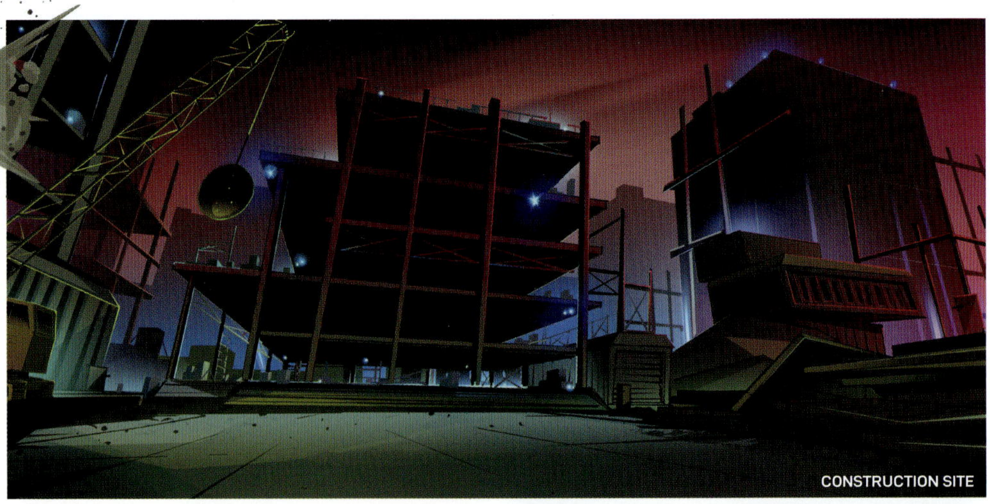
CONSTRUCTION SITE

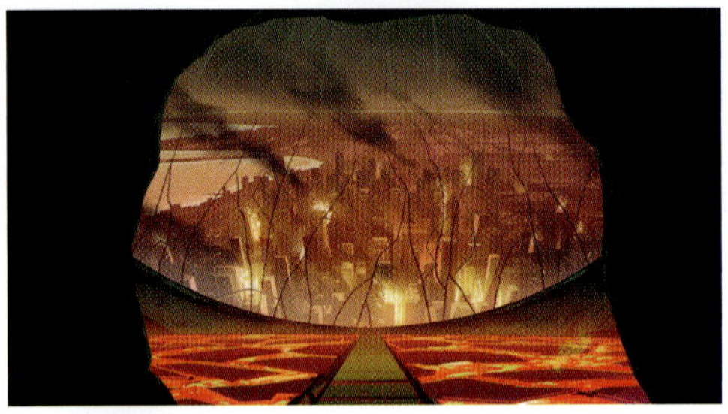

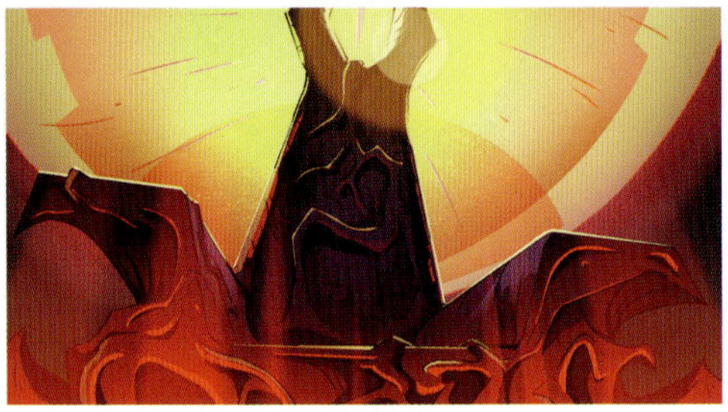

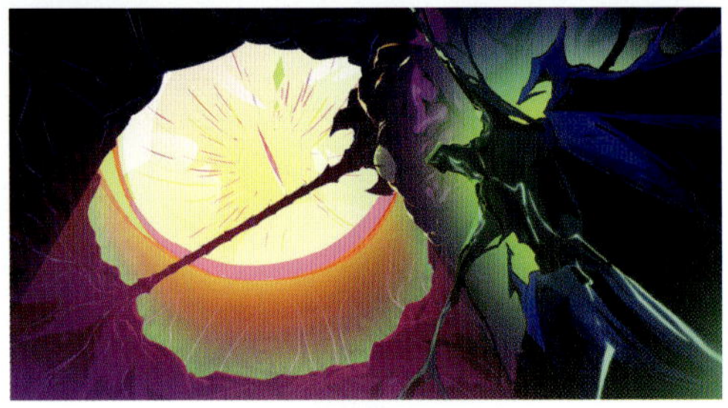

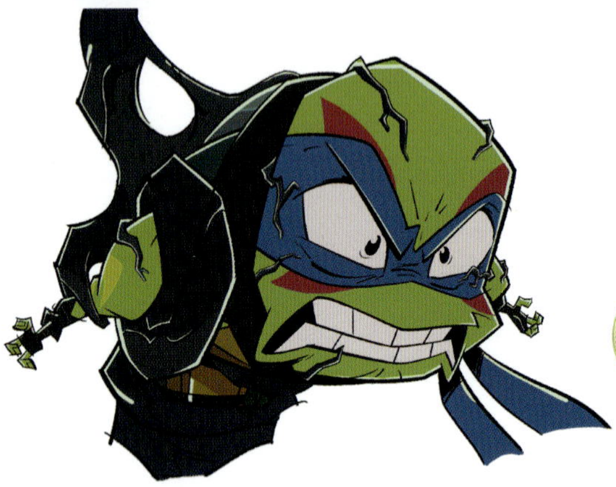

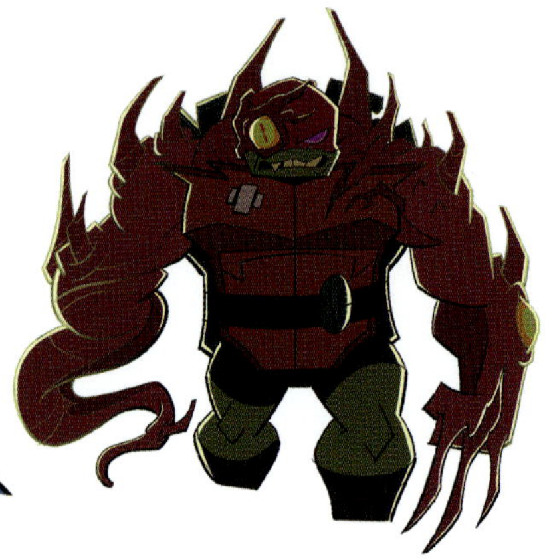

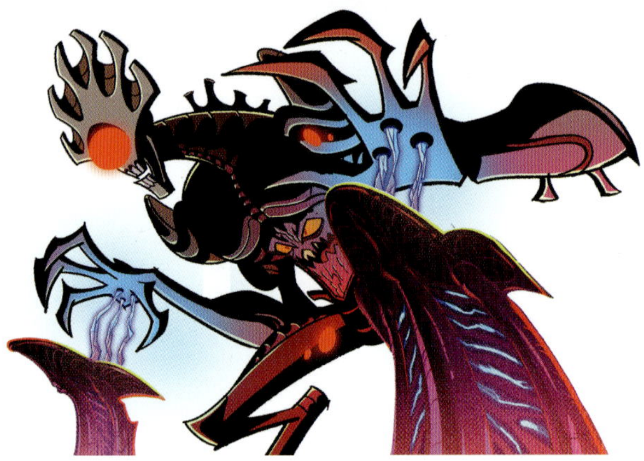

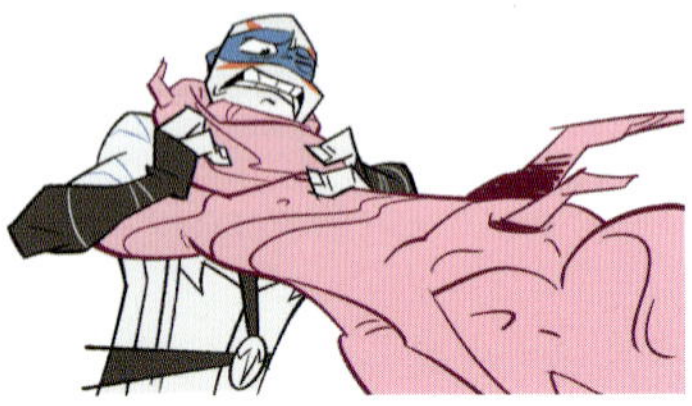

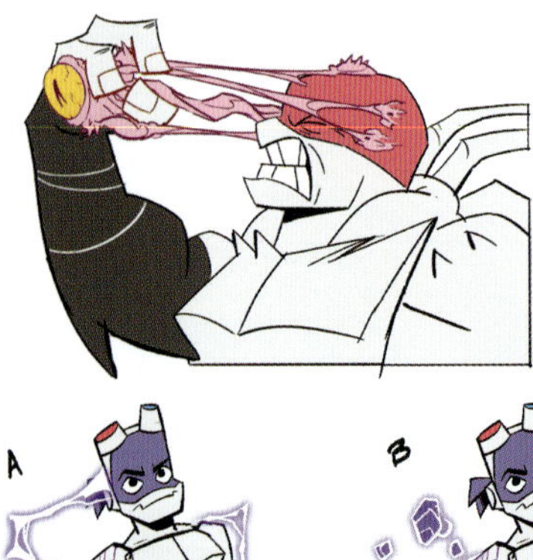

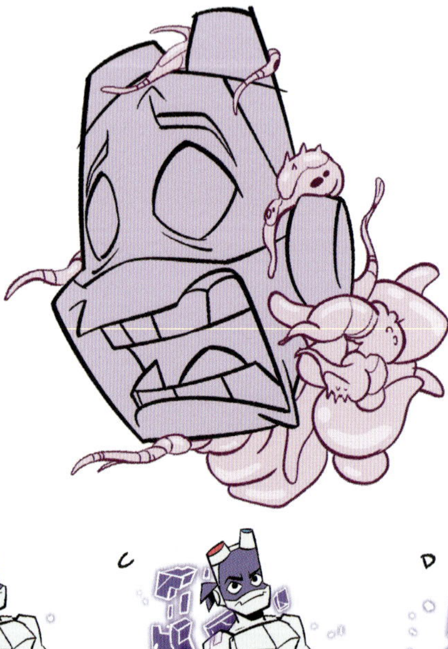

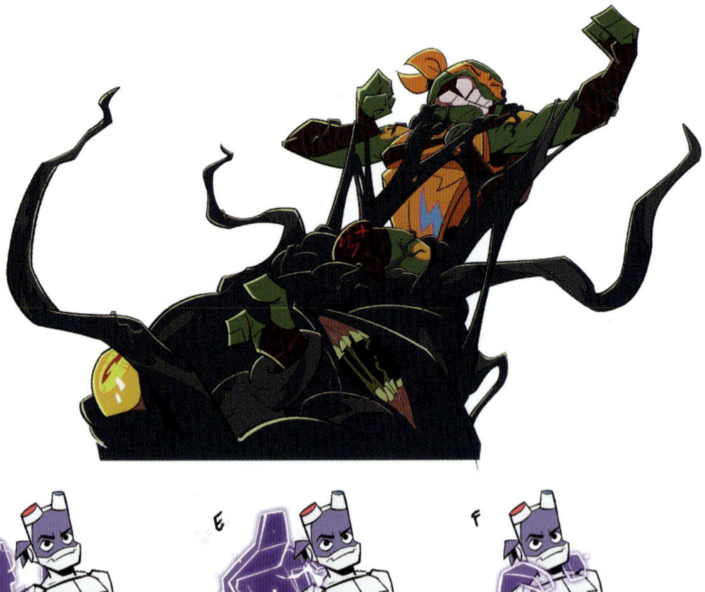

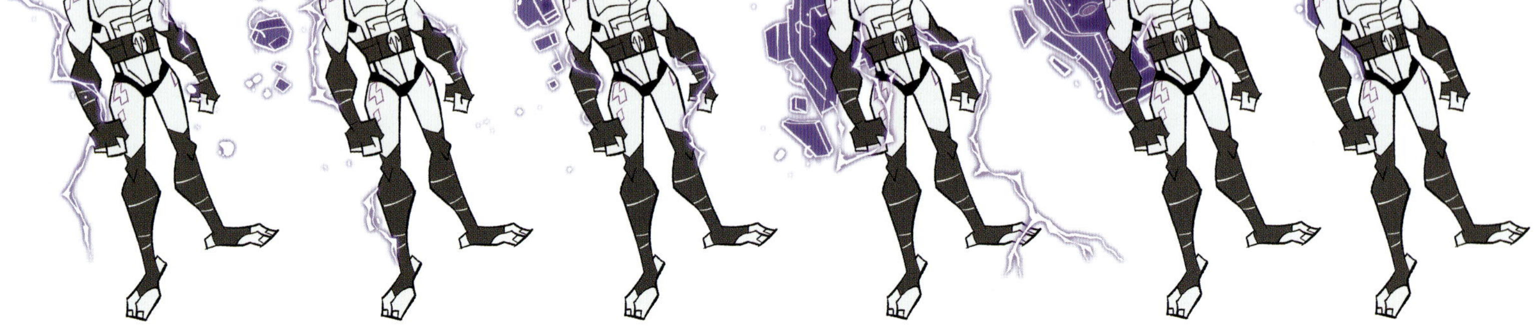

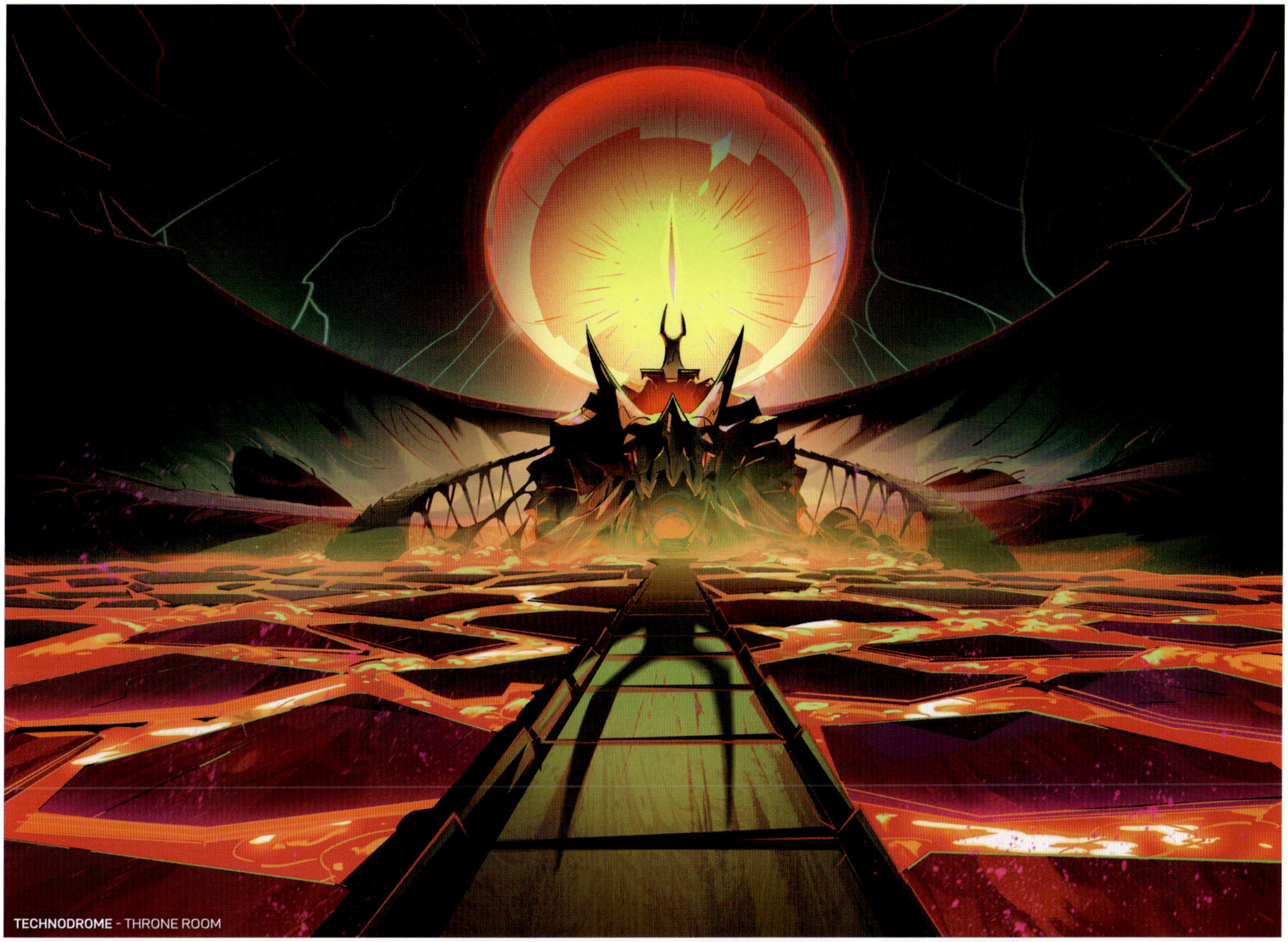

TECHNODROME - THRONE ROOM

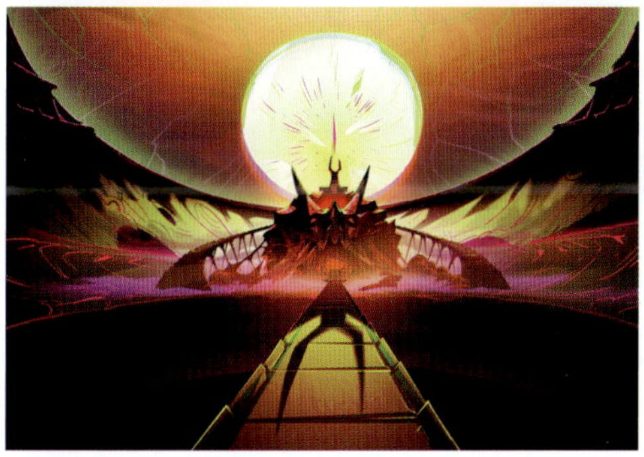

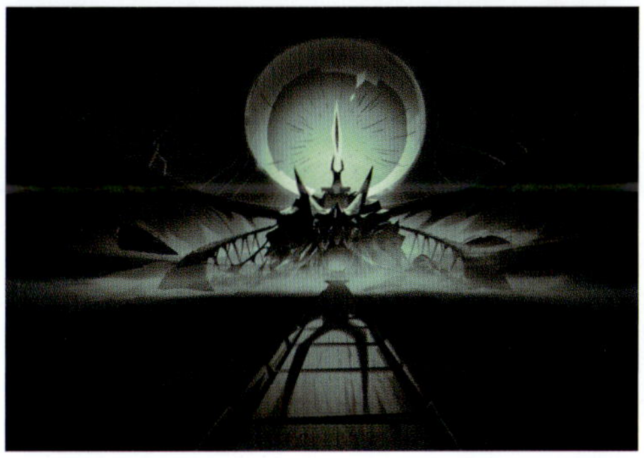

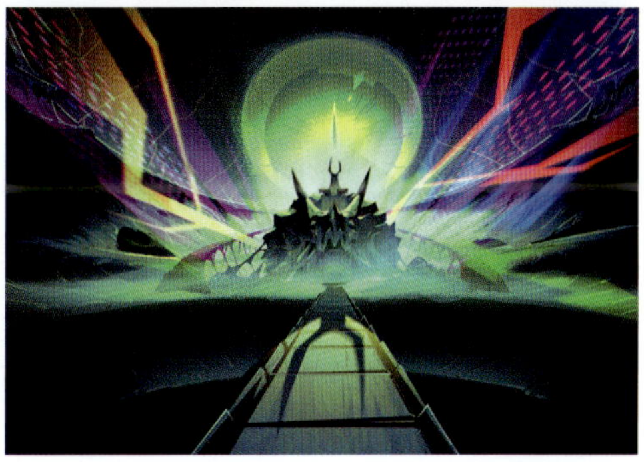

JERMAINE JOSE: The throne in the Technodrome sits atop a Triceraton skull. I wanted the floor membrane to feel like lava, with a noxious gas enveloping the throne. I ended up having to paint four versions for the different lighting changes that would occur.

TONY GAMA-LOBO: In a way, the whole movie comes down to the fight between Leo and Krangified Raph. We knew we needed to bookend the fight they had near the beginning of the movie, but this time Leo has changed. This is where we get to see how Leo has grown into the leader he's meant to become. This is Leo's *Rise* moment. JJ's boards of this fight were perfection. Epic fight, but never lost the emotion. JJ suggested Leo drops his katanas at some point and refuses to fight Raph any more to show how far he's come. And it beautifully pays off when Leo's able to reach Raph deep under that Krangified exterior. And then Kevin's boards of the Turtles all getting their powers back played huge. It was his idea for them to say for the first time who they've become: "The Teenage Mutant Ninja Turtles!"

CARL BEU: This sequence builds up from the most desperate moment, just as our heroes seem done for. We tried to convey that visually as colors getting progressively duller and more desaturated until Leo's lines ignites a burst of color and hope.

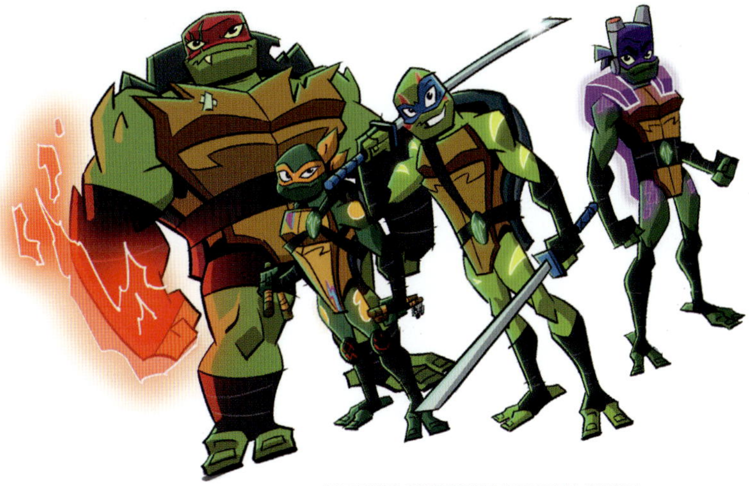

"IF THIS ISN'T THE POSTER SHOT, SOMEONE'S GETTING FIRED"

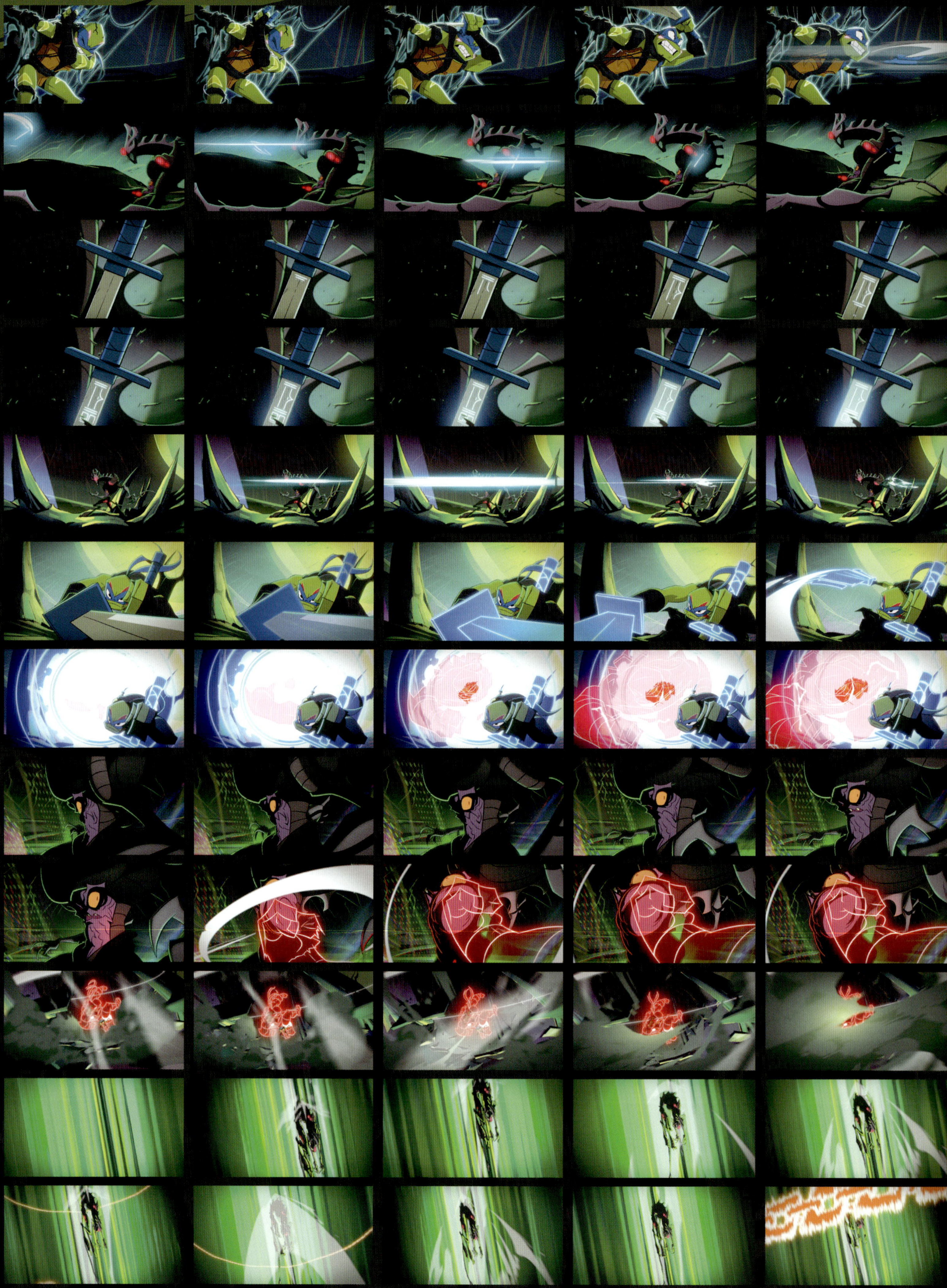

STORYBOARD ARTIST: **KEVIN MOLINA-ORTIZ**

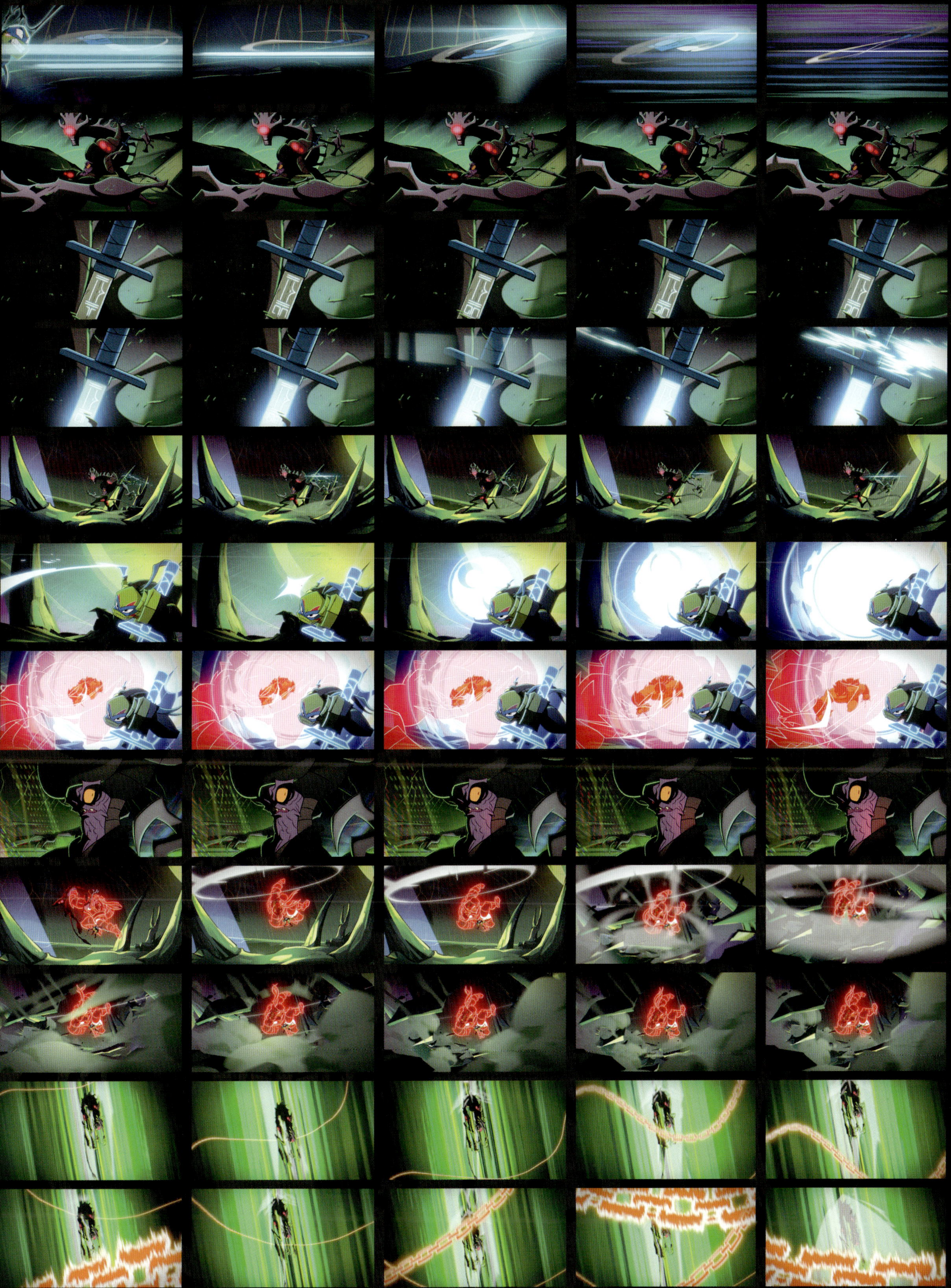

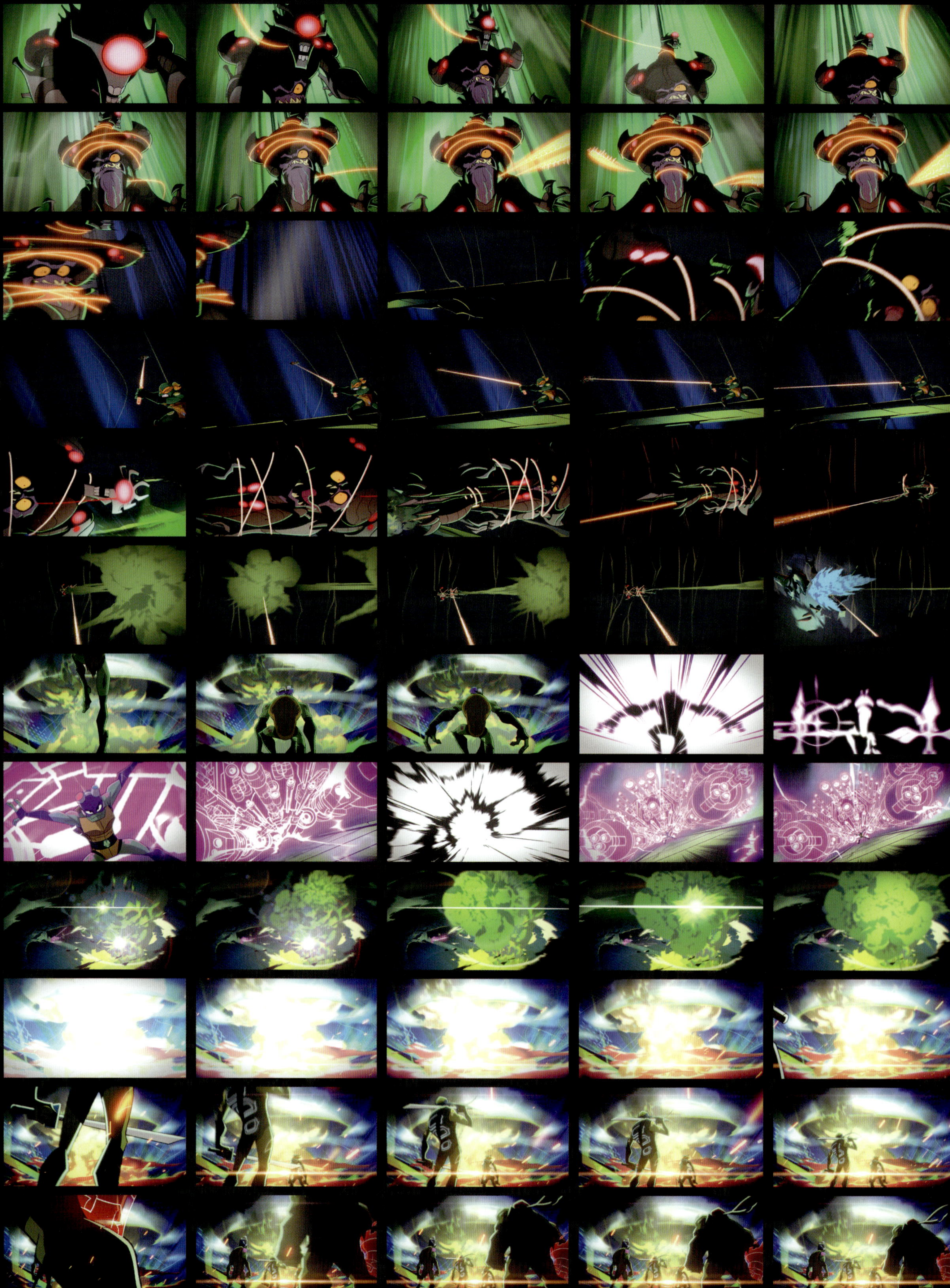

STORYBOARD ARTIST: **KEVIN MOLINA-ORTIZ**

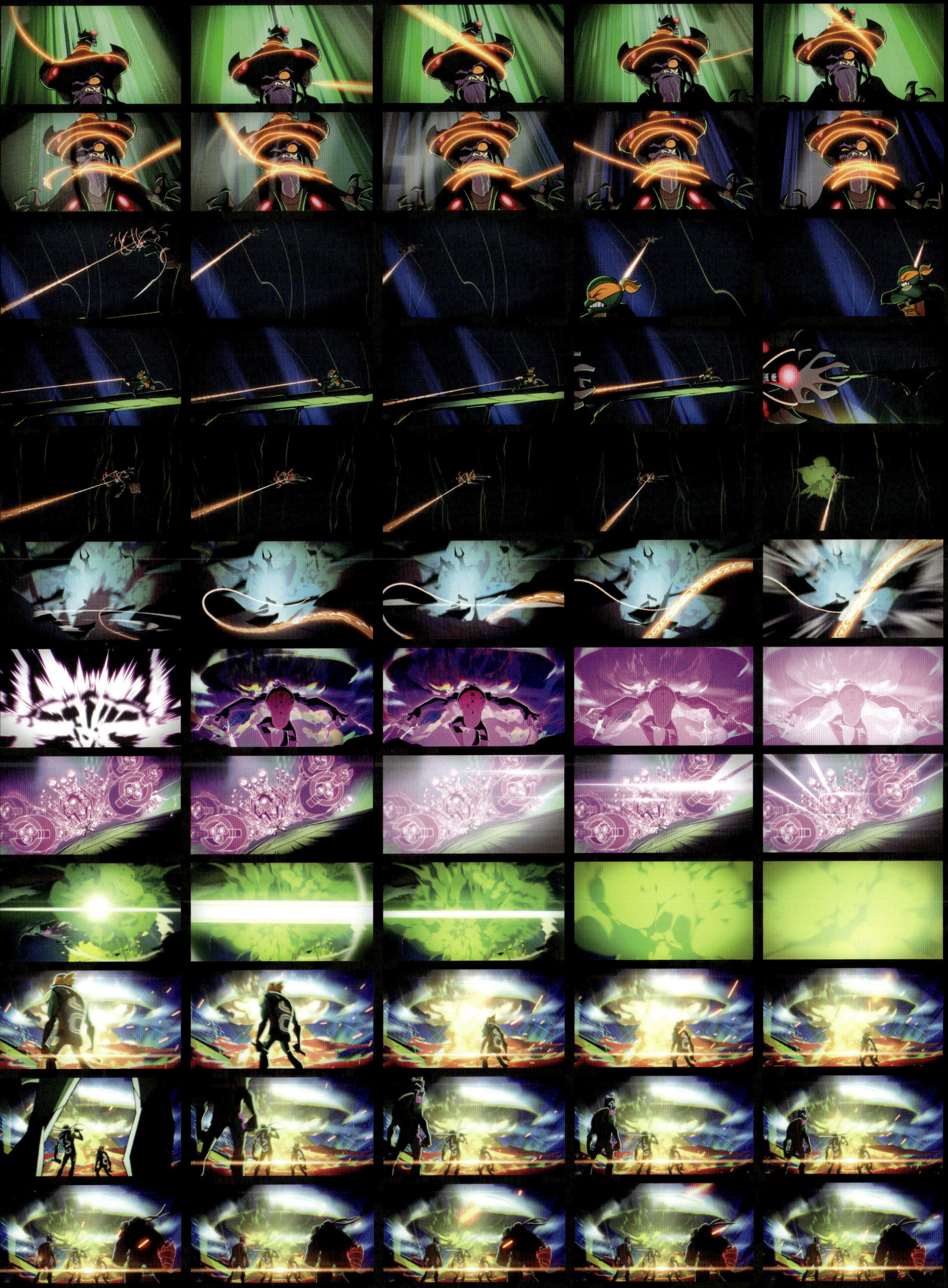

THE FINAL FIGHT

"WE ARE THE TEENAGE MUTANT NINJA TURTLES!"

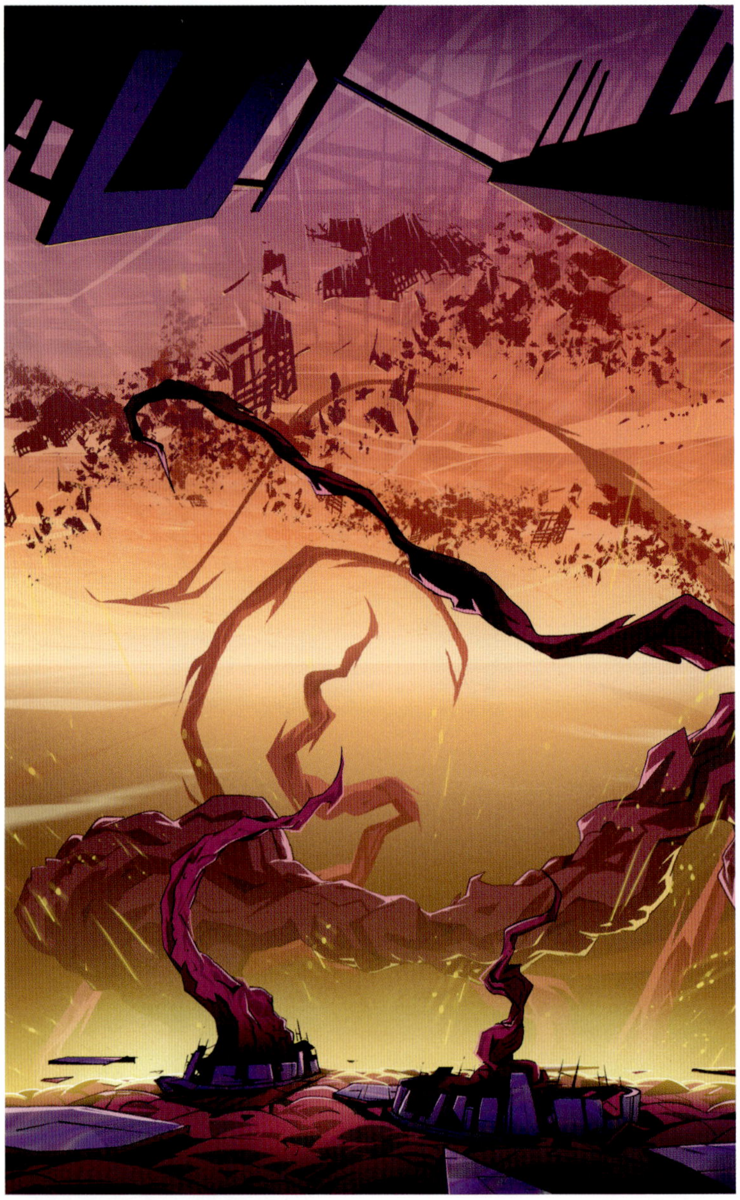

TONY GAMA-LOBO: From a script perspective, this whole section was a complete bear. We knew where we needed to end up, but choreographing six different heroes, three different Krang, on the streets of New York, in the Technodrome and ultimately in the Prison Dimension was extremely difficult. I think at one point we wrote a whole scene of Hypno and Warren showing up to help April trap one of the Krang in some arcade while Mikey and Donnie were operating some big military tech to help get Leo into the Technodrome. It was all too much.

In an earlier version of the script, there was no Technodrome at all. The Krang emerged from under the Brooklyn Bridge, where they had been in stasis for centuries. They proceeded to Krangify the bridge and create a massive Krang castle of sorts. In a more *Lord of the Rings* version, the final battle was the Turtles, Casey, April, and Splinter charging up the Krang Kastle stairs fighting off Krangified orc-like creatures until they reached the top and finally defeated Krang One.

JJ CONWAY: The throwdown between the TMNT and Krang One was the very last thing to be storyboarded. We'd put it off both because we were so busy with the rest of the film, but also because we weren't sure how much screen time we'd actually have for it. But in November of 2020, Kevin's full-time task became storyboarding that fight while I oversaw revisions on the rest of the film, and five weeks later he delivered the incredible final battle with almost no time to spare. Originally clocking in around two and a half minutes, we had to quickly cut it down for time, patch and sew up where we cut, then ship it off for animation.

Once Leo gets Krang into the Prison Dimension, Kevin had an idea and just went for it, delivering a sequence dripping with thematic symbolism. On a character level, Leo has fully realized his arc, and Kevin heartbreakingly shows a leader embracing his fate, at peace knowing that he saved his family and the world.

On the outside, India Swift storyboarded the emotional sequence where all seems lost, but Mikey refuses to give up on Leo and rips open a portal in time and space. India excels at emotional character acting and brings Mikey's sheer determination to life.

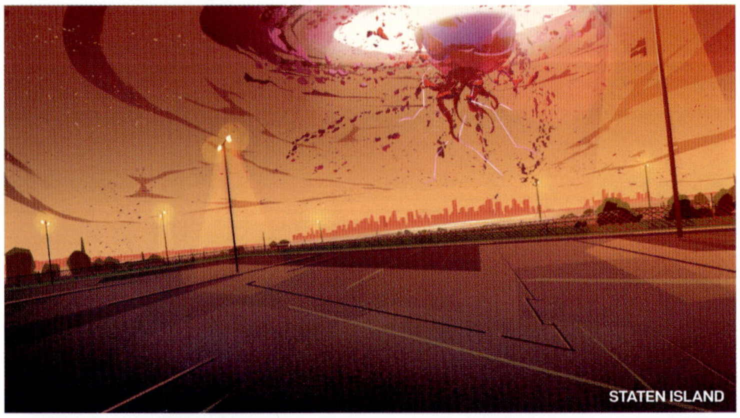

STATEN ISLAND

TONY GAMA-LOBO: I was blown away by the emotion the board team put into Leo's final sacrifice. Sometimes when you're writing you wonder if people can really care about a bunch of animated mutant turtles, but when you watch the boards of this sequence and listen to the performance of the actors, you can't help but be totally sucked in.

One of the things that made the ending so difficult was making sure to give everyone their big moment. Donnie became a spaceship, April and Splinter defeated Krang Two, Casey reached the key and closed the portal, etc. My favorite was Mikey finally able to summon his mystic powers and give us a glimpse of the Mystic Warrior we saw in the prologue opening of the movie. The second he starts to glow, oh man. What a great full circle moment for the audience.

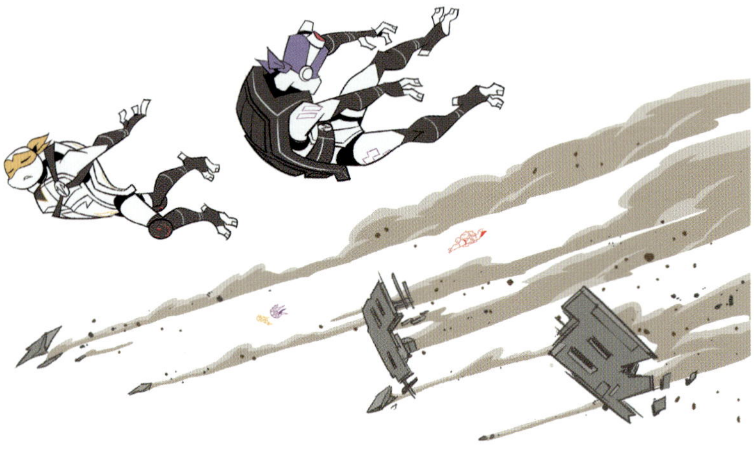

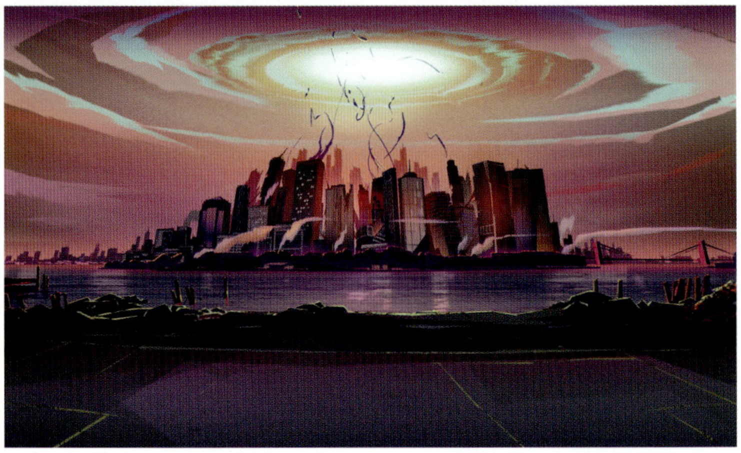

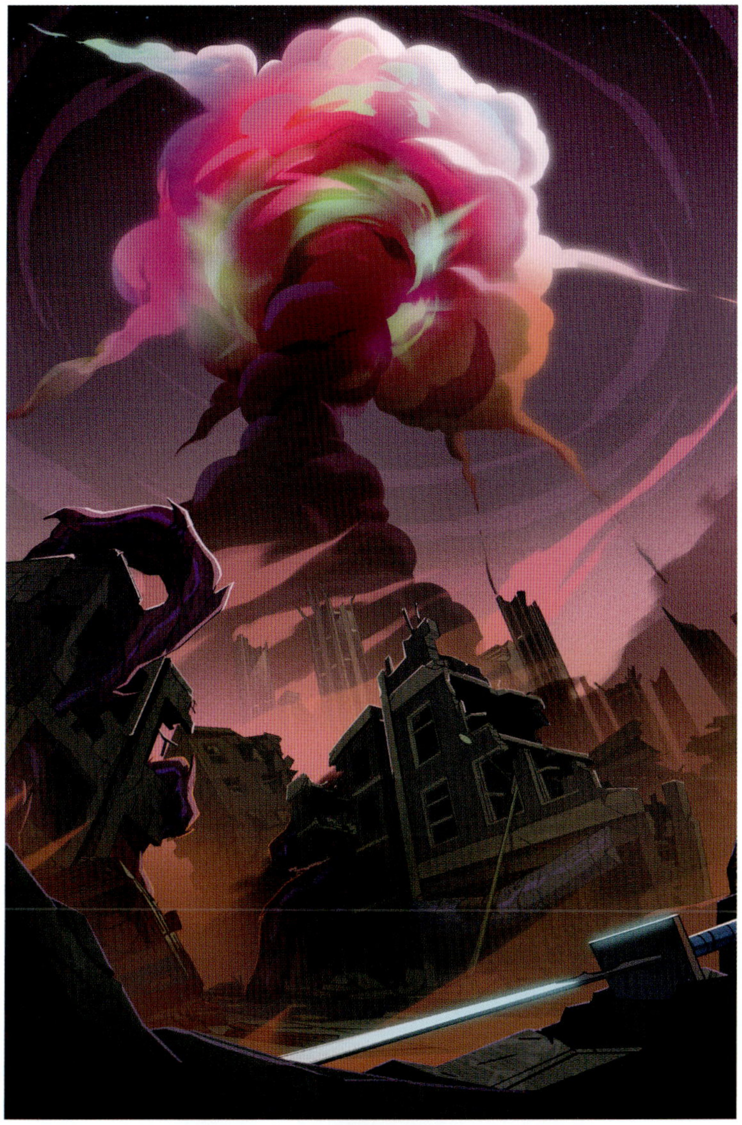

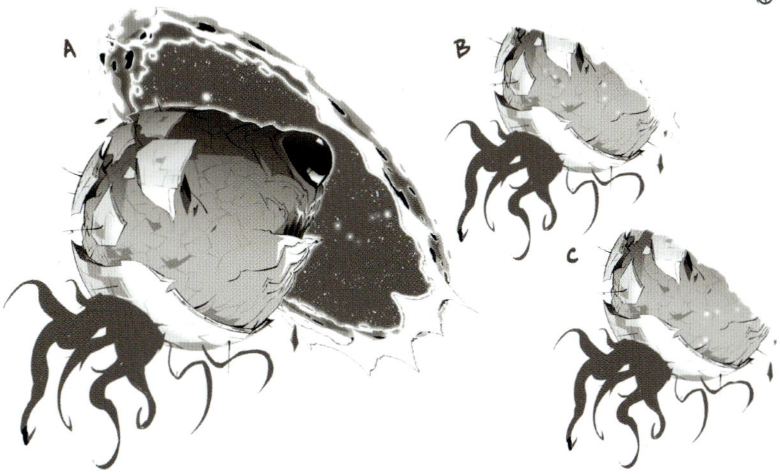

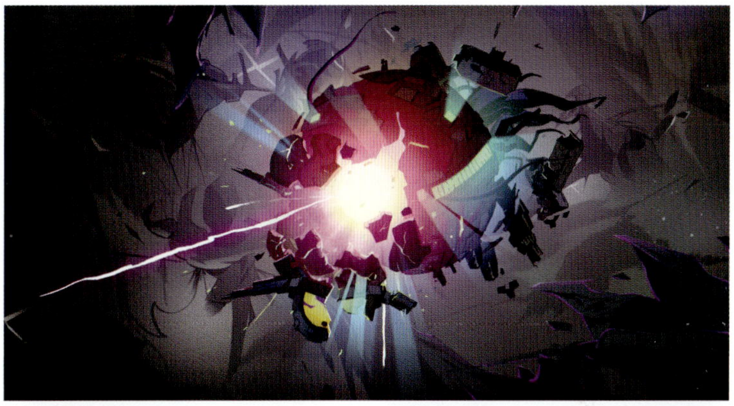

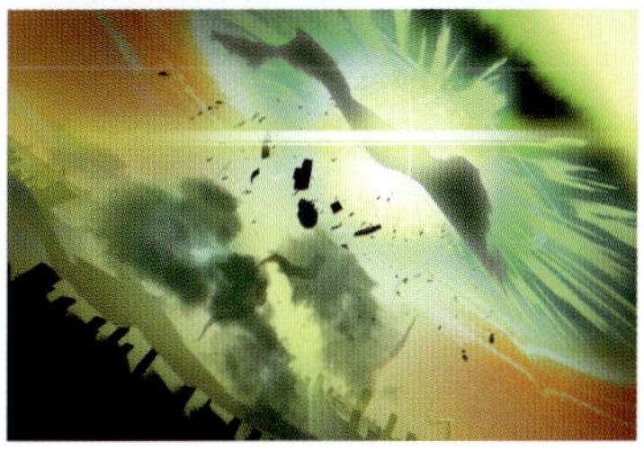

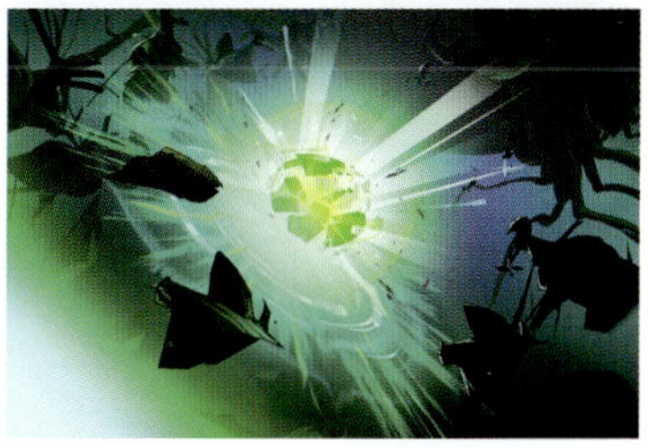

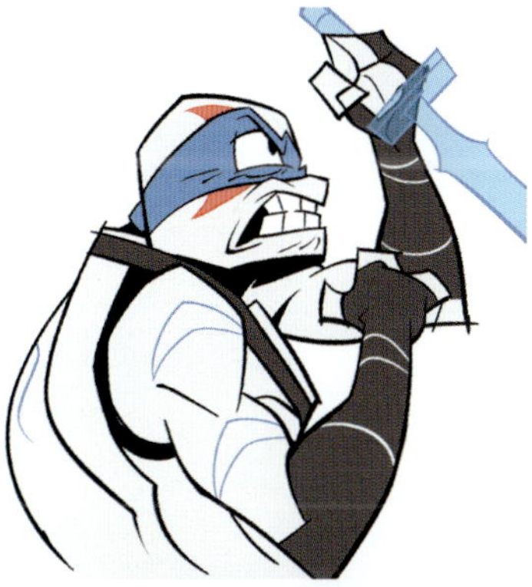

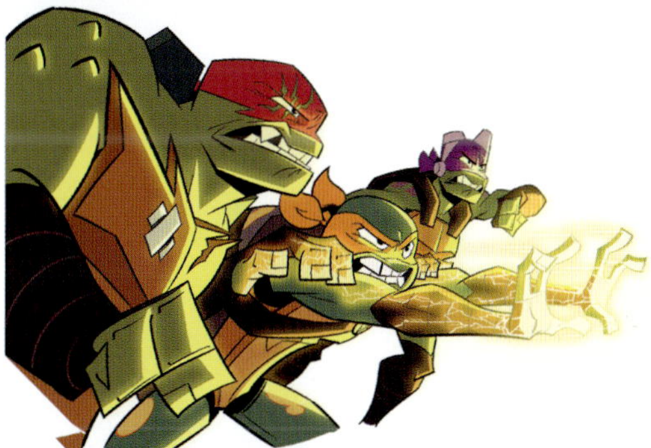

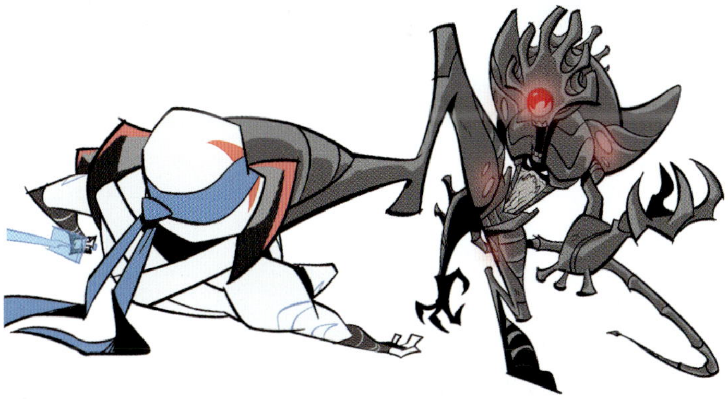

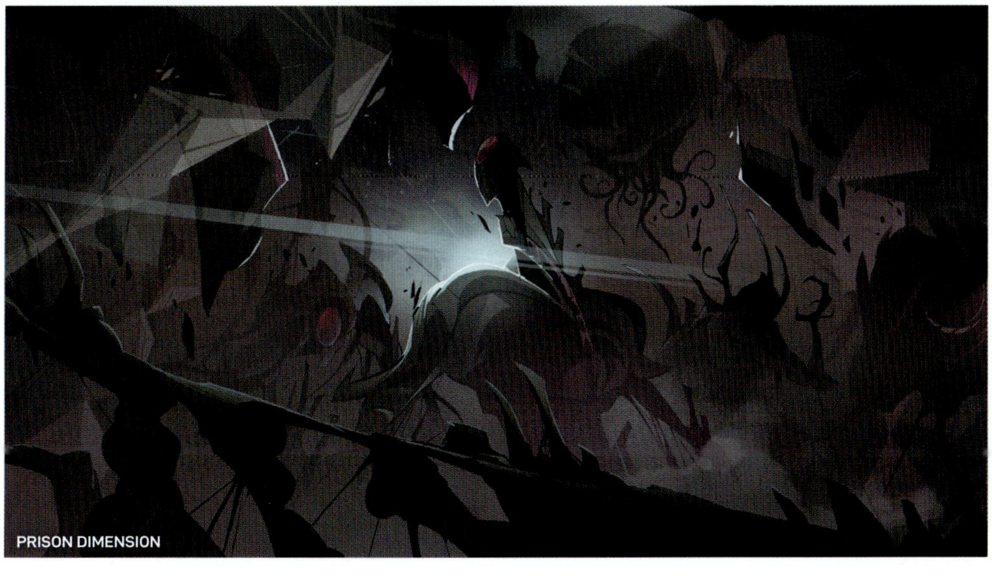

PRISON DIMENSION

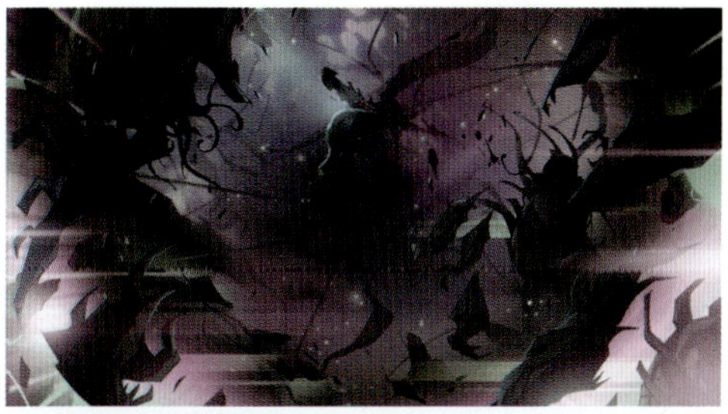

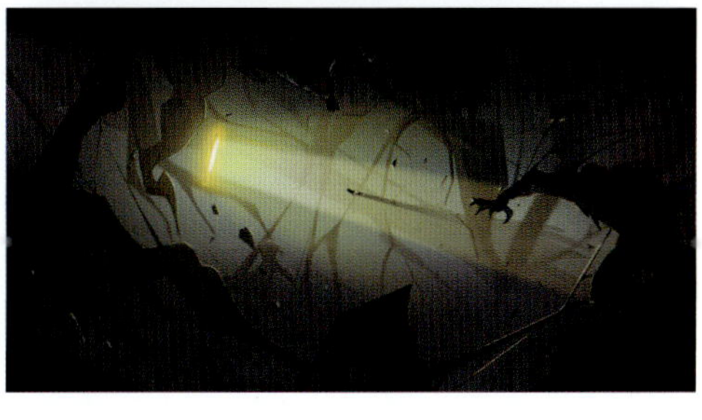

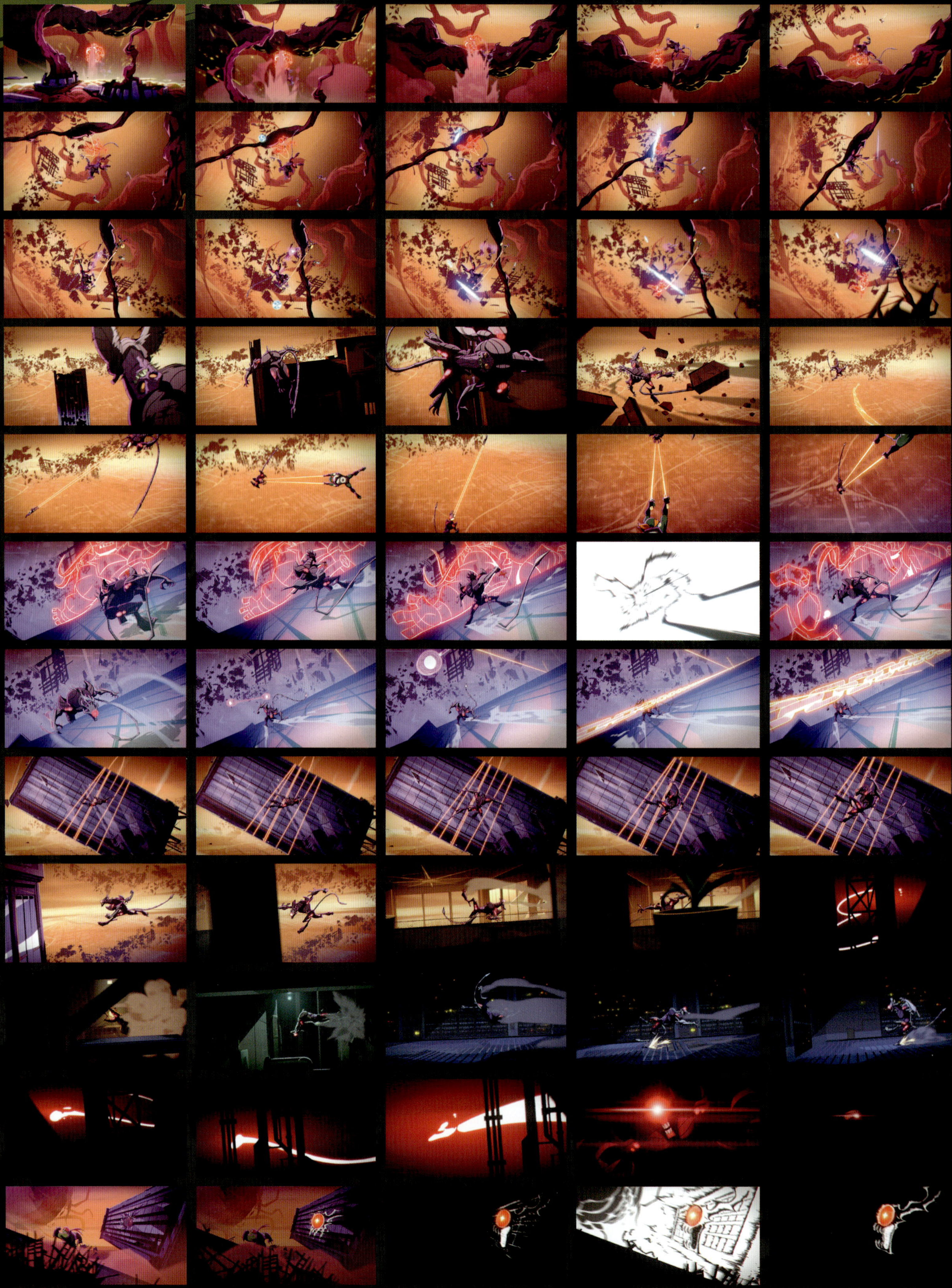

STORYBOARD ARTIST: **KEVIN MOLINA-ORTIZ**

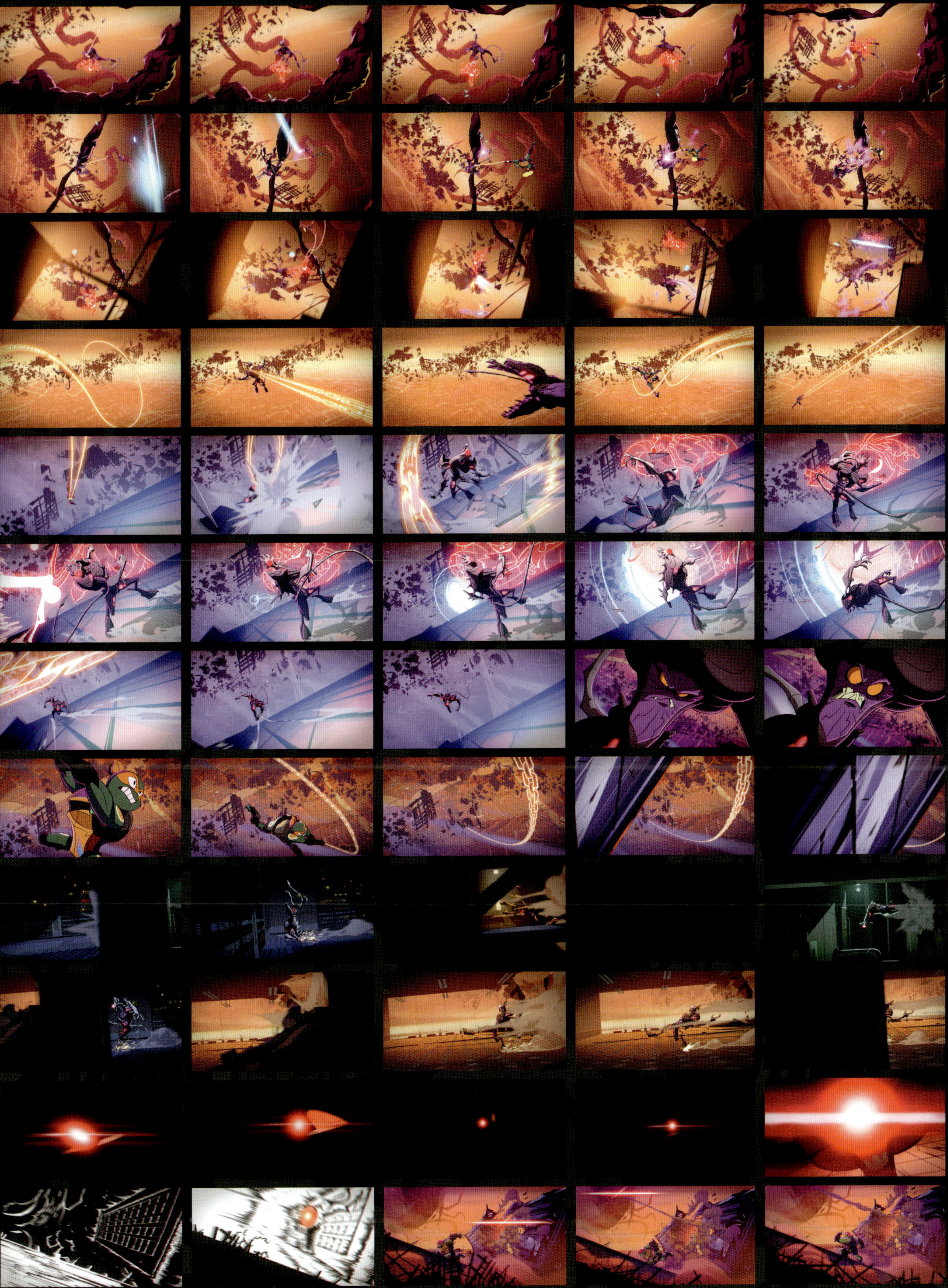

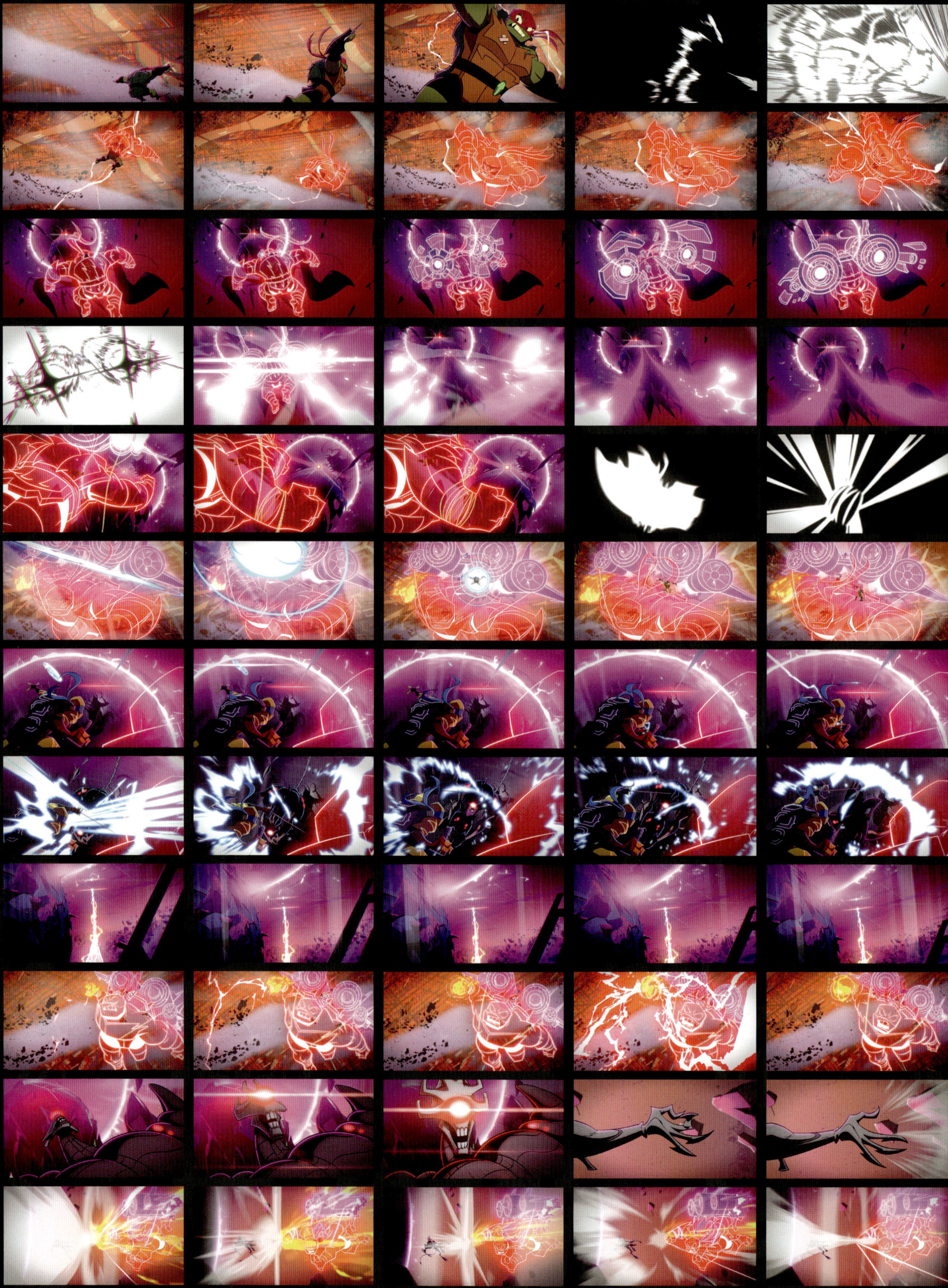

STORYBOARD ARTIST: **KEVIN MOLINA-ORTIZ**

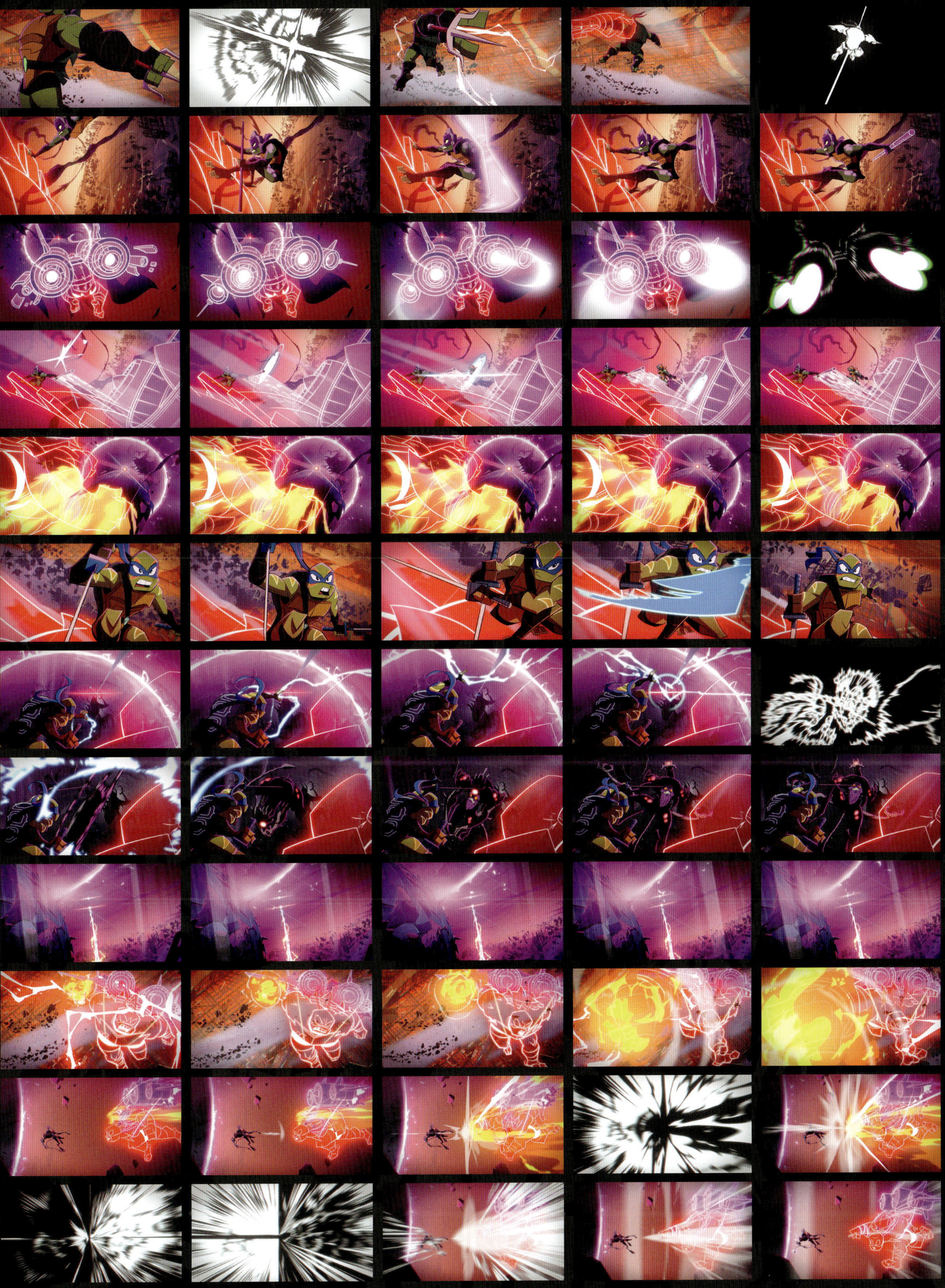

OUR HEROES

"We'll always rise to the challenge."

JJ CONWAY: This was a difficult scene to nail because it had to sum up everything we wanted to say about not just the movie, but *Rise of the TMNT* as a whole. We needed to bring things full circle while also illustrating how all of our characters had grown on their journey through the film.

In general we tried to avoid gratuitous fan service, since screen time was so precious and because we wanted our story to be accessible to anybody who might find it on Netflix. However, we allowed ourselves to indulge with the Cassandra cameo. We only had a precious few seconds but wanted those seconds to embody why she's such a beloved character to both the fans and the crew.

TONY GAMA-LOBO: I wish I could remember who first pitched the gag of Foot Recruit (a.k.a. Cassandra Jones) calling April, and Casey seeing his mom. It made us all laugh so hard. We even tried versions where she would show up and meet her future son, but the time-travel paradox of everything was just too much.

JJ CONWAY: In the end, I think this sequence really succeeds at bidding a heartfelt farewell to our heroes and this iteration of TMNT.

TONY GAMA-LOBO: We had the greatest cast you could ever ask for. They truly were the greatest stewards of these timeless characters. And they cared for them as much as we did. I remember when we first turned in our script, Becky and I got this incredibly thoughtful email from Ben Schwartz thanking us for giving Leo such a great final story. Very grateful for that. It cannot be overstated what Ben, Josh, Omar, Brandon, Kat, and Eric brought to the Turtles, April, and Splinter. Not only did they demonstrate a genius level of comedic talent, but they found a depth of soul that made it impossible not to love them, root for them, and miss them when they were gone.

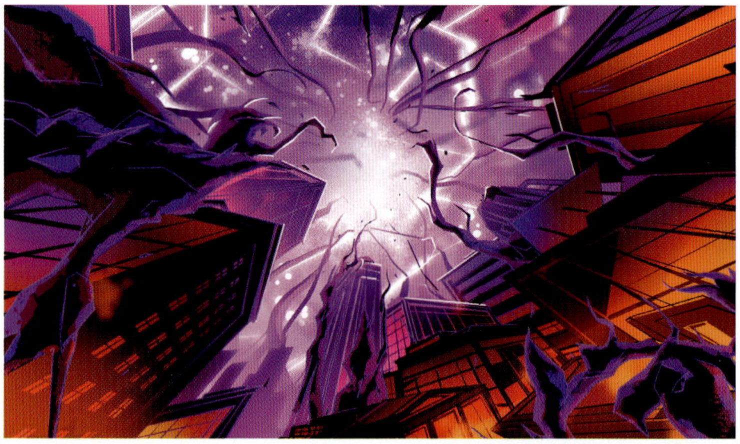

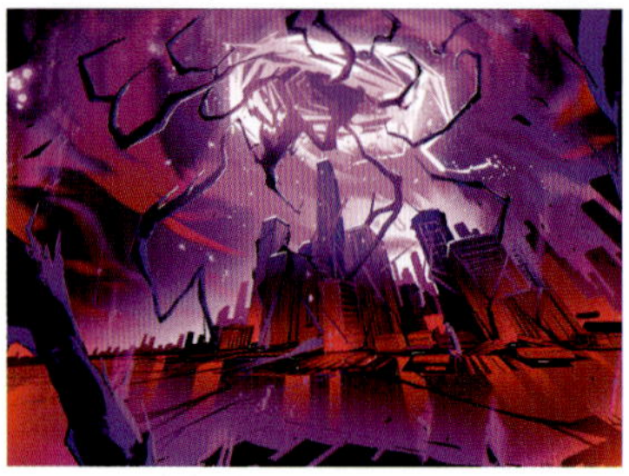

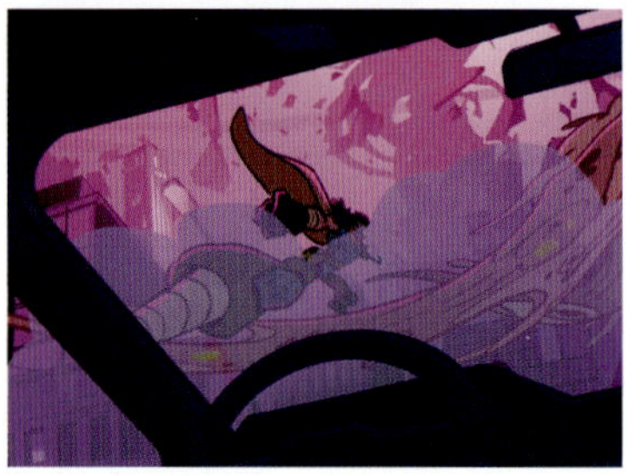

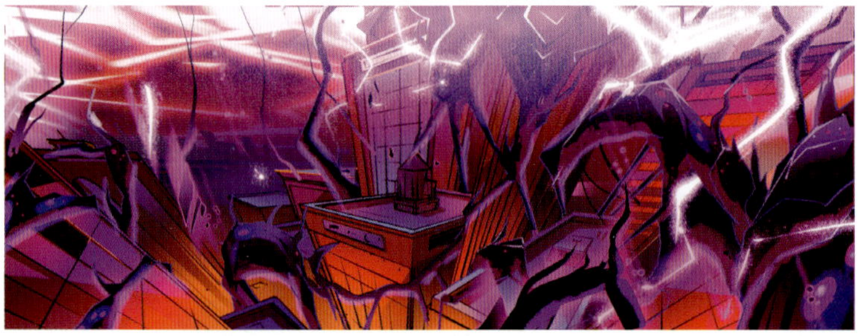

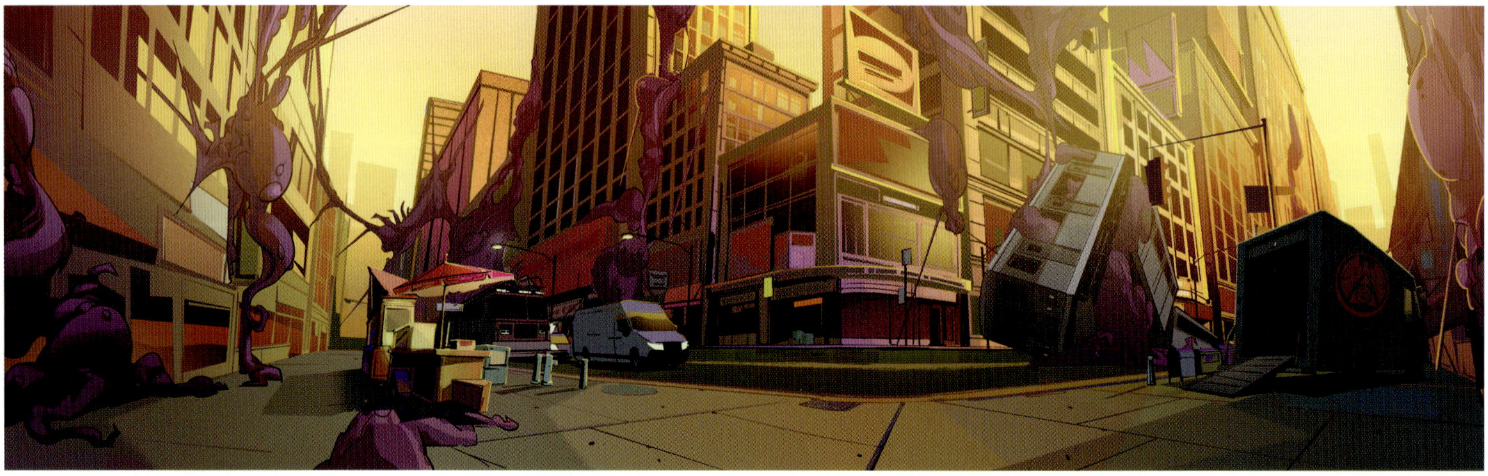

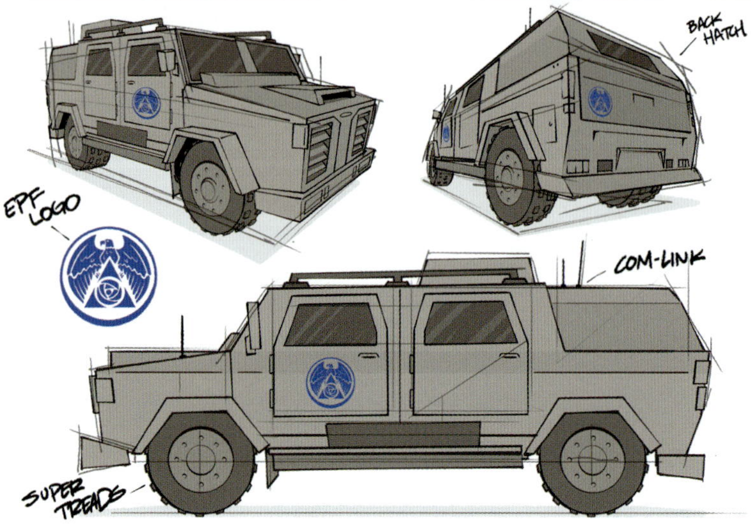

EARTH PROTECTION FORCE
RESPONSE VEHICLE

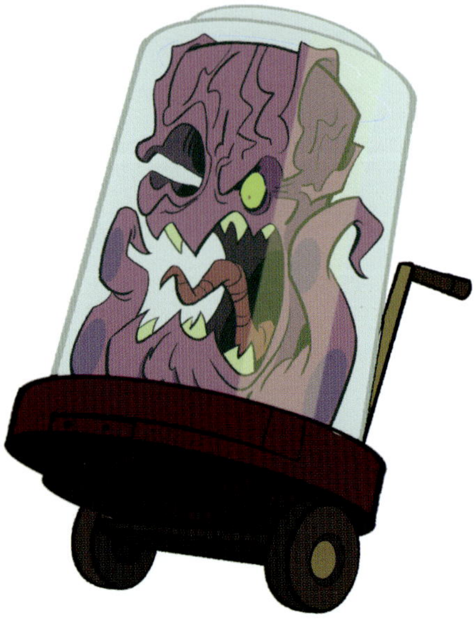

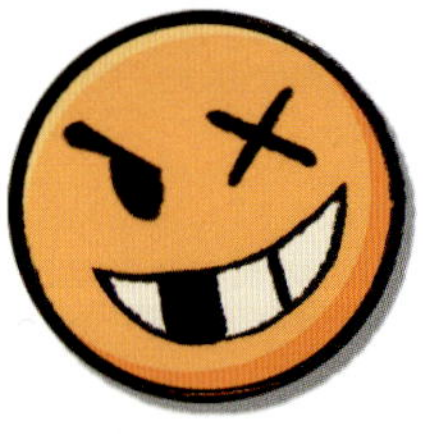

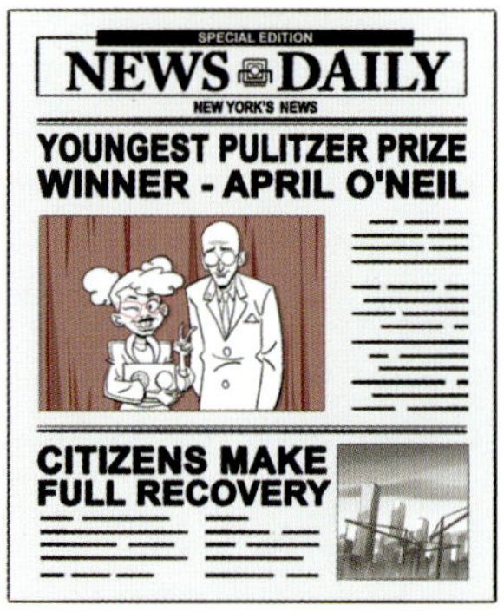
SPECIAL EDITION
NEWS DAILY
NEW YORK'S NEWS
YOUNGEST PULITZER PRIZE WINNER - APRIL O'NEIL
CITIZENS MAKE FULL RECOVERY

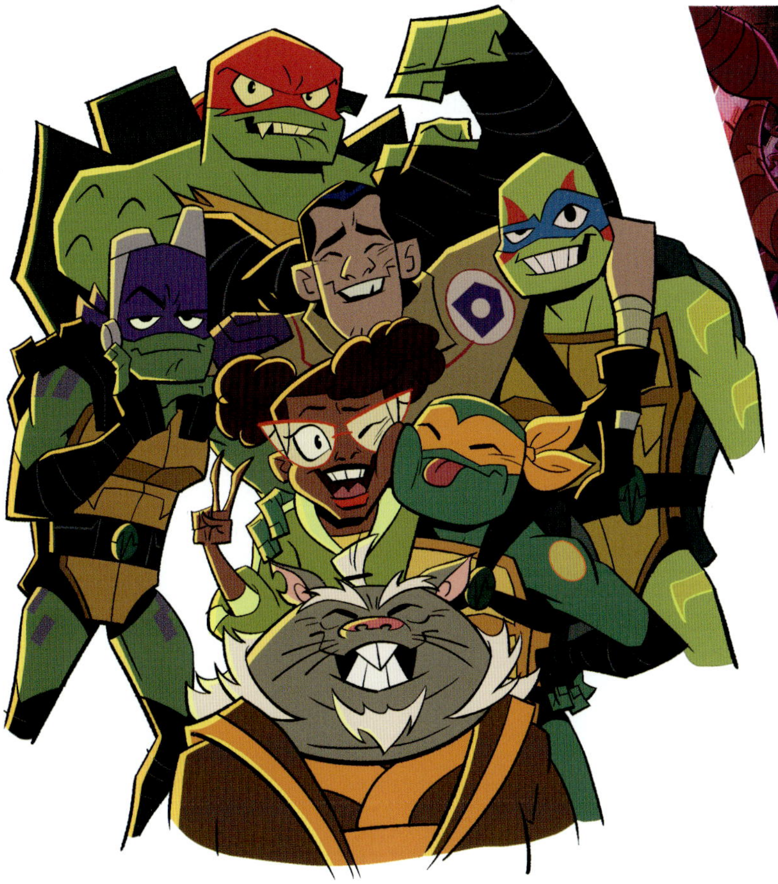

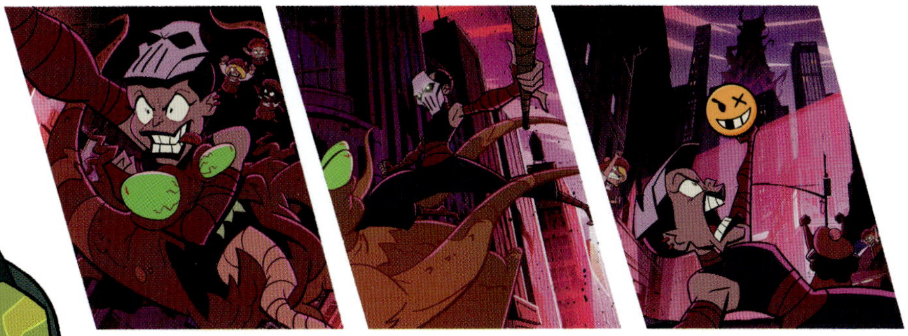

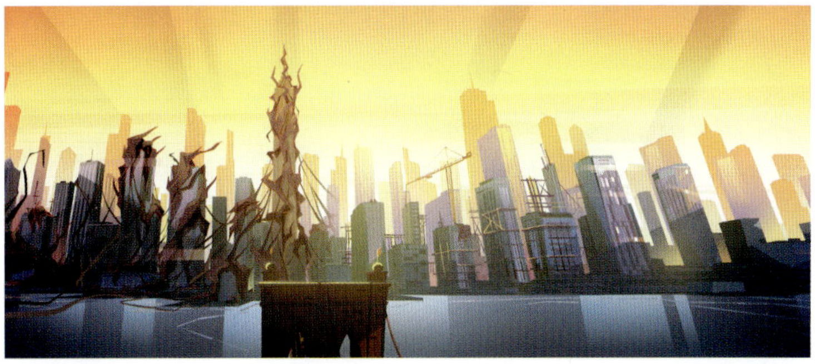

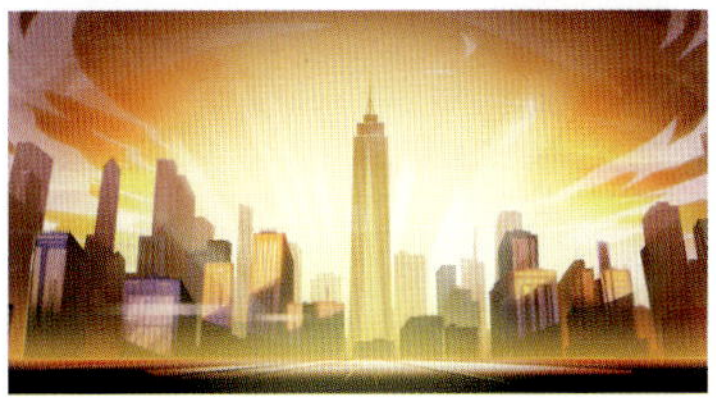

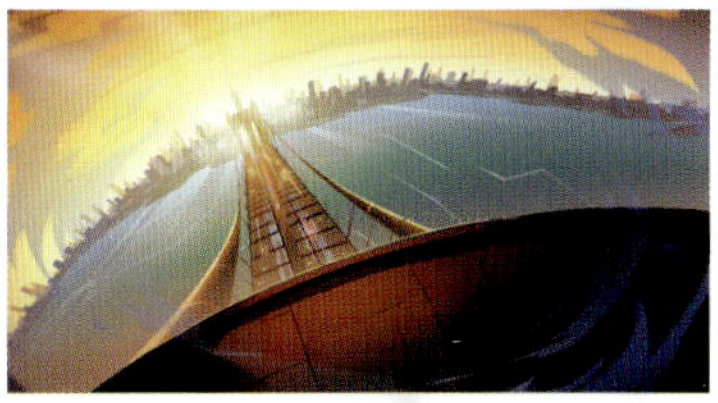

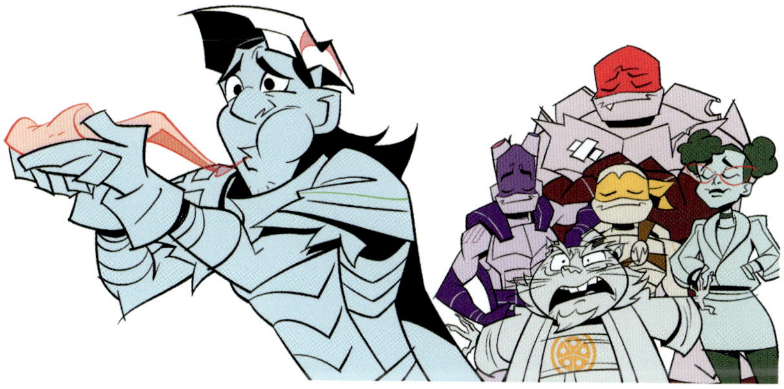

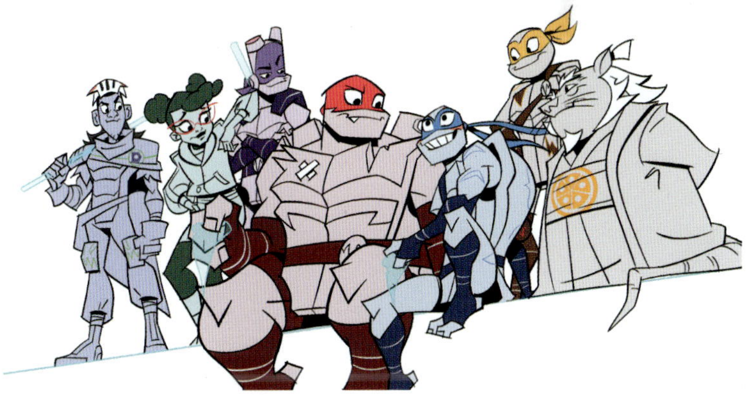

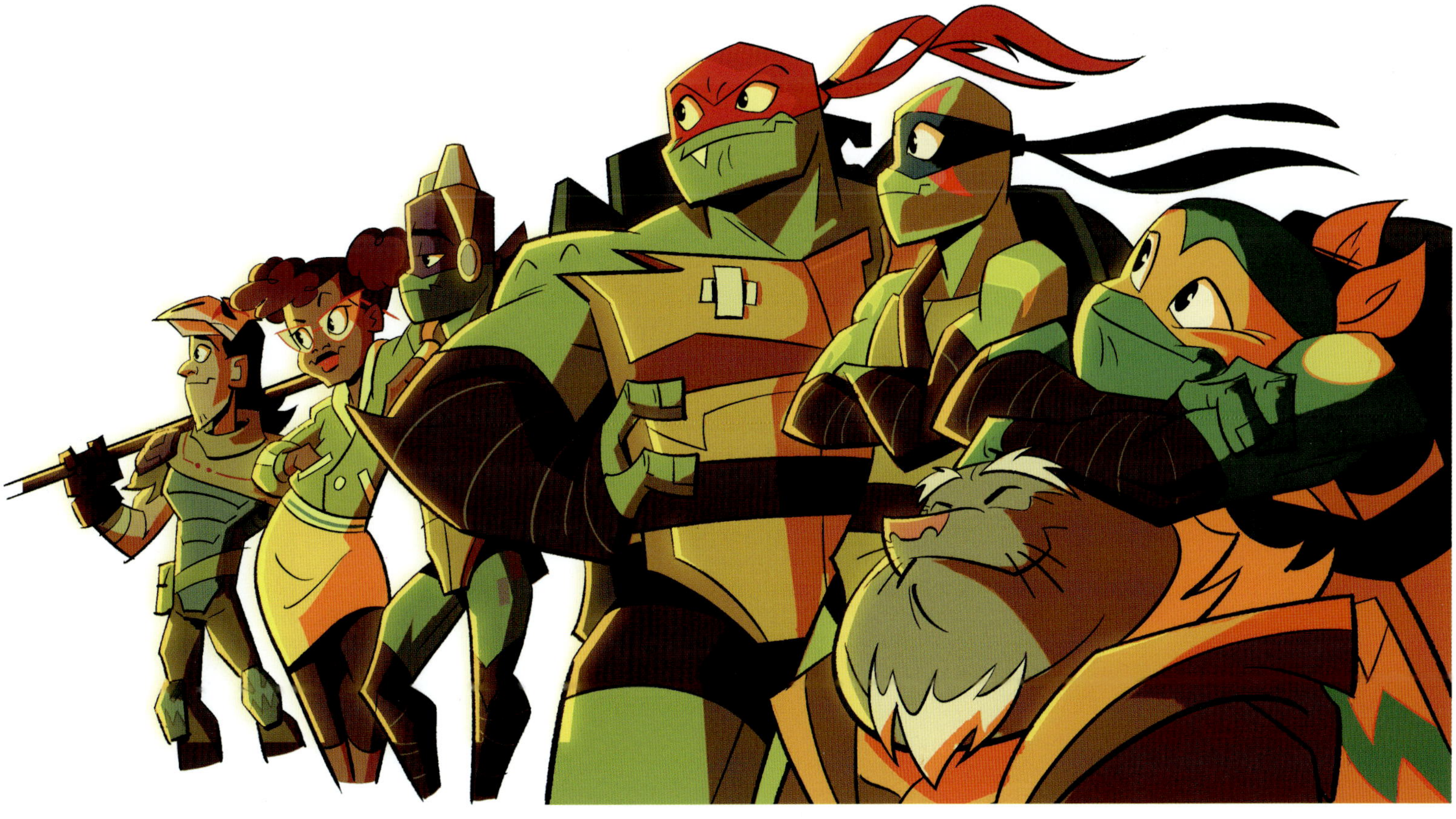

ALTERNATE PROLOGUE

STORYBOARDS BY
ALLISON SMITH, DAVID MAXIMO

JJ CONWAY: The very first assignment was launching Allison Smith and David Maximo on storyboarding an extended prologue in the apocalyptic future. It starts with a chase through the Krang-conquered streets of NYC, leading to an epic last stand at the resistance base under the Statue of Liberty. It was huge, packed with cameos, and everyone died. Unfortunately, it started around seven minutes, and the more we cut from it, the less impact it had. That led us to seriously consider cutting the concept of a prologue altogether, but our writers Tony Gama-Lobo and Rebecca May wanted to take one last crack at it, and they came back with the amazing prologue we have now.

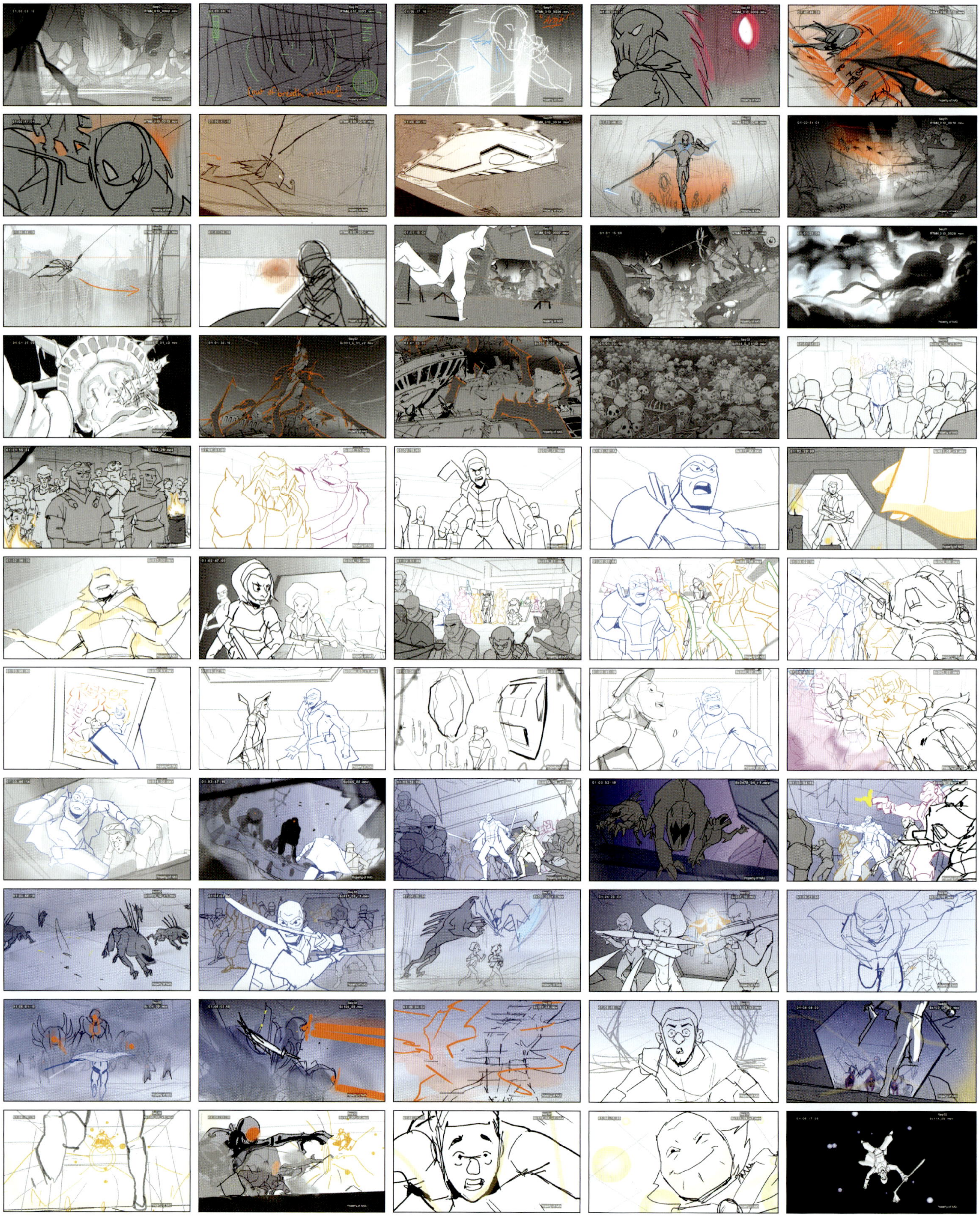

WARREN AND HYPNO HEIST

STORYBOARDS BY **ALLISON SMITH**

JJ CONWAY: In the final film we meet Warren and Hypno right after they've stolen the Krang key. However, we originally saw that whole heist, and the Turtles actually fought Warren and Hypno, showing off all their mystic skills for anybody new to *Rise of the TMNT*. Allison Smith did a really cinematic break-in sequence that was exciting and hilarious. We realized that we didn't have screen time for this whole heist, so we took all of the important setup that had been done in the heist sequence and grafted that into the car chase that Nas Pasha had storyboarded. He gave us a really strong foundation, so it was just a matter of building a few new beats to make sure all the bases were covered.

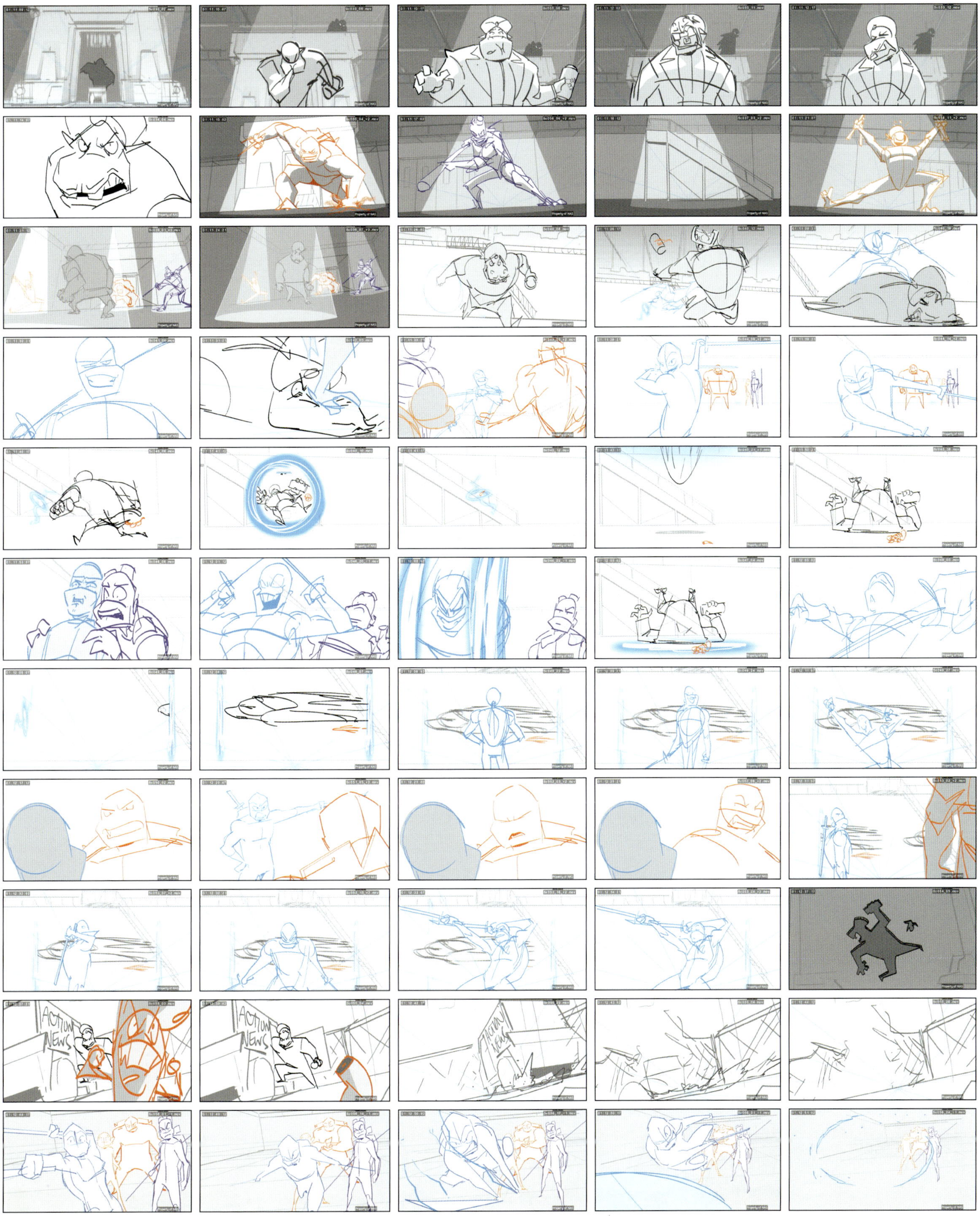

KRANG'S INTERROGATION

STORYBOARDS BY
MATTHEW HUMPHREYS

JJ CONWAY: In the final film, Raph's interrogation ends with Krang One diving into his mind to pull out the location of the lair. Originally this was an extended sequence storyboarded by Matt Humphreys where Raph escapes from the Krang and returns to the lair, but when he tries to warn his brothers they turn into horrifying, decaying versions of themselves, and it's revealed that this whole "escape" was just Krang One manipulating Raph into revealing the location of their lair.

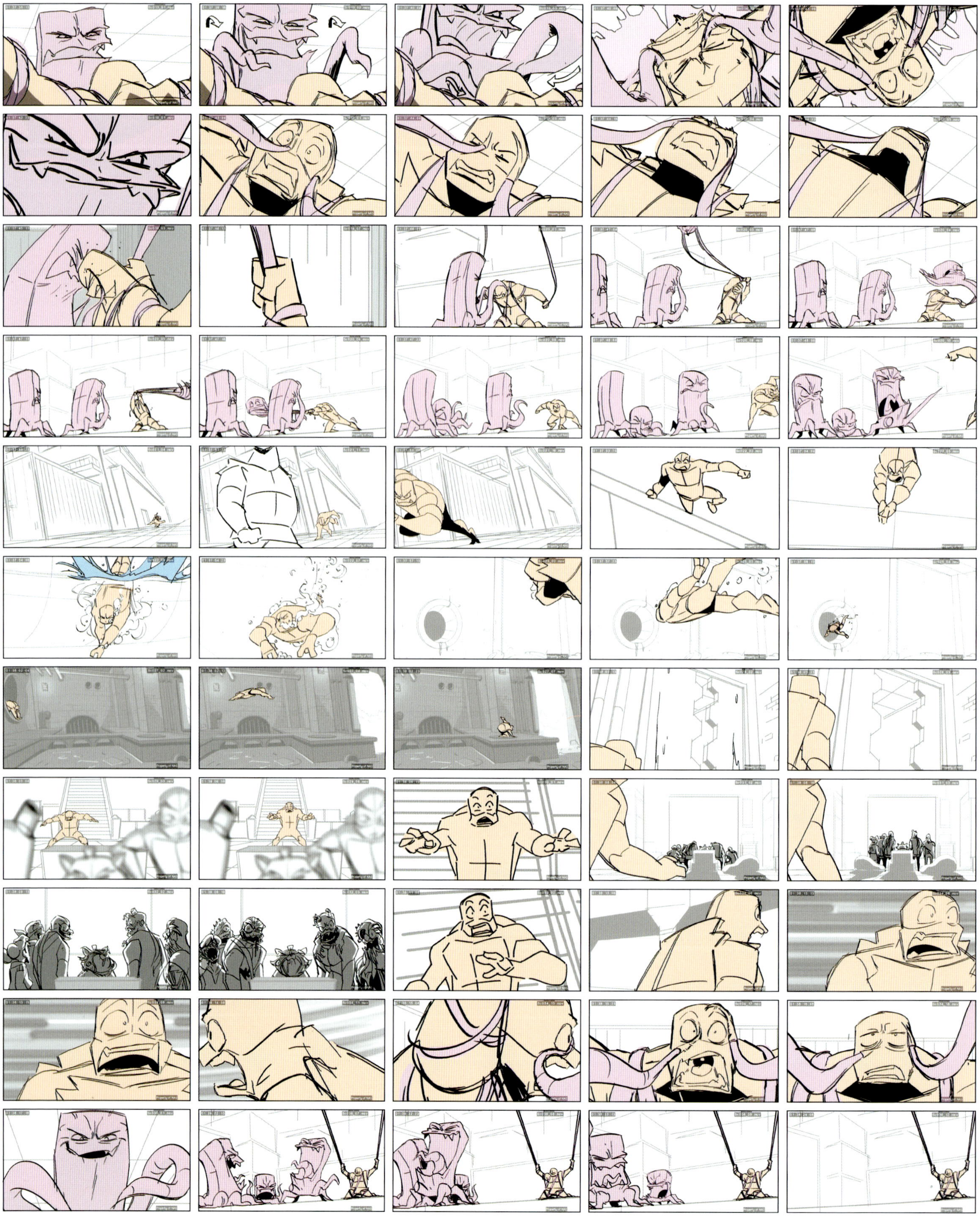

SPLINTER AND APRIL VS THE KEY

STORYBOARDS BY **MADELEINE FLORES**

JJ CONWAY: There was a full sequence storyboarded by Maddie Flores where April and Splinter break into Donnie's lab and use his equipment to try destroying the key. It was hilarious and full of great character moments. It was unfortunately cut for time.

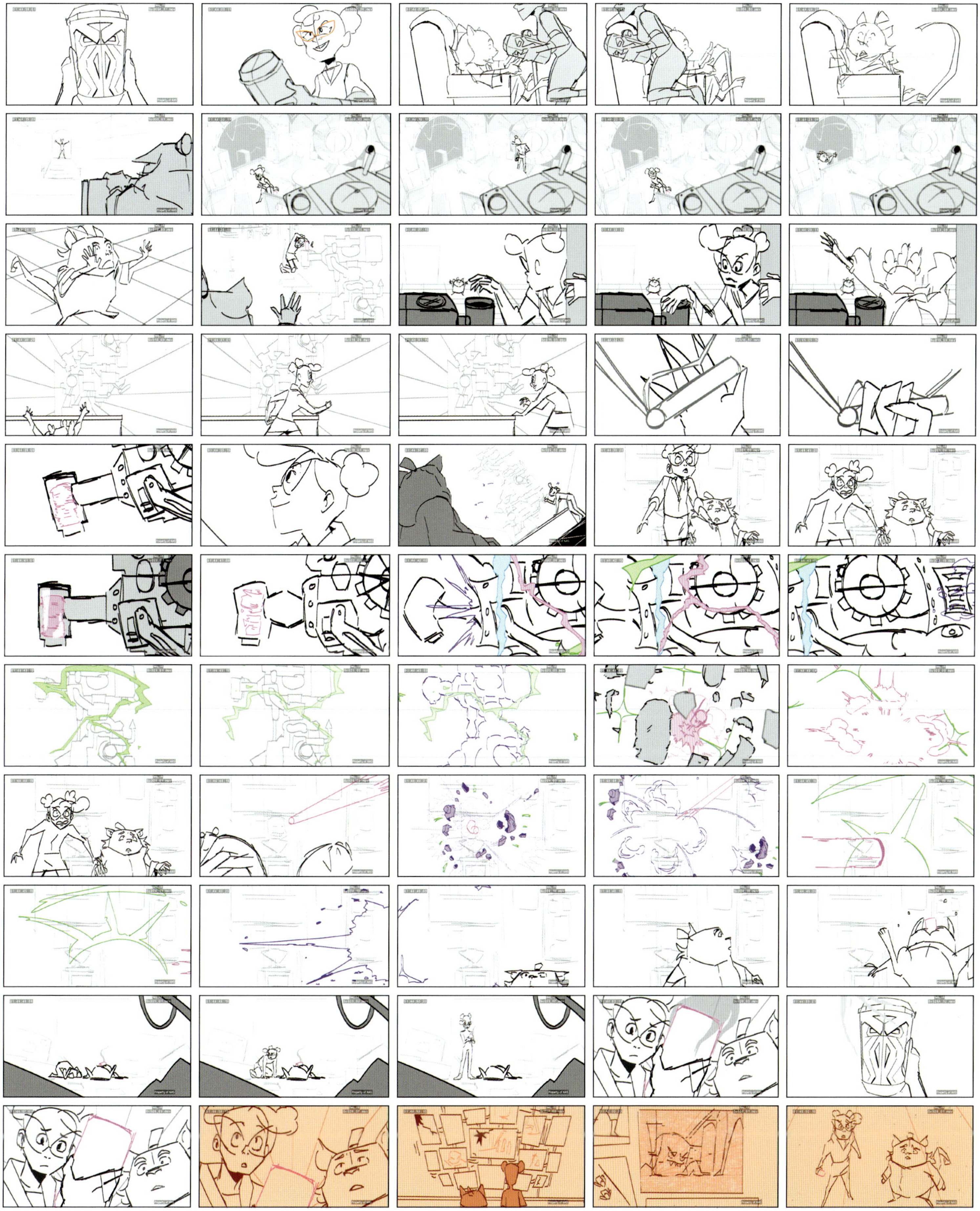

THE NIGHTMARE

STORYBOARDS BY **KEVIN MOLINA-ORTIZ**

JJ CONWAY: This is one of the most stunning sequences Kevin Molina-Ortiz has ever boarded. The entire concept is that Krang One captures the Turtles and tries to mentally break them to his will by digging into their minds and forcing them to see their greatest fears on repeat, with no escape. But through sheer willpower Leo rallies his brothers out of the darkness, leading to them regaining their Ninpō powers and breaking free of Krang One's control.

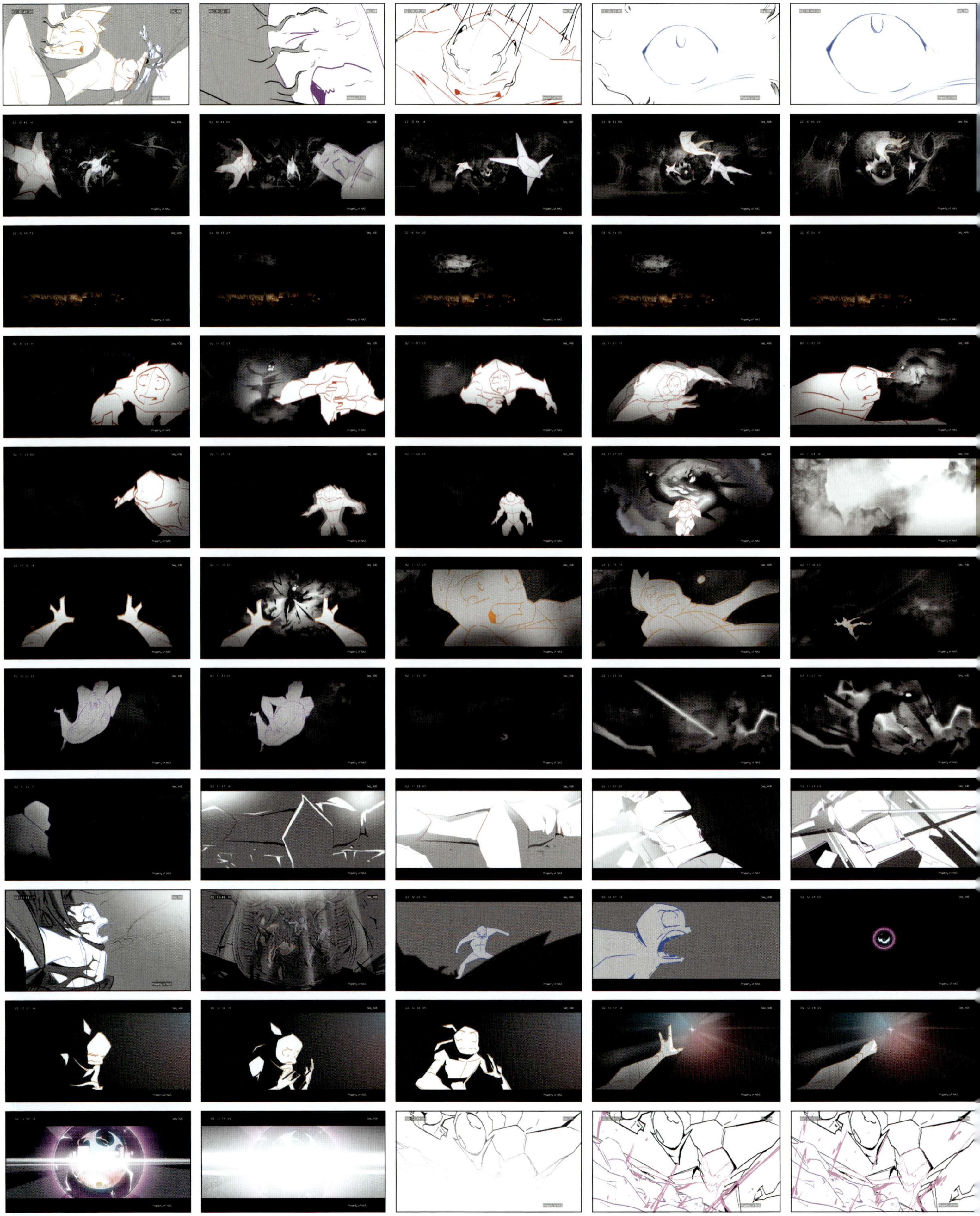

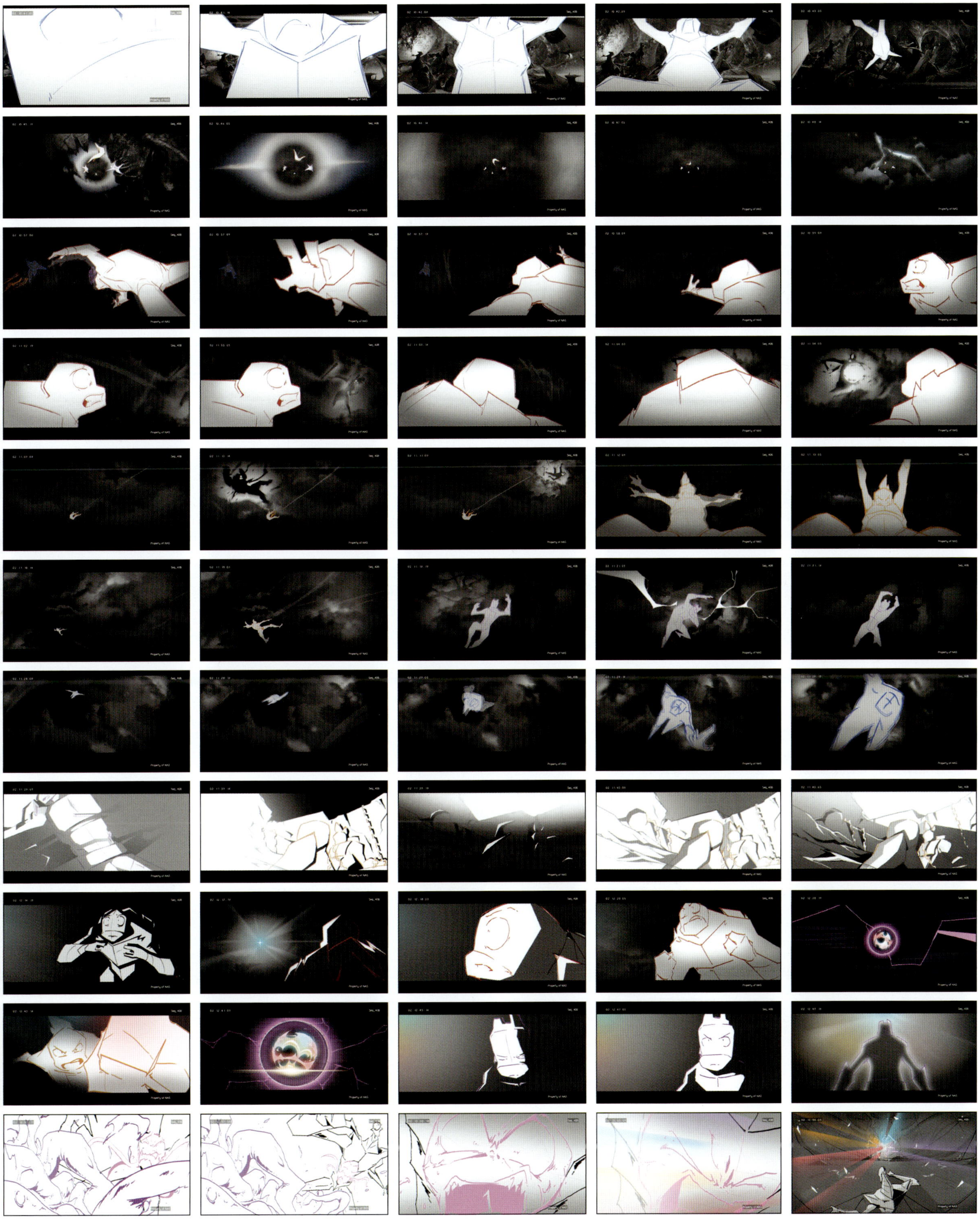

THE BATTLE AT METRO TOWER

STORYBOARDS BY:
MADELEINE FLORES
JJ CONWAY

JJ CONWAY: In the film, Raph is revealed to be under Krang control and the Krang quickly escape with the key. However, originally this was a massive battle storyboarded by Maddie Flores and myself. April was hosing down Krangified New Yorkers with her insecticide, Casey took on the Krangified Foot Lieutenant and Brute, all while Leo and Raph threw down. Originally, Leo saves Raph at this point, and Raph is with the team for all of act III. We always had a feeling that we were saving Raph too early, but we reasoned that you wanted the team together for act III of a TMNT movie. But Netflix called it out, and we knew we needed to do the major overhaul that became the film you see today.

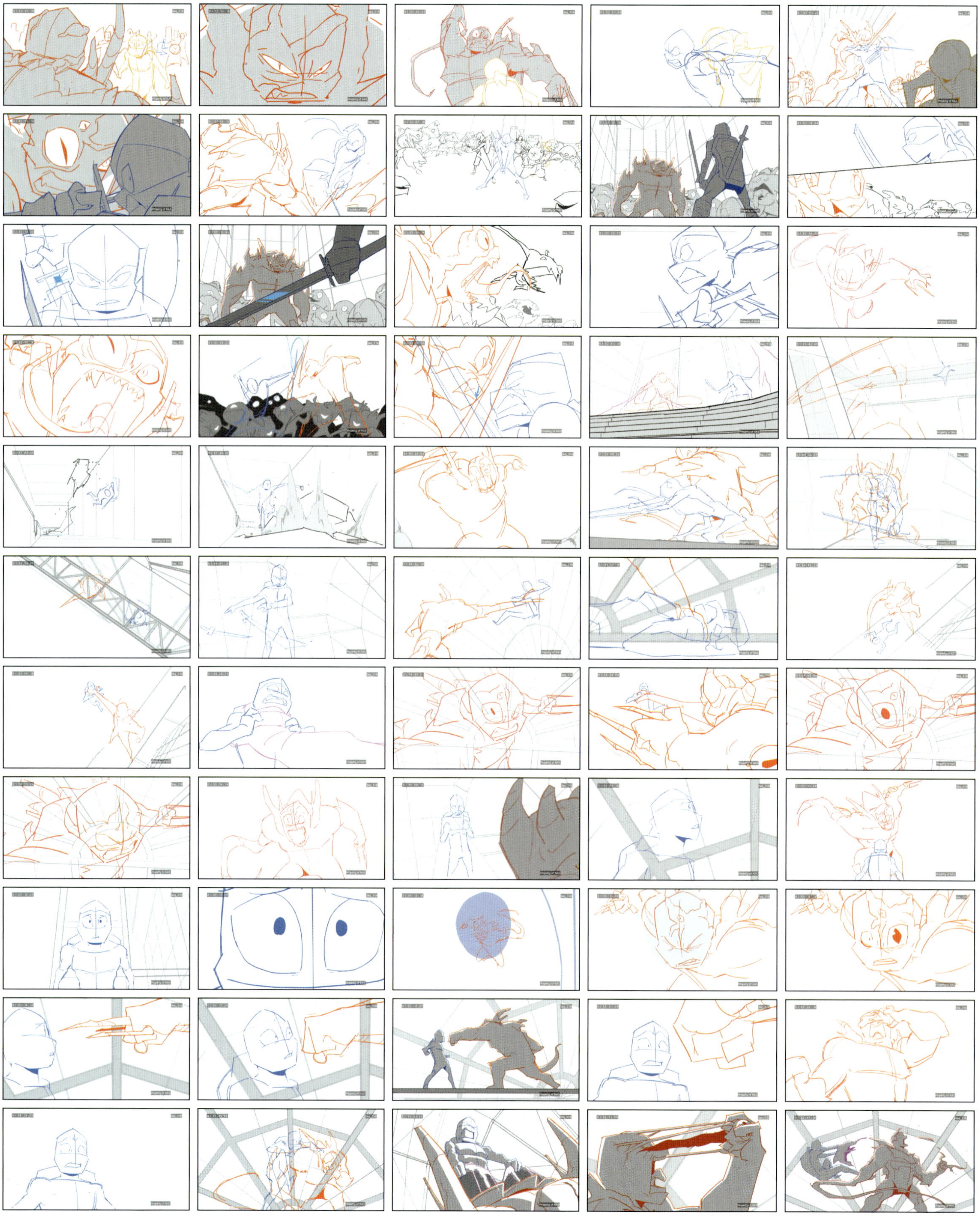

ALTERNATE ENDING

STORYBOARDS BY **LAURA GILLE**

JJ CONWAY: This scene was from that first version. Ant and Andy didn't understand why Casey was leaving or where he was going. So it was rewritten to the new version, which was kind of welcoming him to his new life in New York City. But with that original version, I told Laura Gille to picture it like the last day of summer camp, when you're saying goodbye to this circle of friends you've become so close with over a short period of time but might never see again. Then I think she said when she boarded it, it was like her saying goodbye to the *Rise* Turtles.

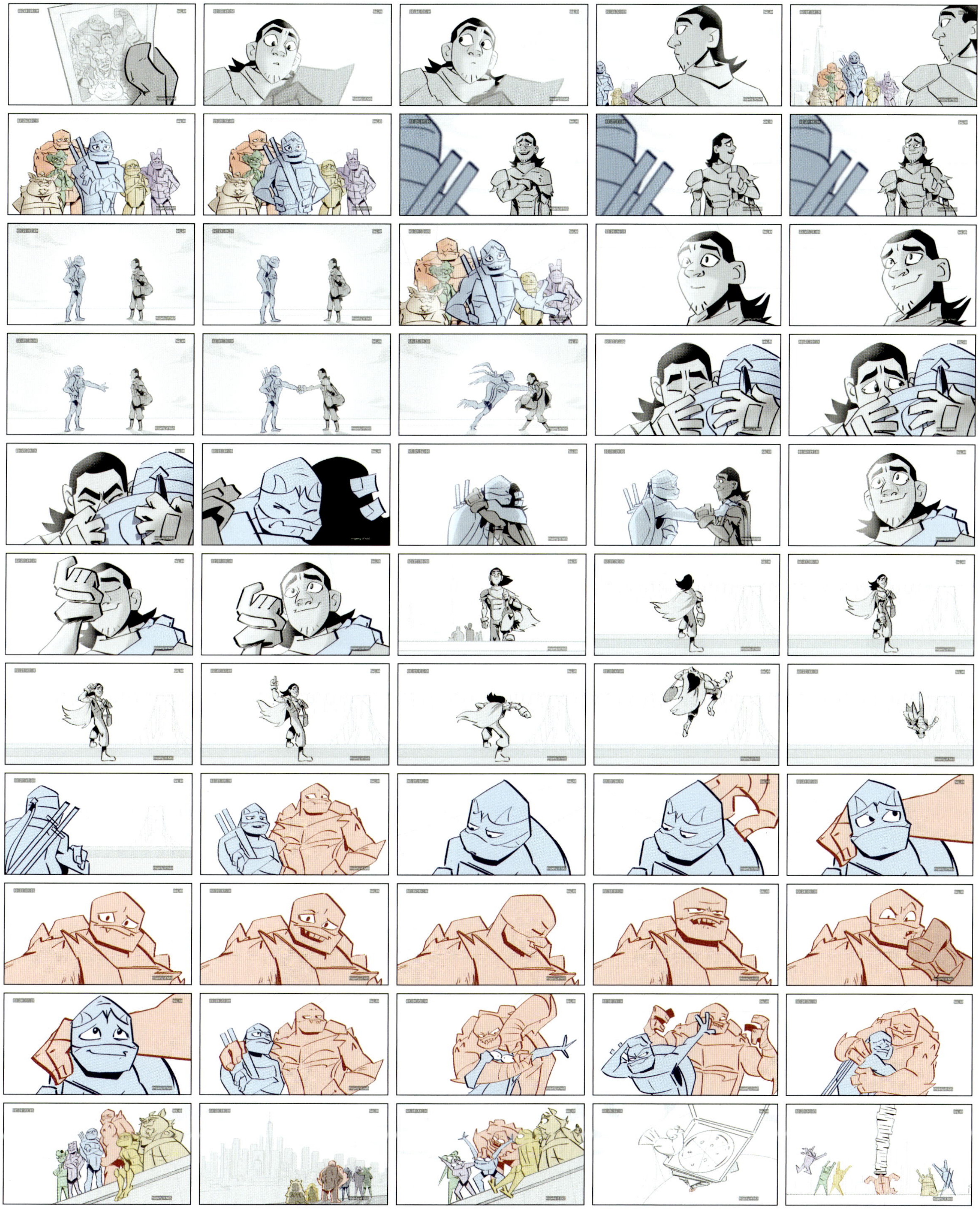

LOST EPISODES & BEYOND

Behind every great show lies a treasure trove of secrets—untold stories, abandoned ideas, and unseen adventures. When *Rise of the Teenage Mutant Ninja Turtles* came to a close, it left behind a wealth of unexplored possibilities.

The episodes you'll discover in this chapter were originally slated to fill the gap between "Battle Nexus: New York" and the series finale. They were meant to be the next chapter in the Turtles' journey, exploring new dynamics and threats before the ultimate showdown with the Shredder.

Imagine Raph and Leo trapped on a tropical island, hunted by a disturbed dentist obsessed with Raph's snaggletooth. Or April caught in the middle of a rivalry between two Warren Stones, each vying for the title of the Turtles' greatest foe. What about Raph's hilarious obsession with his hero Ghostbear or Mikey accidentally unleashing a robotic pet that turns out to be a thief?

As the team shifted focus to crafting an epic finale, these stories were set aside to bring the Turtles' journey to a thrilling close. While the list below includes over a dozen episodes in development, this chapter spotlights the handful for which concept art, storyboards, or written premises still exist. These artifacts offer a rare glimpse into what could have been—a never-before-seen look at the Rise that almost was.

THE LOST EPISODE TITLES:

- 073 - **Wedding Smashers**
- 074 - **Warren Stone 2**
- 077 - **T-Hex**
- 078 - **Psyched Out**
- 079 - **Shred Dead Redemption**
- 080 - **The Island of Dr. Noe**
- 081 - **Toddler Mutant Ninja Turtles**
- 082 - **Dog Dale Afternoon**
- 083 - **Bee Story**
- 084 - **Goyles Just Want To Have Fun**
- 085 - **Rampagin' Raph**
- 086 - **Hot Thrash**
- 087 - **Gourd Almighty**
- 088 - **A Spider's Web Widens**
- 089 - **Hidden City Heroes**
- 090 - **Gone Goat**
- 091 - **The Key (Part 1)**
- 092 - **The Key (Part 2)**

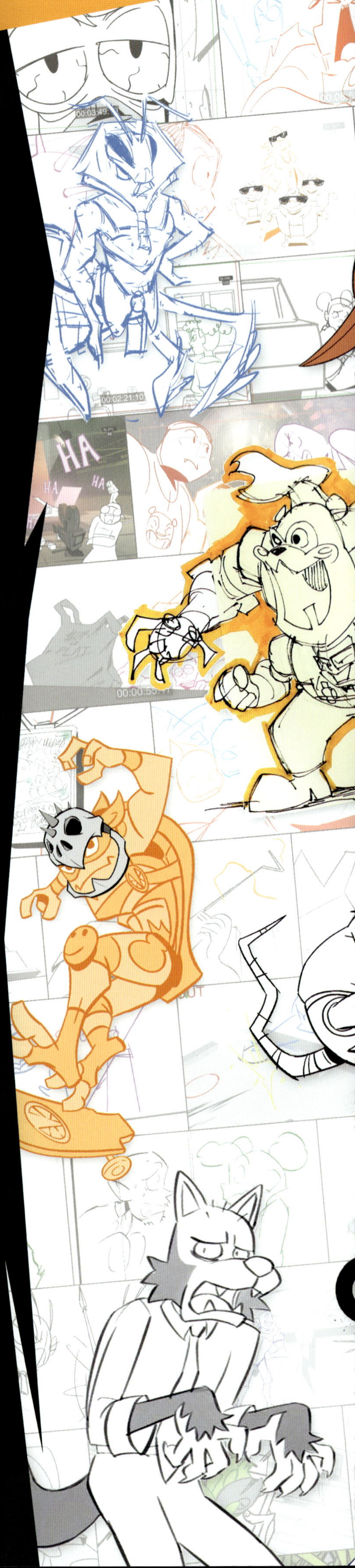

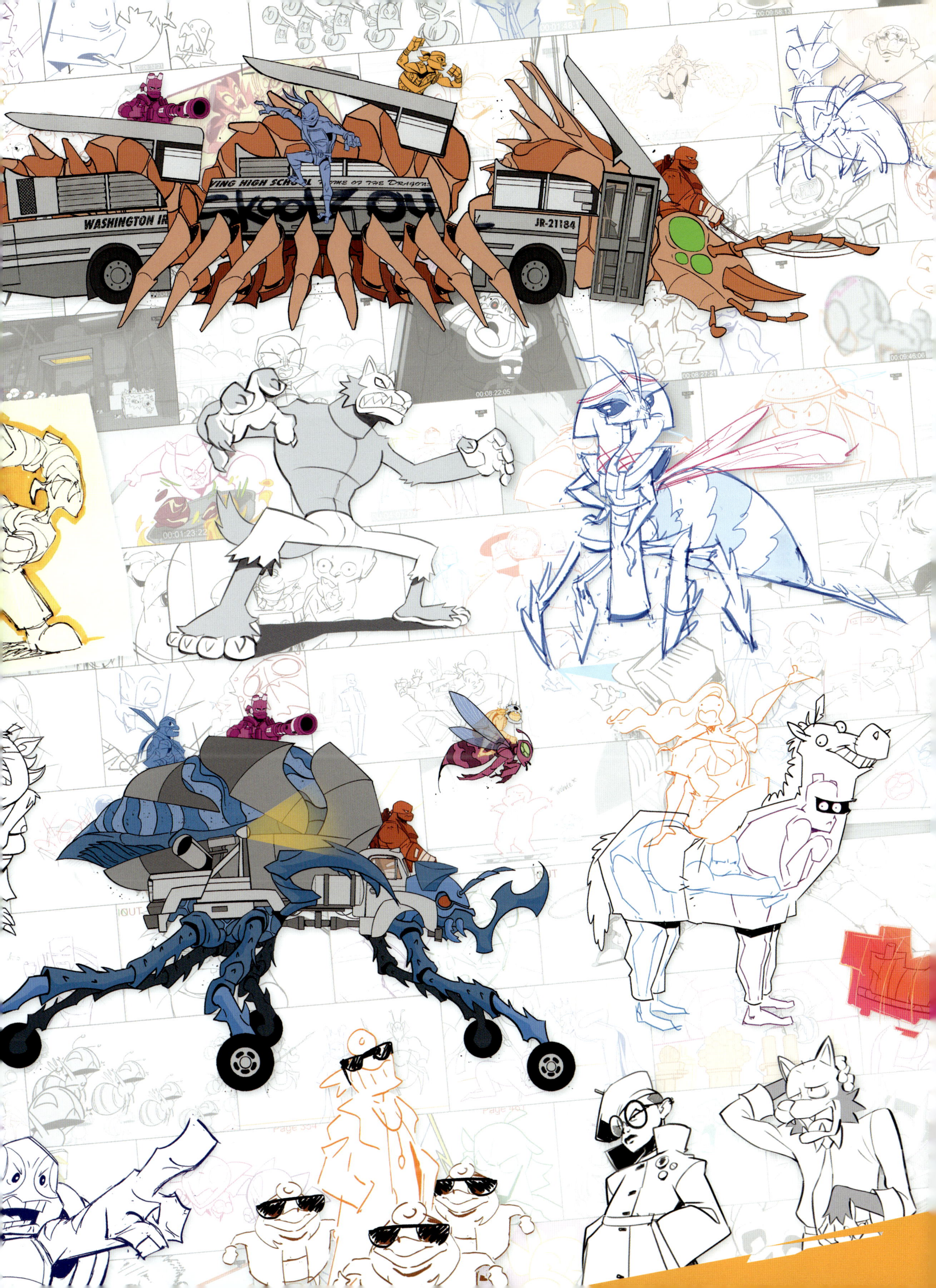
WASHINGTON IR
VING HIGH SCHOOL
JR-21184
00:08:22:05
00:01:23:22
00:09:46:06
00:08:27:21

WEDDING SMASHERS

PRODUCTION CODE: 073

WRITTEN BY **DALE MALINOWSKI**
STORYBOARDS BY **SHELDON VELLA, SAM MONTES, KEVIN MOLINA-ORTIZ**

When Raph accidentally gifts Donnie's Black Hole Generator (mistaken for a toaster) to his wrestling idol, Ghostbear, he and Mikey crash the villain's wedding as fake villains "Shadybug" and "Dr. Rude." Their mission: Retrieve the device before it destroys reality. But chaos erupts when Mikey's "rudeness" escalates—recruiting henchmen and volunteering as Ghostbear's replacement best man after Meat Sweats no-shows.

As vows begin, Raph's cover blows when he tackles Mikey for stealing the best man title: "Raph should be best man!" Their brawl destroys the cake, exposing them. Cornered mid-wrestling match, Raph delivers an impassioned best-man speech from a chandelier: "You're my guy, Ghostbear...bound by the love of wrestling!" Moved, Ghostbear spares them and asks Raph to be best man. Love conquers all as Todd officiates the wedding and cries the hardest.

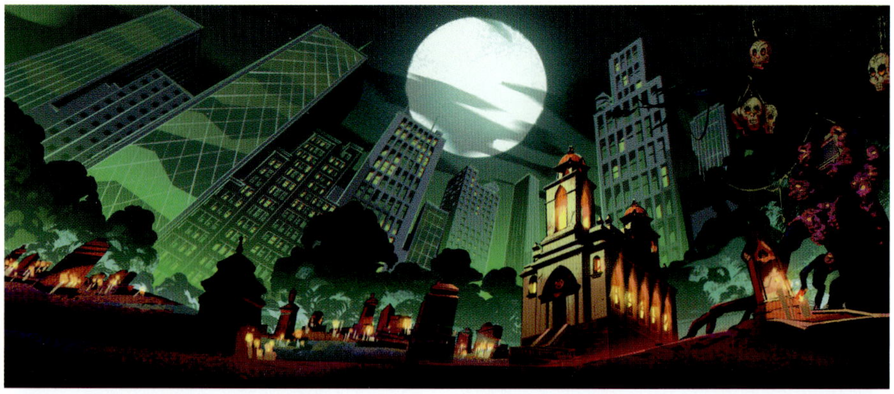

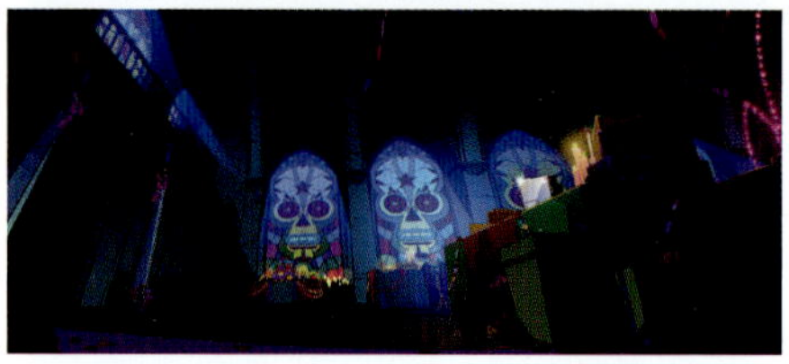

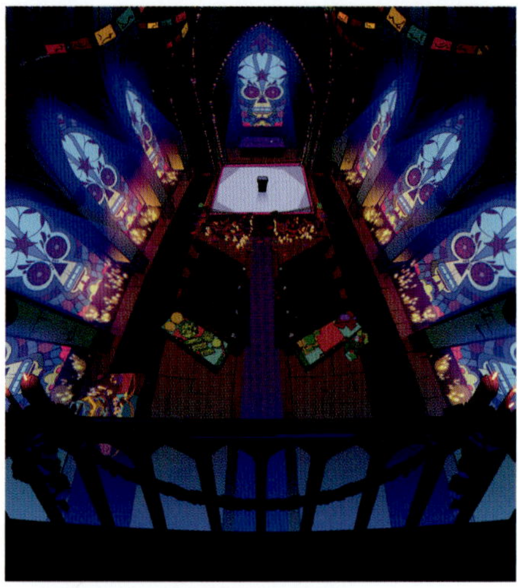

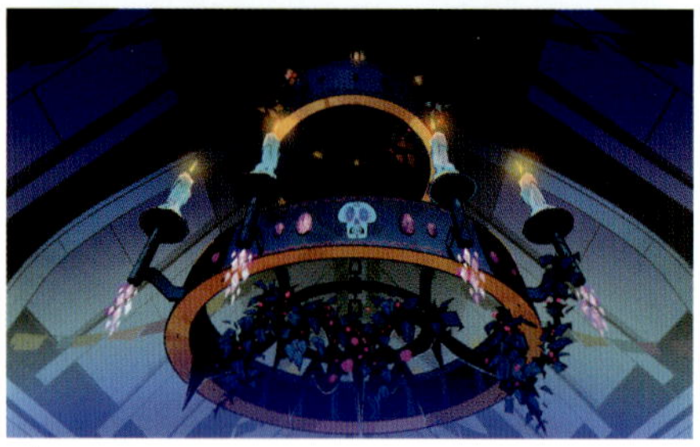

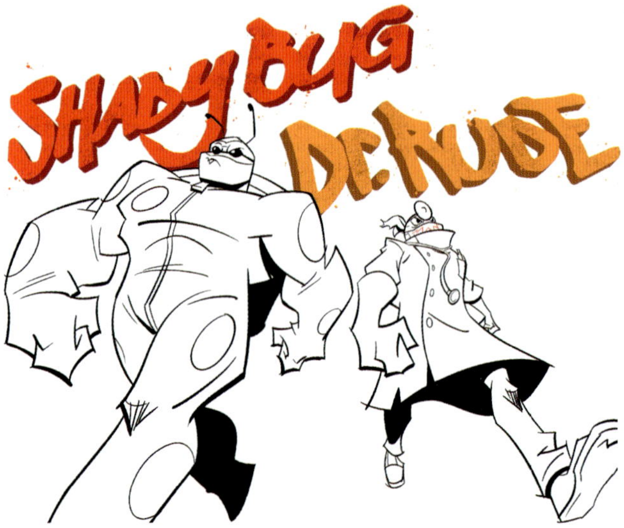

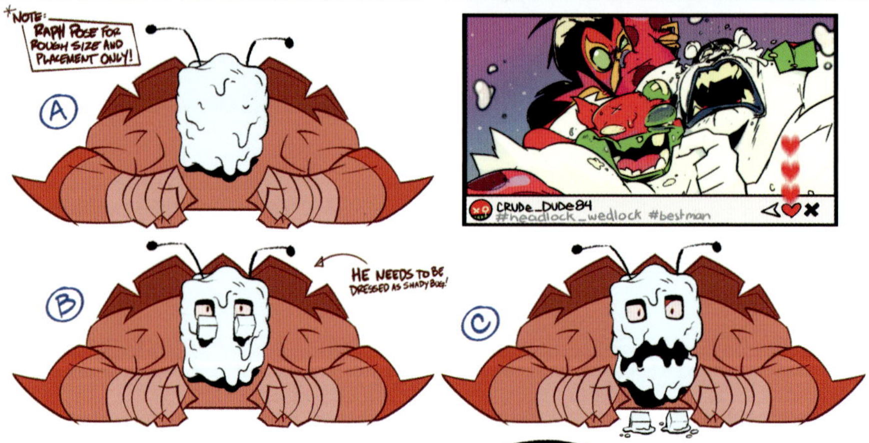

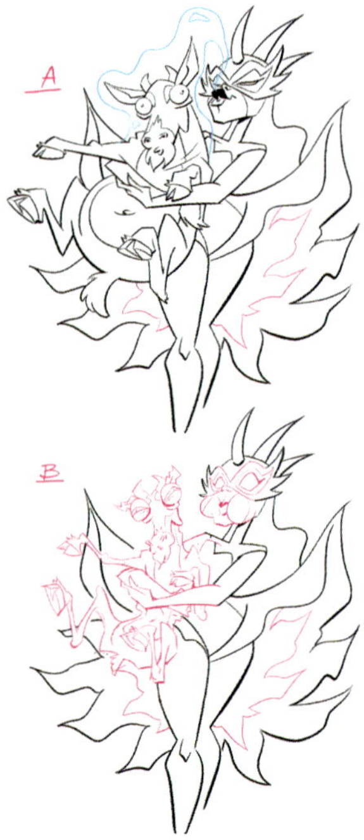

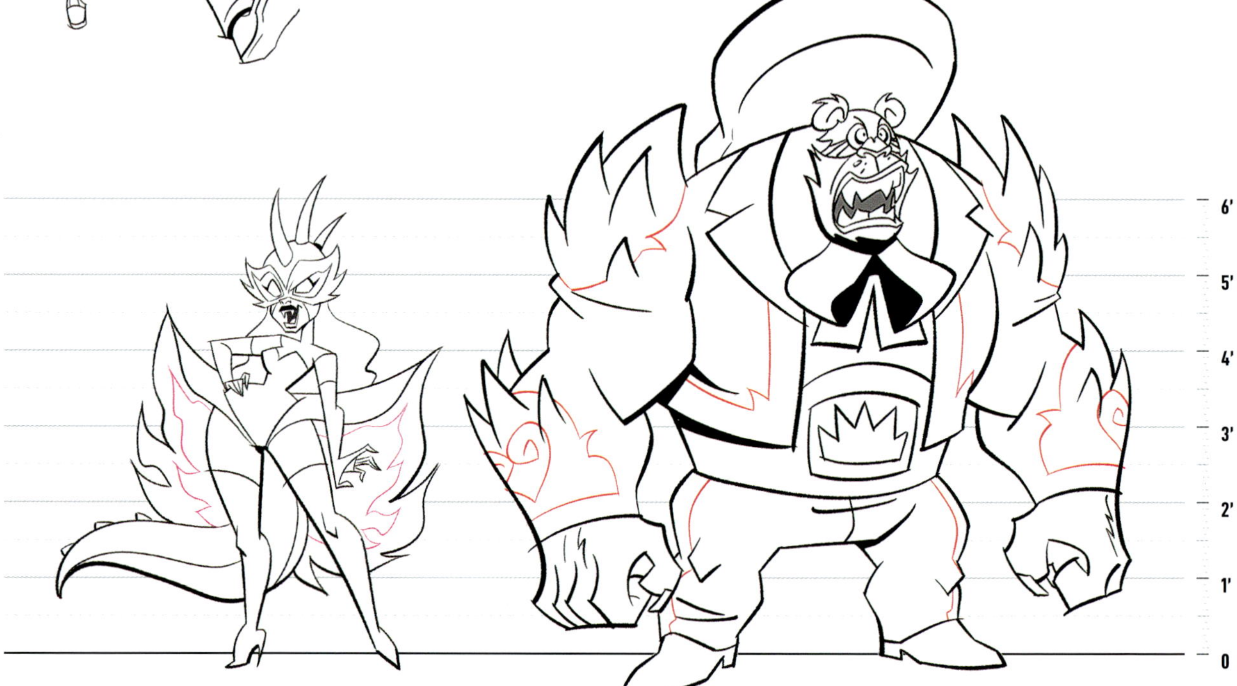

GHOSTPEPPER

GHOSTBEAR
FORMAL WEDDING ATTIRE

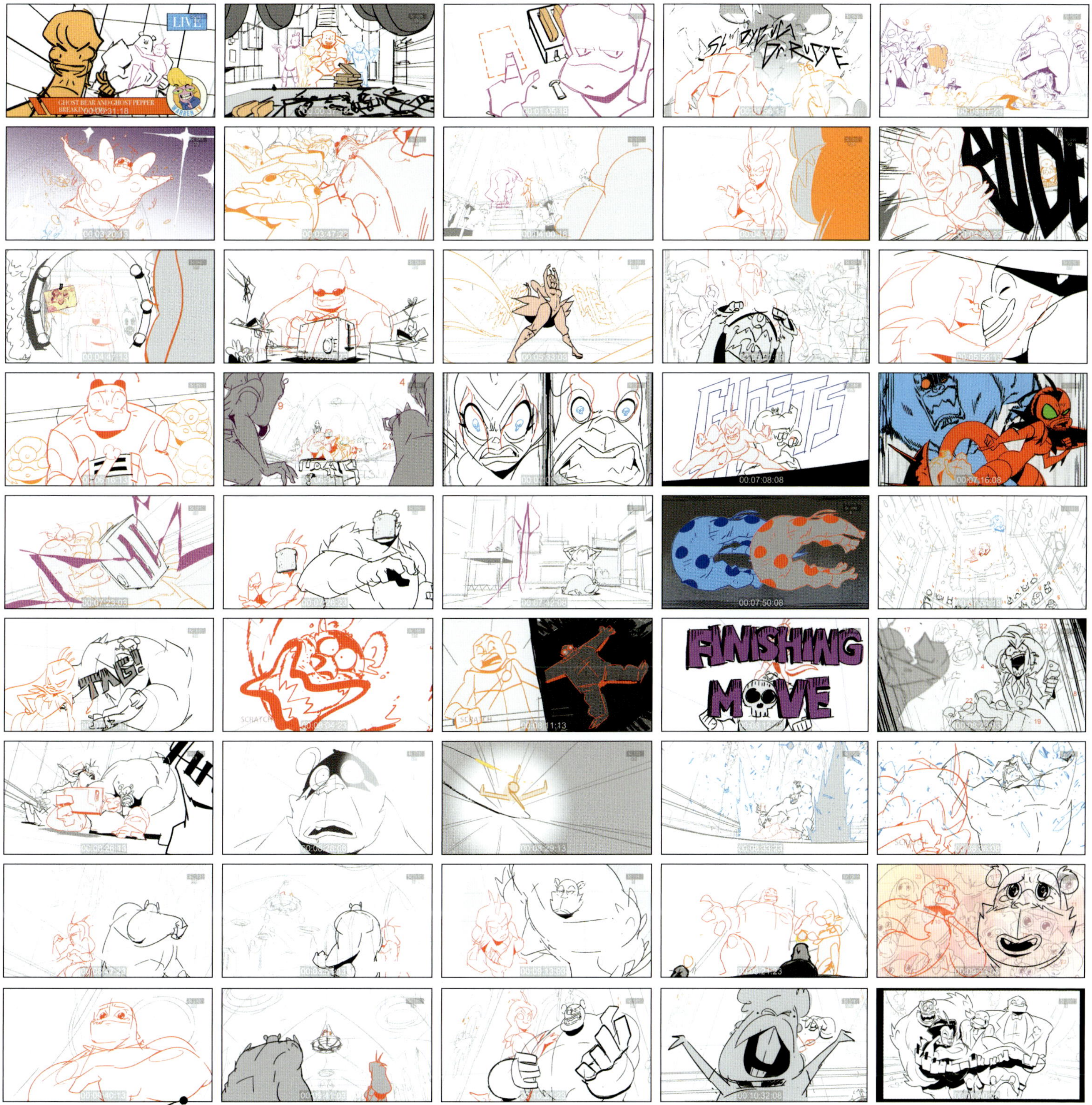
LIVE
RUDE
GHOSTS
00:07:08:08
00:07:50:08
TAG!
FINISHING
MOVE

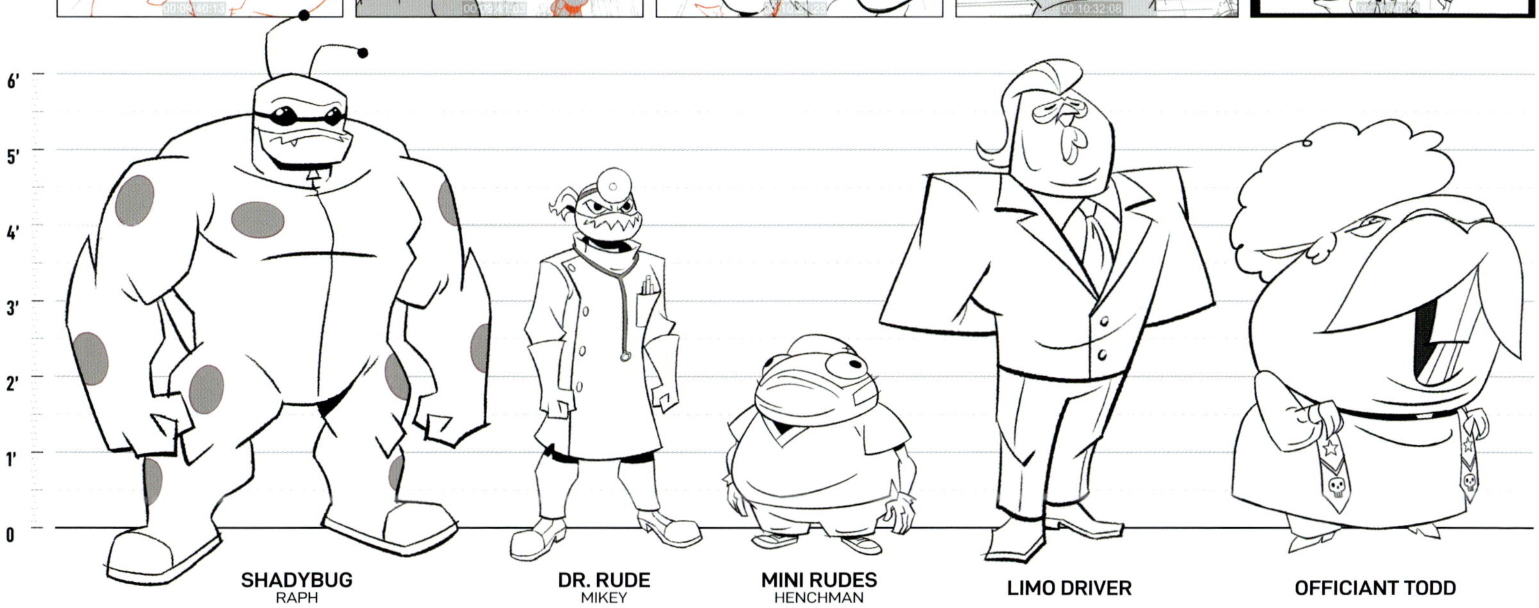
6'
5'
4'
3'
2'
1'
0
SHADYBUG
RAPH
DR. RUDE
MIKEY
MINI RUDES
HENCHMAN
LIMO DRIVER
OFFICIANT TODD

WARREN STONE 2

PRODUCTION CODE: 074
WRITTEN BY **IAN BUSCH**
STORYBOARDS BY **KALEN WHITFIELD, CASSEY KUO, RACHEL NAPIERKOWSKI, KAREN GUO**

BREAKING NEWS! When Warren Stone sets bear traps ("Turtle Traps!") outside Clem's Candy store, the TMNT crash through the wall mid-fight with a surprise foe: Warren Stone 2, a bearded, buff clone grown from Warren's severed arm! "This story just took a shocking turn!" cries Warren 1.

Amid laser blasts, April confesses her secret: She kept the mutant arm, which regenerated into Warren 2. "Then he broke bad... I feel guilty!" Warren 2 captures the Turtles with a mystic lasso, declaring, "Your shells will help me break into WNYNY and become King of the News!" As he flies off with them, Leo shouts, "Feel guilty for getting us kidnaaaaapped!"

Desperate, April recruits a depressed Warren 1: "You're their greatest foe! Help me save my friends!" After "training" (limbo, hair-whipping drills, and extreme stretching), Warren tracks them to the news station, where Warren 2 uses the tied-up Turtles as a wrecking ball to smash into a vault. Warren 1 stretches between lampposts to halt their swing ("We interrupt with a breaking story: ME!"), but Donnie's elastic-recoil warning sends them ricocheting between buildings.

April takes control of the crane while the Warrens duel in a hair-vs.-beard battle. "You're yesterday's news!" taunts Warren 1. When Warren 2 knocks him off a roof, April drops the "Turtle Ball" on the clone, forcing his retreat. "This is Warren Stone 2 signing off...for now."

Leo thanks "Warren Stone" by name. The TMNT hug April...and then bring Warren into the hug. "Don't think hugging makes us friends!"

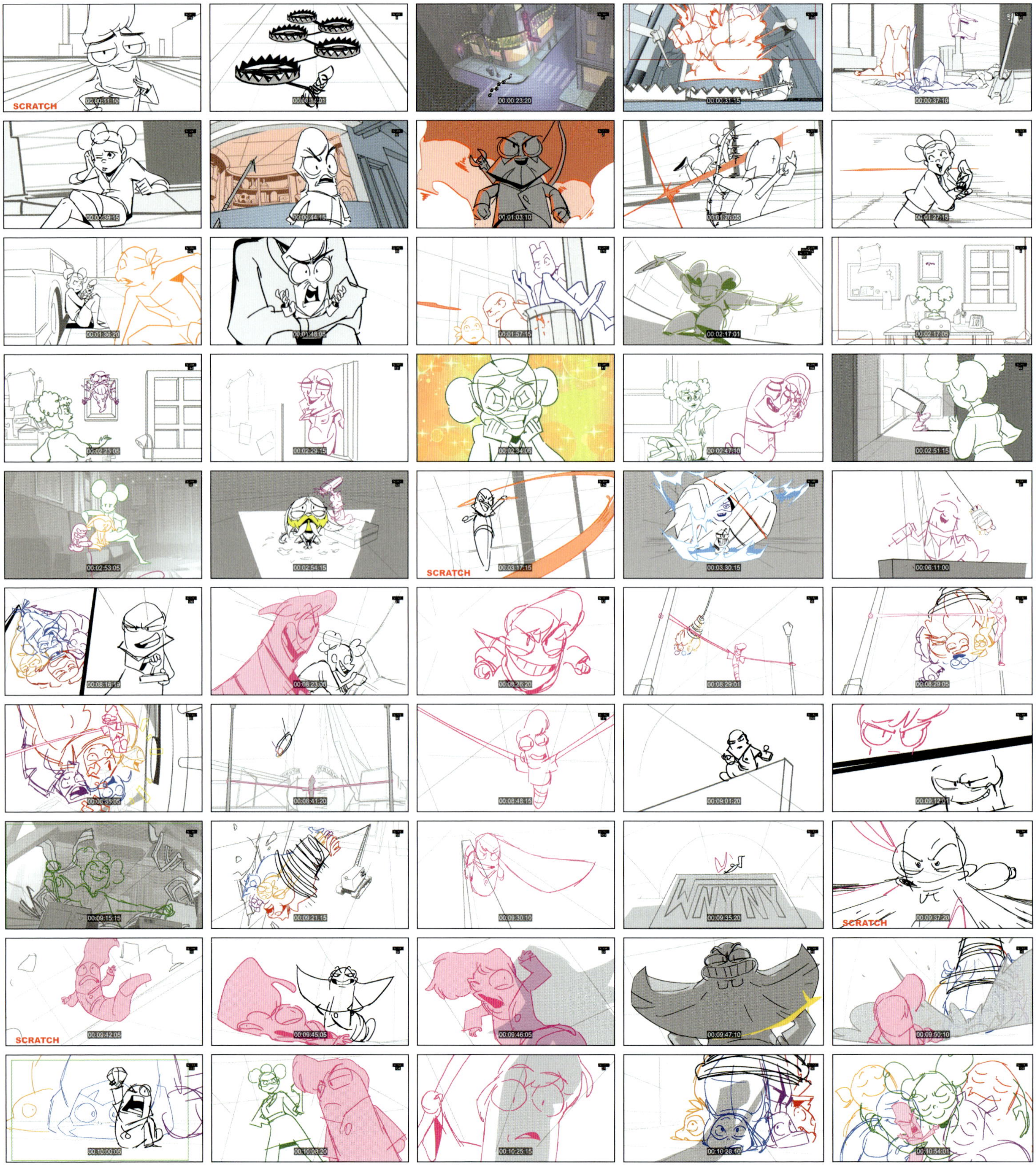

T-HEX

PRODUCTION CODE: 077
WRITTEN BY **RUSS CARNEY & RON CORCILLO**
STORYBOARDS BY **MORGAN HILLEBRAND, ANDREW KIM**

There's a new electronic pet toy, the Tyrannosaurus Hexadecimal, whose boopable snoot is taking NYC by storm! Mikey's dying to get it. He sneaks out to get one and keeps it hidden in his room. When the family awakens the next day, Splinter walks into the kitchen—he can barely talk. It turns out his fabulous gold teeth are gone! What gold teeth, you ask? Well, back in the '80s, when gold teeth were all the rage, action star Lou Jitsu had a set installed, but they went out of style about a minute later, and he's been painting them white ever since.

Donnie accesses his crime database, and it is revealed that precious metals are being stolen around town. In the surveillance footage, T-Hexes appear to be the culprits. All eyes fall on Mikey, who admits that he, in fact, has one. The guys set up a sting operation in the lair, waiting for Mikey's T-Hex to show up and steal a bar of Donnie's gold. What gold, you ask? Donnie casually admits that he has a secret Fort Knox in the lair somewhere.

The T-Hex takes the bait and leads the boys to a toy factory/precious metals processing plant, where the Turtles discover that the T-Hexes are M.O.U.S.E.R.S. in disguise. Raph: "All right, Stockboy, we're shutting down your surprisingly successful self-made business, which for some reason you decided to supplement with crime. Kind of a hat on a hat, if you ask me." Stockboy commands the M.O.U.S.E.R.S. to attack our heroes, but Raph's powered-up tonfa takes them all out of commission with one blow. As the Turtles are prepared to take Stockboy back to the Kid Genius Jail, Stockboy reveals that he's partnered up, Master Blaster–style, with an upgraded, weaponized Albearto. Stockboy hops into a clear laser-cannon cockpit in Albearto's chest and the two villains attack the boys, who suddenly notice Splinter's gold teeth on a conveyor belt leading to a red-hot industrial crucible! An epic battle ensues! Can the Turtles defeat AlBaxter or StockBearto or whatever his name is? Can the Turtles retrieve Splinter's precious gold chompers? Yes!

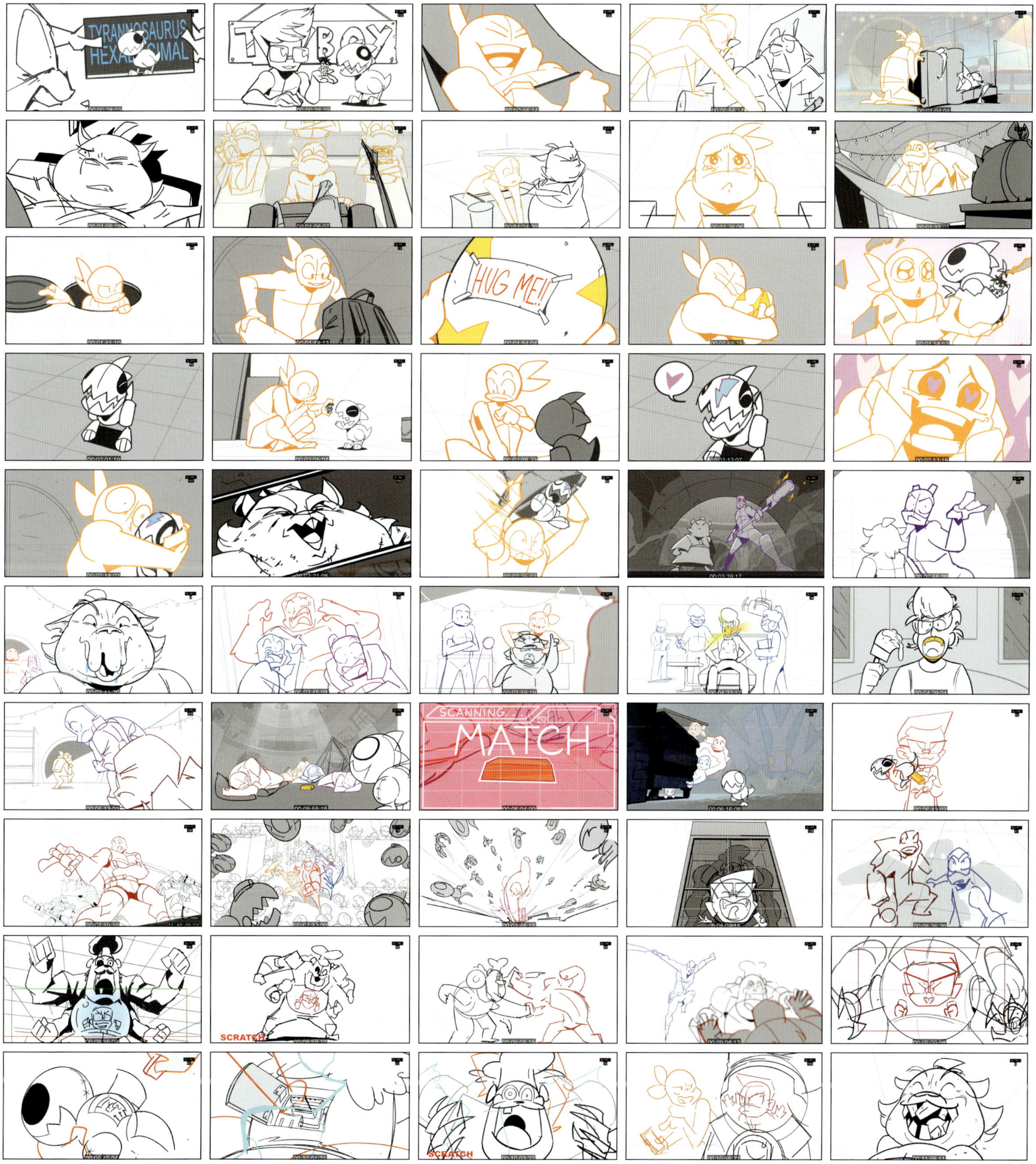

PSYCHED OUT

PRODUCTION CODE: 078
WRITTEN BY **ISABEL GALUPO**
STORYBOARDS BY **ANDREW KIM, ALICIA CHAN**

After letting a "reformed" Meat Sweats go (he claimed the whisk was for meringues), Mikey gets a terrifying prophecy from psychic Madame Future-See: "Everyone you love is in grave danger! Beware the orange orb, purple moon, and clock striking two!" Back in the lair, Mikey spirals into panic—reinforcing skateboards, snipping yo-yo strings, and bubble-wrapping hazards.

His brothers mock him until the prophecy literally unfolds: Leo juggles an orange basketball ("Orb!"), Donnie crashes through a hoop with his purple battle shell ("Moon!"), and Leo's sword nearly impales Raph as the clock chimes two. "We're all in danger!" they shriek in unison.

News breaks: Citywide "evil kitchenware" attacks during Restaurant Week! Though fearing for their "toesies," the Turtles arm themselves in absurd kitchen armor (saucepan helmets, cheese-grater shin guards) to confront Meat Sweats—only to find Mikey already captured at Chez Prétenche Nouveau. The villain reveals his mystic whisk controls every utensil: "You thought bringing kitchenware was a good idea?!" he taunts as their DIY gear attacks them.

Cornered, Mikey has an epiphany: "If we only obsess about bad things, we'll never do good! Live in the present, baby!" Shedding their safety gear, the brothers execute Forbidden Move #1: Rising Spiral Skull-Breaker, destroying the whisk and freeing New York.

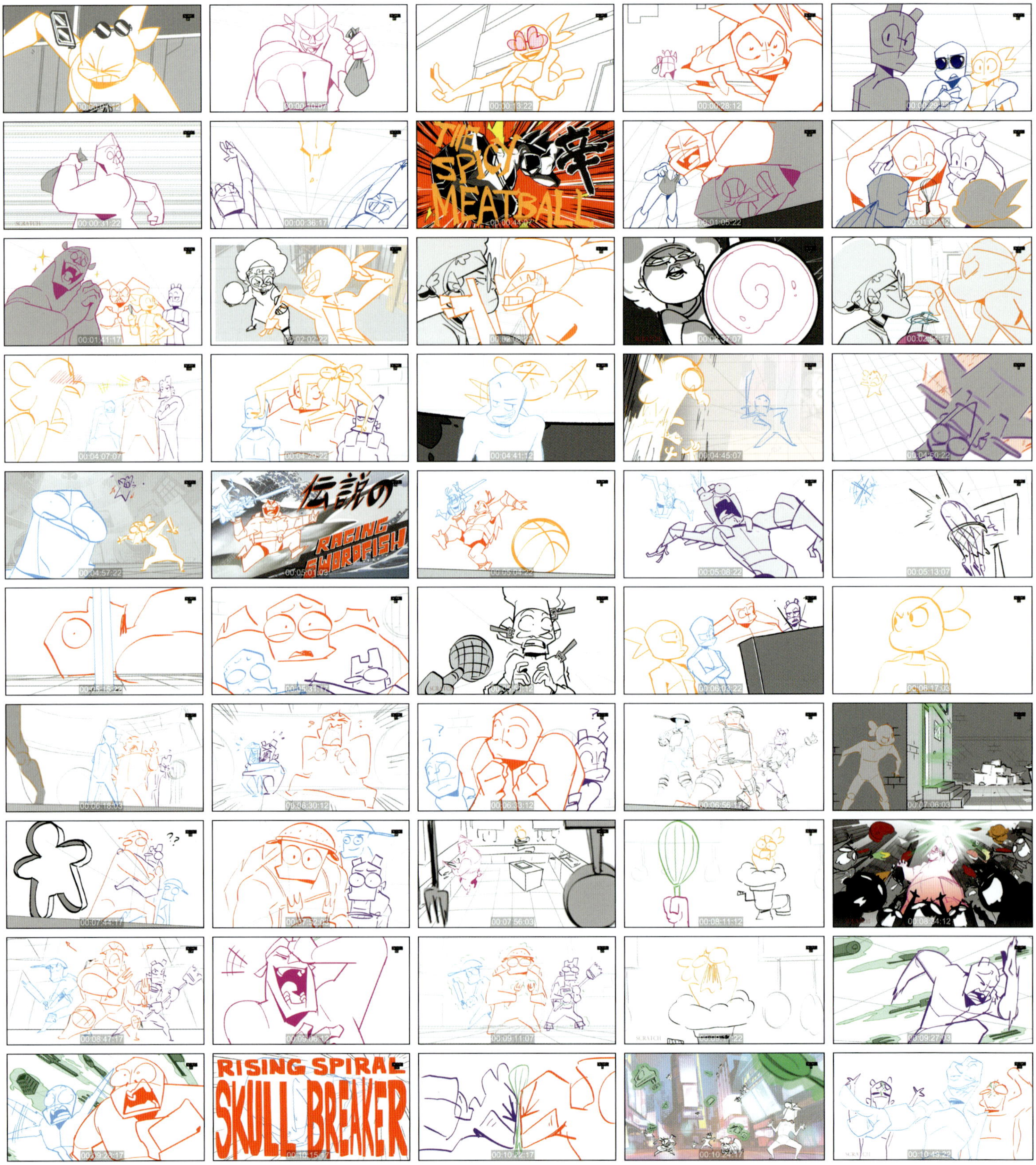

SHRED DEAD REDEMPTION

PRODUCTION CODE: 079
WRITTEN BY **RUSS CARNEY & RON CORCILLO**
STORYBOARDS BY **SHELDON VELLA, SAM MONTES**

Foot Lieutenant and Foot Brute have moved on. After the crushing disappointment of what they still think was a failed attempt to resurrect Shredder at the end of season 1, they've found their true bliss as proprietors of a boutique cupcake shop, Fire and Icing, where they offer a unique line of mystic flaming cupcakes, such as Caramel Monoxide and Cinnamon Smokers. Raph, though, is convinced that there's no way those goons have given up their evil ways. Convinced they must be up to something, he's dragged his brothers along on a stakeout of the perfectly innocent cupcake shop.

The Foot Recruit arrives at the shop and reveals that Shadow Fiend is actually Shredder, but every time she attempts to communicate this to the Foot, they interrupt her with loud bakery equipment. Finally, she KOs them and abducts them to the Hidden City to prove what she saw. Seeing this commotion, Raph is convinced that the Foot are up to something evil and hauls after them in hot pursuit.

At the Battle Nexus "Mandatory Family Fun Day," the Foot wait in the Shadow Fiend's autograph line. Once face-to-face with him, the Foot Lieutenant and Brute realize that Shredder is locked within Shadow Fiend, and they become determined to release him. Their efforts raise an alarm, and a three-way fight begins between the Foot, Big Mama's thugs, and the Turtles. Outmatched, the Foot retreat back to Fire and Icing. An enraged Foot Recruit barks at them, "Silence! You two brought Shredder back improperly, lost him, and didn't even try to find him! I am the one who discovered our master. I am the one who will bring him back. From now on, you will obey me. Ha!"

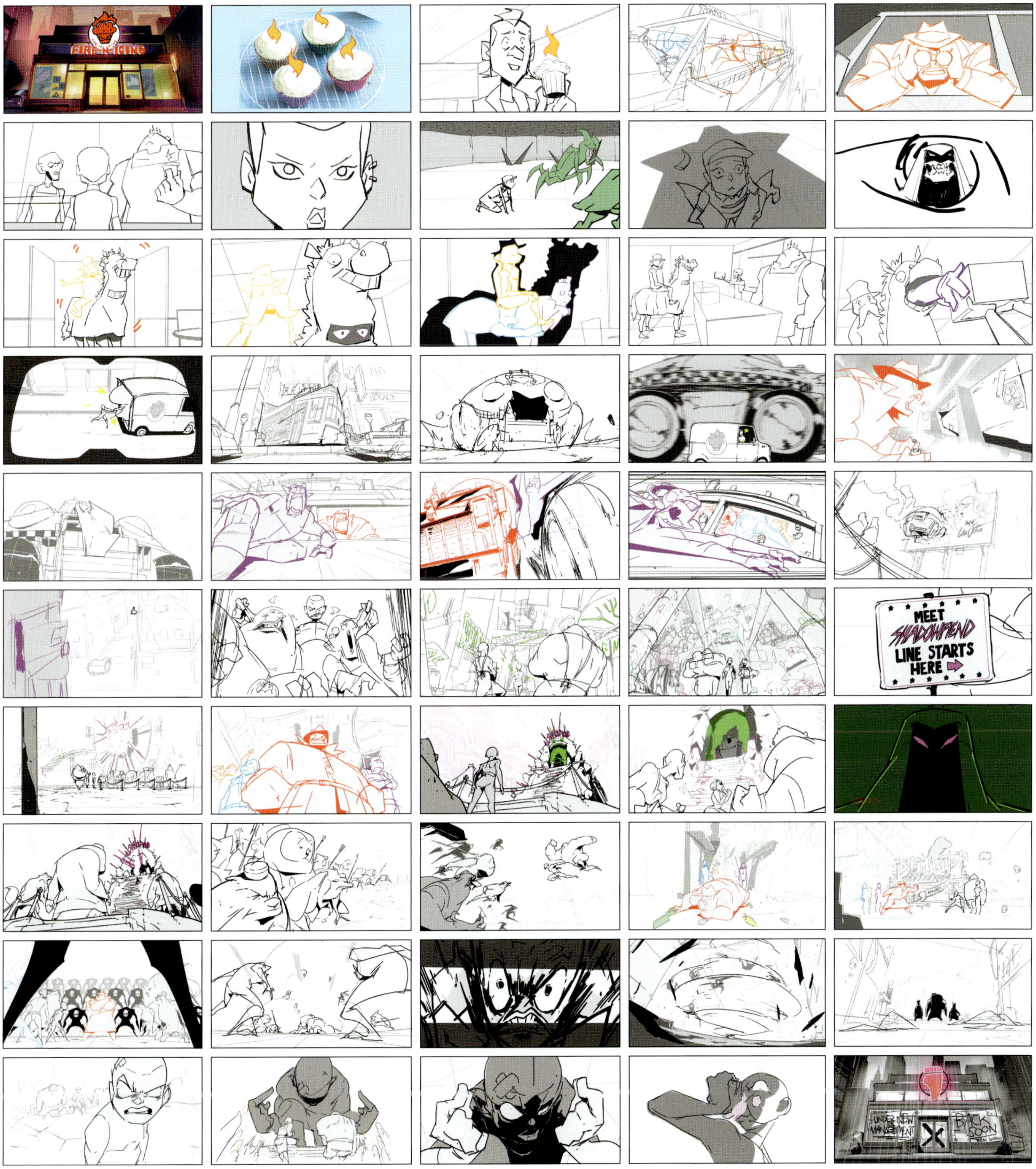

THE ISLAND OF DR. NOE

PRODUCTION CODE: 080
WRITTEN BY **IAN BUSCH**
STORYBOARDS BY **CASSEY KUO, ZANE YARBROUGH, SARAH PARTINGTON**

After foiling Repo Mantis' attempt to tow the Turtle Tank, Raph and Leo take a shortcut that lands them captured by the dastardly dentist Dr. Noe. Trapped on a jungle island, they learn he covets Raph's snaggletooth as a trophy and plans to give Leo kangaroo teeth. "Survive the night and you are free to leave," Dr. Noe declares—before immediately hunting them with his Tooth Fairies and henchpeople, Croc Mouth and Shark Face.

As Dr. Noe pursues them through booby-trapped forests (featuring dental suction hoses and X-ray death rays), Raph spirals into panic over his endangered tooth, frantically building twig armor for protection while Leo watches in disbelief. With Raph incapacitated by fear, Leo reluctantly steps up as "guest leader" and recruits the disgruntled henchpeople by exposing Dr. Noe's disrespect. "It's Clarence—our kidnappee knows my name and you don't?! And you were best man at my wedding!" Croc Mouth protests. Shark Face promptly knocks out Dr. Noe and the hunters.

Leo orchestrates a wild escape: Croc Mouth distracts Dr. Noe with nonsensical idioms while Shark Face silently takes out the remaining hunting party. Leo then pushes the twig-armored Raph into the river as a raft, which smashes through the giant novocaine needles.

Dr. Noe screams after them, "You're gonna regret this!"—but Leo gloats, "You've just been Leo'ed. Guest Mad Dogs ahoy!" As they near Manhattan, Raph commends Leo's leadership. Leo sighs in relief: "Promise I'm not forced into leading again soon. Leading's harrrrrrrrd!"

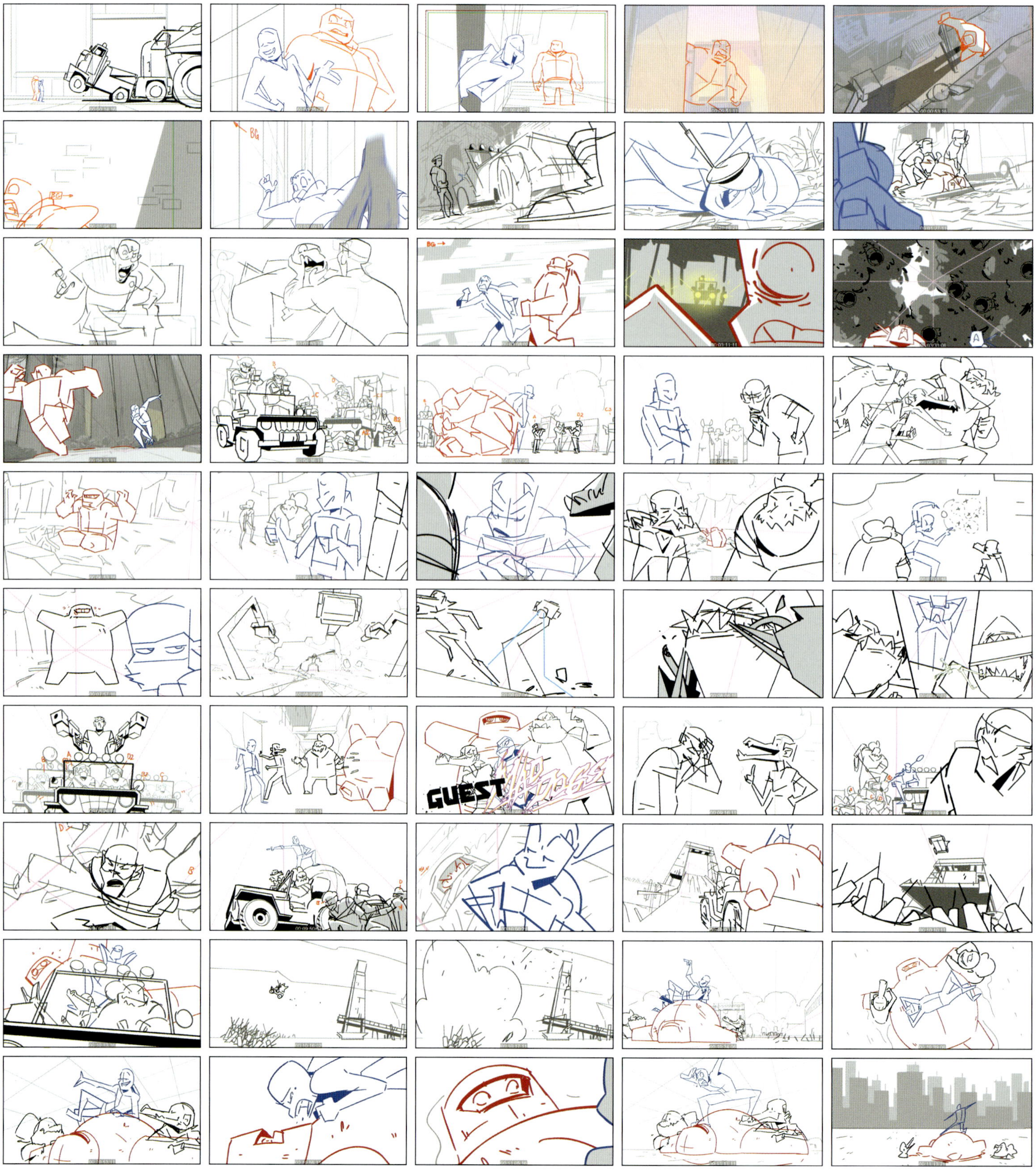

TODDLER MUTANT NINJA TURTLES

PRODUCTION CODE: 081
WRITTEN BY **SAMMIE CROWLEY**
STORYBOARDS BY **CHRISTINE LIU**
DIRECTED BY **JAKE CASTORENA**

Leo passes his Turtle Tank driving test. Donnie declares, "By the power vested in me by the DDMV—Donnie's Department of Motor Vehicles—I hereby declare you have passed!" Mikey slides into the driver's seat ("Is it my turn yet?"), but Donnie shuts him down ("Sweet, innocent, childlike Michelangelo...you're not old enough!"). When the tank's AI alerts to a robbery, they find the mutant jellyfish Kyle smashing jewelry cases, sliding bracelets onto his tentacles. "You dare challenge me? The greatest villain... Kyle!" He stings Leo, Donnie, and Raph, shrinking them into toddlers. Mikey rescues them as Raph shouts, "Mikey, get us out of here!"

Back at the lair, toddler Donnie explains Kyle's de-aging power while Mikey exploits being the eldest—hijacking air hockey, stealing pizza orders, forcing his brothers to watch cooking shows, and imprisoning them in a playpen for his "Oldest Brother Bucket List." While raiding Raph's room, Mikey discovers Raph's "How to Be a Big Brother Like a Boss" notes, realizing his selfishness just as the toddlers escape.

The toddlers hijack the Turtle Tank, swerving wildly to Kyle's next heist. There, Kyle rebrands himself "Jellicon, Conqueror of Worlds" (he's still workshopping it). Mikey redeems himself by trapping Kyle with a chandelier. Chainsaw-wielding Donnie threatens, "I'm hacking off a tentacle to reverse your powers!" A terrified Kyle zaps them back to normal before fleeing. Donnie rewards Mikey with a learner's permit—not a license. Mikey crashes into a dumpster instantly, sighing, "All of my dreams have come true."

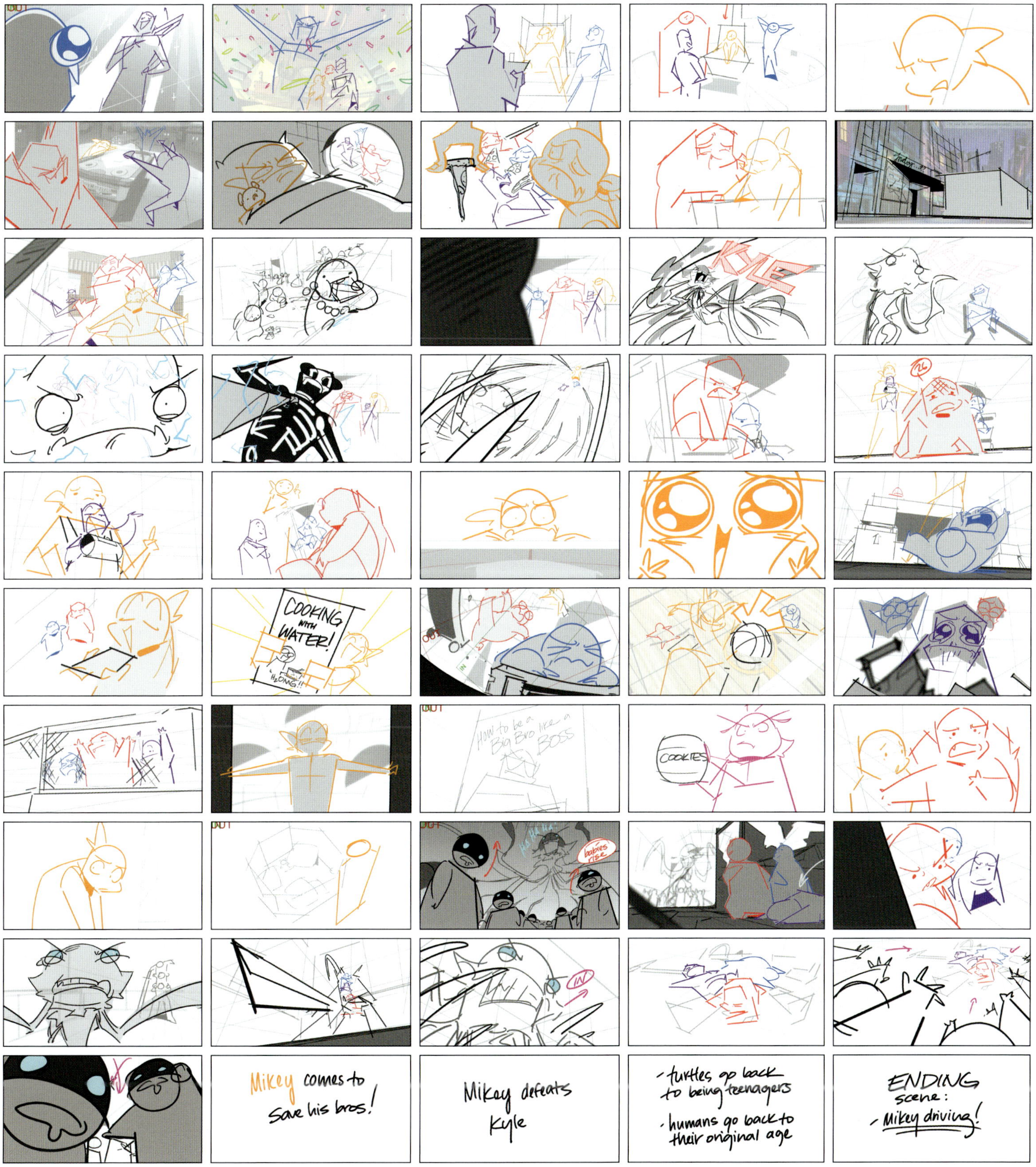

DOG DALE AFTERNOON

PRODUCTION CODE: 082
WRITTEN BY **RUSS CARNEY & RON CORCILLO**
STORYBOARDS BY **MAX COLLINS**
DIRECTED BY **SEBASTIAN MONTES & SAM MONTES**

Dale texts April in a panic! Something's wrong and he needs help. April finds him hiding in his locker. His ears are pointy and he's scratching at fur on his neck. Just then, Donnie appears behind April in a lab coat and surgical mask. He's enrolled in the Medical Magnet program at April's school ("And they are learning a lot from me!"). "Dr." Donnie examines Dale. "Any idea what's wrong, Doc?" Donnie, wanting to keep Dale calm, says, "Oh, it's probably just a little case of growing up, sport!" He then whispers to April that Dale's been hit with some serious magic. Dale explains that he was at a new restaurant, Baba Yaga's Chicken Hut, when he accidentally spilled a milkshake, enraging Yaga. "But then she gave me another milkshake. It tasted like dog hair!"

April and Donnie learn that Baba Yaga is a powerful witch who's cursed Dale into slowly becoming a werewolf. They'll need her secret recipe book to transform him back. Donnie, posing as city health inspector Don Splinterson, and April, as the mustachioed cowboy food critic Clifton Fenugreek, infiltrate the restaurant. Donnie sneaks into the back and locates the safe ("I'll just finesse my way in with the grace of a balleriña"). Then he uses a buzzsaw to open the safe and nabs the book. Our heroes flee with Baba Yaga, in her mortar and pestle, in hot pursuit, followed by her entire chicken hut, which chases after them on large bird legs. A huge fight ensues and the chicken hut is about to stomp our heroes, but Dale, now in full werewolf form, bravely steels himself and flings a rope around the hut's legs, tripping it and saving the day. Later, Dale is transformed back to his "normal" self, with a faint memory that something bad happened, but April convinces him that it was just a fever dream.

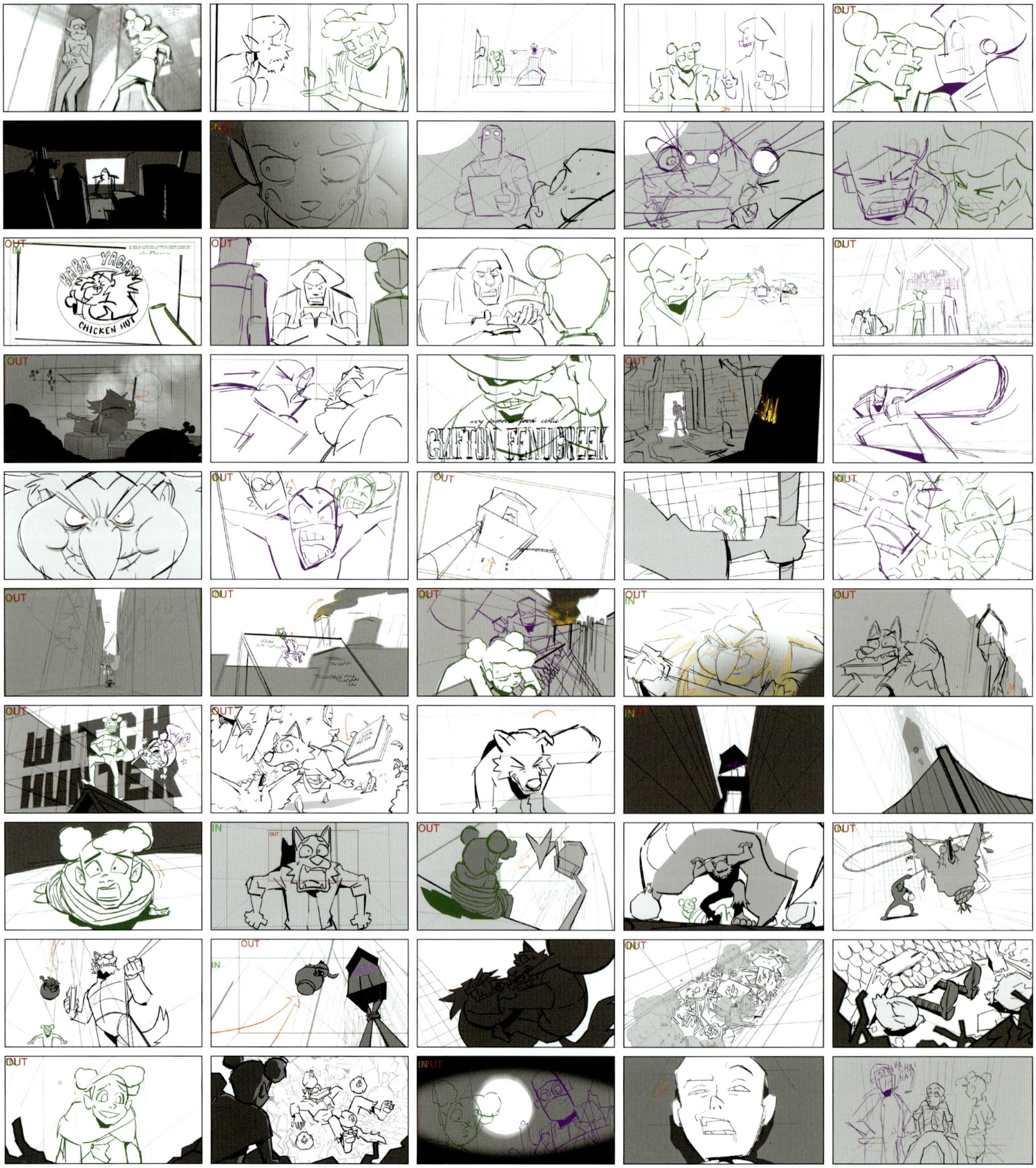

BEE STORY

PRODUCTION CODE: 083
WRITTEN BY **DALE MALINOWSKI**
STORYBOARDS BY **MORGAN HILLEBRAND, CASSEY KUO, CHRISTOPHER LUC**
DIRECTED BY **JJ CONWAY**

The TMNT must replace Splinter's honey after using all of it in the hot tub. Donnie guides them to a colossal Yōkai bee nest in the Hidden City. Leo's impulsive press of the Bee Scout button on the side of the Battle Beetle draws the attention of the territorial Guard Bees. Captured, Leo is declared the prophesied Red Striped King by Queen Beeopatra, while Raph, Donnie, and Mikey are forced into labor building a throne.

While Leo embraces his role as "King Leopatra," his brothers teach the worker bees about fun and start to stage a protest at the coronation. On the day of the ceremony, it's unveiled that Leo has made some changes to the blueprint, making the thrones into a giant statue of himself!

A furious Queen Beeopatra orders it be rebuilt in its original image, but the worker bees declare their vacation and leave the nest, with a devastated queen crying out, "Wha—no—my lovelies! Come back!"

Raph confronts Leo: "It's over, Leo. We gave these bees the gift of fun, now you get us a gift of honey so we can go home." Hearing this confirms Leo only wanted honey, and Queen Beeopatra attacks, shrieking, "You will never have my honey. Ever!" She strikes out at Leo and lunges to finish him. Donnie blocks her and sends his robotic Bee Scout as a decoy. The entire colony returns to defend their queen. Seeing her bees' loyalty, Queen Beeopatra relents: "How much honey would it take to get you four out of here immediately?"

Loaded with honey, they exit through the gift shop—Leo's stunned realization: "Wait, is this a gift shop? We could've just bought honey the whole time?!"

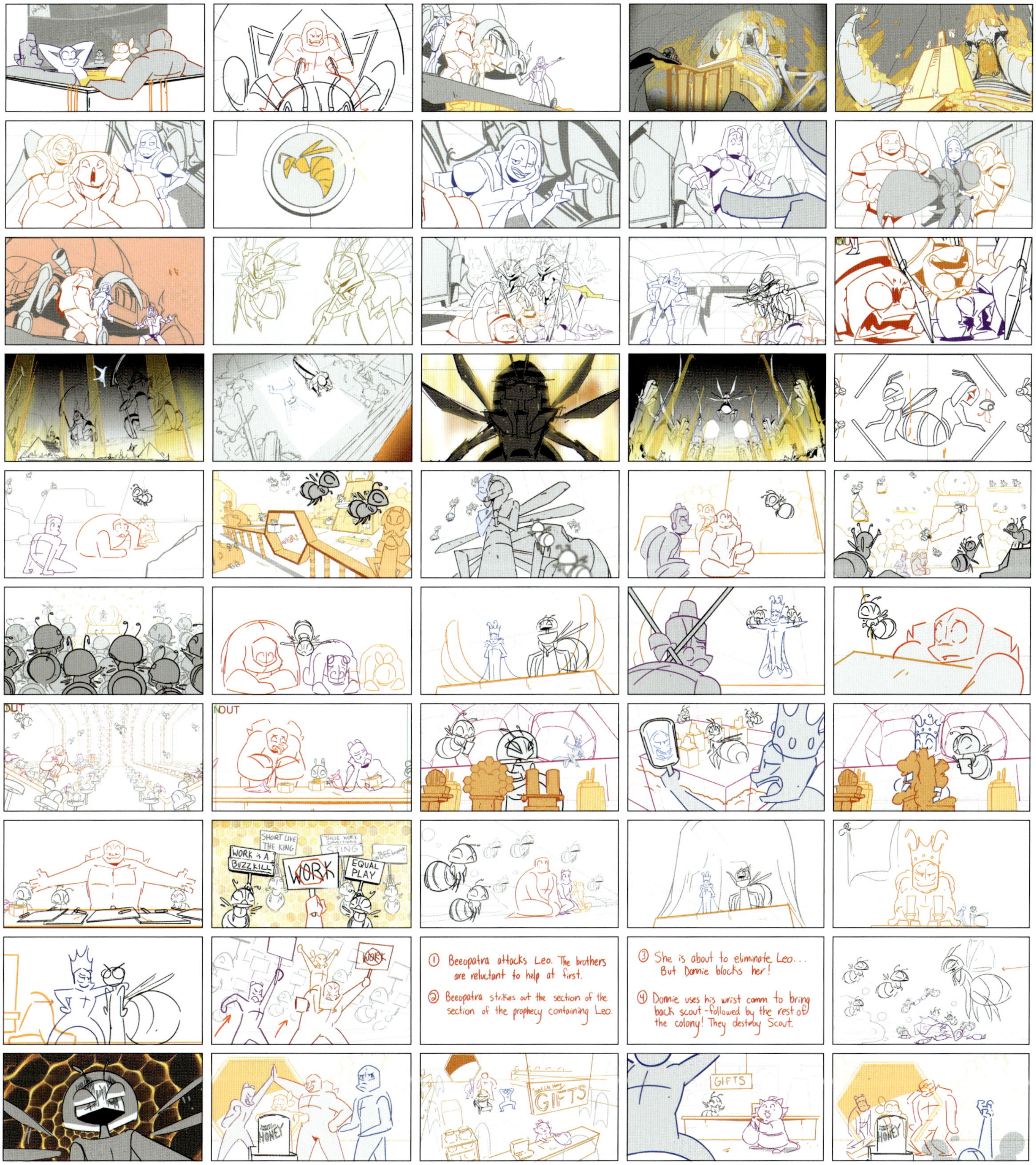

GOYLES JUST WANT TO HAVE FUN

PRODUCTION CODE: 084
WRITTEN BY **RUSS CARNEY & RON CORCILLO**
STORYBOARDS BY **ALICIA CHAN, ASHE JACOBSON, ANDREW KIM**
DIRECTED BY **JAKE CASTORENA**

Huginn and Muninn discover school lunch tickets in a dumpster, leading them to Baron Draxum working in a high school cafeteria. Thrilled to reunite with their cool evil boss, they eagerly assume he's plotting world domination and insist on assisting, citing their lifetime servitude contract. Trapped by their overenthusiastic loyalty, Draxum fabricates a museum scheme—prompting the goyles to reveal their stash of saved oozesquitoes like overprepared henchmen.

In a panicked call to Leo, Draxum confesses: "I've got a bit of a situation. A couple of my 'guys' are here, and they think I'm still 'cool' with the whole mutation thing!" Leo and Donnie stage an elaborate hoax with a robotic TerrorDon, but chaos erupts when Splinter's family outing collides with the act. Mistaking Draxum for a villain, Splinter attacks, shouting "Traitor!" while Raph and Mikey rage-charge the mech. In a spectacular backfire, the well-meaning goyles mutate a sabertooth tiger skeleton into a rampaging mammoth—"Ooh, that's a beaut!"

Cornered, Draxum admits his redemption, only for Huginn to deliver the heartfelt punchline: "Did you think we liked you because you were evil? We liked you because you were smart!" In a moment of pure loyalty, they fly back to his shoulders where they belong, turning disaster into teamwork as they encase the mammoth in amber.

The next day, a clueless docent deadpans, "And here we have the sabertooth mammoth. Which existed. Apparently."

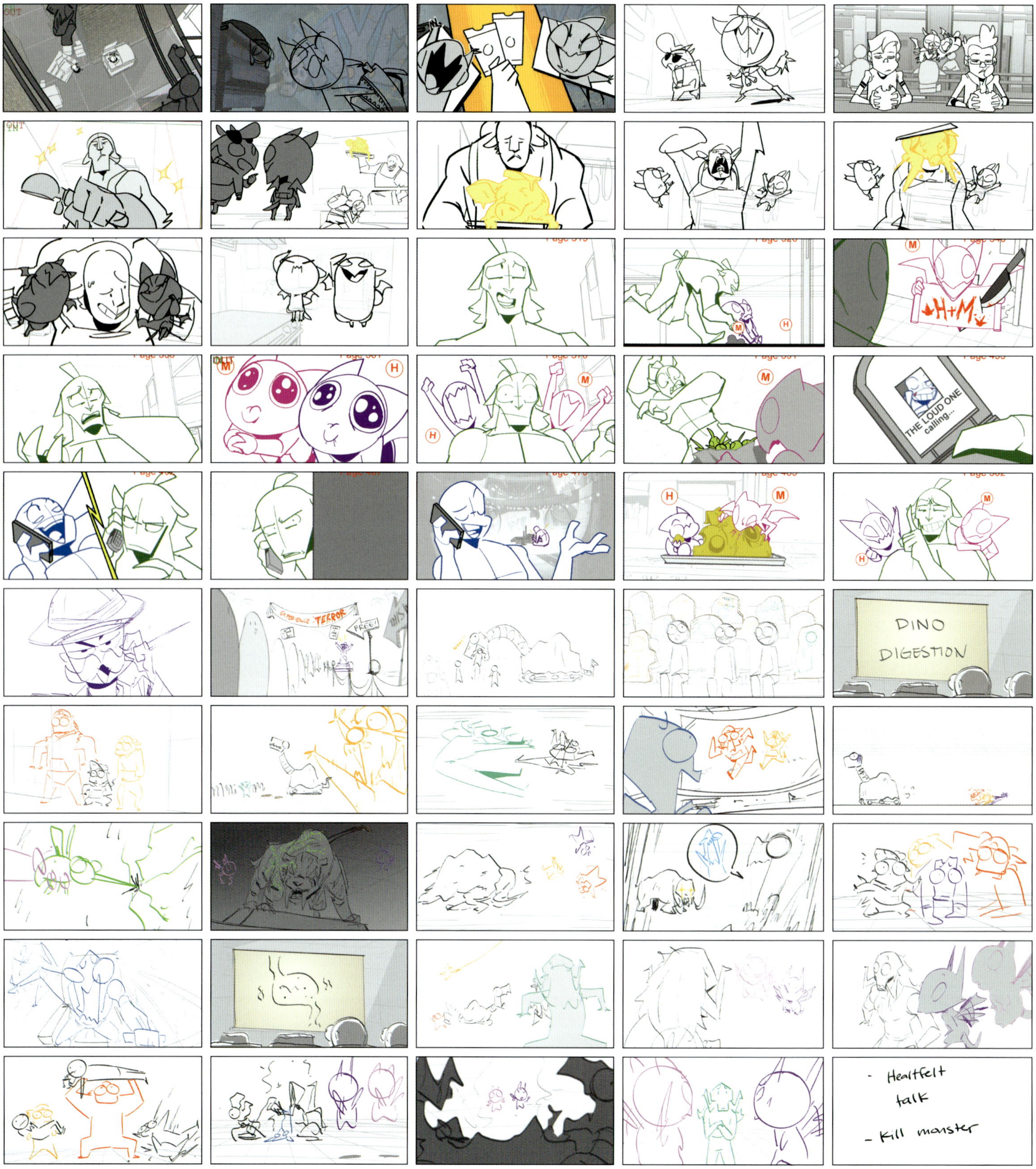

GOURD ALMIGHTY

PRODUCTION CODE: 087
WRITTEN BY **RUSS CARNEY & RON CORCILLO**

Raph, Mikey, and Leo are gathered outside Donnie's lab. An eerie glow comes from within. Raph knocks on the door: "Donnie! You've been in there for...(checks watch)...six months! You sure you're okay?" Donnie: "Yes! Just slide my nutritional paste through the slot in the door." Leo: "Can't we come in?" Donnie: "No! There's too much UV radiation. You'll be melted alive!" Mikey: "What are you doing in there, anyway?" Donnie: "Patience, patience, all will be revealed in time...(BEAT) Aaand, it is time." The lights go out, the door unlocks. Mikey waves them inside.

Donnie: "Gentlemen, prepare to witness the spawn of my blood, sweat, and blatant disregard for genetic ethics! I give you the most gigantic, curvaceous, and perfectly symmetrical (inside and out) pumpkin the world has ever seen!" The lights come on, revealing an intensely sun-tanned Donnie. The brothers are blown away by the enormous pumpkin. Raph: "Wow! Donnie, I have a lot of questions. Starting with... Why?" Donnie: "Why? WHY? This is why!" He holds up a flyer for... "Halloween GourdFest?" Donnie: "I know, I know, you all think of me as the mechanics and thermodynamics guy, but my muse, my true passion this week, is BOTANY!" Donnie explains that he's incredibly excited to finally win the premier pumpkin festival in NYC after being thwarted year after year by that smug Ethel Crabtree and her all-organic claptrap. Raph: "Okay, my next question is...How are we going to get it there? The door's way too small." Donnie: "Oh, sweet Raphael, did you think I would create a giant pumpkin without having a way to get it out of my lab?" Donnie back-handsprings into the seat of a DONNIE-TECH CANNON and grabs the controls. The others leap for cover as KA-BOOM! the wall of Donnie's lab collapses into rubble! Raph stirs. "All right, let's drag that thing over to the Turtle Tank!" Donnie: "Drag? Drag?! We must not sully her pristine skin!"

QUICK BEATS: The TMNT struggle to move the giant pumpkin to the surface without damaging it:

1. Donnie zips off-screen and returns driving a forklift that carries the pumpkin on a massive velvet pillow. He lowers the pumpkin gently on top of the Turtle Tank. The tank shudders, then collapses under its weight. FLIP TO:
2. In the vertical sewer shaft from Shadow of Evil, the Turtles struggle to lift the pumpkin, which still sits on the cushion, up the shaft. Exterior shot: On an NYC street, a manhole cover and the surrounding asphalt bulge as the TMNT try to force it out from underneath. Back in the shaft, the exhausted boys lose their grip and fall. The pumpkin and cushion land on them. The pumpkin is fine, they are not. FLIP TO:
3. The boys sail through the sewers on the pumpkin. They're cruising along, until they approach a grate across the opening where the sewer empties into the Hudson. Donnie tries to stop the pumpkin, but it bumps into the grate, sending the brothers flying through the grate and into the river.

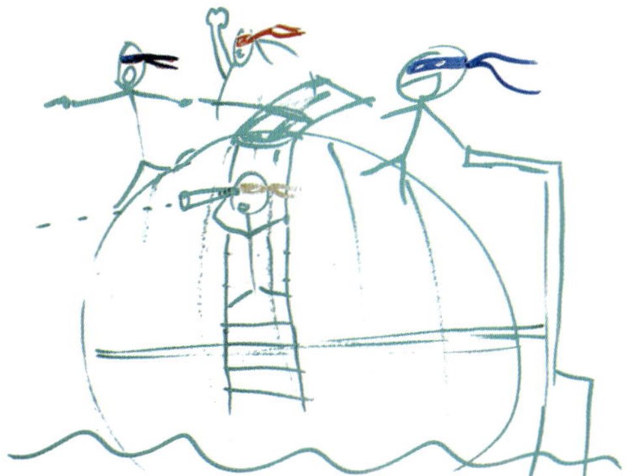

The boys drag themselves onto the banks of the river. Leo: "That's it. I'm portalling this thing right to the festival!" Donnie: "Nononononono!" But before he can stop him, Leo makes a gigantic portal that sucks in the pumpkin. CUT TO: The Van Pelt household living room. A wispy-haired old man with a powder-blue blanket sits on the sofa when the massive pumpkin portals into the middle of the room. The man's eyes go wide with excitement! "Sally! Sally, it's finally here!" A toilet flushes off-screen. The TMNT appear through the portal, apologize for the disturbance, and portal away. Sally rushes into the room only to find no giant pumpkin. She folds her arms and shakes her head at her husband crossly. He hangs his head.

In the park, the TMNT roll the pumpkin on logs up to the entrance to Halloween GourdFest. Raph: "Donnie, couldn't we use a cart or something?" Donnie: "No, Raph. This is how the ancient Egyptians rolled their giant pumpkins to the pyramids." They arrive at their display booth, where people assume they're in Halloween costumes just like everybody else. A festival judge approaches the pumpkin and slaps a number on its side. She blows a whistle, then: "Okay, contestants, you'll have an hour to carve your pumpkin." Donnie: "What?! Carve this spectacle of modern fertilization?! What about the biggest pumpkin contest? The heaviest pumpkin contest? Most symmetrical? Orangest? Tallest? Roundest?!" Judge: "Yeah, we used to do all that until last year when some crazy kid threw a tantrum after not winning any of the prizes." In Donnie's thought bubble, a FLASHBACK of Donnie frantically arguing with the judges last year, stretching out a measuring tape, pointing to a clipboard of data, kicking over a chair, and running away crying his eyes out. BACK TO SCENE: The other Turtles saw the flashback in Donnie's thought bubble. Raph: "I guess some people just don't take criticism well." The judge heads off: "Remember, one hour."

Donnie is torn. He doesn't want to harm his pristine creation. Leo: "Great, we spent all day humping this pumpkin around for nothing. I say we schlep it home and make the world's biggest pumpkin pie." Mikey whispers: "It's 90 percent poison!" Donnie: "I mean, what kind of philistine would even ask me to deface my greatest— Is that the Taj Mahal?!" ON ETHEL CRABTREE: She sits quietly beside her majestically carved pumpkin, with a smug smile on her face. Donnie: "Oh, Ethel, you have poked the wrong bear." He steels himself, whips out his Tech-Bō chainsaw, and jams it in the pumpkin. INSIDE PUMPKIN: The gourd, seeds, and guts SHAKE over the sound of the chainsaw.

Inside the Horticultural Garden's greenhouse, among some ivy, we see an eyeball spring open. STINKBOMB awakens! "I feel a great disturbance! As if millions of seeds suddenly cried out in terror!" He springs to his "feet" and races off-screen.

BACK AT GOURDFEST, in a REVERSE ANGLE: Donnie works intensely. Mikey: "You know, Donnie, I've got a couple of really great designs that we could use for—" Donnie: "No! I know just how to make this a champion jack-of-the-lantern!" He continues sawing, then we reveal his carving masterpiece. Raph: "Two triangles and a circle? Oh, good luck, buddy." Leo: "Yeah, you really should've gone with Mikey's idea." Donnie: "I think the judges will really appreciate the simplicity and Euclidean perfection." Leo: "You mean based on your zero years of winning?"

Just then, Stinkbomb darts onto the festival grounds: "Gape in awe, spawn of evil! The Stinkbomb has come to punish you for your wrongdoings!" Mikey: "Uh-oh, it's Stinkbomb!" Stinkbomb is furious about the atrocity of pumpkin carving. Contestants flee as Stinkbomb shoots his goo bombs. Stinkbomb looks at Donnie's pumpkin: "Symmetry. Largeness. A perfect specimen!" Donnie: "Thank you, it's about time someone—" Stinkbomb: "Clearly the work of a gene-twisting MADMAN!" Leo, Raph, and Mikey attack, but he pelts them with goo. As they regroup, Stinkbomb places his vine hands on the face of Donnie's pumpkin and closes his eyes: "My mind to your mind. My thoughts to your thoughts!" Raph: "I've seen this in a Jupiter Jim comic. He's doing the Vegetonian fruit meld!" Donnie's giant pumpkin grows vines and stands at full height. Its innocuous face becomes grotesque. It grabs Donnie, who screams before he gets flung into a tree trunk! Mikey: "Whoa! Two Triangles and a Circle just got wayyy scarier!" The guys battle the pumpkin. Stinkbomb brings more decorative pumpkins to life, which also attack the guys. Two Triangles pulls a long strand of seed goop out of his mouth and uses it as nunchucks! The other pumpkins attack with various props from around the festival, including carving knives, crates, chairs, whatever.

As the guys struggle to fend off the enemies, Donnie recruits Mikey to trap the giant pumpkin with the GourdFest banner. But their efforts fail after Two Triangles grabs the banner, scoops them up in it, and flings them like a slingshot through crates full of pumpkins. Ouch! Raph gets fed up, insisting that Donnie has to destroy Two Triangles. Donnie protests. "Oh right, the mad scientist has to destroy his out-of-control creation, is that your plan? Well, I don't do tropes! No, we'll have to take out Stinkbomb!" He hands Mikey a wad of cash. "Mikey, here's $6,500 (stuffs cash in his hand) go to every car wash in town and bring back all the air fresheners!" Raph: "Donnie, we don't have time for that! Raph's got a simpler plan! <OVERLY LONG SELF-SATISFIED LAUGH> Leo: "We don't have time for the plan, but we have time for that laugh?" Raph: "Donnie, do you remember that bee costume you made for S.H.E.L.L.D.O.N. on Halloween?" Donnie: "Ah, of course!" He taps his wrist tablet. In the lab, S.H.E.L.L.D.O.N., in a metal bee costume, awakens and rockets out of the lair and to the festival. Donnie pilots S.H.E.L.L.D.O.N. toward Stinkbomb, who takes notice: "What's this? A tasty little pollinator? Come to Papa!" S.H.E.L.L.D.O.N. flies into Stinkbomb's mouth, and Donnie works the controls to beat and batter Stinkbomb from the inside. Stinkbomb is KO'ed, and the telepathic link between him, Two Triangles, and the lesser pumpkins is severed. The giant pumpkin returns to normal, then deflates like a basketball. Our heroes have won! Raph: "Now what are we gonna do with this thing?"

Later that evening, the guys sit on top of the Turtle Tank near the riverbank. Donnie works a remote control. In the distance, his quadcopters haul the massive pumpkin in a net over a grassy island in the East River. Donnie: "And once again, the four of us—all four of us equally—learned a valuable lesson about monkeying with mother nature." Raph: "Donnie, just dump the moldy pumpkin." Donnie hits a button, releasing the pumpkin from the net. It hits the ground with a splort. TIGHT ON THE PUMPKIN EYE: A single seed pops out and looks around. It gestures and runs off. A BEAT, and a whole lot of seeds dart out and plant themselves in the grass.

THE END.

RISE OF THE TEENAGE MUTANT NINJA TURTLES COMICS COVER GALLERY

PUBLISHED BY IDW PUBLISHING

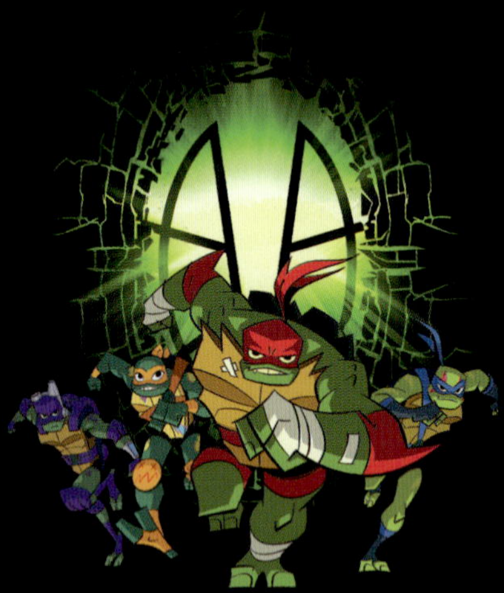

RISE OF THE TMNT #0
CONVENTION EDITION

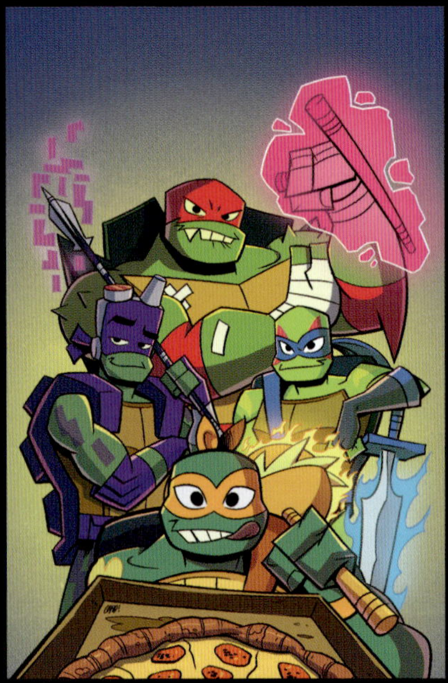

RISE OF THE TMNT #0
COVER RI BY CHAD THOMAS

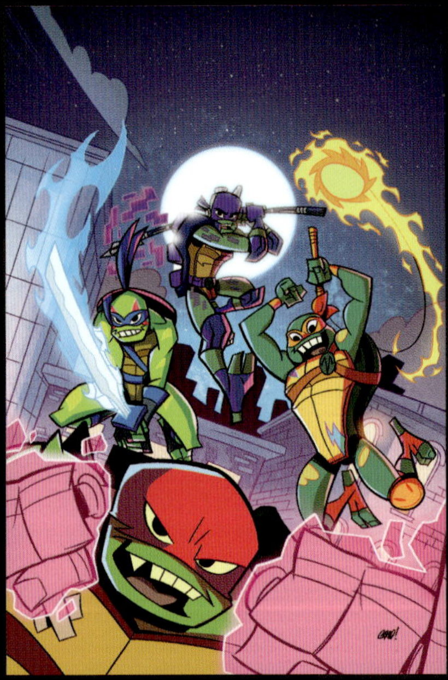

RISE OF THE TMNT #1
COVER RI BY CHAD THOMAS

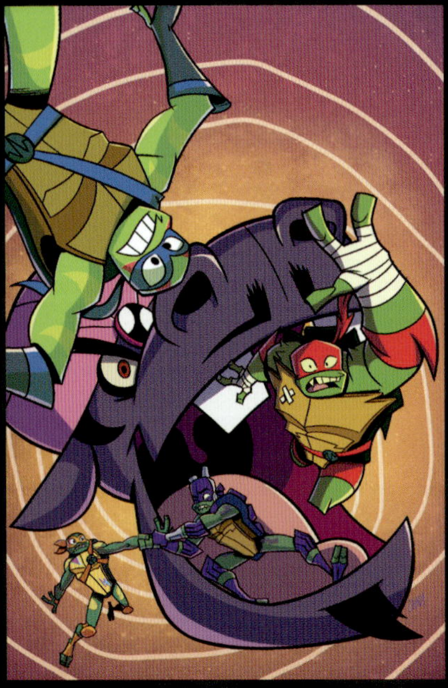

RISE OF THE TMNT #2
COVER RI BY CHAD THOMAS

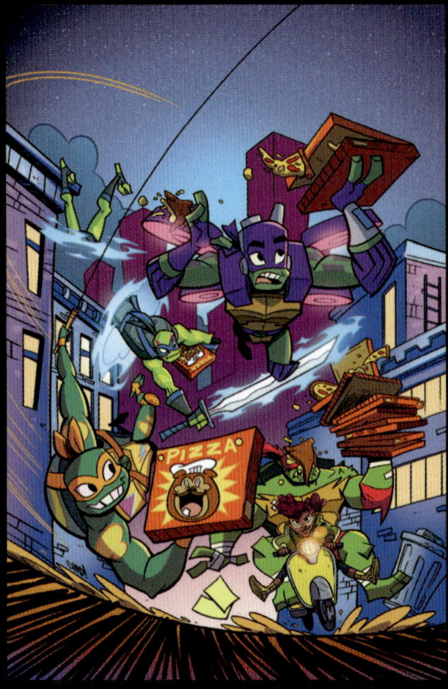

RISE OF THE TMNT #3
COVER RI BY CHAD THOMAS

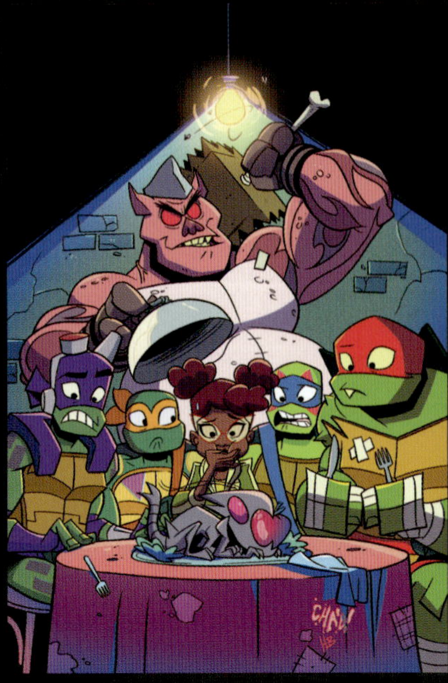

RISE OF THE TMNT #4
COVER RI BY CHAD THOMAS

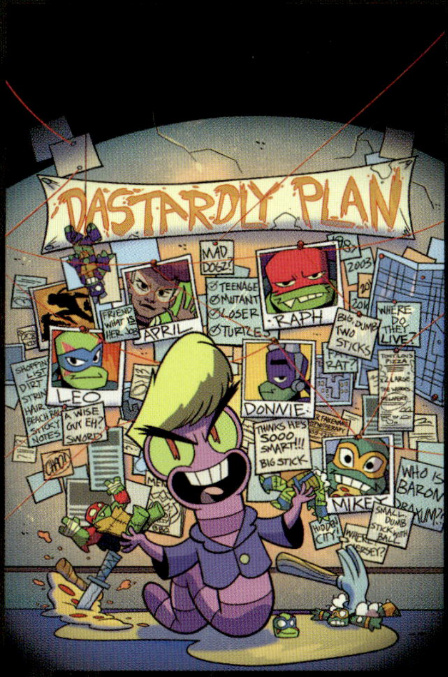

RISE OF THE TMNT #5
COVER RI BY CHAD THOMAS

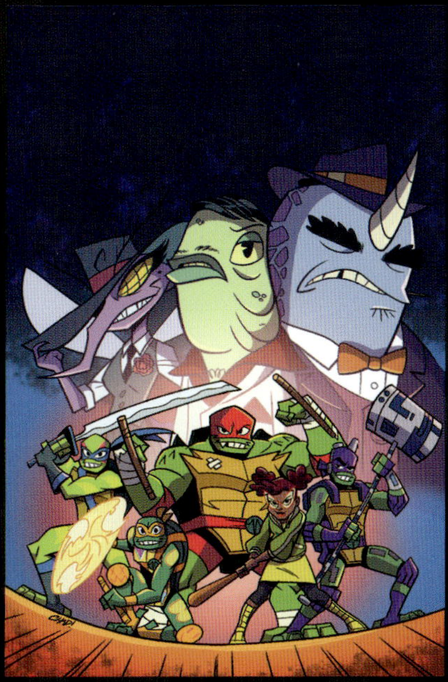

RISE OF THE TMNT: SOUND OFF! #1
COVER A BY CHAD THOMAS

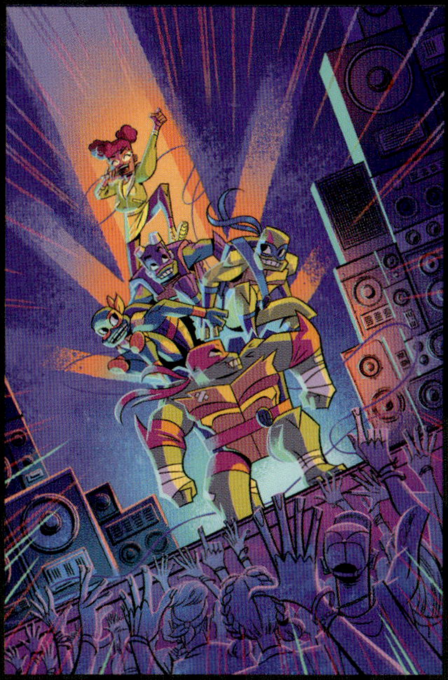

RISE OF THE TMNT: SOUND OFF! #1
COVER RI BY GEORGE CALTSOUDAS

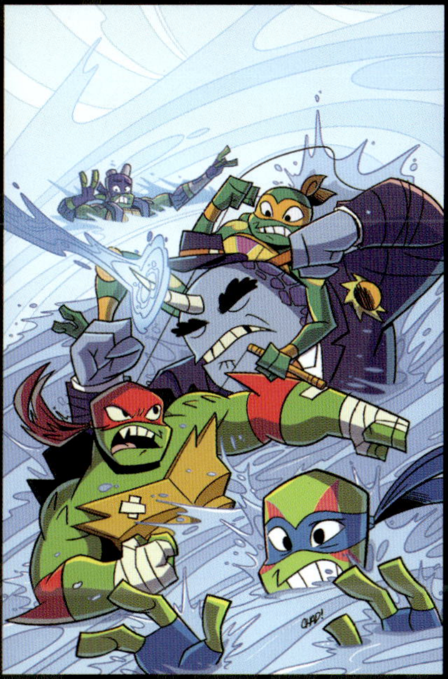

RISE OF THE TMNT: SOUND OFF! #2
COVER A BY CHAD THOMAS

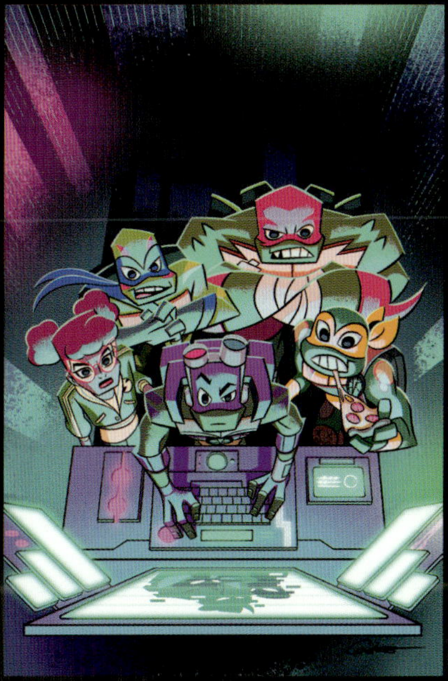

RISE OF THE TMNT: SOUND OFF! #2
COVER RI BY GEORGE CALTSOUDAS

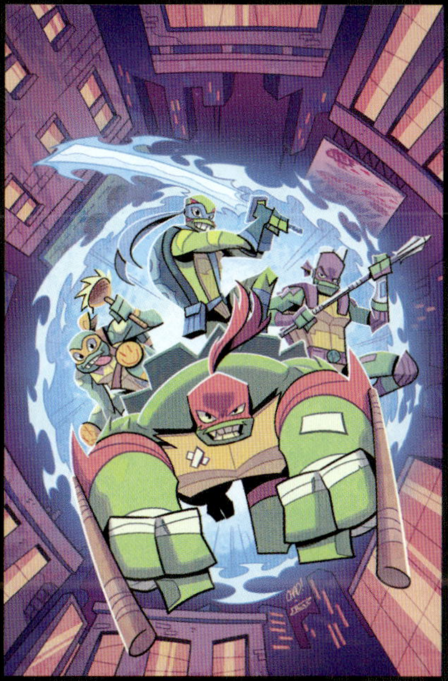

RISE OF THE TMNT: SOUND OFF! #3
COVER A BY CHAD THOMAS

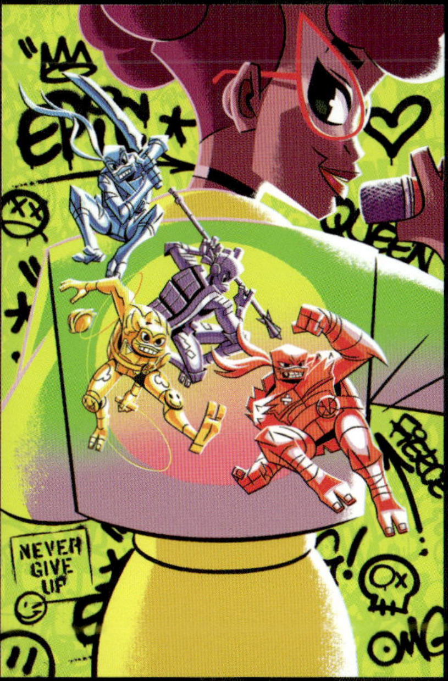

RISE OF THE TMNT: SOUND OFF! #3
COVER RI BY GEORGE CALTSOUDAS

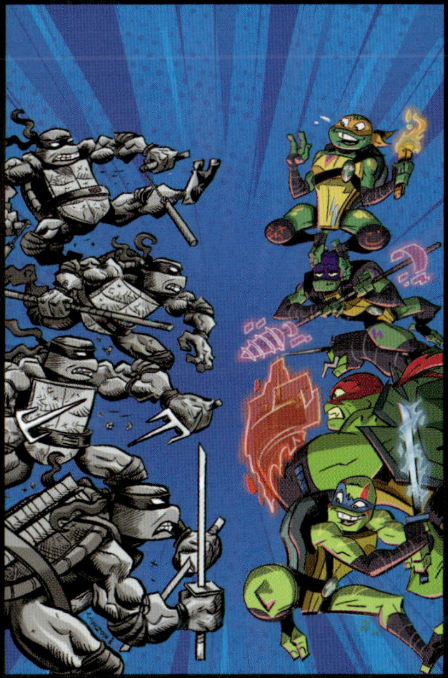

TEENAGE MUTANT NINJA TURTLES: BATTLE NEXUS #3
COVER C BY JIM LAWSON AND ANDY SURIANO

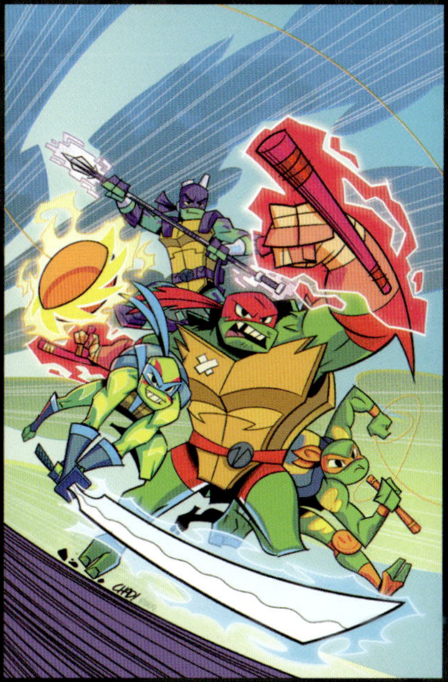

TEENAGE MUTANT NINJA TURTLES: TURTLE POWER PACK, VOL. 4
COVER BY CHAD THOMAS; COLORS BY NICK FILARDI

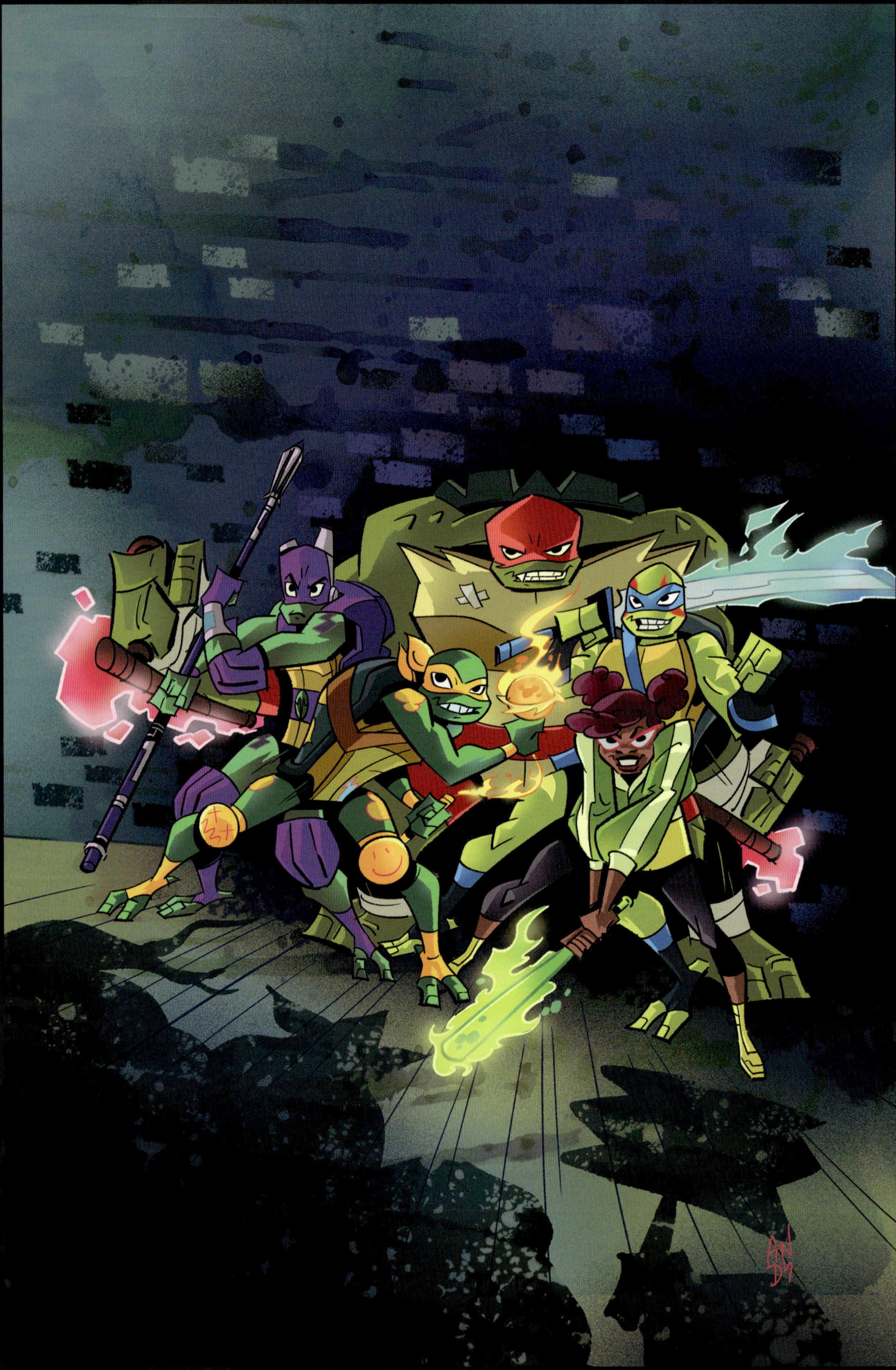

RISE OF THE TEENAGE MUTANT NINJA TURTLES - PROMO

COVER A BY ANDY SURIANO

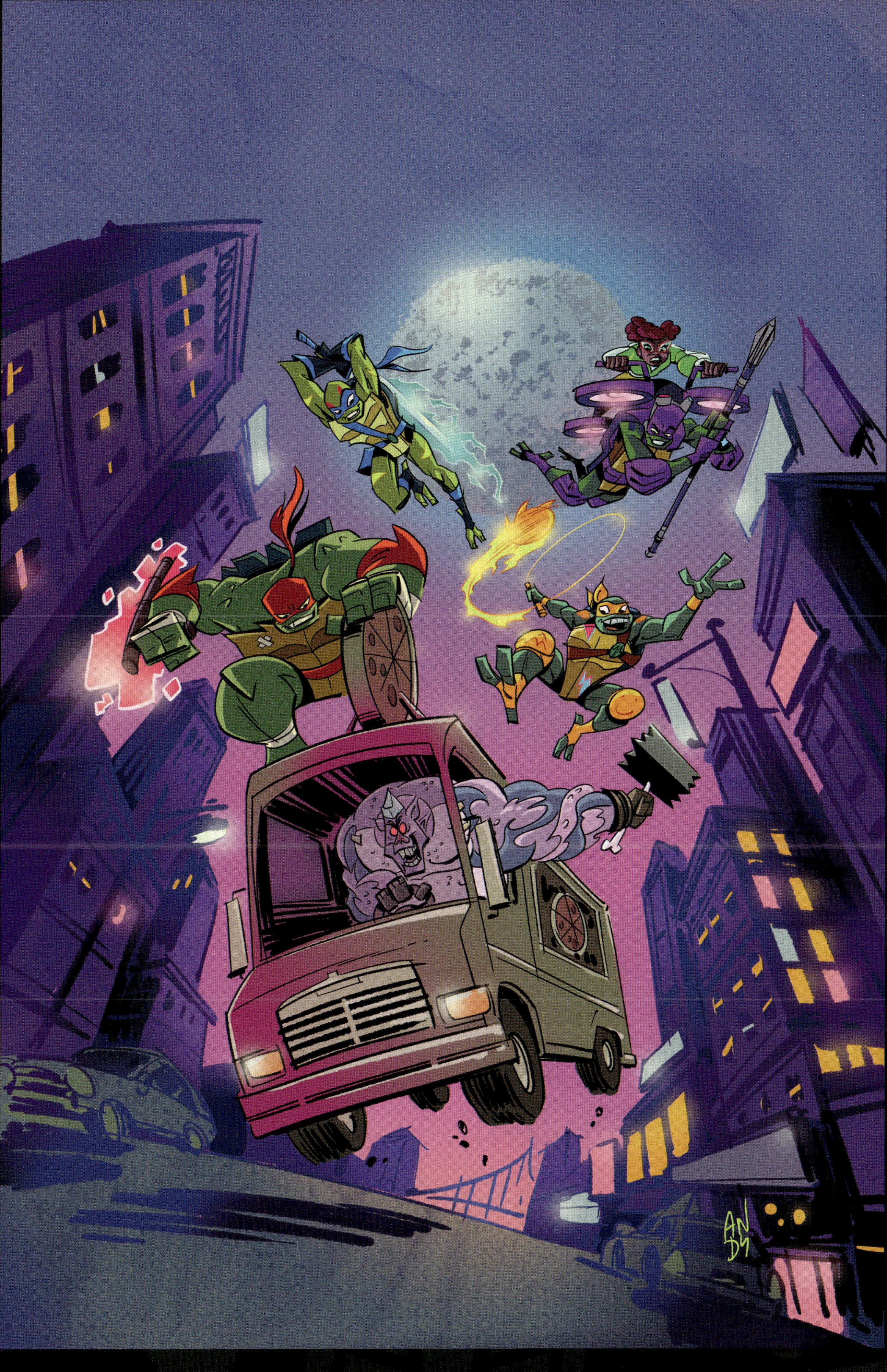

RISE OF THE TEENAGE MUTANT NINJA TURTLES - PROMO

COVER B BY ANDY SURIANO

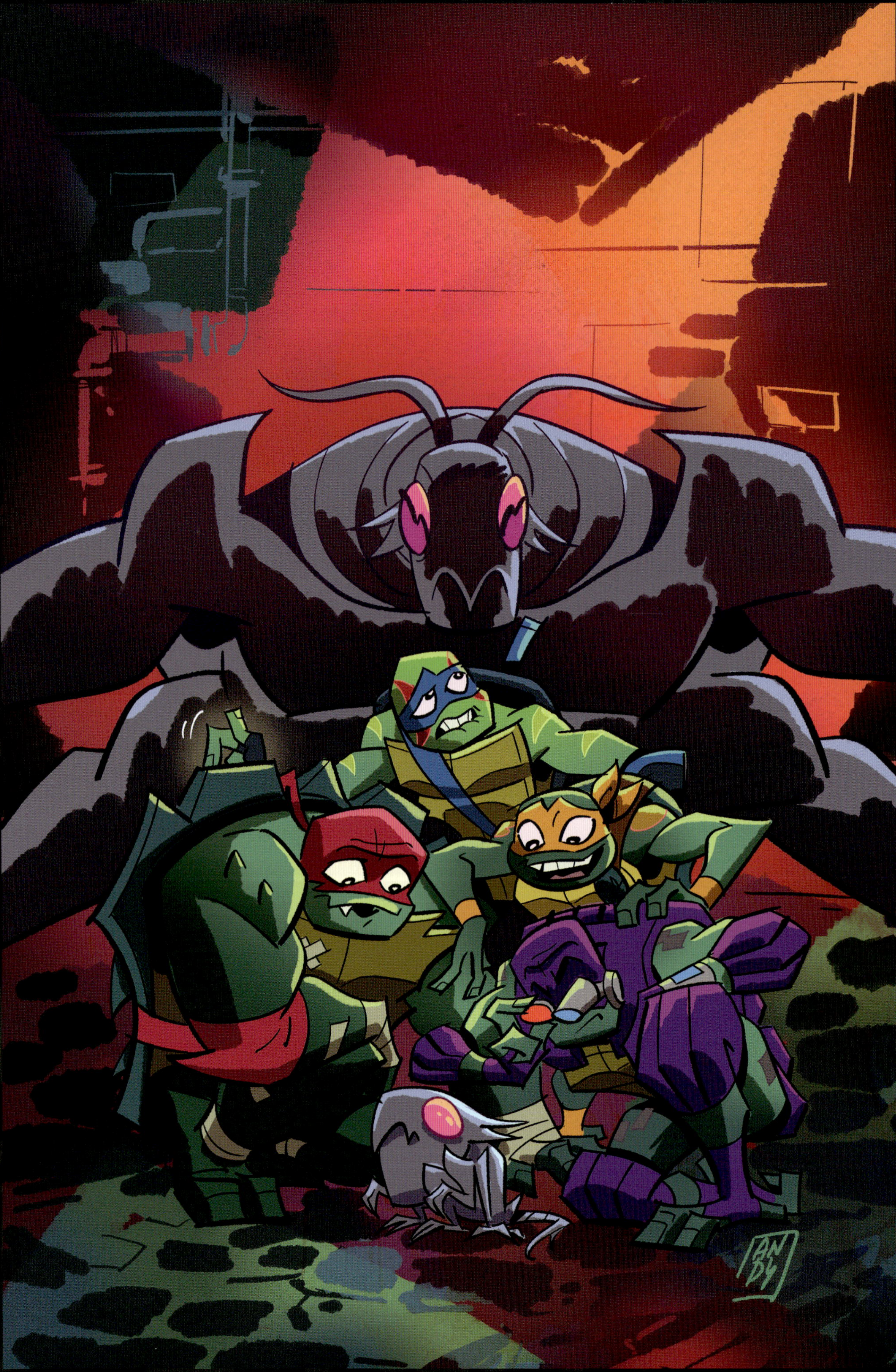

TEENAGE MUTANT NINJA TURTLES: RISE OF THE TMNT #0

COVER RI BY ANDY SURIANO

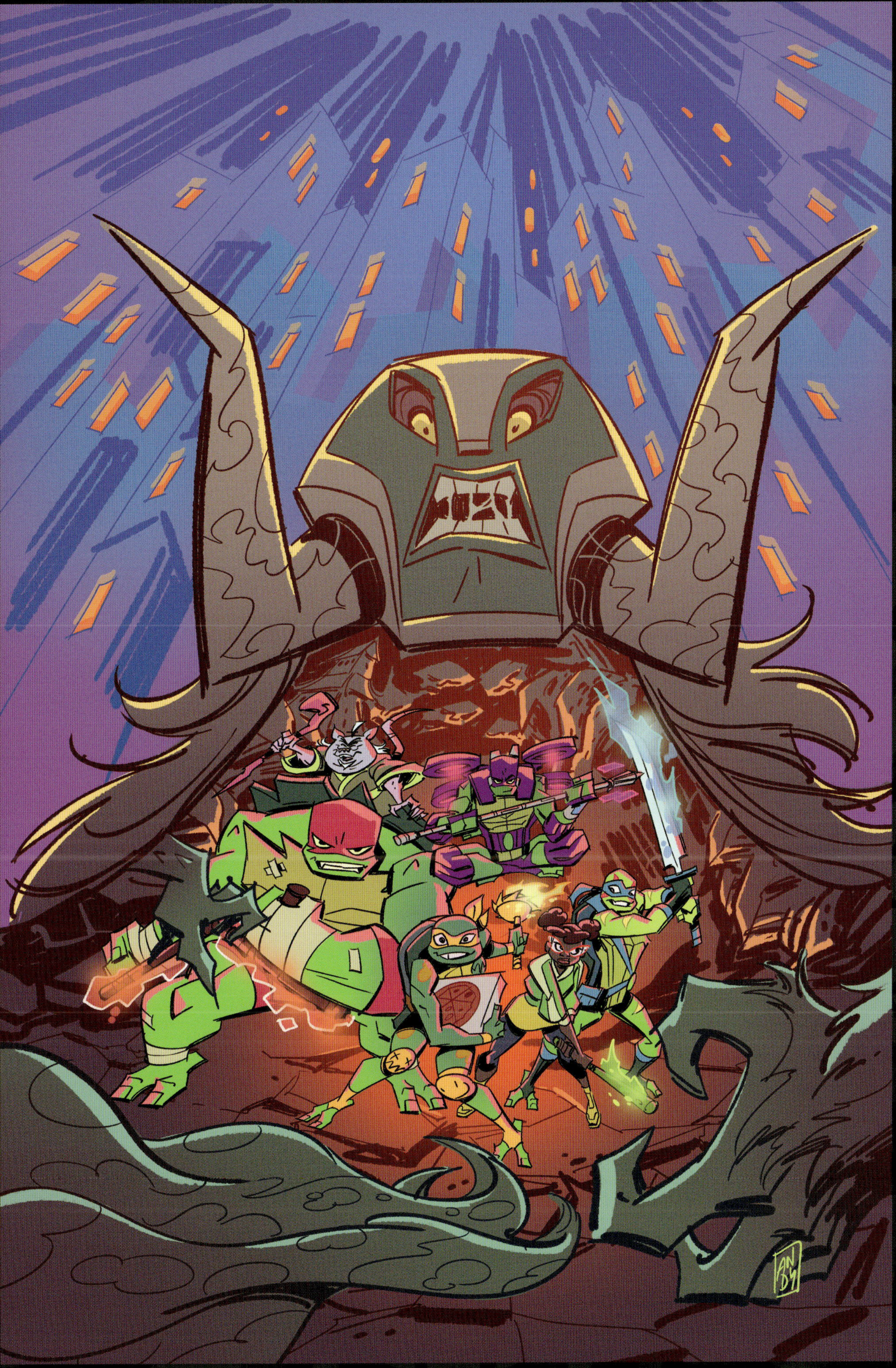

TEENAGE MUTANT NINJA TURTLES: RISE OF THE TMNT #1
COVER A BY ANDY SURIANO

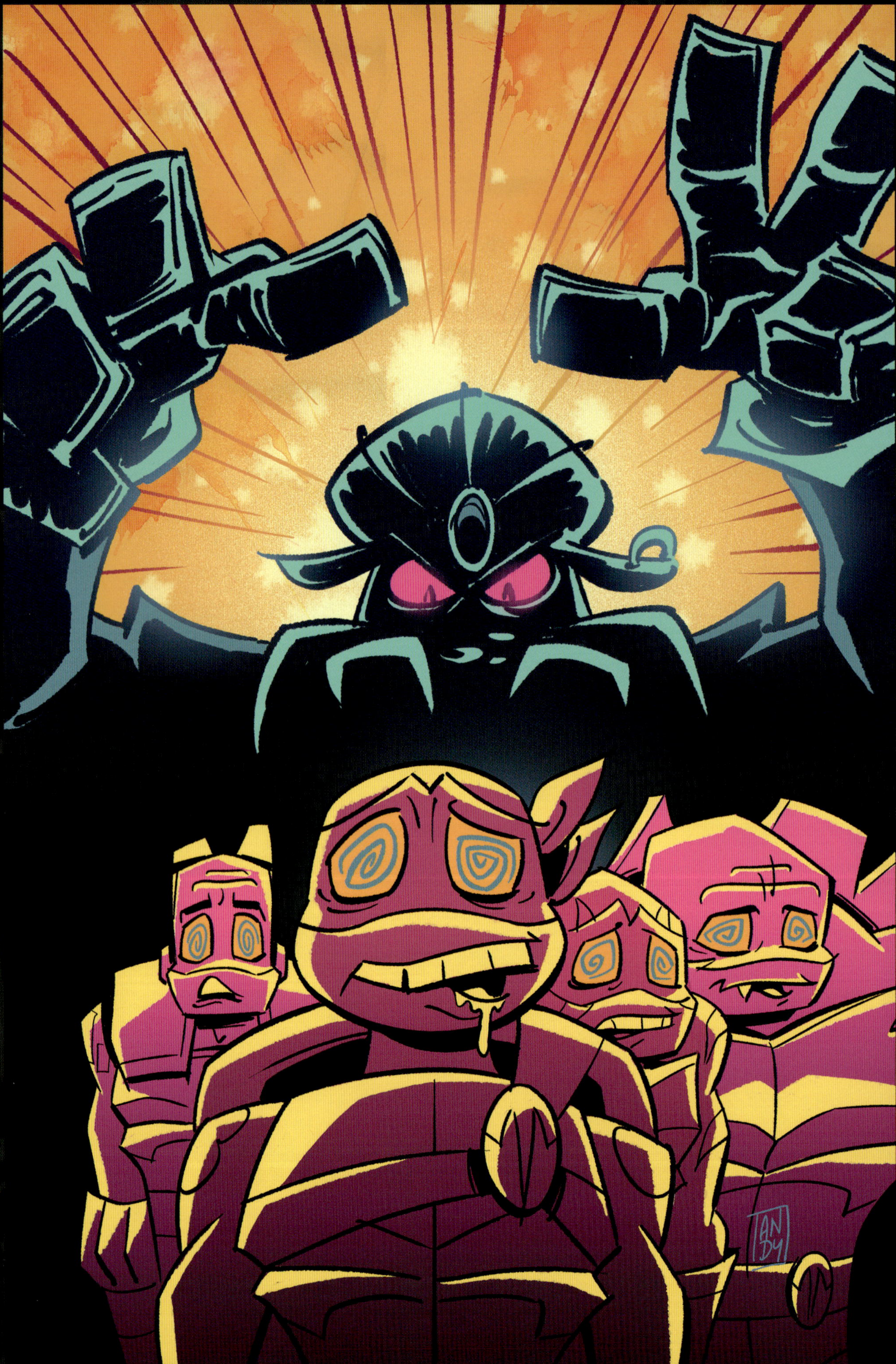

TEENAGE MUTANT NINJA TURTLES: RISE OF THE TMNT #2
COVER A BY ANDY SURIANO

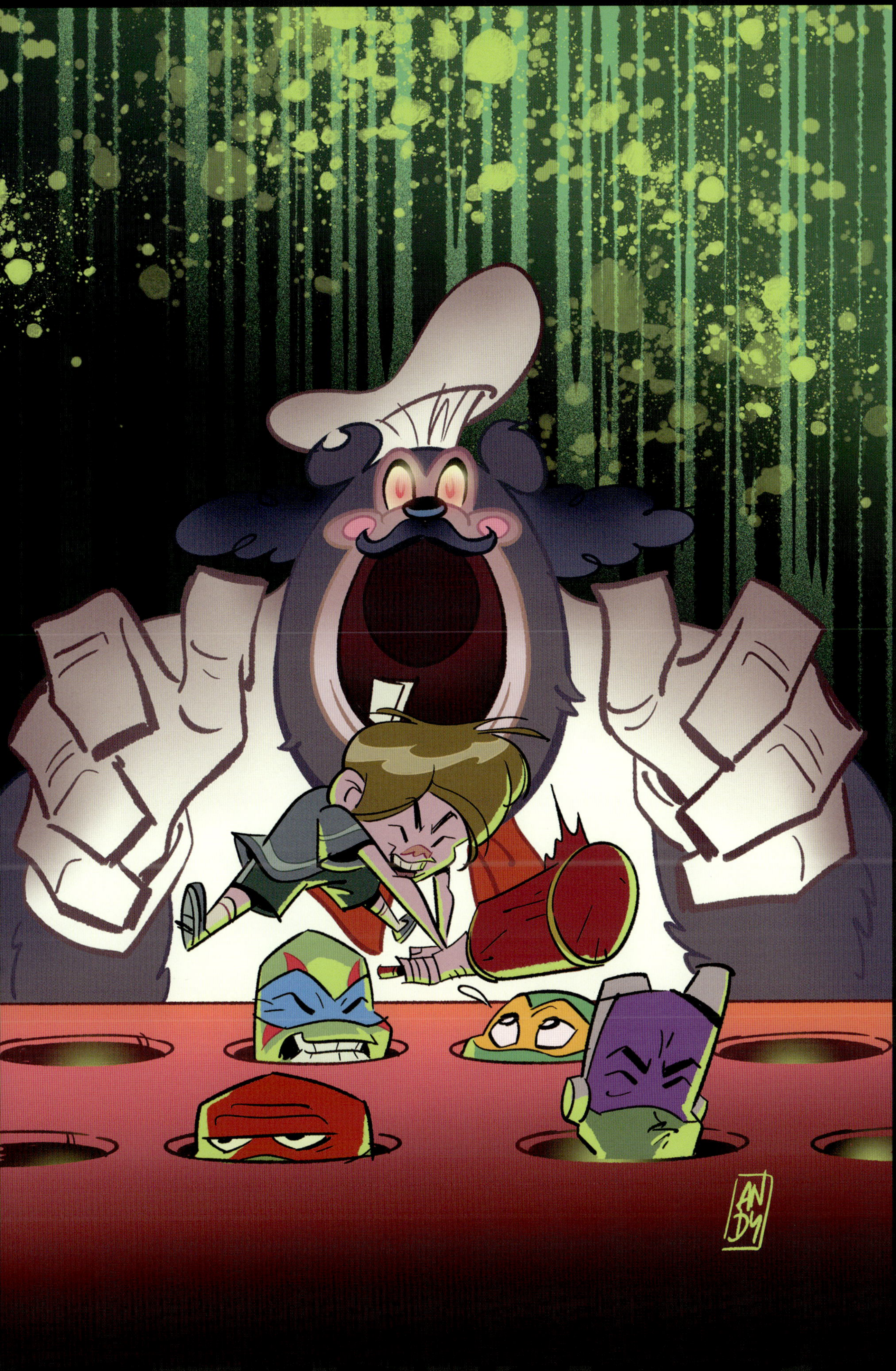

TEENAGE MUTANT NINJA TURTLES: RISE OF THE TMNT #3
COVER A BY ANDY SURIANO

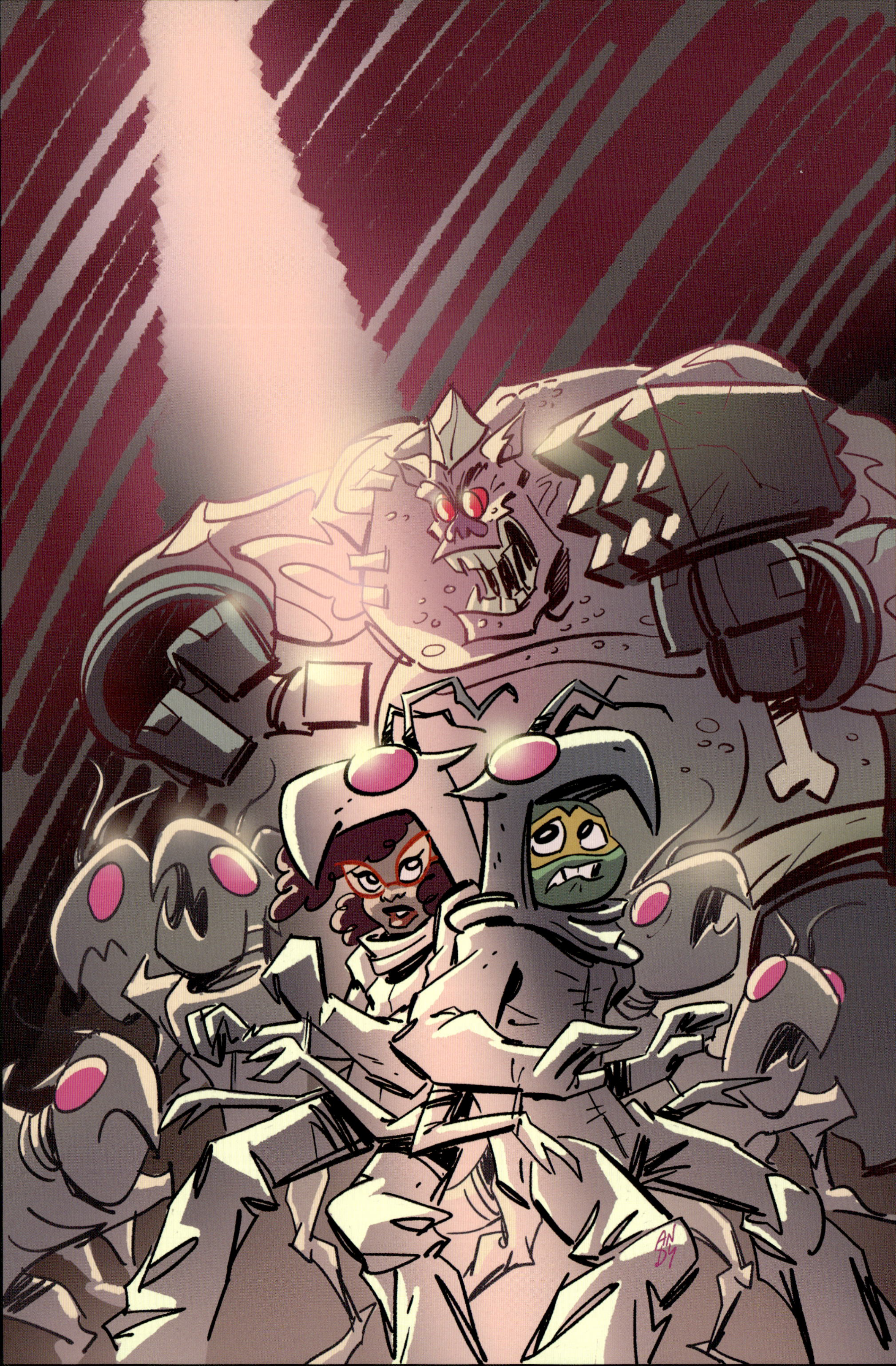

TEENAGE MUTANT NINJA TURTLES: RISE OF THE TMNT #4

COVER A BY ANDY SURIANO

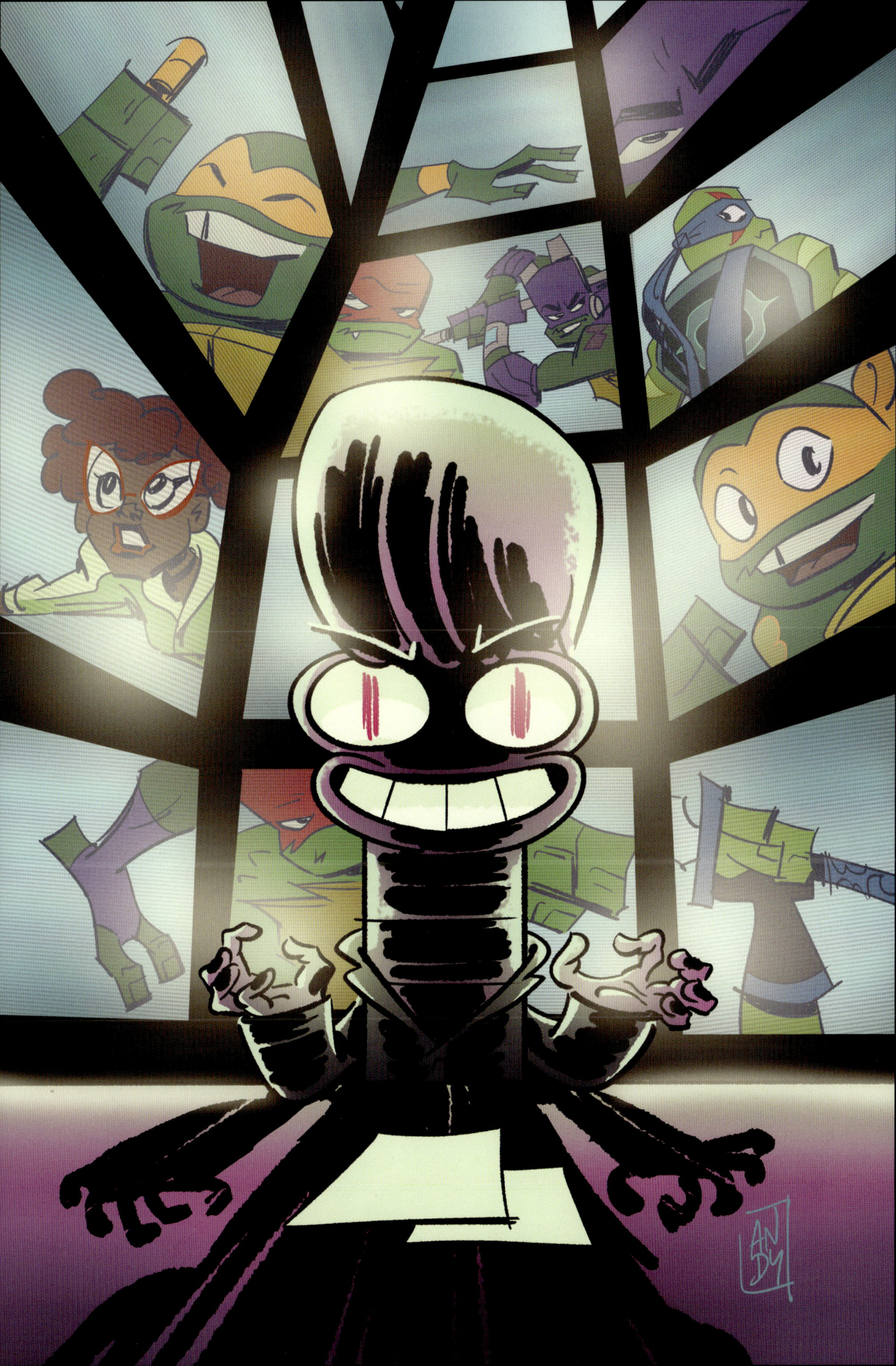

TEENAGE MUTANT NINJA TURTLES: RISE OF THE TMNT #5

COVER A BY ANDY SURIANO

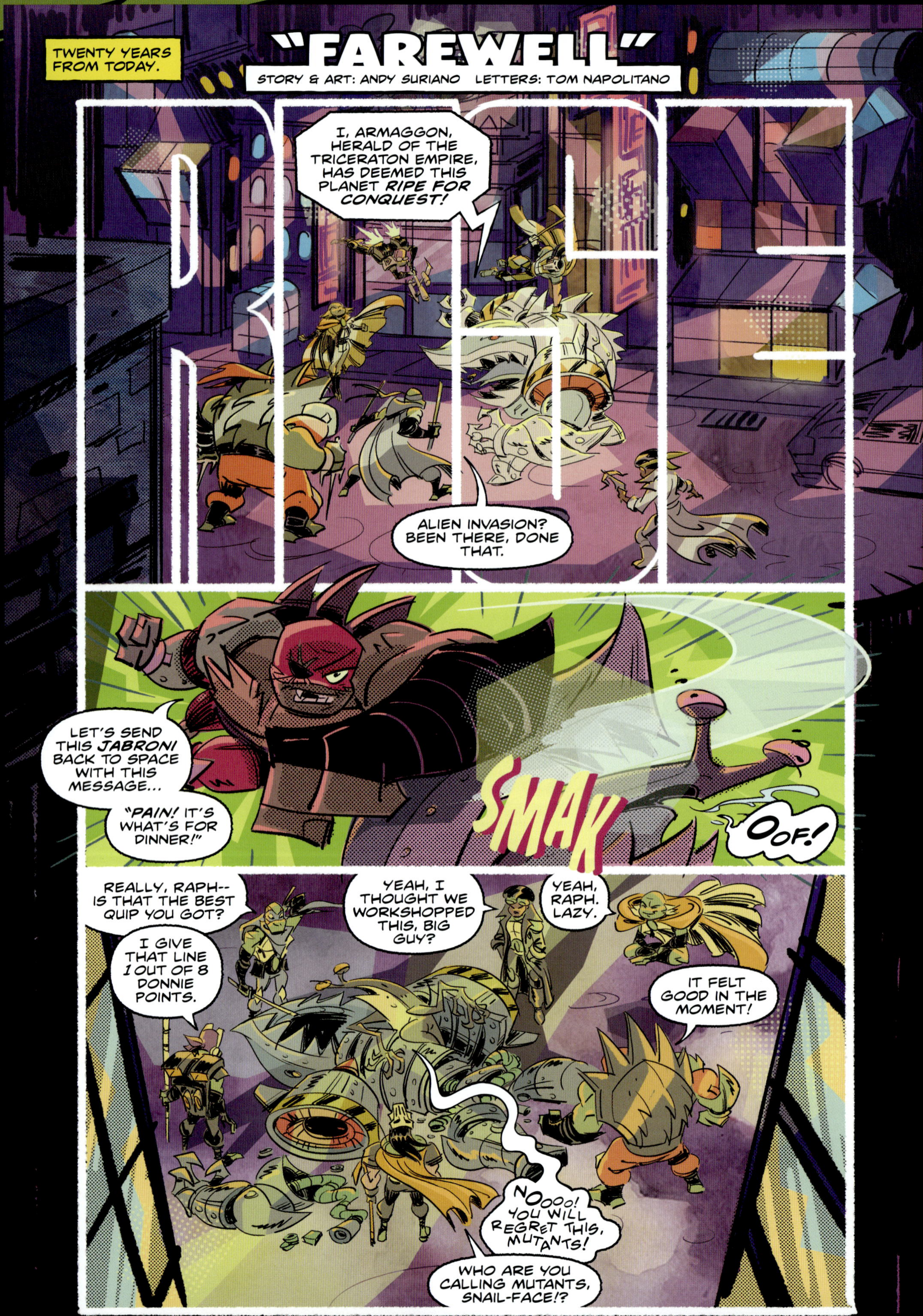
TWENTY YEARS FROM TODAY.
"FAREWELL"
STORY & ART: ANDY SURIANO LETTERS: TOM NAPOLITANO
I, ARMAGGON, HERALD OF THE TRICERATON EMPIRE, HAS DEEMED THIS PLANET RIPE FOR CONQUEST!
ALIEN INVASION? BEEN THERE, DONE THAT.
LET'S SEND THIS JABRONI BACK TO SPACE WITH THIS MESSAGE...
"PAIN! IT'S WHAT'S FOR DINNER!"
SMAK
OOF!
REALLY, RAPH-- IS THAT THE BEST QUIP YOU GOT?
I GIVE THAT LINE 1 OUT OF 8 DONNIE POINTS.
YEAH, I THOUGHT WE WORKSHOPPED THIS, BIG GUY?
YEAH, RAPH. LAZY.
IT FELT GOOD IN THE MOMENT!
NOOOO! YOU WILL REGRET THIS, MUTANTS!
WHO ARE YOU CALLING MUTANTS, SNAIL-FACE!?

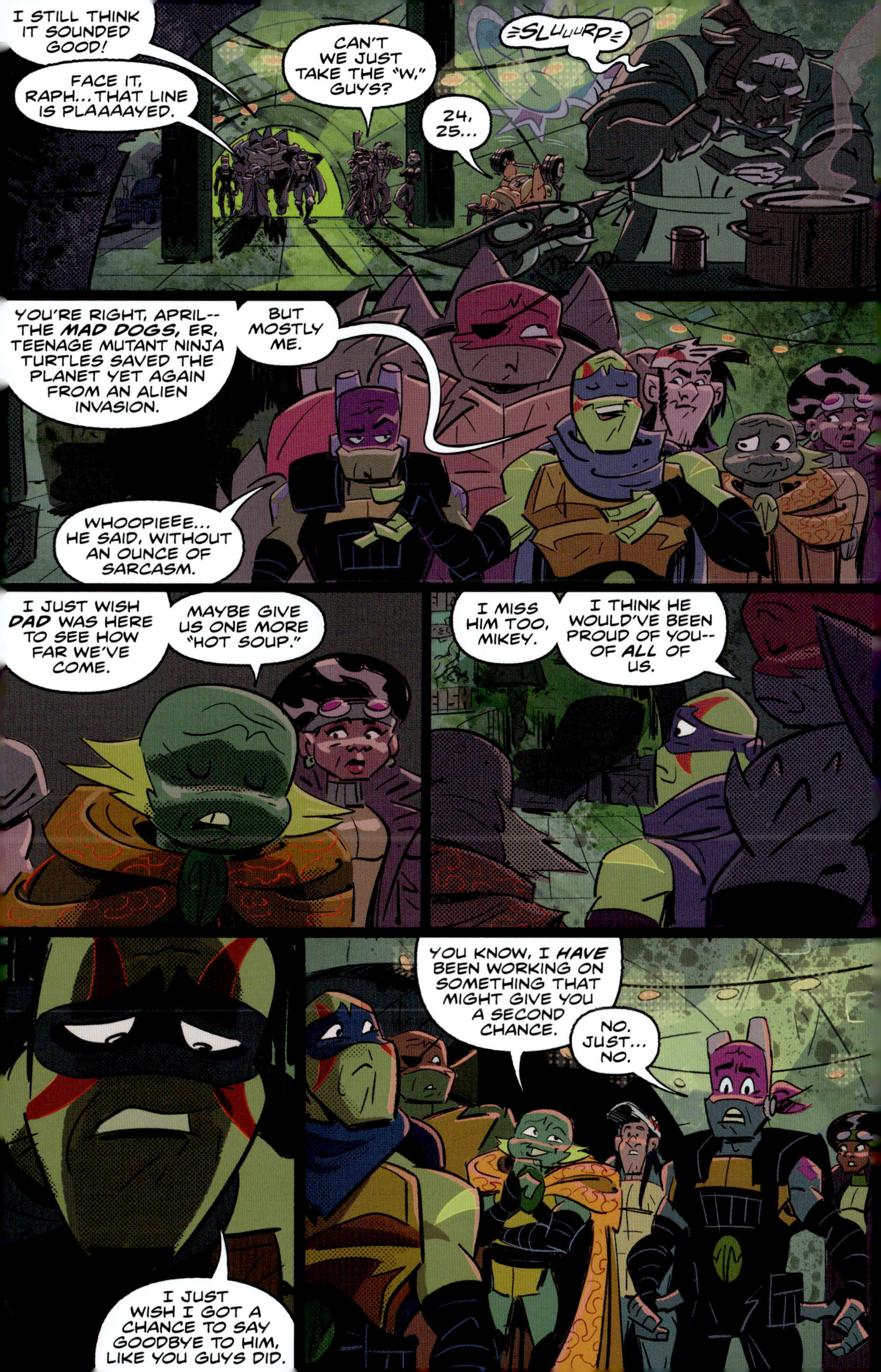
I STILL THINK IT SOUNDED GOOD!
FACE IT, RAPH... THAT LINE IS PLAAAAYED.
CAN'T WE JUST TAKE THE "W," GUYS?
24, 25...
SLUUURP
YOU'RE RIGHT, APRIL-- THE MAD DOGS, ER, TEENAGE MUTANT NINJA TURTLES SAVED THE PLANET YET AGAIN FROM AN ALIEN INVASION.
BUT MOSTLY ME.
WHOOPIEEE... HE SAID, WITHOUT AN OUNCE OF SARCASM.
I JUST WISH DAD WAS HERE TO SEE HOW FAR WE'VE COME.
MAYBE GIVE US ONE MORE "HOT SOUP."
I MISS HIM TOO, MIKEY.
I THINK HE WOULD'VE BEEN PROUD OF YOU-- OF ALL OF US.
I JUST WISH I GOT A CHANCE TO SAY GOODBYE TO HIM, LIKE YOU GUYS DID.
YOU KNOW, I HAVE BEEN WORKING ON SOMETHING THAT MIGHT GIVE YOU A SECOND CHANCE.
NO. JUST... NO.

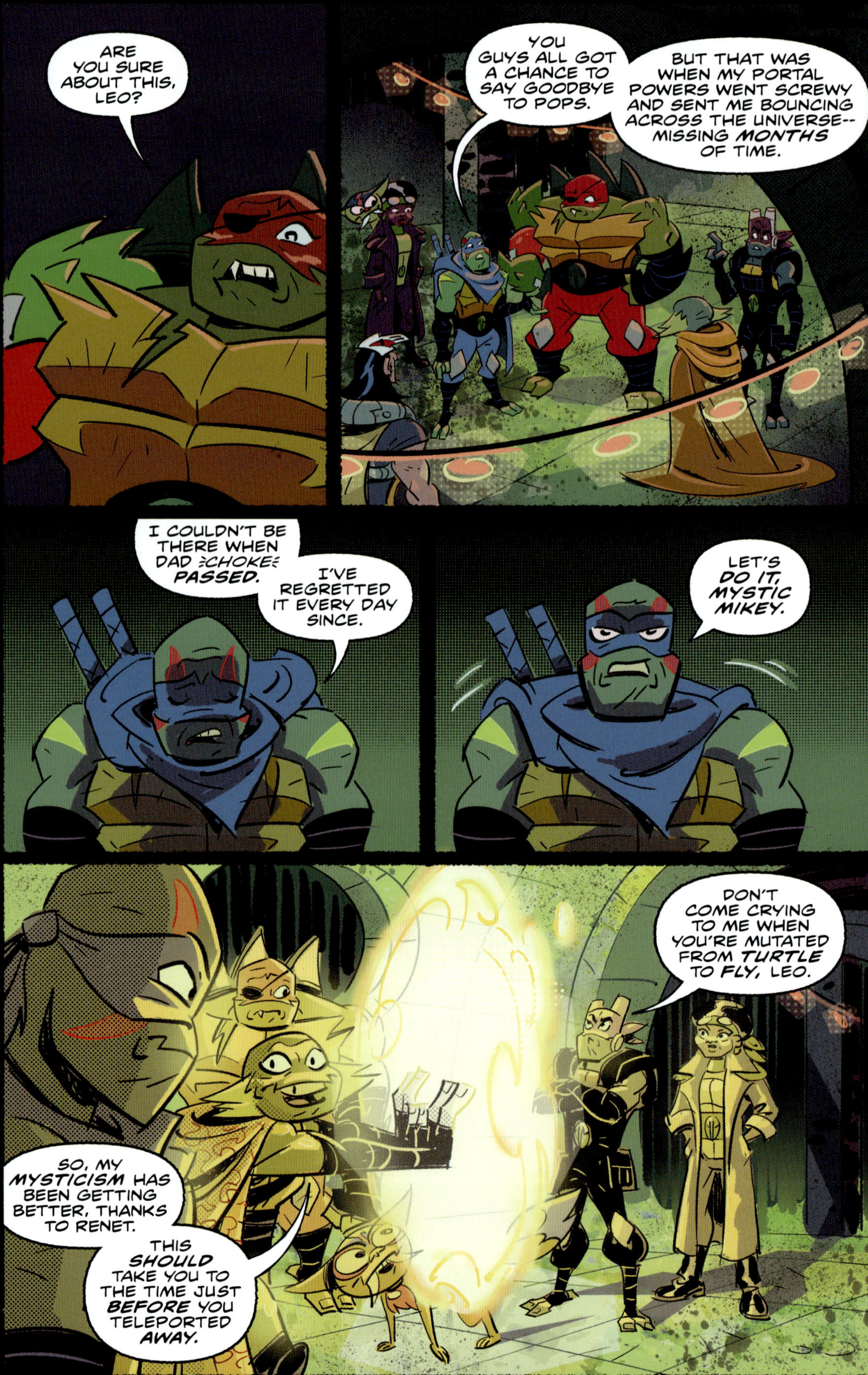
ARE YOU SURE ABOUT THIS, LEO?
YOU GUYS ALL GOT A CHANCE TO SAY GOODBYE TO POPS.
BUT THAT WAS WHEN MY PORTAL POWERS WENT SCREWY AND SENT ME BOUNCING ACROSS THE UNIVERSE-- MISSING MONTHS OF TIME.
I COULDN'T BE THERE WHEN DAD *CHOKE* PASSED.
I'VE REGRETTED IT EVERY DAY SINCE.
LET'S DO IT, MYSTIC MIKEY.
SO, MY MYSTICISM HAS BEEN GETTING BETTER, THANKS TO RENET.
THIS SHOULD TAKE YOU TO THE TIME JUST BEFORE YOU TELEPORTED AWAY.
DON'T COME CRYING TO ME WHEN YOU'RE MUTATED FROM TURTLE TO FLY, LEO.

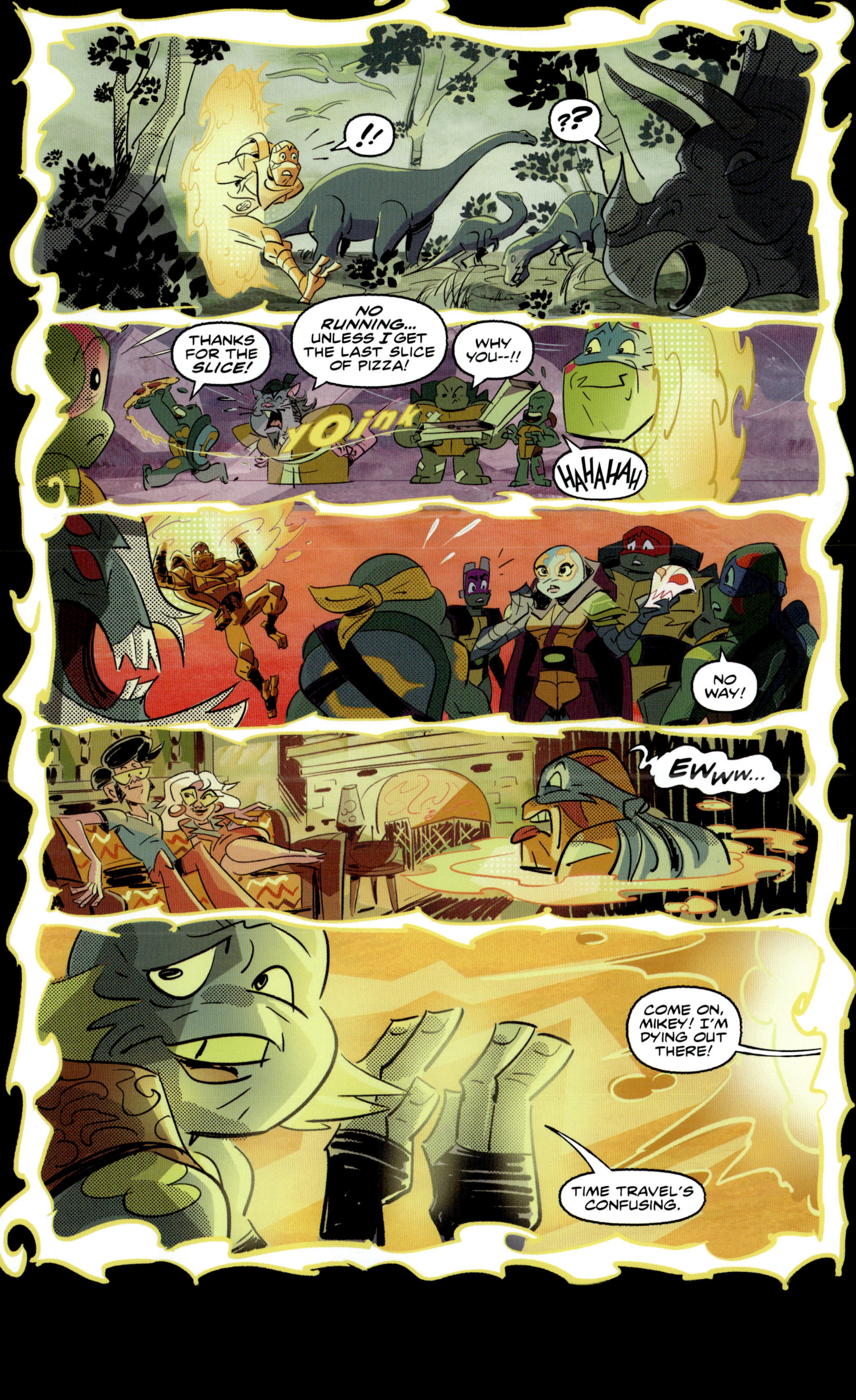
!!
??
THANKS FOR THE SLICE!
NO RUNNING... UNLESS I GET THE LAST SLICE OF PIZZA!
WHY YOU--!!
YOink
HAHAHAH
NO WAY!
EWWW...
COME ON, MIKEY! I'M DYING OUT THERE!
TIME TRAVEL'S CONFUSING.

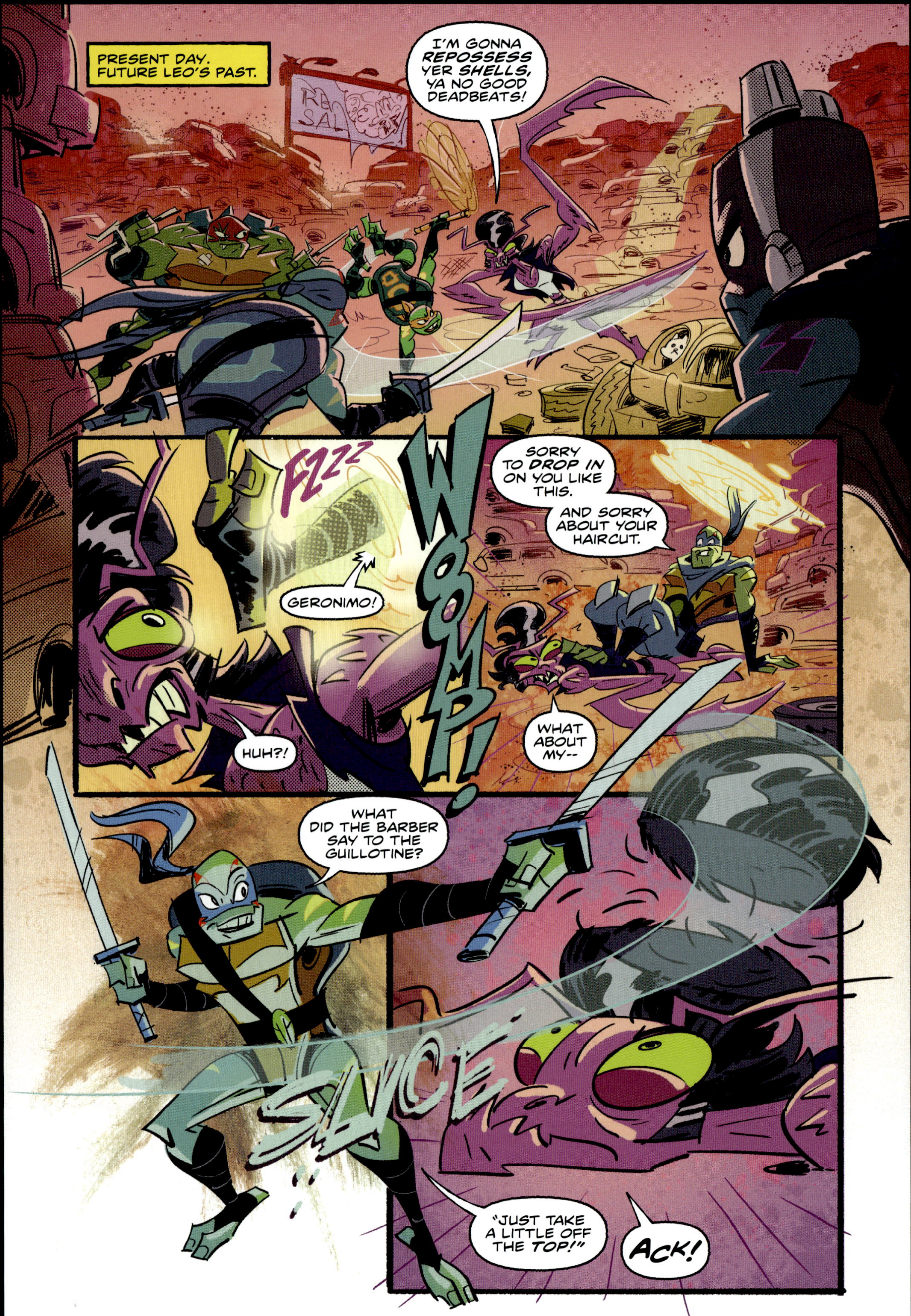
PRESENT DAY.
FUTURE LEO'S PAST.
I'M GONNA REPOSSESS YER SHELLS, YA NO GOOD DEADBEATS!
FZZZ
GERONIMO!
WOOMP!!
SORRY TO DROP IN ON YOU LIKE THIS.
AND SORRY ABOUT YOUR HAIRCUT.
HUH?!
WHAT ABOUT MY--
WHAT DID THE BARBER SAY TO THE GUILLOTINE?
SLICE
"JUST TAKE A LITTLE OFF THE TOP!"
ACK!

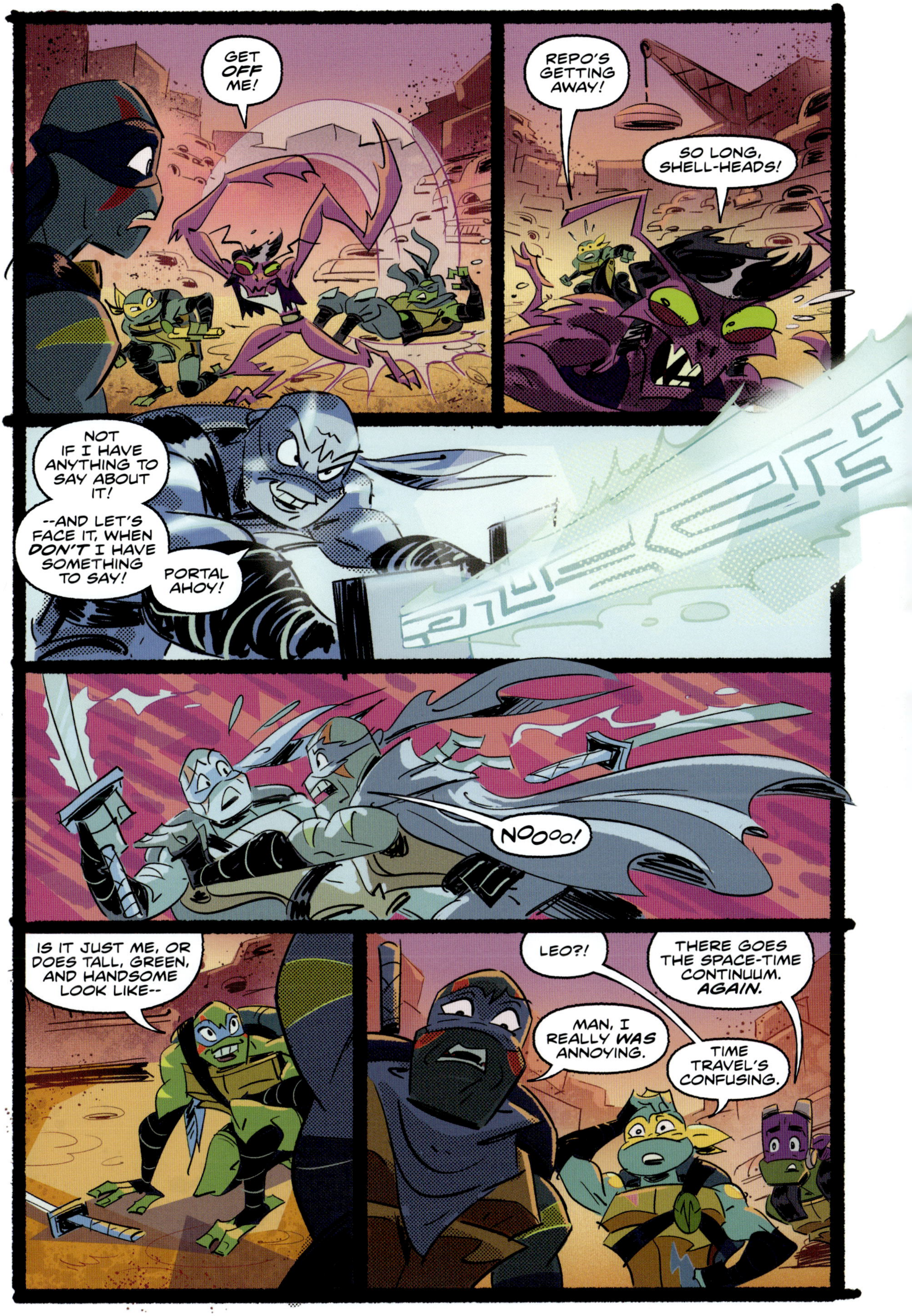
GET OFF ME!
REPO'S GETTING AWAY!
SO LONG, SHELL-HEADS!
NOT IF I HAVE ANYTHING TO SAY ABOUT IT!
--AND LET'S FACE IT, WHEN DON'T I HAVE SOMETHING TO SAY!
PORTAL AHOY!
NOOOO!
IS IT JUST ME, OR DOES TALL, GREEN, AND HANDSOME LOOK LIKE--
LEO?!
THERE GOES THE SPACE-TIME CONTINUUM. AGAIN.
MAN, I REALLY WAS ANNOYING.
TIME TRAVEL'S CONFUSING.

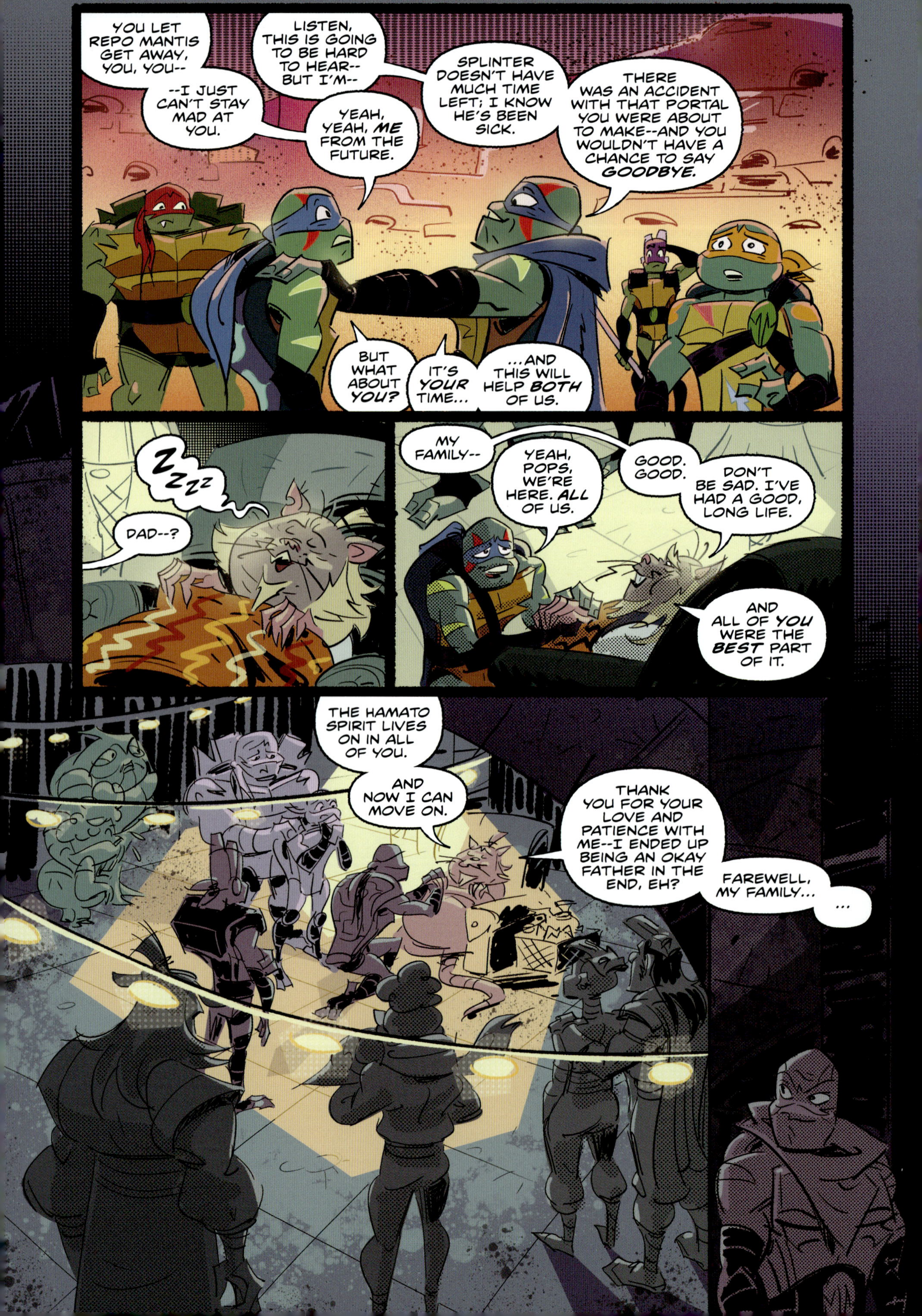
YOU LET REPO MANTIS GET AWAY, YOU, YOU--
--I JUST CAN'T STAY MAD AT YOU.
LISTEN, THIS IS GOING TO BE HARD TO HEAR--BUT I'M--
YEAH, YEAH, ME FROM THE FUTURE.
SPLINTER DOESN'T HAVE MUCH TIME LEFT; I KNOW HE'S BEEN SICK.
THERE WAS AN ACCIDENT WITH THAT PORTAL YOU WERE ABOUT TO MAKE--AND YOU WOULDN'T HAVE A CHANCE TO SAY GOODBYE.
BUT WHAT ABOUT YOU?
IT'S YOUR TIME...
...AND THIS WILL HELP BOTH OF US.
ZZZZ
DAD--?
MY FAMILY--
YEAH, POPS, WE'RE HERE. ALL OF US.
GOOD. GOOD.
DON'T BE SAD. I'VE HAD A GOOD, LONG LIFE.
AND ALL OF YOU WERE THE BEST PART OF IT.
THE HAMATO SPIRIT LIVES ON IN ALL OF YOU.
AND NOW I CAN MOVE ON.
THANK YOU FOR YOUR LOVE AND PATIENCE WITH ME--I ENDED UP BEING AN OKAY FATHER IN THE END, EH?
FAREWELL, MY FAMILY...
...

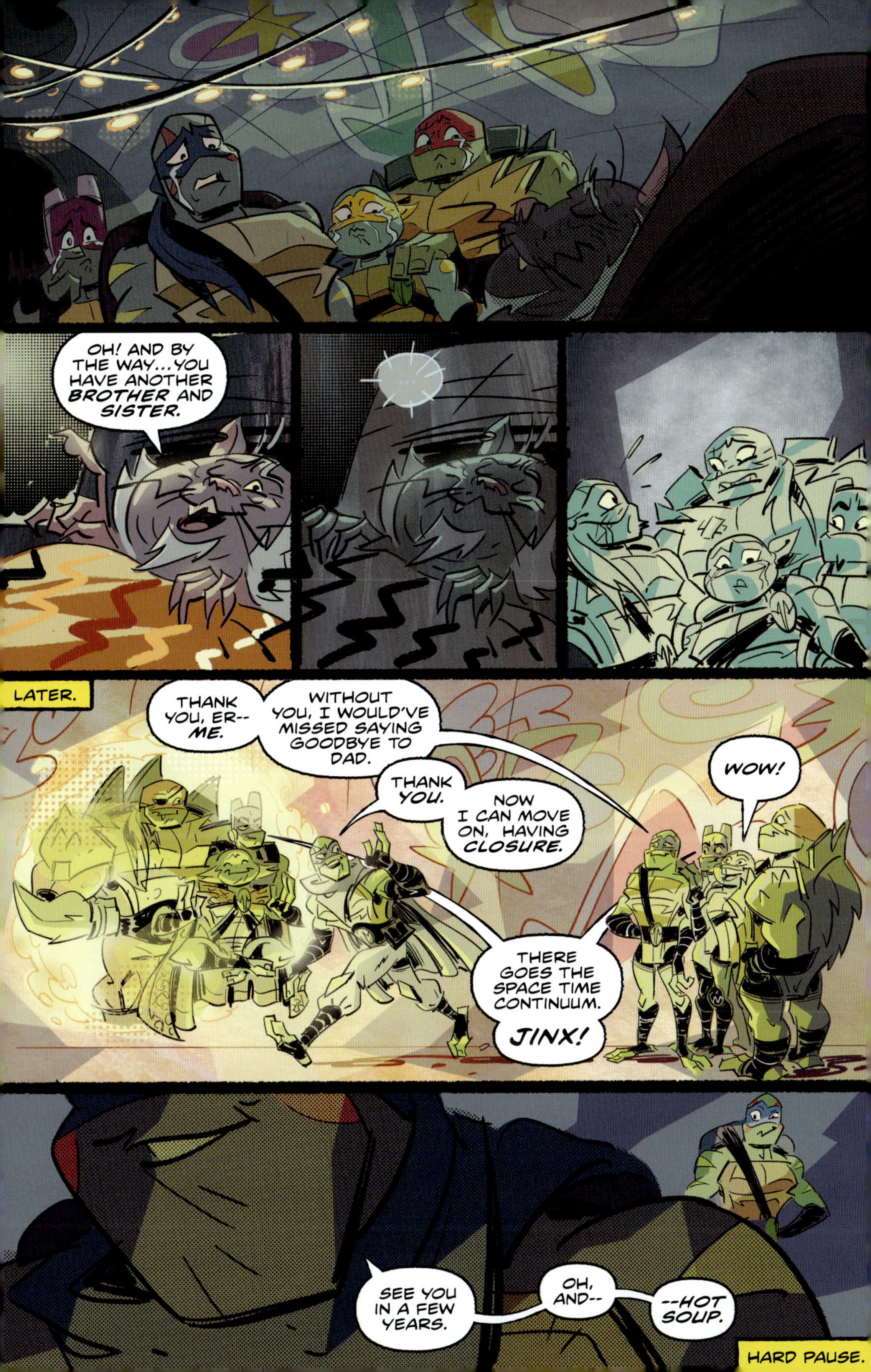
OH! AND BY THE WAY...YOU HAVE ANOTHER BROTHER AND SISTER.
LATER.
THANK YOU, ER-- ME.
WITHOUT YOU, I WOULD'VE MISSED SAYING GOODBYE TO DAD.
THANK YOU.
NOW I CAN MOVE ON, HAVING CLOSURE.
WOW!
THERE GOES THE SPACE TIME CONTINUUM.
JINX!
SEE YOU IN A FEW YEARS.
OH, AND--
--HOT SOUP.
HARD PAUSE.

LOOKING BACK

REFLECTIONS ON THE MAKING OF *RISE*

ANDY SURIANO: Oh, the places we were going to go! Ant and I always had a blueprint of where we were taking the series, so after we'd outlined an entire season 3 (and getting it greenlit), we were so excited to share the culmination of storylines we'd set up since Day One.

Had season 2 continued as planned, we would've been introduced to Karai much sooner, giving viewers ample time to get invested in her. The payoff of Big Mama's assistant would reveal that she would indeed be another turtle sibling, and we would get to see what being raised by a spider mama would do to a teenaged mutant vs. the warmth of Splinter's (albeit controversial) parenting style. We had even set this up by showing *six* baby turtles initially, of the four Splinter/Lou Jitsu was able to save (did anyone catch that?).

Six? Yes. There was indeed a no-nonsense eldest brother out there as well that would shake up the family dynamics further, especially for Raph and Leo. Baron Draxum would reveal that indeed there were two more siblings out there, one right under their nose in Big Mama's Battle Nexus, while another was trapped across space and possibly another dimension (opening further Krang storylines). Season 2 was going to end with these revelations, while season 3 would start off with our team(s) being separated into two groups led by Splinter and Baron Draxum to rescue their long-lost family members. Just think of the toys we could've gotten...

To say *Rise* was a career high point for me would be an understatement. Nickelodeon allowed me the freedom to flex all of my creative muscles. I had always said if I had a show, I'd make sure artists knew they were more than a wrist, and I had the opportunity to employ that theory. I feel proud of how Ant and I ran the production(s), of how we empowered everyone on the crew (and Flying Bark) to contribute, giving them a stake in what their hard labor yielded. It was fun watching our crazy experiment come to life—and to continue taking the creative risks we set out to do. We could've made just another TMNT series that everyone knew and expected, but Ant and I are storytellers and artists and used this opportunity to push ourselves and challenge an audience's expectations and, at times, comfort level. We told stories from the heart, from our own experiences as fathers, sons, brothers, and friends, and we got to tell them with an incredible backdrop of hidden cities, battle nexuses, and bonkers action sequences. We fought for a path to tell surprising, exciting new stories with unexpected outcomes to characters audiences were all too familiar with for years.

I'd say a high note from the entire experience for me was surprisingly at our lowest point of production, when Ant and I presented our talented, hardworking team with the unfortunate news that the series was prematurely ending and that we could either ride out the remainder of time and contracts doing nothing but looking for new jobs or attempt to do the near impossible: Wrap up two-plus seasons of stories in four episodes with half the time to do them. The response is one I will cherish forever—every single crew member emphatically wanted to stay and do the monumental task of giving our heroes an exciting, emotional send-off they deserved. In my nearly 30 years in this industry, this was completely unheard of. That is how much this show meant to us and how much the fervent fans and supporters inspired us to keep taking the more challenging, ambitious road over and over. We did this for us as artists and creators, we did this for the fans, and finally, we did this for the Mad Dogs.

ANT WARD: The development of *Rise* was really a once-in-a-lifetime opportunity. Andy and I were on the same page from the beginning of what we wanted to do. We were able to assemble one of the best teams in the industry to help us create it, and we had incredible support during development from Nickelodeon, which allowed us to have fun, be playful, and take the franchise in a unique direction. Mad Dogs for life!

We were only getting started to explore the wonderfully unique world of *Rise*. There was a larger arc that we were beginning to lean into, setting up a season 3. The Krang would have played a much larger role, as we would have resolved most of the Splinter and Hamato story. The stakes would have gotten bigger on a galactic scale while also maintaining *Rise's* boisterous and out-of-this-world style.

It might sound silly, but I stick with the old motto "Go big or go home" and swing for the fences. It would have been easy for Andy and me to take a path creating this show that was far more traditional for TMNT, but in doing so, we would just be retreading what had already been done by so many incredible TMNT creators before us. It was always important to us that *Rise* stood unique alongside its franchise peers. This was never a reboot but rather a reimagining. To the future generation of artists and storytellers, stick to your guns, tell the stories you want to tell, and don't let the Hollywood machine beat you down.

While it is heartbreaking that we won't be making more *Rise*, I don't think it's really fair to say a true goodbye to the series, as it still finds new fans every day, inspires, and gives hope to so many around the world. We have an incredible fan base and have had the most astonishing crew that any creator could have the fortune to collaborate with. I hope to see the fan base grow in the future as more people find the show and are open to the new ideas it presents.

OMAR BENSON MILLER: Thank you all so much for accepting me and giving me a chance to entertain you all and your kids. I still keep in contact with the legion of *Rise* fans via social media and conventions, and believe me I feel the love. I'm gonna keep Raph alive... LIKE A BOSS!!!

BEN SCHWARTZ: I would say thank you to that incredible crew. The writing, directing, and animation on *Rise* was unbelievable. And I would say thank you to the fans. I know it's not easy when a new version of a series everyone loves comes into the zeitgeist, but after we showed you what we wanted to do and how Andy and Ant were going to put it all together, people really started to fall in love and support the show. I really wish we had more episodes to show you what else we were capable of, but thrilled that we got to play as much as we did and love that new people are finding the show every day. Thanks for all of the support. Turtle Power.

JOSH BRENER: Man, I really, really miss working on *Rise*. Tony Gama-Lobo, the brilliant and hilarious head writer behind the series, and I will regularly text things to each other like "We really didn't know how good we had it back then." And it's so true. It was just the most fun, joyous project with the absolute best people. And those were really the good old days. Back before the pandemic, we all got to be together every week to record the show...all the voice actors, all the writers, our amazing casting team, and the GOAT, Rob Paulsen, voice directing. I mean, we would just laugh our...shells...off, and then occasionally get some work done. The best! And of course, that kind of magic always starts at the top. Andy and Ant just built this incredible creative environment, and produced such a funny, amazing, delightfully bonkers show. Here's hoping Donnie creates a time machine so we can all go back!

BRANDON MYCHAL SMITH: This show impacted me in ways I can't even explain and can only be represented by a phrase I coined and created during the series run, which I think speaks to the emotions of everyone who was an integral part of this legacy property, *Rise of the Teenage Mutant Ninja Turtles*, and that is "OMIIIIIIIGOOOOOOOOOSSSH." What a ride, what a time, what a humbling journey together we had with the sensational producers, writers, animators, crew members, and fearless executives at the most amazing network on the planet, Nickelodeon. Thank you from Michelangelo, a.k.a. Brandon Mychal Smith! COWAAAAABUNGAAAA, BABY!!!

JOSH RILEY BROWN: *Rise* was a show about brotherhood, and the spirit of that was very much a part of the writers room. There were jokes, shenanigans, a tower made out of trash, and a real sense that the people in that room always had your back. Ron, Russ, Ian, Dale, and Tony were very much the same sort of colorful, goofy, supportive characters they were writing about. They found me as a baby turtle and welcomed me into their sewer lair because that's what *Rise* was all about.

JEFFRY CHOZON: It really was an honor and privilege to work on both the show and the movie. TMNT will always be special, but the crew is the heart and soul of the production. I helped a bit in the middle and end of the series, and we almost single-handedly made this entire movie during one of the toughest times in history—the pandemic. It was such an accomplishment made possible by a stellar production team who had to design a work-from-home pipeline from scratch. I still remember one Friday, we were instructed to move our workstations home to test out the new system for a week, but then we never came back in until years later after the movie was wrapped. The studio was a time capsule. Carl was an amazing AD, and developing the style with the team while building upon the marvel of the series was tremendously fun! I learned a ton on this production and will always be grateful for the support of the people who challenged me artistically and of course to the fans who we made the show for! Cheers to you!

THANH DANG: *Rise* has always been a special project to me. I'm so proud to have been part of a team I truly admired—everyone was really talented. Andy knew how to bring together a great team and set us all up to win. I'll always remember the laughs, the hustle, and the magic we made together. *Rise* was also a love letter to the fans. We honored the generations of Turtles before us and proudly carried the torch (and the nunchucks) during our turn. From pushing the designs to bring out each Turtle's personality to telling stories that deepened their bonds, every episode was crafted with love and passion. We tucked Easter eggs into every corner of the show, hoping fans would be as excited to find them as we were to hide them. Home is where you find the most comfort. For the Turtles, it was the sewer, the smell of pizza, and 122 1/8 (you're probably stepping on it). For me, it was *Rise*.

IAN BUSCH: *Rise* was such a beautiful show, with so many talented artists and writers dreaming up such an embarrassment of riches. I consider myself so fortunate to have been included in the creative process and I'm still elated I got to put so much of my creative self up on the screen. I look back on both the people and the final product with never-ending pride. Cheers to all.

RUSS CARNEY: Working on *Rise* was one of the most creatively satisfying experiences of my career to date. Ant, Andy, and Tony gave us so much creative freedom: freedom to get goofy, freedom to take chances with the characters, and freedom to, essentially, manage all of our episodes from start to finish, from voice records to dialogue edit sessions. I really feel like my own personality and sense of humor are inherent to this version of the Turtles, April, Splinter, and all the rest. It was a phenomenal experience for me, and I very much enjoyed working with all of the creative people in our crew, and I learned a lot from the experience. I'm also immensely grateful to our fans, who are not only consistently supportive of the series, but they are also so supportive and kind to one another! Thank you all!

RON CORCILLO: The *Rise* cast and crew was the greatest group I've ever worked with, from our fellow writers and script coordinators to the amazingly talented cast and the phenomenal artists who brought it all to life. But even more incredible was getting to know the fandom that grew and grew even long after the show was done. It's amazing how committed the fans are, not just to the show, but also to supporting each other and everyone who worked on the project. We love you, *Rise* stans!

MORGAN HILLEBRAND: *Rise* was my very first job in the animation industry. I began as a storyboard revisionist on my team's first episode, and I felt so unbelievably excited and grateful to be surrounded by such talented and kind people. Because everyone on the team was always inspiring each other, I evolved so much as an artist over the course of the show. We put so many long and hard hours into every moment of each episode, and the team really grew and bonded through that. Some of my fondest memories on *Rise* were our weekly Thursday game nights. A bunch of us would gather around the PlayStation after work and play all sorts of horror and choice-based story games, laughing and shouting over each other. To this day, many of them remain my closest and most cherished friends. I'm so happy that we've continued to work together on various projects, play many more games, and even travel together. It's a cheesy saying, but it really does feel like the real treasure was the friends we made along the way.

TONY GAMA-LOBO: I will be forever grateful to Ant and Andy for bringing me onto *Rise*. Coming from the world of prime-time adult comedy, I kinda thought it was going to be just this fun, goofy kids show. I could not have been more wrong. The stories and characters were both hilarious and moving, the designs and animation were jaw-dropping, and the world was truly inspiring. Honestly, I was not prepared for the talented people I would work with—starting at the top with Ant and Andy to the board artists, designers, directors, editors, and god-tier cast. Everyone blew my mind on a daily basis. I learned so much about the creative process from the whole crew. Above all else I will cherish my time with the writers: Ron, Russ, Ian, Dale, and Josh. A truly tremendous group with boundless creativity and a deep love of storytelling. *Rise* was a very special show that ended too soon. I was lucky to continue with the movie, which I co-wrote with my extraordinarily gifted writing partner, Becky May. We got to be with the boys until the very end. The four-part finale and movie are some of the work I'm most proud of in my career. And I miss it constantly.

ALICIA CHAN: My time on *Rise* was a very formative point in my career as an artist! I learned so much from my peers and directors creatively and had the opportunity to try new things as a board artist that can be hard to pull off in the TV pipeline. Working with Flying Bark as an animation studio was amazing, and getting to see them elevate our work even further was always inspiring to see! Every facet of the *Rise* crew (story, art, production, writing) was full of incredibly talented, wonderful people that brought a lot of enthusiasm and fun to the day-to-day work as well! I made a lot of lifelong friends from my time on *Rise*, and I am grateful every day that it brought us together.

Thank you to all the fans of *Rise* who saw the fun and passion we put into our work on the show! No one achieves anything alone—the support and love you all have given to the show is just as powerful as the work we put in to create it.

JJ CONWAY: *Rise of the TMNT* was the most formative experience of my career. Ant, Andy, and Alan put so much trust in me, allowing me to grow into the artist I am today. I'll never be able to express the full depth of my gratitude towards them, but I'll carry the lessons they taught me about storytelling and leadership with me for the rest of my life.

Not only was it one of the most creatively rewarding shows I've ever worked on, it has one of the most talented fan bases I've ever seen. Their bottomless creativity will never cease to amaze and inspire me. It's an honor to have been a part of such a lightning-in-a-bottle crew and series.

JERMAINE JOSE: *Rise* was a rush the whole way through. Making it, being a fan of it, I'm incredibly grateful to have been a part of it. It was a wild take on the franchise and exactly the kind of show I would have loved as a kid. It's bold, dynamic, silly, and heartfelt! The crew was an amazing group of people to work with, and Ant and Andy gave us such a creative atmosphere it eventually all felt like play. But even then, I felt like I had to step up my game to earn my place. New style, new format, new way of doing things. It challenged me to the core, but I was so glad to hang out with these Turtles again and meet so many amazing people along the way. Cheers to the *Rise* crew, everyone who had a hand in the making—y'all are incredible, and can't wait to work with you again in the future. HOT SOUP!

IDA HEM: *Rise of the TMNT* was my very first job as a character designer, and it was quite a surreal experience to work alongside such phenomenal talent! Everybody loved the work that was being made, and we were all more and more impressed by the animation coming in each episode. The show has a special place in my heart and has given me amazing memories and lifelong friends I will cherish forever! Hot Soup!

ALEXIS PAGE: Being on *Rise* was such a unique experience, and I will never forget it. I am so, so grateful for all the friends I've made during my time. This was a really formative time in my career, and I'm so glad I was able to experience it with my teammates on *Rise*. And thank you to Andy for taking a chance on me.

CARL BEU: I have so much gratitude for *Rise* and the people I got to know along this journey. I hope seeing our creative process here inspires you in a small way to take your own artistic risks and dare something great.

SEBASTIAN MONTES: *Rise* was one of the most talented and driven crews I have ever had the pleasure of working with. And this book serves as a love letter for all the hard work they have put in. Thank you for this, Colin. And thank you to all the fans who have enjoyed our wacky show.

NANCY RAMIREZ: In all my years working in animation production, *Rise of the TMNT* is hands down the best, most fun and wildest show I've ever had the pleasure to work on. At the very start of it all, I was one of the first production members to roll onto the show in season 1. I got to see everyone come on the show one by one and grow into this incredible production crew—a dream production crew! It was my first time working on an action-adventure show and I didn't know what to expect. During my time on the show, I learned so much under Ant and Andy's leadership. I also learned a lot from the best management and production team! Thank you, Vlad, Stephanie, and Tanya! You all made every workday fun. I can honestly say I looked forward to coming to work every day. We became a family, and I miss working with this amazing team. Watching back the series and the movie, you can just tell that so much love and passion was poured into this. I hope that the fandom will cherish the artwork and the show for years to come. Please enjoy! It honestly makes me so happy seeing there's still so much love and respect for this show. Thank you for keeping this show alive! I love seeing everyone's reels and compilations online. It warms my heart! Forever a Turtle! Bootyshaker9000!!!

TANYA MELENDEZ: My time on *Rise of the Teenage Mutant Ninja Turtles* was an absolute career highlight that has left an indelible mark both personally and professionally. While the show and movie themselves are incredibly beautiful, entertaining, heartfelt, and additive to the already full world of TMNT, the people who worked on the projects and gave it their all left a lasting impact on everyone involved. For my part, I was able to grow so much during my time on *Rise*, starting as a production assistant and coordinator, and becoming the production manager on the series and later associate producer on the *Rise* movie. I wasn't alone; it was wonderful to see so many people grow and thrive during their *Rise* journey, which wouldn't have been possible without such supportive and open-minded leadership (shout-out to Andy and Ant!). I also got the opportunity to test for a Color Design opening on the series, and while it was tremendously intimidating to put myself out there artistically, it was a risk that paid off and opened the door for much color work to come, including providing the color design for the majority of the *Rise* movie.

Contributing to the world of *Rise* in a variety of ways allowed me a multifaceted view of what made it shine and a greater appreciation for all its moving parts and invaluable team players. The integration of so many talented, hardworking, and collaborative individuals was truly lightning in a bottle; the team would come away from crew screenings and design reviews invigorated, inspired to get back to work. It was an energizing experience full of mutual respect and genuine joy. This passion is mirrored by the wonderful and talented fans the show and movie have garnered through the years.

The series came to a close during the first year of the pandemic, while the movie was simultaneously ramping up, and the team met every new challenge with a can-do spirit and the determination to deliver an amazing product, even during such trying times. When we came together in-person to screen the movie quite a while later, the pride, camaraderie, and appreciation were palpable. I will always be immensely grateful for my time on *Rise*—nothing will ever compare to it. I'm so happy we got to do the incredible work that we did, and hopefully the fans will continue to enjoy the property for years to come.

CINDY Y. AVILA: I've been lucky enough to have worked on three adaptations of the Teenage Mutant Ninja Turtles so far in my career and, like many, grew up loving the original. Each take holds something dear to the fans. With *Rise*, this was a very imaginative take on the TMNT universe, taking the familiar story we all grew up knowing and reworking it in the most unique way I've ever seen it! Andy, Ant, and our writers weren't afraid to reach beyond what we've seen before, add new intriguing characters, push the style and even change up the structure of our heroes, and the immensely talented team, week after week, would put their vision into fruition that was just so much fun! I am so very thankful to have even played a small part in the making of this series and movie, and every time I think back to the *Rise* days, I can't help but smile, and I am forever proud of the entire crew and the outcome of the work we all put into it together. I love you, *Rise* team!

CHELSEA JAUREGUI: Getting to work on *Rise* was just "wow!" This was my first time working on an action show, and from Day One I was blown away by everyone's talent, the show's complexity, and how visually stunning every element was, from the boards, to the designs, color, and animation! Everyone really gave it their all! I feel incredibly lucky to have been a part the Production team, and I'm forever grateful to Ant and Andy for taking a chance on me as an artist as well. I truly had the time of my life on this show, and I'll always miss working with the amazing people who made it all so special!

THE REAL MAD DOGS

AARON MCDONALD - Inbetween Animator
ABE AUDISH - Director
ADAM ARNOLD - Animatic Editor
ADAM DIX - Character Designer
ADAM GUNN - Background Design
ADELINE JIE - Inbetween Animator
ADRIAN FIJALEK - FX Animator
ADRIANA DURAN - Technical Animator
AGATHA OZDOWSKA - Production Coordinator
AGGELOS PAPANTONIOU - Key Animator
AHMED ALI AL HASNAWI - Character Layout Artist
ALAN LOPEZ - Inbetween Animator, Key Animator
ALAN RUIVIVAR LOPEZ - Inbetween Animator
ALAN WAN - Supervising Director, Main Title Design, Director, Supervising Producer, Storyboard Artist
ALEX DELIGIANNIS - Color Stylist
ALEXA PASZTOR - Character Layout Artist
ALEXIA GATES-FOALE - Supervising Producer
ALEXIS NADINE MOUTON PAGE - Character Designer
ALICIA CHAN - Storyboard Artist
ALLAN CORTEZ - Key Animator
ALLISON SMITH - Storyboard Artist
ALY EL DIN - Inbetween Animator, Key Animator
ALYSHA CHUA - FX Animator, Cleanup Ink and Paint Artist, Technical Animator
AMANDA TRAN - Production Assistant
ANASTASIA TURAEVA - Key Animator
ANDREA BEDELIS - Production Manager, Production Coordinator, Associate Line Producer
ANDREA HENNEN - Casting Director
ANDREW BATTYE - Compositing
ANDREW KIM - Storyboard Revisionist, Storyboard Artist
ANDREW LEBLANC - FX Animator
ANDY SURIANO - Co-Executive Producer, Art Director, Main Character Design, Development, Director
ANGELO VILAR - Background Layout Designer, Character Designer
ANNA MARTINO - Senior Manager, Archive and Resource Library
ANNA NICOLSON - Technical Animator
ANNABELLE LUICIEN - Inbetween Animator
ANNE CHIEM - Technical Animator
ANNE-FLORE AUSSANT - Line Producer
ANT WARD - Co-Executive Producer, Main Title Design, Development, Director
ASHE JACOBSON - Storyboard Artist, Assistant Director
ASHLEIGH CHOW - Animation Coordinator, Production Coordinator
AYON BHAKTA - Cleanup, Ink and Paint Artist, Technical Animator, Inbetween Animator
BACHIR KAZZI - CG Generalist
BARBARA STEPHEN - Managing Director
BEN CHOI - Storyboard Artist
BEN GRIMSHAW - FX Animator
BEN LEE - Background Design Supervisor
BENEDITO ANTONIO DE OLIVEIRA SILVA - Inbetween Animator
BENJAMIN FORMAKER-OLIVAS - Archive and Resource Library
BENJAMIN JONES - Inbetween Animator
BILL NORTHCOTT - Key Animator
BILLY MARTIN - Character Designer
BILLY MPETHA - Key Animator
BILLY WEBER - Editor
BOBBY THAYER - Casting Assistant
BOBBY WALKER - Background Painter
BOOM BOX POST - Post-Production Sound Services
BOY LACAMPUENGA - Inbetween Animator
BRAD MEYER - Sound Editor
BRANDON CHUNG - Inbetween Animator, Key Animator
BRANDON CUELLAR - Background Layout Designer
BRANDON DENMARK - Inbetween Animator, Key Animator
BRANDON HOANG - Current Series Management
BRANDON MCKINNEY - Storyboard Artist
BRENDAN CLOGHER - Director
BRANDON CUELLAR - Background Design and Paint
BRENT SKINNER - Animation Technical Assistant, Cleanup, Ink and Paint Artist, Technical Animator
BRIAN HILL - Production Assistant
BRIAN KAUFMAN - Inbetween Animator, Key Animator
BRITANY VALDEZ - Archivist
BRYCE COLLINS - Character Designer
BRYCE PEMBERTON - Inbetween Animator
C.J. KINYON - Machine Room
CARINA GALVAO - Key Animator
CARL BEU - Color Supervisor, Art Director
CARLOS PEREZ - Character Layout Artist
CARLOS VASQUEZ - Production Assistant
CAROL MA - Foley Editor
CARTOON CONRAD PRODUCTIONS INC. - Animation Services
CASSEY KUO - Storyboard Revisionist, Storyboard Artist
CHEEKS CHICO REQUIERON - Cleanup Ink and Paint Artist, Key Animator, Inbetween Animator
CHELSEA JAUREGUI - Production Assistant, Production Coordinator, Color Stylist
CHERIE HAGUE - CG Generalist
CHRIS CHAPMAN - Key Animator, FX Animator
CHRIS HULL - Cleanup, Ink and Paint Artist
CHRIS PURDIN - Key Animator, Inbetween Animator
CHRIS SPEARS - Animation Technology
CHRISTIAN BARKEL - Animation Supervisor, Main Title Animation
CHRISTINA "KIKI" MANRIQUE - Storyboard Artist
CHRISTINA KNORR - Archive and Resource Library
CHRISTINE FELLMETH - Inbetween Animator, Key Animator
CHRISTINE LIU - Storyboard Artist
CHRISTINE WILSON - Key Animator, Character Layout Artist
CHRISTOPHER LUC - Storyboard Artist, Assistant Director
CHU-HUI SONG - Background Painter
CINDY Y. AVILA - Production Coordinator
CRAIG CAMPBELL - Inbetween Animator, Animation Technical Assistant, Cleanup, Ink and Paint Artist, Technical Animator
CRAIG LEE CAMPBELL - Inbetween Animator, Technical Animator
CRISTINA DE MANUEL LOPEZ - Key Animator
CYNTHIA HALLEY - Background Layout Designer
CYNTHIA Z. JAVIER - Inbetween Animator
D.J. LYNCH - Re-recording Mixer
DALE MALINOWSKI - Script Coordinator, Staff Writer
DAN ELDER - FX Animator
DAN HERMELIN - Colorist
DAN HOLLAND - Character Designer
DANA VASQUEZ-EBERHARDT - Executive in Charge for Nickelodeon
DANIEL ELDER - FX Animator
DANIEL SACHS - Background Design
DARRYL CHEN - Technical Animator
DAVID LOPEZ - Key Animator
DAVID MAJMAN - Reuse Manager
DAVID MAXIMO - Storyboard Artist
DAVID MUSSEL - Key Animator
DEAN HOFF - Vice President of Animation Production
DEBBIE STEER - Producer, Supervising Producer
DENNIS MORAN - FX Animator
DEREK KOSOL - Background Layout Designer
DIANA LUU - Production Coordinator, Production Assistant
DIGITOONZ MEDIA & ENTERTAINMENT - Animation Services
DONAVAN FOO - Character Layout Artist, Key Animator
EDGARDO SANTIAGO - Key Animator
EDWIN VAN BEEK - Key Animator
EKATERINA MAXIMOVA - Key Animator
ELENA STAMOULIS - Character Layout Artist
ELLEN WILLIS - Executive Assistant
ELMER S. SALES - Key Animator
ENOC CASTANEDA JR. - Key Animator
ERAY BALUNCA - Key Animator
ERIC BRAVO - Production Assistant, Script Coordinator
ERIC SWANBORG - Vice President, Animation Technology
ERIC TERLATO - Inbetween Animator
ERIK ELIZARREZ - Prop Designer
ERIK STEINMAN - Executive Assistant, Script Coordinator
ERIN SLYNEY - Production Coordinator
EVAN ELEY - Production Assistant
EVANILDO SANTOS - Key Animator
EWA OTWINOWSKA - Production Coordinator
FLYING BARK PRODUCTIONS - Animation Services
F.M. DE MARCO - Writer
FRAN GONZALEZ - Key Animator
FRANK SUMMERS - Inbetween Animator, Key Animator
GENE VASSILAROS - Original Casting, Voice Director
GENER FACUNDO ESPIRITU - Key Animator
GERARD PROUST - Cleanup Ink and Paint Lead, Inbetween Animator, Inbetween Lead
GIANCARLO VOLPE - Storyboard Artist
GLADYFAITH ABCEDE - Storyboard Revisionist, Storyboard Artist
GLENN WONG - Character Designer
GRACE LIM - Production Coordinator, Production Manager
GRACE REIN - Production Coordinator
GREGORY MITCHELL - Machine Room
GUY CHARNAUX - Key Animator
HAEIN KIM - Key Animator, Inbetween Animator
HAILEY LAIN - Inbetween Animator, Key Animator
HANNAH JUDD - Inbetween Animator
HAYDEN BROWNE - Key Animator
HECTOR AMAVIZCA - Inbetween Animator
HOGEOL LEE - CG Generalist
HUNTER HILL - Production Assistant
HUSAIN UNTORO - FX Animator
IAN BUSCH - Staff Writer
IAN HOWARD - Assistant Sound Editor, Sound Editors
IDA HEM - Character Designer, Lead Character Designer
IFESINACHI ORJIEKWE - Storyboard Artist
INDIA SWIFT - Storyboard Artist
ISABEL GALUPO - Current Series Management
ISABELLA (FUZ) BUCKLEY - Inbetween Animator
ISABELLA SPAGNOLO - Inbetween Animator, Key Animator
IVAN FREIRE - Character Layout Artist
IVAN KO - Cleanup, Ink and Paint Artist
JACK ROSSI - Prop Designer
JACK TEA - Inbetween Animator, Technical Animator, Background Design
JACOB COOK - Re-Recording Mixer
JACQUELYN PENNAY - Data Assistant, Production Assistant, Production Coordinator
JAIDON POWELL - Key Animator, Inbetween Animator, Animation Supervisor
JAKE CASTORENA - Storyboard Artist, Director
JAMES HORNER - Cleanup, Ink and Paint Artist, Inbetween Animator, Key Animator
JAMES MARSH - Inbetween Animator, Cleanup, Ink and Paint Artist, Inbetween Lead, Key Animator
JAMIE VICKERS - Director, Assistant Director
JASMINE AUCHTERLONIE - Inbetween Animator
JASON MEIER - Writer
JASON PIEMNOPPAKAO - Post-Production Assistant, Post-Production Coordinator
JAYDEN DOWLER - Inbetween Animator, Key Animator
JAZON PAUL E. PIÑEDA - Inbetween Animator, Key Animator
JEAN PAUL FERNANDEZ - Archive and Resource Library Coordinator, Archivist
JEFF SHIFFMAN - Supervising Sound Editor, Re-Recording Mixer
JEFFERSON BASTIDA - Key Animator

JEFFRY CHOZON - Background Painter
JEN DICKINSON - Key Animator, Animation Supervisor, Background Lead
JENNIFER KATIPUNAN - Technical Animator
JENNIFER QUACH - Inbetween Animator
JENNY TAN - Background Design
JEREMY LE - Inbetween Animator
JERMAINE JOSE - Background Painter
JESSE GORDON - Staff Writer
JESSEY DRAKE - Sound Editor
JESSICA CHEN - Inbetween Animator, Technical Animator
JESSICA ZAMMIT - Storyboard Artist
JJ CONWAY - Assistant Director, Storyboard Artist, Director
JOANNE LEE-JUNG - Technical Animator
JOEL BUHAIN - CG Generalist
JOEL SURDICH - Technical Animator
JOEL WILLIAMS - Inbetween Animator
JOHN DELIGIANNIS - Dialogue Editor
JOHN OLDROYD - Compositing
JOSE ANTONIO CERRO - Inbetween Animator
JOSH RILEY BROWN - Script Coordinator, Staff Writer
JOSHUA REH - Background Design, Background Layout Lead
JOSHUA WOLSKI - Cleanup Ink and Paint Lead
JUAN GALICIA - Key Animator
JULES BRIDGERS - Storyboard Artist
JULIA BRAID - Storyboard Artist
JULIE LY - Cleanup, Ink and Paint Artist, Animation Technical Assistant, Technical Animator
JUSTIN BRINSFIELD - Director of Audio Production, Recording Engineer
JUVENSIA J - Inbetween Animator
KAI JIANG - Storyboard Artist
KAI LYNN JIANG - Storyboard Artist
KATIE MITCHELL - Production Coordinator
KEVIN MOLINA-ORTIZ - Main Title Design, Storyboard Artist, Director, Assistant Director
KHANG LE - Background Design
KIARA FRANKLIN - Production Assistant
KIMBERLY MADORE - Animation Technology, Director, Animation Technology
KIT RIGBY - Background Design, Background Supervisor, Background Lead, Background Layout Consultant
KURT PARTON - Background Design, Character Layout Artist, Animation Supervisor
KYLIE SUN - Inbetween Animator, Cleanup Ink and Paint Artist, Key Animator
LACHLAN PINI - Inbetween Animator, Cleanup Ink and Paint Artist, Key Animator
LAURA BULLEN - Production Manager
LAURA GALLAGHER - Background Design
LAURA GILLE - Storyboard Artist
LAURA PIUNTI - Inbetween Animator
LAURA SREEBNY - Writer
LEANNE LEE - Key Animator
LESTER CHAN - Cleanup, Ink and Paint Artist
LETICIA WOLF - Main Title Theme Composer
LIANNA COHEN - Current Series Management
LIEM NGUYEN - Inbetween Animator, Cleanup, Ink and Paint Artist, Key Animator
LINDY LOU - Inbetween Animator
LING SIU - Background Design
LOGAN NIBLOCK - Inbetween Animator, Cleanup, Ink and Paint Artist, Key Animator
LORENZO ESTRADA - Key Animator, Inbetween Animator
LUCIE JULLIAT - Inbetween Animator
LUCY ZHANG - Background Design
MADELEINE FLORES - Storyboard Artist
MAGALY PYLIPEC - Compositing
MANNY GRIJALVA - Recording Engineer
MANUEL BERNARDO RAMOS ORTIZ - Key Animator
MARDINE J. POURYOUSEF - Animation Technology, Pipeline Technical Director
MARIA DE LEON - Cleanup, Ink and Paint Artist, Inbetween Animator, Key Animator
MARISKA NATHAN - Key Animator, Inbetween Animator
MARK INGRAM - Inbetween Animator, Key Animator
MARK JUSTISON - Pipeline Technical Director
MARTA BERTOLUCCI - Production Assistant, Production Coordinator
MATIAS BERGARA - Flashback Sequence Visual Development
MATTHEW HUMPHREYS - Storyboard Artist
MATT MAHAFFEY - Composer, Main Title Theme Composer, Main Title Theme Performer
MATTHEW FEINMAN - Editor
MATTHEW GILLIGAN - Inbetween Animator
MATTHEW VOYSEY - Cleanup, Ink and Paint Artist
MAX CAJAZERIRAS - Inbetween Animator
MAX COLLINS - Storyboard Artist
MAYUMI NOSE - Storyboard Revisionist
MEGAN CASEY - Executive in Charge for Nickelodeon
MEGHAN BURLESON - Animatic Editor
MEL ROUEN - Background Design, Background Color Lead, Background Supervisor
MELANIE SHIN - Key Animator
MELISSA LUGO - Animatic Editor
MELVIN YOUNG JR. - Production Coordinator
MEREDITH LAYNE - Casting Director
MICHAEL DEGRANDIS - Production Assistant, Script Coordinator
MICHAEL PAZMINO - Archive and Resource Library
MICHAEL TEBBLE - CG Generalist
MIHO TOMIMASU - Background Painter
MILENA GONÇALEZ - FX Animator
MIN LEE - Cleanup Ink and Paint Artist
MIRAN MLANG - Inbetween Animator
MOLLY MILLER - Casting Assistant
MOLLY MINUS - Post-Production Supervisor
MONICA DESTEFANO - Animatic Editor
MORGAN HILLEBRAND - Storyboard Revisionist, Storyboard Artist
NANCY COVARRUBIAS RAMIREZ - Production Coordinator
NANCY RAMIREZ - Production Coordinator
NAOKI ARAIZA - FX Animator
NAS PASHA - Storyboard Artist
NASSER LUCENADA - Inbetween Animator
NATHAN MENDEL - Key Animator
NETTA LAHAV - Key Animator
NICHOLAS GOOCH - Inbetween Animator
NICHOLAS MASTELLO - Background Design
NICHOLAS RALPH - Edit Assistant
NICHOLS MANIQUIS - Background Design
NICK LEONG - Key Animator, Inbetween Animator
NICOLE HEKEL - Compositing
NIKHIL MARKALE - Key Animator, Inbetween Animator
NIKITA CHAN - Background Design and Paint
NINA MANCUSO - Character Layout Artist
NIRALI SOMAIA - Inbetween Animator, Key Animator
NITSAN MILEIKOWSKI - Inbetween Animator, Character Layout Artist
NOAH HOLDEN - Background Design
OLGA GRECHANOVA - Inbetween Animator, Key Animator
OLGA PERMIAKOVA - Key Animator
OLIVER PEARCE - Director of Post-Production
OLIVIER MALRIC - FX Animator
OTTO FERRENE - Supervising Picture Editor
PAIGE MCINTOSH - Character Layout Artist
PAUL RHODES - Inbetween Animator, Key Animator
PAUL SCHWARZ - Inbetween Animator, Key Animator
PETER BOTEV - Inbetween Animator
PHUI JING LING - Inbetween Animator, Key Animator
PIERO PILUSO - Storyboard Artist
PIP FRANCIS - Animation Coordinator, Production Coordinator
POLYNA KIM - Storyboard Artist
RACHEL TOH - Inbetween Animator
RALPH EUSEBIO - Supervising Picture Editor
RAMIRO FRANQUEIRA - Compositing
REBECCA MAY - Writer, Consulting Producer
REY SANTIAGO - Inbetween Animator
RICHARD CHHOA - Key Animator, Animation Supervisor
RICHARD TAN - Key Animator
RICK DOMINICUS - Assistant Picture Editor
RICK HERRERA - Background Design and Paint
RIDVAN CEVIK - Key Animator
ROB PAULSEN - Voice Director
RODEL GRAVO - Background Layout Designer
RODNEY MARCH - CG Generalist
RODRIGO TELLO - Background Design and Paint
RON CORCILLO - Staff Writer
ROSE HAMMER - Inbetween Animator, Key Animator
ROXANNE ESCATEL - Casting Manager
ROXANNE MCAULEY - FX Animator
RUSS CARNEY - Staff Writer
RYAN GREENE - Recording Engineer
RYAN HOSKIN - Cleanup, Ink and Paint Artist, Inbetween Animator, Key Animator
RYLEY MILLER - Inbetween Animator, Key Animator
SAM BUSEKRUS - Sound Editor
SAM MONTES - Storyboard Artist, Assistant Director
SAM SZYMANSKI - Storyboard Artist, Character Designer
SAMIRA ONGCHUA - Storyboard Artist
SAMUEL SATHLER - Key Animator
SARAH HARPER - Background Supervisor, Main Title Animation, Inbetween Lead, Animation Supervisor, Key Animator
SARAH WILLIAMS - Casting Assistant
SEAN MUNDY - Cleanup, Ink and Paint Artist, Inbetween Animator
SEBASTIAN MONTES - Director, Storyboard Artist
SHAWN KOSTANIAN - Vice President of Post-Production
SHAWNA MILLS - Storyboard Artist
SHAZ LYM - Inbetween Animator, Key Animator
SHELDON VELLA - Storyboard Artist
SHIONDRE AUSTIN - Original Casting
SKYE HENWOOD - Inbetween Animator, Cleanup Ink and Paint Artist, Key Animator
SOFIA IFFLA - Production Manager, Line Producer
STEPHANIE CHACON - Production Manager
STEPHEN DESTEFANO - Character Designer
STEPHEN MCDERMOTT - FX Animator
STEVE EAT - Background Painter
STUART GEDDIS - FX Animator
SUN-MIN LEE - Cleanup, Ink and Paint Artist, Inbetween Animator, Key Animator
SUSANNA WANG - Inbetween Animator, Key Animator
TANYA MELENDEZ - Production Coordinator, Color Stylist, Production Manager, Associate Producer
TERRY TRINH - Inbetween Animator, Key Animator
TESSA BRIGHT - Key Animator, Animation Supervisor
THANH DANG - Color Stylist
TIM ANDREWS - Animation Technical Assistant, Technical Animator, FX Animator, Reuse Manager
TIM CANT - Technical Animator
TIM VINDIGNI - Assistant Sound Editor
TOBIAS ANKER - FX Animator
TOM BARKEL - Main Title Animation by, Animation Supervisor, Animation Director
TOM DE GROOT - Inbetween Animator
TOM MURRAY - Inbetween Animator
TOM WOOD - Production Coordinator
TOMASZ PILARSKI - Key Animator
TOÑO LEON - Key Animator
TONY GAMA-LOBO - Writer, Story Editor, Consulting Producer
TONY UNSER - FX Animator
TOP DRAW ANIMATION INC. - Animation Services
TRYSTIN SINNOTT - Background Design
TYLER CHAN - FX Animator
VICTOR BOLO OLIVEIRA - Key Animator
VICTORIA DINH - Inbetween Animator, Key Animator
VICTORIA MAZZEI - Character Layout Artist
VLADIMIR RADEV - Producer, Line Producer
WILL RUZICKA - Storyboard Artist
XIANG TANG - Key Animator
XINYUE YU - Dialogue Editor
YANGLEI WU - Background Design
YASMIN MOINI - Key Animator, Inbetween Animator
YI FU - Background Design
YINING XIA - Inbetween Animator, Key Animator
ZAK PLUCINSKI - Character Designer
ZANE YARBROUGH - Storyboard Artist
ZHE XIANG TANG - Key Animator, Animation Supervisor, Inbetween Animator
ZHENG QU - Background Design

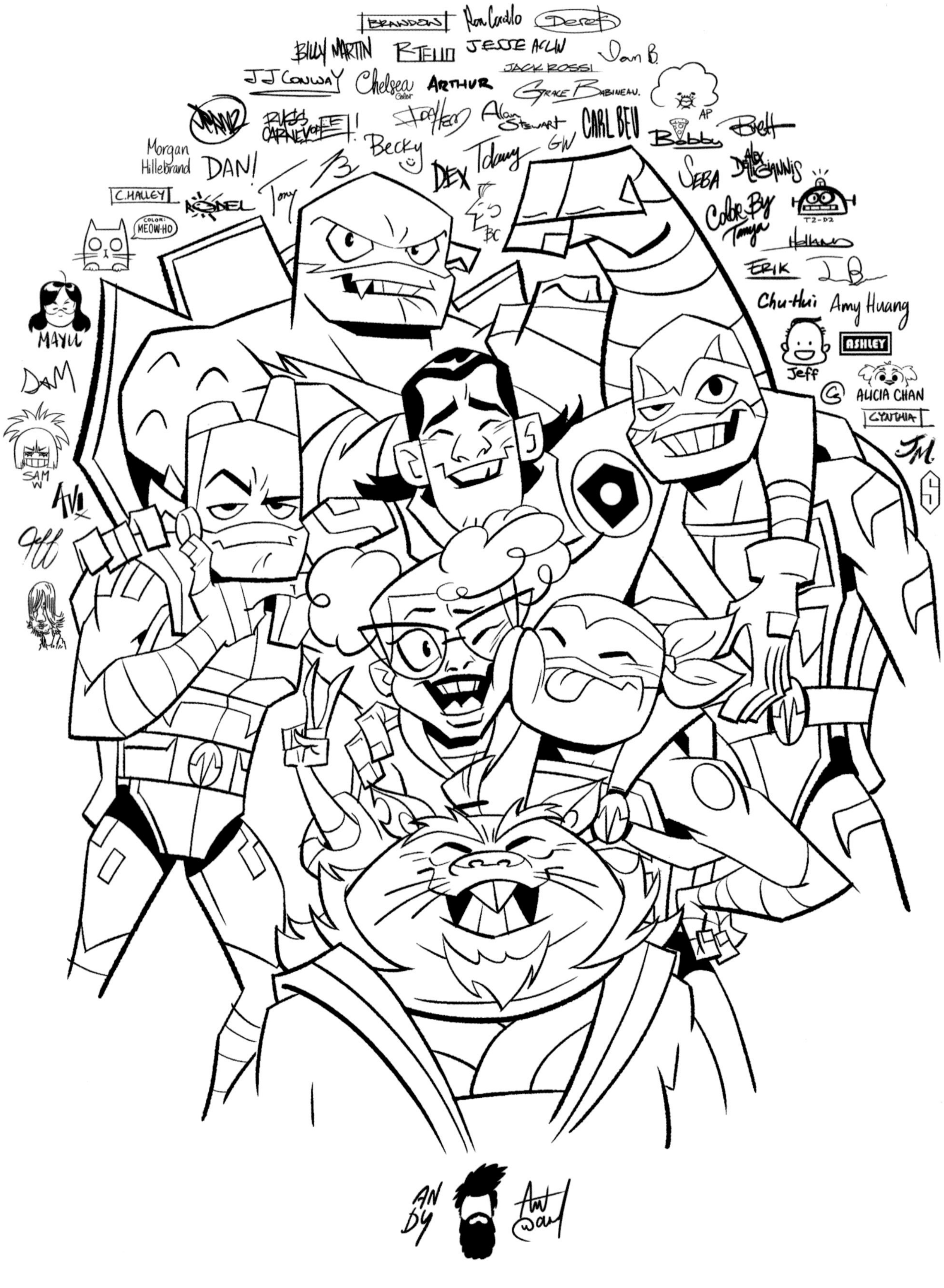
BRANDON
Ron Caudillo
BILLY MARTIN
JESSE ACLIN
Dan B.
JACK ROSSI
JJ CONWAY
Chelsea
Color
ARTHUR
GRACE BABINEAU.
AP
RUSS CARNEVALE!
Alan Stewart
CARL BEU
Bobby
Brett
Morgan Hillebrand
DAN!
Becky
DEX
GW
SEBA
Alex Delligiannis
C.HALLEY
Tony
BC
Color By Tamya
T2-D2
COLOR: MEOW-HO
ERIK
Chu-Hui
Amy Huang
MAYU
ASHLEY
Jeff
ALICIA CHAN
CYNTHIA
DAM
JM.
SAM
AN DY

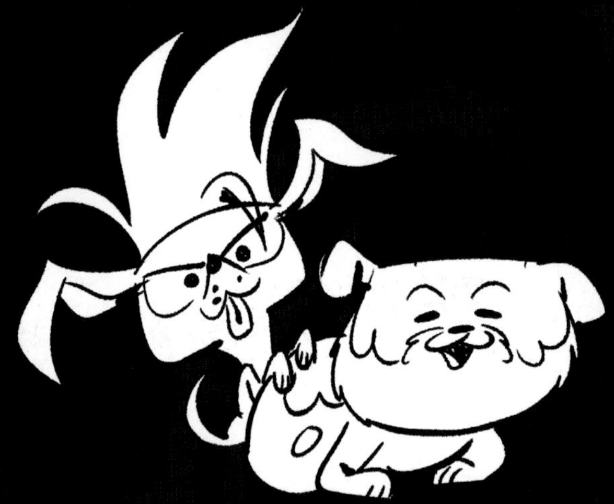